FIRST-ORDER METHODS IN OPTIMIZATION

MOS-SIAM Series on Optimization

This series is published jointly by the Mathematical Optimization Society and the Society for Industrial and Applied Mathematics. It includes research monographs, books on applications, textbooks at all levels, and tutorials. Besides being of high scientific quality, books in the series must advance the understanding and practice of optimization. They must also be written clearly and at an appropriate level for the intended audience.

Editor-in-Chief

Katya Scheinberg
Lehigh University

Editorial Board

Santanu S. Dey, *Georgia Institute of Technology*
Maryam Fazel, *University of Washington*
Andrea Lodi, *University of Bologna*
Arkadi Nemirovski, *Georgia Institute of Technology*
Stefan Ulbrich, *Technische Universität Darmstadt*
Luis Nunes Vicente, *University of Coimbra*
David Williamson, *Cornell University*
Stephen J. Wright, *University of Wisconsin*

Series Volumes

Beck, Amir, *First-Order Methods in Optimization*
Terlaky, Tamás, Anjos, Miguel F., and Ahmed, Shabbir, editors, *Advances and Trends in Optimization with Engineering Applications*
Todd, Michael J., *Minimum-Volume Ellipsoids: Theory and Algorithms*
Bienstock, Daniel, *Electrical Transmission System Cascades and Vulnerability: An Operations Research Viewpoint*
Koch, Thorsten, Hiller, Benjamin, Pfetsch, Marc E., and Schewe, Lars, editors, *Evaluating Gas Network Capacities*
Corberán, Ángel, and Laporte, Gilbert, *Arc Routing: Problems, Methods, and Applications*
Toth, Paolo, and Vigo, Daniele, *Vehicle Routing: Problems, Methods, and Applications, Second Edition*
Beck, Amir, *Introduction to Nonlinear Optimization: Theory, Algorithms, and Applications with MATLAB*
Attouch, Hedy, Buttazzo, Giuseppe, and Michaille, Gérard, *Variational Analysis in Sobolev and BV Spaces: Applications to PDEs and Optimization, Second Edition*
Shapiro, Alexander, Dentcheva, Darinka, and Ruszczynski, Andrzej, *Lectures on Stochastic Programming: Modeling and Theory, Second Edition*
Locatelli, Marco and Schoen, Fabio, *Global Optimization: Theory, Algorithms, and Applications*
De Loera, Jesús A., Hemmecke, Raymond, and Köppe, Matthias, *Algebraic and Geometric Ideas in the Theory of Discrete Optimization*
Blekherman, Grigoriy, Parrilo, Pablo A., and Thomas, Rekha R., editors, *Semidefinite Optimization and Convex Algebraic Geometry*
Delfour, M. C., *Introduction to Optimization and Semidifferential Calculus*
Ulbrich, Michael, *Semismooth Newton Methods for Variational Inequalities and Constrained Optimization Problems in Function Spaces*
Biegler, Lorenz T., *Nonlinear Programming: Concepts, Algorithms, and Applications to Chemical Processes*
Shapiro, Alexander, Dentcheva, Darinka, and Ruszczynski, Andrzej, *Lectures on Stochastic Programming: Modeling and Theory*
Conn, Andrew R., Scheinberg, Katya, and Vicente, Luis N., *Introduction to Derivative-Free Optimization*
Ferris, Michael C., Mangasarian, Olvi L., and Wright, Stephen J., *Linear Programming with MATLAB*
Attouch, Hedy, Buttazzo, Giuseppe, and Michaille, Gérard, *Variational Analysis in Sobolev and BV Spaces: Applications to PDEs and Optimization*
Wallace, Stein W. and Ziemba, William T., editors, *Applications of Stochastic Programming*
Grötschel, Martin, editor, *The Sharpest Cut: The Impact of Manfred Padberg and His Work*
Renegar, James, *A Mathematical View of Interior-Point Methods in Convex Optimization*
Ben-Tal, Aharon and Nemirovski, Arkadi, *Lectures on Modern Convex Optimization: Analysis, Algorithms, and Engineering Applications*
Conn, Andrew R., Gould, Nicholas I. M., and Toint, Phillippe L., *Trust-Region Methods*

FIRST-ORDER METHODS IN OPTIMIZATION

Amir Beck

Tel-Aviv University
Tel-Aviv
Israel

Society for Industrial and Applied Mathematics
Philadelphia

Mathematical Optimization Society
Philadelphia

Publisher	Kivmars Bowling
Acquisitions Editor	Paula Callaghan
Developmental Editor	Gina Rinelli Harris
Managing Editor	Kelly Thomas
Production Editor	Louis R. Primus
Copy Editor	Bruce Owens
Production Manager	Donna Witzleben
Production Coordinator	Cally Shrader
Compositor	Cheryl Hufnagle
Graphic Designer	Lois Sellers

Library of Congress Cataloging-in-Publication Data
Names: Beck, Amir, author.
Title: First-order methods in optimization / Amir Beck, Technion-Israel
    Institute for Technology, Technion, Haifa, Israel.
Description: Philadelphia : Society for Industrial and Applied Mathematics ;
    Philadelphia : Mathematical Optimization Society, [2017] | Series:
    MOS-SIAM series on optimization ; 25 | Includes bibliographical references
    and index.
Identifiers: LCCN 2017026859 (print) | LCCN 2017042114 (ebook) | ISBN
    9781611974997 (e-book) | ISBN 9781611974980 (print)
Subjects: LCSH: Mathematical optimization. | Convergence.
Classification: LCC QA402.5 (ebook) | LCC QA402.5 .B42238 2017 (print) | DDC
    519.6–dc23
LC record available at *https://lccn.loc.gov/2017026859*

 is a registered trademark.

 Mathematical Optimization Society is a registered trademark.

For
My wife, Nili
My daughters, Noy and Vered
My parents, Nili and Itzhak

Contents

Preface

This book, as the title suggests, is about first-order methods, namely, methods that exploit information on values and gradients/subgradients (but not Hessians) of the functions comprising the model under consideration. First-order methods go back to 1847 with the work of Cauchy on the steepest descent method. With the increase in the amount of applications that can be modeled as large- or even huge-scale optimization problems, there has been a revived interest in using simple methods that require low iteration cost as well as low memory storage.

The primary goal of the book is to provide in a self-contained manner a comprehensive study of the main first-order methods that are frequently used in solving large-scale problems. This is done by gathering and reorganizing in a unified manner many results that are currently scattered throughout the literature. Special emphasis is placed on rates of convergence and complexity analysis. Although the name of the book is "first-order methods in optimization," two disclaimers are in order. First, we will actually also consider methods that exploit additional operations at each iteration such as prox evaluations, linear oracles, exact minimization w.r.t. blocks of variables, and more, so perhaps a more suitable name would have been "simple methods in optimization." Second, in order to be truly self-contained, the first part of the book (Chapters 1–7) is actually purely theoretical and contains essential topics that are crucial for the developments in the algorithmic part (Chapters 8–15).

The book is intended for students and researchers with a background in advanced calculus and linear algebra, as well as prior knowledge in the fundamentals of optimization (some convex analysis, optimality conditions, and duality). A MATLAB toolbox implementing many of the algorithms described in the book was developed by the author and Nili Guttmann-Beck and can be found at www.siam.org/books/mo25.

The outline of the book is as follows. Chapter 1 reviews important facts about vector spaces. Although the material is quite fundamental, it is advisable not to skip this chapter since many of the conventions regarding the underlying spaces used in the book are explained. Chapter 2 focuses on extended real-valued functions with a special emphasis on properties such as convexity, closedness, and continuity. Chapter 3 covers the topic of subgradients starting from basic definitions, continuing with directional derivatives, differentiability, and subdifferentiability and ending with calculus rules. Optimality conditions are derived for convex problems (Fermat's optimality condition), but also for the nonconvex composite model, which will be discussed extensively throughout the book. Conjugate functions are the subject of Chapter 4, which covers several issues, such as Fenchel's inequality, the biconjugate, calculus rules, conjugate subgradient theorem, relations with the infimal convolution, and Fenchel's duality theorem. Chapter 5 covers two different but closely related subjects: smoothness and strong convexity—several characterizations of each of these concepts are given, and their relation via the conjugate correspondence theorem is established. The proximal operator is discussed in Chapter 6, which includes a large amount of prox computations as well as calculus rules. The basic properties of the proximal mapping (first and second prox theorems and Moreau decomposition) are proved, and the Moreau envelope concludes the theoretical part of the chapter. The first part of the book ends with Chapter 7, which contains a study of symmetric spectral functions. The second, algorithmic part of the book starts with Chapter 8 with primal and dual projected subgradient methods. Several stepsize rules are discussed, and complexity results for both the convex and the strongly convex cases are established. The chapter also includes discussions on the stochastic as well as the incremental projected subgradient methods. The non-Euclidean version of the projected subgradient method, a.k.a. the mirror descent method, is discussed in Chapter 9. Chapter 10 is concerned with the proximal gradient method as well as its many variants and extensions. The chapter also studies several theoretical results concerning the so-called gradient mapping, which plays an important part in the convergence analysis of proximal gradient–based methods. The extension of the proximal gradient method to the *block* proximal gradient method is discussed in Chapter 11, while Chapter 12 considers the dual proximal gradient method and contains a result on a primal-dual relation that allows one to transfer rate of convergence results from the dual problem to the primal problem. The generalized conditional gradient method is the topic of Chapter 13, which contains the basic rate of convergence results of the method, as well as its block version, and discusses the effect of strong convexity assumptions on the model. The alternating minimization method is the subject of Chapter 14, where its convergence (as well as divergence) in many settings is established and illustrated. The book concludes with a discussion on the ADMM method in Chapter 15.

My deepest thanks to Marc Teboulle, whose fundamental works in first-order methods form the basis of many of the results in the book. Marc introduced me to the world of optimization, and he is a constant source and inspiration and admiration. I would like to thank Luba Tetruashvili for reading the book and for her helpful remarks. It has been a pleasure to work with the extremely devoted and efficient SIAM staff. Finally, I would like to acknowledge the support of the Israel Science Foundation for supporting me while writing this book.

Chapter 1

Vector Spaces

This chapter reviews several important facts about different aspects of vectors spaces that will be used throughout the book. More comprehensive and detailed accounts of these subjects can be found in advanced linear algebra books.

1.1 Definition

A *vector space* $\mathbb{E}$ over $\mathbb{R}$ (or a "real vector space") is a set of elements called *vectors* such that the following holds.

(A) For any two vectors $\mathbf{x}, \mathbf{y} \in \mathbb{E}$, there corresponds a vector $\mathbf{x} + \mathbf{y}$, called the *sum* of $\mathbf{x}$ and $\mathbf{y}$, satisfying the following properties:

    1. $\mathbf{x} + \mathbf{y} = \mathbf{y} + \mathbf{x}$ for any $\mathbf{x}, \mathbf{y} \in \mathbb{E}$.

    2. $\mathbf{x} + (\mathbf{y} + \mathbf{z}) = (\mathbf{x} + \mathbf{y}) + \mathbf{z}$ for any $\mathbf{x}, \mathbf{y}, \mathbf{z} \in \mathbb{E}$.

    3. There exists in $\mathbb{E}$ a unique vector $\mathbf{0}$ (called the *zeros vector*) such that $\mathbf{x} + \mathbf{0} = \mathbf{x}$ for any $\mathbf{x}$.

    4. For any $\mathbf{x} \in \mathbb{E}$, there exists a vector $-\mathbf{x} \in \mathbb{E}$ such that $\mathbf{x} + (-\mathbf{x}) = \mathbf{0}$.

(B) For any real number (also called *scalar*) $\alpha \in \mathbb{R}$ and $\mathbf{x} \in \mathbb{E}$, there corresponds a vector $\alpha \mathbf{x}$ called the *scalar multiplication* of α and $\mathbf{x}$ satisfying the following properties:

    1. $\alpha(\beta \mathbf{x}) = (\alpha \beta)\mathbf{x}$ for any $\alpha, \beta \in \mathbb{R}, \mathbf{x} \in \mathbb{E}$.

    2. $1\mathbf{x} = \mathbf{x}$ for any $\mathbf{x} \in \mathbb{E}$.

(C) The two operations (summation, scalar multiplication) satisfy the following properties:

    1. $\alpha(\mathbf{x} + \mathbf{y}) = \alpha \mathbf{x} + \alpha \mathbf{y}$ for any $\alpha \in \mathbb{R}, \mathbf{x}, \mathbf{y} \in \mathbb{E}$.

    2. $(\alpha + \beta)\mathbf{x} = \alpha \mathbf{x} + \beta \mathbf{x}$ for any $\alpha, \beta \in \mathbb{R}, \mathbf{x} \in \mathbb{E}$.

1.2   Dimension

A set of vectors $\{\mathbf{v}_1, \mathbf{v}_2, \ldots, \mathbf{v}_n\}$ in a vector space $\mathbb{E}$ is called *linearly independent* or just *independent* if the linear system

$$\sum_{i=1}^{n} \alpha_i \mathbf{v}_i = \mathbf{0}$$

implies that $\alpha_1 = \alpha_2 = \cdots = \alpha_n = 0$. In other words, there does not exist a nontrivial linear combination of vectors that is equal to the zeros vector. A set of vectors $\{\mathbf{v}_1, \mathbf{v}_2, \ldots, \mathbf{v}_n\}$ is said to *span* $\mathbb{E}$ if for any $\mathbf{x} \in \mathbb{E}$, there exist $\beta_1, \beta_2, \ldots, \beta_n \in \mathbb{R}$ such that

$$\mathbf{x} = \sum_{i=1}^{n} \beta_i \mathbf{v}_i.$$

A *basis* of a vector space $\mathbb{E}$ is an independent set of vectors that spans $\mathbb{E}$. It is well known that the number of vectors in all the bases of a vector space $\mathbb{E}$ is the same; this number is called the *dimension* of the space and is denoted by $\dim(\mathbb{E})$. In this book we will discuss only vector spaces with a finite dimension, namely, *finite-dimensional vector spaces*.

1.3   Norms

A *norm* $\|\cdot\|$ on a vector space $\mathbb{E}$ is a function $\|\cdot\| : \mathbb{E} \to \mathbb{R}$ satisfying the following properties:

1. **(nonnegativity)** $\|\mathbf{x}\| \geq 0$ for any $\mathbf{x} \in \mathbb{E}$ and $\|\mathbf{x}\| = 0$ if and only if $\mathbf{x} = \mathbf{0}$.

2. **(positive homogeneity)** $\|\lambda \mathbf{x}\| = |\lambda| \cdot \|\mathbf{x}\|$ for any $\mathbf{x} \in \mathbb{E}$ and $\lambda \in \mathbb{R}$.

3. **(triangle inequality)** $\|\mathbf{x} + \mathbf{y}\| \leq \|\mathbf{x}\| + \|\mathbf{y}\|$ for any $\mathbf{x}, \mathbf{y} \in \mathbb{E}$.

We will sometimes denote the norm of a space $\mathbb{E}$ by $\|\cdot\|_\mathbb{E}$ to emphasize the identity of the space and to distinguish it from other norms. The *open ball* with center $\mathbf{c} \in \mathbb{E}$ and radius $r > 0$ is denoted by $B(\mathbf{c}, r)$ and defined by

$$B(\mathbf{c}, r) = \{\mathbf{x} \in \mathbb{E} : \|\mathbf{x} - \mathbf{c}\| < r\}.$$

The *closed ball* with center $\mathbf{c} \in \mathbb{E}$ and radius $r > 0$ is denoted by $B[\mathbf{c}, r]$ and defined by

$$B[\mathbf{c}, r] = \{\mathbf{x} \in \mathbb{E} : \|\mathbf{x} - \mathbf{c}\| \leq r\}.$$

We will sometimes use the notation $B_{\|\cdot\|}[\mathbf{c}, r]$ or $B_{\|\cdot\|}(\mathbf{c}, r)$ to identify the specific norm that is being used.

1.4   Inner Products

An *inner product* of a real vector space $\mathbb{E}$ is a function that associates to each pair of vectors $\mathbf{x}, \mathbf{y}$ a real number, which is denoted by $\langle \mathbf{x}, \mathbf{y} \rangle$ and satisfies the following properties:

1. **(commutativity)** $\langle \mathbf{x}, \mathbf{y} \rangle = \langle \mathbf{y}, \mathbf{x} \rangle$ for any $\mathbf{x}, \mathbf{y} \in \mathbb{E}$.

2. **(linearity)** $\langle \alpha_1 \mathbf{x}_1 + \alpha_2 \mathbf{x}_2, \mathbf{y} \rangle = \alpha_1 \langle \mathbf{x}_1, \mathbf{y} \rangle + \alpha_2 \langle \mathbf{x}_2, \mathbf{y} \rangle$ for any $\alpha_1, \alpha_2 \in \mathbb{R}$ and $\mathbf{x}_1, \mathbf{x}_2, \mathbf{y} \in \mathbb{E}$.

3. **(positive definiteness)** $\langle \mathbf{x}, \mathbf{x} \rangle \geq 0$ for any $\mathbf{x} \in \mathbb{E}$ and $\langle \mathbf{x}, \mathbf{x} \rangle = 0$ if and only if $\mathbf{x} = \mathbf{0}$.

A vector space endowed with an inner product is also called an *inner product space*. At this point we would like to make the following important note:

Underlying Spaces: In this book the underlying vector spaces, usually denoted by $\mathbb{V}$ or $\mathbb{E}$, are always finite dimensional real inner product spaces with endowed inner product $\langle \cdot, \cdot \rangle$ and endowed norm $\| \cdot \|$.

1.5 Affine Sets and Convex Sets

Given a real vector space $\mathbb{E}$, a set $S \subseteq \mathbb{E}$ is called *affine* if for any $\mathbf{x}, \mathbf{y} \in S$ and $\lambda \in \mathbb{R}$, the inclusion $\lambda \mathbf{x} + (1 - \lambda)\mathbf{y} \in S$ holds. For a set $S \subseteq \mathbb{E}$, the *affine hull* of S, denoted by aff(S), is the intersection of all affine sets containing S. Clearly, aff(S) is by itself an affine set, and it is the smallest affine set containing S (w.r.t. inclusion). A *hyperplane* is a subset of $\mathbb{E}$ given by

$$H_{\mathbf{a},b} = \{ \mathbf{x} \in \mathbb{E} : \langle \mathbf{a}, \mathbf{x} \rangle = b \},$$

where $\mathbf{a} \in \mathbb{E}$ and $b \in \mathbb{R}$. It is an easy exercise to show that hyperplanes are affine sets.

A set $C \subseteq \mathbb{E}$ is called *convex* if for any $\mathbf{x}, \mathbf{y} \in C$ and $\lambda \in [0, 1]$ it holds that $\lambda \mathbf{x} + (1 - \lambda)\mathbf{y} \in C$. Evidently, affine sets are always convex. Open and closed balls are always convex regardless of the choice of norm. For given $\mathbf{x}, \mathbf{y} \in \mathbb{E}$, the *closed line segment* between $\mathbf{x}$ and $\mathbf{y}$ is a subset of $\mathbb{E}$ denoted by $[\mathbf{x}, \mathbf{y}]$ and defined as

$$[\mathbf{x}, \mathbf{y}] = \{ \alpha \mathbf{x} + (1 - \alpha)\mathbf{y} : \alpha \in [0, 1] \} .$$

The *open line segment* $(\mathbf{x}, \mathbf{y})$ is similarly defined as

$$(\mathbf{x}, \mathbf{y}) = \{ \alpha \mathbf{x} + (1 - \alpha)\mathbf{y} : \alpha \in (0, 1) \}$$

when $\mathbf{x} \neq \mathbf{y}$ and is the empty set $\emptyset$ when $\mathbf{x} = \mathbf{y}$. Closed and open line segments are convex sets. Another example of convex sets are *half-spaces*, which are sets of the form

$$H_{\mathbf{a},b}^{-} = \{ \mathbf{x} \in \mathbb{E} : \langle \mathbf{a}, \mathbf{x} \rangle \leq b \},$$

where $\mathbf{a} \in \mathbb{E}$ and $b \in \mathbb{R}$.

1.6 Euclidean Spaces

A finite dimensional real vector space equipped with an inner product $\langle \cdot, \cdot \rangle$ is called a *Euclidean space* if it is endowed with the norm $\|\mathbf{x}\| = \sqrt{\langle \mathbf{x}, \mathbf{x} \rangle}$, which is referred to as the *Euclidean norm*.

1.7   The Space $\mathbb{R}^n$

The vector space $\mathbb{R}^n$ (n being a positive integer) is the set of n-dimensional column vectors with real components endowed with the component-wise addition operator,

$$
\begin{pmatrix} x_1 \\ x_2 \\ \vdots \\ x_n \end{pmatrix} + \begin{pmatrix} y_1 \\ y_2 \\ \vdots \\ y_n \end{pmatrix} = \begin{pmatrix} x_1 + y_1 \\ x_2 + y_2 \\ \vdots \\ x_n + y_n \end{pmatrix},
$$

and the scalar-vector product,

$$
\lambda \begin{pmatrix} x_1 \\ x_2 \\ \vdots \\ x_n \end{pmatrix} = \begin{pmatrix} \lambda x_1 \\ \lambda x_2 \\ \vdots \\ \lambda x_n \end{pmatrix},
$$

where in the above $x_1, x_2, \ldots, x_n, \lambda$ are real numbers. We will denote the standard basis of $\mathbb{R}^n$ by $\mathbf{e}_1, \mathbf{e}_2, \ldots, \mathbf{e}_n$, where $\mathbf{e}_i$ is the n-length column vector whose ith component is one while all the others are zeros. The column vectors of all ones and all zeros will be denoted by $\mathbf{e}$ and $\mathbf{0}$, respectively, where the length of the vectors will be clear from the context.

By far the most used inner product in $\mathbb{R}^n$ is the *dot product* defined by

$$
\langle \mathbf{x}, \mathbf{y} \rangle = \sum_{i=1}^{n} x_i y_i.
$$

Inner Product in $\mathbb{R}^n$: In this book, unless otherwise stated, the endowed inner product in $\mathbb{R}^n$ is the dot product.

Of course, the dot product is not the only possible inner product that can be defined over $\mathbb{R}^n$. Another useful option is the $\mathbf{Q}$-inner product, which is defined as

$$
\langle \mathbf{x}, \mathbf{y} \rangle_{\mathbf{Q}} = \mathbf{x}^T \mathbf{Q} \mathbf{y},
$$

where $\mathbf{Q}$ is a positive definite $n \times n$ matrix. Obviously, the $\mathbf{Q}$-inner product amounts to the dot product when $\mathbf{Q} = \mathbf{I}$. If $\mathbb{R}^n$ is endowed with the dot product, then the associated Euclidean norm is the l_2-norm

$$
\|\mathbf{x}\|_2 = \sqrt{\langle \mathbf{x}, \mathbf{x} \rangle} = \sqrt{\sum_{i=1}^{n} x_i^2}.
$$

If $\mathbb{R}^n$ is endowed with the $\mathbf{Q}$-inner product, then the associated Euclidean norm is the $\mathbf{Q}$-*norm*

$$
\|\mathbf{x}\|_{\mathbf{Q}} = \sqrt{\mathbf{x}^T \mathbf{Q} \mathbf{x}}.
$$

For a given $p \geq 1$, the l_p-norm on $\mathbb{R}^n$ is given by the formula

$$\|\mathbf{x}\|_p = \sqrt[p]{\sum_{i=1}^{n} |x_i|^p}.$$

The l_∞-norm on $\mathbb{R}^n$ is defined by

$$\|\mathbf{x}\|_\infty = \max_{i=1,2,\ldots,n} |x_i|.$$

1.7.1 Subsets of $\mathbb{R}^n$

The *nonnegative orthant* is the subset of $\mathbb{R}^n$ consisting of all vectors in $\mathbb{R}^n$ with nonnegative components and is denoted by $\mathbb{R}_+^n$:

$$\mathbb{R}_+^n = \left\{ (x_1, x_2, \ldots, x_n)^T : x_1, x_2, \ldots, x_n \geq 0 \right\}.$$

Similarly, the *positive orthant* consists of all the vectors in $\mathbb{R}^n$ with positive components and is denoted by $\mathbb{R}_{++}^n$:

$$\mathbb{R}_{++}^n = \left\{ (x_1, x_2, \ldots, x_n)^T : x_1, x_2, \ldots, x_n > 0 \right\}.$$

The *unit simplex*, denoted by Δ_n, is the subset of $\mathbb{R}^n$ comprising all nonnegative vectors whose components sum up to one:

$$\Delta_n = \left\{ \mathbf{x} \in \mathbb{R}^n : \mathbf{x} \geq \mathbf{0}, \mathbf{e}^T \mathbf{x} = 1 \right\}.$$

Given two vectors $\boldsymbol{\ell}, \mathbf{u} \in \mathbb{R}^n$ that satisfy $\boldsymbol{\ell} \leq \mathbf{u}$, the *box* with lower bounds $\boldsymbol{\ell}$ and upper bounds $\mathbf{u}$ is denoted by $\mathrm{Box}[\boldsymbol{\ell}, \mathbf{u}]$ and defined as

$$\mathrm{Box}[\boldsymbol{\ell}, \mathbf{u}] = \{\mathbf{x} \in \mathbb{R}^n : \boldsymbol{\ell} \leq \mathbf{x} \leq \mathbf{u}\}.$$

Thus, for example, $\mathrm{Box}[-\mathbf{e}, \mathbf{e}] = [-1, 1]^n$.

1.7.2 Operations on Vectors in $\mathbb{R}^n$

There are several operations on vectors in $\mathbb{R}^n$ that will be frequently used in the book. For a given vector $\mathbf{x} \in \mathbb{R}^n$, the vector $[\mathbf{x}]_+$ is the *nonnegative part* of $\mathbf{x}$ defined by $[\mathbf{x}]_+ = (\max\{x_i, 0\})_{i=1}^n$. For a given $\mathbf{x} \in \mathbb{R}^n$, the vector $|\mathbf{x}|$ is the vector of component-wise absolute values $(|x_i|)_{i=1}^n$, and the vector $\mathrm{sgn}(\mathbf{x})$ is defined as

$$\mathrm{sgn}(\mathbf{x})_i = \begin{cases} 1, & x_i \geq 0, \\ -1, & x_i < 0. \end{cases}$$

For two vectors $\mathbf{a}, \mathbf{b} \in \mathbb{R}^n$, their *Hadamard product*, denoted by $\mathbf{a} \odot \mathbf{b}$, is the vector comprising the component-wise products: $\mathbf{a} \odot \mathbf{b} = (a_i b_i)_{i=1}^n$.

1.8   The Space $\mathbb{R}^{m \times n}$

The set of all real-valued $m \times n$ matrices is denoted by $\mathbb{R}^{m \times n}$. This is a vector space with the component-wise addition as the summation operation and the component-wise scalar multiplication as the "scalar-vector multiplication" operation. The *dot product* in $\mathbb{R}^{m \times n}$ is defined by

$$\langle \mathbf{A}, \mathbf{B} \rangle = \text{Tr}(\mathbf{A}^T \mathbf{B}) = \sum_{i=1}^{m} \sum_{j=1}^{n} A_{ij} B_{ij}, \quad \mathbf{A}, \mathbf{B} \in \mathbb{R}^{m \times n}.$$

The space $\mathbb{R}^{m \times n}$ is sometimes associated with the space $\mathbb{R}^{mn}$ in the sense that each matrix in $\mathbb{R}^{m \times n}$ corresponds to the mn-length vector constructed by stacking the columns of the matrix. Unless otherwise stated, we will assume that the inner product in $\mathbb{R}^{m \times n}$ is the dot product.

Inner Product in $\mathbb{R}^{m \times n}$: In this book, unless otherwise stated, the endowed inner product in $\mathbb{R}^{m \times n}$ is the dot product.

1.8.1   Subsets of $\mathbb{R}^{n \times n}$

The set of all $n \times n$ symmetric matrices is denoted by $\mathbb{S}^n$:

$$\mathbb{S}^n = \left\{ \mathbf{A} \in \mathbb{R}^{n \times n} : \mathbf{A} = \mathbf{A}^T \right\}.$$

Note that $\mathbb{S}^n$ is also a vector space with the same summation and scalar multiplication operations as in $\mathbb{R}^{n \times n}$. The inner product in $\mathbb{S}^n$, unless otherwise stated, is the dot product.

The set of all $n \times n$ positive semidefinite matrices is denoted by $\mathbb{S}^n_+$:

$$\mathbb{S}^n_+ = \left\{ \mathbf{A} \in \mathbb{R}^{n \times n} : \mathbf{A} \succeq \mathbf{0} \right\}.$$

The set of all $n \times n$ positive definite matrices is denoted by $\mathbb{S}^n_{++}$:

$$\mathbb{S}^n_{++} = \left\{ \mathbf{A} \in \mathbb{R}^{n \times n} : \mathbf{A} \succ \mathbf{0} \right\}.$$

Obviously, the inclusion $\mathbb{S}^n_{++} \subseteq \mathbb{S}^n_+ \subseteq \mathbb{S}^n$ holds. Similarly, $\mathbb{S}^n_-$ is the set of all $n \times n$ negative semidefinite matrices, and $\mathbb{S}^n_{--}$ is the set of all $n \times n$ negative definite matrices:

$$\mathbb{S}^n_- = \left\{ \mathbf{A} \in \mathbb{R}^{n \times n} : \mathbf{A} \preceq \mathbf{0} \right\},$$
$$\mathbb{S}^n_{--} = \left\{ \mathbf{A} \in \mathbb{R}^{n \times n} : \mathbf{A} \prec \mathbf{0} \right\}.$$

The set of all $n \times n$ orthogonal matrices is denoted by $\mathbb{O}^n$:

$$\mathbb{O}^n = \left\{ \mathbf{A} \in \mathbb{R}^{n \times n} : \mathbf{A} \mathbf{A}^T = \mathbf{A}^T \mathbf{A} = \mathbf{I} \right\}.$$

1.8.2   Norms in $\mathbb{R}^{m \times n}$

If $\mathbb{R}^{m \times n}$ is endowed with the dot product, then the corresponding Euclidean norm is the *Frobenius norm* defined by

$$\|\mathbf{A}\|_F = \sqrt{\text{Tr}(\mathbf{A}^T \mathbf{A})} = \sqrt{\sum_{i=1}^{m} \sum_{j=1}^{n} A_{ij}^2}, \quad \mathbf{A} \in \mathbb{R}^{m \times n}.$$

Many examples of matrix norms are generated by using the concept of induced norms, which we now describe. Given a matrix $\mathbf{A} \in \mathbb{R}^{m \times n}$ and two norms $\| \cdot \|_a$ and $\| \cdot \|_b$ on $\mathbb{R}^n$ and $\mathbb{R}^m$, respectively, the *induced matrix norm* $\|\mathbf{A}\|_{a,b}$ is defined by

$$\|\mathbf{A}\|_{a,b} = \max_{\mathbf{x}}\{\|\mathbf{A}\mathbf{x}\|_b : \|\mathbf{x}\|_a \leq 1\}.$$

It can be easily shown that the above definition implies that for any $\mathbf{x} \in \mathbb{R}^n$, the inequality

$$\|\mathbf{A}\mathbf{x}\|_b \leq \|\mathbf{A}\|_{a,b}\|\mathbf{x}\|_a$$

holds. We refer to the matrix norm $\| \cdot \|_{a,b}$ as the (a, b)-norm. When $a = b$, we will simply refer to it as an a-norm and omit one of the subscripts in its notation, that is, use the notation $\| \cdot \|_a$ instead of $\| \cdot \|_{a,a}$.

Example 1.1 (spectral norm). If $\| \cdot \|_a = \| \cdot \|_b = \| \cdot \|_2$, then the induced norm of a matrix $\mathbf{A} \in \mathbb{R}^{m \times n}$ is the maximum singular value of $\mathbf{A}$:

$$\|\mathbf{A}\|_2 = \|\mathbf{A}\|_{2,2} = \sqrt{\lambda_{\max}(\mathbf{A}^T \mathbf{A})} \equiv \sigma_{\max}(\mathbf{A}). \quad \blacksquare$$

Example 1.2 (1-norm). When $\| \cdot \|_a = \| \cdot \|_b = \| \cdot \|_1$, the induced matrix norm of a matrix $\mathbf{A} \in \mathbb{R}^{m \times n}$ is given by

$$\|\mathbf{A}\|_1 = \max_{j=1,2,\ldots,n} \sum_{i=1}^{m} |A_{i,j}|.$$

This norm is also called the *maximum absolute column sum norm*. $\quad \blacksquare$

Example 1.3 (∞-norm). When $\| \cdot \|_a = \| \cdot \|_b = \| \cdot \|_\infty$, the induced matrix norm of a matrix $\mathbf{A} \in \mathbb{R}^{m \times n}$ is given by

$$\|\mathbf{A}\|_\infty = \max_{i=1,2,\ldots,m} \sum_{j=1}^{n} |A_{i,j}|.$$

This norm is also called the *maximum absolute row sum norm*. $\quad \blacksquare$

1.9 Cartesian Product of Vector Spaces

Given m vector spaces $\mathbb{E}_1, \mathbb{E}_2, \ldots, \mathbb{E}_m$ equipped with inner products $\langle \cdot, \cdot \rangle_{\mathbb{E}_i}$, their Cartesian product $\mathbb{E}_1 \times \mathbb{E}_2 \times \cdots \times \mathbb{E}_m$ is the vector space of all m-tuples $(\mathbf{v}_1, \mathbf{v}_2, \ldots, \mathbf{v}_m)$ equipped with the component-wise addition between vectors:

$$(\mathbf{v}_1, \mathbf{v}_2, \ldots, \mathbf{v}_m) + (\mathbf{w}_1, \mathbf{w}_2, \ldots, \mathbf{w}_m) = (\mathbf{v}_1 + \mathbf{w}_1, \mathbf{v}_2 + \mathbf{w}_2, \ldots, \mathbf{v}_m + \mathbf{w}_m)$$

and the scalar-vector multiplication operation given by

$$\alpha(\mathbf{v}_1, \mathbf{v}_2, \ldots, \mathbf{v}_m) = (\alpha\mathbf{v}_1, \alpha\mathbf{v}_2, \ldots, \alpha\mathbf{v}_m).$$

The inner product in the Cartesian product space is defined as

$$\langle (\mathbf{v}_1, \mathbf{v}_2, \ldots, \mathbf{v}_m), (\mathbf{w}_1, \mathbf{w}_2, \ldots, \mathbf{w}_m) \rangle_{\mathbb{E}_1 \times \mathbb{E}_2 \times \cdots \times \mathbb{E}_m} = \sum_{i=1}^{m} \langle \mathbf{v}_i, \mathbf{w}_i \rangle_{\mathbb{E}_i}. \quad (1.1)$$

The space $\mathbb{R} \times \mathbb{R}$, for example, consists of all two-dimensional row vectors, so in that respect it is different than $\mathbb{R}^2$, which comprises all two-dimensional *column* vectors. However, with only a slight abuse of notation, we will occasionally refer to $\mathbb{R} \times \mathbb{R}$ as $\mathbb{R}^2$.

Suppose that $\mathbb{E}_1, \mathbb{E}_2, \ldots, \mathbb{E}_m$ are vector spaces with endowed norms $\| \cdot \|_{\mathbb{E}_1}, \| \cdot \|_{\mathbb{E}_2}, \ldots, \| \cdot \|_{\mathbb{E}_m}$, respectively. There are many ways to define a norm on the Cartesian product space $\mathbb{E}_1 \times \mathbb{E}_2 \times \cdots \times \mathbb{E}_m$. For example, for any $p \geq 1$, we can define the composite l_p-norm as

$$\|(\mathbf{u}_1, \mathbf{u}_2, \ldots, \mathbf{u}_m)\| = \sqrt[p]{\sum_{i=1}^{m} \|\mathbf{u}_i\|_{\mathbb{E}_i}^p}.$$

Another norm is a composite weighted l_2-norm:

$$\|(\mathbf{u}_1, \mathbf{u}_2, \ldots, \mathbf{u}_m)\| = \sqrt{\sum_{i=1}^{m} \omega_i \|\mathbf{u}_i\|_{\mathbb{E}_i}^2},$$

where $\omega_1, \omega_2, \ldots, \omega_m$ are given positive real numbers.

We will use the convention that if $\mathbb{E}_1, \mathbb{E}_2, \ldots, \mathbb{E}_m$ are Euclidean spaces, then $\mathbb{E}_1 \times \mathbb{E}_2 \times \cdots \times \mathbb{E}_m$ is also a Euclidean space, and consequently, by the definition (1.1) of the inner product in product spaces,

$$\|(\mathbf{u}_1, \mathbf{u}_2, \ldots, \mathbf{u}_m)\|_{\mathbb{E}_1 \times \mathbb{E}_2 \times \cdots \times \mathbb{E}_m} = \sqrt{\sum_{i=1}^{m} \|\mathbf{u}_i\|_{\mathbb{E}_i}^2}.$$

1.10   Linear Transformations

Given two vector spaces $\mathbb{E}$ and $\mathbb{V}$, a function $\mathcal{A} : \mathbb{E} \to \mathbb{V}$ is called a *linear transformation* if the following property holds for any $\mathbf{x}, \mathbf{y} \in \mathbb{E}$ and $\alpha, \beta \in \mathbb{R}$:

$$\mathcal{A}(\alpha \mathbf{x} + \beta \mathbf{y}) = \alpha \mathcal{A}(\mathbf{x}) + \beta \mathcal{A}(\mathbf{y}).$$

All linear transformations from $\mathbb{R}^n$ to $\mathbb{R}^m$ have the form

$$\mathcal{A}(\mathbf{x}) = \mathbf{A}\mathbf{x}$$

for some matrix $\mathbf{A} \in \mathbb{R}^{m \times n}$. All linear transformations from $\mathbb{R}^{m \times n}$ to $\mathbb{R}^k$ have the form

$$\mathcal{A}(\mathbf{X}) = \begin{pmatrix} \mathrm{Tr}(\mathbf{A}_1^T \mathbf{X}) \\ \mathrm{Tr}(\mathbf{A}_2^T \mathbf{X}) \\ \vdots \\ \mathrm{Tr}(\mathbf{A}_k^T \mathbf{X}) \end{pmatrix}$$

for some $\mathbf{A}_1, \mathbf{A}_2, \ldots, \mathbf{A}_k \in \mathbb{R}^{m \times n}$. The *identity transformation*, denoted by $\mathcal{I}$, is defined by the relation $\mathcal{I}(\mathbf{x}) = \mathbf{x}$ for all $\mathbf{x} \in \mathbb{E}$.

1.11 The Dual Space

A *linear functional* on a vector space $\mathbb{E}$ is a linear transformation from $\mathbb{E}$ to $\mathbb{R}$. Given a vector space $\mathbb{E}$, the set of all linear functionals on $\mathbb{E}$ is called the *dual space* and is denoted by $\mathbb{E}^*$. For inner product spaces, it is known that given a linear functional $f \in \mathbb{E}^*$, there always exists $\mathbf{v} \in \mathbb{E}$ such that

$$f(\mathbf{x}) = \langle \mathbf{v}, \mathbf{x} \rangle. \tag{1.2}$$

For the sake of simplicity of notation, we will represent the linear functional f given in (1.2) by the vector $\mathbf{v}$. This correspondence between linear functionals and elements in $\mathbb{E}$ leads us to consider the elements in $\mathbb{E}^*$ as exactly the same as those in $\mathbb{E}$. The inner product in $\mathbb{E}^*$ is the same as the inner product in $\mathbb{E}$. Essentially, the only difference between $\mathbb{E}$ and $\mathbb{E}^*$ will be in the choice of norms of each of the spaces. Suppose that $\mathbb{E}$ is endowed with a norm $\|\cdot\|$. Then the norm of the dual space, called the *dual norm*, is given by

$$\|\mathbf{y}\|_* \equiv \max_{\mathbf{x}} \{ \langle \mathbf{y}, \mathbf{x} \rangle : \|\mathbf{x}\| \leq 1 \}, \quad \mathbf{y} \in \mathbb{E}^*. \tag{1.3}$$

It is not difficult to show that the dual norm is indeed a norm. A useful property is that the maximum in (1.3) can be taken over the unit sphere rather than over the unit ball, meaning that the following formula is valid:

$$\|\mathbf{y}\|_* = \max_{\mathbf{x}} \{ \langle \mathbf{y}, \mathbf{x} \rangle : \|\mathbf{x}\| = 1 \}, \quad \mathbf{y} \in \mathbb{E}^*.$$

The definition of the dual norm readily implies the following generalized version of the Cauchy–Schwarz inequality.

Lemma 1.4 (generalized Cauchy–Schwarz inequality). *Let $\mathbb{E}$ be an inner product vector space endowed with a norm $\|\cdot\|$. Then*

$$|\langle \mathbf{y}, \mathbf{x} \rangle| \leq \|\mathbf{y}\|_* \|\mathbf{x}\| \text{ for any } \mathbf{y} \in \mathbb{E}^*, \mathbf{x} \in \mathbb{E}. \tag{1.4}$$

Proof. If $\mathbf{x} = \mathbf{0}$, the inequality is trivially satisfied. Otherwise, take $\tilde{\mathbf{x}} = \frac{\mathbf{x}}{\|\mathbf{x}\|}$. Obviously, $\|\tilde{\mathbf{x}}\| = 1$, and hence, by the definition of the dual norm, we have

$$\|\mathbf{y}\|_* \geq \langle \mathbf{y}, \tilde{\mathbf{x}} \rangle = \frac{1}{\|\mathbf{x}\|} \langle \mathbf{y}, \mathbf{x} \rangle,$$

showing that $\langle \mathbf{y}, \mathbf{x} \rangle \leq \|\mathbf{y}\|_* \|\mathbf{x}\|$. Plugging $-\mathbf{x}$ instead of $\mathbf{x}$ in the latter inequality, we obtain that $\langle \mathbf{y}, \mathbf{x} \rangle \geq -\|\mathbf{y}\|_* \|\mathbf{x}\|$, thus showing the validity of inequality (1.4). $\quad\square$

Another important result is that Euclidean norms are self-dual, meaning that $\|\cdot\| = \|\cdot\|_*$. Here of course we use our convention that the elements in the dual space $\mathbb{E}^*$ are the same as the elements in $\mathbb{E}$. We can thus write, in only a slight abuse of notation,[1] that for any Euclidean space $\mathbb{E}$, $\mathbb{E} = \mathbb{E}^*$.

---

[1] Disregarding the fact that the members of $\mathbb{E}^*$ are actually linear functionals on $\mathbb{E}$.

Example 1.5 (l_p-norms). Consider the space $\mathbb{R}^n$ endowed with the l_p-norm. When $p > 1$, the dual norm is the l_q-norm, where $q > 1$ is the number satisfying $\frac{1}{p} + \frac{1}{q} = 1$. When $p = 1$, the dual norm is the l_∞-norm, and vice versa—the dual norm of the l_∞-norm is the l_1-norm. ∎

Example 1.6 (Q-norms). Consider the space $\mathbb{R}^n$ endowed with the $\mathbf{Q}$-norm, where $\mathbf{Q} \in \mathbb{S}^n_{++}$. The dual norm of $\|\cdot\|_{\mathbf{Q}}$ is $\|\cdot\|_{\mathbf{Q}^{-1}}$, meaning

$$\|\mathbf{x}\|_{\mathbf{Q}^{-1}} = \sqrt{\mathbf{x}^T \mathbf{Q}^{-1} \mathbf{x}}.$$

As an example, consider the case where $\mathbf{Q}$ is diagonal: $\mathbf{Q} = \mathrm{diag}(w_1, w_2, \dots, w_n)$ with $w_1, w_2, \dots, w_n > 0$. The $\mathbf{Q}$-norm in this case takes the form

$$\|\mathbf{x}\| = \sqrt{\sum_{i=1}^n w_i x_i^2},$$

and its dual norm is

$$\|\mathbf{x}\|_* = \sqrt{\sum_{i=1}^n \frac{1}{w_i} x_i^2}. \quad ∎$$

Example 1.7 (dual norm of Cartesian products of spaces). Consider the space $\mathbb{E} = \mathbb{E}_1 \times \mathbb{E}_1 \times \cdots \times \mathbb{E}_m$, where $\mathbb{E}_1, \mathbb{E}_2, \dots, \mathbb{E}_m$ are inner product vector spaces with norms $\|\cdot\|_{\mathbb{E}_1}, \|\cdot\|_{\mathbb{E}_2}, \dots, \|\cdot\|_{\mathbb{E}_m}$, respectively. Recall that we assume that the inner product in the product space is given by

$$\langle (\mathbf{v}_1, \mathbf{v}_2, \dots, \mathbf{v}_m), (\mathbf{w}_1, \mathbf{w}_2, \dots, \mathbf{w}_m) \rangle = \sum_{i=1}^m \langle \mathbf{v}_i, \mathbf{w}_i \rangle.$$

The dual space to $\mathbb{E}_1 \times \mathbb{E}_2 \times \cdots \times \mathbb{E}_m$ is the product space $\mathbb{E}_1^* \times \mathbb{E}_2^* \times \cdots \times \mathbb{E}_m^*$ with endowed norm defined as usual in dual spaces. For example, suppose that the norm on the product space is the composite weighted l_2-norm:

$$\|(\mathbf{u}_1, \mathbf{u}_2, \dots, \mathbf{u}_m)\| = \sqrt{\sum_{i=1}^m \omega_i \|\mathbf{u}_i\|_{\mathbb{E}_i}^2}, \quad \mathbf{u}_i \in \mathbb{E}_i, i = 1, 2, \dots, p,$$

where $\omega_1, \omega_2, \dots, \omega_m > 0$ are given positive weights. Then it is simple to show that the dual norm in this case is given by

$$\|(\mathbf{v}_1, \mathbf{v}_2, \dots, \mathbf{v}_m)\|_* = \sqrt{\sum_{i=1}^m \frac{1}{\omega_i} \|\mathbf{v}_i\|_{\mathbb{E}_i^*}^2}, \quad \mathbf{v}_i \in \mathbb{E}_i^*, i = 1, 2, \dots, p.$$

where $\|\cdot\|_{\mathbb{E}_i^*}$ is the dual norm to $\|\cdot\|_{\mathbb{E}_i}$, namely, the norm of the dual space $\mathbb{E}_i^*$. ∎

1.12   The Bidual Space

Given a vector space $\mathbb{E}$, the dual space $\mathbb{E}^*$ is also a vector space, and we can also consider its dual space, namely, $\mathbb{E}^{**}$. This is the so-called *bidual* space. In the setting of finite dimensional spaces, the bidual space is the same as the original space (under our convention that the elements in the dual space are the same as the elements in the original space), and the corresponding norm (bidual norm) is the same as the original norm.

1.13 Adjoint Transformations

Given two inner product vector spaces $\mathbb{E}, \mathbb{V}$ and a linear transformation $\mathcal{A}$ from $\mathbb{V}$ to $\mathbb{E}$, the *adjoint transformation*, denoted by $\mathcal{A}^T$, is the transformation from $\mathbb{E}^*$ to $\mathbb{V}^*$ defined by the relation

$$\langle \mathbf{y}, \mathcal{A}(\mathbf{x}) \rangle = \langle \mathcal{A}^T(\mathbf{y}), \mathbf{x} \rangle$$

for any $\mathbf{x} \in \mathbb{V}, \mathbf{y} \in \mathbb{E}^*$. When $\mathbb{V} = \mathbb{R}^n, \mathbb{E} = \mathbb{R}^m$ (endowed with the dot product), and $\mathcal{A}(\mathbf{x}) = \mathbf{A}\mathbf{x}$ for some matrix $\mathbf{A} \in \mathbb{R}^{m \times n}$, then the adjoint transformation is given by $\mathcal{A}^T(\mathbf{x}) = \mathbf{A}^T\mathbf{x}$.

Example 1.8 (adjoint of a transformation from $\mathbb{R}^{m \times n}$ to $\mathbb{R}^k$). Consider now a linear transformation from the space $\mathbb{R}^{m \times n}$ to $\mathbb{R}^k$. As was already mentioned in Section 1.10, such a transformation has the form

$$\mathcal{A}(\mathbf{X}) = \begin{pmatrix} \mathrm{Tr}(\mathbf{A}_1^T \mathbf{X}) \\ \mathrm{Tr}(\mathbf{A}_2^T \mathbf{X}) \\ \vdots \\ \mathrm{Tr}(\mathbf{A}_k^T \mathbf{X}) \end{pmatrix},$$

where $\mathbf{A}_i \in \mathbb{R}^{m \times n}$ are given matrices. The adjoint transformation $\mathcal{A}^T$ will be a transformation from $\mathbb{R}^k$ to $\mathbb{R}^{m \times n}$. To find it, let us write the defining relation of the adjoint operator:

$$\langle \mathbf{y}, \mathcal{A}(\mathbf{X}) \rangle = \langle \mathcal{A}^T(\mathbf{y}), \mathbf{X} \rangle \text{ for all } \mathbf{X} \in \mathbb{R}^{m \times n}, \mathbf{y} \in \mathbb{R}^k,$$

which is the same as (recall that unless otherwise stated, the inner products in $\mathbb{R}^{m \times n}$ and $\mathbb{R}^k$ are the dot products)

$$\sum_{i=1}^{k} y_i \mathrm{Tr}(\mathbf{A}_i^T \mathbf{X}) = \langle \mathcal{A}^T(\mathbf{y}), \mathbf{X} \rangle \text{ for all } \mathbf{X} \in \mathbb{R}^{m \times n}, \mathbf{y} \in \mathbb{R}^k,$$

that is,

$$\mathrm{Tr}\left(\left[\sum_{i=1}^{k} y_i \mathbf{A}_i \right]^T \mathbf{X} \right) = \langle \mathcal{A}^T(\mathbf{y}), \mathbf{X} \rangle \text{ for all } \mathbf{X} \in \mathbb{R}^{m \times n}, \mathbf{y} \in \mathbb{R}^k.$$

Obviously, the above relation implies that the adjoint transformation is given by

$$\mathcal{A}^T(\mathbf{y}) = \sum_{i=1}^{k} y_i \mathbf{A}_i. \quad \blacksquare$$

The adjoint of the adjoint transformation is the original transformation: $(\mathcal{A}^T)^T$ $= \mathcal{A}$. It also holds that whenever $\mathcal{A}$ is an invertible transformation,

$$(\mathcal{A}^T)^{-1} = (\mathcal{A}^{-1})^T.$$

1.14   Norms of Linear Transformations

Let $\mathcal{A} : \mathbb{E} \to \mathbb{V}$ be a linear transformation from a vector space $\mathbb{E}$ to a vector space $\mathbb{V}$. Assume that $\mathbb{E}$ and $\mathbb{V}$ are endowed with the norms $\|\cdot\|_\mathbb{E}$ and $\|\cdot\|_\mathbb{V}$, respectively. The norm of the linear transformation is defined by

$$\|\mathcal{A}\| \equiv \max\{\|\mathcal{A}(\mathbf{x})\|_\mathbb{V} : \|\mathbf{x}\|_\mathbb{E} \leq 1\}.$$

It is not difficult to show that $\|\mathcal{A}\| = \|\mathcal{A}^T\|$. There is a close connection between the notion of induced norms discussed in Section 1.8.2 and norms of linear transformations. Specifically, suppose that $\mathcal{A}$ is a linear transformation from $\mathbb{R}^n$ to $\mathbb{R}^m$ given by

$$\mathcal{A}(\mathbf{x}) = \mathbf{Ax}, \tag{1.5}$$

where $\mathbf{A} \in \mathbb{R}^{m \times n}$, and assume that $\mathbb{R}^n$ and $\mathbb{R}^m$ are endowed with the norms $\|\cdot\|_a$ and $\|\cdot\|_b$, respectively. Then $\|\mathcal{A}\| = \|\mathbf{A}\|_{a,b}$, meaning that the induced norm of a matrix is actually the norm of the corresponding linear transformation given by the relation (1.5).

Chapter 2

Extended Real-Valued Functions

> **Underlying Space:** Recall that in this book, the underlying spaces (denoted usually by $\mathbb{E}$ or $\mathbb{V}$) are finite-dimensional inner product vector spaces with inner product $\langle \cdot, \cdot \rangle$ and norm $\| \cdot \|$.

2.1 Extended Real-Valued Functions and Closedness

An *extended real-valued function* is a function defined over the entire underlying space that can take any real value, as well as the infinite values $-\infty$ and ∞. Since infinite values are allowed, we also define the appropriate arithmetic operations with $-\infty$ and ∞ as follows:

$$a + \infty = \infty + a \ \ = \infty \quad (-\infty < a < \infty),$$

$$a - \infty = -\infty + a \ \ = -\infty \quad (-\infty < a < \infty),$$

$$a \cdot \infty = \infty \cdot a \ \ = \infty \quad (0 < a < \infty),$$

$$a \cdot (-\infty) = (-\infty) \cdot a \ \ = -\infty \quad (0 < a < \infty),$$

$$a \cdot \infty = \infty \cdot a \ \ = -\infty \quad (-\infty < a < 0),$$

$$a \cdot (-\infty) = (-\infty) \cdot a \ \ = \infty \quad (-\infty < a < 0),$$

$$0 \cdot \infty = \infty \cdot 0 = 0 \cdot (-\infty) = (-\infty) \cdot 0 \ \ = 0.$$

In a sense, the only "unnatural" rule is the last one, since the expression "$0 \cdot \infty$" is considered to be undefined in some branches of mathematics, but in the context of extended real-valued functions, defining it as zero is the "correct" choice in the sense of consistency. We will also use the following natural order between finite and infinite numbers:

$$\infty > a \quad (-\infty \le a < \infty),$$
$$-\infty < a \quad (-\infty < a \le \infty).$$

For an extended real-valued function $f : \mathbb{E} \to [-\infty, \infty]$, the *effective domain* or just the *domain* is the set

$$\text{dom}(f) = \{\mathbf{x} \in \mathbb{E} : f(\mathbf{x}) < \infty\}.$$

The notation "$f : \mathbb{E} \to [-\infty, \infty]$" means that f is (potentially) extended real-valued (even if not explicitly stated). The notation "$f : \mathbb{E} \to (-\infty, \infty]$" means that f is extended real-valued and does not attain the value $-\infty$.

The simplest examples of extended real-valued functions are indicators.

Example 2.1 (indicator functions). For any subset $C \subseteq \mathbb{E}$, the *indicator function* of C is defined to be the extended real-valued function

$$\delta_C(\mathbf{x}) = \begin{cases} 0, & \mathbf{x} \in C, \\ \infty, & \mathbf{x} \notin C. \end{cases} \qquad \blacksquare$$

We obviously have

$$\text{dom}(\delta_C) = C.$$

The *epigraph* of an extended real-valued function $f : \mathbb{E} \to [-\infty, \infty]$ is defined by

$$\text{epi}(f) = \{(\mathbf{x}, y) : f(\mathbf{x}) \leq y, \mathbf{x} \in \mathbb{E}, y \in \mathbb{R}\}.$$

The epigraph is a subset of $\mathbb{E} \times \mathbb{R}$. Note that if $(\mathbf{x}, y) \in \text{epi}(f)$, then obviously $\mathbf{x} \in \text{dom}(f)$. A function $f : \mathbb{E} \to [-\infty, \infty]$ is called *proper* if it does not attain the value $-\infty$ and there exists at least one $\mathbf{x} \in \mathbb{E}$ such that $f(\mathbf{x}) < \infty$, meaning that $\text{dom}(f)$ is nonempty.

The notion of closedness will play an important role in much of the analysis in this book.

Definition 2.2 (closed functions). *A function $f : \mathbb{E} \to [-\infty, \infty]$ is* **closed** *if its epigraph is closed.*

The indicator function δ_C is closed if and only if its underlying set C is closed.

Proposition 2.3 (closedness of indicators of closed sets). *The indicator function δ_C is closed if and only if C is a closed set.*

Proof. The epigraph of δ_C is given by

$$\text{epi}(\delta_C) = \{(\mathbf{x}, y) \in \mathbb{E} \times \mathbb{R} : \delta_C(\mathbf{x}) \leq y\} = C \times \mathbb{R}_+,$$

which is evidently closed if and only if C is closed. $\quad\square$

We thus obtained in particular that the domain of a closed indicator function is necessarily a closed set. However, in general, the domain of a closed function might not be closed. A classical example for this observation is given below.

Example 2.4. Consider the function $f : \mathbb{R} \to [-\infty, \infty]$ given by

$$f(x) = \begin{cases} \frac{1}{x}, & x > 0, \\ \infty, & \text{else.} \end{cases}$$

The domain of the function, which is the open interval $(0, \infty)$, is obviously not closed, but the function is closed since its epigraph

$$\mathrm{epi}(f) = \{(x, y) : xy \geq 1, x > 0\}$$

is a closed set; see Figure 2.1. ∎

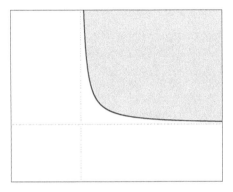

Figure 2.1. *The epigraph of the function $f(x) = \frac{1}{x}$ for $x > 0$ and ∞ otherwise.*

A property that will be later shown to be equivalent to closedness is *lower semicontinuity*.

Definition 2.5 (lower semicontinuity). *A function $f : \mathbb{E} \to [-\infty, \infty]$ is called* **lower semicontinuous at** $\mathbf{x} \in \mathbb{E}$ *if*

$$f(\mathbf{x}) \leq \liminf_{n \to \infty} f(\mathbf{x}_n)$$

for any sequence $\{\mathbf{x}_n\}_{n \geq 1} \subseteq \mathbb{E}$ for which $\mathbf{x}_n \to \mathbf{x}$ as $n \to \infty$. A function $f : \mathbb{E} \to [-\infty, \infty]$ is called **lower semicontinuous** *if it is lower semicontinuous at each point in $\mathbb{E}$.*

For any $\alpha \in \mathbb{R}$, the α-*level set* of a function $f : \mathbb{E} \to [-\infty, \infty]$ is the set

$$\mathrm{Lev}(f, \alpha) = \{\mathbf{x} \in \mathbb{E} : f(\mathbf{x}) \leq \alpha\}.$$

The following theorem shows that closedness and lower semicontinuity are equivalent properties, and they are both equivalent to the property that all the level sets of the function are closed.

Theorem 2.6 (equivalence of closedness, lower semicontinuity, and closedness of level sets). *Let $f : \mathbb{E} \to [-\infty, \infty]$. Then the following three claims are equivalent:*

(i) *f is lower semicontinuous.*

(ii) *f is closed.*

(iii) *For any $\alpha \in \mathbb{R}$, the level set*

$$\mathrm{Lev}(f, \alpha) = \{\mathbf{x} \in \mathbb{E} : f(\mathbf{x}) \leq \alpha\}$$

is closed.

Proof. (i $\Rightarrow$ ii) Suppose that f is lower semicontinuous. We will show that $\mathrm{epi}(f)$ is closed. For that, take $\{(\mathbf{x}_n, y_n)\}_{n \geq 1} \subseteq \mathrm{epi}(f)$ such that $(\mathbf{x}_n, y_n) \to (\mathbf{x}^*, y^*)$ as $n \to \infty$. Then for any $n \geq 1$,

$$f(\mathbf{x}_n) \leq y_n.$$

Therefore, by the lower semicontinuity of f at $\mathbf{x}^*$, we have

$$f(\mathbf{x}^*) \leq \liminf_{n \to \infty} f(\mathbf{x}_n) \leq \liminf_{n \to \infty} y_n = y^*,$$

showing that $(\mathbf{x}^*, y^*) \in \mathrm{epi}(f)$ and hence that f is closed.

(ii $\Rightarrow$ iii) Suppose that f is closed, namely, that $\mathrm{epi}(f)$ is closed. Let $\alpha \in \mathbb{R}$. We will show that $\mathrm{Lev}(f, \alpha)$ is closed. If $\mathrm{Lev}(f, \alpha) = \emptyset$, we are done. Otherwise, take a sequence $\{\mathbf{x}_n\}_{n \geq 1} \subseteq \mathrm{Lev}(f, \alpha)$ that converges to $\bar{\mathbf{x}}$. Obviously $(\mathbf{x}_n, \alpha) \in \mathrm{epi}(f)$ for any n and $(\mathbf{x}_n, \alpha) \to (\bar{\mathbf{x}}, \alpha)$ as $n \to \infty$. By the closedness of $\mathrm{epi}(f)$, it follows that $(\bar{\mathbf{x}}, \alpha) \in \mathrm{epi}(f)$, establishing the fact that $\bar{\mathbf{x}} \in \mathrm{Lev}(f, \alpha)$.

(iii $\Rightarrow$ i) Suppose that all the level sets of f are closed. We will show that it is lower semicontinuous. Assume by contradiction that f is not lower semicontinuous, meaning that there exists $\mathbf{x}^* \in \mathbb{E}$ and $\{\mathbf{x}_n\}_{n \geq 1} \subseteq \mathbb{E}$ such that $\mathbf{x}_n \to \mathbf{x}^*$ and $\liminf_{n \to \infty} f(\mathbf{x}_n) < f(\mathbf{x}^*)$. Take α that satisfies

$$\liminf_{n \to \infty} f(\mathbf{x}_n) < \alpha < f(\mathbf{x}^*). \tag{2.1}$$

Then there exists a subsequence $\{\mathbf{x}_{n_k}\}_{k \geq 1}$ such that $f(\mathbf{x}_{n_k}) \leq \alpha$ for all $k \geq 1$. By the closedness of the level set $\mathrm{Lev}(f, \alpha)$ and the fact that $\mathbf{x}_{n_k} \to \mathbf{x}^*$ as $k \to \infty$, it follows that $f(\mathbf{x}^*) \leq \alpha$, which is a contradiction to (2.1), showing that (iii) implies (i). $\quad\square$

The next result shows that closedness of functions is preserved under affine change of variables, summation, multiplication by a nonnegative number, and maximization. Before stating the theorem, we note that in this book we will not use the inf/sup notation but rather use only the min/max notation, where the usage of this notation does not imply that the maximum or minimum is actually attained.

Theorem 2.7 (operations preserving closedness).

(a) *Let* $\mathcal{A} : \mathbb{E} \to \mathbb{V}$ *be a linear transformation from* $\mathbb{E}$ *to* $\mathbb{V}$ *and* $\mathbf{b} \in \mathbb{V}$ *and let* $f : \mathbb{V} \to [-\infty, \infty]$ *be an extended real-valued closed function. Then the function* $g : \mathbb{E} \to [-\infty, \infty]$ *given by*

$$g(\mathbf{x}) = f(\mathcal{A}(\mathbf{x}) + \mathbf{b})$$

is closed.

(b) *Let* $f_1, f_2, \ldots, f_m : \mathbb{E} \to (-\infty, \infty]$ *be extended real-valued closed functions and let* $\alpha_1, \alpha_2, \ldots, \alpha_m \in \mathbb{R}_+$. *Then the function* $f = \sum_{i=1}^{m} \alpha_i f_i$ *is closed.*

(c) *Let* $f_i : \mathbb{E} \to (-\infty, \infty], i \in I$ *be extended real-valued closed functions, where* I *is a given index set. Then the function*

$$f(\mathbf{x}) = \max_{i \in I} f_i(\mathbf{x})$$

is closed.

Proof. (a) To show that g is closed, take a sequence $\{(\mathbf{x}_n, y_n)\}_{n \geq 1} \subseteq \mathrm{epi}(g)$ such that $(\mathbf{x}_n, y_n) \to (\mathbf{x}^*, y^*)$ as $n \to \infty$, where $\mathbf{x}^* \in \mathbb{E}$ and $y^* \in \mathbb{R}$. The relation $\{(\mathbf{x}_n, y_n)\}_{n \geq 1} \subseteq \mathrm{epi}(g)$ can be written equivalently as

$$f(\mathcal{A}(\mathbf{x}_n) + \mathbf{b}) \leq y_n \text{ for all } n \geq 1.$$

Therefore, $(\mathcal{A}(\mathbf{x}_n) + \mathbf{b}, y_n) \in \mathrm{epi}(f)$. Hence, since f is closed and $\mathcal{A}(\mathbf{x}_n) + \mathbf{b} \to \mathcal{A}(\mathbf{x}^*) + \mathbf{b}, y_n \to y^*$ as $n \to \infty$ (by the continuity of linear transformations), it follows that $(\mathcal{A}(\mathbf{x}^*) + \mathbf{b}, y^*) \in \mathrm{epi}(f)$, meaning that

$$f(\mathcal{A}(\mathbf{x}^*) + \mathbf{b}) \leq y^*,$$

which is the same as the relation $(\mathbf{x}^*, y^*) \in \mathrm{epi}(g)$. We have shown that $\mathrm{epi}(g)$ is closed or, equivalently, that g is closed.

(b) We will prove that f is lower semicontinuous, which by Theorem 2.6 is equivalent to the closedness of f. Let $\{\mathbf{x}_n\}_{n \geq 1}$ be a sequence converging to $\mathbf{x}^*$. Then by the lower semicontinuity of f_i, for any $i = 1, 2, \ldots, m$,

$$f_i(\mathbf{x}^*) \leq \liminf_{n \to \infty} f_i(\mathbf{x}_n).$$

Multiplying the above inequality by α_i and summing for $i = 1, 2, \ldots, m$ gives

$$\left(\sum_{i=1}^{m} \alpha_i f_i \right) (\mathbf{x}^*) \leq \sum_{i=1}^{m} \liminf_{n \to \infty} \alpha_i f_i(\mathbf{x}_n) \leq \liminf_{n \to \infty} \left(\sum_{i=1}^{m} \alpha_i f_i \right) (\mathbf{x}_n),$$

where in the last inequality we used the fact that for any two sequences of real numbers $\{a_n\}_{n \geq 1}$ and $\{b_n\}_{n \geq 1}$, it holds that

$$\liminf_{n \to \infty} a_n + \liminf_{n \to \infty} b_n \leq \liminf_{n \to \infty} (a_n + b_n).$$

A simple induction argument shows that this property holds for an arbitrary number of sequences. We have thus established the lower semicontinuity and hence closedness of $\sum_{i=1}^{m} \alpha_i f_i$.

(c) Since f_i is closed for any $i \in I$, it follows that $\mathrm{epi}(f_i)$ is closed for any i, and hence $\mathrm{epi}(f) = \bigcap_{i \in I} \mathrm{epi}(f_i)$ is closed as an intersection of closed sets, implying that f is closed. $\square$

2.2   Closedness versus Continuity

A relation between continuity and closedness is described in the following theorem stating that if an extended real-valued function is continuous over its domain,[2] which is assumed to be closed, then it is closed.

Theorem 2.8. *Let $f : \mathbb{E} \to (-\infty, \infty]$ be an extended real-valued function that is continuous over its domain and suppose that $\mathrm{dom}(f)$ is closed. Then f is closed.*

Proof. To show that $\mathrm{epi}(f)$ is closed (which is the same as saying that f is closed), take a sequence $\{(\mathbf{x}_n, y_n)\}_{n\geq 1} \subseteq \mathrm{epi}(f)$ for which $(\mathbf{x}_n, y_n) \to (\mathbf{x}^*, y^*)$ as $n \to \infty$ for some $\mathbf{x}^* \in \mathbb{E}$ and $y \in \mathbb{R}$. Since $\{\mathbf{x}_n\}_{n\geq 1} \subseteq \mathrm{dom}(f)$, $\mathbf{x}_n \to \mathbf{x}^*$ and $\mathrm{dom}(f)$ is closed, it follows that $\mathbf{x}^* \in \mathrm{dom}(f)$. By the definition of the epigraph, we have for all $n \geq 1$,

$$f(\mathbf{x}_n) \leq y_n. \tag{2.2}$$

Since f is continuous over $\mathrm{dom}(f)$, and in particular at $\mathbf{x}^*$, it follows by taking n to ∞ in (2.2) that

$$f(\mathbf{x}^*) \leq y^*,$$

showing that $(\mathbf{x}^*, y^*) \in \mathrm{epi}(f)$, thus establishing the closedness of $\mathrm{epi}(f)$. $\square$

In particular, any real-valued continuous function over $\mathbb{E}$ is closed.

Corollary 2.9. *Let $f : \mathbb{E} \to \mathbb{R}$ be continuous. Then f is closed.*

The above results demonstrate that there is a connection between continuity and closedness. However, these two notions are different, as the following example illustrates.

Example 2.10. Consider the function $f_\alpha : \mathbb{R} \to (-\infty, \infty]$ given by

$$f_\alpha(x) = \begin{cases} \alpha, & x = 0, \\ x, & 0 < x \leq 1, \\ \infty, & \text{else.} \end{cases}$$

---

[2]A function $g : \mathbb{E} \to (-\infty, \infty]$ is *continuous over its domain* if for any sequence $\{\mathbf{x}_n\}_{n\geq 1} \subseteq \mathrm{dom}(g)$ satisfying $\mathbf{x}_n \to \mathbf{x}^*$ as $n \to \infty$ for some $\mathbf{x}^* \in \mathrm{dom}(g)$, it holds that $g(\mathbf{x}_n) \to g(\mathbf{x}^*)$ as $n \to \infty$.

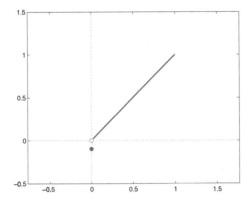

Figure 2.2. *An example of a closed function, which is not continuous over its domain.*

This function is closed if and only if $\alpha \leq 0$, and it is continuous over its domain if and only if $\alpha = 0$. Thus, the function $f_{-0.1}$, plotted in Figure 2.2, is closed but not continuous over its domain. ∎

Example 2.11 (l_0-norm). Consider the l_0-norm function $f : \mathbb{R}^n \to \mathbb{R}$ given by

$$f(\mathbf{x}) = \|\mathbf{x}\|_0 \equiv \#\{i : x_i \neq 0\}.$$

That is, $\|\mathbf{x}\|_0$ is the number of nonzero elements in $\mathbf{x}$. Note the l_0-norm is actually not a norm. It does not satisfy the homogeneity property. Nevertheless, this terminology is widely used in the literature, and we will therefore adopt it. Although f is obviously not continuous, it is closed. To show this, note that

$$f(\mathbf{x}) = \sum_{i=1}^{n} I(x_i),$$

where $I : \mathbb{R} \to \{0, 1\}$ is given by

$$I(y) = \begin{cases} 0, & y = 0, \\ 1, & y \neq 0. \end{cases}$$

The function I is closed since its level sets, which are given by

$$\mathrm{Lev}(I, \alpha) = \begin{cases} \emptyset, & \alpha < 0, \\ \{0\}, & \alpha \in [0, 1), \\ \mathbb{R}, & \alpha \geq 1, \end{cases}$$

are closed sets. Therefore, f, as a sum of closed functions, is closed (Theorem 2.7(b)). ∎

It is well known that a continuous function over a nonempty compact[3] set attains a minimum. This is the well-known Weierstrass theorem. We will now show that this property also holds for closed functions.

Theorem 2.12 (Weierstrass theorem for closed functions). *Let $f : \mathbb{E} \to (-\infty, \infty]$ be a proper closed function and assume that C is a compact set satisfying $C \cap \mathrm{dom}(f) \neq \emptyset$. Then*

(a) *f is bounded below over C.*

(b) *f attains its minimal value over C.*

Proof. (a) Suppose by contradiction that f is not bounded below over C. Then there exists a sequence $\{\mathbf{x}_n\}_{n \geq 1} \subseteq C$ such that

$$\lim_{n \to \infty} f(\mathbf{x}_n) = -\infty. \tag{2.3}$$

By the Bolzano–Weierstrass theorem, since C is compact, there exists a subsequence $\{\mathbf{x}_{n_k}\}_{k \geq 1}$ that converges to a point $\bar{\mathbf{x}} \in C$. By Theorem 2.6, f is lower semicontinuous, and hence

$$f(\bar{\mathbf{x}}) \leq \liminf_{k \to \infty} f(\mathbf{x}_{n_k}),$$

which is a contradiction to (2.3).

(b) Denote by f_{opt} the minimal value of f over C. Then there exists a sequence $\{\mathbf{x}_n\}_{n \geq 1}$ for which $f(\mathbf{x}_n) \to f_{\mathrm{opt}}$ as $n \to \infty$. As before, take a subsequence $\{\mathbf{x}_{n_k}\}_{k \geq 1}$ that converges to some point $\bar{\mathbf{x}} \in C$. By the lower semicontinuity of f, it follows that

$$f(\bar{\mathbf{x}}) \leq \lim_{k \to \infty} f(\mathbf{x}_{n_k}) = f_{\mathrm{opt}},$$

showing that $\bar{\mathbf{x}}$ is a minimizer of f over C.   □

When the set C in the premise of Theorem 2.12 is not compact, the Weierstrass theorem does not guarantee the attainment of a minimizer, but attainment of a minimizer can be shown when the compactness of C is replaced by closedness if the function has a property called *coerciveness*.

Definition 2.13 (coerciveness). *A proper function $f : \mathbb{E} \to (-\infty, \infty]$ is called* **coercive** *if*

$$\lim_{\|\mathbf{x}\| \to \infty} f(\mathbf{x}) = \infty.$$

An important property of closed coercive functions is that they possess a minimizer on any closed set that has a nonempty intersection with the domain of the function.

Theorem 2.14 (attainment under coerciveness). *Let $f : \mathbb{E} \to (-\infty, \infty]$ be a proper closed and coercive function and let $S \subseteq \mathbb{E}$ be a nonempty closed set satisfying $S \cap \mathrm{dom}(f) \neq \emptyset$. Then f attains its minimal value over S.*

---

[3]A set is called *compact* if it is closed and bounded.

Proof. Let $\mathbf{x}_0$ be an arbitrary point in $S \cap \mathrm{dom}(f)$. By the coerciveness of f, there exists an $M > 0$ such that

$$f(\mathbf{x}) > f(\mathbf{x}_0) \text{ for any } \mathbf{x} \text{ satisfying } \|\mathbf{x}\| > M. \qquad (2.4)$$

Since any minimizer $\mathbf{x}^*$ of f over S satisfies $f(\mathbf{x}^*) \leq f(\mathbf{x}_0)$, it follows from (2.4) that the set of minimizers of f over S is the same as the set of minimizers of f over $S \cap B_{\|\cdot\|}[\mathbf{0}, M]$, which is compact (both sets are closed, and $B_{\|\cdot\|}[\mathbf{0}, M]$ is bounded) and nonempty (as it contains $\mathbf{x}_0$). Therefore, by the Weierstrass theorem for closed functions (Theorem 2.12), there exists a minimizer of f over $S \cap B[\mathbf{0}, M]$ and hence also over S. $\square$

2.3 Convex Functions

2.3.1 Definition and Basic Properties

Like closedness, the definition of convexity for extended real-valued functions can be written in terms of the epigraph.

Definition 2.15 (convex functions). *An extended real-valued function $f : \mathbb{E} \to [-\infty, \infty]$ is called* **convex** *if* $\mathrm{epi}(f)$ *is a convex set.*

It is not difficult to show that a proper extended real-valued function $f : \mathbb{E} \to (-\infty, \infty]$ is convex if and only if $\mathrm{dom}(f)$ is convex and the restriction of f to $\mathrm{dom}(f)$ is convex over $\mathrm{dom}(f)$ in the sense of convexity of real-valued functions over convex domains. Using this observation, we conclude that a proper extended real-valued function f is convex if and only if

$$f(\lambda \mathbf{x} + (1 - \lambda)\mathbf{y}) \leq \lambda f(\mathbf{x}) + (1 - \lambda)f(\mathbf{y}) \text{ for all } \mathbf{x}, \mathbf{y} \in \mathbb{E}, \lambda \in [0, 1], \qquad (2.5)$$

or, equivalently, if and only if $\mathrm{dom}(f)$ is convex and (2.5) is satisfied for any $\mathbf{x}, \mathbf{y} \in \mathrm{dom}(f)$ and $\lambda \in [0, 1]$. Inequality (2.5) is a special case of *Jensen's inequality*, stating that for any $\mathbf{x}_1, \mathbf{x}_2, \ldots, \mathbf{x}_k \in \mathbb{E}$ and $\boldsymbol{\lambda} \in \Delta_k$, the following inequality holds:

$$f\left(\sum_{i=1}^{k} \lambda_i \mathbf{x}_i\right) \leq \sum_{i=1}^{k} \lambda_i f(\mathbf{x}_i).$$

There are several operations that preserve convexity of extended real-valued convex functions. Some of them are summarized in Theorem 2.16 below. The proof can be easily deduced by combining two facts: (i) the same properties are known to hold for real-valued convex functions defined on a given convex domain, and (ii) the observation that a proper extended real-valued function is convex if and only if its domain is convex and its restriction to its domain is a real-valued convex function.

Theorem 2.16 (operations preserving convexity).

(a) *Let $\mathcal{A} : \mathbb{E} \to \mathbb{V}$ be a linear transformation from $\mathbb{E}$ to $\mathbb{V}$ (two underlying vector spaces) and $\mathbf{b} \in \mathbb{V}$, and let $f : \mathbb{V} \to (-\infty, \infty]$ be an extended real-valued* *convex function. Then the extended real-valued function $g : \mathbb{E} \to (-\infty, \infty]$ given by*

$$g(\mathbf{x}) = f(\mathcal{A}(\mathbf{x}) + \mathbf{b})$$

is convex.

(b) *Let $f_1, f_2, \ldots, f_m : \mathbb{E} \to (-\infty, \infty]$ be extended real-valued convex functions, and let $\alpha_1, \alpha_2, \ldots, \alpha_m \in \mathbb{R}_+$. Then the function $\sum_{i=1}^m \alpha_i f_i$ is convex.*

(c) *Let $f_i : \mathbb{E} \to (-\infty, \infty], i \in I$, be extended real-valued convex functions, where I is a given index set. Then the function*

$$f(\mathbf{x}) = \max_{i \in I} f_i(\mathbf{x})$$

is convex.

Given a nonempty set $C \subseteq \mathbb{E}$, the *distance function to C* is defined by

$$d_C(\mathbf{x}) = \min_{\mathbf{y} \in C} \|\mathbf{x} - \mathbf{y}\|.$$

The next example shows that for Euclidean spaces, the function $\frac{1}{2} \left(\|\mathbf{x}\|^2 - d_C^2(\mathbf{x}) \right)$ is always convex, regardless of whether C is convex or not.

Example 2.17.[4] Suppose that the underlying space $\mathbb{E}$ is Euclidean (meaning that $\|\cdot\| = \sqrt{\langle \cdot, \cdot \rangle}$). Let $C \subseteq \mathbb{E}$ be a nonempty set, and consider the function

$$\varphi_C(\mathbf{x}) = \frac{1}{2} \left(\|\mathbf{x}\|^2 - d_C^2(\mathbf{x}) \right).$$

To show that φ_C is convex, note that

$$d_C^2(\mathbf{x}) = \min_{\mathbf{y} \in C} \|\mathbf{x} - \mathbf{y}\|^2 = \|\mathbf{x}\|^2 - \max_{\mathbf{y} \in C}[2\langle \mathbf{y}, \mathbf{x} \rangle - \|\mathbf{y}\|^2].$$

Hence,

$$\varphi_C(\mathbf{x}) = \max_{\mathbf{y} \in C} \left[\langle \mathbf{y}, \mathbf{x} \rangle - \frac{1}{2}\|\mathbf{y}\|^2 \right]. \tag{2.6}$$

Therefore, since φ_C is a maximization of affine—and hence convex—functions, by Theorem 2.16(c), it is necessarily convex. ∎

Another operation that preserves convexity is partial minimization of jointly convex functions.

Theorem 2.18 (convexity under partial minimization). *Let $f : \mathbb{E} \times \mathbb{V} \to (-\infty, \infty]$ be a convex function satisfying the following property:*

$$\text{for any } \mathbf{x} \in \mathbb{E} \text{ there exists } \mathbf{y} \in \mathbb{V} \text{ for which } f(\mathbf{x}, \mathbf{y}) < \infty. \tag{2.7}$$

---

[4]Example 2.17 is from Hiriart-Urruty and Lemaréchal [67, Example 2.1.4].

Let[5] $g : \mathbb{E} \to [-\infty, \infty)$ be defined by

$$g(\mathbf{x}) \equiv \min_{\mathbf{y} \in \mathbb{E}} f(\mathbf{x}, \mathbf{y}).$$

Then g is convex.

Proof. Let $\mathbf{x}_1, \mathbf{x}_2 \in \mathbb{E}$ and $\lambda \in [0,1]$. To show the convexity of g, we will prove that

$$g(\lambda \mathbf{x}_1 + (1 - \lambda)\mathbf{x}_2) \leq \lambda g(\mathbf{x}_1) + (1 - \lambda)g(\mathbf{x}_2). \qquad (2.8)$$

The inequality is obvious if $\lambda = 0$ or 1. We will therefore assume that $\lambda \in (0,1)$. The proof is split into two cases.

Case I: Here we assume that $g(\mathbf{x}_1), g(\mathbf{x}_2) > -\infty$. Take $\varepsilon > 0$. Then there exist $\mathbf{y}_1, \mathbf{y}_2 \in \mathbb{V}$ such that

$$f(\mathbf{x}_1, \mathbf{y}_1) \leq g(\mathbf{x}_1) + \varepsilon, \qquad (2.9)$$
$$f(\mathbf{x}_2, \mathbf{y}_2) \leq g(\mathbf{x}_2) + \varepsilon. \qquad (2.10)$$

By the convexity of f, we have

$$
\begin{aligned}
f(\lambda \mathbf{x}_1 + (1 - \lambda)\mathbf{x}_2, \lambda \mathbf{y}_1 + (1 - \lambda)\mathbf{y}_2) \quad &\leq \quad \lambda f(\mathbf{x}_1, \mathbf{y}_1) + (1 - \lambda)f(\mathbf{x}_2, \mathbf{y}_2) \\
&\overset{(2.9),(2.10)}{\leq} \quad \lambda(g(\mathbf{x}_1) + \varepsilon) + (1 - \lambda)(g(\mathbf{x}_2) + \varepsilon) \\
&= \quad \lambda g(\mathbf{x}_1) + (1 - \lambda)g(\mathbf{x}_2) + \varepsilon.
\end{aligned}
$$

Therefore, by the definition of g, we can conclude that

$$g(\lambda \mathbf{x}_1 + (1 - \lambda)\mathbf{x}_2) \leq \lambda g(\mathbf{x}_1) + (1 - \lambda)g(\mathbf{x}_2) + \varepsilon.$$

Since the above inequality holds for any $\varepsilon > 0$, it follows that (2.8) holds.

Case II: Assume that at least one of the values $g(\mathbf{x}_1), g(\mathbf{x}_2)$ is equal $-\infty$. We will assume without loss of generality that $g(\mathbf{x}_1) = -\infty$. In this case, (2.8) is equivalent to saying that $g(\lambda \mathbf{x}_1 + (1 - \lambda)\mathbf{x}_2) = -\infty$. Take any $M \in \mathbb{R}$. Then since $g(\mathbf{x}_1) = -\infty$, it follows that there exists $\mathbf{y}_1 \in \mathbb{V}$ for which

$$f(\mathbf{x}_1, \mathbf{y}_1) \leq M.$$

By property (2.7), there exists $\mathbf{y}_2 \in \mathbb{V}$ for which $f(\mathbf{x}_2, \mathbf{y}_2) < \infty$. Using the convexity of f, we obtain that

$$
\begin{aligned}
f(\lambda \mathbf{x}_1 + (1 - \lambda)\mathbf{x}_2, \lambda \mathbf{y}_1 + (1 - \lambda)\mathbf{y}_2) &\leq \lambda f(\mathbf{x}_1, \mathbf{y}_1) + (1 - \lambda)f(\mathbf{x}_2, \mathbf{y}_2) \\
&\leq \lambda M + (1 - \lambda)f(\mathbf{x}_2, \mathbf{y}_2),
\end{aligned}
$$

which by the definition of g implies the inequality

$$g(\lambda \mathbf{x}_1 + (1 - \lambda)\mathbf{x}_2) \leq \lambda M + (1 - \lambda)f(\mathbf{x}_2, \mathbf{y}_2).$$

Since the latter inequality holds for any $M \in \mathbb{R}$ and since $f(\mathbf{x}_2, \mathbf{y}_2) < \infty$, it follows that $g(\lambda \mathbf{x}_1 + (1 - \lambda)\mathbf{x}_2) = -\infty$, proving the result for the second case. $\square$

---

[5]The fact that g does not attain the value ∞ is a direct consequence of property (2.7).

2.3.2   The Infimal Convolution

Let $h_1, h_2 : \mathbb{E} \to (-\infty, \infty]$ be two proper functions. The *infimal convolution* of h_1, h_2 is defined by the following formula:

$$(h_1 \square h_2)(\mathbf{x}) \equiv \min_{\mathbf{u} \in \mathbb{E}} \{h_1(\mathbf{u}) + h_2(\mathbf{x} - \mathbf{u})\}.$$

A direct consequence of Theorem 2.18 is the following result stating that the infimal convolution of a proper convex function and a real-valued convex function is always convex.

Theorem 2.19 (convexity of the infimal convolution). *Let $h_1 : \mathbb{E} \to (-\infty, \infty]$ be a proper convex function and let $h_2 : \mathbb{E} \to \mathbb{R}$ be a real-valued convex function. Then $h_1 \square h_2$ is convex.*

Proof. Define $f(\mathbf{x}, \mathbf{y}) \equiv h_1(\mathbf{y}) + h_2(\mathbf{x} - \mathbf{y})$. The convexity of h_1 and h_2 implies that f is convex. In addition, property (2.7) holds since for any $\mathbf{x} \in \mathbb{E}$, we can pick any $\mathbf{y} \in \text{dom}(h_1)$ and obtain that $f(\mathbf{x}, \mathbf{y}) = h_1(\mathbf{y}) + h_2(\mathbf{x} - \mathbf{y}) < \infty$. Thus, by Theorem 2.18, the function $h_1 \square h_2$, as a partial minimization function of $f(\cdot, \cdot)$ w.r.t. the second argument is a convex function. $\square$

Example 2.20 (convexity of the distance function). Let $C \subseteq \mathbb{E}$ be a nonempty convex set. The distance function can be written as the following infimal convolution:

$$d_C(\mathbf{x}) = \min_{\mathbf{y}} \{\|\mathbf{x} - \mathbf{y}\| : \mathbf{y} \in C\} = \min_{\mathbf{y} \in \mathbb{E}} \{\delta_C(\mathbf{y}) + \|\mathbf{x} - \mathbf{y}\|\} = (\delta_C \square h_1)(\mathbf{x}),$$

where $h_1(\cdot) = \|\cdot\|$. Since δ_C is proper and convex and h_1 is real-valued convex, it follows by Theorem 2.19 that d_C is convex.   ∎

2.3.3   Continuity of Convex Functions

It is well known that convex functions are continuous at points in the interior of their domain. This is explicitly recalled in the next result, which actually states a stronger property of convex functions—local Lipschitz continuity.

Theorem 2.21 (local Lipschitz continuity of convex functions [10, Theorem 7.36]). *Let $f : \mathbb{E} \to (-\infty, \infty]$ be convex. Let $\mathbf{x}_0 \in \text{int}(\text{dom}(f))$. Then there exist $\varepsilon > 0$ and $L > 0$ such that $B[\mathbf{x}_0, \varepsilon] \subseteq C$ and*

$$|f(\mathbf{x}) - f(\mathbf{x}_0)| \leq L\|\mathbf{x} - \mathbf{x}_0\| \tag{2.11}$$

for all $\mathbf{x} \in B[\mathbf{x}_0, \varepsilon]$.

Convex functions are not necessarily continuous at boundary points. Continuity is not guaranteed even when the function at hand is closed and convex (cf. Example 2.32). However, for univariate functions we will now show that closed and convex functions are continuous.

Theorem 2.22 (continuity of closed convex univariate functions). *Let $f : \mathbb{R} \to (-\infty, \infty]$ be a proper closed and convex function. Then f is continuous over $\mathrm{dom}(f)$.*

Proof. Since f is convex, its domain is some interval $I = \mathrm{dom}(f)$. If $\mathrm{int}(I) = \emptyset$, then I is a singleton, and consequently the continuity of f over I is obvious. Assume then that $\mathrm{int}(I) \neq \emptyset$. The fact that f is continuous over $\mathrm{int}(I)$ follows from Theorem 2.21. We only need to show the continuity of f at the endpoints of I (if they exist). For that, we can assume without loss of generality that the interval I has a left endpoint a, and we will prove the right continuity of f at a. We begin by showing that $\lim_{t \to a^+} f(t)$ exists. Let $c > a$ be an arbitrary scalar in I and define the function

$$g(t) \equiv \frac{f(c-t) - f(c)}{t}.$$

Obviously, g is defined on $(0, c-a]$. We will show that g is nondecreasing and upper bounded over $(0, c-a]$. For that, take $0 < t \leq s \leq c-a$. Then

$$c - t = \left(1 - \frac{t}{s}\right)c + \frac{t}{s}(c-s),$$

and hence, by the convexity of f,

$$f(c-t) \leq \left(1 - \frac{t}{s}\right)f(c) + \frac{t}{s}f(c-s),$$

which after some rearrangement of terms can be seen to be equivalent to

$$\frac{f(c-t) - f(c)}{t} \leq \frac{f(c-s) - f(c)}{s}.$$

Thus,
$$g(t) \leq g(s) \text{ for any } 0 < t \leq s \leq c-a. \tag{2.12}$$

Namely, g is nondecreasing over $(0, c-a]$. To show the upper boundedness, just plug $s = c - a$ into (2.12) and obtain that

$$g(t) \leq g(c-a) \text{ for any } t \in (0, c-a]. \tag{2.13}$$

We can thus conclude that $\lim_{t \to (c-a)^-} g(t)$ exists and is equal to some real number ℓ. Hence,

$$f(c-t) = f(c) + tg(t) \to f(c) + (c-a)\ell,$$

as $t \to (c-a)^-$, and consequently $\lim_{t \to a^+} f(t)$ exists and is equal to $f(c) + (c-a)\ell$. Using (2.13), we obtain that for any $t \in (0, c-a]$,

$$f(c-t) = f(c) + tg(t) \leq f(c) + (c-a)g(c-a) = f(c) + (c-a)\frac{f(a) - f(c)}{c-a} = f(a),$$

implying the inequality $\lim_{t \to a^+} f(t) \leq f(a)$. On the other hand, since f is closed, it is also lower semicontinuous (Theorem 2.6), and thus $\lim_{t \to a^+} f(t) \geq f(a)$. Consequently, $\lim_{t \to a^+} f(t) = f(a)$, proving the right continuity of f at a. $\quad\square$

2.4   Support Functions

Let $C \subseteq \mathbb{E}$ be a nonempty set. Then the *support function* of C is the function $\sigma_C : \mathbb{E}^* \to (-\infty, \infty]$ given by

$$\sigma_C(\mathbf{y}) = \max_{\mathbf{x} \in C} \langle \mathbf{y}, \mathbf{x} \rangle.$$

For a fixed $\mathbf{x}$, the linear function $\mathbf{y} \mapsto \langle \mathbf{y}, \mathbf{x} \rangle$ is obviously closed and convex. Therefore, by Theorems 2.7(c) and 2.16(c), the support function, as a maximum of closed and convex functions, is always closed and convex, regardless of whether C is closed and/or convex. We summarize this property in the next lemma.

Lemma 2.23 (closedness and convexity of support functions). *Let $C \subseteq \mathbb{E}$ be a nonempty set. Then σ_C is a closed and convex function.*

In most of our discussions on support functions in this chapter, the fact that σ_C operates on the dual space $\mathbb{E}^*$ instead of $\mathbb{E}$ will have no importance—recall that we use the convention that the elements of $\mathbb{E}^*$ and $\mathbb{E}$ are the same. However, when norms will be involved, naturally, the dual norm will have to be used (cf. Example 2.31).

Additional properties of support functions that follow directly by definition are given in Lemma 2.24 below. Note that for two sets A, B that reside in the same space, the sum $A + B$ stands for the *Minkowski sum* given by

$$A + B = \{ \mathbf{a} + \mathbf{b} : \mathbf{a} \in A, \mathbf{b} \in B \}.$$

Also, for a scalar $\alpha \in \mathbb{R}$ and a set $A \subseteq \mathbb{E}$, the set αA is

$$\alpha A = \{ \alpha \mathbf{a} : \mathbf{a} \in A \}.$$

Lemma 2.24.

(a) **(positive homogeneity)** *For any nonempty set $C \subseteq \mathbb{E}, \mathbf{y} \in \mathbb{E}^*$ and $\alpha \geq 0$,*

$$\sigma_C(\alpha \mathbf{y}) = \alpha \sigma_C(\mathbf{y}).$$

(b) **(subadditivity)** *For any nonempty set $C \subseteq \mathbb{E}$ and $\mathbf{y}_1, \mathbf{y}_2 \in \mathbb{E}^*$,*

$$\sigma_C(\mathbf{y}_1 + \mathbf{y}_2) \leq \sigma_C(\mathbf{y}_1) + \sigma_C(\mathbf{y}_2).$$

(c) *For any nonempty set $C \subseteq \mathbb{E}, \mathbf{y} \in \mathbb{E}^*$ and $\alpha \geq 0$,*

$$\sigma_{\alpha C}(\mathbf{y}) = \alpha \sigma_C(\mathbf{y}).$$

(d) *For any two nonempty sets $A, B \subseteq \mathbb{E}$ and $\mathbf{y} \in \mathbb{E}^*$,*

$$\sigma_{A+B}(\mathbf{y}) = \sigma_A(\mathbf{y}) + \sigma_B(\mathbf{y}).$$

Proof. (a) $\sigma_C(\alpha\mathbf{y}) = \max_{\mathbf{x}\in C}\langle\alpha\mathbf{y},\mathbf{x}\rangle = \alpha\max_{\mathbf{x}\in C}\langle\mathbf{y},\mathbf{x}\rangle = \alpha\sigma_C(\mathbf{y})$.

(b)

$$\sigma_C(\mathbf{y}_1+\mathbf{y}_2) = \max_{\mathbf{x}\in C}\langle\mathbf{y}_1+\mathbf{y}_2,\mathbf{x}\rangle = \max_{\mathbf{x}\in C}\left[\langle\mathbf{y}_1,\mathbf{x}\rangle+\langle\mathbf{y}_2,\mathbf{x}\rangle\right]$$
$$\leq \max_{\mathbf{x}\in C}\langle\mathbf{y}_1,\mathbf{x}\rangle + \max_{\mathbf{x}\in C}\langle\mathbf{y}_2,\mathbf{x}\rangle = \sigma_C(\mathbf{y}_1)+\sigma_C(\mathbf{y}_2).$$

(c)

$$\sigma_{\alpha C}(\mathbf{y}) = \max_{\mathbf{x}\in\alpha C}\langle\mathbf{y},\mathbf{x}\rangle = \max_{\mathbf{x}_1\in C}\langle\mathbf{y},\alpha\mathbf{x}_1\rangle = \alpha\max_{\mathbf{x}_1\in C}\langle\mathbf{y},\mathbf{x}_1\rangle = \alpha\sigma_C(\mathbf{y}).$$

(d)

$$\sigma_{A+B}(\mathbf{y}) = \max_{\mathbf{x}\in A+B}\langle\mathbf{y},\mathbf{x}\rangle = \max_{\mathbf{x}_1\in A,\mathbf{x}_2\in B}\langle\mathbf{y},\mathbf{x}_1+\mathbf{x}_2\rangle$$
$$= \max_{\mathbf{x}_1\in A,\mathbf{x}_2\in B}\left[\langle\mathbf{y},\mathbf{x}_1\rangle+\langle\mathbf{y},\mathbf{x}_2\rangle\right] = \max_{\mathbf{x}_1\in A}\langle\mathbf{y},\mathbf{x}_1\rangle + \max_{\mathbf{x}_2\in B}\langle\mathbf{y},\mathbf{x}_2\rangle$$
$$= \sigma_A(\mathbf{y})+\sigma_B(\mathbf{y}). \qquad \Box$$

Following are some basic examples of support functions.

Example 2.25 (support functions of finite sets). Suppose that

$$C = \{\mathbf{b}_1,\mathbf{b}_2,\ldots,\mathbf{b}_m\},$$

where $\mathbf{b}_1,\mathbf{b}_2,\ldots,\mathbf{b}_m \in \mathbb{E}$. Then

$$\sigma_C(\mathbf{y}) = \max\{\langle\mathbf{b}_1,\mathbf{y}\rangle,\langle\mathbf{b}_2,\mathbf{y}\rangle,\ldots,\langle\mathbf{b}_m,\mathbf{y}\rangle\}.$$

■

Recall that $S\subseteq\mathbb{E}$ is called a *cone* if it satisfies the following property: for any $\mathbf{x}\in S$ and $\lambda\geq 0$, the inclusion $\lambda\mathbf{x}\in S$ holds.

Example 2.26 (support functions of cones). Let $K\subseteq\mathbb{E}$ be a cone. Define the polar cone of K as

$$K^\circ = \{\mathbf{y}\in\mathbb{E}^* : \langle\mathbf{y},\mathbf{x}\rangle \leq 0 \text{ for all } \mathbf{x}\in K\}.$$

We will show that

$$\sigma_K(\mathbf{y}) = \delta_{K^\circ}(\mathbf{y}). \qquad (2.14)$$

Indeed, if $\mathbf{y}\in K^\circ$, then $\langle\mathbf{y},\mathbf{x}\rangle \leq 0$ for all $\mathbf{x}\in K$ and for $\mathbf{x}=\mathbf{0}$, $\langle\mathbf{y},\mathbf{x}\rangle = 0$. Therefore,

$$\sigma_K(\mathbf{y}) = \max_{\mathbf{x}\in K}\langle\mathbf{y},\mathbf{x}\rangle = 0.$$

If $\mathbf{y}\notin K^\circ$, then there exists $\tilde{\mathbf{x}}\in K$ such that $\langle\mathbf{y},\tilde{\mathbf{x}}\rangle > 0$. Since $\lambda\tilde{\mathbf{x}}\in K$ for all $\lambda\geq 0$, it follows that

$$\sigma_K(\mathbf{y}) \geq \langle\mathbf{y},\lambda\tilde{\mathbf{x}}\rangle = \lambda\langle\mathbf{y},\tilde{\mathbf{x}}\rangle \text{ for all } \lambda\geq 0.$$

Taking $\lambda\to\infty$, we obtain that $\sigma_K(\mathbf{y}) = \infty$ for $\mathbf{y}\notin K^\circ$, and hence formula (2.14) is proven. ■

Example 2.27 (support function of the nonnegative orthant). Consider the space $\mathbb{E} = \mathbb{R}^n$. As a special case of Example 2.26, since $(\mathbb{R}^n_+)^\circ = \mathbb{R}^n_-$, it follows that

$$\sigma_{\mathbb{R}^n_+}(\mathbf{y}) = \delta_{\mathbb{R}^n_-}(\mathbf{y}).$$

■

The next example uses Farkas's lemma,[6] which we now recall.

Lemma 2.28 (Farkas's lemma—second formulation). *Let* $\mathbf{c} \in \mathbb{R}^n$ *and* $\mathbf{A} \in \mathbb{R}^{m \times n}$. *Then the following two claims are equivalent:*

A. *The implication* $\mathbf{A}\mathbf{x} \leq \mathbf{0} \Rightarrow \mathbf{c}^T\mathbf{x} \leq 0$ *holds true.*

B. *There exists* $\mathbf{y} \in \mathbb{R}^m_+$ *such that* $\mathbf{A}^T\mathbf{y} = \mathbf{c}$.

Example 2.29 (support functions of convex polyhedral cones). Let the underlying space be $\mathbb{E} = \mathbb{R}^n$ and let $\mathbf{A} \in \mathbb{R}^{m \times n}$. Define the set

$$S = \{\mathbf{x} \in \mathbb{R}^n : \mathbf{A}\mathbf{x} \leq \mathbf{0}\}.$$

Since S is a cone, we can use Example 2.26 to conclude that

$$\sigma_S(\mathbf{y}) = \delta_{S^\circ}(\mathbf{y}).$$

Note that $\mathbf{y} \in S^\circ$ if and only if

$$\langle \mathbf{y}, \mathbf{x} \rangle \leq 0 \text{ for any } \mathbf{x} \text{ satisfying } \mathbf{A}\mathbf{x} \leq \mathbf{0}. \tag{2.15}$$

By Farkas's lemma (Lemma 2.28), (2.15) is equivalent to the statement

$$\text{there exists } \boldsymbol{\lambda} \in \mathbb{R}^m_+ \text{ such that } \mathbf{A}^T\boldsymbol{\lambda} = \mathbf{y}.$$

Hence,

$$S^\circ = \left\{\mathbf{A}^T\boldsymbol{\lambda} : \boldsymbol{\lambda} \in \mathbb{R}^m_+\right\}.$$

To conclude,

$$\sigma_S(\mathbf{y}) = \delta_{\{\mathbf{A}^T\boldsymbol{\lambda}:\boldsymbol{\lambda}\in\mathbb{R}^m_+\}}(\mathbf{y}).$$

■

Example 2.30 (support functions of affine sets). Let the underlying space be $\mathbb{E} = \mathbb{R}^n$ and let $\mathbf{B} \in \mathbb{R}^{m \times n}, \mathbf{b} \in \mathbb{R}^m$. Define the affine set

$$C = \{\mathbf{x} \in \mathbb{R}^n : \mathbf{B}\mathbf{x} = \mathbf{b}\}.$$

---

[6]The lemma and its proof can be found, for example, in [10, Lemma 10.3].

We assume that C is nonempty, namely, that there exists $\mathbf{x}_0 \in \mathbb{R}^n$ for which $\mathbf{B}\mathbf{x}_0 = \mathbf{b}$. The support function is obviously given by

$$\sigma_C(\mathbf{y}) = \max_{\mathbf{x}} \left\{ \langle \mathbf{y}, \mathbf{x} \rangle : \mathbf{B}\mathbf{x} = \mathbf{b} \right\}.$$

Making the change of variables $\mathbf{x} = \mathbf{z} + \mathbf{x}_0$, we obtain that the support function can be rewritten as

$$\begin{aligned}
\sigma_C(\mathbf{y}) &= \max_{\mathbf{z}} \left\{ \langle \mathbf{y}, \mathbf{z} \rangle + \langle \mathbf{y}, \mathbf{x}_0 \rangle : \mathbf{B}\mathbf{z} = \mathbf{0} \right\} \\
&= \langle \mathbf{y}, \mathbf{x}_0 \rangle + \max_{\mathbf{z}} \left\{ \langle \mathbf{y}, \mathbf{z} \rangle : \mathbf{B}\mathbf{z} = \mathbf{0} \right\} \\
&= \langle \mathbf{y}, \mathbf{x}_0 \rangle + \sigma_{\tilde{C}}(\mathbf{y}),
\end{aligned} \tag{2.16}$$

where $\tilde{C} = \{ \mathbf{x} \in \mathbb{R}^n : \mathbf{B}\mathbf{x} = \mathbf{0} \}$. The set $\tilde{C}$ is a convex polyhedral cone that can be written as

$$\tilde{C} = \{ \mathbf{x} \in \mathbb{R}^n : \mathbf{A}\mathbf{x} \leq \mathbf{0} \},$$

where $\mathbf{A} = \left(\begin{smallmatrix} \mathbf{B} \\ -\mathbf{B} \end{smallmatrix} \right)$. By Example 2.29, it follows that

$$\sigma_{\tilde{C}} = \delta_{\tilde{C}^\circ}, \tag{2.17}$$

where $\tilde{C}^\circ$ is the polar cone of $\tilde{C}$, which is given by

$$\tilde{C}^\circ = \left\{ \mathbf{B}^T \boldsymbol{\lambda}_1 - \mathbf{B}^T \boldsymbol{\lambda}_2 : \boldsymbol{\lambda}_1, \boldsymbol{\lambda}_2 \in \mathbb{R}_+^m \right\}.$$

We will show that

$$\tilde{C}^\circ = \text{Range}(\mathbf{B}^T). \tag{2.18}$$

Indeed, if $\mathbf{v} \in \tilde{C}^\circ$, then there exists $\boldsymbol{\lambda}_1, \boldsymbol{\lambda}_2 \in \mathbb{R}_+^m$ for which $\mathbf{v} = \mathbf{B}^T \boldsymbol{\lambda}_1 - \mathbf{B}^T \boldsymbol{\lambda}_2 = \mathbf{B}^T (\boldsymbol{\lambda}_1 - \boldsymbol{\lambda}_2) \in \text{Range}(\mathbf{B}^T)$. In the other direction, if $\mathbf{v} \in \text{Range}(\mathbf{B}^T)$, then there exists $\boldsymbol{\lambda} \in \mathbb{R}^m$ for which $\mathbf{v} = \mathbf{B}^T \boldsymbol{\lambda}$. Defining $\boldsymbol{\lambda}_1 = [\boldsymbol{\lambda}]_+, \boldsymbol{\lambda}_2 = [-\boldsymbol{\lambda}]_+$, we obtain that $\boldsymbol{\lambda} = \boldsymbol{\lambda}_1 - \boldsymbol{\lambda}_2$ with $\boldsymbol{\lambda}_1, \boldsymbol{\lambda}_2 \in \mathbb{R}_+^m$, and hence

$$\mathbf{v} = \mathbf{B}^T \boldsymbol{\lambda} = \mathbf{B}^T (\boldsymbol{\lambda}_1 - \boldsymbol{\lambda}_2) = \mathbf{B}^T \boldsymbol{\lambda}_1 - \mathbf{B}^T \boldsymbol{\lambda}_2 \in \tilde{C}^\circ.$$

Combining (2.16), (2.17), and (2.18), we finally conclude that

$$\boxed{\sigma_C(\mathbf{y}) = \langle \mathbf{y}, \mathbf{x}_0 \rangle + \delta_{\text{Range}(\mathbf{B}^T)}(\mathbf{y}).}$$

∎

Example 2.31 (support functions of unit balls). Suppose that $\mathbb{E}$ is the underlying space endowed with a norm $\| \cdot \|$. Consider the unit ball given by

$$B_{\|\cdot\|}[\mathbf{0}, 1] = \{ \mathbf{x} \in \mathbb{E} : \|\mathbf{x}\| \leq 1 \}.$$

By the definition of the dual norm, we have for any $\mathbf{y} \in \mathbb{E}^*$

$$\sigma_{B_{\|\cdot\|}[0,1]}(\mathbf{y}) = \max_{\|\mathbf{x}\|\leq 1} \langle \mathbf{y}, \mathbf{x}\rangle = \|\mathbf{y}\|_*.$$

Thus, for example, for the space $\mathbb{R}^n$ we have

$$\sigma_{B_{\|\cdot\|_p}[0,1]}(\mathbf{y}) = \|\mathbf{y}\|_q \quad \left(1 \leq p \leq \infty, \frac{1}{p} + \frac{1}{q} = 1\right),$$

$$\sigma_{B_{\|\cdot\|_{\mathbf{Q}}}[0,1]}(\mathbf{y}) = \|\mathbf{y}\|_{\mathbf{Q}^{-1}} \quad (\mathbf{Q} \in \mathbb{S}_{++}^n).$$

In the first formula we use the convention that $p = 1/\infty$ corresponds to $q = \infty/1$.
∎

The next example is also an example of a closed and convex function that is not continuous (recall that such an example does not exist for one-dimensional functions; see Theorem 2.22).

Example 2.32.[7] Consider the following set in $\mathbb{R}^2$:

$$C = \left\{(x_1, x_2)^T : x_1 + \frac{x_2^2}{2} \leq 0\right\}.$$

Then the support function of C is given by

$$\sigma_C(\mathbf{y}) = \max_{x_1, x_2} \left\{y_1 x_1 + y_2 x_2 : x_1 + \frac{x_2^2}{2} \leq 0\right\}. \tag{2.19}$$

Obviously, $\sigma_C(\mathbf{0}) = 0$. We will compute the support function at $\mathbf{y} \neq \mathbf{0}$. In this case, it is easy to see that the maximum of problem (2.19) is attained at the boundary of C.[8] Therefore,

$$\sigma_C(\mathbf{y}) = \max_{x_1, x_2} \left\{y_1 x_1 + y_2 x_2 : x_1 + \frac{x_2^2}{2} = 0\right\} = \max_{x_2} \left\{-\frac{y_1}{2}x_2^2 + y_2 x_2\right\}.$$

If $y_1 < 0$, then the maximal value is ∞. If $y_1 = 0$ and $y_2 \neq 0$, then the maximal value is also ∞. If $y_1 > 0$, the maximum is attained at $x_2 = \frac{y_2}{y_1}$, and the corresponding maximal value is $\frac{y_2^2}{2y_1}$. Thus, the support function is given by

$$\sigma_C(\mathbf{y}) = \begin{cases} \frac{y_2^2}{2y_1}, & y_1 > 0, \\ 0, & y_1 = y_2 = 0, \\ \infty & \text{else.} \end{cases}$$

---

[7]Example 2.32 is from Rockafellar [108, p. 83].

[8]This fact can be shown by contradiction. If the maximum was attained at an interior point of C, then the gradient of the objective function, meaning $\mathbf{y}$, would be the zeros vector, which is a contradiction to the assumption that $\mathbf{y} \neq \mathbf{0}$.

By Lemma 2.23, σ_C is closed and convex. However, it is not continuous at $(y_1, y_2) = (0,0)$. Indeed, taking for any $\alpha > 0$ the path $y_1(t) = \frac{t^2}{2\alpha}, y_2(t) = t (t > 0)$, we obtain that

$$\sigma_C(y_1(t), y_2(t)) = \alpha,$$

and hence the limit of $\sigma_C(y_1(t), y_2(t))$ as $t \to 0^+$ is α, which combined with the fact that $\sigma_C(0,0) = 0$ implies the discontinuity of f at $(0,0)$. The contour lines of σ_C are plotted in Figure 2.3. ■

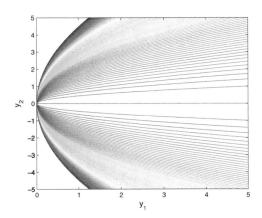

Figure 2.3. *Contour lines of the closed, convex, and noncontinuous function from Example 2.32.*

An important property of support functions is that they are completely determined by their underlying sets as long as these sets are closed and convex. The proof of this result requires the strict separation theorem,[9] which is now recalled.

Theorem 2.33 (strict separation theorem). *Let $C \subseteq \mathbb{E}$ be a nonempty closed and convex set, and let $\mathbf{y} \notin C$. Then there exist $\mathbf{p} \in \mathbb{E}^* \backslash \{\mathbf{0}\}$ and $\alpha \in \mathbb{R}$ such that*

$$\langle \mathbf{p}, \mathbf{y} \rangle > \alpha$$

and

$$\langle \mathbf{p}, \mathbf{x} \rangle \leq \alpha \text{ for all } \mathbf{x} \in C.$$

Lemma 2.34. *Let $A, B \subseteq \mathbb{E}$ be nonempty closed and convex sets. Then $A = B$ if and only if $\sigma_A = \sigma_B$.*

Proof. If $A = B$, then obviously $\sigma_A = \sigma_B$. Suppose now that $\sigma_A = \sigma_B$. We will prove that $A = B$. Assume by contradiction that this is not the case, and without loss of generality suppose that there exists $\mathbf{y} \in A$ such that $\mathbf{y} \notin B$. Since $\mathbf{y} \notin B$ and B is nonempty closed and convex, by the strict separation theorem, there exists a

---

[9]The theorem and its proof can be found, for example, in [10, Theorem 10.1].

hyperplane separating $\mathbf{y}$ from B, meaning that there exists $\mathbf{p} \in \mathbb{E}^* \setminus \{\mathbf{0}\}$ and α such that

$$\langle \mathbf{p}, \mathbf{x} \rangle \leq \alpha < \langle \mathbf{p}, \mathbf{y} \rangle \text{ for any } \mathbf{x} \in B.$$

Taking the maximum over $\mathbf{x} \in B$, we conclude that $\sigma_B(\mathbf{p}) \leq \alpha < \langle \mathbf{p}, \mathbf{y} \rangle \leq \sigma_A(\mathbf{y})$, a contradiction to the assertion that the support functions are the same. $\square$

A related result states that the support function stays the same under the operations of closure and convex hull of the underlying set.

Lemma 2.35. *Let $A \subseteq \mathbb{E}$ be nonempty. Then*

(a) $\sigma_A = \sigma_{\mathrm{cl}(A)}$;

(b) $\sigma_A = \sigma_{\mathrm{conv}(A)}$.

Proof. (a) Since $A \subseteq \mathrm{cl}(A)$,

$$\sigma_A(\mathbf{y}) \leq \sigma_{\mathrm{cl}(A)}(\mathbf{y}) \text{ for any } \mathbf{y} \in \mathbb{E}^*. \tag{2.20}$$

We will show the reverse inequality. Let $\mathbf{y} \in \mathbb{E}^*$. Then by the definition of the support function, there exists a sequence $\{\mathbf{x}^k\}_{k \geq 1} \subseteq \mathrm{cl}(A)$ such that

$$\langle \mathbf{y}, \mathbf{x}^k \rangle \to \sigma_{\mathrm{cl}(A)}(\mathbf{y}) \text{ as } k \to \infty. \tag{2.21}$$

By the definition of the closure, it follows that there exists a sequence $\{\mathbf{z}^k\}_{k \geq 1} \subseteq A$ such that $\|\mathbf{z}^k - \mathbf{x}^k\| \leq \frac{1}{k}$ for all k, and hence

$$\mathbf{z}^k - \mathbf{x}^k \to 0 \text{ as } k \to \infty. \tag{2.22}$$

Now, since $\mathbf{z}^k \in A$,

$$\sigma_A(\mathbf{y}) \geq \langle \mathbf{y}, \mathbf{z}^k \rangle = \langle \mathbf{y}, \mathbf{x}^k \rangle + \langle \mathbf{y}, \mathbf{z}^k - \mathbf{x}^k \rangle.$$

Taking $k \to \infty$ and using (2.21), (2.22), we obtain that

$$\sigma_A(\mathbf{y}) \geq \sigma_{\mathrm{cl}(A)}(\mathbf{y}) + 0 = \sigma_{\mathrm{cl}(A)}(\mathbf{y}),$$

which combined with (2.20) yields the desired result $\sigma_A = \sigma_{\mathrm{cl}(A)}$.

(b) Since $A \subseteq \mathrm{conv}(A)$, we have that $\sigma_A(\mathbf{y}) \leq \sigma_{\mathrm{conv}(A)}(\mathbf{y})$ for any $\mathbf{y} \in \mathbb{E}^*$. We will show the reverse inequality. Let $\mathbf{y} \in \mathbb{E}^*$. Then by the definition of the support function, there exists a sequence $\{\mathbf{x}^k\}_{k \geq 1} \subseteq \mathrm{conv}(A)$ such that

$$\langle \mathbf{y}, \mathbf{x}^k \rangle \to \sigma_{\mathrm{conv}(A)}(\mathbf{y}) \text{ as } k \to \infty. \tag{2.23}$$

By the definition of the convex hull, it follows that for any k, there exist vectors $\mathbf{z}_1^k, \mathbf{z}_2^k, \ldots, \mathbf{z}_{n_k}^k \in A$ (n_k is a positive integer) and $\boldsymbol{\lambda}^k \in \Delta_{n_k}$ such that

$$\mathbf{x}^k = \sum_{i=1}^{n_k} \lambda_i^k \mathbf{z}_i^k.$$

Now,

$$\langle \mathbf{y}, \mathbf{x}^k \rangle = \left\langle \mathbf{y}, \sum_{i=1}^{n_k} \lambda_i^k \mathbf{z}_i^k \right\rangle = \sum_{i=1}^{n_k} \lambda_i^k \langle \mathbf{y}, \mathbf{z}_i^k \rangle \leq \sum_{i=1}^{n_k} \lambda_i^k \sigma_A(\mathbf{y}) = \sigma_A(\mathbf{y}),$$

where the inequality follows by the fact that $\mathbf{z}_i^k \in A$. Taking the limit as $k \to \infty$ and using (2.23), we obtain that $\sigma_{\mathrm{conv}(A)}(\mathbf{y}) \leq \sigma_A(\mathbf{y})$. $\square$

Example 2.36 (support of the unit simplex). Suppose that the underlying space is $\mathbb{R}^n$ and consider the unit simplex set $\Delta_n = \{\mathbf{x} \in \mathbb{R}^n : \mathbf{e}^T \mathbf{x} = 1, \mathbf{x} \geq \mathbf{0}\}$. Since the unit simplex can be written as the convex hull of the standard basis of $\mathbb{R}^n$,

$$\Delta_n = \mathrm{conv}\{\mathbf{e}_1, \mathbf{e}_2, \dots, \mathbf{e}_n\},$$

it follows by Lemma 2.35(b) that

$$\sigma_{\Delta_n}(\mathbf{y}) = \sigma_{\{\mathbf{e}_1, \dots, \mathbf{e}_n\}}(\mathbf{y}) = \max\{\langle \mathbf{e}_1, \mathbf{y} \rangle, \langle \mathbf{e}_2, \mathbf{y} \rangle, \dots, \langle \mathbf{e}_n, \mathbf{y} \rangle\}.$$

Since we always assume (unless otherwise stated) that $\mathbb{R}^n$ is endowed with the dot product, the support function is

$$\boxed{\sigma_{\Delta_n}(\mathbf{y}) = \max\{y_1, y_2, \dots, y_n\}.}$$

■

The table below summarizes the main support function computations that were considered in this section.

C	$\sigma_C(\mathbf{y})$	Assumptions	Reference
$\{\mathbf{b}_1, \mathbf{b}_2, \dots, \mathbf{b}_n\}$	$\max_{i=1,2,\dots,n} \langle \mathbf{b}_i, \mathbf{y} \rangle$	$\mathbf{b}_i \in \mathbb{E}$	Example 2.25
K	$\delta_{K^\circ}(\mathbf{y})$	K—cone	Example 2.26
$\mathbb{R}^n_+$	$\delta_{\mathbb{R}^n_-}(\mathbf{y})$	$\mathbb{E} = \mathbb{R}^n$	Example 2.27
Δ_n	$\max\{y_1, y_2, \dots, y_n\}$	$\mathbb{E} = \mathbb{R}^n$	Example 2.36
$\{\mathbf{x} \in \mathbb{R}^n : \mathbf{A}\mathbf{x} \leq \mathbf{0}\}$	$\delta_{\{\mathbf{A}^T \boldsymbol{\lambda}: \boldsymbol{\lambda} \in \mathbb{R}^m_+\}}(\mathbf{y})$	$\mathbb{E} = \mathbb{R}^n$, $\mathbf{A} \in \mathbb{R}^{m \times n}$	Example 2.29
$\{\mathbf{x} \in \mathbb{R}^n : \mathbf{B}\mathbf{x} = \mathbf{b}\}$	$\langle \mathbf{y}, \mathbf{x}_0 \rangle + \delta_{\mathrm{Range}(\mathbf{B}^T)}(\mathbf{y})$	$\mathbb{E} = \mathbb{R}^n$, $\mathbf{B} \in \mathbb{R}^{m \times n}$, $\mathbf{b} \in \mathbb{R}^m$, $\mathbf{B}\mathbf{x}_0 = \mathbf{b}$	Example 2.30
$B_{\|\cdot\|}[\mathbf{0}, 1]$	$\|\mathbf{y}\|_*$	-	Example 2.31

Chapter 3

Subgradients

3.1 Definitions and First Examples

Definition 3.1 (subgradient). *Let $f : \mathbb{E} \to (-\infty, \infty]$ be a proper function and let $\mathbf{x} \in \mathrm{dom}(f)$. A vector $\mathbf{g} \in \mathbb{E}^*$ is called* **a subgradient** *of f at $\mathbf{x}$ if*

$$f(\mathbf{y}) \geq f(\mathbf{x}) + \langle \mathbf{g}, \mathbf{y} - \mathbf{x} \rangle \text{ for all } \mathbf{y} \in \mathbb{E}. \tag{3.1}$$

Recall (see Section 1.11) that we use in this book the convention that the elements of $\mathbb{E}^*$ are exactly the elements of $\mathbb{E}$, whereas the asterisk just marks the fact that the endowed norm on $\mathbb{E}^*$ is the dual norm $\|\cdot\|_*$ rather than the endowed norm $\|\cdot\|$ on $\mathbb{E}$.

The inequality (3.1) is also called *the subgradient inequality*. It actually says that each subgradient is associated with an underestimate affine function, which is tangent to the surface of the function at $\mathbf{x}$. Since the subgradient inequality (3.1) is trivial for $\mathbf{y} \notin \mathrm{dom}(f)$, it is frequently restricted to points in $\mathrm{dom}(f)$ and is thus written as

$$f(\mathbf{y}) \geq f(\mathbf{x}) + \langle \mathbf{g}, \mathbf{y} - \mathbf{x} \rangle \text{ for all } \mathbf{y} \in \mathrm{dom}(f).$$

Given a point $\mathbf{x} \in \mathrm{dom}(f)$, there might be more than one subgradient of f at $\mathbf{x}$, and the set of all subgradients is called the *subdifferential*.

Definition 3.2 (subdifferential). *The set of all subgradients of f at $\mathbf{x}$ is called* **the subdifferential** *of f at $\mathbf{x}$ and is denoted by $\partial f(\mathbf{x})$:*

$$\partial f(\mathbf{x}) \equiv \{\mathbf{g} \in \mathbb{E}^* : f(\mathbf{y}) \geq f(\mathbf{x}) + \langle \mathbf{g}, \mathbf{y} - \mathbf{x} \rangle \text{ for all } \mathbf{y} \in \mathbb{E}\}.$$

When $\mathbf{x} \notin \mathrm{dom}(f)$, we define $\partial f(\mathbf{x}) = \emptyset$. Actually, for proper functions, this is a direct consequence of the definition of the subdifferential set since the subgradient inequality (3.1) does not hold for $\mathbf{x} \notin \mathrm{dom} f$ and $\mathbf{y} \in \mathrm{dom} f$.

Example 3.3 (subdifferential of norms at 0). Let $f : \mathbb{E} \to \mathbb{R}$ be given by $f(\mathbf{x}) = \|\mathbf{x}\|$, where $\|\cdot\|$ is the endowed norm on $\mathbb{E}$. We will show that the subdifferential of f at $\mathbf{x} = \mathbf{0}$ is the dual norm unit ball:

$$\partial f(\mathbf{0}) = B_{\|\cdot\|_*}[\mathbf{0}, 1] = \{\mathbf{g} \in \mathbb{E}^* : \|\mathbf{g}\|_* \leq 1\}. \tag{3.2}$$

To show (3.2), note that $\mathbf{g} \in \partial f(\mathbf{0})$ if and only if

$$f(\mathbf{y}) \geq f(\mathbf{0}) + \langle \mathbf{g}, \mathbf{y} - \mathbf{0} \rangle \text{ for all } \mathbf{y} \in \mathbb{E},$$

which is the same as

$$\|\mathbf{y}\| \geq \langle \mathbf{g}, \mathbf{y} \rangle \text{ for all } \mathbf{y} \in \mathbb{E}. \tag{3.3}$$

We will prove that the latter holds true if and only if $\|\mathbf{g}\|_* \leq 1$. Indeed, if $\|\mathbf{g}\|_* \leq 1$, then by the generalized Cauchy–Schwarz inequality (Lemma 1.4),

$$\langle \mathbf{g}, \mathbf{y} \rangle \leq \|\mathbf{g}\|_* \|\mathbf{y}\| \leq \|\mathbf{y}\| \text{ for any } \mathbf{y} \in \mathbb{E},$$

implying (3.3). In the reverse direction, assume that (3.3) holds. Taking the maximum of both sides of (3.3) over all $\mathbf{y}$ satisfying $\|\mathbf{y}\| \leq 1$, we get

$$\|\mathbf{g}\|_* = \max_{\mathbf{y}:\|\mathbf{y}\|\leq 1} \langle \mathbf{g}, \mathbf{y} \rangle \leq \max_{\mathbf{y}:\|\mathbf{y}\|\leq 1} \|\mathbf{y}\| = 1.$$

We have thus established the equivalence between (3.3) and the inequality $\|\mathbf{g}\|_* \leq 1$, which is the same as the result (3.2). ∎

Example 3.4 (subdifferential of the l_1-norm at 0). Let $f : \mathbb{R}^n \to \mathbb{R}$ be given by $f(\mathbf{x}) = \|\mathbf{x}\|_1$. Then, since this is a special case of Example 3.3 with $\|\cdot\| = \|\cdot\|_1$, and since the l_∞-norm is the dual of the l_1-norm, it follows that

$$\partial f(\mathbf{0}) = B_{\|\cdot\|_\infty}[\mathbf{0}, 1] = [-1, 1]^n.$$

In particular, when $n = 1$, then $f(x) = |x|$, and we have

$$\partial f(0) = [-1, 1].$$

The linear underestimators that correspond to $-0.8, -0.3$, and $0.7 \in \partial f(0)$, meaning $-0.8x, -0.3x$, and $0.7x$, are described in Figure 3.1. ∎

For the next example, we need the definition of the *normal cone*. Given a set $S \subseteq \mathbb{E}$ and a point $\mathbf{x} \in S$, the normal cone of S at $\mathbf{x}$ is defined as

$$N_S(\mathbf{x}) = \{\mathbf{y} \in \mathbb{E}^* : \langle \mathbf{y}, \mathbf{z} - \mathbf{x} \rangle \leq 0 \text{ for any } \mathbf{z} \in S\}.$$

The normal cone, in addition to being a cone, is closed and convex as an intersection of half-spaces. When $\mathbf{x} \notin S$, we define $N_S(\mathbf{x}) = \emptyset$.

Example 3.5 (subdifferential of indicator functions). Suppose that $S \subseteq \mathbb{E}$ is nonempty and consider the indicator function δ_S. Then for any $\mathbf{x} \in S$, we have that $\mathbf{y} \in \partial \delta_S(\mathbf{x})$ if and only if

$$\delta_S(\mathbf{z}) \geq \delta_S(\mathbf{x}) + \langle \mathbf{y}, \mathbf{z} - \mathbf{x} \rangle \text{ for all } \mathbf{z} \in S,$$

which is the same as

$$\langle \mathbf{y}, \mathbf{z} - \mathbf{x} \rangle \leq 0 \text{ for all } \mathbf{z} \in S.$$

Therefore, we have that

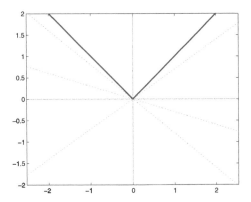

Figure 3.1. *The linear underestimators of* $|x|$ *corresponding to* -0.8, -0.3, $0.7 \in \partial f(0)$; *see Example* 3.4.

$$\partial \delta_S(\mathbf{x}) = N_S(\mathbf{x}) \text{ for all } \mathbf{x} \in S. \tag{3.4}$$

For $\mathbf{x} \notin S$, $\partial \delta_S(\mathbf{x}) = N_S(\mathbf{x}) = \emptyset$ by convention, so we obtain that (3.4) holds also for $\mathbf{x} \notin S$. ∎

Example 3.6 (subdifferential of the indicator function of the unit ball). As a special case of Example 3.5, let

$$S = B[\mathbf{0}, 1] = \{\mathbf{x} \in \mathbb{E} : \|\mathbf{x}\| \leq 1\}.$$

Then $\partial \delta_S(\mathbf{x}) = N_S(\mathbf{x})$, where $N_S(\mathbf{x})$ is given by

$$N_S(\mathbf{x}) = \{\mathbf{y} \in \mathbb{E}^* : \langle \mathbf{y}, \mathbf{z} - \mathbf{x} \rangle \leq 0 \text{ for all } \mathbf{z} \in S\}.$$

We will find a more explicit representation for $N_S(\mathbf{x})$. If $\mathbf{x} \notin S$, then $N_S(\mathbf{x}) = \emptyset$. Suppose that $\|\mathbf{x}\| \leq 1$. A vector $\mathbf{y} \in \mathbb{E}^*$ satisfies $\mathbf{y} \in N_S(\mathbf{x})$ if and only if

$$\langle \mathbf{y}, \mathbf{z} - \mathbf{x} \rangle \leq 0 \text{ for any } \mathbf{z} \text{ satisfying } \|\mathbf{z}\| \leq 1,$$

which is the same as the inequality,

$$\max_{\mathbf{z}:\|\mathbf{z}\| \leq 1} \langle \mathbf{y}, \mathbf{z} \rangle \leq \langle \mathbf{y}, \mathbf{x} \rangle.$$

Using the definition of the dual norm, we obtain that the latter can be rewritten as

$$\|\mathbf{y}\|_* \leq \langle \mathbf{y}, \mathbf{x} \rangle.$$

Therefore,

$$\partial \delta_{B[0,1]}(\mathbf{x}) = N_{B[0,1]}(\mathbf{x}) = \begin{cases} \{\mathbf{y} \in \mathbb{E}^* : \|\mathbf{y}\|_* \leq \langle \mathbf{y}, \mathbf{x} \rangle\}, & \|\mathbf{x}\| \leq 1, \\ \emptyset, & \|\mathbf{x}\| > 1. \end{cases}$$

∎

Example 3.7 (subgradient of the dual function). Consider the minimization problem

$$\min\{f(\mathbf{x}) : \mathbf{g}(\mathbf{x}) \leq \mathbf{0}, \mathbf{x} \in X\}, \tag{3.5}$$

where $\emptyset \neq X \subseteq \mathbb{E}$, $f : \mathbb{E} \to \mathbb{R}$ and $\mathbf{g} : \mathbb{E} \to \mathbb{R}^m$ is a vector-valued function. The Lagrangian dual objective function is given by

$$q(\boldsymbol{\lambda}) = \min_{\mathbf{x} \in X} \left\{ L(\mathbf{x}; \boldsymbol{\lambda}) \equiv f(\mathbf{x}) + \boldsymbol{\lambda}^T \mathbf{g}(\mathbf{x}) \right\}.$$

The dual problem consists of maximizing q on its effective domain, which is given by

$$\text{dom}(-q) = \{\boldsymbol{\lambda} \in \mathbb{R}^m_+ : q(\boldsymbol{\lambda}) > -\infty\}.$$

No matter whether the primal problem (3.5) is convex or not, the dual problem

$$\max_{\boldsymbol{\lambda} \in \mathbb{R}^m} \{q(\boldsymbol{\lambda}) : \boldsymbol{\lambda} \in \text{dom}(-q)\}$$

is always convex, meaning that q is a concave function and $\text{dom}(-q)$ is a convex set. Let $\boldsymbol{\lambda}_0 \in \text{dom}(-q)$ and assume that the minimum in the minimization problem defining $q(\boldsymbol{\lambda}_0)$,

$$q(\boldsymbol{\lambda}_0) = \min_{\mathbf{x} \in X} \left\{ f(\mathbf{x}) + \boldsymbol{\lambda}_0^T \mathbf{g}(\mathbf{x}) \right\},$$

is attained at $\mathbf{x}_0 \in X$, that is,

$$L(\mathbf{x}_0; \boldsymbol{\lambda}_0) = f(\mathbf{x}_0) + \boldsymbol{\lambda}_0^T \mathbf{g}(\mathbf{x}_0) = q(\boldsymbol{\lambda}_0).$$

We seek to find a subgradient of the convex function $-q$ at $\boldsymbol{\lambda}_0$. For that, note that for any $\boldsymbol{\lambda} \in \text{dom}(-q)$,

$$\begin{aligned} q(\boldsymbol{\lambda}) &= \min_{\mathbf{x} \in X} \left\{ f(\mathbf{x}) + \boldsymbol{\lambda}^T \mathbf{g}(\mathbf{x}) \right\} \\ &\leq f(\mathbf{x}_0) + \boldsymbol{\lambda}^T \mathbf{g}(\mathbf{x}_0) \\ &= f(\mathbf{x}_0) + \boldsymbol{\lambda}_0^T \mathbf{g}(\mathbf{x}_0) + (\boldsymbol{\lambda} - \boldsymbol{\lambda}_0)^T \mathbf{g}(\mathbf{x}_0) \\ &= q(\boldsymbol{\lambda}_0) + \mathbf{g}(\mathbf{x}_0)^T (\boldsymbol{\lambda} - \boldsymbol{\lambda}_0). \end{aligned}$$

Thus,

$$-q(\boldsymbol{\lambda}) \geq -q(\boldsymbol{\lambda}_0) + (-\mathbf{g}(\mathbf{x}_0))^T (\boldsymbol{\lambda} - \boldsymbol{\lambda}_0) \text{ for any } \boldsymbol{\lambda} \in \text{dom}(-q),$$

concluding that

$$-\mathbf{g}(\mathbf{x}_0) \in \partial(-q)(\boldsymbol{\lambda}_0).$$

∎

Example 3.8 (subgradient of the maximum eigenvalue function). Consider the function $f : \mathbb{S}^n \to \mathbb{R}$ given by $f(\mathbf{X}) = \lambda_{\max}(\mathbf{X})$ (recall that $\mathbb{S}^n$ is the set of all $n \times n$ symmetric matrices). Let $\mathbf{X} \in \mathbb{S}^n$ and let $\mathbf{v}$ be a normalized eigenvector of $\mathbf{X}$ ($\|\mathbf{v}\|_2 = 1$) associated with the maximum eigenvalue of $\mathbf{X}$. We will establish the relation

$$\mathbf{v}\mathbf{v}^T \in \partial f(\mathbf{X}). \tag{3.6}$$

To show this, note that for any $\mathbf{Y} \in \mathbb{S}^n$,

$$
\begin{aligned}
\lambda_{\max}(\mathbf{Y}) &= \max_{\mathbf{u}}\{\mathbf{u}^T\mathbf{Y}\mathbf{u} : \|\mathbf{u}\|_2 = 1\} \\
&\geq \mathbf{v}^T\mathbf{Y}\mathbf{v} \\
&= \mathbf{v}^T\mathbf{X}\mathbf{v} + \mathbf{v}^T(\mathbf{Y} - \mathbf{X})\mathbf{v} \\
&= \lambda_{\max}(\mathbf{X})\|\mathbf{v}\|_2^2 + \mathrm{Tr}(\mathbf{v}^T(\mathbf{Y} - \mathbf{X})\mathbf{v}) \\
&= \lambda_{\max}(\mathbf{X}) + \mathrm{Tr}(\mathbf{v}\mathbf{v}^T(\mathbf{Y} - \mathbf{X})) \\
&= \lambda_{\max}(\mathbf{X}) + \langle \mathbf{v}\mathbf{v}^T, \mathbf{Y} - \mathbf{X} \rangle,
\end{aligned}
$$

establishing (3.6). ■

There is an intrinsic difference between the results in Examples 3.7 and 3.8 and the results in Examples 3.3, 3.4, 3.5, and 3.6. Only one subgradient is computed in Examples 3.7 and 3.8; such results are referred to as *weak results*. On the other hand, in Examples 3.3, 3.4, 3.5, and 3.6 the entire subdifferential set is characterized—such results are called *strong results*.

3.2 Properties of the Subdifferential Set

Note that the subdifferential sets computed in the previous section are all closed and convex. This is not a coincidence. Subdifferential sets are *always* closed and convex.

Theorem 3.9 (closedness and convexity of the subdifferential set). *Let* $f : \mathbb{E} \to (-\infty, \infty]$ *be a proper function. Then the set* $\partial f(\mathbf{x})$ *is closed and convex for any* $\mathbf{x} \in \mathbb{E}$.

Proof. For any $\mathbf{x} \in \mathbb{E}$, the subdifferential set can be represented as

$$\partial f(\mathbf{x}) = \bigcap_{\mathbf{y} \in \mathbb{E}} H_{\mathbf{y}},$$

where $H_{\mathbf{y}} = \{\mathbf{g} \in \mathbb{E}^* : f(\mathbf{y}) \geq f(\mathbf{x}) + \langle \mathbf{g}, \mathbf{y} - \mathbf{x} \rangle\}$. Since the sets $H_{\mathbf{y}}$ are half-spaces and, in particular, closed and convex, it follows that $\partial f(\mathbf{x})$ is closed and convex. □

The subdifferential set $\partial f(\mathbf{x})$ may be empty. When it is nonempty at a given $\mathbf{x} \in \mathbb{E}$, the function f is called *subdifferentiable* at $\mathbf{x}$.

Definition 3.10 (subdifferentiability). *A proper function* $f : \mathbb{E} \to (-\infty, \infty]$ *is called* **subdifferentiable** *at* $\mathbf{x} \in \mathrm{dom}(f)$ *if* $\partial f(\mathbf{x}) \neq \emptyset$.

The collection of points of subdifferentiability is denoted by $\mathrm{dom}(\partial f)$:

$$\mathrm{dom}(\partial f) = \{\mathbf{x} \in \mathbb{E} : \partial f(\mathbf{x}) \neq \emptyset\}.$$

We will now show that if a function is subdifferentiable at any point in its domain, which is assumed to be convex, then it is necessarily convex.

Lemma 3.11 (nonemptiness of subdifferential sets $\Rightarrow$ convexity). *Let $f :$ $\mathbb{E} \rightarrow (-\infty, \infty]$ be a proper function and assume that $\mathrm{dom}(f)$ is convex. Suppose that for any $\mathbf{x} \in \mathrm{dom}(f)$, the set $\partial f(\mathbf{x})$ is nonempty. Then f is convex.*

Proof. Let $\mathbf{x}, \mathbf{y} \in \mathrm{dom}(f)$ and $\alpha \in [0, 1]$. Define $\mathbf{z}_\alpha = (1 - \alpha)\mathbf{x} + \alpha\mathbf{y}$. By the convexity of $\mathrm{dom}(f)$, $\mathbf{z}_\alpha \in \mathrm{dom}(f)$, and hence there exists $\mathbf{g} \in \partial f(\mathbf{z}_\alpha)$, which in particular implies the following two inequalities:

$$f(\mathbf{y}) \geq f(\mathbf{z}_\alpha) + \langle \mathbf{g}, \mathbf{y} - \mathbf{z}_\alpha \rangle = f(\mathbf{z}_\alpha) + (1 - \alpha)\langle \mathbf{g}, \mathbf{y} - \mathbf{x} \rangle,$$
$$f(\mathbf{x}) \geq f(\mathbf{z}_\alpha) + \langle \mathbf{g}, \mathbf{x} - \mathbf{z}_\alpha \rangle = f(\mathbf{z}_\alpha) - \alpha\langle \mathbf{g}, \mathbf{y} - \mathbf{x} \rangle.$$

Multiplying the first inequality by α, the second by $1 - \alpha$, and summing them yields

$$f((1 - \alpha)\mathbf{x} + \alpha\mathbf{y}) = f(\mathbf{z}_\alpha) \leq (1 - \alpha)f(\mathbf{x}) + \alpha f(\mathbf{y}).$$

Since the latter holds for any $\mathbf{x}, \mathbf{y} \in \mathrm{dom}(f)$ with $\mathrm{dom}(f)$ being convex, it follows that the function f is convex. $\Box$

We have thus shown that if a function is subdifferentiable at any point in its (assumed to be) convex domain, then it is convex. However, this does not mean that the reverse direction is correct. The next example describes a convex function, which is not subdifferentiable at one of the points in its domain.

Example 3.12. Consider the convex function $f : \mathbb{R} \rightarrow (-\infty, \infty]$ defined by

$$f(x) = \begin{cases} -\sqrt{x}, & x \geq 0, \\ \infty, & \text{else.} \end{cases}$$

The function is plotted in Figure 3.2. It is not subdifferentiable at $x = 0$. To show this, suppose by contradiction that there exists $g \in \mathbb{R}$ such that $g \in \partial f(0)$. Then

$$f(y) \geq f(0) + g(y - 0) \text{ for any } y \geq 0,$$

which is the same as

$$-\sqrt{y} \geq gy \text{ for any } y \geq 0. \tag{3.7}$$

The above is impossible since substituting $y = 1$, we obtain that $g \leq -1$ (and in particular $g < 0$), while substituting $y = \frac{1}{2g^2}$ in (3.7) yields the inequality

$$-\sqrt{1/(2g^2)} \geq 1/(2g),$$

which is equivalent to the impossible inequality (utilizing the fact that $g < 0$)

$$\frac{1}{2g^2} \leq \frac{1}{4g^2}. \quad \blacksquare$$

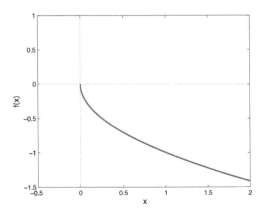

Figure 3.2. *The function $f(x) = -\sqrt{x}$ with $\mathrm{dom}(f) = \mathbb{R}_+$. The function is not subdifferentiable at $x = 0$.*

Although, as demonstrated in Example 3.12, convex functions are not necessarily subdifferentiable at any point in their domain, they must be subdifferentiable at any point in the interior of their domain. This is stated in Theorem 3.14 below, which also shows the boundedness of the subdifferential set in this setting. The proof of the theorem strongly relies on the supporting hyperplane theorem stated explicitly below.

Theorem 3.13 (supporting hyperplane theorem [29, Proposition 2.4.1]). *Let $\emptyset \neq C \subseteq \mathbb{E}$ be a convex set, and let $\mathbf{y} \notin \mathrm{int}(C)$. Then there exists $\mathbf{0} \neq \mathbf{p} \in \mathbb{E}^*$ such that*

$$\langle \mathbf{p}, \mathbf{x} \rangle \leq \langle \mathbf{p}, \mathbf{y} \rangle \text{ for any } \mathbf{x} \in C.$$

Theorem 3.14 (nonemptiness and boundedness of the subdifferential set at interior points of the domain). *Let $f : \mathbb{E} \to (-\infty, \infty]$ be a proper convex function, and assume that $\tilde{\mathbf{x}} \in \mathrm{int}(\mathrm{dom}(f))$. Then $\partial f(\tilde{\mathbf{x}})$ is nonempty and bounded.*

Proof. Recall that the inner product in the product space $\mathbb{E} \times \mathbb{R}$ is defined as (see Section 1.9)

$$\langle (\mathbf{y}_1, \beta_1), (\mathbf{y}_2, \beta_2) \rangle \equiv \langle \mathbf{y}_1, \mathbf{y}_2 \rangle + \beta_1 \beta_2, \quad (\mathbf{y}_1, \beta_1), (\mathbf{y}_2, \beta_2) \in \mathbb{E} \times \mathbb{R}.$$

Since $(\tilde{\mathbf{x}}, f(\tilde{\mathbf{x}}))$ is on the boundary of $\mathrm{epi}(f) \subseteq \mathbb{E} \times \mathbb{R}$, it follows by the supporting hyperplane theorem (Theorem 3.13) that there exists a separating hyperplane between $(\tilde{\mathbf{x}}, f(\tilde{\mathbf{x}}))$ and $\mathrm{epi}(f)$, meaning that there exists a nonzero vector $(\mathbf{p}, -\alpha) \in \mathbb{E}^* \times \mathbb{R}$ for which

$$\langle \mathbf{p}, \tilde{\mathbf{x}} \rangle - \alpha f(\tilde{\mathbf{x}}) \geq \langle \mathbf{p}, \mathbf{x} \rangle - \alpha t \text{ for any } (\mathbf{x}, t) \in \mathrm{epi}(f). \tag{3.8}$$

Note that $\alpha \geq 0$ since $(\tilde{\mathbf{x}}, f(\tilde{\mathbf{x}}) + 1) \in \mathrm{epi}(f)$, and hence plugging $\mathbf{x} = \tilde{\mathbf{x}}$ and $t = f(\tilde{\mathbf{x}}) + 1$ into (3.8) yields

$$\langle \mathbf{p}, \tilde{\mathbf{x}} \rangle - \alpha f(\tilde{\mathbf{x}}) \geq \langle \mathbf{p}, \tilde{\mathbf{x}} \rangle - \alpha(f(\tilde{\mathbf{x}}) + 1),$$

implying that $\alpha \geq 0$. Since $\tilde{\mathbf{x}} \in \mathrm{int}(\mathrm{dom}(f))$, it follows by the local Lipschitz continuity property of convex functions (Theorem 2.21) that there exist $\varepsilon > 0$ and $L > 0$ such that $B_{\|\cdot\|}[\tilde{\mathbf{x}}, \varepsilon] \subseteq \mathrm{dom}(f)$ and

$$|f(\mathbf{x}) - f(\tilde{\mathbf{x}})| \leq L\|\mathbf{x} - \tilde{\mathbf{x}}\| \text{ for any } \mathbf{x} \in B_{\|\cdot\|}[\tilde{\mathbf{x}}, \varepsilon]. \tag{3.9}$$

Since $B_{\|\cdot\|}[\tilde{\mathbf{x}}, \varepsilon] \subseteq \mathrm{dom}(f)$, it follows that $(\mathbf{x}, f(\mathbf{x})) \in \mathrm{epi}(f)$ for any $\mathbf{x} \in B_{\|\cdot\|}[\tilde{\mathbf{x}}, \varepsilon]$. Therefore, plugging $t = f(\mathbf{x})$ into (3.8), yields that

$$\langle \mathbf{p}, \mathbf{x} - \tilde{\mathbf{x}} \rangle \leq \alpha(f(\mathbf{x}) - f(\tilde{\mathbf{x}})) \text{ for any } \mathbf{x} \in B_{\|\cdot\|}[\tilde{\mathbf{x}}, \varepsilon]. \tag{3.10}$$

Combining (3.9) and (3.10), we obtain that for any $\mathbf{x} \in B_{\|\cdot\|}[\tilde{\mathbf{x}}, \varepsilon]$,

$$\langle \mathbf{p}, \mathbf{x} - \tilde{\mathbf{x}} \rangle \leq \alpha(f(\mathbf{x}) - f(\tilde{\mathbf{x}})) \leq \alpha L\|\mathbf{x} - \tilde{\mathbf{x}}\|. \tag{3.11}$$

Take $\mathbf{p}^{\dagger} \in \mathbb{E}$ satisfying $\langle \mathbf{p}, \mathbf{p}^{\dagger} \rangle = \|\mathbf{p}\|_*$ and $\|\mathbf{p}^{\dagger}\| = 1$. Since $\tilde{\mathbf{x}} + \varepsilon \mathbf{p}^{\dagger} \in B_{\|\cdot\|}[\tilde{\mathbf{x}}, \varepsilon]$, we can plug $\mathbf{x} = \tilde{\mathbf{x}} + \varepsilon \mathbf{p}^{\dagger}$ into (3.11) and obtain that

$$\varepsilon\|\mathbf{p}\|_* = \varepsilon \langle \mathbf{p}, \mathbf{p}^{\dagger} \rangle \leq \alpha L \varepsilon\|\mathbf{p}^{\dagger}\| = \alpha L \varepsilon.$$

Therefore, $\alpha > 0$, since otherwise we would have $\alpha = 0$ and $\mathbf{p} = \mathbf{0}$, which is impossible by the fact that the vector $(\mathbf{p}, \alpha)$ is not the zeros vector. Taking $t = f(\mathbf{x})$ in (3.8) and dividing by α yields

$$f(\mathbf{x}) \geq f(\tilde{\mathbf{x}}) + \langle \mathbf{g}, \mathbf{x} - \tilde{\mathbf{x}} \rangle \text{ for all } \mathbf{x} \in \mathrm{dom}(f), \tag{3.12}$$

where $\mathbf{g} = \mathbf{p}/\alpha$. Thus, $\mathbf{g} \in \partial f(\tilde{\mathbf{x}})$, establishing the nonemptiness of $\partial f(\tilde{\mathbf{x}})$. To show the boundedness of $\partial f(\tilde{\mathbf{x}})$, let $\mathbf{g} \in \partial f(\tilde{\mathbf{x}})$, meaning that (3.12) holds. Take $\mathbf{g}^{\dagger} \in \mathbb{E}$ for which $\|\mathbf{g}\|_* = \langle \mathbf{g}, \mathbf{g}^{\dagger} \rangle$ and $\|\mathbf{g}^{\dagger}\| = 1$. Then plugging $\mathbf{x} = \tilde{\mathbf{x}} + \varepsilon \mathbf{g}^{\dagger}$ in (3.12) yields

$$\varepsilon\|\mathbf{g}\|_* = \varepsilon \langle \mathbf{g}, \mathbf{g}^{\dagger} \rangle = \langle \mathbf{g}, \mathbf{x} - \tilde{\mathbf{x}} \rangle \leq f(\mathbf{x}) - f(\tilde{\mathbf{x}}) \overset{(3.9)}{\leq} L\|\mathbf{x} - \tilde{\mathbf{x}}\| = L\varepsilon,$$

showing that $\partial f(\tilde{\mathbf{x}}) \subseteq B_{\|\cdot\|_*}[\mathbf{0}, L]$, and hence establishing the boundedness of $\partial f(\tilde{\mathbf{x}})$. $\square$

The result of Theorem 3.14 can be stated as the following inclusion relation:

$$\mathrm{int}(\mathrm{dom}(f)) \subseteq \mathrm{dom}(\partial f).$$

A direct consequence of Theorem 3.14 is that real-valued convex functions (namely, convex functions f with $\mathrm{dom}(f) = \mathbb{E}$) are subdifferentiable at any point.

Corollary 3.15 (subdifferentiability of real-valued convex functions). *Let $f : \mathbb{E} \rightarrow \mathbb{R}$ be a convex function. Then f is subdifferentiable over $\mathbb{E}$.*

We can extend the boundedness result of Theorem 3.14 and show that the set of all subgradients of points in a given compact set contained in the interior of the domain is always bounded.

Theorem 3.16 (boundedness of subgradients over compact sets). *Let $f : \mathbb{E} \rightarrow (-\infty, \infty]$ be a proper convex function, and assume that $X \subseteq \mathrm{int}(\mathrm{dom}(f))$ is nonempty and compact. Then $Y = \bigcup_{\mathbf{x} \in X} \partial f(\mathbf{x})$ is nonempty and bounded.*

Proof. The set Y is nonempty, since by Theorem 3.14 $\partial f(\mathbf{x}) \neq \emptyset$ for any $\mathbf{x} \in X$. To prove the boundedness, assume by contradiction that there exists a sequence $\{\mathbf{x}_k\}_{k \geq 1} \subseteq X$ and $\mathbf{g}_k \in \partial f(\mathbf{x}_k)$ such that $\|\mathbf{g}_k\|_* \to \infty$ as $k \to \infty$. For any k, let $\mathbf{g}_k^\dagger$ be a vector satisfying $\langle \mathbf{g}_k, \mathbf{g}_k^\dagger \rangle = \|\mathbf{g}_k\|_*$ and $\|\mathbf{g}_k^\dagger\| = 1$. Since X is compact, $(\text{int}(\text{dom}(f)))^c$ (the complement of $\text{int}(\text{dom}(f)))$ is closed, and $X \cap (\text{int}(\text{dom}(f)))^c = \emptyset$, it follows that the distance between the two sets is nonempty, meaning in particular that there exists an $\varepsilon > 0$ for which[10]

$$\|\mathbf{x} - \mathbf{y}\| \geq \varepsilon \text{ for any } \mathbf{x} \in X, \mathbf{y} \notin \text{int}(\text{dom}(f)). \tag{3.13}$$

The relation $\mathbf{g}_k \in \partial f(\mathbf{x}_k)$ implies in particular that

$$f\left(\mathbf{x}_k + \frac{\varepsilon}{2}\mathbf{g}_k^\dagger\right) - f(\mathbf{x}_k) \geq \frac{\varepsilon}{2}\langle \mathbf{g}_k, \mathbf{g}_k^\dagger \rangle = \frac{\varepsilon}{2}\|\mathbf{g}_k\|_*, \tag{3.14}$$

where we used the fact that by (3.13), $\mathbf{x}_k + \frac{\varepsilon}{2}\mathbf{g}_k^\dagger \in \text{int}(\text{dom}(f))$. We will show that the left-hand side of (3.14) is bounded. Suppose by contradiction that it is not bounded. Then there exist subsequences $\{\mathbf{x}_k\}_{k \in T}$, $\{\mathbf{g}_k^\dagger\}_{k \in T}$ (T being the set of indices of the subsequences) for which

$$f\left(\mathbf{x}_k + \frac{\varepsilon}{2}\mathbf{g}_k^\dagger\right) - f(\mathbf{x}_k) \to \infty \text{ as } k \xrightarrow{T} \infty. \tag{3.15}$$

Since both $\{\mathbf{x}_k\}_{k \in T}$ and $\{\mathbf{g}_k^\dagger\}_{k \in T}$ are bounded, it follows that there exist convergent subsequences $\{\mathbf{x}_k\}_{k \in S}$, $\{\mathbf{g}_k^\dagger\}_{k \in S}$ ($S \subseteq T$) whose limits will be denoted by $\bar{\mathbf{x}}$ and $\bar{\mathbf{g}}$. Consequently, $\mathbf{x}_k + \frac{\varepsilon}{2}\mathbf{g}_k^\dagger \to \bar{\mathbf{x}} + \frac{\varepsilon}{2}\bar{\mathbf{g}}$ as $k \xrightarrow{S} \infty$. Since $\mathbf{x}_k, \mathbf{x}_k + \frac{\varepsilon}{2}\mathbf{g}_k^\dagger, \bar{\mathbf{x}} + \frac{\varepsilon}{2}\bar{\mathbf{g}}$ are all[11] in $\text{int}(\text{dom}(f))$, it follows by the continuity of f over $\text{int}(\text{dom}(f))$ (Theorem 2.21) that

$$f\left(\mathbf{x}_k + \frac{\varepsilon}{2}\mathbf{g}_k^\dagger\right) - f(\mathbf{x}_k) \to f\left(\bar{\mathbf{x}} + \frac{\varepsilon}{2}\bar{\mathbf{g}}^\dagger\right) - f(\bar{\mathbf{x}}) \text{ as } k \xrightarrow{S} \infty,$$

which is a contradiction of (3.15). We can thus conclude that the left-hand side of (3.14) is bounded and hence that the right-hand side of (3.14) is also bounded, in contradiction to our assumption that $\|\mathbf{g}_k\|_*$ goes to ∞ as $k \to \infty$. $\square$

Subdifferentiability can be guaranteed for points that are not necessarily in the interior of the domain but are in the interior of the domain w.r.t. its affine hull. This is the notion of *relative interior* that we now recall:

$$\text{ri}(S) = \{\mathbf{x} \in \text{aff}(S) : B[\mathbf{x}, \varepsilon] \cap \text{aff}(S) \subseteq S \text{ for some } \varepsilon > 0\}.$$

One key property of the relative interior is that it is nonempty for convex sets.

Theorem 3.17 (nonemptiness of the relative interior [108, Theorem 6.2]). *Let $C \subseteq \mathbb{E}$ be a nonempty convex set. Then $\text{ri}(C)$ is nonempty.*

---

[10]The proof of (3.13) is simple. Suppose by contradiction that there exist sequences $\{\mathbf{x}_k\}_{k \geq 1} \subseteq X$ and $\{\mathbf{y}_k\}_{k \geq 1} \subseteq (\text{int}(\text{dom}(f)))^c$ satisfying $\|\mathbf{x}_k - \mathbf{y}_k\| \to 0$ as $k \to \infty$. Since $\{\mathbf{x}_k\}_{k \geq 1}$ is bounded, there exists $M > 0$ for which $\|\mathbf{x}_k\| \leq M$ for all k. Therefore, $\|\mathbf{y}_k\| \leq \|\mathbf{x}_k - \mathbf{y}_k\| + \|\mathbf{x}_k\| \leq \|\mathbf{x}_k - \mathbf{y}_k\| + M$, and we can conclude by the boundedness of $\{\|\mathbf{x}_k - \mathbf{y}_k\|\}_{k \geq 1}$ that $\{\mathbf{y}_k\}_{k \geq 1}$ is bounded. By the Bolzano–Weierstrass theorem, there exist convergent subsequences $\mathbf{x}_{k_j} \to \bar{\mathbf{x}}, \mathbf{y}_{k_j} \to \bar{\mathbf{y}}$, and by the closedness of X and $(\text{int}(\text{dom}(f)))^c$, we have that $\bar{\mathbf{x}} \in X, \bar{\mathbf{y}} \in (\text{int}(\text{dom}(f)))^c$. The limit $\|\mathbf{x}_{k_j} - \mathbf{y}_{k_j}\| \to 0$ as $j \to \infty$ now brings us to the impossible equality $\bar{\mathbf{x}} = \bar{\mathbf{y}}$.

[11]The fact that $\bar{\mathbf{x}} + \frac{\varepsilon}{2}\bar{\mathbf{g}} \in \text{int}(\text{dom}(f))$ follows by (3.13) and the relations $\bar{\mathbf{x}} \in X$ and $\|\bar{\mathbf{g}}\| = 1$.

A well-known result is that a proper convex function is always subdifferentiable at relative interior points of its domain. We state this result without a proof.

Theorem 3.18 (nonemptiness of the subdifferential set at relative interior points [108, Theorem 23.4]). *Let $f : \mathbb{E} \to (-\infty, \infty]$ be a proper convex function, and let $\tilde{\mathbf{x}} \in \mathrm{ri}(\mathrm{dom}(f))$. Then $\partial f(\tilde{\mathbf{x}})$ is nonempty.*

The result stated in Theorem 3.18 can be written as the inclusion

$$\mathrm{ri}(\mathrm{dom}(f)) \subseteq \mathrm{dom}(\partial f).$$

Since the relative interior of $\mathrm{dom}(f)$ is always nonempty (Theorem 3.17), we can conclude that there always exists a point in the domain for which the subdifferential set is nonempty.

Corollary 3.19. *Let $f : \mathbb{E} \to (-\infty, \infty]$ be a proper convex function. Then there exists $\mathbf{x} \in \mathrm{dom}(f)$ for which $\partial f(\mathbf{x})$ is nonempty.*

One instance in which the subdifferential set $\partial f(\mathbf{x})$ is guaranteed to be *unbounded* is when the dimension of the domain of the function is strictly smaller than the dimension of the underlying space $\mathbb{E}$.

Theorem 3.20 (unboundedness of the subdifferential set when $\dim(\mathrm{dom}(f)) < \dim(\mathbb{E})$). *Let $f : \mathbb{E} \to (-\infty, \infty]$ be a proper convex function. Suppose that $\dim(\mathrm{dom}(f)) < \dim(\mathbb{E})$ and let $\mathbf{x} \in \mathrm{dom}(f)$. If $\partial f(\mathbf{x}) \neq \emptyset$, then $\partial f(\mathbf{x})$ is unbounded.*

Proof. Let $\boldsymbol{\eta}$ be an arbitrary vector in $\partial f(\mathbf{x})$. The set[12] $\mathbb{V} \equiv \mathrm{aff}(\mathrm{dom}(f)) - \{\mathbf{x}\}$ is a vector space. The dimension condition translates to $\dim(\mathbb{V}) < \dim(\mathbb{E})$, which in particular implies that there exists a nonzero vector $\mathbf{v} \in \mathbb{E}$ such that $\langle \mathbf{v}, \mathbf{w} \rangle = 0$ for any $\mathbf{w} \in \mathbb{V}$. Take any $\beta \in \mathbb{R}$. For any $\mathbf{y} \in \mathrm{dom}(f)$,

$$f(\mathbf{y}) \geq f(\mathbf{x}) + \langle \boldsymbol{\eta}, \mathbf{y} - \mathbf{x} \rangle = f(\mathbf{x}) + \langle \boldsymbol{\eta} + \beta \mathbf{v}, \mathbf{y} - \mathbf{x} \rangle,$$

where the equality is due to the fact that $\mathbf{y} - \mathbf{x} \in \mathbb{V}$. We thus obtained that $\boldsymbol{\eta} + \beta \mathbf{v} \in \partial f(\mathbf{x})$ for any β, implying the unboundedness of $\partial f(\mathbf{x})$. $\quad\square$

3.3   Directional Derivatives

3.3.1   Definition and Basic Properties

Let $f : \mathbb{E} \to (-\infty, \infty]$ be a proper function and let $\mathbf{x} \in \mathrm{int}(\mathrm{dom}(f))$. The *directional derivative* of f at $\mathbf{x}$ in a given direction $\mathbf{d} \in \mathbb{E}$, if it exists, is defined by

$$f'(\mathbf{x}; \mathbf{d}) \equiv \lim_{\alpha \to 0^+} \frac{f(\mathbf{x} + \alpha \mathbf{d}) - f(\mathbf{x})}{\alpha}.$$

A well-known result states that convex functions have directional derivatives in all directions at points in the interior of their domains.

---

[12]Here the notation "$-$" stands for the Minkowski difference.

Theorem 3.21 ([108, Theorem 23.1][13]). *Let $f : \mathbb{E} \to (-\infty, \infty]$ be a proper convex function and let $\mathbf{x} \in \text{int}(\text{dom}(f))$. Then for any $\mathbf{d} \in \mathbb{E}$, the directional derivative $f'(\mathbf{x}; \mathbf{d})$ exists.*

It is important to establish some basic properties of the function $\mathbf{d} \mapsto f'(\mathbf{x}; \mathbf{d})$. The next theorem shows that it is convex and homogeneous of degree 1.

Lemma 3.22 (convexity and homogeneity of $\mathbf{d} \mapsto f'(\mathbf{x}; \mathbf{d})$). *Let $f : \mathbb{E} \to (-\infty, \infty]$ be a proper convex function and let $\mathbf{x} \in \text{int}(\text{dom}(f))$. Then*

(a) *the function $\mathbf{d} \mapsto f'(\mathbf{x}; \mathbf{d})$ is convex;*

(b) *for any $\lambda \geq 0$ and $\mathbf{d} \in \mathbb{E}$, it holds that $f'(\mathbf{x}; \lambda \mathbf{d}) = \lambda f'(\mathbf{x}; \mathbf{d})$.*

Proof. (a) To show that the function $g(\mathbf{d}) \equiv f'(\mathbf{x}; \mathbf{d})$ is convex, take $\mathbf{d}_1, \mathbf{d}_2 \in \mathbb{E}$ and $\lambda \in [0, 1]$. Then

$$
\begin{aligned}
f'(\mathbf{x}; \lambda \mathbf{d}_1 + (1 - \lambda)\mathbf{d}_2) \\
&= \lim_{\alpha \to 0^+} \frac{f(\mathbf{x} + \alpha[\lambda \mathbf{d}_1 + (1 - \lambda)\mathbf{d}_2]) - f(\mathbf{x})}{\alpha} \\
&= \lim_{\alpha \to 0^+} \frac{f(\lambda(\mathbf{x} + \alpha \mathbf{d}_1) + (1 - \lambda)(\mathbf{x} + \alpha \mathbf{d}_2)) - f(\mathbf{x})}{\alpha} \\
&\leq \lim_{\alpha \to 0^+} \frac{\lambda f(\mathbf{x} + \alpha \mathbf{d}_1) + (1 - \lambda)f(\mathbf{x} + \alpha \mathbf{d}_2) - f(\mathbf{x})}{\alpha} \\
&= \lambda \lim_{\alpha \to 0^+} \frac{f(\mathbf{x} + \alpha \mathbf{d}_1) - f(\mathbf{x})}{\alpha} + (1 - \lambda) \lim_{\alpha \to 0^+} \frac{f(\mathbf{x} + \alpha \mathbf{d}_2) - f(\mathbf{x})}{\alpha} \\
&= \lambda f'(\mathbf{x}; \mathbf{d}_1) + (1 - \lambda)f'(\mathbf{x}; \mathbf{d}_2),
\end{aligned}
$$

where the inequality follows from Jensen's inequality for convex functions.
(b) If $\lambda = 0$, the claim is trivial. Take $\lambda > 0$. Then

$$
f'(\mathbf{x}; \lambda \mathbf{d}) = \lim_{\alpha \to 0^+} \frac{f(\mathbf{x} + \alpha \lambda \mathbf{d}) - f(\mathbf{x})}{\alpha} = \lambda \lim_{\alpha \to 0^+} \frac{f(\mathbf{x} + \alpha \lambda \mathbf{d}) - f(\mathbf{x})}{\alpha \lambda} = \lambda f'(\mathbf{x}; \mathbf{d}).
$$

$\square$

The next result highlights a connection between function values and directional derivatives under a convexity assumption.

Lemma 3.23. *Let $f : \mathbb{E} \to (-\infty, \infty]$ be a proper convex function, and let $\mathbf{x} \in \text{int}(\text{dom}(f))$. Then*

$$
f(\mathbf{y}) \geq f(\mathbf{x}) + f'(\mathbf{x}; \mathbf{y} - \mathbf{x}) \text{ for all } \mathbf{y} \in \text{dom}(f).
$$

---

[13]See also [10, Theorem 7.37].

Proof. By the definition of the directional derivative,

$$
\begin{aligned}
f'(\mathbf{x}; \mathbf{y} - \mathbf{x}) &= \lim_{\alpha \to 0^+} \frac{f(\mathbf{x} + \alpha(\mathbf{y} - \mathbf{x})) - f(\mathbf{x})}{\alpha} \\
&= \lim_{\alpha \to 0^+} \frac{f((1 - \alpha)\mathbf{x} + \alpha\mathbf{y}) - f(\mathbf{x})}{\alpha} \\
&\leq \lim_{\alpha \to 0^+} \frac{-\alpha f(\mathbf{x}) + \alpha f(\mathbf{y})}{\alpha} \\
&= f(\mathbf{y}) - f(\mathbf{x}),
\end{aligned}
$$

where the inequality follows by Jensen's inequality. $\square$

A useful "calculus" rule for directional derivatives shows how to compute the directional derivative of maximum of a finite collection of functions without any convexity assumptions.

Theorem 3.24 (directional derivative of maximum of functions). *Suppose that $f(\mathbf{x}) = \max\{f_1(\mathbf{x}), f_2(\mathbf{x}), \ldots, f_m(\mathbf{x})\}$, where $f_1, f_2, \ldots, f_m : \mathbb{E} \to (-\infty, \infty]$ are proper functions. Let $\mathbf{x} \in \bigcap_{i=1}^{m} \operatorname{int}(\operatorname{dom}(f_i))$ and $\mathbf{d} \in \mathbb{E}$. Assume that $f_i'(\mathbf{x}; \mathbf{d})$ exist for any $i \in \{1, 2, \ldots, m\}$. Then*

$$
f'(\mathbf{x}; \mathbf{d}) = \max_{i \in I(\mathbf{x})} f_i'(\mathbf{x}; \mathbf{d}),
$$

where $I(\mathbf{x}) = \{i : f_i(\mathbf{x}) = f(\mathbf{x})\}$.

Proof. For any $i \in \{1, 2, \ldots, m\}$,

$$
\lim_{t \to 0^+} f_i(\mathbf{x} + t\mathbf{d}) = \lim_{t \to 0^+} \left[t \frac{f_i(\mathbf{x} + t\mathbf{d}) - f_i(\mathbf{x})}{t} + f_i(\mathbf{x}) \right] = 0 \cdot f_i'(\mathbf{x}; \mathbf{d}) + f_i(\mathbf{x}) = f_i(\mathbf{x}).
$$

$$(3.16)$$

By the definition of $I(\mathbf{x})$, $f_i(\mathbf{x}) > f_j(\mathbf{x})$ for any $i \in I(\mathbf{x}), j \notin I(\mathbf{x})$. Utilizing (3.16), it follows that there exists an $\varepsilon > 0$ such that $f_i(\mathbf{x} + t\mathbf{d}) > f_j(\mathbf{x} + t\mathbf{d})$ for any $i \in I(\mathbf{x}), j \notin I(\mathbf{x})$ and $t \in (0, \varepsilon]$. Therefore, for any $t \in (0, \varepsilon]$,

$$
f(\mathbf{x} + t\mathbf{d}) = \max_{i=1,2,\ldots,m} f_i(\mathbf{x} + t\mathbf{d}) = \max_{i \in I(\mathbf{x})} f_i(\mathbf{x} + t\mathbf{d}).
$$

Consequently, for any $t \in (0, \varepsilon]$,

$$
\frac{f(\mathbf{x} + t\mathbf{d}) - f(\mathbf{x})}{t} = \frac{\max_{i \in I(\mathbf{x})} f_i(\mathbf{x} + t\mathbf{d}) - f(\mathbf{x})}{t} = \max_{i \in I(\mathbf{x})} \frac{f_i(\mathbf{x} + t\mathbf{d}) - f_i(\mathbf{x})}{t},
$$

where the last equality follows from the fact that $f(\mathbf{x}) = f_i(\mathbf{x})$ for any $i \in I(\mathbf{x})$. Finally, taking $t \to 0^+$, we obtain that

$$
\begin{aligned}
f'(\mathbf{x}; \mathbf{d}) &= \lim_{t \to 0^+} \frac{f(\mathbf{x} + t\mathbf{d}) - f(\mathbf{x})}{t} \\
&= \lim_{t \to 0^+} \max_{i \in I(\mathbf{x})} \frac{f_i(\mathbf{x} + t\mathbf{d}) - f_i(\mathbf{x})}{t} \\
&= \max_{i \in I(\mathbf{x})} \lim_{t \to 0^+} \frac{f_i(\mathbf{x} + t\mathbf{d}) - f_i(\mathbf{x})}{t} \\
&= \max_{i \in I(\mathbf{x})} f_i'(\mathbf{x}; \mathbf{d}).   \square
\end{aligned}
$$

Note that an assumption of Theorem 3.24 is that the directional derivatives $f_i'(\mathbf{x}; \mathbf{d})$ exist. This assumption is automatically satisfied when the functions $f_1, f_2, \ldots, f_m$ are convex. We can thus write the next corollary that replaces the condition on the existence of the directional derivatives by a convexity assumption.

Corollary 3.25 (directional derivative of maximum of functions—convex case). *Suppose that $f(\mathbf{x}) = \max\{f_1(\mathbf{x}), f_2(\mathbf{x}), \ldots, f_m(\mathbf{x})\}$, where $f_1, f_2, \ldots, f_m : \mathbb{E} \to (-\infty, \infty]$ are proper convex functions. Let $\mathbf{x} \in \bigcap_{i=1}^m \mathrm{int}(\mathrm{dom}(f_i))$ and $\mathbf{d} \in \mathbb{E}$. Then*

$$f'(\mathbf{x}; \mathbf{d}) = \max_{i \in I(\mathbf{x})} f_i'(\mathbf{x}; \mathbf{d}),$$

where $I(\mathbf{x}) = \{i : f_i(\mathbf{x}) = f(\mathbf{x})\}$.

3.3.2 The Max Formula

We will now prove an extremely important and useful result, known as the *max formula*, that connects subgradients and directional derivatives.

Theorem 3.26 (max formula). *Let $f : \mathbb{E} \to (-\infty, \infty]$ be a proper convex function. Then for any $\mathbf{x} \in \mathrm{int}(\mathrm{dom}(f))$ and $\mathbf{d} \in \mathbb{E}$,*

$$f'(\mathbf{x}; \mathbf{d}) = \max\{\langle \mathbf{g}, \mathbf{d} \rangle : \mathbf{g} \in \partial f(\mathbf{x})\}. \tag{3.17}$$

Proof. Let $\mathbf{x} \in \mathrm{int}(\mathrm{dom}(f))$ and $\mathbf{d} \in \mathbb{E}$. By the subgradient inequality, we have that for any $\mathbf{g} \in \partial f(\mathbf{x})$,

$$f'(\mathbf{x}; \mathbf{d}) = \lim_{\alpha \to 0^+} \frac{1}{\alpha}(f(\mathbf{x} + \alpha \mathbf{d}) - f(\mathbf{x})) \geq \lim_{\alpha \to 0^+} \langle \mathbf{g}, \mathbf{d} \rangle = \langle \mathbf{g}, \mathbf{d} \rangle \tag{3.18}$$

and, consequently,

$$f'(\mathbf{x}; \mathbf{d}) \geq \max\{\langle \mathbf{g}, \mathbf{d} \rangle : \mathbf{g} \in \partial f(\mathbf{x})\}. \tag{3.19}$$

All that is left is to show the reverse direction of the above inequality. For that, define the function $h(\mathbf{w}) \equiv f'(\mathbf{x}; \mathbf{w})$. Then by Theorem 3.21 and Lemma 3.22(a), h is a real-valued convex function and is thus subdifferentiable over $\mathbb{E}$ (Corollary 3.15). Let $\tilde{\mathbf{g}} \in \partial h(\mathbf{d})$. Then for any $\mathbf{v} \in \mathbb{E}$ and $\alpha \geq 0$, using the homogeneity of h (Lemma 3.22(b)),

$$\alpha f'(\mathbf{x}; \mathbf{v}) = f'(\mathbf{x}; \alpha \mathbf{v}) = h(\alpha \mathbf{v}) \geq h(\mathbf{d}) + \langle \tilde{\mathbf{g}}, \alpha \mathbf{v} - \mathbf{d} \rangle = f'(\mathbf{x}; \mathbf{d}) + \langle \tilde{\mathbf{g}}, \alpha \mathbf{v} - \mathbf{d} \rangle.$$

Therefore,

$$\alpha(f'(\mathbf{x}; \mathbf{v}) - \langle \tilde{\mathbf{g}}, \mathbf{v} \rangle) \geq f'(\mathbf{x}; \mathbf{d}) - \langle \tilde{\mathbf{g}}, \mathbf{d} \rangle. \tag{3.20}$$

Since the above inequality holds for any $\alpha \geq 0$, it follows that the coefficient of α in the left-hand side expression is nonnegative (otherwise, inequality (3.20) would be violated for large enough α), meaning that

$$f'(\mathbf{x}; \mathbf{v}) \geq \langle \tilde{\mathbf{g}}, \mathbf{v} \rangle.$$

Thus, by Lemma 3.23, for any $\mathbf{y} \in \mathrm{dom}(f)$,

$$f(\mathbf{y}) \geq f(\mathbf{x}) + f'(\mathbf{x}; \mathbf{y} - \mathbf{x}) \geq f(\mathbf{x}) + \langle \tilde{\mathbf{g}}, \mathbf{y} - \mathbf{x} \rangle,$$

showing that $\tilde{\mathbf{g}} \in \partial f(\mathbf{x})$. Taking $\alpha = 0$ in (3.20), we have that $f'(\mathbf{x}; \mathbf{d}) \leq \langle \tilde{\mathbf{g}}, \mathbf{d} \rangle$, so that

$$f'(\mathbf{x}; \mathbf{d}) \leq \langle \tilde{\mathbf{g}}, \mathbf{d} \rangle \leq \max\{\langle \mathbf{g}, \mathbf{d} \rangle : \mathbf{g} \in \partial f(\mathbf{x})\},$$

establishing the desired result. $\square$

Remark 3.27. *The max formula (3.17) can also be rewritten using the support function notation as follows:*

$$f'(\mathbf{x}; \mathbf{d}) = \sigma_{\partial f(\mathbf{x})}(\mathbf{d}).$$

3.3.3   Differentiability

Definition 3.28 (differentiability). *Let* $f : \mathbb{E} \to (-\infty, \infty]$ *and* $\mathbf{x} \in \text{int}(\text{dom} f)$. *The function* f *is said to be* **differentiable** *at* $\mathbf{x}$ *if there exists* $\mathbf{g} \in \mathbb{E}^*$ *such that*

$$\lim_{\mathbf{h} \to \mathbf{0}} \frac{f(\mathbf{x} + \mathbf{h}) - f(\mathbf{x}) - \langle \mathbf{g}, \mathbf{h} \rangle}{\|\mathbf{h}\|} = 0. \tag{3.21}$$

The unique[14] *vector* $\mathbf{g}$ *satisfying (3.21) is called the* **gradient** *of* f *at* $\mathbf{x}$ *and is denoted by* $\nabla f(\mathbf{x})$.

The above is actually a definition of Fréchet differentiability, which is the one used in this book.

If f is differentiable at $\mathbf{x} \in \text{int}(\text{dom} f)$, then the directional derivative has a simple formula.

Theorem 3.29 (directional derivatives at points of differentiability). *Let* $f : \mathbb{E} \to (-\infty, \infty]$ *be proper, and suppose that* f *is differentiable at* $\mathbf{x} \in \text{int}(\text{dom} f)$. *Then for any* $\mathbf{d} \in \mathbb{E}$

$$f'(\mathbf{x}; \mathbf{d}) = \langle \nabla f(\mathbf{x}), \mathbf{d} \rangle. \tag{3.22}$$

Proof. The formula is obviously correct for $\mathbf{d} = \mathbf{0}$. Suppose that $\mathbf{d} \neq \mathbf{0}$. The differentiability of f implies that

$$0 = \lim_{\alpha \to 0^+} \frac{f(\mathbf{x} + \alpha \mathbf{d}) - f(\mathbf{x}) - \langle \nabla f(\mathbf{x}), \alpha \mathbf{d} \rangle}{\|\alpha \mathbf{d}\|}$$

$$= \lim_{\alpha \to 0^+} \left[\frac{f(\mathbf{x} + \alpha \mathbf{d}) - f(\mathbf{x})}{\alpha \|\mathbf{d}\|} - \frac{\langle \nabla f(\mathbf{x}), \mathbf{d} \rangle}{\|\mathbf{d}\|} \right].$$

Therefore,

$$f'(\mathbf{x}; \mathbf{d}) = \lim_{\alpha \to 0^+} \frac{f(\mathbf{x} + \alpha \mathbf{d}) - f(\mathbf{x})}{\alpha}$$

$$= \lim_{\alpha \to 0^+} \left\{ \|\mathbf{d}\| \left[\frac{f(\mathbf{x} + \alpha \mathbf{d}) - f(\mathbf{x})}{\alpha \|\mathbf{d}\|} - \frac{\langle \nabla f(\mathbf{x}), \mathbf{d} \rangle}{\|\mathbf{d}\|} \right] + \langle \nabla f(\mathbf{x}), \mathbf{d} \rangle \right\}$$

$$= \langle \nabla f(\mathbf{x}), \mathbf{d} \rangle. \quad \square$$

---

[14]The uniqueness can be shown by the following argument. Suppose that (3.21) is satisfied by both $\mathbf{g} = \mathbf{g}_1$ and $\mathbf{g} = \mathbf{g}_2$. Then by subtracting the two limits, we obtain that $\lim_{\mathbf{h} \to \mathbf{0}} \langle \mathbf{g}_1 - \mathbf{g}_2, \mathbf{h} \rangle / \|\mathbf{h}\| = 0$, which immediately shows that $\mathbf{g}_1 = \mathbf{g}_2$.

Example 3.30 (directional derivative of maximum of differentiable functions). Consider the function $f(\mathbf{x}) = \max_{i=1,2,\ldots,m} f_i(\mathbf{x})$, where $f_i : \mathbb{E} \to (-\infty, \infty]$ are proper functions. Assume that $f_1, f_2, \ldots, f_m$ are differentiable at a given point $\mathbf{x} \in \cap_{i=1}^{m} \mathrm{int}(\mathrm{dom}(f_i))$. Then by Theorem 3.29, for any $\mathbf{d} \in \mathbb{E}$, $f_i'(\mathbf{x}; \mathbf{d}) = \langle \nabla f_i(\mathbf{x}), \mathbf{d} \rangle$. Therefore, invoking Theorem 3.24,

$$f'(\mathbf{x}; \mathbf{d}) = \max_{i \in I(\mathbf{x})} f_i'(\mathbf{x}; \mathbf{d}) = \max_{i \in I(\mathbf{x})} \langle \nabla f_i(\mathbf{x}), \mathbf{d} \rangle,$$

where $I(\mathbf{x}) = \{i : f_i(\mathbf{x}) = f(\mathbf{x})\}$. ■

Example 3.31 (gradient of $\frac{1}{2} d_C^2(\cdot)$).[15] Suppose that $\mathbb{E}$ is a Euclidean space, and let $C \subseteq \mathbb{E}$ be nonempty closed and convex set. Consider the function $\varphi_C : \mathbb{E} \to \mathbb{R}$ given by $\varphi_C(\mathbf{x}) \equiv \frac{1}{2} d_C^2(\mathbf{x}) = \frac{1}{2} \|\mathbf{x} - P_C(\mathbf{x})\|^2$, where P_C is the so-called *orthogonal projection* mapping defined by

$$P_C(\mathbf{x}) \equiv \mathrm{argmin}_{\mathbf{y} \in C} \|\mathbf{y} - \mathbf{x}\|.$$

It is well known that P_C is well defined (exists and unique) when the underlying set C is nonempty, closed, and convex.[16] We will show that for any $\mathbf{x} \in \mathbb{E}$,

$$\nabla \varphi_C(\mathbf{x}) = \mathbf{x} - P_C(\mathbf{x}). \tag{3.23}$$

For that, fix $\mathbf{x} \in \mathbb{E}$ and define the function $g_\mathbf{x}$ by

$$g_\mathbf{x}(\mathbf{d}) \equiv \varphi_C(\mathbf{x} + \mathbf{d}) - \varphi_C(\mathbf{x}) - \langle \mathbf{d}, \mathbf{z_x} \rangle,$$

where $\mathbf{z_x} = \mathbf{x} - P_C(\mathbf{x})$. By the definition of the gradient, to show (3.23), it is enough to establish that

$$\frac{g_\mathbf{x}(\mathbf{d})}{\|\mathbf{d}\|} \to 0 \text{ as } \mathbf{d} \to \mathbf{0}. \tag{3.24}$$

To prove (3.24), note that by the definition of the orthogonal projection, we have for any $\mathbf{d} \in \mathbb{E}$

$$\|\mathbf{x} + \mathbf{d} - P_C(\mathbf{x} + \mathbf{d})\|^2 \le \|\mathbf{x} + \mathbf{d} - P_C(\mathbf{x})\|^2,$$

which implies that for any $\mathbf{d} \in \mathbb{E}$,

$$\begin{aligned} g_\mathbf{x}(\mathbf{d}) &= \frac{1}{2} \|\mathbf{x} + \mathbf{d} - P_C(\mathbf{x} + \mathbf{d})\|^2 - \frac{1}{2} \|\mathbf{x} - P_C(\mathbf{x})\|^2 - \langle \mathbf{d}, \mathbf{z_x} \rangle \\ &\le \frac{1}{2} \|\mathbf{x} + \mathbf{d} - P_C(\mathbf{x})\|^2 - \frac{1}{2} \|\mathbf{x} - P_C(\mathbf{x})\|^2 - \langle \mathbf{d}, \mathbf{z_x} \rangle \\ &= \frac{1}{2} \|\mathbf{x} - P_C(\mathbf{x})\|^2 + \langle \mathbf{d}, \mathbf{x} - P_C(\mathbf{x}) \rangle + \frac{1}{2} \|\mathbf{d}\|^2 - \frac{1}{2} \|\mathbf{x} - P_C(\mathbf{x})\|^2 - \langle \mathbf{d}, \mathbf{z_x} \rangle \\ &= \frac{1}{2} \|\mathbf{d}\|^2. \end{aligned} \tag{3.25}$$

In particular, we also have

$$g_\mathbf{x}(-\mathbf{d}) \le \frac{1}{2} \|\mathbf{d}\|^2. \tag{3.26}$$

---

[15]The proof in Example 3.31 follows Beck and Teboulle [20, proof of Theorem 4.1].

[16]See, for example, [10, Theorem 8.8]. In addition, see Section 6.4.

Since φ_C is convex, so is $g_\mathbf{x}$. Therefore, by Jensen's inequality, and noting that $g_\mathbf{x}(\mathbf{0}) = 0$,

$$0 = g_\mathbf{x}(\mathbf{0}) = g_\mathbf{x}\left(\frac{\mathbf{d} + (-\mathbf{d})}{2}\right) \leq \frac{1}{2}(g_\mathbf{x}(\mathbf{d}) + g_\mathbf{x}(-\mathbf{d})). \tag{3.27}$$

Combining (3.26) and (3.27), we get

$$g_\mathbf{x}(\mathbf{d}) \geq -g_\mathbf{x}(-\mathbf{d}) \geq -\frac{1}{2}\|\mathbf{d}\|^2. \tag{3.28}$$

Finally, by (3.25) and (3.28), it follows that $|g_\mathbf{x}(\mathbf{d})| \leq \frac{1}{2}\|\mathbf{d}\|^2$, from which the limit (3.24) follows and hence also the desired result (3.23). ∎

Remark 3.32 (what is the gradient?). *We will now illustrate the fact that the gradient depends on the choice of the inner product in the underlying space. Let $\mathbb{E} = \mathbb{R}^n$ be endowed with the dot product. By Theorem 3.29 we know that when f is differentiable at $\mathbf{x}$, then*

$$(\nabla f(\mathbf{x}))_i = \langle \nabla f(\mathbf{x}), \mathbf{e}_i \rangle = f'(\mathbf{x}; \mathbf{e}_i);$$

that is, in this case, the ith component of $\nabla f(\mathbf{x})$ is equal to $\frac{\partial f}{\partial x_i}(\mathbf{x}) = f'(\mathbf{x}; \mathbf{e}_i)$ —the ith partial derivative of f at $\mathbf{x}$—so that $\nabla f(\mathbf{x}) = D_f(\mathbf{x})$, where

$$D_f(\mathbf{x}) \equiv \begin{pmatrix} \frac{\partial f}{\partial x_1}(\mathbf{x}) \\ \frac{\partial f}{\partial x_2}(\mathbf{x}) \\ \vdots \\ \frac{\partial f}{\partial x_n}(\mathbf{x}) \end{pmatrix}. \tag{3.29}$$

Note that the definition of the directional derivative does not depend on the choice of the inner product in the underlying space, so we can arbitrarily choose the inner product in the formula (3.22) as the dot product and obtain (recalling that in this case $\nabla f(\mathbf{x}) = D_f(\mathbf{x})$)

$$f'(\mathbf{x}; \mathbf{d}) = D_f(\mathbf{x})^T \mathbf{d} = \sum_{i=1}^{n} \frac{\partial f}{\partial x_i}(\mathbf{x})d_i. \tag{3.30}$$

Formula (3.30) holds for any choice of inner product in the space. However, $\nabla f(\mathbf{x})$ is not necessarily equal to $D_f(\mathbf{x})$ when the endowed inner product is not the dot product. For example, suppose that the inner product is given by

$$\langle \mathbf{x}, \mathbf{y} \rangle = \mathbf{x}^T \mathbf{H} \mathbf{y}, \tag{3.31}$$

where $\mathbf{H}$ is a given $n \times n$ positive definite matrix. In this case,

$$(\nabla f(\mathbf{x}))_i = \nabla f(\mathbf{x})^T \mathbf{e}_i = \nabla f(\mathbf{x})^T \mathbf{H}\left(\mathbf{H}^{-1}\mathbf{e}_i\right)$$

$$= \langle \nabla f(\mathbf{x}), \mathbf{H}^{-1}\mathbf{e}_i \rangle \qquad [by\ (3.31)]$$

$$= f'(\mathbf{x}; \mathbf{H}^{-1}\mathbf{e}_i) \qquad [by\ (3.22)]$$

$$= D_f(\mathbf{x})^T \mathbf{H}^{-1}\mathbf{e}_i. \qquad [by\ (3.30)]$$

Hence, we obtain that with respect to the inner product (3.31), *the gradient is actually a "scaled"/"weighted" gradient:*

$$\nabla f(\mathbf{x}) = \mathbf{H}^{-1} D_f(\mathbf{x}).$$

Now consider the space $\mathbb{E} = \mathbb{R}^{m \times n}$ *of all* $m \times n$ *real-valued matrices with the dot product as the endowed inner product:*

$$\langle \mathbf{x}, \mathbf{y} \rangle = \operatorname{Tr}(\mathbf{x}^T \mathbf{y}) \text{ for any } \mathbf{x}, \mathbf{y} \in \mathbb{R}^{m \times n}.$$

Given a proper function $f : \mathbb{R}^{m \times n} \to (-\infty, \infty]$ *and* $\mathbf{x} \in \operatorname{int}(\operatorname{dom}(f))$, *the gradient, if it exists, is given by* $\nabla f(\mathbf{x}) = D_f(\mathbf{x})$, *where* $D_f(\mathbf{x})$ *is the* $m \times n$ *matrix*

$$D_f(\mathbf{x}) = \left(\frac{\partial f}{\partial x_{ij}}(\mathbf{x}) \right)_{i,j}.$$

If the inner product is replaced by

$$\langle \mathbf{x}, \mathbf{y} \rangle = \operatorname{Tr}(\mathbf{x}^T \mathbf{H} \mathbf{y}),$$

where $\mathbf{H}$ *is a given* $m \times m$ *positive definite matrix, then a similar argument to the one given previously shows that*

$$\nabla f(\mathbf{x}) = \mathbf{H}^{-1} D_f(\mathbf{x}).$$

We will now show that when a convex function is differentiable at a point in the interior of its domain, then the subdifferential set is the singleton (i.e., a set containing a single vector) consisting of the gradient at the point. The reverse is also correct in the sense that if the subdifferential set is a singleton $\{\mathbf{g}\}$, then the function is differentiable at the given point with $\mathbf{g}$ being its gradient.

Theorem 3.33 (the subdifferential at points of differentiability). *Let* $f : \mathbb{E} \to (-\infty, \infty]$ *be a proper convex function, and let* $\mathbf{x} \in \operatorname{int}(\operatorname{dom}(f))$. *If* f *is differentiable at* $\mathbf{x}$, *then* $\partial f(\mathbf{x}) = \{\nabla f(\mathbf{x})\}$. *Conversely, if* f *has a unique subgradient at* $\mathbf{x}$, *then it is differentiable at* $\mathbf{x}$ *and* $\partial f(\mathbf{x}) = \{\nabla f(\mathbf{x})\}$.

Proof. Let $\mathbf{x} \in \operatorname{int}(\operatorname{dom}(f))$ and assume that f is differentiable at $\mathbf{x}$. Then by Theorem 3.29 it follows that for any $\mathbf{d} \in \mathbb{E}$,

$$f'(\mathbf{x}; \mathbf{d}) = \langle \nabla f(\mathbf{x}), \mathbf{d} \rangle. \tag{3.32}$$

Let $\mathbf{g} \in \partial f(\mathbf{x})$. We will show that $\mathbf{g} = \nabla f(\mathbf{x})$. Combining (3.32) with the max formula (Theorem 3.26) we have

$$\langle \nabla f(\mathbf{x}), \mathbf{d} \rangle = f'(\mathbf{x}; \mathbf{d}) \geq \langle \mathbf{g}, \mathbf{d} \rangle,$$

so that

$$\langle \mathbf{g} - \nabla f(\mathbf{x}), \mathbf{d} \rangle \leq 0.$$

Taking the maximum over all $\mathbf{d}$ satisfying $\|\mathbf{d}\| \leq 1$, we obtain that $\|\mathbf{g} - \nabla f(\mathbf{x})\|_* \leq 0$ and consequently that $\nabla f(\mathbf{x}) = \mathbf{g}$. We have thus shown that the only possible subgradient in $\partial f(\mathbf{x})$ is $\nabla f(\mathbf{x})$. Combining this with the fact that the subdifferential set is nonempty (Theorem 3.14) yields the desired result $\partial f(\mathbf{x}) = \{\nabla f(\mathbf{x})\}$.

For the reverse direction, suppose that f has a unique subgradient $\mathbf{g}$ at $\mathbf{x} \in \operatorname{int}(\operatorname{dom}(f))$. Consider the convex function

$$h(\mathbf{u}) \equiv f(\mathbf{x} + \mathbf{u}) - f(\mathbf{x}) - \langle \mathbf{g}, \mathbf{u} \rangle.$$

We will show that

$$\lim_{\mathbf{u} \to \mathbf{0}} \frac{h(\mathbf{u})}{\|\mathbf{u}\|} = 0.$$

This will establish (by definition) that $\mathbf{g} = \nabla f(\mathbf{x})$. Obviously, $\mathbf{0}$ is the unique subgradient of h at $\mathbf{0}$ and $\mathbf{0} \in \operatorname{int}(\operatorname{dom}(h))$, and hence by the max formula (Theorem 3.26), for any $\mathbf{d} \in \mathbb{E}$,

$$h'(\mathbf{0}; \mathbf{d}) = \sigma_{\partial h(\mathbf{0})}(\mathbf{d}) = 0.$$

We can thus conclude that for any $\mathbf{d} \in \mathbb{E}$,

$$0 = h'(\mathbf{0}; \mathbf{d}) = \lim_{\alpha \to 0^+} \frac{h(\alpha \mathbf{d}) - h(\mathbf{0})}{\alpha} = \lim_{\alpha \to 0^+} \frac{h(\alpha \mathbf{d})}{\alpha}. \tag{3.33}$$

Let $\{\mathbf{v}_1, \mathbf{v}_2, \ldots, \mathbf{v}_k\}$ be an orthonormal basis of $\mathbb{E}$. Since $\mathbf{0} \in \operatorname{int}(\operatorname{dom}(h))$, there exists $\varepsilon \in (0, 1)$ such that $\varepsilon \mathbf{v}_i, -\varepsilon \mathbf{v}_i \in \operatorname{dom}(h)$ for any $i = 1, 2, \ldots, k$. Therefore, since $\operatorname{dom}(h)$ is convex, the set

$$D = \operatorname{conv}\left(\{\pm \varepsilon \mathbf{v}_i\}_{i=1}^k\right)$$

satisfies $D \subseteq \operatorname{dom}(h)$. Let $\|\cdot\| = \sqrt{\langle \cdot, \cdot \rangle}$ be the Euclidean norm corresponding to the endowed inner product on $\mathbb{E}$. Note that $B_{\|\cdot\|}[\mathbf{0}, \gamma] \subseteq D$, where $\gamma = \frac{\varepsilon}{k}$. Indeed, let $\mathbf{w} \in B_{\|\cdot\|}[\mathbf{0}, \gamma]$. Then since $\{\mathbf{v}_1, \mathbf{v}_2, \ldots, \mathbf{v}_k\}$ is an orthonormal basis of $\mathbb{E}$, we have

$$\mathbf{w} = \sum_{i=1}^k \langle \mathbf{w}, \mathbf{v}_i \rangle \mathbf{v}_i$$

as well as

$$\|\mathbf{w}\|^2 = \sum_{i=1}^k \langle \mathbf{w}, \mathbf{v}_i \rangle^2. \tag{3.34}$$

Since $\|\mathbf{w}\|^2 \le \gamma^2$, it follows by (3.34) that $|\langle \mathbf{w}, \mathbf{v}_i \rangle| \le \gamma$, and hence

$$\mathbf{w} = \sum_{i=1}^k \langle \mathbf{w}, \mathbf{v}_i \rangle \mathbf{v}_i = \sum_{i=1}^k \frac{|\langle \mathbf{w}, \mathbf{v}_i \rangle|}{\varepsilon} [\operatorname{sgn}(\langle \mathbf{w}, \mathbf{v}_i \rangle) \varepsilon \mathbf{v}_i] + \left(1 - \sum_{i=1}^k \frac{|\langle \mathbf{w}, \mathbf{v}_i \rangle|}{\varepsilon}\right) \cdot \mathbf{0} \in D,$$

where the membership in D follows by the fact that $\mathbf{0}, \pm \varepsilon \mathbf{v}_i \in D$ and $\sum_{i=1}^k \frac{|\langle \mathbf{w}, \mathbf{v}_i \rangle|}{\varepsilon} \le \frac{k\gamma}{\varepsilon} = 1$. We have therefore established the inclusion $B_{\|\cdot\|}[\mathbf{0}, \gamma] \subseteq D$. Denote the $2k$ vectors $\{\pm \varepsilon \mathbf{v}_i\}_{i=1}^k$ by $\mathbf{z}_1, \mathbf{z}_2, \ldots, \mathbf{z}_{2k}$. Take $\mathbf{0} \ne \mathbf{u} \in B_{\|\cdot\|}[\mathbf{0}, \gamma^2]$. We have that $\gamma \frac{\mathbf{u}}{\|\mathbf{u}\|} \in B_{\|\cdot\|}[\mathbf{0}, \gamma] \subseteq D$, and hence there exists $\boldsymbol{\lambda} \in \Delta_{2k}$ such that

$$\gamma \frac{\mathbf{u}}{\|\mathbf{u}\|} = \sum_{i=1}^{2k} \lambda_i \mathbf{z}_i.$$

Therefore,

$$\frac{h(\mathbf{u})}{\|\mathbf{u}\|} = \frac{h\left(\frac{\|\mathbf{u}\|}{\gamma}\gamma\frac{\mathbf{u}}{\|\mathbf{u}\|}\right)}{\|\mathbf{u}\|} = \frac{h\left(\sum_{i=1}^{2k}\lambda_i\frac{\|\mathbf{u}\|}{\gamma}\mathbf{z}_i\right)}{\|\mathbf{u}\|}$$

$$\leq \sum_{i=1}^{2k}\lambda_i\frac{h\left(\|\mathbf{u}\|\frac{\mathbf{z}_i}{\gamma}\right)}{\|\mathbf{u}\|}$$

$$\leq \max_{i=1,2,\ldots,2k}\left\{\frac{h\left(\|\mathbf{u}\|\frac{\mathbf{z}_i}{\gamma}\right)}{\|\mathbf{u}\|}\right\}, \tag{3.35}$$

where the first inequality follows by the convexity of h and by the fact that $\|\mathbf{u}\|\frac{\mathbf{z}_i}{\gamma} \in B_{\|\cdot\|}[\mathbf{0},\gamma] \subseteq D \subseteq \text{dom}(h)$. By (3.33),

$$\lim_{\mathbf{u}\to\mathbf{0}}\frac{h\left(\|\mathbf{u}\|\frac{\mathbf{z}_i}{\gamma}\right)}{\|\mathbf{u}\|} = \lim_{\|\mathbf{u}\|\to 0}\frac{h\left(\|\mathbf{u}\|\frac{\mathbf{z}_i}{\gamma}\right)}{\|\mathbf{u}\|} = \lim_{\alpha\to 0^+}\frac{h\left(\alpha\frac{\mathbf{z}_i}{\gamma}\right)}{\alpha} = 0,$$

which, combined with (3.35), implies that $\frac{h(\mathbf{u})}{\|\mathbf{u}\|} \to 0$ as $\mathbf{u} \to \mathbf{0}$, proving the desired result. $\square$

Example 3.34 (subdifferential of the l_2-norm). Let $f : \mathbb{R}^n \to \mathbb{R}$ be given by $f(\mathbf{x}) = \|\mathbf{x}\|_2$. Then the subdifferential set of f at $\mathbf{x} = \mathbf{0}$ was already computed in Example 3.3. When $\mathbf{x} \neq \mathbf{0}$, the function is differentiable with gradient $\frac{\mathbf{x}}{\|\mathbf{x}\|_2}$. Thus, using Theorem 3.33, we can summarize and write the subdifferential set as

$$\partial f(\mathbf{x}) = \begin{cases} \left\{\frac{\mathbf{x}}{\|\mathbf{x}\|_2}\right\}, & \mathbf{x} \neq \mathbf{0}, \\ B_{\|\cdot\|_2}[\mathbf{0},1], & \mathbf{x} = \mathbf{0}. \end{cases}$$

In particular, when considering the case $n = 1$, we obtain that for the one-dimensional function $g(x) = |x|$, we have

$$\partial g(x) = \begin{cases} \{\text{sgn}(x)\}, & x \neq 0, \\ [-1,1], & x = 0. \end{cases} \qquad \blacksquare$$

3.4 Computing Subgradients

This section establishes several useful calculus rules for subgradients and subdifferentials. Some of the results are "weak results" (rules for computing some of the subgradients in the subdifferential set), and some are "strong" (full characterization of the subdifferential set).

3.4.1   Multiplication by a Positive Scalar

Theorem 3.35. *Let* $f : \mathbb{E} \to (-\infty, \infty]$ *be a proper function and let* $\alpha > 0$. *Then for any* $\mathbf{x} \in \mathrm{dom}(f)$

$$\partial(\alpha f)(\mathbf{x}) = \alpha \partial f(\mathbf{x}).$$

Proof. We have that $\mathbf{g} \in \partial f(\mathbf{x})$ if and only if

$$f(\mathbf{y}) \geq f(\mathbf{x}) + \langle \mathbf{g}, \mathbf{y} - \mathbf{x} \rangle \text{ for any } \mathbf{y} \in \mathrm{dom}(f).$$

Multiplying the inequality by $\alpha > 0$, we can conclude that the above inequality holds if and only if

$$\alpha f(\mathbf{y}) \geq \alpha f(\mathbf{x}) + \langle \alpha \mathbf{g}, \mathbf{y} - \mathbf{x} \rangle \text{ for any } \mathbf{y} \in \mathrm{dom}(\alpha f), \tag{3.36}$$

where we used the obvious fact that $\mathrm{dom}(\alpha f) = \mathrm{dom}(f)$. The statement (3.36) is equivalent to the relation $\alpha \mathbf{g} \in \partial(\alpha f)(\mathbf{x})$. $\square$

3.4.2   Summation

The following result contains both weak and strong results on the subdifferential set of a sum of functions. The weak result is also "weak" in the sense that its proof only requires the definition of the subgradient. The strong result utilizes the max formula.

Theorem 3.36. *Let* $f_1, f_2 : \mathbb{E} \to (-\infty, \infty]$ *be proper convex functions, and let* $\mathbf{x} \in \mathrm{dom}(f_1) \cap \mathrm{dom}(f_2)$.

(a) *The following inclusion holds:*

$$\partial f_1(\mathbf{x}) + \partial f_2(\mathbf{x}) \subseteq \partial(f_1 + f_2)(\mathbf{x}).$$

(b) *If* $\mathbf{x} \in \mathrm{int}(\mathrm{dom}(f_1)) \cap \mathrm{int}(\mathrm{dom}(f_2))$, *then*

$$\partial(f_1 + f_2)(\mathbf{x}) = \partial f_1(\mathbf{x}) + \partial f_2(\mathbf{x}).$$

Proof. (a) Let $\mathbf{g} \in \partial f_1(\mathbf{x}) + \partial f_2(\mathbf{x})$. Then there exist $\mathbf{g}_1 \in \partial f_1(\mathbf{x})$ and $\mathbf{g}_2 \in \partial f_2(\mathbf{x})$ such that $\mathbf{g} = \mathbf{g}_1 + \mathbf{g}_2$. By the definition of $\mathbf{g}_1$ and $\mathbf{g}_2$, it follows that for any $\mathbf{y} \in \mathrm{dom}(f_1) \cap \mathrm{dom}(f_2)$,

$$f_1(\mathbf{y}) \geq f_1(\mathbf{x}) + \langle \mathbf{g}_1, \mathbf{y} - \mathbf{x} \rangle,$$
$$f_2(\mathbf{y}) \geq f_2(\mathbf{x}) + \langle \mathbf{g}_2, \mathbf{y} - \mathbf{x} \rangle.$$

Summing the two inequalities, we obtain that for any $\mathbf{y} \in \mathrm{dom}(f_1) \cap \mathrm{dom}(f_2)$,

$$f_1(\mathbf{y}) + f_2(\mathbf{y}) \geq f_1(\mathbf{x}) + f_2(\mathbf{x}) + \langle \mathbf{g}_1 + \mathbf{g}_2, \mathbf{y} - \mathbf{x} \rangle,$$

that is, $\mathbf{g} = \mathbf{g}_1 + \mathbf{g}_2 \in \partial(f_1 + f_2)(\mathbf{x})$.

(b) Let $\mathbf{d} \in \mathbb{E}$ and define $f \equiv f_1 + f_2$. Then since $\mathbf{x} \in \text{int}(\text{dom}(f)) = \text{int}(\text{dom}(f_1)) \cap \text{int}(\text{dom}(f_2))$, it follows by the max formula (Theorem 3.26) that

$$\sigma_{\partial f(\mathbf{x})}(\mathbf{d}) = \max\left\{\langle \mathbf{g}, \mathbf{d}\rangle : \mathbf{g} \in \partial f(\mathbf{x})\right\} = f'(\mathbf{x}; \mathbf{d}).$$

Using the additivity of the directional derivative and the max formula (again), we also obtain

$$
\begin{aligned}
\sigma_{\partial f(\mathbf{x})}(\mathbf{d}) &= f'(\mathbf{x}; \mathbf{d}) \\
&= f_1'(\mathbf{x}; \mathbf{d}) + f_2'(\mathbf{x}; \mathbf{d}) \\
&= \max\left\{\langle \mathbf{g}_1, \mathbf{d}\rangle : \mathbf{g}_1 \in \partial f_1(\mathbf{x})\right\} + \max\left\{\langle \mathbf{g}_2, \mathbf{d}\rangle : \mathbf{g}_2 \in \partial f_2(\mathbf{x})\right\} \\
&= \max\left\{\langle \mathbf{g}_1 + \mathbf{g}_2, \mathbf{d}\rangle : \mathbf{g}_1 \in \partial f_1(\mathbf{x}), \mathbf{g}_2 \in \partial f_2(\mathbf{x})\right\} \\
&= \sigma_{\partial f_1(\mathbf{x}) + \partial f_2(\mathbf{x})}(\mathbf{d}).
\end{aligned}
$$

By Theorems 3.9 and 3.14, $\partial f(\mathbf{x})$, $\partial f_1(\mathbf{x})$, and $\partial f_2(\mathbf{x})$ are nonempty compact convex sets, which also implies (simple exercise) that $\partial f_1(\mathbf{x}) + \partial f_2(\mathbf{x})$ is nonempty compact and convex. Finally, invoking Lemma 2.34, it follows that $\partial f(\mathbf{x}) = \partial f_1(\mathbf{x}) + \partial f_2(\mathbf{x})$. $\quad\square$

Remark 3.37. *Note that the proof of part* (a) *of Theorem* 3.36 *does not require a convexity assumption on f_1 and f_2.*

A simple induction argument can be used to generalize the last result to an arbitrary number of functions.

Corollary 3.38. *Let $f_1, f_2, \ldots, f_m : \mathbb{E} \to (-\infty, \infty]$ be proper convex functions, and let $\mathbf{x} \in \cap_{i=1}^m \text{dom}(f_i)$.*

(a) **(weak sum rule of subdifferential calculus)** *The following inclusion holds:*

$$\sum_{i=1}^m \partial f_i(\mathbf{x}) \subseteq \partial\left(\sum_{i=1}^m f_i\right)(\mathbf{x}).$$

(b) *If $\mathbf{x} \in \cap_{i=1}^m \text{int}(\text{dom}(f_i))$, then*

$$\partial\left(\sum_{i=1}^m f_i\right)(\mathbf{x}) = \sum_{i=1}^m \partial f_i(\mathbf{x}). \tag{3.37}$$

Another direct consequence is that if $f_1, f_2, \ldots, f_m$ are real-valued, meaning that their domain is the entire space $\mathbb{E}$, then the sum formula (3.37) holds.

Corollary 3.39. *Let $f_1, f_2, \ldots, f_m : \mathbb{E} \to \mathbb{R}$ be real-valued convex functions. Then for any $\mathbf{x} \in \mathbb{E}$*

$$\partial\left(\sum_{i=1}^m f_i\right)(\mathbf{x}) = \sum_{i=1}^m \partial f_i(\mathbf{x}).$$

A result with a less restrictive assumption than the one in Corollary 3.38(b) states that if the intersection $\cap_{i=1}^{m} \mathrm{ri}(\mathrm{dom}(f_i))$ is nonempty, then the sum formula is correct at *any* point. We state this result without a proof.

Theorem 3.40 (sum rule of subdifferential calculus [108, Theorem 23.8]). *Let $f_1, f_2, \ldots, f_m : \mathbb{E} \to (-\infty, \infty]$ be proper convex functions, and assume that $\cap_{i=1}^{m} \mathrm{ri}(\mathrm{dom}(f_i)) \neq \emptyset$. Then for any $\mathbf{x} \in \mathbb{E}$*

$$\partial \left(\sum_{i=1}^{m} f_i \right) (\mathbf{x}) = \sum_{i=1}^{m} \partial f_i(\mathbf{x}).$$

Example 3.41 (subdifferential set of the l_1-norm function—strong result). Consider the function $f : \mathbb{R}^n \to \mathbb{R}$ given by $f(\mathbf{x}) = \|\mathbf{x}\|_1 = \sum_{i=1}^{n} |x_i|$. Then $f = \sum_{i=1}^{n} f_i$, where $f_i(\mathbf{x}) \equiv |x_i|$. We have (see also Example 3.34)

$$\partial f_i(\mathbf{x}) = \begin{cases} \{\mathrm{sgn}(x_i)\mathbf{e}_i\}, & x_i \neq 0, \\ [-\mathbf{e}_i, \mathbf{e}_i], & x_i = 0. \end{cases}$$

Thus, by Corollary 3.39,

$$\partial f(\mathbf{x}) = \sum_{i=1}^{n} \partial f_i(\mathbf{x}) = \sum_{i \in I_{\neq}(\mathbf{x})} \mathrm{sgn}(x_i)\mathbf{e}_i + \sum_{i \in I_0(\mathbf{x})} [-\mathbf{e}_i, \mathbf{e}_i],$$

where

$$I_{\neq}(\mathbf{x}) = \{i : x_i \neq 0\}, \ I_0(\mathbf{x}) = \{i : x_i = 0\},$$

and hence

$$\partial f(\mathbf{x}) = \{\mathbf{z} \in \mathbb{R}^n : z_i = \mathrm{sgn}(x_i), i \in I_{\neq}(\mathbf{x}), |z_j| \leq 1, j \in I_0(\mathbf{x})\}.$$

∎

Example 3.42 (a subgradient of the l_1-norm function—weak result). Using the formula for the subdifferential set described in Example 3.41, we can readily conclude that

$$\mathrm{sgn}(\mathbf{x}) \in \partial f(\mathbf{x}).$$

∎

3.4.3 Affine Transformation

The following theorem states strong and weak results on the subdifferential set of a composition of a convex function with an affine transformation.

Theorem 3.43. *Let $f : \mathbb{E} \to (-\infty, \infty]$ be a proper convex function and $\mathcal{A} : \mathbb{V} \to \mathbb{E}$ be a linear transformation. Let $h(\mathbf{x}) = f(\mathcal{A}(\mathbf{x}) + \mathbf{b})$ with $\mathbf{b} \in \mathbb{E}$. Assume that h is proper, meaning that*

$$\mathrm{dom}(h) = \{\mathbf{x} \in \mathbb{V} : \mathcal{A}(\mathbf{x}) + \mathbf{b} \in \mathrm{dom}(f)\} \neq \emptyset.$$

(a) **(weak affine transformation rule of subdifferential calculus)** *For any* $\mathbf{x} \in \mathrm{dom}(h)$,

$$\mathcal{A}^T(\partial f(\mathcal{A}(\mathbf{x}) + \mathbf{b})) \subseteq \partial h(\mathbf{x}).$$

(b) **(affine transformation rule of subdifferential calculus)** *If* $\mathbf{x} \in \mathrm{int}(\mathrm{dom}(h))$ *and* $\mathcal{A}(\mathbf{x}) + \mathbf{b} \in \mathrm{int}(\mathrm{dom}(f))$, *then*

$$\partial h(\mathbf{x}) = \mathcal{A}^T(\partial f(\mathcal{A}(\mathbf{x}) + \mathbf{b})).$$

Proof. (a) Let $\mathbf{x} \in \mathrm{dom}(h)$ and assume that $\mathbf{g} \in \mathcal{A}^T(\partial f(\mathcal{A}(\mathbf{x}) + \mathbf{b}))$. Then there exists $\mathbf{d} \in \mathbb{E}^*$ for which $\mathbf{g} = \mathcal{A}^T(\mathbf{d})$, where

$$\mathbf{d} \in \partial f(\mathcal{A}(\mathbf{x}) + \mathbf{b}). \tag{3.38}$$

For any $\mathbf{y} \in \mathrm{dom}(h)$, we have $\mathcal{A}(\mathbf{y}) + \mathbf{b} \in \mathrm{dom}(f)$, and hence, by (3.38),

$$f(\mathcal{A}(\mathbf{y}) + \mathbf{b}) \geq f(\mathcal{A}(\mathbf{x}) + \mathbf{b}) + \langle \mathbf{d}, \mathcal{A}(\mathbf{y}) + \mathbf{b} - \mathcal{A}(\mathbf{x}) - \mathbf{b} \rangle,$$

and therefore

$$h(\mathbf{y}) \geq h(\mathbf{x}) + \langle \mathcal{A}^T(\mathbf{d}), \mathbf{y} - \mathbf{x} \rangle \text{ for all } \mathbf{y} \in \mathrm{dom}(h).$$

Hence, $\mathbf{g} = \mathcal{A}^T(\mathbf{d}) \in \partial h(\mathbf{x})$, proving that $\mathcal{A}^T(\partial f(\mathcal{A}(\mathbf{x}) + \mathbf{b})) \subseteq \partial h(\mathbf{x})$.

(b) Since $\mathbf{x} \in \mathrm{int}(\mathrm{dom}(h))$, then for any $\mathbf{d} \in \mathbb{V}$, by the max formula (Theorem 3.26),

$$h'(\mathbf{x}; \mathbf{d}) = \sigma_{\partial h(\mathbf{x})}(\mathbf{d}). \tag{3.39}$$

In addition, by the definition of the directional derivative, we have

$$
\begin{aligned}
h'(\mathbf{x}; \mathbf{d}) &= \lim_{\alpha \to 0^+} \frac{h(\mathbf{x} + \alpha \mathbf{d}) - h(\mathbf{x})}{\alpha} \\
&= \lim_{\alpha \to 0^+} \frac{f(\mathcal{A}(\mathbf{x}) + \mathbf{b} + \alpha \mathcal{A}(\mathbf{d})) - f(\mathcal{A}(\mathbf{x}) + \mathbf{b})}{\alpha} \\
&= f'(\mathcal{A}(\mathbf{x}) + \mathbf{b}; \mathcal{A}(\mathbf{d})),
\end{aligned}
$$

which, combined with (3.39), yields

$$\sigma_{\partial h(\mathbf{x})}(\mathbf{d}) = f'(\mathcal{A}(\mathbf{x}) + \mathbf{b}; \mathcal{A}(\mathbf{d})).$$

Therefore, using the max formula again and the assumption that $\mathcal{A}(\mathbf{x}) + \mathbf{b} \in \mathrm{int}(\mathrm{dom}(f))$, we obtain that

$$
\begin{aligned}
\sigma_{\partial h(\mathbf{x})}(\mathbf{d}) &= f'(\mathcal{A}(\mathbf{x}) + \mathbf{b}; \mathcal{A}(\mathbf{d})) \\
&= \max_{\mathbf{g}} \left\{ \langle \mathbf{g}, \mathcal{A}(\mathbf{d}) \rangle : \mathbf{g} \in \partial f(\mathcal{A}(\mathbf{x}) + \mathbf{b}) \right\} \\
&= \max_{\mathbf{g}} \left\{ \langle \mathcal{A}^T(\mathbf{g}), \mathbf{d} \rangle : \mathbf{g} \in \partial f(\mathcal{A}(\mathbf{x}) + \mathbf{b}) \right\} \\
&= \max_{\tilde{\mathbf{g}}} \left\{ \langle \tilde{\mathbf{g}}, \mathbf{d} \rangle : \tilde{\mathbf{g}} \in \mathcal{A}^T(\partial f(\mathcal{A}(\mathbf{x}) + \mathbf{b})) \right\} \\
&= \sigma_{\mathcal{A}^T(\partial f(\mathcal{A}(\mathbf{x}) + \mathbf{b}))}(\mathbf{d}).
\end{aligned}
$$

Since $\mathbf{x} \in \text{int}(\text{dom}(h))$, it follows by Theorems 3.9 and 3.14 that $\partial h(\mathbf{x})$ is nonempty compact and convex. Similarly, since $\mathcal{A}(\mathbf{x}) + \mathbf{b} \in \text{int}(\text{dom}(f))$, the set $\partial f(\mathcal{A}(\mathbf{x}) + \mathbf{b})$ is nonempty, compact, and convex, which implies that $\mathcal{A}^T(\partial f(\mathcal{A}(\mathbf{x}) + \mathbf{b}))$ is also nonempty, compact, and convex. Finally, invoking Lemma 2.34, we obtain that $\partial h(\mathbf{x}) = \mathcal{A}^T(\partial f(\mathcal{A}(\mathbf{x}) + \mathbf{b})).$ $\square$

Example 3.44 (subdifferential of $\|\mathbf{Ax} + \mathbf{b}\|_1$). Let $f : \mathbb{R}^n \to \mathbb{R}$ be the function given by $f(\mathbf{x}) = \|\mathbf{Ax} + \mathbf{b}\|_1$, where $\mathbf{A} \in \mathbb{R}^{m \times n}, \mathbf{b} \in \mathbb{R}^m$. Then $f(\mathbf{x}) = g(\mathbf{Ax} + \mathbf{b})$ with $g : \mathbb{R}^m \to \mathbb{R}$ given by $g(\mathbf{y}) = \|\mathbf{y}\|_1$. By the affine transformation rule of subdifferential calculus (Theorem 3.43(b)), we have that

$$\partial f(\mathbf{x}) = \mathbf{A}^T \partial g(\mathbf{Ax} + \mathbf{b}). \tag{3.40}$$

Denote the ith row of $\mathbf{A}$ by $\mathbf{a}_i^T$ and define

$$I_{\neq}(\mathbf{x}) = \{i : \mathbf{a}_i^T \mathbf{x} + b_i \neq 0\},$$
$$I_0(\mathbf{x}) = \{i : \mathbf{a}_i^T \mathbf{x} + b_i = 0\}.$$

In this terminology, by Example 3.41,

$$\partial g(\mathbf{Ax} + \mathbf{b}) = \sum_{i \in I_{\neq}(\mathbf{x})} \text{sgn}(\mathbf{a}_i^T \mathbf{x} + b_i)\mathbf{e}_i + \sum_{i \in I_0(\mathbf{x})} [-\mathbf{e}_i, \mathbf{e}_i].$$

Thus, by (3.40),

$$\partial f(\mathbf{x}) = \mathbf{A}^T \partial g(\mathbf{Ax} + \mathbf{b})$$
$$= \sum_{i \in I_{\neq}(\mathbf{x})} \text{sgn}(\mathbf{a}_i^T \mathbf{x} + b_i)\mathbf{A}^T \mathbf{e}_i + \sum_{i \in I_0(\mathbf{x})} [-\mathbf{A}^T \mathbf{e}_i, \mathbf{A}^T \mathbf{e}_i].$$

Using the relation $\mathbf{A}^T \mathbf{e}_i = \mathbf{a}_i$, we finally conclude that

$$\boxed{\partial f(\mathbf{x}) = \sum_{i \in I_{\neq}(\mathbf{x})} \text{sgn}(\mathbf{a}_i^T \mathbf{x} + b_i)\mathbf{a}_i + \sum_{i \in I_0(\mathbf{x})} [-\mathbf{a}_i, \mathbf{a}_i].}$$

The above is a strong result characterizing the entire subdifferential set. A weak result indicating one possible subgradient is

$$\mathbf{A}^T \text{sgn}(\mathbf{Ax} + \mathbf{b}) \in \partial f(\mathbf{x}). \quad \blacksquare$$

Example 3.45 (subdifferential of $\|\mathbf{Ax} + \mathbf{b}\|_2$). Let $f : \mathbb{R}^n \to \mathbb{R}$ be the function $f(\mathbf{x}) = \|\mathbf{Ax} + \mathbf{b}\|_2$, where $\mathbf{A} \in \mathbb{R}^{m \times n}, \mathbf{b} \in \mathbb{R}^m$. Then $f(\mathbf{x}) = g(\mathbf{Ax} + \mathbf{b})$ with $g : \mathbb{R}^m \to \mathbb{R}$ given by $g(\mathbf{y}) = \|\mathbf{y}\|_2$. By Example 3.34,

$$\partial g(\mathbf{Ax} + \mathbf{b}) = \begin{cases} \dfrac{\mathbf{Ax} + \mathbf{b}}{\|\mathbf{Ax} + \mathbf{b}\|_2}, & \mathbf{Ax} + \mathbf{b} \neq \mathbf{0}, \\ B_{\|\cdot\|_2}[\mathbf{0}, 1], & \mathbf{Ax} + \mathbf{b} = \mathbf{0}. \end{cases}$$

Thus, by the affine transformation rule of subdifferential calculus (Theorem 3.43(b)),

$$\partial f(\mathbf{x}) = \mathbf{A}^T \partial g(\mathbf{A}\mathbf{x} + \mathbf{b}) = \begin{cases} \frac{\mathbf{A}^T(\mathbf{A}\mathbf{x}+\mathbf{b})}{\|\mathbf{A}\mathbf{x}+\mathbf{b}\|_2}, & \mathbf{A}\mathbf{x}+\mathbf{b} \neq \mathbf{0}, \\ \mathbf{A}^T B_{\|\cdot\|_2}[\mathbf{0},1], & \mathbf{A}\mathbf{x}+\mathbf{b} = \mathbf{0}, \end{cases}$$

Note that at a vector $\mathbf{x}$ satisfying $\mathbf{A}\mathbf{x} + \mathbf{b} = \mathbf{0}$, the subdifferential set can be explicitly written as

$$\partial f(\mathbf{x}) = \mathbf{A}^T B_{\|\cdot\|_2}[\mathbf{0},1] = \left\{ \mathbf{A}^T \mathbf{y} : \|\mathbf{y}\|_2 \leq 1 \right\}.$$

If a weak result is required, then since $\mathbf{0} \in B_{\|\cdot\|_2}[\mathbf{0},1]$, we can write $\mathbf{0} = \mathbf{A}^T \mathbf{0} \in \partial f(\mathbf{x})$ for any $\mathbf{x}$ satisfying $\mathbf{A}\mathbf{x} + \mathbf{b} = \mathbf{0}$. ∎

3.4.4 Composition

The derivative of a composition of differentiable functions can be computed by using the well-known chain rule. We recall here the classical result on the derivative of the composition of two one-dimensional functions. The result is a small variation of the result from [112, Theorem 5.5].

Theorem 3.46. *Suppose that f is continuous on $[a,b]$ $(a < b)$ and that $f'_+(a)$ exists. Let g be a function defined on an open interval I which contains the range of f, and assume that g is differentiable at $f(a)$. Then the function*

$$h(t) = g(f(t)) \quad (a \leq t \leq b)$$

is right differentiable at $t = a$ and

$$h'_+(a) = g'(f(a))f'_+(a).$$

Proof.

$$\begin{aligned} h'_+(a) &= \lim_{t \to a^+} \frac{g(f(t)) - g(f(a))}{t - a} \\ &= \lim_{t \to a^+} \frac{g(f(t)) - g(f(a))}{f(t) - f(a)} \cdot \frac{f(t) - f(a)}{t - a} = g'(f(a))f'_+(a). \quad \square \end{aligned}$$

We will now show how the one-dimensional chain rule can be used with the help of the max formula (Theorem 3.26) to show a multidimensional version of the chain rule.

Theorem 3.47 (chain rule of subdifferential calculus). *Let $f : \mathbb{E} \to \mathbb{R}$ be a convex function and $g : \mathbb{R} \to \mathbb{R}$ be a nondecreasing convex function. Let $\mathbf{x} \in \mathbb{E}$, and suppose that g is differentiable at the point $f(\mathbf{x})$. Let $h = g \circ f$. Then*

$$\partial h(\mathbf{x}) = g'(f(\mathbf{x}))\partial f(\mathbf{x}).$$

Proof. For any $\mathbf{d} \in \mathbb{E}$, define the following one-dimensional functions:

$$\begin{aligned} f_{\mathbf{x},\mathbf{d}}(t) &= f(\mathbf{x} + t\mathbf{d}), \quad t \in \mathbb{R}, \\ h_{\mathbf{x},\mathbf{d}}(t) &= h(\mathbf{x} + t\mathbf{d}), \quad t \in \mathbb{R}. \end{aligned}$$

We have the following simple relation between $f_{\mathbf{x},\mathbf{d}}$ and $h_{\mathbf{x},\mathbf{d}}$:

$$h_{\mathbf{x},\mathbf{d}}(t) = h(\mathbf{x} + t\mathbf{d}) = g(f(\mathbf{x} + t\mathbf{d})) = g(f_{\mathbf{x},\mathbf{d}}(t)), \quad t \in \mathbb{R}. \tag{3.41}$$

The function f is convex by the premise of the theorem, and h is convex since it is a composition of a nondecreasing convex function with a convex function. Therefore, the directional derivatives of f and h exist in every direction (Theorem 3.21), and we have by the definition of the directional derivative that

$$(f_{\mathbf{x},\mathbf{d}})'_+(0) = f'(\mathbf{x}; \mathbf{d}), \tag{3.42}$$

$$(h_{\mathbf{x},\mathbf{d}})'_+(0) = h'(\mathbf{x}; \mathbf{d}). \tag{3.43}$$

Since $h_{\mathbf{x},\mathbf{d}} = g \circ f_{\mathbf{x},\mathbf{d}}$ (by (3.41)), $f_{\mathbf{x},\mathbf{d}}$ is right differentiable at 0, and g is differentiable at $f_{\mathbf{x},\mathbf{d}}(0) = f(\mathbf{x})$, it follows by the chain rule for one-dimensional functions (Theorem 3.46) that

$$(h_{\mathbf{x},\mathbf{d}})'_+(0) = g'(f(\mathbf{x}))(f_{\mathbf{x};\mathbf{d}})'_+(0).$$

Plugging (3.42) and (3.43) into the latter equality, we obtain

$$h'(\mathbf{x}; \mathbf{d}) = g'(f(\mathbf{x}))f'(\mathbf{x}; \mathbf{d}).$$

By the max formula (Theorem 3.26), since f and h are convex and $\mathbf{x} \in \operatorname{int}(\operatorname{dom}(f)) = \operatorname{int}(\operatorname{dom}(h)) = \mathbb{E}$,

$$h'(\mathbf{x}; \mathbf{d}) = \sigma_{\partial h(\mathbf{x})}(\mathbf{d}), \ f'(\mathbf{x}; \mathbf{d}) = \sigma_{\partial f(\mathbf{x})}(\mathbf{d}),$$

and hence

$$\sigma_{\partial h(\mathbf{x})}(\mathbf{d}) = h'(\mathbf{x}; \mathbf{d}) = g'(f(\mathbf{x}))f'(\mathbf{x}; \mathbf{d}) = g'(f(\mathbf{x}))\sigma_{\partial f(\mathbf{x})}(\mathbf{d}) = \sigma_{g'(f(\mathbf{x}))\partial f(\mathbf{x})}(\mathbf{d}),$$

where the last equality is due to Lemma 2.24(c) and the fact that $g'(f(\mathbf{x})) \geq 0$. Finally, by Theorems 3.9 and 3.14 the sets $\partial h(\mathbf{x}), \partial f(\mathbf{x})$ are nonempty, closed, and convex, and thus by Lemma 2.34

$$\partial h(\mathbf{x}) = g'(f(\mathbf{x}))\partial f(\mathbf{x}). \quad \square$$

Example 3.48 (subdifferential of $\| \cdot \|_1^2$). Consider the function $h : \mathbb{R}^n \to \mathbb{R}$ given by $h(\mathbf{x}) = \|\mathbf{x}\|_1^2$, which can be written as the composition $h = g \circ f$, where $f(\mathbf{x}) = \|\mathbf{x}\|_1$ and $g(t) = [t]_+^2 = \max\{t, 0\}^2$. Both f and g are real-valued convex functions, and g is nondecreasing and differentiable over $\mathbb{R}$ with derivative $g'(t) = 2[t]_+$. Therefore, by the chain rule of subdifferential calculus (Theorem 3.47), for any $\mathbf{x} \in \mathbb{R}^n$,

$$\partial h(\mathbf{x}) = g'(f(\mathbf{x}))\partial f(\mathbf{x}) = 2\left[\|\mathbf{x}\|_1\right]_+ \partial f(\mathbf{x}) = 2\|\mathbf{x}\|_1\partial f(\mathbf{x}).$$

Using the general form of $\partial f(\mathbf{x})$ as derived in Example 3.41, we can write $\partial h(\mathbf{x})$ explicitly as follows:

$$\partial h(\mathbf{x}) = 2\|\mathbf{x}\|_1 \left\{ \mathbf{z} \in \mathbb{R}^n : z_i = \operatorname{sgn}(x_i), i \in I_{\neq}(\mathbf{x}), |z_j| \leq 1, j \in I_0(\mathbf{x}) \right\},$$

where $I_{\neq}(\mathbf{x}) = \{i : x_i \neq 0\}, I_0(\mathbf{x}) = \{i : x_i = 0\}$.

Plugging $\mathbf{x} = \mathbf{0}$ into the above formula, we obtain that

$$\partial h(\mathbf{0}) = \{\mathbf{0}\}.$$

Since h has a unique subgradient at $\mathbf{x} = \mathbf{0}$, it follows by Theorem 3.33 that h is differentiable at $\mathbf{x} = \mathbf{0}$ and $\nabla h(\mathbf{0}) = \mathbf{0}$. Note that the function is obviously not differentiable over $\mathbb{R}^n$. For example, when $n = 2$, the nondifferentiability points are $\{(x_1, 0)^T : x_1 \neq 0\} \cup \{(0, x_2)^T : x_2 \neq 0\}$, as illustrated in Figure 3.3. ∎

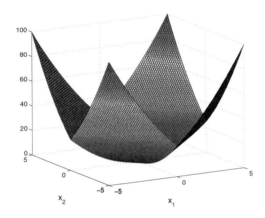

Figure 3.3. *Surface plot of the function* $f(x_1, x_2) = (|x_1| + |x_2|)^2$.

Example 3.49 (subdifferential of $d_C(\cdot)$). Suppose that $\mathbb{E}$ is a Euclidean space, and let $C \subseteq \mathbb{E}$ be a nonempty closed and convex set. The distance function d_C is convex (see Example 2.20). We will show that

$$\partial d_C(\mathbf{x}) = \begin{cases} \left\{ \frac{\mathbf{x} - P_C(\mathbf{x})}{d_C(\mathbf{x})} \right\}, & \mathbf{x} \notin C, \\ N_C(\mathbf{x}) \cap B[\mathbf{0}, 1], & \mathbf{x} \in C. \end{cases}$$

By Example 3.31, we know that the function $\varphi_C(\mathbf{x}) = \frac{1}{2} d_C^2(\mathbf{x})$ is differentiable and

$$\partial \varphi_C(\mathbf{x}) = \{\mathbf{x} - P_C(\mathbf{x})\} \tag{3.44}$$

for any $\mathbf{x} \in \mathbb{E}$. Note that $\varphi_C = g \circ d_C$, where $g(t) = \frac{1}{2}[t]_+^2$ is a nondecreasing real-valued convex differentiable function. Then by the chain rule of subdifferential calculus (Theorem 3.47),

$$\partial \varphi_C(\mathbf{x}) = g'(d_C(\mathbf{x})) \partial d_C(\mathbf{x}) = [d_C(\mathbf{x})]_+ \partial d_C(\mathbf{x}) = d_C(\mathbf{x}) \partial d_C(\mathbf{x}). \tag{3.45}$$

If $\mathbf{x} \notin C$, then $d_C(\mathbf{x}) \neq 0$, and thus by (3.44) and (3.45),

$$\partial d_C(\mathbf{x}) = \left\{ \frac{\mathbf{x} - P_C(\mathbf{x})}{d_C(\mathbf{x})} \right\} \text{ for any } \mathbf{x} \notin C.$$

Since $\partial d_C(\mathbf{x})$ is a singleton for any $\mathbf{x} \notin C$, it follows in particular, by Theorem 3.33, that d_C is differentiable at points outside C.

Now assume that $\mathbf{x} \in C$. We will show that

$$\partial d_C(\mathbf{x}) = N_C(\mathbf{x}) \cap B[\mathbf{0}, 1].$$

Indeed, if $\mathbf{d} \in \partial d_C(\mathbf{x})$, then

$$d_C(\mathbf{y}) \geq \langle \mathbf{d}, \mathbf{y} - \mathbf{x} \rangle \text{ for any } \mathbf{y} \in \mathbb{E}. \tag{3.46}$$

This means in particular that for any $\mathbf{y} \in C$

$$\langle \mathbf{d}, \mathbf{y} - \mathbf{x} \rangle \leq 0,$$

that is, $\mathbf{d} \in N_C(\mathbf{x})$. In addition, taking $\mathbf{y} = \mathbf{x} + \mathbf{d}$ in (3.46), we get

$$\|\mathbf{d}\|^2 = \langle \mathbf{d}, \mathbf{x} + \mathbf{d} - \mathbf{x} \rangle \leq d_C(\mathbf{x} + \mathbf{d}) \leq \|\mathbf{x} + \mathbf{d} - \mathbf{x}\| = \|\mathbf{d}\|,$$

which readily implies that $\|\mathbf{d}\| \leq 1$. We conclude that $\partial d_C(\mathbf{x}) \subseteq N_C(\mathbf{x}) \cap B[\mathbf{0}, 1]$. To show the reverse direction, take $\mathbf{d} \in N_C(\mathbf{x}) \cap B[\mathbf{0}, 1]$. Then for any $\mathbf{y} \in \mathbb{E}$,

$$\langle \mathbf{d}, \mathbf{y} - \mathbf{x} \rangle = \langle \mathbf{d}, \mathbf{y} - P_C(\mathbf{y}) \rangle + \langle \mathbf{d}, P_C(\mathbf{y}) - \mathbf{x} \rangle. \tag{3.47}$$

Since $\mathbf{d} \in N_C(\mathbf{x})$ and $P_C(\mathbf{y}) \in C$, it follows by the definition of the normal cone that $\langle \mathbf{d}, P_C(\mathbf{y}) - \mathbf{x} \rangle \leq 0$, which, combined with (3.47), the Cauchy–Schwarz inequality, and the assertion that $\|\mathbf{d}\| \leq 1$, implies that for any $\mathbf{y} \in \mathbb{E}$

$$\langle \mathbf{d}, \mathbf{y} - \mathbf{x} \rangle \leq \langle \mathbf{d}, \mathbf{y} - P_C(\mathbf{y}) \rangle \leq \|\mathbf{d}\| \cdot \|\mathbf{y} - P_C(\mathbf{y})\| \leq \|\mathbf{y} - P_C(\mathbf{y})\| = d_C(\mathbf{y}),$$

and hence $\mathbf{d} \in \partial d_C(\mathbf{x})$. ∎

3.4.5 Maximization

The following result shows how to compute the subdifferential set of a maximum of a finite collection of convex functions.

Theorem 3.50 (max rule of subdifferential calculus). *Let* $f_1, f_2, \ldots, f_m :$ $\mathbb{E} \to (-\infty, \infty]$ *be proper convex functions, and define*

$$f(\mathbf{x}) = \max\{f_1(\mathbf{x}), f_2(\mathbf{x}), \ldots, f_m(\mathbf{x})\}.$$

Let $\mathbf{x} \in \bigcap_{i=1}^m \text{int}(\text{dom}(f_i))$. *Then*

$$\partial f(\mathbf{x}) = \text{conv}\left(\cup_{i \in I(\mathbf{x})} \partial f_i(\mathbf{x}) \right),$$

where $I(\mathbf{x}) = \{i \in \{1, 2, \ldots, m\} : f_i(\mathbf{x}) = f(\mathbf{x})\}$.

Proof. First note that f, as a maximum of convex functions, is convex (see Theorem 2.16(c)) and that by Corollary 3.25 for any $\mathbf{d} \in \mathbb{E}$,

$$f'(\mathbf{x}; \mathbf{d}) = \max_{i \in I(\mathbf{x})} f_i'(\mathbf{x}; \mathbf{d}).$$

For the sake of simplicity of notation, we will assume that $I(\mathbf{x}) = \{1, 2, \ldots, k\}$ for some $k \in \{1, 2, \ldots, m\}$. Now, using the max formula (Theorem 3.26), we obtain

$$f'(\mathbf{x}; \mathbf{d}) = \max_{i=1,2,\ldots,k} f_i'(\mathbf{x}; \mathbf{d}) = \max_{i=1,2,\ldots,k} \max_{\mathbf{g}_i \in \partial f_i(\mathbf{x})} \langle \mathbf{g}_i, \mathbf{d} \rangle. \qquad (3.48)$$

Using the fact that for any $a_1, a_2, \ldots, a_k \in \mathbb{R}$ the identity

$$\max\{a_1, a_2, \ldots, a_k\} = \max_{\boldsymbol{\lambda} \in \Delta_k} \sum_{i=1}^{k} \lambda_i a_i$$

holds, we can continue (3.48) and write

$$f'(\mathbf{x}; \mathbf{d}) = \max_{\boldsymbol{\lambda} \in \Delta_k} \left\{ \sum_{i=1}^{k} \lambda_i \max\{\langle \mathbf{g}_i, \mathbf{d} \rangle : \mathbf{g}_i \in \partial f_i(\mathbf{x})\} \right\}$$

$$= \max \left\{ \left\langle \sum_{i=1}^{k} \lambda_i \mathbf{g}_i, \mathbf{d} \right\rangle : \mathbf{g}_i \in \partial f_i(\mathbf{x}), \boldsymbol{\lambda} \in \Delta_k \right\}$$

$$= \max \left\{ \langle \mathbf{g}, \mathbf{d} \rangle : \mathbf{g} \in \mathrm{conv}\left(\cup_{i=1}^{k} \partial f_i(\mathbf{x})\right) \right\}$$

$$= \sigma_A(\mathbf{d}),$$

where $A = \mathrm{conv}\left(\cup_{i=1}^{k} \partial f_i(\mathbf{x})\right)$. By the max formula (Theorem 3.26), since $\mathbf{x} \in \mathrm{int}(\mathrm{dom}(f))$,

$$f'(\mathbf{x}; \mathbf{d}) = \sigma_{\partial f(\mathbf{x})}(\mathbf{d}),$$

and hence

$$\sigma_A(\mathbf{d}) = \sigma_{\partial f(\mathbf{x})}(\mathbf{d}) \text{ for any } \mathbf{d} \in \mathbb{E}. \qquad (3.49)$$

The set $\partial f(\mathbf{x})$ is closed and convex by Theorem 3.9, and since $\mathbf{x} \in \mathrm{int}(\mathrm{dom}(f))$, it is also nonempty and bounded by Theorem 3.14. Similarly, $\partial f_i(\mathbf{x}), i = 1, 2, \ldots, k$, are nonempty and compact sets, and hence also is $\cup_{i=1}^{k} \partial f_i(\mathbf{x})$. We can conclude that the set $A = \mathrm{conv}(\cup_{i=1}^{k} \partial f_i(\mathbf{x}))$, as a convex hull of a nonempty compact set, is also nonempty and compact.[17] In addition, by the definition of the convex hull, A is convex.

To conclude, both A and $\partial f(\mathbf{x})$ are nonempty closed and convex, and thus (3.49) implies by Lemma 2.34 that

$$\partial f(\mathbf{x}) = A,$$

which is the desired result. $\square$

Example 3.51 (subdifferential of the max function). Let $f : \mathbb{R}^n \to \mathbb{R}$ be given by $f(\mathbf{x}) = \max\{x_1, x_2, \ldots, x_n\}$. Obviously, $f(\mathbf{x}) = \max\{f_1(\mathbf{x}), f_2(\mathbf{x}), \ldots, f_n(\mathbf{x})\}$, where $f_i(\mathbf{x}) = x_i$, and hence $\partial f_i(\mathbf{x}) = \{\mathbf{e}_i\}$ for any $i = 1, 2, \ldots, n$. Denote

$$I(\mathbf{x}) = \{i : f(\mathbf{x}) = x_i\}.$$

---

[17]This follows by [10, Proposition 6.31].

Then by the max rule of subdifferential calculus (Theorem 3.50),

$$\partial f(\mathbf{x}) = \text{conv}(\cup_{i \in I(\mathbf{x})} \partial f_i(\mathbf{x})) = \text{conv}(\cup_{i \in I(\mathbf{x})} \{\mathbf{e}_i\}),$$

and hence

$$\partial f(\mathbf{x}) = \left\{ \sum_{i \in I(\mathbf{x})} \lambda_i \mathbf{e}_i : \sum_{i \in I(\mathbf{x})} \lambda_i = 1, \lambda_j \geq 0, j \in I(\mathbf{x}) \right\}.$$

In particular,

$$\partial f(\alpha \mathbf{e}) = \Delta_n \text{ for any } \alpha \in \mathbb{R}. \quad \blacksquare$$

Example 3.52 (subdifferential of the l_∞-norm). Let $f : \mathbb{R}^n \to \mathbb{R}$ be given by $f(\mathbf{x}) = \|\mathbf{x}\|_\infty$. There are two options. If $\mathbf{x} = \mathbf{0}$, then by Example 3.3 $\partial f(\mathbf{0})$ is the dual-norm unit ball, and in this case,

$$\partial f(\mathbf{0}) = B_{\|\cdot\|_1}[\mathbf{0}, 1] = \{\mathbf{x} \in \mathbb{R}^n : \|\mathbf{x}\|_1 \leq 1\}.$$

Suppose that $\mathbf{x} \neq \mathbf{0}$. Note that $f(\mathbf{x}) = \max\{f_1(\mathbf{x}), f_2(\mathbf{x}), \ldots, f_n(\mathbf{x})\}$ with $f_i(\mathbf{x}) = |x_i|$ and set

$$I(\mathbf{x}) = \{i : |x_i| = \|\mathbf{x}\|_\infty\}.$$

For any $i \in I(\mathbf{x})$ we have $x_i \neq 0$, and hence for any such i, $\partial f_i(\mathbf{x}) = \{\text{sgn}(x_i)\mathbf{e}_i\}$. Thus, by the max rule of subdifferential calculus (Theorem 3.50),

$$\partial f(\mathbf{x}) = \text{conv}\left(\cup_{i \in I(\mathbf{x})} \partial f_i(\mathbf{x})\right)$$

$$= \text{conv}\left(\cup_{i \in I(\mathbf{x})} \{\text{sgn}(x_i)\mathbf{e}_i\}\right)$$

$$= \left\{ \sum_{i \in I(\mathbf{x})} \lambda_i \text{sgn}(x_i)\mathbf{e}_i : \sum_{i \in I(\mathbf{x})} \lambda_i = 1, \lambda_j \geq 0, j \in I(\mathbf{x}) \right\}.$$

To conclude,

$$\partial f(\mathbf{x}) = \begin{cases} B_{\|\cdot\|_1}[\mathbf{0}, 1], & \mathbf{x} = \mathbf{0}, \\ \left\{ \sum_{i \in I(\mathbf{x})} \lambda_i \text{sgn}(x_i)\mathbf{e}_i : \sum_{i \in I(\mathbf{x})} \lambda_i = 1, \lambda_j \geq 0, j \in I(\mathbf{x}) \right\}, & \mathbf{x} \neq \mathbf{0}. \end{cases}$$

$$\blacksquare$$

Example 3.53 (subdifferential of piecewise linear functions). Consider the piecewise linear function $f : \mathbb{R}^n \to \mathbb{R}$ given by

$$f(\mathbf{x}) = \max_{i=1,2,\ldots,m} \{\mathbf{a}_i^T \mathbf{x} + b_i\},$$

where $\mathbf{a}_i \in \mathbb{R}^n, b_i \in \mathbb{R}, i = 1, 2, \ldots, m$. The function f can be written as $f(\mathbf{x}) = \max\{f_1(\mathbf{x}), f_2(\mathbf{x}), \ldots, f_m(\mathbf{x})\}$, where $f_i(\mathbf{x}) = \mathbf{a}_i^T \mathbf{x} + b_i$, $i = 1, 2, \ldots, m$. Obviously, $\partial f_i(\mathbf{x}) = \{\mathbf{a}_i\}$. Thus, by the max rule of subdifferential calculus (Theorem 3.50),

$$\partial f(\mathbf{x}) = \left\{ \sum_{i\in I(\mathbf{x})} \lambda_i \mathbf{a}_i : \sum_{i\in I(\mathbf{x})} \lambda_i = 1, \lambda_j \geq 0, j \in I(\mathbf{x}) \right\},$$
where $I(\mathbf{x}) = \{i : f(\mathbf{x}) = \mathbf{a}_i^T \mathbf{x} + b_i\}$.

∎

Example 3.54 (subdifferential of $\|\mathbf{Ax} + \mathbf{b}\|_\infty$). Consider the function $f : \mathbb{R}^n \to \mathbb{R}$ given by $f(\mathbf{x}) = \|\mathbf{Ax} + \mathbf{b}\|_\infty$, where $\mathbf{A} \in \mathbb{R}^{m\times n}$ and $\mathbf{b} \in \mathbb{R}^m$. Then $f(\mathbf{x}) = g(\mathbf{Ax} + \mathbf{b})$, where $g : \mathbb{R}^m \to \mathbb{R}$ is given by $g(\mathbf{y}) = \|\mathbf{y}\|_\infty$. By Example 3.52, we have, for any $\mathbf{y} \in \mathbb{R}^m$,

$$\partial g(\mathbf{y}) = \begin{cases} B_{\|\cdot\|_1}[\mathbf{0}, 1], & \mathbf{y} = \mathbf{0}, \\ \left\{ \sum_{i\in I(\mathbf{y})} \lambda_i \mathrm{sgn}(y_i)\mathbf{e}_i : \sum_{i\in I(\mathbf{y})} \lambda_i = 1, \lambda_j \geq 0, j \in I(\mathbf{y}) \right\}, & \mathbf{y} \neq \mathbf{0}, \end{cases}$$

where
$$I(\mathbf{y}) = \{i \in \{1,2,\ldots,m\} : |y_i| = \|\mathbf{y}\|_\infty\}.$$

We can thus use the affine transformation rule of subdifferential calculus (Theorem 3.43(b)) to conclude that $\partial f(\mathbf{x}) = \mathbf{A}^T \partial g(\mathbf{Ax} + \mathbf{b})$ is given by

$$\partial f(\mathbf{x}) = \begin{cases} \mathbf{A}^T B_{\|\cdot\|_1}[\mathbf{0}, 1], & \mathbf{Ax} + \mathbf{b} = \mathbf{0}, \\ \left\{ \sum_{i\in I_\mathbf{x}} \lambda_i \mathrm{sgn}(\mathbf{a}_i^T \mathbf{x} + b_i)\mathbf{a}_i : \sum_{i\in I_\mathbf{x}} \lambda_i = 1, \lambda_j \geq 0, j \in I_\mathbf{x} \right\}, & \mathbf{Ax} + \mathbf{b} \neq \mathbf{0}, \end{cases}$$

where $\mathbf{a}_1^T, \mathbf{a}_2^T, \ldots, \mathbf{a}_m^T$ are the rows of $\mathbf{A}$ and $I_\mathbf{x} = I(\mathbf{Ax} + \mathbf{b})$. ∎

When the index set is arbitrary (for example, infinite), it is still possible to prove a weak subdifferential calculus rule.

Theorem 3.55 (weak maximum rule of subdifferential calculus). *Let I be an arbitrary set, and suppose that any $i \in I$ is associated with a proper convex function $f_i : \mathbb{E} \to (-\infty, \infty]$. Let*

$$f(\mathbf{x}) = \max_{i\in I} f_i(\mathbf{x}). \tag{3.50}$$

Then for any $\mathbf{x} \in \mathrm{dom}(f)$

$$\mathrm{conv}\left(\cup_{i\in I(\mathbf{x})} \partial f_i(\mathbf{x})\right) \subseteq \partial f(\mathbf{x}), \tag{3.51}$$

where $I(\mathbf{x}) = \{i \in I : f(\mathbf{x}) = f_i(\mathbf{x})\}$.

Proof. Let $\mathbf{x} \in \mathrm{dom}(f)$. Then for any $\mathbf{z} \in \mathrm{dom}(f), i \in I(\mathbf{x})$ and $\mathbf{g} \in \partial f_i(\mathbf{x})$,

$$f(\mathbf{z}) \geq f_i(\mathbf{z}) \geq f_i(\mathbf{x}) + \langle \mathbf{g}, \mathbf{z} - \mathbf{x} \rangle = f(\mathbf{x}) + \langle \mathbf{g}, \mathbf{z} - \mathbf{x} \rangle, \tag{3.52}$$

where the first inequality follows from (3.50), the second inequality is the subgradient inequality, and the equality is due to the assertion that $i \in I(\mathbf{x})$. Since (3.52) holds for any $\mathbf{z} \in \mathrm{dom}(f)$, we can conclude that $\mathbf{g} \in \partial f(\mathbf{x})$. Thus, $\partial f_i(\mathbf{x}) \subseteq \partial f(\mathbf{x})$. Finally, by the convexity of $\partial f(\mathbf{x})$ (Theorem 3.9), the result (3.51) follows. $\quad\Box$

Example 3.56 (subgradient of $\lambda_{\max}(\mathbf{A}_0 + \sum_{i=1}^m x_i \mathbf{A}_i)$). Let $\mathbf{A}_0, \mathbf{A}_1, \ldots, \mathbf{A}_m \in \mathbb{S}^n$. Let $\mathcal{A} : \mathbb{R}^m \to \mathbb{S}^n$ be the affine transformation given by

$$\mathcal{A}(\mathbf{x}) = \mathbf{A}_0 + \sum_{i=1}^m x_i \mathbf{A}_i \text{ for any } \mathbf{x} \in \mathbb{R}^m.$$

Consider the function $f : \mathbb{R}^m \to \mathbb{R}$ given by $f(\mathbf{x}) = \lambda_{\max}(\mathcal{A}(\mathbf{x}))$. Since for any $\mathbf{x} \in \mathbb{R}^m$,

$$f(\mathbf{x}) = \max_{\mathbf{y} \in \mathbb{R}^n : \|\mathbf{y}\|_2 = 1} \mathbf{y}^T \mathcal{A}(\mathbf{x}) \mathbf{y}, \tag{3.53}$$

and since the function

$$f_{\mathbf{y}}(\mathbf{x}) \equiv \mathbf{y}^T \mathcal{A}(\mathbf{x}) \mathbf{y} = \mathbf{y}^T \mathbf{A}_0 \mathbf{y} + \sum_{i=1}^m (\mathbf{y}^T \mathbf{A}_i \mathbf{y}) x_i$$

is affine in $\mathbf{x}$, and in particular convex in $\mathbf{x}$, it follows by Theorem 2.16(c) that f is convex. For a given $\mathbf{x} \in \mathbb{R}^n$, the maximum in (3.53) is attained at normalized eigenvectors which correspond to the maximum eigenvalue of $\mathcal{A}(\mathbf{x})$. Let $\tilde{\mathbf{y}}$ be such a normalized eigenvector. Then it follows by the weak maximum rule of subdifferential calculus (Theorem 3.55) that a subgradient of the affine function $f_{\tilde{\mathbf{y}}}$ at $\mathbf{x}$ is a subgradient of f at $\mathbf{x}$, that is,

$$(\tilde{\mathbf{y}}^T \mathbf{A}_1 \tilde{\mathbf{y}}, \tilde{\mathbf{y}}^T \mathbf{A}_2 \tilde{\mathbf{y}}, \ldots, \tilde{\mathbf{y}}^T \mathbf{A}_m \tilde{\mathbf{y}})^T \in \partial f(\mathbf{x}), \tag{3.54}$$

where $\tilde{\mathbf{y}}$ is a normalized eigenvector of $\mathcal{A}(\mathbf{x})$ corresponding to the maximum eigenvalue.

It is interesting to note that the result (3.54) can also be deduced by the affine transformation rule of subdifferential calculus (Theorem 3.43(b)). Indeed, let $\tilde{\mathbf{y}}$ be as defined above. The function f can be written as $f(\mathbf{x}) = g(\mathcal{B}(\mathbf{x}) + \mathbf{A}_0)$, where $\mathcal{B}(\mathbf{x}) \equiv \sum_{i=1}^m x_i \mathbf{A}_i$ and $g(\mathbf{X}) \equiv \lambda_{\max}(\mathbf{X})$. Then by the affine transformation rule of subdifferential calculus,

$$\partial f(\mathbf{x}) = \mathcal{B}^T(\partial g(\mathcal{B}(\mathbf{x}) + \mathbf{A}_0)). \tag{3.55}$$

By Example 3.8, we know that $\tilde{\mathbf{y}} \tilde{\mathbf{y}}^T \in \partial g(\mathcal{B}(\mathbf{x}) + \mathbf{A}_0)$, and hence, by (3.55),

$$\mathcal{B}^T(\tilde{\mathbf{y}} \tilde{\mathbf{y}}^T) \in \partial f(\mathbf{x}).$$

The result now follows by noting that

$$\mathcal{B}^T(\tilde{\mathbf{y}} \tilde{\mathbf{y}}^T) = (\mathrm{Tr}(\mathbf{A}_1 \tilde{\mathbf{y}} \tilde{\mathbf{y}}^T), \mathrm{Tr}(\mathbf{A}_2 \tilde{\mathbf{y}} \tilde{\mathbf{y}}^T), \ldots, \mathrm{Tr}(\mathbf{A}_m \tilde{\mathbf{y}} \tilde{\mathbf{y}}^T))^T$$
$$= (\tilde{\mathbf{y}}^T \mathbf{A}_1 \tilde{\mathbf{y}}, \tilde{\mathbf{y}}^T \mathbf{A}_2 \tilde{\mathbf{y}}, \ldots, \tilde{\mathbf{y}}^T \mathbf{A}_m \tilde{\mathbf{y}})^T. \quad\blacksquare$$

3.5 The Value Function[18]

Consider the minimization problem

$$f_{\text{opt}} = \min_{\mathbf{x} \in X}\{f(\mathbf{x}) : g_i(\mathbf{x}) \leq 0, i = 1, 2, \ldots, m, \mathbf{Ax} + \mathbf{b} = \mathbf{0}\}, \qquad (3.56)$$

where $f, g_1, g_2, \ldots, g_m : \mathbb{E} \to (-\infty, \infty]$ are extended real-valued functions, $X \subseteq \mathbb{E}$ a nonempty set, $\mathbf{A} \in \mathbb{R}^{p \times n}$, and $\mathbf{b} \in \mathbb{R}^p$. We will define the vector-valued function $\mathbf{g} : \mathbb{E} \to \mathbb{R}^m$ as

$$\mathbf{g}(\mathbf{x}) \equiv (g_1(\mathbf{x}), g_2(\mathbf{x}), \ldots, g_m(\mathbf{x}))^T,$$

so that problem (3.56) can be rewritten more compactly as

$$\min_{\mathbf{x} \in X}\{f(\mathbf{x}) : \mathbf{g}(\mathbf{x}) \leq \mathbf{0}, \mathbf{Ax} + \mathbf{b} = \mathbf{0}\}.$$

The *value function* associated with problem (3.56) is the function $v : \mathbb{R}^m \times \mathbb{R}^p \to [-\infty, \infty]$ given by

$$v(\mathbf{u}, \mathbf{t}) = \min_{\mathbf{x} \in X}\{f(\mathbf{x}) : g(\mathbf{x}) \leq \mathbf{u}, \mathbf{Ax} + \mathbf{b} = \mathbf{t}\}. \qquad (3.57)$$

The feasible set of the minimization problem in (3.57) will be denoted by

$$C(\mathbf{u}, \mathbf{t}) = \{\mathbf{x} \in X : g(\mathbf{x}) \leq \mathbf{u}, \mathbf{Ax} + \mathbf{b} = \mathbf{t}\},$$

so that the value function can also be rewritten as $v(\mathbf{u}, \mathbf{t}) = \min\{f(\mathbf{x}) : \mathbf{x} \in C(\mathbf{u}, \mathbf{t})\}$. By convention $v(\mathbf{u}, \mathbf{t}) = \infty$ if $C(\mathbf{u}, \mathbf{t})$ is empty. A simple property of the value function $v(\cdot, \cdot)$ is that it is monotone w.r.t. its first argument.

Lemma 3.57 (monotonicity of the value function). *Let $f, g_1, g_2, \ldots, g_m : \mathbb{E} \to (-\infty, \infty]$ be extended real-valued functions, $X \subseteq \mathbb{E}$ a nonempty set, $\mathbf{A} \in \mathbb{R}^{p \times n}$, and $\mathbf{b} \in \mathbb{R}^p$. Let v be the value function given in (3.57). Then*

$$v(\mathbf{u}, \mathbf{t}) \geq v(\mathbf{w}, \mathbf{t}) \text{ for any } \mathbf{u}, \mathbf{w} \in \mathbb{R}^m, \mathbf{t} \in \mathbb{R}^p \text{ satisfying } \mathbf{u} \leq \mathbf{w}.$$

Proof. Follows by the obvious fact that $C(\mathbf{u}, \mathbf{t}) \subseteq C(\mathbf{w}, \mathbf{t})$ whenever $\mathbf{u} \leq \mathbf{w}$. $\quad\square$

From now on we will also assume in addition that $f, g_1, g_2, \ldots, g_m$, and X are convex. With these additional assumptions, we now show that the value function is convex as long as it is proper.

Lemma 3.58 (convexity of the value function). *Let $f, g_1, g_2, \ldots, g_m : \mathbb{E} \to (-\infty, \infty]$ be convex functions, $X \subseteq \mathbb{E}$ a nonempty convex set, $\mathbf{A} \in \mathbb{R}^{p \times n}$, and $\mathbf{b} \in \mathbb{R}^p$. Suppose that the value function v given in (3.57) is proper. Then v is convex over $\mathbb{R}^m \times \mathbb{R}^p$.*

Proof. Let $(\mathbf{u}, \mathbf{t}), (\mathbf{w}, \mathbf{s}) \in \text{dom}(v)$ and $\lambda \in [0, 1]$. Since v is proper, to prove the convexity, we need to show that

$$v(\lambda\mathbf{u} + (1 - \lambda)\mathbf{w}, \lambda\mathbf{t} + (1 - \lambda)\mathbf{s}) \leq \lambda v(\mathbf{u}, \mathbf{t}) + (1 - \lambda)v(\mathbf{w}, \mathbf{s}).$$

---

[18]Section 3.5, excluding Theorem 3.60, follows Hiriart-Urruty and Lemaréchal [67, Section VII.3.3].

By the definition of the value function v, there exist sequences $\{\mathbf{x}_k\}_{k \geq 1}, \{\mathbf{y}_k\}_{k \geq 1}$ satisfying

$$\mathbf{x}_k \in C(\mathbf{u}, \mathbf{t}), \mathbf{y}_k \in C(\mathbf{w}, \mathbf{s}), f(\mathbf{x}_k) \to v(\mathbf{u}, \mathbf{t}), f(\mathbf{y}_k) \to v(\mathbf{w}, \mathbf{s}) \text{ as } k \to \infty.$$

Since $\mathbf{x}_k \in C(\mathbf{u}, \mathbf{t})$ and $\mathbf{y}_k \in C(\mathbf{w}, \mathbf{s})$, we have $\mathbf{g}(\mathbf{x}_k) \leq \mathbf{u}, \mathbf{g}(\mathbf{y}_k) \leq \mathbf{w}$. Therefore, by the convexity of the components of $\mathbf{g}$,

$$\mathbf{g}(\lambda \mathbf{x}_k + (1 - \lambda)\mathbf{y}_k) \leq \lambda \mathbf{g}(\mathbf{x}_k) + (1 - \lambda)\mathbf{g}(\mathbf{y}_k) \leq \lambda \mathbf{u} + (1 - \lambda)\mathbf{w}. \qquad (3.58)$$

Moreover,

$$\mathbf{A}(\lambda \mathbf{x}_k + (1 - \lambda)\mathbf{y}_k) + \mathbf{b} = \lambda(\mathbf{A}\mathbf{x}_k + \mathbf{b}) + (1 - \lambda)(\mathbf{A}\mathbf{y}_k + \mathbf{b}) = \lambda \mathbf{s} + (1 - \lambda)\mathbf{t}. \quad (3.59)$$

Combining (3.58) and (3.59), we conclude that

$$\lambda \mathbf{x}_k + (1 - \lambda)\mathbf{y}_k \in C(\lambda \mathbf{u} + (1 - \lambda)\mathbf{w}, \lambda \mathbf{s} + (1 - \lambda)\mathbf{t}). \qquad (3.60)$$

By the convexity of f,

$$f(\lambda \mathbf{x}_k + (1 - \lambda)\mathbf{y}_k) \leq \lambda f(\mathbf{x}_k) + (1 - \lambda)f(\mathbf{y}_k). \qquad (3.61)$$

Since $\lambda f(\mathbf{x}_k) + (1 - \lambda)f(\mathbf{y}_k) \to \lambda v(\mathbf{u}, \mathbf{t}) + (1 - \lambda)v(\mathbf{w}, \mathbf{s})$ as $k \to \infty$, by (3.61) we have

$$\liminf_{k \to \infty} f(\lambda \mathbf{x}_k + (1 - \lambda)\mathbf{y}_k) \leq \lambda v(\mathbf{u}, \mathbf{t}) + (1 - \lambda)v(\mathbf{w}, \mathbf{s}). \qquad (3.62)$$

Finally, since (3.60) holds, by the definition of v, for all k,

$$v(\lambda \mathbf{u} + (1 - \lambda)\mathbf{w}, \lambda \mathbf{t} + (1 - \lambda)\mathbf{s}) \leq f(\lambda \mathbf{x}_k + (1 - \lambda)\mathbf{y}_k),$$

and hence

$$v(\lambda \mathbf{u} + (1 - \lambda)\mathbf{w}, \lambda \mathbf{t} + (1 - \lambda)\mathbf{s}) \leq \liminf_{k \to \infty} f(\lambda \mathbf{x}_k + (1 - \lambda)\mathbf{y}_k),$$

which, combined with (3.62), yields the inequality

$$v(\lambda \mathbf{u} + (1 - \lambda)\mathbf{w}, \lambda \mathbf{t} + (1 - \lambda)\mathbf{s}) \leq \lambda v(\mathbf{u}, \mathbf{t}) + (1 - \lambda)v(\mathbf{w}, \mathbf{s}),$$

establishing the convexity of v. $\square$

The dual objective function $q : \mathbb{R}_+^m \times \mathbb{R}^q \to [-\infty, \infty)$ of problem (3.56) is

$$q(\mathbf{y}, \mathbf{z}) = \min_{\mathbf{x} \in X} \left\{ L(\mathbf{x}; \mathbf{y}, \mathbf{z}) = f(\mathbf{x}) + \mathbf{y}^T \mathbf{g}(\mathbf{x}) + \mathbf{z}^T (\mathbf{A}\mathbf{x} + \mathbf{b}) \right\}, \mathbf{y} \in \mathbb{R}_+^m, \mathbf{z} \in \mathbb{R}^p.$$

The dual problem consists of maximizing q on its effective domain given by

$$\text{dom}(-q) = \{(\mathbf{y}, \mathbf{z}) \in \mathbb{R}_+^m \times \mathbb{R}^p : q(\mathbf{y}, \mathbf{z}) > -\infty\}.$$

The dual problem

$$q_{\text{opt}} = \max_{\mathbf{y} \in \mathbb{R}_+^m, \mathbf{z} \in \mathbb{R}^p} \{q(\mathbf{y}, \mathbf{z}) : (\mathbf{y}, \mathbf{z}) \in \text{dom}(-q)\} \qquad (3.63)$$

is convex in the sense that it consists of maximizing the concave function q over the convex feasible set $\mathrm{dom}(-q)$. We are now ready to show the main result of this section, which is a relation between the subdifferential set of the value function at the zeros vector and the set of optimal solutions of the dual problem. The result is established under the assumption that strong duality holds, meaning under the assumptions that the optimal values of the primal and dual problems are finite and equal ($f_{\mathrm{opt}} = q_{\mathrm{opt}}$) and the optimal set of the dual problem is nonempty. By the strong duality theorem stated as Theorem A.1 in the appendix, it follows that these assumptions are met if the optimal value of problem (3.56) is finite, and if there exists a feasible solution $\bar{\mathbf{x}}$ satisfying $\mathbf{g}(\bar{\mathbf{x}}) < \mathbf{0}$ and a vector $\hat{\mathbf{x}} \in \mathrm{ri}(X)$ satisfying $\mathbf{A}\hat{\mathbf{x}} + \mathbf{b} = \mathbf{0}$.

Theorem 3.59 (characterization of the subdifferential of the value function at 0). *Let $f, g_1, g_2, \ldots, g_m : \mathbb{E} \to (-\infty, \infty]$ be convex functions, $X \subseteq \mathbb{E}$ a nonempty convex set, $\mathbf{A} \in \mathbb{R}^{p \times n}$, and $\mathbf{b} \in \mathbb{R}^p$. Let v be the value function given by (3.57). Suppose that $f_{\mathrm{opt}} = q_{\mathrm{opt}} \in (-\infty, \infty)$ and that the optimal set of the dual problem is nonempty. Then*

(a) *v is proper and convex;*

(b) *$(\mathbf{y}, \mathbf{z})$ is an optimal solution of problem (3.63) if and only if $-(\mathbf{y}, \mathbf{z}) \in \partial v(\mathbf{0}, \mathbf{0})$.*

Proof. Let $(\mathbf{y}, \mathbf{z}) \in \mathrm{dom}(-q)$ be an optimal solution of the dual problem. Then (recalling that $v(\mathbf{0}, \mathbf{0}) = f_{\mathrm{opt}}$)

$$L(\mathbf{x}; \mathbf{y}, \mathbf{z}) \geq \min_{\mathbf{w} \in X} L(\mathbf{w}; \mathbf{y}, \mathbf{z}) = q(\mathbf{y}, \mathbf{z}) = q_{\mathrm{opt}} = f_{\mathrm{opt}} = v(\mathbf{0}, \mathbf{0}) \text{ for all } \mathbf{x} \in X.$$

Therefore, for any $\mathbf{x} \in C(\mathbf{u}, \mathbf{t})$,

$$\begin{aligned}
v(\mathbf{0}, \mathbf{0}) - \mathbf{y}^T \mathbf{u} - \mathbf{z}^T \mathbf{t} &\leq L(\mathbf{x}; \mathbf{y}, \mathbf{z}) - \mathbf{y}^T \mathbf{u} - \mathbf{z}^T \mathbf{t} \\
&= f(\mathbf{x}) + \mathbf{y}^T \mathbf{g}(\mathbf{x}) + \mathbf{z}^T (\mathbf{A}\mathbf{x} + \mathbf{b}) - \mathbf{y}^T \mathbf{u} - \mathbf{z}^T \mathbf{t} \\
&= f(\mathbf{x}) + \mathbf{y}^T (\mathbf{g}(\mathbf{x}) - \mathbf{u}) + \mathbf{z}^T (\mathbf{A}\mathbf{x} + \mathbf{b} - \mathbf{t}) \\
&\leq f(\mathbf{x}),
\end{aligned}$$

where the last inequality follows from the facts that $\mathbf{g}(\mathbf{x}) \leq \mathbf{u}, \mathbf{y} \geq \mathbf{0}$, and $\mathbf{A}\mathbf{x} + \mathbf{b} = \mathbf{t}$. We thus obtained the bound

$$f(\mathbf{x}) \geq v(\mathbf{0}, \mathbf{0}) - \mathbf{y}^T \mathbf{u} - \mathbf{z}^T \mathbf{t} \text{ for any } \mathbf{x} \in C(\mathbf{u}, \mathbf{t}).$$

Minimizing the left-hand side w.r.t. $\mathbf{x} \in C(\mathbf{u}, \mathbf{t})$ yields

$$v(\mathbf{u}, \mathbf{t}) \geq v(\mathbf{0}, \mathbf{0}) - \mathbf{y}^T \mathbf{u} - \mathbf{z}^T \mathbf{t}, \tag{3.64}$$

which is equivalent to saying that $-(\mathbf{y}, \mathbf{z}) \in \partial v(\mathbf{0}, \mathbf{0})$. We actually showed one direction of claim (b), as well as the properness of v since by (3.64), $v(\mathbf{u}, \mathbf{t}) > -\infty$ for any $(\mathbf{u}, \mathbf{t}) \in \mathbb{R}^m \times \mathbb{R}^p$, and by the premise of the theorem, $v(\mathbf{0}, \mathbf{0}) = f_{\mathrm{opt}} < \infty$. Invoking Lemma 3.58, it follows that v is convex, establishing claim (a).

All that is left is to show the reverse direction of claim (b). Assume that $-(\mathbf{y}, \mathbf{z}) \in \partial v(\mathbf{0}, \mathbf{0})$, meaning that

$$v(\mathbf{u}, \mathbf{t}) \geq v(\mathbf{0}, \mathbf{0}) - \mathbf{y}^T \mathbf{u} - \mathbf{z}^T \mathbf{t} \text{ for any } (\mathbf{u}, \mathbf{t}) \in \mathbb{R}^m \times \mathbb{R}^p. \tag{3.65}$$

Let $\mathbf{x} \in X$. Then

$$f(\mathbf{x}) \geq v(\mathbf{g}(\mathbf{x}), \mathbf{A}\mathbf{x} + \mathbf{b}) \overset{(3.65)}{\geq} v(\mathbf{0}, \mathbf{0}) - \mathbf{y}^T \mathbf{g}(\mathbf{x}) - \mathbf{z}^T (\mathbf{A}\mathbf{x} + \mathbf{b}).$$

Therefore,

$$v(\mathbf{0}, \mathbf{0}) \leq f(\mathbf{x}) + \mathbf{y}^T \mathbf{g}(\mathbf{x}) + \mathbf{z}^T (\mathbf{A}\mathbf{x} + \mathbf{b}) = L(\mathbf{x}; \mathbf{y}, \mathbf{z}) \text{ for any } \mathbf{x} \in X.$$

Minimizing the right-hand side w.r.t. $\mathbf{x} \in X$ yields

$$v(\mathbf{0}, \mathbf{0}) \leq \min_{\mathbf{x} \in X} L(\mathbf{x}; \mathbf{y}, \mathbf{z}) = q(\mathbf{y}, \mathbf{z}). \tag{3.66}$$

Let $j \in \{1, 2, \ldots, m\}$. Plugging $\mathbf{u} = \mathbf{e}_j, \mathbf{t} = \mathbf{0}$ into (3.65), we obtain

$$y_j \geq v(\mathbf{0}, \mathbf{0}) - v(\mathbf{e}_j, \mathbf{0}) \geq 0,$$

where the second inequality follows from the monotonicity property of the value function stated in Lemma 3.57. We thus obtained that $\mathbf{y} \geq \mathbf{0}$, and we can consequently write using (3.66)

$$q_{\text{opt}} = f_{\text{opt}} = v(\mathbf{0}, \mathbf{0}) \leq q(\mathbf{y}, \mathbf{z}) \leq q_{\text{opt}},$$

showing that $q(\mathbf{y}, \mathbf{z}) = q_{\text{opt}}$, meaning that $(\mathbf{y}, \mathbf{z})$ is an optimal solution of the dual problem. $\square$

Theorem 3.59 can be used to prove a result concerning an optimality measure of problem (3.56). Consider the following expression:

$$D(\mathbf{x}) \equiv f(\mathbf{x}) - f_{\text{opt}} + \rho_1 \|[\mathbf{g}(\mathbf{x})]_+\|_2 + \rho_2 \|\mathbf{A}\mathbf{x} + \mathbf{b}\|_2.$$

Now assume that

$$D(\tilde{\mathbf{x}}) \leq \delta \tag{3.67}$$

for some $\tilde{\mathbf{x}} \in X$ and a small $\delta > 0$. The question that now arises is whether (3.67) implies that the expressions $f(\tilde{\mathbf{x}}) - f_{\text{opt}}$ as well as $\|[\mathbf{g}(\tilde{\mathbf{x}})]_+\|_2$ and $\|\mathbf{A}\tilde{\mathbf{x}} + \mathbf{b}\|_2$ are also "small" in the sense that they are smaller than a constant times δ. In general, the answer is no. The vector $\tilde{\mathbf{x}}$ is not guaranteed to be feasible, and therefore, in principle, $f(\tilde{\mathbf{x}}) - f_{\text{opt}}$ might be very small (and negative), and $\|[\mathbf{g}(\tilde{\mathbf{x}})]_+\|_2$ and $\|\mathbf{A}\tilde{\mathbf{x}} + \mathbf{b}\|_2$ can be very large. However, we will show in the next theorem that if ρ_1 and ρ_2 are chosen to be large enough, then under the setting of Theorem 3.59, such a conclusion can be drawn.

Theorem 3.60.[19] *Let $f, g_1, g_2, \ldots, g_m : \mathbb{E} \to (-\infty, \infty]$ be convex functions, $X \subseteq \mathbb{E}$ a nonempty convex set, $\mathbf{A} \in \mathbb{R}^{p \times n}$, and $\mathbf{b} \in \mathbb{R}^p$. Let f_{opt} and q_{opt} be the optimal values of the primal and dual problems (3.56) and (3.63), respectively. Suppose that $f_{\text{opt}} = q_{\text{opt}} \in (-\infty, \infty)$ and that the optimal set of the dual problem is nonempty. Let $(\mathbf{y}^*, \mathbf{z}^*)$ be an optimal solution of the dual problem. Assume that $\tilde{\mathbf{x}} \in X$ satisfies*

$$f(\tilde{\mathbf{x}}) - f_{\text{opt}} + \rho_1 \|[\mathbf{g}(\tilde{\mathbf{x}})]_+\|_2 + \rho_2 \|\mathbf{A}\tilde{\mathbf{x}} + \mathbf{b}\|_2 \leq \delta, \tag{3.68}$$

---

[19]Theorem 3.60 is a slight extension of Lemma 6 from Lan [78].

where $\delta > 0$ and ρ_1, ρ_2 are constants satisfying $\rho_1 \geq 2\|\mathbf{y}^*\|_2, \rho_2 \geq 2\|\mathbf{z}^*\|_2$. Then

$$f(\tilde{\mathbf{x}}) - f_{\text{opt}} \leq \delta,$$

$$\|[\mathbf{g}(\tilde{\mathbf{x}})]_+\|_2 \leq \frac{2}{\rho_1}\delta,$$

$$\|\mathbf{A}\tilde{\mathbf{x}} + \mathbf{b}\|_2 \leq \frac{2}{\rho_2}\delta.$$

Proof. The inequality $f(\tilde{\mathbf{x}}) - f_{\text{opt}} \leq \delta$ trivially follows from (3.68) and the fact that the expressions $\rho_1\|[\mathbf{g}(\tilde{\mathbf{x}})]_+\|_2$ and $\rho_2\|\mathbf{A}\tilde{\mathbf{x}} + \mathbf{b}\|_2$ are nonnegative.

Define the function

$$v(\mathbf{u}, \mathbf{t}) = \min_{\mathbf{x} \in X}\{f(\mathbf{x}) : \mathbf{g}(\mathbf{x}) \leq \mathbf{u}, \mathbf{A}\mathbf{x} + \mathbf{b} = \mathbf{t}\}.$$

Since $(\mathbf{y}^*, \mathbf{z}^*)$ is an optimal solution of the dual problem, it follows by Theorem 3.59 that $(-\mathbf{y}^*, -\mathbf{z}^*) \in \partial v(\mathbf{0}, \mathbf{0})$. Therefore, for any $(\mathbf{u}, \mathbf{t}) \in \text{dom}(v)$,

$$v(\mathbf{u}, \mathbf{t}) - v(\mathbf{0}, \mathbf{0}) \geq \langle -\mathbf{y}^*, \mathbf{u}\rangle + \langle -\mathbf{z}^*, \mathbf{t}\rangle. \tag{3.69}$$

Plugging $\mathbf{u} = \tilde{\mathbf{u}} \equiv [\mathbf{g}(\tilde{\mathbf{x}})]_+$ and $\mathbf{t} = \tilde{\mathbf{t}} \equiv \mathbf{A}\tilde{\mathbf{x}}+\mathbf{b}$ into (3.69), while using the inequality $v(\tilde{\mathbf{u}}, \tilde{\mathbf{t}}) \leq f(\tilde{\mathbf{x}})$ and the equality $v(\mathbf{0}, \mathbf{0}) = f_{\text{opt}}$, we obtain

$$\begin{aligned}(\rho_1 - \|\mathbf{y}^*\|_2)\|\tilde{\mathbf{u}}\|_2 + (\rho_2 - \|\mathbf{z}^*\|_2)\|\tilde{\mathbf{t}}\|_2 &= -\|\mathbf{y}^*\|_2\|\tilde{\mathbf{u}}\|_2 - \|\mathbf{z}^*\|_2\|\tilde{\mathbf{t}}\|_2 + \rho_1\|\tilde{\mathbf{u}}\|_2 + \rho_2\|\tilde{\mathbf{t}}\|_2 \\ &\leq \langle -\mathbf{y}^*, \tilde{\mathbf{u}}\rangle + \langle -\mathbf{z}^*, \tilde{\mathbf{t}}\rangle + \rho_1\|\tilde{\mathbf{u}}\|_2 + \rho_2\|\tilde{\mathbf{t}}\|_2 \\ &\leq v(\tilde{\mathbf{u}}, \tilde{\mathbf{t}}) - v(\mathbf{0}, \mathbf{0}) + \rho_1\|\tilde{\mathbf{u}}\|_2 + \rho_2\|\tilde{\mathbf{t}}\|_2 \\ &\leq f(\tilde{\mathbf{x}}) - f_{\text{opt}} + \rho_1\|\tilde{\mathbf{u}}\|_2 + \rho_2\|\tilde{\mathbf{t}}\|_2 \\ &\leq \delta.\end{aligned}$$

Therefore, since both expressions $(\rho_1 - \|\mathbf{y}^*\|_2)\|\tilde{\mathbf{u}}\|_2$ and $(\rho_2 - \|\mathbf{z}^*\|_2)\|\tilde{\mathbf{t}}\|_2$ are nonnegative, it follows that

$$(\rho_1 - \|\mathbf{y}^*\|_2)\|\tilde{\mathbf{u}}\|_2 \leq \delta,$$
$$(\rho_2 - \|\mathbf{z}^*\|_2)\|\tilde{\mathbf{t}}\|_2 \leq \delta,$$

and hence, using the assumptions that $\rho_1 \geq 2\|\mathbf{y}^*\|_2$ and $\rho_2 \geq 2\|\mathbf{t}^*\|_2$,

$$\|[\mathbf{g}(\tilde{\mathbf{x}})]_+\|_2 = \|\tilde{\mathbf{u}}\|_2 \leq \frac{\delta}{\rho_1 - \|\mathbf{y}^*\|_2} \leq \frac{2}{\rho_1}\delta,$$

$$\|\mathbf{A}\tilde{\mathbf{x}} + \mathbf{b}\|_2 = \|\tilde{\mathbf{t}}\|_2 \leq \frac{\delta}{\rho_2 - \|\mathbf{z}^*\|_2} \leq \frac{2}{\rho_2}\delta. \qquad \square$$

3.6 Lipschitz Continuity and Boundedness of Subgradients

This section considers an important relation between Lipschitz continuity of a convex function and boundedness of its subgradients.

Theorem 3.61 (Lipschitz continuity and boundedness of the subdifferential sets). *Let $f : \mathbb{E} \to (-\infty, \infty]$ be a proper and convex function. Suppose that $X \subseteq \text{int}(\text{dom}f)$. Consider the following two claims:*

(i) $|f(\mathbf{x}) - f(\mathbf{y})| \leq L\|\mathbf{x} - \mathbf{y}\|$ for any $\mathbf{x}, \mathbf{y} \in X$.

(ii) $\|\mathbf{g}\|_* \leq L$ for any $\mathbf{g} \in \partial f(\mathbf{x}), \mathbf{x} \in X$.

Then

(a) *the implication* (ii) $\Rightarrow$ (i) *holds;*

(b) *if X is open, then* (i) *holds if and only if* (ii) *holds.*

Proof. (a) Suppose that (ii) is satisfied and let $\mathbf{x}, \mathbf{y} \in X$. Let $\mathbf{g_x} \in \partial f(\mathbf{x})$ and $\mathbf{g_y} \in \partial f(\mathbf{y})$. The existence of these subgradients is guaranteed by Theorem 3.14. Then by the definitions of $\mathbf{g_x}, \mathbf{g_y}$ and the generalized Cauchy–Schwarz inequality (Lemma 1.4),

$$f(\mathbf{x}) - f(\mathbf{y}) \leq \langle \mathbf{g_x}, \mathbf{x} - \mathbf{y} \rangle \leq \|\mathbf{g_x}\|_* \|\mathbf{x} - \mathbf{y}\| \leq L\|\mathbf{x} - \mathbf{y}\|,$$
$$f(\mathbf{y}) - f(\mathbf{x}) \leq \langle \mathbf{g_y}, \mathbf{y} - \mathbf{x} \rangle \leq \|\mathbf{g_y}\|_* \|\mathbf{x} - \mathbf{y}\| \leq L\|\mathbf{x} - \mathbf{y}\|,$$

showing the validity of (i).

(b) The implication (ii) $\Rightarrow$ (i) was already shown. Now assume that (i) is satisfied. Take $\mathbf{x} \in X$ and $\mathbf{g} \in \partial f(\mathbf{x})$. We will show that $\|\mathbf{g}\|_* \leq L$. Define $\mathbf{g}^\dagger \in \mathbb{E}$ as a vector that satisfies $\|\mathbf{g}^\dagger\| = 1, \langle \mathbf{g}^\dagger, \mathbf{g} \rangle = \|\mathbf{g}\|_*$ (the existence of such a vector is warranted by the definition of the dual norm). Take $\varepsilon > 0$ small enough such that $\mathbf{x} + \varepsilon \mathbf{g}^\dagger \in X$. By the subgradient inequality we have

$$f(\mathbf{x} + \varepsilon \mathbf{g}^\dagger) \geq f(\mathbf{x}) + \langle \mathbf{g}, \varepsilon \mathbf{g}^\dagger \rangle.$$

Thus,

$$\varepsilon \|\mathbf{g}\|_* = \langle \mathbf{g}, \varepsilon \mathbf{g}^\dagger \rangle \leq f(\mathbf{x} + \varepsilon \mathbf{g}^\dagger) - f(\mathbf{x}) \leq L\|\mathbf{x} + \varepsilon \mathbf{g}^\dagger - \mathbf{x}\| = L\varepsilon,$$

showing that $\|\mathbf{g}\|_* \leq L$. $\quad\square$

Recall that by Theorem 3.16, the subgradients of a given convex function f are bounded over compact sets contained in $\mathrm{int}(\mathrm{dom}(f))$. Combining this with Theorem 3.61, we can conclude that convex functions are always Lipschitz continuous over compact sets contained in the interior of their domain.

Corollary 3.62 (Lipschitz continuity of convex functions over compact domains). *Let $f : \mathbb{E} \to (-\infty, \infty]$ be a proper and convex function. Suppose that $X \subseteq \mathrm{int}(\mathrm{dom}(f))$ is compact. Then there exists $L > 0$ for which*

$$|f(\mathbf{x}) - f(\mathbf{y})| \leq L\|\mathbf{x} - \mathbf{y}\| \text{ for any } \mathbf{x}, \mathbf{y} \in X.$$

3.7 Optimality Conditions

3.7.1 Fermat's Optimality Condition

Subdifferential sets are extremely useful in characterizing minima points. Perhaps the most basic optimality condition states that a point is a global minimum of a proper extended real-valued convex function if and only if $\mathbf{0}$ belongs to the subdifferential set at the point. In a sense, this is a generalization of Fermat's optimality condition at points of differentiability ("$\nabla f(\mathbf{x}^*) = \mathbf{0}$"). We will refer to this condition as *Fermat's optimality condition*.

Theorem 3.63 (Fermat's optimality condition). *Let $f : \mathbb{E} \to (-\infty, \infty]$ be a proper convex function. Then*

$$\mathbf{x}^* \in \operatorname{argmin}\{f(\mathbf{x}) : \mathbf{x} \in \mathbb{E}\} \tag{3.70}$$

if and only if $\mathbf{0} \in \partial f(\mathbf{x}^*)$.

Proof. Follows by the definition of the subgradient. Indeed, (3.70) is satisfied if and only if

$$f(\mathbf{x}) \geq f(\mathbf{x}^*) + \langle \mathbf{0}, \mathbf{x} - \mathbf{x}^* \rangle \text{ for any } \mathbf{x} \in \operatorname{dom}(f),$$

which is the same as the inclusion $\mathbf{0} \in \partial f(\mathbf{x}^*)$. $\square$

Example 3.64 (minimizing piecewise linear functions). Consider the problem

$$\min_{\mathbf{x} \in \mathbb{R}^n} \left[f(\mathbf{x}) \equiv \max_{i=1,2,\dots,m} \left\{ \mathbf{a}_i^T \mathbf{x} + b_i \right\} \right], \tag{3.71}$$

where $\mathbf{a}_i \in \mathbb{R}^n, b_i \in \mathbb{R}, i = 1, 2, \dots, m$. Denote

$$I(\mathbf{x}) = \left\{ i : f(\mathbf{x}) = \mathbf{a}_i^T \mathbf{x} + b_i \right\}.$$

Then, by Example 3.53,

$$\partial f(\mathbf{x}) = \left\{ \sum_{i \in I(\mathbf{x})} \lambda_i \mathbf{a}_i : \sum_{i \in I(\mathbf{x})} \lambda_i = 1, \lambda_j \geq 0, j \in I(\mathbf{x}) \right\}.$$

Therefore, since by Fermat's optimality condition $\mathbf{x}^*$ is an optimal solution of (3.71) if and only if $\mathbf{0} \in \partial f(\mathbf{x}^*)$, it follows that $\mathbf{x}^*$ is an optimal solution of problem (3.71) if and only if there exists $\boldsymbol{\lambda} \in \Delta_m$ such that

$$\mathbf{0} = \sum_{i=1}^m \lambda_i \mathbf{a}_i \text{ and } \lambda_j = 0 \text{ for any } j \notin I(\mathbf{x}^*). \tag{3.72}$$

We can rewrite this condition in a more compact way by denoting $\mathbf{A} \in \mathbb{R}^{m \times n}$ to be the matrix whose rows are $\mathbf{a}_1^T, \mathbf{a}_2^T, \dots, \mathbf{a}_m^T$. Then the optimality condition (3.72) can be written as

$$\exists \boldsymbol{\lambda} \in \Delta_m \text{ s.t. } \mathbf{A}^T \boldsymbol{\lambda} = \mathbf{0} \text{ and } \lambda_j(\mathbf{a}_j^T \mathbf{x}^* + b_j - f(\mathbf{x}^*)) = 0, j = 1, 2, \dots, m. \quad \blacksquare$$

Example 3.65 (medians). Suppose that we are given n different[20] and ordered numbers $a_1 < a_2 < \cdots < a_n$. Denote $A = \{a_1, a_2, \dots, a_n\} \subseteq \mathbb{R}$. The *median* of A is a number β that satisfies

$$\#\{i : a_i \leq \beta\} \geq \frac{n}{2} \text{ and } \#\{i : a_i \geq \beta\} \geq \frac{n}{2}.$$

---

[20]The assumption that these are different and ordered numbers is not essential and is made for the sake of simplicity of exposition.

That is, a median of A is a number that satisfies that at least half of the numbers in A are smaller or equal to it and that at least half are larger or equal. It is not difficult to see that if A has an odd number of elements, then the median is the middlemost number. For example, the median of $\{5, 8, 11, 60, 100\}$ is 11. If the number of elements in A is even, then there is no unique median. The set of medians comprises all numbers between the two middle values. For example, if $A = \{5, 8, 11, 20, 60, 100\}$, then the set of medians of A is the interval $[11, 20]$. In general,

$$\text{median}(A) = \begin{cases} a_{\frac{n+1}{2}}, & n \text{ odd}, \\ [a_{\frac{n}{2}}, a_{\frac{n}{2}+1}], & n \text{ even}. \end{cases}$$

From an optimization perspective, the set of possible medians is the optimal solution set of the problem

$$\min \left\{ f(x) \equiv \sum_{i=1}^{n} |x - a_i| \right\}. \tag{3.73}$$

To show this, denote $f_i(x) \equiv |x - a_i|$, so that $f(x) = f_1(x) + f_2(x) + \cdots + f_n(x)$, and note that for any $i \in \{1, 2, \ldots, n\}$,

$$\partial f_i(x) = \begin{cases} 1, & x > a_i, \\ -1, & x < a_i, \\ [-1, 1], & x = a_i. \end{cases}$$

By the sum rule of subdifferential calculus (Theorem 3.40),

$$\begin{aligned} \partial f(x) &= \partial f_1(x) + \partial f_2(x) + \cdots + \partial f_n(x) \\ &= \begin{cases} \#\{i : a_i < x\} - \#\{i : a_i > x\}, & x \notin A, \\ \#\{i : a_i < x\} - \#\{i : a_i > x\} + [-1, 1], & x \in A. \end{cases} \end{aligned}$$

We can further elaborate and write

$$\partial f(x) = \begin{cases} 2i - n, & x \in (a_i, a_{i+1}), \\ 2i - 1 - n + [-1, 1], & x = a_i, \\ -n, & x < a_1, \\ n, & x > a_n. \end{cases} \tag{3.74}$$

Let $i \in \{1, 2, \ldots, n\}$. By (3.74), $0 \in \partial f(a_i)$ if and only if $|2i - 1 - n| \le 1$, which is equivalent to $\frac{n}{2} \le i \le \frac{n}{2} + 1$ and $0 \in \partial f(x)$ for some $x \in (a_i, a_{i+1})$ if and only if $i = \frac{n}{2}$. We can thus conclude that if n is odd, then the only optimal point is $a_{\frac{n+1}{2}}$, and when n is even, the optimal set is the interval $[a_{\frac{n}{2}}, a_{\frac{n}{2}+1}]$, establishing the fact that the optimal set of (3.73) is exactly the set of medians. ∎

Example 3.66 (Fermat–Weber problem). Given m different points in $\mathbb{R}^d$, $\mathcal{A} = \{\mathbf{a}_1, \mathbf{a}_2, \ldots, \mathbf{a}_m\}$, and m positive weights $\omega_1, \omega_2, \ldots, \omega_m$, the *Fermat–Weber problem* is given by

$$\text{(FW)} \quad \min_{\mathbf{x} \in \mathbb{R}^d} \left\{ f(\mathbf{x}) \equiv \sum_{i=1}^{m} \omega_i \|\mathbf{x} - \mathbf{a}_i\|_2 \right\}.$$

The Fermat–Weber problem is actually a weighted multidimensional version of the median problem (3.73) discussed in the previous example and is therefore also referred to in the literature as the *geometric median* problem. Let us write explicitly the optimality conditions for problem (FW). Denote $f_i(\mathbf{x}) = \omega_i g_i(\mathbf{x})$, where $g_i(\mathbf{x}) \equiv \|\mathbf{x} - \mathbf{a}_i\|_2$. Then for any $i \in \{1, 2, \ldots, m\}$

$$\partial f_i(\mathbf{x}) = \begin{cases} \omega_i \dfrac{\mathbf{x} - \mathbf{a}_i}{\|\mathbf{x} - \mathbf{a}_i\|_2}, & \mathbf{x} \neq \mathbf{a}_i, \\[2mm] B_{\|\cdot\|_2}[\mathbf{0}, \omega_i], & \mathbf{x} = \mathbf{a}_i, \end{cases}$$

where here we used Theorems 3.35 ("multiplication by a positive scalar"), the affine transformation rule of subdifferential calculus (Theorem 3.43(b)), and Example 3.34, in which the subdifferential set of the l_2-norm was computed. Obviously, $f = \sum_{i=1}^{m} f_i$, and hence, by the sum rule of subdifferential calculus (Theorem 3.40[21]), we obtain that

$$\partial f(\mathbf{x}) = \sum_{i=1}^{m} \partial f_i(\mathbf{x}) = \begin{cases} \sum_{i=1}^{m} \omega_i \dfrac{\mathbf{x} - \mathbf{a}_i}{\|\mathbf{x} - \mathbf{a}_i\|_2}, & \mathbf{x} \notin \mathcal{A}, \\[2mm] \sum_{i=1, i \neq j}^{m} \omega_i \dfrac{\mathbf{x} - \mathbf{a}_i}{\|\mathbf{x} - \mathbf{a}_i\|_2} + B[\mathbf{0}, \omega_j], & \mathbf{x} = \mathbf{a}_j (j = 1, 2, \ldots, m). \end{cases}$$

Using Fermat's optimality condition (Theorem 3.63), we can conclude that $\mathbf{x}^* \in \mathbb{R}^d$ is an optimal solution of problem (FW) if and only if either

$$\mathbf{x}^* \notin \mathcal{A} \text{ and } \sum_{i=1}^{m} \omega_i \frac{\mathbf{x}^* - \mathbf{a}_i}{\|\mathbf{x}^* - \mathbf{a}_i\|_2} = \mathbf{0}$$

or for some $j \in \{1, 2, \ldots, m\}$

$$\mathbf{x}^* = \mathbf{a}_j \text{ and } \left\| \sum_{i=1, i \neq j}^{m} \omega_i \frac{\mathbf{x}^* - \mathbf{a}_i}{\|\mathbf{x}^* - \mathbf{a}_i\|_2} \right\|_2 \leq \omega_j. \quad \blacksquare$$

3.7.2 Convex Constrained Optimization

Consider the constrained optimization problem

$$\min\{f(\mathbf{x}) : \mathbf{x} \in C\}, \tag{3.75}$$

where f is an extended real-valued convex function and $C \subseteq \mathbb{E}$ is a convex set. Using Fermat's optimality condition (Theorem 3.63) and the convexity assumptions, it is easy to write a necessary and sufficient optimality condition for problem (3.75) in terms of the subdifferential set of f and the normal cone of C.

---

[21]or by Corollary 3.39

Theorem 3.67 (necessary and sufficient optimality conditions for convex constrained optimization). *Let* $f : \mathbb{E} \to (-\infty, \infty]$ *be a proper and convex function, and let* $C \subseteq \mathbb{E}$ *be a convex set for which* $\mathrm{ri}(\mathrm{dom}(f)) \cap \mathrm{ri}(C) \neq \emptyset$. *Then* $\mathbf{x}^* \in C$ *is an optimal solution of* (3.75) *if and only if*

$$\text{there exists } \mathbf{g} \in \partial f(\mathbf{x}^*) \text{ for which } -\mathbf{g} \in N_C(\mathbf{x}^*). \tag{3.76}$$

Proof. Problem (3.75) can be rewritten as

$$\min_{\mathbf{x} \in \mathbb{E}} f(\mathbf{x}) + \delta_C(\mathbf{x}).$$

Since $\mathrm{ri}(\mathrm{dom}(f)) \cap \mathrm{ri}(C) \neq \emptyset$, it follows by the sum rule of subdifferential calculus (Theorem 3.40) that for any $\mathbf{x} \in C$,

$$\partial(f + \delta_C)(\mathbf{x}) = \partial f(\mathbf{x}) + \partial \delta_C(\mathbf{x}).$$

By Example 3.5, $\partial \delta_C(\mathbf{x}) = N_C(\mathbf{x})$, and consequently for any $\mathbf{x} \in C$,

$$\partial(f + \delta_C)(\mathbf{x}) = \partial f(\mathbf{x}) + N_C(\mathbf{x}).$$

Therefore, invoking Fermat's optimality condition (Theorem 3.63), $\mathbf{x}^* \in C$ is an optimal solution of (3.75) if and only if $\mathbf{0} \in \partial f(\mathbf{x}^*) + N_C(\mathbf{x}^*)$, that is, if and only if

$$(-\partial f(\mathbf{x}^*)) \cap N_C(\mathbf{x}^*) \neq \emptyset,$$

which is the same as condition (3.76). $\quad\square$

Using the definition of the normal cone, we can write the optimality condition in a slightly more explicit manner.

Corollary 3.68 (necessary and sufficient optimality conditions for convex constrained optimization—second version). *Let* $f : \mathbb{E} \to (-\infty, \infty]$ *be a proper and convex function, and let* C *be a convex set satisfying* $\mathrm{ri}(\mathrm{dom}(f)) \cap \mathrm{ri}(C) \neq \emptyset$. *Then* $\mathbf{x}^* \in C$ *is an optimal solution of* (3.75) *if and only if*

$$\text{there exists } \mathbf{g} \in \partial f(\mathbf{x}^*) \text{ for which } \langle \mathbf{g}, \mathbf{x} - \mathbf{x}^* \rangle \geq 0 \text{ for any } \mathbf{x} \in C. \tag{3.77}$$

Condition (3.77) is not particularly explicit. We will show in the next example how to write it in an explicit way for the case where $C = \Delta_n$.

Example 3.69 (optimality conditions over the unit simplex). Suppose that the assumptions in Corollary 3.68 hold and that $C = \Delta_n, \mathbb{E} = \mathbb{R}^n$. Given $\mathbf{x}^* \in \Delta_n$, we will show that the condition

$$(\mathrm{I}) \ \mathbf{g}^T(\mathbf{x} - \mathbf{x}^*) \geq 0 \text{ for all } \mathbf{x} \in \Delta_n$$

is satisfied if and only if the following condition is satisfied:

$$(\mathrm{II}) \text{ there exist } \mu \in \mathbb{R} \text{ such that } g_i \begin{cases} = \mu, & x_i^* > 0, \\ \geq \mu, & x_i^* = 0. \end{cases}$$

Assume first that (II) is satisfied. Then for any $\mathbf{x} \in \Delta_n$,

$$
\begin{aligned}
\mathbf{g}^T(\mathbf{x} - \mathbf{x}^*) &= \sum_{i=1}^{n} g_i(x_i - x_i^*) \\
&= \sum_{i:x_i^* > 0} g_i(x_i - x_i^*) + \sum_{i:x_i^* = 0} g_i x_i \\
&\geq \sum_{i:x_i^* > 0} \mu(x_i - x_i^*) + \mu \sum_{i:x_i^* = 0} x_i \\
&= \mu \sum_{i=1}^{n} x_i - \mu \sum_{i:x_i^* > 0} x_i^* = \mu - \mu = 0,
\end{aligned}
$$

proving that condition (I) is satisfied. To show the reverse direction, assume that (I) is satisfied. Let i and j be two different indices for which $x_i^* > 0$. Define the vector $\mathbf{x} \in \Delta_n$ as

$$
x_k = \begin{cases}
x_k^*, & k \notin \{i, j\}, \\
x_i^* - \frac{x_i^*}{2}, & k = i, \\
x_j^* + \frac{x_i^*}{2}, & k = j.
\end{cases}
$$

The inequality $\mathbf{g}^T(\mathbf{x} - \mathbf{x}^*) \geq 0$ then amounts to

$$
-\frac{x_i^*}{2} g_i + \frac{x_i^*}{2} g_j \geq 0,
$$

which by the fact that $x_i^* > 0$ implies that

$$
g_i \leq g_j. \tag{3.78}
$$

In particular, for any two indices $i \neq j$ for which $x_i^*, x_j^* > 0$, the two inequalities $g_i \leq g_j$ and $g_j \leq g_i$ hold, and hence $g_i = g_j$. Therefore, all the components of $\mathbf{g}$ corresponding to positive components of $\mathbf{x}^*$ have the same value, which we will denote by μ. Let i be any index for which $x_i^* > 0$. Then for any index j for which $x_j^* = 0$, the inequality (3.78) holds. Therefore, $g_j \geq \mu$, and condition (II) is thus established. ∎

We summarize the discussion in Example 3.69 with the following corollary.

Corollary 3.70 (necessary and sufficient optimality conditions for convex problems over the unit simplex). *Let $f : \mathbb{E} \to (-\infty, \infty]$ be a proper and convex function. Suppose that $\mathrm{ri}(\Delta_n) \cap \mathrm{ri}(\mathrm{dom}(f)) \neq \emptyset$. Then $\mathbf{x}^* \in \Delta_n$ is an optimal solution of*

$$
\min\{f(\mathbf{x}) : \mathbf{x} \in \Delta_n\}
$$

if and only if there exists $\mathbf{g} \in \partial f(\mathbf{x}^*)$ and $\mu \in \mathbb{R}$ for which

$$
g_i \begin{cases}
= \mu, & x_i^* > 0, \\
\geq \mu, & x_i^* = 0.
\end{cases}
$$

The following example illustrates one instance in which the optimal solution of a convex problem over the unit simplex can be found using Corollary 3.70.

Example 3.71. Consider the problem

$$\min_{\mathbf{x}} \left\{ \sum_{i=1}^{n} x_i \log x_i - \sum_{i=1}^{n} y_i x_i : \mathbf{x} \in \Delta_n \right\}, \tag{3.79}$$

where $\mathbf{y} \in \mathbb{R}^n$ is a given vector. Problem (3.79) can be written as

$$\min\{f(\mathbf{x}) : \mathbf{x} \in \Delta_n\},$$

where $f : \mathbb{R}^n \to (-\infty, \infty]$ is given by

$$f(\mathbf{x}) = \begin{cases} \sum_{i=1}^{n} x_i \log x_i - \sum_{i=1}^{n} y_i x_i, & \mathbf{x} \geq \mathbf{0}, \\ \infty & \text{else.} \end{cases}$$

Let us assume that there exists an optimal solution[22] $\mathbf{x}^*$ satisfying $\mathbf{x}^* > \mathbf{0}$. Then under this assumption, by Corollary 3.70 and the fact that f is differentiable at any positive vector, it follows that there exists $\mu \in \mathbb{R}$ such that for any i, $\frac{\partial f}{\partial x_i}(\mathbf{x}^*) = \mu$, which is the same as $\log x_i^* + 1 - y_i = \mu$. Therefore, for any i,

$$x_i^* = e^{\mu - 1 + y_i} = \alpha e^{y_i}, \quad i = 1, 2, \dots, n$$

where $\alpha = e^{\mu - 1}$. Since $\sum_{i=1}^{n} x_i^* = 1$, it follows that $\alpha = \frac{1}{\sum_{j=1}^{n} e^{y_j}}$. Therefore,

$$x_i^* = \frac{e^{y_i}}{\sum_{j=1}^{n} e^{y_j}}, \quad i = 1, 2, \dots, n.$$

This is indeed an optimal solution of problem (3.79) since it satisfies the conditions of Corollary 3.70, which are (also) sufficient conditions for optimality. ∎

3.7.3   The Nonconvex Composite Model

It is also possible to write a necessary optimality condition for *nonconvex* problems in terms of subgradients. We will write such a condition for problems consisting of minimizing a composite function $f + g$, where f possesses some differentiability properties but is not assumed to be convex while g is convex but not assumed to have any special differentiability properties.

Theorem 3.72 (optimality conditions for the composite problem). *Let $f : \mathbb{E} \to (-\infty, \infty]$ be a proper function, and let $g : \mathbb{E} \to (-\infty, \infty]$ be a proper convex function such that $\mathrm{dom}(g) \subseteq \mathrm{int}(\mathrm{dom}(f))$. Consider the problem*

$$(P) \quad \min_{\mathbf{x} \in \mathbb{E}} f(\mathbf{x}) + g(\mathbf{x}).$$

---

[22]It is not difficult to show a priori that the problem has a unique solution.

(a) **(necessary condition)** *If* $\mathbf{x}^* \in \mathrm{dom}(g)$ *is a local optimal solution of* (P) *and* f *is differentiable at* $\mathbf{x}^*$, *then*

$$-\nabla f(\mathbf{x}^*) \in \partial g(\mathbf{x}^*). \tag{3.80}$$

(b) **(necessary and sufficient condition for convex problems)** *Suppose that* f *is convex. If* f *is differentiable at* $\mathbf{x}^* \in \mathrm{dom}(g)$, *then* $\mathbf{x}^*$ *is a global optimal solution of* (P) *if and only if* (3.80) *is satisfied.*

Proof. (a) Let $\mathbf{y} \in \mathrm{dom}(g)$. Then by the convexity of $\mathrm{dom}(g)$, for any $\lambda \in (0,1)$, the point $\mathbf{x}_\lambda = (1-\lambda)\mathbf{x}^* + \lambda\mathbf{y}$ is in $\mathrm{dom}(g)$, and by the local optimality of $\mathbf{x}^*$, it follows that, for small enough λ,

$$f(\mathbf{x}_\lambda) + g(\mathbf{x}_\lambda) \geq f(\mathbf{x}^*) + g(\mathbf{x}^*).$$

That is,

$$f((1-\lambda)\mathbf{x}^* + \lambda\mathbf{y}) + g((1-\lambda)\mathbf{x}^* + \lambda\mathbf{y}) \geq f(\mathbf{x}^*) + g(\mathbf{x}^*).$$

Using the convexity of g, it follows that

$$f((1-\lambda)\mathbf{x}^* + \lambda\mathbf{y}) + (1-\lambda)g(\mathbf{x}^*) + \lambda g(\mathbf{y}) \geq f(\mathbf{x}^*) + g(\mathbf{x}^*),$$

which is the same as

$$\frac{f((1-\lambda)\mathbf{x}^* + \lambda\mathbf{y}) - f(\mathbf{x}^*)}{\lambda} \geq g(\mathbf{x}^*) - g(\mathbf{y}).$$

Taking $\lambda \to 0^+$ in the last inequality yields

$$f'(\mathbf{x}^*; \mathbf{y} - \mathbf{x}^*) \geq g(\mathbf{x}^*) - g(\mathbf{y}),$$

where we used the fact that since f is differentiable at $\mathbf{x}^*$, its directional derivatives exist. In fact, by Theorem 3.29, we have $f'(\mathbf{x}^*; \mathbf{y} - \mathbf{x}^*) = \langle \nabla f(\mathbf{x}^*), \mathbf{y} - \mathbf{x}^* \rangle$, and hence for any $\mathbf{y} \in \mathrm{dom}(g)$,

$$g(\mathbf{y}) \geq g(\mathbf{x}^*) + \langle -\nabla f(\mathbf{x}^*), \mathbf{y} - \mathbf{x}^* \rangle,$$

showing that indeed $-\nabla f(\mathbf{x}^*) \in \partial g(\mathbf{x}^*)$.

(b) Suppose in addition that f is convex. If $\mathbf{x}^*$ is an optimal solution of (P), then we already proved in part (a) that (3.80) is satisfied. Suppose now that (3.80) is satisfied. Then for any $\mathbf{y} \in \mathrm{dom}(g)$,

$$g(\mathbf{y}) \geq g(\mathbf{x}^*) + \langle -\nabla f(\mathbf{x}^*), \mathbf{y} - \mathbf{x}^* \rangle. \tag{3.81}$$

By the convexity of f, for any $\mathbf{y} \in \mathrm{dom}(g)$,

$$f(\mathbf{y}) \geq f(\mathbf{x}^*) + \langle \nabla f(\mathbf{x}^*), \mathbf{y} - \mathbf{x}^* \rangle. \tag{3.82}$$

Adding (3.81) and (3.82), we obtain that

$$f(\mathbf{y}) + g(\mathbf{y}) \geq f(\mathbf{x}^*) + g(\mathbf{x}^*)$$

for any $\mathbf{y} \in \mathrm{dom}(g)$, meaning that $\mathbf{x}^*$ is an optimal solution of (P). $\square$

The condition (3.80) is an important optimality condition, and we will refer to it as the "stationarity" condition.

Definition 3.73 (stationarity). *Let $f : \mathbb{E} \to (-\infty, \infty]$ be proper and let $g : \mathbb{E} \to (-\infty, \infty]$ be a proper convex function such that $\mathrm{dom}(g) \subseteq \mathrm{int}(\mathrm{dom}(f))$. Consider the problem*

$$(\mathrm{P}) \quad \min_{\mathbf{x} \in \mathbb{E}} f(\mathbf{x}) + g(\mathbf{x}).$$

A point $\mathbf{x}^*$ in which f is differentiable is called a **stationary point** *of* (P) *if*

$$-\nabla f(\mathbf{x}^*) \in \partial g(\mathbf{x}^*).$$

Under the setting of Definition 3.73, $\mathbf{x}^*$ is also called *a stationary point of the function $f + g$*.

We have shown in Theorem 3.72 that stationarity is a necessary local optimality condition for problem (P), and that if f is convex, then stationarity is a necessary and sufficient global optimality condition. The case $g = \delta_C$ deserves a separate discussion.

Example 3.74 (convex constrained nonconvex programming). When $g = \delta_C$ for a nonempty convex set $C \subseteq \mathbb{E}$, problem (P) becomes

$$\min\{f(\mathbf{x}) : \mathbf{x} \in C\},$$

which is a problem consisting of minimizing a (possibly) nonconvex function over a convex set. A point $\mathbf{x}^* \in C$ in which f is differentiable is a stationary point of (P) if and only if

$$-\nabla f(\mathbf{x}^*) \in \partial \delta_C(\mathbf{x}^*) = N_C(\mathbf{x}^*), \tag{3.83}$$

where the equality is due to Example 3.5. By the definition of the normal cone, condition (3.83) can be rewritten as

$$\langle -\nabla f(\mathbf{x}^*), \mathbf{x} - \mathbf{x}^* \rangle \leq 0 \text{ for any } \mathbf{x} \in C,$$

which is the same as

$$\langle \nabla f(\mathbf{x}^*), \mathbf{x} - \mathbf{x}^* \rangle \geq 0 \text{ for any } \mathbf{x} \in C. \quad \blacksquare$$

Example 3.75. Consider the problem

$$\min_{\mathbf{x} \in \mathbb{R}^n} f(\mathbf{x}) + \lambda \|\mathbf{x}\|_1, \tag{3.84}$$

where $f : \mathbb{R}^n \to (-\infty, \infty]$ is an extended real-valued function. A point $\mathbf{x}^* \in \mathrm{int}(\mathrm{dom}(f))$ in which f is differentiable is a stationary point of (3.84) if

$$-\nabla f(\mathbf{x}^*) \in \lambda \partial g(\mathbf{x}^*),$$

where $g(\cdot) = \| \cdot \|_1$. Using the expression for the subdifferential set of the l_1-norm given in Example 3.41, we obtain that $\mathbf{x}^*$ is a stationary point of problem (3.84) if and only if

$$
\frac{\partial f(\mathbf{x}^*)}{\partial x_i}
\begin{cases}
= -\lambda, & x_i^* > 0, \\
= \lambda, & x_i^* < 0, \\
\in [-\lambda, \lambda], & x_i^* = 0.
\end{cases}
\tag{3.85}
$$

By Theorem 3.72, condition (3.85) is a necessary condition for $\mathbf{x}^*$ to be a local minimum of problem (3.84). If f is also convex, then condition (3.85) is a necessary and sufficient condition for $\mathbf{x}^*$ to be a global optimal solution of problem (3.84). ∎

3.7.4   The KKT Conditions

In this section we will show that the KKT conditions for constrained convex problems can be directly deduced by Fermat's optimality condition. For that, we begin by establishing an equivalent reformulation of general inequality constrained problems.

Lemma 3.76. *Let $f, g_1, g_2, \ldots, g_m : \mathbb{E} \to \mathbb{R}$ be real-valued functions. Consider the problem*

$$
\begin{aligned}
\min \quad & f(\mathbf{x}) \\
s.t. \quad & g_i(\mathbf{x}) \le 0, \quad i = 1, 2, \ldots, m.
\end{aligned}
\tag{3.86}
$$

Assume that the minimum value of problem (3.86) is finite and equal to $\bar{f}$. Define the function

$$
F(\mathbf{x}) \equiv \max\{f(\mathbf{x}) - \bar{f}, g_1(\mathbf{x}), g_2(\mathbf{x}), \ldots, g_m(\mathbf{x})\}.
\tag{3.87}
$$

Then the optimal set of problem (3.86) is the same as the set of minimizers of F.

Proof. Let X^* be the optimal set of problem (3.86). To establish the result, we will show that F satisfies the following two properties:

(i) $F(\mathbf{x}) > 0$ for any $\mathbf{x} \notin X^*$.

(ii) $F(\mathbf{x}) = 0$ for any $\mathbf{x} \in X^*$.

To prove property (i), let $\mathbf{x} \notin X^*$. There are two options. Either $\mathbf{x}$ is not feasible, meaning that $g_i(\mathbf{x}) > 0$ for some i, and hence by its definition $F(\mathbf{x}) > 0$. If $\mathbf{x}$ is feasible but not optimal, then $g_i(\mathbf{x}) \le 0$ for all $i = 1, 2, \ldots, m$ and $f(\mathbf{x}) > \bar{f}$, which also implies that $F(\mathbf{x}) > 0$. To prove (ii), suppose that $\mathbf{x} \in X^*$. Then $g_i(\mathbf{x}) \le 0$ for all $i = 1, 2, \ldots, m$ and $f(\mathbf{x}) = \bar{f}$, implying that $F(\mathbf{x}) = 0$.   □

Using Lemma 3.76, we can conclude that problem (3.86) reduces to

$$
\min_{\mathbf{x} \in \mathbb{E}} F(\mathbf{x})
\tag{3.88}
$$

in the sense that the optimal sets of the two problems are the same. Using this equivalence, we can now establish under additional convexity assumptions the well-known Fritz-John optimality conditions for problem (3.86).

Theorem 3.77 (Fritz-John necessary optimality conditions). *Consider the minimization problem*

$$\begin{aligned} \min \quad & f(\mathbf{x}) \\ s.t. \quad & g_i(\mathbf{x}) \leq 0, \quad i = 1, 2, \ldots, m, \end{aligned} \tag{3.89}$$

where $f, g_1, g_2, \ldots, g_m : \mathbb{E} \to \mathbb{R}$ are real-valued convex functions. Let $\mathbf{x}^*$ be an optimal solution of (3.89). Then there exist $\lambda_0, \lambda_1, \ldots, \lambda_m \geq 0$, not all zeros, for which

$$\mathbf{0} \in \lambda_0 \partial f(\mathbf{x}^*) + \sum_{i=1}^{m} \lambda_i \partial g_i(\mathbf{x}^*) \tag{3.90}$$

$$\lambda_i g_i(\mathbf{x}^*) = 0, \quad i = 1, 2, \ldots, m. \tag{3.91}$$

Proof. Let $\mathbf{x}^*$ be an optimal solution of problem (3.89). Denote the optimal value of problem (3.89) by $\bar{f} = f(\mathbf{x}^*)$. Using Lemma 3.76, it follows that $\mathbf{x}^*$ is an optimal solution of the problem

$$\min_{\mathbf{x} \in \mathbb{E}} \{F(\mathbf{x}) \equiv \max\{g_0(\mathbf{x}), g_1(\mathbf{x}), \ldots, g_m(\mathbf{x})\},$$

where $g_0(\mathbf{x}) \equiv f(\mathbf{x}) - \bar{f}$. Obviously, $F(\mathbf{x}^*) = 0$. Since F is a maximum of convex functions, it is convex, and hence, using Fermat's optimality condition (Theorem 3.63),

$$\mathbf{0} \in \partial F(\mathbf{x}^*). \tag{3.92}$$

By the max rule of subdifferential calculus (Theorem 3.50),

$$\partial F(\mathbf{x}^*) = \text{conv}\left((\cup_{i \in I(\mathbf{x}^*)} \partial g_i(\mathbf{x}^*))\right), \tag{3.93}$$

where $I(\mathbf{x}^*) = \{i \in \{0, 1, \ldots, m\} : g_i(\mathbf{x}^*) = 0\}$. Combining (3.92) and (3.93), we can deduce that there exists $\lambda_i \geq 0, i \in I(\mathbf{x}^*)$, such that $\sum_{i \in I(\mathbf{x}^*)} \lambda_i = 1$ for which

$$\mathbf{0} \in \sum_{i \in I(\mathbf{x}^*)} \lambda_i \partial g_i(\mathbf{x}^*). \tag{3.94}$$

Since $g_0(\mathbf{x}^*) = f(\mathbf{x}^*) - \bar{f} = 0$, it follows that $0 \in I(\mathbf{x}^*)$, and hence (3.94) can be rewritten as

$$\mathbf{0} \in \lambda_0 \partial f(\mathbf{x}^*) + \sum_{i \in I(\mathbf{x}^*) \backslash \{0\}} \lambda_i \partial g_i(\mathbf{x}^*).$$

Defining $\lambda_i = 0$ for any $i \in \{1, 2, \ldots, m\} \setminus I(\mathbf{x}^*)$, we conclude that conditions (3.90) and (3.91) are satisfied. Finally, not all the λ_i's are zeros since $\sum_{i \in I(\mathbf{x}^*)} \lambda_i = 1$. $\square$

We will now establish the KKT conditions, which are the same as the Fritz-John conditions, but with $\lambda_0 = 1$. The necessity of these conditions requires the following additional condition, which we refer to as *Slater's condition*:

$$\text{there exists } \bar{\mathbf{x}} \in \mathbb{E} \text{ for which } g_i(\bar{\mathbf{x}}) < 0, \quad i = 1, 2, \ldots, m. \tag{3.95}$$

The sufficiency of the KKT conditions does not require any additional assumptions (besides convexity) and is actually easily derived without using the result on the Fritz-John conditions.

Theorem 3.78 (KKT conditions). *Consider the minimization problem*

$$\begin{aligned} \min \quad & f(\mathbf{x}) \\ s.t. \quad & g_i(\mathbf{x}) \leq 0, \quad i = 1, 2, \ldots, m, \end{aligned} \tag{3.96}$$

where $f, g_1, g_2, \ldots, g_m : \mathbb{E} \to \mathbb{R}$ are real-valued convex functions.

(a) *Let $\mathbf{x}^*$ be an optimal solution of (3.96), and assume that Slater's condition (3.95) is satisfied. Then there exist $\lambda_1, \ldots, \lambda_m \geq 0$ for which*

$$\mathbf{0} \in \partial f(\mathbf{x}^*) + \sum_{i=1}^{m} \lambda_i \partial g_i(\mathbf{x}^*) \tag{3.97}$$

$$\lambda_i g_i(\mathbf{x}^*) = 0, \quad i = 1, 2, \ldots, m. \tag{3.98}$$

(b) *If $\mathbf{x}^* \in \mathbb{E}$ satisfies conditions (3.97) and (3.98) for some $\lambda_1, \lambda_2, \ldots, \lambda_m \geq 0$, then it is an optimal solution of problem (3.96).*

Proof. (a) By the Fritz-John conditions (Theorem 3.77) there exist $\tilde{\lambda}_0, \tilde{\lambda}_1, \ldots, \tilde{\lambda}_m \geq 0$, not all zeros, for which

$$\mathbf{0} \in \tilde{\lambda}_0 \partial f(\mathbf{x}^*) + \sum_{i=1}^{m} \tilde{\lambda}_i \partial g_i(\mathbf{x}^*), \tag{3.99}$$

$$\tilde{\lambda}_i g_i(\mathbf{x}^*) = 0, \quad i = 1, 2, \ldots, m. \tag{3.100}$$

We will show that $\tilde{\lambda}_0 \neq 0$. Assume by contradiction that $\tilde{\lambda}_0 = 0$. Then, by (3.99),

$$\mathbf{0} \in \sum_{i=1}^{m} \tilde{\lambda}_i \partial g_i(\mathbf{x}^*);$$

that is, there exist $\boldsymbol{\xi}_i \in \partial g_i(\mathbf{x}^*), i = 1, 2, \ldots, m$, such that

$$\sum_{i=1}^{m} \tilde{\lambda}_i \boldsymbol{\xi}_i = \mathbf{0}. \tag{3.101}$$

Let $\bar{\mathbf{x}}$ be a point satisfying Slater's condition (3.95). By the subgradient inequality employed on the pair of points $\bar{\mathbf{x}}, \mathbf{x}^*$ w.r.t. the functions $g_i, i = 1, 2, \ldots, m$, we have

$$g_i(\mathbf{x}^*) + \langle \boldsymbol{\xi}_i, \bar{\mathbf{x}} - \mathbf{x}^* \rangle \leq g_i(\bar{\mathbf{x}}), \quad i = 1, 2, \ldots, m.$$

Multiplying the ith inequality by $\tilde{\lambda}_i \geq 0$ and summing over $i = 1, 2, \ldots, m$ yields

$$\sum_{i=1}^{m} \tilde{\lambda}_i g_i(\mathbf{x}^*) + \left\langle \sum_{i=1}^{m} \tilde{\lambda}_i \boldsymbol{\xi}_i, \bar{\mathbf{x}} - \mathbf{x}^* \right\rangle \leq \sum_{i=1}^{m} \tilde{\lambda}_i g_i(\bar{\mathbf{x}}), \quad i = 1, 2, \ldots, m.$$

Using (3.100) and (3.101), we obtain the inequality $\sum_{i=1}^{m} \tilde{\lambda}_i g_i(\bar{\mathbf{x}}) \geq 0$, which is impossible since $\tilde{\lambda}_i \geq 0$ and $g_i(\bar{\mathbf{x}}) < 0$ for any i, and not all the $\tilde{\lambda}_i$'s are zeros. Therefore, $\tilde{\lambda}_0 > 0$, and we can thus divide both the relation (3.99) and the equalities (3.100) by $\tilde{\lambda}_0$ to obtain that (3.97) and (3.98) are satisfied with $\lambda_i = \frac{\tilde{\lambda}_i}{\tilde{\lambda}_0}, i = 1, 2, \ldots, m$.

(b) Suppose then that $\mathbf{x}^*$ satisfies (3.97) and (3.98) for some nonnegative numbers $\lambda_1, \lambda_2, \ldots, \lambda_m$. Let $\hat{\mathbf{x}} \in \mathbb{E}$ be a feasible point of (3.96), meaning that $g_i(\hat{\mathbf{x}}) \leq 0$, $i = 1, 2, \ldots, m$. We will show that $f(\hat{\mathbf{x}}) \geq f(\mathbf{x}^*)$. Define the function

$$h(\mathbf{x}) = f(\mathbf{x}) + \sum_{i=1}^{m} \lambda_i g_i(\mathbf{x}).$$

The function h is convex, and the condition (3.97) along with the sum rule of subdifferential calculus (Theorem 3.40) yields the relation

$$\mathbf{0} \in \partial h(\mathbf{x}^*),$$

which by Fermat's optimality condition (Theorem 3.63) implies that $\mathbf{x}^*$ is a minimizer of h over $\mathbb{E}$. Combining this fact with (3.98) implies that

$$f(\mathbf{x}^*) = f(\mathbf{x}^*) + \sum_{i=1}^{m} \lambda_i g_i(\mathbf{x}^*) = h(\mathbf{x}^*) \leq h(\hat{\mathbf{x}}) = f(\hat{\mathbf{x}}) + \sum_{i=1}^{m} \lambda_i g_i(\hat{\mathbf{x}}) \leq f(\hat{\mathbf{x}}),$$

where the last inequality follows from the facts that $\lambda_i \geq 0$ and $g_i(\hat{\mathbf{x}}) \leq 0$ for $i = 1, 2, \ldots, m$. We have thus proven that $\mathbf{x}^*$ is an optimal solution of (3.96). $\square$

3.8   Summary of Weak and Strong Subgradient Calculus Results

This section contains a summary of most of the rules and results concerning the computation of subdifferential sets (strong results), as well as rules for computing specific subgradients in the subdifferential sets (weak results). Before that, we begin by summarizing the rules of subdifferential calculus.

- **Multiplication by a positive scalar**

  $$\partial(\alpha f)(\mathbf{x}) = \alpha \partial f(\mathbf{x}).$$

  Assumptions: $f : \mathbb{E} \to (-\infty, \infty]$ proper, $\alpha > 0$, $\mathbf{x} \in \text{dom}(f)$. [Theorem 3.35]
- **Differentiability**
  f is differentiable at $\mathbf{x}$ if and only if $\partial f(\mathbf{x})$ is a singleton, and in that case

  $$\partial f(\mathbf{x}) = \{\nabla f(\mathbf{x})\}.$$

  Assumptions: $f : \mathbb{E} \to (-\infty, \infty]$ proper convex, $\mathbf{x} \in \text{int}(\text{dom}(f))$. [Theorem 3.33]
- **Weak sum rule of subdifferential calculus**

  $$\sum_{i=1}^{m} \partial f_i(\mathbf{x}) \subseteq \partial(\sum_{i=1}^{m} f_i)(\mathbf{x}).$$

  Assumptions: $f_1, f_2, \ldots, f_m : \mathbb{E} \to (-\infty, \infty]$ proper convex. [Corollary 3.38(a)]

- **Sum rule of subdifferential calculus**

$$\partial(\textstyle\sum_{i=1}^{m} f_i)(\mathbf{x}) = \sum_{i=1}^{m} \partial f_i(\mathbf{x}).$$

Assumptions: $f_1, f_2, \ldots, f_m : \mathbb{E} \to (-\infty, \infty]$ proper convex, $\cap_{i=1}^{m} \mathrm{ri}(\mathrm{dom}(f_i)) \neq \emptyset$. [Theorem 3.40]

- **Weak affine transformation rule of subdifferential calculus**

$$\mathcal{A}^T(\partial f(\mathcal{A}(\mathbf{x}) + \mathbf{b})) \subseteq \partial h(\mathbf{x}) \quad (h(\mathbf{x}) \equiv f(\mathcal{A}(\mathbf{x}) + \mathbf{b})).$$

Assumptions: $f, h : \mathbb{E} \to (-\infty, \infty]$ proper convex, $\mathbf{x} \in \mathrm{dom}(h)$. [Theorem 3.43(a)]

- **Affine transformation rule of subdifferential calculus**

$$\partial h(\mathbf{x}) = \mathcal{A}^T(\partial f(\mathcal{A}(\mathbf{x}) + \mathbf{b})) \quad (h(\mathbf{x}) \equiv f(\mathcal{A}(\mathbf{x}) + \mathbf{b})).$$

Assumptions: $f, h : \mathbb{E} \to (-\infty, \infty]$ proper convex, $\mathbf{x} \in \mathrm{int}(\mathrm{dom}(h)), \mathcal{A}(\mathbf{x}) + \mathbf{b} \in \mathrm{int}(\mathrm{dom}(f))$. [Theorem 3.43(b)]

- **Chain rule of subdifferential calculus**

$$\partial h(\mathbf{x}) = g'(f(\mathbf{x}))\partial f(\mathbf{x}) \quad (h = g \circ f).$$

Assumptions: $f : \mathbb{E} \to \mathbb{R}$ convex, $g : \mathbb{R} \to \mathbb{R}$ nondecreasing, differentiable and convex. [Theorem 3.47]

- **Max rule of subdifferential calculus**

$$\partial(\max(f_1, f_2, \ldots, f_m))(\mathbf{x}) = \mathrm{conv}\left(\cup_{i \in I(\mathbf{x})}\partial f_i(\mathbf{x})\right),$$

where

$$I(\mathbf{x}) = \{i : f_i(\mathbf{x}) = \max\{f_1(\mathbf{x}), f_2(\mathbf{x}), \ldots, f_m(\mathbf{x})\}\}.$$

Assumptions: $f_1, f_2, \ldots, f_m$ proper, convex, $\mathbf{x} \in \cap_{i=1}^{m}\mathrm{int}(\mathrm{dom}(f_i))$. [Theorem 3.50]

- **Weak max rule of subdifferential calculus**

$$\mathrm{conv}\left(\cup_{i \in I(\mathbf{x})}\partial f_i(\mathbf{x})\right) \subseteq \partial(\max_{i \in I} f_i)(\mathbf{x}),$$

where

$$I(\mathbf{x}) = \{i \in I : f_i(\mathbf{x}) = \max_{i \in I} f_i(\mathbf{x})\}.$$

Assumptions: I = arbitrary index set. $f_i : \mathbb{E} \to (-\infty, \infty]$ $(i \in I)$ proper, convex, $\mathbf{x} \in \cap_{i \in I}\mathrm{dom}(f_i)$. [Theorem 3.55]

The table below contains the main examples from the chapter related to weak results of subgradients computations.

Function	Weak result	Setting	Reference
$-q$ = negative dual function	$-\mathbf{g}(\mathbf{x}_0) \in \partial(-q)(\boldsymbol{\lambda}_0)$	$q(\boldsymbol{\lambda}) = \min_{\mathbf{x} \in X} f(\mathbf{x}) + \boldsymbol{\lambda}^T\mathbf{g}(\mathbf{x})$, $f : \mathbb{E} \to \mathbb{R}$, $\mathbf{g} : \mathbb{E} \to \mathbb{R}^m$, $\mathbf{x}_0$ = a minimizer of $f(\mathbf{x}) + \boldsymbol{\lambda}_0^T\mathbf{g}(\mathbf{x})$ over X	Example 3.7
$f(\mathbf{X}) = \lambda_{\max}(\mathbf{X})$	$\mathbf{v}\mathbf{v}^T \in \partial f(\mathbf{X})$	$f : \mathbb{S}^n \to \mathbb{R}$, $\mathbf{v}$ = normalized maximum eigenvector of $X \in \mathbb{S}^n$	Example 3.8
$f(\mathbf{x}) = \|\mathbf{x}\|_1$	$\mathrm{sgn}(\mathbf{x}) \in \partial f(\mathbf{x})$	$\mathbb{E} = \mathbb{R}^n$	Example 3.42
$f(\mathbf{x}) = \lambda_{\max}(\mathbf{A}_0 + \sum_{i=1}^{m} x_i\mathbf{A}_i)$	$(\tilde{\mathbf{y}}^T\mathbf{A}_i\tilde{\mathbf{y}})_{i=1}^{m} \in \partial f(\mathbf{x})$	$\tilde{\mathbf{y}}$ = normalized maximum eigenvector of $\mathbf{A}_0 + \sum_{i=1}^{m} x_i\mathbf{A}_i$	Example 3.56

The following table contains the main strong results of subdifferential sets computations derived in this chapter.

$f(\mathbf{x})$	$\partial f(\mathbf{x})$	Assumptions	Reference
$\|\mathbf{x}\|$	$B_{\|\cdot\|_*}[\mathbf{0}, 1]$	$\mathbf{x} = \mathbf{0}$	Example 3.3
$\|\mathbf{x}\|_1$	$\left\{ \sum_{i \in I_{\neq}(\mathbf{x})} \mathrm{sgn}(x_i)\mathbf{e}_i + \sum_{i \in I_0(\mathbf{x})} [-\mathbf{e}_i, \mathbf{e}_i] \right\}$	$\mathbb{E} = \mathbb{R}^n$, $I_{\neq}(\mathbf{x}) = \{i \,:\, x_i \neq 0\}$, $I_0(\mathbf{x}) = \{i \,:\, x_i = 0\}$.	Example 3.41
$\|\mathbf{x}\|_2$	$\begin{cases} \left\{ \frac{\mathbf{x}}{\|\mathbf{x}\|_2} \right\}, & \mathbf{x} \neq \mathbf{0}, \\ B_{\|\cdot\|_2}[\mathbf{0}, 1], & \mathbf{x} = \mathbf{0}. \end{cases}$	$\mathbb{E} = \mathbb{R}^n$	Example 3.34
$\|\mathbf{x}\|_\infty$	$\left\{ \sum_{i \in I(\mathbf{x})} \lambda_i \mathrm{sgn}(x_i)\mathbf{e}_i \,:\, \begin{array}{c} \sum_{i \in I(\mathbf{x})} \lambda_i = 1 \\ \lambda_i \geq 0 \end{array} \right\}$	$\mathbb{E} = \mathbb{R}^n$, $I(\mathbf{x}) = \{i : \|\mathbf{x}\|_\infty = |x_i|\}$, $\mathbf{x} \neq \mathbf{0}$	Example 3.52
$\max(\mathbf{x})$	$\left\{ \sum_{i \in I(\mathbf{x})} \lambda_i \mathbf{e}_i \,:\, \sum_{i \in I(\mathbf{x})} \lambda_i = 1, \lambda_i \geq 0 \right\}$	$\mathbb{E} = \mathbb{R}^n$, $I(\mathbf{x}) = \{i : \max(\mathbf{x}) = x_i\}$	Example 3.51
$\max(\mathbf{x})$	Δ_n	$\mathbb{E} = \mathbb{R}^n$, $\mathbf{x} = \alpha\mathbf{e}$ for some $\alpha \in \mathbb{R}$	Example 3.51
$\delta_S(\mathbf{x})$	$N_S(\mathbf{x})$	$\emptyset \neq S \subseteq \mathbb{E}$	Example 3.5
$\delta_{B[\mathbf{0},1]}(\mathbf{x})$	$\begin{cases} \{\mathbf{y} \in \mathbb{E}^* : \|\mathbf{y}\|_* \leq \langle \mathbf{y}, \mathbf{x} \rangle\}, & \|\mathbf{x}\| \leq 1, \\ \emptyset, & \|\mathbf{x}\| > 1. \end{cases}$		Example 3.6
$\|\mathbf{A}\mathbf{x} + \mathbf{b}\|_1$	$\sum_{i \in I_{\neq}(\mathbf{x})} \mathrm{sgn}(\mathbf{a}_i^T\mathbf{x} + b_i)\mathbf{a}_i + \sum_{i \in I_0(\mathbf{x})} [-\mathbf{a}_i, \mathbf{a}_i]$	$\mathbb{E} = \mathbb{R}^n$, $\mathbf{A} \in \mathbb{R}^{m \times n}$, $\mathbf{b} \in \mathbb{R}^m$, $I_{\neq}(\mathbf{x}) = \{i : \mathbf{a}_i^T\mathbf{x} + b_i \neq 0\}$, $I_0(\mathbf{x}) = \{i : \mathbf{a}_i^T\mathbf{x} + b_i = 0\}$	Example 3.44
$\|\mathbf{A}\mathbf{x} + \mathbf{b}\|_2$	$\begin{cases} \frac{\mathbf{A}^T(\mathbf{A}\mathbf{x}+\mathbf{b})}{\|\mathbf{A}\mathbf{x}+\mathbf{b}\|_2}, & \mathbf{A}\mathbf{x}+\mathbf{b} \neq \mathbf{0}, \\ \mathbf{A}^T B_{\|\cdot\|_2}[\mathbf{0}, 1], & \mathbf{A}\mathbf{x}+\mathbf{b} = \mathbf{0}. \end{cases}$	$\mathbb{E} = \mathbb{R}^n$, $\mathbf{A} \in \mathbb{R}^{m \times n}$, $\mathbf{b} \in \mathbb{R}^m$	Example 3.45
$\|\mathbf{A}\mathbf{x} + \mathbf{b}\|_\infty$	$\left\{ \sum_{i \in I_{\mathbf{x}}} \lambda_i \mathrm{sgn}(\mathbf{a}_i^T\mathbf{x} + b_i)\mathbf{a}_i \,:\, \begin{array}{c} \sum_{i \in I_{\mathbf{x}}} \lambda_i = 1 \\ \lambda_i \geq 0 \end{array} \right\}$	$\mathbb{E} = \mathbb{R}^n$, $\mathbf{A} \in \mathbb{R}^{m \times n}$, $\mathbf{b} \in \mathbb{R}^m$, $I_{\mathbf{x}} = \{i \,:\, \|\mathbf{A}\mathbf{x}+\mathbf{b}\|_\infty = |\mathbf{a}_i^T\mathbf{x}+b_i|\}$, $\mathbf{A}\mathbf{x}+\mathbf{b} \neq \mathbf{0}$	Example 3.54
$\|\mathbf{A}\mathbf{x} + \mathbf{b}\|_\infty$	$\mathbf{A}^T B_{\|\cdot\|_1}[\mathbf{0}, 1]$	same as above but with $\mathbf{A}\mathbf{x} + \mathbf{b} = \mathbf{0}$	Example 3.54
$\max_i\{\mathbf{a}_i^T\mathbf{x} + b\}$	$\left\{ \sum_{i \in I(\mathbf{x})} \lambda_i \mathbf{a}_i \,:\, \sum_{i \in I(\mathbf{x})} \lambda_i = 1, \lambda_i \geq 0 \right\}$	$\mathbb{E} = \mathbb{R}^n$, $\mathbf{a}_i \in \mathbb{R}^n$, $b_i \in \mathbb{R}$, $I(\mathbf{x}) = \{i : f(\mathbf{x}) = \mathbf{a}_i^T\mathbf{x} + b_i\}$	Example 3.53
$\frac{1}{2}d_C^2(\mathbf{x})$	$\{\mathbf{x} - P_C(\mathbf{x})\}$	$C = $ nonempty closed and convex, $\mathbb{E} = $ Euclidean	Example 3.31
$d_C(\mathbf{x})$	$\begin{cases} \left\{ \frac{\mathbf{x} - P_C(\mathbf{x})}{d_C(\mathbf{x})} \right\}, & \mathbf{x} \notin C, \\ N_C(\mathbf{x}) \cap B[\mathbf{0}, 1] & \mathbf{x} \in C. \end{cases}$	$C = $ nonempty closed and convex, $\mathbb{E} = $ Euclidean	Example 3.49

Chapter 4

Conjugate Functions

4.1 Definition and Basic Properties

We begin with the definition of the conjugate function.

Definition 4.1 (conjugate functions). *Let $f : \mathbb{E} \to [-\infty, \infty]$ be an extended real-valued function. The function $f^* : \mathbb{E}^* \to [-\infty, \infty]$, defined by*

$$f^*(\mathbf{y}) = \max_{\mathbf{x} \in \mathbb{E}} \{\langle \mathbf{y}, \mathbf{x} \rangle - f(\mathbf{x})\}, \quad \mathbf{y} \in \mathbb{E}^*,$$

is called the **conjugate function of** f.

Example 4.2 (conjugate of indicator functions). Let $f = \delta_C$, where $C \subseteq \mathbb{E}$ is nonempty. Then for any $\mathbf{y} \in \mathbb{E}^*$

$$f^*(\mathbf{y}) = \max_{\mathbf{x} \in \mathbb{E}} \{\langle \mathbf{y}, \mathbf{x} \rangle - \delta_C(\mathbf{x})\} = \max_{\mathbf{x} \in C} \langle \mathbf{y}, \mathbf{x} \rangle = \sigma_C(\mathbf{y}).$$

That is, the conjugate of the indicator function is the support function of the same underlying set:

$$\delta_C^* = \sigma_C.$$

∎

Two fundamental properties of conjugate functions are their convexity and closedness (regardless of whether the original function is closed or convex).

Theorem 4.3 (convexity and closedness of conjugate functions). *Let $f : \mathbb{E} \to (-\infty, \infty]$ be an extended real-valued function. Then the conjugate function f^* is closed and convex.*

Proof. Note that f^* is the pointwise maximum of affine functions, which are convex and closed, and thus, invoking Theorems 2.16(c) and 2.7(c), it follows that f^* is closed and convex. □

87

Example 4.4 (conjugate of $\frac{1}{2}\|\cdot\|^2 + \delta_C$). Suppose that $\mathbb{E}$ is Euclidean and that $C \subseteq \mathbb{E}$ is nonempty. Define $f(\mathbf{x}) = \frac{1}{2}\|\mathbf{x}\|^2 + \delta_C(\mathbf{x})$. Then by Example 2.17 (specifically, (2.6)), it follows that

$$f^*(\mathbf{y}) = \frac{1}{2}\|\mathbf{y}\|^2 - \frac{1}{2}d_C^2(\mathbf{y}).$$

Note that while f is convex only if C is convex, the convexity of f^* is guaranteed regardless of whether C is convex or not. ∎

The next result states that the conjugate function of a proper convex function is also proper.

Theorem 4.5 (properness of conjugate functions). *Let $f : \mathbb{E} \to (-\infty, \infty]$ be a proper convex function. Then f^* is proper.*

Proof. Since f is proper, it follows that there exists $\hat{\mathbf{x}} \in \mathbb{E}$ such that $f(\hat{\mathbf{x}}) < \infty$. By the definition of the conjugate function, for any $\mathbf{y} \in \mathbb{E}^*$,

$$f^*(\mathbf{y}) \geq \langle \mathbf{y}, \hat{\mathbf{x}} \rangle - f(\hat{\mathbf{x}}),$$

and hence $f^*(\mathbf{y}) > -\infty$. What remains in order to establish the properness of f^* is to show that there exists $\mathbf{g} \in \mathbb{E}^*$ such that $f^*(\mathbf{g}) < \infty$. By Corollary 3.19, there exists $\mathbf{x} \in \text{dom}(f)$ such that $\partial f(\mathbf{x}) \neq \emptyset$. Take $\mathbf{g} \in \partial f(\mathbf{x})$. Then by the definition of the subgradient, for any $\mathbf{z} \in \mathbb{E}$,

$$f(\mathbf{z}) \geq f(\mathbf{x}) + \langle \mathbf{g}, \mathbf{z} - \mathbf{x} \rangle.$$

Hence,

$$f^*(\mathbf{g}) = \max_{\mathbf{z} \in \mathbb{E}} \{ \langle \mathbf{g}, \mathbf{z} \rangle - f(\mathbf{z}) \} \leq \langle \mathbf{g}, \mathbf{x} \rangle - f(\mathbf{x}) < \infty,$$

concluding that f^* is a proper function. □

The following result, called *Fenchel's inequality*, is a trivial implication of the definition of conjugacy.

Theorem 4.6 (Fenchel's inequality). *Let $f : \mathbb{E} \to (-\infty, \infty]$ be an extended real-valued proper function. Then for any $\mathbf{x} \in \mathbb{E}$ and $\mathbf{y} \in \mathbb{E}^*$,*

$$f(\mathbf{x}) + f^*(\mathbf{y}) \geq \langle \mathbf{y}, \mathbf{x} \rangle.$$

Proof. By the definition of the conjugate function we have that for any $\mathbf{x} \in \mathbb{E}$ and $\mathbf{y} \in \mathbb{E}^*$,

$$f^*(\mathbf{y}) \geq \langle \mathbf{y}, \mathbf{x} \rangle - f(\mathbf{x}). \tag{4.1}$$

Since f is proper, it follows that $f(\mathbf{x}), f^*(\mathbf{y}) > -\infty$. We can thus add $f(\mathbf{x})$ to both sides of (4.1) and obtain the desired result. □

4.2 The Biconjugate

The conjugacy operation can be invoked twice resulting in the biconjugate operation. Specifically, for a function $f : \mathbb{E} \to [-\infty, \infty]$ we define (recall that in this book $\mathbb{E}$ and $\mathbb{E}^{**}$ are considered to be identical)

$$f^{**}(\mathbf{x}) = \max_{\mathbf{y} \in \mathbb{E}^*} \{\langle \mathbf{x}, \mathbf{y} \rangle - f^*(\mathbf{y})\}, \quad \mathbf{x} \in \mathbb{E}.$$

The biconjugate function is always a lower bound on the original function, as the following result states.

Lemma 4.7 ($f^{**} \leq f$). *Let $f : \mathbb{E} \to [-\infty, \infty]$ be an extended real-valued function. Then $f(\mathbf{x}) \geq f^{**}(\mathbf{x})$ for any $\mathbf{x} \in \mathbb{E}$.*

Proof. By the definition of the conjugate function we have for any $\mathbf{x} \in \mathbb{E}$ and $\mathbf{y} \in \mathbb{E}^*$,

$$f^*(\mathbf{y}) \geq \langle \mathbf{y}, \mathbf{x} \rangle - f(\mathbf{x}).$$

Thus,

$$f(\mathbf{x}) \geq \langle \mathbf{y}, \mathbf{x} \rangle - f^*(\mathbf{y}),$$

implying that

$$f(\mathbf{x}) \geq \max_{\mathbf{y} \in \mathbb{E}^*} \{\langle \mathbf{y}, \mathbf{x} \rangle - f^*(\mathbf{y})\} = f^{**}(\mathbf{x}). \quad \square$$

If we assume that f is proper closed and convex, then the biconjugate is not just a lower bound on f—it is equal to f.

Theorem 4.8 ($f = f^{**}$ for proper closed convex functions). *Let $f : \mathbb{E} \to (-\infty, \infty]$ be a proper closed and convex function. Then $f^{**} = f$.*

Proof. By Lemma 4.7, $f^{**} \leq f$. We thus need to show that $f^{**} \geq f$. Suppose by contradiction that for some $\mathbf{x} \in \mathbb{E}$ we have $f^{**}(\mathbf{x}) < f(\mathbf{x})$. This means that $(\mathbf{x}, f^{**}(\mathbf{x})) \notin \mathrm{epi}(f) \subseteq \mathbb{E} \times \mathbb{R}$. We assume as usual that the product space $\mathbb{V} = \mathbb{E} \times \mathbb{R}$ is endowed with the inner product $\langle (\mathbf{u}, s), (\mathbf{v}, t) \rangle_{\mathbb{V}} = \langle \mathbf{u}, \mathbf{v} \rangle + st$, where $\langle \cdot, \cdot \rangle$ is the inner product associated with $\mathbb{E}$ (see Section 1.9). Since f is proper closed and convex, the set $\mathrm{epi}(f)$ is nonempty closed and convex, and hence, by the strict separation theorem (Theorem 2.33), there exist $\mathbf{a} \in \mathbb{E}^*, b, c_1, c_2 \in \mathbb{R}$ such that

$$\langle \mathbf{a}, \mathbf{z} \rangle + bs \leq c_1 < c_2 \leq \langle \mathbf{a}, \mathbf{x} \rangle + bf^{**}(\mathbf{x}) \text{ for all } (\mathbf{z}, s) \in \mathrm{epi}(f).$$

We can thus conclude that

$$\langle \mathbf{a}, \mathbf{z} - \mathbf{x} \rangle + b(s - f^{**}(\mathbf{x})) \leq c_1 - c_2 \equiv c < 0 \text{ for all } (\mathbf{z}, s) \in \mathrm{epi}(f). \qquad (4.2)$$

The scalar b must be nonpositive, since otherwise, if it was positive, the inequality would have been violated by taking a fixed $\mathbf{z}$ and large enough s. We will now consider two cases.

- If $b < 0$, then dividing (4.2) by $-b$ and taking $\mathbf{y} = -\frac{\mathbf{a}}{b}$, we get

$$\langle \mathbf{y}, \mathbf{z} - \mathbf{x} \rangle - s + f^{**}(\mathbf{x}) \leq \frac{c}{-b} < 0 \text{ for all } (\mathbf{z}, s) \in \mathrm{epi}(f).$$

In particular, taking $s = f(\mathbf{z})$ (which is possible since $(\mathbf{z}, f(\mathbf{z})) \in \operatorname{epi}(f)$), we obtain that

$$\langle \mathbf{y}, \mathbf{z} \rangle - f(\mathbf{z}) - \langle \mathbf{y}, \mathbf{x} \rangle + f^{**}(\mathbf{x}) \leq \frac{c}{-b} < 0 \text{ for all } \mathbf{z} \in \mathbb{E}.$$

Taking the maximum over $\mathbf{z}$ yields the inequality

$$f^*(\mathbf{y}) - \langle \mathbf{y}, \mathbf{x} \rangle + f^{**}(\mathbf{x}) \leq \frac{c}{-b} < 0,$$

which is a contradiction of Fenchel's inequality (Theorem 4.6).

- If $b = 0$, then take some $\hat{\mathbf{y}} \in \operatorname{dom}(f^*)$. Such a vector exists since f^* is proper by the properness and convexity of f (Theorem 4.5). Let $\varepsilon > 0$ and define $\hat{\mathbf{a}} = \mathbf{a} + \varepsilon \hat{\mathbf{y}}$ and $\hat{b} = -\varepsilon$. Then for any $\mathbf{z} \in \operatorname{dom}(f)$,

$$\begin{aligned} \langle \hat{\mathbf{a}}, \mathbf{z} - \mathbf{x} \rangle + \hat{b}(f(\mathbf{z}) - f^{**}(\mathbf{x})) &= \langle \mathbf{a}, \mathbf{z} - \mathbf{x} \rangle + \varepsilon[\langle \hat{\mathbf{y}}, \mathbf{z} \rangle - f(\mathbf{z}) + f^{**}(\mathbf{x}) - \langle \hat{\mathbf{y}}, \mathbf{x} \rangle] \\ &\leq c + \varepsilon[\langle \hat{\mathbf{y}}, \mathbf{z} \rangle - f(\mathbf{z}) + f^{**}(\mathbf{x}) - \langle \hat{\mathbf{y}}, \mathbf{x} \rangle] \\ &\leq c + \varepsilon[f^*(\hat{\mathbf{y}}) - \langle \hat{\mathbf{y}}, \mathbf{x} \rangle + f^{**}(\mathbf{x})], \end{aligned}$$

where the first inequality is due to (4.2) and the second by the definition of $f^*(\hat{\mathbf{y}})$ as the maximum of $\langle \hat{\mathbf{y}}, \mathbf{z} \rangle - f(\mathbf{z})$ over all possible $\mathbf{z} \in \mathbb{E}$. We thus obtained the inequality

$$\langle \hat{\mathbf{a}}, \mathbf{z} - \mathbf{x} \rangle + \hat{b}(f(\mathbf{z}) - f^{**}(\mathbf{x})) \leq \hat{c}, \tag{4.3}$$

where $\hat{c} \equiv c + \varepsilon[f^*(\hat{\mathbf{y}}) - \langle \hat{\mathbf{y}}, \mathbf{x} \rangle + f^{**}(\mathbf{x})]$. Since $c < 0$, we can pick $\varepsilon > 0$ small enough to ensure that $\hat{c} < 0$. At this point we employ exactly the same argument used in the first case. Dividing (4.3) by $-\hat{b}$ and denoting $\tilde{\mathbf{y}} = -\frac{1}{\hat{b}}\hat{\mathbf{a}}$ yields the inequality

$$\langle \tilde{\mathbf{y}}, \mathbf{z} \rangle - f(\mathbf{z}) - \langle \tilde{\mathbf{y}}, \mathbf{x} \rangle + f^{**}(\mathbf{x}) \leq -\frac{\hat{c}}{\hat{b}} < 0 \text{ for any } \mathbf{z} \in \operatorname{dom}(f).$$

Taking the maximum over $\mathbf{z}$ results in

$$f^*(\tilde{\mathbf{y}}) - \langle \tilde{\mathbf{y}}, \mathbf{x} \rangle + f^{**}(\mathbf{x}) \leq \frac{\hat{c}}{-\hat{b}} < 0,$$

which, again, is a contradiction of Fenchel's inequality. $\square$

Example 4.9 (conjugate of support functions). We will now show how to exploit Theorem 4.8 in order to compute the conjugate of support functions. Suppose that $C \subseteq \mathbb{E}$ is a given nonempty set. Since $\operatorname{cl}(\operatorname{conv}(C))$ is closed and convex, it follows that $\delta_{\operatorname{cl}(\operatorname{conv}(C))}$ is closed and convex, and hence, by Example 4.2 and Theorem 4.8,

$$\sigma^*_{\operatorname{cl}(\operatorname{conv}(C))} = (\delta^*_{\operatorname{cl}(\operatorname{conv}(C))})^* = \delta^{**}_{\operatorname{cl}(\operatorname{conv}(C))} = \delta_{\operatorname{cl}(\operatorname{conv}(C))}. \tag{4.4}$$

Finally, by Lemma 2.35,

$$\sigma_C = \sigma_{\operatorname{cl}(\operatorname{conv}(C))},$$

which, combined with (4.4), establishes the result

$$\sigma_C^* = \delta_{\text{cl(conv}(C))}.$$

∎

Example 4.10 (conjugate of the max function). Consider the function $f:$ $\mathbb{R}^n \to \mathbb{R}$ given by $f(\mathbf{x}) = \max\{x_1, x_2, \ldots, x_n\}$. Note that the following elementary identity holds for any $\mathbf{x} \in \mathbb{R}^n$:

$$\max\{x_1, x_2, \ldots, x_n\} = \max_{\mathbf{y} \in \Delta_n} \mathbf{y}^T \mathbf{x} = \sigma_{\Delta_n}(\mathbf{x}).$$

Therefore, using Example 4.9, we can conclude, exploiting the convexity and closedness of Δ_n, that

$$f^* = \delta_{\Delta_n}.$$

∎

Example 4.11 (conjugate of $\frac{1}{2}\|\cdot\|^2 - d_C^2$). Let $\mathbb{E}$ be Euclidean, and let $C \subseteq \mathbb{E}$ be a nonempty closed and convex set. Define $f(\mathbf{x}) = \frac{1}{2}\|\mathbf{x}\|^2 - \frac{1}{2}d_C^2(\mathbf{x})$. By Example 4.4, $f = g^*$, where $g(\mathbf{y}) = \frac{1}{2}\|\mathbf{y}\|^2 + \delta_C(\mathbf{y})$. By the nonemptiness, closedness, and convexity of C, it follows that g is proper closed and convex, and hence, by Theorem 4.8,

$$f^*(\mathbf{y}) = g^{**}(\mathbf{y}) = g(\mathbf{y}) = \frac{1}{2}\|\mathbf{y}\|^2 + \delta_C(\mathbf{y}).$$

∎

4.3 Conjugate Calculus Rules

In this section we present the basic calculus rules for computing conjugate functions. We begin with a very simple rule for separable functions.

Theorem 4.12 (conjugate of separable functions). *Let* $g : \mathbb{E}_1 \times \mathbb{E}_2 \times \cdots \times \mathbb{E}_p \to (-\infty, \infty]$ *be given by* $g(\mathbf{x}_1, \mathbf{x}_2, \ldots, \mathbf{x}_p) = \sum_{i=1}^p f_i(\mathbf{x}_i)$, *where* $f_i : \mathbb{E}_i \to (-\infty, \infty]$ *is a proper function for any* $i = 1, 2, \ldots, p$. *Then*

$$g^*(\mathbf{y}_1, \mathbf{y}_2, \ldots, \mathbf{y}_p) = \sum_{i=1}^p f_i^*(\mathbf{y}_i) \text{ for any } \mathbf{y}_i \in \mathbb{E}_i^*, \quad i = 1, 2, \ldots, p.$$

Proof. For any $(\mathbf{y}_1, \mathbf{y}_2, \ldots, \mathbf{y}_p) \in \mathbb{E}_1^* \times \mathbb{E}_2^* \times \cdots \times \mathbb{E}_p^*$, it holds that

$$g^*(\mathbf{y}_1, \mathbf{y}_2, \ldots, \mathbf{y}_p) = \max_{\mathbf{x}_1, \mathbf{x}_2, \ldots, \mathbf{x}_p} \{\langle (\mathbf{y}_1, \mathbf{y}_2, \ldots, \mathbf{y}_p), (\mathbf{x}_1, \mathbf{x}_2, \ldots, \mathbf{x}_p) \rangle - g(\mathbf{x}_1, \mathbf{x}_2, \ldots, \mathbf{x}_p)\}$$

$$= \max_{\mathbf{x}_1, \mathbf{x}_2, \ldots, \mathbf{x}_p} \left\{ \sum_{i=1}^p \langle \mathbf{y}_i, \mathbf{x}_i \rangle - \sum_{i=1}^p f_i(\mathbf{x}_i) \right\}$$

$$= \sum_{i=1}^p \max_{\mathbf{x}_i} \{\langle \mathbf{y}_i, \mathbf{x}_i \rangle - f_i(\mathbf{x}_i)\}$$

$$= \sum_{i=1}^p f_i^*(\mathbf{y}_i). \quad \square$$

The next result shows how the conjugate operation is affected by invertible affine change of variables as well as by addition of an affine function.

Theorem 4.13 (conjugate of $f(\mathcal{A}(\mathbf{x}-\mathbf{a}))+\langle\mathbf{b},\mathbf{x}\rangle+c$). *Let $f: \mathbb{E} \to (-\infty, \infty]$ be an extended real-valued function, and let $\mathcal{A}: \mathbb{V} \to \mathbb{E}$ be an invertible linear transformation, $\mathbf{a} \in \mathbb{V}$, $\mathbf{b} \in \mathbb{V}^*$, and $c \in \mathbb{R}$. Then the conjugate of the function $g(\mathbf{x}) = f(\mathcal{A}(\mathbf{x}-\mathbf{a}))+\langle\mathbf{b},\mathbf{x}\rangle+c$ is given by*

$$g^*(\mathbf{y}) = f^*\left((\mathcal{A}^T)^{-1}(\mathbf{y}-\mathbf{b})\right)+\langle\mathbf{a},\mathbf{y}\rangle-c-\langle\mathbf{a},\mathbf{b}\rangle, \quad \mathbf{y} \in \mathbb{V}^*.$$

Proof. Making the change of variables $\mathbf{z} = \mathcal{A}(\mathbf{x}-\mathbf{a})$, which is equivalent to $\mathbf{x} = \mathcal{A}^{-1}(\mathbf{z})+\mathbf{a}$, we can write for any $\mathbf{y} \in \mathbb{V}^*$,

$$\begin{aligned}
g^*(\mathbf{y}) &= \max_{\mathbf{x}}\{\langle\mathbf{y},\mathbf{x}\rangle - g(\mathbf{x})\} \\
&= \max_{\mathbf{x}}\{\langle\mathbf{y},\mathbf{x}\rangle - f(\mathcal{A}(\mathbf{x}-\mathbf{a})) - \langle\mathbf{b},\mathbf{x}\rangle - c\} \\
&= \max_{\mathbf{z}}\{\langle\mathbf{y},\mathcal{A}^{-1}(\mathbf{z})+\mathbf{a}\rangle - f(\mathbf{z}) - \langle\mathbf{b},\mathcal{A}^{-1}(\mathbf{z})+\mathbf{a}\rangle - c\} \\
&= \max_{\mathbf{z}}\left\{\langle\mathbf{y}-\mathbf{b},\mathcal{A}^{-1}(\mathbf{z})\rangle - f(\mathbf{z}) + \langle\mathbf{a},\mathbf{y}\rangle - \langle\mathbf{a},\mathbf{b}\rangle - c\right\} \\
&= \max_{\mathbf{z}}\left\{\langle(\mathcal{A}^{-1})^T(\mathbf{y}-\mathbf{b}),\mathbf{z}\rangle - f(\mathbf{z}) + \langle\mathbf{a},\mathbf{y}\rangle - \langle\mathbf{a},\mathbf{b}\rangle - c\right\} \\
&= f^*\left((\mathcal{A}^T)^{-1}(\mathbf{y}-\mathbf{b})\right) + \langle\mathbf{a},\mathbf{y}\rangle - c - \langle\mathbf{a},\mathbf{b}\rangle,
\end{aligned}$$

where in the last equality we also used the fact that $(\mathcal{A}^{-1})^T = (\mathcal{A}^T)^{-1}$.   □

Theorem 4.14 (conjugate of $\alpha f(\cdot)$ and $\alpha f(\cdot/\alpha)$). *Let $f: \mathbb{E} \to (-\infty, \infty]$ be an extended real-valued function and let $\alpha \in \mathbb{R}_{++}$.*

(a) *The conjugate of the function $g(\mathbf{x}) = \alpha f(\mathbf{x})$ is given by*

$$g^*(\mathbf{y}) = \alpha f^*\left(\frac{\mathbf{y}}{\alpha}\right), \quad \mathbf{y} \in \mathbb{E}^*.$$

(b) *The conjugate of the function $h(\mathbf{x}) = \alpha f\left(\frac{\mathbf{x}}{\alpha}\right)$ is given by*

$$h^*(\mathbf{y}) = \alpha f^*(\mathbf{y}), \quad \mathbf{y} \in \mathbb{E}^*.$$

Proof. For any $\mathbf{y} \in \mathbb{E}^*$,

$$\begin{aligned}
g^*(\mathbf{y}) &= \max_{\mathbf{x}}\{\langle\mathbf{y},\mathbf{x}\rangle - g(\mathbf{x})\} \\
&= \max_{\mathbf{x}}\{\langle\mathbf{y},\mathbf{x}\rangle - \alpha f(\mathbf{x})\} \\
&= \alpha \max_{\mathbf{x}}\left\{\langle\frac{\mathbf{y}}{\alpha},\mathbf{x}\rangle - f(\mathbf{x})\right\} \\
&= \alpha f^*\left(\frac{\mathbf{y}}{\alpha}\right),
\end{aligned}$$

proving (a). The proof of (b) follows by the following chain of equalities:

$$
\begin{aligned}
h^*(\mathbf{y}) &= \max_{\mathbf{x}}\{\langle \mathbf{y}, \mathbf{x}\rangle - h(\mathbf{x})\} \\
&= \max_{\mathbf{x}}\left\{\langle \mathbf{y}, \mathbf{x}\rangle - \alpha f\left(\frac{\mathbf{x}}{\alpha}\right)\right\} \\
&= \alpha \max_{\mathbf{x}}\left\{\left\langle \mathbf{y}, \frac{\mathbf{x}}{\alpha}\right\rangle - f\left(\frac{\mathbf{x}}{\alpha}\right)\right\} \\
&\overset{\mathbf{z}\leftarrow\frac{\mathbf{x}}{\alpha}}{=} \alpha \max_{\mathbf{z}}\{\langle \mathbf{y}, \mathbf{z}\rangle - f(\mathbf{z})\} \\
&= \alpha f^*(\mathbf{y}). \qquad \square
\end{aligned}
$$

The table below summarizes the four calculus rules discussed in this section.

$g(\mathbf{x})$	$g^*(\mathbf{y})$	Reference
$\sum_{i=1}^{m} f_i(\mathbf{x}_i)$	$\sum_{i=1}^{m} f_i^*(\mathbf{y}_i)$	Theorem 4.12
$\alpha f(\mathbf{x})\ (\alpha > 0)$	$\alpha f^*(\mathbf{y}/\alpha)$	Theorem 4.14
$\alpha f(\mathbf{x}/\alpha)\ (\alpha > 0)$	$\alpha f^*(\mathbf{y})$	Theorem 4.14
$f(\mathcal{A}(\mathbf{x}-\mathbf{a})) + \langle \mathbf{b}, \mathbf{x}\rangle + c$	$f^*\left((\mathcal{A}^T)^{-1}(\mathbf{y}-\mathbf{b})\right) + \langle \mathbf{a}, \mathbf{y}\rangle - c - \langle \mathbf{a}, \mathbf{b}\rangle$	Theorem 4.13

4.4 Examples

In this section we compute the conjugate functions of several fundamental convex functions. The first examples are one-dimensional, while the rest are multidimensional.

4.4.1 Exponent

Let $f : \mathbb{R} \to \mathbb{R}$ be given by $f(x) = e^x$. Then for any $y \in \mathbb{R}$,

$$f^*(y) = \max_x \{xy - e^x\}. \tag{4.5}$$

If $y < 0$, then the maximum value of the above problem is ∞ (easily seen by taking $x \to -\infty$). If $y = 0$, then obviously the maximal value (which is not attained) is 0. If $y > 0$, the unique maximizer of (4.5) is $x = \tilde{x} \equiv \log y$. Consequently, $f^*(y) = \tilde{x}y - e^{\tilde{x}} = y \log y - y$ for any $y > 0$. Using the convention $0 \log 0 \equiv 0$, we can finally deduce that

$$
f^*(y) = \begin{cases} y \log y - y, & y \geq 0, \\ \infty & \text{else.} \end{cases}
$$

4.4.2 Negative Log

Let $f : \mathbb{R} \to (-\infty, \infty]$ be given by

$$
f(x) = \begin{cases} -\log(x), & x > 0, \\ \infty, & x \leq 0. \end{cases}
$$

For any $y \in \mathbb{R}$,

$$f^*(y) = \max_{x>0}\{xy - f(x)\} = \max_{x>0}\{xy + \log(x)\}. \qquad (4.6)$$

If $y \geq 0$, then the maximum value of the above problem is ∞ (since the objective function in (4.6) goes to ∞ as $x \to \infty$). If $y < 0$, the unique optimal solution of (4.6) is attained at $\tilde{x} = -\frac{1}{y}$, and hence for $y < 0$ we have $f^*(y) = \tilde{x}y + \log(\tilde{x}) = -1 - \log(-y)$. To conclude,

$$f^*(y) = \begin{cases} -1 - \log(-y), & y < 0, \\ \infty, & y \geq 0. \end{cases}$$

4.4.3 Hinge Loss

Consider the one-dimensional function $f : \mathbb{R} \to \mathbb{R}$ given by

$$f(x) = \max\{1 - x, 0\}.$$

Then for any $y \in \mathbb{R}$,

$$f^*(y) = \max_x \left[yx - \max\{1 - x, 0\}\right] = \max_x \left[\min\left\{(1+y)x - 1, yx\right\}\right]. \qquad (4.7)$$

The objective function in the above maximization problem can be rewritten as

$$\min\left\{(1+y)x - 1, yx\right\} = \begin{cases} (1+y)x - 1, & x < 1, \\ yx, & x \geq 1. \end{cases}$$

Thus, the objective function is a continuous piecewise linear function comprising two pieces: a line with slope $1 + y$ over $(-\infty, 1]$ and a line with slope y over $[1, \infty)$. Therefore, a maximizer exists if the slope of the left line is nonnegative ($1 + y \geq 0$) and the slope of the right line is nonpositive ($y \leq 0$). Consequently, a maximizer exists for the problem in (4.7) if and only if $y \in [-1, 0]$, and in that case it is attained at $x = 1$, with y being the corresponding optimal value. To summarize,

$$f^*(y) = y + \delta_{[-1,0]}(y), \quad y \in \mathbb{R}.$$

4.4.4 $\frac{1}{p}|\cdot|^p$ ($p > 1$)

Let $f : \mathbb{R} \to \mathbb{R}$ be given by $f(x) = \frac{1}{p}|x|^p$, where $p > 1$. For any $y \in \mathbb{R}$,

$$f^*(y) = \max_x \left\{xy - \frac{1}{p}|x|^p\right\}. \qquad (4.8)$$

Since the problem in (4.8) consists of maximizing a differentiable concave function over $\mathbb{R}$, its optimal solutions are the points $\tilde{x}$ in which the derivative vanishes:

$$y - \text{sgn}(\tilde{x})|\tilde{x}|^{p-1} = 0.$$

Therefore, $\mathrm{sgn}(\tilde{x}) = \mathrm{sgn}(y)$ and $|\tilde{x}|^{p-1} = |y|$, implying that $\tilde{x} = \mathrm{sgn}(y)|y|^{\frac{1}{p-1}}$. Thus,

$$f^*(y) = \tilde{x}y - \frac{1}{p}|\tilde{x}|^p = |y|^{1+\frac{1}{p-1}} - \frac{1}{p}|y|^{\frac{p}{p-1}} = \left(1 - \frac{1}{p}\right)|y|^{\frac{p}{p-1}} = \frac{1}{q}|y|^q,$$

where q is the positive number satisfying $\frac{1}{p} + \frac{1}{q} = 1$. To summarize,

$$f^*(y) = \frac{1}{q}|y|^q, \quad y \in \mathbb{R}.$$

4.4.5 $-\frac{(\cdot)^p}{p}$ $(0 < p < 1)$

Let $f : \mathbb{R} \to (-\infty, \infty]$ be given by

$$f(x) = \begin{cases} -\frac{x^p}{p}, & x \geq 0, \\ \infty, & x < 0, \end{cases}$$

where $p \in (0, 1)$. For any $y \in \mathbb{R}$,

$$f^*(y) = \max_x \{xy - f(x)\} = \max_{x \geq 0} \left\{ g(x) \equiv xy + \frac{x^p}{p} \right\}.$$

When $y \geq 0$, the value of the above problem is ∞ since $g(x) \to \infty$ as $x \to \infty$. If $y < 0$, then the derivative of $g(x)$ vanishes at $x = \tilde{x} \equiv (-y)^{\frac{1}{p-1}} > 0$, and since g is concave, it follows that $\tilde{x}$ is a global maximizer of g. Therefore,

$$f^*(y) = \tilde{x}y + \frac{\tilde{x}^p}{p} = -(-y)^{\frac{p}{p-1}} + \frac{1}{p}(-y)^{\frac{p}{p-1}} = -\frac{(-y)^q}{q},$$

where q is the negative number for which $\frac{1}{p} + \frac{1}{q} = 1$. To summarize,

$$f^*(y) = \begin{cases} -\frac{(-y)^q}{q}, & y < 0, \\ \infty, & \text{else.} \end{cases}$$

4.4.6 Strictly Convex Quadratic Functions

Let $f : \mathbb{R}^n \to \mathbb{R}$ be given by $f(\mathbf{x}) = \frac{1}{2}\mathbf{x}^T\mathbf{A}\mathbf{x} + \mathbf{b}^T\mathbf{x} + c$, where $\mathbf{A} \in \mathbb{S}_{++}^n$, $\mathbf{b} \in \mathbb{R}^n$, and $c \in \mathbb{R}$. We use our convention that (unless otherwise stated) $\mathbb{R}^n$ is endowed with the dot product, meaning that $\langle \mathbf{x}, \mathbf{y} \rangle = \mathbf{x}^T\mathbf{y}$. For any $\mathbf{y} \in \mathbb{R}^n$,

$$f^*(\mathbf{y}) = \max_{\mathbf{x}} \{\mathbf{y}^T\mathbf{x} - f(\mathbf{x})\}$$

$$= \max_{\mathbf{x}} \left\{ \mathbf{y}^T\mathbf{x} - \frac{1}{2}\mathbf{x}^T\mathbf{A}\mathbf{x} - \mathbf{b}^T\mathbf{x} - c \right\}$$

$$= \max_{\mathbf{x}} \left\{ -\frac{1}{2}\mathbf{x}^T\mathbf{A}\mathbf{x} - (\mathbf{b} - \mathbf{y})^T\mathbf{x} - c \right\}.$$

The maximum in the above problem is attained at $\mathbf{x} = \mathbf{A}^{-1}(\mathbf{y} - \mathbf{b})$, leading to the following expression for the conjugate function:

$$f^*(\mathbf{y}) = \frac{1}{2}(\mathbf{y} - \mathbf{b})^T \mathbf{A}^{-1}(\mathbf{y} - \mathbf{b}) - c.$$

4.4.7 Convex Quadratic Functions

Let $f : \mathbb{R}^n \to \mathbb{R}$ be given by $f(\mathbf{x}) = \frac{1}{2}\mathbf{x}^T \mathbf{A}\mathbf{x} + \mathbf{b}^T \mathbf{x} + c$, where $\mathbf{A} \in \mathbb{S}^n_+$, $\mathbf{b} \in \mathbb{R}^n$ and $c \in \mathbb{R}$. The only difference between this example and the previous one is the fact that here $\mathbf{A}$ is not necessarily positive definite but is assumed to be only positive *semi*definite. For any $\mathbf{y} \in \mathbb{R}^n$,

$$f^*(\mathbf{y}) = \max_{\mathbf{x}}\{\mathbf{y}^T\mathbf{x} - f(\mathbf{x})\} = \max_{\mathbf{x}}\left\{g(\mathbf{x}) \equiv -\frac{1}{2}\mathbf{x}^T\mathbf{A}\mathbf{x} + (\mathbf{y} - \mathbf{b})^T\mathbf{x} - c\right\}.$$

Since g is concave and differentiable over $\mathbb{R}^n$, it follows that the maximizers of the above problem are the points for which the gradient vanishes, namely, points $\mathbf{x}$ satisfying

$$\mathbf{A}\mathbf{x} = \mathbf{y} - \mathbf{b}. \tag{4.9}$$

This system has a solution if and only if $\mathbf{y} \in \mathbf{b} + \text{Range}(\mathbf{A})$, and in that case we can choose one of the solutions to the system (4.9), for example, $\tilde{\mathbf{x}} = \mathbf{A}^\dagger(\mathbf{y} - \mathbf{b})$, where $\mathbf{A}^\dagger$ is the Moore–Penrose pseudoinverse of $\mathbf{A}$. We can now compute $f^*(\mathbf{y})$ as follows:

$$\begin{aligned}
f^*(\mathbf{y}) &= -\frac{1}{2}\tilde{\mathbf{x}}^T\mathbf{A}\tilde{\mathbf{x}} - (\mathbf{b} - \mathbf{y})^T\tilde{\mathbf{x}} - c \\
&= -\frac{1}{2}(\mathbf{y} - \mathbf{b})\mathbf{A}^\dagger\mathbf{A}\mathbf{A}^\dagger(\mathbf{y} - \mathbf{b}) - (\mathbf{b} - \mathbf{y})^T\mathbf{A}^\dagger(\mathbf{y} - \mathbf{b}) - c \\
&= \frac{1}{2}(\mathbf{y} - \mathbf{b})^T\mathbf{A}^\dagger(\mathbf{y} - \mathbf{b}) - c,
\end{aligned}$$

where we used the fact that the Moore–Penrose pseudoinverse of a symmetric matrix is symmetric, as well as the known identity $\mathbf{A}^\dagger\mathbf{A}\mathbf{A}^\dagger = \mathbf{A}^\dagger$. We are left with the case where $\mathbf{y} - \mathbf{b} \notin \text{Range}(\mathbf{A})$. We will show that in this case $f^*(\mathbf{y}) = \infty$. Indeed, since $\text{Range}(\mathbf{A}) = \text{Null}(\mathbf{A})^\perp$, it follows that $\mathbf{y} - \mathbf{b} \notin \text{Null}(\mathbf{A})^\perp$, meaning that there exists a vector $\mathbf{v} \in \text{Null}(\mathbf{A})$ such that $(\mathbf{y} - \mathbf{b})^T\mathbf{v} > 0$. Note that for any $\alpha \in \mathbb{R}$,

$$g(\alpha\mathbf{v}) = \alpha(\mathbf{y} - \mathbf{b})^T\mathbf{v} - c,$$

and hence $g(\alpha\mathbf{v}) \to \infty$ as α tends to ∞, establishing the fact that $f^*(\mathbf{y}) = \infty$ whenever $\mathbf{y} \notin \mathbf{b} + \text{Range}(\mathbf{A})$. To conclude,

$$f^*(\mathbf{y}) = \begin{cases} \frac{1}{2}(\mathbf{y} - \mathbf{b})^T\mathbf{A}^\dagger(\mathbf{y} - \mathbf{b}) - c, & \mathbf{y} \in \mathbf{b} + \text{Range}(\mathbf{A}), \\ \infty & \text{else.} \end{cases}$$

4.4.8 Negative Entropy

Let $f : \mathbb{R}^n \to (-\infty, \infty]$ be given by

$$f(\mathbf{x}) = \begin{cases} \sum_{i=1}^n x_i \log x_i, & \mathbf{x} \geq \mathbf{0}, \\ \infty & \text{else.} \end{cases}$$

Since the function is separable, it is enough to compute the conjugate of the scalar function g defined by $g(t) = t \log t$ for $t \geq 0$ and ∞ for $t < 0$. For any $s \in \mathbb{R}$,

$$g^*(s) = \max_t \{ts - g(t)\} = \max_{t \geq 0} \{ts - t \log t\}.$$

The maximum of the above problem is attained at $t = e^{s-1}$, and hence the conjugate is given by

$$g^*(s) = se^{s-1} - (s-1)e^{s-1} = e^{s-1}.$$

Since $f(\mathbf{x}) = \sum_{i=1}^n g(x_i)$, it follows by Theorem 4.12 that for any $\mathbf{y} \in \mathbb{R}^n$,

$$f^*(\mathbf{y}) = \sum_{i=1}^n g^*(y_i) = \sum_{i=1}^n e^{y_i - 1}.$$

4.4.9 Negative Sum of Logs

Let $f : \mathbb{R}^n \to (-\infty, \infty]$ be given by

$$f(\mathbf{x}) = \begin{cases} -\sum_{i=1}^n \log x_i, & \mathbf{x} > \mathbf{0}, \\ \infty & \text{else.} \end{cases}$$

Note that $f(\mathbf{x}) = \sum_{i=1}^n g(x_i)$, where $g(t) = -\log t$ for $t > 0$ and ∞ for $t \leq 0$. Therefore, invoking Theorem 4.12,

$$f^*(\mathbf{x}) = \sum_{i=1}^n g^*(x_i).$$

By Section 4.4.2, $g^*(y) = -1 - \log(-y)$ for $y < 0$ and ∞ otherwise. Therefore,

$$f^*(\mathbf{y}) = \begin{cases} -n - \sum_{i=1}^n \log(-y_i), & \mathbf{y} < \mathbf{0}, \\ \infty & \text{else.} \end{cases}$$

4.4.10 Negative Entropy over the Unit Simplex

Let $f : \mathbb{R}^n \to (-\infty, \infty]$ be given by

$$f(\mathbf{x}) = \begin{cases} \sum_{i=1}^n x_i \log x_i, & \mathbf{x} \in \Delta_n, \\ \infty & \text{else.} \end{cases} \tag{4.10}$$

For any $\mathbf{y} \in \mathbb{R}^n$,

$$f^*(\mathbf{y}) = \max \left\{ \sum_{i=1}^n y_i x_i - \sum_{i=1}^n x_i \log x_i : \sum_{i=1}^n x_i = 1, x_1, x_2, \dots, x_n \geq 0 \right\}.$$

By Example 3.71, the optimal solution of the above maximization problem is

$$x_i^* = \frac{e^{y_i}}{\sum_{j=1}^n e^{y_j}}, \quad i = 1, 2, \ldots, n,$$

with a corresponding optimal value of

$$f^*(\mathbf{y}) = \sum_{i=1}^n y_i x_i^* - \sum_{i=1}^n x_i^* \log x_i^* = \log \left(\sum_{j=1}^n e^{y_j} \right).$$

That is, the conjugate of the negative entropy is the log-sum-exp function.

4.4.11 log-sum-exp

Let $g : \mathbb{R}^n \to \mathbb{R}$ be given by

$$g(\mathbf{x}) = \log \left(\sum_{j=1}^n e^{x_j} \right).$$

By Section 4.4.10, $g = f^*$, where f is the negative entropy over the unit simplex given by (4.10). Since f is proper closed and convex, it follows by Theorem 4.8 that $f^{**} = f$, and hence

$$g^* = f^{**} = f,$$

meaning that

$$g^*(\mathbf{y}) = \begin{cases} \sum_{i=1}^n y_i \log y_i, & \mathbf{y} \in \Delta_n, \\ \infty & \text{else.} \end{cases}$$

4.4.12 Norms

Let $f : \mathbb{E} \to \mathbb{R}$ be given by $f(\mathbf{x}) = \|\mathbf{x}\|$. Then, by Example 2.31,

$$f = \sigma_{B_{\|\cdot\|_*}[\mathbf{0},1]},$$

where we used the fact that the bidual norm $\|\cdot\|_{**}$ is identical to the norm $\|\cdot\|$. Hence, by Example 4.9,

$$f^* = \delta_{\mathrm{cl}(\mathrm{conv}(B_{\|\cdot\|_*}[\mathbf{0},1]))},$$

but since $B_{\|\cdot\|_*}[\mathbf{0},1]$ is closed and convex, $\mathrm{cl}(\mathrm{conv}(B_{\|\cdot\|_*}[\mathbf{0},1])) = B_{\|\cdot\|_*}[\mathbf{0},1]$, and therefore for any $\mathbf{y} \in \mathbb{E}^*$,

$$f^*(\mathbf{y}) = \delta_{B_{\|\cdot\|_*}[\mathbf{0},1]}(\mathbf{y}) = \begin{cases} 0, & \|\mathbf{y}\|_* \le 1, \\ \infty & \text{else.} \end{cases}$$

4.4.13 Ball-Pen

Let $f : \mathbb{E} \to (-\infty, \infty]$ be given by

$$f(\mathbf{x}) = \begin{cases} -\sqrt{1 - \|\mathbf{x}\|^2}, & \|\mathbf{x}\| \leq 1, \\ \infty & \text{else.} \end{cases}$$

To compute the conjugate function, we begin by rewriting it in a double maximization form:

$$f^*(\mathbf{y}) = \max_{\mathbf{x}} \left\{ \langle \mathbf{y}, \mathbf{x} \rangle + \sqrt{1 - \|\mathbf{x}\|^2} : \|\mathbf{x}\| \leq 1 \right\}$$
$$= \max_{\alpha \in [0,1]} \max_{\mathbf{x}: \|\mathbf{x}\| = \alpha} \left\{ \langle \mathbf{y}, \mathbf{x} \rangle + \sqrt{1 - \alpha^2} \right\}.$$

By the definition of the dual norm, the optimal value of the inner maximization problem is $\alpha \|\mathbf{y}\|_* + \sqrt{1 - \alpha^2}$, and we can therefore write, for any $\mathbf{y} \in \mathbb{E}^*$,

$$f^*(\mathbf{y}) = \max_{\alpha \in [0,1]} \left\{ g(\alpha) \equiv \alpha \|\mathbf{y}\|_* + \sqrt{1 - \alpha^2} \right\}. \qquad (4.11)$$

It is easy to see that the maximizer of g over $[0,1]$ is

$$\tilde{\alpha} = \frac{\|\mathbf{y}\|_*}{\sqrt{\|\mathbf{y}\|_*^2 + 1}}.$$

Plugging $\alpha = \tilde{\alpha}$ into (4.11), we finally obtain that for any $\mathbf{y} \in \mathbb{E}^*$,

$$f^*(\mathbf{y}) = \sqrt{\|\mathbf{y}\|_*^2 + 1}.$$

It is also possible to generalize the result to functions of the form

$$f_\alpha(\mathbf{x}) = \begin{cases} -\sqrt{\alpha^2 - \|\mathbf{x}\|^2}, & \|\mathbf{x}\| \leq \alpha, \\ \infty & \text{else,} \end{cases}$$

where $\alpha \in \mathbb{R}_{++}$. In this notation, $f = f_1$. To compute f_α^*, note that $f_\alpha(\mathbf{x}) = \alpha f\left(\frac{\mathbf{x}}{\alpha}\right)$, and hence by Theorem 4.14(b) it follows that for any $\mathbf{y} \in \mathbb{E}^*$,

$$f_\alpha^*(\mathbf{y}) = \alpha f^*(\mathbf{y}) = \alpha \sqrt{1 + \|\mathbf{y}\|_*^2}.$$

4.4.14 $\sqrt{\alpha^2 + \|\cdot\|^2}$

Consider the function $g_\alpha : \mathbb{E} \to \mathbb{R}$ given by $g_\alpha(\mathbf{x}) = \sqrt{\alpha^2 + \|\mathbf{x}\|^2}$, where $\alpha > 0$. Then $g_\alpha(\mathbf{x}) = \alpha g\left(\frac{\mathbf{x}}{\alpha}\right)$, where $g(\mathbf{x}) = \sqrt{1 + \|\mathbf{x}\|^2}$. By Section 4.4.13, it follows that $g = f^*$, where f is given by

$$f(\mathbf{y}) = \begin{cases} -\sqrt{1 - \|\mathbf{y}\|_*^2}, & \|\mathbf{y}\|_* \leq 1, \\ \infty & \text{else.} \end{cases}$$

Since f is proper closed and convex, it follows by Theorem 4.8 that

$$g^* = f^{**} = f.$$

Finally, invoking Theorem 4.14(b), we conclude that for any $\mathbf{y} \in \mathbb{E}^*$,

$$g_\alpha^*(\mathbf{y}) = \alpha g^*(\mathbf{y}) = \alpha f(\mathbf{y}) = \begin{cases} -\alpha\sqrt{1 - \|\mathbf{y}\|_*^2}, & \|\mathbf{y}\|_* \leq 1, \\ \infty & \text{else.} \end{cases}$$

4.4.15   Squared Norm

Let $f : \mathbb{E} \to \mathbb{R}$ be given by $f(\mathbf{x}) = \frac{1}{2}\|\mathbf{x}\|^2$, where $\|\cdot\|$ is the norm associated with the space $\mathbb{E}$. For any $\mathbf{y} \in \mathbb{E}^*$, we can write $f^*(\mathbf{y})$ as the optimal value of the following double maximization problem:

$$f^*(\mathbf{y}) = \max_{\mathbf{x} \in \mathbb{E}} \left\{ \langle \mathbf{y}, \mathbf{x} \rangle - \frac{1}{2}\|\mathbf{x}\|^2 \right\} = \max_{\alpha \geq 0} \max_{\mathbf{x}:\|\mathbf{x}\|=\alpha} \left\{ \langle \mathbf{y}, \mathbf{x} \rangle - \frac{1}{2}\alpha^2 \right\}.$$

Using the definition of the dual norm, it follows that

$$\max_{\mathbf{x} \in \mathbb{E}:\|\mathbf{x}\|=\alpha} \langle \mathbf{y}, \mathbf{x} \rangle = \alpha\|\mathbf{y}\|_*,$$

Hence,

$$f^*(\mathbf{y}) = \max_{\alpha \geq 0} \left\{ \alpha\|\mathbf{y}\|_* - \frac{1}{2}\alpha^2 \right\} = \frac{1}{2}\|\mathbf{y}\|_*^2.$$

4.4.16 Summary of Conjugate Computations

The table below summarizes all the computations of conjugate functions described in this chapter.

$f(\mathbf{x})$	$\mathrm{dom}(f)$	f^*	Assumptions	Reference
e^x	$\mathbb{R}$	$y\log y - y$ ($\mathrm{dom}(f^*) = \mathbb{R}_+$)	–	Section 4.4.1
$-\log x$	$\mathbb{R}_{++}$	$-1-\log(-y)$ ($\mathrm{dom}(f^*) = \mathbb{R}_{--}$)	–	Section 4.4.2
$\max\{1-x,0\}$	$\mathbb{R}$	$y + \delta_{[-1,0]}(y)$	–	Section 4.4.3
$\frac{1}{p}|x|^p$	$\mathbb{R}$	$\frac{1}{q}|y|^q$	$p>1, \frac{1}{p}+\frac{1}{q}=1$	Section 4.4.4
$-\frac{x^p}{p}$	$\mathbb{R}_+$	$-\frac{(-y)^q}{q}$ ($\mathrm{dom}(f^*) = \mathbb{R}_{--}$)	$0<p<1, \frac{1}{p}+\frac{1}{q}=1$	Section 4.4.5
$\frac{1}{2}\mathbf{x}^T\mathbf{A}\mathbf{x} + \mathbf{b}^T\mathbf{x} + c$	$\mathbb{R}^n$	$\frac{1}{2}(\mathbf{y}-\mathbf{b})^T\mathbf{A}^{-1}(\mathbf{y}-\mathbf{b})-c$	$\mathbf{A}\in\mathbb{S}^n_{++},\ \mathbf{b}\in\mathbb{R}^n, c\in\mathbb{R}$	Section 4.4.6
$\frac{1}{2}\mathbf{x}^T\mathbf{A}\mathbf{x} + \mathbf{b}^T\mathbf{x} + c$	$\mathbb{R}^n$	$\frac{1}{2}(\mathbf{y}-\mathbf{b})^T\mathbf{A}^\dagger(\mathbf{y}-\mathbf{b})-c$ ($\mathrm{dom}(f^*) = \mathbf{b} + \mathrm{Range}(\mathbf{A})$)	$\mathbf{A}\in\mathbb{S}^n_+,\ \mathbf{b}\in\mathbb{R}^n, c\in\mathbb{R}$	Section 4.4.7
$\sum_{i=1}^n x_i\log x_i$	$\mathbb{R}^n_+$	$\sum_{i=1}^n e^{y_i-1}$	–	Section 4.4.8
$\sum_{i=1}^n x_i\log x_i$	Δ_n	$\log\left(\sum_{i=1}^n e^{y_i}\right)$	–	Section 4.4.10
$-\sum_{i=1}^n\log x_i$	$\mathbb{R}^n_{++}$	$-n-\sum_{i=1}^n\log(-y_i)$ ($\mathrm{dom}(f^*) = \mathbb{R}^n_{--}$)	–	Section 4.4.9
$\log\left(\sum_{i=1}^n e^{x_i}\right)$	$\mathbb{R}^n$	$\sum_{i=1}^n y_i\log y_i$ ($\mathrm{dom}(f^*) = \Delta_n$)	–	Section 4.4.11
$\max_i\{x_i\}$	$\mathbb{R}^n$	$\delta_{\Delta_n}(\mathbf{y})$	–	Example 4.10
$\delta_C(\mathbf{x})$	C	$\sigma_C(\mathbf{y})$	$\emptyset\neq C\subseteq\mathbb{E}$	Example 4.2
$\sigma_C(\mathbf{x})$	$\mathrm{dom}(\sigma_C)$	$\delta_{\mathrm{cl}(\mathrm{conv}(C))}(\mathbf{y})$	$\emptyset\neq C\subseteq\mathbb{E}$	Example 4.9
$\|\mathbf{x}\|$	$\mathbb{E}$	$\delta_{B_{\|\cdot\|_*}[0,1]}(\mathbf{y})$	–	Section 4.4.12
$-\sqrt{\alpha^2-\|\mathbf{x}\|^2}$	$B[\mathbf{0},\alpha]$	$\alpha\sqrt{\|\mathbf{y}\|_*^2+1}$	$\alpha>0$	Section 4.4.13
$\sqrt{\alpha^2+\|\mathbf{x}\|^2}$	$\mathbb{E}$	$-\alpha\sqrt{1-\|\mathbf{y}\|_*^2}$ ($\mathrm{dom}f^* = B_{\|\cdot\|_*}[0,1]$)	$\alpha>0$	Section 4.4.14
$\frac{1}{2}\|\mathbf{x}\|^2$	$\mathbb{E}$	$\frac{1}{2}\|\mathbf{y}\|_*^2$	–	Section 4.4.15
$\frac{1}{2}\|\mathbf{x}\|^2 + \delta_C(\mathbf{x})$	C	$\frac{1}{2}\|\mathbf{y}\|^2 - \frac{1}{2}d_C^2(\mathbf{y})$	$\emptyset\neq C\subseteq\mathbb{E}$, $\mathbb{E}$ Euclidean	Example 4.4
$\frac{1}{2}\|\mathbf{x}\|^2 - \frac{1}{2}d_C^2(\mathbf{x})$	$\mathbb{E}$	$\frac{1}{2}\|\mathbf{y}\|^2 + \delta_C(\mathbf{y})$	$\emptyset\neq C\subseteq\mathbb{E}$ closed convex. $\mathbb{E}$ Euclidean	Example 4.11

4.4.17   Fenchel's Duality Theorem

Conjugate functions naturally appear in dual problems most prominently in the celebrated *Fenchel's duality theorem*, which we now recall. Consider the problem

$$\text{(P)} \ \min_{\mathbf{x} \in \mathbb{E}} f(\mathbf{x}) + g(\mathbf{x}).$$

We begin by rewriting the problem as

$$\min_{\mathbf{x}, \mathbf{z} \in \mathbb{E}} \{ f(\mathbf{x}) + g(\mathbf{z}) : \mathbf{x} = \mathbf{z} \}$$

and then constructing the Lagrangian

$$L(\mathbf{x}, \mathbf{z}; \mathbf{y}) = f(\mathbf{x}) + g(\mathbf{z}) + \langle \mathbf{y}, \mathbf{z} - \mathbf{x} \rangle = - \left[\langle \mathbf{y}, \mathbf{x} \rangle - f(\mathbf{x}) \right] - \left[\langle -\mathbf{y}, \mathbf{z} \rangle - g(\mathbf{z}) \right].$$

The dual objective function is computed by minimizing the Lagrangian w.r.t. the primal variables $\mathbf{x}, \mathbf{z}$:

$$q(\mathbf{y}) = \min_{\mathbf{x}, \mathbf{z}} L(\mathbf{x}, \mathbf{z}; \mathbf{y}) = -f^*(\mathbf{y}) - g^*(-\mathbf{y}).$$

We thus obtain the following dual problem, which is also called *Fenchel's dual*:

$$\text{(D)} \ \max_{\mathbf{y} \in \mathbb{E}^*} \{ -f^*(\mathbf{y}) - g^*(-\mathbf{y}) \}.$$

Fenchel's duality theorem, which we recall below, provides conditions under which strong duality holds for the pair of problems (P) and (D).

Theorem 4.15 (Fenchel's duality theorem [108, Theorem 31.1]). *Let $f, g :$ $\mathbb{E} \to (-\infty, \infty]$ be proper convex functions. If $\mathrm{ri}(\mathrm{dom}(f)) \cap \mathrm{ri}(\mathrm{dom}(g)) \neq \emptyset$, then*

$$\min_{\mathbf{x} \in \mathbb{E}} \{ f(\mathbf{x}) + g(\mathbf{x}) \} = \max_{\mathbf{y} \in \mathbb{E}^*} \{ -f^*(\mathbf{y}) - g^*(-\mathbf{y}) \},$$

and the maximum in the right-hand problem is attained whenever it is finite.

4.5   Infimal Convolution and Conjugacy

We will now show that in some sense the operations of addition and infimal convolution are dual to each other under the conjugacy operation. The first result holds under the very mild condition of properness of the functions.

Theorem 4.16 (conjugate of infimal convolution). *For two proper functions $h_1, h_2 : \mathbb{E} \to (-\infty, \infty]$ it holds that*

$$(h_1 \square h_2)^* = h_1^* + h_2^*.$$

Proof. For every $\mathbf{y} \in \mathbb{E}^*$ one has

$$
\begin{aligned}
(h_1 \square h_2)^*(\mathbf{y}) &= \max_{\mathbf{x} \in \mathbb{E}} \{\langle \mathbf{y}, \mathbf{x} \rangle - (h_1 \square h_2)(\mathbf{x})\} \\
&= \max_{\mathbf{x} \in \mathbb{E}} \{\langle \mathbf{y}, \mathbf{x} \rangle - \min_{\mathbf{u} \in \mathbb{E}} \{h_1(\mathbf{u}) + h_2(\mathbf{x} - \mathbf{u})\}\} \\
&= \max_{\mathbf{x} \in \mathbb{E}} \max_{\mathbf{u} \in \mathbb{E}} \{\langle \mathbf{y}, \mathbf{x} \rangle - h_1(\mathbf{u}) - h_2(\mathbf{x} - \mathbf{u})\} \\
&= \max_{\mathbf{x} \in \mathbb{E}} \max_{\mathbf{u} \in \mathbb{E}} \{\langle \mathbf{y}, \mathbf{x} - \mathbf{u} \rangle + \langle \mathbf{y}, \mathbf{u} \rangle - h_1(\mathbf{u}) - h_2(\mathbf{x} - \mathbf{u})\} \\
&= \max_{\mathbf{u} \in \mathbb{E}} \max_{\mathbf{x} \in \mathbb{E}} \{\langle \mathbf{y}, \mathbf{x} - \mathbf{u} \rangle + \langle \mathbf{y}, \mathbf{u} \rangle - h_1(\mathbf{u}) - h_2(\mathbf{x} - \mathbf{u})\} \\
&= \max_{\mathbf{u} \in \mathbb{E}} \{h_2^*(\mathbf{y}) + \langle \mathbf{y}, \mathbf{u} \rangle - h_1(\mathbf{u})\} \\
&= h_1^*(\mathbf{y}) + h_2^*(\mathbf{y}). \qquad \square
\end{aligned}
$$

The second "direction" is a much deeper result requiring additional assumptions like convexity of the functions under consideration.

Theorem 4.17 (conjugate of sum). *Let $h_1 : \mathbb{E} \to (-\infty, \infty]$ be a proper convex function and $h_2 : \mathbb{E} \to \mathbb{R}$ be a real-valued convex function. Then*

$$
(h_1 + h_2)^* = h_1^* \square h_2^*.
$$

Proof. For any $\mathbf{y} \in \mathbb{E}^*$,

$$
\begin{aligned}
(h_1 + h_2)^*(\mathbf{y}) &= \max_{\mathbf{x} \in \mathbb{E}} \{\langle \mathbf{y}, \mathbf{x} \rangle - h_1(\mathbf{x}) - h_2(\mathbf{x})\} \\
&= -\min_{\mathbf{x} \in \mathbb{E}} \{h_1(\mathbf{x}) + h_2(\mathbf{x}) - \langle \mathbf{y}, \mathbf{x} \rangle\} \\
&= -\min_{\mathbf{x} \in \mathbb{E}} \{h_1(\mathbf{x}) + g(\mathbf{x})\}, \tag{4.12}
\end{aligned}
$$

where $g(\mathbf{x}) \equiv h_2(\mathbf{x}) - \langle \mathbf{y}, \mathbf{x} \rangle$. Note that

$$
\operatorname{ri}(\operatorname{dom}(h_1)) \cap \operatorname{ri}(\operatorname{dom}(g)) = \operatorname{ri}(\operatorname{dom}(h_1)) \cap \mathbb{E} = \operatorname{ri}(\operatorname{dom}(h_1)) \neq \emptyset,
$$

and we can thus employ Fenchel's duality theorem (Theorem 4.15) and obtain the following equality:

$$
\min_{\mathbf{x} \in \mathbb{E}} \{h_1(\mathbf{x}) + g(\mathbf{x})\} = \max_{\mathbf{z} \in \mathbb{E}^*} \{-h_1^*(\mathbf{z}) - g^*(-\mathbf{z})\} = \max_{\mathbf{z} \in \mathbb{E}^*} \{-h_1^*(\mathbf{z}) - h_2^*(\mathbf{y} - \mathbf{z})\}. \tag{4.13}
$$

Combining (4.12) and (4.13), we finally obtain that for any $\mathbf{y} \in \mathbb{E}^*$,

$$
(h_1 + h_2)^*(\mathbf{y}) = \min_{\mathbf{z} \in \mathbb{E}^*} \{h_1^*(\mathbf{z}) + h_2^*(\mathbf{y} - \mathbf{z})\} = (h_1^* \square h_2^*)(\mathbf{y}),
$$

establishing the desired result. $\quad \square$

Corollary 4.18. *Let $h_1 : \mathbb{E} \to (-\infty, \infty]$ be a proper closed convex function and $h_2 : \mathbb{E} \to \mathbb{R}$ be a real-valued convex function. Then*

$$
h_1 + h_2 = (h_1^* \square h_2^*)^*.
$$

Proof. The function $h_1 + h_2$ is obviously proper and is closed by the closedness of h_1, h_2 (Theorem 2.7(b)). Therefore, by Theorem 4.8, $(h_1 + h_2)^{**} = h_1 + h_2$, which, combined with Theorem 4.17, yields

$$h_1 + h_2 = (h_1 + h_2)^{**} = [(h_1 + h_2)^*]^* = (h_1^* \square h_2^*)^*. \qquad \square$$

The next result shows a representation of the infimal convolution in terms of the corresponding conjugate functions.

Theorem 4.19 (representation of the infimal convolution by conjugates). *Let $h_1 : \mathbb{E} \to (-\infty, \infty]$ be a proper convex function, and let $h_2 : \mathbb{E} \to \mathbb{R}$ be a real-valued convex function. Suppose that $h_1 \square h_2$ is a real-valued function. Then*

$$h_1 \square h_2 = (h_1^* + h_2^*)^*. \tag{4.14}$$

Proof. By Theorem 4.16,

$$(h_1 \square h_2)^* = h_1^* + h_2^*. \tag{4.15}$$

Since h_1 is proper and convex and h_2 is real-valued and convex, it follows by Theorem 2.19 that $h_1 \square h_2$ is convex. Since $h_1 \square h_2$ is real-valued, it is in particular proper and closed. Therefore, by Theorem 4.8, $(h_1 \square h_2)^{**} = h_1 \square h_2$. Hence, taking the conjugate of both sides of (4.15), the identity (4.14) follows. $\square$

4.6   Subdifferentials of Conjugate Functions

The main result concerning the subdifferential of a conjugate function is the so-called *conjugate subgradient theorem*.

Theorem 4.20 (conjugate subgradient theorem). *Let $f : \mathbb{E} \to (-\infty, \infty]$ be proper and convex. The following two claims are equivalent for any $\mathbf{x} \in \mathbb{E}, \mathbf{y} \in \mathbb{E}^*$:*

(i) $\langle \mathbf{x}, \mathbf{y} \rangle = f(\mathbf{x}) + f^*(\mathbf{y})$.

(ii) $\mathbf{y} \in \partial f(\mathbf{x})$.

If in addition f is closed, then (i) *and* (ii) *are equivalent to*

(iii) $\mathbf{x} \in \partial f^*(\mathbf{y})$.

Proof. The relation $\mathbf{y} \in \partial f(\mathbf{x})$ holds if and only if

$$f(\mathbf{z}) \geq f(\mathbf{x}) + \langle \mathbf{y}, \mathbf{z} - \mathbf{x} \rangle \text{ for all } \mathbf{z} \in \mathbb{E},$$

which is the same as

$$\langle \mathbf{y}, \mathbf{x} \rangle - f(\mathbf{x}) \geq \langle \mathbf{y}, \mathbf{z} \rangle - f(\mathbf{z}) \text{ for all } \mathbf{z} \in \mathbb{E}. \tag{4.16}$$

Taking the maximum over $\mathbf{z}$, we obtain that (4.16) is the same as

$$\langle \mathbf{y}, \mathbf{x} \rangle - f(\mathbf{x}) \geq f^*(\mathbf{y}),$$

which by Fenchel's inequality (Theorem 4.6) is equivalent to the equality $\langle \mathbf{x}, \mathbf{y} \rangle = f(\mathbf{x}) + f^*(\mathbf{y})$. We have thus established the equivalence between (i) and (ii). Assume now that in addition f is closed. Then by Theorem 4.8, $f^{**} = f$, which in particular implies that (i) is equivalent to

$$\langle \mathbf{x}, \mathbf{y} \rangle = g(\mathbf{y}) + g^*(\mathbf{x}),$$

where $g = f^*$. By the same equivalence that was already established between (i) and (ii) (but here employed on g), we conclude that (i) is equivalent to $\mathbf{x} \in \partial g(\mathbf{y}) = \partial f^*(\mathbf{y})$. □

By the definition of the conjugate function, claim (i) in Theorem 4.20 can be rewritten as

$$\mathbf{x} \in \operatorname{argmax}_{\tilde{\mathbf{x}} \in \mathbb{E}} \left\{ \langle \mathbf{y}, \tilde{\mathbf{x}} \rangle - f(\tilde{\mathbf{x}}) \right\},$$

and, when f is closed, also as

$$\mathbf{y} \in \operatorname{argmax}_{\tilde{\mathbf{y}} \in \mathbb{E}^*} \left\{ \langle \mathbf{x}, \tilde{\mathbf{y}} \rangle - f^*(\tilde{\mathbf{y}}) \right\}.$$

Equipped with the above observation, we can conclude that the conjugate subgradient theorem, in the case where f is closed, can also be equivalently formulated as follows.

Corollary 4.21 (conjugate subgradient theorem—second formulation). *Let* $f : \mathbb{E} \to (-\infty, \infty]$ *be a proper closed convex function. Then for any* $\mathbf{x} \in \mathbb{E}, \mathbf{y} \in \mathbb{E}^*$,

$$\partial f(\mathbf{x}) = \operatorname{argmax}_{\tilde{\mathbf{y}} \in \mathbb{E}^*} \left\{ \langle \mathbf{x}, \tilde{\mathbf{y}} \rangle - f^*(\tilde{\mathbf{y}}) \right\}$$

and

$$\partial f^*(\mathbf{y}) = \operatorname{argmax}_{\tilde{\mathbf{x}} \in \mathbb{E}} \left\{ \langle \mathbf{y}, \tilde{\mathbf{x}} \rangle - f(\tilde{\mathbf{x}}) \right\}.$$

In particular, we can also conclude that for any proper closed convex function f,

$$\partial f(0) = \operatorname{argmin}_{\mathbf{y} \in \mathbb{E}^*} f^*(\mathbf{y})$$

and

$$\partial f^*(0) = \operatorname{argmin}_{\mathbf{x} \in \mathbb{E}} f(\mathbf{x}).$$

Example 4.22. Let $f : \mathbb{E} \to \mathbb{R}$ be given by $f(\mathbf{x}) = \|\mathbf{x}\|$. Obviously, f is proper, closed, and convex. By Example 2.31, $f = \sigma_{B_{\|\cdot\|_*}[0,1]}$. Therefore, by Example 4.9, $f^* = \delta_{B_{\|\cdot\|_*}[0,1]}$. We can now use the conjugate subgradient theorem (Corollary 4.21) and compute the subdifferential set of f at $\mathbf{0}$ as follows:

$$\partial f(\mathbf{0}) = \operatorname{argmin}_{\mathbf{y} \in \mathbb{E}^*} f^*(\mathbf{y}) = \operatorname{argmin}_{\mathbf{y} \in \mathbb{E}^*} \delta_{B_{\|\cdot\|_*}[0,1]} = B_{\|\cdot\|_*}[0,1].$$

This result was already established in Example 3.3. ■

A relation between Lipschitz continuity of a function and the boundedness of its subgradients over a given set was established in Theorem 3.61. We end this chapter with a related result showing that Lipschitz continuity over the entire space is also equivalent to boundedness of the domain of the conjugate.

Theorem 4.23 (Lipschitz continuity and boundedness of the domain of the conjugate). *Let $f : \mathbb{E} \to \mathbb{R}$ be convex. Then the following three claims are equivalent for a given constant $L > 0$:*

(i) $|f(\mathbf{x}) - f(\mathbf{y})| \leq L\|\mathbf{x} - \mathbf{y}\|$ *for any* $\mathbf{x}, \mathbf{y} \in \mathbb{E}$.

(ii) $\|\mathbf{g}\|_* \leq L$ *for any* $\mathbf{g} \in \partial f(\mathbf{x}), \mathbf{x} \in \mathbb{E}$.

(iii) $\mathrm{dom}(f^*) \subseteq B_{\|\cdot\|_*}[\mathbf{0}, L]$.

Proof. The equivalence between (i) and (ii) follows from Theorem 3.61. We will show that (iii) implies (ii). Indeed, assume that (iii) holds, that is, $\mathrm{dom}(f^*) \subseteq B_{\|\cdot\|_*}[\mathbf{0}, L]$. Since by the conjugate subgradient theorem (Corollary 4.21) for any $\mathbf{x} \in \mathbb{E}$,

$$\partial f(\mathbf{x}) = \mathrm{argmax}_{\mathbf{y} \in \mathbb{E}^*} \{\langle \mathbf{x}, \mathbf{y} \rangle - f^*(\mathbf{y})\},$$

it follows that $\partial f(\mathbf{x}) \subseteq \mathrm{dom}(f^*)$, and hence in particular $\partial f(\mathbf{x}) \subseteq B_{\|\cdot\|_*}[\mathbf{0}, L]$ for any $\mathbf{x} \in \mathbb{E}$, establishing (ii). In the reverse direction, we will show that the implication (i) $\Rightarrow$ (iii) holds. Suppose that (i) holds. Then in particular

$$f(\mathbf{x}) - f(\mathbf{0}) \leq |f(\mathbf{x}) - f(\mathbf{0})| \leq L\|\mathbf{x}\|,$$

and hence

$$-f(\mathbf{x}) \geq -f(\mathbf{0}) - L\|\mathbf{x}\|.$$

Therefore, for any $\mathbf{y} \in \mathbb{E}^*$,

$$f^*(\mathbf{y}) = \max_{\mathbf{x} \in \mathbb{E}} \{\langle \mathbf{x}, \mathbf{y} \rangle - f(\mathbf{x})\} \geq \max_{\mathbf{x} \in \mathbb{E}} \{\langle \mathbf{x}, \mathbf{y} \rangle - f(\mathbf{0}) - L\|\mathbf{x}\|\}. \quad (4.17)$$

To show (iii), we take $\tilde{\mathbf{y}} \in \mathbb{E}^*$ that satisfies $\|\tilde{\mathbf{y}}\|_* > L$ and show that $\tilde{\mathbf{y}} \notin \mathrm{dom}(f^*)$. Take a vector $\mathbf{y}^\dagger \in \mathbb{E}$ satisfying $\|\mathbf{y}^\dagger\| = 1$ for which $\langle \tilde{\mathbf{y}}, \mathbf{y}^\dagger \rangle = \|\tilde{\mathbf{y}}\|_*$ (such a vector exists by the definition of the dual norm). Define $C = \{\alpha \mathbf{y}^\dagger : \alpha \geq 0\} \subseteq \mathbb{E}$. We can now continue (4.17) (with $\mathbf{y} = \tilde{\mathbf{y}}$) and write

$$
\begin{aligned}
f^*(\tilde{\mathbf{y}}) \quad &\geq \quad \max_{\mathbf{x} \in \mathbb{E}} \{\langle \mathbf{x}, \tilde{\mathbf{y}} \rangle - f(\mathbf{0}) - L\|\mathbf{x}\|\} \\
&\geq \quad \max_{\mathbf{x} \in C} \{\langle \mathbf{x}, \tilde{\mathbf{y}} \rangle - f(\mathbf{0}) - L\|\mathbf{x}\|\} \\
&= \quad \max_{\alpha \geq 0} \{\langle \alpha \tilde{\mathbf{y}}, \mathbf{y}^\dagger \rangle - f(\mathbf{0}) - L\alpha\|\mathbf{y}^\dagger\|\} \\
&= \quad \max_{\alpha \geq 0} \{\alpha\|\tilde{\mathbf{y}}\|_* - f(\mathbf{0}) - L\alpha\} \\
&= \quad \max_{\alpha \geq 0} \{\alpha(\|\tilde{\mathbf{y}}\|_* - L) - f(\mathbf{0})\} \\
&\overset{\|\tilde{\mathbf{y}}\|_* > L}{=} \quad \infty,
\end{aligned}
$$

thus showing that $\tilde{\mathbf{y}} \notin \mathrm{dom}(f^*)$, establishing claim (iii). $\square$

Chapter 5

Smoothness and Strong Convexity

5.1 L-Smooth Functions

We begin with the definition of L-*smoothness*.

Definition 5.1 (L-smoothness). *Let $L \geq 0$. A function $f : \mathbb{E} \to (-\infty, \infty]$ is said to be L-smooth over a set $D \subseteq \mathbb{E}$ if it is differentiable over D and satisfies*

$$\|\nabla f(\mathbf{x}) - \nabla f(\mathbf{y})\|_* \leq L\|\mathbf{x} - \mathbf{y}\| \text{ for all } \mathbf{x}, \mathbf{y} \in D.$$

The constant L is called the **smoothness parameter**.

Obviously, by the definition of differentiability, if f is L-smooth over a set $D \subseteq \mathbb{E}$, this means in particular that $D \subseteq \text{int}(\text{dom} f)$. If a function is L-smooth over $\mathbb{E}$, then we will just refer to it as L-*smooth* (without mentioning the entire space). Another frequent terminology in the literature refers to an L-smooth function over D as "a function with Lipschitz gradient with constant L." The class of L-smooth functions over a set D is denoted by $C_L^{1,1}(D)$. When $D = \mathbb{E}$, the class is often denoted by $C_L^{1,1}$ instead of $C_L^{1,1}(\mathbb{E})$. The class of functions which are L-smooth for some $L \geq 0$ is denoted by $C^{1,1}$.

By the definition of L-smoothness, it is clear that if a function is L_1-smooth, then it is also L_2-smooth for any $L_2 \geq L_1$. It is therefore sometimes interesting to discuss the value of the *smallest* possible smoothness parameter of a given function.

Example 5.2 (smoothness of quadratic functions). Consider the function $f : \mathbb{R}^n \to \mathbb{R}$ given by $f(\mathbf{x}) = \frac{1}{2}\mathbf{x}^T \mathbf{A}\mathbf{x} + \mathbf{b}^T\mathbf{x} + c$, where $\mathbf{A} \in \mathbb{S}^n, \mathbf{b} \in \mathbb{R}^n$, and $c \in \mathbb{R}$. We assume that $\mathbb{R}^n$ is endowed with the l_p-norm ($1 \leq p \leq \infty$). Then, for any $\mathbf{x}, \mathbf{y} \in \mathbb{R}^n$,

$$\|\nabla f(\mathbf{x}) - \nabla f(\mathbf{y})\|_q = \|\mathbf{A}\mathbf{x} - \mathbf{A}\mathbf{y}\|_q \leq \|\mathbf{A}\|_{p,q}\|\mathbf{x} - \mathbf{y}\|_p,$$

where $\|\cdot\|_{p,q}$ is the induced norm given by (see also Section 1.8.2)

$$\|\mathbf{A}\|_{p,q} = \max\{\|\mathbf{A}\mathbf{x}\|_q : \|\mathbf{x}\|_p \leq 1\},$$

with $q \in [1, \infty]$ satisfying $\frac{1}{p} + \frac{1}{q} = 1$. We can thus conclude that f is $\|\mathbf{A}\|_{p,q}$-smooth. We will show that $\|\mathbf{A}\|_{p,q}$ is the smallest smoothness parameter. For that, assume that f is L-smooth. Take a vector $\tilde{\mathbf{x}}$ satisfying $\|\tilde{\mathbf{x}}\|_p = 1$ and $\|\mathbf{A}\tilde{\mathbf{x}}\|_q = \|\mathbf{A}\|_{p,q}$. The existence of such a vector is guaranteed by the definition the induced matrix norm. Then

$$\|\mathbf{A}\|_{p,q} = \|\mathbf{A}\tilde{\mathbf{x}}\|_q = \|\nabla f(\tilde{\mathbf{x}}) - \nabla f(\mathbf{0})\|_q \le L\|\tilde{\mathbf{x}} - \mathbf{0}\|_p = L.$$

We thus showed that if f is L-smooth, then $L \ge \|\mathbf{A}\|_{p,q}$, proving that $\|\mathbf{A}\|_{p,q}$ is indeed the smallest possible smoothness parameter. ∎

Example 5.3 (0-smoothness of affine functions). Let $f : \mathbb{E} \to \mathbb{R}$ be given by $f(\mathbf{x}) = \langle \mathbf{b}, \mathbf{x} \rangle + c$, where $\mathbf{b} \in \mathbb{E}^*$ and $c \in \mathbb{R}$. For any $\mathbf{x}, \mathbf{y} \in \mathbb{E}$,

$$\|\nabla f(\mathbf{x}) - \nabla f(\mathbf{y})\|_* = \|\mathbf{b} - \mathbf{b}\|_* = 0 \le 0\|\mathbf{x} - \mathbf{y}\|,$$

showing that affine functions are 0-smooth. ∎

The next example will utilize a well-known result on the orthogonal projection operator, which was introduced in Example 3.31. A more general result will be shown later on in Theorem 6.42.

Theorem 5.4 (see [10, Theorem 9.9]). *Let $\mathbb{E}$ be a Euclidean space, and let $C \subseteq \mathbb{E}$ be a nonempty closed and convex set. Then*

(a) **(firm nonexpansiveness)** *For any $\mathbf{v}, \mathbf{w} \in \mathbb{E}$,*

$$\langle P_C(\mathbf{v}) - P_C(\mathbf{w}), \mathbf{v} - \mathbf{w} \rangle \ge \|P_C(\mathbf{v}) - P_C(\mathbf{w})\|^2. \qquad (5.1)$$

(b) **(nonexpansiveness)** *For any $\mathbf{v}, \mathbf{w} \in \mathbb{E}$,*

$$\|P_C(\mathbf{v}) - P_C(\mathbf{w})\| \le \|\mathbf{v} - \mathbf{w}\|. \qquad (5.2)$$

Example 5.5 (1-smoothness of $\frac{1}{2}d_C^2$). Suppose that $\mathbb{E}$ is a Euclidean space, and let $C \subseteq \mathbb{E}$ be a nonempty closed and convex set. Consider the function $\varphi_C(\mathbf{x}) = \frac{1}{2}d_C^2(\mathbf{x})$. By Example 3.31, φ_C is differentiable over $\mathbb{E}$ and $\nabla \varphi_C(\mathbf{x}) = \mathbf{x} - P_C(\mathbf{x})$. We will show that φ_C is 1-smooth. Indeed, for any $\mathbf{x}, \mathbf{y} \in \mathbb{E}$,

$$
\begin{aligned}
\|\nabla \varphi_C(\mathbf{x}) - \nabla \varphi_C(\mathbf{y})\|^2 &= \|\mathbf{x} - \mathbf{y} - P_C(\mathbf{x}) + P_C(\mathbf{y})\|^2 \\
&= \|\mathbf{x} - \mathbf{y}\|^2 - 2\langle P_C(\mathbf{x}) - P_C(\mathbf{y}), \mathbf{x} - \mathbf{y} \rangle + \|P_C(\mathbf{x}) - P_C(\mathbf{y})\|^2 \\
&\overset{(*)}{\le} \|\mathbf{x} - \mathbf{y}\|^2 - 2\|P_C(\mathbf{x}) - P_C(\mathbf{y})\|^2 + \|P_C(\mathbf{x}) - P_C(\mathbf{y})\|^2 \\
&= \|\mathbf{x} - \mathbf{y}\|^2 - \|P_C(\mathbf{x}) - P_C(\mathbf{y})\|^2 \\
&\le \|\mathbf{x} - \mathbf{y}\|^2,
\end{aligned}
$$

where the inequality $(*)$ follows by the firm nonexpansivity of the orthogonal projection operator (Theorem 5.4(a)). ∎

Example 5.6 (1-smoothness of $\frac{1}{2}\|\cdot\|^2 - \frac{1}{2}d_C^2$). Suppose that $\mathbb{E}$ is a Euclidean space, and let $C \subseteq \mathbb{E}$ be a nonempty closed convex set. Consider the function

$\psi_C(\mathbf{x}) = \frac{1}{2}\|\mathbf{x}\|^2 - \frac{1}{2}d_C^2(\mathbf{x})$. By Example 2.17, ψ_C is convex.[23] We will now show that it is 1-smooth. By Example 3.31, $\frac{1}{2}d_C^2(\mathbf{x})$ is differentiable over $\mathbb{E}$, and its gradient is given by $\mathbf{x} - P_C(\mathbf{x})$. Therefore,

$$\nabla\psi_C(\mathbf{x}) = \mathbf{x} - (\mathbf{x} - P_C(\mathbf{x})) = P_C(\mathbf{x}).$$

The 1-smoothness of ψ_C now follows by the nonexpansivity of the projection operator (Theorem 5.4(b))—for any $\mathbf{x}, \mathbf{y} \in \mathbb{E}$,

$$\|\nabla\psi_C(\mathbf{x}) - \nabla\psi_C(\mathbf{y})\| = \|P_C(\mathbf{x}) - P_C(\mathbf{y})\| \leq \|\mathbf{x} - \mathbf{y}\|. \quad \blacksquare$$

5.1.1 The Descent Lemma

An extremely useful result on L-smooth functions is the descent lemma, which states that they can be upper bounded by a certain quadratic function.

Lemma 5.7 (descent lemma). *Let $f : \mathbb{E} \to (-\infty, \infty]$ be an L-smooth function ($L \geq 0$) over a given convex set D. Then for any $\mathbf{x}, \mathbf{y} \in D$,*

$$f(\mathbf{y}) \leq f(\mathbf{x}) + \langle\nabla f(\mathbf{x}), \mathbf{y} - \mathbf{x}\rangle + \frac{L}{2}\|\mathbf{x} - \mathbf{y}\|^2. \tag{5.3}$$

Proof. By the fundamental theorem of calculus,

$$f(\mathbf{y}) - f(\mathbf{x}) = \int_0^1 \langle\nabla f(\mathbf{x} + t(\mathbf{y} - \mathbf{x})), \mathbf{y} - \mathbf{x}\rangle dt.$$

Therefore,

$$f(\mathbf{y}) - f(\mathbf{x}) = \langle\nabla f(\mathbf{x}), \mathbf{y} - \mathbf{x}\rangle + \int_0^1 \langle\nabla f(\mathbf{x} + t(\mathbf{y} - \mathbf{x})) - \nabla f(\mathbf{x}), \mathbf{y} - \mathbf{x}\rangle dt.$$

Thus,

$$
\begin{aligned}
|f(\mathbf{y}) - f(\mathbf{x}) - \langle\nabla f(\mathbf{x}), \mathbf{y} - \mathbf{x}\rangle| &= \left|\int_0^1 \langle\nabla f(\mathbf{x} + t(\mathbf{y} - \mathbf{x})) - \nabla f(\mathbf{x}), \mathbf{y} - \mathbf{x}\rangle dt\right| \\
&\leq \int_0^1 |\langle\nabla f(\mathbf{x} + t(\mathbf{y} - \mathbf{x})) - \nabla f(\mathbf{x}), \mathbf{y} - \mathbf{x}\rangle| dt \\
&\overset{(*)}{\leq} \int_0^1 \|\nabla f(\mathbf{x} + t(\mathbf{y} - \mathbf{x})) - \nabla f(\mathbf{x})\|_* \cdot \|\mathbf{y} - \mathbf{x}\| dt \\
&\leq \int_0^1 tL\|\mathbf{y} - \mathbf{x}\|^2 dt \\
&= \frac{L}{2}\|\mathbf{y} - \mathbf{x}\|^2,
\end{aligned}
$$

where in $(*)$ we used the generalized Cauchy–Schwarz inequality (Lemma 1.4). $\quad\square$

---

[23]The convexity of ψ_C actually does not require the convexity of C; see Example 2.17.

5.1.2 Characterizations of L-Smooth Functions

When f is convex, the next result gives several different and equivalent characterizations of the L-smoothness property of f over the entire space. Note that property (5.3) from the descent lemma is one of the mentioned equivalent properties.

Theorem 5.8 (characterizations of L-smoothness). *Let $f : \mathbb{E} \to \mathbb{R}$ be a convex function, differentiable over $\mathbb{E}$, and let $L > 0$. Then the following claims are equivalent:*

(i) *f is L-smooth.*

(ii) *$f(\mathbf{y}) \leq f(\mathbf{x}) + \langle \nabla f(\mathbf{x}), \mathbf{y} - \mathbf{x} \rangle + \frac{L}{2}\|\mathbf{x} - \mathbf{y}\|^2$ for all $\mathbf{x}, \mathbf{y} \in \mathbb{E}$.*

(iii) *$f(\mathbf{y}) \geq f(\mathbf{x}) + \langle \nabla f(\mathbf{x}), \mathbf{y} - \mathbf{x} \rangle + \frac{1}{2L}\|\nabla f(\mathbf{x}) - \nabla f(\mathbf{y})\|_*^2$ for all $\mathbf{x}, \mathbf{y} \in \mathbb{E}$.*

(iv) *$\langle \nabla f(\mathbf{x}) - \nabla f(\mathbf{y}), \mathbf{x} - \mathbf{y} \rangle \geq \frac{1}{L}\|\nabla f(\mathbf{x}) - \nabla f(\mathbf{y})\|_*^2$ for all $\mathbf{x}, \mathbf{y} \in \mathbb{E}$.*

(v) *$f(\lambda\mathbf{x} + (1-\lambda)\mathbf{y}) \geq \lambda f(\mathbf{x}) + (1-\lambda)f(\mathbf{y}) - \frac{L}{2}\lambda(1-\lambda)\|\mathbf{x} - \mathbf{y}\|^2$ for any $\mathbf{x}, \mathbf{y} \in \mathbb{E}$ and $\lambda \in [0, 1]$.*

Proof. (i) $\Rightarrow$ (ii). The fact that (i) implies (ii) is just the descent lemma (Lemma 5.7).

(ii) $\Rightarrow$ (iii). Suppose that (ii) is satisfied. We can assume that $\nabla f(\mathbf{x}) \neq \nabla f(\mathbf{y})$ since otherwise the inequality (iii) is trivial by the convexity of f. For a fixed $\mathbf{x} \in \mathbb{E}$ consider the function

$$g_{\mathbf{x}}(\mathbf{y}) = f(\mathbf{y}) - f(\mathbf{x}) - \langle \nabla f(\mathbf{x}), \mathbf{y} - \mathbf{x} \rangle, \quad \mathbf{y} \in \mathbb{E}.$$

The function $g_{\mathbf{x}}$ also satisfies property (ii). Indeed, for any $\mathbf{y}, \mathbf{z} \in \mathbb{E}$,

$$
\begin{aligned}
g_{\mathbf{x}}(\mathbf{z}) &= f(\mathbf{z}) - f(\mathbf{x}) - \langle \nabla f(\mathbf{x}), \mathbf{z} - \mathbf{x} \rangle \\
&\leq f(\mathbf{y}) + \langle \nabla f(\mathbf{y}), \mathbf{z} - \mathbf{y} \rangle + \frac{L}{2}\|\mathbf{z} - \mathbf{y}\|^2 - f(\mathbf{x}) - \langle \nabla f(\mathbf{x}), \mathbf{z} - \mathbf{x} \rangle \\
&= f(\mathbf{y}) - f(\mathbf{x}) - \langle \nabla f(\mathbf{x}), \mathbf{y} - \mathbf{x} \rangle + \langle \nabla f(\mathbf{y}) - \nabla f(\mathbf{x}), \mathbf{z} - \mathbf{y} \rangle + \frac{L}{2}\|\mathbf{z} - \mathbf{y}\|^2 \\
&= g_{\mathbf{x}}(\mathbf{y}) + \langle \nabla g_{\mathbf{x}}(\mathbf{y}), \mathbf{z} - \mathbf{y} \rangle + \frac{L}{2}\|\mathbf{z} - \mathbf{y}\|^2, \quad\quad\quad\quad (5.4)
\end{aligned}
$$

where we used in the last equality the fact that $\nabla g_{\mathbf{x}}(\mathbf{y}) = \nabla f(\mathbf{y}) - \nabla f(\mathbf{x})$ for any $\mathbf{y} \in \mathbb{E}$. In particular, $\nabla g_{\mathbf{x}}(\mathbf{x}) = \mathbf{0}$, which by the convexity of $g_{\mathbf{x}}$ implies that $\mathbf{x}$ is a global minimizer of g, meaning that

$$g_{\mathbf{x}}(\mathbf{x}) \leq g_{\mathbf{x}}(\mathbf{z}) \text{ for all } \mathbf{z} \in \mathbb{E}. \quad\quad\quad\quad (5.5)$$

Let $\mathbf{y} \in \mathbb{E}$, and let $\mathbf{v} \in \mathbb{E}$ be a vector satisfying $\|\mathbf{v}\| = 1$ and $\langle \nabla g_{\mathbf{x}}(\mathbf{y}), \mathbf{v} \rangle = \|\nabla g_{\mathbf{x}}(\mathbf{y})\|_*$. Substituting

$$\mathbf{z} = \mathbf{y} - \frac{\|\nabla g_{\mathbf{x}}(\mathbf{y})\|_*}{L}\mathbf{v} \quad\quad\quad\quad (5.6)$$

into (5.5) yields

$$0 = g_{\mathbf{x}}(\mathbf{x}) \leq g_{\mathbf{x}}\left(\mathbf{y} - \frac{\|\nabla g_{\mathbf{x}}(\mathbf{y})\|_*}{L}\mathbf{v}\right).$$

Combining the last inequality with (5.4) (using the specific choice of $\mathbf{z}$ given in (5.6)), we obtain

$$
\begin{aligned}
0 &= g_{\mathbf{x}}(\mathbf{x}) \\
&\leq g_{\mathbf{x}}(\mathbf{y}) - \frac{\|\nabla g_{\mathbf{x}}(\mathbf{y})\|_*}{L} \langle \nabla g_{\mathbf{x}}(\mathbf{y}), \mathbf{v} \rangle + \frac{1}{2L}\|\nabla g_{\mathbf{x}}(\mathbf{y})\|_*^2 \cdot \|\mathbf{v}\|^2 \\
&= g_{\mathbf{x}}(\mathbf{y}) - \frac{1}{2L}\|\nabla g_{\mathbf{x}}(\mathbf{y})\|_*^2 \\
&= f(\mathbf{y}) - f(\mathbf{x}) - \langle \nabla f(\mathbf{x}), \mathbf{y} - \mathbf{x} \rangle - \frac{1}{2L}\|\nabla f(\mathbf{x}) - \nabla f(\mathbf{y})\|_*^2,
\end{aligned}
$$

which is claim (iii).

(iii) $\Rightarrow$ (iv). Writing the inequality (iii) for the two pairs $(\mathbf{x}, \mathbf{y}), (\mathbf{y}, \mathbf{x})$ yields

$$
f(\mathbf{y}) \geq f(\mathbf{x}) + \langle \nabla f(\mathbf{x}), \mathbf{y} - \mathbf{x} \rangle + \frac{1}{2L}\|\nabla f(\mathbf{x}) - \nabla f(\mathbf{y})\|_*^2,
$$

$$
f(\mathbf{x}) \geq f(\mathbf{y}) + \langle \nabla f(\mathbf{y}), \mathbf{x} - \mathbf{y} \rangle + \frac{1}{2L}\|\nabla f(\mathbf{x}) - \nabla f(\mathbf{y})\|_*^2.
$$

Adding the two inequalities and rearranging terms results in (iv).

(iv) $\Rightarrow$ (i). The Lipschitz condition

$$
\|\nabla f(\mathbf{x}) - \nabla f(\mathbf{y})\|_* \leq L\|\mathbf{x} - \mathbf{y}\|
$$

is trivial when $\nabla f(\mathbf{x}) = \nabla f(\mathbf{y})$. We will therefore assume that $\nabla f(\mathbf{x}) \neq \nabla f(\mathbf{y})$. By (iv) and the generalized Cauchy–Schwarz inequality (Lemma 1.4) we have for any $\mathbf{x}, \mathbf{y} \in \mathbb{E}$,

$$
\|\nabla f(\mathbf{x}) - \nabla f(\mathbf{y})\|_* \cdot \|\mathbf{x} - \mathbf{y}\| \geq \langle \nabla f(\mathbf{x}) - \nabla f(\mathbf{y}), \mathbf{x} - \mathbf{y} \rangle \geq \frac{1}{L}\|\nabla f(\mathbf{x}) - \nabla f(\mathbf{y})\|_*^2.
$$

Dividing by $\|\nabla f(\mathbf{x}) - \nabla f(\mathbf{y})\|_*$ and multiplying by L, (i) is obtained.

We have just shown the equivalence between (i), (ii), (iii), and (iv). To prove that (v) is also equivalent to each of these four claims, we will establish the equivalence (ii) $\Leftrightarrow$ (v).

(ii) $\Rightarrow$ (v). Let $\mathbf{x}, \mathbf{y} \in \mathbb{E}$ and $\lambda \in [0, 1]$. Denote $\mathbf{x}_\lambda = \lambda \mathbf{x} + (1 - \lambda)\mathbf{y}$. Then by (ii),

$$
f(\mathbf{x}) \leq f(\mathbf{x}_\lambda) + \langle \nabla f(\mathbf{x}_\lambda), \mathbf{x} - \mathbf{x}_\lambda \rangle + \frac{L}{2}\|\mathbf{x} - \mathbf{x}_\lambda\|^2,
$$

$$
f(\mathbf{y}) \leq f(\mathbf{x}_\lambda) + \langle \nabla f(\mathbf{x}_\lambda), \mathbf{y} - \mathbf{x}_\lambda \rangle + \frac{L}{2}\|\mathbf{y} - \mathbf{x}_\lambda\|^2,
$$

which is the same as

$$
f(\mathbf{x}) \leq f(\mathbf{x}_\lambda) + (1 - \lambda)\langle \nabla f(\mathbf{x}_\lambda), \mathbf{x} - \mathbf{y} \rangle + \frac{L(1 - \lambda)^2}{2}\|\mathbf{x} - \mathbf{y}\|^2,
$$

$$
f(\mathbf{y}) \leq f(\mathbf{x}_\lambda) + \lambda\langle \nabla f(\mathbf{x}_\lambda), \mathbf{y} - \mathbf{x} \rangle + \frac{L\lambda^2}{2}\|\mathbf{x} - \mathbf{y}\|^2.
$$

Multiplying the first inequality by λ and the second by $1 - \lambda$ and adding them yields the inequality (iv).

$(v) \Rightarrow (ii)$. Rearranging terms in the inequality (v), we obtain that it is equivalent to

$$f(\mathbf{y}) \le f(\mathbf{x}) + \frac{f(\mathbf{x} + (1-\lambda)(\mathbf{y} - \mathbf{x})) - f(\mathbf{x})}{1 - \lambda} + \frac{L}{2}\lambda\|\mathbf{x} - \mathbf{y}\|^2.$$

Taking $\lambda \to 1^-$, the last inequality becomes

$$f(\mathbf{y}) \le f(\mathbf{x}) + f'(\mathbf{x}; \mathbf{y} - \mathbf{x}) + \frac{L}{2}\|\mathbf{x} - \mathbf{y}\|^2,$$

which, by the fact that $f'(\mathbf{x}; \mathbf{y} - \mathbf{x}) = \langle \nabla f(\mathbf{x}), \mathbf{y} - \mathbf{x} \rangle$ (see Theorem 3.29), implies (ii). $\quad\square$

Remark 5.9 (necessity of convexity in Theorem 5.8). *The convexity assumption in Theorem 5.8 is essential. Consider, for example, the function $f : \mathbb{R}^n \to \mathbb{R}$ given by $f(\mathbf{x}) = -\frac{1}{2}\|\mathbf{x}\|_2^2$, which is 1-smooth w.r.t. the l_2-norm but is not L-smooth for $L < 1$ (see Example 5.2). However, f is concave, and hence*

$$f(\mathbf{y}) \le f(\mathbf{x}) + \langle \nabla f(\mathbf{x}), \mathbf{y} - \mathbf{x} \rangle,$$

which implies that property (ii) of Theorem 5.8 is satisfied with $L = 0$, although the function is obviously not 0-smooth.

The next example will require the linear approximation theorem, which we now recall.

Theorem 5.10 (linear approximation theorem, [10, Theorem 1.24], [101, Fact 3.3.10]). *Let $f : U \to \mathbb{R}$ be a twice continuously differentiable function[24] over an open set $U \subseteq \mathbb{R}^n$, and let $\mathbf{x} \in U, r > 0$ satisfy $B(\mathbf{x}, r) \subseteq U$. Then for any $\mathbf{y} \in B(\mathbf{x}, r)$ there exists $\boldsymbol{\xi} \in [\mathbf{x}, \mathbf{y}]$ such that*

$$f(\mathbf{y}) = f(\mathbf{x}) + \nabla f(\mathbf{x})^T(\mathbf{y} - \mathbf{x}) + \frac{1}{2}(\mathbf{y} - \mathbf{x})^T \nabla^2 f(\boldsymbol{\xi})(\mathbf{y} - \mathbf{x}).$$

Example 5.11 ($(p-1)$-smoothness of the half-squared l_p-norm function).[25] Consider the convex function $f : \mathbb{R}^n \to \mathbb{R}$ given by

$$f(\mathbf{x}) = \frac{1}{2}\|\mathbf{x}\|_p^2 = \frac{1}{2}\left(\sum_{i=1}^n |x_i|^p\right)^{\frac{2}{p}},$$

where $p \in [2, \infty)$. We assume that $\mathbb{R}^n$ is endowed with the l_p-norm and show that f is $(p-1)$-smooth w.r.t. the l_p-norm. The result was already established for the case $p = 2$ in Example 5.2, and we will henceforth assume that $p > 2$. We begin by computing the partial derivatives:

$$\frac{\partial f}{\partial x_i}(\mathbf{x}) = \begin{cases} \text{sgn}(x_i)\frac{|x_i|^{p-1}}{\|\mathbf{x}\|_p^{p-2}}, & \mathbf{x} \ne \mathbf{0}, \\ 0, & \mathbf{x} = \mathbf{0}, \end{cases}$$

---

[24] By "twice continuously differentiable over U," we mean that the function has second-order partial derivatives, which are continuous over U.

[25] The analysis in Example 5.11 follows the derivation of Ben-Tal, Margalit, and Nemirovski [24, Appendix 1].

The partial derivatives are continuous over $\mathbb{R}^n$, and hence f is differentiable over $\mathbb{R}^n$ (in the sense of Definition 3.28).[26] The second-order partial derivatives exist for any $\mathbf{x} \neq \mathbf{0}$ and are given by

$$\frac{\partial^2 f}{\partial x_i \partial x_j}(\mathbf{x}) = \begin{cases} (2-p)\mathrm{sgn}(x_i)\mathrm{sgn}(x_j)\frac{|x_i|^{p-1}|x_j|^{p-1}}{\|\mathbf{x}\|_p^{2p-2}}, & i \neq j, \\ (p-1)\frac{|x_i|^{p-2}}{\|\mathbf{x}\|_p^{p-2}} + (2-p)\frac{|x_i|^{2p-2}}{\|\mathbf{x}\|_p^{2p-2}}, & i = j. \end{cases}$$

It is easy to see that the second-order partial derivatives are continuous for any $\mathbf{x} \neq \mathbf{0}$. We will show that property (ii) of Theorem 5.8 is satisfied with $L = p - 1$. Let $\mathbf{x}, \mathbf{y} \in \mathbb{R}^n$ be such that $\mathbf{0} \notin [\mathbf{x}, \mathbf{y}]$. Then by the linear approximation theorem (Theorem 5.10)—taking U to be some open set containing $[\mathbf{x}, \mathbf{y}]$ but not containing $\mathbf{0}$—there exists $\boldsymbol{\xi} \in [\mathbf{x}, \mathbf{y}]$ for which

$$f(\mathbf{y}) = f(\mathbf{x}) + \nabla f(\mathbf{x})^T(\mathbf{y} - \mathbf{x}) + \frac{1}{2}(\mathbf{y} - \mathbf{x})^T \nabla^2 f(\boldsymbol{\xi})(\mathbf{y} - \mathbf{x}). \tag{5.7}$$

We will show that $\mathbf{d}^T \nabla^2 f(\boldsymbol{\xi}) \mathbf{d} \leq (p-1)\|\mathbf{d}\|_p^2$ for any $\mathbf{d} \in \mathbb{R}^n$. Since $\nabla^2 f(t\boldsymbol{\xi}) = \nabla^2 f(\boldsymbol{\xi})$ for any $t \in \mathbb{R}$, we can assume without loss of generality that $\|\boldsymbol{\xi}\|_p = 1$. Now, for any $\mathbf{d} \in \mathbb{R}^n$,

$$\mathbf{d}^T \nabla^2 f(\boldsymbol{\xi}) \mathbf{d} = (2-p)\|\boldsymbol{\xi}\|_p^{2-2p} \left(\sum_{i=1}^n |\xi_i|^{p-1} \mathrm{sgn}(\xi_i) d_i \right)^2 + (p-1)\|\boldsymbol{\xi}\|_p^{2-p} \sum_{i=1}^n |\xi_i|^{p-2} d_i^2$$

$$\leq (p-1)\|\boldsymbol{\xi}\|_p^{2-p} \sum_{i=1}^n |\xi_i|^{p-2} d_i^2, \tag{5.8}$$

where the last inequality follows by the fact that $p > 2$. Using the generalized Cauchy–Schwarz inequality (Lemma 1.4) with $\|\cdot\| = \|\cdot\|_{\frac{p}{p-2}}$, we have

$$\sum_{i=1}^n |\xi_i|^{p-2} d_i^2 \leq \left(\sum_{i=1}^n (|\xi_i|^{p-2})^{\frac{p}{p-2}} \right)^{\frac{p-2}{p}} \left(\sum_{i=1}^n (d_i^2)^{\frac{p}{2}} \right)^{\frac{2}{p}}$$

$$= \left(\sum_{i=1}^n |\xi_i|^p \right)^{\frac{p-2}{p}} \left(\sum_{i=1}^n |d_i|^p \right)^{\frac{2}{p}}$$

$$= \|\mathbf{d}\|_p^2. \tag{5.9}$$

Combining (5.8) and (5.9), we obtain that for any $\mathbf{d} \in \mathbb{R}^n$,

$$\mathbf{d}^T \nabla^2 f(\boldsymbol{\xi}) \mathbf{d} \leq (p-1)\|\mathbf{d}\|_p^2,$$

and specifically, for $\mathbf{d} = \mathbf{x} - \mathbf{y}$,

$$(\mathbf{y} - \mathbf{x})^T \nabla^2 f(\boldsymbol{\xi})(\mathbf{y} - \mathbf{x}) \leq (p-1)\|\mathbf{x} - \mathbf{y}\|_p^2.$$

Plugging the above inequality into (5.7) implies the inequality

$$f(\mathbf{y}) \leq f(\mathbf{x}) + \nabla f(\mathbf{x})^T(\mathbf{y} - \mathbf{x}) + \frac{p-1}{2}\|\mathbf{x} - \mathbf{y}\|_p^2. \tag{5.10}$$

---

[26] See, for example, [112, Theorem 9.21] for a precise statement of this result.

The inequality (5.10) was proven for any $\mathbf{x}, \mathbf{y} \in \mathbb{R}^n$ that satisfy $\mathbf{0} \notin [\mathbf{x}, \mathbf{y}]$. We can show that it holds for any $\mathbf{x}, \mathbf{y} \in \mathbb{R}^n$ using a continuity argument. Indeed, assume that $\mathbf{0} \in [\mathbf{x}, \mathbf{y}]$. Then we can find a sequence $\{\mathbf{y}_k\}_{k \geq 0}$ converging to $\mathbf{y}$ for which $\mathbf{0} \notin [\mathbf{x}, \mathbf{y}_k]$. Thus, by what was already proven, for any $k \geq 0$,

$$f(\mathbf{y}_k) \leq f(\mathbf{x}) + \nabla f(\mathbf{x})^T(\mathbf{y}_k - \mathbf{x}) + \frac{p-1}{2} \|\mathbf{x} - \mathbf{y}_k\|_p^2.$$

Taking $k \to \infty$ in the last inequality and using the continuity of f, we obtain that (5.10) holds. To conclude, we established that (5.10) holds for any $\mathbf{x}, \mathbf{y} \in \mathbb{R}^n$, and thus by Theorem 5.8 (equivalence between properties (i) and (ii)) and the convexity of f, it follows that f is $(p-1)$-smooth w.r.t. the l_p-norm. ∎

5.1.3 Second-Order Characterization

We will now consider the space $\mathbb{E} = \mathbb{R}^n$ endowed with the l_p-norm ($p \geq 1$). For twice continuously differentiable functions, it is possible to fully characterize the property of L-smoothness via the norm of the Hessian matrix.

Theorem 5.12 (L-smoothness and boundedness of the Hessian). *Let f : $\mathbb{R}^n \to \mathbb{R}$ be a twice continuously differentiable function over $\mathbb{R}^n$. Then for a given $L \geq 0$, the following two claims are equivalent:*

(i) *f is L-smooth w.r.t. the l_p-norm ($p \in [1, \infty]$).*

(ii) *$\|\nabla^2 f(\mathbf{x})\|_{p,q} \leq L$ for any $\mathbf{x} \in \mathbb{R}^n$, where $q \in [1, \infty]$ satisfies $\frac{1}{p} + \frac{1}{q} = 1$.*

Proof. (ii) $\Rightarrow$ (i). Suppose that $\|\nabla^2 f(\mathbf{x})\|_{p,q} \leq L$ for any $\mathbf{x} \in \mathbb{R}^n$. Then by the fundamental theorem of calculus, for all $\mathbf{x}, \mathbf{y} \in \mathbb{R}^n$,

$$\nabla f(\mathbf{y}) = \nabla f(\mathbf{x}) + \int_0^1 \nabla^2 f(\mathbf{x} + t(\mathbf{y} - \mathbf{x}))(\mathbf{y} - \mathbf{x}) dt$$

$$= \nabla f(\mathbf{x}) + \left(\int_0^1 \nabla^2 f(\mathbf{x} + t(\mathbf{y} - \mathbf{x})) dt \right) \cdot (\mathbf{y} - \mathbf{x}).$$

Then

$$\|\nabla f(\mathbf{y}) - \nabla f(\mathbf{x})\|_q = \left\| \left(\int_0^1 \nabla^2 f(\mathbf{x} + t(\mathbf{y} - \mathbf{x})) dt \right) \cdot (\mathbf{y} - \mathbf{x}) \right\|_q$$

$$\leq \left\| \int_0^1 \nabla^2 f(\mathbf{x} + t(\mathbf{y} - \mathbf{x})) dt \right\|_{p,q} \|\mathbf{y} - \mathbf{x}\|_p$$

$$\leq \left(\int_0^1 \|\nabla^2 f(\mathbf{x} + t(\mathbf{y} - \mathbf{x}))\|_{p,q} dt \right) \|\mathbf{y} - \mathbf{x}\|_p$$

$$\leq L \|\mathbf{y} - \mathbf{x}\|_p,$$

establishing (i).

(i) $\Rightarrow$ (ii). Suppose now that f is L-smooth w.r.t. the l_p-norm. Then by the fundamental theorem of calculus, for any $\mathbf{d} \in \mathbb{R}^n$ and $\alpha > 0$,

$$\nabla f(\mathbf{x} + \alpha \mathbf{d}) - \nabla f(\mathbf{x}) = \int_0^\alpha \nabla^2 f(\mathbf{x} + t\mathbf{d}) \mathbf{d} dt.$$

Thus,

$$\left\| \left(\int_0^\alpha \nabla^2 f(\mathbf{x} + t\mathbf{d}) dt \right) \mathbf{d} \right\|_q = \|\nabla f(\mathbf{x} + \alpha \mathbf{d}) - \nabla f(\mathbf{x})\|_q \leq \alpha L \|\mathbf{d}\|_p.$$

Dividing by α and taking the limit $\alpha \to 0^+$, we obtain

$$\left\|\nabla^2 f(\mathbf{x})\mathbf{d}\right\|_q \leq L\|\mathbf{d}\|_p \text{ for any } \mathbf{d} \in \mathbb{R}^n,$$

implying that $\|\nabla^2 f(\mathbf{x})\|_{p,q} \leq L$. $\quad\square$

A direct consequence is that for twice continuously differentiable convex functions, L-smoothness w.r.t. the l_2-norm is equivalent to the property that the maximum eigenvalue of the Hessian matrix is smaller than or equal to L.

Corollary 5.13. *Let $f : \mathbb{R}^n \to \mathbb{R}$ be a twice continuously differentiable convex function over $\mathbb{R}^n$. Then f is L-smooth w.r.t. the l_2-norm if and only if $\lambda_{\max}(\nabla^2 f(\mathbf{x})) \leq L$ for any $\mathbf{x} \in \mathbb{R}^n$.*

Proof. Since f is convex, it follows that $\nabla^2 f(\mathbf{x}) \succeq \mathbf{0}$ for any $\mathbf{x} \in \mathbb{R}^n$. Therefore, in this case,

$$\|\nabla^2 f(\mathbf{x})\|_{2,2} = \sqrt{\lambda_{\max}((\nabla^2 f(\mathbf{x}))^2)} = \lambda_{\max}(\nabla^2 f(\mathbf{x})),$$

which, combined with Theorem 5.12, establishes the desired result. $\quad\square$

Example 5.14 (1-smoothness of $\sqrt{1 + \|\cdot\|_2^2}$ w.r.t. the l_2-norm). Let $f : \mathbb{R}^n \to \mathbb{R}$ be the convex function given by

$$f(\mathbf{x}) = \sqrt{1 + \|\mathbf{x}\|_2^2}.$$

We will show that f is 1-smooth w.r.t. the l_2-norm. For any $\mathbf{x} \in \mathbb{R}^n$,

$$\nabla f(\mathbf{x}) = \frac{\mathbf{x}}{\sqrt{\|\mathbf{x}\|_2^2 + 1}}$$

and

$$\nabla^2 f(\mathbf{x}) = \frac{1}{\sqrt{\|\mathbf{x}\|_2^2 + 1}} \mathbf{I} - \frac{\mathbf{x}\mathbf{x}^T}{(\|\mathbf{x}\|_2^2 + 1)^{3/2}} \preceq \frac{1}{\sqrt{\|\mathbf{x}\|_2^2 + 1}} \mathbf{I} \preceq \mathbf{I}.$$

Therefore, $\lambda_{\max}(\nabla^2 f(\mathbf{x})) \leq 1$ for all $\mathbf{x} \in \mathbb{R}^n$, and hence by Corollary 5.13 it follows that f is 1-smooth w.r.t. the l_2-norm. $\quad\blacksquare$

Example 5.15 (1-smoothness of the log-sum-exp function w.r.t. the l_2, l_∞ norms). Consider the log-sum-exp function $f : \mathbb{R}^n \to \mathbb{R}$ given by

$$f(\mathbf{x}) = \log\left(e^{x_1} + e^{x_2} + \cdots + e^{x_n}\right).$$

We will first show that it is 1-smooth w.r.t. the l_2-norm. The partial derivatives of f are

$$\frac{\partial f}{\partial x_i}(\mathbf{x}) = \frac{e^{x_i}}{\sum_{k=1}^n e^{x_k}}, \quad i = 1, 2, \ldots, n,$$

and the second-order partial derivatives are

$$
\frac{\partial^2 f}{\partial x_i \partial x_j}(\mathbf{x}) = \begin{cases} -\dfrac{e^{x_i} e^{x_j}}{\left(\sum_{k=1}^n e^{x_k}\right)^2}, & i \neq j, \\[3mm] -\dfrac{e^{x_i} e^{x_i}}{\left(\sum_{k=1}^n e^{x_k}\right)^2} + \dfrac{e^{x_i}}{\sum_{k=1}^n e^{x_k}}, & i = j. \end{cases}
$$

We can thus write the Hessian matrix as

$$
\nabla^2 f(\mathbf{x}) = \operatorname{diag}(\mathbf{w}) - \mathbf{w}\mathbf{w}^T,
$$

where $w_i = \frac{e^{x_i}}{\sum_{k=1}^n e^{x_k}}$. To show that f is 1-smooth w.r.t. the l_2-norm, note that for any $\mathbf{x} \in \mathbb{R}^n$,

$$
\nabla^2 f(\mathbf{x}) = \operatorname{diag}(\mathbf{w}) - \mathbf{w}\mathbf{w}^T \preceq \operatorname{diag}(\mathbf{w}) \preceq \mathbf{I},
$$

and hence $\lambda_{\max}(\nabla^2 f(\mathbf{x})) \leq 1$ for any $\mathbf{x} \in \mathbb{R}^n$. Noting that the log-sum-exp function is convex, we can invoke Corollary 5.13 and conclude that f is 1-smooth w.r.t. the l_2-norm.

We will show that f is 1-smooth also w.r.t. the l_∞-norm. For that, we begin by proving that for any $\mathbf{d} \in \mathbb{R}^n$,

$$
\mathbf{d}^T \nabla^2 f(\mathbf{x})\mathbf{d} \leq \|\mathbf{d}\|_\infty^2. \tag{5.11}
$$

Indeed,

$$
\begin{aligned}
\mathbf{d}^T \nabla^2 f(\mathbf{x})\mathbf{d} &= \mathbf{d}^T(\operatorname{diag}(\mathbf{w}) - \mathbf{w}\mathbf{w}^T)\mathbf{d} = \mathbf{d}^T \operatorname{diag}(\mathbf{w})\mathbf{d} - (\mathbf{w}^T\mathbf{d})^2 \\
&\leq \mathbf{d}^T \operatorname{diag}(\mathbf{w})\mathbf{d} \\
&= \sum_{i=1}^n w_i d_i^2 \\
&\leq \|\mathbf{d}\|_\infty^2 \sum_{i=1}^n w_i \\
&= \|\mathbf{d}\|_\infty^2.
\end{aligned}
$$

Now, since f is twice continuously differentiable over $\mathbb{R}^n$, it follows by the linear approximation theorem (Theorem 5.10) that for any $\mathbf{x}, \mathbf{y} \in \mathbb{R}^n$ there exists $\boldsymbol{\xi} \in [\mathbf{x}, \mathbf{y}]$ for which

$$
f(\mathbf{y}) = f(\mathbf{x}) + \nabla f(\mathbf{x})^T(\mathbf{y} - \mathbf{x}) + \frac{1}{2}(\mathbf{y} - \mathbf{x})^T \nabla^2 f(\boldsymbol{\xi})(\mathbf{y} - \mathbf{x}). \tag{5.12}
$$

Combining (5.12) (taking $\mathbf{d} = \mathbf{y} - \mathbf{x}$) and (5.11), we obtain the inequality

$$
f(\mathbf{y}) \leq f(\mathbf{x}) + \nabla f(\mathbf{x})^T(\mathbf{y} - \mathbf{x}) + \frac{1}{2}\|\mathbf{y} - \mathbf{x}\|_\infty^2,
$$

which by Theorem 5.8 (equivalence between properties (i) and (ii)) implies the 1-smoothness of f w.r.t. the l_∞-norm. ∎

5.1.4 Summary of Smoothness Parameter Computations

The table below summarizes the smoothness parameters of the functions discussed in this section. The last function will only be discussed later on in Example 6.62.

$f(\mathbf{x})$	$\mathrm{dom}(f)$	Parameter	Norm	Reference
$\frac{1}{2}\mathbf{x}^T \mathbf{A}\mathbf{x} + \mathbf{b}^T\mathbf{x} + c$ $(\mathbf{A} \in \mathbb{S}^n, \mathbf{b} \in \mathbb{R}^n, c \in \mathbb{R})$	$\mathbb{R}^n$	$\|\mathbf{A}\|_{p,q}$	l_p	Example 5.2
$\langle \mathbf{b}, \mathbf{x} \rangle + c$ $(\mathbf{b} \in \mathbb{E}^*, c \in \mathbb{R})$	$\mathbb{E}$	0	any norm	Example 5.3
$\frac{1}{2}\|\mathbf{x}\|_p^2, \ p \in [2, \infty)$	$\mathbb{R}^n$	$p-1$	l_p	Example 5.11
$\sqrt{1 + \|\mathbf{x}\|_2^2}$	$\mathbb{R}^n$	1	l_2	Example 5.14
$\log(\sum_{i=1}^n e^{x_i})$	$\mathbb{R}^n$	1	l_2, l_∞	Example 5.15
$\frac{1}{2}d_C^2(\mathbf{x})$ $(\emptyset \neq C \subseteq \mathbb{E} \text{ closed convex})$	$\mathbb{E}$	1	Euclidean	Example 5.5
$\frac{1}{2}\|\mathbf{x}\|^2 - \frac{1}{2}d_C^2(\mathbf{x})$ $(\emptyset \neq C \subseteq \mathbb{E} \text{ closed convex})$	$\mathbb{E}$	1	Euclidean	Example 5.6
$H_\mu(\mathbf{x}) \ (\mu > 0)$	$\mathbb{E}$	$\frac{1}{\mu}$	Euclidean	Example 6.62

5.2 Strong Convexity

Definition 5.16 (strong convexity). *A function $f : \mathbb{E} \to (-\infty, \infty]$ is called σ-strongly convex for a given $\sigma > 0$ if $\mathrm{dom}(f)$ is convex and the following inequality holds for any $\mathbf{x}, \mathbf{y} \in \mathrm{dom}(f)$ and $\lambda \in [0,1]$:*

$$f(\lambda\mathbf{x} + (1-\lambda)\mathbf{y}) \leq \lambda f(\mathbf{x}) + (1-\lambda)f(\mathbf{y}) - \frac{\sigma}{2}\lambda(1-\lambda)\|\mathbf{x}-\mathbf{y}\|^2. \qquad (5.13)$$

We will sometimes use the terminology "strongly convex with parameter σ" instead of "σ-strongly convex." It is important to note that the strong convexity parameter σ depends on the underlying norm, and we will therefore sometimes refer to it as the "strong convexity parameter w.r.t. $\|\cdot\|$." Obviously, strongly convex functions are necessarily also convex since their domain is assumed to be convex and inequality (5.13) implies that for any $\mathbf{x}, \mathbf{y} \in \mathrm{dom}(f)$ and $\lambda \in [0,1]$, Jensen's inequality is satisfied:

$$f(\lambda\mathbf{x} + (1-\lambda)\mathbf{y}) \leq \lambda f(\mathbf{x}) + (1-\lambda)f(\mathbf{y}).$$

When the underlying set $\mathbb{E}$ is Euclidean, meaning that $\|\mathbf{x}\| = \sqrt{\langle \mathbf{x}, \mathbf{x} \rangle}$ for any $\mathbf{x} \in \mathbb{E}$, we can write a different and simple property that is equivalent to strong convexity.

Theorem 5.17. *Let $\mathbb{E}$ be a Euclidean space. Then $f : \mathbb{E} \to (-\infty, \infty]$ is a σ-strongly convex function ($\sigma > 0$) if and only if the function $f(\cdot) - \frac{\sigma}{2}\|\cdot\|^2$ is convex.*

Proof. The function $g(\mathbf{x}) \equiv f(\mathbf{x}) - \frac{\sigma}{2}\|\mathbf{x}\|^2$ is convex if and only if its domain $\text{dom}(g) = \text{dom}(f)$ is convex and for any $\mathbf{x}, \mathbf{y} \in \text{dom}(f)$ and $\lambda \in [0, 1]$,

$$g(\lambda\mathbf{x} + (1-\lambda)\mathbf{y}) \leq \lambda g(\mathbf{x}) + (1-\lambda)g(\mathbf{y}).$$

The latter inequality is the same as

$$f(\lambda\mathbf{x}+(1-\lambda)\mathbf{y}) \leq \lambda f(\mathbf{x})+(1-\lambda)f(\mathbf{y})+\frac{\sigma}{2}\left[\|\lambda\mathbf{x} + (1-\lambda)\mathbf{y}\|^2 - \lambda\|\mathbf{x}\|^2 - (1-\lambda)\|\mathbf{y}\|^2\right].$$
$$(5.14)$$

Now, using the identity (which holds since the norm is assumed to be Euclidean)

$$\|\lambda\mathbf{x} + (1-\lambda)\mathbf{y}\|^2 - \lambda\|\mathbf{x}\|^2 - (1-\lambda)\|\mathbf{y}\|^2 = -\lambda(1-\lambda)\|\mathbf{x} - \mathbf{y}\|^2,$$

combined with (5.14), we can conclude that the convexity of g is equivalent to the convexity of $\text{dom}(f)$ and the validity of the inequality

$$f(\lambda\mathbf{x} + (1-\lambda)\mathbf{y}) \leq \lambda f(\mathbf{x}) + (1-\lambda)f(\mathbf{y}) - \frac{\sigma}{2}\lambda(1-\lambda)\|\mathbf{x} - \mathbf{y}\|^2$$

for any $\mathbf{x}, \mathbf{y} \in \text{dom}(f)$ and $\lambda \in [0, 1]$, namely, to the σ-strong convexity of f. $\quad\square$

Remark 5.18. *The assumption that the underlying space is Euclidean is essential in Theorem 5.17. As an example, consider the negative entropy function over the unit simplex*

$$f(\mathbf{x}) \equiv \begin{cases} \sum_{i=1}^n x_i \log x_i, & \mathbf{x} \in \Delta_n, \\ \infty & else. \end{cases}$$

We will later show (in Example 5.27) that f is a 1-strongly convex function with respect to the l_1-norm. Regardless of this fact, note that the function

$$g(\mathbf{x}) = f(\mathbf{x}) - \alpha\|\mathbf{x}\|_1^2$$

is convex for any $\alpha > 0$ since over the domain of f, we have that $\|\mathbf{x}\|_1 = 1$. Obviously, it is impossible that a function will be α-strongly convex for any $\alpha > 0$. Therefore, the characterization of strong convexity in Theorem 5.17 is not correct for any norm.

Note that if a function f is σ_1-strongly convex ($\sigma_1 > 0$), then it is necessarily also σ_2-strongly convex for any $\sigma_2 \in (0, \sigma_1)$. An interesting problem is to find the largest possible strong convexity parameter of a given function.

Example 5.19 (strong convexity of quadratic functions). Suppose that $\mathbb{E} = \mathbb{R}^n$ is endowed with the l_2-norm, and consider the quadratic function $f : \mathbb{R}^n \to \mathbb{R}$ given by

$$f(\mathbf{x}) = \frac{1}{2}\mathbf{x}^T\mathbf{A}\mathbf{x} + \mathbf{b}^T\mathbf{x} + c,$$

where $\mathbf{A} \in \mathbb{S}^n$, $\mathbf{b} \in \mathbb{R}^n$, and $c \in \mathbb{R}$. Then by Theorem 5.17, f is strongly convex with parameter $\sigma > 0$ if and only if the function $\frac{1}{2}\mathbf{x}^T(\mathbf{A} - \sigma\mathbf{I})\mathbf{x}+\mathbf{b}^T\mathbf{x}+c$ is convex, which is equivalent to the matrix inequality $\mathbf{A} - \sigma\mathbf{I} \succeq \mathbf{0}$, namely, to the inequality $\lambda_{\min}(\mathbf{A}) \geq \sigma$. Thus, f is strongly convex if and only if $\mathbf{A}$ is positive definite, and in that case, $\lambda_{\min}(\mathbf{A})$ is its largest possible strong convexity parameter. ∎

A simple result is that the sum of a strongly convex function and a convex function is always a strongly convex function.

Lemma 5.20. *Let $f : \mathbb{E} \to (-\infty, \infty]$ be a σ-strongly convex function ($\sigma > 0$), and let $g : \mathbb{E} \to (-\infty, \infty]$ be convex. Then $f + g$ is σ-strongly convex.*

Proof. Follows directly from the definitions of strong convexity and convexity. Since f and g are convex, both $\mathrm{dom}(f)$ and $\mathrm{dom}(g)$ are convex sets, and hence also $\mathrm{dom}(f + g) = \mathrm{dom}(f) \cap \mathrm{dom}(g)$ is a convex set. Let $\mathbf{x}, \mathbf{y} \in \mathrm{dom}(f) \cap \mathrm{dom}(g)$ and $\lambda \in [0, 1]$. Then by the σ-strong convexity of f,

$$f(\lambda \mathbf{x} + (1 - \lambda)\mathbf{y}) \leq \lambda f(\mathbf{x}) + (1 - \lambda)f(\mathbf{y}) - \frac{\sigma}{2}\lambda(1 - \lambda)\|\mathbf{x} - \mathbf{y}\|^2.$$

Since g is convex,

$$g(\lambda \mathbf{x} + (1 - \lambda)\mathbf{y}) \leq \lambda g(\mathbf{x}) + (1 - \lambda)g(\mathbf{y}).$$

Adding the two inequalities, we obtain

$$(f + g)(\lambda \mathbf{x} + (1 - \lambda)\mathbf{y}) \leq \lambda(f + g)(\mathbf{x}) + (1 - \lambda)(f + g)(\mathbf{y}) - \frac{\sigma}{2}\lambda(1 - \lambda)\|\mathbf{x} - \mathbf{y}\|^2,$$

showing that $f + g$ is σ-strongly convex. $\square$

Example 5.21 (strong convexity of $\frac{1}{2}\|\cdot\|^2 + \delta_C$). Suppose that $\mathbb{E}$ is a Euclidean space, and let $C \subseteq \mathbb{E}$ be a nonempty convex set. The function $\frac{1}{2}\|\mathbf{x}\|^2$ is 1-strongly convex (Theorem 5.17), and by the convexity of C, δ_C is convex. Therefore, by Lemma 5.20, the function $\frac{1}{2}\|\mathbf{x}\|^2 + \delta_C(\mathbf{x})$ is 1-strongly convex. ∎

Theorem 5.24 below describes two properties that are equivalent to σ-strong convexity. The two properties are of a first-order nature in the sense that they are written in terms of the function and its subgradients. The proof uses the following version of the mean-value theorem for one-dimensional functions.

Lemma 5.22 (see [67, p. 26]). *Let $f : \mathbb{R} \to (-\infty, \infty]$ be a closed convex function, and let $[a, b] \subseteq \mathrm{dom}(f)(a < b)$. Then*

$$f(b) - f(a) = \int_a^b h(t)dt,$$

where $h : (a, b) \to \mathbb{R}$ satisfies $h(t) \in \partial f(t)$ for any $t \in (a, b)$.

Another technical lemma that is being used in the proof is the so-called line segment principle.

Lemma 5.23 (line segment principle [108, Theorem 6.1]). *Let C be a convex set. Suppose that $\mathbf{x} \in \mathrm{ri}(C), \mathbf{y} \in \mathrm{cl}(C)$, and let $\lambda \in (0, 1]$. Then $\lambda\mathbf{x} + (1 - \lambda)\mathbf{y} \in \mathrm{ri}(C)$.*

Theorem 5.24 (first-order characterizations of strong convexity). *Let $f : \mathbb{E} \to (-\infty, \infty]$ be a proper closed and convex function. Then for a given $\sigma > 0$, the following three claims are equivalent:*

(i) f is σ-strongly convex.

(ii)
$$f(\mathbf{y}) \geq f(\mathbf{x}) + \langle \mathbf{g}, \mathbf{y} - \mathbf{x} \rangle + \frac{\sigma}{2}\|\mathbf{y} - \mathbf{x}\|^2$$
for any $\mathbf{x} \in \text{dom}(\partial f), \mathbf{y} \in \text{dom}(f)$ and $\mathbf{g} \in \partial f(\mathbf{x})$.

(iii)
$$\langle \mathbf{g_x} - \mathbf{g_y}, \mathbf{x} - \mathbf{y} \rangle \geq \sigma\|\mathbf{x} - \mathbf{y}\|^2 \tag{5.15}$$
for any $\mathbf{x}, \mathbf{y} \in \text{dom}(\partial f)$, and $\mathbf{g_x} \in \partial f(\mathbf{x}), \mathbf{g_y} \in \partial f(\mathbf{y})$.

Proof. (ii) $\Rightarrow$ (i). Assume that (ii) is satisfied. To show (i), take $\mathbf{x}, \mathbf{y} \in \text{dom}(f)$ and $\lambda \in (0,1)$. Take some $\mathbf{z} \in \text{ri}(\text{dom}(f))$. Then for any $\alpha \in (0,1]$, by the line segment principle (Lemma 5.23), the vector $\tilde{\mathbf{x}} = (1-\alpha)\mathbf{x} + \alpha\mathbf{z}$ is in $\text{ri}(\text{dom}(f))$. At this point we fix α. Using the notation $\mathbf{x}_\lambda = \lambda\tilde{\mathbf{x}} + (1-\lambda)\mathbf{y}$, we obtain that $\mathbf{x}_\lambda \in \text{ri}(\text{dom}(f))$ for any $\lambda \in (0,1)$, and hence, by Theorem 3.18, $\partial f(\mathbf{x}_\lambda) \neq \emptyset$, meaning that $\mathbf{x}_\lambda \in \text{dom}(\partial f)$. Take $\mathbf{g} \in \partial f(\mathbf{x}_\lambda)$. Then by (ii),
$$f(\tilde{\mathbf{x}}) \geq f(\mathbf{x}_\lambda) + \langle \mathbf{g}, \tilde{\mathbf{x}} - \mathbf{x}_\lambda \rangle + \frac{\sigma}{2}\|\tilde{\mathbf{x}} - \mathbf{x}_\lambda\|^2,$$
which is the same as
$$f(\tilde{\mathbf{x}}) \geq f(\mathbf{x}_\lambda) + (1-\lambda)\langle \mathbf{g}, \tilde{\mathbf{x}} - \mathbf{y} \rangle + \frac{\sigma(1-\lambda)^2}{2}\|\mathbf{y} - \tilde{\mathbf{x}}\|^2. \tag{5.16}$$
Similarly,
$$f(\mathbf{y}) \geq f(\mathbf{x}_\lambda) + \lambda\langle \mathbf{g}, \mathbf{y} - \tilde{\mathbf{x}} \rangle + \frac{\sigma\lambda^2}{2}\|\mathbf{y} - \tilde{\mathbf{x}}\|^2. \tag{5.17}$$
Multiplying (5.16) by λ and (5.17) by $1-\lambda$ and adding the two resulting inequalities, we obtain that
$$f(\lambda\tilde{\mathbf{x}} + (1-\lambda)\mathbf{y}) \leq \lambda f(\tilde{\mathbf{x}}) + (1-\lambda)f(\mathbf{y}) - \frac{\sigma\lambda(1-\lambda)}{2}\|\tilde{\mathbf{x}} - \mathbf{y}\|^2.$$
Plugging the expression for $\tilde{\mathbf{x}}$ in the above inequality, we obtain that
$$g_1(\alpha) \leq \lambda g_2(\alpha) + (1-\lambda)f(\mathbf{y}) - \frac{\sigma\lambda(1-\lambda)}{2}\|(1-\alpha)\mathbf{x} + \alpha\mathbf{z} - \mathbf{y}\|^2, \tag{5.18}$$
where $g_1(\alpha) \equiv f(\lambda(1-\alpha)\mathbf{x} + (1-\lambda)\mathbf{y} + \lambda\alpha\mathbf{z})$ and $g_2(\alpha) \equiv f((1-\alpha)\mathbf{x} + \alpha\mathbf{z})$. The functions g_1 and g_2 are one-dimensional proper closed and convex functions, and consequently, by Theorem 2.22, they are also continuous over their domain. Thus, taking $\alpha \to 0^+$ in (5.18), it follows that
$$g_1(0) \leq \lambda g_2(0) + (1-\lambda)f(\mathbf{y}) - \frac{\sigma\lambda(1-\lambda)}{2}\|\mathbf{x} - \mathbf{y}\|^2.$$
Finally, since $g_1(0) = f(\lambda\mathbf{x} + (1-\lambda)\mathbf{y})$ and $g_2(0) = f(\mathbf{x})$, we obtain the inequality
$$f(\lambda\mathbf{x} + (1-\lambda)\mathbf{y}) \leq \lambda f(\mathbf{x}) + (1-\lambda)f(\mathbf{y}) - \frac{\sigma\lambda(1-\lambda)}{2}\|\mathbf{x} - \mathbf{y}\|^2,$$
establishing the σ-strong convexity of f.

(i) $\Rightarrow$ (iii). Assume that (i) is satisfied. Let $\mathbf{x}, \mathbf{y} \in \text{dom}(\partial f)$ and $\mathbf{g_x} \in \partial f(\mathbf{x}), \mathbf{g_y} \in \partial f(\mathbf{y})$. We will show that inequality (5.15) is satisfied. Let $\lambda \in [0, 1)$ and denote $\mathbf{x}_\lambda = \lambda \mathbf{x} + (1 - \lambda)\mathbf{y}$. By condition (i),

$$f(\mathbf{x}_\lambda) \leq \lambda f(\mathbf{x}) + (1 - \lambda)f(\mathbf{y}) - \frac{\sigma}{2}\lambda(1 - \lambda)\|\mathbf{x} - \mathbf{y}\|^2,$$

which is the same as

$$\frac{f(\mathbf{x}_\lambda) - f(\mathbf{x})}{1 - \lambda} \leq f(\mathbf{y}) - f(\mathbf{x}) - \frac{\sigma}{2}\lambda\|\mathbf{x} - \mathbf{y}\|^2. \tag{5.19}$$

Since $\mathbf{g_x} \in \partial f(\mathbf{x})$,

$$\frac{f(\mathbf{x}_\lambda) - f(\mathbf{x})}{1 - \lambda} \geq \frac{\langle \mathbf{g_x}, \mathbf{x}_\lambda - \mathbf{x} \rangle}{1 - \lambda} = \langle \mathbf{g_x}, \mathbf{y} - \mathbf{x} \rangle,$$

which, combined with (5.19), yields the inequality

$$\langle \mathbf{g_x}, \mathbf{y} - \mathbf{x} \rangle \leq f(\mathbf{y}) - f(\mathbf{x}) - \frac{\sigma\lambda}{2}\|\mathbf{x} - \mathbf{y}\|^2. \tag{5.20}$$

Inequality (5.20) holds for any $\lambda \in [0, 1)$. Taking the limit $\lambda \to 1^-$, we conclude that

$$\langle \mathbf{g_x}, \mathbf{y} - \mathbf{x} \rangle \leq f(\mathbf{y}) - f(\mathbf{x}) - \frac{\sigma}{2}\|\mathbf{x} - \mathbf{y}\|^2. \tag{5.21}$$

Changing the roles of $\mathbf{x}$ and $\mathbf{y}$ yields the inequality

$$\langle \mathbf{g_y}, \mathbf{x} - \mathbf{y} \rangle \leq f(\mathbf{x}) - f(\mathbf{y}) - \frac{\sigma}{2}\|\mathbf{x} - \mathbf{y}\|^2. \tag{5.22}$$

Adding inequalities (5.21) and (5.22), we can finally conclude that

$$\langle \mathbf{g_x} - \mathbf{g_y}, \mathbf{x} - \mathbf{y} \rangle \geq \sigma\|\mathbf{x} - \mathbf{y}\|^2,$$

which is the desired inequality.

(iii) $\Rightarrow$ (ii) Suppose that (iii) is satisfied, and let $\mathbf{x} \in \text{dom}(\partial f), \mathbf{y} \in \text{dom}(f)$, and $\mathbf{g} \in \partial f(\mathbf{x})$. Let $\mathbf{z}$ be any vector in $\text{ri}(\text{dom}(f))$, and define $\tilde{\mathbf{y}} = (1 - \alpha)\mathbf{y} + \alpha\mathbf{z}$ for some $\alpha \in (0, 1)$, which at this point we fix. By the line segment principle (Lemma 5.23), $\tilde{\mathbf{y}} \in \text{ri}(\text{dom}(f))$. Consider now the one-dimensional function

$$\varphi(\lambda) = f(\mathbf{x}_\lambda), \quad \lambda \in [0, 1],$$

where $\mathbf{x}_\lambda = (1 - \lambda)\mathbf{x} + \lambda\tilde{\mathbf{y}}$. For any $\lambda \in (0, 1)$, let $\mathbf{g}_\lambda \in \partial f(\mathbf{x}_\lambda)$ (whose existence is guaranteed since $\mathbf{x}_\lambda \in \text{ri}(\text{dom}(f))$ by the line segment principle). Then $\langle \mathbf{g}_\lambda, \tilde{\mathbf{y}} - \mathbf{x} \rangle \in \partial\varphi(\lambda)$, and hence by the mean-value theorem (Lemma 5.22),

$$f(\tilde{\mathbf{y}}) - f(\mathbf{x}) = \varphi(1) - \varphi(0) = \int_0^1 \langle \mathbf{g}_\lambda, \tilde{\mathbf{y}} - \mathbf{x} \rangle d\lambda. \tag{5.23}$$

Since $\mathbf{g} \in \partial f(\mathbf{x})$ and $\mathbf{g}_\lambda \in \partial f(\mathbf{x}_\lambda)$, by property (iii),

$$\langle \mathbf{g}_\lambda - \mathbf{g}, \mathbf{x}_\lambda - \mathbf{x} \rangle \geq \sigma\|\mathbf{x}_\lambda - \mathbf{x}\|^2,$$

which is equivalent to

$$\langle \mathbf{g}_\lambda, \tilde{\mathbf{y}} - \mathbf{x} \rangle \geq \langle \mathbf{g}, \tilde{\mathbf{y}} - \mathbf{x} \rangle + \sigma\lambda\|\tilde{\mathbf{y}} - \mathbf{x}\|^2.$$

Plugging the last inequality into (5.23), we obtain that

$$f(\tilde{\mathbf{y}}) - f(\mathbf{x}) \geq \int_0^1 \left[\langle \mathbf{g}, \tilde{\mathbf{y}} - \mathbf{x} \rangle + \sigma\lambda\|\tilde{\mathbf{y}} - \mathbf{x}\|^2 \right] d\lambda$$

$$= \langle \mathbf{g}, \tilde{\mathbf{y}} - \mathbf{x} \rangle + \frac{\sigma}{2}\|\tilde{\mathbf{y}} - \mathbf{x}\|^2.$$

Recalling the definition of $\tilde{\mathbf{y}}$, we obtain that for any $\alpha \in (0, 1)$,

$$f((1 - \alpha)\mathbf{y} + \alpha\mathbf{z}) \geq f(\mathbf{x}) + \langle \mathbf{g}, (1 - \alpha)\mathbf{y} + \alpha\mathbf{z} - \mathbf{x} \rangle + \frac{\sigma}{2}\|(1 - \alpha)\mathbf{y} + \alpha\mathbf{z} - \mathbf{x}\|^2.$$

Taking $\alpha \to 0^+$ and using the continuity of the one-dimensional function $\alpha \mapsto f((1 - \alpha)\mathbf{y} + \alpha\mathbf{z})$ over $[0, 1]$ (follows by invoking Theorem 2.22 and recalling that the one-dimensional function is closed and convex), we obtain the desired result

$$f(\mathbf{y}) \geq f(\mathbf{x}) + \langle \mathbf{g}, \mathbf{y} - \mathbf{x} \rangle + \frac{\sigma}{2}\|\mathbf{y} - \mathbf{x}\|^2. \qquad \square$$

The next theorem states that a proper closed and strongly convex function has a unique minimizer and that it satisfies a certain growth property around its minimizer.

Theorem 5.25 (existence and uniqueness of a minimizer of closed strongly convex functions). *Let $f : \mathbb{E} \to (-\infty, \infty]$ be a proper closed and σ-strongly convex function ($\sigma > 0$). Then*

(a) *f has a unique minimizer;*

(b) *$f(\mathbf{x}) - f(\mathbf{x}^*) \geq \frac{\sigma}{2}\|\mathbf{x} - \mathbf{x}^*\|^2$ for all $\mathbf{x} \in \mathrm{dom}(f)$, where $\mathbf{x}^*$ is the unique minimizer of f.*

Proof. (a) Since $\mathrm{dom}(f)$ is nonempty and convex, it follows that there exists $\mathbf{x}_0 \in \mathrm{ri}(\mathrm{dom}(f))$ (Theorem 3.17), and consequently, by Theorem 3.18, $\partial f(\mathbf{x}_0) \neq \emptyset$. Let $\mathbf{g} \in \partial f(\mathbf{x}_0)$. Then by the equivalence between σ-strong convexity and property (ii) of Theorem 5.24, it follows that

$$f(\mathbf{x}) \geq f(\mathbf{x}_0) + \langle \mathbf{g}, \mathbf{x} - \mathbf{x}_0 \rangle + \frac{\sigma}{2}\|\mathbf{x} - \mathbf{x}_0\|^2 \text{ for all } \mathbf{x} \in \mathbb{E}.$$

Since all norms in finite dimensional spaces are equivalent, there exists a constant $C > 0$ such that

$$\|\mathbf{y}\| \geq \sqrt{C}\|\mathbf{y}\|_a,$$

where $\|\cdot\|_a \equiv \sqrt{\langle \cdot, \cdot \rangle}$ denotes the Euclidean norm associated with the inner product of the space $\mathbb{E}$ (which might be different than the endowed norm $\|\cdot\|$). Therefore,

$$f(\mathbf{x}) \geq f(\mathbf{x}_0) + \langle \mathbf{g}, \mathbf{x} - \mathbf{x}_0 \rangle + \frac{C\sigma}{2}\|\mathbf{x} - \mathbf{x}_0\|_a^2 \text{ for any } \mathbf{x} \in \mathbb{E},$$

which is the same as

$$f(\mathbf{x}) \geq f(\mathbf{x}_0) - \frac{1}{2C\sigma}\|\mathbf{g}\|_a^2 + \frac{C\sigma}{2}\left\|\mathbf{x} - \left(\mathbf{x}_0 - \frac{1}{C\sigma}\mathbf{g}\right)\right\|_a^2 \text{ for any } \mathbf{x} \in \mathbb{E}.$$

In particular, it follows that

$$\mathrm{Lev}(f, f(\mathbf{x}_0)) \subseteq B_{\|\cdot\|_a}\left[\mathbf{x}_0 - \frac{1}{C\sigma}\mathbf{g}, \frac{1}{C\sigma}\|\mathbf{g}\|_a\right].$$

Since f is closed, the above level set is closed (Theorem 2.6), and since it is contained in a ball, it is also bounded. Therefore, $\mathrm{Lev}(f, f(\mathbf{x}_0))$ is compact. We can thus deduce that the optimal set of the problem of minimizing f over $\mathrm{dom}(f)$ is the same as the optimal set of the problem of minimizing f over the nonempty compact set $\mathrm{Lev}(f, f(\mathbf{x}_0))$. Invoking Weierstrass theorem for closed functions (Theorem 2.12), it follows that a minimizer exists. To show the uniqueness, assume that $\tilde{\mathbf{x}}$ and $\hat{\mathbf{x}}$ are minimizers of f. Then $f(\tilde{\mathbf{x}}) = f(\hat{\mathbf{x}}) = f_{\mathrm{opt}}$, where f_{opt} is the minimal value of f. Then by the definition of σ-strong convexity of f,

$$f_{\mathrm{opt}} \leq f\left(\frac{1}{2}\tilde{\mathbf{x}} + \frac{1}{2}\hat{\mathbf{x}}\right) \leq \frac{1}{2}f(\tilde{\mathbf{x}}) + \frac{1}{2}f(\hat{\mathbf{x}}) - \frac{\sigma}{8}\|\tilde{\mathbf{x}} - \hat{\mathbf{x}}\|^2 = f_{\mathrm{opt}} - \frac{\sigma}{8}\|\tilde{\mathbf{x}} - \hat{\mathbf{x}}\|^2,$$

implying that $\tilde{\mathbf{x}} = \hat{\mathbf{x}}$ and hence establishing the uniqueness of the minimizer of f.

(b) Let $\mathbf{x}^*$ be the unique minimizer of f. Then by Fermat's optimality condition (Theorem 3.63), $\mathbf{0} \in \partial f(\mathbf{x}^*)$ and hence by using the equivalence between σ-strong convexity and property (ii) of Theorem 5.24, it follows that

$$f(\mathbf{x}) - f(\mathbf{x}^*) \geq \langle \mathbf{0}, \mathbf{x} - \mathbf{x}^* \rangle + \frac{\sigma}{2}\|\mathbf{x} - \mathbf{x}^*\|^2 = \frac{\sigma}{2}\|\mathbf{x} - \mathbf{x}^*\|^2 \tag{5.24}$$

for any $\mathbf{x} \in \mathbb{E}$, establishing claim (b). $\square$

5.3 Smoothness and Strong Convexity Correspondence

5.3.1 The Conjugate Correspondence Theorem

An extremely useful connection between smoothness and strong convexity is given in the conjugate correspondence theorem that, loosely speaking, states that f is σ-strongly convex if and only if f^* is $\frac{1}{\sigma}$-smooth.

Theorem 5.26 (conjugate correspondence theorem). *Let $\sigma > 0$. Then*

(a) *If $f : \mathbb{E} \to \mathbb{R}$ is a $\frac{1}{\sigma}$-smooth convex function, then f^* is σ-strongly convex w.r.t. the dual norm $\|\cdot\|_*$.*

(b) *If $f : \mathbb{E} \to (-\infty, \infty]$ is a proper closed σ-strongly convex function, then $f^* : \mathbb{E}^* \to \mathbb{R}$ is $\frac{1}{\sigma}$-smooth.*

Proof. (a) Suppose that $f : \mathbb{E} \to \mathbb{R}$ is a $\frac{1}{\sigma}$-smooth convex function. To prove that f^* is σ-strongly convex, take $\mathbf{y}_1, \mathbf{y}_2 \in \mathrm{dom}(\partial f^*)$ and $\mathbf{v}_1 \in \partial f^*(\mathbf{y}_1), \mathbf{v}_2 \in \partial f^*(\mathbf{y}_2)$. Then by the conjugate subgradient theorem (Theorem 4.20), using also the properness closedness and convexity of f, it follows that $\mathbf{y}_1 \in \partial f(\mathbf{v}_1)$ and $\mathbf{y}_2 \in \partial f(\mathbf{v}_2)$, which, by the differentiability of f, implies that $\mathbf{y}_1 = \nabla f(\mathbf{v}_1)$ and $\mathbf{y}_2 = \nabla f(\mathbf{v}_2)$ (see Theorem 3.33). By the equivalence between properties (i) and (iv) in Theorem 5.8, we can write

$$\langle \mathbf{y}_1 - \mathbf{y}_2, \mathbf{v}_1 - \mathbf{v}_2 \rangle \geq \sigma \|\mathbf{y}_1 - \mathbf{y}_2\|_*^2.$$

Since the last inequality holds for any $\mathbf{y}_1, \mathbf{y}_2 \in \mathrm{dom}(\partial f^*)$ and $\mathbf{v}_1 \in \partial f^*(\mathbf{y}_1), \mathbf{v}_2 \in \partial f^*(\mathbf{y}_2)$, it follows by the equivalence between σ-strong convexity and property (iii) of Theorem 5.24 that f^* is a σ-strongly convex function.

(b) Suppose that f is a proper closed σ-strongly convex function. By the conjugate subgradient theorem (Corollary 4.21),

$$\partial f^*(\mathbf{y}) = \mathrm{argmax}_{\mathbf{x} \in \mathbb{E}}\{\langle \mathbf{x}, \mathbf{y} \rangle - f(\mathbf{x})\} \text{ for any } \mathbf{y} \in \mathbb{E}^*.$$

Thus, by the strong convexity and closedness of f, along with Theorem 5.25(a), it follows that $\partial f^*(\mathbf{y})$ is a singleton for any $\mathbf{y} \in \mathbb{E}^*$. Therefore, by Theorem 3.33, f^* is differentiable over the entire dual space $\mathbb{E}^*$. To show the $\frac{1}{\sigma}$-smoothness of f^*, take $\mathbf{y}_1, \mathbf{y}_2 \in \mathbb{E}^*$ and denote $\mathbf{v}_1 = \nabla f^*(\mathbf{y}_1), \mathbf{v}_2 = \nabla f^*(\mathbf{y}_2)$. These relations, by the conjugate subgradient theorem (Theorem 4.20), are equivalent to $\mathbf{y}_1 \in \partial f(\mathbf{v}_1), \mathbf{y}_2 \in \partial f(\mathbf{v}_2)$. Therefore, by Theorem 5.24 (equivalence between properties (i) and (iii)),

$$\langle \mathbf{y}_1 - \mathbf{y}_2, \mathbf{v}_1 - \mathbf{v}_2 \rangle \geq \sigma \|\mathbf{v}_1 - \mathbf{v}_2\|^2,$$

that is,

$$\langle \mathbf{y}_1 - \mathbf{y}_2, \nabla f^*(\mathbf{y}_1) - \nabla f^*(\mathbf{y}_2) \rangle \geq \sigma \|\nabla f^*(\mathbf{y}_1) - \nabla f^*(\mathbf{y}_2)\|^2,$$

which, combined with the generalized Cauchy–Schwarz inequality (Lemma 1.4), implies the inequality

$$\|\nabla f^*(\mathbf{y}_1) - \nabla f^*(\mathbf{y}_2)\| \leq \frac{1}{\sigma}\|\mathbf{y}_1 - \mathbf{y}_2\|_*,$$

proving the $\frac{1}{\sigma}$-smoothness of f^*. $\square$

5.3.2 Examples of Strongly Convex Functions

We can use the conjugate correspondence theorem (Theorem 5.26) to conclude results on the strong convexity of several important functions.

Example 5.27 (negative entropy over the unit simplex). Consider the function $f : \mathbb{R}^n \to (-\infty, \infty]$ given by

$$f(\mathbf{x}) = \begin{cases} \sum_{i=1}^n x_i \log x_i, & \mathbf{x} \in \Delta_n, \\ \infty & \text{else.} \end{cases}$$

Then, by Section 4.4.10, the conjugate of this function is the log-sum-exp function $f^*(\mathbf{y}) = \log\left(\sum_{i=1}^{n} e^{y_i}\right)$, which, by Example 5.15, is a 1-smooth function w.r.t. both the l_∞- and l_2-norms. Consequently, by the conjugate correspondence theorem, f is 1-strongly convex w.r.t. both the l_1- and l_2-norms. ∎

Example 5.28 (squared p-norm for $p \in (1, 2]$). Consider the function $f :$ $\mathbb{R}^n \to \mathbb{R}$ given by $f(\mathbf{x}) = \frac{1}{2}\|\mathbf{x}\|_p^2$ ($p \in (1, 2]$). Then, by Section 4.4.15, $f^*(\mathbf{y}) = \frac{1}{2}\|\mathbf{y}\|_q^2$, where $q \geq 2$ is determined by the relation $\frac{1}{p} + \frac{1}{q} = 1$. By Example 5.11, f^* is a $(q-1)$-smooth function w.r.t. the l_q-norm, which, by the conjugate correspondence theorem, implies that the function f is $\frac{1}{q-1}$-strongly convex w.r.t. the l_p-norm. Since $\frac{1}{q-1} = p - 1$, we conclude that f is $(p-1)$-strongly convex w.r.t. the l_p-norm. ∎

Example 5.29 (l_2 ball-pen function). Consider the ball-pen function $f : \mathbb{R}^n \to (-\infty, \infty]$ given by

$$f(\mathbf{x}) = \begin{cases} -\sqrt{1 - \|\mathbf{x}\|_2^2}, & \|\mathbf{x}\|_2 \leq 1, \\ \infty & \text{else.} \end{cases}$$

By Section 4.4.13, the conjugate of f is

$$f^*(\mathbf{y}) = \sqrt{\|\mathbf{y}\|_2^2 + 1},$$

which, by Example 5.14, is known to be 1-smooth w.r.t. the l_2-norm, and hence, by the conjugate correspondence theorem, f is 1-strongly convex w.r.t. the l_2-norm. ∎

The table below contains all the strongly convex functions described in this chapter.

$f(\mathbf{x})$	dom(f)	Strong convexity parameter	Norm	Reference
$\frac{1}{2}\mathbf{x}^T\mathbf{A}\mathbf{x} + 2\mathbf{b}^T\mathbf{x} + c$ ($\mathbf{A} \in \mathbb{S}_{++}^n, \mathbf{b} \in \mathbb{R}^n, c \in \mathbb{R}$)	$\mathbb{R}^n$	$\lambda_{\min}(\mathbf{A})$	l_2	Example 5.19
$\frac{1}{2}\|\mathbf{x}\|^2 + \delta_C(\mathbf{x})$ ($\emptyset \neq C \subseteq \mathbb{E}$ convex)	C	1	Euclidean	Example 5.21
$-\sqrt{1 - \|\mathbf{x}\|_2^2}$	$B_{\|\cdot\|_2}[0, 1]$	1	l_2	Example 5.29
$\frac{1}{2}\|\mathbf{x}\|_p^2$ ($p \in (1, 2]$)	$\mathbb{R}^n$	$p - 1$	l_p	Example 5.28
$\sum_{i=1}^{n} x_i \log x_i$	Δ_n	1	l_2 or l_1	Example 5.27

5.3.3 Smoothness and Differentiability of the Infimal Convolution

We will now show that under appropriate conditions, the infimal convolution of a convex function and an L-smooth convex function is also L-smooth; in addition, we will derive an expression for the gradient. The proof of the result is based on the conjugate correspondence theorem.

Theorem 5.30 (smoothness of the infimal convolution). *Let $f : \mathbb{E} \to (-\infty, \infty]$ be a proper closed and convex function, and let $\omega : \mathbb{E} \to \mathbb{R}$ be an L-smooth convex function. Assume that $f \square \omega$ is real-valued. Then the following hold:*

(a) *$f \square \omega$ is L-smooth.*

(b) *Let $\mathbf{x} \in \mathbb{E}$, and assume that $\mathbf{u}(\mathbf{x})$ is a minimizer of*

$$\min_{\mathbf{u}} \left\{ f(\mathbf{u}) + \omega(\mathbf{x} - \mathbf{u}) \right\}. \tag{5.25}$$

Then $\nabla(f \square \omega)(\mathbf{x}) = \nabla \omega(\mathbf{x} - \mathbf{u}(\mathbf{x}))$.

Proof. (a) By Theorem 4.19,

$$f \square \omega = (f^* + \omega^*)^*.$$

Since f and ω are proper closed and convex, then so are f^*, ω^* (Theorems 4.3, 4.5). In addition, by the conjugate correspondence theorem (Theorem 5.26), ω^* is $\frac{1}{L}$-strongly convex. Therefore, by Lemma 5.20, $f^* + \omega^*$ is $\frac{1}{L}$-strongly convex, and it is also closed as a sum of closed functions; we will prove that it is also proper. Indeed, by Theorem 4.16,

$$(f \square \omega)^* = f^* + \omega^*.$$

Since $f \square \omega$ is convex (by Theorem 2.19) and proper, it follows that $f^* + \omega^*$ is proper as a conjugate of a proper and convex function (Theorem 4.5). Thus, since $f^* + \omega^*$ is proper closed and $\frac{1}{L}$-strongly convex function, by the conjugate correspondence theorem, it follows that $f \square \omega = (f^* + \omega^*)^*$ is L-smooth.

(b) Let $\mathbf{x} \in \mathbb{E}$ be such that $\mathbf{u}(\mathbf{x})$ is a minimizer of (5.25), namely,

$$(f \square \omega)(\mathbf{x}) = f(\mathbf{u}(\mathbf{x})) + \omega(\mathbf{x} - \mathbf{u}(\mathbf{x})). \tag{5.26}$$

For convenience, define $\mathbf{z} \equiv \nabla \omega(\mathbf{x} - \mathbf{u}(\mathbf{x}))$. Our objective is to show that $\nabla(f \square \omega)(\mathbf{x}) = \mathbf{z}$. This means that we have to show that for any $\boldsymbol{\xi} \in \mathbb{E}$, $\lim_{\|\boldsymbol{\xi}\| \to 0} |\phi(\boldsymbol{\xi})|/\|\boldsymbol{\xi}\| = 0$, where $\phi(\boldsymbol{\xi}) \equiv (f \square \omega)(\mathbf{x} + \boldsymbol{\xi}) - (f \square \omega)(\mathbf{x}) - \langle \boldsymbol{\xi}, \mathbf{z} \rangle$. By the definition of the infimal convolution,

$$(f \square \omega)(\mathbf{x} + \boldsymbol{\xi}) \leq f(\mathbf{u}(\mathbf{x})) + \omega(\mathbf{x} + \boldsymbol{\xi} - \mathbf{u}(\mathbf{x})), \tag{5.27}$$

which, combined with (5.26), yields

$$\phi(\boldsymbol{\xi}) = (f\square\omega)(\mathbf{x}+\boldsymbol{\xi}) - (f\square\omega)(\mathbf{x}) - \langle\boldsymbol{\xi},\mathbf{z}\rangle$$

$$\leq \omega(\mathbf{x}+\boldsymbol{\xi}-\mathbf{u}(\mathbf{x})) - \omega(\mathbf{x}-\mathbf{u}(\mathbf{x})) - \langle\boldsymbol{\xi},\mathbf{z}\rangle \qquad [(5.26),(5.27)]$$

$$\leq \langle\boldsymbol{\xi},\nabla\omega(\mathbf{x}+\boldsymbol{\xi}-\mathbf{u}(\mathbf{x}))\rangle - \langle\boldsymbol{\xi},\mathbf{z}\rangle, \qquad [\text{gradient inequality for } \omega]$$

$$= \langle\boldsymbol{\xi},\nabla\omega(\mathbf{x}+\boldsymbol{\xi}-\mathbf{u}(\mathbf{x})) - \nabla\omega(\mathbf{x}-\mathbf{u}(\mathbf{x}))\rangle \qquad [\text{substitution of } \mathbf{z}]$$

$$\leq \|\boldsymbol{\xi}\| \cdot \|\nabla\omega(\mathbf{x}+\boldsymbol{\xi}-\mathbf{u}(\mathbf{x})) - \nabla\omega(\mathbf{x}-\mathbf{u}(\mathbf{x}))\|_* \qquad [\text{generalized Cauchy–Schwarz}]$$

$$\leq L\|\boldsymbol{\xi}\|^2. \qquad [L\text{-smoothness of } \omega]$$

To complete the proof, it is enough to show that we also have $\phi(\boldsymbol{\xi}) \geq -L\|\boldsymbol{\xi}\|^2$. Since $f\square\omega$ is convex, so is ϕ, which, along the fact that $\phi(\mathbf{0}) = 0$, implies that $\phi(\boldsymbol{\xi}) \geq -\phi(-\boldsymbol{\xi})$, and hence the desired result follows. $\square$

Example 5.31 (revisiting the 1-smoothness of $\frac{1}{2}d_C^2$). Suppose that $\mathbb{E}$ is a Euclidean space and let $C \subseteq \mathbb{E}$ be a nonempty closed and convex set. Consider the function $\varphi_C(\mathbf{x}) = \frac{1}{2}d_C^2(\mathbf{x})$. We have already shown in Example 5.5 that it is 1-smooth. We will provide here a second proof for this result, which is based on Theorem 5.30. Note that $\varphi_C = \delta_C \square h$, where $h(\mathbf{x}) = \frac{1}{2}\|\mathbf{x}\|^2$. Since h is a real-valued 1-smooth convex function, and since δ_C is proper closed and convex, it follows by Theorem 5.30 that φ_C is 1-smooth. $\blacksquare$

Chapter 6

The Proximal Operator

> **Underlying Space:** In this chapter $\mathbb{E}$ is a Euclidean space, meaning a finite dimensional space endowed with an inner product $\langle \cdot, \cdot \rangle$ and the Euclidean norm $\| \cdot \| = \sqrt{\langle \cdot, \cdot \rangle}$.

This chapter is devoted to the study of the proximal mapping, which will be fundamental in many of the algorithms that will be explored later in the book. The operator and its properties were first studied by Moreau, and hence it is also referred to as "Moreau's proximal mapping."

6.1 Definition, Existence, and Uniqueness

Definition 6.1 (proximal mapping). *Given a function $f : \mathbb{E} \to (-\infty, \infty]$, the* **proximal mapping** *of f is the operator given by*

$$\operatorname{prox}_f(\mathbf{x}) = \operatorname{argmin}_{\mathbf{u} \in \mathbb{E}} \left\{ f(\mathbf{u}) + \frac{1}{2} \|\mathbf{u} - \mathbf{x}\|^2 \right\} \quad \text{for any } \mathbf{x} \in \mathbb{E}.$$

We will often use the term "prox" instead of "proximal." The mapping prox_f takes a vector $\mathbf{x} \in \mathbb{E}$ and maps it into a subset of $\mathbb{E}$, which might be empty, a singleton, or a set with multiple vectors as the following example illustrates.

Example 6.2. Consider the following three functions from $\mathbb{R}$ to $\mathbb{R}$:

$$g_1(x) \equiv 0,$$

$$g_2(x) = \begin{cases} 0, & x \neq 0, \\ -\lambda, & x = 0, \end{cases}$$

$$g_3(x) = \begin{cases} 0, & x \neq 0, \\ \lambda, & x = 0, \end{cases}$$

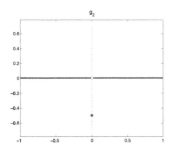
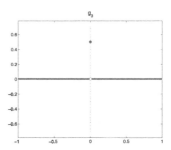

Figure 6.1. *The left and right images are the plots of the functions g_2 and g_3, respectively, with $\lambda = 0.5$ from Example 6.2.*

where $\lambda > 0$ is a given constant. The plots of the noncontinuous functions g_2 and g_3 are given in Figure 6.1. The prox of g_1 can computed as follows:

$$\mathrm{prox}_{g_1}(x) = \mathrm{argmin}_{u\in\mathbb{R}}\left\{g_1(u) + \frac{1}{2}(u-x)^2\right\} = \mathrm{argmin}_{u\in\mathbb{R}}\left\{\frac{1}{2}(u-x)^2\right\} = \{x\}.$$

To compute the prox of g_2, note that $\mathrm{prox}_{g_2}(x) = \mathrm{argmin}_{u\in\mathbb{R}}\tilde{g}_2(u,x)$, where

$$\tilde{g}_2(u,x) \equiv g_2(u) + \frac{1}{2}(u-x)^2 = \begin{cases} -\lambda + \frac{x^2}{2}, & u = 0, \\ \frac{1}{2}(u-x)^2, & u \neq 0. \end{cases}$$

For $x \neq 0$, the minimum of $\frac{1}{2}(u-x)^2$ over $\mathbb{R}\setminus\{0\}$ is attained at $u = x(\neq 0)$ with a minimal value of 0. Therefore, in this case, if $0 > -\lambda + \frac{x^2}{2}$, then the unique minimizer of $\tilde{g}_2(\cdot,x)$ is $u = 0$, and if $0 < -\lambda + \frac{x^2}{2}$, then $u = x$ is the unique minimizer of $\tilde{g}_2(\cdot,x)$; finally, if $0 = -\lambda + \frac{x^2}{2}$, then 0 and x are the two minimizers $\tilde{g}_2(\cdot,x)$. When $x = 0$, the minimizer of $\tilde{g}_2(\cdot,0)$ is $u = 0$. To conclude,

$$\mathrm{prox}_{g_2}(x) = \begin{cases} \{0\}, & |x| < \sqrt{2\lambda}, \\ \{x\}, & |x| > \sqrt{2\lambda}, \\ \{0,x\}, & |x| = \sqrt{2\lambda}. \end{cases}$$

Similar arguments show that

$$\mathrm{prox}_{g_3}(x) = \begin{cases} \{x\}, & x \neq 0, \\ \emptyset, & x = 0. \quad\blacksquare \end{cases}$$

The next theorem, called the *first prox theorem*, states that if f is proper closed and convex, then $\mathrm{prox}_f(\mathbf{x})$ is always a singleton, meaning that the prox exists and is unique. This is the reason why in the last example only g_1, which was proper closed and convex, had a unique prox at any point.

Theorem 6.3 (first prox theorem). *Let $f : \mathbb{E} \to (-\infty, \infty]$ be a proper closed and convex function. Then $\mathrm{prox}_f(\mathbf{x})$ is a singleton for any $\mathbf{x} \in \mathbb{E}$.*

Proof. For any $\mathbf{x} \in \mathbb{E}$,

$$\mathrm{prox}_f(\mathbf{x}) = \mathrm{argmin}_{\mathbf{u} \in \mathbb{E}} \tilde{f}(\mathbf{u}, \mathbf{x}), \tag{6.1}$$

where $\tilde{f}(\mathbf{u}, \mathbf{x}) \equiv f(\mathbf{u}) + \frac{1}{2}\|\mathbf{u} - \mathbf{x}\|^2$. The function $\tilde{f}(\cdot, \mathbf{x})$ is a closed and strongly convex function as a sum of the closed and strongly convex function $\frac{1}{2}\|\cdot -\mathbf{x}\|^2$ and the closed and convex function f (see Lemma 5.20 and Theorem 2.7(b)). The properness of $\tilde{f}(\cdot, \mathbf{x})$ immediately follows from the properness of f. Therefore, by Theorem 5.25(a), there exists a unique minimizer to the problem in (6.1). $\qquad\square$

When f is proper closed and convex, the last result shows that $\mathrm{prox}_f(\mathbf{x})$ is a singleton for any $\mathbf{x} \in \mathbb{E}$. In these cases, which will constitute the vast majority of cases that will be discussed in this chapter, we will treat prox_f as a single-valued mapping from $\mathbb{E}$ to $\mathbb{E}$, meaning that we will write $\mathrm{prox}_f(\mathbf{x}) = \mathbf{y}$ and not $\mathrm{prox}_f(\mathbf{x}) = \{\mathbf{y}\}$.

If we relax the assumptions in the first prox theorem and only require closedness of the function, then it is possible to show under some coerciveness assumptions that $\mathrm{prox}_f(\mathbf{x})$ is never an empty set.

Theorem 6.4 (nonemptiness of the prox under closedness and coerciveness). *Let $f : \mathbb{E} \to (-\infty, \infty]$ be a proper closed function, and assume that the following condition is satisfied:*

$$\text{the function } \mathbf{u} \mapsto f(\mathbf{u}) + \frac{1}{2}\|\mathbf{u} - \mathbf{x}\|^2 \text{ is coercive for any } \mathbf{x} \in \mathbb{E}. \tag{6.2}$$

Then $\mathrm{prox}_f(\mathbf{x})$ is nonempty for any $\mathbf{x} \in \mathbb{E}$.

Proof. For any $\mathbf{x} \in \mathbb{E}$, the proper function $h(\mathbf{u}) \equiv f(\mathbf{u}) + \frac{1}{2}\|\mathbf{u} - \mathbf{x}\|^2$ is closed as a sum of two closed functions. Since by the premise of the theorem it is also coercive, it follows by Theorem 2.14 (with $S = \mathbb{E}$) that $\mathrm{prox}_f(\mathbf{x})$, which consists of the minimizers of h, is nonempty. $\qquad\square$

Example 6.2 actually gave an illustration of Theorem 6.4 since although both g_2 and g_3 satisfy the coercivity assumption (6.2), only g_2 was closed, and thus the fact that $\mathrm{prox}_{g_3}(x)$ was empty for a certain value of x, as opposed to $\mathrm{prox}_{g_2}(x)$, which was never empty, is not surprising.

6.2   First Set of Examples of Proximal Mappings

Equipped just with the definition of the proximal mapping, we will now compute the proximal mapping of several proper closed and convex functions.

6.2.1   Constant

If $f \equiv c$ for some $c \in \mathbb{R}$, then

$$\text{prox}_f(\mathbf{x}) = \text{argmin}_{\mathbf{u} \in \mathbb{E}} \left\{ c + \frac{1}{2}\|\mathbf{u} - \mathbf{x}\|^2 \right\} = \mathbf{x}.$$

Therefore,

$$\text{prox}_f(\mathbf{x}) = \mathbf{x}$$

is the identity mapping.

6.2.2   Affine

Let $f(\mathbf{x}) = \langle \mathbf{a}, \mathbf{x} \rangle + b$, where $\mathbf{a} \in \mathbb{E}$ and $b \in \mathbb{R}$. Then

$$\begin{aligned} \text{prox}_f(\mathbf{x}) &= \text{argmin}_{\mathbf{u} \in \mathbb{E}} \left\{ \langle \mathbf{a}, \mathbf{u} \rangle + b + \frac{1}{2}\|\mathbf{u} - \mathbf{x}\|^2 \right\} \\ &= \text{argmin}_{\mathbf{u} \in \mathbb{E}} \left\{ \langle \mathbf{a}, \mathbf{x} \rangle + b - \frac{1}{2}\|\mathbf{a}\|^2 + \frac{1}{2}\|\mathbf{u} - (\mathbf{x} - \mathbf{a})\|^2 \right\} \\ &= \mathbf{x} - \mathbf{a}. \end{aligned}$$

Therefore,

$$\text{prox}_f(\mathbf{x}) = \mathbf{x} - \mathbf{a}$$

is a translation mapping.

6.2.3   Convex Quadratic

Let $f : \mathbb{R}^n \to \mathbb{R}$ be given by $f(\mathbf{x}) = \frac{1}{2}\mathbf{x}^T\mathbf{A}\mathbf{x} + \mathbf{b}^T\mathbf{x} + c$, where $\mathbf{A} \in \mathbb{S}_+^n, \mathbf{b} \in \mathbb{R}^n$, and $c \in \mathbb{R}$. The vector $\text{prox}_f(\mathbf{x})$ is the minimizer of the problem

$$\min_{\mathbf{u} \in \mathbb{E}} \left\{ \frac{1}{2}\mathbf{u}^T\mathbf{A}\mathbf{u} + \mathbf{b}^T\mathbf{u} + c + \frac{1}{2}\|\mathbf{u} - \mathbf{x}\|^2 \right\}.$$

The optimal solution of the last problem is attained when the gradient of the objective function vanishes:

$$\mathbf{A}\mathbf{u} + \mathbf{b} + \mathbf{u} - \mathbf{x} = \mathbf{0},$$

that is, when

$$(\mathbf{A} + \mathbf{I})\mathbf{u} = \mathbf{x} - \mathbf{b},$$

and hence

$$\text{prox}_f(\mathbf{x}) = (\mathbf{A} + \mathbf{I})^{-1}(\mathbf{x} - \mathbf{b}).$$

6.2.4   One-Dimensional Examples

The following lemma contains several prox computations of one-dimensional functions.

Lemma 6.5. *The following are pairs of proper closed and convex functions and their prox mappings:*

$$g_1(x) = \begin{cases} \mu x, & x \geq 0, \\ \infty, & x < 0, \end{cases} \qquad \mathrm{prox}_{g_1}(x) = [x - \mu]_+,$$

$$g_2(x) = \lambda|x|, \qquad \mathrm{prox}_{g_2}(x) = [|x| - \lambda]_+ \mathrm{sgn}(x),$$

$$g_3(x) = \begin{cases} \lambda x^3, & x \geq 0, \\ \infty, & x < 0, \end{cases} \qquad \mathrm{prox}_{g_3}(x) = \frac{-1+\sqrt{1+12\lambda[x]_+}}{6\lambda},$$

$$g_4(x) = \begin{cases} -\lambda \log x, & x > 0, \\ \infty, & x \leq 0, \end{cases} \qquad \mathrm{prox}_{g_4}(x) = \frac{x+\sqrt{x^2+4\lambda}}{2},$$

$$g_5(x) = \delta_{[0,\eta]\cap\mathbb{R}}(x), \qquad \mathrm{prox}_{g_5}(x) = \min\{\max\{x,0\},\eta\},$$

where $\lambda \in \mathbb{R}_+, \eta \in [0,\infty],$ *and* $\mu \in \mathbb{R}$.

Proof. The proofs repeatedly use the following trivial arguments: (i) if $f'(u) = 0$ for a convex function f, then u must be one of its minimizers; (ii) if a minimizer of a convex function exists and is *not* attained at any point of differentiability, then it must be attained at a point of nondifferentiability.

[prox of g_1] By definition, $\mathrm{prox}_{g_1}(x)$ is the minimizer of the function

$$f(u) = \begin{cases} \infty, & u < 0, \\ f_1(u), & u \geq 0, \end{cases}$$

where $f_1(u) = \mu u + \frac{1}{2}(u-x)^2$. First note that $f_1'(u) = 0$ if and only if $u = x - \mu$. If $x > \mu$, then $f'(x-\mu) = f_1'(x-\mu) = 0$, implying that in this case $\mathrm{prox}_{g_1}(x) = x - \mu$. Otherwise, if $x \leq \mu$, the minimizer of f is not attained at a point of differentiability, meaning that it has to be attained at 0, which is the only point of nondifferentiability in the domain of f, so that $\mathrm{prox}_{g_1}(x) = 0$.

[prox of g_2] $\mathrm{prox}_{g_2}(x)$ is the minimizer of the function

$$h(u) = \begin{cases} h_1(u) \equiv \lambda u + \frac{1}{2}(u-x)^2, & u > 0, \\ h_2(u) \equiv -\lambda u + \frac{1}{2}(u-x)^2, & u \leq 0. \end{cases}$$

If the minimizer is attained at $u > 0$, then $0 = h_1'(u) = \lambda + u - x$, meaning that $u = x - \lambda$. Therefore, if $x > \lambda$, then $\mathrm{prox}_{g_2}(x) = x - \lambda$. The same argument shows that if $x < -\lambda$, then $\mathrm{prox}_{g_2}(x) = x + \lambda$. If $|x| \leq \lambda$, then $\mathrm{prox}_{g_2}(x)$ must be the only point of nondifferentiability of h, namely, 0.

[prox of g_3] $\text{prox}_{g_3}(x)$ is the minimizer of the function

$$s(u) = \begin{cases} \lambda u^3 + \frac{1}{2}(u - x)^2, & u \geq 0, \\ \infty, & u < 0. \end{cases}$$

If the minimizer is positive, then $\tilde{u} = \text{prox}_{g_3}(x)$ satisfies $s'(\tilde{u}) = 0$, that is,

$$3\lambda\tilde{u}^2 + \tilde{u} - x = 0.$$

The above equation has a positive root if and only if $x > 0$, and in this case the (unique) positive root is $\text{prox}_{g_3}(x) = \tilde{u} = \frac{-1+\sqrt{1+12\lambda x}}{6\lambda}$. If $x \leq 0$, the minimizer of s is attained at the only point of nondifferentiability of s in its domain, that is, at 0.

[prox of g_4] $\tilde{u} = \text{prox}_{g_4}(x)$ is a minimizer over $\mathbb{R}_{++}$ of

$$t(u) = -\lambda \log u + \frac{1}{2}(u - x)^2,$$

which is determined by the condition that the derivative vanishes:

$$-\frac{\lambda}{\tilde{u}} + (\tilde{u} - x) = 0,$$

that is,

$$\tilde{u}^2 - \tilde{u}x - \lambda = 0.$$

Therefore (taking the positive root),

$$\text{prox}_{g_4}(x) = \tilde{u} = \frac{x + \sqrt{x^2 + 4\lambda}}{2}.$$

[prox of g_5] We will first assume that $\eta < \infty$. Note that $\tilde{u} = \text{prox}_{g_5}(x)$ is the minimizer of

$$w(u) = \frac{1}{2}(u - x)^2$$

over $[0, \eta]$. The minimizer of w over $\mathbb{R}$ is $u = x$. Therefore, if $0 \leq x \leq \eta$, then $\tilde{u} = x$. If $x < 0$, then w is increasing over $[0, \eta]$, and hence $\tilde{u} = 0$. Finally, if $x > \eta$, then w is decreasing over $[0, \eta]$, and thus $\tilde{u} = \eta$. To conclude,

$$\text{prox}_{g_5}(x) = \tilde{u} = \begin{cases} x, & 0 \leq x \leq \eta, \\ 0, & x < 0, \\ \eta, & x > \eta, \end{cases} = \min\{\max\{x, 0\}, \eta\}.$$

For $\eta = \infty$, $g_5(x) = \delta_{[0,\infty)}(x)$, and in this case, g_5 is identical to g_1 with $\mu = 0$, implying that $\text{prox}_{g_5}(x) = [x]_+$, which can also be written as

$$\text{prox}_{g_5}(x) = \min\{\max\{x, 0\}, \infty\}. \quad \square$$

6.3   Prox Calculus Rules

In this section we gather several important results on the calculus of proximal mappings. Note that some of the results do not require any convexity/closedness assumptions.

Theorem 6.6 (prox of separable functions). *Suppose that* $f : \mathbb{E}_1 \times \mathbb{E}_2 \times \cdots \times \mathbb{E}_m \to (-\infty, \infty]$ *is given by*

$$f(\mathbf{x}_1, \mathbf{x}_2, \ldots, \mathbf{x}_m) = \sum_{i=1}^{m} f_i(\mathbf{x}_i) \text{ for any } \mathbf{x}_i \in \mathbb{E}_i, \quad i = 1, 2, \ldots, m.$$

Then for any $\mathbf{x}_1 \in \mathbb{E}_1, \mathbf{x}_2 \in \mathbb{E}_2, \ldots, \mathbf{x}_m \in \mathbb{E}_m,$

$$\text{prox}_f(\mathbf{x}_1, \mathbf{x}_2, \ldots, \mathbf{x}_m) = \text{prox}_{f_1}(\mathbf{x}_1) \times \text{prox}_{f_2}(\mathbf{x}_2) \times \cdots \times \text{prox}_{f_m}(\mathbf{x}_m). \quad (6.3)$$

Proof. Formula (6.3) is a result of the following chain of equalities:

$$\text{prox}_f(\mathbf{x}_1, \mathbf{x}_2, \ldots, \mathbf{x}_m) = \text{argmin}_{\mathbf{y}_1, \mathbf{y}_2, \ldots, \mathbf{y}_m} \sum_{i=1}^{m} \left[\frac{1}{2} \|\mathbf{y}_i - \mathbf{x}_i\|^2 + f_i(\mathbf{y}_i) \right]$$

$$= \prod_{i=1}^{m} \text{argmin}_{\mathbf{y}_i} \left[\frac{1}{2} \|\mathbf{y}_i - \mathbf{x}_i\|^2 + f_i(\mathbf{y}_i) \right]$$

$$= \prod_{i=1}^{m} \text{prox}_{f_i}(\mathbf{x}_i). \quad \square$$

Remark 6.7. *If* $f : \mathbb{R}^n \to \mathbb{R}$ *is proper closed convex and separable,*

$$f(\mathbf{x}) = \sum_{i=1}^{n} f_i(x_i),$$

with f_i *being proper closed and convex univariate functions, then the result of Theorem 6.6 can be rewritten as*

$$\text{prox}_f(\mathbf{x}) = (\text{prox}_{f_i}(x_i))_{i=1}^{n}.$$

Example 6.8 (l_1-norm). Suppose that $g : \mathbb{R}^n \to \mathbb{R}$ is given by $g(\mathbf{x}) = \lambda \|\mathbf{x}\|_1$, where $\lambda > 0$. Then

$$g(\mathbf{x}) = \sum_{i=1}^{n} \varphi(x_i), \quad (6.4)$$

where $\varphi(t) = \lambda |t|$. By Lemma 6.5 (computation of prox_{g_2}), $\text{prox}_\varphi(s) = \mathcal{T}_\lambda(s)$, where $\mathcal{T}_\lambda$ is defined as

$$\mathcal{T}_\lambda(y) = [|y| - \lambda]_+ \text{sgn}(y) = \begin{cases} y - \lambda, & y \geq \lambda, \\ 0, & |y| < \lambda, \\ y + \lambda, & y \leq -\lambda. \end{cases}$$

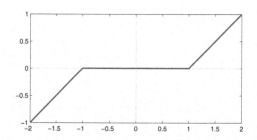

Figure 6.2. *The soft thresholding function* $\mathcal{T}_1$.

The function $\mathcal{T}_\lambda$ is called the *soft thresholding* function, and its description is given in Figure 6.2.

By Theorem 6.6,

$$\text{prox}_g(\mathbf{x}) = (\mathcal{T}_\lambda(x_j))_{j=1}^n.$$

We will expand the definition of the soft thresholding function for vectors by applying it componentwise, that is, for any $\mathbf{x} \in \mathbb{R}^n$,

$$\mathcal{T}_\lambda(\mathbf{x}) \equiv (\mathcal{T}_\lambda(x_j))_{j=1}^n = [|\mathbf{x}| - \lambda \mathbf{e}]_+ \odot \text{sgn}(\mathbf{x}).$$

In this notation,

$$\text{prox}_g(\mathbf{x}) = \mathcal{T}_\lambda(\mathbf{x}).$$

∎

Example 6.9 (negative sum of logs). Let $g : \mathbb{R}^n \to (-\infty, \infty]$ be given by

$$g(\mathbf{x}) = \begin{cases} -\lambda \sum_{j=1}^n \log x_j, & \mathbf{x} > \mathbf{0}, \\ \infty & \text{else}, \end{cases}$$

where $\lambda > 0$. Then $g(\mathbf{x}) = \sum_{i=1}^n \varphi(x_i)$, where

$$\varphi(t) = \begin{cases} -\lambda \log t, & t > 0, \\ \infty, & t < 0. \end{cases}$$

By Lemma 6.5 (computation of prox_{g_4}),

$$\text{prox}_\varphi(s) = \frac{s + \sqrt{s^2 + 4\lambda}}{2}.$$

Thus, by Theorem 6.6,

$$\text{prox}_g(\mathbf{x}) = (\text{prox}_\varphi(x_j))_{j=1}^n = \left(\frac{x_j + \sqrt{x_j^2 + 4\lambda}}{2} \right)_{j=1}^n.$$

∎

Example 6.10 (l_0-norm). Let $f : \mathbb{R}^n \to \mathbb{R}$ be given by $f(\mathbf{x}) = \lambda\|\mathbf{x}\|_0$, where $\lambda > 0$ and $\|\mathbf{x}\|_0 = \#\{i : x_i \neq 0\}$ is the l_0-norm discussed in Example 2.11. For any $\mathbf{x} \in \mathbb{R}^n$,

$$f(\mathbf{x}) = \sum_{i=1}^n I(x_i),$$

where

$$I(t) = \begin{cases} \lambda, & t \neq 0, \\ 0, & t = 0. \end{cases}$$

Note that $I(\cdot) = J(\cdot) + \lambda$, where

$$J(t) = \begin{cases} 0, & t \neq 0, \\ -\lambda, & t = 0, \end{cases}$$

and that by Example 6.2,

$$\text{prox}_J(s) = \begin{cases} \{0\}, & |s| < \sqrt{2\lambda}, \\ \{s\}, & |s| > \sqrt{2\lambda}, \\ \{0, s\}, & |s| = \sqrt{2\lambda}. \end{cases} \tag{6.5}$$

We can write the above as $\text{prox}_J(s) = \mathcal{H}_{\sqrt{2\lambda}}(s)$, where $\mathcal{H}_\alpha$ is the so-called *hard thresholding* operator defined by

$$\mathcal{H}_\alpha(s) \equiv \begin{cases} \{0\}, & |s| < \alpha, \\ \{s\}, & |s| > \alpha, \\ \{0, s\}, & |s| = \alpha. \end{cases}$$

The operators prox_J and prox_I are the same since for any $s \in \mathbb{R}$,

$$\text{prox}_I(s) = \text{argmin}_t \left\{ I(t) + \frac{1}{2}(t - s)^2 \right\}$$

$$= \text{argmin}_t \left\{ J(t) + \lambda + \frac{1}{2}(t - s)^2 \right\}$$

$$= \text{argmin}_t \left\{ J(t) + \frac{1}{2}(t - s)^2 \right\}$$

$$= \text{prox}_J(s).$$

Thus, invoking Theorem 6.6, it follows that[27]

$$\text{prox}_g(\mathbf{x}) = \mathcal{H}_{\sqrt{2\lambda}}(x_1) \times \mathcal{H}_{\sqrt{2\lambda}}(x_2) \times \cdots \times \mathcal{H}_{\sqrt{2\lambda}}(x_n).$$

∎

Theorem 6.11 (scaling and translation). *Let* $g : \mathbb{E} \to (-\infty, \infty]$ *be a proper function. Let* $\lambda \neq 0$ *and* $\mathbf{a} \in \mathbb{E}$*. Define* $f(\mathbf{x}) = g(\lambda\mathbf{x} + \mathbf{a})$*. Then*

$$\text{prox}_f(\mathbf{x}) = \frac{1}{\lambda} \left[\text{prox}_{\lambda^2 g}(\lambda\mathbf{x} + \mathbf{a}) - \mathbf{a} \right]. \tag{6.6}$$

Proof. By definition of the prox,

$$\text{prox}_f(\mathbf{x}) = \text{argmin}_\mathbf{u} \left\{ f(\mathbf{u}) + \frac{1}{2}\|\mathbf{u} - \mathbf{x}\|^2 \right\}$$

$$= \text{argmin}_\mathbf{u} \left\{ g(\lambda\mathbf{u} + \mathbf{a}) + \frac{1}{2}\|\mathbf{u} - \mathbf{x}\|^2 \right\}. \tag{6.7}$$

Making the change of variables

$$\mathbf{z} = \lambda\mathbf{u} + \mathbf{a}, \tag{6.8}$$

the objective function in the minimization problem (6.7) becomes

$$g(\mathbf{z}) + \frac{1}{2}\left\| \frac{1}{\lambda}(\mathbf{z} - \mathbf{a}) - \mathbf{x} \right\|^2 = \frac{1}{\lambda^2}\left[\lambda^2 g(\mathbf{z}) + \frac{1}{2}\|\mathbf{z} - (\lambda\mathbf{x} + \mathbf{a})\|^2 \right]. \tag{6.9}$$

The minimizer of (6.9) is $\mathbf{z} = \text{prox}_{\lambda^2 g}(\lambda\mathbf{x} + \mathbf{a})$, and hence by (6.8), it follows that (6.6) holds. □

Theorem 6.12 (prox of $\lambda g(\cdot/\lambda)$**).** *Let* $g : \mathbb{E} \to (-\infty, \infty]$ *be proper, and let* $\lambda > 0$*. Define* $f(\mathbf{x}) = \lambda g(\mathbf{x}/\lambda)$*. Then*

$$\text{prox}_f(\mathbf{x}) = \lambda\text{prox}_{g/\lambda}(\mathbf{x}/\lambda).$$

Proof. Note that

$$\text{prox}_f(\mathbf{x}) = \text{argmin}_\mathbf{u} \left\{ f(\mathbf{u}) + \frac{1}{2}\|\mathbf{u} - \mathbf{x}\|^2 \right\} = \text{argmin}_\mathbf{u} \left\{ \lambda g\left(\frac{\mathbf{u}}{\lambda} \right) + \frac{1}{2}\|\mathbf{u} - \mathbf{x}\|^2 \right\}.$$

---

[27]Actually, $\text{prox}_g(\mathbf{x})$ should be a subset of $\mathbb{R}^n$, meaning the space of n-length *column* vectors, but here we practice some abuse of notation and represent $\text{prox}_g(\mathbf{x})$ as a set of n-length *row* vectors.

Making the change of variables $\mathbf{z} = \frac{\mathbf{u}}{\lambda}$, we can continue to write

$$
\begin{aligned}
\operatorname{prox}_f(\mathbf{x}) &= \lambda \operatorname{argmin}_{\mathbf{z}} \left\{ \lambda g(\mathbf{z}) + \frac{1}{2} \|\lambda \mathbf{z} - \mathbf{x}\|^2 \right\} \\
&= \lambda \operatorname{argmin}_{\mathbf{z}} \left\{ \lambda^2 \left[\frac{g(\mathbf{z})}{\lambda} + \frac{1}{2} \left\| \mathbf{z} - \frac{\mathbf{x}}{\lambda} \right\|^2 \right] \right\} \\
&= \lambda \operatorname{argmin}_{\mathbf{z}} \left\{ \frac{g(\mathbf{z})}{\lambda} + \frac{1}{2} \left\| \mathbf{z} - \frac{\mathbf{x}}{\lambda} \right\|^2 \right\} \\
&= \lambda \operatorname{prox}_{g/\lambda}(\mathbf{x}/\lambda). \quad \square
\end{aligned}
$$

Theorem 6.13 (quadratic perturbation). *Let $g : \mathbb{E} \to (-\infty, \infty]$ be proper, and let $f(\mathbf{x}) = g(\mathbf{x}) + \frac{c}{2}\|\mathbf{x}\|^2 + \langle \mathbf{a}, \mathbf{x} \rangle + \gamma$, where $c \geq 0, \mathbf{a} \in \mathbb{E}$, and $\gamma \in \mathbb{R}$. Then*

$$
\operatorname{prox}_f(\mathbf{x}) = \operatorname{prox}_{\frac{1}{c+1}g} \left(\frac{\mathbf{x} - \mathbf{a}}{c+1} \right).
$$

Proof. Follows by the following simple computation:

$$
\begin{aligned}
\operatorname{prox}_f(\mathbf{x}) &= \operatorname{argmin}_{\mathbf{u}} \left\{ f(\mathbf{u}) + \frac{1}{2}\|\mathbf{u} - \mathbf{x}\|^2 \right\} \\
&= \operatorname{argmin}_{\mathbf{u}} \left\{ g(\mathbf{u}) + \frac{c}{2}\|\mathbf{u}\|^2 + \langle \mathbf{a}, \mathbf{u} \rangle + \gamma + \frac{1}{2}\|\mathbf{u} - \mathbf{x}\|^2 \right\} \\
&= \operatorname{argmin}_{\mathbf{u}} \left\{ g(\mathbf{u}) + \frac{c+1}{2} \left\| \mathbf{u} - \left(\frac{\mathbf{x} - \mathbf{a}}{c+1} \right) \right\|^2 \right\} \\
&= \operatorname{prox}_{\frac{1}{c+1}g} \left(\frac{\mathbf{x} - \mathbf{a}}{c+1} \right). \quad \square
\end{aligned}
$$

Example 6.14. Consider the function $f : \mathbb{R} \to (-\infty, \infty]$ given for any $x \in \mathbb{R}$ by

$$
f(x) = \begin{cases} \mu x, & 0 \leq x \leq \alpha, \\ \infty & \text{else}, \end{cases}
$$

where $\mu \in \mathbb{R}$ and $\alpha \in [0, \infty]$. To compute the prox of f, note first that f can be represented as

$$
f(x) = \delta_{[0,\alpha] \cap \mathbb{R}}(x) + \mu x.
$$

By Lemma 6.5 (computation of $\operatorname{prox}_{g_5}$), $\operatorname{prox}_{\delta_{[0,\alpha] \cap \mathbb{R}}}(x) = \min\{\max\{x, 0\}, \alpha\}$. Therefore, using Theorem 6.13 with $c = 0, \mathbf{a} = \mu, \gamma = 0$, we obtain that for any $x \in \mathbb{R}$,

$$
\operatorname{prox}_f(x) = \operatorname{prox}_g(x - \mu) = \min\{\max\{x - \mu, 0\}, \alpha\}.
$$

■

Unfortunately, there is no useful calculus rule for computing the prox mapping of a composition of a function with a general affine mapping. However, if the associated linear transformation satisfies a certain orthogonality condition, such a rule exists.

Theorem 6.15 (composition with an affine mapping). *Let $g : \mathbb{R}^m \to (-\infty, \infty]$ be a proper closed convex function, and let $f(\mathbf{x}) = g(\mathcal{A}(\mathbf{x}) + \mathbf{b})$, where $\mathbf{b} \in \mathbb{R}^m$ and $\mathcal{A} : \mathbb{V} \to \mathbb{R}^m$ is a linear transformation satisfying[28] $\mathcal{A} \circ \mathcal{A}^T = \alpha \mathcal{I}$ for some constant $\alpha > 0$. Then for any $\mathbf{x} \in \mathbb{V}$,*

$$\mathrm{prox}_f(\mathbf{x}) = \mathbf{x} + \frac{1}{\alpha}\mathcal{A}^T(\mathrm{prox}_{\alpha g}(\mathcal{A}(\mathbf{x}) + \mathbf{b}) - \mathcal{A}(\mathbf{x}) - \mathbf{b}).$$

Proof. By definition, $\mathrm{prox}_f(\mathbf{x})$ is the optimal solution of

$$\min_{\mathbf{u} \in \mathbb{V}} \left\{ f(\mathbf{u}) + \frac{1}{2}\|\mathbf{u} - \mathbf{x}\|^2 \right\},$$

which can be rewritten as

$$\min_{\mathbf{u} \in \mathbb{V}} \left\{ g(\mathcal{A}(\mathbf{u}) + \mathbf{b}) + \frac{1}{2}\|\mathbf{u} - \mathbf{x}\|^2 \right\}.$$

The above problem can be formulated as the following constrained problem:

$$\begin{aligned} \min_{\mathbf{u} \in \mathbb{V}, \mathbf{z} \in \mathbb{R}^m} \quad & g(\mathbf{z}) + \frac{1}{2}\|\mathbf{u} - \mathbf{x}\|^2 \\ \text{s.t.} \quad & \mathbf{z} = \mathcal{A}(\mathbf{u}) + \mathbf{b}. \end{aligned} \tag{6.10}$$

Denote the optimal solution of (6.10) by $(\tilde{\mathbf{z}}, \tilde{\mathbf{u}})$ (the existence and uniqueness of $\tilde{\mathbf{z}}$ and $\tilde{\mathbf{u}}$ follow by the underlying assumption that g is proper closed and convex). Note that $\tilde{\mathbf{u}} = \mathrm{prox}_f(\mathbf{x})$. Fixing $\mathbf{z} = \tilde{\mathbf{z}}$, we obtain that $\tilde{\mathbf{u}}$ is the optimal solution of

$$\begin{aligned} \min_{\mathbf{u} \in \mathbb{V}} \quad & \frac{1}{2}\|\mathbf{u} - \mathbf{x}\|^2 \\ \text{s.t.} \quad & \mathcal{A}(\mathbf{u}) = \tilde{\mathbf{z}} - \mathbf{b}. \end{aligned} \tag{6.11}$$

Since strong duality holds for problem (6.11) (see Theorem A.1), by Theorem A.2, it follows that there exists $\mathbf{y} \in \mathbb{R}^m$ for which

$$\tilde{\mathbf{u}} \in \mathrm{argmin}_{\mathbf{u} \in \mathbb{V}} \left\{ \frac{1}{2}\|\mathbf{u} - \mathbf{x}\|^2 + \langle \mathbf{y}, \mathcal{A}(\mathbf{u}) - \tilde{\mathbf{z}} + \mathbf{b} \rangle \right\} \tag{6.12}$$

$$\mathcal{A}(\tilde{\mathbf{u}}) = \tilde{\mathbf{z}} - \mathbf{b}. \tag{6.13}$$

By (6.12),

$$\tilde{\mathbf{u}} = \mathbf{x} - \mathcal{A}^T(\mathbf{y}). \tag{6.14}$$

---

[28]The identity transformation $\mathcal{I}$ was defined in Section 1.10.

Substituting this expression of $\tilde{\mathbf{u}}$ into (6.13), we obtain

$$\mathcal{A}(\mathbf{x} - \mathcal{A}^T(\mathbf{y})) = \tilde{\mathbf{z}} - \mathbf{b},$$

and hence, using the assumption that $\mathcal{A} \circ \mathcal{A}^T = \alpha \mathcal{I}$,

$$\alpha \mathbf{y} = \mathcal{A}(\mathbf{x}) + \mathbf{b} - \tilde{\mathbf{z}},$$

which, combined with (6.14), yields an explicit expression for $\tilde{\mathbf{u}} = \text{prox}_f(\mathbf{x})$ in terms of $\tilde{\mathbf{z}}$:

$$\text{prox}_f(\mathbf{x}) = \tilde{\mathbf{u}} = \mathbf{x} + \frac{1}{\alpha}\mathcal{A}^T(\tilde{\mathbf{z}} - \mathcal{A}(\mathbf{x}) - \mathbf{b}). \qquad (6.15)$$

Substituting $\mathbf{u} = \tilde{\mathbf{u}}$ in the minimization problem (6.10), we obtain that $\tilde{\mathbf{z}}$ is given by

$$\begin{aligned}
\tilde{\mathbf{z}} &= \text{argmin}_{\mathbf{z} \in \mathbb{R}^m} \left\{ g(\mathbf{z}) + \frac{1}{2} \left\| \mathbf{x} + \frac{1}{\alpha}\mathcal{A}^T(\mathbf{z} - \mathcal{A}(\mathbf{x}) - \mathbf{b}) - \mathbf{x} \right\|^2 \right\} \\
&= \text{argmin}_{\mathbf{z} \in \mathbb{R}^m} \left\{ g(\mathbf{z}) + \frac{1}{2\alpha^2} \|\mathcal{A}^T(\mathbf{z} - \mathcal{A}(\mathbf{x}) - \mathbf{b})\|^2 \right\} \\
&\overset{(*)}{=} \text{argmin}_{\mathbf{z} \in \mathbb{R}^m} \left\{ \alpha g(\mathbf{z}) + \frac{1}{2} \|\mathbf{z} - \mathcal{A}(\mathbf{x}) - \mathbf{b}\|^2 \right\} \\
&= \text{prox}_{\alpha g}(\mathcal{A}(\mathbf{x}) + \mathbf{b}),
\end{aligned}$$

where the equality $(*)$ uses the assumption that $\mathcal{A} \circ \mathcal{A}^T = \alpha \mathcal{I}$. Plugging the expression for $\tilde{\mathbf{z}}$ into (6.15) produces the desired result. $\square$

Example 6.16. Let $g : \mathbb{E} \to (-\infty, \infty]$ be proper closed and convex where $\mathbb{E} = \mathbb{R}^d$, and let $f : \mathbb{E}^m \to (-\infty, \infty]$ be defined as

$$f(\mathbf{x}_1, \mathbf{x}_2, \ldots, \mathbf{x}_m) = g(\mathbf{x}_1 + \mathbf{x}_2 + \cdots + \mathbf{x}_m).$$

The above can be written as $f(\mathbf{x}_1, \mathbf{x}_2, \ldots, \mathbf{x}_m) = g(\mathcal{A}(\mathbf{x}_1, \mathbf{x}_2, \ldots, \mathbf{x}_m))$, where $\mathcal{A} : \mathbb{E}^m \to \mathbb{E}$ is the linear transformation

$$\mathcal{A}(\mathbf{x}_1, \mathbf{x}_2, \ldots, \mathbf{x}_m) = \mathbf{x}_1 + \mathbf{x}_2 + \cdots + \mathbf{x}_m.$$

Obviously, the adjoint operator $\mathcal{A}^T : \mathbb{E} \to \mathbb{E}^m$ is given by

$$\mathcal{A}^T(\mathbf{x}) = (\mathbf{x}, \mathbf{x}, \ldots, \mathbf{x}),$$

and for any $\mathbf{x} \in \mathbb{E}$,

$$\mathcal{A}(\mathcal{A}^T(\mathbf{x})) = m\mathbf{x}.$$

Thus, the conditions of Theorem 6.15 are satisfied with $\alpha = m$ and $\mathbf{b} = 0$, and consequently, for any $(\mathbf{x}_1, \mathbf{x}_2, \ldots, \mathbf{x}_m) \in \mathbb{E}^m$,

$$\text{prox}_f(\mathbf{x}_1, \mathbf{x}_2, \ldots, \mathbf{x}_m)_j = \mathbf{x}_j + \frac{1}{m}\left(\text{prox}_{mg}\left(\sum_{i=1}^{m}\mathbf{x}_i\right) - \sum_{i=1}^{m}\mathbf{x}_i\right), \quad j = 1, 2, \ldots, m.$$

■

Example 6.17. Let $f : \mathbb{R}^n \to \mathbb{R}$ be given by $f(\mathbf{x}) = |\mathbf{a}^T\mathbf{x}|$, where $\mathbf{a} \in \mathbb{R}^n \setminus \{\mathbf{0}\}$. We can write f as $f(\mathbf{x}) = g(\mathbf{a}^T\mathbf{x})$, where $g(t) = |t|$. By Lemma 6.5 (prox_{g_2} computation), $\text{prox}_{\lambda g} = \mathcal{T}_\lambda$, with $\mathcal{T}_\lambda(x) = [|x| - \lambda]_+\text{sgn}(x)$ being the soft thresholding operator defined in Example 6.8. Invoking Theorem 6.15 with $\alpha = \|\mathbf{a}\|^2$, $\mathbf{b} = 0$, and $\mathcal{A}$ defined as the transformation $\mathbf{x} \mapsto \mathbf{a}^T\mathbf{x}$, we obtain that

$$\text{prox}_f(\mathbf{x}) = \mathbf{x} + \frac{1}{\|\mathbf{a}\|^2}\left(\mathcal{T}_{\|\mathbf{a}\|^2}(\mathbf{a}^T\mathbf{x}) - \mathbf{a}^T\mathbf{x}\right)\mathbf{a}.$$

■

Theorem 6.18 (norm composition). *Let* $f : \mathbb{E} \to \mathbb{R}$ *be given by* $f(\mathbf{x}) = g(\|\mathbf{x}\|)$, *where* $g : \mathbb{R} \to (-\infty, \infty]$ *is a proper closed and convex function satisfying* $\text{dom}(g) \subseteq [0, \infty)$. *Then*

$$\text{prox}_f(\mathbf{x}) = \begin{cases} \text{prox}_g(\|\mathbf{x}\|)\frac{\mathbf{x}}{\|\mathbf{x}\|}, & \mathbf{x} \neq \mathbf{0}, \\ \{\mathbf{u} \in \mathbb{E} : \|\mathbf{u}\| = \text{prox}_g(0)\}, & \mathbf{x} = \mathbf{0}. \end{cases} \tag{6.16}$$

Proof. By definition, $\text{prox}_f(\mathbf{0})$ is the set of minimizers of the problem

$$\min_{\mathbf{u} \in \mathbb{E}}\left\{f(\mathbf{u}) + \frac{1}{2}\|\mathbf{u}\|^2\right\} = \min_{\mathbf{u} \in \mathbb{E}}\left\{g(\|\mathbf{u}\|) + \frac{1}{2}\|\mathbf{u}\|^2\right\}.$$

Making the change of variables $w = \|\mathbf{u}\|$, the problem reduces to (recalling that $\text{dom}(g) \subseteq [0, \infty)$)

$$\min_{w \in \mathbb{R}}\left\{g(w) + \frac{1}{2}w^2\right\}.$$

The optimal set of the above problem is $\text{prox}_g(0)$, and hence $\text{prox}_f(\mathbf{0})$ is the set of vectors $\mathbf{u}$ satisfying $\|\mathbf{u}\| = \text{prox}_g(0)$. We will now compute $\text{prox}_f(\mathbf{x})$ for $\mathbf{x} \neq \mathbf{0}$. The optimization problem associated with the prox computation can be rewritten as the following double minimization problem:

$$\min_{\mathbf{u} \in \mathbb{E}}\left\{g(\|\mathbf{u}\|) + \frac{1}{2}\|\mathbf{u} - \mathbf{x}\|^2\right\} = \min_{\mathbf{u} \in \mathbb{E}}\left\{g(\|\mathbf{u}\|) + \frac{1}{2}\|\mathbf{u}\|^2 - \langle\mathbf{u}, \mathbf{x}\rangle + \frac{1}{2}\|\mathbf{x}\|^2\right\}$$

$$= \min_{\alpha \in \mathbb{R}_+}\min_{\mathbf{u} \in \mathbb{E}:\|\mathbf{u}\|=\alpha}\left\{g(\alpha) + \frac{1}{2}\alpha^2 - \langle\mathbf{u}, \mathbf{x}\rangle + \frac{1}{2}\|\mathbf{x}\|^2\right\}.$$

Using the Cauchy–Schwarz inequality, it is easy to see that the minimizer of the inner minimization problem is

$$\mathbf{u} = \alpha \frac{\mathbf{x}}{\|\mathbf{x}\|}, \tag{6.17}$$

and the corresponding optimal value is

$$g(\alpha) + \frac{1}{2}\alpha^2 - \alpha\|\mathbf{x}\| + \frac{1}{2}\|\mathbf{x}\|^2 = g(\alpha) + \frac{1}{2}(\alpha - \|\mathbf{x}\|)^2.$$

Therefore, $\mathrm{prox}_f(\mathbf{x})$ is given by $\mathbf{u}$ in (6.17) with α given by

$$\alpha = \mathrm{argmin}_{\alpha \in \mathbb{R}_+} \left\{ g(\alpha) + \frac{1}{2}(\alpha - \|\mathbf{x}\|)^2 \right\}$$

$$= \mathrm{argmin}_{\alpha \in \mathbb{R}} \left\{ g(\alpha) + \frac{1}{2}(\alpha - \|\mathbf{x}\|)^2 \right\}$$

$$= \mathrm{prox}_g(\|\mathbf{x}\|),$$

where the second equality is due to the assumption that $\mathrm{dom}(g) \subseteq [0, \infty)$. Thus, $\mathrm{prox}_f(\mathbf{x}) = \mathrm{prox}_g(\|\mathbf{x}\|)\frac{\mathbf{x}}{\|\mathbf{x}\|}$. $\quad\square$

Example 6.19 (prox of Euclidean norm). Let $f : \mathbb{E} \to \mathbb{R}$ be given by $f(\mathbf{x}) = \lambda\|\mathbf{x}\|$, where $\lambda > 0$ and $\|\cdot\|$ is the underlying Euclidean norm (recall that in this section we assume that the underlying space is Euclidean). Then $f(\mathbf{x}) = g(\|\mathbf{x}\|)$, where

$$g(t) = \begin{cases} \lambda t, & t \geq 0, \\ \infty, & t < 0. \end{cases}$$

Then by Theorem 6.18, for any $\mathbf{x} \in \mathbb{E}$,

$$\mathrm{prox}_f(\mathbf{x}) = \begin{cases} \mathrm{prox}_g(\|\mathbf{x}\|)\frac{\mathbf{x}}{\|\mathbf{x}\|}, & \mathbf{x} \neq \mathbf{0}, \\ \{\mathbf{u} \in \mathbb{E} : \|\mathbf{u}\| = \mathrm{prox}_g(0)\}, & \mathbf{x} = \mathbf{0}. \end{cases}$$

By Lemma 6.5 (computation of prox_{g_1}), $\mathrm{prox}_g(t) = [t - \lambda]_+$. Thus, $\mathrm{prox}_g(0) = 0$ and $\mathrm{prox}_g(\|\mathbf{x}\|) = [\|\mathbf{x}\| - \lambda]_+$, and therefore

$$\mathrm{prox}_f(\mathbf{x}) = \begin{cases} [\|\mathbf{x}\| - \lambda]_+ \frac{\mathbf{x}}{\|\mathbf{x}\|}, & \mathbf{x} \neq \mathbf{0}, \\ \mathbf{0}, & \mathbf{x} = \mathbf{0}. \end{cases}$$

Finally, we can write the above formula in the following compact form:

$$\boxed{\mathrm{prox}_{\lambda\|\cdot\|}(\mathbf{x}) = \left(1 - \frac{\lambda}{\max\{\|\mathbf{x}\|, \lambda\}}\right)\mathbf{x}.}$$

Example 6.20 (prox of cubic Euclidean norm). Let $f(\mathbf{x}) = \lambda\|\mathbf{x}\|^3$, where $\lambda > 0$. Then $f(\mathbf{x}) = g(\|\mathbf{x}\|)$, where

$$g(t) = \begin{cases} \lambda t^3, & t \geq 0, \\ \infty, & t < 0. \end{cases}$$

Then by Theorem 6.18, for any $\mathbf{x} \in \mathbb{R}$,

$$\text{prox}_f(\mathbf{x}) = \begin{cases} \text{prox}_g(\|\mathbf{x}\|)\frac{\mathbf{x}}{\|\mathbf{x}\|}, & \mathbf{x} \neq \mathbf{0}, \\ \{\mathbf{u} \in \mathbb{E} : \|\mathbf{u}\| = \text{prox}_g(0)\}, & \mathbf{x} = \mathbf{0}. \end{cases}$$

By Lemma 6.5 (computation of prox_{g_3}), $\text{prox}_g(t) = \frac{-1+\sqrt{1+12\lambda[t]_+}}{6\lambda}$.   Therefore, $\text{prox}_g(0) = 0$ and

$$\text{prox}_f(\mathbf{x}) = \begin{cases} \frac{-1+\sqrt{1+12\lambda\|\mathbf{x}\|}}{6\lambda}\frac{\mathbf{x}}{\|\mathbf{x}\|}, & \mathbf{x} \neq \mathbf{0}, \\ \mathbf{0}, & \mathbf{x} = \mathbf{0}, \end{cases}$$

and thus

$$\boxed{\text{prox}_{\lambda\|\cdot\|^3}(\mathbf{x}) = \frac{2}{1 + \sqrt{1 + 12\lambda\|\mathbf{x}\|}}\mathbf{x}.}$$

■

Example 6.21 (prox of negative Euclidean norm). Let $f : \mathbb{E} \to \mathbb{R}$ be given by $f(\mathbf{x}) = -\lambda\|\mathbf{x}\|$, where $\lambda > 0$. Since f is not convex, we do not expect the prox to be a single-valued mapping. However, since f is closed, and since the function $\mathbf{u} \mapsto f(\mathbf{u}) + \frac{1}{2}\|\mathbf{u} - \mathbf{x}\|^2$ is coercive for any $\mathbf{x} \in \mathbb{E}$, it follows by Theorem 6.4 that the set $\text{prox}_f(\mathbf{x})$ is always nonempty. To compute the prox, note that $f(\mathbf{x}) = g(\|\mathbf{x}\|)$, where

$$g(t) = \begin{cases} -\lambda t, & t \geq 0, \\ \infty, & t < 0. \end{cases}$$

By Theorem 6.18, for any $\mathbf{x} \in \mathbb{R}$,

$$\text{prox}_f(\mathbf{x}) = \begin{cases} \text{prox}_g(\|\mathbf{x}\|)\frac{\mathbf{x}}{\|\mathbf{x}\|}, & \mathbf{x} \neq \mathbf{0}, \\ \{\mathbf{u} \in \mathbb{E} : \|\mathbf{u}\| = \text{prox}_g(0)\}, & \mathbf{x} = \mathbf{0}. \end{cases}$$

By Lemma 6.5 (computation of prox_{g_1}), $\text{prox}_g(t) = [t+\lambda]_+$. Therefore, $\text{prox}_g(0) = \lambda$ and

$$\text{prox}_{-\lambda\|\cdot\|}(\mathbf{x}) = \begin{cases} \left(1 + \frac{\lambda}{\|\mathbf{x}\|}\right)\mathbf{x}, & \mathbf{x} \neq \mathbf{0}, \\ \{\mathbf{u} : \|\mathbf{u}\| = \lambda\}, & \mathbf{x} = \mathbf{0}. \end{cases}$$

∎

Example 6.22 (prox of absolute value over symmetric intervals). Consider the function $f : \mathbb{R} \to (-\infty, \infty]$ given by

$$f(x) = \begin{cases} \lambda|x|, & |x| \leq \alpha, \\ \infty & \text{else,} \end{cases}$$

where $\lambda \in [0, \infty)$ and $\alpha \in [0, \infty]$. Then $f(x) = g(|x|)$, where

$$g(x) = \begin{cases} \lambda x, & 0 \leq x \leq \alpha, \\ \infty & \text{else.} \end{cases}$$

Thus, by Theorem 6.18, for any x,

$$\text{prox}_f(\mathbf{x}) = \begin{cases} \text{prox}_g(|x|)\frac{x}{|x|}, & x \neq 0, \\ \{u \in \mathbb{R} : |u| = \text{prox}_g(0)\}, & x = 0. \end{cases} \tag{6.18}$$

By Example 6.14, $\text{prox}_g(x) = \min\{\max\{x - \lambda, 0\}, \alpha\}$, which, combined with (6.18) and the fact that $\frac{x}{|x|} = \text{sgn}(x)$ for any $x \neq 0$, yields the formula

$$\text{prox}_{\lambda|\cdot|+\delta_{[-\alpha,\alpha]}}(x) = \min\{\max\{|x| - \lambda, 0\}, \alpha\}\text{sgn}(x).$$

∎

Using the previous example, we can compute the prox of weighted l_1-norms over boxes.

Example 6.23 (prox of weighted l_1 over a box). Consider the function $f : \mathbb{R}^n \to \mathbb{R}$ given by

$$f(\mathbf{x}) = \begin{cases} \sum_{i=1}^n \omega_i|x_i|, & -\boldsymbol{\alpha} \leq \mathbf{x} \leq \boldsymbol{\alpha}, \\ \infty, & \text{else,} \end{cases}$$

for any $\mathbf{x} \in \mathbb{R}^n$, where $\boldsymbol{\omega} \in \mathbb{R}^n_+$ and $\boldsymbol{\alpha} \in [0, \infty]^n$. Then $f = \sum_{i=1}^n f_i$, where

$$f_i(x) = \begin{cases} w_i|x|, & -\alpha_i \leq x \leq \alpha_i, \\ \infty, & \text{else.} \end{cases}$$

Using Example 6.22 and invoking Theorem 6.6, we finally obtain that

$$\text{prox}_f(\mathbf{x}) = (\min\{\max\{|x_i| - \omega_i, 0\}, \alpha_i\}\text{sgn}(x_i))_{i=1}^n.$$

∎

The table below summarizes the main prox calculus rules discussed in this section.

$f(\mathbf{x})$	$\text{prox}_f(\mathbf{x})$	Assumptions	Reference
$\sum_{i=1}^m f_i(\mathbf{x}_i)$	$\text{prox}_{f_1}(\mathbf{x}_1) \times \cdots \times \text{prox}_{f_m}(\mathbf{x}_m)$		Theorem 6.6
$g(\lambda\mathbf{x} + \mathbf{a})$	$\frac{1}{\lambda}\left[\text{prox}_{\lambda^2 g}(\lambda\mathbf{x} + \mathbf{a}) - \mathbf{a}\right]$	$\lambda \neq 0, \mathbf{a} \in \mathbb{E}, g$ proper	Theorem 6.11
$\lambda g(\mathbf{x}/\lambda)$	$\lambda\text{prox}_{g/\lambda}(\mathbf{x}/\lambda)$	$\lambda > 0, g$ proper	Theorem 6.12
$g(\mathbf{x}) + \frac{c}{2}\|\mathbf{x}\|^2 + \langle\mathbf{a}, \mathbf{x}\rangle + \gamma$	$\text{prox}_{\frac{1}{c+1}g}\left(\frac{\mathbf{x}-\mathbf{a}}{c+1}\right)$	$\mathbf{a} \in \mathbb{E}, c \geq 0,$ $\gamma \in \mathbb{R}, g$ proper	Theorem 6.13
$g(\mathcal{A}(\mathbf{x}) + \mathbf{b})$	$\mathbf{x} + \frac{1}{\alpha}\mathcal{A}^T(\text{prox}_{\alpha g}(\mathcal{A}(\mathbf{x}) + \mathbf{b}) - \mathcal{A}(\mathbf{x}) - \mathbf{b})$	$\mathbf{b} \in \mathbb{R}^m,$ $\mathcal{A} : \mathbb{V} \to \mathbb{R}^m,$ g proper closed convex, $\mathcal{A} \circ \mathcal{A}^T = \alpha I,$ $\alpha > 0$	Theorem 6.15
$g(\|\mathbf{x}\|)$	$\text{prox}_g(\|\mathbf{x}\|)\frac{\mathbf{x}}{\|\mathbf{x}\|}, \quad \mathbf{x} \neq \mathbf{0}$ $\{\mathbf{u} : \|\mathbf{u}\| = \text{prox}_g(0)\}, \quad \mathbf{x} = \mathbf{0}$	g proper closed convex, $\text{dom}(g) \subseteq [0, \infty)$	Theorem 6.18

6.4   Prox of Indicators—Orthogonal Projections

6.4.1   The First Projection Theorem

Let $g : \mathbb{E} \to (-\infty, \infty]$ be given by $g(\mathbf{x}) = \delta_C(\mathbf{x})$, where C is a nonempty set. Then

$$\text{prox}_g(\mathbf{x}) = \text{argmin}_{\mathbf{u}\in\mathbb{E}}\left\{\delta_C(\mathbf{u}) + \frac{1}{2}\|\mathbf{u} - \mathbf{x}\|^2\right\} = \text{argmin}_{\mathbf{u}\in C}\|\mathbf{u} - \mathbf{x}\|^2 = P_C(\mathbf{x}).$$

Thus, the proximal mapping of the indicator function of a given set is the orthogonal projection[29] operator onto the same set.

Theorem 6.24. *Let $C \subseteq \mathbb{E}$ be nonempty. Then $\text{prox}_{\delta_C}(\mathbf{x}) = P_C(\mathbf{x})$ for any $\mathbf{x} \in \mathbb{E}$.*

If C is closed and convex, in addition to being nonempty, the indicator function δ_C is proper closed and convex, and hence by the first prox theorem (Theorem 6.3), the orthogonal projection mapping (which coincides with the proximal mapping) exists and is unique. This is the first projection theorem.

---

[29]The orthogonal projection operator was introduced in Example 3.31.

Theorem 6.25 (first projection theorem). *Let $C \subseteq \mathbb{E}$ be a nonempty closed convex set. Then $P_C(\mathbf{x})$ is a singleton for any $\mathbf{x} \in \mathbb{E}$.*

6.4.2 First Examples in $\mathbb{R}^n$

We begin by recalling[30] several known expressions for the orthogonal projection onto some basic subsets of $\mathbb{R}^n$. Since the assumption made throughout the book is that (unless otherwise stated) $\mathbb{R}^n$ is endowed with the dot product, and since the standing assumption in this chapter is that the underlying space is Euclidean, it follows that the endowed norm is the l_2-norm.

Lemma 6.26 (projection onto subsets of $\mathbb{R}^n$). *Following are pairs of nonempty closed and convex sets and their corresponding orthogonal projections:*

nonnegative orthant	$C_1 = \mathbb{R}^n_+,$	$[\mathbf{x}]_+,$
box	$C_2 = \text{Box}[\boldsymbol{\ell}, \mathbf{u}],$	$(\min\{\max\{x_i, \ell_i\}, u_i\})^n_{i=1},$
affine set	$C_3 = \{\mathbf{x} \in \mathbb{R}^n : \mathbf{A}\mathbf{x} = \mathbf{b}\},$	$\mathbf{x} - \mathbf{A}^T(\mathbf{A}\mathbf{A}^T)^{-1}(\mathbf{A}\mathbf{x} - \mathbf{b}),$
l_2 ball	$C_4 = B_{\|\cdot\|_2}[\mathbf{c}, r],$	$\mathbf{c} + \frac{r}{\max\{\|\mathbf{x}-\mathbf{c}\|_2, r\}}(\mathbf{x} - \mathbf{c}),$
half-space	$C_5 = \{\mathbf{x} : \mathbf{a}^T\mathbf{x} \leq \alpha\},$	$\mathbf{x} - \frac{[\mathbf{a}^T\mathbf{x}-\alpha]_+}{\|\mathbf{a}\|^2}\mathbf{a},$

where $\boldsymbol{\ell} \in [-\infty, \infty)^n, \mathbf{u} \in (-\infty, \infty]^n$ are such that $\boldsymbol{\ell} \leq \mathbf{u}$, $\mathbf{A} \in \mathbb{R}^{m \times n}$ has full row rank, $\mathbf{b} \in \mathbb{R}^m$, $\mathbf{c} \in \mathbb{R}^n$, $r > 0$, $\mathbf{a} \in \mathbb{R}^n \setminus \{\mathbf{0}\}$, and $\alpha \in \mathbb{R}$.

Note that we extended the definition of box sets given in Section 1.7.1 to include unbounded intervals, meaning that $\text{Box}[\boldsymbol{\ell}, \mathbf{u}]$ is also defined when the components of $\boldsymbol{\ell}$ might also take the value $-\infty$, and the components of $\mathbf{u}$ might take the value ∞. However, boxes are always subsets of $\mathbb{R}^n$, and the formula

$$\text{Box}[\boldsymbol{\ell}, \mathbf{u}] = \{\mathbf{x} \in \mathbb{R}^n : \boldsymbol{\ell} \leq \mathbf{x} \leq \mathbf{u}\}$$

still holds. For example, $\text{Box}[\mathbf{0}, \infty\mathbf{e}] = \mathbb{R}^n_+$.

6.4.3 Projection onto the Intersection of a Hyperplane and a Box

The next result develops an expression for the orthogonal projection onto another subset of $\mathbb{R}^n$—the intersection of an hyperplane and a box.

Theorem 6.27 (projection onto the intersection of a hyperplane and a box). *Let $C \subseteq \mathbb{R}^n$ be given by*

$$C = H_{\mathbf{a},b} \cap \text{Box}[\boldsymbol{\ell}, \mathbf{u}] = \{\mathbf{x} \in \mathbb{R}^n : \mathbf{a}^T\mathbf{x} = b, \boldsymbol{\ell} \leq \mathbf{x} \leq \mathbf{u}\},$$

where $\mathbf{a} \in \mathbb{R}^n \setminus \{\mathbf{0}\}, b \in \mathbb{R}, \boldsymbol{\ell} \in [-\infty, \infty)^n, \mathbf{u} \in (-\infty, \infty]^n$. Assume that $C \neq \emptyset$. Then

$$P_C(\mathbf{x}) = P_{\text{Box}[\boldsymbol{\ell}, \mathbf{u}]}(\mathbf{x} - \mu^*\mathbf{a}),$$

---

[30]The derivations of the orthogonal projection expressions in Lemma 6.26 can be found, for example, in [10].

where $\text{Box}[\boldsymbol{\ell}, \mathbf{u}] = \{\mathbf{y} \in \mathbb{R}^n : \ell_i \leq y_i \leq u_i, i = 1, 2, \ldots, n\}$ *and* μ^* *is a solution of the equation*

$$\mathbf{a}^T P_{\text{Box}[\boldsymbol{\ell}, \mathbf{u}]}(\mathbf{x} - \mu \mathbf{a}) = b. \tag{6.19}$$

Proof. The orthogonal projection of $\mathbf{x}$ onto C is the unique optimal solution of

$$\min_{\mathbf{y}} \left\{ \frac{1}{2} \|\mathbf{y} - \mathbf{x}\|_2^2 : \mathbf{a}^T \mathbf{y} = b, \boldsymbol{\ell} \leq \mathbf{y} \leq \mathbf{u} \right\}. \tag{6.20}$$

A Lagrangian of the problem is

$$L(\mathbf{y}; \mu) = \frac{1}{2} \|\mathbf{y} - \mathbf{x}\|_2^2 + \mu(\mathbf{a}^T \mathbf{y} - b) = \frac{1}{2} \|\mathbf{y} - (\mathbf{x} - \mu \mathbf{a})\|_2^2 - \frac{\mu^2}{2} \|\mathbf{a}\|_2^2 + \mu(\mathbf{a}^T \mathbf{x} - b). \tag{6.21}$$

Since strong duality holds for problem (6.20) (see Theorem A.1), it follows by Theorem A.2 that $\mathbf{y}^*$ is an optimal solution of problem (6.20) if and only if there exists $\mu^* \in \mathbb{R}$ (which will actually be an optimal solution of the dual problem) for which

$$\mathbf{y}^* \in \text{argmin}_{\boldsymbol{\ell} \leq \mathbf{y} \leq \mathbf{u}} L(\mathbf{y}; \mu^*), \tag{6.22}$$

$$\mathbf{a}^T \mathbf{y}^* = b. \tag{6.23}$$

Using the expression of the Lagrangian given in (6.21), the relation (6.22) can be equivalently written as

$$\mathbf{y}^* = P_{\text{Box}[\boldsymbol{\ell}, \mathbf{u}]}(\mathbf{x} - \mu^* \mathbf{a}).$$

The feasibility condition (6.23) can then be rewritten as

$$\mathbf{a}^T P_{\text{Box}[\boldsymbol{\ell}, \mathbf{u}]}(\mathbf{x} - \mu^* \mathbf{a}) = b. \qquad \square$$

Remark 6.28. *The projection onto the box* $\text{Box}[\boldsymbol{\ell}, \mathbf{u}]$ *is extremely simple and is done component-wise as described in Lemma 6.26. Note also that (6.19) actually consists in finding a root of the nonincreasing function* $\varphi(\mu) = \mathbf{a}^T P_{\text{Box}}(\mathbf{x} - \mu \mathbf{a}) - b$, *which is a task that can be performed efficiently even by simple procedures such as bisection. The fact that* φ *is nonincreasing follows from the observation that* $\varphi(\mu) = \sum_{i=1}^n a_i \min\{\max\{x_i - \mu a_i, \ell_i\}, u_i\} - b$ *and the fact that* $\mu \mapsto a_i \min\{\max\{x_i - \mu a_i, \ell_i\}, u_i\}$ *is a nonincreasing function for any* i.

A direct consequence of Theorem 6.27 is an expression for the orthogonal projection onto the unit simplex.

Corollary 6.29 (orthogonal projection onto the unit simplex). *For any* $\mathbf{x} \in \mathbb{R}^n$,

$$P_{\Delta_n}(\mathbf{x}) = [\mathbf{x} - \mu^* \mathbf{e}]_+,$$

where μ^* *is a root of the equation*

$$\mathbf{e}^T [\mathbf{x} - \mu^* \mathbf{e}]_+ - 1 = 0.$$

Proof. Invoking Theorem 6.27 with $\mathbf{a} = \mathbf{e}$, $b = 1$, $\ell_i = 0$, $u_i = \infty$, $i = 1, 2, \ldots, n$, and noting that in this case $P_{\text{Box}[\boldsymbol{\ell},\mathbf{u}]}(\mathbf{x}) = [\mathbf{x}]_+$, the result follows. □

In order to expend the variety of sets on which we will be able to find simple expressions for the orthogonal projection mapping, in the next two subsections, we will discuss how to project onto level sets and epigraphs.

6.4.4   Projection onto Level Sets

Theorem 6.30 (orthogonal projection onto level sets). *Let* $C = Lev(f, \alpha) = \{\mathbf{x} \in \mathbb{E} : f(\mathbf{x}) \leq \alpha\}$, *where* $f : \mathbb{E} \to (-\infty, \infty]$ *is proper closed and convex, and* $\alpha \in \mathbb{R}$. *Assume that there exists* $\hat{\mathbf{x}} \in \mathbb{E}$ *for which* $f(\hat{\mathbf{x}}) < \alpha$. *Then*

$$P_C(\mathbf{x}) = \begin{cases} P_{\text{dom}(f)}(\mathbf{x}), & f(P_{\text{dom}(f)}(\mathbf{x})) \leq \alpha, \\[2mm] \text{prox}_{\lambda^* f}(\mathbf{x}) & else, \end{cases} \tag{6.24}$$

where λ^* *is any positive root of the equation*

$$\varphi(\lambda) \equiv f(\text{prox}_{\lambda f}(\mathbf{x})) - \alpha = 0.$$

In addition, the function φ *is nonincreasing.*

Proof. The orthogonal projection of $\mathbf{x}$ onto C is the optimal solution of the problem

$$\min_{\mathbf{y} \in \mathbb{E}} \left\{ \frac{1}{2} \|\mathbf{y} - \mathbf{x}\|^2 : f(\mathbf{y}) \leq \alpha, \mathbf{y} \in X \right\},$$

where $X = \text{dom}(f)$. A Lagrangian of the problem is ($\lambda \geq 0$)

$$L(\mathbf{y}; \lambda) = \frac{1}{2} \|\mathbf{y} - \mathbf{x}\|^2 + \lambda f(\mathbf{y}) - \alpha\lambda. \tag{6.25}$$

Since the problem is convex and satisfies Slater's condition, strong duality holds (see Theorem A.1), and therefore it follows by the optimality conditions in Theorem A.2 that $\mathbf{y}^*$ is an optimal solution of problem (6.25) if and only if there exists $\lambda^* \in \mathbb{R}_+$ for which

$$\mathbf{y}^* \in \operatorname{argmin}_{\mathbf{y} \in X} L(\mathbf{y}; \lambda^*), \tag{6.26}$$
$$f(\mathbf{y}^*) \leq \alpha, \tag{6.27}$$
$$\lambda^*(f(\mathbf{y}^*) - \alpha) = 0. \tag{6.28}$$

There are two cases. If $P_X(\mathbf{x})$ exists and $f(P_X(\mathbf{x})) \leq \alpha$, then $\mathbf{y}^* = P_X(\mathbf{x})$, and $\lambda^* = 0$ is a solution to the system (6.26), (6.27), (6.28). Otherwise, if $P_X(\mathbf{x})$ does not exist or $f(P_X(\mathbf{x})) > \alpha$, then $\lambda^* > 0$, and in this case the system (6.26), (6.27), (6.28) reduces to $\mathbf{y}^* = \text{prox}_{\lambda^* f}(\mathbf{x})$ and $f(\text{prox}_{\lambda^* f}(\mathbf{x})) = \alpha$, which yields the formula (6.24).

To prove that φ is nonincreasing, recall that

$$\text{prox}_{\lambda f}(\mathbf{x}) = \operatorname{argmin}_{\mathbf{y} \in X} \left\{ \frac{1}{2} \|\mathbf{y} - \mathbf{x}\|^2 + \lambda(f(\mathbf{y}) - \alpha) \right\}.$$

Take $0 \leq \lambda_1 < \lambda_2$. Then denoting $\mathbf{v}_1 = \text{prox}_{\lambda_1 f}(\mathbf{x})$ and $\mathbf{v}_2 = \text{prox}_{\lambda_2 f}(\mathbf{x})$, we have

$$\frac{1}{2}\|\mathbf{v}_2 - \mathbf{x}\|^2 + \lambda_2(f(\mathbf{v}_2) - \alpha)$$

$$= \frac{1}{2}\|\mathbf{v}_2 - \mathbf{x}\|^2 + \lambda_1(f(\mathbf{v}_2) - \alpha) + (\lambda_2 - \lambda_1)(f(\mathbf{v}_2) - \alpha)$$

$$\geq \frac{1}{2}\|\mathbf{v}_1 - \mathbf{x}\|^2 + \lambda_1(f(\mathbf{v}_1) - \alpha) + (\lambda_2 - \lambda_1)(f(\mathbf{v}_2) - \alpha)$$

$$= \frac{1}{2}\|\mathbf{v}_1 - \mathbf{x}\|^2 + \lambda_2(f(\mathbf{v}_1) - \alpha) + (\lambda_2 - \lambda_1)(f(\mathbf{v}_2) - f(\mathbf{v}_1))$$

$$\geq \frac{1}{2}\|\mathbf{v}_2 - \mathbf{x}\|^2 + \lambda_2(f(\mathbf{v}_2) - \alpha) + (\lambda_2 - \lambda_1)(f(\mathbf{v}_2) - f(\mathbf{v}_1)).$$

Therefore, $(\lambda_2 - \lambda_1)(f(\mathbf{v}_2) - f(\mathbf{v}_1)) \leq 0$. Since $\lambda_1 < \lambda_2$, we can conclude that $f(\mathbf{v}_2) \leq f(\mathbf{v}_1)$. Finally,

$$\varphi(\lambda_2) = f(\mathbf{v}_2) - \alpha \leq f(\mathbf{v}_1) - \alpha = \varphi(\lambda_1),$$

establishing the monotonicity of φ. $\square$

Remark 6.31. *Note that in Theorem 6.30 f is assumed to be closed, but this does not necessarily imply that $\text{dom}(f)$ is closed. In cases where $\text{dom}(f)$ is not closed, it might happen that $P_{\text{dom}(f)}(\mathbf{x})$ does not exist and formula (6.24) amounts to $P_C(\mathbf{x}) = \text{prox}_{\lambda^* f}(\mathbf{x})$.*

Example 6.32 (projection onto the intersection of a half-space and a box).
Consider the set

$$C = H_{\mathbf{a},b}^- \cap \text{Box}[\boldsymbol{\ell}, \mathbf{u}] = \{\mathbf{x} \in \mathbb{R}^n : \mathbf{a}^T\mathbf{x} \leq b, \boldsymbol{\ell} \leq \mathbf{x} \leq \mathbf{u}\},$$

where $\mathbf{a} \in \mathbb{R}^n \setminus \{\mathbf{0}\}, b \in \mathbb{R}$, $\boldsymbol{\ell} \in [-\infty, \infty)^n$ and $\mathbf{u} \in (-\infty, \infty]^n$. Assume that $C \neq \emptyset$. Then $C = \text{Lev}(f, b)$, where $f(\mathbf{x}) = \mathbf{a}^T\mathbf{x} + \delta_{\text{Box}[\boldsymbol{\ell}, \mathbf{u}]}(\mathbf{x})$. For any $\lambda > 0$,

$$\text{prox}_{\lambda f}(\mathbf{x}) = \text{prox}_{\lambda \mathbf{a}^T(\cdot) + \delta_{\text{Box}[\boldsymbol{\ell}, \mathbf{u}]}(\cdot)}(\mathbf{x}) \overset{(*)}{=} \text{prox}_{\delta_{\text{Box}[\boldsymbol{\ell}, \mathbf{u}]}}(\mathbf{x} - \lambda\mathbf{a}) = P_{\text{Box}[\boldsymbol{\ell}, \mathbf{u}]}(\mathbf{x} - \lambda\mathbf{a}),$$

where in the equality $(*)$ we used Theorem 6.13. Invoking Theorem 6.30, we obtain the following formula for the projection on C:

$$P_C(\mathbf{x}) = \begin{cases} P_{\text{Box}[\boldsymbol{\ell}, \mathbf{u}]}(\mathbf{x}), & \mathbf{a}^T P_{\text{Box}[\boldsymbol{\ell}, \mathbf{u}]}(\mathbf{x}) \leq b, \\ P_{\text{Box}[\boldsymbol{\ell}, \mathbf{u}]}(\mathbf{x} - \lambda^*\mathbf{a}), & \mathbf{a}^T P_{\text{Box}[\boldsymbol{\ell}, \mathbf{u}]}(\mathbf{x}) > b, \end{cases}$$

where λ^* is any positive root of the nonincreasing function

$$\varphi(\lambda) = \mathbf{a}^T P_{\text{Box}[\boldsymbol{\ell}, \mathbf{u}]}(\mathbf{x} - \lambda\mathbf{a}) - b.$$

∎

Example 6.33 (projection onto the l_1 ball). Let $C = B_{\|\cdot\|_1}[\mathbf{0}, \alpha] = \{\mathbf{x} \in \mathbb{R}^n : \|\mathbf{x}\|_1 \leq \alpha\}$, where $\alpha > 0$. Then $C = \mathrm{Lev}(f, \alpha)$ with $f(\mathbf{x}) = \|\mathbf{x}\|_1$. The prox of $\lambda f = \lambda \|\cdot\|_1$ for any $\lambda > 0$ was computed in Example 6.8, where it was shown that

$$\mathrm{prox}_{\lambda f}(\mathbf{x}) = \mathcal{T}_\lambda(\mathbf{x}) \text{ for all } \mathbf{x} \in \mathbb{R}^n$$

with $\mathcal{T}_\lambda$ being the soft thresholding operator given by $\mathcal{T}_\lambda(\mathbf{x}) = [\mathbf{x} - \lambda \mathbf{e}]_+ \odot \mathrm{sgn}(\mathbf{x})$. Invoking Theorem 6.30, we obtain that

$$P_{B_{\|\cdot\|_1}[\mathbf{0},\alpha]}(\mathbf{x}) = \begin{cases} \mathbf{x}, & \|\mathbf{x}\|_1 \leq \alpha, \\ \mathcal{T}_{\lambda^*}(\mathbf{x}), & \|\mathbf{x}\|_1 > \alpha, \end{cases}$$

where λ^* is any positive root of the nonincreasing function

$$\varphi(\lambda) = \|\mathcal{T}_\lambda(\mathbf{x})\|_1 - \alpha.$$

∎

The next example uses a generalization of the soft thresholding mapping, which will be called the *two-sided soft thresholding* operator, and is defined for any $\mathbf{a}, \mathbf{b} \in (-\infty, \infty]^n$ as

$$\mathcal{S}_{\mathbf{a},\mathbf{b}}(\mathbf{x}) = (\min\{\max\{|x_i| - a_i, 0\}, b_i\}\mathrm{sgn}(x_i))_{i=1}^n, \quad \mathbf{x} \in \mathbb{R}^n.$$

Obviously,

$$\mathcal{S}_{\lambda \mathbf{e}, \infty \mathbf{e}} = \mathcal{T}_\lambda.$$

Here $\infty \mathbf{e}$ is the n-dimensional column vector whose elements are all ∞. A plot of the function $t \mapsto \mathcal{S}_{1,2}(t)$ is given in Figure 6.3.

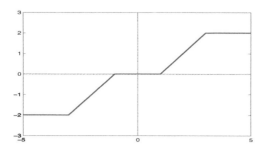

Figure 6.3. *The two-sided soft thresholding function $t \mapsto \mathcal{S}_{1,2}(t) = \min\{\max\{|t| - 1, 0\}, 2\}\mathrm{sgn}(t)$.*

Example 6.34 (projection onto the intersection of weighted l_1 ball and a box). Let $C \subseteq \mathbb{R}^n$ be given by

$$C = \left\{ \mathbf{x} \in \mathbb{R}^n : \sum_{i=1}^n \omega_i |x_i| \leq \beta, -\boldsymbol{\alpha} \leq \mathbf{x} \leq \boldsymbol{\alpha} \right\},$$

where $\boldsymbol{\omega} \in \mathbb{R}^n_+$, $\boldsymbol{\alpha} \in [0, \infty]^n$, and $\beta \in \mathbb{R}_{++}$. Then obviously $C = \text{Lev}(f, \beta)$, where

$$f(\mathbf{x}) = \boldsymbol{\omega}^T |\mathbf{x}| + \delta_{\text{Box}[-\boldsymbol{\alpha}, \boldsymbol{\alpha}]}(\mathbf{x}) = \begin{cases} \sum_{i=1}^n \omega_i |x_i|, & -\boldsymbol{\alpha} \leq \mathbf{x} \leq \boldsymbol{\alpha}, \\ \infty & \text{else} \end{cases}$$

for any $\mathbf{x} \in \mathbb{R}^n$. By Example 6.23, for any $\lambda > 0$ and $\mathbf{x} \in \mathbb{R}^n$,

$$\text{prox}_{\lambda f}(\mathbf{x}) = (\min\{\max\{|x_i| - \lambda \omega_i, 0\}, \alpha_i\} \text{sgn}(x_i))_{i=1}^n = \mathcal{S}_{\lambda \boldsymbol{\omega}, \boldsymbol{\alpha}}(\mathbf{x}).$$

Therefore, invoking Theorem 6.30, we obtain that

$$P_C(\mathbf{x}) = \begin{cases} P_{\text{Box}[-\boldsymbol{\alpha}, \boldsymbol{\alpha}]}(\mathbf{x}), & \boldsymbol{\omega}^T |P_{\text{Box}[-\boldsymbol{\alpha}, \boldsymbol{\alpha}]}(\mathbf{x})| \leq \beta, \\ \mathcal{S}_{\lambda^* \boldsymbol{\omega}, \boldsymbol{\alpha}}(\mathbf{x}), & \boldsymbol{\omega}^T |P_{\text{Box}[-\boldsymbol{\alpha}, \boldsymbol{\alpha}]}(\mathbf{x})| > \beta, \end{cases}$$

where λ^* is any positive root of the nonincreasing function

$$\varphi(\lambda) = \boldsymbol{\omega}^T |\mathcal{S}_{\lambda \boldsymbol{\omega}, \boldsymbol{\alpha}}(\mathbf{x})| - \beta.$$

∎

As a final illustration of Theorem 6.30, we give an example in which the domain of f is not closed.

Example 6.35. Let
$$C = \left\{ \mathbf{x} \in \mathbb{R}^n_{++} : \Pi_{i=1}^n x_i \geq \alpha \right\},$$
where $\alpha > 0$. The key property that will allow us to compute the orthogonal projection onto C is the fact that it can be rewritten as

$$C = \left\{ \mathbf{x} \in \mathbb{R}^n_{++} : -\sum_{i=1}^n \log x_i \leq -\log \alpha \right\}.$$

Thus, $C = \text{Lev}(f, -\log \alpha)$, where $f : \mathbb{R}^n \to (-\infty, \infty]$ is the negative sum of logs function:

$$f(\mathbf{x}) = \begin{cases} -\sum_{i=1}^n \log x_i, & \mathbf{x} \in \mathbb{R}^n_{++}, \\ \infty & \text{else.} \end{cases}$$

In Example 6.9 it was shown that for any $\mathbf{x} \in \mathbb{R}^n$,

$$\text{prox}_{\lambda f}(\mathbf{x}) = \left(\frac{x_j + \sqrt{x_j^2 + 4\lambda}}{2} \right)_{j=1}^n.$$

We can now invoke Theorem 6.30 to obtain a formula (up to a single parameter that can be found by a one-dimensional search) for the projection onto C, but there is one issue that needs to be treated delicately. If $\mathbf{x} \notin \mathbb{R}^n_{++}$, meaning that it has at least one nonpositive element, then $P_{\mathbb{R}^n_{++}}(\mathbf{x})$ does not exist. In this case only the second part of (6.24) is relevant, meaning that $P_C(\mathbf{x}) = \text{prox}_{\lambda^* f}(\mathbf{x})$. To conclude,

$$P_C(\mathbf{x}) = \begin{cases} \mathbf{x}, & \mathbf{x} \in C, \\ \left(\frac{x_j + \sqrt{x_j^2 + 4\lambda^*}}{2} \right)_{j=1}^{n}, & \mathbf{x} \notin C, \end{cases}$$

where λ^* is any positive root of the nonincreasing function

$$\varphi(\lambda) = -\sum_{j=1}^{n} \log\left(\frac{x_j + \sqrt{x_j^2 + 4\lambda}}{2} \right) + \log \alpha.$$

∎

6.4.5 Projection onto Epigraphs

We can use Theorem 6.30 to prove a theorem on the projection onto epigraphs of convex functions.

Theorem 6.36 (orthogonal projection onto epigraphs). *Let*

$$C = \mathrm{epi}(g) = \{(\mathbf{x}, t) \in \mathbb{E} \times \mathbb{R} : g(\mathbf{x}) \le t\},$$

where $g : \mathbb{E} \to \mathbb{R}$ *is convex. Then*

$$P_C((\mathbf{x}, s)) = \begin{cases} (\mathbf{x}, s), & g(\mathbf{x}) \le s, \\ (\mathrm{prox}_{\lambda^* g}(\mathbf{x}), s + \lambda^*), & g(\mathbf{x}) > s, \end{cases}$$

where λ^* *is any positive root of the function*

$$\psi(\lambda) = g(\mathrm{prox}_{\lambda g}(\mathbf{x})) - \lambda - s.$$

In addition, ψ *is nonincreasing.*

Proof. Define $f : \mathbb{E} \times \mathbb{R} \to \mathbb{R}$ as $f(\mathbf{x}, t) \equiv g(\mathbf{x}) - t$. By definition of the prox,

$$\mathrm{prox}_{\lambda f}(\mathbf{x}, s) = \mathrm{argmin}_{\mathbf{y}, t} \left\{ \frac{1}{2} \|\mathbf{y} - \mathbf{x}\|^2 + \frac{1}{2}(t - s)^2 + \lambda f(\mathbf{y}, t) \right\}$$

$$= \mathrm{argmin}_{\mathbf{y}, t} \left\{ \frac{1}{2} \|\mathbf{y} - \mathbf{x}\|^2 + \frac{1}{2}(t - s)^2 + \lambda g(\mathbf{y}) - \lambda t \right\}.$$

The above problem is separable in $\mathbf{y}$ and $\mathbf{t}$, and thus

$$\mathrm{prox}_{\lambda f}(\mathbf{x}, s) = \left(\mathrm{argmin}_{\mathbf{y}} \left\{ \frac{1}{2} \|\mathbf{y} - \mathbf{x}\|^2 + \lambda g(\mathbf{y}) \right\}, \mathrm{argmin}_t \left\{ \frac{1}{2}(t - s)^2 - \lambda t \right\} \right)$$

$$= \left(\mathrm{prox}_{\lambda g}(\mathbf{x}), \mathrm{prox}_{\lambda h}(s) \right),$$

where $h(t) \equiv -t$. Since λh is linear, then by Section 6.2.2, $\mathrm{prox}_{\lambda h}(z) = z + \lambda$ for any $z \in \mathbb{R}$. Thus,

$$\mathrm{prox}_{\lambda f}(\mathbf{x}, s) = \left(\mathrm{prox}_{\lambda g}(\mathbf{x}), s + \lambda \right).$$

Since $\text{epi}(g) = \text{Lev}(f, 0)$, we can invoke Theorem 6.30 (noting that $\text{dom}(f) = \mathbb{E}$) and obtain that

$$P_C((\mathbf{x}, s)) = \begin{cases} (\mathbf{x}, s), & g(\mathbf{x}) \leq s, \\ (\text{prox}_{\lambda^* g}(\mathbf{x}), s + \lambda^*), & g(\mathbf{x}) > s, \end{cases}$$

where λ^* is any positive root of the function

$$\psi(\lambda) = g(\text{prox}_{\lambda g}(\mathbf{x})) - \lambda - s,$$

which by Theorem 6.30 is nonincreasing.   □

Example 6.37 (projection onto the Lorentz cone). Consider the *Lorentz cone*, which is given by $L^n = \{(\mathbf{x}, t) \in \mathbb{R}^n \times \mathbb{R} : \|\mathbf{x}\|_2 \leq t\}$. We will show that for any $(\mathbf{x}, s) \in \mathbb{R}^n \times \mathbb{R}$,

$$P_{L^n}(\mathbf{x}, s) = \begin{cases} \left(\frac{\|\mathbf{x}\|_2 + s}{2\|\mathbf{x}\|_2}\mathbf{x}, \frac{\|\mathbf{x}\|_2 + s}{2}\right), & \|\mathbf{x}\|_2 \geq |s|, \\ (\mathbf{0}, 0), & s < \|\mathbf{x}\|_2 < -s, \\ (\mathbf{x}, s), & \|\mathbf{x}\|_2 \leq s. \end{cases}$$

To show the above,[31] we invoke Theorem 6.36 to obtain the formula

$$P_{L^n}((\mathbf{x}, s)) = \begin{cases} (\mathbf{x}, s), & \|\mathbf{x}\|_2 \leq s, \\ (\text{prox}_{\lambda^* \|\cdot\|_2}(\mathbf{x}), s + \lambda^*), & \|\mathbf{x}\|_2 > s, \end{cases}$$

where λ^* is any positive root of the nonincreasing function

$$\psi(\lambda) = \|\text{prox}_{\lambda\|\cdot\|_2}(\mathbf{x})\|_2 - \lambda - s. \tag{6.29}$$

Let $(\mathbf{x}, s) \in \mathbb{R}^n \times \mathbb{R}$ be such that $\|\mathbf{x}\|_2 > s$. Recall that by Example 6.19,

$$\text{prox}_{\lambda\|\cdot\|_2}(\mathbf{x}) = \left[1 - \frac{\lambda}{\max\{\|\mathbf{x}\|_2, \lambda\}}\right]_+ \mathbf{x}.$$

Plugging the above into the expression of ψ in (6.29) yields

$$\psi(\lambda) = \begin{cases} \|\mathbf{x}\|_2 - 2\lambda - s, & \lambda \leq \|\mathbf{x}\|_2, \\ -\lambda - s, & \lambda \geq \|\mathbf{x}\|_2. \end{cases}$$

The unique positive root λ^* of the piecewise linear function ψ is

$$\lambda^* = \begin{cases} \frac{\|\mathbf{x}\|_2 - s}{2}, & \|\mathbf{x}\|_2 \geq -s, \\ -s, & \|\mathbf{x}\|_2 < -s. \end{cases}$$

[31]Actually, the formula for $P_C(\mathbf{x})$ when $\|\mathbf{x}\|_2 = s$ appears twice in the formula, but in both cases it amounts to $(\mathbf{x}, s)$.

Thus, in the case $\|\mathbf{x}\|_2 > s$ (noting that $\|\mathbf{x}\|_2 \geq -s$ corresponds to the case where $\|\mathbf{x}\|_2 \geq \lambda^*$ and $\|\mathbf{x}\|_2 < -s$ corresponds to $\|\mathbf{x}\|_2 \leq \lambda^*$),

$$(\text{prox}_{\lambda^*\|\cdot\|_2}(\mathbf{x}), s + \lambda^*) = \left(\left[1 - \frac{\lambda^*}{\max\{\|\mathbf{x}\|_2, \lambda^*\}}\right]_+ \mathbf{x}, s + \lambda^*\right),$$

$$= \begin{cases} \left(\left[1 - \frac{\|\mathbf{x}\|_2 - s}{2\|\mathbf{x}\|_2}\right]_+ \mathbf{x}, \frac{\|\mathbf{x}\|_2 + s}{2}\right), & \|\mathbf{x}\|_2 \geq -s, \\ (\mathbf{0}, 0), & \|\mathbf{x}\|_2 < -s. \end{cases}$$

$$= \begin{cases} \left(\frac{\|\mathbf{x}\|_2 + s}{2\|\mathbf{x}\|_2}\mathbf{x}, \frac{\|\mathbf{x}\|_2 + s}{2}\right), & \|\mathbf{x}\|_2 \geq -s, \\ (\mathbf{0}, 0), & \|\mathbf{x}\|_2 < -s. \end{cases}$$

Recalling that $\|\mathbf{x}\|_2 > s$, we have thus established that $P_{L^n}(\mathbf{x}, s) = (\mathbf{0}, 0)$ when $s < \|\mathbf{x}\|_2 < -s$ and that whenever $(\mathbf{x}, s)$ satisfies $\|\mathbf{x}\|_2 > s$ and $\|\mathbf{x}\|_2 \geq -s$, the formula

$$P_{L^n}(\mathbf{x}, s) = \left(\frac{\|\mathbf{x}\|_2 + s}{2\|\mathbf{x}\|_2}\mathbf{x}, \frac{\|\mathbf{x}\|_2 + s}{2}\right) \tag{6.30}$$

holds. The result now follows by noting that

$$\{(\mathbf{x}, s) : \|\mathbf{x}\|_2 \geq |s|\} = \{(\mathbf{x}, s) : \|\mathbf{x}\|_2 > s, \|\mathbf{x}\|_2 \geq -s\} \cup \{(\mathbf{x}, s) : \|\mathbf{x}\|_2 = s\},$$

and that formula (6.30) is trivial for the case $\|\mathbf{x}\|_2 = s$ (amounts to $P_{L^n}(\mathbf{x}, s) = (\mathbf{x}, s)$). ∎

Example 6.38 (projection onto the epigraph of the l_1-norm). Let

$$C = \{(\mathbf{y}, t) \in \mathbb{R}^n \times \mathbb{R} : \|\mathbf{y}\|_1 \leq t\}.$$

Invoking Theorem 6.36 and recalling that for any $\lambda > 0$, $\text{prox}_{\lambda\|\cdot\|_1} = \mathcal{T}_\lambda$, where $\mathcal{T}_\lambda$ is the soft thresholding operator (see Example 6.8), it follows that

$$P_C((\mathbf{x}, s)) = \begin{cases} (\mathbf{x}, s), & \|\mathbf{x}\|_1 \leq s, \\ (\mathcal{T}_{\lambda^*}(\mathbf{x}), s + \lambda^*), & \|\mathbf{x}\|_1 > s, \end{cases}$$

where λ^* is any positive root of the nonincreasing function

$$\varphi(\lambda) = \|\mathcal{T}_\lambda(\mathbf{x})\|_1 - \lambda - s.$$

∎

6.4.6   Summary of Orthogonal Projection Computations

Table 6.1 describes all the examples of orthogonal projection computations onto subsets of $\mathbb{R}^n$ and $\mathbb{R}^n \times \mathbb{R}$ that were discussed so far.

Table 6.1. *The following notation is used in the table.* $[\mathbf{x}]_+$ *is the non-negative part of* $\mathbf{x}$, $\mathcal{T}_\lambda(\mathbf{y}) = ([|y_i| - \lambda]_+ \mathrm{sgn}(y_i))_{i=1}^n$, *and* $\mathcal{S}_{\mathbf{a},\mathbf{b}}(\mathbf{x}) = (\min\{\max\{|x_i| - a_i, 0\}, b_i\}\mathrm{sgn}(x_i))_{i=1}^n$.

set (C)	$P_C(\mathbf{x})$	Assumptions	Reference
$\mathbb{R}_+^n$	$[\mathbf{x}]_+$	$-$	Lemma 6.26
$\mathrm{Box}[\boldsymbol{\ell}, \mathbf{u}]$	$P_C(\mathbf{x})_i = \min\{\max\{x_i, \ell_i\}, u_i\}$	$\ell_i \leq u_i$	Lemma 6.26
$B_{\|\cdot\|_2}[\mathbf{c}, r]$	$\mathbf{c} + \frac{r}{\max\{\|\mathbf{x}-\mathbf{c}\|_2, r\}}(\mathbf{x} - \mathbf{c})$	$\mathbf{c} \in \mathbb{R}^n, r > 0$	Lemma 6.26
$\{\mathbf{x} : \mathbf{A}\mathbf{x} = \mathbf{b}\}$	$\mathbf{x} - \mathbf{A}^T(\mathbf{A}\mathbf{A}^T)^{-1}(\mathbf{A}\mathbf{x} - \mathbf{b})$	$\mathbf{A} \in \mathbb{R}^{m\times n}$, $\mathbf{b} \in \mathbb{R}^m$, $\mathbf{A}$ full row rank	Lemma 6.26
$\{\mathbf{x} : \mathbf{a}^T\mathbf{x} \leq b\}$	$\mathbf{x} - \frac{[\mathbf{a}^T\mathbf{x}-b]_+}{\|\mathbf{a}\|^2}\mathbf{a}$	$\mathbf{0} \neq \mathbf{a} \in \mathbb{R}^n, b \in \mathbb{R}$	Lemma 6.26
Δ_n	$[\mathbf{x} - \mu^*\mathbf{e}]_+$ where $\mu^* \in \mathbb{R}$ satisfies $\mathbf{e}^T[\mathbf{x} - \mu^*\mathbf{e}]_+ = 1$		Corollary 6.29
$H_{\mathbf{a},b} \cap \mathrm{Box}[\boldsymbol{\ell}, \mathbf{u}]$	$P_{\mathrm{Box}[\boldsymbol{\ell},\mathbf{u}]}(\mathbf{x} - \mu^*\mathbf{a})$ where $\mu^* \in \mathbb{R}$ satisfies $\mathbf{a}^T P_{\mathrm{Box}[\boldsymbol{\ell},\mathbf{u}]}(\mathbf{x} - \mu^*\mathbf{a}) = b$	$\mathbf{a} \in \mathbb{R}^n \setminus \{\mathbf{0}\}$, $b \in \mathbb{R}$	Theorem 6.27
$H_{\mathbf{a},b}^- \cap \mathrm{Box}[\boldsymbol{\ell}, \mathbf{u}]$	$\begin{cases} P_{\mathrm{Box}[\boldsymbol{\ell},\mathbf{u}]}(\mathbf{x}), & \mathbf{a}^T\mathbf{v_x} \leq b, \\ P_{\mathrm{Box}[\boldsymbol{\ell},\mathbf{u}]}(\mathbf{x} - \lambda^*\mathbf{a}), & \mathbf{a}^T\mathbf{v_x} > b, \end{cases}$ $\mathbf{v_x} = P_{\mathrm{Box}[\boldsymbol{\ell},\mathbf{u}]}(\mathbf{x})$, $\mathbf{a}^T P_{\mathrm{Box}[\boldsymbol{\ell},\mathbf{u}]}(\mathbf{x} - \lambda^*\mathbf{a}) = b, \lambda^* > 0$	$\mathbf{a} \in \mathbb{R}^n \setminus \{\mathbf{0}\}$, $b \in \mathbb{R}$	Example 6.32
$B_{\|\cdot\|_1}[\mathbf{0}, \alpha]$	$\begin{cases} \mathbf{x}, & \|\mathbf{x}\|_1 \leq \alpha, \\ \mathcal{T}_{\lambda^*}(\mathbf{x}), & \|\mathbf{x}\|_1 > \alpha, \end{cases}$ $\|\mathcal{T}_{\lambda^*}(\mathbf{x})\|_1 = \alpha, \lambda^* > 0$	$\alpha > 0$	Example 6.33
$\{\mathbf{x} : \boldsymbol{\omega}^T|\mathbf{x}| \leq \beta,$ $-\boldsymbol{\alpha} \leq \mathbf{x} \leq \boldsymbol{\alpha}\}$	$\begin{cases} \mathbf{v_x}, & \boldsymbol{\omega}^T|\mathbf{v_x}| \leq \beta, \\ \mathcal{S}_{\lambda^*\boldsymbol{\omega},\boldsymbol{\alpha}}(\mathbf{x}), & \boldsymbol{\omega}^T|\mathbf{v_x}| > \beta, \end{cases}$ $\mathbf{v_x} = P_{\mathrm{Box}[-\boldsymbol{\alpha},\boldsymbol{\alpha}]}(\mathbf{x})$, $\boldsymbol{\omega}^T|\mathcal{S}_{\lambda^*\boldsymbol{\omega},\boldsymbol{\alpha}}(\mathbf{x})| = \beta, \lambda^* > 0$	$\boldsymbol{\omega} \in \mathbb{R}_+^n$, $\boldsymbol{\alpha} \in [0,\infty]^n$, $\beta \in \mathbb{R}_{++}$	Example 6.34
$\{\mathbf{x} > 0 : \Pi x_i \geq \alpha\}$	$\begin{cases} \mathbf{x}, & \mathbf{x} \in C, \\ \left(\frac{x_j + \sqrt{x_j^2 + 4\lambda^*}}{2}\right)_{j=1}^n, & \mathbf{x} \notin C, \end{cases}$ $\Pi_{j=1}^n\left((x_j + \sqrt{x_j^2 + 4\lambda^*})/2\right) = \alpha, \lambda^* > 0$	$\alpha > 0$	Example 6.35
$\{(\mathbf{x}, s) : \|\mathbf{x}\|_2 \leq s\}$	$\left(\frac{\|\mathbf{x}\|_2+s}{2\|\mathbf{x}\|_2}\mathbf{x}, \frac{\|\mathbf{x}\|_2+s}{2}\right)$ if $\|\mathbf{x}\|_2 \geq |s|$ $(\mathbf{0}, 0)$ if $s < \|\mathbf{x}\|_2 < -s,$ $(\mathbf{x}, s)$ if $\|\mathbf{x}\|_2 \leq s$.		Example 6.37
$\{(\mathbf{x}, s) : \|\mathbf{x}\|_1 \leq s\}$	$\begin{cases} (\mathbf{x}, s), & \|\mathbf{x}\|_1 \leq s, \\ (\mathcal{T}_{\lambda^*}(\mathbf{x}), s + \lambda^*), & \|\mathbf{x}\|_1 > s, \end{cases}$ $\|\mathcal{T}_{\lambda^*}(\mathbf{x})\|_1 - \lambda^* - s = 0, \lambda^* > 0$		Example 6.38

6.5 The Second Prox Theorem

We can use Fermat's optimality condition (Theorem 3.63) in order to prove the second prox theorem.

Theorem 6.39 (second prox theorem). *Let $f : \mathbb{E} \to (-\infty, \infty]$ be a proper closed and convex function. Then for any $\mathbf{x}, \mathbf{u} \in \mathbb{E}$, the following three claims are equivalent:*

(i) $\mathbf{u} = \mathrm{prox}_f(\mathbf{x})$.

(ii) $\mathbf{x} - \mathbf{u} \in \partial f(\mathbf{u})$.

(iii) $\langle \mathbf{x} - \mathbf{u}, \mathbf{y} - \mathbf{u} \rangle \leq f(\mathbf{y}) - f(\mathbf{u})$ *for any* $\mathbf{y} \in \mathbb{E}$.

Proof. By definition, $\mathbf{u} = \mathrm{prox}_f(\mathbf{x})$ if and only if $\mathbf{u}$ is the minimizer of the problem

$$\min_{\mathbf{v}} \left\{ f(\mathbf{v}) + \frac{1}{2} \|\mathbf{v} - \mathbf{x}\|^2 \right\},$$

which, by Fermat's optimality condition (Theorem 3.63) and the sum rule of subdifferential calculus (Theorem 3.40), is equivalent to the relation

$$\mathbf{0} \in \partial f(\mathbf{u}) + \mathbf{u} - \mathbf{x}. \tag{6.31}$$

We have thus shown the equivalence between claims (i) and (ii). Finally, by the definition of the subgradient, the membership relation of claim (ii) is equivalent to (iii). □

A direct consequence of the second prox theorem is that for a proper closed and convex function, $\mathbf{x} = \mathrm{prox}_f(\mathbf{x})$ if and only $\mathbf{x}$ is a minimizer of f.

Corollary 6.40. *Let f be a proper closed and convex function. Then $\mathbf{x}$ is a minimizer of f if and only if $\mathbf{x} = \mathrm{prox}_f(\mathbf{x})$.*

Proof. $\mathbf{x}$ is a minimizer of f if and only if $\mathbf{0} \in \partial f(\mathbf{x})$, that is, if and only if $\mathbf{x} - \mathbf{x} \in \partial f(\mathbf{x})$, which by the second prox theorem (equivalence between (i) and (ii)) is the same as $\mathbf{x} = \mathrm{prox}_f(\mathbf{x})$. □

When $f = \delta_C$, with C being a nonempty closed and convex set, the equivalence between claims (i) and (iii) in the second prox theorem amounts to the second projection theorem.

Theorem 6.41 (second projection theorem). *Let $C \subseteq \mathbb{E}$ be a nonempty closed and convex set. Let $\mathbf{u} \in C$. Then $\mathbf{u} = P_C(\mathbf{x})$ if and only if*

$$\langle \mathbf{x} - \mathbf{u}, \mathbf{y} - \mathbf{u} \rangle \leq 0 \text{ for any } \mathbf{y} \in C.$$

Another rather direct result of the second prox theorem is the firm nonexpansivity of the prox operator.

Theorem 6.42 (firm nonexpansivity of the prox operator). *Let f be a proper closed and convex function. Then for any $\mathbf{x}, \mathbf{y} \in \mathbb{E}$,*

(a) **(firm nonexpansivity)**

$$\langle \mathbf{x} - \mathbf{y}, \operatorname{prox}_f(\mathbf{x}) - \operatorname{prox}_f(\mathbf{y}) \rangle \geq \| \operatorname{prox}_f(\mathbf{x}) - \operatorname{prox}_f(\mathbf{y}) \|^2.$$

(b) **(nonexpansivity)**

$$\| \operatorname{prox}_f(\mathbf{x}) - \operatorname{prox}_f(\mathbf{y}) \| \leq \| \mathbf{x} - \mathbf{y} \|.$$

Proof. (a) Denoting $\mathbf{u} = \operatorname{prox}_f(\mathbf{x}), \mathbf{v} = \operatorname{prox}_f(\mathbf{y})$, by the equivalence of (i) and (ii) in the second prox theorem (Theorem 6.39), it follows that

$$\mathbf{x} - \mathbf{u} \in \partial f(\mathbf{u}), \mathbf{y} - \mathbf{v} \in \partial f(\mathbf{v}).$$

Thus, by the subgradient inequality,

$$f(\mathbf{v}) \geq f(\mathbf{u}) + \langle \mathbf{x} - \mathbf{u}, \mathbf{v} - \mathbf{u} \rangle,$$
$$f(\mathbf{u}) \geq f(\mathbf{v}) + \langle \mathbf{y} - \mathbf{v}, \mathbf{u} - \mathbf{v} \rangle.$$

Summing the above two inequalities, we obtain

$$0 \geq \langle \mathbf{y} - \mathbf{x} + \mathbf{u} - \mathbf{v}, \mathbf{u} - \mathbf{v} \rangle,$$

which is the same as

$$\langle \mathbf{x} - \mathbf{y}, \mathbf{u} - \mathbf{v} \rangle \geq \| \mathbf{u} - \mathbf{v} \|^2,$$

that is,

$$\langle \mathbf{x} - \mathbf{y}, \operatorname{prox}_f(\mathbf{x}) - \operatorname{prox}_f(\mathbf{y}) \rangle \geq \| \operatorname{prox}_f(\mathbf{x}) - \operatorname{prox}_f(\mathbf{y}) \|^2.$$

(b) If $\operatorname{prox}_f(\mathbf{x}) = \operatorname{prox}_f(\mathbf{y})$, then the inequality is obvious. Assume that $\operatorname{prox}_f(\mathbf{x}) \neq \operatorname{prox}_f(\mathbf{y})$. Using (a) and the Cauchy–Schwarz inequality, it follows that

$$\| \operatorname{prox}_f(\mathbf{x}) - \operatorname{prox}_f(\mathbf{y}) \|^2 \leq \langle \operatorname{prox}_h(\mathbf{x}) - \operatorname{prox}_h(\mathbf{y}), \mathbf{x} - \mathbf{y} \rangle$$
$$\leq \| \operatorname{prox}_h(\mathbf{x}) - \operatorname{prox}_h(\mathbf{y}) \| \cdot \| \mathbf{x} - \mathbf{y} \|.$$

Dividing by $\| \operatorname{prox}_h(\mathbf{x}) - \operatorname{prox}_h(\mathbf{y}) \|$, the desired result is established.   □

The following result shows how to compute the prox of the distance function to a nonempty closed and convex set. The proof is heavily based on the second prox theorem.

Lemma 6.43 (prox of the distance function). *Let $C \subseteq \mathbb{E}$ be a nonempty, closed, and convex set. Let $\lambda > 0$. Then for any $\mathbf{x} \in \mathbb{E}$,*

$$\operatorname{prox}_{\lambda d_C}(\mathbf{x}) = \begin{cases} (1 - \theta)\mathbf{x} + \theta P_C(\mathbf{x}), & d_C(\mathbf{x}) > \lambda, \\ P_C(\mathbf{x}), & d_C(\mathbf{x}) \leq \lambda, \end{cases} \tag{6.32}$$

where[32]

$$\theta = \frac{\lambda}{d_C(\mathbf{x})}. \tag{6.33}$$

Proof. Let $\mathbf{u} = \text{prox}_{\lambda d_C}(\mathbf{x})$. By the second prox theorem (Theorem 6.39),

$$\mathbf{x} - \mathbf{u} \in \lambda \partial d_C(\mathbf{u}). \tag{6.34}$$

We will split the analysis into two cases.

Case I. $\mathbf{u} \notin C$. By Example 3.49, (6.34) is the same as

$$\mathbf{x} - \mathbf{u} = \lambda \frac{\mathbf{u} - P_C(\mathbf{u})}{d_C(\mathbf{u})}.$$

Denoting $\alpha = \frac{\lambda}{d_C(\mathbf{u})}$, the last equality can be rewritten as

$$\mathbf{u} = \frac{1}{\alpha + 1} \mathbf{x} + \frac{\alpha}{\alpha + 1} P_C(\mathbf{u}) \tag{6.35}$$

or as

$$\mathbf{x} - P_C(\mathbf{u}) = (\alpha + 1)(\mathbf{u} - P_C(\mathbf{u})). \tag{6.36}$$

By the second projection theorem (Theorem 6.41), in order to show that $P_C(\mathbf{u}) = P_C(\mathbf{x})$, it is enough to show that

$$\langle \mathbf{x} - P_C(\mathbf{u}), \mathbf{y} - P_C(\mathbf{u}) \rangle \leq 0 \text{ for any } \mathbf{y} \in C. \tag{6.37}$$

Using (6.36), we can deduce that (6.37) is equivalent to

$$(\alpha + 1)\langle \mathbf{u} - P_C(\mathbf{u}), \mathbf{y} - P_C(\mathbf{u}) \rangle \leq 0 \text{ for any } \mathbf{y} \in C,$$

which is a valid inequality by the second projection theorem, and hence $P_C(\mathbf{u}) = P_C(\mathbf{x})$. Using this fact and taking the norm in both sides of (6.36), we obtain that

$$d_C(\mathbf{x}) = (\alpha + 1)d_C(\mathbf{u}) = d_C(\mathbf{u}) + \lambda,$$

which also shows that in this case $d_C(\mathbf{x}) > \lambda$ (since $d_C(\mathbf{u}) > 0$) and that

$$\frac{1}{\alpha + 1} = \frac{d_C(\mathbf{u})}{\lambda + d_C(\mathbf{u})} = \frac{d_C(\mathbf{x}) - \lambda}{d_C(\mathbf{x})} = 1 - \theta,$$

where θ is given in (6.33). Therefore, (6.35) can also be written as (recalling also that $P_C(\mathbf{u}) = P_C(\mathbf{x})$)

$$\text{prox}_{\lambda d_C}(\mathbf{x}) = (1 - \theta)\mathbf{x} + \theta P_C(\mathbf{x}). \tag{6.38}$$

Case II. If $\mathbf{u} \in C$, then $\mathbf{u} = P_C(\mathbf{x})$. To show this, let $\mathbf{v} \in C$. Since $\mathbf{u} = \text{prox}_{\lambda d_C}(\mathbf{x})$, it follows in particular that

$$\lambda d_C(\mathbf{u}) + \frac{1}{2}\|\mathbf{u} - \mathbf{x}\|^2 \leq \lambda d_C(\mathbf{v}) + \frac{1}{2}\|\mathbf{v} - \mathbf{x}\|^2,$$

---

[32]Since θ is used only when $\mathbf{x} \notin C$, it follows that $d_C(\mathbf{x}) > 0$, so that θ is well defined.

and hence, since $d_C(\mathbf{u}) = d_C(\mathbf{v}) = 0$,

$$\|\mathbf{u} - \mathbf{x}\| \leq \|\mathbf{v} - \mathbf{x}\|.$$

Therefore,

$$\mathbf{u} = \operatorname{argmin}_{\mathbf{v} \in C} \|\mathbf{v} - \mathbf{x}\| = P_C(\mathbf{x}).$$

By Example 3.49, the optimality condition (6.34) becomes

$$\frac{\mathbf{x} - P_C(\mathbf{x})}{\lambda} \in N_C(\mathbf{u}) \cap B[\mathbf{0}, 1],$$

which in particular implies that

$$\left\| \frac{\mathbf{x} - P_C(\mathbf{x})}{\lambda} \right\| \leq 1,$$

that is,

$$d_C(\mathbf{x}) = \|P_C(\mathbf{x}) - \mathbf{x}\| \leq \lambda.$$

Since the first case in which (6.38) holds corresponds to vectors satisfying $d_C(\mathbf{x}) > \lambda$, while the second case in which $\operatorname{prox}_{\lambda d_C}(\mathbf{x}) = P_C(\mathbf{x})$ corresponds to vectors satisfying $d_C(\mathbf{x}) \leq \lambda$, the desired result (6.32) is established. $\square$

6.6   Moreau Decomposition

A key property of the prox operator is the so-called Moreau decomposition theorem, which connects the prox operator of proper closed convex functions and their conjugates.

Theorem 6.44 (Moreau decomposition).   *Let* $f : \mathbb{E} \to (-\infty, \infty]$ *be proper closed and convex. Then for any* $\mathbf{x} \in \mathbb{E}$,

$$\operatorname{prox}_f(\mathbf{x}) + \operatorname{prox}_{f^*}(\mathbf{x}) = \mathbf{x}.$$

Proof. Let $\mathbf{x} \in \mathbb{E}$ and denote $\mathbf{u} = \operatorname{prox}_f(\mathbf{x})$. Then by the equivalence between claims (i) and (ii) in the second prox theorem (Theorem 6.39), it follows that $\mathbf{x} - \mathbf{u} \in \partial f(\mathbf{u})$, which by the conjugate subgradient theorem (Theorem 4.20) is equivalent to $\mathbf{u} \in \partial f^*(\mathbf{x} - \mathbf{u})$. Using the second prox theorem again, we conclude that $\mathbf{x} - \mathbf{u} = \operatorname{prox}_{f^*}(\mathbf{x})$. Therefore,

$$\operatorname{prox}_f(\mathbf{x}) + \operatorname{prox}_{f^*}(\mathbf{x}) = \mathbf{u} + (\mathbf{x} - \mathbf{u}) = \mathbf{x}.   \square$$

The next result is a useful extension of the Moreau decomposition theorem.

Theorem 6.45 (extended Moreau decomposition).   *Let* $f : \mathbb{E} \to (-\infty, \infty]$ *be proper closed and convex, and let* $\lambda > 0$. *Then for any* $\mathbf{x} \in \mathbb{E}$,

$$\operatorname{prox}_{\lambda f}(\mathbf{x}) + \lambda \operatorname{prox}_{\lambda^{-1} f^*}(\mathbf{x}/\lambda) = \mathbf{x}. \tag{6.39}$$

Proof. Using Moreau decomposition, for any $\mathbf{x} \in \mathbb{E}$,

$$\text{prox}_{\lambda f}(\mathbf{x}) = \mathbf{x} - \text{prox}_{(\lambda f)^*}(\mathbf{x}) = \mathbf{x} - \text{prox}_{\lambda f^*(\cdot/\lambda)}(\mathbf{x}), \qquad (6.40)$$

where the second equality follows by Theorem 4.14(a). By Theorem 6.12,

$$\text{prox}_{\lambda f^*(\cdot/\lambda)}(\mathbf{x}) = \lambda \text{prox}_{\lambda^{-1} f^*}(\mathbf{x}/\lambda),$$

which, combined with (6.40), yields (6.39). □

6.6.1 Support Functions

Using Moreau decomposition, we can develop a formula for computing the prox of a support function of a given nonempty closed and convex set in terms of the orthogonal projection operator.

Theorem 6.46 (prox of support functions). *Let $C \subseteq \mathbb{E}$ be a nonempty closed and convex set, and let $\lambda > 0$. Then for any $\mathbf{x} \in \mathbb{E}$,*

$$\text{prox}_{\lambda \sigma_C}(\mathbf{x}) = \mathbf{x} - \lambda P_C(\mathbf{x}/\lambda). \qquad (6.41)$$

Proof. A direct consequence of the extended Moreau decomposition formula (Theorem 6.45) along with the fact that $(\sigma_C)^* = \delta_C$ (Example 4.9). □

Following are several examples of prox computations using formula (6.41).

Example 6.47 (prox of norms). Let $f : \mathbb{E} \to \mathbb{R}$ be given by $f(\mathbf{x}) = \lambda \|\mathbf{x}\|_\alpha$, where $\lambda > 0$ and $\|\cdot\|_\alpha$ is any norm on $\mathbb{E}$. Note that $\|\cdot\|_\alpha$ is not necessarily the endowed norm on $\mathbb{E}$, which is denoted by $\|\cdot\|$ and in this chapter is always assumed to be the Euclidean norm. We know by Example 2.31 that

$$\|\mathbf{x}\|_\alpha = \sigma_C(\mathbf{x}),$$

where

$$C = B_{\|\cdot\|_{\alpha,*}}[\mathbf{0}, 1] = \{\mathbf{x} \in \mathbb{E} : \|\mathbf{x}\|_{\alpha,*} \leq 1\}$$

with $\|\cdot\|_{\alpha,*}$ being the dual norm of $\|\cdot\|_\alpha$. Invoking Theorem 6.46, we obtain

$$\text{prox}_{\lambda\|\cdot\|_\alpha}(\mathbf{x}) = \mathbf{x} - \lambda P_{B_{\|\cdot\|_{\alpha,*}}[\mathbf{0},1]}(\mathbf{x}/\lambda).$$

■

Example 6.48 (prox of l_∞-norm). By Example 6.47 we have for all $\lambda > 0$ and $\mathbf{x} \in \mathbb{R}^n$,

$$\text{prox}_{\lambda\|\cdot\|_\infty}(\mathbf{x}) = \mathbf{x} - \lambda P_{B_{\|\cdot\|_1}[\mathbf{0},1]}(\mathbf{x}/\lambda).$$

The projection onto the l_1 unit ball can be easily computed by finding a root of a nonincreasing one-dimensional function; see Example 6.33. ∎

Example 6.49 (prox of the max function). Consider the max function g : $\mathbb{R}^n \to \mathbb{R}$ given by $g(\mathbf{x}) = \max(\mathbf{x}) \equiv \max\{x_1, x_2, \ldots, x_n\}$. It is easy to see that the max function is actually the support function of the unit simplex:

$$\max(\mathbf{x}) = \sigma_{\Delta_n}(\mathbf{x}).$$

Therefore, by Theorem 6.46, for any $\lambda > 0$ and $\mathbf{x} \in \mathbb{R}^n$,

$$\mathrm{prox}_{\lambda \max(\cdot)}(\mathbf{x}) = \mathbf{x} - \lambda P_{\Delta_n}(\mathbf{x}/\lambda).$$

The projection onto the unit simplex can be efficiently computed by finding a root of a nonincreasing one-dimensional function; see Corollary 6.29. ∎

Example 6.50 (prox of the sum-of-k-largest-values function). Let $f : \mathbb{R}^n \to \mathbb{R}$ be given by

$$f(\mathbf{x}) = x_{[1]} + x_{[2]} + \cdots + x_{[k]},$$

where $k \in \{1, 2, \ldots, n\}$ and for any i, $x_{[i]}$ denotes ith largest value in the vector $\mathbf{x}$. It is not difficult to show that $f = \sigma_C$, where

$$C = \{\mathbf{y} \in \mathbb{R}^n : \mathbf{e}^T\mathbf{y} = k, \mathbf{0} \leq \mathbf{y} \leq \mathbf{e}\}.$$

Therefore, by Theorem 6.46,

$$\mathrm{prox}_{\lambda f}(\mathbf{x}) = \mathbf{x} - \lambda P_C(\mathbf{x}/\lambda).$$

That is, for any $\mathbf{x} \in \mathbb{R}^n$,

$$\mathrm{prox}_{\lambda f}(\mathbf{x}) = \mathbf{x} - \lambda P_{\{\mathbf{y}:\mathbf{e}^T\mathbf{y}=k,\mathbf{0}\leq\mathbf{y}\leq\mathbf{e}\}}(\mathbf{x}/\lambda).$$

As in the previous examples, computing the projection onto C amounts to finding a root of a monotone one-dimensional function; see Theorem 6.27. ∎

Example 6.51 (prox of the sum-of-k-largest-absolute-values function). Let $f : \mathbb{R}^n \to \mathbb{R}$ be given by

$$f(\mathbf{x}) = \sum_{i=1}^{k} |x_{\langle i \rangle}|,$$

where $k \in \{1, 2, \ldots, n\}$ and $x_{\langle i \rangle}$ is the component of $\mathbf{x}$ with the ith largest absolute value, meaning in particular that $|x_{\langle 1 \rangle}| \geq |x_{\langle 2 \rangle}| \geq \cdots \geq |x_{\langle n \rangle}|$. Then

$$f(\mathbf{x}) = \max\left\{\sum_{i=1}^{n} z_i x_i : \|\mathbf{z}\|_1 \leq k, -\mathbf{e} \leq \mathbf{z} \leq \mathbf{e}\right\}.$$

Therefore, $f = \sigma_C$, where

$$C = \{\mathbf{z} \in \mathbb{R}^n : \|\mathbf{z}\|_1 \leq k, -\mathbf{e} \leq \mathbf{z} \leq \mathbf{e}\},$$

and consequently, by Theorem 6.46,

$$\mathrm{prox}_{\lambda f}(\mathbf{x}) = \mathbf{x} - \lambda P_C(\mathbf{x}/\lambda).$$

That is, for any $\mathbf{x} \in \mathbb{R}^n$,

$$\mathrm{prox}_{\lambda f}(\mathbf{x}) = \mathbf{x} - \lambda P_{\{\mathbf{y}: \|\mathbf{y}\|_1 \le k, -\mathbf{e} \le \mathbf{y} \le \mathbf{e}\}}(\mathbf{x}/\lambda).$$

The orthogonal projection in the above formula amounts to finding a root of a nonincreasing one-dimensional function; see Example 6.34. ∎

6.7 The Moreau Envelope

6.7.1 Definition and Basic Properties

Definition 6.52 (Moreau envelope). *Given a proper closed convex function* $f : \mathbb{E} \to (-\infty, \infty]$ *and* $\mu > 0$, *the* **Moreau envelope** *of* f *is the function*

$$M_f^\mu(\mathbf{x}) = \min_{\mathbf{u} \in \mathbb{E}} \left\{ f(\mathbf{u}) + \frac{1}{2\mu} \|\mathbf{x} - \mathbf{u}\|^2 \right\}. \tag{6.42}$$

The parameter μ is called the *smoothing parameter*. The explanation for this terminology will be given in Section 6.7.2. By the first prox theorem (Theorem 6.3), the minimization problem in (6.42) has a unique solution, given by $\mathrm{prox}_{\mu f}(\mathbf{x})$. Therefore, $M_f^\mu(\mathbf{x})$ is always a real number and

$$M_f^\mu(\mathbf{x}) = f(\mathrm{prox}_{\mu f}(\mathbf{x})) + \frac{1}{2\mu} \|\mathbf{x} - \mathrm{prox}_{\mu f}(\mathbf{x})\|^2.$$

Example 6.53 (Moreau envelope of indicators). Let $f = \delta_C$, where $C \subseteq \mathbb{E}$ is a nonempty closed and convex set. By Theorem 6.24, $\mathrm{prox}_{\mu f}(\mathbf{x}) = P_C(\mathbf{x})$. Thus, for any $\mathbf{x} \in \mathbb{E}$,

$$M_f^\mu(\mathbf{x}) = \delta_C(P_C(\mathbf{x})) + \frac{1}{2\mu} \|\mathbf{x} - P_C(\mathbf{x})\|^2,$$

and hence

$$M_{\delta_C}^\mu = \frac{1}{2\mu} d_C^2.$$

∎

The next example will show that the Moreau envelope of the (Euclidean) norm is the so-called *Huber function* defined as

$$H_\mu(\mathbf{x}) = \begin{cases} \frac{1}{2\mu} \|\mathbf{x}\|^2, & \|\mathbf{x}\| \le \mu, \\ \|\mathbf{x}\| - \frac{\mu}{2}, & \|\mathbf{x}\| > \mu. \end{cases} \tag{6.43}$$

The one-dimensional Huber function is plotted in Figure 6.4, where it is illustrated that the function becomes smoother as μ becomes larger.

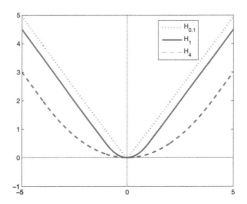

Figure 6.4. *The Huber function with parameters* $\mu = 0.1, 1, 4$. *The function becomes smoother as μ gets larger.*

Example 6.54 (Huber function). Let $f : \mathbb{E} \to \mathbb{R}$ be given by $f(\mathbf{x}) = \|\mathbf{x}\|$. Then by Example 6.19, for any $\mathbf{x} \in \mathbb{E}$ and $\mu > 0$,

$$\operatorname{prox}_{\mu f}(\mathbf{x}) = \left(1 - \frac{\mu}{\max\{\|\mathbf{x}\|, \mu\}}\right)\mathbf{x}.$$

Therefore,

$$M_f^{\mu}(\mathbf{x}) = \|\operatorname{prox}_{\mu f}(\mathbf{x})\| + \frac{1}{2\mu}\|\mathbf{x} - \operatorname{prox}_{\mu f}(\mathbf{x})\|^2 = \begin{cases} \frac{1}{2\mu}\|\mathbf{x}\|^2, & \|\mathbf{x}\| \leq \mu, \\ \|\mathbf{x}\| - \frac{\mu}{2}, & \|\mathbf{x}\| > \mu. \end{cases}$$

Thus, for any $\mu > 0$,

$$M_{\|\cdot\|}^{\mu} = H_{\mu}.$$

■

Note that the Moreau envelope function is actually a result of an infimal convolution operation between the function f and the function

$$\omega_{\mu}(\mathbf{x}) = \frac{1}{2\mu}\|\mathbf{x}\|^2. \tag{6.44}$$

That is,

$$M_f^{\mu} = f \square \omega_{\mu}.$$

One consequence of this observation is that by Theorem 2.19, if f is a proper closed[33] and convex function, then M_f^{μ} is convex. We summarize the above discussion in the following theorem.

---

[33] Actually, closedness is not necessary in order to establish the convexity of the Moreau envelope.

Theorem 6.55. *Let* $f : \mathbb{E} \to (-\infty, \infty]$ *be a proper closed and convex function, and let* ω_μ *be given in* (6.44), *where* $\mu > 0$. *Then*

(a) $M_f^\mu = f \Box \omega_\mu$;

(b) $M_f^\mu : \mathbb{E} \to \mathbb{R}$ *is real-valued and convex.*

We can immediately conclude from Theorem 6.55(a) along with the formula for the conjugate of the infimal convolution (Theorem 4.16) an expression for the conjugate of the Moreau envelope.

Corollary 6.56. *Let* $f : \mathbb{E} \to (-\infty, \infty]$ *be a proper closed and convex function and let* ω_μ *be given in* (6.44), *where* $\mu > 0$. *Then*

$$(M_f^\mu)^* = f^* + \omega_{\frac{1}{\mu}}.$$

Another useful algebraic property of the Moreau envelope is described in the following result.

Lemma 6.57. *Let* $f : \mathbb{E} \to (-\infty, \infty]$ *be a proper closed and convex function, and let* $\lambda, \mu > 0$. *Then for any* $\mathbf{x} \in \mathbb{E}$,

$$\lambda M_f^\mu(\mathbf{x}) = M_{\lambda f}^{\mu/\lambda}(\mathbf{x}). \tag{6.45}$$

Proof. For any $\mathbf{x} \in \mathbb{E}$,

$$\lambda M_f^\mu(\mathbf{x}) = \lambda \min_{\mathbf{u}} \left\{ f(\mathbf{u}) + \frac{1}{2\mu} \|\mathbf{u} - \mathbf{x}\|^2 \right\}$$
$$= \min_{\mathbf{u}} \left\{ \lambda f(\mathbf{u}) + \frac{1}{2\mu/\lambda} \|\mathbf{u} - \mathbf{x}\|^2 \right\}$$
$$= M_{\lambda f}^{\mu/\lambda}(\mathbf{x}). \quad \square$$

A simple calculus rule states that the Moreau envelope of a separable sum of functions is the sum of the corresponding Moreau envelopes.

Theorem 6.58 (Moreau envelope of sum of separable functions). *Suppose that* $\mathbb{E} = \mathbb{E}_1 \times \mathbb{E}_2 \times \cdots \times \mathbb{E}_m$, *and let* $f : \mathbb{E} \to (-\infty, \infty]$ *be given by*

$$f(\mathbf{x}_1, \mathbf{x}_2, \ldots, \mathbf{x}_m) = \sum_{i=1}^m f_i(\mathbf{x}_i), \quad \mathbf{x}_1 \in \mathbb{E}_1, \mathbf{x}_2 \in \mathbb{E}_2, \ldots, \mathbf{x}_m \in \mathbb{E}_m,$$

with $f_i : \mathbb{E}_i \to (-\infty, \infty]$ *being a proper closed and convex function for any* i. *Then given* $\mu > 0$, *for any* $\mathbf{x}_1 \in \mathbb{E}_1, \mathbf{x}_2 \in \mathbb{E}_2, \ldots, \mathbf{x}_m \in \mathbb{E}_m$,

$$M_f^\mu(\mathbf{x}_1, \mathbf{x}_2, \ldots, \mathbf{x}_m) = \sum_{i=1}^m M_{f_i}^\mu(\mathbf{x}_i).$$

Proof. For any $\mathbf{x}_1 \in \mathbb{E}_1, \mathbf{x}_2 \in \mathbb{E}_2, \ldots, \mathbf{x}_m \in \mathbb{E}_m$, denoting $\mathbf{x} = (\mathbf{x}_1, \mathbf{x}_2, \ldots, \mathbf{x}_m)$, we have

$$
\begin{aligned}
M_f^\mu(\mathbf{x}) &= \min_{\mathbf{u}_i \in \mathbb{E}_i, i=1,2,\ldots,m} \left\{ f(\mathbf{u}_1, \mathbf{u}_2, \ldots, \mathbf{u}_m) + \frac{1}{2\mu} \|(\mathbf{u}_1, \mathbf{u}_2, \ldots, \mathbf{u}_m) - \mathbf{x}\|^2 \right\} \\
&= \min_{\mathbf{u}_i \in \mathbb{E}_i, i=1,2,\ldots,m} \left\{ \sum_{i=1}^m f_i(\mathbf{u}_i) + \frac{1}{2\mu} \sum_{i=1}^m \|\mathbf{u}_i - \mathbf{x}_i\|^2 \right\} \\
&= \sum_{i=1}^m \min_{\mathbf{u}_i \in \mathbb{E}_i} \left\{ f_i(\mathbf{u}_i) + \frac{1}{2\mu} \|\mathbf{u}_i - \mathbf{x}_i\|^2 \right\} \\
&= \sum_{i=1}^m M_{f_i}^\mu(\mathbf{x}_i). \qquad \square
\end{aligned}
$$

Example 6.59 (Moreau envelope of the l_1-norm). Consider the function $f : \mathbb{R}^n \to \mathbb{R}$ given by $f(\mathbf{x}) = \|\mathbf{x}\|_1$. Note that

$$
f(\mathbf{x}) = \|\mathbf{x}\|_1 = \sum_{i=1}^n g(x_i),
$$

where $g(t) = |t|$. By Example 6.54, $M_g^\mu = H_\mu$. Thus, invoking Theorem 6.58, we obtain that for any $\mathbf{x} \in \mathbb{R}^n$,

$$
M_f^\mu(\mathbf{x}) = \sum_{i=1}^n M_g^\mu(x_i) = \sum_{i=1}^n H_\mu(x_i). \qquad \blacksquare
$$

6.7.2   Differentiability of the Moreau Envelope

The main differentiability properties of the Moreau envelope function are stated in the next result.

Theorem 6.60 (smoothness of the Moreau envelope). *Let $f : \mathbb{E} \to (-\infty, \infty]$ be a proper closed and convex function. Let $\mu > 0$. Then M_f^μ is $\frac{1}{\mu}$-smooth over $\mathbb{E}$, and for any $\mathbf{x} \in \mathbb{E}$,*

$$
\nabla M_f^\mu(\mathbf{x}) = \frac{1}{\mu} \left(\mathbf{x} - \mathrm{prox}_{\mu f}(\mathbf{x}) \right).
$$

Proof. By Theorem 6.55(a), $M_f^\mu = f \square \omega_\mu$, where $\omega_\mu = \frac{1}{2\mu} \| \cdot \|^2$. We can therefore invoke Theorem 5.30, whose assumptions are satisfied (taking $\omega = \omega_\mu$ and $L = \frac{1}{\mu}$), and conclude that M_f^μ is $\frac{1}{\mu}$-smooth. In addition, since

$$
\mathrm{prox}_{\mu f}(\mathbf{x}) = \mathrm{argmin}_{\mathbf{u} \in \mathbb{E}} \left\{ f(\mathbf{u}) + \frac{1}{2\mu} \|\mathbf{u} - \mathbf{x}\|^2 \right\},
$$

it follows that the vector $\mathbf{u}(\mathbf{x})$ defined in Theorem 5.30 is equal to $\mathrm{prox}_{\mu f}(\mathbf{x})$ and that

$$
\nabla M_f^\mu(\mathbf{x}) = \nabla \omega_\mu(\mathbf{x} - \mathbf{u}(\mathbf{x})) = \frac{1}{\mu}(\mathbf{x} - \mathrm{prox}_{\mu f}(\mathbf{x})). \qquad \square
$$

Example 6.61 (1-smoothness of $\frac{1}{2}d_C^2$). Let $C \subseteq \mathbb{E}$ be a nonempty closed and convex set. Recall that by Example 6.53, $\frac{1}{2}d_C^2 = M_{\delta_C}^1$. Then by Theorem 6.60, $\frac{1}{2}d_C^2$ is 1-smooth and

$$\nabla \left(\frac{1}{2}d_C^2\right)(\mathbf{x}) = \mathbf{x} - \mathrm{prox}_{\delta_C}(\mathbf{x}) = \mathbf{x} - P_C(\mathbf{x}).$$

Note that the above expression for the gradient was already derived in Example 3.31 and that the 1-smoothness of $\frac{1}{2}d_C^2$ was already established twice in Examples 5.5 and 5.31. ∎

Example 6.62 (smoothness of the Huber function). Recall that the Huber function is given by

$$H_\mu(\mathbf{x}) = \begin{cases} \frac{1}{2\mu}\|\mathbf{x}\|^2, & \|\mathbf{x}\| \leq \mu, \\ \|\mathbf{x}\| - \frac{\mu}{2}, & \|\mathbf{x}\| > \mu. \end{cases}$$

By Example 6.54, $H_\mu = M_f^\mu$, where $f(\mathbf{x}) = \|\mathbf{x}\|$. Then, by Theorem 6.60, H_μ is $\frac{1}{\mu}$-smooth and

$$\nabla H_\mu(\mathbf{x}) = \frac{1}{\mu}\left(\mathbf{x} - \mathrm{prox}_{\mu f}(\mathbf{x})\right)$$

$$\overset{(*)}{=} \frac{1}{\mu}\left(\mathbf{x} - \left(1 - \frac{\mu}{\max\{\|\mathbf{x}\|, \mu\}}\right)\mathbf{x}\right)$$

$$= \begin{cases} \frac{1}{\mu}\mathbf{x}, & \|\mathbf{x}\| \leq \mu, \\ \frac{\mathbf{x}}{\|\mathbf{x}\|}, & \|\mathbf{x}\| > \mu, \end{cases}$$

where the equality $(*)$ uses the expression for $\mathrm{prox}_{\mu f}$ developed in Example 6.19. ∎

6.7.3 Prox of the Moreau Envelope

An interesting and important result states that if we can compute the prox of a proper closed and convex function f, then we can also compute the prox of its Moreau envelope.

Theorem 6.63 (prox of Moreau envelope). *Let $f : \mathbb{E} \to (-\infty, \infty]$ be a proper closed and convex function, and let $\mu > 0$. Then for any $\mathbf{x} \in \mathbb{E}$,*

$$\mathrm{prox}_{M_f^\mu}(\mathbf{x}) = \mathbf{x} + \frac{1}{\mu+1}\left(\mathrm{prox}_{(\mu+1)f}(\mathbf{x}) - \mathbf{x}\right).$$

Proof. First note that

$$\min_{\mathbf{u}}\left\{M_f^\mu(\mathbf{u}) + \frac{1}{2}\|\mathbf{u} - \mathbf{x}\|^2\right\} = \min_{\mathbf{u}}\min_{\mathbf{y}}\left\{f(\mathbf{y}) + \frac{1}{2\mu}\|\mathbf{u} - \mathbf{y}\|^2 + \frac{1}{2}\|\mathbf{u} - \mathbf{x}\|^2\right\}.$$
$$\tag{6.46}$$

Exchanging the order of minimizations, we obtain the following problem:

$$\min_{\mathbf{y}} \min_{\mathbf{u}} \left\{ f(\mathbf{y}) + \frac{1}{2\mu}\|\mathbf{u}-\mathbf{y}\|^2 + \frac{1}{2}\|\mathbf{u}-\mathbf{x}\|^2 \right\}. \tag{6.47}$$

The optimal solution of the inner minimization problem in $\mathbf{u}$ is attained when the gradient w.r.t. $\mathbf{u}$ vanishes:

$$\frac{1}{\mu}(\mathbf{u}-\mathbf{y}) + (\mathbf{u}-\mathbf{x}) = \mathbf{0},$$

that is, when

$$\mathbf{u} = \mathbf{u}_\mu \equiv \frac{\mu\mathbf{x}+\mathbf{y}}{\mu+1}. \tag{6.48}$$

Therefore, the optimal value of the inner minimization problem in (6.47) is

$$f(\mathbf{y}) + \frac{1}{2\mu}\|\mathbf{u}_\mu - \mathbf{y}\|^2 + \frac{1}{2}\|\mathbf{u}_\mu - \mathbf{x}\|^2 = f(\mathbf{y}) + \frac{1}{2\mu}\left\|\frac{\mu\mathbf{x}-\mu\mathbf{y}}{\mu+1}\right\|^2 + \frac{1}{2}\left\|\frac{\mathbf{y}-\mathbf{x}}{\mu+1}\right\|^2$$

$$= f(\mathbf{y}) + \frac{1}{2(\mu+1)}\|\mathbf{x}-\mathbf{y}\|^2.$$

Therefore, the optimal solution of (6.46) is given by (6.48), where $\mathbf{y}$ is the solution of

$$\min_{\mathbf{y}} \left\{ f(\mathbf{y}) + \frac{1}{2(\mu+1)}\|\mathbf{x}-\mathbf{y}\|^2 \right\},$$

that is, $\mathbf{y} = \operatorname{prox}_{(\mu+1)f}(\mathbf{x})$. To summarize,

$$\operatorname{prox}_{M_f^\mu}(\mathbf{x}) = \frac{1}{\mu+1}\left(\mu\mathbf{x} + \operatorname{prox}_{(\mu+1)f}(\mathbf{x})\right). \qquad \square$$

Combining Theorem 6.63 with Lemma 6.57 leads to the following corollary.

Corollary 6.64. *Let* $f : \mathbb{E} \to (-\infty, \infty]$ *be a proper closed and convex function, and let* $\lambda, \mu > 0$. *Then for any* $\mathbf{x} \in \mathbb{E}$,

$$\operatorname{prox}_{\lambda M_f^\mu}(\mathbf{x}) = \mathbf{x} + \frac{\lambda}{\mu+\lambda}\left(\operatorname{prox}_{(\mu+\lambda)f}(\mathbf{x}) - \mathbf{x}\right).$$

Proof. $\operatorname{prox}_{\lambda M_f^\mu}(\mathbf{x}) = \operatorname{prox}_{M_{\lambda f}^{\mu/\lambda}}(\mathbf{x}) = \mathbf{x} + \frac{\lambda}{\mu+\lambda}\left(\operatorname{prox}_{(\mu+\lambda)f}(\mathbf{x}) - \mathbf{x}\right).$ $\qquad \square$

Example 6.65 (prox of $\frac{\lambda}{2}d_C^2$). Let $C \subseteq \mathbb{E}$ be a nonempty closed and convex set, and let $\lambda > 0$. Consider the function $f = \frac{1}{2}d_C^2$. Then, by Example 6.53, $f = M_g^1$, where $g = \delta_C$. Recall that $\operatorname{prox}_g = P_C$. Therefore, invoking Corollary 6.64, we obtain that for any $\mathbf{x} \in \mathbb{E}$,

$$\operatorname{prox}_{\lambda f}(\mathbf{x}) = \operatorname{prox}_{\lambda M_g^1}(\mathbf{x}) = \mathbf{x} + \frac{\lambda}{\lambda+1}\left(\operatorname{prox}_{(\lambda+1)g}(\mathbf{x}) - \mathbf{x}\right) = \mathbf{x} + \frac{\lambda}{\lambda+1}\left(P_C(\mathbf{x}) - \mathbf{x}\right).$$

To conclude,

$$\text{prox}_{\frac{\lambda}{2} d_C^2}(\mathbf{x}) = \frac{\lambda}{\lambda + 1} P_C(\mathbf{x}) + \frac{1}{\lambda + 1} \mathbf{x}.$$

∎

Example 6.66 (prox of the Huber function). Consider the function

$$f(\mathbf{x}) = \lambda H_\mu(\mathbf{x}),$$

where H_μ is the Huber function with a smoothing parameter $\mu > 0$ given in (6.43). By Example 6.54, $H_\mu = M_g^\mu$, where $g(\mathbf{x}) = \|\mathbf{x}\|$. Therefore, by Corollary 6.64, it follows that for any $\lambda > 0$ and $\mathbf{x} \in \mathbb{E}$ (recalling the expression for the prox of the Euclidean norm derived in Example 6.19),

$$\text{prox}_{\lambda H_\mu}(\mathbf{x}) = \text{prox}_{\lambda M_g^\mu}(\mathbf{x}) = \mathbf{x} + \frac{\lambda}{\mu + \lambda} \left(\text{prox}_{(\mu + \lambda)g}(\mathbf{x}) - \mathbf{x} \right)$$

$$= \mathbf{x} + \frac{\lambda}{\mu + \lambda} \left(\left(1 - \frac{\mu + \lambda}{\max\{\|\mathbf{x}\|, \mu + \lambda\}} \right) \mathbf{x} - \mathbf{x} \right),$$

which, after some algebraic cancellations, reduces to

$$\text{prox}_{\lambda H_\mu}(\mathbf{x}) = \left(1 - \frac{\lambda}{\max\{\|\mathbf{x}\|, \mu + \lambda\}} \right) \mathbf{x}.$$

∎

Similarly to the Moreau decomposition formula for the prox operator (Theorem 6.45), we can obtain a decomposition formula for the Moreau envelope function.

Theorem 6.67 (Moreau envelope decomposition). *Let* $f : \mathbb{E} \to (-\infty, \infty]$ *be a proper closed and convex function, and let* $\mu > 0$. *Then for any* $\mathbf{x} \in \mathbb{E}$,

$$M_f^\mu(\mathbf{x}) + M_{f^*}^{1/\mu}(\mathbf{x}/\mu) = \frac{1}{2\mu} \|\mathbf{x}\|^2.$$

Proof. Recall that for any $\mathbf{x} \in \mathbb{E}$,

$$M_f^\mu(\mathbf{x}) = \min_{\mathbf{u} \in \mathbb{E}} \{ f(\mathbf{u}) + \psi(\mathbf{u}) \},$$

where $\psi(\mathbf{u}) \equiv \frac{1}{2\mu} \|\mathbf{u} - \mathbf{x}\|^2$. By Fenchel's duality theorem (Theorem 4.15), we have

$$M_f^\mu(\mathbf{x}) = \max_{\mathbf{v} \in \mathbb{E}} \{ -f^*(\mathbf{v}) - \psi^*(-\mathbf{v}) \} = - \min_{\mathbf{v} \in \mathbb{E}} \{ f^*(\mathbf{v}) + \psi^*(-\mathbf{v}) \}.$$

Denote $\phi(\cdot) = \frac{1}{2} \| \cdot - \mathbf{x} \|^2$. Then

$$\phi^*(\mathbf{v}) = \frac{1}{2} \|\mathbf{v}\|^2 + \langle \mathbf{x}, \mathbf{v} \rangle.$$

Since $\psi = \frac{1}{\mu}\phi$, it follows by Theorem 4.14 that

$$\psi^*(\mathbf{v}) = \frac{1}{\mu}\phi^*(\mu\mathbf{v}) = \frac{\mu}{2}\|\mathbf{v}\|^2 + \langle \mathbf{x}, \mathbf{v} \rangle.$$

Therefore,

$$M_f^\mu(\mathbf{x}) = -\min_{\mathbf{v}\in\mathbb{E}}\left\{ f^*(\mathbf{v}) + \frac{\mu}{2}\|\mathbf{v}\|^2 - \langle \mathbf{x}, \mathbf{v} \rangle \right\},$$

and hence

$$M_f^\mu(\mathbf{x}) = -\min_{\mathbf{v}\in\mathbb{E}}\left\{ f^*(\mathbf{v}) + \frac{\mu}{2}\|\mathbf{v} - \mathbf{x}/\mu\|^2 - \frac{1}{2\mu}\|\mathbf{x}\|^2 \right\} = \frac{1}{2\mu}\|\mathbf{x}\|^2 - M_{f^*}^{1/\mu}(\mathbf{x}/\mu),$$

establishing the desired result. $\square$

6.8   Miscellaneous Prox Computations

In this section we gather several examples of prox computations that are not linked to any specific result established in this chapter.

6.8.1   Norm of a Linear Transformation over $\mathbb{R}^n$

Lemma 6.68. *Let $f : \mathbb{R}^n \to \mathbb{R}$ be given by $f(\mathbf{x}) = \|\mathbf{A}\mathbf{x}\|_2$, where $\mathbf{A} \in \mathbb{R}^{m\times n}$ is with full row rank, and let $\lambda > 0$. Then*

$$\mathrm{prox}_{\lambda f}(\mathbf{x}) = \begin{cases} \mathbf{x} - \mathbf{A}^T(\mathbf{A}\mathbf{A}^T)^{-1}\mathbf{A}\mathbf{x}, & \|(\mathbf{A}\mathbf{A}^T)^{-1}\mathbf{A}\mathbf{x}\|_2 \le \lambda, \\ \mathbf{x} - \mathbf{A}^T(\mathbf{A}\mathbf{A}^T + \alpha^*\mathbf{I})^{-1}\mathbf{A}\mathbf{x}, & \|(\mathbf{A}\mathbf{A}^T)^{-1}\mathbf{A}\mathbf{x}\|_2 > \lambda, \end{cases}$$

where α^* is the unique positive root of the decreasing function

$$g(\alpha) = \|(\mathbf{A}\mathbf{A}^T + \alpha\mathbf{I})^{-1}\mathbf{A}\mathbf{x}\|_2^2 - \lambda^2.$$

Proof. The vector $\mathrm{prox}_{\lambda f}(\mathbf{x})$ is the unique optimal solution to

$$\min_{\mathbf{u}\in\mathbb{R}^n}\left\{ \lambda\|\mathbf{A}\mathbf{u}\|_2 + \frac{1}{2}\|\mathbf{u} - \mathbf{x}\|_2^2 \right\},$$

which can also be rewritten as

$$\min_{\mathbf{u}\in\mathbb{R}^n, \mathbf{z}\in\mathbb{R}^m}\left\{ \frac{1}{2}\|\mathbf{u} - \mathbf{x}\|_2^2 + \lambda\|\mathbf{z}\|_2 : \mathbf{z} = \mathbf{A}\mathbf{u} \right\}. \tag{6.49}$$

To construct a Lagrangian dual problem, we first form the Lagrangian:

$$\begin{aligned} L(\mathbf{u}, \mathbf{z}; \mathbf{y}) &= \frac{1}{2}\|\mathbf{u} - \mathbf{x}\|_2^2 + \lambda\|\mathbf{z}\|_2 + \mathbf{y}^T(\mathbf{z} - \mathbf{A}\mathbf{u}) \\ &= \left[\frac{1}{2}\|\mathbf{u} - \mathbf{x}\|_2^2 - (\mathbf{A}^T\mathbf{y})^T\mathbf{u}\right] + \left[\lambda\|\mathbf{z}\|_2 + \mathbf{y}^T\mathbf{z}\right]. \end{aligned}$$

Since the Lagrangian is separable w.r.t. $\mathbf{u}$ and $\mathbf{z}$, the dual objective function can be rewritten as

$$\min_{\mathbf{u},\mathbf{z}} L(\mathbf{u},\mathbf{z};\mathbf{y}) = \min_{\mathbf{u}} \left[\frac{1}{2}\|\mathbf{u}-\mathbf{x}\|_2^2 - (\mathbf{A}^T\mathbf{y})^T\mathbf{u}\right] + \min_{\mathbf{z}}\left[\lambda\|\mathbf{z}\|_2 + \mathbf{y}^T\mathbf{z}\right]. \qquad (6.50)$$

The minimizer of the minimization problem in $\mathbf{u}$ is $\tilde{\mathbf{u}} = \mathbf{x} + \mathbf{A}^T\mathbf{y}$ with a corresponding optimal value of

$$\min_{\mathbf{u}} \left[\frac{1}{2}\|\mathbf{u}-\mathbf{x}\|_2^2 - (\mathbf{A}^T\mathbf{y})^T\mathbf{u}\right] = \frac{1}{2}\|\tilde{\mathbf{u}}-\mathbf{x}\|_2^2 - (\mathbf{A}^T\mathbf{y})^T\tilde{\mathbf{u}}$$
$$= -\frac{1}{2}\mathbf{y}^T\mathbf{A}\mathbf{A}^T\mathbf{y} - (\mathbf{A}\mathbf{x})^T\mathbf{y}. \qquad (6.51)$$

As for the second minimization problem, note that

$$\min_{\mathbf{z}} \left[\lambda\|\mathbf{z}\|_2 + \mathbf{y}^T\mathbf{z}\right] = -\max_{\mathbf{z}}[(-\mathbf{y})^T\mathbf{z} - \lambda\|\mathbf{z}\|_2] = -g^*(-\mathbf{y}),$$

where $g(\cdot) = \lambda\|\cdot\|_2$. Since $g^*(\mathbf{w}) = \lambda\delta_{B_{\|\cdot\|_2}[0,1]}(\mathbf{w}/\lambda) = \delta_{B_{\|\cdot\|_2}[0,\lambda]}$ (see Section 4.4.12 and Theorem 4.14), we can conclude that

$$\min_{\mathbf{z}} \left[\lambda\|\mathbf{z}\|_2 + \mathbf{y}^T\mathbf{z}\right] = \begin{cases} 0, & \|\mathbf{y}\|_2 \leq \lambda, \\ -\infty, & \|\mathbf{y}\|_2 > \lambda. \end{cases}$$

Combining this with (6.51), we obtain the following dual problem:

$$\max_{\mathbf{y}\in\mathbb{R}^m} \left\{-\frac{1}{2}\mathbf{y}^T\mathbf{A}\mathbf{A}^T\mathbf{y} - (\mathbf{A}\mathbf{x})^T\mathbf{y} : \|\mathbf{y}\|_2 \leq \lambda\right\}. \qquad (6.52)$$

Note that strong duality holds for the primal-dual pair of problems (6.49) and (6.52) (see Theorem A.1). To solve problem (6.52), we will first rewrite it as a minimization problem:

$$\min_{\mathbf{y}\in\mathbb{R}^m} \left\{\frac{1}{2}\mathbf{y}^T\mathbf{A}\mathbf{A}^T\mathbf{y} + (\mathbf{A}\mathbf{x})^T\mathbf{y} : \|\mathbf{y}\|_2^2 \leq \lambda^2\right\}. \qquad (6.53)$$

So far we have shown that

$$\mathrm{prox}_{\lambda f}(\mathbf{x}) = \mathbf{x} + \mathbf{A}^T\mathbf{y}, \qquad (6.54)$$

where $\mathbf{y}$ is an optimal solution of problem (6.53). Since problem (6.53) is convex and satisfies Slater's condition, it follows by the KKT conditions that $\mathbf{y}$ is an optimal solution of (6.53) if and only if there exists α^* (optimal dual variable) for which

$$(\mathbf{A}\mathbf{A}^T + \alpha^*\mathbf{I})\mathbf{y} + \mathbf{A}\mathbf{x} = \mathbf{0}, \qquad (6.55)$$
$$\alpha^*(\|\mathbf{y}\|_2^2 - \lambda^2) = 0, \qquad (6.56)$$
$$\|\mathbf{y}\|_2^2 \leq \lambda^2, \qquad (6.57)$$
$$\alpha^* \geq 0. \qquad (6.58)$$

There are two options. In the first, $\alpha^* = 0$, and then by (6.55),

$$\mathbf{y} = -(\mathbf{A}\mathbf{A}^T)^{-1}\mathbf{A}\mathbf{x}. \qquad (6.59)$$

Since (6.56) and (6.58) are automatically satisfied for $\alpha^* = 0$, we can conclude that $\mathbf{y}$ given in (6.59) is the optimal solution of (6.53) if and only if (6.57) is satisfied, meaning if and only if $\|(\mathbf{A}\mathbf{A}^T)^{-1}\mathbf{A}\mathbf{x}\|_2 \leq \lambda$. In this case, by (6.54), $\operatorname{prox}_{\lambda f}(\mathbf{x}) = \mathbf{x} - \mathbf{A}^T(\mathbf{A}\mathbf{A}^T)^{-1}\mathbf{A}\mathbf{x}$.

On the other hand, if $\|(\mathbf{A}\mathbf{A}^T)^{-1}\mathbf{A}\mathbf{x}\|_2 > \lambda$, then $\alpha^* > 0$, and hence by the complementary slackness condition (6.56),

$$\|\mathbf{y}\|_2^2 = \lambda^2. \tag{6.60}$$

By (6.55),

$$\mathbf{y} = -(\mathbf{A}\mathbf{A}^T + \alpha^*\mathbf{I})^{-1}\mathbf{A}\mathbf{x}.$$

Using (6.60), we can conclude that α^* can be uniquely determined as the positive root of the function

$$g(\alpha) = \|(\mathbf{A}\mathbf{A}^T + \alpha\mathbf{I})^{-1}\mathbf{A}\mathbf{x}\|_2^2 - \lambda^2.$$

It is easy to see that g is strictly decreasing for $\alpha \geq 0$, and therefore g has a unique root. □

6.8.2   Squared l_1-Norm

The prox of the l_1-norm has a simple formula. In this section we will show how to compute the prox of the squared l_1-norm. We will require the following lemma that expresses $\|\mathbf{x}\|_1^2$ as the optimal value of an optimization problem written in terms of the function

$$\varphi(s,t) = \begin{cases} \frac{s^2}{t}, & t > 0, \\ 0, & s = 0, t = 0, \\ \infty & \text{else.} \end{cases} \tag{6.61}$$

By Example 2.32, φ is closed and convex (even though it is not continuous at $(s,t) = (0,0)$).

Lemma 6.69 (variational representation of $\|\cdot\|_1^2$). *For any $\mathbf{x} \in \mathbb{R}^n$ the following holds:*

$$\min_{\boldsymbol{\lambda} \in \Delta_n} \sum_{j=1}^n \varphi(x_j, \lambda_j) = \|\mathbf{x}\|_1^2, \tag{6.62}$$

where φ is defined in (6.61). An optimal solution of the minimization problem in (6.62) is given by

$$\tilde{\lambda}_j = \begin{cases} \frac{|x_j|}{\|\mathbf{x}\|_1}, & \mathbf{x} \neq \mathbf{0}, \\ \frac{1}{n}, & \mathbf{x} = \mathbf{0}, \end{cases} \quad j = 1, 2, \ldots, n. \tag{6.63}$$

Proof. Since problem (6.62) consists of minimizing a closed and convex function (by Example 2.32) over a compact set, then by the Weierstrass theorem for closed functions (Theorem 2.12), it possesses an optimal solution, which we denote by $\boldsymbol{\lambda}^* \in \Delta_n$. Define

$$I_0 = \{i \in \{1, 2, \ldots, n\} : \lambda_i^* = 0\},$$
$$I_1 = \{i \in \{1, 2, \ldots, n\} : \lambda_i^* > 0\}.$$

By the definitions of I_0 and I_1, we have

$$\sum_{i \in I_1} \lambda_j^* = \sum_{i=1}^n \lambda_j^* = 1. \tag{6.64}$$

It holds that $x_i = 0$ for any $i \in I_0$, since otherwise we will have that $\varphi(x_i, \lambda_i^*) = \infty$, which is a clear contradiction to the optimality of $\boldsymbol{\lambda}^*$. Therefore, using the Cauchy–Schwarz inequality,

$$\sum_{j=1}^n |x_j| = \sum_{j \in I_1} |x_j| = \sum_{j \in I_1} \frac{|x_j|}{\sqrt{\lambda_j^*}} \sqrt{\lambda_j^*} \leq \sqrt{\sum_{j \in I_1} \frac{x_j^2}{\lambda_j^*}} \cdot \sqrt{\sum_{j \in I_1} \lambda_j^*} \overset{(6.64)}{=} \sqrt{\sum_{j \in I_1} \frac{x_j^2}{\lambda_j^*}}.$$

We can thus conclude that

$$\sum_{j=1}^n \varphi(x_j, \lambda_j^*) = \sum_{j \in I_1} \varphi(x_j, \lambda_j^*) = \sum_{j \in I_1} \frac{x_j^2}{\lambda_j^*} \geq \|\mathbf{x}\|_1^2. \tag{6.65}$$

On the other hand, since $\boldsymbol{\lambda}^*$ is an optimal solution of the problem in (6.62),

$$\sum_{j=1}^n \varphi(x_j, \lambda_j^*) \leq \sum_{j=1}^n \varphi(x_j, \tilde{\lambda}_j) = \|\mathbf{x}\|_1^2, \tag{6.66}$$

where $\tilde{\boldsymbol{\lambda}}$ is given by (6.63). Combining (6.65) and (6.66), we finally conclude that the optimal value of the minimization problem in (6.62) is $\|\mathbf{x}\|_1^2$ and that $\tilde{\boldsymbol{\lambda}}$ is an optimal solution. □

Lemma 6.70 (prox of $\|\cdot\|_1^2$).[34] *Let $f : \mathbb{R}^n \to \mathbb{R}$ be given by $f(\mathbf{x}) = \|\mathbf{x}\|_1^2$, and let $\rho > 0$. Then*

$$\mathrm{prox}_{\rho f}(\mathbf{x}) = \begin{cases} \left(\dfrac{\lambda_i x_i}{\lambda_i + 2\rho} \right)_{i=1}^n, & \mathbf{x} \neq \mathbf{0}, \\ \mathbf{0}, & \mathbf{x} = \mathbf{0}, \end{cases}$$

where $\lambda_i = \left[\dfrac{\sqrt{\rho}|x_i|}{\sqrt{\mu^*}} - 2\rho \right]_+$ with μ^* being any positive root of the nonincreasing function

$$\psi(\mu) = \sum_{i=1}^n \left[\frac{\sqrt{\rho}|x_i|}{\sqrt{\mu}} - 2\rho \right]_+ - 1.$$

---

[34]The computation of the prox of the squared l_1-norm is due to Evgeniou, Pontil, Spinellis, and Nassuphis [54].

Proof. If $\mathbf{x} = \mathbf{0}$, then obviously $\text{prox}_{\rho f}(\mathbf{x}) = \text{argmin}_{\mathbf{u}} \left\{ \frac{1}{2} \|\mathbf{u}\|_2^2 + \rho \|\mathbf{u}\|_1^2 \right\} = \mathbf{0}$. Assume that $\mathbf{x} \neq \mathbf{0}$. By Lemma 6.69, $\mathbf{u} = \text{prox}_{\rho f}(\mathbf{x})$ if and only if it is the $\mathbf{u}$-part of the optimal solution of

$$\min_{\mathbf{u} \in \mathbb{R}^n, \boldsymbol{\lambda} \in \Delta_n} \left\{ \frac{1}{2} \|\mathbf{u} - \mathbf{x}\|_2^2 + \rho \sum_{i=1}^{n} \varphi(u_i, \lambda_i) \right\},$$

where φ is defined in (6.61). Minimizing first with respect to $\mathbf{u}$, we obtain that $u_i = \frac{\lambda_i x_i}{\lambda_i + 2\rho}$, and the problem thus reduces to

$$
\begin{aligned}
\min_{\boldsymbol{\lambda}} \quad & \sum_{i=1}^{n} \frac{\rho x_i^2}{\lambda_i + 2\rho} \\
\text{s.t.} \quad & \mathbf{e}^T \boldsymbol{\lambda} = 1, \\
& \boldsymbol{\lambda} \geq \mathbf{0}.
\end{aligned}
\tag{6.67}
$$

By Theorem A.1, strong duality holds for problem (6.67) (taking the underlying set as $X = \mathbb{R}_+^n$). Associating a Lagrange multiplier μ to the equality constraint, the Lagrangian is

$$L(\boldsymbol{\lambda}; \mu) = \sum_{i=1}^{n} \left(\frac{\rho x_i^2}{\lambda_i + 2\rho} + \lambda_i \mu \right) - \mu.$$

By Theorem A.2, $\boldsymbol{\lambda}^*$ is an optimal solution of (6.67) if and only if there exists μ^* for which

$$\boldsymbol{\lambda}^* \in \text{argmin}_{\boldsymbol{\lambda} \geq \mathbf{0}} L(\boldsymbol{\lambda}; \mu^*), \tag{6.68}$$

$$\mathbf{e}^T \boldsymbol{\lambda}^* = 1. \tag{6.69}$$

Since the minimum in (6.68) is finite and attained, and since $\mathbf{x} \neq \mathbf{0}$, it follows that $\mu^* > 0$ (otherwise, if $\mu^* = 0$, the minimum in (6.68) would not be attained). Exploiting the separability of the Lagrangian, it follows that (6.68) is the same as

$$\lambda_i^* = \left[\frac{\sqrt{\rho} |x_i|}{\sqrt{\mu^*}} - 2\rho \right]_+.$$

The dual optimal variable μ^* is chosen to satisfy (6.69):

$$\sum_{i=1}^{n} \left[\frac{\sqrt{\rho} |x_i|}{\sqrt{\mu^*}} - 2\rho \right]_+ = 1. \quad \square$$

6.8.3   Projection onto the Set of s-Sparse Vectors

Let $s \in \{1, 2, \ldots, n\}$ and consider the set

$$C_s = \{\mathbf{x} \in \mathbb{R}^n : \|\mathbf{x}\|_0 \leq s\}.$$

The set C_s comprises all *s-sparse vectors*, meaning all vectors with at most s nonzero elements. Obviously C_s is not convex; for example, for $n = 2$, $(0, 1)^T, (1, 0)^T \in C_1$, but $(0.5, 0.5)^T = 0.5(0, 1)^T + 0.5(1, 0)^T \notin C_1$. The set C_s is closed as a level set of the closed function $\|\cdot\|_0$ (see Example 2.11). Therefore, by Theorem 6.4, $P_{C_s} = \text{prox}_{\delta_{C_s}}$ is nonempty; however, the nonconvexity of C_s implies that $P_{C_s}(\mathbf{x})$ is not necessarily a singleton.

The set $P_{C_s}(\mathbf{x})$ is described in Lemma 6.71 below. The description requires some additional notation. For a vector $\mathbf{x} \in \mathbb{R}^n$ and a set of indices $S \subseteq \{1, 2, \ldots, n\}$, the vector $\mathbf{x}_S$ is the subvector of $\mathbf{x}$ that corresponds to the indices in S. For example, for $n = 4$, if $\mathbf{x} = (4, 3, 5, -1)^T$, then $\mathbf{x}_{\{1,4\}} = (4, -1)^T, \mathbf{x}_{\{2,3\}} = (3, 5)^T$. For a given indices set $S \subseteq \{1, 2, \ldots, n\}$, the matrix $\mathbf{U}_S$ is the submatrix of the identity matrix $\mathbf{I}_n$ comprising the columns corresponding to the indices in S. For example, for $n = 3$,

$$
\mathbf{U}_{\{1,3\}} = \begin{pmatrix} 1 & 0 \\ 0 & 0 \\ 0 & 1 \end{pmatrix}, \qquad \mathbf{U}_{\{2\}} = \begin{pmatrix} 0 \\ 1 \\ 0 \end{pmatrix}.
$$

For a given indices set $S \subseteq \{1, 2, \ldots, n\}$, the complement set S^c is given by $S^c = \{1, 2, \ldots, n\} \setminus S$.

Finally, we recall our notation (that was also used in Example 6.51) that for a given $\mathbf{x} \in \mathbb{R}^n$, $x_{\langle i \rangle}$ is the ith largest value among $|x_1|, |x_2|, \ldots, |x_n|$. Therefore, in particular, $|x_{\langle 1 \rangle}| \geq |x_{\langle 2 \rangle}| \geq \cdots \geq |x_{\langle n \rangle}|$. Lemma 6.71 shows that $P_{C_s}(\mathbf{x})$ comprises all vectors consisting of the s components of $\mathbf{x}$ with the largest absolute values and with zeros elsewhere. There may be several choices for the s components with largest absolute values, and this is why $P_{C_s}(\mathbf{x})$ might consist of several vectors. Note that in the statement of the lemma, we characterize the property of an index set S to "comprise s indices corresponding to the s largest absolute values in $\mathbf{x}$" by the relation

$$
S \subseteq \{1, 2, \ldots, n\}, \quad |S| = s, \quad \sum_{i \in S} |x_i| = \sum_{i=1}^{s} |x_{\langle i \rangle}|.
$$

Lemma 6.71 (projection onto C_s). *Let $s \in \{1, 2, \ldots, n\}$ and $\mathbf{x} \in \mathbb{R}^n$. Then*

$$
P_{C_s}(\mathbf{x}) = \left\{ \mathbf{U}_S \mathbf{x}_S : |S| = s, S \subseteq \{1, 2, \ldots, n\}, \sum_{i \in S} |x_i| = \sum_{i=1}^{s} |x_{\langle i \rangle}| \right\}.
$$

Proof. Since C_s consists of all s-sparse vectors, it can be represented as the following union:

$$
C_s = \bigcup_{S \subseteq \{1, 2, \ldots, n\}, |S| = s} A_S,
$$

where $A_S = \{\mathbf{x} \in \mathbb{R}^n : \mathbf{x}_{S^c} = \mathbf{0}\}$. Therefore,[35]

$$
P_{C_s}(\mathbf{x}) \subseteq \bigcup_{S \subseteq \{1, 2, \ldots, n\}, |S| = s} \{P_{A_S}(\mathbf{x})\}. \tag{6.70}
$$

---

[35]Since A_S is convex, we treat $P_{A_S}(\mathbf{x})$ as a vector and not as a singleton set. The inclusion (6.70) holds since if $B_1, B_2, \ldots, B_m$ are closed convex sets, then $P_{\cup_{i=1}^{m} B_i}(\mathbf{x}) \subseteq \cup_{i=1}^{m} \{P_{B_i}(\mathbf{x})\}$ for any $\mathbf{x}$.

The vectors in $P_{C_s}(\mathbf{x})$ will be the vectors $P_{A_S}(\mathbf{x})$ with the smallest possible value of $\|P_{A_S}(\mathbf{x}) - \mathbf{x}\|^2$. The vector $P_{A_S}(\mathbf{x})$ is the optimal solution of the problem

$$\min_{\mathbf{y} \in \mathbb{R}^n} \left\{ \|\mathbf{y} - \mathbf{x}\|_2^2 : \mathbf{y}_{S^c} = \mathbf{0} \right\},$$

which can be rewritten as

$$\min_{\mathbf{y} \in \mathbb{R}^n} \left\{ \|\mathbf{y}_S - \mathbf{x}_S\|_2^2 + \|\mathbf{x}_{S^c}\|_2^2 : \mathbf{y}_{S^c} = \mathbf{0} \right\}.$$

The optimal solution of the above problem is obviously given by $\mathbf{y}_S = \mathbf{x}_S, \mathbf{y}_{S^c} = \mathbf{0}$, that is, $\mathbf{y} = \mathbf{U}_S \mathbf{x}_S$, and the optimal value is $\|\mathbf{x}_{S^c}\|_2^2$. The vectors in $P_{C_s}(\mathbf{x})$ will therefore be of the form $\mathbf{U}_S \mathbf{x}_S$, with indices sets S with cardinality s and with minimal value $\|\mathbf{x}_{S^c}\|_2^2$, which is equivalent to the condition that S consists of s indices corresponding to the s largest absolute values in $\mathbf{x}$. $\square$

Example 6.72. Suppose that $n = 4$. Then

$$P_{C_2}[(2, 3, -2, 1)^T] = \{(2, 3, 0, 0)^T, (0, 3, -2, 0)^T\}. \quad \blacksquare$$

6.9 Summary of Prox Computations

$f(\mathbf{x})$	$\mathrm{dom}(f)$	$\mathrm{prox}_f(\mathbf{x})$	Assumptions	Reference
$\frac{1}{2}\mathbf{x}^T\mathbf{A}\mathbf{x} + \mathbf{b}^T\mathbf{x} + c$	$\mathbb{R}^n$	$(\mathbf{A}+\mathbf{I})^{-1}(\mathbf{x}-\mathbf{b})$	$\mathbf{A}\in\mathbb{S}^n_+,\ \mathbf{b}\in\mathbb{R}^n,\ c\in\mathbb{R}$	Section 6.2.3
λx^3	$\mathbb{R}_+$	$\frac{-1+\sqrt{1+12\lambda[x]_+}}{6\lambda}$	$\lambda>0$	Lemma 6.5
μx	$[0,\alpha]\cap\mathbb{R}$	$\min\{\max\{x-\mu,0\},\alpha\}$	$\mu\in\mathbb{R},\ \alpha\in[0,\infty]$	Example 6.14
$\lambda\|\mathbf{x}\|$	$\mathbb{E}$	$\left(1-\frac{\lambda}{\max\{\|\mathbf{x}\|,\lambda\}}\right)\mathbf{x}$	$\|\cdot\|$—Euclidean norm, $\lambda>0$	Example 6.19
$-\lambda\|\mathbf{x}\|$	$\mathbb{E}$	$\left(1+\frac{\lambda}{\|\mathbf{x}\|}\right)\mathbf{x},\quad \mathbf{x}\neq\mathbf{0},$ $\{\mathbf{u}:\|\mathbf{u}\|=\lambda\},\quad \mathbf{x}=\mathbf{0}.$	$\|\cdot\|$—Euclidean norm, $\lambda>0$	Example 6.21
$\lambda\|\mathbf{x}\|_1$	$\mathbb{R}^n$	$\mathcal{T}_\lambda(\mathbf{x})=[|\mathbf{x}|-\lambda\mathbf{e}]_+\odot\mathrm{sgn}(\mathbf{x})$	$\lambda>0$	Example 6.8
$\|\boldsymbol{\omega}\odot\mathbf{x}\|_1$	$\mathrm{Box}[-\boldsymbol{\alpha},\boldsymbol{\alpha}]$	$\mathcal{S}_{\boldsymbol{\omega},\boldsymbol{\alpha}}(\mathbf{x})$	$\boldsymbol{\alpha}\in[0,\infty]^n,\ \boldsymbol{\omega}\in\mathbb{R}^n_+$	Example 6.23
$\lambda\|\mathbf{x}\|_\infty$	$\mathbb{R}^n$	$\mathbf{x}-\lambda P_{B_{\|\cdot\|_1}[\mathbf{0},1]}(\mathbf{x}/\lambda)$	$\lambda>0$	Example 6.48
$\lambda\|\mathbf{x}\|_a$	$\mathbb{E}$	$\mathbf{x}-\lambda P_{B_{\|\cdot\|_{a,*}}[\mathbf{0},1]}(\mathbf{x}/\lambda)$	$\|\mathbf{x}\|_a$—arbitrary norm, $\lambda>0$	Example 6.47
$\lambda\|\mathbf{x}\|_0$	$\mathbb{R}^n$	$\mathcal{H}_{\sqrt{2\lambda}}(x_1)\times\cdots\times\mathcal{H}_{\sqrt{2\lambda}}(x_n)$	$\lambda>0$	Example 6.10
$\lambda\|\mathbf{x}\|^3$	$\mathbb{E}$	$\frac{2}{1+\sqrt{1+12\lambda\|\mathbf{x}\|}}\mathbf{x}$	$\|\cdot\|$—Euclidean norm, $\lambda>0$,	Example 6.20
$-\lambda\sum_{j=1}^n\log x_j$	$\mathbb{R}^n_{++}$	$\left(\frac{x_j+\sqrt{x_j^2+4\lambda}}{2}\right)^n_{j=1}$	$\lambda>0$	Example 6.9
$\delta_C(\mathbf{x})$	$\mathbb{E}$	$P_C(\mathbf{x})$	$\emptyset\neq C\subseteq\mathbb{E}$	Theorem 6.24
$\lambda\sigma_C(\mathbf{x})$	$\mathbb{E}$	$\mathbf{x}-\lambda P_C(\mathbf{x}/\lambda)$	$\lambda>0,\ C\neq\emptyset$ closed convex	Theorem 6.46
$\lambda\max\{x_i\}$	$\mathbb{R}^n$	$\mathbf{x}-\lambda P_{\Delta_n}(\mathbf{x}/\lambda)$	$\lambda>0$	Example 6.49
$\lambda\sum_{i=1}^k x_{[i]}$	$\mathbb{R}^n$	$\mathbf{x}-\lambda P_C(\mathbf{x}/\lambda),$ $C=H_{\mathbf{e},k}\cap\mathrm{Box}[\mathbf{0},\mathbf{e}]$	$\lambda>0$	Example 6.50
$\lambda\sum_{i=1}^k |x_{\langle i\rangle}|$	$\mathbb{R}^n$	$\mathbf{x}-\lambda P_C(\mathbf{x}/\lambda),$ $C=B_{\|\cdot\|_1}[\mathbf{0},k]\cap\mathrm{Box}[-\mathbf{e},\mathbf{e}]$	$\lambda>0$	Example 6.51
$\lambda M_f^\mu(\mathbf{x})$	$\mathbb{E}$	$\mathbf{x}+$ $\frac{\lambda}{\mu+\lambda}\left(\mathrm{prox}_{(\mu+\lambda)f}(\mathbf{x})-\mathbf{x}\right)$	$\lambda,\mu>0,\ f$ proper closed convex	Corollary 6.64
$\lambda d_C(\mathbf{x})$	$\mathbb{E}$	$\mathbf{x}+$ $\min\left\{\frac{\lambda}{d_C(\mathbf{x})},1\right\}(P_C(\mathbf{x})-\mathbf{x})$	$\emptyset\neq C$ closed convex, $\lambda>0$	Lemma 6.43
$\frac{\lambda}{2}d_C^2(\mathbf{x})$	$\mathbb{E}$	$\frac{\lambda}{\lambda+1}P_C(\mathbf{x})+\frac{1}{\lambda+1}\mathbf{x}$	$\emptyset\neq C$ closed convex, $\lambda>0$	Example 6.65
$\lambda H_\mu(\mathbf{x})$	$\mathbb{E}$	$\left(1-\frac{\lambda}{\max\{\|\mathbf{x}\|,\mu+\lambda\}}\right)\mathbf{x}$	$\lambda,\mu>0$	Example 6.66
$\rho\|\mathbf{x}\|_1^2$	$\mathbb{R}^n$	$\left(\frac{v_i x_i}{v_i+2\rho}\right)^n_{i=1},\ \mathbf{v}=$ $\left[\sqrt{\frac{\rho}{\mu}}|\mathbf{x}|-2\rho\right]_+,\mathbf{e}^T\mathbf{v}=1\ (\mathbf{0}$ when $\mathbf{x}=\mathbf{0})$	$\rho>0$	Lemma 6.70
$\lambda\|\mathbf{A}\mathbf{x}\|_2$	$\mathbb{R}^n$	$\mathbf{x}-\mathbf{A}^T(\mathbf{A}\mathbf{A}^T+\alpha^*\mathbf{I})^{-1}\mathbf{A}\mathbf{x},$ $\alpha^*=0$ if $\|\mathbf{v}_0\|_2\leq\lambda$; otherwise, $\|\mathbf{v}_{\alpha^*}\|_2=\lambda;\ \mathbf{v}_\alpha\equiv(\mathbf{A}\mathbf{A}^T+\alpha\mathbf{I})^{-1}\mathbf{A}\mathbf{x}$	$\mathbf{A}\in\mathbb{R}^{m\times n}$ with full row rank, $\lambda>0$	Lemma 6.68

Chapter 7

Spectral Functions

In this chapter we will concentrate on spectral functions, which are functions of matrices that depend only on their singular values or on their eigenvalues. The underlying spaces in this chapter are all Euclidean. We start by defining the notion of *symmetry* w.r.t. a given set of orthogonal matrices.

7.1 Symmetric Functions

7.1.1 Definition and Examples

Definition 7.1 (symmetric functions). *Let $\mathcal{A} \subseteq \mathbb{O}^n$ be a set of orthogonal matrices. A proper function $f : \mathbb{R}^n \to (-\infty, \infty]$ is called* **symmetric** *w.r.t. $\mathcal{A}$ if*

$$f(\mathbf{A}\mathbf{x}) = f(\mathbf{x}) \text{ for all } \mathbf{x} \in \mathbb{R}^n, \mathbf{A} \in \mathcal{A}.$$

The following are five types of symmetric functions, each one dictated by the choice of orthogonal matrices in $\mathcal{A}$.

Example 7.2 (even functions). If $\mathcal{A} = \{-\mathbf{I}\}$, then $f : \mathbb{R}^n \to (-\infty, \infty]$ is symmetric w.r.t. $\mathcal{A}$ if

$$f(\mathbf{x}) = f(-\mathbf{x}) \text{ for all } \mathbf{x} \in \mathbb{R}^n.$$

Such functions will be called *even functions.* ∎

Example 7.3 (absolutely symmetric functions). Take $\mathcal{A} = \{\mathbf{D}_1, \mathbf{D}_2, \ldots, \mathbf{D}_n\} \subseteq \mathbb{R}^{n \times n}$, where $\mathbf{D}_i$ is the diagonal matrix whose diagonal elements are all ones except for the (i, i) component which is equal to -1. Then a proper function $f : \mathbb{R}^n \to (-\infty, \infty]$ is symmetric w.r.t. $\mathcal{A}$ if and only if

$$f(\mathbf{x}) = f(|\mathbf{x}|) \text{ for all } \mathbf{x} \in \mathbb{R}^n.$$

We will call such a function an *absolutely symmetric function.* It is easy to show that f is absolutely symmetric if and only if there exists a function $g : \mathbb{R}^n_+ \to (-\infty, \infty]$ such that $f(\mathbf{x}) = g(|\mathbf{x}|)$ for all $\mathbf{x} \in \mathbb{R}^n$. ∎

179

Example 7.4 (norm-dependent functions). A proper function $f : \mathbb{R}^n \to (-\infty, \infty]$ is symmetric w.r.t. $\mathcal{A} = \mathbb{O}^n$ if and only if

$$f(\mathbf{x}) = f(\mathbf{U}\mathbf{x}) \text{ for all } \mathbf{x} \in \mathbb{R}^n, \mathbf{U} \in \mathbb{O}^n.$$

The above holds if and only if there exists a proper function $g : \mathbb{R} \to (-\infty, \infty]$ such that

$$f(\mathbf{x}) = g(\|\mathbf{x}\|_2) \text{ for all } \mathbf{x} \in \mathbb{R}^n.$$

A function satisfying the above is called a *norm-dependent function*. ∎

We will require some additional notation before describing the next two examples. For a given vector $\mathbf{x} \in \mathbb{R}^n$, the vector $\mathbf{x}^{\downarrow}$ is the vector $\mathbf{x}$ reordered nonincreasingly. For example, if $\mathbf{x} = (2, -9, 2, 10)^T$, then $\mathbf{x}^{\downarrow} = (10, 2, 2, -9)^T$.

Definition 7.5 (permutation matrices). *An $n \times n$ matrix is called a* **permutation matrix** *if all its components are either 0 or 1 and each row and each column has exactly one nonzero element. The set of all $n \times n$ permutation matrices is denoted by Λ_n.*

Definition 7.6 (generalized permutation matrices). *An $n \times n$ matrix is called a* **generalized permutation matrix** *if all its components are either 0, 1, or -1 and each row and each column has exactly one nonzero element. The set of all $n \times n$ generalized permutation matrices is denoted by Λ_n^{G}.*

Thus, for example,

$$\begin{pmatrix} 0 & 1 & 0 \\ 1 & 0 & 0 \\ 0 & 0 & 1 \end{pmatrix} \in \Lambda_3, \qquad \begin{pmatrix} 0 & -1 & 0 \\ 1 & 0 & 0 \\ 0 & 0 & -1 \end{pmatrix} \in \Lambda_3^{\mathrm{G}}.$$

By the definition of permutation and generalized permutation matrices, it is easy to see that for any $\mathbf{x} \in \mathbb{R}^n$ there exists a permutation matrix $\mathbf{P} \in \Lambda_n$ for which $\mathbf{P}\mathbf{x} = \mathbf{x}^{\downarrow}$ and a generalized permutation matrix $\mathbf{Q} \in \Lambda_n^{\mathrm{G}}$ for which $\mathbf{Q}\mathbf{x} = |\mathbf{x}|^{\downarrow}$. It can be readily verified that permutation matrices, as well as generalized permutation matrices, are orthogonal.

Example 7.7 (permutation symmetric functions). A proper function $f : \mathbb{R}^n \to (-\infty, \infty]$ is symmetric w.r.t. Λ_n if and only if

$$f(\mathbf{x}) = f(\mathbf{P}\mathbf{x}) \text{ for all } \mathbf{x} \in \mathbb{R}^n, \mathbf{P} \in \Lambda_n.$$

Such a function will be called a *permutation symmetric function*. It is easy to show that f is permutation symmetric if and only if

$$f(\mathbf{x}) = f(\mathbf{x}^{\downarrow}) \text{ for all } \mathbf{x} \in \mathbb{R}^n. \quad ∎$$

Example 7.8 (absolutely permutation symmetric functions). A proper function $f : \mathbb{R}^n \to (-\infty, \infty]$ is symmetric w.r.t. Λ_n^{G} if and only if

$$f(\mathbf{x}) = f(\mathbf{P}\mathbf{x}) \text{ for all } \mathbf{x} \in \mathbb{R}^n, \mathbf{P} \in \Lambda_n^{\mathrm{G}}.$$

Such a function will be called an *absolutely permutation symmetric function*. It is easy to show that f is absolutely permutation symmetric if and only if

$$f(\mathbf{x}) = f(|\mathbf{x}|^{\downarrow}) \text{ for all } \mathbf{x} \in \mathbb{R}^n. \quad \blacksquare$$

7.1.2 The Symmetric Conjugate Theorem

We will now show that the conjugate of a symmetric function w.r.t. a set of orthogonal matrices is always symmetric w.r.t. the same set of matrices.

Theorem 7.9 (symmetric conjugate theorem).[36] *Let* $f : \mathbb{R}^n \to (-\infty, \infty]$ *be a proper function which is symmetric w.r.t. a set of orthogonal matrices* $\mathcal{A} \subseteq \mathbb{O}^n$. *Then* f^* *is symmetric w.r.t.* $\mathcal{A}$.

Proof. Let $\mathbf{A} \in \mathcal{A}$. Then by the symmetry assumption, $h = f$, where $h(\mathbf{x}) \equiv f(\mathbf{A}\mathbf{x})$. Thus,

$$f^*(\mathbf{y}) = h^*(\mathbf{y}) \text{ for all } \mathbf{y} \in \mathbb{R}^n. \quad (7.1)$$

By Theorem 4.13 and the orthogonality of $\mathbf{A}$, for any $\mathbf{y} \in \mathbb{R}^n$,

$$h^*(\mathbf{y}) = f^*((\mathbf{A}^T)^{-1}\mathbf{y}) = f^*(\mathbf{A}\mathbf{y}),$$

which, combined with (7.1), yields

$$f^*(\mathbf{y}) = f^*(\mathbf{A}\mathbf{y}) \text{ for all } \mathbf{y} \in \mathbb{R}^n.$$

Since the above holds for any $\mathbf{A} \in \mathcal{A}$, it follows that f^* is symmetric w.r.t. $\mathcal{A}$. $\quad\square$

Example 7.10. In this example we will illustrate the symmetric conjugate theorem by verifying that the types of symmetries satisfied by the functions in the table of Section 4.4.16 also hold for their conjugates.

- **even functions**

$f(\mathbf{x})$	$\mathrm{dom}(f)$	$f^*(\mathbf{y})$	Assumptions	Reference
$\frac{1}{p}|x|^p$	$\mathbb{R}$	$\frac{1}{q}|y|^q$	$p > 1, \frac{1}{p} + \frac{1}{q} = 1$	Section 4.4.4
$\frac{1}{2}\mathbf{x}^T\mathbf{A}\mathbf{x} + c$	$\mathbb{R}^n$	$\frac{1}{2}\mathbf{y}^T\mathbf{A}^{-1}\mathbf{y} - c$	$\mathbf{A} \in \mathbb{S}^n_{++}, c \in \mathbb{R}$	Section 4.4.6

- **permutation symmetric functions**

$f(\mathbf{x})$	$\mathrm{dom}(f)$	$f^*(\mathbf{y})$	Reference
$\sum_{i=1}^n x_i \log x_i$	$\mathbb{R}^n_+$	$\sum_{i=1}^n e^{y_i - 1}$	Section 4.4.8
$\sum_{i=1}^n x_i \log x_i$	Δ_n	$\log\left(\sum_{i=1}^n e^{y_i}\right)$	Section 4.4.10
$\log\left(\sum_{i=1}^n e^{x_i}\right)$	$\mathbb{R}^n$	$\sum_{i=1}^n y_i \log y_i$ $(\mathrm{dom}(f^*) = \Delta_n)$	Section 4.4.11
$\max_i\{x_i\}$	$\mathbb{R}^n$	$\delta_{\Delta_n}(\mathbf{y})$	Example 4.10

---

[36]The symmetric conjugate theorem (Theorem 7.9) is from Rockafellar [108, Corollary 12.3.1].

- **absolutely permutation symmetric functions**

$f(\mathbf{x})$	$\operatorname{dom}(f)$	$f^*(\mathbf{y})$	Reference
$\|\mathbf{x}\|_p$	$\mathbb{R}^n$	$\delta_{B_{\|\cdot\|_q}[\mathbf{0},1]}(\mathbf{y})$	Section 4.4.12
$\frac{1}{2}\|\mathbf{x}\|_p^2$	$\mathbb{E}$	$\frac{1}{2}\|\mathbf{y}\|_q^2$	Section 4.4.15

where $p,q \in [1,\infty]$, $\frac{1}{p}+\frac{1}{q}=1$ (with the convention that if $p=1,\infty$, then $q=\infty,1$, respectively).

- **norm-dependent functions**

f	$\operatorname{dom}(f)$	f^*	Reference
$\|\mathbf{x}\|_2$	$\mathbb{R}^n$	$\delta_{B_{\|\cdot\|_2}[\mathbf{0},1]}(\mathbf{y})$	Section 4.4.12
$-\sqrt{\alpha^2-\|\mathbf{x}\|_2^2}$ $(\alpha>0)$	$B_{\|\cdot\|_2}[\mathbf{0},\alpha]$	$\alpha\sqrt{\|\mathbf{y}\|_2^2+1}$	Section 4.4.13
$\sqrt{\alpha^2+\|\mathbf{x}\|_2^2}$ $(\alpha>0)$	$\mathbb{R}^n$	$-\alpha\sqrt{1-\|\mathbf{y}\|_2^2}$ $(\operatorname{dom}f^* = B_{\|\cdot\|_2}[\mathbf{0},1])$	Section 4.4.14
$\frac{1}{2}\|\mathbf{x}\|_2^2$	$\mathbb{R}^n$	$\frac{1}{2}\|\mathbf{y}\|_2^2$	Section 4.4.15

■

7.2   Symmetric Spectral Functions over $\mathbb{S}^{n}$ [37]

The main concern of this chapter are functions of matrices that are defined on either the set of symmetric matrices $\mathbb{S}^n$ or the set of matrices $\mathbb{R}^{m\times n}$. We will deal only with functions that depend either on the eigenvalues of their argument (if the underlying space is $\mathbb{S}^n$) or on the singular values (if the underlying space is $\mathbb{R}^{m\times n}$). Such functions are called *spectral functions*. We first consider functions over $\mathbb{S}^n$. Given a matrix $\mathbf{X} \in \mathbb{S}^n$, its eigenvalues ordered nonincreasingly are denoted by

$$\lambda_1(\mathbf{X}) \ge \lambda_2(\mathbf{X}) \ge \cdots \ge \lambda_n(\mathbf{X}).$$

The eigenvalues function $\boldsymbol{\lambda} : \mathbb{S}^n \to \mathbb{R}^n$ is defined as

$$\boldsymbol{\lambda}(\mathbf{X}) \equiv (\lambda_1(\mathbf{X}), \lambda_2(\mathbf{X}), \ldots, \lambda_n(\mathbf{X}))^T.$$

A key fact from linear algebra is that any symmetric matrix $\mathbf{X} \in \mathbb{S}^n$ has a *spectral decomposition*, meaning an orthogonal matrix $\mathbf{U} \in \mathbb{O}^n$ for which $\mathbf{X} = \mathbf{U}\operatorname{diag}(\boldsymbol{\lambda}(\mathbf{X}))\mathbf{U}^T$. We begin by formally defining the notion of spectral functions over $\mathbb{S}^n$.

Definition 7.11 (spectral functions over $\mathbb{S}^n$). *A proper function $g : \mathbb{S}^n \to (-\infty,\infty]$ is called a **spectral function** over $\mathbb{S}^n$ if there exists a proper function $f : \mathbb{R}^n \to (-\infty,\infty]$ for which $g = f \circ \boldsymbol{\lambda}$.*

---

[37]Sections 7.2 and 7.3, excluding the spectral proximal theorem, are based on the seminal papers of Lewis [80, 81] on unitarily invariant functions. The spectral proximal formulas can be found in Parikh and Boyd [102].

If $g = f \circ \boldsymbol{\lambda}$, we will refer to f (which is actually not necessarily unique) as the *associated function*. Our main interest will be to study spectral functions whose associated functions are permutation symmetric.

Definition 7.12 (symmetric spectral functions over $\mathbb{S}^n$). *A proper function* $f : \mathbb{S}^n \to (-\infty, \infty]$ *is called a* **symmetric spectral function over $\mathbb{S}^n$** *if there exists a proper permutation symmetric function* $f : \mathbb{R}^n \to (-\infty, \infty]$ *for which* $g = f \circ \boldsymbol{\lambda}$.

Example 7.13. Following is a list of permutation symmetric functions along with their associated symmetric spectral functions.

#	$f(\mathbf{x})$	dom(f)	$f(\boldsymbol{\lambda}(\mathbf{X}))$	dom$(f \circ \boldsymbol{\lambda})$
1	$\sum_{i=1}^n x_i$	$\mathbb{R}^n$	$\mathrm{Tr}(\mathbf{X})$	$\mathbb{S}^n$
2	$\max_{i=1,2,\ldots,n} x_i$	$\mathbb{R}^n$	$\lambda_{\max}(\mathbf{X})$	$\mathbb{S}^n$
3	$\alpha\|\mathbf{x}\|_2 \ (\alpha \in \mathbb{R})$	$\mathbb{R}^n$	$\alpha\|\mathbf{X}\|_F$	$\mathbb{S}^n$
4	$\alpha\|\mathbf{x}\|_2^2 \ (\alpha \in \mathbb{R})$	$\mathbb{R}^n$	$\alpha\|\mathbf{X}\|_F^2$	$\mathbb{S}^n$
5	$\alpha\|\mathbf{x}\|_\infty \ (\alpha \in \mathbb{R})$	$\mathbb{R}^n$	$\alpha\|\mathbf{X}\|_{2,2}$	$\mathbb{S}^n$
6	$\alpha\|\mathbf{x}\|_1 \ (\alpha \in \mathbb{R})$	$\mathbb{R}^n$	$\alpha\|\mathbf{X}\|_{S_1}$	$\mathbb{S}^n$
7	$-\sum_{i=1}^n \log(x_i)$	$\mathbb{R}^n_{++}$	$-\log\det(\mathbf{X})$	$\mathbb{S}^n_{++}$
8	$\sum_{i=1}^n x_i \log(x_i)$	$\mathbb{R}^n_+$	$\sum_{i=1}^n \lambda_i(\mathbf{X})\log(\lambda_i(\mathbf{X}))$	$\mathbb{S}^n_+$
9	$\sum_{i=1}^n x_i \log(x_i)$	Δ_n	$\sum_{i=1}^n \lambda_i(\mathbf{X})\log(\lambda_i(\mathbf{X}))$	Υ_n

The domain of the last function in the above table is the *spectahedron* set given by
$$\Upsilon_n = \{\mathbf{X} \in \mathbb{S}^n_+ : \mathrm{Tr}(\mathbf{X}) = 1\}.$$

The norm used in the sixth function is the Schatten 1-norm whose expression for symmetric matrices is given by
$$\|\mathbf{X}\|_{S_1} = \sum_{i=1}^n |\lambda_i(\mathbf{X})|, \quad \mathbf{X} \in \mathbb{S}^n.$$

Schatten p-norms will be discussed in detail in Section 7.3 ∎

A fundamental inequality that will be a key argument in establishing the main results of this section is the so-called Fan inequality stating that the inner product of two symmetric matrices is upper bounded by the inner product of their eigenvalues vectors and that equality holds if and only if the two matrices are simultaneously orthogonally diagonalizable.

Theorem 7.14 (Fan's Inequality [32, 119]). *For any two symmetric matrices* $\mathbf{X}, \mathbf{Y} \in \mathbb{S}^n$ *it holds that*
$$\mathrm{Tr}(\mathbf{XY}) \le \langle \boldsymbol{\lambda}(\mathbf{X}), \boldsymbol{\lambda}(\mathbf{Y}) \rangle,$$

and equality holds if and only if there exists $\mathbf{V} \in \mathbb{O}^n$ for which

$$\mathbf{X} = \mathbf{V}\mathrm{diag}(\lambda(\mathbf{X}))\mathbf{V}^T,$$
$$\mathbf{Y} = \mathbf{V}\mathrm{diag}(\lambda(\mathbf{Y}))\mathbf{V}^T.$$

7.2.1   The Spectral Conjugate Formula

A rather direct result of Fan's inequality is the spectral conjugate formula that shows how to compute the conjugate of a symmetric spectral function over $\mathbb{S}^n$ in terms of the conjugate of its associated function.

Theorem 7.15 (spectral conjugate formula over $\mathbb{S}^n$).   *Let $f : \mathbb{E} \to (-\infty, \infty]$ be a permutation symmetric function. Then*

$$(f \circ \lambda)^* = f^* \circ \lambda.$$

Proof. Let $\mathbf{Y} \in \mathbb{S}^n$. Then

$$
\begin{aligned}
(f \circ \lambda)^*(\mathbf{Y}) &= \max_{\mathbf{X} \in \mathbb{S}^n} \{ \mathrm{Tr}(\mathbf{XY}) - f(\lambda(\mathbf{X})) \} \\
&\le \max_{\mathbf{X} \in \mathbb{S}^n} \{ \langle \lambda(\mathbf{X}), \lambda(\mathbf{Y}) \rangle - f(\lambda(\mathbf{X})) \} \\
&\le \max_{\mathbf{x} \in \mathbb{R}^n} \{ \langle \mathbf{x}, \lambda(\mathbf{Y}) \rangle - f(\mathbf{x}) \} \\
&= (f^* \circ \lambda)(\mathbf{Y}),
\end{aligned}
$$

where Fan's inequality (Theorem 7.14) was used in the first inequality. To show the reverse inequality, take a spectral decomposition of $\mathbf{Y}$:

$$\mathbf{Y} = \mathbf{U}\mathrm{diag}(\lambda(\mathbf{Y}))\mathbf{U}^T \ (\mathbf{U} \in \mathbb{O}^n).$$

Then

$$
\begin{aligned}
(f^* \circ \lambda)(\mathbf{Y}) &= \max_{\mathbf{x} \in \mathbb{R}^n} \{ \langle \mathbf{x}, \lambda(\mathbf{Y}) \rangle - f(\mathbf{x}) \} \\
&= \max_{\mathbf{x} \in \mathbb{R}^n} \{ \mathrm{Tr}(\mathrm{diag}(\mathbf{x})\mathrm{diag}(\lambda(\mathbf{Y}))) - f(\mathbf{x}) \} \\
&= \max_{\mathbf{x} \in \mathbb{R}^n} \{ \mathrm{Tr}(\mathrm{diag}(\mathbf{x})\mathbf{U}^T\mathbf{Y}\mathbf{U}) - f(\mathbf{x}^{\downarrow}) \} \\
&= \max_{\mathbf{x} \in \mathbb{R}^n} \{ \mathrm{Tr}(\mathrm{diag}(\mathbf{x})\mathbf{U}^T\mathbf{Y}\mathbf{U}) - f(\lambda(\mathbf{U}\mathrm{diag}(\mathbf{x})\mathbf{U}^T)) \} \\
&= \max_{\mathbf{x} \in \mathbb{R}^n} \{ \mathrm{Tr}(\mathbf{U}\mathrm{diag}(\mathbf{x})\mathbf{U}^T\mathbf{Y}) - f(\lambda(\mathbf{U}\mathrm{diag}(\mathbf{x})\mathbf{U}^T)) \} \\
&\le \max_{\mathbf{Z} \in \mathbb{S}^n} \{ \mathrm{Tr}(\mathbf{ZY}) - f(\lambda(\mathbf{Z})) \} \\
&= (f \circ \lambda)^*(\mathbf{Y}). \quad \square
\end{aligned}
$$

Example 7.16. Using the spectral conjugate formula, we can compute the conjugates of the functions from the table of Example 7.13. The conjugates appear in the following table, which also includes references to the corresponding results for functions over $\mathbb{R}^n$. The numbering is the same as in the table of Example 7.13.

#	$g(\mathbf{X})$	dom(g)	$g^*(\mathbf{Y})$	dom(g^*)	Reference
1	$\mathrm{Tr}(\mathbf{X})$	$\mathbb{S}^n$	$\delta_{\{\mathbf{I}\}}(\mathbf{Y})$	$\{\mathbf{I}\}$	Section 4.4.7
2	$\lambda_{\max}(\mathbf{X})$	$\mathbb{S}^n$	$\delta_{\Upsilon_n}(\mathbf{Y})$	Υ_n	Example 4.10
3	$\alpha\|\mathbf{X}\|_F$ $(\alpha > 0)$	$\mathbb{S}^n$	$\delta_{B_{\|\cdot\|_F}[\mathbf{0},\alpha]}(\mathbf{Y})$	$B_{\|\cdot\|_F}[\mathbf{0},\alpha]$	Section 4.4.12
4	$\alpha\|\mathbf{X}\|_F^2$ $(\alpha > 0)$	$\mathbb{S}^n$	$\frac{1}{4\alpha}\|\mathbf{Y}\|_F^2$	$\mathbb{S}^n$	Section 4.4.6
5	$\alpha\|\mathbf{X}\|_{2,2}$ $(\alpha > 0)$	$\mathbb{S}^n$	$\delta_{B_{\|\cdot\|_{S_1}}[\mathbf{0},\alpha]}(\mathbf{Y})$	$B_{\|\cdot\|_{S_1}}[\mathbf{0},\alpha]$	Section 4.4.12
6	$\alpha\|\mathbf{X}\|_{S_1}$ $(\alpha > 0)$	$\mathbb{S}^n$	$\delta_{B_{\|\cdot\|_{2,2}}[\mathbf{0},\alpha]}(\mathbf{Y})$	$B_{\|\cdot\|_{2,2}}[\mathbf{0},\alpha]$	Section 4.4.12
7	$-\log\det(\mathbf{X})$	$\mathbb{S}^n_{++}$	$-n - \log\det(-\mathbf{Y})$	$\mathbb{S}^n_{--}$	Section 4.4.9
8	$\sum_{i=1}^n \lambda_i(\mathbf{X})\log(\lambda_i(\mathbf{X}))$	$\mathbb{S}^n_+$	$\sum_{i=1}^n e^{\lambda_i(\mathbf{Y})-1}$	$\mathbb{S}^n$	Section 4.4.8
9	$\sum_{i=1}^n \lambda_i(\mathbf{X})\log(\lambda_i(\mathbf{X}))$	Υ_n	$\log\left(\sum_{i=1}^n e^{\lambda_i(\mathbf{Y})}\right)$	$\mathbb{S}^n$	Section 4.4.10

∎

The spectral conjugate formula has several important consequences, one of which is the following theorem stating that a symmetric spectral function is closed and convex if and only if its associated function is closed and convex.

Theorem 7.17 (closedness and convexity of symmetric spectral functions over $\mathbb{S}^n$). *Let $F : \mathbb{S}^n \to (-\infty,\infty]$ be given by $F = f \circ \boldsymbol{\lambda}$, where $f : \mathbb{R}^n \to (-\infty,\infty]$ is a permutation symmetric proper function. Then F is closed and convex if and only if f is closed and convex.*

Proof. By the spectral conjugate formula (Theorem 7.15),

$$F^* = (f \circ \boldsymbol{\lambda})^* = f^* \circ \boldsymbol{\lambda}.$$

Since by the symmetric conjugate theorem (Theorem 7.9) f^* is permutation symmetric, we can invoke once again the spectral conjugate formula to obtain

$$F^{**} = (f^* \circ \boldsymbol{\lambda})^* = f^{**} \circ \boldsymbol{\lambda}. \tag{7.2}$$

If f is closed and convex, then by Theorem 4.8 (taking also into account the properness of f), it follows that $f^{**} = f$. Therefore, by (7.2),

$$F^{**} = f \circ \boldsymbol{\lambda} = F.$$

Thus, since F is a conjugate of another function (F^*), it follows by Theorem 4.3 that it is closed and convex. Now assume that F is closed and convex. Since F is in addition proper, it follows by Theorem 4.8 that $F^{**} = F$, which, combined with (7.2), yields the equality

$$f \circ \boldsymbol{\lambda} = F = F^{**} = f^{**} \circ \boldsymbol{\lambda}.$$

Therefore, for any $\mathbf{x} \in \mathbb{R}^n$

$$f(\mathbf{x}^{\downarrow}) = f(\boldsymbol{\lambda}(\mathrm{diag}(\mathbf{x}))) = f^{**}(\boldsymbol{\lambda}(\mathrm{diag}(\mathbf{x}))) = f^{**}(\mathbf{x}^{\downarrow}).$$

By the permutation symmetry property of both f and f^{**}, it follows that $f(\mathbf{x}^{\downarrow}) = f(\mathbf{x})$ and $f^{**}(\mathbf{x}^{\downarrow}) = f^{**}(\mathbf{x})$, and we thus obtained that $f(\mathbf{x}) = f^{**}(\mathbf{x})$ for any

$\mathbf{x} \in \mathbb{R}^n$, meaning that $f = f^{**}$. Therefore, f, as a conjugate of another function (f^*) is closed and convex. $\square$

7.2.2 The Proximal Operator of Symmetric Spectral Functions over $\mathbb{S}^n$

The next result shows a simple formula for computing the prox operator of a symmetric spectral function over $\mathbb{S}^n$ which is also proper closed and convex. The prox is expressed in terms of the spectral decomposition of the argument and the prox operator of the associated function.

Theorem 7.18 (spectral prox formula over $\mathbb{S}^n$). *Let $F : \mathbb{S}^n \rightarrow (-\infty, \infty]$ be given by $F = f \circ \boldsymbol{\lambda}$, where $f : \mathbb{R}^n \rightarrow (-\infty, \infty]$ is a permutation symmetric proper closed and convex function. Let $\mathbf{X} \in \mathbb{S}^n$, and suppose that $\mathbf{X} = \mathbf{U}\mathrm{diag}(\boldsymbol{\lambda}(\mathbf{X}))\mathbf{U}^T$, where $\mathbf{U} \in \mathbb{O}^n$. Then*

$$\mathrm{prox}_F(\mathbf{X}) = \mathbf{U}\mathrm{diag}(\mathrm{prox}_f(\boldsymbol{\lambda}(\mathbf{X})))\mathbf{U}^T.$$

Proof. Recall that

$$\mathrm{prox}_F(\mathbf{X}) = \mathrm{argmin}_{\mathbf{Z} \in \mathbb{S}^n} \left\{ F(\mathbf{Z}) + \frac{1}{2}\|\mathbf{Z} - \mathbf{X}\|_F^2 \right\}. \tag{7.3}$$

Denoting $\mathbf{D} = \mathrm{diag}(\boldsymbol{\lambda}(\mathbf{X}))$, we note that for any $\mathbf{Z} \in \mathbb{S}^n$,

$$F(\mathbf{Z}) + \frac{1}{2}\|\mathbf{Z} - \mathbf{X}\|_F^2 = F(\mathbf{Z}) + \frac{1}{2}\|\mathbf{Z} - \mathbf{U}\mathbf{D}\mathbf{U}^T\|_F^2 \overset{(*)}{=} F(\mathbf{U}^T\mathbf{Z}\mathbf{U}) + \frac{1}{2}\|\mathbf{U}^T\mathbf{Z}\mathbf{U} - \mathbf{D}\|_F^2,$$

where the transition $(*)$ is due to the fact that $F(\mathbf{Z}) = f(\boldsymbol{\lambda}(\mathbf{Z})) = f(\boldsymbol{\lambda}(\mathbf{U}^T\mathbf{Z}\mathbf{U})) = F(\mathbf{U}^T\mathbf{Z}\mathbf{U})$. Making the change of variables $\mathbf{W} = \mathbf{U}^T\mathbf{Z}\mathbf{U}$, we conclude that the optimal solution of (7.3) is given by

$$\mathbf{Z} = \mathbf{U}\mathbf{W}^*\mathbf{U}^T, \tag{7.4}$$

where $\mathbf{W}^* \in \mathbb{S}^n$ is the unique optimal solution of

$$\min_{\mathbf{W} \in \mathbb{S}^n} \left\{ G(\mathbf{W}) \equiv F(\mathbf{W}) + \frac{1}{2}\|\mathbf{W} - \mathbf{D}\|_F^2 \right\}. \tag{7.5}$$

We will prove that $\mathbf{W}^*$ is diagonal. Let $i \in \{1, 2, \ldots, n\}$. Take $\mathbf{V}_i$ to be the diagonal matrix whose diagonal elements are all ones except for the (i, i)th component, which is -1. Define $\widetilde{\mathbf{W}}_i = \mathbf{V}_i\mathbf{W}^*\mathbf{V}_i^T$. Obviously, by the fact that $\mathbf{V}_i \in \mathbb{O}^n$,

$$F(\mathbf{V}_i\mathbf{W}^*\mathbf{V}_i^T) = f(\boldsymbol{\lambda}(\mathbf{V}_i\mathbf{W}^*\mathbf{V}_i^T)) = f(\boldsymbol{\lambda}(\mathbf{W}^*)) = F(\mathbf{W}^*),$$

and we thus obtain

$$\begin{aligned} G(\widetilde{\mathbf{W}}_i) &= F(\widetilde{\mathbf{W}}_i) + \frac{1}{2}\|\widetilde{\mathbf{W}}_i - \mathbf{D}\|_F^2 \\ &= F(\mathbf{V}_i\mathbf{W}^*\mathbf{V}_i^T) + \frac{1}{2}\|\mathbf{V}_i\mathbf{W}^*\mathbf{V}_i^T - \mathbf{D}\|_F^2 \\ &= F(\mathbf{W}^*) + \frac{1}{2}\|\mathbf{W}^* - \mathbf{V}_i^T\mathbf{D}\mathbf{V}_i\|_F^2 \\ &\overset{(**)}{=} F(\mathbf{W}^*) + \frac{1}{2}\|\mathbf{W}^* - \mathbf{D}\|_F^2, \\ &= G(\mathbf{W}^*), \end{aligned}$$

where (**) follows from the fact that $\mathbf{V}_i$ and $\mathbf{D}$ are both diagonal, and hence $\mathbf{V}_i^T \mathbf{D} \mathbf{V}_i = \mathbf{V}_i^T \mathbf{V}_i \mathbf{D} = \mathbf{D}$. We conclude that $\widetilde{\mathbf{W}}_i$ is also an optimal solution, but by the uniqueness of the optimal solution of problem (7.5), it follows that $\mathbf{W}^* = \mathbf{V}_i \mathbf{W}^* \mathbf{V}_i^T$. Comparing the ith rows of the two matrices, we deduce that $W_{ij}^* = 0$ for any $j \neq i$. Since this argument is valid for any $i \in \{1, 2, \ldots, n\}$, it follows that $\mathbf{W}^*$ is a diagonal matrix, and consequently the optimal solution of (7.5) is given by $\mathbf{W}^* = \text{diag}(\mathbf{w}^*)$, where $\mathbf{w}^*$ is the optimal solution of

$$\min_{\mathbf{w}} \left\{ F(\text{diag}(\mathbf{w})) + \frac{1}{2} \|\text{diag}(\mathbf{w}) - \mathbf{D}\|_F^2 \right\}.$$

Since $F(\text{diag}(\mathbf{w})) = f(\mathbf{w}^\downarrow) = f(\mathbf{w})$ and $\|\text{diag}(\mathbf{w}) - \mathbf{D}\|_F^2 = \|\mathbf{w} - \boldsymbol{\lambda}(\mathbf{X})\|_2^2$, it follows that $\mathbf{w}^*$ is given by

$$\mathbf{w}^* = \text{argmin}_{\mathbf{w}} \left\{ f(\mathbf{w}) + \frac{1}{2} \|\mathbf{w} - \boldsymbol{\lambda}(\mathbf{X})\|_2^2 \right\} = \text{prox}_f(\boldsymbol{\lambda}(\mathbf{X})).$$

Therefore, $\mathbf{W}^* = \text{diag}(\text{prox}_f(\boldsymbol{\lambda}(\mathbf{X})))$, which, along with (7.4), establishes the desired result. $\quad\square$

Example 7.19. Using the spectral prox formula, we can compute the prox of symmetric spectral functions in terms of the prox of their associated functions. Using this observation, we present in the table below expressions of prox operators of several functions. The parameter α is always assumed to be positive, and $\mathbf{U}$ is assumed to be an orthogonal matrix satisfying $\mathbf{X} = \mathbf{U}\text{diag}(\boldsymbol{\lambda}(\mathbf{X}))\mathbf{U}^T$. The table also includes references to the corresponding results for the associated functions, which are always defined over $\mathbb{R}^n$.

$F(\mathbf{X})$	$\text{dom}(F)$	$\text{prox}_F(\mathbf{X})$	Reference
$\alpha\|\mathbf{X}\|_F^2$	$\mathbb{S}^n$	$\frac{1}{1+2\alpha}\mathbf{X}$	Section 6.2.3
$\alpha\|\mathbf{X}\|_F$	$\mathbb{S}^n$	$\left(1 - \frac{\alpha}{\max\{\|\mathbf{X}\|_F, \alpha\}}\right)\mathbf{X}$	Example 6.19
$\alpha\|\mathbf{X}\|_{S_1}$	$\mathbb{S}^n$	$\mathbf{U}\text{diag}(\mathcal{T}_\alpha(\boldsymbol{\lambda}(\mathbf{X})))\mathbf{U}^T$	Example 6.8
$\alpha\|\mathbf{X}\|_{2,2}$	$\mathbb{S}^n$	$\mathbf{U}\text{diag}(\boldsymbol{\lambda}(\mathbf{X}) - \alpha P_{B_{\|\cdot\|_1}[\mathbf{0},1]}(\boldsymbol{\lambda}(\mathbf{X})/\alpha))\mathbf{U}^T$	Example 6.48
$-\alpha\log\det(\mathbf{X})$	$\mathbb{S}^n_{++}$	$\mathbf{U}\text{diag}\left(\frac{\lambda_j(\mathbf{X}) + \sqrt{\lambda_j(\mathbf{X})^2 + 4\alpha}}{2}\right)\mathbf{U}^T$	Example 6.9
$\alpha\lambda_1(\mathbf{X})$	$\mathbb{S}^n$	$\mathbf{U}\text{diag}(\boldsymbol{\lambda}(\mathbf{X}) - \alpha P_{\Delta_n}(\boldsymbol{\lambda}(\mathbf{X})/\alpha))\mathbf{U}^T$	Example 6.49
$\alpha\sum_{i=1}^k \lambda_i(\mathbf{X})$	$\mathbb{S}^n$	$\mathbf{X} - \alpha\mathbf{U}\text{diag}(P_C(\boldsymbol{\lambda}(\mathbf{X})/\alpha))\mathbf{U}^T$, $C = H_{\mathbf{e},k} \cap \text{Box}[\mathbf{0}, \mathbf{e}]$	Example 6.50

$\blacksquare$

A set $T \subseteq \mathbb{S}^n$ is called a *symmetric spectral set* in $\mathbb{S}^n$ if the indicator function δ_T is a symmetric spectral function over $\mathbb{S}^n$, meaning that it has the form $\delta_T = \delta_C \circ \boldsymbol{\lambda}$, where δ_C is a permutation symmetric function. The set $C \subseteq \mathbb{R}^n$ is the *associated set*. Since $\text{prox}_{\delta_T} = P_T$ and $\text{prox}_{\delta_C} = P_C$, it follows by the spectral prox formula that if C is nonempty closed and convex, then

$$P_T(\mathbf{X}) = \mathbf{U}\mathrm{diag}(P_C(\boldsymbol{\lambda}(\mathbf{X})))\mathbf{U}^T, \ \mathbf{X} \in \mathbb{S}^n, \tag{7.6}$$

where $\mathbf{U}$ is an orthogonal matrix satisfying $\mathbf{X} = \mathbf{U}\mathrm{diag}(\boldsymbol{\lambda}(\mathbf{X}))\mathbf{U}^T$.

Example 7.20. Using formula (7.6), we present in the following table expressions for the orthogonal projection onto several symmetric spectral sets in $\mathbb{S}^n$. The table also includes references to the corresponding results on orthogonal projections onto the associated subsets of $\mathbb{R}^n$. The matrix $\mathbf{U}$ is assumed to be an orthogonal matrix satisfying $\mathbf{X} = \mathbf{U}\mathrm{diag}(\boldsymbol{\lambda}(\mathbf{X}))\mathbf{U}^T$.

set (T)	$P_T(\mathbf{X})$	Assumptions	Reference
$\mathbb{S}^n_+$	$\mathbf{U}\mathrm{diag}([\boldsymbol{\lambda}(\mathbf{X})]_+)\mathbf{U}^T$	–	Lemma 6.26
$\{\mathbf{X} : \ell\mathbf{I} \preceq \mathbf{X} \preceq u\mathbf{I}\}$	$\mathbf{U}\mathrm{diag}(\mathbf{v})\mathbf{U}^T,$ $v_i = \min\{\max\{\lambda_i(\mathbf{X}), \ell\}, u\}$	$\ell \leq u$	Lemma 6.26
$B_{\|\cdot\|_F}[0, r]$	$\frac{r}{\max\{\|\mathbf{X}\|_F, r\}}\mathbf{X}$	$r > 0$	Lemma 6.26
$\{\mathbf{X} : \mathrm{Tr}(\mathbf{X}) \leq b\}$	$\mathbf{U}\mathrm{diag}(\mathbf{v})\mathbf{U}^T, \ \mathbf{v} = \boldsymbol{\lambda}(\mathbf{X}) - \frac{[\mathbf{e}^T\boldsymbol{\lambda}(\mathbf{X})-b]_+}{n}\mathbf{e}$	$b \in \mathbb{R}$	Lemma 6.26
Υ_n	$\mathbf{U}\mathrm{diag}(\mathbf{v})\mathbf{U}^T, \ \mathbf{v} = [\boldsymbol{\lambda}(\mathbf{X}) - \mu^*\mathbf{e}]_+$ where $\mu^* \in \mathbb{R}$ satisfies $\mathbf{e}^T[\boldsymbol{\lambda}(\mathbf{X}) - \mu^*\mathbf{e}]_+ = 1$	–	Corollary 6.29
$B_{\|\cdot\|_{S_1}}[0, \alpha]$	$\begin{cases} \mathbf{X}, & \|\mathbf{X}\|_{S_1} \leq \alpha, \\ \mathbf{U}\mathrm{diag}(\mathcal{T}_{\beta^*}(\boldsymbol{\lambda}(\mathbf{X})))\mathbf{U}^T, & \|\mathbf{X}\|_{S_1} > \alpha, \end{cases}$ $\|\mathcal{T}_{\beta^*}(\boldsymbol{\lambda}(\mathbf{X}))\|_1 = \alpha, \ \beta^* > 0$	$\alpha > 0$	Example 6.33

∎

7.3 Symmetric Spectral Functions over $\mathbb{R}^{m \times n}$

Let m, n be two positive integers and $r = \min\{m, n\}$. We will denote by $\boldsymbol{\sigma} : \mathbb{R}^{m \times n} \to \mathbb{R}^r$ the singular values function that assigns to each matrix $\mathbf{X} \in \mathbb{R}^{m \times n}$ the vector of singular values $(\sigma_1(\mathbf{X}), \sigma_2(\mathbf{X}), \dots, \sigma_r(\mathbf{X}))^T$, where $\sigma_1(\mathbf{X}) \geq \sigma_2(\mathbf{X}) \geq \dots \geq \sigma_r(\mathbf{X}) \geq 0$. We will also require the following notation. For a vector $\mathbf{v} \in \mathbb{R}^r$, the matrix $\mathrm{dg}(\mathbf{v})$ is the $m \times n$ matrix defined by

$$\mathrm{dg}(\mathbf{v})_{i,j} = \begin{cases} v_i, & i = j, \\ 0 & \text{else.} \end{cases}$$

The operator $\mathrm{dg}(\cdot)$ maps r-dimensional vectors to generalized[38] $m \times n$ diagonal matrices. The integers m and n (and hence also r) will be fixed throughout this section, and hence there is no need to indicate their values in the operator dg. We do not use the "diag" notation since it is reserved to square diagonal matrices.

It is well known (see Golub and Van Loan [60, Theorem 2.5.2]) that any matrix $\mathbf{X} \in \mathbb{R}^{m \times n}$ has a *singular value decomposition*, meaning matrices $\mathbf{U} \in \mathbb{O}^m, \mathbf{V} \in \mathbb{O}^n$ for which $\mathbf{X} = \mathbf{U}\mathrm{dg}(\boldsymbol{\sigma}(\mathbf{X}))\mathbf{V}^T$.

---

[38]A matrix $\mathbf{X} \in \mathbb{R}^{m \times n}$ is a *generalized diagonal matrix* if $X_{ij} = 0$ for any $i \neq j$.

The analysis in this section uses very similar arguments to those used in the previous section; however, for the sake of completeness we will provide the results with their complete proofs.

We begin by formally defining the notion of spectral functions over $\mathbb{R}^{m\times n}$.

Definition 7.21 (spectral functions over $\mathbb{R}^{m\times n}$). *A proper function $g :$ $\mathbb{R}^{m\times n} \to (-\infty, \infty]$ is called a **spectral function over** $\mathbb{R}^{m\times n}$ if there exists a proper function $f : \mathbb{R}^r \to (-\infty, \infty]$ for which $g = f \circ \boldsymbol{\sigma}$.*

Similarly to the notation in Section 7.2, if $g = f \circ \boldsymbol{\sigma}$, we will refer to f (which is actually not necessarily unique) as the *associated function*. Our main interest will be with spectral functions whose associated functions are absolutely permutation symmetric.

Definition 7.22 (symmetric spectral functions over $\mathbb{R}^{m\times n}$). *A proper function $f : \mathbb{R}^{m\times n} \to (-\infty, \infty]$ is called a **symmetric spectral function over** $\mathbb{R}^{m\times n}$ if there exists a proper absolutely permutation symmetric function $f : \mathbb{R}^r \to (-\infty, \infty]$ for which $g = f \circ \boldsymbol{\sigma}$.*

Example 7.23 (Schatten p-norms). Let $p \in [1, \infty]$. Then the *Schatten p-norm* is the norm defined by

$$\|\mathbf{X}\|_{S_p} \equiv \|\boldsymbol{\sigma}(\mathbf{X})\|_p, \ \mathbf{X} \in \mathbb{R}^{m\times n}.$$

It is well known[39] that $\|\cdot\|_{S_p}$ is indeed a norm for any $p \in [1, \infty]$. Specific examples are the following:

- **trace-norm** (Schatten 1-norm)—also called the **nuclear norm**:

$$\|\mathbf{X}\|_{S_1} = \sum_{i=1}^{r} \sigma_i(\mathbf{X}).$$

- **spectral norm** (Schatten ∞-norm):

$$\|\mathbf{X}\|_{S_\infty} = \sigma_1(\mathbf{X}) = \|\mathbf{X}\|_{2,2}.$$

- **Frobenius norm** (Schatten 2-norm):

$$\|\mathbf{X}\|_{S_2} = \sqrt{\sum_{i=1}^{r} \sigma_i(\mathbf{X})^2} = \sqrt{\mathrm{Tr}(\mathbf{X}^T\mathbf{X})}.$$

The Schatten p-norm is a symmetric spectral function over $\mathbb{R}^{m\times n}$ whose associated function is the l_p-norm on $\mathbb{R}^r$, which is obviously an absolutely permutation symmetric function. ∎

---

[39]See, for example, Horn and Johnson [70].

Example 7.24 (Ky Fan k-norms). Recall the notation from Example 6.51—given a vector $\mathbf{x} \in \mathbb{R}^r$, $x_{\langle i \rangle}$ is the component of $\mathbf{x}$ with the ith largest absolute value, meaning in particular that

$$|x_{\langle 1 \rangle}| \geq |x_{\langle 2 \rangle}| \geq \cdots \geq |x_{\langle r \rangle}|.$$

The function $f_k(\mathbf{x}) = \sum_{i=1}^{k} |x_{\langle i \rangle}|$ is an absolutely permutation symmetric function. The corresponding symmetric spectral function is the so-called *Ky Fan k-norm* given by

$$\|\mathbf{X}\|_{\langle k \rangle} = f_k(\sigma(\mathbf{X})) = \sum_{i=1}^{k} \sigma_i(\mathbf{X}).$$

Obviously, $\| \cdot \|_{\langle 1 \rangle}$ is the spectral norm, which is also the Schatten ∞-norm; the norm $\| \cdot \|_{\langle r \rangle}$ is the trace-norm, which is also the Schatten 1-norm. ∎

A key inequality that is used in the analysis of spectral functions over $\mathbb{R}^{m \times n}$ is an inequality bounding the inner product of two matrices via the inner product of their singular vectors. The inequality, which is credited to von Neumann, is in a sense the "$\mathbb{R}^{m \times n}$-counterpart" of Fan's inequality (Theorem 7.14).

Theorem 7.25 (von Neumann's trace inequality [123]). *For any two matrices* $\mathbf{X}, \mathbf{Y} \in \mathbb{R}^{m \times n}$, *the inequality*

$$\langle \mathbf{X}, \mathbf{Y} \rangle \leq \langle \boldsymbol{\sigma}(\mathbf{X}), \boldsymbol{\sigma}(\mathbf{Y}) \rangle$$

holds. Equality holds if and only if there exists a simultaneous nonincreasing singular value decomposition of $\mathbf{X}, \mathbf{Y}$, *meaning that there exist* $\mathbf{U} \in \mathbb{O}^m$ *and* $\mathbf{V} \in \mathbb{O}^n$ *for which*

$$\mathbf{X} = \mathbf{U} \mathrm{dg}(\boldsymbol{\sigma}(\mathbf{X})) \mathbf{V}^T,$$
$$\mathbf{Y} = \mathbf{U} \mathrm{dg}(\boldsymbol{\sigma}(\mathbf{Y})) \mathbf{V}^T.$$

7.3.1   The Spectral Conjugate Formula

A direct result of von Neumann's trace inequality is the spectral conjugate formula over $\mathbb{R}^{m \times n}$.

Theorem 7.26 (spectral conjugate formula over $\mathbb{R}^{m \times n}$). *Let* $f : \mathbb{E} \to (-\infty, \infty]$ *be an absolutely permutation symmetric function. Then*

$$(f \circ \boldsymbol{\sigma})^* = f^* \circ \boldsymbol{\sigma}.$$

Proof. Let $\mathbf{Y} \in \mathbb{R}^{m \times n}$. Then

$$
\begin{aligned}
(f \circ \boldsymbol{\sigma})^*(\mathbf{Y}) &= \max_{\mathbf{X} \in \mathbb{R}^{m \times n}} \{\mathrm{Tr}(\mathbf{XY}) - f(\boldsymbol{\sigma}(\mathbf{X}))\} \\
&\leq \max_{\mathbf{X} \in \mathbb{R}^{m \times n}} \{\langle \boldsymbol{\sigma}(\mathbf{X}), \boldsymbol{\sigma}(\mathbf{Y}) \rangle - f(\boldsymbol{\sigma}(\mathbf{X}))\} \\
&\leq \max_{\mathbf{x} \in \mathbb{R}^r} \{\langle \mathbf{x}, \boldsymbol{\sigma}(\mathbf{Y}) \rangle - f(\mathbf{x})\} \\
&= (f^* \circ \boldsymbol{\sigma})(\mathbf{Y}),
\end{aligned}
$$

where Von Neumann's trace inequality (Theorem 7.25) was used in the first inequality. To show the reverse inequality, take a singular value decomposition of $\mathbf{Y}$:

$$\mathbf{Y} = \mathbf{U}\mathrm{dg}(\boldsymbol{\sigma}(\mathbf{Y}))\mathbf{V}^T \ (\mathbf{U} \in \mathbb{O}^m, \mathbf{V} \in \mathbb{O}^n).$$

Then

$$
\begin{aligned}
(f^* \circ \boldsymbol{\sigma})(\mathbf{Y}) &= \max_{\mathbf{x} \in \mathbb{R}^r} \{\langle \mathbf{x}, \boldsymbol{\sigma}(\mathbf{Y}) \rangle - f(\mathbf{x})\} \\
&= \max_{\mathbf{x} \in \mathbb{R}^r} \{\mathrm{Tr}(\mathrm{dg}(\mathbf{x})^T \mathrm{dg}(\boldsymbol{\sigma}(\mathbf{Y}))) - f(\mathbf{x})\} \\
&= \max_{\mathbf{x} \in \mathbb{R}^r} \{\mathrm{Tr}(\mathrm{dg}(\mathbf{x})^T \mathbf{U}^T \mathbf{Y} \mathbf{V}) - f(\mathbf{x}^\downarrow)\} \\
&= \max_{\mathbf{x} \in \mathbb{R}^r} \{\mathrm{Tr}(\mathrm{dg}(\mathbf{x})^T \mathbf{U}^T \mathbf{Y} \mathbf{V}) - f(\boldsymbol{\sigma}(\mathbf{U}\mathrm{dg}(\mathbf{x})\mathbf{V}^T))\} \\
&= \max_{\mathbf{x} \in \mathbb{R}^r} \{\mathrm{Tr}(\mathbf{V}\mathrm{dg}(\mathbf{x})^T \mathbf{U}^T \mathbf{Y}) - f(\boldsymbol{\sigma}(\mathbf{U}\mathrm{dg}(\mathbf{x})\mathbf{V}^T))\} \\
&\leq \max_{\mathbf{Z} \in \mathbb{R}^{m \times n}} \{\mathrm{Tr}(\mathbf{Z}^T \mathbf{Y}) - f(\boldsymbol{\sigma}(\mathbf{Z}))\} \\
&= (f \circ \boldsymbol{\sigma})^*(\mathbf{Y}). \quad \square
\end{aligned}
$$

Example 7.27. Using the spectral conjugate formula over $\mathbb{R}^{m \times n}$, we present below expressions for the conjugate functions of several symmetric spectral functions over $\mathbb{R}^{m \times n}$ (all with full domain). The table also includes the references to the corresponding results on functions over $\mathbb{R}^r$. The constant α is assumed to be positive.

$g(\mathbf{X})$	$\mathrm{dom}(g)$	$g^*(\mathbf{Y})$	$\mathrm{dom}(g^*)$	Reference
$\alpha\sigma_1(\mathbf{X})$ $(\alpha > 0)$	$\mathbb{R}^{m \times n}$	$\delta_{B_{\|\cdot\|_{S_1}}[0,\alpha]}(\mathbf{Y})$	$B_{\|\cdot\|_{S_1}}[\mathbf{0}, \alpha]$	Section 4.4.12
$\alpha\|\mathbf{X}\|_F$ $(\alpha > 0)$	$\mathbb{R}^{m \times n}$	$\delta_{B_{\|\cdot\|_F}[0,\alpha]}(\mathbf{Y})$	$B_{\|\cdot\|_F}[\mathbf{0}, \alpha]$	Section 4.4.12
$\alpha\|\mathbf{X}\|_F^2$ $(\alpha > 0)$	$\mathbb{R}^{m \times n}$	$\frac{1}{4\alpha}\|\mathbf{Y}\|_F^2$	$\mathbb{R}^{m \times n}$	Section 4.4.6
$\alpha\|\mathbf{X}\|_{S_1}$ $(\alpha > 0)$	$\mathbb{R}^{m \times n}$	$\delta_{B_{\|\cdot\|_{S_\infty}}[0,\alpha]}(\mathbf{Y})$	$B_{\|\cdot\|_{S_\infty}}[\mathbf{0}, \alpha]$	Section 4.4.12

∎

The spectral conjugate formula can be used to show that a symmetric spectral function over $\mathbb{R}^{m \times n}$ is closed and convex if and only if its associated function is closed and convex.

Theorem 7.28 (closedness and convexity of symmetric spectral functions over $\mathbb{R}^{m \times n}$). *Let $F : \mathbb{R}^{m \times n} \to (-\infty, \infty]$ be given by $F = f \circ \boldsymbol{\sigma}$, where $f : \mathbb{R}^r \to (-\infty, \infty]$ is an absolutely permutation symmetric proper function. Then F is closed and convex if and only if f is closed and convex.*

Proof. By the spectral conjugate formula (Theorem 7.26),

$$F^* = (f \circ \boldsymbol{\sigma})^* = f^* \circ \boldsymbol{\sigma}.$$

Since by the symmetric conjugate theorem (Theorem 7.9) f^* is absolutely permutation symmetric, we can invoke once again the spectral conjugate formula to obtain

$$F^{**} = (f^* \circ \boldsymbol{\sigma})^* = f^{**} \circ \boldsymbol{\sigma}. \tag{7.7}$$

If f is closed and convex, then by Theorem 4.8 (taking also in account the properness of f) it follows that $f^{**} = f$. Therefore, by (7.7),

$$F^{**} = f \circ \boldsymbol{\sigma} = F.$$

Thus, since F is a conjugate of another function (F^*), it follows by Theorem 4.3 that it is closed and convex. Now assume that F is closed and convex. Since F is in addition proper, it follows by Theorem 4.8 that $F^{**} = F$, which, combined with (7.7), yields the equality

$$f \circ \boldsymbol{\sigma} = F = F^{**} = f^{**} \circ \boldsymbol{\sigma}.$$

Therefore, for any $\mathbf{x} \in \mathbb{R}^r$,

$$f(|\mathbf{x}|^{\downarrow}) = f(\boldsymbol{\sigma}(\mathrm{dg}(\mathbf{x}))) = f^{**}(\boldsymbol{\sigma}(\mathrm{dg}(\mathbf{x}))) = f^{**}(|\mathbf{x}|^{\downarrow}).$$

By the absolutely permutation symmetry property of both f and f^{**}, it follows that $f(|\mathbf{x}|^{\downarrow}) = f(\mathbf{x})$ and $f^{**}(|\mathbf{x}|^{\downarrow}) = f^{**}(\mathbf{x})$, and therefore $f(\mathbf{x}) = f^{**}(\mathbf{x})$ for any $\mathbf{x} \in \mathbb{R}^r$, meaning that $f = f^{**}$. Therefore, f, as a conjugate of another function (f^*), is closed and convex. $\square$

7.3.2 The Proximal Operator of Symmetric Spectral Functions over $\mathbb{R}^{m \times n}$

The next result shows a simple formula for computing the prox operator of a symmetric spectral function over $\mathbb{R}^{m \times n}$, which is also proper closed and convex. The prox is expressed in terms of the singular value decomposition of the argument and the prox operator of the associated function.

Theorem 7.29 (spectral prox formula over $\mathbb{R}^{m \times n}$). *Let $F : \mathbb{R}^{m \times n} \to (-\infty, \infty]$ be given by $F = f \circ \boldsymbol{\sigma}$, where $f : \mathbb{R}^r \to (-\infty, \infty]$ is an absolutely permutation symmetric proper closed and convex function. Let $\mathbf{X} \in \mathbb{R}^{m \times n}$, and suppose that $\mathbf{X} = \mathbf{U} \mathrm{dg}(\boldsymbol{\sigma}(\mathbf{X})) \mathbf{V}^T$, where $\mathbf{U} \in \mathbb{O}^m, \mathbf{V} \in \mathbb{O}^n$. Then*

$$\mathrm{prox}_F(\mathbf{X}) = \mathbf{U} \mathrm{dg}(\mathrm{prox}_f(\boldsymbol{\sigma}(\mathbf{X}))) \mathbf{V}^T.$$

Proof. Recall that

$$\mathrm{prox}_F(\mathbf{X}) = \mathrm{argmin}_{\mathbf{Z} \in \mathbb{R}^{m \times n}} \left\{ F(\mathbf{Z}) + \frac{1}{2} \|\mathbf{Z} - \mathbf{X}\|_F^2 \right\}. \tag{7.8}$$

Denoting $\mathbf{D} = \mathrm{dg}(\boldsymbol{\sigma}(\mathbf{X}))$, we note that for any $\mathbf{Z} \in \mathbb{R}^{m \times n}$,

$$F(\mathbf{Z}) + \frac{1}{2}\|\mathbf{Z} - \mathbf{X}\|_F^2 = F(\mathbf{Z}) + \frac{1}{2}\|\mathbf{Z} - \mathbf{U}\mathbf{D}\mathbf{V}^T\|_F^2 \overset{(*)}{=} F(\mathbf{U}^T \mathbf{Z}\mathbf{V}) + \frac{1}{2}\|\mathbf{U}^T\mathbf{Z}\mathbf{V} - \mathbf{D}\|_F^2,$$

where the transition $(*)$ is due to the fact that $F(\mathbf{Z}) = f(\boldsymbol{\sigma}(\mathbf{Z})) = f(\boldsymbol{\sigma}(\mathbf{U}^T\mathbf{Z}\mathbf{V})) = F(\mathbf{U}^T\mathbf{Z}\mathbf{V})$. Making the change of variables $\mathbf{W} = \mathbf{U}^T\mathbf{Z}\mathbf{V}$, we conclude that the unique optimal solution of (7.8) is given by

$$\mathbf{Z} = \mathbf{U}\mathbf{W}^*\mathbf{V}^T, \tag{7.9}$$

where $\mathbf{W}^*$ is the unique optimal solution of

$$\min_{\mathbf{W} \in \mathbb{R}^{m \times n}} \left\{ G(\mathbf{W}) \equiv F(\mathbf{W}) + \frac{1}{2} \|\mathbf{W} - \mathbf{D}\|_F^2 \right\}. \tag{7.10}$$

We will prove that $\mathbf{W}^*$ is a generalized diagonal matrix (meaning that all off-diagonal components are zeros). Let $i \in \{1, 2, \ldots, r\}$. Take $\mathbf{\Sigma}_i^{(1)} \in \mathbb{R}^{m \times m}$ and $\mathbf{\Sigma}_i^{(2)} \in \mathbb{R}^{n \times n}$ to be the $m \times m$ and $n \times n$ diagonal matrices whose diagonal elements are all ones except for the (i, i)th component, which is -1. Define $\widetilde{\mathbf{W}}_i = \mathbf{\Sigma}_i^{(1)} \mathbf{W}^* \mathbf{\Sigma}_i^{(2)}$. Obviously, by the fact that $\mathbf{\Sigma}_i^{(1)} \in \mathbb{O}^m, \mathbf{\Sigma}_i^{(2)} \in \mathbb{O}^n$,

$$F(\mathbf{\Sigma}_i^{(1)} \mathbf{W}^* \mathbf{\Sigma}_i^{(2)}) = f(\boldsymbol{\sigma}(\mathbf{\Sigma}_i^{(1)} \mathbf{W}^* \mathbf{\Sigma}_i^{(2)})) = f(\boldsymbol{\sigma}(\mathbf{W}^*)) = F(\mathbf{W}^*),$$

and we thus obtain

$$\begin{aligned}
G(\widetilde{\mathbf{W}}_i) &= F(\widetilde{\mathbf{W}}_i) + \frac{1}{2} \|\widetilde{\mathbf{W}}_i - \mathbf{D}\|_F^2 \\
&= F(\mathbf{\Sigma}_i^{(1)} \mathbf{W}^* \mathbf{\Sigma}_i^{(2)}) + \frac{1}{2} \|\mathbf{\Sigma}_i^{(1)} \mathbf{W}^* \mathbf{\Sigma}_i^{(2)} - \mathbf{D}\|_F^2 \\
&= F(\mathbf{W}^*) + \frac{1}{2} \|\mathbf{W}^* - \mathbf{\Sigma}_i^{(1)} \mathbf{D} \mathbf{\Sigma}_i^{(2)}\|_F^2 \\
&= F(\mathbf{W}^*) + \frac{1}{2} \|\mathbf{W}^* - \mathbf{D}\|_F^2, \\
&= G(\mathbf{W}^*).
\end{aligned}$$

Consequently, $\widetilde{\mathbf{W}}_i$ is also an optimal solution of (7.10), but by the uniqueness of the optimal solution of problem (7.10), we conclude that $\mathbf{W}^* = \mathbf{\Sigma}_i^{(1)} \mathbf{W}^* \mathbf{\Sigma}_i^{(2)}$. Comparing the ith rows and columns of the two matrices we obtain that $W_{ij}^* = 0$ and $W_{ji}^* = 0$ for any $j \neq i$. Since this argument is valid for any $i \in \{1, 2, \ldots, r\}$, it follows that $\mathbf{W}^*$ is a generalized diagonal matrix, and consequently the optimal solution of (7.10) is given by $\mathbf{W}^* = \mathrm{dg}(\mathbf{w}^*)$, where $\mathbf{w}^*$ is the optimal solution of

$$\min_{\mathbf{w}} \left\{ F(\mathrm{dg}(\mathbf{w})) + \frac{1}{2} \|\mathrm{dg}(\mathbf{w}) - \mathbf{D}\|_F^2 \right\}.$$

Since $F(\mathrm{dg}(\mathbf{w})) = f(|\mathbf{w}|^{\downarrow}) = f(\mathbf{w})$ and $\|\mathrm{dg}(\mathbf{w}) - \mathbf{D}\|_F^2 = \|\mathbf{w} - \boldsymbol{\sigma}(\mathbf{X})\|_2^2$, it follows that $\mathbf{w}^*$ is given by

$$\mathbf{w}^* = \mathrm{argmin}_{\mathbf{w}} \left\{ f(\mathbf{w}) + \frac{1}{2} \|\mathbf{w} - \boldsymbol{\sigma}(\mathbf{X})\|_2^2 \right\} = \mathrm{prox}_f(\boldsymbol{\sigma}(\mathbf{X})).$$

Therefore, $\mathbf{W}^* = \mathrm{dg}(\mathrm{prox}_f(\boldsymbol{\sigma}(\mathbf{X})))$, which, along with (7.9), establishes the desired result. $\square$

Example 7.30. Using the spectral prox formula over $\mathbb{R}^{m \times n}$, we can compute the prox of symmetric spectral functions in terms of the prox of their associated functions. Using this observation, we present in the table below expressions of prox operators of several functions. The parameter α is always assumed to be positive, and $\mathbf{U} \in \mathbb{O}^m, \mathbf{V} \in \mathbb{O}^n$ are assumed to satisfy $\mathbf{X} = \mathbf{U} \mathrm{dg}(\boldsymbol{\sigma}(\mathbf{X})) \mathbf{V}^T$. The table also includes a reference to the corresponding results for the associated functions, which are always defined over $\mathbb{R}^r$.

$F(\mathbf{X})$	$\mathrm{prox}_F(\mathbf{X})$	Reference
$\alpha\|\mathbf{X}\|_F^2$	$\frac{1}{1+2\alpha}\mathbf{X}$	Section 6.2.3
$\alpha\|\mathbf{X}\|_F$	$\left(1 - \frac{\alpha}{\max\{\|\mathbf{X}\|_F, \alpha\}}\right)\mathbf{X}$	Example 6.19
$\alpha\|\mathbf{X}\|_{S_1}$	$\mathbf{U}\mathrm{dg}(\mathcal{T}_\alpha(\boldsymbol{\sigma}(\mathbf{X})))\mathbf{V}^T$	Example 6.8
$\alpha\|\mathbf{X}\|_{S_\infty}$	$\mathbf{X} - \alpha\mathbf{U}\mathrm{dg}(P_{B_{\|\cdot\|_1}[\mathbf{0},1]}(\boldsymbol{\sigma}(\mathbf{X})/\alpha))\mathbf{V}^T$	Example 6.48
$\alpha\|\mathbf{X}\|_{\langle k\rangle}$	$\mathbf{X} - \alpha\mathbf{U}\mathrm{dg}(P_C(\boldsymbol{\sigma}(\mathbf{X})/\alpha))\mathbf{V}^T$,	Example 6.51
	$C = B_{\|\cdot\|_1}[\mathbf{0},k] \cap B_{\|\cdot\|_\infty}[\mathbf{0},1]$	

Note that $\|\mathbf{X}\|_{S_\infty}$ can be written as either $\sigma_1(\mathbf{X})$ or $\|\mathbf{X}\|_{2,2}$. ∎

A set $T \subseteq \mathbb{R}^{m\times n}$ is called a *symmetric spectral set* in $\mathbb{R}^{m\times n}$ if the indicator function δ_T is a symmetric spectral function over $\mathbb{R}^{m\times n}$, meaning that it has the form $\delta_T = \delta_C \circ \boldsymbol{\sigma}$, where δ_C is an absolutely permutation symmetric function. The set $C \subseteq \mathbb{R}^{m\times n}$ is the *associated set*. Since $\mathrm{prox}_{\delta_T} = P_T$ and $\mathrm{prox}_{\delta_C} = P_C$, it follows by the spectral prox formula that if C is nonempty closed and convex, then

$$P_T(\mathbf{X}) = \mathbf{U}\mathrm{dg}(P_C(\boldsymbol{\sigma}(\mathbf{X})))\mathbf{V}^T, \ \mathbf{X} \in \mathbb{R}^{m\times n}, \tag{7.11}$$

where $\mathbf{U} \in \mathbb{O}^m, \mathbf{V} \in \mathbb{O}^n$ are assumed to satisfy $\mathbf{X} = \mathbf{U}\mathrm{dg}(\boldsymbol{\sigma}(\mathbf{X}))\mathbf{V}^T$.

Example 7.31. Using formula (7.11), we present in the following table expressions for the orthogonal projection onto several symmetric spectral sets in $\mathbb{R}^{m\times n}$. The table also includes references to the corresponding results on the orthogonal projection onto the associated subset of $\mathbb{R}^r$. The matrices $\mathbf{U} \in \mathbb{O}^m, \mathbf{V} \in \mathbb{O}^n$ are assumed to satisfy $\mathbf{X} = \mathbf{U}\mathrm{dg}(\boldsymbol{\sigma}(\mathbf{X}))\mathbf{V}^T$.

set (T)	$P_T(\mathbf{X})$	Assumptions	Reference
$B_{\|\cdot\|_{S_\infty}}[\mathbf{0},\alpha]$	$\mathbf{U}\mathrm{dg}(\mathbf{v})\mathbf{V}^T, \ v_i = \min\{\sigma_i(\mathbf{X}),\alpha\}$	$\alpha > 0$	Lemma 6.26
$B_{\|\cdot\|_F}[\mathbf{0},r]$	$\frac{r}{\max\{\|\mathbf{X}\|_F, r\}}\mathbf{X}$	$r > 0$	Lemma 6.26
$B_{\|\cdot\|_{S_1}}[\mathbf{0},\alpha]$	$\begin{cases} \mathbf{X}, & \|\mathbf{X}\|_{S_1} \leq \alpha, \\ \mathbf{U}\mathrm{dg}(\mathcal{T}_{\beta^*}(\boldsymbol{\sigma}(\mathbf{X})))\mathbf{V}^T, & \|\mathbf{X}\|_{S_1} > \alpha, \end{cases}$ $\|\mathcal{T}_{\beta^*}(\boldsymbol{\sigma}(\mathbf{X}))\|_1 = \alpha, \ \beta^* > 0$	$\alpha > 0$	Example 6.33

∎

Chapter 8

Primal and Dual Projected Subgradient Methods

Underlying Space: In this chapter $\mathbb{E}$ is a Euclidean space, meaning a finite dimensional space endowed with an inner product $\langle \cdot, \cdot \rangle$ and the Euclidean norm $\| \cdot \| = \sqrt{\langle \cdot, \cdot \rangle}$.

8.1 From Gradient Descent to Subgradient Descent

8.1.1 Descent Directions?

Consider the unconstrained problem

$$\text{(P)} \quad \min\{f(\mathbf{x}) : \mathbf{x} \in \mathbb{E}\}.$$

If f is differentiable over $\mathbb{E}$, then a well-known method for solving problem (P) is the *gradient method*, also known as *steepest descent*, which takes the form

$$\mathbf{x}^{k+1} = \mathbf{x}^k - t_k \nabla f(\mathbf{x}^k), \tag{8.1}$$

where t_k is an appropriately chosen stepsize. A key property of the direction of the negative of the gradient is that it is a *descent direction*, a notion that is now recalled.

Definition 8.1 (descent direction). *Let $f : \mathbb{E} \to (-\infty, \infty]$ be an extended real-valued function, and let $\mathbf{x} \in \text{int}(\text{dom}(f))$. A vector $\mathbf{0} \neq \mathbf{d} \in \mathbb{E}$ is called a **descent direction** of f at $\mathbf{x}$ if the directional derivative $f'(\mathbf{x}; \mathbf{d})$ exists and is negative.*

An important property of descent directions, which can be directly deduced from their definition, is that taking small enough steps along these directions leads to a decrease in function value.

Lemma 8.2 (descent property of descent directions [10, Lemma 4.2]). *Let $f : \mathbb{E} \to (-\infty, \infty]$ be an extended real-valued function. Let $\mathbf{x} \in \text{int}(\text{dom}(f))$, and assume that $\mathbf{0} \neq \mathbf{d} \in \mathbb{E}$ is a descent direction of f at $\mathbf{x}$. Then there exists $\varepsilon > 0$ such that $\mathbf{x} + t\mathbf{d} \in \text{dom}(f)$ and*

$$f(\mathbf{x} + t\mathbf{d}) < f(\mathbf{x})$$

for any $t \in (0, \varepsilon]$.

Coming back to the gradient method, we note that the directional derivative of f at $\mathbf{x}^k$ in the direction of $-\nabla f(\mathbf{x}^k)$ is negative as long as $\nabla f(\mathbf{x}^k) \neq \mathbf{0}$:

$$f'(\mathbf{x}^k; -\nabla f(\mathbf{x}^k)) = \langle \nabla f(\mathbf{x}^k), -\nabla f(\mathbf{x}^k) \rangle = -\|\nabla f(\mathbf{x}^k)\|^2 < 0, \qquad (8.2)$$

where Theorem 3.29 was used in the first equality. We have thus shown that $-\nabla f(\mathbf{x}^k)$ is a *descent direction* of f at $\mathbf{x}^k$, which by Lemma 8.2 implies that there exists $\varepsilon > 0$ such that $f(\mathbf{x}^k - t\nabla f(\mathbf{x}^k)) < f(\mathbf{x}^k)$ for any $t \in (0, \varepsilon]$. In particular, this means that t_k can always be chosen in a way that guarantees a decrease in the function value from one iteration to the next. For example, one choice of stepsize that guarantees descent is the *exact line search* strategy in which t_k is chosen as

$$t_k \in \operatorname{argmin}_{t \geq 0} f(\mathbf{x}^k - t\nabla f(\mathbf{x}^k)).$$

If f is not differentiable, then scheme (8.1) is not well defined. Under a convexity assumption, a natural generalization to the nonsmooth case will consist in replacing the gradient by a subgradient (assuming that it exists):

$$\mathbf{x}^{k+1} = \mathbf{x}^k - t_k \mathbf{g}^k, \quad \mathbf{g}^k \in \partial f(\mathbf{x}^k), \qquad (8.3)$$

where we assume that the choice of the subgradient from $\partial f(\mathbf{x}^k)$ is arbitrary. The scheme (8.3) is called the *subgradient method*. One substantial difference between the gradient and subgradient methods is that the direction of minus the subgradient is not necessarily a descent direction. This means that t_k cannot be chosen in a way that will guarantee a descent property in function values of the scheme (8.3).

Example 8.3 (non-descent subgradient direction).[40] Consider the function $f : \mathbb{R} \times \mathbb{R} \to \mathbb{R}$ given by $f(x_1, x_2) = |x_1| + 2|x_2|$. Then

$$\partial f(1, 0) = \{(1, x) : |x| \leq 2\}.$$

In particular, $(1, 2) \in \partial f(1, 0)$. However, the direction $-(1, 2)$ is not a descent direction. To show this, note that for any $t > 0$,

$$g(t) \equiv f((1,0) - t(1,2)) = f(1-t, -2t) = |1-t| + 4t = \begin{cases} 1 + 3t, & t \in (0, 1], \\ 5t - 1, & t \geq 1. \end{cases} \qquad (8.4)$$

In particular,

$$f'((1,0); -(1,2)) = g'_+(0) = 3 > 0,$$

showing that $-(1, 2)$ is not a descent direction. It is also interesting to note that by (8.4), it holds that

$$f((1,0) - t(1,2)) \geq 1 = f(1,0) \text{ for any } t > 0,$$

which actually shows that there is no point in the ray $\{(1,0) - t(1,2) : t > 0\}$ with a smaller function value than $(1, 0)$. ∎

---

[40] Example 8.3 is taken from Vandenberghe's lecture notes [122].

8.1.2 Wolfe's Example

To better understand the effect of nonsmoothness, we recall a famous example of Wolfe. The example deals with the gradient method employed on a nonsmooth convex function with stepsizes chosen by exact line search. The function is differentiable at all the iterate vectors generated by the method, which in particular means that all the directions picked by the method are descent directions, and the sequence of function values strictly decreases. However, although it seems that the nonsmoothness is "bypassed," this is hardly the case. The sequence generated by the method converges to a nonoptimal point.

Let $\gamma > 1$, and consider the function $f : \mathbb{R} \times \mathbb{R} \to \mathbb{R}$ given by

$$f(x_1, x_2) = \begin{cases} \sqrt{x_1^2 + \gamma x_2^2}, & |x_2| \leq x_1, \\ \frac{x_1 + \gamma |x_2|}{\sqrt{1+\gamma}} & \text{else.} \end{cases} \qquad (8.5)$$

We begin by showing in Lemma 8.5 below that the function f is closed and convex and describe its subdifferential set at any point in $\mathbb{R} \times \mathbb{R}$. For that, we will prove that f is actually a support function of a closed and convex set.[41] The proof of Lemma 8.5 uses the following simple technical lemma, whose trivial proof is omitted.

Lemma 8.4. *Consider the problem*

$$\text{(P)} \quad \max\{g(\mathbf{y}) : f_1(\mathbf{y}) \leq 0, f_2(\mathbf{y}) \leq 0\},$$

where $g : \mathbb{E} \to \mathbb{R}$ is concave and $f_1, f_2 : \mathbb{E} \to \mathbb{R}$ are convex. Assume that the problem $\max\{g(\mathbf{y}) : f_1(\mathbf{y}) \leq 0\}$ has a unique solution $\tilde{\mathbf{y}}$. Let Y^* be the optimal set of problem (P). Then exactly one of the following two options holds:

(i) $f_2(\tilde{\mathbf{y}}) \leq 0$, *and in this case* $Y^* = \{\tilde{\mathbf{y}}\}$.

(ii) $f_2(\tilde{\mathbf{y}}) > 0$, *and in this case* $Y^* = \text{argmax}\{g(\mathbf{y}) : f_1(\mathbf{y}) \leq 0, f_2(\mathbf{y}) = 0\}$.

Lemma 8.5. *Let f be given by (8.5). Then*

(a) $f = \sigma_C$, *where*

$$C = \left\{ (y_1, y_2) \in \mathbb{R} \times \mathbb{R} : y_1^2 + \frac{y_2^2}{\gamma} \leq 1, y_1 \geq \frac{1}{\sqrt{1+\gamma}} \right\};$$

(b) f *is closed and convex;*

(c)

$$\partial f(x_1, x_2) = \begin{cases} C, & x_1 = x_2 = 0, \\ \frac{(x_1, \gamma x_2)}{\sqrt{x_1^2 + \gamma x_2^2}}, & |x_2| \leq x_1, x_1 \neq 0, \\ \left(\frac{1}{\sqrt{1+\gamma}}, \frac{\gamma \text{sgn}(x_2)}{\sqrt{1+\gamma}} \right), & |x_2| > x_1, x_2 \neq 0, \\ \left\{ \frac{1}{\sqrt{\gamma+1}} \right\} \times \left[-\frac{\gamma}{\sqrt{1+\gamma}}, \frac{\gamma}{\sqrt{1+\gamma}} \right], & x_2 = 0, x_1 < 0. \end{cases}$$

---

[41] Recall that support functions of nonempty sets are always closed and convex (Lemma 2.23).

Proof. By the definition of support functions,

$$\sigma_C(x_1, x_2) = \max_{y_1, y_2} \left\{ x_1 y_1 + x_2 y_2 : y_1^2 + \frac{y_2^2}{\gamma} \leq 1, y_1 \geq \frac{1}{\sqrt{1+\gamma}} \right\}. \tag{8.6}$$

Note that if $(x_1, x_2) = (0, 0)$, then $\sigma_C(x_1, x_2) = 0$ and

$$\text{argmax}_{y_1, y_2} \left\{ x_1 y_1 + x_2 y_2 : y_1^2 + \frac{y_2^2}{\gamma} \leq 1, y_1 \geq \frac{1}{\sqrt{1+\gamma}} \right\} = C.$$

Assume that $(x_1, x_2) \neq (0, 0)$. Denoting $g(y_1, y_2) = x_1 y_1 + x_2 y_2$, $f_1(y_1, y_2) = y_1^2 + \frac{y_2^2}{\gamma} - 1$ and $f_2(y_1, y_2) = -y_1 + \frac{1}{\sqrt{1+\gamma}}$, problem (8.6) becomes

$$\max_{y_1, y_2} \{ g(y_1, y_2) : f_1(y_1, y_2) \leq 0, f_2(y_1, y_2) \leq 0 \}.$$

The assumptions made in Lemma 8.4 are all met: g is concave, f_1, f_2 are convex, and the optimal solution of

$$\max_{y_1, y_2} \{ g(y_1, y_2) : f_1(y_1, y_2) \leq 0 \}$$

is unique and equal to $(\tilde{y}_1, \tilde{y}_2) = \frac{(x_1, \gamma x_2)}{\sqrt{x_1^2 + \gamma x_2^2}}$. Thus, by Lemma 8.4, there are two options:

Case I: $f_2(\tilde{y}_1, \tilde{y}_2) \leq 0$, meaning that $\frac{x_1}{\sqrt{x_1^2 + \gamma x_2^2}} \geq \frac{1}{\sqrt{1+\gamma}}$. It can be easily seen that the last inequality is equivalent to the condition $|x_2| \leq x_1$. Under this condition, by Lemma 8.4, $(\tilde{y}_1, \tilde{y}_2) = \frac{(x_1, \gamma x_2)}{\sqrt{x_1^2 + \gamma x_2^2}}$ is the unique optimal solution of problem (8.6) with a corresponding function value of $\sigma_C(x_1, x_2) = \sqrt{x_1^2 + \gamma x_2^2}$.

Case II: $f_2(\tilde{y}_1, \tilde{y}_2) > 0$, which is the same as $x_1 < |x_2|$. In this case, by Lemma 8.4, all the optimal solutions of problem (8.6) satisfy $y_1 = \frac{1}{\sqrt{1+\gamma}}$, and the problem thus amounts to

$$\max_{y_2} \left\{ \frac{1}{\sqrt{1+\gamma}} x_1 + x_2 y_2 : y_2^2 \leq \frac{\gamma^2}{1+\gamma} \right\}.$$

The set of maximizers of the above problem is either $\left\{ \frac{\gamma \text{sgn}(x_2)}{\sqrt{1+\gamma}} \right\}$ if $x_2 \neq 0$ or $\left[-\frac{\gamma}{\sqrt{1+\gamma}}, \frac{\gamma}{\sqrt{1+\gamma}} \right]$ if $x_2 = 0$. In both options, $\sigma_C(x_1, x_2) = \frac{x_1 + \gamma |x_2|}{\sqrt{1+\gamma}}$.

To summarize, we have shown that

$$\sigma_C(x_1, x_2) = \begin{cases} \sqrt{x_1^2 + \gamma x_2^2}, & |x_2| \leq x_1, \\ \frac{x_1 + \gamma |x_2|}{\sqrt{1+\gamma}} & \text{else,} \end{cases}$$

establishing part (a), meaning that $f = \sigma_C$. Therefore, f, as a support function, is a closed and convex function, and we have thus established part (b) as well. To prove part (c), note that we also showed that

$$\operatorname{argmax}_{y_1,y_2}\{x_1y_1 + x_2y_2 : (y_1,y_2) \in C\}$$

$$= \begin{cases} C, & x_1 = x_2 = 0, \\ \frac{(x_1,\gamma x_2)}{\sqrt{x_1^2+\gamma x_2^2}}, & |x_2| \le x_1, x_1 \ne 0, \\ \left(\frac{1}{\sqrt{1+\gamma}}, \frac{\gamma \operatorname{sgn}(x_2)}{\sqrt{1+\gamma}}\right), & |x_2| > x_1, x_2 \ne 0, \\ \left\{\frac{1}{\sqrt{\gamma+1}}\right\} \times \left[-\frac{\gamma}{\sqrt{1+\gamma}}, \frac{\gamma}{\sqrt{1+\gamma}}\right], & x_2 = 0, x_1 < 0. \end{cases}$$

Combining this with the conjugate subgradient theorem (Corollary 4.21), as well as Example 4.9 and the closedness and convexity of C, implies

$$\partial f(x_1,x_2) = \partial \sigma_C(x_1,x_2)$$
$$= \operatorname{argmax}_{y_1,y_2}\{x_1y_1 + x_2y_2 - \sigma_C^*(y_1,y_2)\}$$
$$= \operatorname{argmax}_{y_1,y_2}\{x_1y_1 + x_2y_2 - \delta_C(y_1,y_2)\}$$
$$= \operatorname{argmax}_{y_1,y_2}\{x_1y_1 + x_2y_2 : (y_1,y_2) \in C\}$$

$$= \begin{cases} C, & x_1 = x_2 = 0, \\ \frac{(x_1,\gamma x_2)}{\sqrt{x_1^2+\gamma x_2^2}}, & |x_2| \le x_1, x_1 \ne 0, \\ \left(\frac{1}{\sqrt{1+\gamma}}, \frac{\gamma \operatorname{sgn}(x_2)}{\sqrt{1+\gamma}}\right), & |x_2| > x_1, x_2 \ne 0, \\ \left\{\frac{1}{\sqrt{\gamma+1}}\right\} \times \left[-\frac{\gamma}{\sqrt{1+\gamma}}, \frac{\gamma}{\sqrt{1+\gamma}}\right], & x_2 = 0, x_1 < 0. \end{cases} \qquad \square$$

Note that a direct result of part (c) of Lemma 8.5 and Theorem 3.33 is that f is not differentiable only at the nonpositive part of the x_1 axis.

In the next result we will show that the gradient method with exact line search employed on f with a certain initialization converges to the nonoptimal point $(0,0)$ even though all the points generated by the gradient method are points in which f is differentiable.

Lemma 8.6. *Let* $\{(x_1^{(k)}, x_2^{(k)})\}_{k \ge 0}$ *be the sequence generated by the gradient method with exact line search employed on f with initial point $(x_1^0, x_2^0) = (\gamma, 1)$, where $\gamma > 1$. Then for any $k \ge 0$,*

(a) *f is differentiable at $(x_1^{(k)}, x_2^{(k)})$;*

(b) *$|x_2^{(k)}| \le x_1^{(k)}$ and $x_1^{(k)} \ne 0$;*

(c) *$(x_1^{(k)}, x_2^{(k)}) = \left(\gamma\left(\frac{\gamma-1}{\gamma+1}\right)^k, \left(-\frac{\gamma-1}{\gamma+1}\right)^k\right).$*

Proof. We only need to show part (c) since part (b) follows directly from the expression of $(x_1^{(k)}, x_2^{(k)})$ given in (c), and part (a) is then a consequence of Lemma 8.5(c).

We will prove part (c) by induction. The claim is obviously correct for $k = 0$ by the choice of initial point. Assume that the claim is correct for k, that is,

$$(x_1^{(k)}, x_2^{(k)}) = \left(\gamma \left(\frac{\gamma - 1}{\gamma + 1} \right)^k, \left(-\frac{\gamma - 1}{\gamma + 1} \right)^k \right).$$

We will prove that it is correct for $k + 1$, meaning that

$$(x_1^{(k+1)}, x_2^{(k+1)}) = (\beta_k, \gamma_k), \tag{8.7}$$

where

$$\beta_k = \gamma \left(\frac{\gamma - 1}{\gamma + 1} \right)^{k+1}, \gamma_k = \left(-\frac{\gamma - 1}{\gamma + 1} \right)^{k+1}.$$

Since $|x_2^{(k)}| \leq x_1^{(k)}$ and $x_1^{(k)} \neq 0$, we have $f(x_1^{(k)}, x_2^{(k)}) = \sqrt{(x_1^{(k)})^2 + \gamma(x_2^{(k)})^2}$, and by Lemma 8.5(c), f is differentiable at $(x_1^{(k)}, x_2^{(k)})$ with

$$\nabla f(x_1^{(k)}, x_2^{(k)}) = \frac{1}{\sqrt{(x_1^{(k)})^2 + \gamma(x_2^{(k)})^2}} (x_1^{(k)}, \gamma x_2^{(k)}).$$

What is important in the above formula is that $\nabla f(x_1^{(k)}, x_2^{(k)})$ can be written in the form

$$\nabla f(x_1^{(k)}, x_2^{(k)}) = \alpha_k (x_1^{(k)}, \gamma x_2^{(k)}) \tag{8.8}$$

for some positive constant α_k. To show the validity of (8.7), we will define $g(t) \equiv f((x_1^{(k)}, x_2^{(k)}) - t(x_1^{(k)}, \gamma x_2^{(k)}))$ and prove the following two statements:

(A) $(\beta_k, \gamma_k) = (x_1^{(k)}, x_2^{(k)}) - \frac{2}{\gamma+1}(x_1^{(k)}, \gamma x_2^{(k)})$.

(B) $g'\left(\frac{2}{\gamma+1} \right) = 0$.

(A) and (B) are enough to show (8.7) since g is strictly convex. The proof of (A) follows by the computations below:

$$x_1^{(k)} - \frac{2}{\gamma+1}x_1^{(k)} = \frac{\gamma - 1}{\gamma + 1}x_1^{(k)} = \frac{\gamma - 1}{\gamma + 1}\gamma \left(\frac{\gamma - 1}{\gamma + 1} \right)^k = \gamma \left(\frac{\gamma - 1}{\gamma + 1} \right)^{k+1} = \beta_k,$$

$$x_2^{(k)} - \frac{2\gamma}{\gamma+1}x_2^{(k)} = \frac{-\gamma + 1}{\gamma + 1}x_2^{(k)} = \frac{-\gamma + 1}{\gamma + 1} \left(-\frac{\gamma - 1}{\gamma + 1} \right)^k = \left(-\frac{\gamma - 1}{\gamma + 1} \right)^{k+1} = \gamma_k.$$

To prove (B), note that

$$g(t) = f\left((x_1^{(k)}, x_2^{(k)}) - t(x_1^{(k)}, \gamma x_2^{(k)}) \right) = f((1-t)x_1^{(k)}, (1 - \gamma t)x_2^{(k)})$$

$$= \sqrt{(1-t)^2(x_1^{(k)})^2 + \gamma(1 - \gamma t)^2(x_2^{(k)})^2}.$$

Therefore,

$$g'(t) = \frac{(t-1)(x_1^{(k)})^2 + \gamma^2(\gamma t - 1)(x_2^{(k)})^2}{\sqrt{(1-t)^2(x_1^{(k)})^2 + \gamma(1 - \gamma t)^2(x_2^{(k)})^2}}. \tag{8.9}$$

To prove that $g'\left(\frac{2}{\gamma+1}\right) = 0$, it is enough to show that the nominator in the last expression is equal to zero at $t = \frac{2}{\gamma+1}$. Indeed,

$$\left(\frac{2}{\gamma+1} - 1\right)(x_1^{(k)})^2 + \gamma^2 \left(\gamma \cdot \frac{2}{\gamma+1} - 1\right)(x_2^{(k)})^2$$

$$= \left(-\frac{\gamma-1}{\gamma+1}\right)\gamma^2 \left(\frac{\gamma-1}{\gamma+1}\right)^{2k} + \gamma^2 \left(\frac{\gamma-1}{\gamma+1}\right)\left(-\frac{\gamma-1}{\gamma+1}\right)^{2k}$$

$$= 0. \quad \square$$

Obviously, by Lemma 8.6, the sequence generated by the gradient method with exact line search and initial point $(\gamma, 1)$ converges to $(0, 0)$, which is not a minimizer of f since f is not bounded below (take $x_2 = 0$ and $x_1 \to -\infty$). Actually, $(-1, 0)$ is a descent direction of f at $(0, 0)$. The contour lines of the function along with the iterates of the gradient method are described in Figure 8.1.

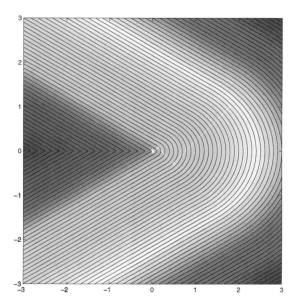

Figure 8.1. *Contour lines of Wolfe's function with $\gamma = \frac{16}{9}$ along with the iterates of the gradient method with exact line search.*

8.2 The Projected Subgradient Method

The main model that will be discussed in this section is

$$\min\{f(\mathbf{x}) : \mathbf{x} \in C\}, \tag{8.10}$$

where the following assumption will be made throughout this section.

Assumption 8.7.

(A) $f : \mathbb{E} \to (-\infty, \infty]$ *is proper closed and convex.*

(B) $C \subseteq \mathbb{E}$ *is nonempty closed and convex.*

(C) $C \subseteq \operatorname{int}(\operatorname{dom}(f))$.

(D) *The optimal set of* (8.10) *is nonempty and denoted by* X^*. *The optimal value of the problem is denoted by* f_{opt}.

Remark 8.8 (subdifferentiability of f and closedness of X^*). *Since f is convex and $C \subseteq \operatorname{int}(\operatorname{dom}(f))$, it follows by Theorem 3.14 that f is subdifferentiable over C. Also, since f is closed,*

$$X^* = C \cap \operatorname{Lev}(f, f_{\mathrm{opt}})$$

is closed. This means in particular that for any $\mathbf{x} \notin X^*$ the distance $d_{X^*}(\mathbf{x})$ is positive.

From now on, we will use the following notation: $f'(\mathbf{x})$ will denote a certain subgradient of f at $\mathbf{x}$, meaning a member in $\partial f(\mathbf{x})$. Thus, f' is actually a function from C to $\mathbb{E}^*$. The rule for choosing $f'(\mathbf{x})$ out of the members of $\partial f(\mathbf{x})$ can be arbitrary but has to be deterministic, meaning that if $f'(\mathbf{x})$ is evaluated twice, the results have to be the same.

Equipped with the observations of the previous section, we can speculate that a method which utilizes subgradients rather than gradients will not necessarily be a descent method and will not have to be based on a line search procedure for choosing its stepsizes. We will see that this is indeed the case for the projected subgradient method.

8.2.1   The Method

Each iteration of the projected subgradient method consists of a step taken toward the negative of the chosen subgradient followed by an orthogonal projection onto the underlying set C.

Projected Subgradient Method

Initialization: pick $\mathbf{x}^0 \in C$ arbitrarily.
General step: for any $k = 0, 1, 2, \ldots$ execute the following steps:

  (a) pick a stepsize $t_k > 0$ and a subgradient $f'(\mathbf{x}^k) \in \partial f(\mathbf{x}^k)$;

  (b) set $\mathbf{x}^{k+1} = P_C(\mathbf{x}^k - t_k f'(\mathbf{x}^k))$.

The sequence generated by the projected subgradient method is $\{\mathbf{x}^k\}_{k \geq 0}$, while the sequence of function values generated by the method is $\{f(\mathbf{x}^k)\}_{k \geq 0}$. As was already discussed, the sequence of function values is not necessarily monotone, and we will be also interested in the sequence of best achieved function values, which is defined by

$$f_{\text{best}}^k \equiv \min_{n=0,1,\ldots,k} f(\mathbf{x}^n). \tag{8.11}$$

Obviously, the sequence $\{f_{\text{best}}^k\}_{k\geq 0}$ is nonincreasing.

Remark 8.9 (stopping criterion for the projected subgradient method). *In actual implementations of the projected subgradient method, a stopping criterion has to be incorporated, but as a rule, we will not deal in this book with stopping criteria but rather concentrate on issues of convergence.*

Remark 8.10 (zero subgradients). *In the unlikely case where $f'(\mathbf{x}^k) = \mathbf{0}$ for some k, then by Fermat's optimality condition (Theorem 3.63), $\mathbf{x}^k$ is a minimizer of f over $\mathbb{E}$, and since $\mathbf{x}^k \in C$, it is also a minimizer of f over C. In this situation, the method is "stuck" at the optimal solution $\mathbf{x}^k$ from iteration k onward, meaning that $\mathbf{x}^n = \mathbf{x}^k$ for all $n \geq k$.*

The analysis of the projected subgradient method relies on the following simple technical lemma.

Lemma 8.11 (fundamental inequality for projected subgradient). *Suppose that Assumption 8.7 holds. Let $\{\mathbf{x}^k\}_{k\geq 0}$ be the sequence generated by the projected subgradient method. Then for any $\mathbf{x}^* \in X^*$ and $k \geq 0$,*

$$\|\mathbf{x}^{k+1} - \mathbf{x}^*\|^2 \leq \|\mathbf{x}^k - \mathbf{x}^*\|^2 - 2t_k(f(\mathbf{x}^k) - f_{\text{opt}}) + t_k^2\|f'(\mathbf{x}^k)\|^2. \tag{8.12}$$

Proof.

$$
\begin{aligned}
\|\mathbf{x}^{k+1} - \mathbf{x}^*\|^2 &= \|P_C(\mathbf{x}^k - t_k f'(\mathbf{x}^k)) - P_C(\mathbf{x}^*)\|^2 \\
&\overset{(*)}{\leq} \|\mathbf{x}^k - t_k f'(\mathbf{x}^k) - \mathbf{x}^*\|^2 \\
&= \|\mathbf{x}^k - \mathbf{x}^*\|^2 - 2t_k\langle f'(\mathbf{x}^k), \mathbf{x}^k - \mathbf{x}^*\rangle + t_k^2\|f'(\mathbf{x}^k)\|^2 \\
&\overset{(**)}{\leq} \|\mathbf{x}^k - \mathbf{x}^*\|^2 - 2t_k(f(\mathbf{x}^k) - f_{\text{opt}}) + t_k^2\|f'(\mathbf{x}^k)\|^2,
\end{aligned}
$$

where the inequality $(*)$ is due to the nonexpansiveness of the orthogonal projection operator (Theorem 6.42), and $(**)$ follows by the subgradient inequality. $\square$

8.2.2 Convergence under Polyak's Stepsize Rule

We will require an assumption in addition to Assumption 8.7 in order to prove convergence of the sequence of function values generated by the projected subgradient method.

Assumption 8.12. *There exists a constant $L_f > 0$ for which $\|\mathbf{g}\| \leq L_f$ for all $\mathbf{g} \in \partial f(\mathbf{x}), \mathbf{x} \in C$.*

Since $C \subseteq \text{int}(\text{dom}(f))$ (Assumption 8.7(C)), it follows by Theorem 3.61 that Assumption 8.12 implies that f is Lipschitz continuous over C with constant L_f:

$$|f(\mathbf{x}) - f(\mathbf{y})| \leq L_f \|\mathbf{x} - \mathbf{y}\| \text{ for all } \mathbf{x}, \mathbf{y} \in C.$$

In addition, since (again) $C \subseteq \text{int}(\text{dom}(f))$, it follows by Theorem 3.16 that Assumption 8.12 holds if C is assumed to be compact.

One natural way to choose the stepsize t_k is by taking it as the minimizer of the right-hand side of (8.12) over $t_k \geq 0$:

$$t_k = \frac{f(\mathbf{x}^k) - f_{\text{opt}}}{\|f'(\mathbf{x}^k)\|^2}.$$

When $f'(\mathbf{x}^k) = \mathbf{0}$, the above formula is not defined, and by Remark 8.10, $\mathbf{x}^k$ is an optimal solution of (8.10). We will artificially define $t_k = 1$ (any other positive number could also have been chosen). The complete formula is therefore

$$t_k = \begin{cases} \frac{f(\mathbf{x}^k) - f_{\text{opt}}}{\|f'(\mathbf{x}^k)\|^2}, & f'(\mathbf{x}^k) \neq \mathbf{0}, \\ 1, & f'(\mathbf{x}^k) = \mathbf{0}. \end{cases} \tag{8.13}$$

We will refer to this stepsize rule as *Polyak's stepsize rule.*[42]

The main convergence result of the projected subgradient method with Polyak's stepsize rule is given in the next theorem.

Theorem 8.13 (convergence of projected subgradient with Polyak's stepsize). *Suppose that Assumptions 8.7 and 8.12 hold. Let $\{\mathbf{x}^k\}_{k \geq 0}$ be the sequence generated by the projected subgradient method with Polyak's stepsize rule (8.13). Then*

(a) $\|\mathbf{x}^{k+1} - \mathbf{x}^*\|^2 \leq \|\mathbf{x}^k - \mathbf{x}^*\|^2$ *for any $k \geq 0$ and $\mathbf{x}^* \in X^*$;*

(b) $f(\mathbf{x}^k) \to f_{\text{opt}}$ *as $k \to \infty$;*

(c) $f_{\text{best}}^k - f_{\text{opt}} \leq \frac{L_f d_{X^*}(\mathbf{x}^0)}{\sqrt{k+1}}$ *for any $k \geq 0$.*

Proof. Let n be a nonnegative integer and $\mathbf{x}^* \in X^*$. By Lemma 8.11,

$$\|\mathbf{x}^{n+1} - \mathbf{x}^*\|^2 \leq \|\mathbf{x}^n - \mathbf{x}^*\|^2 - 2t_n(f(\mathbf{x}^n) - f_{\text{opt}}) + t_n^2 \|f'(\mathbf{x}^n)\|^2. \tag{8.14}$$

If $f'(\mathbf{x}^n) \neq \mathbf{0}$, then by substituting $t_n = \frac{f(\mathbf{x}^n) - f_{\text{opt}}}{\|f'(\mathbf{x}^n)\|^2}$ into (8.14), it follows that

$$\|\mathbf{x}^{n+1} - \mathbf{x}^*\|^2 \leq \|\mathbf{x}^n - \mathbf{x}^*\|^2 - \frac{(f(\mathbf{x}^n) - f_{\text{opt}})^2}{\|f'(\mathbf{x}^n)\|^2}.$$

---

[42]As the name suggests, this stepsize was first suggested by Boris T. Polyak; see, for example, [104].

Using the bound $\|f'(\mathbf{x}^n)\| \leq L_f$, we thus obtain

$$\|\mathbf{x}^{n+1} - \mathbf{x}^*\|^2 \leq \|\mathbf{x}^n - \mathbf{x}^*\|^2 - \frac{(f(\mathbf{x}^n) - f_{\text{opt}})^2}{L_f^2}. \tag{8.15}$$

Inequality (8.15) also holds when $f'(\mathbf{x}^n) = \mathbf{0}$, since in this case $f(\mathbf{x}^n) = f_{\text{opt}}$ and $\mathbf{x}^{n+1} = \mathbf{x}^n$. A direct result of (8.15) is that

$$\|\mathbf{x}^{n+1} - \mathbf{x}^*\|^2 \leq \|\mathbf{x}^n - \mathbf{x}^*\|^2,$$

and part (a) is thus proved (by plugging $n = k$). Summing inequality (8.15) over $n = 0, 1, \ldots, k$, we obtain that

$$\frac{1}{L_f^2} \sum_{n=0}^{k} (f(\mathbf{x}^n) - f_{\text{opt}})^2 \leq \|\mathbf{x}^0 - \mathbf{x}^*\|^2 - \|\mathbf{x}^{k+1} - \mathbf{x}^*\|^2,$$

and thus

$$\sum_{n=0}^{k} (f(\mathbf{x}^n) - f_{\text{opt}})^2 \leq L_f^2 \|\mathbf{x}^0 - \mathbf{x}^*\|^2.$$

Since the above inequality holds for any $\mathbf{x}^* \in X^*$, it follows that

$$\sum_{n=0}^{k} (f(\mathbf{x}^n) - f_{\text{opt}})^2 \leq L_f^2 d_{X^*}^2(\mathbf{x}^0), \tag{8.16}$$

which in particular implies that $f(\mathbf{x}^n) - f_{\text{opt}} \to 0$ as $n \to \infty$, and the validity of (b) is established. To prove part (c), note that since $f(\mathbf{x}^n) \geq f_{\text{best}}^k$ for any $n = 0, 1, \ldots, k$, it follows that

$$\sum_{n=0}^{k} (f(\mathbf{x}^n) - f_{\text{opt}})^2 \geq (k+1)(f_{\text{best}}^k - f_{\text{opt}})^2,$$

which, combined with (8.16), yields

$$(k+1)(f_{\text{best}}^k - f_{\text{opt}})^2 \leq L_f^2 d_{X^*}^2(\mathbf{x}^0),$$

and hence

$$f_{\text{best}}^k - f_{\text{opt}} \leq \frac{L_f d_{X^*}(\mathbf{x}^0)}{\sqrt{k+1}}. \qquad \square$$

Remark 8.14. *Note that in the convergence result of Theorem 8.13 we can replace the constant L_f with $\max_{n=0,1,\ldots,k} \|f'(\mathbf{x}^n)\|$.*

The property of the sequence generated by the projected subgradient method described in part (a) of Theorem 8.13 is known as *Fejér monotonicity*.

Definition 8.15 (Fejér monotonicity). *A sequence $\{\mathbf{x}^k\}_{k \geq 0} \subseteq \mathbb{E}$ is called **Fejér monotone** w.r.t. a set $S \subseteq \mathbb{E}$ if*

$$\|\mathbf{x}^{k+1} - \mathbf{y}\| \leq \|\mathbf{x}^k - \mathbf{y}\| \text{ for all } k \geq 0 \text{ and } \mathbf{y} \in S.$$

Since Fejér monotonicity w.r.t. a set S implies that for all $k \geq 0$ and any $\mathbf{y} \in S$, $\|\mathbf{x}^k - \mathbf{y}\| \leq \|\mathbf{x}^0 - \mathbf{y}\|$, it follows that Fejér monotone sequences are always bounded. We will now prove that sequences which are Fejér monotone w.r.t. sets containing all their limit points are convergent.

Theorem 8.16 (convergence under Fejér monotonicity). *Let* $\{\mathbf{x}^k\}_{k \geq 0} \subseteq \mathbb{E}$ *be a sequence, and let* S *be a set satisfying* $D \subseteq S$, *where* D *is the set comprising all the limit points of* $\{\mathbf{x}^k\}_{k \geq 0}$. *If* $\{\mathbf{x}^k\}_{k \geq 0}$ *is Fejér monotone w.r.t.* S, *then it converges to a point in* D.

Proof. Since $\{\mathbf{x}^k\}_{k \geq 0}$ is Fejér monotone, it is also bounded and hence has limit points. Let $\tilde{\mathbf{x}}$ be a limit point of the sequence $\{\mathbf{x}^k\}_{k \geq 0}$, meaning that there exists a subsequence $\{\mathbf{x}^{k_j}\}_{j \geq 0}$ such that $\mathbf{x}^{k_j} \to \tilde{\mathbf{x}}$. Since $\tilde{\mathbf{x}} \in D \subseteq S$, it follows by the Fejér monotonicity w.r.t. S that for any $k \geq 0$,

$$\|\mathbf{x}^{k+1} - \tilde{\mathbf{x}}\| \leq \|\mathbf{x}^k - \tilde{\mathbf{x}}\|.$$

Thus, $\{\|\mathbf{x}^k - \tilde{\mathbf{x}}\|\}_{k \geq 0}$ is a nonincreasing sequence which is bounded below (by zero) and hence convergent. Since $\|\mathbf{x}^{k_j} - \tilde{\mathbf{x}}\| \to 0$ as $j \to \infty$, it follows that the whole sequence $\{\|\mathbf{x}^k - \tilde{\mathbf{x}}\|\}_{k \geq 0}$ converges to zero, and consequently $\mathbf{x}^k \to \tilde{\mathbf{x}}$ as $k \to \infty$. □

Equipped with the last theorem, we can now prove convergence of the sequence generated by the projected subgradient method with Polyak's stepsize rule.

Theorem 8.17 (convergence of the sequence generated by projected subgradient with Polyak's stepsize rule). *Suppose that Assumptions 8.7 and 8.12 hold. Let* $\{\mathbf{x}^k\}_{k \geq 0}$ *be the sequence generated by the projected subgradient method with Polyak's stepsize rule (8.13). Then* $\{\mathbf{x}^k\}_{k \geq 0}$ *converges to a point in* X^*.

Proof. By Theorem 8.13(a), the sequence is Fejér monotone w.r.t. X^*. Therefore, by Theorem 8.16, to show convergence to a point in X^*, it is enough to show that any limit point of the sequence is necessarily in X^* (that is, an optimal solution of the problem). Let then $\tilde{\mathbf{x}}$ be a limit point of the sequence. Then there exists a subsequence $\{\mathbf{x}^{k_j}\}_{j \geq 0}$ converging to $\tilde{\mathbf{x}}$. By the closedness of C, $\tilde{\mathbf{x}} \in C$. By Theorem 8.13(b),

$$f(\mathbf{x}^{k_j}) \to f_{\mathrm{opt}} \text{ as } j \to \infty. \tag{8.17}$$

Since $\tilde{\mathbf{x}} \in C \subseteq \mathrm{int}(\mathrm{dom}(f))$, it follows by Theorem 2.21 that f is continuous at $\tilde{\mathbf{x}}$, which, combined with (8.17), implies that $f(\tilde{\mathbf{x}}) = f_{\mathrm{opt}}$, meaning that $\tilde{\mathbf{x}} \in X^*$. □

Part (c) of Theorem 8.13 provides an upper bound on the *rate of convergence* in which the sequence $\{f_{\mathrm{best}}^k\}_{k \geq 0}$ converges to f_{opt}. Specifically, the result shows that the distance of f_{best}^k to f_{opt} is bounded above by a constant factor of $\frac{1}{\sqrt{k+1}}$ with k being the iteration index. We will sometimes refer to it as an "$O(1/\sqrt{k})$ rate of convergence result" with a slight abuse of the "big O" notation (which actually refers to asymptotic results). We can also write the rate of convergence result as a *complexity* result. For that, we first introduce the concept of an ε-optimal solution. A vector $\mathbf{x} \in C$ is called an ε-*optimal solution* of problem (8.10) if $f(\mathbf{x}) - f_{\mathrm{opt}} \leq \varepsilon$. In complexity analysis, the following question is asked: *how many iterations are* *required to obtain an ε-optimal solution?* That is, how many iterations are required to obtain the condition

$$f_{\text{best}}^k - f_{\text{opt}} \leq \varepsilon? \tag{8.18}$$

Using Theorem 8.13(c), it follows that a sufficient condition for (8.18) to hold is the following inequality:

$$\frac{L_f d_{X^*}(\mathbf{x}^0)}{\sqrt{k+1}} \leq \varepsilon, \tag{8.19}$$

which is the same as

$$k \geq \frac{L_f^2 d_{X^*}^2(\mathbf{x}^0)}{\varepsilon^2} - 1.$$

Therefore, an order of $\frac{1}{\varepsilon^2}$ iterations is required to obtain an ε-optimal solution. We summarize the discussion in the following theorem.

Theorem 8.18 (complexity of projected subgradient with Polyak's step-size). *Suppose that Assumptions 8.7 and 8.12 hold. Let $\{\mathbf{x}^k\}_{k \geq 0}$ be the sequence generated by the projected subgradient method with Polyak's stepsize rule (8.13). Then for any nonnegative integer k satisfying*

$$k \geq \frac{L_f^2 d_{X^*}^2(\mathbf{x}^0)}{\varepsilon^2} - 1,$$

it holds that

$$f_{\text{best}}^k - f_{\text{opt}} \leq \varepsilon.$$

Example 8.19. Consider the problem

$$\min_{x_1, x_2} \left\{ f(x_1, x_2) = |x_1 + 2x_2| + |3x_1 + 4x_2| \right\}.$$

Since in this chapter the underlying spaces are Euclidean, it follows that the underlying space in this example is $\mathbb{R}^2$ endowed with the dot product and the l_2-norm. The optimal solution of the problem is $(x_1, x_2) = (0, 0)$, and the optimal value is $f_{\text{opt}} = 0$. Clearly, both Assumptions 8.7 and 8.12 hold. Since $f(\mathbf{x}) = \|\mathbf{A}\mathbf{x}\|_1$, where $\mathbf{A} = \begin{pmatrix} 1 & 2 \\ 3 & 4 \end{pmatrix}$, it follows that for any $\mathbf{x} \in \mathbb{R}^2$,

$$\partial f(\mathbf{x}) = \mathbf{A}^T \partial h(\mathbf{A}\mathbf{x}),$$

where $h(\mathbf{x}) = \|\mathbf{x}\|_1$. By Example 3.41, for any $\mathbf{w} \in \mathbb{R}^2$,

$$\partial h(\mathbf{w}) = \left\{ \mathbf{z} \in \mathbb{R}^2 : z_i = \text{sgn}(w_i), i \in I_{\neq}(\mathbf{w}), |z_j| \leq 1, j \in I_0(\mathbf{w}) \right\},$$

where

$$I_0(\mathbf{w}) = \{i : w_i = 0\}, I_{\neq}(\mathbf{w}) = \{i : w_i \neq 0\}.$$

Hence, if $\boldsymbol{\eta} \in \partial h(\mathbf{A}\mathbf{x})$, then $\boldsymbol{\eta} \in [-1, 1] \times [-1, 1]$, and, in particular, $\|\boldsymbol{\eta}\|_2 \leq \sqrt{2}$. Therefore, since any $\mathbf{g} \in \partial f(\mathbf{x})$ can be written as $\mathbf{g} = \mathbf{A}^T \boldsymbol{\eta}$ for some $\boldsymbol{\eta} \in \partial h(\mathbf{A}\mathbf{x})$, we have

$$\|\mathbf{g}\|_2 = \|\mathbf{A}^T \boldsymbol{\eta}\|_2 \leq \|\mathbf{A}^T\|_{2,2} \|\boldsymbol{\eta}\|_2 \leq \|\mathbf{A}^T\|_{2,2} \cdot \sqrt{2} = 7.7287.$$

We can thus choose $L_f = 7.7287$.

The subgradient method update step with Polyak's stepsize rule takes the form

$$
\begin{pmatrix} x_1^{k+1} \\ x_2^{k+1} \end{pmatrix} = \begin{pmatrix} x_1^k \\ x_2^k \end{pmatrix} - \frac{|x_1^k + 2x_2^k| + |3x_1^k + 4x_2^k|}{\|\mathbf{v}(x_1^k, x_2^k)\|_2^2} \mathbf{v}(x_1^k, x_2^k),
$$

where we choose

$$
\mathbf{v}(x_1, x_2) = \begin{pmatrix} \mathrm{sgn}(x_1 + 2x_2) + 3\mathrm{sgn}(3x_1 + 4x_2) \\ 2\mathrm{sgn}(x_1 + 2x_2) + 4\mathrm{sgn}(3x_1 + 4x_2) \end{pmatrix} \in \partial f(x_1, x_2).
$$

Note that in the terminology of this book $\mathrm{sgn}(0) = 1$ (see Section 1.7.2), which dictates the choice of the subgradient among the vectors in the subdifferential set in cases where f is not differentiable at the given point. We can immediately see that there are actually only four possible choices of directions $\mathbf{v}(x_1, x_2)$ depending on the two possible values of $\mathrm{sgn}(x_1 + 2x_2)$ and the two possible choices of $\mathrm{sgn}(3x_1 + 4x_2)$. The four possible directions are

$$
\mathbf{u}_1 = \begin{pmatrix} -4 \\ -6 \end{pmatrix}, \quad \mathbf{u}_2 = \begin{pmatrix} 2 \\ 2 \end{pmatrix}, \quad \mathbf{u}_3 = \begin{pmatrix} -2 \\ -2 \end{pmatrix}, \quad \mathbf{u}_4 = \begin{pmatrix} 4 \\ 6 \end{pmatrix}.
$$

By Remark 8.14, the constant L_f can be chosen as $\max_i\{\|\mathbf{u}_i\|_2\} = 7.2111$, which is a slightly better bound than 7.7287. The first 100 iterations of the method with a starting point $(1, 2)^T$ are described in Figure 8.2. Note that the sequence of function values is indeed not monotone (although convergence to f_{opt} is quite apparent) and that actually only two directions are being used by the method: $(-2, -2)^T$, $(4, 6)^T$. ∎

8.2.3   The Convex Feasibility Problem

Let $S_1, S_2, \ldots, S_m \subseteq \mathbb{E}$ be closed and convex sets. Assume that

$$
S \equiv \bigcap_{i=1}^m S_i \neq \emptyset. \tag{8.20}
$$

The *convex feasibility problem* is the problem of finding a point $\mathbf{x}$ in the intersection $\bigcap_{i=1}^m S_i$. We can formulate the problem as the following minimization problem:

$$
\min_{\mathbf{x}} \left\{ f(\mathbf{x}) \equiv \max_{i=1,2,\ldots,m} d_{S_i}(\mathbf{x}) \right\}. \tag{8.21}
$$

Since we assume that the intersection is nonempty, we have that $f_{\mathrm{opt}} = 0$ and that the optimal set is S. Another property of f is that it is Lipschitz continuous with constant 1.

Lemma 8.20. *Let $S_1, S_2, \ldots, S_m$ be nonempty closed and convex sets. Then the function f given in (8.21) is Lipschitz continuous with constant 1.*

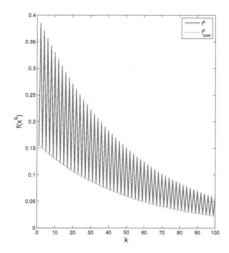 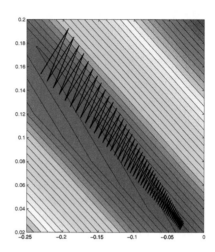

Figure 8.2. *First* 100 *iterations of the subgradient method applied to the function* $f(x_1, x_2) = |x_1 + 2x_2| + |3x_1 + 4x_2|$ *with Polyak's stepsize rule and starting point* $(1, 2)^T$. *The left image describes the function values at each iteration, and the right image shows the contour lines along with the iterations.*

Proof. Let $i \in \{1, 2, \ldots, m\}$, and let $\mathbf{x}, \mathbf{y} \in \mathbb{E}$. Then

$$d_{S_i}(\mathbf{x}) = \|\mathbf{x} - P_{S_i}(\mathbf{x})\|$$

$$\leq \|\mathbf{x} - P_{S_i}(\mathbf{y})\| \qquad [\|\mathbf{x} - P_{S_i}(\mathbf{x})\| = \mathrm{argmin}_{\mathbf{v} \in S_i} \|\mathbf{x} - \mathbf{v}\|]$$

$$\leq \|\mathbf{x} - \mathbf{y}\| + \|\mathbf{y} - P_{S_i}(\mathbf{y})\| \quad \text{[triangle inequality]}$$

$$= \|\mathbf{x} - \mathbf{y}\| + d_{S_i}(\mathbf{y}). \qquad [d_{S_i}(\mathbf{y}) = \|\mathbf{y} - P_{S_i}(\mathbf{y})\|]$$

Thus,

$$d_{S_i}(\mathbf{x}) - d_{S_i}(\mathbf{y}) \leq \|\mathbf{x} - \mathbf{y}\|. \tag{8.22}$$

Replacing the roles of $\mathbf{x}$ and $\mathbf{y}$, we obtain that

$$d_{S_i}(\mathbf{y}) - d_{S_i}(\mathbf{x}) \leq \|\mathbf{x} - \mathbf{y}\|,$$

which, combined with (8.22), yields the inequality

$$|d_{S_i}(\mathbf{x}) - d_{S_i}(\mathbf{y})| \leq \|\mathbf{x} - \mathbf{y}\|. \tag{8.23}$$

Finally, for any $\mathbf{x}, \mathbf{y} \in \mathbb{E}$,

$$|f(\mathbf{x}) - f(\mathbf{y})| = \left| \max_{i=1,2,\ldots,m} d_{S_i}(\mathbf{x}) - \max_{i=1,2,\ldots,m} d_{S_i}(\mathbf{y}) \right| = |\|\mathbf{v}_\mathbf{x}\|_\infty - \|\mathbf{v}_\mathbf{y}\|_\infty|, \tag{8.24}$$

where $\mathbf{v_x} = (d_{S_i}(\mathbf{x}))_{i=1}^m \in \mathbb{R}^m$ and $\mathbf{v_y} = (d_{S_i}(\mathbf{y}))_{i=1}^m \in \mathbb{R}^m$. Using the triangle inequality for norms, we can continue (8.24) and obtain

$$
\begin{aligned}
|f(\mathbf{x}) - f(\mathbf{y})| &\leq |\|\mathbf{v_x}\|_\infty - \|\mathbf{v_y}\|_\infty| \\
&\leq \|\mathbf{v_x} - \mathbf{v_y}\|_\infty \\
&= \max_{i=1,2,\ldots,m} |d_{S_i}(\mathbf{x}) - d_{S_i}(\mathbf{y})| \\
&\overset{(8.23)}{\leq} \|\mathbf{x} - \mathbf{y}\|. \quad \square
\end{aligned}
$$

Let us write explicitly the projected subgradient method with Polyak's stepsize rule as applied to problem (8.21). The method starts with an arbitrary $\mathbf{x}^0 \in \mathbb{E}$. If the kth iteration satisfies $\mathbf{x}^k \in S$, then we can pick $f'(\mathbf{x}^k) = \mathbf{0}$ and hence $\mathbf{x}^{k+1} = \mathbf{x}^k$. Otherwise, we take a step toward minus of the subgradient with Polyak's stepsize. By Theorem 3.50, to compute a subgradient of the objective function at the kth iterate, we can use the following procedure:

(i) compute $i_k \in \operatorname{argmax}_{i=1,2,\ldots,m} d_{S_i}(\mathbf{x}^k)$;

(ii) take any $\mathbf{g}^k \in \partial d_{S_{i_k}}(\mathbf{x}^k)$.

By Example 3.49, the only subgradient in $\partial d_{S_{i_k}}(\mathbf{x}^k)$ is $\mathbf{g}^k = \dfrac{\mathbf{x}^k - P_{S_{i_k}}(\mathbf{x}^k)}{d_{S_{i_k}}(\mathbf{x}^k)}$, and the update step becomes

$$
\begin{aligned}
\mathbf{x}^{k+1} &= \mathbf{x}^k - \frac{d_{S_{i_k}}(\mathbf{x}^k) - f_{\mathrm{opt}}}{\|\mathbf{g}^k\|^2} \cdot \frac{\mathbf{x}^k - P_{S_{i_k}}(\mathbf{x}^k)}{d_{S_{i_k}}(\mathbf{x}^k)} \\
&= \mathbf{x}^k - d_{S_{i_k}}(\mathbf{x}^k) \frac{\mathbf{x}^k - P_{S_{i_k}}(\mathbf{x}^k)}{d_{S_{i_k}}(\mathbf{x}^k)} \\
&= P_{S_{i_k}}(\mathbf{x}^k),
\end{aligned}
$$

where we used in the above the facts that $f_{\mathrm{opt}} = 0$ and $\|\mathbf{g}^k\| = 1$. What we actually obtained is the *greedy projection algorithm*, which at each iteration projects the current iterate $\mathbf{x}^k$ onto the farthest set among $S_1, S_2, \ldots, S_m$. The algorithm is summarized below.

Greedy Projection Algorithm

Input: m nonempty closed and convex sets $S_1, S_2, \ldots, S_m$.
Initialization: pick $\mathbf{x}^0 \in \mathbb{E}$.
General step: for any $k = 0, 1, 2, \ldots$, execute the step

$$
\mathbf{x}^{k+1} = P_{S_{i_k}}(\mathbf{x}^k),
$$

where $i_k \in \operatorname{argmax}_{i=1,2,\ldots,m} d_{S_i}(\mathbf{x}^k)$.

We can invoke Theorems 8.13 and 8.17 to obtain the following convergence result of the algorithm.

Theorem 8.21 (convergence of the greedy projection algorithm). *Let $S_1, S_2, \ldots, S_m \subseteq \mathbb{E}$ be closed and convex sets such that $S \equiv \bigcap_{i=1}^m S_i \neq \emptyset$. Let $\{\mathbf{x}^k\}_{k \geq 0}$ be the sequence generated by the greedy projection algorithm.*

(a) *For any $k \geq 0$,*

$$\min_{n=0,1,2,\ldots,k} \left\{ \max_{i=1,2,\ldots,m} d(\mathbf{x}^n, S_i) \right\} \leq \frac{d_S(\mathbf{x}^0)}{\sqrt{k+1}}. \tag{8.25}$$

(b) *There exists $\mathbf{x}^* \in S$ such that $\mathbf{x}^k \to \mathbf{x}^*$ as $k \to \infty$.*

Proof. To prove part (a), define $f(\mathbf{x}) \equiv \max_{i=1,2,\ldots,m} d(\mathbf{x}, S_i)$ and $C = \mathbb{E}$. Then the optimal set of the problem

$$\min\{f(\mathbf{x}) : \mathbf{x} \in C\}$$

is $X^* = S$. Assumption 8.7 is satisfied since f is proper closed and convex and $C = \mathbb{E}$ is obviously nonempty closed and convex and contained in $\text{int}(\text{dom}(f)) = \mathbb{E}$. The optimal set $X^* = S$ is nonempty by the assumption in the premise of the theorem. Assumption 8.12 is satisfied with $L_f = 1$ by Lemma 8.20 and Theorem 3.61. Therefore, all the assumptions of Theorem 8.13 are satisfied, and hence, since the greedy projection algorithm is the same as the projected subgradient method with Polyak's stepsize rule, the result (8.25) holds, as it is exactly part (c) of Theorem 8.13. Part (b) follows by invoking Theorem 8.17. $\square$

When $m = 2$, the algorithm amounts to the *alternating projection method*, which is described below.

Alternating Projection Method

Input: two nonempty closed and convex sets S_1, S_2.
Initialization: pick $\mathbf{x}^0 \in S_2$ arbitrarily.
General step: for any $k = 0, 1, 2, \ldots$, execute the following step:

$$\mathbf{x}^{k+1} = P_{S_2}(P_{S_1}(\mathbf{x}^k)).$$

If $S_1 \cap S_2 \neq \emptyset$, by Theorem 8.21, the sequence generated by the alternating projection method converges to a point in $S_1 \cap S_2$.

Corollary 8.22 (convergence of alternating projection). *Let S_1, S_2 be closed and convex sets such that $S \equiv S_1 \cap S_2 \neq \emptyset$. Let $\{\mathbf{x}^k\}_{k \geq 0}$ be the sequence generated by the alternating projection method with initial point $\mathbf{x}^0 \in S_2$. Then*

(a) *for any $k \geq 0$,*

$$\min_{n=0,1,2,\dots,k} d(\mathbf{x}^n, S_1) \leq \frac{d_S(\mathbf{x}^0)}{\sqrt{k+1}};$$

(b) *there exists $\mathbf{x}^* \in S$ such that $\mathbf{x}^k \to \mathbf{x}^*$ as $k \to \infty$.*

Example 8.23 (solution of linear feasibility problems). Consider the following system of linear equalities and inequalities:

$$\mathbf{Ax} = \mathbf{b}, \mathbf{x} \geq \mathbf{0}, \tag{8.26}$$

where $\mathbf{A} \in \mathbb{R}^{m \times n}$ has full row rank and $\mathbf{b} \in \mathbb{R}^m$. The system (8.26) is one of the standard forms of feasible sets of linear programming problems. One way to solve the problem of finding a solution to (8.26) is by employing the alternating projection method. Define

$$S_1 = \{\mathbf{x} \in \mathbb{R}^n : \mathbf{Ax} = \mathbf{b}\}, \quad S_2 = \mathbb{R}_+^n.$$

The projections on S_1 and S_2 have analytic expressions (see Lemma 6.26):

$$P_{S_1}(\mathbf{x}) = \mathbf{x} - \mathbf{A}^T (\mathbf{AA}^T)^{-1} (\mathbf{Ax} - \mathbf{b}), \quad P_{S_2}(\mathbf{x}) = [\mathbf{x}]_+.$$

The alternating projection method for finding a solution to (8.26) takes the following form:

Algorithm 1

- **Initialization:** pick $\mathbf{x}^0 \in \mathbb{R}_+^n$.

- **General step ($k \geq 0$):** $\mathbf{x}^{k+1} = \left[\mathbf{x}^k - \mathbf{A}^T (\mathbf{AA}^T)^{-1} (\mathbf{Ax}^k - \mathbf{b}) \right]_+$.

The general step of the above scheme involves the computation of the expression $(\mathbf{AA}^T)^{-1} (\mathbf{Ax}^k - \mathbf{b})$, which requires the computation of the matrix $\mathbf{AA}^T$, as well as the solution of the linear system $(\mathbf{AA}^T)\mathbf{z} = \mathbf{Ax}^k - \mathbf{b}$. In cases when these computations are too demanding (e.g., when the dimension is large), we can employ a different projection algorithm that avoids the necessity of solving a linear system. Specifically, denoting the ith row of $\mathbf{A}$ by $\mathbf{a}_i^T$ and defining

$$T_i = \{\mathbf{x} \in \mathbb{R}^n : \mathbf{a}_i^T \mathbf{x} = b_i\}, \ i = 1, 2, \dots, m, \quad T_{m+1} = \mathbb{R}_+^n,$$

we obtain that finding a solution to (8.26) is the same as finding a point in the intersection $\bigcap_{i=1}^{m+1} T_i$. Note that (see Lemma 6.26)

$$P_{T_i}(\mathbf{x}) = \mathbf{x} - \frac{\mathbf{a}_i^T \mathbf{x} - b_i}{\|\mathbf{a}_i\|_2^2} \mathbf{a}_i, \ i = 1, 2, \dots, m.$$

Hence,

$$d_{T_i}(\mathbf{x}) = \|\mathbf{x} - P_{T_i}(\mathbf{x})\| = \frac{|\mathbf{a}_i^T \mathbf{x} - b_i|}{\|\mathbf{a}_i\|_2}.$$

We can now invoke the greedy projection method that has the following form:

Algorithm 2

- **Initialization:** pick $\mathbf{x}^0 \in \mathbb{E}$.

- **General step $(k = 0, 1, \ldots)$:**

  - compute $i_k \in \operatorname{argmax}_{i=1,2,\ldots,m} \frac{|\mathbf{a}_i^T \mathbf{x}^k - b_i|}{\|\mathbf{a}_i\|_2}$.

  - if $\frac{|\mathbf{a}_{i_k}^T \mathbf{x}^k - b_{i_k}|}{\|\mathbf{a}_{i_k}\|_2} > \|\mathbf{x}^k - [\mathbf{x}^k]_+\|_2$, then

  $$\mathbf{x}^{k+1} = \mathbf{x}^k - \frac{\mathbf{a}_{i_k}^T \mathbf{x}^k - b_{i_k}}{\|\mathbf{a}_{i_k}\|_2^2} \mathbf{a}_{i_k}.$$

  else,
  $$\mathbf{x}^{k+1} = [\mathbf{x}^k]_+.$$

Algorithm 2 is simpler than Algorithm 1 in the sense that it requires much less operations per iteration. However, simplicity has its cost. Consider, for example, the instance

$$\mathbf{A} = \begin{pmatrix} 0 & 6 & -7 & 1 \\ -1 & 2 & 10 & -1 \end{pmatrix}, \quad \mathbf{b} = \begin{pmatrix} 0 \\ 10 \end{pmatrix}.$$

Figure 8.3 shows the constraint violation of the two sequences generated by the two algorithms initialized with the zeros vector in the first 20 iterations. Obviously, in this case, Algorithm 1 (alternating projection) reached substantially better accuracies than Algorithm 2 (greedy projection). ∎

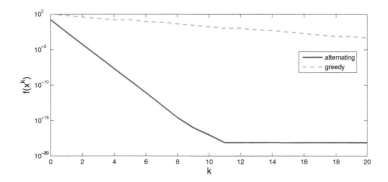

Figure 8.3. *Constraints violation of alternating and greedy projection methods. Here* $f(\mathbf{x}) = \max\left\{ \frac{|\mathbf{a}_1^T \mathbf{x} - b_1|}{\|\mathbf{a}_1\|_2}, \frac{|\mathbf{a}_2^T \mathbf{x} - b_2|}{\|\mathbf{a}_2\|_2}, \|\mathbf{x} - [\mathbf{x}]_+\|_2 \right\}$, *where* $\mathbf{a}_1^T = (0, 6, -7, 1)$, $\mathbf{a}_2^T = (-1, 2, 10, -1)$, *and* $\mathbf{b} = (0, 10)^T$.

8.2.4 Projected Subgradient with Dynamic Stepsizes

Polyak's stepsize is optimal in the sense that it minimizes the upper bound given in the fundamental inequality (8.12). However, a major disadvantage of this rule is that usually the optimal value f_{opt} is unknown, and in these (frequent) cases, the stepsize is incomputable. In this section we will show how to find computable stepsize rules that still maintain the $O(1/\sqrt{k})$ rate of convergence result of the projected subgradient method. Theorem 8.25 below describes a simple condition on the stepsizes under which convergence of f_{best}^k to f_{opt} is guaranteed. The result uses the following technical lemma.

Lemma 8.24. *Suppose that Assumption 8.7 holds. Let $\{\mathbf{x}^k\}_{k\geq 0}$ be the sequence generated by the projected subgradient method with positive stepsizes $\{t_k\}_{k\geq 0}$. Then for any $\mathbf{x}^* \in X^*$ and nonnegative integer k,*

$$\sum_{n=0}^{k} t_n(f(\mathbf{x}^n) - f_{\text{opt}}) \leq \frac{1}{2}\|\mathbf{x}^0 - \mathbf{x}^*\|^2 + \frac{1}{2}\sum_{n=0}^{k} t_n^2 \|f'(\mathbf{x}^n)\|^2. \qquad (8.27)$$

Proof. By Lemma 8.11, for any $n \geq 0$ and $\mathbf{x}^* \in X^*$,

$$\frac{1}{2}\|\mathbf{x}^{n+1} - \mathbf{x}^*\|^2 \leq \frac{1}{2}\|\mathbf{x}^n - \mathbf{x}^*\|^2 - t_n(f(\mathbf{x}^n) - f_{\text{opt}}) + \frac{t_n^2}{2}\|f'(\mathbf{x}^n)\|^2.$$

Summing the above inequality over $n = 0, 1, \ldots, k$ and arranging terms yields the following inequality:

$$\sum_{n=0}^{k} t_n(f(\mathbf{x}^n) - f_{\text{opt}}) \leq \frac{1}{2}\|\mathbf{x}^0 - \mathbf{x}^*\|^2 - \frac{1}{2}\|\mathbf{x}^{k+1} - \mathbf{x}^*\|^2 + \sum_{n=0}^{k} \frac{t_n^2}{2}\|f'(\mathbf{x}^n)\|^2$$

$$\leq \frac{1}{2}\|\mathbf{x}^0 - \mathbf{x}^*\|^2 + \frac{1}{2}\sum_{n=0}^{k} t_n^2\|f'(\mathbf{x}^n)\|^2. \qquad \square$$

Theorem 8.25 (stepsize conditions warranting convergence of projected subgradient). *Suppose that Assumptions 8.7 and 8.12 hold. Let $\{\mathbf{x}^k\}_{k\geq 0}$ be the sequence generated by the projected subgradient method with positive stepsizes $\{t_k\}_{k\geq 0}$. If*

$$\frac{\sum_{n=0}^{k} t_n^2}{\sum_{n=0}^{k} t_n} \to 0 \text{ as } k \to \infty, \qquad (8.28)$$

then

$$f_{\text{best}}^k - f_{\text{opt}} \to 0 \text{ as } k \to \infty, \qquad (8.29)$$

where $\{f_{\text{best}}^k\}_{k\geq 0}$ is the sequence of best achieved values defined in (8.11).

Proof. Let L_f be a constant for which $\|\mathbf{g}\| \leq L_f$ for any $\mathbf{g} \in \partial f(\mathbf{x}), \mathbf{x} \in C$ whose existence is warranted by Assumption 8.12. Employing Lemma 8.24 and using the inequalities $\|f'(\mathbf{x}^n)\| \leq L_f$ and $f(\mathbf{x}^n) \geq f_{\text{best}}^k$ for $n \leq k$, we obtain

$$\left(\sum_{n=0}^{k} t_n\right)(f_{\text{best}}^k - f_{\text{opt}}) \leq \frac{1}{2}\|\mathbf{x}^0 - \mathbf{x}^*\|^2 + \frac{L_f^2}{2}\sum_{n=0}^{k} t_n^2.$$

Therefore,

$$f_{\text{best}}^k - f_{\text{opt}} \leq \frac{1}{2}\frac{\|\mathbf{x}^0 - \mathbf{x}^*\|^2}{\sum_{n=0}^{k} t_n} + \frac{L_f^2}{2}\frac{\sum_{n=0}^{k} t_n^2}{\sum_{n=0}^{k} t_n}.$$

The result (8.29) now follows by (8.28), and the fact that (8.28) implies the limit $\sum_{n=0}^{k} t_n \to \infty$ as $k \to \infty$. $\square$

By Theorem 8.25, we can pick, for example, the stepsizes as $t_k = \frac{1}{\sqrt{k+1}}$, and convergence of function values to f_{opt} will be guaranteed since $\sum_{n=0}^{k} \frac{1}{\sqrt{n+1}}$ is of the order of $\sqrt{k}$ and $\sum_{n=0}^{k} \frac{1}{n+1}$ is of the order of $\log(k)$. We will analyze the convergence rate of the projected subgradient method when the stepsizes are chosen as $t_k = \frac{1}{\|f'(\mathbf{x}^k)\|\sqrt{k+1}}$ in Theorem 8.28 below. Note that in addition to proving the limit $f_{\mathrm{best}}^k \to f_{\mathrm{opt}}$, we will further show that the function values of a certain sequence of averages also converges to the optimal value. Such a result is called an *ergodic convergence result*.

To prove the result, we will need to upper and lower bound sums of sequences of real numbers. For that, we will use the following technical lemma from calculus.

Lemma 8.26. *Let $f : [a - 1, b + 1] \to \mathbb{R}$ be a continuous nonincreasing function over $[a - 1, b + 1]$, where a and b are integer numbers satisfying $a \le b$. Then*

$$\int_a^{b+1} f(t)dt \le f(a) + f(a + 1) + \cdots + f(b) \le \int_{a-1}^{b} f(t)dt.$$

Using Lemma 8.26, we can prove the following lemma that will be useful in proving Theorem 8.28, as well as additional results in what follows.

Lemma 8.27. *Let $D \in \mathbb{R}$. Then*

(a) *for any $k \ge 1$,*

$$\frac{D + \sum_{n=0}^{k} \frac{1}{n+1}}{\sum_{n=0}^{k} \frac{1}{\sqrt{n+1}}} \le \frac{D + 1 + \log(k+1)}{\sqrt{k+1}}; \tag{8.30}$$

(b) *for any $k \ge 2$,*

$$\frac{D + \sum_{n=\lceil k/2 \rceil}^{k} \frac{1}{n+1}}{\sum_{n=\lceil k/2 \rceil}^{k} \frac{1}{\sqrt{n+1}}} \le \frac{4(D + \log(3))}{\sqrt{k+2}}. \tag{8.31}$$

Proof. (a) Using Lemma 8.26, we obtain the following inequalities:

$$\sum_{n=0}^{k} \frac{1}{n+1} = 1 + \sum_{n=1}^{k} \frac{1}{n+1} \le 1 + \int_0^k \frac{1}{x+1}dx = 1 + \log(k+1), \tag{8.32}$$

$$\sum_{n=0}^{k} \frac{1}{\sqrt{n+1}} \ge \int_0^{k+1} \frac{1}{\sqrt{x+1}}dx = 2\sqrt{k+2} - 2 \ge \sqrt{k+1}, \tag{8.33}$$

where the last inequality holds for all $k \ge 1$. The result (8.30) now follows immediately from (8.32) and (8.33).

(b) Using Lemma 8.26, we obtain the following inequalities for any $k \geq 2$:

$$\sum_{n=\lceil k/2 \rceil}^{k} \frac{1}{n+1} \leq \int_{\lceil k/2 \rceil - 1}^{k} \frac{dt}{t+1} = \log(k+1) - \log(\lceil k/2 \rceil)$$

$$= \log\left(\frac{k+1}{\lceil 0.5k \rceil}\right) \leq \log\left(\frac{k+1}{0.5k}\right) = \log\left(2 + \frac{2}{k}\right)$$

$$\leq \log(3) \tag{8.34}$$

and

$$\sum_{n=\lceil k/2 \rceil}^{k} \frac{1}{\sqrt{n+1}} \geq \int_{\lceil k/2 \rceil}^{k+1} \frac{dt}{\sqrt{t+1}} = 2\sqrt{k+2} - 2\sqrt{\lceil k/2 \rceil + 1}$$

$$\geq 2\sqrt{k+2} - 2\sqrt{k/2 + 2} = \frac{4(k+2) - 4(0.5k+2)}{2\sqrt{k+2} + 2\sqrt{0.5k+2}}$$

$$= \frac{k}{\sqrt{k+2} + \sqrt{0.5k+2}} \geq \frac{k}{2\sqrt{k+2}}$$

$$\geq \frac{1}{4}\sqrt{k+2}, \tag{8.35}$$

where the last inequality holds since $k \geq 2$. The result (8.31) now follows by combining (8.34) and (8.35). □

We are now ready to prove the convergence result.

Theorem 8.28 ($O(\log(k)/\sqrt{k})$ rate of convergence of projected subgradient). *Suppose that Assumptions 8.7 and 8.12 hold. Let $\{\mathbf{x}^k\}_{k\geq 0}$ be the sequence generated by the projected subgradient method with stepsizes $t_k = \frac{1}{\|f'(\mathbf{x}^k)\|\sqrt{k+1}}$ if $f'(\mathbf{x}^k) \neq 0$ and $t_k = \frac{1}{L_f}$ otherwise. Then*

(a) *for any $k \geq 1$,*

$$f_{\text{best}}^k - f_{\text{opt}} \leq \frac{L_f}{2} \frac{\|\mathbf{x}^0 - \mathbf{x}^*\|^2 + 1 + \log(k+1)}{\sqrt{k+1}},$$

where $\{f_{\text{best}}^k\}_{k\geq 0}$ is the sequence of best achieved values defined in (8.11);

(b) *for any $k \geq 1$,*

$$f(\mathbf{x}^{(k)}) - f_{\text{opt}} \leq \frac{L_f}{2} \frac{\|\mathbf{x}^0 - \mathbf{x}^*\|^2 + 1 + \log(k+1)}{\sqrt{k+1}},$$

where

$$\mathbf{x}^{(k)} = \frac{1}{\sum_{n=0}^{k} t_n} \sum_{n=0}^{k} t_n \mathbf{x}^n.$$

Proof. Using (8.27) along with the inequality $f(\mathbf{x}^n) \geq f_{\text{best}}^k$ for any $n = 0, 1, 2, \ldots, k$, we obtain

$$f_{\text{best}}^k - f_{\text{opt}} \leq \frac{1}{2} \frac{\|\mathbf{x}^0 - \mathbf{x}^*\|^2 + \sum_{n=0}^{k} t_n^2 \|f'(\mathbf{x}^n)\|^2}{\sum_{n=0}^{k} t_n}. \tag{8.36}$$

Alternatively, by Jensen's inequality

$$f(\mathbf{x}^{(k)}) \leq \frac{1}{\sum_{n=0}^{k} t_n} \sum_{n=0}^{k} t_n f(\mathbf{x}^n),$$

which, along with (8.27), yields

$$f(\mathbf{x}^{(k)}) - f_{\mathrm{opt}} \leq \frac{1}{2} \frac{\|\mathbf{x}^0 - \mathbf{x}^*\|^2 + \sum_{n=0}^{k} t_n^2 \|f'(\mathbf{x}^n)\|^2}{\sum_{n=0}^{k} t_n}. \tag{8.37}$$

Therefore, combining (8.36) and (8.37), we have

$$\max\{f_{\mathrm{best}}^k - f_{\mathrm{opt}}, f(\mathbf{x}^{(k)}) - f_{\mathrm{opt}}\} \leq \frac{1}{2} \frac{\|\mathbf{x}^0 - \mathbf{x}^*\|^2 + \sum_{n=0}^{k} t_n^2 \|f'(\mathbf{x}^n)\|^2}{\sum_{n=0}^{k} t_n}.$$

By the definition of t_n, $t_n^2 \|f'(\mathbf{x}^n)\|^2 \leq \frac{1}{n+1}$ (satisfied as equality when $f'(\mathbf{x}^n) \neq \mathbf{0}$ and as a strict inequality when $f'(\mathbf{x}^n) = \mathbf{0}$); in addition, since $\|f'(\mathbf{x}^n)\| \leq L_f$, we have $t_n \geq \frac{1}{L_f \sqrt{n+1}}$. Therefore,

$$\max\{f_{\mathrm{best}}^k - f_{\mathrm{opt}}, f(\mathbf{x}^{(k)}) - f_{\mathrm{opt}}\} \leq \frac{L_f}{2} \frac{\|\mathbf{x}^0 - \mathbf{x}^*\|^2 + \sum_{n=0}^{k} \frac{1}{n+1}}{\sum_{n=0}^{k} \frac{1}{\sqrt{n+1}}}. \tag{8.38}$$

Invoking Lemma 8.27(a) with $D = \|\mathbf{x}^0 - \mathbf{x}^*\|^2$ implies the inequality

$$\max\{f_{\mathrm{best}}^k - f_{\mathrm{opt}}, f(\mathbf{x}^{(k)}) - f_{\mathrm{opt}}\} \leq \frac{L_f}{2} \frac{\|\mathbf{x}^0 - \mathbf{x}^*\|^2 + 1 + \log(k+1)}{\sqrt{k+1}},$$

which is equivalent to the validity of the two claims (a) and (b).   □

Remark 8.29. *The sequence of averages* $\mathbf{x}^{(k)}$ *as defined in Theorem 8.28 can be computed in an adaptive way by noting that the following simple recursion relation holds:*

$$\mathbf{x}^{(k+1)} = \frac{T_k}{T_{k+1}} \mathbf{x}^{(k)} + \frac{t_{k+1}}{T_{k+1}} \mathbf{x}^{k+1},$$

where $T_k \equiv \sum_{n=0}^{k} t_n$ *can be computed by the obvious recursion relation* $T_{k+1} = T_k + t_{k+1}$.

The $O(\log(k)/\sqrt{k})$ rate of convergence proven in Theorem 8.28 is worse than the $O(1/\sqrt{k})$ rate established in Theorem 8.13 for the version of the projected subgradient method with Polyak's stepsize. It is possible to prove an $O(1/\sqrt{k})$ rate of convergence if we assume in addition that the feasible set C is compact. Note that by Theorem 3.16, the compactness of C implies the validity of Assumption 8.12, but we will nonetheless explicitly state it in the following result.

Theorem 8.30 ($O(1/\sqrt{k})$ rate of convergence of projected subgradient).
Suppose that Assumptions 8.7 and 8.12 hold and assume that C is compact. Let Θ be an upper bound on the half-squared diameter of C:

$$\Theta \geq \max_{\mathbf{x}, \mathbf{y} \in C} \frac{1}{2} \|\mathbf{x} - \mathbf{y}\|^2.$$

Let $\{\mathbf{x}^k\}_{k\geq 0}$ be the sequence generated by the projected subgradient method with stepsizes chosen as either

$$t_k = \frac{\sqrt{2\Theta}}{L_f\sqrt{k+1}} \tag{8.39}$$

or

$$t_k = \begin{cases} \frac{\sqrt{2\Theta}}{\|f'(\mathbf{x}^k)\|\sqrt{k+1}}, & f'(\mathbf{x}^k) \neq \mathbf{0}, \\ \frac{\sqrt{2\Theta}}{L_f\sqrt{k+1}}, & f'(\mathbf{x}^k) = \mathbf{0}. \end{cases} \tag{8.40}$$

Then for all $k \geq 2$,

$$f_{\text{best}}^k - f_{\text{opt}} \leq \frac{\delta L_f\sqrt{2\Theta}}{\sqrt{k+2}},$$

where $\delta = 2(1 + \log(3))$ and f_{best}^k is the sequence of best achieved values defined in (8.11).

Proof. By Lemma 8.11, for any $n \geq 0$,

$$\frac{1}{2}\|\mathbf{x}^{n+1} - \mathbf{x}^*\|^2 \leq \frac{1}{2}\|\mathbf{x}^n - \mathbf{x}^*\|^2 - t_n(f(\mathbf{x}^n) - f_{\text{opt}}) + \frac{t_n^2}{2}\|f'(\mathbf{x}^n)\|^2.$$

Summing the above inequality over $n = \lceil k/2\rceil, \lceil k/2\rceil + 1, \ldots, k$, we obtain

$$\sum_{n=\lceil k/2\rceil}^{k} t_n(f(\mathbf{x}^n) - f_{\text{opt}}) \leq \frac{1}{2}\|\mathbf{x}^{\lceil k/2\rceil} - \mathbf{x}^*\|^2 - \frac{1}{2}\|\mathbf{x}^{k+1} - \mathbf{x}^*\|^2 + \sum_{n=\lceil k/2\rceil}^{k} \frac{t_n^2}{2}\|f'(\mathbf{x}^n)\|^2$$

$$\leq \Theta + \sum_{n=\lceil k/2\rceil}^{k} \frac{t_n^2}{2}\|f'(\mathbf{x}^n)\|^2$$

$$\leq \Theta + \Theta \sum_{n=\lceil k/2\rceil}^{k} \frac{1}{n+1}, \tag{8.41}$$

where the last inequality is due to the fact that in either of the definitions of the stepsizes (8.39), (8.40), $t_n^2\|f'(\mathbf{x}^n)\|^2 \leq \frac{2\Theta}{n+1}$.

Since $t_n \geq \frac{\sqrt{2\Theta}}{L_f\sqrt{n+1}}$ and $f(\mathbf{x}^n) \geq f_{\text{best}}^k$ for all $n \leq k$, it follows that

$$\sum_{n=\lceil k/2\rceil}^{k} t_n(f(\mathbf{x}^n) - f_{\text{opt}}) \geq \left(\sum_{n=\lceil k/2\rceil}^{k} \frac{\sqrt{2\Theta}}{L_f\sqrt{n+1}}\right)(f_{\text{best}}^k - f_{\text{opt}}). \tag{8.42}$$

Therefore, combining (8.41) and (8.42) yields

$$f_{\text{best}}^k - f_{\text{opt}} \leq \frac{L_f\sqrt{\Theta}}{\sqrt{2}} \frac{1 + \sum_{n=\lceil k/2\rceil}^{k} \frac{1}{n+1}}{\sum_{n=\lceil k/2\rceil}^{k} \frac{1}{\sqrt{n+1}}}, \tag{8.43}$$

which, combined with Lemma 8.27(b), yields the desired result. $\square$

8.2.5   The Strongly Convex Case[43]

We will now show that if f is in addition strongly convex, then the $O(1/\sqrt{k})$ rate of convergence result can be improved to a rate of $O(1/k)$. The stepsizes used in order to achieve this improved rate diminish at an order of $1/k$. We will also use the growth property of strongly convex functions described in Theorem 5.25(b) in order to show a result on the rate of convergence of the sequence $\{\mathbf{x}^k\}_{k \geq 0}$ to an optimal solution.

Theorem 8.31 ($O(1/k)$ rate of convergence of projected subgradient for strongly convex functions). *Suppose that Assumptions 8.7 and 8.12 hold. Assume in addition that f is σ-strongly convex for some $\sigma > 0$, and let $\mathbf{x}^*$ be its unique minimizer. Let $\{\mathbf{x}^k\}_{k \geq 0}$ be the sequence generated by the projected subgradient method with stepsize $t_k = \frac{2}{\sigma(k+1)}$.*

(a) *Let $\{f_{\mathrm{best}}^k\}_{k \geq 0}$ be the sequence of best achieved values defined in (8.11). Then for any $k \geq 0$,*

$$f_{\mathrm{best}}^k - f_{\mathrm{opt}} \leq \frac{2L_f^2}{\sigma(k+1)}. \tag{8.44}$$

In addition,

$$\|\mathbf{x}^{i_k} - \mathbf{x}^*\| \leq \frac{2L_f}{\sigma\sqrt{k+1}}, \tag{8.45}$$

where $i_k \in \operatorname{argmin}_{i=0,1,\dots,k} f(\mathbf{x}^i)$.

(b) *Define the sequence of averages:*

$$\mathbf{x}^{(k)} = \sum_{n=0}^{k} \alpha_n^k \mathbf{x}^n,$$

where $\alpha_n^k \equiv \frac{2n}{k(k+1)}$. Then for all $k \geq 0$,

$$f(\mathbf{x}^{(k)}) - f_{\mathrm{opt}} \leq \frac{2L_f^2}{\sigma(k+1)}. \tag{8.46}$$

In addition,

$$\|\mathbf{x}^{(k)} - \mathbf{x}^*\| \leq \frac{2L_f}{\sigma\sqrt{k+1}}. \tag{8.47}$$

Proof. (a) Repeating the arguments in the proof of Lemma 8.11, we can write for any $n \geq 0$

$$\begin{aligned}
\|\mathbf{x}^{n+1} - \mathbf{x}^*\|^2 &= \|P_C(\mathbf{x}^n - t_n f'(\mathbf{x}^n)) - P_C(\mathbf{x}^*)\|^2 \\
&\leq \|\mathbf{x}^n - t_n f'(\mathbf{x}^n) - \mathbf{x}^*\|^2 \\
&= \|\mathbf{x}^n - \mathbf{x}^*\|^2 - 2t_n \langle f'(\mathbf{x}^n), \mathbf{x}^n - \mathbf{x}^* \rangle + t_n^2 \|f'(\mathbf{x}^n)\|^2. \tag{8.48}
\end{aligned}$$

---

[43]The analysis of the stochastic and deterministic projected subgradient method in the strongly convex case is based on the work of Lacoste-Julien, Schmidt, and Bach [77].

Since f is σ-strongly convex, it follows by Theorem 5.24 that

$$f(\mathbf{x}^*) \geq f(\mathbf{x}^n) + \langle f'(\mathbf{x}^n), \mathbf{x}^* - \mathbf{x}^n \rangle + \frac{\sigma}{2} \|\mathbf{x}^n - \mathbf{x}^*\|^2.$$

That is,

$$\langle f'(\mathbf{x}^n), \mathbf{x}^n - \mathbf{x}^* \rangle \geq f(\mathbf{x}^n) - f_{\text{opt}} + \frac{\sigma}{2} \|\mathbf{x}^n - \mathbf{x}^*\|^2.$$

Plugging the above into (8.48), we obtain that

$$\|\mathbf{x}^{n+1} - \mathbf{x}^*\|^2 \leq (1 - \sigma t_n) \|\mathbf{x}^n - \mathbf{x}^*\|^2 - 2t_n(f(\mathbf{x}^n) - f_{\text{opt}}) + t_n^2 \|f'(\mathbf{x}^n)\|^2.$$

Rearranging terms, dividing by $2t_n$, and using the bound $\|f'(\mathbf{x}^n)\| \leq L_f$ leads to the following inequality:

$$f(\mathbf{x}^n) - f_{\text{opt}} \leq \frac{1}{2}(t_n^{-1} - \sigma) \|\mathbf{x}^n - \mathbf{x}^*\|^2 - \frac{1}{2} t_n^{-1} \|\mathbf{x}^{n+1} - \mathbf{x}^*\|^2 + \frac{t_n}{2} L_f^2.$$

Plugging $t_n = \frac{2}{\sigma(n+1)}$ into the latter inequality, we obtain

$$f(\mathbf{x}^n) - f_{\text{opt}} \leq \frac{\sigma(n-1)}{4} \|\mathbf{x}^n - \mathbf{x}^*\|^2 - \frac{\sigma(n+1)}{4} \|\mathbf{x}^{n+1} - \mathbf{x}^*\|^2 + \frac{1}{\sigma(n+1)} L_f^2.$$

Multiplying the above by n yields the following inequality:

$$n(f(\mathbf{x}^n) - f_{\text{opt}}) \leq \frac{\sigma n(n-1)}{4} \|\mathbf{x}^n - \mathbf{x}^*\|^2 - \frac{\sigma(n+1)n}{4} \|\mathbf{x}^{n+1} - \mathbf{x}^*\|^2 + \frac{n}{\sigma(n+1)} L_f^2.$$

Summing over $n = 0, 1, \ldots, k$, we conclude that

$$\sum_{n=0}^{k} n(f(\mathbf{x}^n) - f_{\text{opt}}) \leq 0 - \frac{\sigma}{4} k(k+1) \|\mathbf{x}^{k+1} - \mathbf{x}^*\|^2 + \frac{L_f^2}{\sigma} \sum_{n=0}^{k} \frac{n}{n+1} \leq \frac{L_f^2 k}{\sigma}. \quad (8.49)$$

Therefore, using the inequality $f(\mathbf{x}^n) \geq f_{\text{best}}^k$ for all $n = 0, 1, \ldots, k$, it follows that

$$\left(\sum_{n=0}^{k} n \right) (f_{\text{best}}^k - f_{\text{opt}}) \leq \frac{L_f^2 k}{\sigma},$$

which by the known identity $\sum_{n=0}^{k} n = \frac{k(k+1)}{2}$ shows that

$$f_{\text{best}}^k - f_{\text{opt}} \leq \frac{2L_f^2}{\sigma(k+1)}, \quad (8.50)$$

meaning that (8.44) holds. To prove (8.45), note that $f_{\text{best}}^k = f(\mathbf{x}^{i_k})$, and hence by Theorem 5.25(b) employed on the σ-strongly convex function $f + \delta_C$ and (8.50),

$$\frac{\sigma}{2} \|\mathbf{x}^{i_k} - \mathbf{x}^*\|^2 \leq f_{\text{best}}^k - f_{\text{opt}} \leq \frac{2L_f^2}{\sigma(k+1)},$$

which is the same as

$$\|\mathbf{x}^{i_k} - \mathbf{x}^*\| \leq \frac{2L_f}{\sigma\sqrt{k+1}}.$$

(b) To establish the ergodic convergence, we begin by dividing (8.49) by $\frac{k(k+1)}{2}$ to obtain

$$\sum_{n=0}^{k} \alpha_n^k (f(\mathbf{x}^n) - f_{\text{opt}}) \leq \frac{2L_f^2}{\sigma(k+1)}.$$

By Jensen's inequality (utilizing the fact that $(\alpha_n^k)_{n=0}^k \in \Delta_{k+1}$),

$$f(\mathbf{x}^{(k)}) - f_{\text{opt}} = f\left(\sum_{n=0}^{k} \alpha_n^k \mathbf{x}^n\right) - f_{\text{opt}} \leq \sum_{n=0}^{k} \alpha_n^k (f(\mathbf{x}^n) - f_{\text{opt}}) \leq \frac{2L_f^2}{\sigma(k+1)},$$

meaning that (8.46) holds. The result (8.47) now follows by the same arguments used to prove (8.45) in part (a). □

Remark 8.32. *The sequence of averages $\mathbf{x}^{(k)}$ as defined in Theorem 8.31 can be computed in an adaptive way by noting that the following simple recursion relation holds:*

$$\mathbf{x}^{(k+1)} = \frac{k}{k+2} \mathbf{x}^{(k)} + \frac{2}{k+2} \mathbf{x}^{k+1}.$$

The $O(1/k)$ rate of convergence of the sequence of function values naturally leads to the observation that to obtain an ε-optimal solution, an order of $1/\varepsilon$ iterations is required. The proof is trivial and follows the argument of the proof of Theorem 8.18.

Theorem 8.33 (complexity of projected subgradient for strongly convex functions). *Under the setting and assumptions of Theorem 8.31, for any nonnegative integer k satisfying*

$$k \geq \frac{2L_f^2}{\sigma\varepsilon} - 1,$$

it holds that

$$f_{\text{best}}^k - f_{\text{opt}} \leq \varepsilon$$

and

$$f(\mathbf{x}^{(k)}) - f_{\text{opt}} \leq \varepsilon.$$

8.3 The Stochastic Projected Subgradient Method

8.3.1 Setting and Method

In this section we still study the model (8.10) under Assumption 8.7. The main difference will be that at each iteration we do not necessarily utilize a subgradient at the current iterate $\mathbf{x}^k$ as the update direction vector, but rather a random estimator $\mathbf{g}^k$ of a subgradient of f at $\mathbf{x}^k$ (a precise characterization will be given in Assumption 8.34). The method is therefore given as follows.

The Stochastic Projected Subgradient Method

Initialization: pick $\mathbf{x}^0 \in C$ arbitrarily.
General step: for any $k = 0, 1, 2, \ldots$ execute the following steps:

(A) pick a stepsize $t_k > 0$ and a random vector $\mathbf{g}^k \in \mathbb{E}$;

(B) set $\mathbf{x}^{k+1} = P_C(\mathbf{x}^k - t_k \mathbf{g}^k)$.

Obviously, since the vectors $\mathbf{g}^k$ are random vectors, so are the iterate vectors $\mathbf{x}^k$. The exact assumptions on the random vectors $\mathbf{g}^k$ are given below.

Assumption 8.34.

(A) **(unbiasedness)** *For any $k \geq 0$, $\mathsf{E}(\mathbf{g}^k | \mathbf{x}^k) \in \partial f(\mathbf{x}^k)$.*

(B) **(boundedness)** *There exists a constant $\tilde{L}_f > 0$ such that for any $k \geq 0$,* $\mathsf{E}(\|\mathbf{g}^k\|^2 | \mathbf{x}^k) \leq \tilde{L}_f^2$.

Part (A) of the assumption says that $\mathbf{g}^k$ is an *unbiased estimator* of a subgradient at $\mathbf{x}^k$. This assumption can also be written as

$$f(\mathbf{z}) \geq f(\mathbf{x}^k) + \langle \mathsf{E}(\mathbf{g}^k | \mathbf{x}^k), \mathbf{z} - \mathbf{x}^k \rangle \text{ for all } \mathbf{z} \in \mathrm{dom}(f).$$

The constant $\tilde{L}_f$ from part (B) of Assumption 8.34 is not necessarily a Lipschitz constant of f as in the deterministic case.

8.3.2 Analysis

The analysis of the stochastic projected subgradient is almost identical to the analysis of the deterministic method. We gather the main results in the following theorem.

Theorem 8.35 (convergence of stochastic projected gradient). *Suppose that Assumptions 8.7 and 8.34 hold. Let $\{\mathbf{x}^k\}_{k \geq 0}$ be the sequence generated by the stochastic projected subgradient method with positive stepsizes $\{t_k\}_{k \geq 0}$, and let $\{f_{\mathrm{best}}^k\}_{k \geq 0}$ be the sequence of best achieved values defined in (8.11).*

(a) *If $\frac{\sum_{n=0}^k t_n^2}{\sum_{n=0}^k t_n} \to 0$ as $k \to \infty$, then $\mathsf{E}(f_{\mathrm{best}}^k) \to f_{\mathrm{opt}}$ as $k \to \infty$.*

(b) *Assume that C is compact. Let $\tilde{L}_f$ be the positive constant defined in Assumption 8.34, and let Θ be an upper bound on the half-squared diameter of C:*

$$\Theta \geq \max_{\mathbf{x}, \mathbf{y} \in C} \frac{1}{2} \|\mathbf{x} - \mathbf{y}\|^2. \tag{8.51}$$

If $t_k = \frac{\sqrt{2\Theta}}{\tilde{L}_f \sqrt{k+1}}$, then for all $k \geq 2$,

$$\mathsf{E}(f_{\mathrm{best}}^k) - f_{\mathrm{opt}} \leq \frac{\delta \tilde{L}_f \sqrt{2\Theta}}{\sqrt{k+2}},$$

where $\delta = 2(1 + \log(3))$.

Proof. We have for any $n \geq 0$,

$$\begin{aligned}
\mathsf{E}\left(\|\mathbf{x}^{n+1} - \mathbf{x}^*\|^2 \,|\, \mathbf{x}^n\right) &= \mathsf{E}\left(\|P_C(\mathbf{x}^n - t_n\mathbf{g}^n) - P_C(\mathbf{x}^*)\|^2 \,|\, \mathbf{x}^n\right) \\
&\overset{(*)}{\leq} \mathsf{E}\left(\|\mathbf{x}^n - t_n\mathbf{g}^n - \mathbf{x}^*\|^2 \,|\, \mathbf{x}^n\right) \\
&= \|\mathbf{x}^n - \mathbf{x}^*\|^2 - 2t_n\mathsf{E}\left(\langle\mathbf{g}^n, \mathbf{x}^n - \mathbf{x}^*\rangle \,|\, \mathbf{x}^n\right) + t_n^2\mathsf{E}\left(\|\mathbf{g}^n\|^2 \,|\, \mathbf{x}^n\right) \\
&= \|\mathbf{x}^n - \mathbf{x}^*\|^2 - 2t_n\langle\mathsf{E}(\mathbf{g}^n|\mathbf{x}^n), \mathbf{x}^n - \mathbf{x}^*\rangle + t_n^2\mathsf{E}\left(\|\mathbf{g}^n\|^2 \,|\, \mathbf{x}^n\right) \\
&\overset{(**)}{\leq} \|\mathbf{x}^n - \mathbf{x}^*\|^2 - 2t_n\langle\mathsf{E}(\mathbf{g}^n|\mathbf{x}^n), \mathbf{x}^n - \mathbf{x}^*\rangle + t_n^2\tilde{L}_f^2 \\
&\overset{(***)}{\leq} \|\mathbf{x}^n - \mathbf{x}^*\|^2 - 2t_n(f(\mathbf{x}^n) - f_{\mathrm{opt}}) + t_n^2\tilde{L}_f^2,
\end{aligned}$$

where $(*)$ follows by the nonexpansiveness property of the orthogonal projection operator (Theorem 6.42), and $(**)$ and $(***)$ follow by Assumption 8.34.

Taking expectation w.r.t. $\mathbf{x}^n$, we obtain

$$\mathsf{E}\left(\|\mathbf{x}^{n+1} - \mathbf{x}^*\|^2\right) \leq \mathsf{E}\left(\|\mathbf{x}^n - \mathbf{x}^*\|^2\right) - 2t_n(\mathsf{E}(f(\mathbf{x}^n)) - f_{\mathrm{opt}}) + t_n^2\tilde{L}_f^2.$$

Summing over $n = m, m+1, \ldots, k$ (where m is an integer satisfying $m \leq k$),

$$\mathsf{E}\left(\|\mathbf{x}^{k+1} - \mathbf{x}^*\|^2\right) \leq \mathsf{E}\left(\|\mathbf{x}^m - \mathbf{x}^*\|^2\right) - 2\sum_{n=m}^k t_n(\mathsf{E}(f(\mathbf{x}^n)) - f_{\mathrm{opt}}) + \tilde{L}_f^2\sum_{n=m}^k t_n^2.$$

Therefore,

$$\sum_{n=m}^k t_n(\mathsf{E}(f(\mathbf{x}^n)) - f_{\mathrm{opt}}) \leq \frac{1}{2}\left[\mathsf{E}\left(\|\mathbf{x}^m - \mathbf{x}^*\|^2\right) + \tilde{L}_f^2\sum_{n=m}^k t_n^2\right],$$

which implies

$$\left(\sum_{n=m}^k t_n\right)\left(\min_{n=m,m+1,\ldots,k}\mathsf{E}(f(\mathbf{x}^n)) - f_{\mathrm{opt}}\right) \leq \frac{1}{2}\left[\mathsf{E}\left(\|\mathbf{x}^m - \mathbf{x}^*\|^2\right) + \tilde{L}_f^2\sum_{n=m}^k t_n^2\right].$$

Using the inequality[44]

$$\mathsf{E}(f_{\mathrm{best}}^k) \leq \mathsf{E}\left(\min_{n=m,m+1,\ldots,k} f(\mathbf{x}^n)\right) \leq \min_{n=m,m+1,\ldots,k}\mathsf{E}(f(\mathbf{x}^n)),$$

we can conclude that

$$\mathsf{E}(f_{\mathrm{best}}^k) - f_{\mathrm{opt}} \leq \frac{\mathsf{E}(\|\mathbf{x}^m - \mathbf{x}^*\|^2) + \tilde{L}_f^2\sum_{n=m}^k t_n^2}{2\sum_{n=m}^k t_n}. \tag{8.52}$$

Plugging $m = 0$ in (8.52), we obtain

$$\mathsf{E}(f_{\mathrm{best}}^k) - f_{\mathrm{opt}} \leq \frac{\|\mathbf{x}^0 - \mathbf{x}^*\|^2 + \tilde{L}_f^2\sum_{n=0}^k t_n^2}{2\sum_{n=0}^k t_n}.$$

---

[44]The fact that for any p random variables $\mathsf{E}(\min\{X_1, X_2, \ldots, X_p\}) \leq \min_{i=1,2,\ldots,p}\mathsf{E}(X_i)$ follows by the following argument: for any $i = 1, 2, \ldots, p$, the inequality $\min\{X_1, X_2, \ldots, X_p\} \leq X_i$ holds. Taking expectation leads to the inequality $\mathsf{E}(\min\{X_1, X_2, \ldots, X_p\}) \leq \mathsf{E}(X_i)$ for any i, from which the desired inequality $\mathsf{E}(\min\{X_1, X_2, \ldots, X_p\}) \leq \min_{i=1,2,\ldots,p}\mathsf{E}(X_i)$ follows.

Therefore, if $\frac{\sum_{n=0}^{k} t_n^2}{\sum_{n=0}^{k} t_n} \to 0$, then $\mathsf{E}(f_{\text{best}}^k) \to f_{\text{opt}}$ as $k \to \infty$, proving claim (a). To show the validity of claim (b), use (8.52) with $m = \lceil k/2 \rceil$ and the bound (8.51) to obtain

$$\mathsf{E}(f_{\text{best}}^k) - f_{\text{opt}} \leq \frac{\Theta + \frac{\tilde{L}_f^2}{2} \sum_{n=\lceil k/2 \rceil}^{k} t_n^2}{\sum_{n=\lceil k/2 \rceil}^{k} t_n}.$$

Taking $t_n = \frac{\sqrt{2\Theta}}{\tilde{L}_f \sqrt{n+1}}$, we get

$$\mathsf{E}(f_{\text{best}}^k) - f_{\text{opt}} \leq \frac{\tilde{L}_f \sqrt{2\Theta}}{2} \frac{1 + \sum_{n=\lceil k/2 \rceil}^{k} \frac{1}{n+1}}{\sum_{n=\lceil k/2 \rceil}^{k} \frac{1}{\sqrt{n+1}}},$$

which, combined with Lemma 8.27(b), yields the desired result. $\square$

Example 8.36 (minimization of sum of convex functions). Consider the optimization model

$$\text{(P)} \quad \min \left\{ f(\mathbf{x}) \equiv \sum_{i=1}^{m} f_i(\mathbf{x}) : \mathbf{x} \in C \right\},$$

where $f_1, f_2, \ldots, f_m : \mathbb{E} \to (-\infty, \infty]$ are proper closed and convex functions. Suppose that Assumption 8.7 holds and that C is compact, which in particular implies the validity of Assumption 8.12 with some constant L_f. By Theorem 3.61 L_f is a Lipschitz constant of f over C. Let Θ be some upper bound on the half-squared diameter of C:

$$\frac{1}{2} \max_{\mathbf{x}, \mathbf{y} \in C} \|\mathbf{x} - \mathbf{y}\|^2 \leq \Theta.$$

In addition, we will assume that for any $i = 1, 2, \ldots, m$, there exists a constant L_{f_i} for which

$$\|\mathbf{g}\| \leq L_{f_i} \text{ for all } \mathbf{g} \in \partial f_i(\mathbf{x}), \mathbf{x} \in C.$$

By Theorem 3.61, L_{f_i} is a Lipschitz constant of f_i over C. We can consider two options for solving the main problem (P). The first is to employ the projected subgradient method (we assume that $f'(\mathbf{x}^k) \neq \mathbf{0}$):

Algorithm 1

- **Initialization:** pick $\mathbf{x}^0 \in C$.

- **General step** $(k \geq 0)$: choose $f_i'(\mathbf{x}^k) \in \partial f_i(\mathbf{x}^k), i = 1, 2, \ldots, m$, and compute

$$\mathbf{x}^{k+1} = P_C \left(\mathbf{x}^k - \frac{\sqrt{2\Theta}}{\| \sum_{i=1}^{m} f_i'(\mathbf{x}^k) \| \sqrt{k+1}} \left(\sum_{i=1}^{m} f_i'(\mathbf{x}^k) \right) \right).$$

By Theorem 8.30, the following efficiency estimate holds for any $k \geq 2$:

$$f_{\text{best}}^k - f_{\text{opt}} \leq \frac{\delta L_f \sqrt{2\Theta}}{\sqrt{k+2}}, \tag{8.53}$$

where $\delta = 2(1+\log(3))$. A direct consequence is that in order to obtain an ε-optimal solution,

$$N_1 = \max\left\{\frac{2\delta^2 L_f^2 \Theta}{\varepsilon^2} - 2, 2\right\}$$

iterations are sufficient. Since the computation of the subgradient of f at $\mathbf{x}^k$ by the formula $\sum_{i=1}^m f_i'(\mathbf{x}^k)$ might be too expensive in cases where m is large, we can alternatively employ the stochastic projected subgradient method where at iteration k, we define the unbiased estimate of $f'(\mathbf{x}^k)$ as

$$\mathbf{g}^k = m f_{i_k}'(\mathbf{x}^k),$$

where i_k is randomly picked from $\{1, 2, \ldots, m\}$ via a uniform distribution. Obviously,

$$\mathsf{E}(\mathbf{g}^k|\mathbf{x}^k) = \sum_{i=1}^m \frac{1}{m} m f_i'(\mathbf{x}^k) = \sum_{i=1}^m f_i'(\mathbf{x}^k) \in \partial f(\mathbf{x}^k),$$

where the inclusion in $\partial f(\mathbf{x}^k)$ follows by the sum rule of subdifferential calculus (Corollary 3.38). Also,

$$\mathsf{E}(\|\mathbf{g}^k\|^2|\mathbf{x}^k) = \frac{1}{m}\sum_{i=1}^m m^2 \|f_i'(\mathbf{x}^k)\|^2 \le m\sum_{i=1}^m L_{f_i}^2 \equiv \tilde{L}_f^2.$$

The stochastic projected subgradient method employed on problem (P) therefore takes the following form:

Algorithm 2

- **Initialization:** pick $\mathbf{x}^0 \in C$.

- **General step** $(k \ge 0)$:

  - pick $i_k \in \{1, 2, \ldots, m\}$ randomly via a uniform distribution and $f_{i_k}'(\mathbf{x}^k) \in \partial f_{i_k}(\mathbf{x}^k)$;
  - compute

    $$\mathbf{x}^{k+1} = P_C\left(\mathbf{x}^k - \frac{\sqrt{2\Theta}m}{\tilde{L}_f\sqrt{k+1}}f_{i_k}'(\mathbf{x}^k)\right),$$

    where $\tilde{L}_f = \sqrt{m}\sqrt{\sum_{i=1}^m L_{f_i}^2}$.

Invoking Theorem 8.35, we obtain that

$$\mathsf{E}(f_{\text{best}}^k) - f_{\text{opt}} \le \frac{\delta\sqrt{m}\sqrt{\sum_{i=1}^m L_{f_i}^2}\sqrt{2\Theta}}{\sqrt{k+2}}. \tag{8.54}$$

In particular,

$$N_2 = \max\left\{\frac{2\delta^2 m\Theta \sum_{i=1}^m L_{f_i}^2}{\varepsilon^2} - 2, 2\right\}$$

iterations are sufficient in order to ensure that an ε-optimal solution in expectation is reached. The natural question that arises is, *is it possible to compare between the two algorithms?* The answer is actually not clear. We can compare the two quantities N_2 and N_1, but there are two major flaws in such a comparison. First, in a sense this is like comparing apples and oranges since N_1 considers a sequence of function values, while N_2 refers to a sequence of expected function values. In addition, recall that N_2 and N_1 only provide upper bounds on the amount of iterations required to obtain an ε-optimal solution (deterministically or in expectation). Comparison of *upper bounds* might be influenced dramatically by the tightness of the upper bounds. Disregarding these drawbacks, estimating the ratio between N_2 and N_1, while neglecting the constant terms, which do not depend on ε, we get

$$\frac{N_2}{N_1} \approx \frac{\frac{2\delta^2 m \Theta \sum_{i=1}^m L_{f_i}^2}{\varepsilon^2}}{\frac{2\delta^2 L_f^2 \Theta}{\varepsilon^2}} = \frac{m \sum_{i=1}^m L_{f_i}^2}{L_f^2} \equiv \beta.$$

The value of β obviously depends on the specific problem at hand. Let us, for example, consider the instance in which $f_i(\mathbf{x}) = |\mathbf{a}_i^T \mathbf{x} + b_i|$, $i = 1, 2, \ldots, m$, where $\mathbf{a}_i \in \mathbb{R}^n, b_i \in \mathbb{R}$, and $C = B_{\|\cdot\|_2}[\mathbf{0}, 1]$. In this case,

$$f(\mathbf{x}) = \|\mathbf{A}\mathbf{x} + \mathbf{b}\|_1,$$

where $\mathbf{A}$ is the $m \times n$ matrix whose rows are $\mathbf{a}_i^T$ and $\mathbf{b} = (b_i)_{i=1}^m$. Since

$$\partial f_i(\mathbf{x}) = \begin{cases} \mathbf{a}_i, & \mathbf{a}_i^T \mathbf{x} + b_i > 0, \\ -\mathbf{a}_i, & \mathbf{a}_i^T \mathbf{x} + b_i < 0, \\ \{\xi \mathbf{a}_i : \xi \in [-1, 1]\}, & \mathbf{a}_i^T \mathbf{x} + b_i = 0, \end{cases}$$

it follows that we can choose $L_{f_i} = \|\mathbf{a}_i\|_2$. To estimate L_f, note that by Example 3.44, any $\mathbf{g} \in \partial f(\mathbf{x})$ has the form $\mathbf{g} = \mathbf{A}^T \boldsymbol{\eta}$ for some $\boldsymbol{\eta} \in [-1, 1]^m$, which in particular implies that $\|\boldsymbol{\eta}\|_2 \leq \sqrt{m}$. Thus,

$$\|\mathbf{g}\|_2 = \|\mathbf{A}^T \boldsymbol{\eta}\|_2 \leq \|\mathbf{A}^T\|_{2,2} \|\boldsymbol{\eta}\|_2 \leq \sqrt{m} \|\mathbf{A}^T\|_{2,2},$$

where $\|\cdot\|_{2,2}$ is the spectral norm. We can therefore choose $L_f = \sqrt{m} \|\mathbf{A}^T\|_{2,2}$. Thus,

$$\beta = \frac{m \sum_{i=1}^m \|\mathbf{a}_i\|_2^2}{m \|\mathbf{A}^T\|_{2,2}^2} = \frac{\|\mathbf{A}^T\|_F^2}{\|\mathbf{A}^T\|_{2,2}^2} = \frac{\sum_{i=1}^n \lambda_i(\mathbf{A}\mathbf{A}^T)}{\max_{i=1,2,\ldots,n} \lambda_i(\mathbf{A}\mathbf{A}^T)},$$

where $\lambda_1(\mathbf{A}\mathbf{A}^T) \geq \lambda_2(\mathbf{A}\mathbf{A}^T) \geq \cdots \geq \lambda_n(\mathbf{A}\mathbf{A}^T)$ are the eigenvalues of $\mathbf{A}\mathbf{A}^T$ ordered nonincreasingly. Using the fact that for any nonnegative numbers $\alpha_1, \alpha_2, \ldots, \alpha_m$ the inequalities

$$\max_{i=1,2,\ldots,m} \alpha_i \leq \sum_{i=1}^m \alpha_i \leq m \max_{i=1,2,\ldots,m} \alpha_i$$

hold, we obtain that $1 \leq \beta \leq m$. The extreme case $\beta = m$ is actually quite logical in the sense that the number of subgradient computations per iteration in Algorithm 1 is m times larger than what is required in Algorithm 2, and it is thus not surprising that the amount of iterations of Algorithm 2 might be m times larger than what is required by Algorithm 1 to obtain the same level of accuracy. What is much less intuitive is the case when β is close 1. In these instances, the two algorithms require (modulo the faults of this comparison) the same order of iterations to obtain the same order of accuracy. For example, when $\mathbf{A}$ is "close" to be of rank one, then β will be close to 1. In these cases, the two algorithms should perform similarly, although Algorithm 2 is much less computationally demanding. We can explain this result by the fact that in this instance the vectors $\mathbf{a}_i$ are "almost" proportional to each other, and thus all the subgradient directions $f_i'(\mathbf{x}^k)$ are similar. ∎

8.3.3 Stochastic Projected Subgradient—The Strongly Convex Case

The analysis of the stochastic projected subgradient method is almost identical to the one presented for the deterministic case in Theorem 8.31, but for the sake of completeness we present the result and its complete proof.

Theorem 8.37 (convergence of stochastic projected subgradient for strongly convex functions). *Suppose that Assumptions 8.7 and 8.34 hold. Let $\tilde{L}_f$ be the positive constant defined in Assumption 8.34. Assume in addition that f is σ-strongly convex for some $\sigma > 0$. Let $\{\mathbf{x}^k\}_{k \geq 0}$ be the sequence generated by the stochastic projected subgradient method with stepsizes $t_k = \frac{2}{\sigma(k+1)}$.*

(a) *Let $\{f_{\text{best}}^k\}_{k \geq 0}$ be the sequence of best achieved function values defined in (8.11). Then for any $k \geq 0$,*

$$\mathsf{E}(f_{\text{best}}^k) - f_{\text{opt}} \leq \frac{2\tilde{L}_f^2}{\sigma(k+1)}.$$

(b) *Define the sequence of averages*

$$\mathbf{x}^{(k)} = \sum_{n=0}^{k} \alpha_n^k \mathbf{x}^n,$$

where $\alpha_n^k \equiv \frac{2n}{k(k+1)}$. Then

$$\mathsf{E}(f(\mathbf{x}^{(k)})) - f_{\text{opt}} \leq \frac{2\tilde{L}_f^2}{\sigma(k+1)}.$$

Proof. (a) For any $\mathbf{x}^* \in X^*$ and $n \geq 0$,

$$\begin{aligned}
\mathsf{E}\left(\|\mathbf{x}^{n+1} - \mathbf{x}^*\|^2 | \mathbf{x}^n\right) &= \mathsf{E}\left(\|P_C(\mathbf{x}^n - t_n \mathbf{g}^n) - P_C(\mathbf{x}^*)\|^2 | \mathbf{x}^n\right) \\
&\leq \mathsf{E}\left(\|\mathbf{x}^n - t_n \mathbf{g}^n - \mathbf{x}^*\|^2 | \mathbf{x}^n\right) \\
&= \|\mathbf{x}^n - \mathbf{x}^*\|^2 - 2t_n \langle \mathsf{E}(\mathbf{g}^n | \mathbf{x}^n), \mathbf{x}^n - \mathbf{x}^* \rangle \\
&\quad + t_n^2 \mathsf{E}(\|\mathbf{g}^n\|^2 | \mathbf{x}^n).
\end{aligned} \tag{8.55}$$

Since f is σ-strongly convex and $\mathsf{E}(\mathbf{g}^n | \mathbf{x}^n) \in \partial f(\mathbf{x}^n)$, it follows by Theorem 5.24(ii) that

$$f(\mathbf{x}^*) \geq f(\mathbf{x}^n) + \langle \mathsf{E}(\mathbf{g}^n | \mathbf{x}^n), \mathbf{x}^* - \mathbf{x}^n \rangle + \frac{\sigma}{2}\|\mathbf{x}^n - \mathbf{x}^*\|^2.$$

That is,

$$\langle \mathsf{E}(\mathbf{g}^n|\mathbf{x}^n), \mathbf{x}^n - \mathbf{x}^* \rangle \geq f(\mathbf{x}^n) - f_{\mathrm{opt}} + \frac{\sigma}{2}\|\mathbf{x}^n - \mathbf{x}^*\|^2.$$

Plugging the above into (8.55), we obtain that

$$\mathsf{E}\left(\|\mathbf{x}^{n+1} - \mathbf{x}^*\|^2|\mathbf{x}^n\right) \leq (1 - \sigma t_n)\|\mathbf{x}^n - \mathbf{x}^*\|^2 - 2t_n(f(\mathbf{x}^n) - f_{\mathrm{opt}}) + t_n^2\mathsf{E}(\|\mathbf{g}^n\|^2|\mathbf{x}^n).$$

Rearranging terms, dividing by $2t_n$, and using the bound $\mathsf{E}(\|\mathbf{g}^n\|^2|\mathbf{x}^n) \leq \tilde{L}_f^2$ leads to the following inequality:

$$f(\mathbf{x}^n) - f_{\mathrm{opt}} \leq \frac{1}{2}(t_n^{-1} - \sigma)\|\mathbf{x}^n - \mathbf{x}^*\|^2 - \frac{1}{2}t_n^{-1}\mathsf{E}(\|\mathbf{x}^{n+1} - \mathbf{x}^*\|^2|\mathbf{x}^n) + \frac{t_n}{2}\tilde{L}_f^2.$$

Plugging $t_n = \frac{2}{\sigma(n+1)}$ into the last inequality, we obtain

$$f(\mathbf{x}^n) - f_{\mathrm{opt}} \leq \frac{\sigma(n-1)}{4}\|\mathbf{x}^n - \mathbf{x}^*\|^2 - \frac{\sigma(n+1)}{4}\mathsf{E}(\|\mathbf{x}^{n+1} - \mathbf{x}^*\|^2|\mathbf{x}^n) + \frac{1}{\sigma(n+1)}\tilde{L}_f^2.$$

Multiplying the above by n and taking expectation w.r.t. $\mathbf{x}^n$ yields the following inequality:

$$n(\mathsf{E}(f(\mathbf{x}^n)) - f_{\mathrm{opt}}) \leq \frac{\sigma n(n-1)}{4}\mathsf{E}(\|\mathbf{x}^n - \mathbf{x}^*\|^2) - \frac{\sigma(n+1)n}{4}\mathsf{E}(\|\mathbf{x}^{n+1} - \mathbf{x}^*\|^2)$$
$$+ \frac{n}{\sigma(n+1)}\tilde{L}_f^2.$$

Summing over $n = 0, 1, \ldots, k$,

$$\sum_{n=0}^{k} n(\mathsf{E}(f(\mathbf{x}^n)) - f_{\mathrm{opt}}) \leq 0 - \frac{\sigma}{4}k(k+1)\mathsf{E}(\|\mathbf{x}^{k+1} - \mathbf{x}^*\|^2) + \frac{\tilde{L}_f^2}{\sigma}\sum_{n=0}^{k}\frac{n}{n+1} \leq \frac{\tilde{L}_f^2 k}{\sigma}.$$
$$(8.56)$$

Therefore, using the inequality $\mathsf{E}(f(\mathbf{x}^n)) \geq \mathsf{E}(f_{\mathrm{best}}^k)$ for all $n = 0, 1, \ldots, k$, it follows that

$$\left(\sum_{n=0}^{k} n\right)(\mathsf{E}(f_{\mathrm{best}}^k) - f_{\mathrm{opt}}) \leq \frac{\tilde{L}_f^2 k}{\sigma},$$

which, by the identity $\sum_{n=0}^{k} n = \frac{k(k+1)}{2}$, implies that

$$\mathsf{E}(f_{\mathrm{best}}^k) - f_{\mathrm{opt}} \leq \frac{2\tilde{L}_f^2}{\sigma(k+1)}.$$

(b) Divide (8.56) by $\frac{k(k+1)}{2}$ to obtain

$$\sum_{n=0}^{k}\alpha_n^k(\mathsf{E}(f(\mathbf{x}^n)) - f_{\mathrm{opt}}) \leq \frac{2L_f^2}{\sigma(k+1)}.$$

By Jensen's inequality (utilizing the fact that $(\alpha_n^k)_{n=0}^k \in \Delta_{k+1}$), we finally obtain

$$\mathsf{E}(f(\mathbf{x}^{(k)})) - f_{\mathrm{opt}} = \mathsf{E}\left(f\left(\sum_{n=0}^{k}\alpha_n^k\mathbf{x}^n\right)\right) - f_{\mathrm{opt}} \leq \sum_{n=0}^{k}\alpha_n^k(\mathsf{E}(f(\mathbf{x}^n)) - f_{\mathrm{opt}})$$
$$\leq \frac{2\tilde{L}_f^2}{\sigma(k+1)}. \qquad \square$$

8.4   The Incremental Projected Subgradient Method

Consider the main model (8.10), where f has the form $f(\mathbf{x}) = \sum_{i=1}^{m} f_i(\mathbf{x})$. That is, we consider the problem

$$\min \left\{ f(\mathbf{x}) = \sum_{i=1}^{m} f_i(\mathbf{x}) : \mathbf{x} \in C \right\}. \tag{8.57}$$

In addition to Assumption 8.7, we make the following assumption.

Assumption 8.38.

(a) f_i *is proper closed and convex for any* $i = 1, 2, \ldots, m$.

(b) *There exists* $L > 0$ *for which* $\|\mathbf{g}\| \leq L$ *for any* $\mathbf{g} \in \partial f_i(\mathbf{x}), i = 1, 2, \ldots, m$, $\mathbf{x} \in C$.

In Example 8.36 the same model was also considered, and a projected subgradient method that takes a step toward a direction of the form $-f'_{i_k}(\mathbf{x}^k)$ was analyzed. The index i_k was chosen in Example 8.36 randomly by a uniform distribution over the indices $\{1, 2, \ldots, m\}$, and the natural question that arises is whether we can obtain similar convergence results when i_k is chosen in a deterministic manner. We will consider the variant in which the indices are chosen in a deterministic cyclic order. The resulting method is called the *incremental projected subgradient method*. We will show that although the analysis is much more involved, it is still possible to obtain similar rates of convergence (albeit with worse constants).

An iteration of the incremental projected subgradient method is divided into subiterations. Let $\mathbf{x}^k$ be the kth iterate vector. Then we define $\mathbf{x}^{k,0} = \mathbf{x}^k$ and produce m subiterations $\mathbf{x}^{k,1}, \mathbf{x}^{k,2}, \ldots, \mathbf{x}^{k,m}$ by the rule that $\mathbf{x}^{k,i+1} = P_C(\mathbf{x}^{k,i} - t_k \mathbf{g}^{k,i})$, where $\mathbf{g}^{k,i} \in \partial f_{i+1}(\mathbf{x}^{k,i})$ and $t_k > 0$ is a positive stepsize. Finally, the next iterate is defined by $\mathbf{x}^{k+1} = \mathbf{x}^{k,m}$.

The Incremental Projected Subgradient Method

Initialization: pick $\mathbf{x}^0 \in C$ arbitrarily.
General step: for any $k = 0, 1, 2, \ldots$ execute the following steps:

(a) set $\mathbf{x}^{k,0} = \mathbf{x}^k$ and pick a stepsize $t_k > 0$;

(b) for any $i = 0, 1, \ldots, m-1$ compute

$$\mathbf{x}^{k,i+1} = P_C(\mathbf{x}^{k,i} - t_k \mathbf{g}^{k,i}),$$

where $\mathbf{g}^{k,i} \in \partial f_{i+1}(\mathbf{x}^{k,i})$;

(c) set $\mathbf{x}^{k+1} = \mathbf{x}^{k,m}$.

The fundamental inequality from which convergence results can be deduced is proven in the following lemma. The result is similar to the result in Lemma 8.11, but the proof is considerably more complicated.

Lemma 8.39 (fundamental inequality for the incremental projected subgradient method).[45] *Suppose that Assumptions 8.7 and 8.38 hold, and let $\{\mathbf{x}^k\}_{k \geq 0}$ be the sequence generated by the incremental projected subgradient method with positive stepsizes $\{t_k\}_{k \geq 0}$. Then for any $k \geq 0$,*

$$\|\mathbf{x}^{k+1} - \mathbf{x}^*\|^2 \leq \|\mathbf{x}^k - \mathbf{x}^*\|^2 - 2t_k(f(\mathbf{x}^k) - f_{\text{opt}}) + t_k^2 m^2 L^2. \tag{8.58}$$

Proof. For any $\mathbf{x}^* \in X^*$, $k \geq 0$ and $i \in \{0, 1, \ldots, m-1\}$,

$$
\begin{aligned}
\|\mathbf{x}^{k,i+1} - \mathbf{x}^*\|^2 &= \|P_C(\mathbf{x}^{k,i} - t_k \mathbf{g}^{k,i}) - \mathbf{x}^*\|^2 \\
&= \|P_C(\mathbf{x}^{k,i} - t_k \mathbf{g}^{k,i}) - P_C(\mathbf{x}^*)\|^2 \\
&\stackrel{(*)}{\leq} \|\mathbf{x}^{k,i} - t_k \mathbf{g}^{k,i} - \mathbf{x}^*\|^2 \\
&\stackrel{(**)}{\leq} \|\mathbf{x}^{k,i} - \mathbf{x}^*\|^2 - 2t_k \langle \mathbf{g}^{k,i}, \mathbf{x}^{k,i} - \mathbf{x}^* \rangle + t_k^2 L^2 \\
&\stackrel{(***)}{\leq} \|\mathbf{x}^{k,i} - \mathbf{x}^*\|^2 - 2t_k (f_{i+1}(\mathbf{x}^{k,i}) - f_{i+1}(\mathbf{x}^*)) + t_k^2 L^2,
\end{aligned}
$$

where $(*)$ follows by the nonexpansivity property of the orthogonal projection operator (Theorem 6.42(b)), $(**)$ by Assumption 8.38(b), and $(***)$ by the subgradient inequality. Summing the inequality over $i = 0, 1, \ldots, m-1$ and using the identities $\mathbf{x}^{k,0} = \mathbf{x}^k, \mathbf{x}^{k,m} = \mathbf{x}^{k+1}$, we obtain that for any $\mathbf{x}^* \in X^*$,

$$
\begin{aligned}
\|\mathbf{x}^{k+1} - \mathbf{x}^*\|^2 &\leq \|\mathbf{x}^k - \mathbf{x}^*\|^2 - 2t_k \sum_{i=0}^{m-1} \left(f_{i+1}(\mathbf{x}^{k,i}) - f_{i+1}(\mathbf{x}^*) \right) + t_k^2 m L^2 \\
&= \|\mathbf{x}^k - \mathbf{x}^*\|^2 - 2t_k \left(f(\mathbf{x}^k) - f_{\text{opt}} + \sum_{i=0}^{m-1} (f_{i+1}(\mathbf{x}^{k,i}) - f_{i+1}(\mathbf{x}^k)) \right) + t_k^2 m L^2 \\
&\leq \|\mathbf{x}^k - \mathbf{x}^*\|^2 - 2t_k(f(\mathbf{x}^k) - f_{\text{opt}}) + 2t_k \sum_{i=0}^{m-1} L \|\mathbf{x}^{k,i} - \mathbf{x}^k\| + t_k^2 m L^2, \tag{8.59}
\end{aligned}
$$

where in the last inequality we used the fact that by Assumptions 8.7 and 8.38, $C \subseteq \text{int}(\text{dom}(f)) \subseteq \text{int}(\text{dom}(f_{i+1}))$ and $\|\mathbf{g}\| \leq L$ for all $\mathbf{g} \in \partial f_{i+1}(\mathbf{x}), \mathbf{x} \in C$, and thus, by Theorem 3.61, f_{i+1} is Lipschitz with constant L over C.

Now, using the nonexpansivity of the orthogonal projection operator,

$$\|\mathbf{x}^{k,1} - \mathbf{x}^k\| = \|P_C(\mathbf{x}^{k,0} - t_k \mathbf{g}^{k,0}) - P_C(\mathbf{x}^k)\| \leq t_k \|\mathbf{g}^{k,0}\| \leq t_k L.$$

Similarly,

$$\|\mathbf{x}^{k,2} - \mathbf{x}^k\| = \|P_C(\mathbf{x}^{k,1} - t_k \mathbf{g}^{k,1}) - P_C(\mathbf{x}^k)\| \leq \|\mathbf{x}^{k,1} - \mathbf{x}^k\| + t_k \|\mathbf{g}^{k,1}\| \leq 2t_k L.$$

In general, for any $i = 0, 1, 2, \ldots, m-1$,

$$\|\mathbf{x}^{k,i} - \mathbf{x}^k\| \leq t_k i L,$$

and we can thus continue (8.59) and deduce that

$$
\begin{aligned}
\|\mathbf{x}^{k+1} - \mathbf{x}^*\|^2 &\leq \|\mathbf{x}^k - \mathbf{x}^*\|^2 - 2t_k(f(\mathbf{x}^k) - f_{\text{opt}}) + 2t_k^2 \sum_{i=0}^{m-1} i L^2 + t_k^2 m L^2 \\
&= \|\mathbf{x}^k - \mathbf{x}^*\|^2 - 2t_k(f(\mathbf{x}^k) - f_{\text{opt}}) + t_k^2 m^2 L^2. \qquad \square
\end{aligned}
$$

---

[45]The fundamental inequality for the incremental projected subgradient method is taken from Nedić and Bertsekas [89].

From this point, equipped with Lemma 8.39, we can use the same techniques used in the proofs of Theorems 8.25 and 8.30, for example, and establish the following result, whose proof is detailed here for the sake of completeness.

Theorem 8.40 (convergence of incremental projected subgradient). *Suppose that Assumptions 8.7 and 8.38 hold. Let $\{\mathbf{x}^k\}_{k\geq 0}$ be the sequence generated by the incremental projected subgradient method with positive stepsizes $\{t_k\}_{k\geq 0}$, and let $\{f_{\text{best}}^k\}_{k\geq 0}$ be the sequence of best achieved values defined in (8.11).*

(a) *If $\frac{\sum_{n=0}^{k} t_n^2}{\sum_{n=0}^{k} t_n} \to 0$ as $k \to \infty$, then $f_{\text{best}}^k \to f_{\text{opt}}$ as $k \to \infty$.*

(b) *Assume that C is compact. Let Θ be an upper bound on the half-squared diameter of C:*

$$\Theta \geq \max_{\mathbf{x},\mathbf{y}\in C} \frac{1}{2}\|\mathbf{x}-\mathbf{y}\|^2.$$

If $t_k = \frac{\sqrt{\Theta}}{Lm\sqrt{k+1}}$, then for all $k \geq 2$,

$$f_{\text{best}}^k - f_{\text{opt}} \leq \frac{\delta mL\sqrt{\Theta}}{\sqrt{k+2}},$$

where $\delta = 2(2+\log(3))$.

Proof. By Lemma 8.39, for any $n \geq 0$,

$$\|\mathbf{x}^{n+1}-\mathbf{x}^*\|^2 \leq \|\mathbf{x}^n-\mathbf{x}^*\|^2 - 2t_n(f(\mathbf{x}^n)-f_{\text{opt}}) + L^2m^2t_n^2. \qquad (8.60)$$

Summing (8.60) over $n = p, p+1, \ldots, k$, we obtain

$$\|\mathbf{x}^{k+1}-\mathbf{x}^*\|^2 \leq \|\mathbf{x}^p-\mathbf{x}^*\|^2 - 2\sum_{n=p}^{k} t_n(f(\mathbf{x}^n)-f_{\text{opt}}) + L^2m^2\sum_{n=p}^{k} t_n^2.$$

Therefore,

$$2\sum_{n=p}^{k} t_n(f(\mathbf{x}^n)-f_{\text{opt}}) \leq \|\mathbf{x}^p-\mathbf{x}^*\|^2 + L^2m^2\sum_{n=p}^{k} t_n^2,$$

and hence

$$f_{\text{best}}^k - f_{\text{opt}} \leq \frac{\|\mathbf{x}^p-\mathbf{x}^*\|^2 + L^2m^2\sum_{n=p}^{k} t_n^2}{2\sum_{n=p}^{k} t_n}. \qquad (8.61)$$

Plugging $p = 0$ into (8.61), we obtain

$$f_{\text{best}}^k - f_{\text{opt}} \leq \frac{\|\mathbf{x}^0-\mathbf{x}^*\|^2 + L^2m^2\sum_{n=0}^{k} t_n^2}{2\sum_{n=0}^{k} t_n}.$$

Therefore, if $\frac{\sum_{n=0}^{k} t_n^2}{\sum_{n=0}^{k} t_n} \to 0$ as $k \to \infty$, then $f_{\text{best}}^k \to f_{\text{opt}}$ as $k \to \infty$, proving claim (a). To show the validity of claim (b), use (8.61) with $p = \lceil k/2 \rceil$ to obtain

$$f_{\text{best}}^k - f_{\text{opt}} \leq \frac{2\Theta + L^2m^2\sum_{n=\lceil k/2 \rceil}^{k} t_n^2}{2\sum_{n=\lceil k/2 \rceil}^{k} t_n}.$$

Take $t_n = \frac{\sqrt{\Theta}}{Lm\sqrt{n+1}}$. Then we get

$$f_{\text{best}}^k - f_{\text{opt}} \leq \frac{Lm\sqrt{\Theta}}{2} \frac{2 + \sum_{n=\lceil k/2 \rceil}^{k} \frac{1}{n+1}}{\sum_{n=\lceil k/2 \rceil}^{k} \frac{1}{\sqrt{n+1}}},$$

which, combined with Lemma 8.27(b) (with $D = 2$), yields the desired result. □

8.5   The Dual Projected Subgradient Method

8.5.1   The Dual Problem

Consider the problem

$$\begin{aligned} f_{\text{opt}} = \quad &\min \quad f(\mathbf{x}) \\ &\text{s.t.} \quad \mathbf{g}(\mathbf{x}) \leq \mathbf{0}, \\ &\qquad \mathbf{x} \in X, \end{aligned} \tag{8.62}$$

where the following assumptions are made.

Assumption 8.41.

(A) $X \subseteq \mathbb{E}$ *is convex.*

(B) $f : \mathbb{E} \to \mathbb{R}$ *is convex.*

(C) $\mathbf{g}(\cdot) = (g_1(\cdot), g_2(\cdot), \dots, g_m(\cdot))^T$, *where* $g_1, g_2, \dots, g_m : \mathbb{E} \to \mathbb{R}$ *are convex.*

(D) *The problem has a finite optimal value denoted by* f_{opt}, *and the optimal set, denoted by* X^*, *is nonempty.*

(E) *There exists* $\bar{\mathbf{x}} \in X$ *for which* $\mathbf{g}(\bar{\mathbf{x}}) < \mathbf{0}$.

(F) *For any* $\boldsymbol{\lambda} \in \mathbb{R}_+^m$, *the problem* $\min_{\mathbf{x} \in X}\{f(\mathbf{x}) + \boldsymbol{\lambda}^T \mathbf{g}(\mathbf{x})\}$ *has an optimal solution.*

The Lagrangian dual objective function of problem (8.62) is given by

$$q(\boldsymbol{\lambda}) = \min_{\mathbf{x} \in X} \left\{ L(\mathbf{x}; \boldsymbol{\lambda}) \equiv f(\mathbf{x}) + \boldsymbol{\lambda}^T \mathbf{g}(\mathbf{x}) \right\}. \tag{8.63}$$

By Assumption 8.41(F), the minimization problem in (8.63) possesses a solution, and thus, in particular, $q(\boldsymbol{\lambda})$ is finite for any $\boldsymbol{\lambda} \in \mathbb{R}_+^m$. Recall that q is concave over $\mathbb{R}_+^m$ (as a minimum of affine and, in particular, concave functions), and hence the dual problem, which is given by

$$q_{\text{opt}} = \max\{q(\boldsymbol{\lambda}) : \boldsymbol{\lambda} \in \mathbb{R}_+^m\}, \tag{8.64}$$

is a convex problem, as it consists of maximizing a concave function over a convex set. We note that the dual problem is defined in the space $\mathbb{R}^m$, which we assume in this context to be endowed with the dot product and the l_2-norm.

By Theorem A.1 and Assumption 8.41, it follows that strong duality holds for the primal-dual pair of problems (8.62) and (8.64), namely,

$$f_{\text{opt}} = q_{\text{opt}}$$

and the optimal solution of the dual problem is attained. We will denote the optimal set of the dual problem as Λ^*.

An interesting property of the dual problem under the Slater-type assumption (part (E) of Assumption 8.41) is that its superlevel sets are bounded.

Theorem 8.42 (boundedness of superlevel sets of the dual objective function).[46] *Suppose that Assumption 8.41 holds. Let $\bar{\mathbf{x}} \in X$ be a point satisfying $\mathbf{g}(\bar{\mathbf{x}}) < 0$ whose existence is warranted by Assumption 8.41(E). Let $\mu \in \mathbb{R}$. Then for any $\boldsymbol{\lambda} \in S_\mu \equiv \{\boldsymbol{\lambda} \in \mathbb{R}_+^m : q(\boldsymbol{\lambda}) \geq \mu\}$,*

$$\|\boldsymbol{\lambda}\|_2 \leq \frac{f(\bar{\mathbf{x}}) - \mu}{\min_{j=1,2,\ldots,m}\{-g_j(\bar{\mathbf{x}})\}}.$$

Proof. Since $\boldsymbol{\lambda} \in S_\mu$, we have

$$\mu \leq q(\boldsymbol{\lambda}) \leq f(\bar{\mathbf{x}}) + \boldsymbol{\lambda}^T \mathbf{g}(\bar{\mathbf{x}}) = f(\bar{\mathbf{x}}) + \sum_{j=1}^m \lambda_j g_j(\bar{\mathbf{x}}).$$

Therefore,

$$-\sum_{j=1}^m \lambda_j g_j(\bar{\mathbf{x}}) \leq f(\bar{\mathbf{x}}) - \mu,$$

which, by the facts that $\lambda_j \geq 0$ and $g_j(\bar{\mathbf{x}}) < 0$ for all j, implies that

$$\sum_{j=1}^m \lambda_j \leq \frac{f(\bar{\mathbf{x}}) - \mu}{\min_{j=1,2,\ldots,m}\{-g_j(\bar{\mathbf{x}})\}}.$$

Finally, since $\boldsymbol{\lambda} \geq \mathbf{0}$, we have that $\|\boldsymbol{\lambda}\|_2 \leq \sum_{j=1}^m \lambda_j$, and the desired result is established. $\square$

Taking $\mu = f_{\text{opt}} = q_{\text{opt}}$, we have $S_\mu = \Lambda^*$, and Theorem 8.42 amounts to the following corollary describing a bound on the dual optimal set.

Corollary 8.43 (boundedness of the optimal dual set). *Suppose that Assumption 8.41 holds, and let Λ^* be the optimal set of the dual problem (8.64). Let $\bar{\mathbf{x}} \in X$ be a point satisfying $\mathbf{g}(\bar{\mathbf{x}}) < 0$ whose existence is warranted by Assumption 8.41(E). Then for any $\boldsymbol{\lambda} \in \Lambda^*$,*

$$\|\boldsymbol{\lambda}\|_2 \leq \frac{f(\bar{\mathbf{x}}) - f_{\text{opt}}}{\min_{j=1,2,\ldots,m}\{-g_j(\bar{\mathbf{x}})\}}.$$

---

[46]Theorem 8.42 is Lemma 1 from Nedić and Ozdaglar [90].

8.5.2   The Dual Projected Subgradient Method

We begin by recalling how to compute a subgradient of minus of the dual objective function. By Example 3.7, if for a given $\boldsymbol{\lambda} \in \mathbb{R}_+^m$ the minimum of the problem defining $q(\boldsymbol{\lambda})$ is attained at $\mathbf{x}_{\boldsymbol{\lambda}} \in X$, meaning if $q(\boldsymbol{\lambda}) = f(\mathbf{x}_{\boldsymbol{\lambda}}) + \boldsymbol{\lambda}^T \mathbf{g}(\mathbf{x}_{\boldsymbol{\lambda}})$, then $-\mathbf{g}(\mathbf{x}_{\boldsymbol{\lambda}}) \in \partial(-q)(\boldsymbol{\lambda})$.

Using the above expression for the subgradient of $-q$, we can define the projected subgradient method employed on the dual problem.

The Dual Projected Subgradient Method

Initialization: pick $\boldsymbol{\lambda}^0 \in \mathbb{R}_+^m$ arbitrarily.
General step: for any $k = 0, 1, 2, \ldots$ execute the following steps:

(a) pick a positive number γ_k;

(b) compute $\mathbf{x}^k \in \operatorname{argmin}_{\mathbf{x} \in X} \left\{ f(\mathbf{x}) + (\boldsymbol{\lambda}^k)^T \mathbf{g}(\mathbf{x}) \right\}$;

(c) if $\mathbf{g}(\mathbf{x}^k) = \mathbf{0}$, then **terminate** with an output $\mathbf{x}^k$; otherwise,

$$\boldsymbol{\lambda}^{k+1} = \left[\boldsymbol{\lambda}^k + \gamma_k \frac{\mathbf{g}(\mathbf{x}^k)}{\|\mathbf{g}(\mathbf{x}^k)\|_2} \right]_+.$$

The stepsize $\frac{\gamma_k}{\|\mathbf{g}(\mathbf{x}^k)\|_2}$ is similar in form to the normalized stepsizes considered in Section 8.2.4. The fact that the condition $\mathbf{g}(\mathbf{x}^k) = \mathbf{0}$ guarantees that $\mathbf{x}^k$ is an optimal solution of problem (8.62) is established in the following lemma.

Lemma 8.44. *Suppose that Assumption 8.41 holds. Let $\bar{\boldsymbol{\lambda}} \in \mathbb{R}_+^m$, and let $\bar{\mathbf{x}} \in X$ be such that*

$$\bar{\mathbf{x}} \in \operatorname{argmin}_{\mathbf{x} \in X} \left\{ f(\mathbf{x}) + \bar{\boldsymbol{\lambda}}^T \mathbf{g}(\mathbf{x}) \right\} \tag{8.65}$$

and $\mathbf{g}(\bar{\mathbf{x}}) = \mathbf{0}$. Then $\bar{\mathbf{x}}$ is an optimal solution of problem (8.62).

Proof. Let $\mathbf{x}$ be a feasible point of problem (8.62), meaning that $\mathbf{x} \in X$ and $\mathbf{g}(\mathbf{x}) \le \mathbf{0}$. Then

$$\begin{aligned} f(\mathbf{x}) &\ge f(\mathbf{x}) + \bar{\boldsymbol{\lambda}}^T \mathbf{g}(\mathbf{x}) && [\mathbf{g}(\mathbf{x}) \le \mathbf{0}, \bar{\boldsymbol{\lambda}} \ge \mathbf{0}] \\ &\ge f(\bar{\mathbf{x}}) + \bar{\boldsymbol{\lambda}}^T \mathbf{g}(\bar{\mathbf{x}}) && [(8.65)] \\ &= f(\bar{\mathbf{x}}), && [g(\bar{\mathbf{x}}) = \mathbf{0}] \end{aligned}$$

establishing the optimality of $\bar{\mathbf{x}}$. $\square$

8.5.3   Convergence Analysis

Proving convergence of the *dual* objective function sequence $\{q(\boldsymbol{\lambda}^k)\}_{k \ge 0}$ under various choices of the parameters $\{\gamma_k\}_{k \ge 0}$ is an easy task since such results were already proven in the previous sections. The more interesting question is whether we can prove convergence in some sense of a primal sequence. The answer is yes, but perhaps quite surprisingly the sequence $\{\mathbf{x}^k\}_{k \geq 0}$ is not the "correct" primal sequence. We will consider the following two possible definitions of the primal sequence that involve averaging of the sequence $\{\mathbf{x}^k\}_{k \geq 0}$.

- **Full averaging sequence.** In this option, we perform averaging of the entire history of iterates:

$$\mathbf{x}^{(k)} = \sum_{n=0}^{k} \mu_n^k \mathbf{x}^n \tag{8.66}$$

with μ_n^k defined by

$$\mu_n^k = \frac{\gamma_n / \|\mathbf{g}(\mathbf{x}^n)\|_2}{\sum_{j=0}^{k} \frac{\gamma_j}{\|\mathbf{g}(\mathbf{x}^j)\|_2}}, \quad n = 0, 1, \ldots, k. \tag{8.67}$$

- **Partial averaging sequence.** Here, at iteration k, we only perform averaging of iterations $\lceil k/2 \rceil, \lceil k/2 \rceil + 1, \ldots, k$:

$$\mathbf{x}^{\langle k \rangle} = \sum_{n=\lceil k/2 \rceil}^{k} \eta_n^k \mathbf{x}^n \tag{8.68}$$

with η_n^k defined by

$$\eta_n^k = \frac{\gamma_n / \|\mathbf{g}(\mathbf{x}^n)\|_2}{\sum_{j=\lceil k/2 \rceil}^{k} \frac{\gamma_j}{\|\mathbf{g}(\mathbf{x}^j)\|_2}}, \quad n = \lceil k/2 \rceil, \ldots, k. \tag{8.69}$$

Our underlying assumption will be that the method did not terminate, meaning that $\mathbf{g}(\mathbf{x}^k) \neq \mathbf{0}$ for any k.

Lemma 8.45. *Suppose that Assumption 8.41 holds, and assume further that there exists $L > 0$ such that $\|\mathbf{g}(\mathbf{x})\|_2 \leq L$ for any $\mathbf{x} \in X$. Let $\rho > 0$ be some positive number, and let $\{\mathbf{x}^k\}_{k \geq 0}$ and $\{\boldsymbol{\lambda}^k\}_{k \geq 0}$ be the sequences generated by the dual projected subgradient method. Then for any $k \geq 2$,*

$$f(\mathbf{x}^{(k)}) - f_{\text{opt}} + \rho\|[\mathbf{g}(\mathbf{x}^{(k)})]_+\|_2 \leq \frac{L}{2} \frac{(\|\boldsymbol{\lambda}^0\|_2 + \rho)^2 + \sum_{n=0}^{k} \gamma_n^2}{\sum_{n=0}^{k} \gamma_n} \tag{8.70}$$

and

$$f(\mathbf{x}^{\langle k \rangle}) - f_{\text{opt}} + \rho\|[\mathbf{g}(\mathbf{x}^{\langle k \rangle})]_+\|_2 \leq \frac{L}{2} \frac{(\|\boldsymbol{\lambda}^{\lceil k/2 \rceil}\|_2 + \rho)^2 + \sum_{n=\lceil k/2 \rceil}^{k} \gamma_n^2}{\sum_{n=\lceil k/2 \rceil}^{k} \gamma_n}, \tag{8.71}$$

where $\mathbf{x}^{(k)}$ and $\mathbf{x}^{\langle k \rangle}$ are given in (8.66) and (8.68), respectively.

Proof. Let $\bar{\boldsymbol{\lambda}} \in \mathbb{R}_+^m$. Then for every $n \geq 0$,

$$
\|\boldsymbol{\lambda}^{n+1} - \bar{\boldsymbol{\lambda}}\|_2^2 = \left\| \left[\boldsymbol{\lambda}^n + \gamma_n \frac{\mathbf{g}(\mathbf{x}^n)}{\|\mathbf{g}(\mathbf{x}^n)\|_2} \right]_+ - [\bar{\boldsymbol{\lambda}}]_+ \right\|_2^2
$$

$$
\leq \left\| \boldsymbol{\lambda}^n + \gamma_n \frac{\mathbf{g}(\mathbf{x}^n)}{\|\mathbf{g}(\mathbf{x}^n)\|_2} - \bar{\boldsymbol{\lambda}} \right\|_2^2
$$

$$
= \|\boldsymbol{\lambda}^n - \bar{\boldsymbol{\lambda}}\|_2^2 + \gamma_n^2 + \frac{2\gamma_n}{\|\mathbf{g}(\mathbf{x}^n)\|_2} \mathbf{g}(\mathbf{x}^n)^T (\boldsymbol{\lambda}^n - \bar{\boldsymbol{\lambda}}),
$$

where the inequality follows by the nonexpansivity of the orthogonal projection operator (Theorem 6.42(b)). Let $p \in \{0, 1, 2, \ldots, k\}$. Summing the above inequality for $n = p, p+1, \ldots, k$, we obtain that

$$
\|\boldsymbol{\lambda}^{k+1} - \bar{\boldsymbol{\lambda}}\|_2^2 \leq \|\boldsymbol{\lambda}^p - \bar{\boldsymbol{\lambda}}\|_2^2 + \sum_{n=p}^{k} \gamma_n^2 + 2 \sum_{n=p}^{k} \frac{\gamma_n}{\|\mathbf{g}(\mathbf{x}^n)\|_2} \mathbf{g}(\mathbf{x}^n)^T (\boldsymbol{\lambda}^n - \bar{\boldsymbol{\lambda}}).
$$

Therefore,

$$
2 \sum_{n=p}^{k} \frac{\gamma_n}{\|\mathbf{g}(\mathbf{x}^n)\|_2} \mathbf{g}(\mathbf{x}^n)^T (\bar{\boldsymbol{\lambda}} - \boldsymbol{\lambda}^n) \leq \|\boldsymbol{\lambda}^p - \bar{\boldsymbol{\lambda}}\|_2^2 + \sum_{n=p}^{k} \gamma_n^2. \tag{8.72}
$$

To facilitate the proof of the lemma, we will define for any $p \in \{0, 1, \ldots, k\}$

$$
\mathbf{x}^{k,p} \equiv \sum_{n=p}^{k} \alpha_n^{k,p} \mathbf{x}^n, \tag{8.73}
$$

where

$$
\alpha_n^{k,p} = \frac{\frac{\gamma_n}{\|\mathbf{g}(\mathbf{x}^n)\|_2}}{\sum_{j=p}^{k} \frac{\gamma_j}{\|\mathbf{g}(\mathbf{x}^j)\|_2}}.
$$

In particular, the sequences $\{\mathbf{x}^{k,0}\}_{k \geq 0}, \{\mathbf{x}^{k,\lceil k/2 \rceil}\}_{k \geq 0}$ are the same as the sequences $\{\mathbf{x}^{(k)}\}_{k \geq 0}$ and $\{\mathbf{x}^{\langle k \rangle}\}_{k \geq 0}$, respectively. Using the above definition of $\alpha_n^{k,p}$ and the fact that $\|\mathbf{g}(\mathbf{x}^n)\|_2 \leq L$, we conclude that (8.72) implies the following inequality:

$$
\sum_{n=p}^{k} \alpha_n^{k,p} \mathbf{g}(\mathbf{x}^n)^T (\bar{\boldsymbol{\lambda}} - \boldsymbol{\lambda}^n) \leq \frac{L}{2} \frac{\|\boldsymbol{\lambda}^p - \bar{\boldsymbol{\lambda}}\|_2^2 + \sum_{n=p}^{k} \gamma_n^2}{\sum_{n=p}^{k} \gamma_n}. \tag{8.74}
$$

By the definition of $\mathbf{x}^n$, we have for any $\mathbf{x}^* \in X^*$,

$$
f(\mathbf{x}^*) \geq f(\mathbf{x}^*) + (\boldsymbol{\lambda}^n)^T \mathbf{g}(\mathbf{x}^*) \qquad [\boldsymbol{\lambda}^n \geq \mathbf{0}, \mathbf{g}(\mathbf{x}^*) \leq \mathbf{0}]
$$

$$
\geq f(\mathbf{x}^n) + (\boldsymbol{\lambda}^n)^T \mathbf{g}(\mathbf{x}^n). \qquad [\mathbf{x}^n \in \operatorname{argmin}_{\mathbf{x} \in X} \{f(\mathbf{x}) + (\boldsymbol{\lambda}^n)^T \mathbf{g}(\mathbf{x})\}]
$$

Thus,

$$
-(\boldsymbol{\lambda}^n)^T \mathbf{g}(\mathbf{x}^n) \geq f(\mathbf{x}^n) - f_{\text{opt}},
$$

and hence

$$\sum_{n=p}^{k} \alpha_n^{k,p} \mathbf{g}(\mathbf{x}^n)^T (\bar{\boldsymbol{\lambda}} - \boldsymbol{\lambda}^n) \geq \sum_{n=p}^{k} \alpha_n^{k,p} \mathbf{g}(\mathbf{x}^n)^T \bar{\boldsymbol{\lambda}} + \sum_{n=p}^{k} \alpha_n^{k,p} f(\mathbf{x}^n) - \sum_{n=p}^{k} \alpha_n^{k,p} f_{\text{opt}}$$

$$\geq \bar{\boldsymbol{\lambda}}^T \mathbf{g}\left(\mathbf{x}^{k,p}\right) + f\left(\mathbf{x}^{k,p}\right) - f_{\text{opt}}, \tag{8.75}$$

where the last inequality follows by Jensen's inequality (recalling that f and the components of $\mathbf{g}$ are convex) and the definition (8.73) of $\mathbf{x}^{k,p}$. Combining (8.74) and (8.75), while using the obvious inequality $\|\boldsymbol{\lambda}^p - \bar{\boldsymbol{\lambda}}\|_2 \leq \|\boldsymbol{\lambda}^p\|_2 + \|\bar{\boldsymbol{\lambda}}\|_2$, we obtain

$$f(\mathbf{x}^{k,p}) - f_{\text{opt}} + \bar{\boldsymbol{\lambda}}^T \mathbf{g}(\mathbf{x}^{k,p}) \leq \frac{L}{2} \frac{\left(\|\boldsymbol{\lambda}^p\|_2 + \|\bar{\boldsymbol{\lambda}}\|_2\right)^2 + \sum_{n=p}^{k} \gamma_n^2}{\sum_{n=p}^{k} \gamma_n}. \tag{8.76}$$

Plugging

$$\bar{\boldsymbol{\lambda}} = \begin{cases} \rho \frac{[\mathbf{g}(\mathbf{x}^{k,p})]_+}{\|[\mathbf{g}(\mathbf{x}^{k,p})]_+\|_2}, & [\mathbf{g}(\mathbf{x}^{k,p})]_+ \neq \mathbf{0}, \\ \mathbf{0}, & [\mathbf{g}(\mathbf{x}^{k,p})]_+ = \mathbf{0} \end{cases}$$

into (8.76), we obtain the inequality

$$f(\mathbf{x}^{k,p}) - f_{\text{opt}} + \rho \|[\mathbf{g}(\mathbf{x}^{k,p})]_+\|_2 \leq \frac{L}{2} \frac{\left(\|\boldsymbol{\lambda}^p\|_2 + \rho\right)^2 + \sum_{n=p}^{k} \gamma_n^2}{\sum_{n=p}^{k} \gamma_n}. \tag{8.77}$$

Substituting $p = 0$ and $p = \lceil k/2 \rceil$ in (8.77) yields the inequalities (8.70) and (8.71), respectively. $\quad\square$

Analysis of the Full Averaging Scheme

We begin by developing a convergence rate related to the sequence $\{\mathbf{x}^{(k)}\}_{k \geq 0}$ given by (8.66). Similarly to the analysis for the primal projected subgradient method, choosing $\gamma_k = \frac{1}{\sqrt{k+1}}$ will imply that the right-hand side of (8.70) will converge to zero. In principle, the fact that the left-hand side of (8.70) converges to zero does not necessarily imply that both the expression for the distance to optimality in function values $f(\mathbf{x}^{(k)}) - f_{\text{opt}}$ and the expression for the constraints violation $\|[\mathbf{g}(\mathbf{x}^{(k)})]_+\|_2$ converge to zero. However, using Theorem 3.60, we can show the convergence of these terms as long as ρ is chosen appropriately.

Theorem 8.46 ($O(\log(k)/\sqrt{k})$ rate of convergence of the full averaging sequence). *Suppose that Assumption 8.41 holds, and assume further that there exists $L > 0$ for which $\|\mathbf{g}(\mathbf{x})\|_2 \leq L$ for any $\mathbf{x} \in X$. Let $\{\mathbf{x}^k\}_{k \geq 0}$, and let $\{\boldsymbol{\lambda}^k\}_{k \geq 0}$ be the sequences generated by the dual projected subgradient method with $\gamma_k = \frac{1}{\sqrt{k+1}}$. Then for any $k \geq 1$,*

$$f(\mathbf{x}^{(k)}) - f_{\text{opt}} \leq \frac{L}{2} \frac{\left(\|\boldsymbol{\lambda}^0\|_2 + 2\alpha\right)^2 + 1 + \log(k+1)}{\sqrt{k+1}}, \tag{8.78}$$

$$\|[\mathbf{g}(\mathbf{x}^{(k)})]_+\|_2 \leq \frac{L}{2\alpha} \frac{\left(\|\boldsymbol{\lambda}^0\|_2 + 2\alpha\right)^2 + 1 + \log(k+1)}{\sqrt{k+1}}, \tag{8.79}$$

where $\{\mathbf{x}^{(k)}\}_{k\geq 0}$ is given in (8.66) and

$$\alpha = \frac{f(\bar{\mathbf{x}}) - f_{\text{opt}}}{\min_{j=1,2,\dots,m}\{-g_j(\bar{\mathbf{x}})\}},$$

with $\bar{\mathbf{x}}$ being a Slater point whose existence is guaranteed by Assumption 8.41(E).

Proof. Employing Lemma 8.45 with $\rho = 2\alpha$, and substituting $\gamma_n = \frac{1}{\sqrt{n+1}}$, we have

$$f(\mathbf{x}^{(k)}) - f_{\text{opt}} + 2\alpha\|[\mathbf{g}(\mathbf{x}^{(k)})]_+\|_2 \leq \frac{L}{2}\frac{(\|\boldsymbol{\lambda}^0\|_2 + 2\alpha)^2 + \sum_{n=0}^{k}\frac{1}{n+1}}{\sum_{n=0}^{k}\frac{1}{\sqrt{n+1}}}. \tag{8.80}$$

Using Lemma 8.27(a), we have

$$\frac{(\|\boldsymbol{\lambda}^0\|_2 + 2\alpha)^2 + \sum_{n=0}^{k}\frac{1}{n+1}}{\sum_{n=0}^{k}\frac{1}{\sqrt{n+1}}} \leq \frac{(\|\boldsymbol{\lambda}^0\|_2 + 2\alpha)^2 + 1 + \log(k+1)}{\sqrt{k+1}},$$

which, combined with (8.80), yields the inequality

$$f(\mathbf{x}^{(k)}) - f_{\text{opt}} + 2\alpha\|[\mathbf{g}(\mathbf{x}^{(k)})]_+\|_2 \leq \frac{L}{2}\frac{(\|\boldsymbol{\lambda}^0\|_2 + 2\alpha)^2 + 1 + \log(k+1)}{\sqrt{k+1}}. \tag{8.81}$$

Since by Corollary 8.43, 2α is an upper bound on twice the l_2-norm of any dual optimal solution, it follows by Theorem 3.60 that the inequality (8.81) implies the two inequalities (8.78) and (8.79). $\quad\square$

Analysis of the Partial Averaging Scheme

We will now show an $O(1/\sqrt{k})$ rate of convergence in terms of function values as well as constraint violation of the partial averaging sequence given in (8.68). The proof is similar to the proof of Theorem 8.46 and utilizes inequality (8.71) but in addition utilizes the boundedness of the sequence of dual variables—a fact established in the next lemma.

Lemma 8.47.[47] *Suppose that Assumption 8.41 holds and assume further that there exists $L > 0$ for which $\|\mathbf{g}(\mathbf{x})\|_2 \leq L$ for any $\mathbf{x} \in X$. Let $\{\mathbf{x}^k\}_{k\geq 0}$ and $\{\boldsymbol{\lambda}^k\}_{k\geq 0}$ be the sequences generated by the dual projected subgradient method with positive stepsizes γ_k satisfying $\gamma_k \leq \gamma_0$ for all $k \geq 0$. Then*

$$\|\boldsymbol{\lambda}^k\|_2 \leq M, \tag{8.82}$$

where[48]

$$M = \left\{\|\boldsymbol{\lambda}^0\|_2 + 2\alpha, \frac{f(\bar{\mathbf{x}}) - q_{\text{opt}}}{\beta} + \frac{\gamma_0 L}{2\beta} + 2\alpha + \gamma_0\right\}, \tag{8.83}$$

---

[47] Lemma 8.47 is Lemma 3 from Nedić and Ozdaglar [90].
[48] Recall that in our setting $q_{\text{opt}} = f_{\text{opt}}$.

with

$$\alpha = \frac{f(\bar{\mathbf{x}}) - f_{\text{opt}}}{\min_{j=1,2,\ldots,m}\{-g_j(\bar{\mathbf{x}})\}}, \qquad \beta = \min_{j=1,2,\ldots,m}\{-g_j(\bar{\mathbf{x}})\},$$

where $\bar{\mathbf{x}}$ is a Slater point of problem (8.62) whose existence is guaranteed by Assumption 8.41(E).

Proof. Let $\boldsymbol{\lambda}^*$ be an optimal solution of the dual problem (8.64). We begin by showing by induction on k that for any $k \geq 0$,

$$\|\boldsymbol{\lambda}^k - \boldsymbol{\lambda}^*\|_2 \leq \max\left\{\|\boldsymbol{\lambda}^0 - \boldsymbol{\lambda}^*\|_2, \frac{f(\bar{\mathbf{x}}) - q_{\text{opt}}}{\beta} + \frac{\gamma_0 L}{2\beta} + \|\boldsymbol{\lambda}^*\|_2 + \gamma_0\right\}. \qquad (8.84)$$

The inequality holds trivially for $k = 0$. Assume that it holds for k, and we will show that it holds for $k + 1$. We will consider two cases.

Case I. Assume that $q(\boldsymbol{\lambda}^k) \geq q_{\text{opt}} - \frac{\gamma_k L}{2}$. Then, by Theorem 8.42,

$$\|\boldsymbol{\lambda}^k\|_2 \leq \frac{f(\bar{\mathbf{x}}) - q_{\text{opt}} + \frac{\gamma_k L}{2}}{\beta},$$

where $\beta = \min_{i=1,2,\ldots,m}\{-g_i(\bar{\mathbf{x}})\}$. Therefore,

$$\begin{aligned}
\|\boldsymbol{\lambda}^{k+1} - \boldsymbol{\lambda}^*\|_2 &\leq \left\|\boldsymbol{\lambda}^k + \frac{\gamma_k}{\|\mathbf{g}(\mathbf{x}^k)\|_2}\mathbf{g}(\mathbf{x}^k) - \boldsymbol{\lambda}^*\right\|_2 \\
&\leq \|\boldsymbol{\lambda}^k\|_2 + \|\boldsymbol{\lambda}^*\|_2 + \gamma_k \\
&\leq \frac{f(\bar{\mathbf{x}}) - q_{\text{opt}}}{\beta} + \frac{\gamma_k L}{2\beta} + \|\boldsymbol{\lambda}^*\|_2 + \gamma_k \\
&\leq \frac{f(\bar{\mathbf{x}}) - q_{\text{opt}}}{\beta} + \frac{\gamma_0 L}{2\beta} + \|\boldsymbol{\lambda}^*\|_2 + \gamma_0.
\end{aligned}$$

Case II. Now assume that $q(\boldsymbol{\lambda}^k) < q_{\text{opt}} - \frac{\gamma_k L}{2}$. In this case we can write

$$\begin{aligned}
\|\boldsymbol{\lambda}^{k+1} - \boldsymbol{\lambda}^*\|_2^2 &= \left\|\left[\boldsymbol{\lambda}^k + \frac{\gamma_k}{\|\mathbf{g}(\mathbf{x}^k)\|_2}\mathbf{g}(\mathbf{x}^k)\right]_+ - \boldsymbol{\lambda}^*\right\|_2^2 \\
&\leq \left\|\boldsymbol{\lambda}^k - \boldsymbol{\lambda}^* + \frac{\gamma_k}{\|\mathbf{g}(\mathbf{x}^k)\|_2}\mathbf{g}(\mathbf{x}^k)\right\|_2^2 \\
&= \|\boldsymbol{\lambda}^k - \boldsymbol{\lambda}^*\|_2^2 + 2\frac{\gamma_k}{\|\mathbf{g}(\mathbf{x}^k)\|_2}(\boldsymbol{\lambda}^k - \boldsymbol{\lambda}^*)^T\mathbf{g}(\mathbf{x}^k) + \gamma_k^2. \qquad (8.85)
\end{aligned}$$

Since $-\mathbf{g}(\mathbf{x}^k) \in \partial(-q)(\boldsymbol{\lambda}^k)$ (Example 3.7), it follows by the subgradient inequality that

$$-q_{\text{opt}} \geq -q(\boldsymbol{\lambda}^k) - \mathbf{g}(\mathbf{x}^k)^T(\boldsymbol{\lambda}^* - \boldsymbol{\lambda}^k).$$

Therefore, continuing (8.85),

$$\|\boldsymbol{\lambda}^{k+1} - \boldsymbol{\lambda}^*\|^2 \leq \|\boldsymbol{\lambda}^k - \boldsymbol{\lambda}^*\|_2^2 + 2\frac{\gamma_k}{\|\mathbf{g}(\mathbf{x}^k)\|_2}(q(\boldsymbol{\lambda}^k) - q_{\text{opt}}) + \gamma_k^2$$

$$\leq \|\boldsymbol{\lambda}^k - \boldsymbol{\lambda}^*\|_2^2 + 2\frac{\gamma_k}{L}(q(\boldsymbol{\lambda}^k) - q_{\text{opt}}) + \gamma_k^2$$

$$= \|\boldsymbol{\lambda}^k - \boldsymbol{\lambda}^*\|_2^2 + 2\frac{\gamma_k}{L}\left(q(\boldsymbol{\lambda}^k) - q_{\text{opt}} + \frac{\gamma_k L}{2}\right)$$

$$< \|\boldsymbol{\lambda}^k - \boldsymbol{\lambda}^*\|_2^2,$$

where in the last inequality we used our assumption that $q(\boldsymbol{\lambda}^k) < q_{\text{opt}} - \frac{\gamma_k L}{2}$. We can now use the induction hypothesis and conclude that

$$\|\boldsymbol{\lambda}^{k+1} - \boldsymbol{\lambda}^*\|_2 \leq \max\left\{\|\boldsymbol{\lambda}^0 - \boldsymbol{\lambda}^*\|_2, \frac{f(\bar{\mathbf{x}}) - q_{\text{opt}}}{\beta} + \frac{\gamma_0 L}{2\beta} + \|\boldsymbol{\lambda}^*\|_2 + \gamma_0\right\}.$$

We have thus established the validity of (8.84) for all $k \geq 0$. The result (8.82) now follows by recalling that by Corollary 8.43, $\|\boldsymbol{\lambda}^*\|_2 \leq \alpha$, and hence

$$\|\boldsymbol{\lambda}^k\|_2 \leq \|\boldsymbol{\lambda}^k - \boldsymbol{\lambda}^*\|_2 + \|\boldsymbol{\lambda}^*\|_2$$

$$\leq \max\left\{\|\boldsymbol{\lambda}^0 - \boldsymbol{\lambda}^*\|_2, \frac{f(\bar{\mathbf{x}}) - q_{\text{opt}}}{\beta} + \frac{\gamma_0 L}{2\beta} + \|\boldsymbol{\lambda}^*\|_2 + \gamma_0\right\} + \|\boldsymbol{\lambda}^*\|_2$$

$$\leq \max\left\{\|\boldsymbol{\lambda}^0\|_2 + 2\alpha, \frac{f(\bar{\mathbf{x}}) - q_{\text{opt}}}{\beta} + \frac{\gamma_0 L}{2\beta} + 2\alpha + \gamma_0\right\}. \quad \square$$

Equipped with the upper bound on the sequence of dual variables, we can prove, using a similar argument to the one used in the proof of Theorem 8.46, an $O(1/\sqrt{k})$ rate of convergence related to the partial averaging sequence generated by the dual projected subgradient method.

Theorem 8.48 ($O(1/\sqrt{k})$ rate of convergence of the partial averaging sequence). *Suppose that Assumption 8.41 holds, and assume further that there exists $L > 0$ for which $\|\mathbf{g}(\mathbf{x})\|_2 \leq L$ for any $\mathbf{x} \in X$. Let $\{\mathbf{x}^k\}_{k\geq 0}$, and let $\{\boldsymbol{\lambda}^k\}_{k\geq 0}$ be the sequences generated by the dual projected subgradient method with $\gamma_k = \frac{1}{\sqrt{k+1}}$. Then for any $k \geq 2$,*

$$f(\mathbf{x}^{\langle k \rangle}) - f_{\text{opt}} \leq \frac{2L((M + 2\alpha)^2 + \log(3))}{\sqrt{k+2}}, \tag{8.86}$$

$$\|[\mathbf{g}(\mathbf{x}^{\langle k \rangle})]_+\|_2 \leq \frac{2L((M + 2\alpha)^2 + \log(3))}{\alpha\sqrt{k+2}}, \tag{8.87}$$

where $\{\mathbf{x}^{\langle k \rangle}\}_{k\geq 0}$ is given in (8.68), M in (8.83), and

$$\alpha = \frac{f(\bar{\mathbf{x}}) - f_{\text{opt}}}{\min_{j=1,2,\ldots,m}\{-g_j(\bar{\mathbf{x}})\}}$$

with $\bar{\mathbf{x}}$ being a Slater point whose existence is guaranteed by Assumption 8.41(E).

Proof. Employing Lemma 8.45 with $\rho = 2\alpha$, and substituting $\gamma_n = \frac{1}{\sqrt{n+1}}$, we have

$$f(\mathbf{x}^{\langle k \rangle}) - f_{\text{opt}} + 2\alpha \|[\mathbf{g}(\mathbf{x}^{\langle k \rangle})]_+\|_2 \le \frac{L}{2} \frac{(\|\boldsymbol{\lambda}^{\lceil k/2 \rceil}\|_2 + 2\alpha)^2 + \sum_{n=\lceil k/2 \rceil}^{k} \frac{1}{n+1}}{\sum_{n=\lceil k/2 \rceil}^{k} \frac{1}{\sqrt{n+1}}}$$

$$\le \frac{L}{2} \frac{(M + 2\alpha)^2 + \sum_{n=\lceil k/2 \rceil}^{k} \frac{1}{n+1}}{\sum_{n=\lceil k/2 \rceil}^{k} \frac{1}{\sqrt{n+1}}}, \qquad (8.88)$$

where in the last inequality we used the bound on the dual iterates given in Lemma 8.47. Now, using Lemma 8.27(b), we have

$$\frac{(M + 2\alpha)^2 + \sum_{n=\lceil k/2 \rceil}^{k} \frac{1}{n+1}}{\sum_{n=\lceil k/2 \rceil}^{k} \frac{1}{\sqrt{n+1}}} \le \frac{4((M + 2\alpha)^2 + \log(3))}{\sqrt{k+2}},$$

which, combined with (8.88), yields the inequality

$$f(\mathbf{x}^{\langle k \rangle}) - f_{\text{opt}} + 2\alpha \|[\mathbf{g}(\mathbf{x}^{\langle k \rangle})]_+\|_2 \le \frac{2L((M + 2\alpha)^2 + \log(3))}{\sqrt{k+2}}. \qquad (8.89)$$

Since, by Corollary 8.43, 2α is an upper bound on twice the l_2-norm of any dual optimal solution, it follows by Theorem 3.60 that the inequality (8.89) implies the two inequalities (8.86) and (8.87). $\square$

To derive a complexity result for the dual projected subgradient method, we should first note that the primal sequence is not feasible, as it does not necessarily satisfy the inequality constraints $\mathbf{g}(\mathbf{x}) \le \mathbf{0}$. Therefore, there is no point in asking how many iterations are required to obtain an ε-optimal solution. Instead, we will consider the related concept of an ε-optimal and feasible solution. A vector $\mathbf{x} \in X$ is called an *ε-optimal and feasible solution* of problem (8.62) if $f(\mathbf{x}) - f_{\text{opt}} \le \varepsilon$ and $\|[\mathbf{g}(\mathbf{x})]_+\|_2 \le \varepsilon$. Theorem 8.48 immediately implies a complexity result stating that an order of $\frac{1}{\varepsilon^2}$ iterations are required to obtain an ε-optimal and feasible solution.

Corollary 8.49 ($O(1/\varepsilon^2)$ complexity result for the dual projected subgradient method). *Under the setting of Theorem 8.48, if $k \ge 2$ satisfies*

$$k \ge \frac{4L^2((M + 2\alpha)^2 + \log(3))^2}{\min\{\alpha^2, 1\}\varepsilon^2} - 2,$$

then

$$f(\mathbf{x}^{\langle k \rangle}) - f_{\text{opt}} \le \varepsilon,$$
$$\|[\mathbf{g}(\mathbf{x}^{\langle k \rangle})]_+\|_2 \le \varepsilon.$$

Example 8.50 (linear programming example). Consider the linear programming problem

$$\min \quad \mathbf{c}^T \mathbf{x}$$

$$(\text{LP}) \quad \text{s.t.} \quad \mathbf{A}\mathbf{x} \le \mathbf{b},$$

$$\mathbf{x} \in \Delta_n,$$

where $\mathbf{c} \in \mathbb{R}^n, \mathbf{A} \in \mathbb{R}^{m \times n}$, and $\mathbf{b} \in \mathbb{R}^m$. We will consider the dual projected subgradient method when the underlying set X is Δ_n and $\mathbf{g}(\mathbf{x}) \equiv \mathbf{A}\mathbf{x} - \mathbf{b}$. The vector $\mathbf{x}^k$ is calculated by the update rule $\mathbf{x}^k \in \operatorname{argmin}_{\mathbf{x} \in \Delta_n}(\mathbf{c} + \mathbf{A}^T \boldsymbol{\lambda}^k)^T \mathbf{x}$. It is easy to see that an optimal solution of this subproblem is given by $\mathbf{e}_i$, where i is an index for which $(\mathbf{c} + \mathbf{A}^T \boldsymbol{\lambda}^k)_i$ is minimal. Therefore, the algorithm (with $\gamma_k = \frac{1}{\sqrt{k+1}}$) takes the following form:

Dual Projected Subgradient for solving (LP)

- **Initialization:** pick $\boldsymbol{\lambda}^0 \in \mathbb{R}_+^m$.

- **General step ($k \geq 0$):**

$$i_k \in \operatorname{argmin}_{i=1,2,\ldots,n} v_i; \quad \mathbf{v} = \mathbf{c} + \mathbf{A}^T \boldsymbol{\lambda}^k,$$

$$\mathbf{x}^k = \mathbf{e}_{i_k},$$

$$\boldsymbol{\lambda}^{k+1} = \left[\boldsymbol{\lambda}^k + \frac{1}{\sqrt{k+1}} \frac{\mathbf{A}\mathbf{x}^k - \mathbf{b}}{\|\mathbf{A}\mathbf{x}^k - \mathbf{b}\|_2}\right]_+.$$

Note that we make the implicit assumption that $\mathbf{A}\mathbf{x}^k \neq \mathbf{b}$. The above description of the dual projected subgradient method illustrates the fact that the sequence $\{\mathbf{x}^k\}_{k \geq 0}$ is not the "correct" primal sequence. Indeed, in this case, the vectors $\mathbf{x}^k$ are always unit vectors, and there is no particular reason why the solution of (LP) should be attained at a unit vector. As a specific example, consider the problem

$$
\begin{aligned}
\min \quad & x_1 + 3x_2 + 2x_3 \\
\text{s.t.} \quad & 3x_1 + 2x_2 - x_3 \leq 1, \\
& -2x_3 \leq 2, \\
& x_1 + x_2 + x_3 = 1, \\
& x_1, x_2, x_3 \geq 0,
\end{aligned}
\tag{8.90}
$$

which fits problem (LP) with

$$
\mathbf{A} = \begin{pmatrix} 3 & 2 & -1 \\ 0 & 0 & -2 \end{pmatrix}, \quad \mathbf{b} = \begin{pmatrix} 1 \\ 2 \end{pmatrix}, \quad \mathbf{c} = \begin{pmatrix} 1 \\ 3 \\ 2 \end{pmatrix}.
$$

The optimal solution of problem (8.90) is $(\frac{1}{2}, 0, \frac{1}{2})$. We employed the dual projected subgradient method as described above with $\boldsymbol{\lambda}^0 = \mathbf{0}$ and compared the behavior of the full and partial averaging schemes during the first 100 iterations. The results are described in Figure 8.4. Obviously, the partial averaging scheme exhibits superior behavior compared to the full averaging scheme. ∎

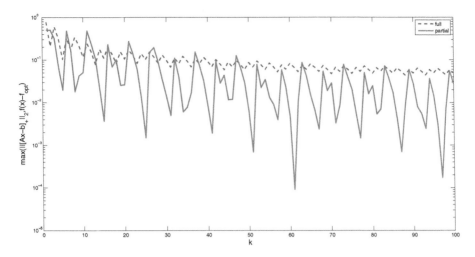

Figure 8.4. *First* 100 *iterations of the dual projected subgradient method employed on problem (8.90). The y-axis describes (in log scale) the quantities* $\max\{f(\mathbf{x}^{(k)}) - f_{\mathrm{opt}}, \|[\mathbf{A}\mathbf{x}^{(k)} - \mathbf{b}]_+\|_2\}$ *and* $\max\{f(\mathbf{x}^{\langle k \rangle}) - f_{\mathrm{opt}}, \|[\mathbf{A}\mathbf{x}^{(k)} - \mathbf{b}]_+\|_2\}$.

8.5.4 Example—Network Utility Maximization

Consider a network that consists of a set $\mathcal{S} = \{1, 2, \ldots, S\}$ of sources and a set $\mathcal{L} = \{1, 2, \ldots, L\}$ of links, where a link ℓ has a capacity c_ℓ. For each source $s \in \mathcal{S}$, we denote by $\mathcal{L}(s) \subseteq \mathcal{L}$ the set of all links used by source s. Similarly, for a given link $\ell \in \mathcal{L}$, the set $\mathcal{S}(\ell) \subseteq \mathcal{S}$ comprises all sources that use link ℓ. In particular, for a pair $\ell \in \mathcal{L}$ and $s \in \mathcal{S}$, the relation $s \in \mathcal{S}(\ell)$ holds if and only if $\ell \in \mathcal{L}(s)$. Each source $s \in \mathcal{S}$ is associated with a concave utility function $u_s : \mathbb{R} \to \mathbb{R}$, meaning that if source s sends data at a rate x_s, it gains a utility $u_s(x_s)$. We also assume that the rate of source s is constrained to be in the interval $I_s = [0, M_s]$, where $M_s \in \mathbb{R}_{++}$. The goal of the network utility maximization problem (abbreviated NUM) is to allocate the source rates as the optimal solution of the following convex problem:

$$
\begin{aligned}
\max \quad & \sum_{s \in \mathcal{S}} u_s(x_s) \\
\text{s.t.} \quad & \sum_{s \in \mathcal{S}(\ell)} x_s \leq c_\ell, \quad \ell \in \mathcal{L}, \\
& x_s \in I_s, \quad s \in \mathcal{S}.
\end{aligned}
\tag{8.91}
$$

Problem (8.91) in its minimization form is a convex problem and fits the main model (8.62) with

$$
\begin{aligned}
\mathbf{g}(\mathbf{x}) &= \left(\sum_{s \in \mathcal{S}(\ell)} x_s - c_\ell \right)_{\ell = 1, 2, \ldots, L}, \\
X &= I_1 \times I_2 \times \cdots \times I_S, \\
f(\mathbf{x}) &= -\sum_{s=1}^{S} u_s(x_s).
\end{aligned}
$$

At iteration k, the vector $\mathbf{x}^k$ is picked as an optimal solution of the problem $\min_{\mathbf{x} \in X}\{f(\mathbf{x}) + (\boldsymbol{\lambda}^k)^T \mathbf{g}(\mathbf{x})\}$, meaning

$$\mathbf{x}^k \in \operatorname{argmin}_{\mathbf{x} \in X}\left\{f(\mathbf{x}) + (\boldsymbol{\lambda}^k)^T \mathbf{g}(\mathbf{x})\right\}$$

$$= \operatorname{argmin}_{\mathbf{x} \in X}\left\{-\sum_{s=1}^{S} u_s(x_s) + \sum_{\ell=1}^{L} \lambda_\ell^k \left[\sum_{s \in \mathcal{S}(\ell)} x_s - c_\ell\right]\right\}$$

$$= \operatorname{argmin}_{\mathbf{x} \in X}\left\{-\sum_{s=1}^{S} u_s(x_s) + \sum_{\ell=1}^{L} \sum_{s \in \mathcal{S}(\ell)} \lambda_\ell^k x_s\right\}$$

$$= \operatorname{argmin}_{\mathbf{x} \in X}\left\{-\sum_{s=1}^{S} u_s(x_s) + \sum_{s=1}^{S} \left[\sum_{\ell \in \mathcal{L}(s)} \lambda_\ell^k\right] x_s\right\}.$$

The above minimization problem is separable w.r.t. the decision variables $x_1, x_2, \ldots,$ x_S. Therefore, the sth element of $\mathbf{x}^k$ can be chosen via the update rule (returning to the max form),

$$x_s^k \in \operatorname{argmax}_{x_s \in I_s}\left\{u_s(x_s) - \left[\sum_{\ell \in \mathcal{L}(s)} \lambda_\ell^k\right] x_s\right\}.$$

The dual projected subgradient method employed on problem (8.91) with stepsizes α_k and initialization $\boldsymbol{\lambda}^0 = \mathbf{0}$ therefore takes the form below. Note that we do not consider here a normalized stepsize (actually, in many practical scenarios, a constant stepsize is used).

Dual Projected Subgradient Method for Solving the NUM Problem (8.91)

Initialization: define $\lambda_\ell^0 = 0$ for all $\ell \in \mathcal{L}$.

(A) **Source-rate update:**

$$x_s^k = \operatorname{argmax}_{x_s \in I_s}\left\{u_s(x_s) - \left[\sum_{\ell \in \mathcal{L}(s)} \lambda_\ell^k\right] x_s\right\}, \qquad s \in \mathcal{S}. \qquad (8.92)$$

(B) **Link-price update:**

$$\lambda_\ell^{k+1} = \left[\lambda_\ell^k + \alpha_k \left(\sum_{s \in \mathcal{S}(\ell)} x_s^k - c_\ell\right)\right]_+, \qquad \ell \in \mathcal{L}.$$

The multipliers λ_ℓ^k can actually be seen as prices that are associated with the links. The algorithm above can be implemented in a distributed manner in the following sense:

(a) Each source s needs to solve the optimization problem (8.92) involving only its own utility function u_s and the multipliers (i.e., prices) associated with the links that it uses, meaning $\lambda_\ell^k, \ell \in \mathcal{L}(s)$.

(b) The price (i.e., multiplier) at each link ℓ is updated according to the rates of the sources that use the link ℓ, meaning $x_s, s \in \mathcal{S}(\ell)$.

Therefore, the algorithm only requires *local* communication between sources and links and can be implemented in a decentralized manner by letting both the sources and the links cooperatively seek an optimal solution of the problem by following the source-rate/price-link update scheme described above. This is one example of a *distributed optimization* method.

Chapter 9

Mirror Descent

This chapter is devoted to the study of the mirror descent method and some of its variations. The method is essentially a generalization of the projected subgradient method to the non-Euclidean setting. Therefore, naturally, we will *not* assume in the chapter that the underlying space is Euclidean.

9.1   From Projected Subgradient to Mirror Descent

Consider the optimization problem

$$(P) \quad \min\{f(\mathbf{x}) : \mathbf{x} \in C\}, \tag{9.1}$$

where we assume the following.[49]

Assumption 9.1.

(A) $f : \mathbb{E} \to (-\infty, \infty]$ *is proper closed and convex.*

(B) $C \subseteq \mathbb{E}$ *is nonempty closed and convex.*

(C) $C \subseteq \operatorname{int}(\operatorname{dom}(f))$.

(D) *The optimal set of* (P) *is nonempty and denoted by* X^*. *The optimal value of the problem is denoted by* f_{opt}.

The projected subgradient method for solving problem (P) was studied in Chapter 8. One of the basic assumptions made in Chapter 8, which was used throughout the analysis, is that the underlying space is Euclidean, meaning that $\| \cdot \| = \sqrt{\langle \cdot, \cdot \rangle}$. Recall that the general update step of the projected subgradient method has the form

$$\mathbf{x}^{k+1} = P_C(\mathbf{x}^k - t_k f'(\mathbf{x}^k)), \quad f'(\mathbf{x}^k) \in \partial f(\mathbf{x}^k), \tag{9.2}$$

for an appropriately chosen stepsize t_k. When the space is non-Euclidean, there is actually a "philosophical" problem with the update rule (9.2)—the vectors $\mathbf{x}^k$ and

---

[49] Assumption 9.1 is the same as Assumption 8.7 from Chapter 8.

$f'(\mathbf{x}^k)$ are in different spaces; one is in $\mathbb{E}$, while the other in $\mathbb{E}^*$. This issue is of course not really problematic since we can use our convention that the vectors in $\mathbb{E}$ and $\mathbb{E}^*$ are the same, and the only difference is in the norm associated with each of the spaces. Nonetheless, this issue is one of the motivations for seeking generalizations of the projected subgradient method better suited to the non-Euclidean setting.

To understand the role of the Euclidean norm in the definition of the projected subgradient method, we will consider the following reformulation of the update step (9.2):

$$\mathbf{x}^{k+1} = \operatorname{argmin}_{\mathbf{x} \in C} \left\{ f(\mathbf{x}^k) + \langle f'(\mathbf{x}^k), \mathbf{x} - \mathbf{x}^k \rangle + \frac{1}{2t_k} \|\mathbf{x} - \mathbf{x}^k\|^2 \right\}, \qquad (9.3)$$

which actually shows that $\mathbf{x}^{k+1}$ is constructed by minimizing a linearization of the objective function plus a quadratic proximity term. The equivalence between the two forms (9.2) and (9.3) in the Euclidean case is evident by the following identity:

$$f(\mathbf{x}^k) + \langle f'(\mathbf{x}^k), \mathbf{x} - \mathbf{x}^k \rangle + \frac{1}{2t_k} \|\mathbf{x} - \mathbf{x}^k\|^2 = \frac{1}{2t_k} \left\|\mathbf{x} - \left[\mathbf{x}^k - t_k f'(\mathbf{x}^k)\right]\right\|^2 + D,$$

where D is a constant (i.e., does not depend on $\mathbf{x}$).

Coming back to the non-Euclidean case, the idea will be to replace the Euclidean "distance" function $\frac{1}{2}\|\mathbf{x} - \mathbf{y}\|^2$ in (9.3) by a different distance, which is not based on the Euclidean norm. The non-Euclidean distances that we will use are *Bregman distances*.

Definition 9.2 (Bregman distance).   *Let $\omega : \mathbb{E} \to (-\infty, \infty]$ be a proper closed and convex function that is differentiable over $\operatorname{dom}(\partial \omega)$. The **Bregman distance** associated with ω is the function $B_\omega : \operatorname{dom}(\omega) \times \operatorname{dom}(\partial \omega) \to \mathbb{R}$ given by*

$$B_\omega(\mathbf{x}, \mathbf{y}) = \omega(\mathbf{x}) - \omega(\mathbf{y}) - \langle \nabla \omega(\mathbf{y}), \mathbf{x} - \mathbf{y} \rangle.$$

The assumptions on ω (given a set C) are gathered in the following.

Assumption 9.3 (properties of ω).

- ω *is proper closed and convex.*

- ω *is differentiable over* $\operatorname{dom}(\partial \omega)$.

- $C \subseteq \operatorname{dom}(\omega)$.

- $\omega + \delta_C$ *is σ-strongly convex ($\sigma > 0$).*

A Bregman distance is actually not necessarily a distance. It is nonnegative and equal to zero if and only if its two arguments coincide, but other than that, in general it is not symmetric and does not satisfy the triangle inequality. The properties of Bregman distances that do hold are summarized in the following lemma.

Lemma 9.4 (basic properties of Bregman distances). *Suppose that $C \subseteq \mathbb{E}$ is nonempty closed and convex and that ω satisfies the properties in Assumption 9.3. Let B_ω be the Bregman distance associated with ω. Then*

(a) $B_\omega(\mathbf{x}, \mathbf{y}) \geq \frac{\sigma}{2}\|\mathbf{x} - \mathbf{y}\|^2$ *for all* $\mathbf{x} \in C, \mathbf{y} \in C \cap \mathrm{dom}(\partial\omega)$.

(b) *Let* $\mathbf{x} \in C$ *and* $\mathbf{y} \in C \cap \mathrm{dom}(\partial\omega)$. *Then*

    – $B_\omega(\mathbf{x}, \mathbf{y}) \geq 0$;

    – $B_\omega(\mathbf{x}, \mathbf{y}) = 0$ *if and only if* $\mathbf{x} = \mathbf{y}$.

Proof. Part (a) follows by the first-order characterization of strongly convex functions described in Theorem 5.24(ii). Part (b) is a direct consequence of part (a). $\square$

Assume that $\mathbf{x}^k \in C \cap \mathrm{dom}(\partial\omega)$. Replacing the term $\frac{1}{2}\|\mathbf{x} - \mathbf{x}^k\|^2$ in formula (9.3) by a Bregman distance $B_\omega(\mathbf{x}, \mathbf{x}^k)$ leads to the following update step:

$$\mathbf{x}^{k+1} = \mathrm{argmin}_{\mathbf{x} \in C} \left\{ f(\mathbf{x}^k) + \langle f'(\mathbf{x}^k), \mathbf{x} - \mathbf{x}^k \rangle + \frac{1}{t_k} B_\omega(\mathbf{x}, \mathbf{x}^k) \right\}. \qquad (9.4)$$

Omitting constant terms, (9.4) becomes

$$\mathbf{x}^{k+1} = \mathrm{argmin}_{\mathbf{x} \in C} \left\{ \langle f'(\mathbf{x}^k), \mathbf{x} \rangle + \frac{1}{t_k} B_\omega(\mathbf{x}, \mathbf{x}^k) \right\}. \qquad (9.5)$$

Further simplification of the update formula can be achieved by noting the following simple identity:

$$\langle f'(\mathbf{x}^k), \mathbf{x} \rangle + \frac{1}{t_k} B_\omega(\mathbf{x}, \mathbf{x}^k)$$

$$= \frac{1}{t_k} \left[\langle t_k f'(\mathbf{x}^k) - \nabla\omega(\mathbf{x}^k), \mathbf{x} \rangle + \omega(\mathbf{x}) \right] \underbrace{- \frac{1}{t_k}\omega(\mathbf{x}^k) + \frac{1}{t_k}\langle \nabla\omega(\mathbf{x}^k), \mathbf{x}^k \rangle}_{\text{constant}}.$$

Therefore, the update formula in its most simplified form reads as

$$\mathbf{x}^{k+1} = \mathrm{argmin}_{\mathbf{x} \in C} \left\{ \langle t_k f'(\mathbf{x}^k) - \nabla\omega(\mathbf{x}^k), \mathbf{x} \rangle + \omega(\mathbf{x}) \right\}.$$

We are now ready to define the mirror descent method.

The Mirror Descent Method

Initialization: pick $\mathbf{x}^0 \in C \cap \mathrm{dom}(\partial\omega)$.
General step: for any $k = 0, 1, 2, \ldots$ execute the following steps:

(a) pick a stepsize $t_k > 0$ and a subgradient $f'(\mathbf{x}^k) \in \partial f(\mathbf{x}^k)$;

(b) set
$$\mathbf{x}^{k+1} = \mathrm{argmin}_{\mathbf{x} \in C} \left\{ \langle t_k f'(\mathbf{x}^k) - \nabla\omega(\mathbf{x}^k), \mathbf{x} \rangle + \omega(\mathbf{x}) \right\}. \qquad (9.6)$$

Remark 9.5. *Although (9.6) is the most simplified form of the update step of the mirror descent method, the formula (9.5), which can also be written as*

$$\mathbf{x}^{k+1} = \mathrm{argmin}_{\mathbf{x}\in C}\left\{\langle t_k f'(\mathbf{x}^k),\mathbf{x}\rangle + B_\omega(\mathbf{x},\mathbf{x}^k)\right\}, \tag{9.7}$$

will also prove itself to be useful.

Remark 9.6. *Defining $\tilde{\omega} = \omega + \delta_C$, we can write the step (9.6) as*

$$\mathbf{x}^{k+1} = \mathrm{argmin}_{\mathbf{x}\in\mathbb{E}}\left\{\langle t_k f'(\mathbf{x}^k) - \nabla\omega(\mathbf{x}^k),\mathbf{x}\rangle + \tilde{\omega}(\mathbf{x})\right\}. \tag{9.8}$$

Since $\nabla\omega(\mathbf{x}^k) \in \partial\tilde{\omega}(\mathbf{x}^k)$, we can write it as $\tilde{\omega}'(\mathbf{x}^k)$, so (9.8) becomes

$$\mathbf{x}^{k+1} = \mathrm{argmin}_{\mathbf{x}\in\mathbb{E}}\left\{\langle t_k f'(\mathbf{x}^k) - \tilde{\omega}'(\mathbf{x}^k),\mathbf{x}\rangle + \tilde{\omega}(\mathbf{x})\right\}. \tag{9.9}$$

Finally, by the conjugate correspondence theorem (Theorem 5.26), whose assumptions hold (properness, closedness, and strong convexity of $\tilde{\omega}$), $\tilde{\omega}^*$ is differentiable, which, combined with the conjugate subgradient theorem (Corollary 4.21), yields that (9.9) is equivalent to the following known formula for the mirror descent method:

$$\mathbf{x}^{k+1} = \nabla\tilde{\omega}^*(\tilde{\omega}'(\mathbf{x}^k) - t_k f'(\mathbf{x}^k)).$$

The basic step of the mirror descent method (9.6) is of the form

$$\min_{\mathbf{x}\in C}\left\{\langle \mathbf{a},\mathbf{x}\rangle + \omega(\mathbf{x})\right\} \tag{9.10}$$

for some $\mathbf{a} \in \mathbb{E}^*$. To show that the method is well defined, Theorem 9.8 below establishes the fact that the minimum of problem (9.10) is uniquely attained at a point in $C \cap \mathrm{dom}(\partial\omega)$. The reason why it is important to show that the minimizer is in $\mathrm{dom}(\partial\omega)$ is that the method requires computing the gradient of ω at the new iterate vector (recall that ω is assumed to be differentiable over $\mathrm{dom}(\partial\omega)$). We will prove a more general lemma that will also be useful in other contexts.

Lemma 9.7. *Assume the following:*

- *$\omega : \mathbb{E} \to (-\infty,\infty]$ is a proper closed and convex function differentiable over $\mathrm{dom}(\partial\omega)$.*

- *$\psi : \mathbb{E} \to (-\infty,\infty]$ is a proper closed and convex function satisfying $\mathrm{dom}(\psi) \subseteq \mathrm{dom}(\omega)$.*

- *$\omega + \delta_{\mathrm{dom}(\psi)}$ is σ-strongly convex ($\sigma > 0$).*

Then the minimizer of the problem

$$\min_{\mathbf{x}\in\mathbb{E}}\left\{\psi(\mathbf{x}) + \omega(\mathbf{x})\right\} \tag{9.11}$$

is uniquely attained at a point in $\mathrm{dom}(\psi) \cap \mathrm{dom}(\partial\omega)$.

Proof. Problem (9.11) is the same as

$$\min_{\mathbf{x}\in\mathbb{E}}\varphi(\mathbf{x}), \tag{9.12}$$

where $\varphi = \psi + \omega$. The function φ is closed since both ψ and ω are closed; it is proper by the fact that $\text{dom}(\varphi) = \text{dom}(\psi) \neq \emptyset$. Since $\omega + \delta_{\text{dom}(\psi)}$ is σ-strongly convex and ψ is convex, their sum $\psi + \omega + \delta_{\text{dom}(\psi)} = \psi + \omega = \varphi$ is σ-strongly convex. To conclude, φ is proper closed and σ-strongly convex, and hence, by Theorem 5.25(a), problem (9.12) has a unique minimizer $\mathbf{x}^*$ in $\text{dom}(\varphi) = \text{dom}(\psi)$. To show that $\mathbf{x}^* \in \text{dom}(\partial \omega)$, note that by Fermat's optimality condition (Theorem 3.63), $\mathbf{0} \in \partial \varphi(\mathbf{x}^*)$, and in particular $\partial \varphi(\mathbf{x}^*) \neq \emptyset$. Therefore, since by the sum rule of subdifferential calculus (Theorem 3.40), $\partial \varphi(\mathbf{x}^*) = \partial \psi(\mathbf{x}^*) + \partial \omega(\mathbf{x}^*)$, it follows in particular that $\partial \omega(\mathbf{x}^*) \neq \emptyset$, meaning that $\mathbf{x}^* \in \text{dom}(\partial \omega)$. $\square$

The fact that the mirror descent method is well defined can now be easily deduced.

Theorem 9.8 (mirror descent is well defined). *Suppose that Assumptions 9.1 and 9.3 hold. Let $\mathbf{a} \in \mathbb{E}^*$. Then the problem*

$$\min_{\mathbf{x} \in C} \{\langle \mathbf{a}, \mathbf{x} \rangle + \omega(\mathbf{x})\}$$

has a unique minimizer in $C \cap \text{dom}(\partial \omega)$.

Proof. The proof follows by invoking Lemma 9.7 with $\psi(\mathbf{x}) \equiv \langle \mathbf{a}, \mathbf{x} \rangle + \delta_C(\mathbf{x})$. $\square$

Two very common choices of strongly convex functions are described below.

Example 9.9 (squared Euclidean norm). Suppose that Assumption 9.1 holds and that $\mathbb{E}$ is Euclidean, meaning that its norm satisfies $\|\cdot\| = \sqrt{\langle \cdot, \cdot \rangle}$. Define

$$\omega(\mathbf{x}) = \frac{1}{2}\|\mathbf{x}\|^2.$$

Then ω obviously satisfies the properties listed in Assumption 9.3—it is proper closed and 1-strongly convex. Since $\nabla \omega(\mathbf{x}) = \mathbf{x}$, then the general update step of the mirror descent method reads as

$$\mathbf{x}^{k+1} = \text{argmin}_{\mathbf{x} \in C} \left\{ \langle t_k f'(\mathbf{x}^k) - \mathbf{x}^k, \mathbf{x} \rangle + \frac{1}{2}\|\mathbf{x}\|^2 \right\},$$

which is the same as the projected subgradient update step: $\mathbf{x}^{k+1} = P_C(\mathbf{x}^k - t_k f'(\mathbf{x}^k))$. This is of course not a surprise since the method was constructed as a generalization of the projected subgradient method. ∎

Example 9.10 (negative entropy over the unit simplex). Suppose that Assumption 9.1 holds with $\mathbb{E} = \mathbb{R}^n$ endowed with the l_1-norm and $C = \Delta_n$. We will take ω to be the negative entropy over the nonnegative orthant:

$$\omega(\mathbf{x}) = \begin{cases} \sum_{i=1}^n x_i \log x_i, & \mathbf{x} \in \mathbb{R}^n_+, \\ \infty & \text{else.} \end{cases}$$

As usual, we use the convention that $0 \log 0 = 0$. By Example 5.27, $\omega + \delta_{\Delta_n}$ is 1-strongly convex w.r.t. the l_1-norm. In this case,

$$\text{dom}(\partial \omega) = \mathbb{R}^n_{++},$$

on which ω is indeed differentiable. Thus, all the properties of Assumption 9.3 hold. The associated Bregman distance is given for any $\mathbf{x} \in \Delta_n$ and $\mathbf{y} \in \Delta_n^+ \equiv \{\mathbf{x} \in \mathbb{R}_{++}^n : \mathbf{e}^T \mathbf{x} = 1\}$ by

$$
\begin{aligned}
B_\omega(\mathbf{x}, \mathbf{y}) &= \sum_{i=1}^n x_i \log x_i - \sum_{i=1}^n y_i \log y_i - \sum_{i=1}^n (\log(y_i) + 1)(x_i - y_i) \\
&= \sum_{i=1}^n x_i \log(x_i/y_i) + \sum_{i=1}^n y_i - \sum_{i=1}^n x_i \\
&= \sum_{i=1}^n x_i \log(x_i/y_i),
\end{aligned}
\tag{9.13}
$$

which is the so-called Kullback-Leibler divergence distance measure. The general update step of the mirror descent method has the form ($f_i'(\mathbf{x}^k)$ is the ith component of $f'(\mathbf{x}^k)$),

$$
\mathbf{x}^{k+1} = \text{argmin}_{\mathbf{x} \in \Delta_n} \left\{ \sum_{i=1}^n (t_k f_i'(\mathbf{x}^k) - 1 - \log(x_i^k)) x_i + \sum_{i=1}^n x_i \log x_i \right\}. \tag{9.14}
$$

By Example 3.71, the optimal solution of problem (9.14) is

$$
x_i^{k+1} = \frac{e^{\log(x_i^k) + 1 - t_k f_i'(\mathbf{x}^k)}}{\sum_{j=1}^n e^{\log(x_j^k) + 1 - t_k f_j'(\mathbf{x}^k)}}, \quad i = 1, 2, \ldots, n,
$$

which can be simplified into the following:

$$
x_i^{k+1} = \frac{x_i^k e^{-t_k f_i'(\mathbf{x}^k)}}{\sum_{j=1}^n x_j^k e^{-t_k f_j'(\mathbf{x}^k)}}, \quad i = 1, 2, \ldots, n. \quad \blacksquare
$$

The natural question that arises is how to choose the stepsizes. The convergence analysis that will be developed in the next section will reveal some possible answers to this question.

9.2   Convergence Analysis

9.2.1   The Toolbox

The following identity, also known as the *three-points lemma*, is essential in the analysis of the mirror descent lemma.

Lemma 9.11 (three-points lemma).[50] *Suppose that $\omega : \mathbb{E} \to (-\infty, \infty]$ is proper closed and convex. Suppose in addition that ω is differentiable over $\text{dom}(\partial \omega)$. Assume that $\mathbf{a}, \mathbf{b} \in \text{dom}(\partial \omega)$ and $\mathbf{c} \in \text{dom}(\omega)$. Then the following equality holds:*

$$
\langle \nabla \omega(\mathbf{b}) - \nabla \omega(\mathbf{a}), \mathbf{c} - \mathbf{a} \rangle = B_\omega(\mathbf{c}, \mathbf{a}) + B_\omega(\mathbf{a}, \mathbf{b}) - B_\omega(\mathbf{c}, \mathbf{b}).
$$

---

[50]The three-points lemma was proven by Chen and Teboulle in [43].

Proof. By definition of B_ω,

$$B_\omega(\mathbf{c}, \mathbf{a}) = \omega(\mathbf{c}) - \omega(\mathbf{a}) - \langle \nabla\omega(\mathbf{a}), \mathbf{c} - \mathbf{a} \rangle,$$
$$B_\omega(\mathbf{a}, \mathbf{b}) = \omega(\mathbf{a}) - \omega(\mathbf{b}) - \langle \nabla\omega(\mathbf{b}), \mathbf{a} - \mathbf{b} \rangle,$$
$$B_\omega(\mathbf{c}, \mathbf{b}) = \omega(\mathbf{c}) - \omega(\mathbf{b}) - \langle \nabla\omega(\mathbf{b}), \mathbf{c} - \mathbf{b} \rangle.$$

Hence,

$$B_\omega(\mathbf{c}, \mathbf{a}) + B_\omega(\mathbf{a}, \mathbf{b}) - B_\omega(\mathbf{c}, \mathbf{b}) = -\langle \nabla\omega(\mathbf{a}), \mathbf{c} - \mathbf{a} \rangle - \langle \nabla\omega(\mathbf{b}), \mathbf{a} - \mathbf{b} \rangle + \langle \nabla\omega(\mathbf{b}), \mathbf{c} - \mathbf{b} \rangle$$
$$= \langle \nabla\omega(\mathbf{b}) - \nabla\omega(\mathbf{a}), \mathbf{c} - \mathbf{a} \rangle. \quad \square$$

Another key lemma is an extension of the second prox theorem (Theorem 6.39) to the case of non-Euclidean distances.

Theorem 9.12 (non-Euclidean second prox theorem). *Let*

- $\omega : \mathbb{E} \to (-\infty, \infty]$ *be a proper closed and convex function differentiable over* $\mathrm{dom}(\partial\omega)$;

- $\psi : \mathbb{E} \to (-\infty, \infty]$ *be a proper closed and convex function satisfying* $\mathrm{dom}(\psi) \subseteq \mathrm{dom}(\omega)$;

- $\omega + \delta_{\mathrm{dom}(\psi)}$ *be σ-strongly convex ($\sigma > 0$).*

Assume that $\mathbf{b} \in \mathrm{dom}(\partial\omega)$, *and let* $\mathbf{a}$ *be defined by*

$$\mathbf{a} = \mathrm{argmin}_{\mathbf{x} \in \mathbb{E}} \{\psi(\mathbf{x}) + B_\omega(\mathbf{x}, \mathbf{b})\}. \tag{9.15}$$

Then $\mathbf{a} \in \mathrm{dom}(\partial\omega)$ *and for all* $\mathbf{u} \in \mathrm{dom}(\psi)$,

$$\langle \nabla\omega(\mathbf{b}) - \nabla\omega(\mathbf{a}), \mathbf{u} - \mathbf{a} \rangle \leq \psi(\mathbf{u}) - \psi(\mathbf{a}). \tag{9.16}$$

Proof. Using the definition of B_ω, (9.15) can be rewritten as

$$\mathbf{a} = \mathrm{argmin}_{\mathbf{x} \in \mathbb{E}} \{\psi(\mathbf{x}) - \langle \nabla\omega(\mathbf{b}), \mathbf{x} \rangle + \omega(\mathbf{x})\}. \tag{9.17}$$

The fact that $\mathbf{a} \in \mathrm{dom}(\partial\omega)$ follows by invoking Lemma 9.7 with $\psi(\mathbf{x}) - \langle \nabla\omega(\mathbf{b}), \mathbf{x} \rangle$ taking the role of $\psi(\mathbf{x})$. Using Fermat's optimality condition (Theorem 3.63), it follows by (9.17) that there exists $\psi'(\mathbf{a}) \in \partial\psi(\mathbf{a})$ for which

$$\psi'(\mathbf{a}) + \nabla\omega(\mathbf{a}) - \nabla\omega(\mathbf{b}) = \mathbf{0}.$$

Hence, by the subgradient inequality, for any $\mathbf{u} \in \mathrm{dom}(\psi)$,

$$\langle \nabla\omega(\mathbf{b}) - \nabla\omega(\mathbf{a}), \mathbf{u} - \mathbf{a} \rangle = \langle \psi'(\mathbf{a}), \mathbf{u} - \mathbf{a} \rangle \leq \psi(\mathbf{u}) - \psi(\mathbf{a}),$$

proving the desired result. $\quad \square$

Using the non-Euclidean second prox theorem and the three-points lemma, we can now establish a fundamental inequality satisfied by the sequence generated by the mirror descent method. The inequality can be seen as a generalization of Lemma 8.11.

Lemma 9.13 (fundamental inequality for mirror descent). *Suppose that Assumptions* 9.1 *and* 9.3 *hold. Let* $\{\mathbf{x}^k\}_{k\geq 0}$ *be the sequence generated by the mirror descent method with positive stepsizes* $\{t_k\}_{k\geq 0}$. *Then for any* $\mathbf{x}^* \in X^*$ *and* $k \geq 0$,

$$t_k(f(\mathbf{x}^k) - f_{\text{opt}}) \leq B_\omega(\mathbf{x}^*, \mathbf{x}^k) - B_\omega(\mathbf{x}^*, \mathbf{x}^{k+1}) + \frac{t_k^2}{2\sigma}\|f'(\mathbf{x}^k)\|_*^2.$$

Proof. By the update formula (9.7) for $\mathbf{x}^{k+1}$ and the non-Euclidean second prox theorem (Theorem 9.12) invoked with $\mathbf{b} = \mathbf{x}^k$ and $\psi(\mathbf{x}) \equiv t_k\langle f'(\mathbf{x}^k), \mathbf{x}\rangle + \delta_C(\mathbf{x})$ (and hence $\mathbf{a} = \mathbf{x}^{k+1}$), we have for any $\mathbf{u} \in C$,

$$\langle \nabla\omega(\mathbf{x}^k) - \nabla\omega(\mathbf{x}^{k+1}), \mathbf{u} - \mathbf{x}^{k+1}\rangle \leq t_k\langle f'(\mathbf{x}^k), \mathbf{u} - \mathbf{x}^{k+1}\rangle. \tag{9.18}$$

By the three-points lemma (with $\mathbf{a} = \mathbf{x}^{k+1}, \mathbf{b} = \mathbf{x}^k$, and $\mathbf{c} = \mathbf{u}$),

$$\langle \nabla\omega(\mathbf{x}^k) - \nabla\omega(\mathbf{x}^{k+1}), \mathbf{u} - \mathbf{x}^{k+1}\rangle = B_\omega(\mathbf{u}, \mathbf{x}^{k+1}) + B_\omega(\mathbf{x}^{k+1}, \mathbf{x}^k) - B_\omega(\mathbf{u}, \mathbf{x}^k),$$

which, combined with (9.18), gives

$$B_\omega(\mathbf{u}, \mathbf{x}^{k+1}) + B_\omega(\mathbf{x}^{k+1}, \mathbf{x}^k) - B_\omega(\mathbf{u}, \mathbf{x}^k) \leq t_k\langle f'(\mathbf{x}^k), \mathbf{u} - \mathbf{x}^{k+1}\rangle.$$

Therefore,

$$\begin{aligned}
&t_k\langle f'(\mathbf{x}^k), \mathbf{x}^k - \mathbf{u}\rangle \\
&\leq B_\omega(\mathbf{u}, \mathbf{x}^k) - B_\omega(\mathbf{u}, \mathbf{x}^{k+1}) - B_\omega(\mathbf{x}^{k+1}, \mathbf{x}^k) + t_k\langle f'(\mathbf{x}^k), \mathbf{x}^k - \mathbf{x}^{k+1}\rangle \\
&\overset{(*)}{\leq} B_\omega(\mathbf{u}, \mathbf{x}^k) - B_\omega(\mathbf{u}, \mathbf{x}^{k+1}) - \frac{\sigma}{2}\|\mathbf{x}^{k+1} - \mathbf{x}^k\|^2 + t_k\langle f'(\mathbf{x}^k), \mathbf{x}^k - \mathbf{x}^{k+1}\rangle \\
&= B_\omega(\mathbf{u}, \mathbf{x}^k) - B_\omega(\mathbf{u}, \mathbf{x}^{k+1}) - \frac{\sigma}{2}\|\mathbf{x}^{k+1} - \mathbf{x}^k\|^2 + \left\langle \frac{t_k}{\sqrt{\sigma}}f'(\mathbf{x}^k), \sqrt{\sigma}(\mathbf{x}^k - \mathbf{x}^{k+1})\right\rangle \\
&\overset{(**)}{\leq} B_\omega(\mathbf{u}, \mathbf{x}^k) - B_\omega(\mathbf{u}, \mathbf{x}^{k+1}) - \frac{\sigma}{2}\|\mathbf{x}^{k+1} - \mathbf{x}^k\|^2 + \frac{t_k^2}{2\sigma}\|f'(\mathbf{x}^k)\|_*^2 + \frac{\sigma}{2}\|\mathbf{x}^{k+1} - \mathbf{x}^k\|^2 \\
&= B_\omega(\mathbf{u}, \mathbf{x}^k) - B_\omega(\mathbf{u}, \mathbf{x}^{k+1}) + \frac{t_k^2}{2\sigma}\|f'(\mathbf{x}^k)\|_*^2,
\end{aligned}$$

where the inequality $(*)$ follows by Lemma 9.4(a) and $(**)$ by Fenchel's inequality (Theorem 4.6) employed on the function $\frac{1}{2}\|\mathbf{x}\|^2$ (whose conjugate is $\frac{1}{2}\|\mathbf{y}\|_*^2$—see Section 4.4.15). Plugging in $\mathbf{u} = \mathbf{x}^*$ and using the subgradient inequality, we obtain

$$t_k(f(\mathbf{x}^k) - f_{\text{opt}}) \leq B_\omega(\mathbf{x}^*, \mathbf{x}^k) - B_\omega(\mathbf{x}^*, \mathbf{x}^{k+1}) + \frac{t_k^2}{2\sigma}\|f'(\mathbf{x}^k)\|_*^2. \qquad \square$$

Under a boundedness assumption on $B_\omega(\mathbf{x}, \mathbf{x}^0)$ over C, we can deduce a useful bound on the sequence of best achieved function values defined by

$$f_{\text{best}}^k \equiv \min_{n=0,1,\ldots,k} f(\mathbf{x}^n). \tag{9.19}$$

Lemma 9.14. *Suppose that Assumptions 9.1 and 9.3 hold and that $\|f'(\mathbf{x})\|_* \leq L_f$ for all $\mathbf{x} \in C$, where $L_f > 0$. Suppose that $B_\omega(\mathbf{x}, \mathbf{x}^0)$ is bounded over C, and let $\Theta(\mathbf{x}^0)$ satisfy*

$$\Theta(\mathbf{x}^0) \geq \max_{\mathbf{x} \in C} B_\omega(\mathbf{x}, \mathbf{x}^0).$$

Let $\{\mathbf{x}^k\}_{k \geq 0}$ be the sequence generated by the mirror descent method with positive stepsizes $\{t_k\}_{k \geq 0}$. Then for any $N \geq 0$,

$$f_{\text{best}}^N - f_{\text{opt}} \leq \frac{\Theta(\mathbf{x}^0) + \frac{L_f^2}{2\sigma} \sum_{k=0}^N t_k^2}{\sum_{k=0}^N t_k}, \tag{9.20}$$

where f_{best}^N is defined in (9.19).

Proof. Let $\mathbf{x}^* \in X^*$. By Lemma 9.13 it follows that for any $k \geq 0$,

$$t_k(f(\mathbf{x}^k) - f_{\text{opt}}) \leq B_\omega(\mathbf{x}^*, \mathbf{x}^k) - B_\omega(\mathbf{x}^*, \mathbf{x}^{k+1}) + \frac{t_k^2}{2\sigma}\|f'(\mathbf{x}^k)\|_*^2. \tag{9.21}$$

Summing (9.21) over $k = 0, 1, \ldots, N$, we obtain

$$\sum_{k=0}^N t_k(f(\mathbf{x}^k) - f_{\text{opt}}) \leq B_\omega(\mathbf{x}^*, \mathbf{x}^0) - B_\omega(\mathbf{x}^*, \mathbf{x}^{N+1}) + \sum_{k=0}^N \frac{t_k^2}{2\sigma}\|f'(\mathbf{x}^k)\|_*^2$$

$$= \Theta(\mathbf{x}^0) + \frac{L_f^2}{2\sigma} \sum_{k=0}^N t_k^2,$$

which, combined with the inequality $(\sum_{k=0}^n t_k)(f_{\text{best}}^N - f_{\text{opt}}) \leq \sum_{k=0}^N t_k(f(\mathbf{x}^k) - f_{\text{opt}})$, yields the result (9.20). $\square$

9.2.2 Fixed Number of Iterations

Let us begin by fixing the number of iterations N and deduce what the "optimal" stepsizes are in the sense that they bring the right-hand side of (9.20) to a minimum. For that, we will prove the following technical lemma.

Lemma 9.15. *The optimal solution of the problem*

$$\min_{t_1, \ldots, t_m > 0} \frac{\alpha + \beta \sum_{k=1}^m t_k^2}{\sum_{k=1}^m t_k}, \tag{9.22}$$

where $\alpha, \beta > 0$, is given by $t_k = \sqrt{\frac{\alpha}{\beta m}}$, $k = 1, 2, \ldots, m$. The optimal value is $2\sqrt{\frac{\alpha\beta}{m}}$.

Proof. Denote the objective function of (9.22) by

$$\phi(\mathbf{t}) \equiv \frac{\alpha + \beta \sum_{k=1}^m t_k^2}{\sum_{k=1}^m t_k}.$$

Note that ϕ is a permutation symmetric function, meaning that $\phi(\mathbf{t}) = \phi(\mathbf{Pt})$ for any permutation matrix $\mathbf{P} \in \Lambda_m$ (see Definition 7.5). A consequence of this observation is that if problem (9.22) has an optimal solution, then it necessarily has an optimal solution in which all the variables are the same. To show this, take an arbitrary optimal solution $\mathbf{t}^*$ and a permutation matrix $\mathbf{P} \in \Lambda_m$. Since $\phi(\mathbf{Pt}^*) = \phi(\mathbf{t}^*)$, it follows that $\mathbf{Pt}^*$ is also an optimal solution of (9.22). Therefore, since ϕ is convex over the positive orthant,[51] it follows that

$$\frac{1}{m!} \sum_{\mathbf{P} \in \Lambda_m} \mathbf{Pt}^* = \frac{1}{m} \begin{pmatrix} \mathbf{e}^T \mathbf{t} \\ \vdots \\ \mathbf{e}^T \mathbf{t} \end{pmatrix}$$

is also an optimal solution, showing that there always exists an optimal solution with equal components. Problem (9.22) therefore reduces to (after substituting $t_1 = t_2 = \cdots = t_m = t$)

$$\min_{t > 0} \frac{\alpha + \beta m t^2}{mt},$$

whose optimal solution is $t = \sqrt{\frac{\alpha}{\beta m}}$, and thus an optimal solution of problem (9.22) is given by $t_k = \sqrt{\frac{\alpha}{\beta m}}$, $k = 1, 2, \ldots, m$. Substituting this value into ϕ, we obtain that the optimal value is $2\sqrt{\frac{\alpha \beta}{m}}$. $\square$

Using Lemma 9.15 with $\alpha = \Theta(\mathbf{x}^0)$, $\beta = \frac{L_f^2}{2\sigma}$ and $m = N+1$, we conclude that the minimum of the right-hand side of (9.20) is attained at $t_k = \frac{\sqrt{2\Theta(\mathbf{x}^0)\sigma}}{L_f \sqrt{N+1}}$. The $O(1/\sqrt{N})$ rate of convergence follows immediately.

Theorem 9.16 ($O(1/\sqrt{N})$ rate of convergence of mirror descent with fixed amount of iterations). *Suppose that Assumptions 9.1 and 9.3 hold and that $\|f'(\mathbf{x})\|_* \leq L_f$ for all $\mathbf{x} \in C$ for some $L_f > 0$. Assume that $B_\omega(\mathbf{x}, \mathbf{x}^0)$ is bounded over C, and let $\Theta(\mathbf{x}^0)$ satisfy*

$$\Theta(\mathbf{x}^0) \geq \max_{\mathbf{x} \in C} B_\omega(\mathbf{x}, \mathbf{x}^0).$$

Let N be a positive integer, and let $\{\mathbf{x}^k\}_{k \geq 0}$ be the sequence generated by the mirror descent method with

$$t_k = \frac{\sqrt{2\Theta(\mathbf{x}^0)\sigma}}{L_f \sqrt{N+1}}, \quad k = 0, 1, \ldots, N. \tag{9.23}$$

Then

$$f_{\text{best}}^N - f_{\text{opt}} \leq \frac{\sqrt{2\Theta(\mathbf{x}^0)} L_f}{\sqrt{\sigma} \sqrt{N+1}},$$

where f_{best}^N is defined in (9.19).

---

[51]See, for example, [10, Example 7.18].

Proof. By Lemma 9.14,

$$f_{\text{best}}^N - f_{\text{opt}} \le \frac{\Theta(\mathbf{x}^0) + \frac{L_f^2}{2\sigma}\sum_{k=0}^N t_k^2}{\sum_{k=0}^N t_k}.$$

Plugging the expression (9.23) for the stepsizes into the above inequality, the result follows. □

Example 9.17 (optimization over the unit simplex). Consider the problem

$$\min\{f(\mathbf{x}) : \mathbf{x} \in \Delta_n\},$$

where $f : \mathbb{R}^n \to (-\infty, \infty]$ is proper closed convex and satisfies $\Delta_n \subseteq \text{int}(\text{dom}(f))$. Consider two possible algorithms.

- **Euclidean setting.** We assume that the underlying norm on $\mathbb{R}^n$ is the l_2-norm and $\omega(\mathbf{x}) = \frac{1}{2}\|\mathbf{x}\|_2^2$, which is 1-strongly convex w.r.t. the l_2-norm. In this case, the mirror descent algorithm is the same as the projected subgradient method:

$$\mathbf{x}^{k+1} = P_{\Delta_n}(\mathbf{x}^k - t_k f'(\mathbf{x}^k)).$$

We will assume that the method starts with the vector $\mathbf{x}^0 = \frac{1}{n}\mathbf{e}$. For this choice,

$$\max_{\mathbf{x}\in\Delta_n} B_\omega(\mathbf{x},\mathbf{x}^0) = \max_{\mathbf{x}\in\Delta_n} \frac{1}{2}\left\|\mathbf{x} - \frac{1}{n}\mathbf{e}\right\|_2^2 = \frac{1}{2}\left(1 - \frac{1}{n}\right),$$

and we will take $\Theta(\mathbf{x}^0) = 1$. By Theorem 9.16, we have that given a positive integer N, by appropriately choosing the stepsizes, we obtain that

$$f_{\text{best}}^N - f_{\text{opt}} \le \underbrace{\frac{\sqrt{2}L_{f,2}}{\sqrt{N+1}}}_{C_e^f}, \tag{9.24}$$

where $L_{f,2} = \max_{\mathbf{x}\in\Delta_n}\|f'(\mathbf{x})\|_2$.

- **Non-Euclidean setting.** Here we assume that the underlying norm on $\mathbb{R}^n$ is the l_1-norm and that the convex function ω is chosen as the negative entropy function

$$\omega(\mathbf{x}) = \begin{cases} \sum_{i=1}^n x_i \log(x_i), & \mathbf{x} \in \mathbb{R}_+^n, \\ \infty & \text{else.} \end{cases} \tag{9.25}$$

By Example 5.27, $\omega+\delta_{\Delta_n}$ is 1-strongly convex w.r.t. the l_1-norm. By Example 9.10, the mirror descent method takes the form

$$x_i^{k+1} = \frac{x_i^k e^{-t_k f_i'(\mathbf{x}^k)}}{\sum_{j=1}^n x_j^k e^{-t_k f_j'(\mathbf{x}^k)}}, \quad i = 1, 2, \ldots, n.$$

As in the Euclidean setting, we will also initialize the method with $\mathbf{x}^0 = \frac{1}{n}\mathbf{e}$. For this choice, using the fact that the Bregman distance coincides with the Kullback–Leibler divergence (see (9.13)), we obtain

$$\max_{\mathbf{x}\in\Delta_n} B_\omega\left(\mathbf{x}, \frac{1}{n}\mathbf{e}\right) = \max_{\mathbf{x}\in\Delta_n} \sum_{i=1}^{n} x_i \log(nx_i) = \log(n) + \max_{\mathbf{x}\in\Delta_n} \sum_{i=1}^{n} x_i \log x_i$$
$$= \log(n).$$

We will thus take $\Theta(\mathbf{x}^0) = \log(n)$. By Theorem 9.16, we have that given a positive integer N, by appropriately choosing the stepsizes, we obtain that

$$f_{\text{best}}^N - f_{\text{opt}} \leq \underbrace{\frac{\sqrt{2\log(n)}L_{f,\infty}}{\sqrt{N+1}}}_{C_{\text{ne}}^f}, \tag{9.26}$$

where $L_{f,\infty} = \max_{\mathbf{x}\in\Delta_n} \|f'(\mathbf{x})\|_\infty$.

The ratio of the two upper bounds in (9.24) and (9.26) is given by

$$\rho^f = \frac{C_{\text{ne}}^f}{C_{\text{e}}^f} = \sqrt{\log(n)}\frac{L_{f,\infty}}{L_{f,2}}.$$

Whether or not ρ^f is greater than 1 (superiority of the Euclidean setting) or smaller than 1 (superiority of the non-Euclidean setting) depends on the properties of the function f. In any case, since $\|\mathbf{y}\|_\infty \leq \|\mathbf{y}\|_2 \leq \sqrt{n}\|\mathbf{y}\|_\infty$ for all $\mathbf{y} \in \mathbb{R}^n$, it follows that

$$\frac{1}{\sqrt{n}} \leq \frac{L_{f,\infty}}{L_{f,2}} \leq 1,$$

and hence that

$$\frac{\sqrt{\log(n)}}{\sqrt{n}} \leq \rho^f \leq \sqrt{\log(n)}.$$

Therefore, the ratio between the efficiency estimates ranges between $\frac{\sqrt{\log(n)}}{\sqrt{n}}$ (superiority of the non-Euclidean setting) and $\sqrt{\log(n)}$ (slight superiority of the Euclidean setting). ∎

9.2.3 Dynamic Stepsize Rule

The constant stepsize rule is relatively easy to analyze but has the disadvantage of requiring the a priori knowledge of the total number of iterations employed by the method. In practical situations, the number of iterations is not fixed a priori, and a stopping criteria different than merely fixing the total number of iterations is usually imposed. This is why dynamic (namely, nonconstant) stepsize rules are important. Similarly to the analysis in Chapter 8 for the projected subgradient method, it is possible to use the fundamental inequality for the mirror descent method (Lemma 9.13) to establish convergence results under dynamic stepsize rules.

Theorem 9.18 (convergence of mirror descent with dynamic stepsizes).
Suppose that Assumptions 9.1 and 9.3 hold and that $\|f'(\mathbf{x})\|_* \leq L_f$ for any $\mathbf{x} \in C$

for some $L_f > 0$. Let $\{\mathbf{x}^k\}_{k \geq 0}$ be the sequence generated by the mirror descent method with positive stepsizes $\{t_k\}_{k \geq 0}$, and let $\{f_{\text{best}}^k\}_{k \geq 0}$ be the sequence of best achieved values defined in (9.19).

(a) *If $\frac{\sum_{n=0}^k t_n^2}{\sum_{n=0}^k t_n} \to 0$ as $k \to \infty$, then $f_{\text{best}}^k \to f_{\text{opt}}$ as $k \to \infty$.*

(b) *If t_k is chosen as either* (**predefined diminishing stepsize**)

$$t_k = \frac{\sqrt{2\sigma}}{L_f \sqrt{k+1}}$$

or (**adaptive stepsize**)

$$t_k = \begin{cases} \frac{\sqrt{2\sigma}}{\|f'(\mathbf{x}^k)\|_* \sqrt{k+1}}, & f'(\mathbf{x}^k) \neq \mathbf{0}, \\ \frac{\sqrt{2\sigma}}{L_f \sqrt{k+1}}, & f'(\mathbf{x}^k) = \mathbf{0}, \end{cases}$$

then for all $k \geq 1$,

$$f_{\text{best}}^k - f_{\text{opt}} \leq \frac{L_f}{\sqrt{2\sigma}} \frac{B_\omega(\mathbf{x}^*, \mathbf{x}^0) + 1 + \log(k+1)}{\sqrt{k+1}}.$$

Proof. By the fundamental inequality for mirror descent (Lemma 9.13), we have, for all $n \geq 0$,

$$t_n(f(\mathbf{x}^n) - f_{\text{opt}}) \leq B_\omega(\mathbf{x}^*, \mathbf{x}^n) - B_\omega(\mathbf{x}^*, \mathbf{x}^{n+1}) + \frac{t_n^2}{2\sigma} \|f'(\mathbf{x}^n)\|_*^2.$$

Summing the above inequality over $n = 0, 1, \ldots, k$ gives

$$\sum_{n=0}^k t_n(f(\mathbf{x}^n) - f_{\text{opt}}) \leq B_\omega(\mathbf{x}^*, \mathbf{x}^0) - B_\omega(\mathbf{x}^*, \mathbf{x}^{k+1}) + \frac{1}{2\sigma} \sum_{n=0}^k t_n^2 \|f'(\mathbf{x}^n)\|_*^2.$$

Using the inequalities $B_\omega(\mathbf{x}^*, \mathbf{x}^{k+1}) \geq 0$ and $f(\mathbf{x}^n) \geq f_{\text{best}}^k$ $(n \leq k)$, we obtain

$$f_{\text{best}}^k - f_{\text{opt}} \leq \frac{B_\omega(\mathbf{x}^*, \mathbf{x}^0) + \frac{1}{2\sigma} \sum_{n=0}^k t_n^2 \|f'(\mathbf{x}^n)\|_*^2}{\sum_{n=0}^k t_n}. \tag{9.27}$$

Since $\|f'(\mathbf{x}^n)\|_* \leq L_f$, we can deduce that

$$f_{\text{best}}^k - f_{\text{opt}} \leq \frac{B_\omega(\mathbf{x}^*, \mathbf{x}^0) + \frac{L_f^2}{2\sigma} \sum_{n=0}^k t_n^2}{\sum_{n=0}^k t_n}.$$

Therefore, if $\frac{\sum_{n=0}^k t_n^2}{\sum_{n=0}^k t_n} \to 0$, then $f_{\text{best}}^k \to f_{\text{opt}}$ as $k \to \infty$, proving claim (a).

To show the validity of claim (b), note that for both stepsize rules we have $t_n^2 \|f'(\mathbf{x}^n)\|_*^2 \leq \frac{2\sigma}{n+1}$ and $t_n \geq \frac{\sqrt{2\sigma}}{L_f \sqrt{n+1}}$. Hence, by (9.27),

$$f_{\text{best}}^k - f_{\text{opt}} \leq \frac{L_f}{\sqrt{2\sigma}} \frac{B_\omega(\mathbf{x}^*, \mathbf{x}^0) + \sum_{n=0}^k \frac{1}{n+1}}{\sum_{n=0}^k \frac{1}{\sqrt{n+1}}},$$

which, combined with Lemma 8.27(a), yields the desired result. $\square$

Example 9.19 (mirror descent vs. projected subgradient—numerical example). Consider the problem

$$\min \left\{ \|\mathbf{A}\mathbf{x} - \mathbf{b}\|_1 : \mathbf{x} \in \Delta_n \right\}, \tag{9.28}$$

where $\mathbf{A} \in \mathbb{R}^{n \times n}$ and $\mathbf{b} \in \mathbb{R}^n$. Following Example 9.17, we consider two methods. The first is the projected subgradient method where $\mathbb{R}^n$ is assumed to be endowed with the Euclidean l_2-norm. The update formula is given by

$$\mathbf{x}^{k+1} = P_{\Delta_n}(\mathbf{x}^k - t_k f'(\mathbf{x}^k)),$$

with $f'(\mathbf{x}^k)$ taken as $\mathbf{A}^T \mathrm{sgn}(\mathbf{A}\mathbf{x}^k - \mathbf{b})$ and the stepsize t_k chosen by the adaptive stepsize rule (in practice, $f'(\mathbf{x}^k)$ is never the zeros vector):

$$t_k = \frac{\sqrt{2}}{\|f'(\mathbf{x}^k)\|_2 \sqrt{k+1}}.$$

The second method is mirror descent in which the underlying norm on $\mathbb{R}^n$ is the l_1-norm and ω is chosen to be the negative entropy function given in (9.25). In this case, the method has the form (see Example 9.17)

$$x_i^{k+1} = \frac{x_i^k e^{-t_k f_i'(\mathbf{x}^k)}}{\sum_{j=1}^n x_j^k e^{-t_k f_j'(\mathbf{x}^k)}}, \quad i = 1, 2, \ldots, n,$$

where here we take

$$t_k = \frac{\sqrt{2}}{\|f'(\mathbf{x}^k)\|_\infty \sqrt{k+1}}.$$

Note that the strong convexity parameter is $\sigma = 1$ in both settings. We created an instance of problem (9.28) with $n = 100$ by generating the components of $\mathbf{A}$ and $\mathbf{b}$ independently via a standard normal distribution. The values of $f(\mathbf{x}^k) - f_{\mathrm{opt}}$ and $f_{\mathrm{best}}^k - f_{\mathrm{opt}}$ for both methods are described in Figure 9.1. Evidently, the non-Euclidean method, referred to as md, is superior to the Euclidean projected subgradient method (ps). ∎

9.3   Mirror Descent for the Composite Model[52]

In this section we will consider a more general model than model (9.1), which was discussed in Sections 9.1 and 9.2. Consider the problem

$$\min_{\mathbf{x} \in \mathbb{E}} \{ F(\mathbf{x}) \equiv f(\mathbf{x}) + g(\mathbf{x}) \}, \tag{9.29}$$

where the following set of assumptions is made on f and g.

Assumption 9.20 (properties of f and g).

(A) $f, g : \mathbb{E} \to (-\infty, \infty]$ *are proper closed and convex.*

(B) $\mathrm{dom}(g) \subseteq \mathrm{int}(\mathrm{dom}(f))$.

---

[52]The analysis of the mirror-C method is based on the work of Duchi, Shalev-Shwartz, Singer, and Tewari [49], where the algorithm is introduced in an online and stochastic setting.

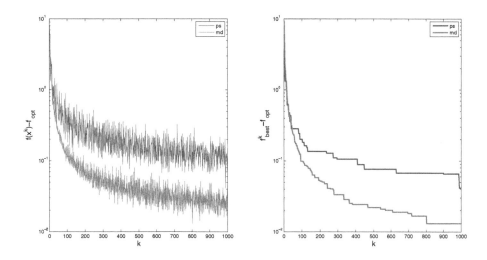

Figure 9.1. *The values $f(\mathbf{x}^k) - f_{\mathrm{opt}}$ and $f_{\mathrm{best}}^k - f_{\mathrm{opt}}$ generated by the mirror descent and projected subgradient methods.*

(C) $\|f'(\mathbf{x})\|_* \leq L_f$ *for any* $\mathbf{x} \in \mathrm{dom}(g)$ $(L_f > 0)$.[53]

(D) *The optimal set of* (9.29) *is nonempty and denoted by* X^*. *The optimal value of the problem is denoted by* F_{opt}.

We will also assume, as usual, that we have at our disposal a convex function ω that satisfies the following properties, which are a slight adjustment of the properties in Assumption 9.3.

Assumption 9.21 (properties of ω).

- ω *is proper closed and convex.*

- ω *is differentiable over* $\mathrm{dom}(\partial\omega)$.

- $\mathrm{dom}(g) \subseteq \mathrm{dom}(\omega)$.

- $\omega + \delta_{\mathrm{dom}(g)}$ *is σ-strongly convex* $(\sigma > 0)$.

We can obviously ignore the composite structure of problem (9.29) and just try to employ the mirror descent method on the function $F = f + g$ with $\mathrm{dom}(g)$ taking the role of C:

$$\mathbf{x}^{k+1} = \mathrm{argmin}_{\mathbf{x} \in C} \left\{ \langle f'(\mathbf{x}^k) + g'(\mathbf{x}^k), \mathbf{x} \rangle + \frac{1}{t_k} B_\omega(\mathbf{x}, \mathbf{x}^k) \right\}. \tag{9.30}$$

---

[53]Recall that we assume that f' represents some rule that takes any $\mathbf{x} \in \mathrm{dom}(\partial f)$ to a vector $f'(\mathbf{x}) \in \partial f(\mathbf{x})$.

However, employing the above scheme might be problematic. First, we did not assume that $C = \text{dom}(g)$ is closed, and thus the argmin in (9.30) might be empty. Second, even if the update step is well defined, we did not assume that g is Lipschitz over C like we did on f in Assumption 9.20(C); this is a key element in the convergence analysis of the mirror descent method. Finally, even if g is Lipschitz over C, it might be that the Lipschitz constant of the sum function $F = f + g$ is much larger than the Lipschitz constant of f, and our objective will be to define a method whose efficiency estimate will depend only on the Lipschitz constant of f over $\text{dom}(g)$.

Instead of linearizing both f and g, as is done in (9.30), we will linearize f and keep g as it is. This leads to the following scheme:

$$\mathbf{x}^{k+1} = \text{argmin}_{\mathbf{x}} \left\{ \langle f'(\mathbf{x}^k), \mathbf{x} \rangle + g(\mathbf{x}) + \frac{1}{t_k} B_\omega(\mathbf{x}, \mathbf{x}^k) \right\}, \qquad (9.31)$$

which can also be written as

$$\mathbf{x}^{k+1} = \text{argmin}_{\mathbf{x}} \left\{ \langle t_k f'(\mathbf{x}^k) - \nabla \omega(\mathbf{x}^k), \mathbf{x} \rangle + t_k g(\mathbf{x}) + \omega(\mathbf{x}) \right\}.$$

The algorithm that performs the above update step will be called the *mirror-C* method.

The Mirror-C Method

Initialization: pick $\mathbf{x}^0 \in \text{dom}(g) \cap \text{dom}(\partial \omega)$.
General step: for any $k = 0, 1, 2, \ldots$ execute the following steps:

(a) pick a stepsize $t_k > 0$ and a subgradient $f'(\mathbf{x}^k) \in \partial f(\mathbf{x}^k)$;

(b) set

$$\mathbf{x}^{k+1} = \text{argmin}_{\mathbf{x}} \left\{ \langle t_k f'(\mathbf{x}^k) - \nabla \omega(\mathbf{x}^k), \mathbf{x} \rangle + t_k g(\mathbf{x}) + \omega(\mathbf{x}) \right\}. \qquad (9.32)$$

Remark 9.22. *The update formula* (9.32) *can also be rewritten as*

$$\mathbf{x}^{k+1} = \text{argmin}_{\mathbf{x}} \left\{ \langle t_k f'(\mathbf{x}^k), \mathbf{x} \rangle + t_k g(\mathbf{x}) + B_\omega(\mathbf{x}, \mathbf{x}^k) \right\}. \qquad (9.33)$$

Remark 9.23 (Euclidean setting—proximal subgradient method). *When the underlying space $\mathbb{E}$ is Euclidean and $\omega(\mathbf{x}) = \frac{1}{2} \|\mathbf{x}\|^2$, then the update formula* (9.33) *reduces to*

$$\mathbf{x}^{k+1} = \text{argmin}_{\mathbf{x}} \left\{ \langle t_k f'(\mathbf{x}^k), \mathbf{x} \rangle + t_k g(\mathbf{x}) + \frac{1}{2} \|\mathbf{x} - \mathbf{x}^k\|^2 \right\},$$

which, after some rearrangement of terms and removal of constant terms, takes the form

$$\mathbf{x}^{k+1} = \text{argmin}_{\mathbf{x}} \left\{ t_k g(\mathbf{x}) + \frac{1}{2} \left\| \mathbf{x} - [\mathbf{x}^k - t_k f'(\mathbf{x}^k)] \right\|^2 \right\}.$$

By the definition of the prox operator (see Chapter 6), the last equation can be rewritten as

$$\mathbf{x}^{k+1} = \text{prox}_{t_k g}(\mathbf{x}^k - t_k f'(\mathbf{x}^k)).$$

Thus, at each iteration the method takes a step toward minus of the subgradient followed by a prox step. The resulting method is called the proximal subgradient method. *The method will be discussed extensively in Chapter 10 in the case where f possesses some differentiability properties.*

Of course, the mirror-C method coincides with the mirror descent method when taking $g = \delta_C$ with C being a nonempty closed and convex set. We begin by showing that the mirror-C method is well defined, meaning that the minimum in (9.32) is uniquely attained at $\text{dom}(g) \cap \text{dom}(\partial\omega)$.

Theorem 9.24 (mirror-C is well defined). *Suppose that Assumptions 9.20 and 9.21 hold. Let $\mathbf{a} \in \mathbb{E}^*$. Then the problem*

$$\min_{\mathbf{x}\in\mathbb{E}}\{\langle\mathbf{a},\mathbf{x}\rangle + g(\mathbf{x}) + \omega(\mathbf{x})\}$$

has a unique minimizer in $\text{dom}(g) \cap \text{dom}(\partial\omega)$.

Proof. The proof follows by invoking Lemma 9.7 with $\psi(\mathbf{x}) \equiv \langle\mathbf{a},\mathbf{x}\rangle + g(\mathbf{x})$. $\square$

The analysis of the mirror-C method is based on arguments similar to those used in Section 9.2 to analyze the mirror descent method. We begin by proving a technical lemma establishing an inequality similar to the one derived in Lemma 9.14. Note that in addition to our basic assumptions, we assume that g is a nonnegative function and that the stepsizes are nonincreasing.

Lemma 9.25. *Suppose that Assumptions 9.20 and 9.21 hold and that g is a nonnegative function. Let $\{\mathbf{x}^k\}_{k\geq 0}$ be the sequence generated by the mirror-C method with positive nonincreasing stepsizes $\{t_k\}_{k\geq 0}$. Then for any $\mathbf{x}^* \in X^*$ and $k \geq 0$,*

$$\min_{n=0,1,\dots,k} F(\mathbf{x}^n) - F_{\text{opt}} \leq \frac{t_0 g(\mathbf{x}^0) + B_\omega(\mathbf{x}^*,\mathbf{x}^0) + \frac{1}{2\sigma}\sum_{n=0}^{k} t_n^2 \|f'(\mathbf{x}^n)\|_*^2}{\sum_{n=0}^{k} t_n}. \quad (9.34)$$

Proof. By the update formula (9.33) and the non-Euclidean second prox theorem (Theorem 9.12) invoked with $\mathbf{b} = \mathbf{x}^n, \mathbf{a} = \mathbf{x}^{n+1}$, and $\psi(\mathbf{x}) \equiv t_n\langle f'(\mathbf{x}^n),\mathbf{x}\rangle + t_n g(\mathbf{x})$, we have

$$\langle\nabla\omega(\mathbf{x}^n) - \nabla\omega(\mathbf{x}^{n+1}), \mathbf{u} - \mathbf{x}^{n+1}\rangle \leq t_n\langle f'(\mathbf{x}^n),\mathbf{u}-\mathbf{x}^{n+1}\rangle + t_n g(\mathbf{u}) - t_n g(\mathbf{x}^{n+1}). \quad (9.35)$$

Invoking the three-points lemma (Lemma 9.11) with $\mathbf{a} = \mathbf{x}^{n+1}, \mathbf{b} = \mathbf{x}^n$, and $\mathbf{c} = \mathbf{u}$ yields

$$\langle\nabla\omega(\mathbf{x}^n) - \nabla\omega(\mathbf{x}^{n+1}), \mathbf{u} - \mathbf{x}^{n+1}\rangle = B_\omega(\mathbf{u},\mathbf{x}^{n+1}) + B_\omega(\mathbf{x}^{n+1},\mathbf{x}^n) - B_\omega(\mathbf{u},\mathbf{x}^n),$$

which, combined with (9.35), gives

$$B_\omega(\mathbf{u},\mathbf{x}^{n+1}) + B_\omega(\mathbf{x}^{n+1},\mathbf{x}^n) - B_\omega(\mathbf{u},\mathbf{x}^n) \leq t_n\langle f'(\mathbf{x}^n),\mathbf{u}-\mathbf{x}^{n+1}\rangle + t_n g(\mathbf{u}) - t_n g(\mathbf{x}^{n+1}).$$

Therefore,

$$t_n \langle f'(\mathbf{x}^n), \mathbf{x}^n - \mathbf{u} \rangle + t_n g(\mathbf{x}^{n+1}) - t_n g(\mathbf{u})$$
$$\leq B_\omega(\mathbf{u}, \mathbf{x}^n) - B_\omega(\mathbf{u}, \mathbf{x}^{n+1}) - B_\omega(\mathbf{x}^{n+1}, \mathbf{x}^n) + t_n \langle f'(\mathbf{x}^n), \mathbf{x}^n - \mathbf{x}^{n+1} \rangle$$
$$\leq B_\omega(\mathbf{u}, \mathbf{x}^n) - B_\omega(\mathbf{u}, \mathbf{x}^{n+1}) - \frac{\sigma}{2} \|\mathbf{x}^{n+1} - \mathbf{x}^n\|^2 + t_n \langle f'(\mathbf{x}^n), \mathbf{x}^n - \mathbf{x}^{n+1} \rangle$$
$$= B_\omega(\mathbf{u}, \mathbf{x}^n) - B_\omega(\mathbf{u}, \mathbf{x}^{n+1}) - \frac{\sigma}{2} \|\mathbf{x}^{n+1} - \mathbf{x}^n\|^2 + \left\langle \frac{t_n}{\sqrt{\sigma}} f'(\mathbf{x}^n), \sqrt{\sigma}(\mathbf{x}^n - \mathbf{x}^{n+1}) \right\rangle$$
$$\leq B_\omega(\mathbf{u}, \mathbf{x}^n) - B_\omega(\mathbf{u}, \mathbf{x}^{n+1}) - \frac{\sigma}{2} \|\mathbf{x}^{n+1} - \mathbf{x}^n\|^2 + \frac{t_n^2}{2\sigma} \|f'(\mathbf{x}^n)\|_*^2 + \frac{\sigma}{2} \|\mathbf{x}^{n+1} - \mathbf{x}^n\|^2$$
$$= B_\omega(\mathbf{u}, \mathbf{x}^n) - B_\omega(\mathbf{u}, \mathbf{x}^{n+1}) + \frac{t_n^2}{2\sigma} \|f'(\mathbf{x}^n)\|_*^2.$$

Plugging in $\mathbf{u} = \mathbf{x}^*$ and using the subgradient inequality, we obtain

$$t_n \left[f(\mathbf{x}^n) + g(\mathbf{x}^{n+1}) - F_{\text{opt}} \right] \leq B_\omega(\mathbf{x}^*, \mathbf{x}^n) - B_\omega(\mathbf{x}^*, \mathbf{x}^{n+1}) + \frac{t_n^2}{2\sigma} \|f'(\mathbf{x}^n)\|_*^2.$$

Summing the above over $n = 0, 1, \ldots, k$,

$$\sum_{n=0}^{k} t_n \left[f(\mathbf{x}^n) + g(\mathbf{x}^{n+1}) - F_{\text{opt}} \right] \leq B_\omega(\mathbf{x}^*, \mathbf{x}^0) - B_\omega(\mathbf{x}^*, \mathbf{x}^{k+1}) + \frac{1}{2\sigma} \sum_{n=0}^{k} t_n^2 \|f'(\mathbf{x}^n)\|_*^2.$$

Adding the term $t_0 g(\mathbf{x}^0) - t_k g(\mathbf{x}^{k+1})$ to both sides and using the nonnegativity of the Bregman distance, we get

$$t_0(F(\mathbf{x}^0) - F_{\text{opt}}) + \sum_{n=1}^{k} [t_n f(\mathbf{x}^n) + t_{n-1} g(\mathbf{x}^n) - t_n F_{\text{opt}}]$$
$$\leq t_0 g(\mathbf{x}^0) - t_k g(\mathbf{x}^{k+1}) + B_\omega(\mathbf{x}^*, \mathbf{x}^0) + \frac{1}{2\sigma} \sum_{n=0}^{k} t_n^2 \|f'(\mathbf{x}^n)\|_*^2.$$

Using the fact that $t_n \leq t_{n-1}$ and the nonnegativity of $g(\mathbf{x}^{k+1})$, we conclude that

$$\sum_{n=0}^{k} t_n \left[F(\mathbf{x}^n) - F_{\text{opt}} \right] \leq t_0 g(\mathbf{x}^0) + B_\omega(\mathbf{x}^*, \mathbf{x}^0) + \frac{1}{2\sigma} \sum_{n=0}^{k} t_n^2 \|f'(\mathbf{x}^n)\|_*^2,$$

which, combined with the fact that

$$\left(\sum_{n=0}^{k} t_n \right) \left(\min_{n=0,1,\ldots,k} F(\mathbf{x}^n) - F_{\text{opt}} \right) \leq \sum_{n=0}^{k} t_n \left[F(\mathbf{x}^n) - F_{\text{opt}} \right],$$

implies the inequality (9.34). $\square$

Using Lemma 9.25, it is now easy to derive a convergence result under the assumption that the number of iterations is fixed.

Theorem 9.26 ($O(1/\sqrt{N})$ rate of convergence of mirror-C with fixed amount of iterations). *Suppose that Assumptions 9.20 and 9.21 hold and that* *g is nonnegative. Assume that $B_\omega(\mathbf{x}, \mathbf{x}^0)$ is bounded above over* $\mathrm{dom}(g)$, *and let* $\Theta(\mathbf{x}^0)$ *satisfy*

$$\Theta(\mathbf{x}^0) \geq \max_{\mathbf{x} \in \mathrm{dom}(g)} B_\omega(\mathbf{x}, \mathbf{x}^0).$$

Suppose that $g(\mathbf{x}^0) = 0$. Let N be a positive integer, and let $\{\mathbf{x}^k\}_{k \geq 0}$ be the sequence generated by the mirror-C method with constant stepsize

$$t_k = \frac{\sqrt{2\Theta(\mathbf{x}^0)\sigma}}{L_f\sqrt{N}}. \tag{9.36}$$

Then

$$\min_{n=0,1,\ldots,N-1} F(\mathbf{x}^n) - F_{\mathrm{opt}} \leq \frac{\sqrt{2\Theta(\mathbf{x}^0)}L_f}{\sqrt{\sigma}\sqrt{N}}.$$

Proof. By Lemma 9.25, using the fact that $g(\mathbf{x}^0) = 0$ and the inequalities $\|f'(\mathbf{x}^n)\|_* \leq L_f$ and $B_\omega(\mathbf{x}^*, \mathbf{x}^0) \leq \Theta(\mathbf{x}^0)$, we have

$$\min_{n=0,1,\ldots,N-1} F(\mathbf{x}^n) - F_{\mathrm{opt}} \leq \frac{\Theta(\mathbf{x}^0) + \frac{L_f^2}{2\sigma}\sum_{n=0}^{N-1} t_n^2}{\sum_{n=0}^{N-1} t_n}.$$

Plugging the expression (9.36) for the stepsizes into the above inequality, the result follows. $\quad\square$

We can also establish a rate of convergence of the mirror-C method with a dynamic stepsize rule.

Theorem 9.27 ($O(\log k/\sqrt{k})$ rate of convergence of mirror-C with dynamic stepsizes). *Suppose that Assumptions 9.20 and 9.21 hold and that g is nonnegative. Let $\{\mathbf{x}^k\}_{k \geq 0}$ be the sequence generated by the mirror-C method with stepsizes $\{t_k\}_{k \geq 0}$ chosen as*

$$t_k = \frac{\sqrt{2\sigma}}{L_f\sqrt{k+1}}.$$

Then for all $k \geq 1$,

$$\min_{n=0,1,\ldots,k} F(\mathbf{x}^n) - F_{\mathrm{opt}} \leq \frac{L_f}{\sqrt{2\sigma}} \frac{B_\omega(\mathbf{x}^*, \mathbf{x}^0) + \frac{\sqrt{2\sigma}}{L_f}g(\mathbf{x}^0) + 1 + \log(k+1)}{\sqrt{k+1}}. \tag{9.37}$$

Proof. By Lemma 9.25, taking into account the fact that $t_0 = \frac{\sqrt{2\sigma}}{L_f}$,

$$\min_{n=0,1,\ldots,k} F(\mathbf{x}^n) - F_{\mathrm{opt}} \leq \frac{B_\omega(\mathbf{x}^*, \mathbf{x}^0) + \frac{\sqrt{2\sigma}}{L_f}g(\mathbf{x}^0) + \frac{1}{2\sigma}\sum_{n=0}^{k} t_n^2 \|f'(\mathbf{x}^n)\|_*^2}{\sum_{n=0}^{k} t_n}, \tag{9.38}$$

which, along with the relations $t_n^2 \|f'(\mathbf{x}^n)\|_*^2 \leq \frac{2\sigma}{n+1}$ and $t_n = \frac{\sqrt{2\sigma}}{L_f\sqrt{n+1}}$, yields the inequality

$$\min_{n=0,1,\ldots,k} F(\mathbf{x}^n) - f_{\mathrm{opt}} \leq \frac{L_f}{\sqrt{2\sigma}} \frac{B_\omega(\mathbf{x}^*, \mathbf{x}^0) + \frac{\sqrt{2\sigma}}{L_f}g(\mathbf{x}^0) + \sum_{n=0}^{k} \frac{1}{n+1}}{\sum_{n=0}^{k} \frac{1}{\sqrt{n+1}}}.$$

The result (9.37) now follows by invoking Lemma 8.27(a). $\quad\square$

Example 9.28. Suppose that the underlying space is $\mathbb{R}^n$ endowed with the Euclidean l_2-norm. Let $f : \mathbb{R}^n \to \mathbb{R}$ be a convex function, which is Lipschitz over $\mathbb{R}^n$, implying that there exists $L_f > 0$ for which $\|f'(\mathbf{x})\|_2 \leq L_f$ for all $\mathbf{x} \in \mathbb{R}^n$. Now consider the problem

$$\min_{\mathbf{x} \in \mathbb{R}^n_{++}} \left\{ F(\mathbf{x}) \equiv f(\mathbf{x}) + \sum_{i=1}^n \frac{1}{x_i} \right\}$$

with ω chosen as $\omega(\mathbf{x}) = \frac{1}{2}\|\mathbf{x}\|_2^2$. In this case, the mirror descent and mirror-C methods coincide with the projected subgradient and proximal subgradient methods, respectively. It is not possible to employ the projected subgradient method on the problem—it is not even clear what is the feasible set C. If we take it as the open set $\mathbb{R}^n_{++}$, then the orthogonal projection onto C is not well defined. In any case, since F is obviously not Lipschitz, no convergence is guaranteed. On the other hand, employing the proximal subgradient method is definitely possible by taking $g(\mathbf{x}) \equiv \sum_{i=1}^n \frac{1}{x_i} + \delta_{\mathbb{R}^n_{++}}$. Both Assumptions 9.20 and 9.21 hold for f, g and $\omega(\mathbf{x}) = \frac{1}{2}\|\mathbf{x}\|^2$, and in addition g is nonnegative. The resulting method is

$$\mathbf{x}^{k+1} = \text{prox}_{t_k g}\left(\mathbf{x}^k - t_k f'(\mathbf{x}^k)\right).$$

The computation of $\text{prox}_{t_k g}$ amounts to solving n cubic scalar equations. ∎

Example 9.29 (projected subgradient vs. proximal subgradient). Suppose that the underlying space is $\mathbb{R}^n$ endowed with the Euclidean l_2-norm and consider the problem

$$\min_{\mathbf{x} \in \mathbb{R}^n} \left\{ F(\mathbf{x}) \equiv \|\mathbf{A}\mathbf{x} - \mathbf{b}\|_1 + \lambda\|\mathbf{x}\|_1 \right\}, \tag{9.39}$$

where $\mathbf{A} \in \mathbb{R}^{m \times n}, \mathbf{b} \in \mathbb{R}^m$, and $\lambda > 0$. We will consider two possible methods to solve the problem:

- **projected subgradient** employed on problem (9.39), where here $C = \mathbb{R}^n$. The method takes the form (when making the choice of the subgradient of $\|\mathbf{y}\|_1$ as $\text{sgn}(\mathbf{y})$)

$$\mathbf{x}^{k+1} = \mathbf{x}^k - t_k(\mathbf{A}^T \text{sgn}(\mathbf{A}\mathbf{x}^k - \mathbf{b}) + \lambda\text{sgn}(\mathbf{x})).$$

The stepsize is chosen according to Theorem 8.28 as $t_k = \frac{1}{\|F'(\mathbf{x}^k)\|_2 \sqrt{k+1}}$.

- **proximal subgradient**, where we take $f(\mathbf{x}) = \|\mathbf{A}\mathbf{x} - \mathbf{b}\|_1$ and $g(\mathbf{x}) = \lambda\|\mathbf{x}\|_1$, so that $F = f + g$. The method then takes the form

$$\mathbf{x}^{k+1} = \text{prox}_{s_k g}(\mathbf{x}^k - s_k\mathbf{A}^T\text{sgn}(\mathbf{A}\mathbf{x}^k - \mathbf{b})).$$

Since $g(\mathbf{x}) = \lambda\|\mathbf{x}\|_1$, it follows that $\text{prox}_{s_k g}$ is a soft thresholding operator. Specifically, by Example 6.8, $\text{prox}_{s_k g} = \mathcal{T}_{\lambda s_k}$, and hence the general update rule becomes

$$\mathbf{x}^{k+1} = \mathcal{T}_{\lambda s_k}(\mathbf{x}^k - s_k\mathbf{A}^T\text{sgn}(\mathbf{A}\mathbf{x}^k - \mathbf{b})).$$

The stepsize is chosen as $s_k = \frac{1}{\|f'(\mathbf{x}^k)\|_2 \sqrt{k+1}}$.

A priori it seems that the proximal subgradient method should have an advantage over the projected subgradient method since the efficiency estimate bound of the proximal subgradient method depends on L_f, while the corresponding constant for the projected subgradient method depends on the larger constant L_F. This observation is also quite apparent in practice. We created an instance of problem (9.39) with $m = 10, n = 15$ by generating the components of $\mathbf{A}$ and $\mathbf{b}$ independently via a standard normal distribution. The values of $F(\mathbf{x}^k) - F_{\mathrm{opt}}$ for both methods are described in Figure 9.2. Evidently, in this case, the proximal subgradient method is better by orders of magnitude than the projected subgradient method. ∎

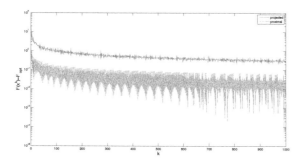

Figure 9.2. *First* 1000 *iterations of the projected and proximal subgradient methods employed on problem* (9.39)*. The y-axis describes (in log scale) the quantity* $F(\mathbf{x}^k) - F_{\mathrm{opt}}$*.*

Chapter 10

The Proximal Gradient Method

Underlying Space: In this chapter, with the exception of Section 10.9, $\mathbb{E}$ is a Euclidean space, meaning a finite dimensional space endowed with an inner product $\langle \cdot, \cdot \rangle$ and the Euclidean norm $\| \cdot \| = \sqrt{\langle \cdot, \cdot \rangle}$.

10.1 The Composite Model

In this chapter we will be mostly concerned with the composite model

$$\min_{\mathbf{x} \in \mathbb{E}} \{ F(\mathbf{x}) \equiv f(\mathbf{x}) + g(\mathbf{x}) \}, \tag{10.1}$$

where we assume the following.

Assumption 10.1.

(A) $g : \mathbb{E} \to (-\infty, \infty]$ *is proper closed and convex.*

(B) $f : \mathbb{E} \to (-\infty, \infty]$ *is proper and closed,* $\mathrm{dom}(f)$ *is convex,* $\mathrm{dom}(g) \subseteq \mathrm{int}(\mathrm{dom}(f))$, *and* f *is* L_f*-smooth over* $\mathrm{int}(\mathrm{dom}(f))$.

(C) *The optimal set of problem* (10.1) *is nonempty and denoted by* X^*. *The optimal value of the problem is denoted by* F_{opt}.

Three special cases of the general model (10.1) are gathered in the following example.

Example 10.2.

- **Smooth unconstrained minimization.** If $g \equiv 0$ and $\mathrm{dom}(f) = \mathbb{E}$, then (10.1) reduces to the unconstrained smooth minimization problem

$$\min_{\mathbf{x} \in \mathbb{E}} f(\mathbf{x}),$$

  where $f : \mathbb{E} \to \mathbb{R}$ is an L_f-smooth function.

269

- **Convex constrained smooth minimization.** If $g = \delta_C$, where C is a nonempty closed and convex set, then (10.1) amounts to the problem of minimizing a differentiable function over a nonempty closed and convex set:

$$\min_{\mathbf{x} \in C} f(\mathbf{x}),$$

  where here f is L_f-smooth over $\mathrm{int}(\mathrm{dom}(f))$ and $C \subseteq \mathrm{int}(\mathrm{dom}(f))$.

- **l_1-regularized minimization.** Taking $g(\mathbf{x}) = \lambda\|\mathbf{x}\|_1$ for some $\lambda > 0$, (10.1) amounts to the l_1-regularized problem

$$\min_{\mathbf{x} \in \mathbb{E}} \{f(\mathbf{x}) + \lambda\|\mathbf{x}\|_1\}$$

  with f being an L_f-smooth function over the entire space $\mathbb{E}$.   ∎

10.2   The Proximal Gradient Method

To understand the idea behind the method for solving (10.1) we are about to study, we begin by revisiting the projected gradient method for solving (10.1) in the case where $g = \delta_C$ with C being a nonempty closed and convex set. In this case, the problem takes the form

$$\min\{f(\mathbf{x}) : \mathbf{x} \in C\}. \tag{10.2}$$

The general update step of the projected gradient method for solving (10.2) takes the form

$$\mathbf{x}^{k+1} = P_C(\mathbf{x}^k - t_k \nabla f(\mathbf{x}^k)),$$

where t_k is the stepsize at iteration k. It is easy to verify that the update step can be also written as (see also Section 9.1 for a similar discussion on the projected subgradient method)

$$\mathbf{x}^{k+1} = \mathrm{argmin}_{\mathbf{x} \in C} \left\{ f(\mathbf{x}^k) + \langle \nabla f(\mathbf{x}^k), \mathbf{x} - \mathbf{x}^k \rangle + \frac{1}{2t_k}\|\mathbf{x} - \mathbf{x}^k\|^2 \right\}.$$

That is, the next iterate is the minimizer over C of the sum of the linearization of the smooth part around the current iterate plus a quadratic prox term.

Back to the more general model (10.1), it is natural to generalize the above idea and to define the next iterate as the minimizer of the sum of the linearization of f around $\mathbf{x}^k$, the nonsmooth function g, and a quadratic prox term:

$$\mathbf{x}^{k+1} = \mathrm{argmin}_{\mathbf{x} \in \mathbb{E}} \left\{ f(\mathbf{x}^k) + \langle \nabla f(\mathbf{x}^k), \mathbf{x} - \mathbf{x}^k \rangle + g(\mathbf{x}) + \frac{1}{2t_k}\|\mathbf{x} - \mathbf{x}^k\|^2 \right\}. \tag{10.3}$$

After some simple algebraic manipulation and cancellation of constant terms, we obtain that (10.3) can be rewritten as

$$\mathbf{x}^{k+1} = \mathrm{argmin}_{\mathbf{x} \in \mathbb{E}} \left\{ t_k g(\mathbf{x}) + \frac{1}{2} \left\| \mathbf{x} - (\mathbf{x}^k - t_k \nabla f(\mathbf{x}^k)) \right\|^2 \right\},$$

which by the definition of the proximal operator is the same as

$$\mathbf{x}^{k+1} = \mathrm{prox}_{t_k g}(\mathbf{x}^k - t_k \nabla f(\mathbf{x}^k)).$$

The above method is called the *proximal gradient method*, as it consists of a gradient step followed by a proximal mapping. From now on, we will take the stepsizes as $t_k = \frac{1}{L_k}$, leading to the following description of the method.

The Proximal Gradient Method

Initialization: pick $\mathbf{x}^0 \in \text{int}(\text{dom}(f))$.
General step: for any $k = 0, 1, 2, \ldots$ execute the following steps:

(a) pick $L_k > 0$;

(b) set $\mathbf{x}^{k+1} = \text{prox}_{\frac{1}{L_k}g}\left(\mathbf{x}^k - \frac{1}{L_k}\nabla f(\mathbf{x}^k)\right)$.

The general update step of the proximal gradient method can be compactly written as

$$\mathbf{x}^{k+1} = T_{L_k}^{f,g}(\mathbf{x}^k),$$

where $T_L^{f,g} : \text{int}(\text{dom}(f)) \to \mathbb{E}$ $(L > 0)$ is the so-called *prox-grad operator* defined by

$$T_L^{f,g}(\mathbf{x}) \equiv \text{prox}_{\frac{1}{L}g}\left(\mathbf{x} - \frac{1}{L}\nabla f(\mathbf{x})\right).$$

When the identities of f and g are clear from the context, we will often omit the superscripts f, g and write $T_L(\cdot)$ instead of $T_L^{f,g}(\cdot)$.

Later on, we will consider two stepsize strategies, constant and backtracking, where the meaning of "backtracking" slightly changes under the different settings that will be considered, and hence several backtracking procedures will be defined.

Example 10.3. The table below presents the explicit update step of the proximal gradient method when applied to the three particular models discussed in Example 10.2.[54] The exact assumptions on the models are described in Example 10.2.

Model	Update step	Name of method
$\min_{\mathbf{x}\in\mathbb{E}} f(\mathbf{x})$	$\mathbf{x}^{k+1} = \mathbf{x}^k - t_k\nabla f(\mathbf{x}^k)$	gradient
$\min_{\mathbf{x}\in C} f(\mathbf{x})$	$\mathbf{x}^{k+1} = P_C(\mathbf{x}^k - t_k\nabla f(\mathbf{x}^k))$	projected gradient
$\min_{\mathbf{x}\in\mathbb{E}}\{f(\mathbf{x}) + \lambda\|\mathbf{x}\|_1\}$	$\mathbf{x}^{k+1} = \mathcal{T}_{\lambda t_k}(\mathbf{x}^k - t_k\nabla f(\mathbf{x}^k))$	ISTA

The third method is known as the *iterative shrinkage-thresholding algorithm* (ISTA) in the literature, since at each iteration a soft-thresholding operation (also known as "shrinkage") is performed. ∎

---

[54]Here we use the facts that $\text{prox}_{t_k g_0} = \mathcal{I}, \text{prox}_{t_k \delta_C} = P_C$ and $\text{prox}_{t_k \lambda\|\cdot\|_1} = \mathcal{T}_{\lambda t_k}$, where $g_0(\mathbf{x}) \equiv 0$.

10.3   Analysis of the Proximal Gradient Method— The Nonconvex Case[55]

10.3.1   Sufficient Decrease

To establish the convergence of the proximal gradient method, we will prove a sufficient decrease lemma for composite functions.

Lemma 10.4 (sufficient decrease lemma). *Suppose that f and g satisfy properties* (A) *and* (B) *of Assumption 10.1. Let $F = f + g$ and $T_L \equiv T_L^{f,g}$. Then for any $\mathbf{x} \in \mathrm{int}(\mathrm{dom}(f))$ and $L \in \left(\frac{L_f}{2}, \infty\right)$ the following inequality holds:*

$$F(\mathbf{x}) - F(T_L(\mathbf{x})) \geq \frac{L - \frac{L_f}{2}}{L^2} \left\| G_L^{f,g}(\mathbf{x}) \right\|^2, \tag{10.4}$$

where $G_L^{f,g} : \mathrm{int}(\mathrm{dom}(f)) \to \mathbb{E}$ is the operator defined by $G_L^{f,g}(\mathbf{x}) = L(\mathbf{x} - T_L(\mathbf{x}))$ for all $\mathbf{x} \in \mathrm{int}(\mathrm{dom}(f))$.

Proof. For the sake of simplicity, we use the shorthand notation $\mathbf{x}^+ = T_L(\mathbf{x})$. By the descent lemma (Lemma 5.7), we have that

$$f(\mathbf{x}^+) \leq f(\mathbf{x}) + \langle \nabla f(\mathbf{x}), \mathbf{x}^+ - \mathbf{x} \rangle + \frac{L_f}{2} \| \mathbf{x} - \mathbf{x}^+ \|^2. \tag{10.5}$$

By the second prox theorem (Theorem 6.39), since $\mathbf{x}^+ = \mathrm{prox}_{\frac{1}{L}g}\left(\mathbf{x} - \frac{1}{L}\nabla f(\mathbf{x})\right)$, we have

$$\left\langle \mathbf{x} - \frac{1}{L}\nabla f(\mathbf{x}) - \mathbf{x}^+, \mathbf{x} - \mathbf{x}^+ \right\rangle \leq \frac{1}{L}g(\mathbf{x}) - \frac{1}{L}g(\mathbf{x}^+),$$

from which it follows that

$$\langle \nabla f(\mathbf{x}), \mathbf{x}^+ - \mathbf{x} \rangle \leq -L \left\| \mathbf{x}^+ - \mathbf{x} \right\|^2 + g(\mathbf{x}) - g(\mathbf{x}^+),$$

which, combined with (10.5), yields

$$f(\mathbf{x}^+) + g(\mathbf{x}^+) \leq f(\mathbf{x}) + g(\mathbf{x}) + \left(-L + \frac{L_f}{2}\right) \left\| \mathbf{x}^+ - \mathbf{x} \right\|^2.$$

Hence, taking into account the definitions of $\mathbf{x}^+, G_L^{f,g}(\mathbf{x})$ and the identities $F(\mathbf{x}) = f(\mathbf{x}) + g(\mathbf{x}), F(\mathbf{x}^+) = f(\mathbf{x}^+) + g(\mathbf{x}^+)$, the desired result follows. $\square$

10.3.2   The Gradient Mapping

The operator $G_L^{f,g}$ that appears in the right-hand side of (10.4) is an important mapping that can be seen as a generalization of the notion of the gradient.

Definition 10.5 (gradient mapping). *Suppose that f and g satisfy properties* (A) *and* (B) *of Assumption 10.1. Then the **gradient mapping** is the operator*

---

[55]The analysis of the proximal gradient method in Sections 10.3 and 10.4 mostly follows the presentation of Beck and Teboulle in [18] and [19].

$G_L^{f,g} : \text{int}(\text{dom}(f)) \to \mathbb{E}$ *defined by*

$$G_L^{f,g}(\mathbf{x}) \equiv L\left(\mathbf{x} - T_L^{f,g}(\mathbf{x})\right)$$

for any $\mathbf{x} \in \text{int}(\text{dom}(f))$.

When the identities of f and g will be clear from the context, we will use the notation G_L instead of $G_L^{f,g}$. With the terminology of the gradient mapping, the update step of the proximal gradient method can be rewritten as

$$\mathbf{x}^{k+1} = \mathbf{x}^k - \frac{1}{L_k}G_{L_k}(\mathbf{x}^k).$$

In the special case where $L = L_f$, the sufficient decrease inequality (10.4) takes a simpler form.

Corollary 10.6. *Under the setting of Lemma* 10.4, *the following inequality holds for any* $\mathbf{x} \in \text{int}(\text{dom}(f))$:

$$F(\mathbf{x}) - F(T_{L_f}(\mathbf{x})) \geq \frac{1}{2L_f}\left\|G_{L_f}(\mathbf{x})\right\|^2.$$

The next result shows that the gradient mapping is a generalization of the "usual" gradient operator $\mathbf{x} \mapsto \nabla f(\mathbf{x})$ in the sense that they coincide when $g \equiv 0$ and that, for a general g, the points in which the gradient mapping vanishes are the stationary points of the problem of minimizing $f + g$. Recall (see Definition 3.73) that a point $\mathbf{x}^* \in \text{dom}(g)$ is a stationary point of problem (10.1) if and only if $-\nabla f(\mathbf{x}^*) \in \partial g(\mathbf{x}^*)$ and that this condition is a necessary optimality condition for local optimal points (see Theorem 3.72).

Theorem 10.7. *Let f and g satisfy properties* (A) *and* (B) *of Assumption* 10.1 *and let $L > 0$. Then*

(a) $G_L^{f,g_0}(\mathbf{x}) = \nabla f(\mathbf{x})$ *for any* $\mathbf{x} \in \text{int}(\text{dom}(f))$, *where* $g_0(\mathbf{x}) \equiv 0$;

(b) *for* $\mathbf{x}^* \in \text{int}(\text{dom}(f))$, *it holds that* $G_L^{f,g}(\mathbf{x}^*) = \mathbf{0}$ *if and only if* $\mathbf{x}^*$ *is a stationary point of problem* (10.1).

Proof. (a) Since $\text{prox}_{\frac{1}{L}g_0}(\mathbf{y}) = \mathbf{y}$ for all $\mathbf{y} \in \mathbb{E}$, it follows that

$$G_L^{f,g_0}(\mathbf{x}) = L(\mathbf{x} - T_L^{f,g_0}(\mathbf{x})) = L\left(\mathbf{x} - \text{prox}_{\frac{1}{L}g_0}\left(\mathbf{x} - \frac{1}{L}\nabla f(\mathbf{x})\right)\right)$$

$$= L\left(\mathbf{x} - \left(\mathbf{x} - \frac{1}{L}\nabla f(\mathbf{x})\right)\right) = \nabla f(\mathbf{x}).$$

(b) $G_L^{f,g}(\mathbf{x}^*) = \mathbf{0}$ if and only if $\mathbf{x}^* = \text{prox}_{\frac{1}{L}g}\left(\mathbf{x}^* - \frac{1}{L}\nabla f(\mathbf{x}^*)\right)$. By the second prox theorem (Theorem 6.39), the latter relation holds if and only if

$$\mathbf{x}^* - \frac{1}{L}\nabla f(\mathbf{x}^*) - \mathbf{x}^* \in \frac{1}{L}\partial g(\mathbf{x}^*),$$

that is, if and only if
$$-\nabla f(\mathbf{x}^*) \in \partial g(\mathbf{x}^*),$$
which is exactly the condition for stationarity.   □

If in addition f is convex, then stationarity is a necessary and sufficient optimality condition (Theorem 3.72(b)), which leads to the following corollary.

Corollary 10.8 (necessary and sufficient optimality condition under convexity). *Let f and g satisfy properties* (A) *and* (B) *of Assumption 10.1, and let $L > 0$. Suppose that in addition f is convex. Then for $\mathbf{x}^* \in \mathrm{dom}(g)$, $G_L^{f,g}(\mathbf{x}^*) = \mathbf{0}$ if and only if $\mathbf{x}^*$ is an optimal solution of problem (10.1).*

We can think of the quantity $\|G_L(\mathbf{x})\|$ as an "optimality measure" in the sense that it is always nonnegative, and equal to zero if and only if $\mathbf{x}$ is a stationary point. The next result establishes important monotonicity properties of $\|G_L(\mathbf{x})\|$ w.r.t. the parameter L.

Theorem 10.9 (monotonicity of the gradient mapping). *Suppose that f and g satisfy properties* (A) *and* (B) *of Assumption 10.1 and let $G_L \equiv G_L^{f,g}$. Suppose that $L_1 \geq L_2 > 0$. Then*
$$\|G_{L_1}(\mathbf{x})\| \geq \|G_{L_2}(\mathbf{x})\| \tag{10.6}$$
and
$$\frac{\|G_{L_1}(\mathbf{x})\|}{L_1} \leq \frac{\|G_{L_2}(\mathbf{x})\|}{L_2} \tag{10.7}$$
for any $\mathbf{x} \in \mathrm{int}(\mathrm{dom}(f))$.

Proof. Recall that by the second prox theorem (Theorem 6.39), for any $\mathbf{v}, \mathbf{w} \in \mathbb{E}$ and $L > 0$, the following inequality holds:
$$\langle \mathbf{v} - \mathrm{prox}_{\frac{1}{L}g}(\mathbf{v}), \mathrm{prox}_{\frac{1}{L}g}(\mathbf{v}) - \mathbf{w} \rangle \geq \frac{1}{L} g\left(\mathrm{prox}_{\frac{1}{L}g}(\mathbf{v})\right) - \frac{1}{L}g(\mathbf{w}).$$

Plugging $L = L_1, \mathbf{v} = \mathbf{x} - \frac{1}{L_1}\nabla f(\mathbf{x})$, and $\mathbf{w} = \mathrm{prox}_{\frac{1}{L_2}g}\left(\mathbf{x} - \frac{1}{L_2}\nabla f(\mathbf{x})\right) = T_{L_2}(\mathbf{x})$ into the last inequality, it follows that
$$\left\langle \mathbf{x} - \frac{1}{L_1}\nabla f(\mathbf{x}) - T_{L_1}(\mathbf{x}), T_{L_1}(\mathbf{x}) - T_{L_2}(\mathbf{x}) \right\rangle \geq \frac{1}{L_1}g(T_{L_1}(\mathbf{x})) - \frac{1}{L_1}g(T_{L_2}(\mathbf{x}))$$
or
$$\left\langle \frac{1}{L_1}G_{L_1}(\mathbf{x}) - \frac{1}{L_1}\nabla f(\mathbf{x}), \frac{1}{L_2}G_{L_2}(\mathbf{x}) - \frac{1}{L_1}G_{L_1}(\mathbf{x}) \right\rangle \geq \frac{1}{L_1}g(T_{L_1}(\mathbf{x})) - \frac{1}{L_1}g(T_{L_2}(\mathbf{x})).$$
Exchanging the roles of L_1 and L_2 yields the following inequality:
$$\left\langle \frac{1}{L_2}G_{L_2}(\mathbf{x}) - \frac{1}{L_2}\nabla f(\mathbf{x}), \frac{1}{L_1}G_{L_1}(\mathbf{x}) - \frac{1}{L_2}G_{L_2}(\mathbf{x}) \right\rangle \geq \frac{1}{L_2}g(T_{L_2}(\mathbf{x})) - \frac{1}{L_2}g(T_{L_1}(\mathbf{x})).$$
Multiplying the first inequality by L_1 and the second by L_2 and adding them, we obtain
$$\left\langle G_{L_1}(\mathbf{x}) - G_{L_2}(\mathbf{x}), \frac{1}{L_2}G_{L_2}(\mathbf{x}) - \frac{1}{L_1}G_{L_1}(\mathbf{x}) \right\rangle \geq 0,$$

which after some expansion of terms can be seen to be the same as

$$\frac{1}{L_1}\|G_{L_1}(\mathbf{x})\|^2 + \frac{1}{L_2}\|G_{L_2}(\mathbf{x})\|^2 \le \left(\frac{1}{L_1} + \frac{1}{L_2}\right)\langle G_{L_1}(\mathbf{x}), G_{L_2}(\mathbf{x})\rangle.$$

Using the Cauchy–Schwarz inequality, we obtain that

$$\frac{1}{L_1}\|G_{L_1}(\mathbf{x})\|^2 + \frac{1}{L_2}\|G_{L_2}(\mathbf{x})\|^2 \le \left(\frac{1}{L_1} + \frac{1}{L_2}\right)\|G_{L_1}(\mathbf{x})\| \cdot \|G_{L_2}(\mathbf{x})\|. \qquad (10.8)$$

Note that if $G_{L_2}(\mathbf{x}) = \mathbf{0}$, then by the last inequality, $G_{L_1}(\mathbf{x}) = \mathbf{0}$, implying that in this case the inequalities (10.6) and (10.7) hold trivially. Assume then that $G_{L_2}(\mathbf{x}) \ne \mathbf{0}$ and define $t = \frac{\|G_{L_1}(\mathbf{x})\|}{\|G_{L_2}(\mathbf{x})\|}$. Then, by (10.8),

$$\frac{1}{L_1}t^2 - \left(\frac{1}{L_1} + \frac{1}{L_2}\right)t + \frac{1}{L_2} \le 0.$$

Since the roots of the quadratic function on the left-hand side of the above inequality are $t = 1, \frac{L_1}{L_2}$, we obtain that

$$1 \le t \le \frac{L_1}{L_2},$$

showing that

$$\|G_{L_2}(\mathbf{x})\| \le \|G_{L_1}(\mathbf{x})\| \le \frac{L_1}{L_2}\|G_{L_2}(\mathbf{x})\|. \qquad \square$$

A straightforward result of the nonexpansivity of the prox operator and the L_f-smoothness of f over $\operatorname{int}(\operatorname{dom}(f))$ is that $G_L(\cdot)$ is Lipschitz continuous with constant $2L + L_f$. Indeed, for any $\mathbf{x}, \mathbf{y} \in \operatorname{int}(\operatorname{dom}(f))$,

$$\|G_L(\mathbf{x}) - G_L(\mathbf{y})\| = L\left\|\mathbf{x} - \operatorname{prox}_{\frac{1}{L}g}\left(\mathbf{x} - \frac{1}{L}\nabla f(\mathbf{x})\right) - \mathbf{y} + \operatorname{prox}_{\frac{1}{L}g}\left(\mathbf{y} - \frac{1}{L}\nabla f(\mathbf{y})\right)\right\|$$

$$\le L\|\mathbf{x} - \mathbf{y}\| + L\left\|\operatorname{prox}_{\frac{1}{L}g}\left(\mathbf{x} - \frac{1}{L}\nabla f(\mathbf{x})\right) - \operatorname{prox}_{\frac{1}{L}g}\left(\mathbf{y} - \frac{1}{L}\nabla f(\mathbf{y})\right)\right\|$$

$$\le L\|\mathbf{x} - \mathbf{y}\| + L\left\|\left(\mathbf{x} - \frac{1}{L}\nabla f(\mathbf{x})\right) - \left(\mathbf{y} - \frac{1}{L}\nabla f(\mathbf{y})\right)\right\|$$

$$\le 2L\|\mathbf{x} - \mathbf{y}\| + \|\nabla f(\mathbf{x}) - \nabla f(\mathbf{y})\|$$

$$\le (2L + L_f)\|\mathbf{x} - \mathbf{y}\|.$$

In particular, for $L = L_f$, we obtain the inequality

$$\|G_{L_f}(\mathbf{x}) - G_{L_f}(\mathbf{y})\| \le 3L_f\|\mathbf{x} - \mathbf{y}\|.$$

The above discussion is summarized in the following lemma.

Lemma 10.10 (Lipschitz continuity of the gradient mapping). *Let f and g satisfy properties* (A) *and* (B) *of Assumption* 10.1. *Let $G_L = G_L^{f,g}$. Then*

(a) $\|G_L(\mathbf{x}) - G_L(\mathbf{y})\| \le (2L + L_f)\|\mathbf{x} - \mathbf{y}\|$ *for any $\mathbf{x}, \mathbf{y} \in \operatorname{int}(\operatorname{dom}(f))$;*

(b) $\|G_{L_f}(\mathbf{x}) - G_{L_f}(\mathbf{y})\| \le 3L_f\|\mathbf{x} - \mathbf{y}\|$ *for any $\mathbf{x}, \mathbf{y} \in \operatorname{int}(\operatorname{dom}(f))$.*

Lemma 10.11 below shows that when f is assumed to be convex and L_f-smooth over the entire space, then the operator $\frac{3}{4L_f} G_{L_f}$ is firmly nonexpansive. A direct consequence is that G_{L_f} is Lipschitz continuous with constant $\frac{4L_f}{3}$.

Lemma 10.11 (firm nonexpansivity of $\frac{3}{4L_f} \mathbf{G_{L_f}}$). *Let f be a convex and L_f-smooth function ($L_f > 0$), and let $g : \mathbb{E} \to (-\infty, \infty]$ be a proper closed and convex function. Then*

(a) *the gradient mapping $G_{L_f} \equiv G_{L_f}^{f,g}$ satisfies the relation*

$$\langle G_{L_f}(\mathbf{x}) - G_{L_f}(\mathbf{y}), \mathbf{x} - \mathbf{y} \rangle \geq \frac{3}{4L_f} \left\| G_{L_f}(\mathbf{x}) - G_{L_f}(\mathbf{y}) \right\|^2 \qquad (10.9)$$

for any $\mathbf{x}, \mathbf{y} \in \mathbb{E}$;

(b) $\left\| G_{L_f}(\mathbf{x}) - G_{L_f}(\mathbf{y}) \right\| \leq \frac{4L_f}{3} \|\mathbf{x} - \mathbf{y}\|$ *for any $\mathbf{x}, \mathbf{y} \in \mathbb{E}$.*

Proof. Part (b) is a direct consequence of (a) and the Cauchy–Schwarz inequality. We will therefore prove (a). To simplify the presentation, we will use the notation $L = L_f$. By the firm nonexpansivity of the prox operator (Theorem 6.42(a)), it follows that for any $\mathbf{x}, \mathbf{y} \in \mathbb{E}$,

$$\left\langle T_L(\mathbf{x}) - T_L(\mathbf{y}), \left(\mathbf{x} - \frac{1}{L} \nabla f(\mathbf{x}) \right) - \left(\mathbf{y} - \frac{1}{L} \nabla f(\mathbf{y}) \right) \right\rangle \geq \| T_L(\mathbf{x}) - T_L(\mathbf{y}) \|^2,$$

where $T_L \equiv T_L^{f,g}$ is the prox-grad mapping. Since $T_L = \mathcal{I} - \frac{1}{L} G_L$, we obtain that

$$\left\langle \left(\mathbf{x} - \frac{1}{L} G_L(\mathbf{x}) \right) - \left(\mathbf{y} - \frac{1}{L} G_L(\mathbf{y}) \right), \left(\mathbf{x} - \frac{1}{L} \nabla f(\mathbf{x}) \right) - \left(\mathbf{y} - \frac{1}{L} \nabla f(\mathbf{y}) \right) \right\rangle$$
$$\geq \left\| \left(\mathbf{x} - \frac{1}{L} G_L(\mathbf{x}) \right) - \left(\mathbf{y} - \frac{1}{L} G_L(\mathbf{y}) \right) \right\|^2,$$

which is the same as

$$\left\langle \left(\mathbf{x} - \frac{1}{L} G_L(\mathbf{x}) \right) - \left(\mathbf{y} - \frac{1}{L} G_L(\mathbf{y}) \right), (G_L(\mathbf{x}) - \nabla f(\mathbf{x})) - (G_L(\mathbf{y}) - \nabla f(\mathbf{y})) \right\rangle \geq 0.$$

Therefore,

$$\langle G_L(\mathbf{x}) - G_L(\mathbf{y}), \mathbf{x} - \mathbf{y} \rangle \geq \frac{1}{L} \| G_L(\mathbf{x}) - G_L(\mathbf{y}) \|^2 + \langle \nabla f(\mathbf{x}) - \nabla f(\mathbf{y}), \mathbf{x} - \mathbf{y} \rangle$$
$$- \frac{1}{L} \langle G_L(\mathbf{x}) - G_L(\mathbf{y}), \nabla f(\mathbf{x}) - \nabla f(\mathbf{y}) \rangle.$$

Since f is L-smooth, it follows from Theorem 5.8 (equivalence between (i) and (iv)) that

$$\langle \nabla f(\mathbf{x}) - \nabla f(\mathbf{y}), \mathbf{x} - \mathbf{y} \rangle \geq \frac{1}{L} \|\nabla f(\mathbf{x}) - \nabla f(\mathbf{y})\|^2.$$

Consequently,

$$L \langle G_L(\mathbf{x}) - G_L(\mathbf{y}), \mathbf{x} - \mathbf{y} \rangle \geq \| G_L(\mathbf{x}) - G_L(\mathbf{y}) \|^2 + \|\nabla f(\mathbf{x}) - \nabla f(\mathbf{y})\|^2$$
$$- \langle G_L(\mathbf{x}) - G_L(\mathbf{y}), \nabla f(\mathbf{x}) - \nabla f(\mathbf{y}) \rangle.$$

From the Cauchy–Schwarz inequality we get

$$L \langle G_L(\mathbf{x}) - G_L(\mathbf{y}), \mathbf{x} - \mathbf{y} \rangle \geq \|G_L(\mathbf{x}) - G_L(\mathbf{y})\|^2 + \|\nabla f(\mathbf{x}) - \nabla f(\mathbf{y})\|^2$$
$$- \|G_L(\mathbf{x}) - G_L(\mathbf{y})\| \cdot \|\nabla f(\mathbf{x}) - \nabla f(\mathbf{y})\|. \quad (10.10)$$

By denoting $\alpha = \|G_L(\mathbf{x}) - G_L(\mathbf{y})\|$ and $\beta = \|\nabla f(\mathbf{x}) - \nabla f(\mathbf{y})\|$, the right-hand side of (10.10) reads as $\alpha^2 + \beta^2 - \alpha\beta$ and satisfies

$$\alpha^2 + \beta^2 - \alpha\beta = \frac{3}{4}\alpha^2 + \left(\frac{\alpha}{2} - \beta\right)^2 \geq \frac{3}{4}\alpha^2,$$

which, combined with (10.10), yields the inequality

$$L \langle G_L(\mathbf{x}) - G_L(\mathbf{y}), \mathbf{x} - \mathbf{y} \rangle \geq \frac{3}{4}\|G_L(\mathbf{x}) - G_L(\mathbf{y})\|^2.$$

Thus, (10.9) holds. □

The next result shows a different kind of a monotonicity property of the gradient mapping norm under the setting of Lemma 10.11—the norm of the gradient mapping does not increase if a prox-grad step is employed on its argument.

Lemma 10.12 (monotonicity of the norm of the gradient mapping w.r.t. the prox-grad operator).[56] *Let f be a convex and L_f-smooth function ($L_f > 0$), and let $g : \mathbb{E} \to (-\infty, \infty]$ be a proper closed and convex function. Then for any $\mathbf{x} \in \mathbb{E}$,*

$$\|G_{L_f}(T_{L_f}(\mathbf{x}))\| \leq \|G_{L_f}(\mathbf{x})\|,$$

where $G_{L_f} \equiv G_{L_f}^{f,g}$ and $T_{L_f} \equiv T_{L_f}^{f,g}$.

Proof. Let $\mathbf{x} \in \mathbb{E}$. We will use the shorthand notation $\mathbf{x}^+ = T_{L_f}(\mathbf{x})$. By Theorem 5.8 (equivalence between (i) and (iv)), it follows that

$$\|\nabla f(\mathbf{x}^+) - \nabla f(\mathbf{x})\|^2 \leq L_f \langle \nabla f(\mathbf{x}^+) - \nabla f(\mathbf{x}), \mathbf{x}^+ - \mathbf{x} \rangle. \quad (10.11)$$

Denoting $\mathbf{a} = \nabla f(\mathbf{x}^+) - \nabla f(\mathbf{x})$ and $\mathbf{b} = \mathbf{x}^+ - \mathbf{x}$, inequality (10.11) can be rewritten as $\|\mathbf{a}\|^2 \leq L_f \langle \mathbf{a}, \mathbf{b} \rangle$, which is the same as

$$\left\|\mathbf{a} - \frac{L_f}{2}\mathbf{b}\right\|^2 \leq \frac{L_f^2}{4}\|\mathbf{b}\|^2$$

and as

$$\left\|\frac{1}{L_f}\mathbf{a} - \frac{1}{2}\mathbf{b}\right\| \leq \frac{1}{2}\|\mathbf{b}\|.$$

Using the triangle inequality,

$$\left\|\frac{1}{L_f}\mathbf{a} - \mathbf{b}\right\| = \left\|\frac{1}{L_f}\mathbf{a} - \frac{1}{2}\mathbf{b} - \frac{1}{2}\mathbf{b}\right\| \leq \left\|\frac{1}{L_f}\mathbf{a} - \frac{1}{2}\mathbf{b}\right\| + \frac{1}{2}\|\mathbf{b}\| \leq \|\mathbf{b}\|.$$

---

[56]Lemma 10.12 is a minor variation of Lemma 2.4 from Necoara and Patrascu [88].

Plugging the expressions for **a** and **b** into the above inequality, we obtain that

$$\left\| \mathbf{x} - \frac{1}{L_f}\nabla f(\mathbf{x}) - \mathbf{x}^+ + \frac{1}{L_f}\nabla f(\mathbf{x}^+) \right\| \le \|\mathbf{x}^+ - \mathbf{x}\|.$$

Combining the above inequality with the nonexpansivity of the prox operator (Theorem 6.42(b)), we finally obtain

$$\|G_{L_f}(T_{L_f}(\mathbf{x}))\| = \|G_{L_f}(\mathbf{x}^+)\| = L_f\|\mathbf{x}^+ - T_{L_f}(\mathbf{x}^+)\| = L_f\|T_{L_f}(\mathbf{x}) - T_{L_f}(\mathbf{x}^+)\|$$

$$= L_f \left\| \mathrm{prox}_{\frac{1}{L_f}g}\left(\mathbf{x} - \frac{1}{L_f}\nabla f(\mathbf{x})\right) - \mathrm{prox}_{\frac{1}{L_f}g}\left(\mathbf{x}^+ - \frac{1}{L_f}\nabla f(\mathbf{x}^+)\right) \right\|$$

$$\le L_f \left\| \mathbf{x} - \frac{1}{L_f}\nabla f(\mathbf{x}) - \mathbf{x}^+ + \frac{1}{L_f}\nabla f(\mathbf{x}^+) \right\|$$

$$\le L_f\|\mathbf{x}^+ - \mathbf{x}\| = L_f\|T_{L_f}(\mathbf{x}) - \mathbf{x}\| = \|G_{L_f}(\mathbf{x})\|,$$

which is the desired result. $\square$

10.3.3   Convergence of the Proximal Gradient Method— The Nonconvex Case

We will now analyze the convergence of the proximal gradient method under the validity of Assumption 10.1. Note that we do not assume at this stage that f is convex. The two stepsize strategies that will be considered are constant and backtracking.

- **Constant.** $L_k = \bar{L} \in \left(\frac{L_f}{2}, \infty\right)$ for all k.

- **Backtracking procedure B1.** The procedure requires three parameters (s, γ, η), where $s > 0, \gamma \in (0,1)$, and $\eta > 1$. The choice of L_k is done as follows. First, L_k is set to be equal to the initial guess s. Then, while

$$F(\mathbf{x}^k) - F(T_{L_k}(\mathbf{x}^k)) < \frac{\gamma}{L_k}\|G_{L_k}(\mathbf{x}^k)\|^2,$$

  we set $L_k := \eta L_k$. In other words, L_k is chosen as $L_k = s\eta^{i_k}$, where i_k is the smallest nonnegative integer for which the condition

$$F(\mathbf{x}^k) - F(T_{s\eta^{i_k}}(\mathbf{x}^k)) \ge \frac{\gamma}{s\eta^{i_k}}\|G_{s\eta^{i_k}}(\mathbf{x}^k)\|^2$$

  is satisfied.

Remark 10.13. *Note that the backtracking procedure is finite under Assumption 10.1. Indeed, plugging* $\mathbf{x} = \mathbf{x}^k$ *into (10.4), we obtain*

$$F(\mathbf{x}^k) - F(T_L(\mathbf{x}^k)) \ge \frac{L - \frac{L_f}{2}}{L^2}\left\|G_L(\mathbf{x}^k)\right\|^2. \tag{10.12}$$

If $L \geq \frac{L_f}{2(1-\gamma)}$, then $\frac{L - \frac{L_f}{2}}{L} \geq \gamma$, and hence, by (10.12), the inequality

$$F(\mathbf{x}^k) - F(T_L(\mathbf{x}^k)) \geq \frac{\gamma}{L}\|G_L(\mathbf{x}^k)\|^2$$

holds, implying that the backtracking procedure must end when $L_k \geq \frac{L_f}{2(1-\gamma)}$.

We can also compute an upper bound on L_k: either L_k is equal to s, or the backtracking procedure is invoked, meaning that $\frac{L_k}{\eta}$ did not satisfy the backtracking condition, which by the above discussion implies that $\frac{L_k}{\eta} < \frac{L_f}{2(1-\gamma)}$, so that $L_k < \frac{\eta L_f}{2(1-\gamma)}$. To summarize, in the backtracking procedure B1, the parameter L_k satisfies

$$L_k \leq \max\left\{ s, \frac{\eta L_f}{2(1-\gamma)} \right\}. \tag{10.13}$$

The convergence of the proximal gradient method in the nonconvex case is heavily based on the sufficient decrease lemma (Lemma 10.4). We begin with the following lemma showing that consecutive function values of the sequence generated by the proximal gradient method decrease by at least a constant times the squared norm of the gradient mapping.

Lemma 10.14 (sufficient decrease of the proximal gradient method). *Suppose that Assumption 10.1 holds. Let $\{\mathbf{x}^k\}_{k \geq 0}$ be the sequence generated by the proximal gradient method for solving problem (10.1) with either a constant stepsize defined by $L_k = \bar{L} \in \left(\frac{L_f}{2}, \infty\right)$ or with a stepsize chosen by the backtracking procedure B1 with parameters (s, γ, η), where $s > 0, \gamma \in (0,1), \eta > 1$. Then for any $k \geq 0$,*

$$F(\mathbf{x}^k) - F(\mathbf{x}^{k+1}) \geq M\|G_d(\mathbf{x}^k)\|^2, \tag{10.14}$$

where

$$M = \begin{cases} \frac{\bar{L} - \frac{L_f}{2}}{(\bar{L})^2}, & \text{constant stepsize,} \\ \frac{\gamma}{\max\left\{ s, \frac{\eta L_f}{2(1-\gamma)} \right\}}, & \text{backtracking,} \end{cases} \tag{10.15}$$

and

$$d = \begin{cases} \bar{L}, & \text{constant stepsize,} \\ s, & \text{backtracking.} \end{cases} \tag{10.16}$$

Proof. The result for the constant stepsize setting follows by plugging $L = \bar{L}$ and $\mathbf{x} = \mathbf{x}^k$ into (10.4). As for the case where the backtracking procedure is used, by its definition we have

$$F(\mathbf{x}^k) - F(\mathbf{x}^{k+1}) \geq \frac{\gamma}{L_k}\|G_{L_k}(\mathbf{x}^k)\|^2 \geq \frac{\gamma}{\max\left\{ s, \frac{\eta L_f}{2(1-\gamma)} \right\}}\|G_{L_k}(\mathbf{x}^k)\|^2,$$

where the last inequality follows from the upper bound on L_k given in (10.13). The result for the case where the backtracking procedure is invoked now follows by the monotonicity property of the gradient mapping (Theorem 10.9) along with the bound $L_k \geq s$, which imply the inequality $\|G_{L_k}(\mathbf{x}^k)\| \geq \|G_s(\mathbf{x}^k)\|$. $\square$

We are now ready to prove the convergence of the norm of the gradient mapping to zero and that limit points of the sequence generated by the method are stationary points of problem (10.1).

Theorem 10.15 (convergence of the proximal gradient method—nonconvex case). *Suppose that Assumption 10.1 holds and let $\{\mathbf{x}^k\}_{k\geq 0}$ be the sequence generated by the proximal gradient method for solving problem (10.1) either with a constant stepsize defined by $L_k = \bar{L} \in \left(\frac{L_f}{2}, \infty\right)$ or with a stepsize chosen by the backtracking procedure B1 with parameters (s, γ, η), where $s > 0, \gamma \in (0, 1)$, and $\eta > 1$. Then*

(a) *the sequence $\{F(\mathbf{x}^k)\}_{k\geq 0}$ is nonincreasing. In addition, $F(\mathbf{x}^{k+1}) < F(\mathbf{x}^k)$ if and only if $\mathbf{x}^k$ is not a stationary point of (10.1);*

(b) *$G_d(\mathbf{x}^k) \to \mathbf{0}$ as $k \to \infty$, where d is given in (10.16);*

(c)

$$\min_{n=0,1,\ldots,k} \|G_d(\mathbf{x}^n)\| \leq \frac{\sqrt{F(\mathbf{x}^0) - F_{\text{opt}}}}{\sqrt{M(k+1)}}, \tag{10.17}$$

where M is given in (10.15);

(d) *all limit points of the sequence $\{\mathbf{x}^k\}_{k\geq 0}$ are stationary points of problem (10.1).*

Proof. (a) By Lemma 10.14 we have that

$$F(\mathbf{x}^k) - F(\mathbf{x}^{k+1}) \geq M\|G_d(\mathbf{x}^k)\|^2, \tag{10.18}$$

from which it readily follows that $F(\mathbf{x}^k) \geq F(\mathbf{x}^{k+1})$. If $\mathbf{x}^k$ is not a stationary point of problem (10.1), then $G_d(\mathbf{x}^k) \neq \mathbf{0}$, and hence, by (10.18), $F(\mathbf{x}^k) > F(\mathbf{x}^{k+1})$. If $\mathbf{x}^k$ is a stationary point of problem (10.1), then $G_{L_k}(\mathbf{x}^k) = \mathbf{0}$, from which it follows that $\mathbf{x}^{k+1} = \mathbf{x}^k - \frac{1}{L_k}G_{L_k}(\mathbf{x}^k) = \mathbf{x}^k$, and consequently $F(\mathbf{x}^k) = F(\mathbf{x}^{k+1})$.

(b) Since the sequence $\{F(\mathbf{x}^k)\}_{k\geq 0}$ is nonincreasing and bounded below, it converges. Thus, in particular, $F(\mathbf{x}^k) - F(\mathbf{x}^{k+1}) \to 0$ as $k \to \infty$, which, combined with (10.18), implies that $\|G_d(\mathbf{x}^k)\| \to 0$ as $k \to \infty$.

(c) Summing the inequality

$$F(\mathbf{x}^n) - F(\mathbf{x}^{n+1}) \geq M\|G_d(\mathbf{x}^n)\|^2$$

over $n = 0, 1, \ldots, k$, we obtain

$$F(\mathbf{x}^0) - F(\mathbf{x}^{k+1}) \geq M \sum_{n=0}^{k} \|G_d(\mathbf{x}^n)\|^2 \geq M(k+1) \min_{n=0,1,\ldots,k} \|G_d(\mathbf{x}^n)\|^2.$$

Using the fact that $F(\mathbf{x}^{k+1}) \geq F_{\text{opt}}$, the inequality (10.17) follows.

(d) Let $\bar{\mathbf{x}}$ be a limit point of $\{\mathbf{x}^k\}_{k\geq 0}$. Then there exists a subsequence $\{\mathbf{x}^{k_j}\}_{j\geq 0}$ converging to $\bar{\mathbf{x}}$. For any $j \geq 0$,

$$\|G_d(\bar{\mathbf{x}})\| \leq \|G_d(\mathbf{x}^{k_j}) - G_d(\bar{\mathbf{x}})\| + \|G_d(\mathbf{x}^{k_j})\| \leq (2d + L_f)\|\mathbf{x}^{k_j} - \bar{\mathbf{x}}\| + \|G_d(\mathbf{x}^{k_j})\|, \tag{10.19}$$

where Lemma 10.10(a) was used in the second inequality. Since the right-hand side of (10.19) goes to 0 as $j \to \infty$, it follows that $G_d(\bar{\mathbf{x}}) = \mathbf{0}$, which by Theorem 10.7(b) implies that $\bar{\mathbf{x}}$ is a stationary point of problem (10.1). $\square$

10.4 Analysis of the Proximal Gradient Method— The Convex Case

10.4.1 The Fundamental Prox-Grad Inequality

The analysis of the proximal gradient method in the case where f is convex is based on the following key inequality (which actually does not assume that f is convex).

Theorem 10.16 (fundamental prox-grad inequality). *Suppose that f and g satisfy properties* (A) *and* (B) *of Assumption* 10.1. *For any* $\mathbf{x} \in \mathbb{E}$, $\mathbf{y} \in \text{int}(\text{dom}(f))$ *and* $L > 0$ *satisfying*

$$f(T_L(\mathbf{y})) \leq f(\mathbf{y}) + \langle \nabla f(\mathbf{y}), T_L(\mathbf{y}) - \mathbf{y} \rangle + \frac{L}{2}\|T_L(\mathbf{y}) - \mathbf{y}\|^2, \tag{10.20}$$

it holds that

$$F(\mathbf{x}) - F(T_L(\mathbf{y})) \geq \frac{L}{2}\|\mathbf{x} - T_L(\mathbf{y})\|^2 - \frac{L}{2}\|\mathbf{x} - \mathbf{y}\|^2 + \ell_f(\mathbf{x}, \mathbf{y}), \tag{10.21}$$

where

$$\ell_f(\mathbf{x}, \mathbf{y}) = f(\mathbf{x}) - f(\mathbf{y}) - \langle \nabla f(\mathbf{y}), \mathbf{x} - \mathbf{y} \rangle.$$

Proof. Consider the function

$$\varphi(\mathbf{u}) = f(\mathbf{y}) + \langle \nabla f(\mathbf{y}), \mathbf{u} - \mathbf{y} \rangle + g(\mathbf{u}) + \frac{L}{2}\|\mathbf{u} - \mathbf{y}\|^2.$$

Since φ is an L-strongly convex function and $T_L(\mathbf{y}) = \text{argmin}_{\mathbf{u} \in \mathbb{E}}\varphi(\mathbf{u})$, it follows by Theorem 5.25(b) that

$$\varphi(\mathbf{x}) - \varphi(T_L(\mathbf{y})) \geq \frac{L}{2}\|\mathbf{x} - T_L(\mathbf{y})\|^2. \tag{10.22}$$

Note that by (10.20),

$$\varphi(T_L(\mathbf{y})) = f(\mathbf{y}) + \langle \nabla f(\mathbf{y}), T_L(\mathbf{y}) - \mathbf{y} \rangle + \frac{L}{2}\|T_L(\mathbf{y}) - \mathbf{y}\|^2 + g(T_L(\mathbf{y}))$$
$$\geq f(T_L(\mathbf{y})) + g(T_L(\mathbf{y})) = F(T_L(\mathbf{y})),$$

and thus (10.22) implies that for any $\mathbf{x} \in \mathbb{E}$,

$$\varphi(\mathbf{x}) - F(T_L(\mathbf{y})) \geq \frac{L}{2}\|\mathbf{x} - T_L(\mathbf{y})\|^2.$$

Plugging the expression for $\varphi(\mathbf{x})$ into the above inequality, we obtain

$$f(\mathbf{y}) + \langle \nabla f(\mathbf{y}), \mathbf{x} - \mathbf{y} \rangle + g(\mathbf{x}) + \frac{L}{2}\|\mathbf{x} - \mathbf{y}\|^2 - F(T_L(\mathbf{y})) \geq \frac{L}{2}\|\mathbf{x} - T_L(\mathbf{y})\|^2,$$

which is the same as the desired result:

$$F(\mathbf{x}) - F(T_L(\mathbf{y})) \geq \frac{L}{2}\|\mathbf{x} - T_L(\mathbf{y})\|^2 - \frac{L}{2}\|\mathbf{x} - \mathbf{y}\|^2$$
$$+ f(\mathbf{x}) - f(\mathbf{y}) - \langle \nabla f(\mathbf{y}), \mathbf{x} - \mathbf{y} \rangle. \qquad \square$$

Remark 10.17. *Obviously, by the descent lemma, (10.20) is satisfied for $L = L_f$, and hence, for any $\mathbf{x} \in \mathbb{E}$ and $\mathbf{y} \in \mathrm{int}(\mathrm{dom}(f))$, the inequality*

$$F(\mathbf{x}) - F(T_{L_f}(\mathbf{y})) \geq \frac{L_f}{2}\|\mathbf{x} - T_{L_f}(\mathbf{y})\|^2 - \frac{L_f}{2}\|\mathbf{x} - \mathbf{y}\|^2 + \ell_f(\mathbf{x}, \mathbf{y})$$

holds.

A direct consequence of Theorem 10.16 is another version of the sufficient decrease lemma (Lemma 10.4). This is accomplished by substituting $\mathbf{y} = \mathbf{x}$ in the fundamental prox-grad inequality.

Corollary 10.18 (sufficient decrease lemma—second version). *Suppose that f and g satisfy properties* (A) *and* (B) *of Assumption 10.1. For any $\mathbf{x} \in \mathrm{int}(\mathrm{dom}(f))$ for which*

$$f(T_L(\mathbf{x})) \leq f(\mathbf{x}) + \langle \nabla f(\mathbf{x}), T_L(\mathbf{x}) - \mathbf{x} \rangle + \frac{L}{2}\|T_L(\mathbf{x}) - \mathbf{x}\|^2,$$

it holds that

$$F(\mathbf{x}) - F(T_L(\mathbf{x})) \geq \frac{1}{2L}\|G_L(\mathbf{x})\|^2.$$

10.4.2   Stepsize Strategies in the Convex Case

When f is also convex, we will consider, as in the nonconvex case, both constant and backtracking stepsize strategies. The backtracking procedure, which we will refer to as "backtracking procedure B2," will be slightly different than the one considered in the nonconvex case, and it will aim to find a constant L_k satisfying

$$f(\mathbf{x}^{k+1}) \leq f(\mathbf{x}^k) + \langle \nabla f(\mathbf{x}^k), \mathbf{x}^{k+1} - \mathbf{x}^k \rangle + \frac{L_k}{2}\|\mathbf{x}^{k+1} - \mathbf{x}^k\|^2. \qquad (10.23)$$

In the special case where $g \equiv 0$, the proximal gradient method reduces to the gradient method $\mathbf{x}^{k+1} = \mathbf{x}^k - \frac{1}{L_k}\nabla f(\mathbf{x}^k)$, and condition (10.23) reduces to

$$f(\mathbf{x}^k) - f(\mathbf{x}^{k+1}) \geq \frac{1}{2L_k}\|\nabla f(\mathbf{x}^k)\|^2,$$

which is similar to the sufficient decrease condition described in Lemma 10.4, and this is why condition (10.23) can also be viewed as a "sufficient decrease condition."

- **Constant.** $L_k = L_f$ for all k.

- **Backtracking procedure B2.** The procedure requires two parameters (s, η), where $s > 0$ and $\eta > 1$. Define $L_{-1} = s$. At iteration k ($k \geq 0$) the choice of L_k is done as follows. First, L_k is set to be equal to L_{k-1}. Then, while

$$f(T_{L_k}(\mathbf{x}^k)) > f(\mathbf{x}^k) + \langle \nabla f(\mathbf{x}^k), T_{L_k}(\mathbf{x}^k) - \mathbf{x}^k \rangle + \frac{L_k}{2} \|T_{L_k}(\mathbf{x}^k) - \mathbf{x}^k\|^2,$$

  we set $L_k := \eta L_k$. In other words, L_k is chosen as $L_k = L_{k-1}\eta^{i_k}$, where i_k is the smallest nonnegative integer for which the condition

$$f(T_{L_{k-1}\eta^{i_k}}(\mathbf{x}^k)) \leq f(\mathbf{x}^k) + \langle \nabla f(\mathbf{x}^k), T_{L_{k-1}\eta^{i_k}}(\mathbf{x}^k) - \mathbf{x}^k \rangle + $$
$$\frac{L_k}{2} \|T_{L_{k-1}\eta^{i_k}}(\mathbf{x}^k) - \mathbf{x}^k\|^2$$

  is satisfied.

Remark 10.19 (upper and lower bounds on L_k). *Under Assumption 10.1 and by the descent lemma (Lemma 5.7), it follows that both stepsize rules ensure that the sufficient decrease condition (10.23) is satisfied at each iteration. In addition, the constants L_k that the backtracking procedure B2 produces satisfy the following bounds for all $k \geq 0$:*

$$s \leq L_k \leq \max\{\eta L_f, s\}. \tag{10.24}$$

The inequality $s \leq L_k$ is obvious. To understand the inequality $L_k \leq \max\{\eta L_f, s\}$, note that there are two options. Either $L_k = s$ or $L_k > s$, and in the latter case there exists an index $0 \leq k' \leq k$ for which the inequality (10.23) is not satisfied with $k = k'$ and $\frac{L_k}{\eta}$ replacing L_k. By the descent lemma, this implies in particular that $\frac{L_k}{\eta} < L_f$, and we have thus shown that $L_k \leq \max\{\eta L_f, s\}$. We also note that the bounds on L_k can be rewritten as

$$\beta L_f \leq L_k \leq \alpha L_f,$$

where

$$\alpha = \begin{cases} 1, & constant, \\ \max\left\{\eta, \frac{s}{L_f}\right\}, & backtracking, \end{cases} \qquad \beta = \begin{cases} 1, & constant, \\ \frac{s}{L_f}, & backtracking. \end{cases} \tag{10.25}$$

Remark 10.20 (monotonicity of the proximal gradient method). *Since condition (10.23) holds for both stepsize rules, for any $k \geq 0$, we can invoke the fundamental prox-grad inequality (10.21) with $\mathbf{y} = \mathbf{x} = \mathbf{x}^k, L = L_k$ and obtain the inequality*

$$F(\mathbf{x}^k) - F(\mathbf{x}^{k+1}) \geq \frac{L_k}{2} \|\mathbf{x}^k - \mathbf{x}^{k+1}\|^2,$$

which in particular implies that $F(\mathbf{x}^k) \geq F(\mathbf{x}^{k+1})$, meaning that the method produces a nonincreasing sequence of function values.

10.4.3   Convergence Analysis in the Convex Case

We will assume in addition to Assumption 10.1 that f is convex. We begin by establishing an $O(1/k)$ rate of convergence of the generated sequence of function values to the optimal value. Such rate of convergence is called a *sublinear rate*. This is of course an improvement over the $O(1/\sqrt{k})$ rate that was established for the projected subgradient and mirror descent methods. It is also not particularly surprising that an improved rate of convergence can be established since additional properties are assumed on the objective function.

Theorem 10.21 ($O(1/k)$ rate of convergence of proximal gradient). *Suppose that Assumption* 10.1 *holds and that in addition f is convex. Let $\{\mathbf{x}^k\}_{k\geq 0}$ be the sequence generated by the proximal gradient method for solving problem* (10.1) *with either a constant stepsize rule in which $L_k \equiv L_f$ for all $k \geq 0$ or the backtracking procedure B2. Then for any $\mathbf{x}^* \in X^*$ and $k \geq 0$,*

$$F(\mathbf{x}^k) - F_{\mathrm{opt}} \leq \frac{\alpha L_f \|\mathbf{x}^0 - \mathbf{x}^*\|^2}{2k}, \tag{10.26}$$

where $\alpha = 1$ in the constant stepsize setting and $\alpha = \max\left\{\eta, \frac{s}{L_f}\right\}$ if the backtracking rule is employed.

Proof. For any $n \geq 0$, substituting $L = L_n$, $\mathbf{x} = \mathbf{x}^*$, and $\mathbf{y} = \mathbf{x}^n$ in the fundamental prox-grad inequality (10.21) and taking into account the fact that in both stepsize rules condition (10.20) is satisfied, we obtain

$$\frac{2}{L_n}(F(\mathbf{x}^*) - F(\mathbf{x}^{n+1})) \geq \|\mathbf{x}^* - \mathbf{x}^{n+1}\|^2 - \|\mathbf{x}^* - \mathbf{x}^n\|^2 + \frac{2}{L_n}\ell_f(\mathbf{x}^*, \mathbf{x}^n)$$

$$\geq \|\mathbf{x}^* - \mathbf{x}^{n+1}\|^2 - \|\mathbf{x}^* - \mathbf{x}^n\|^2,$$

where the convexity of f was used in the last inequality. Summing the above inequality over $n = 0, 1, \ldots, k-1$ and using the bound $L_n \leq \alpha L_f$ for all $n \geq 0$ (see Remark 10.19), we obtain

$$\frac{2}{\alpha L_f}\sum_{n=0}^{k-1}(F(\mathbf{x}^*) - F(\mathbf{x}^{n+1})) \geq \|\mathbf{x}^* - \mathbf{x}^k\|^2 - \|\mathbf{x}^* - \mathbf{x}^0\|^2.$$

Thus,

$$\sum_{n=0}^{k-1}(F(\mathbf{x}^{n+1}) - F_{\mathrm{opt}}) \leq \frac{\alpha L_f}{2}\|\mathbf{x}^* - \mathbf{x}^0\|^2 - \frac{\alpha L_f}{2}\|\mathbf{x}^* - \mathbf{x}^k\|^2 \leq \frac{\alpha L_f}{2}\|\mathbf{x}^* - \mathbf{x}^0\|^2.$$

By the monotonicity of $\{F(\mathbf{x}^n)\}_{n\geq 0}$ (see Remark 10.20), we can conclude that

$$k(F(\mathbf{x}^k) - F_{\mathrm{opt}}) \leq \sum_{n=0}^{k-1}(F(\mathbf{x}^{n+1}) - F_{\mathrm{opt}}) \leq \frac{\alpha L_f}{2}\|\mathbf{x}^* - \mathbf{x}^0\|^2.$$

Consequently,

$$F(\mathbf{x}^k) - F_{\mathrm{opt}} \leq \frac{\alpha L_f \|\mathbf{x}^* - \mathbf{x}^0\|^2}{2k}. \qquad \square$$

Remark 10.22. *Note that we did not utilize in the proof of Theorem 10.21 the fact that procedure B2 produces a nondecreasing sequence of constants $\{L_k\}_{k\geq0}$. This implies in particular that the monotonicity of this sequence of constants is not essential, and we can actually prove the same convergence rate for any backtracking procedure that guarantees the validity of condition (10.23) and the bound $L_k \leq \alpha L_f$.*

We can also prove that the generated sequence is Fejér monotone, from which convergence of the sequence to an optimal solution readily follows.

Theorem 10.23 (Fejér monotonicity of the sequence generated by the proximal gradient method). *Suppose that Assumption 10.1 holds and that in addition f is convex. Let $\{\mathbf{x}^k\}_{k\geq0}$ be the sequence generated by the proximal gradient method for solving problem (10.1) with either a constant stepsize rule in which $L_k \equiv L_f$ for all $k \geq 0$ or the backtracking procedure B2. Then for any $\mathbf{x}^* \in X^*$ and $k \geq 0$,*

$$\|\mathbf{x}^{k+1} - \mathbf{x}^*\| \leq \|\mathbf{x}^k - \mathbf{x}^*\|. \tag{10.27}$$

Proof. We will repeat some of the arguments used in the proof of Theorem 10.21. Substituting $L = L_k$, $\mathbf{x} = \mathbf{x}^*$, and $\mathbf{y} = \mathbf{x}^k$ in the fundamental prox-grad inequality (10.21) and taking into account the fact that in both stepsize rules condition (10.20) is satisfied, we obtain

$$\frac{2}{L_k}(F(\mathbf{x}^*) - F(\mathbf{x}^{k+1})) \geq \|\mathbf{x}^* - \mathbf{x}^{k+1}\|^2 - \|\mathbf{x}^* - \mathbf{x}^k\|^2 + \frac{2}{L_k}\ell_f(\mathbf{x}^*, \mathbf{x}^k)$$

$$\geq \|\mathbf{x}^* - \mathbf{x}^{k+1}\|^2 - \|\mathbf{x}^* - \mathbf{x}^k\|^2,$$

where the convexity of f was used in the last inequality. The result (10.27) now follows by the inequality $F(\mathbf{x}^*) - F(\mathbf{x}^{k+1}) \leq 0$. $\square$

Thanks to the Fejér monotonicity property, we can now establish the convergence of the sequence generated by the proximal gradient method.

Theorem 10.24 (convergence of the sequence generated by the proximal gradient method). *Suppose that Assumption 10.1 holds and that in addition f is convex. Let $\{\mathbf{x}^k\}_{k\geq0}$ be the sequence generated by the proximal gradient method for solving problem (10.1) with either a constant stepsize rule in which $L_k \equiv L_f$ for all $k \geq 0$ or the backtracking procedure B2. Then the sequence $\{\mathbf{x}^k\}_{k\geq0}$ converges to an optimal solution of problem (10.1).*

Proof. By Theorem 10.23, the sequence is Fejér monotone w.r.t. X^*. Therefore, by Theorem 8.16, to show convergence to a point in X^*, it is enough to show that any limit point of the sequence $\{\mathbf{x}^k\}_{k\geq0}$ is necessarily in X^*. Let then $\tilde{\mathbf{x}}$ be a limit point of the sequence. Then there exists a subsequence $\{\mathbf{x}^{k_j}\}_{j\geq0}$ converging to $\tilde{\mathbf{x}}$. By Theorem 10.21,

$$F(\mathbf{x}^{k_j}) \to F_{\text{opt}} \text{ as } j \to \infty. \tag{10.28}$$

Since F is closed, it is also lower semicontinuous, and hence $F(\tilde{\mathbf{x}}) \leq \lim_{j\to\infty} F(\mathbf{x}^{k_j}) = F_{\text{opt}}$, implying that $\tilde{\mathbf{x}} \in X^*$. $\square$

To derive a complexity result for the proximal gradient method, we will assume that $\|\mathbf{x}^0 - \mathbf{x}^*\| \leq R$ for some $\mathbf{x}^* \in X^*$ and some constant $R > 0$; for example, if $\text{dom}(g)$ is bounded, then R might be taken as its diameter. By inequality (10.26) it follows that in order to obtain an ε-optimal solution of problem (10.1), it is enough to require that

$$\frac{\alpha L_f R^2}{2k} \leq \varepsilon,$$

which is the same as

$$k \geq \frac{\alpha L_f R^2}{2\varepsilon}.$$

Thus, to obtain an ε-optimal solution, an order of $\frac{1}{\varepsilon}$ iterations is required, which is an improvement of the result for the projected subgradient method in which an order of $\frac{1}{\varepsilon^2}$ iterations is needed (see, for example, Theorem 8.18). We summarize the above observations in the following theorem.

Theorem 10.25 (complexity of the proximal gradient method). *Under the setting of Theorem* 10.21, *for any k satisfying*

$$k \geq \left\lceil \frac{\alpha L_f R^2}{2\varepsilon} \right\rceil,$$

it holds that $F(\mathbf{x}^k) - F_{\text{opt}} \leq \varepsilon$, where R is an upper bound on $\|\mathbf{x}^* - \mathbf{x}^0\|$ for some $\mathbf{x}^* \in X^*$.

In the nonconvex case (meaning when f is not necessarily convex), an $O(1/\sqrt{k})$ rate of convergence of the norm of the gradient mapping was established in Theorem 10.15(c). We will now show that with the additional convexity assumption on f, this rate can be improved to $O(1/k)$.

Theorem 10.26 ($O(1/k)$ rate of convergence of the minimal norm of the gradient mapping). *Suppose that Assumption* 10.1 *holds and that in addition f is convex. Let $\{\mathbf{x}^k\}_{k \geq 0}$ be the sequence generated by the proximal gradient method for solving problem* (10.1) *with either a constant stepsize rule in which $L_k \equiv L_f$ for all $k \geq 0$ or the backtracking procedure B2. Then for any $\mathbf{x}^* \in X^*$ and $k \geq 1$,*

$$\min_{n=0,1,\ldots,k} \|G_{\alpha L_f}(\mathbf{x}^n)\| \leq \frac{2\alpha^{1.5} L_f \|\mathbf{x}^0 - \mathbf{x}^*\|}{\sqrt{\beta k}}, \qquad (10.29)$$

where $\alpha = \beta = 1$ in the constant stepsize setting and $\alpha = \max\{\eta, \frac{s}{L_f}\}, \beta = \frac{s}{L_f}$ if the backtracking rule is employed.

Proof. By the sufficient decrease lemma (Corollary 10.18), for any $n \geq 0$,

$$F(\mathbf{x}^n) - F(\mathbf{x}^{n+1}) = F(\mathbf{x}^n) - F(T_{L_n}(\mathbf{x}^n)) \geq \frac{1}{2L_n} \|G_{L_n}(\mathbf{x}^n)\|^2. \qquad (10.30)$$

By Theorem 10.9 and the fact that $\beta L_f \leq L_n \leq \alpha L_f$ (see Remark 10.19), it follows that

$$\frac{1}{2L_n} \|G_{L_n}(\mathbf{x}^n)\|^2 = \frac{L_n}{2} \frac{\|G_{L_n}(\mathbf{x}^n)\|^2}{L_n^2} \geq \frac{\beta L_f}{2} \frac{\|G_{\alpha L_f}(\mathbf{x}^n)\|^2}{\alpha^2 L_f^2} = \frac{\beta}{2\alpha^2 L_f} \|G_{\alpha L_f}(\mathbf{x}^n)\|^2.$$

$$\qquad (10.31)$$

Therefore, combining (10.30) and (10.31),

$$F(\mathbf{x}^n) - F_{\text{opt}} \geq F(\mathbf{x}^{n+1}) - F_{\text{opt}} + \frac{\beta}{2\alpha^2 L_f} \|G_{\alpha L_f}(\mathbf{x}^n)\|^2. \tag{10.32}$$

Let p be a positive integer. Summing (10.32) over $n = p, p+1, \ldots, 2p-1$ yields

$$F(\mathbf{x}^p) - F_{\text{opt}} \geq F(\mathbf{x}^{2p}) - F_{\text{opt}} + \frac{\beta}{2\alpha^2 L_f} \sum_{n=p}^{2p-1} \|G_{\alpha L_f}(\mathbf{x}^n)\|^2. \tag{10.33}$$

By Theorem 10.21, $F(\mathbf{x}^p) - F_{\text{opt}} \leq \frac{\alpha L_f \|\mathbf{x}^0 - \mathbf{x}^*\|^2}{2p}$, which, combined with the fact that $F(\mathbf{x}^{2p}) - F_{\text{opt}} \geq 0$ and (10.33), implies

$$\frac{\beta p}{2\alpha^2 L_f} \min_{n=0,1,\ldots,2p-1} \|G_{\alpha L_f}(\mathbf{x}^n)\|^2 \leq \frac{\beta}{2\alpha^2 L_f} \sum_{n=p}^{2p-1} \|G_{\alpha L_f}(\mathbf{x}^n)\|^2 \leq \frac{\alpha L_f \|\mathbf{x}^0 - \mathbf{x}^*\|^2}{2p}.$$

Thus,

$$\min_{n=0,1,\ldots,2p-1} \|G_{\alpha L_f}(\mathbf{x}^n)\|^2 \leq \frac{\alpha^3 L_f^2 \|\mathbf{x}^0 - \mathbf{x}^*\|^2}{\beta p^2} \tag{10.34}$$

and also

$$\min_{n=0,1,\ldots,2p} \|G_{\alpha L_f}(\mathbf{x}^n)\|^2 \leq \frac{\alpha^3 L_f^2 \|\mathbf{x}^0 - \mathbf{x}^*\|^2}{\beta p^2}. \tag{10.35}$$

We conclude that for any $k \geq 1$,

$$\min_{n=0,1,\ldots,k} \|G_{\alpha L_f}(\mathbf{x}^n)\|^2 \leq \frac{\alpha^3 L_f^2 \|\mathbf{x}^0 - \mathbf{x}^*\|^2}{\beta \min\{(k/2)^2, ((k+1)/2)^2\}} = \frac{4\alpha^3 L_f^2 \|\mathbf{x}^0 - \mathbf{x}^*\|^2}{\beta k^2}. \qquad \Box$$

When we assume further that f is L_f-smooth over the entire space $\mathbb{E}$, we can use Lemma 10.12 to obtain an improved result in the case of a constant stepsize.

Theorem 10.27 ($O(1/k)$ rate of convergence of the norm of the gradient mapping under the constant stepsize rule). *Suppose that Assumption* 10.1 *holds and that in addition f is convex and L_f-smooth over $\mathbb{E}$. Let $\{\mathbf{x}^k\}_{k\geq 0}$ be the sequence generated by the proximal gradient method for solving problem* (10.1) *with a constant stepsize rule in which $L_k \equiv L_f$ for all $k \geq 0$. Then for any $\mathbf{x}^* \in X^*$,*

(a) $\|G_{L_f}(\mathbf{x}^{k+1})\| \leq \|G_{L_f}(\mathbf{x}^k)\|$ *for any $k \geq 0$;*

(b) $\|G_{L_f}(\mathbf{x}^k)\| \leq \frac{2L_f \|\mathbf{x}^0 - \mathbf{x}^*\|}{k}$ *for any $k \geq 1$.*

Proof. Invoking Lemma 10.12 with $\mathbf{x} = \mathbf{x}^k$, we obtain (a). Part (b) now follows by substituting $\alpha = \beta = 1$ in the result of Theorem 10.26 and noting that by part (a), $\|G_{L_f}(\mathbf{x}^k)\| = \min_{n=0,1,\ldots,k} \|G_{L_f}(\mathbf{x}^n)\|$. $\quad \Box$

10.5   The Proximal Point Method

Consider the problem

$$\min_{\mathbf{x}\in\mathbb{E}} g(\mathbf{x}), \tag{10.36}$$

where $g : \mathbb{E} \to (-\infty, \infty]$ is a proper closed and convex function. Problem (10.36) is actually a special case of the composite problem (10.1) with $f \equiv 0$. The update step of the proximal gradient method in this case takes the form

$$\mathbf{x}^{k+1} = \text{prox}_{\frac{1}{L_k}g}(\mathbf{x}^k).$$

Taking $L_k = \frac{1}{c}$ for some $c > 0$, we obtain the *proximal point method*.

The Proximal Point Method

Initialization: pick $\mathbf{x}^0 \in \mathbb{E}$ and $c > 0$.
General step $(k \geq 0)$:
$$\mathbf{x}^{k+1} = \text{prox}_{cg}(\mathbf{x}^k).$$

The proximal point method is actually not a practical algorithm since the general step asks to minimize the function $g(\mathbf{x}) + \frac{c}{2}\|\mathbf{x} - \mathbf{x}^k\|^2$, which in general is as hard to accomplish as solving the original problem of minimizing g. Since the proximal point method is a special case of the proximal gradient method, we can deduce its main convergence results from the corresponding results on the proximal gradient method. Specifically, since the smooth part $f \equiv 0$ is 0-smooth, we can take any constant stepsize to guarantee convergence and Theorems 10.21 and 10.24 imply the following result.

Theorem 10.28 (convergence of the proximal point method). *Let $g : \mathbb{E} \to (-\infty, \infty]$ be a proper closed and convex function. Assume that problem*

$$\min_{\mathbf{x}\in\mathbb{E}} g(\mathbf{x})$$

has a nonempty optimal set X^*, and let the optimal value be given by g_{opt}. Let $\{\mathbf{x}^k\}_{k\geq 0}$ be the sequence generated by the proximal point method with parameter $c > 0$. Then

(a) $g(\mathbf{x}^k) - g_{\text{opt}} \leq \frac{\|\mathbf{x}^0 - \mathbf{x}^*\|^2}{2ck}$ *for any $\mathbf{x}^* \in X^*$ and $k \geq 0$;*

(b) *the sequence $\{\mathbf{x}^k\}_{k\geq 0}$ converges to some point in X^*.*

10.6   Convergence of the Proximal Gradient Method—The Strongly Convex Case

In the case where f is assumed to be σ-strongly convex for some $\sigma > 0$, the sublinear rate of convergence can be improved into a *linear rate* of convergence, meaning a rate of the form $O(q^k)$ for some $q \in (0, 1)$. Throughout the analysis of the strongly convex case we denote the unique optimal solution of problem (10.1) by $\mathbf{x}^*$.

Theorem 10.29 (linear rate of convergence of the proximal gradient method—strongly convex case). *Suppose that Assumption 10.1 holds and that in addition f is σ-strongly convex ($\sigma > 0$). Let $\{\mathbf{x}^k\}_{k \geq 0}$ be the sequence generated by the proximal gradient method for solving problem* (10.1) *with either a constant stepsize rule in which $L_k \equiv L_f$ for all $k \geq 0$ or the backtracking procedure B2. Let*

$$
\alpha = \begin{cases} 1, & \text{constant stepsize,} \\ \max\left\{\eta, \frac{s}{L_f}\right\}, & \text{backtracking.} \end{cases}
$$

Then for any $k \geq 0$,

(a) $\|\mathbf{x}^{k+1} - \mathbf{x}^*\|^2 \leq \left(1 - \frac{\sigma}{\alpha L_f}\right)\|\mathbf{x}^k - \mathbf{x}^*\|^2$;

(b) $\|\mathbf{x}^k - \mathbf{x}^*\|^2 \leq \left(1 - \frac{\sigma}{\alpha L_f}\right)^k \|\mathbf{x}^0 - \mathbf{x}^*\|^2$;

(c) $F(\mathbf{x}^{k+1}) - F_{\text{opt}} \leq \frac{\alpha L_f}{2}\left(1 - \frac{\sigma}{\alpha L_f}\right)^{k+1}\|\mathbf{x}^0 - \mathbf{x}^*\|^2$.

Proof. Plugging $L = L_k$, $\mathbf{x} = \mathbf{x}^*$, and $\mathbf{y} = \mathbf{x}^k$ into the fundamental prox-grad inequality (10.21) and taking into account the fact that in both stepsize rules condition (10.20) is satisfied, we obtain

$$
F(\mathbf{x}^*) - F(\mathbf{x}^{k+1}) \geq \frac{L_k}{2}\|\mathbf{x}^* - \mathbf{x}^{k+1}\|^2 - \frac{L_k}{2}\|\mathbf{x}^* - \mathbf{x}^k\|^2 + \ell_f(\mathbf{x}^*, \mathbf{x}^k).
$$

Since f is σ-strongly convex, it follows by Theorem 5.24(ii) that

$$
\ell_f(\mathbf{x}^*, \mathbf{x}^k) = f(\mathbf{x}^*) - f(\mathbf{x}^k) - \langle \nabla f(\mathbf{x}^k), \mathbf{x}^* - \mathbf{x}^k \rangle \geq \frac{\sigma}{2}\|\mathbf{x}^k - \mathbf{x}^*\|^2.
$$

Thus,

$$
F(\mathbf{x}^*) - F(\mathbf{x}^{k+1}) \geq \frac{L_k}{2}\|\mathbf{x}^* - \mathbf{x}^{k+1}\|^2 - \frac{L_k - \sigma}{2}\|\mathbf{x}^* - \mathbf{x}^k\|^2. \qquad (10.37)
$$

Since $\mathbf{x}^*$ is a minimizer of F, $F(\mathbf{x}^*) - F(\mathbf{x}^{k+1}) \leq 0$, and hence, by (10.37) and the fact that $L_k \leq \alpha L_f$ (see Remark 10.19),

$$
\|\mathbf{x}^{k+1} - \mathbf{x}^*\|^2 \leq \left(1 - \frac{\sigma}{L_k}\right)\|\mathbf{x}^k - \mathbf{x}^*\|^2 \leq \left(1 - \frac{\sigma}{\alpha L_f}\right)\|\mathbf{x}^k - \mathbf{x}^*\|^2,
$$

establishing part (a). Part (b) follows immediately by (a). To prove (c), note that by (10.37),

$$
\begin{aligned}
F(\mathbf{x}^{k+1}) - F_{\text{opt}} &\leq \frac{L_k - \sigma}{2}\|\mathbf{x}^k - \mathbf{x}^*\|^2 - \frac{L_k}{2}\|\mathbf{x}^{k+1} - \mathbf{x}^*\|^2 \\
&\leq \frac{\alpha L_f - \sigma}{2}\|\mathbf{x}^k - \mathbf{x}^*\|^2 \\
&= \frac{\alpha L_f}{2}\left(1 - \frac{\sigma}{\alpha L_f}\right)\|\mathbf{x}^k - \mathbf{x}^*\|^2 \\
&\leq \frac{\alpha L_f}{2}\left(1 - \frac{\sigma}{\alpha L_f}\right)^{k+1}\|\mathbf{x}^0 - \mathbf{x}^*\|^2,
\end{aligned}
$$

where part (b) was used in the last inequality. $\qquad \square$

Theorem 10.29 immediately implies that in the strongly convex case, the proximal gradient method requires an order of $\log(\frac{1}{\varepsilon})$ iterations to obtain an ε-optimal solution.

Theorem 10.30 (complexity of the proximal gradient method—The strongly convex case). *Under the setting of Theorem 10.29, for any $k \geq 1$ satisfying*

$$k \geq \alpha \kappa \log\left(\frac{1}{\varepsilon}\right) + \alpha \kappa \log\left(\frac{\alpha L_f R^2}{2}\right),$$

it holds that $F(\mathbf{x}^k) - F_{\text{opt}} \leq \varepsilon$, where R is an upper bound on $\|\mathbf{x}^0 - \mathbf{x}^*\|$ and $\kappa = \frac{L_f}{\sigma}$.

Proof. Let $k \geq 1$. By Theorem 10.29 and the definition of κ, a sufficient condition for the inequality $F(\mathbf{x}^k) - F_{\text{opt}} \leq \varepsilon$ to hold is that

$$\frac{\alpha L_f}{2}\left(1 - \frac{1}{\alpha \kappa}\right)^k R^2 \leq \varepsilon,$$

which is the same as

$$k \log\left(1 - \frac{1}{\alpha \kappa}\right) \leq \log\left(\frac{2\varepsilon}{\alpha L_f R^2}\right). \tag{10.38}$$

Since $\log(1 - x) \leq -x$ for any[57] $x \leq 1$, it follows that a sufficient condition for (10.38) to hold is that

$$-\frac{1}{\alpha \kappa}k \leq \log\left(\frac{2\varepsilon}{\alpha L_f R^2}\right),$$

namely, that

$$k \geq \alpha \kappa \log\left(\frac{1}{\varepsilon}\right) + \alpha \kappa \log\left(\frac{\alpha L_f R^2}{2}\right). \qquad \square$$

10.7   The Fast Proximal Gradient Method—FISTA

10.7.1   The Method

The proximal gradient method achieves an $O(1/k)$ rate of convergence in function values to the optimal value. In this section we will show how to accelerate the method in order to obtain a rate of $O(1/k^2)$ in function values. The method is known as the "fast proximal gradient method," but we will also refer to it as "FISTA," which is an acronym for "fast iterative shrinkage-thresholding algorithm"; see Example 10.37 for further explanations. The method was devised and analyzed by Beck and Teboulle in the paper [18], from which the convergence analysis is taken.

We will assume that f is convex and that it is L_f-smooth, meaning that it is L_f-smooth over the entire space $\mathbb{E}$. We gather all the required properties in the following assumption.

---

[57]The inequality also holds for $x = 1$ since in that case the left-hand side is $-\infty$.

Assumption 10.31.

(A) $g : \mathbb{E} \to (-\infty, \infty]$ *is proper closed and convex.*

(B) $f : \mathbb{E} \to \mathbb{R}$ *is L_f-smooth and convex.*

(C) *The optimal set of problem* (10.1) *is nonempty and denoted by X^*. The optimal value of the problem is denoted by F_{opt}.*

The description of FISTA now follows.

FISTA

Input: $(f, g, \mathbf{x}^0)$, where f and g satisfy properties (A) and (B) in Assumption 10.31 and $\mathbf{x}^0 \in \mathbb{E}$.
Initialization: set $\mathbf{y}^0 = \mathbf{x}^0$ and $t_0 = 1$.
General step: for any $k = 0, 1, 2, \dots$ execute the following steps:

(a) pick $L_k > 0$;

(b) set $\mathbf{x}^{k+1} = \mathrm{prox}_{\frac{1}{L_k} g} \left(\mathbf{y}^k - \frac{1}{L_k} \nabla f(\mathbf{y}^k) \right)$;

(c) set $t_{k+1} = \frac{1 + \sqrt{1 + 4t_k^2}}{2}$;

(d) compute $\mathbf{y}^{k+1} = \mathbf{x}^{k+1} + \left(\frac{t_k - 1}{t_{k+1}} \right) (\mathbf{x}^{k+1} - \mathbf{x}^k)$.

As usual, we will consider two options for the choice of L_k: constant and backtracking. The backtracking procedure for choosing the stepsize is referred to as "backtracking procedure B3" and is identical to procedure B2 with the sole difference that it is invoked on the vector $\mathbf{y}^k$ rather than on $\mathbf{x}^k$.

- **Constant.** $L_k = L_f$ for all k.

- **Backtracking procedure B3.** The procedure requires two parameters (s, η), where $s > 0$ and $\eta > 1$. Define $L_{-1} = s$. At iteration k ($k \geq 0$) the choice of L_k is done as follows: First, L_k is set to be equal to L_{k-1}. Then, while (recall that $T_L(\mathbf{y}) \equiv T_L^{f,g}(\mathbf{y}) = \mathrm{prox}_{\frac{1}{L} g} (\mathbf{y} - \frac{1}{L} \nabla f(\mathbf{y})))$,

$$f(T_{L_k}(\mathbf{y}^k)) > f(\mathbf{y}^k) + \langle \nabla f(\mathbf{y}^k), T_{L_k}(\mathbf{y}^k) - \mathbf{y}^k \rangle + \frac{L_k}{2} \|T_{L_k}(\mathbf{y}^k) - \mathbf{y}^k\|^2,$$

  we set $L_k := \eta L_k$. In other words, the stepsize is chosen as $L_k = L_{k-1} \eta^{i_k}$, where i_k is the smallest nonnegative integer for which the condition

$$f(T_{L_{k-1} \eta^{i_k}}(\mathbf{y}^k)) \leq f(\mathbf{y}^k) + \langle \nabla f(\mathbf{y}^k), T_{L_{k-1} \eta^{i_k}}(\mathbf{y}^k) - \mathbf{y}^k \rangle$$
$$+ \frac{L_k}{2} \|T_{L_{k-1} \eta^{i_k}}(\mathbf{y}^k) - \mathbf{y}^k\|^2$$

  is satisfied.

In both stepsize rules, the following inequality is satisfied for any $k \geq 0$:

$$f(T_{L_k}(\mathbf{y}^k)) \leq f(\mathbf{y}^k) + \langle \nabla f(\mathbf{y}^k), T_{L_k}(\mathbf{y}^k) - \mathbf{y}^k \rangle + \frac{L_k}{2}\|T_{L_k}(\mathbf{y}^k) - \mathbf{y}^k\|^2. \quad (10.39)$$

Remark 10.32. *Since the backtracking procedure B3 is identical to the* B2 *procedure (only employed on* $\mathbf{y}^k$ *), the arguments of Remark 10.19 are still valid, and we have that*

$$\beta L_f \leq L_k \leq \alpha L_f,$$

where α *and* β *are given in* (10.25).

The next lemma shows an important lower bound on the sequence $\{t_k\}_{k\geq 0}$ that will be used in the convergence proof.

Lemma 10.33. *Let* $\{t_k\}_{k\geq 0}$ *be the sequence defined by*

$$t_0 = 1, \ t_{k+1} = \frac{1 + \sqrt{1 + 4t_k^2}}{2}, \quad k \geq 0.$$

Then $t_k \geq \frac{k+2}{2}$ *for all* $k \geq 0$.

Proof. The proof is by induction on k. Obviously, for $k = 0$, $t_0 = 1 \geq \frac{0+2}{2}$. Suppose that the claim holds for k, meaning $t_k \geq \frac{k+2}{2}$. We will prove that $t_{k+1} \geq \frac{k+3}{2}$. By the recursive relation defining the sequence and the induction assumption,

$$t_{k+1} = \frac{1 + \sqrt{1 + 4t_k^2}}{2} \geq \frac{1 + \sqrt{1 + (k+2)^2}}{2} \geq \frac{1 + \sqrt{(k+2)^2}}{2} = \frac{k+3}{2}. \quad \square$$

10.7.2   Convergence Analysis of FISTA

Theorem 10.34 ($O(1/k^2)$ rate of convergence of FISTA). *Suppose that Assumption 10.31 holds. Let* $\{\mathbf{x}^k\}_{k\geq 0}$ *be the sequence generated by FISTA for solving problem* (10.1) *with either a constant stepsize rule in which* $L_k \equiv L_f$ *for all* $k \geq 0$ *or the backtracking procedure B3. Then for any* $\mathbf{x}^* \in X^*$ *and* $k \geq 1$,

$$F(\mathbf{x}^k) - F_{\text{opt}} \leq \frac{2\alpha L_f \|\mathbf{x}^0 - \mathbf{x}^*\|^2}{(k+1)^2},$$

where $\alpha = 1$ *in the constant stepsize setting and* $\alpha = \max\left\{\eta, \frac{s}{L_f}\right\}$ *if the backtracking rule is employed.*

Proof. Let $k \geq 1$. Substituting $\mathbf{x} = t_k^{-1}\mathbf{x}^* + (1 - t_k^{-1})\mathbf{x}^k$, $\mathbf{y} = \mathbf{y}^k$, and $L = L_k$ in the fundamental prox-grad inequality (10.21), taking into account that inequality

(10.39) is satisfied and that f is convex, we obtain that

$$F(t_k^{-1}\mathbf{x}^* + (1 - t_k^{-1})\mathbf{x}^k) - F(\mathbf{x}^{k+1})$$

$$\geq \frac{L_k}{2}\|\mathbf{x}^{k+1} - (t_k^{-1}\mathbf{x}^* + (1 - t_k^{-1})\mathbf{x}^k)\|^2 - \frac{L_k}{2}\|\mathbf{y}^k - (t_k^{-1}\mathbf{x}^* + (1 - t_k^{-1})\mathbf{x}^k)\|^2$$

$$= \frac{L_k}{2t_k^2}\|t_k\mathbf{x}^{k+1} - (\mathbf{x}^* + (t_k - 1)\mathbf{x}^k)\|^2 - \frac{L_k}{2t_k^2}\|t_k\mathbf{y}^k - (\mathbf{x}^* + (t_k - 1)\mathbf{x}^k)\|^2. \quad (10.40)$$

By the convexity of F,

$$F(t_k^{-1}\mathbf{x}^* + (1 - t_k^{-1})\mathbf{x}^k) \leq t_k^{-1}F(\mathbf{x}^*) + (1 - t_k^{-1})F(\mathbf{x}^k).$$

Therefore, using the notation $v_n \equiv F(\mathbf{x}^n) - F_{\mathrm{opt}}$ for any $n \geq 0$,

$$F(t_k^{-1}\mathbf{x}^* + (1 - t_k^{-1})\mathbf{x}^k) - F(\mathbf{x}^{k+1}) \leq (1 - t_k^{-1})(F(\mathbf{x}^k) - F(\mathbf{x}^*)) - (F(\mathbf{x}_{k+1}) - F(\mathbf{x}^*))$$

$$= (1 - t_k^{-1})v_k - v_{k+1}. \quad (10.41)$$

On the other hand, using the relation $\mathbf{y}^k = \mathbf{x}^k + \left(\frac{t_{k-1}-1}{t_k}\right)(\mathbf{x}^k - \mathbf{x}^{k-1})$,

$$\|t_k\mathbf{y}^k - (\mathbf{x}^* + (t_k - 1)\mathbf{x}^k)\|^2 = \|t_k\mathbf{x}^k + (t_{k-1} - 1)(\mathbf{x}^k - \mathbf{x}^{k-1}) - (\mathbf{x}^* + (t_k - 1)\mathbf{x}^k)\|^2$$

$$= \|t_{k-1}\mathbf{x}^k - (\mathbf{x}^* + (t_{k-1} - 1)\mathbf{x}^{k-1})\|^2. \quad (10.42)$$

Combining (10.40), (10.41), and (10.42), we obtain that

$$(t_k^2 - t_k)v_k - t_k^2 v_{k+1} \geq \frac{L_k}{2}\|\mathbf{u}^{k+1}\|^2 - \frac{L_k}{2}\|\mathbf{u}^k\|^2,$$

where we use the notation $\mathbf{u}^n = t_{n-1}\mathbf{x}^n - (\mathbf{x}^* + (t_{n-1} - 1)\mathbf{x}^{n-1})$ for any $n \geq 0$. By the update rule of t_{k+1}, we have $t_k^2 - t_k = t_{k-1}^2$, and hence

$$\frac{2}{L_k}t_{k-1}^2 v_k - \frac{2}{L_k}t_k^2 v_{k+1} \geq \|\mathbf{u}^{k+1}\|^2 - \|\mathbf{u}^k\|^2.$$

Since $L_k \geq L_{k-1}$, we can conclude that

$$\frac{2}{L_{k-1}}t_{k-1}^2 v_k - \frac{2}{L_k}t_k^2 v_{k+1} \geq \|\mathbf{u}^{k+1}\|^2 - \|\mathbf{u}^k\|^2.$$

Thus,

$$\|\mathbf{u}^{k+1}\|^2 + \frac{2}{L_k}t_k^2 v_{k+1} \leq \|\mathbf{u}^k\|^2 + \frac{2}{L_{k-1}}t_{k-1}^2 v_k,$$

and hence, for any $k \geq 1$,

$$\|\mathbf{u}^k\|^2 + \frac{2}{L_{k-1}}t_{k-1}^2 v_k \leq \|\mathbf{u}^1\|^2 + \frac{2}{L_0}t_0^2 v_1 = \|\mathbf{x}^1 - \mathbf{x}^*\|^2 + \frac{2}{L_0}(F(\mathbf{x}^1) - F_{\mathrm{opt}}) \quad (10.43)$$

Substituting $\mathbf{x} = \mathbf{x}^*, \mathbf{y} = \mathbf{y}^0$, and $L = L_0$ in the fundamental prox-grad inequality (10.21), taking into account the convexity of f yields

$$\frac{2}{L_0}(F(\mathbf{x}^*) - F(\mathbf{x}^1)) \geq \|\mathbf{x}^1 - \mathbf{x}^*\|^2 - \|\mathbf{y}^0 - \mathbf{x}^*\|^2,$$

which, along with the fact that $\mathbf{y}^0 = \mathbf{x}^0$, implies the bound

$$\|\mathbf{x}^1 - \mathbf{x}^*\|^2 + \frac{2}{L_0}(F(\mathbf{x}^1) - F_{\mathrm{opt}}) \leq \|\mathbf{x}^0 - \mathbf{x}^*\|^2.$$

Combining the last inequality with (10.43), we get

$$\frac{2}{L_{k-1}}t_{k-1}^2 v_k \leq \|\mathbf{u}^k\|^2 + \frac{2}{L_{k-1}}t_{k-1}^2 v_k \leq \|\mathbf{x}^0 - \mathbf{x}^*\|^2.$$

Thus, using the bound $L_{k-1} \leq \alpha L_f$, the definition of v_k, and Lemma 10.33,

$$F(\mathbf{x}^k) - F_{\text{opt}} \leq \frac{L_{k-1}\|\mathbf{x}^0 - \mathbf{x}^*\|^2}{2t_{k-1}^2} \leq \frac{2\alpha L_f\|\mathbf{x}^0 - \mathbf{x}^*\|^2}{(k+1)^2}. \qquad \square$$

Remark 10.35 (alternative choice for t_k). *A close inspection of the proof of Theorem 10.34 reveals that the result is correct if $\{t_k\}_{k\geq 0}$ is any sequence satisfying the following two properties for any $k \geq 0$: (a) $t_k \geq \frac{k+2}{2}$; (b) $t_{k+1}^2 - t_{k+1} \leq t_k^2$. The choice $t_k = \frac{k+2}{2}$ also satisfies these two properties. The validity of (a) is obvious; to show (b), note that*

$$t_{k+1}^2 - t_{k+1} = t_{k+1}(t_{k+1} - 1) = \frac{k+3}{2} \cdot \frac{k+1}{2} = \frac{k^2 + 4k + 3}{4}$$
$$\leq \frac{k^2 + 4k + 4}{4} = \frac{(k+2)^2}{4} = t_k^2.$$

Remark 10.36. *Note that FISTA has an $O(1/k^2)$ rate of convergence in function values, while the proximal gradient method has an $O(1/k)$ rate of convergence. This improvement was achieved despite the fact that the dominant computational steps at each iteration of both methods are essentially the same: one gradient evaluation and one prox computation.*

10.7.3 Examples

Example 10.37. Consider the following model, which was already discussed in Example 10.2:

$$\min_{\mathbf{x}\in\mathbb{R}^n} f(\mathbf{x}) + \lambda\|\mathbf{x}\|_1,$$

where $\lambda > 0$ and $f : \mathbb{R}^n \to \mathbb{R}$ is assumed to be convex and L_f-smooth. The update formula of the proximal gradient method with constant stepsize $\frac{1}{L_f}$ has the form

$$\mathbf{x}^{k+1} = \mathcal{T}_{\frac{\lambda}{L_f}}\left(\mathbf{x}^k - \frac{1}{L_f}\nabla f(\mathbf{x}^k)\right).$$

As was already noted in Example 10.3, since at each iteration one shrinkage/soft-thresholding operation is performed, this method is also known as the *iterative shrinkage-thresholding algorithm* (ISTA). The general update step of the accelerated proximal gradient method discussed in this section takes the following form:

(a) set $\mathbf{x}^{k+1} = \mathcal{T}_{\frac{\lambda}{L_f}}\left(\mathbf{y}^k - \frac{1}{L_f}\nabla f(\mathbf{y}^k)\right)$;

(b) set $t_{k+1} = \frac{1+\sqrt{1+4t_k^2}}{2}$;

(c) compute $\mathbf{y}^{k+1} = \mathbf{x}^{k+1} + \left(\frac{t_k-1}{t_{k+1}}\right)(\mathbf{x}^{k+1} - \mathbf{x}^k)$.

The above scheme truly deserves to be called "fast iterative shrinkage/thresholding algorithm" (FISTA) since it is an accelerated method that performs at each iteration a thresholding step. In this book we adopt the convention and use the acronym FISTA as the name of the fast proximal gradient method for a general nonsmooth part g. ∎

Example 10.38 (l_1-regularized least squares). As a special instance of Example 10.37, consider the problem

$$\min_{\mathbf{x}\in\mathbb{R}^n} \frac{1}{2}\|\mathbf{A}\mathbf{x} - \mathbf{b}\|_2^2 + \lambda\|\mathbf{x}\|_1, \tag{10.44}$$

where $\mathbf{A} \in \mathbb{R}^{m\times n}, \mathbf{b} \in \mathbb{R}^m$, and $\lambda > 0$. The problem fits model (10.1) with $f(\mathbf{x}) = \frac{1}{2}\|\mathbf{A}\mathbf{x} - \mathbf{b}\|_2^2$ and $g(\mathbf{x}) = \lambda\|\mathbf{x}\|_1$. The function f is L_f-smooth with $L_f = \|\mathbf{A}^T\mathbf{A}\|_{2,2} = \lambda_{\max}(\mathbf{A}^T\mathbf{A})$ (see Example 5.2). The update step of FISTA has the following form:

(a) set $\mathbf{x}^{k+1} = \mathcal{T}_{\frac{\lambda}{L_k}}\left(\mathbf{y}^k - \frac{1}{L_k}\mathbf{A}^T(\mathbf{A}\mathbf{y}^k - \mathbf{b})\right)$;

(b) set $t_{k+1} = \frac{1+\sqrt{1+4t_k^2}}{2}$;

(c) compute $\mathbf{y}^{k+1} = \mathbf{x}^{k+1} + \left(\frac{t_k-1}{t_{k+1}}\right)(\mathbf{x}^{k+1} - \mathbf{x}^k)$.

The update step of the proximal gradient method, which in this case is the same as ISTA, is

$$\mathbf{x}^{k+1} = \mathcal{T}_{\frac{\lambda}{L_k}}\left(\mathbf{x}^k - \frac{1}{L_k}\mathbf{A}^T(\mathbf{A}\mathbf{x}^k - \mathbf{b})\right).$$

The stepsizes in both methods can be chosen to be the constant $L_k \equiv \lambda_{\max}(\mathbf{A}^T\mathbf{A})$.

To illustrate the difference in the actual performance of ISTA and FISTA, we generated an instance of the problem with $\lambda = 1$ and $\mathbf{A} \in \mathbb{R}^{100\times 110}$. The components of $\mathbf{A}$ were independently generated using a standard normal distribution. The "true" vector is $\mathbf{x}_{\text{true}} = \mathbf{e}_3 - \mathbf{e}_7$, and $\mathbf{b}$ was chosen as $\mathbf{b} = \mathbf{A}\mathbf{x}_{\text{true}}$. We ran 200 iterations of ISTA and FISTA in order to solve problem (10.44) with initial vector $\mathbf{x} = \mathbf{e}$, the vector of all ones. It is well known that the l_1-norm element in the objective function is a regularizer that promotes sparsity, and we thus expect that the optimal solution of (10.44) will be close to the "true" sparse vector $\mathbf{x}_{\text{true}}$. The distances to optimality in terms of function values of the sequences generated by the two methods as a function of the iteration index are plotted in Figure 10.1, where it is apparent that FISTA is far superior to ISTA.

In Figure 10.2 we plot the vectors that were obtained by the two methods. Obviously, the solution produced by 200 iterations of FISTA is much closer to the optimal solution (which is very close to $\mathbf{e}_3 - \mathbf{e}_7$) than the solution obtained after 200 iterations of ISTA. ∎

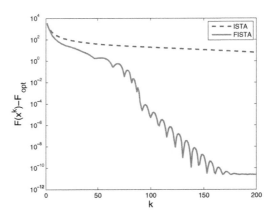

Figure 10.1. *Results of* 200 *iterations of ISTA and FISTA on an* l_1-*regularized least squares problem.*

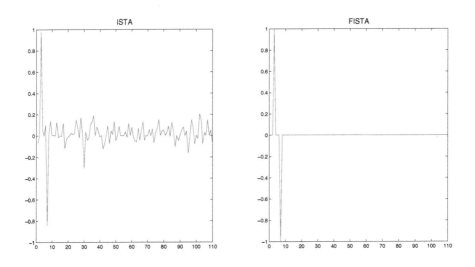

Figure 10.2. *Solutions obtained by ISTA (left) and FISTA (right).*

10.7.4   MFISTA[58]

FISTA is not a monotone method, meaning that the sequence of function values it produces is not necessarily nonincreasing. It is possible to define a monotone version of FISTA, which we call MFISTA, which is a descent method and at the same time preserves the same rate of convergence as FISTA.

---

[58]MFISTA and its convergence analysis are from the work of Beck and Teboulle [17].

MFISTA

Input: $(f, g, \mathbf{x}^0)$, where f and g satisfy properties (A) and (B) in Assumption 10.31 and $\mathbf{x}^0 \in \mathbb{E}$.
Initialization: set $\mathbf{y}^0 = \mathbf{x}^0$ and $t_0 = 1$.
General step: for any $k = 0, 1, 2, \ldots$ execute the following steps:

(a) pick $L_k > 0$;

(b) set $\mathbf{z}^k = \operatorname{prox}_{\frac{1}{L_k} g}\left(\mathbf{y}^k - \frac{1}{L_k}\nabla f(\mathbf{y}^k)\right)$;

(c) choose $\mathbf{x}^{k+1} \in \mathbb{E}$ such that $F(\mathbf{x}^{k+1}) \leq \min\{F(\mathbf{z}^k), F(\mathbf{x}^k)\}$;

(d) set $t_{k+1} = \frac{1+\sqrt{1+4t_k^2}}{2}$;

(e) compute $\mathbf{y}^{k+1} = \mathbf{x}^{k+1} + \frac{t_k}{t_{k+1}}(\mathbf{z}^k - \mathbf{x}^{k+1}) + \left(\frac{t_k - 1}{t_{k+1}}\right)(\mathbf{x}^{k+1} - \mathbf{x}^k)$.

Remark 10.39. *The choice $\mathbf{x}^{k+1} \in \operatorname{argmin}\{F(\mathbf{x}) : \mathbf{x} = \mathbf{x}^k, \mathbf{z}^k\}$ is a very simple rule ensuring the condition $F(\mathbf{x}^{k+1}) \leq \min\{F(\mathbf{z}^k), F(\mathbf{x}^k)\}$. We also note that the convergence established in Theorem 10.40 only requires the condition $F(\mathbf{x}^{k+1}) \leq F(\mathbf{z}^k)$.*

The convergence result of MFISTA, whose proof is a minor adjustment of the proof of Theorem 10.34, is given below.

Theorem 10.40 ($O(1/k^2)$ rate of convergence of MFISTA). *Suppose that Assumption 10.31 holds. Let $\{\mathbf{x}^k\}_{k \geq 0}$ be the sequence generated by MFISTA for solving problem (10.1) with either a constant stepsize rule in which $L_k \equiv L_f$ for all $k \geq 0$ or the backtracking procedure B3. Then for any $\mathbf{x}^* \in X^*$ and $k \geq 1$,*

$$F(\mathbf{x}^k) - F_{\mathrm{opt}} \leq \frac{2\alpha L_f \|\mathbf{x}^0 - \mathbf{x}^*\|^2}{(k+1)^2},$$

where $\alpha = 1$ in the constant stepsize setting and $\alpha = \max\left\{\eta, \frac{s}{L_f}\right\}$ if the backtracking rule is employed.

Proof. Let $k \geq 1$. Substituting $\mathbf{x} = t_k^{-1}\mathbf{x}^* + (1 - t_k^{-1})\mathbf{x}^k$, $\mathbf{y} = \mathbf{y}^k$, and $L = L_k$ in the fundamental prox-grad inequality (10.21), taking into account that inequality (10.39) is satisfied and that f is convex, we obtain that

$$F(t_k^{-1}\mathbf{x}^* + (1 - t_k^{-1})\mathbf{x}^k) - F(\mathbf{z}^k)$$
$$\geq \frac{L_k}{2}\|\mathbf{z}^k - (t_k^{-1}\mathbf{x}^* + (1 - t_k^{-1})\mathbf{x}^k)\|^2 - \frac{L_k}{2}\|\mathbf{y}^k - (t_k^{-1}\mathbf{x}^* + (1 - t_k^{-1})\mathbf{x}^k)\|^2$$
$$= \frac{L_k}{2t_k^2}\|t_k\mathbf{z}^k - (\mathbf{x}^* + (t_k - 1)\mathbf{x}^k)\|^2 - \frac{L_k}{2t_k^2}\|t_k\mathbf{y}^k - (\mathbf{x}^* + (t_k - 1)\mathbf{x}^k)\|^2. \quad (10.45)$$

By the convexity of F,

$$F(t_k^{-1}\mathbf{x}^* + (1 - t_k^{-1})\mathbf{x}^k) \leq t_k^{-1}F(\mathbf{x}^*) + (1 - t_k^{-1})F(\mathbf{x}^k).$$

Therefore, using the notation $v_n \equiv F(\mathbf{x}^n) - F_{\mathrm{opt}}$ for any $n \geq 0$ and the fact that $F(\mathbf{x}^{k+1}) \leq F(\mathbf{z}^k)$, it follows that

$$F(t_k^{-1}\mathbf{x}^* + (1 - t_k^{-1})\mathbf{x}^k) - F(\mathbf{z}^k) \leq (1 - t_k^{-1})(F(\mathbf{x}^k) - F(\mathbf{x}^*)) - (F(\mathbf{x}_{k+1}) - F(\mathbf{x}^*))$$
$$= (1 - t_k^{-1})v_k - v_{k+1}. \tag{10.46}$$

On the other hand, using the relation $\mathbf{y}^k = \mathbf{x}^k + \frac{t_{k-1}}{t_k}(\mathbf{z}^{k-1} - \mathbf{x}^k) + \left(\frac{t_{k-1}-1}{t_k}\right)(\mathbf{x}^k - \mathbf{x}^{k-1})$, we have

$$t_k \mathbf{y}^k - (\mathbf{x}^* + (t_k - 1)\mathbf{x}^k) = t_{k-1}\mathbf{z}^{k-1} - (\mathbf{x}^* + (t_{k-1} - 1)\mathbf{x}^{k-1}). \tag{10.47}$$

Combining (10.45), (10.46), and (10.47), we obtain that

$$(t_k^2 - t_k)v_k - t_k^2 v_{k+1} \geq \frac{L_k}{2}\|\mathbf{u}^{k+1}\|^2 - \frac{L_k}{2}\|\mathbf{u}^k\|^2,$$

where we use the notation $\mathbf{u}^n = t_{n-1}\mathbf{z}^{n-1} - (\mathbf{x}^* + (t_{n-1} - 1)\mathbf{x}^{n-1})$ for any $n \geq 0$. By the update rule of t_{k+1}, we have $t_k^2 - t_k = t_{k-1}^2$, and hence

$$\frac{2}{L_k}t_{k-1}^2 v_k - \frac{2}{L_k}t_k^2 v_{k+1} \geq \|\mathbf{u}^{k+1}\|^2 - \|\mathbf{u}^k\|^2.$$

Since $L_k \geq L_{k-1}$, we can conclude that

$$\frac{2}{L_{k-1}}t_{k-1}^2 v_k - \frac{2}{L_k}t_k^2 v_{k+1} \geq \|\mathbf{u}^{k+1}\|^2 - \|\mathbf{u}^k\|^2.$$

Thus,

$$\|\mathbf{u}^{k+1}\|^2 + \frac{2}{L_k}t_k^2 v_{k+1} \leq \|\mathbf{u}^k\|^2 + \frac{2}{L_{k-1}}t_{k-1}^2 v_k,$$

and hence, for any $k \geq 1$,

$$\|\mathbf{u}^k\|^2 + \frac{2}{L_{k-1}}t_{k-1}^2 v_k \leq \|\mathbf{u}^1\|^2 + \frac{2}{L_0}t_0^2 v_1 = \|\mathbf{z}^0 - \mathbf{x}^*\|^2 + \frac{2}{L_0}(F(\mathbf{x}^1) - F_{\mathrm{opt}}). \tag{10.48}$$

Substituting $\mathbf{x} = \mathbf{x}^*, \mathbf{y} = \mathbf{y}^0$, and $L = L_0$ in the fundamental prox-grad inequality (10.21), taking into account the convexity of f, yields

$$\frac{2}{L_0}(F(\mathbf{x}^*) - F(\mathbf{z}^0)) \geq \|\mathbf{z}^0 - \mathbf{x}^*\|^2 - \|\mathbf{y}^0 - \mathbf{x}^*\|^2,$$

which, along with the facts that $\mathbf{y}^0 = \mathbf{x}^0$ and $F(\mathbf{x}^1) \leq F(\mathbf{z}^0)$, implies the bound

$$\|\mathbf{z}^0 - \mathbf{x}^*\|^2 + \frac{2}{L_0}(F(\mathbf{x}^1) - F_{\mathrm{opt}}) \leq \|\mathbf{x}^0 - \mathbf{x}^*\|^2.$$

Combining the last inequality with (10.48), we get

$$\frac{2}{L_{k-1}}t_{k-1}^2 v_k \leq \|\mathbf{u}^k\|^2 + \frac{2}{L_{k-1}}t_{k-1}^2 v_k \leq \|\mathbf{x}^0 - \mathbf{x}^*\|^2.$$

Thus, using the bound $L_{k-1} \leq \alpha L_f$, the definition of v_k, and Lemma 10.33,

$$F(\mathbf{x}^k) - F_{\mathrm{opt}} \leq \frac{L_{k-1}\|\mathbf{x}^0 - \mathbf{x}^*\|^2}{2t_{k-1}^2} \leq \frac{2\alpha L_f \|\mathbf{x}^0 - \mathbf{x}^*\|^2}{(k+1)^2}. \qquad \square$$

10.7.5 Weighted FISTA

Consider the main composite model (10.1) under Assumption 10.31. Suppose that $\mathbb{E} = \mathbb{R}^n$. Recall that a standing assumption in this chapter is that the underlying space is Euclidean, but this does not mean that the endowed inner product is the dot product. Assume that the endowed inner product is the $\mathbf{Q}$-inner product: $\langle \mathbf{x}, \mathbf{y} \rangle = \mathbf{x}^T \mathbf{Q} \mathbf{y}$, where $\mathbf{Q} \in \mathbb{S}_{++}^n$. In this case, as explained in Remark 3.32, the gradient is given by

$$\nabla f(\mathbf{x}) = \mathbf{Q}^{-1} D_f(\mathbf{x}),$$

where

$$D_f(\mathbf{x}) = \begin{pmatrix} \frac{\partial f}{\partial x_1}(\mathbf{x}) \\ \frac{\partial f}{\partial x_2}(\mathbf{x}) \\ \vdots \\ \frac{\partial f}{\partial x_n}(\mathbf{x}) \end{pmatrix}.$$

We will use a Lipschitz constant of ∇f w.r.t. the $\mathbf{Q}$-norm, which we will denote by $L_f^{\mathbf{Q}}$. The constant is essentially defined by the relation

$$\|\mathbf{Q}^{-1} D_f(\mathbf{x}) - \mathbf{Q}^{-1} D_f(\mathbf{y})\|_{\mathbf{Q}} \le L_f^{\mathbf{Q}} \|\mathbf{x} - \mathbf{y}\|_{\mathbf{Q}} \text{ for any } \mathbf{x}, \mathbf{y} \in \mathbb{R}^n.$$

The general update rule for FISTA with a constant stepsize in this case will have the following form:

(a) set $\mathbf{x}^{k+1} = \mathrm{prox}_{\frac{1}{L_f^{\mathbf{Q}}} g}\left(\mathbf{y}^k - \frac{1}{L_f^{\mathbf{Q}}} \mathbf{Q}^{-1} D_f(\mathbf{y}^k)\right)$;

(b) set $t_{k+1} = \frac{1 + \sqrt{1 + 4t_k^2}}{2}$;

(c) compute $\mathbf{y}^{k+1} = \mathbf{x}^{k+1} + \left(\frac{t_k - 1}{t_{k+1}}\right)(\mathbf{x}^{k+1} - \mathbf{x}^k)$.

Obviously, the prox operator in step (a) is computed in terms of the $\mathbf{Q}$-norm, meaning that

$$\mathrm{prox}_h(\mathbf{x}) = \mathrm{argmin}_{\mathbf{u} \in \mathbb{R}^n}\left\{h(\mathbf{u}) + \frac{1}{2}\|\mathbf{u} - \mathbf{x}\|_{\mathbf{Q}}^2\right\}.$$

The convergence result of Theorem 10.34 will also be written in terms of the $\mathbf{Q}$-norm:

$$F(\mathbf{x}^k) - F_{\mathrm{opt}} \le \frac{2 L_f^{\mathbf{Q}} \|\mathbf{x}^0 - \mathbf{x}^*\|_{\mathbf{Q}}^2}{(k+1)^2}.$$

10.7.6 Restarting FISTA in the Strongly Convex Case

We will now assume that in addition to Assumption 10.31, f is σ-strongly convex for some $\sigma > 0$. Recall that by Theorem 10.30, the proximal gradient method attains an ε-optimal solution after an order of $O(\kappa \log(\frac{1}{\varepsilon}))$ iterations ($\kappa = \frac{L_f}{\sigma}$). The natural question is obviously how the complexity result improves when using FISTA instead of the proximal gradient method. Perhaps surprisingly, one option for obtaining such an improved result is by considering a version of FISTA that incorporates a restarting of the method after a constant amount of iterations.

Restarted FISTA

Initialization: pick $\mathbf{z}^{-1} \in \mathbb{E}$ and a positive integer N. Set $\mathbf{z}^0 = T_{L_f}(\mathbf{z}^{-1})$.

General step $(k \geq 0)$:

- run N iterations of FISTA with constant stepsize $(L_k \equiv L_f)$ and input $(f, g, \mathbf{z}^k)$ and obtain a sequence $\{\mathbf{x}^n\}_{n=0}^N$;

- set $\mathbf{z}^{k+1} = \mathbf{x}^N$.

The algorithm essentially consists of "outer" iterations, and each one employs N iterations of FISTA. To avoid confusion, the outer iterations will be called *cycles*. Theorem 10.41 below shows that an order of $O(\sqrt{\kappa} \log(\frac{1}{\varepsilon}))$ FISTA iterations are enough to guarantee that an ε-optimal solution is attained.

Theorem 10.41 ($O(\sqrt{\kappa} \log(\frac{1}{\varepsilon}))$ complexity of restarted FISTA). *Suppose that Assumption 10.31 holds and that f is σ-strongly convex ($\sigma > 0$). Let $\{\mathbf{z}^k\}_{k \geq 0}$ be the sequence generated by the restarted FISTA method employed with $N = \lceil \sqrt{8\kappa} - 1 \rceil$, where $\kappa = \frac{L_f}{\sigma}$. Let R be an upper bound on $\|\mathbf{z}^{-1} - \mathbf{x}^*\|$, where $\mathbf{x}^*$ is the unique optimal solution of problem (10.1). Then*[59]

(a) *for any $k \geq 0$,*

$$F(\mathbf{z}^k) - F_{\mathrm{opt}} \leq \frac{L_f R^2}{2} \left(\frac{1}{2}\right)^k;$$

(b) *after k iterations of FISTA with k satisfying*

$$k \geq \sqrt{8\kappa} \left(\frac{\log(\frac{1}{\varepsilon})}{\log(2)} + \frac{\log(L_f R^2)}{\log(2)}\right),$$

an ε-optimal solution is obtained at the end of the last completed cycle. That is,

$$F(\mathbf{z}^{\lfloor \frac{k}{N} \rfloor}) - F_{\mathrm{opt}} \leq \varepsilon.$$

Proof. (a) By Theorem 10.34, for any $n \geq 0$,

$$F(\mathbf{z}^{n+1}) - F_{\mathrm{opt}} \leq \frac{2L_f \|\mathbf{z}^n - \mathbf{x}^*\|^2}{(N+1)^2}. \tag{10.49}$$

Since f is σ-strongly convex, it follows by Theorem 5.25(b) that

$$F(\mathbf{z}^n) - F_{\mathrm{opt}} \geq \frac{\sigma}{2} \|\mathbf{z}^n - \mathbf{x}^*\|^2,$$

which, combined with (10.49), yields (recalling that $\kappa = L_f/\sigma$)

$$F(\mathbf{z}^{n+1}) - F_{\mathrm{opt}} \leq \frac{4\kappa(F(\mathbf{z}^n) - F_{\mathrm{opt}})}{(N+1)^2}. \tag{10.50}$$

---

[59]Note that the index k in part (a) stands for the number of cycles, while in part (b) it is the number of FISTA iterations.

Since $N \geq \sqrt{8\kappa} - 1$, it follows that $\frac{4\kappa}{(N+1)^2} \leq \frac{1}{2}$, and hence by (10.50)

$$F(\mathbf{z}^{n+1}) - F_{\mathrm{opt}} \leq \frac{1}{2}(F(\mathbf{z}^n) - F_{\mathrm{opt}}).$$

Employing the above inequality for $n = 0, 1, \ldots, k-1$, we conclude that

$$F(\mathbf{z}^k) - F_{\mathrm{opt}} \leq \left(\frac{1}{2}\right)^k (F(\mathbf{z}^0) - F_{\mathrm{opt}}). \tag{10.51}$$

Note that $\mathbf{z}^0 = T_{L_f}(\mathbf{z}^{-1})$. Invoking the fundamental prox-grad inequality (10.21) with $\mathbf{x} = \mathbf{x}^*, \mathbf{y} = \mathbf{z}^{-1}$, $L = L_f$, and taking into account the convexity of f, we obtain

$$F(\mathbf{x}^*) - F(\mathbf{z}^0) \geq \frac{L_f}{2}\|\mathbf{x}^* - \mathbf{z}^0\|^2 - \frac{L_f}{2}\|\mathbf{x}^* - \mathbf{z}^{-1}\|^2,$$

and hence

$$F(\mathbf{z}^0) - F_{\mathrm{opt}} \leq \frac{L_f}{2}\|\mathbf{x}^* - \mathbf{z}^{-1}\|^2 \leq \frac{L_f R^2}{2}. \tag{10.52}$$

Combining (10.51) and (10.52), we obtain

$$F(\mathbf{z}^k) - F_{\mathrm{opt}} \leq \frac{L_f R^2}{2}\left(\frac{1}{2}\right)^k.$$

(b) If k iterations of FISTA were employed, then $\lfloor \frac{k}{N} \rfloor$ cycles were completed. By part (a),

$$F(\mathbf{z}^{\lfloor \frac{k}{N} \rfloor}) - F_{\mathrm{opt}} \leq \frac{L_f R^2}{2}\left(\frac{1}{2}\right)^{\lfloor \frac{k}{N} \rfloor} \leq L_f R^2 \left(\frac{1}{2}\right)^{\frac{k}{N}}.$$

Therefore, a sufficient condition for the inequality $F(\mathbf{z}^{\lfloor \frac{k}{N} \rfloor}) - F_{\mathrm{opt}} \leq \varepsilon$ to hold is that

$$L_f R^2 \left(\frac{1}{2}\right)^{\frac{k}{N}} \leq \varepsilon,$$

which is equivalent to the inequality

$$k \geq N \left(\frac{\log(\frac{1}{\varepsilon})}{\log(2)} + \frac{\log(L_f R^2)}{\log(2)}\right).$$

The claim now follows by the fact that $N = \lceil \sqrt{8\kappa} - 1 \rceil \leq \sqrt{8\kappa}$. $\square$

10.7.7 The Strongly Convex Case (Once Again)—Variation on FISTA

As in the previous section, we will assume that in addition to Assumption 10.31, f is σ-strongly convex for some $\sigma > 0$. We will define a variant of FISTA, called V-FISTA, that will exhibit the improved linear rate of convergence of the restarted FISTA. This rate is established without any need of restarting of the method.

V-FISTA

Input: $(f, g, \mathbf{x}^0)$, where f and g satisfy properties (A) and (B) in Assumption 10.31, f is σ-strongly convex $(\sigma > 0)$, and $\mathbf{x}^0 \in \mathbb{E}$.

Initialization: set $\mathbf{y}^0 = \mathbf{x}^0, t_0 = 1$ and $\kappa = \frac{L_f}{\sigma}$.

General step: for any $k = 0, 1, 2, \ldots$ execute the following steps:

(a) set $\mathbf{x}^{k+1} = \text{prox}_{\frac{1}{L_f} g} \left(\mathbf{y}^k - \frac{1}{L_f} \nabla f(\mathbf{y}^k) \right)$;

(b) compute $\mathbf{y}^{k+1} = \mathbf{x}^{k+1} + \left(\frac{\sqrt{\kappa}-1}{\sqrt{\kappa}+1} \right) (\mathbf{x}^{k+1} - \mathbf{x}^k)$.

The improved linear rate of convergence is established in the next result, whose proof is a variation on the proof of the rate of convergence of FISTA for the non-strongly convex case (Theorem 10.34).

Theorem 10.42 ($O((1 - 1/\sqrt{\kappa})^k)$ rate of convergence of V-FISTA).[60] *Suppose that Assumption 10.31 holds and that f is σ-strongly convex $(\sigma > 0)$. Let $\{\mathbf{x}^k\}_{k \geq 0}$ be the sequence generated by V-FISTA for solving problem (10.1). Then for any $\mathbf{x}^* \in X^*$ and $k \geq 0$,*

$$F(\mathbf{x}^k) - F_{\text{opt}} \leq \left(1 - \frac{1}{\sqrt{\kappa}} \right)^k \left(F(\mathbf{x}^0) - F_{\text{opt}} + \frac{\sigma}{2} \|\mathbf{x}^0 - \mathbf{x}^*\|^2 \right), \qquad (10.53)$$

where $\kappa = \frac{L_f}{\sigma}$.

Proof. By the fundamental prox-grad inequality (Theorem 10.16) and the σ-strong convexity of f (invoking Theorem 5.24), it follows that for any $\mathbf{x}, \mathbf{y} \in \mathbb{E}$,

$$F(\mathbf{x}) - F(T_{L_f}(\mathbf{y})) \geq \frac{L_f}{2} \|\mathbf{x} - T_{L_f}\mathbf{y}\|^2 - \frac{L_f}{2} \|\mathbf{x} - \mathbf{y}\|^2 + f(\mathbf{x}) - f(\mathbf{y}) - \langle \nabla f(\mathbf{y}), \mathbf{x} - \mathbf{y} \rangle$$

$$\geq \frac{L_f}{2} \|\mathbf{x} - T_{L_f}(\mathbf{y})\|^2 - \frac{L_f}{2} \|\mathbf{x} - \mathbf{y}\|^2 + \frac{\sigma}{2} \|\mathbf{x} - \mathbf{y}\|^2.$$

Therefore,

$$F(\mathbf{x}) - F(T_{L_f}(\mathbf{y})) \geq \frac{L_f}{2} \|\mathbf{x} - T_{L_f}(\mathbf{y})\|^2 - \frac{L_f - \sigma}{2} \|\mathbf{x} - \mathbf{y}\|^2. \qquad (10.54)$$

Let $k \geq 0$ and $t = \sqrt{\kappa} = \sqrt{\frac{L_f}{\sigma}}$. Substituting $\mathbf{x} = t^{-1}\mathbf{x}^* + (1 - t^{-1})\mathbf{x}^k$ and $\mathbf{y} = \mathbf{y}^k$ into (10.54), we obtain that

$$F(t^{-1}\mathbf{x}^* + (1 - t^{-1})\mathbf{x}^k) - F(\mathbf{x}^{k+1})$$

$$\geq \frac{L_f}{2} \|\mathbf{x}^{k+1} - (t^{-1}\mathbf{x}^* + (1 - t^{-1})\mathbf{x}^k)\|^2 - \frac{L_f - \sigma}{2} \|\mathbf{y}^k - (t^{-1}\mathbf{x}^* + (1 - t^{-1})\mathbf{x}^k)\|^2$$

$$= \frac{L_f}{2t^2} \|t\mathbf{x}^{k+1} - (\mathbf{x}^* + (t - 1)\mathbf{x}^k)\|^2 - \frac{L_f - \sigma}{2t^2} \|t\mathbf{y}^k - (\mathbf{x}^* + (t - 1)\mathbf{x}^k)\|^2. \qquad (10.55)$$

---

[60]The proof of Theorem 10.42 follows the proof of Theorem 4.10 from the review paper of Chambolle and Pock [42].

By the σ-strong convexity of F,

$$F(t^{-1}\mathbf{x}^* + (1-t^{-1})\mathbf{x}^k) \leq t^{-1}F(\mathbf{x}^*) + (1-t^{-1})F(\mathbf{x}^k) - \frac{\sigma}{2}t^{-1}(1-t^{-1})\|\mathbf{x}^k - \mathbf{x}^*\|^2.$$

Therefore, using the notation $v_n \equiv F(\mathbf{x}^n) - F_{\mathrm{opt}}$ for any $n \geq 0$,

$$F(t^{-1}\mathbf{x}^* + (1-t^{-1})\mathbf{x}^k) - F(\mathbf{x}^{k+1})$$

$$\leq (1-t^{-1})(F(\mathbf{x}^k) - F(\mathbf{x}^*)) - (F(\mathbf{x}_{k+1}) - F(\mathbf{x}^*)) - \frac{\sigma}{2}t^{-1}(1-t^{-1})\|\mathbf{x}^k - \mathbf{x}^*\|^2$$

$$= (1-t^{-1})v_k - v_{k+1} - \frac{\sigma}{2}t^{-1}(1-t^{-1})\|\mathbf{x}^k - \mathbf{x}^*\|^2,$$

which, combined with (10.55), yields the inequality

$$t(t-1)v_k + \frac{L_f - \sigma}{2}\|t\mathbf{y}^k - (\mathbf{x}^* + (t-1)\mathbf{x}^k)\|^2 - \frac{\sigma(t-1)}{2}\|\mathbf{x}^k - \mathbf{x}^*\|^2$$

$$\geq t^2 v_{k+1} + \frac{L_f}{2}\|t\mathbf{x}^{k+1} - (\mathbf{x}^* + (t-1)\mathbf{x}^k)\|^2. \tag{10.56}$$

We will use the following identity that holds for any $\mathbf{a}, \mathbf{b} \in \mathbb{E}$ and $\beta \in [0,1)$:

$$\|\mathbf{a} + \mathbf{b}\|^2 - \beta\|\mathbf{a}\|^2 = (1-\beta)\left\|\mathbf{a} + \frac{1}{1-\beta}\mathbf{b}\right\|^2 - \frac{\beta}{1-\beta}\|\mathbf{b}\|^2.$$

Plugging $\mathbf{a} = \mathbf{x}^k - \mathbf{x}^*$, $\mathbf{b} = t(\mathbf{y}^k - \mathbf{x}^k)$, and $\beta = \frac{\sigma(t-1)}{L_f - \sigma}$ into the above inequality, we obtain

$$\frac{L_f - \sigma}{2}\|t(\mathbf{y}^k - \mathbf{x}^k) + \mathbf{x}^k - \mathbf{x}^*\|^2 - \frac{\sigma(t-1)}{2}\|\mathbf{x}^k - \mathbf{x}^*\|^2$$

$$= \frac{L_f - \sigma}{2}\left[\|t(\mathbf{y}^k - \mathbf{x}^k) + \mathbf{x}^k - \mathbf{x}^*\|^2 - \frac{\sigma(t-1)}{L_f - \sigma}\|\mathbf{x}^k - \mathbf{x}^*\|^2\right]$$

$$= \frac{L_f - \sigma}{2}\left[\frac{L_f - \sigma t}{L_f - \sigma}\left\|\mathbf{x}^k - \mathbf{x}^* + \frac{L_f - \sigma}{L_f - \sigma t}t(\mathbf{y}^k - \mathbf{x}^k)\right\|^2 - \frac{\sigma(t-1)t^2}{L_f - \sigma t}\|\mathbf{x}^k - \mathbf{y}^k\|^2\right]$$

$$\leq \frac{L_f - \sigma t}{2}\left\|\mathbf{x}^k - \mathbf{x}^* + \frac{L_f - \sigma}{L_f - \sigma t}t(\mathbf{y}^k - \mathbf{x}^k)\right\|^2.$$

We can therefore conclude from the above inequality and (10.56) that

$$t(t-1)v_k + \frac{L_f - \sigma t}{2}\left\|\mathbf{x}^k - \mathbf{x}^* + \frac{L_f - \sigma}{L_f - \sigma t}t(\mathbf{y}^k - \mathbf{x}^k)\right\|^2$$

$$\geq t^2 v_{k+1} + \frac{L_f}{2}\|t\mathbf{x}^{k+1} - (\mathbf{x}^* + (t-1)\mathbf{x}^k)\|^2. \tag{10.57}$$

If $k \geq 1$, then using the relations $\mathbf{y}^k = \mathbf{x}^k + \frac{\sqrt{\kappa}-1}{\sqrt{\kappa}+1}(\mathbf{x}^k - \mathbf{x}^{k-1})$ and $t = \sqrt{\kappa} = \sqrt{\frac{L_f}{\sigma}}$, we obtain

$$\mathbf{x}^k - \mathbf{x}^* + \frac{L_f - \sigma}{L_f - \sigma t}t(\mathbf{y}^k - \mathbf{x}^k) = \mathbf{x}^k - \mathbf{x}^* + \frac{L_f - \sigma}{L_f - \sigma t}\frac{t(t-1)}{t+1}(\mathbf{x}^k - \mathbf{x}^{k-1})$$

$$= \mathbf{x}^k - \mathbf{x}^* + \frac{\kappa - 1}{\kappa - \sqrt{\kappa}}\frac{\sqrt{\kappa}(\sqrt{\kappa}-1)}{\sqrt{\kappa}+1}(\mathbf{x}^k - \mathbf{x}^{k-1})$$

$$= \mathbf{x}^k - \mathbf{x}^* + (\sqrt{\kappa}-1)(\mathbf{x}^k - \mathbf{x}^{k-1})$$

$$= t\mathbf{x}^k - (\mathbf{x}^* + (t-1)\mathbf{x}^{k-1}),$$

and obviously, for the case $k = 0$ (recalling that $\mathbf{y}^0 = \mathbf{x}^0$),

$$\mathbf{x}^0 - \mathbf{x}^* + \frac{L_f - \sigma}{L_f - \sigma t} t(\mathbf{y}^0 - \mathbf{x}^0) = \mathbf{x}^0 - \mathbf{x}^*.$$

We can thus deduce that (10.57) can be rewritten as (after division by t^2 and using again the definition of t as $t = \sqrt{\frac{L_f}{\sigma}}$)

$$v_{k+1} + \frac{\sigma}{2}\|t\mathbf{x}^{k+1} - (\mathbf{x}^* + (t-1)\mathbf{x}^k)\|^2$$
$$\leq \begin{cases} \left(1 - \frac{1}{t}\right)\left[v_k + \frac{\sigma}{2}\|t\mathbf{x}^k - (\mathbf{x}^* + (t-1)\mathbf{x}^{k-1})\|^2\right], & k \geq 1, \\ \left(1 - \frac{1}{t}\right)\left[v_0 + \frac{\sigma}{2}\|\mathbf{x}^0 - \mathbf{x}^*\|^2\right], & k = 0. \end{cases}$$

We can thus conclude that for any $k \geq 0$,

$$v_k \leq \left(1 - \frac{1}{t}\right)^k \left(v_0 + \frac{\sigma}{2}\|\mathbf{x}^0 - \mathbf{x}^*\|^2\right),$$

which is the desired result (10.53). $\Box$

10.8   Smoothing[61]

10.8.1   Motivation

In Chapters 8 and 9 we considered methods for solving nonsmooth convex optimization problems with complexity $O(1/\varepsilon^2)$, meaning that an order of $1/\varepsilon^2$ iterations were required in order to obtain an ε-optimal solution. On the other hand, FISTA requires $O(1/\sqrt{\varepsilon})$ iterations in order to find an ε-optimal solution of the composite model

$$\min_{\mathbf{x} \in \mathbb{E}} f(\mathbf{x}) + g(\mathbf{x}), \tag{10.58}$$

where f is L_f-smooth and convex and g is a proper closed and convex function. In this section we will show how FISTA can be used to devise a method for more general nonsmooth convex problems in an improved complexity of $O(1/\varepsilon)$. In particular, the model that will be considered includes an additional third term to (10.58):

$$\min\{f(\mathbf{x}) + h(\mathbf{x}) + g(\mathbf{x}) : \mathbf{x} \in \mathbb{E}\}. \tag{10.59}$$

The function h will be assumed to be real-valued and convex; we will not assume that it is easy to compute its prox operator (as is implicitly assumed on g), and hence solving it directly using FISTA with smooth and nonsmooth parts taken as $(f, g + h)$ is not a practical solution approach. The idea will be to find a smooth approximation of h, say $\tilde{h}$, and solve the problem via FISTA with smooth and nonsmooth parts taken as $(f + \tilde{h}, g)$. This simple idea will be the basis for the improved $O(1/\varepsilon)$ complexity. To be able to describe the method, we will need to study in more detail the notions of *smooth approximations* and *smoothability*.

---

[61]The idea of producing an $O(1/\varepsilon)$ complexity result for nonsmooth problems by employing an accelerated gradient method was first presented and developed by Nesterov in [95]. The extension presented in Section 10.8 to the three-part composite model and to the setting of more general smooth approximations was developed by Beck and Teboulle in [20], where additional results and extensions can also be found.

10.8.2   Smoothable Functions and Smooth Approximations

Definition 10.43 (smoothable functions). *A convex function* $h : \mathbb{E} \to \mathbb{R}$ *is called* (α, β)**-smoothable** $(\alpha, \beta > 0)$ *if for any* $\mu > 0$ *there exists a convex differentiable function* $h_\mu : \mathbb{E} \to \mathbb{R}$ *such that the following holds:*

(a) $h_\mu(\mathbf{x}) \leq h(\mathbf{x}) \leq h_\mu(\mathbf{x}) + \beta\mu$ *for all* $\mathbf{x} \in \mathbb{E}$.

(b) h_μ *is* $\frac{\alpha}{\mu}$*-smooth.*

The function h_μ *is called a* $\frac{1}{\mu}$**-smooth approximation** *of* h *with parameters* (α, β).

Example 10.44 (smooth approximation of $\|\mathbf{x}\|_2$). Consider the function $h : \mathbb{R}^n \to \mathbb{R}$ given by $h(\mathbf{x}) = \|\mathbf{x}\|_2$. For any $\mu > 0$, define $h_\mu(\mathbf{x}) \equiv \sqrt{\|\mathbf{x}\|_2^2 + \mu^2} - \mu$. Then for any $\mathbf{x} \in \mathbb{R}^n$,

$$h_\mu(\mathbf{x}) = \sqrt{\|\mathbf{x}\|_2^2 + \mu^2} - \mu \leq \|\mathbf{x}\|_2 + \mu - \mu = \|\mathbf{x}\|_2 = h(\mathbf{x}),$$

$$h(\mathbf{x}) = \|\mathbf{x}\|_2 \leq \sqrt{\|\mathbf{x}\|_2^2 + \mu^2} = h_\mu(\mathbf{x}) + \mu,$$

showing that property (a) in the definition of smoothable functions holds with $\beta = 1$. To show that property (b) holds with $\alpha = 1$, note that by Example 5.14, the function $\varphi(\mathbf{x}) \equiv \sqrt{\|\mathbf{x}\|_2^2 + 1}$ is 1-smooth, and hence $h_\mu(\mathbf{x}) = \mu\varphi(\mathbf{x}/\mu) - \mu$ is $\frac{1}{\mu}$-smooth. We conclude that h_μ is a $\frac{1}{\mu}$-smooth approximation of h with parameters $(1, 1)$. In the terminology described in Definition 10.43, we showed that h is $(1, 1)$-smoothable. ∎

Example 10.45 (smooth approximation of $\max_i\{x_i\}$). Consider the function $h : \mathbb{R}^n \to \mathbb{R}$ given by $h(\mathbf{x}) = \max\{x_1, x_2, \ldots, x_n\}$. For any $\mu > 0$, define the function

$$h_\mu(\mathbf{x}) = \mu \log \left(\sum_{i=1}^n e^{x_i/\mu} \right) - \mu \log n.$$

Then for any $\mathbf{x} \in \mathbb{R}^n$,

$$h_\mu(\mathbf{x}) = \mu \log \left(\sum_{i=1}^n e^{x_i/\mu} \right) - \mu \log n$$

$$\leq \mu \log \left(n e^{\max_i\{x_i\}/\mu} \right) - \mu \log n = h(\mathbf{x}), \tag{10.60}$$

$$h(\mathbf{x}) = \max_i\{x_i\} \leq \mu \log \left(\sum_{i=1}^n e^{x_i/\mu} \right) = h_\mu(\mathbf{x}) + \mu \log n. \tag{10.61}$$

By Example 5.15, the function $\varphi(\mathbf{x}) = \log(\sum_{i=1}^n e^{x_i})$ is 1-smooth, and hence the function $h_\mu(\mathbf{x}) = \mu\varphi(\mathbf{x}/\mu) - \mu \log n$ is $\frac{1}{\mu}$-smooth. Combining this with (10.60) and (10.61), it follows that h_μ is a $\frac{1}{\mu}$-smooth approximation of h with parameters $(1, \log n)$. We conclude in particular that h is $(1, \log n)$-smoothable. ∎

The following result describes two important calculus rules of smooth approximations.

Theorem 10.46 (calculus of smooth approximations).

(a) *Let $h^1, h^2 : \mathbb{E} \to \mathbb{R}$ be convex functions, and let γ_1, γ_2 be nonnegative numbers. Suppose that for a given $\mu > 0$, h_μ^i is a $\frac{1}{\mu}$-smooth approximation of h^i with parameters (α_i, β_i) for $i = 1, 2$. Then $\gamma_1 h_\mu^1 + \gamma_2 h_\mu^2$ is a $\frac{1}{\mu}$-smooth approximation of $\gamma_1 h^1 + \gamma_2 h^2$ with parameters $(\gamma_1 \alpha_1 + \gamma_2 \alpha_2, \gamma_1 \beta_1 + \gamma_2 \beta_2)$.*

(b) *Let $\mathcal{A} : \mathbb{E} \to \mathbb{V}$ be a linear transformation between the Euclidean spaces $\mathbb{E}$ and $\mathbb{V}$. Let $h : \mathbb{V} \to \mathbb{R}$ be a convex function and define*

$$q(\mathbf{x}) \equiv h(\mathcal{A}(\mathbf{x}) + \mathbf{b}),$$

where $\mathbf{b} \in \mathbb{V}$. Suppose that for a given $\mu > 0$, h_μ is a $\frac{1}{\mu}$-smooth approximation of h with parameters (α, β). Then the function $q_\mu(\mathbf{x}) \equiv h_\mu(\mathcal{A}(\mathbf{x}) + \mathbf{b})$ is a $\frac{1}{\mu}$-smooth approximation of q with parameters $(\alpha \|\mathcal{A}\|^2, \beta)$.

Proof. (a) By its definition, h_μ^i $(i = 1, 2)$ is convex, $\frac{\alpha_i}{\mu}$-smooth and satisfies $h_\mu^i(\mathbf{x}) \leq h^i(\mathbf{x}) \leq h_\mu^i(\mathbf{x}) + \beta_i \mu$ for any $\mathbf{x} \in \mathbb{E}$. We can thus conclude that $\gamma_1 h_\mu^1 + \gamma_2 h_\mu^2$ is convex and that for any $\mathbf{x}, \mathbf{y} \in \mathbb{E}$,

$$\gamma_1 h_\mu^1(\mathbf{x}) + \gamma_2 h_\mu^2(\mathbf{x}) \leq \gamma_1 h^1(\mathbf{x}) + \gamma_2 h^2(\mathbf{x}) \leq \gamma_1 h_\mu^1(\mathbf{x}) + \gamma_2 h_\mu^2(\mathbf{x}) + (\gamma_1 \beta_1 + \gamma_2 \beta_2)\mu,$$

as well as

$$
\begin{aligned}
\|\nabla(\gamma_1 h_\mu^1 + \gamma_2 h_\mu^2)(\mathbf{x}) - \nabla(\gamma_1 h_\mu^1 + \gamma_2 h_\mu^2)(\mathbf{y})\| &\leq \gamma_1 \|\nabla h_\mu^1(\mathbf{x}) - \nabla h_\mu^1(\mathbf{y})\| \\
&\quad + \gamma_2 \|\nabla h_\mu^2(\mathbf{x}) - \nabla h_\mu^2(\mathbf{y})\| \\
&\leq \gamma_1 \frac{\alpha_1}{\mu} \|\mathbf{x} - \mathbf{y}\| + \gamma_2 \frac{\alpha_2}{\mu} \|\mathbf{x} - \mathbf{y}\| \\
&= \frac{\gamma_1 \alpha_1 + \gamma_2 \alpha_2}{\mu} \|\mathbf{x} - \mathbf{y}\|,
\end{aligned}
$$

establishing the fact that $\gamma_1 h_\mu^1 + \gamma_2 h_\mu^2$ is a $\frac{1}{\mu}$-smooth approximation of $\gamma_1 h^1 + \gamma_2 h^2$ with parameters $(\gamma_1 \alpha_1 + \gamma_2 \alpha_2, \gamma_1 \beta_1 + \gamma_2 \beta_2)$.

(b) Since h_μ is a $\frac{1}{\mu}$-smooth approximation of h with parameters (α, β), it follows that h_μ is convex, $\frac{\alpha}{\mu}$-smooth and for any $\mathbf{y} \in \mathbb{V}$,

$$h_\mu(\mathbf{y}) \leq h(\mathbf{y}) \leq h_\mu(\mathbf{y}) + \beta\mu. \tag{10.62}$$

Let $\mathbf{x} \in \mathbb{E}$. Plugging $\mathbf{y} = \mathcal{A}(\mathbf{x}) + \mathbf{b}$ into (10.62), we obtain that

$$q_\mu(\mathbf{x}) \leq q(\mathbf{x}) \leq q_\mu(\mathbf{x}) + \beta\mu. \tag{10.63}$$

In addition, by the $\frac{\alpha}{\mu}$-smoothness of h_μ, we have for any $\mathbf{x}, \mathbf{y} \in \mathbb{E}$,

$$
\begin{aligned}
\|\nabla q_\mu(\mathbf{x}) - \nabla q_\mu(\mathbf{y})\| &= \|\mathcal{A}^T \nabla h_\mu(\mathcal{A}(\mathbf{x}) + \mathbf{b}) - \mathcal{A}^T \nabla h_\mu(\mathcal{A}(\mathbf{y}) + \mathbf{b})\| \\
&\leq \|\mathcal{A}^T\| \cdot \|\nabla h_\mu(\mathcal{A}(\mathbf{x}) + \mathbf{b}) - \nabla h_\mu(\mathcal{A}(\mathbf{y}) + \mathbf{b})\| \\
&\leq \frac{\alpha}{\mu} \|\mathcal{A}^T\| \cdot \|\mathcal{A}(\mathbf{x}) + \mathbf{b} - \mathcal{A}(\mathbf{y}) - \mathbf{b}\| \\
&\leq \frac{\alpha}{\mu} \|\mathcal{A}^T\| \cdot \|\mathcal{A}\| \cdot \|\mathbf{x} - \mathbf{y}\| \\
&= \frac{\alpha \|\mathcal{A}\|^2}{\mu} \|\mathbf{x} - \mathbf{y}\|,
\end{aligned}
$$

where the last equality follows by the fact that $\|\mathcal{A}\| = \|\mathcal{A}^T\|$ (see Section 1.14). We have thus shown that the convex function h_μ is $\frac{\alpha\|\mathcal{A}\|^2}{\mu}$-smooth and satisfies (10.63) for any $\mathbf{x} \in \mathbb{E}$, establishing the desired result. $\quad\square$

A direct result of Theorem 10.46 is the following corollary stating the preservation of smoothability under nonnegative linear combinations and affine transformations of variables.

Corollary 10.47 (operations preserving smoothability).

(a) *Let $h^1, h^2 : \mathbb{E} \to \mathbb{R}$ be convex functions which are (α_1, β_1)- and (α_2, β_2)-smoothable, respectively, and let γ_1, γ_2 be nonnegative numbers. Then $\gamma_1 h^1 + \gamma_2 h^2$ is a $(\gamma_1 \alpha_1 + \gamma_2 \alpha_2, \gamma_1 \beta_1 + \gamma_2 \beta_2)$-smoothable function.*

(b) *Let $\mathcal{A} : \mathbb{E} \to \mathbb{V}$ be a linear transformation between the Euclidean spaces $\mathbb{E}$ and $\mathbb{V}$. Let $h : \mathbb{V} \to \mathbb{R}$ be a convex (α, β)-smoothable function and define*

$$q(\mathbf{x}) \equiv h(\mathcal{A}(\mathbf{x}) + \mathbf{b}),$$

where $\mathbf{b} \in \mathbb{V}$. Then q is $(\alpha\|\mathcal{A}\|^2, \beta)$-smoothable.

Example 10.48 (smooth approximation of $\|\mathbf{Ax} + \mathbf{b}\|_2$). Let $q : \mathbb{R}^n \to \mathbb{R}$ be given by $q(\mathbf{x}) = \|\mathbf{Ax}+\mathbf{b}\|_2$, where $\mathbf{A} \in \mathbb{R}^{m \times n}$ and $\mathbf{b} \in \mathbb{R}^m$. Then $q(\mathbf{x}) = g(\mathbf{Ax}+\mathbf{b})$, where $g : \mathbb{R}^m \to \mathbb{R}$ is given by $g(\mathbf{y}) = \|\mathbf{y}\|_2$. Let $\mu > 0$. By Example 10.44, $g_\mu(\mathbf{y}) = \sqrt{\|\mathbf{y}\|_2^2 + \mu^2} - \mu$ is a $\frac{1}{\mu}$-smooth approximation of g with parameters $(1,1)$, and hence, by Theorem 10.46(b),

$$q_\mu(\mathbf{x}) \equiv g_\mu(\mathbf{Ax} + \mathbf{b}) = \sqrt{\|\mathbf{Ax} + \mathbf{b}\|_2^2 + \mu^2} - \mu$$

is a $\frac{1}{\mu}$-smooth approximation of q with parameters $(\|\mathbf{A}\|_{2,2}^2, 1)$. $\quad\blacksquare$

Example 10.49 (smooth approximation of piecewise affine functions). Let $q : \mathbb{R}^n \to \mathbb{R}$ be given by $q(\mathbf{x}) = \max_{i=1,\dots,m}\{\mathbf{a}_i^T\mathbf{x} + b_i\}$, where $\mathbf{a}_i \in \mathbb{R}^n$ and $b_i \in \mathbb{R}$ for any $i = 1, 2, \dots, m$. Then $q(\mathbf{x}) = g(\mathbf{Ax}+\mathbf{b})$, where $g(\mathbf{y}) = \max\{y_1, y_2, \dots, y_m\}$, $\mathbf{A}$ is the matrix whose rows are $\mathbf{a}_1^T, \mathbf{a}_2^T, \dots, \mathbf{a}_m^T$, and $\mathbf{b} = (b_1, b_2, \dots, b_m)^T$. Let $\mu > 0$. By Example 10.45, $g_\mu(\mathbf{y}) = \mu \log\left(\sum_{i=1}^m e^{y_i/\mu}\right) - \mu \log m$ is a $\frac{1}{\mu}$-smooth approximation of g with parameters $(1, \log m)$. Therefore, by Theorem 10.46(b), the function

$$q_\mu(\mathbf{x}) \equiv g_\mu(\mathbf{Ax} + \mathbf{b}) = \mu \log\left(\sum_{i=1}^m e^{(\mathbf{a}_i^T\mathbf{x}+b_i)/\mu}\right) - \mu \log m$$

is a $\frac{1}{\mu}$-smooth approximation of q with parameters $(\|\mathbf{A}\|_{2,2}^2, \log m)$. $\quad\blacksquare$

Example 10.50 (tightness of the smoothing parameters). Consider the absolute value function $q : \mathbb{R} \to \mathbb{R}$ given by $q(x) = |x|$. By Example 10.44, for any $\mu > 0$ the function $\sqrt{x^2 + \mu^2} - \mu$ is a $\frac{1}{\mu}$-smooth approximation of q with parameters $(1,1)$. Let us consider an alternative way to construct a smooth approximation of

q using Theorem 10.46. Note that $q(x) = \max\{x, -x\}$. Thus, by Example 10.49 the function $q_\mu(x) = \mu \log(e^{x/\mu} + e^{-x/\mu}) - \mu \log 2$ is a $\frac{1}{\mu}$-smooth approximation of q with parameters $(\|\mathbf{A}\|_{2,2}^2, \log 2)$, where $\mathbf{A} = \left(\begin{smallmatrix} 1 \\ -1 \end{smallmatrix}\right)$. Since $\|\mathbf{A}\|_{2,2}^2 = 2$, we conclude that q_μ is a $\frac{1}{\mu}$-smooth approximation of q with parameters $(2, \log 2)$. The question that arises is whether these parameters are tight, meaning whether they are the smallest ones possible. The β-parameter is indeed tight (since $\lim_{x\to\infty} q(x) - q_\mu(x) = \mu \log(2)$); however, the α-parameter is not tight. To see this, note that for any $x \in \mathbb{R}$,

$$q_1''(x) = \frac{4}{(e^x + e^{-x})^2}.$$

Therefore, for any $x \in \mathbb{R}$, it holds that $|q_1''(x)| \leq 1$, and hence, by Theorem 5.12, q_1 is 1-smooth. Consequently, q_μ, which can also be written as $q_\mu(\mathbf{x}) = \mu q_1(\mathbf{x}/\mu)$, is $\frac{1}{\mu}$-smooth. We conclude that q_μ, is a $\frac{1}{\mu}$-smooth approximation of q with parameters $(1, \log 2)$. ∎

10.8.3 The Moreau Envelope Revisited

A natural $\frac{1}{\mu}$-smooth approximation of a given real-valued convex function $h : \mathbb{E} \to \mathbb{R}$ is its Moreau envelope M_h^μ, which was discussed in detail in Section 6.7. Recall that the Moreau envelope of h is given by

$$M_h^\mu(\mathbf{x}) = \min_{\mathbf{u}\in\mathbb{E}} \left\{ h(\mathbf{u}) + \frac{1}{2\mu}\|\mathbf{x} - \mathbf{u}\|^2 \right\}.$$

We will now show that whenever h is in addition Lipschitz, the Moreau envelope is indeed a $\frac{1}{\mu}$-smooth approximation.

Theorem 10.51 (smoothability of real-valued Lipschitz convex functions). *Let $h : \mathbb{E} \to \mathbb{R}$ be a convex function satisfying*

$$|h(\mathbf{x}) - h(\mathbf{y})| \leq \ell_h\|\mathbf{x} - \mathbf{y}\| \text{ for all } \mathbf{x}, \mathbf{y} \in \mathbb{E}.$$

Then for any $\mu > 0$, M_h^μ is a $\frac{1}{\mu}$-smooth approximation of h with parameters $(1, \frac{\ell_h^2}{2})$.

Proof. By Theorem 6.60, M_h^μ is $\frac{1}{\mu}$-smooth. For any $\mathbf{x} \in \mathbb{E}$,

$$M_h^\mu(\mathbf{x}) = \min_{\mathbf{u}\in\mathbb{E}} \left\{ h(\mathbf{u}) + \frac{1}{2\mu}\|\mathbf{u} - \mathbf{x}\|^2 \right\} \leq h(\mathbf{x}) + \frac{1}{2\mu}\|\mathbf{x} - \mathbf{x}\|^2 = h(\mathbf{x}).$$

Let $\mathbf{g_x} \in \partial h(\mathbf{x})$. Since h is Lipschitz with constant ℓ_h, it follows by Theorem 3.61 that $\|\mathbf{g_x}\| \leq \ell_h$, and hence

$$M_h^\mu(\mathbf{x}) - h(\mathbf{x}) = \min_{\mathbf{u}\in\mathbb{E}} \left\{ h(\mathbf{u}) - h(\mathbf{x}) + \frac{1}{2\mu}\|\mathbf{u} - \mathbf{x}\|^2 \right\}$$
$$\geq \min_{\mathbf{u}\in\mathbb{E}} \left\{ \langle \mathbf{g_x}, \mathbf{u} - \mathbf{x} \rangle + \frac{1}{2\mu}\|\mathbf{u} - \mathbf{x}\|^2 \right\}$$
$$= -\frac{\mu}{2}\|\mathbf{g_x}\|^2$$
$$\geq -\frac{\ell_h^2}{2}\mu,$$

where the subgradient inequality was used in the first inequality. To summarize, we obtained that the convex function M_h^μ is $\frac{1}{\mu}$-smooth and satisfies

$$M_h^\mu(\mathbf{x}) \le h(\mathbf{x}) \le M_h^\mu(\mathbf{x}) + \frac{\ell_h^2}{2}\mu,$$

showing that M_h^μ is a $\frac{1}{\mu}$-smooth approximation of h with parameters $(1, \frac{\ell_h^2}{2})$. $\square$

Corollary 10.52. *Let $h : \mathbb{E} \to \mathbb{R}$ be convex and Lipschitz with constant ℓ_h. Then h is $(1, \frac{\ell_h^2}{2})$-smoothable.*

Example 10.53 (smooth approximation of the l_2-norm). Consider the function $h : \mathbb{R}^n \to \mathbb{R}$ given by $h(\mathbf{x}) = \|\mathbf{x}\|_2$. Then h is convex and Lipschitz with constant $\ell_h = 1$. Hence, by Theorem 10.51, for any $\mu > 0$, the function (see Example 6.54)

$$M_h^\mu(\mathbf{x}) = H_\mu(\mathbf{x}) = \begin{cases} \frac{1}{2\mu}\|\mathbf{x}\|_2^2, & \|\mathbf{x}\|_2 \le \mu, \\[2mm] \|\mathbf{x}\|_2 - \frac{\mu}{2}, & \|\mathbf{x}\|_2 > \mu, \end{cases}$$

is a $\frac{1}{\mu}$-smooth approximation of h with parameters $(1, \frac{1}{2})$. ∎

Example 10.54 (smooth approximation of the l_1-norm). Consider the function $h : \mathbb{R}^n \to \mathbb{R}$ given by $h(\mathbf{x}) = \|\mathbf{x}\|_1$. Then h is convex and Lipschitz with constant $\ell_h = \sqrt{n}$. Hence, by Theorem 10.51, for any $\mu > 0$, the Moreau envelope of h given by

$$M_h^\mu(\mathbf{x}) = \sum_{i=1}^n H_\mu(x_i)$$

is a $\frac{1}{\mu}$-smooth approximation of h with parameters $(1, \frac{n}{2})$. ∎

Example 10.55 (smooth approximations of the absolute value function). Let us consider again the absolute value function $h(x) = |x|$. In our discussions we actually considered three possible $\frac{1}{\mu}$-smooth approximations of h, which are detailed below along with their parameters:

- **(Example 10.44)** $h_\mu^1(x) = \sqrt{x^2 + \mu^2} - \mu$, $(\alpha, \beta) = (1, 1)$.

- **(Example 10.50)** $h_\mu^2(x) = \mu \log(e^{x/\mu} + e^{-x/\mu}) - \mu \log 2$, $(\alpha, \beta) = (1, \log 2)$.

- **(Example 10.53)** $h_\mu^3(x) = H_\mu(x)$, $(\alpha, \beta) = (1, \frac{1}{2})$.

Obviously, the Huber function is the best $\frac{1}{\mu}$-smooth approximation out of the three functions since all the functions have the same α-parameter, but h_μ^3 has the smallest β-parameter. This phenomenon is illustrated in Figure 10.3, where the three functions are plotted (for the case $\mu = 0.2$). ∎

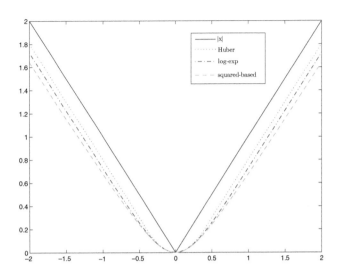

Figure 10.3. *The absolute value function along with its three 5-smooth approximations ($\mu = 0.2$). "squared-based" is the function $h^1_\mu(x) = \sqrt{x^2 + \mu^2} - \mu$, "log-exp" is $h^2_\mu(x) = \mu \log(e^{x/\mu} + e^{-x/\mu}) - \mu \log 2$, and "Huber" is $h^3_\mu(x) = H_\mu(x)$.*

10.8.4   The S-FISTA Method

The optimization model that we consider is

$$\min_{\mathbf{x} \in \mathbb{E}} \{H(\mathbf{x}) \equiv f(\mathbf{x}) + h(\mathbf{x}) + g(\mathbf{x})\}, \tag{10.64}$$

where the following assumptions are made.

Assumption 10.56.

(A) $f : \mathbb{E} \to \mathbb{R}$ *is L_f-smooth ($L_f \geq 0$).*

(B) $h : \mathbb{E} \to \mathbb{R}$ *is (α, β)-smoothable ($\alpha, \beta > 0$). For any $\mu > 0$, h_μ denotes a $\frac{1}{\mu}$-smooth approximation of h with parameters (α, β).*

(C) $g : \mathbb{E} \to (-\infty, \infty]$ *is proper closed and convex.*

(D) *H has bounded level sets. Specifically, for any $\delta > 0$, there exists $R_\delta > 0$ such that*

$$\|\mathbf{x}\| \leq R_\delta \text{ for any } \mathbf{x} \text{ satisfying } H(\mathbf{x}) \leq \delta.$$

(E) *The optimal set of problem (10.64) is nonempty and denoted by X^*. The optimal value of the problem is denoted by H_{opt}.*

Assumption (E) is actually a consequence of assumptions (A)–(D). The idea is to consider the smoothed version of (10.64),

$$\min_{\mathbf{x}\in\mathbb{E}}\{H_\mu(\mathbf{x}) \equiv \underbrace{f(\mathbf{x}) + h_\mu(\mathbf{x})}_{F_\mu(\mathbf{x})} + g(\mathbf{x})\}, \tag{10.65}$$

for some *smoothing parameter* $\mu > 0$, and solve it using an accelerated method with convergence rate of $O(1/k^2)$ in function values. Actually, *any* accelerated method can be employed, but we will describe the version in which FISTA with constant stepsize is employed on (10.65) with the smooth and nonsmooth parts taken as F_μ and g, respectively. The method is described in detail below. Note that a Lipschitz constant of the gradient of F_μ is $L_f + \frac{\alpha}{\mu}$, and thus the stepsize is taken as $\frac{1}{L_f + \frac{\alpha}{\mu}}$.

S-FISTA

Input: $\mathbf{x}^0 \in \mathrm{dom}(g)$, $\mu > 0$.
Initialization: set $\mathbf{y}^0 = \mathbf{x}^0, t_0 = 1$; construct h_μ—a $\frac{1}{\mu}$-smooth approximation of h with parameters (α, β); set $F_\mu = f + h_\mu$, $\tilde{L} = L_f + \frac{\alpha}{\mu}$.
General step: for any $k = 0, 1, 2, \ldots$ execute the following steps:

(a) set $\mathbf{x}^{k+1} = \mathrm{prox}_{\frac{1}{\tilde{L}}g}\left(\mathbf{y}^k - \frac{1}{\tilde{L}}\nabla F_\mu(\mathbf{y}^k)\right)$;

(b) set $t_{k+1} = \frac{1+\sqrt{1+4t_k^2}}{2}$;

(c) compute $\mathbf{y}^{k+1} = \mathbf{x}^{k+1} + \left(\frac{t_k-1}{t_{k+1}}\right)(\mathbf{x}^{k+1} - \mathbf{x}^k)$.

The next result shows how, given an accuracy level $\varepsilon > 0$, the parameter μ can be chosen to ensure that an ε-optimal solution of the original problem (10.64) is reached in $O(1/\varepsilon)$ iterations.

Theorem 10.57 ($O(1/\varepsilon)$ complexity of S-FISTA). *Suppose that Assumption 10.56 holds. Let $\varepsilon \in (0, \bar{\varepsilon})$ for some fixed $\bar{\varepsilon} > 0$. Let $\{\mathbf{x}^k\}_{k\geq 0}$ be the sequence generated by S-FISTA with smoothing parameter*

$$\mu = \sqrt{\frac{\alpha}{\beta}}\frac{\varepsilon}{\sqrt{\alpha\beta} + \sqrt{\alpha\beta + L_f\varepsilon}}.$$

Then for any k satisfying

$$k \geq 2\sqrt{2\alpha\beta\Gamma}\frac{1}{\varepsilon} + \sqrt{2L_f\Gamma}\frac{1}{\sqrt{\varepsilon}},$$

where $\Gamma = (R_{H(\mathbf{x}^0)+\frac{\bar{\varepsilon}}{2}} + \|\mathbf{x}^0\|)^2$, it holds that $H(\mathbf{x}^k) - H_{\mathrm{opt}} \leq \varepsilon$.

Proof. By definition of S-FISTA, $\{\mathbf{x}^k\}_{k\geq 0}$ is the sequence generated by FISTA employed on problem (10.65) with input $(F_\mu, g, \mathbf{x}^0)$. Note that

$$\mathrm{argmin}_{\mathbf{x}\in\mathbb{E}}H_\mu(\mathbf{x}) = \mathrm{argmin}_{\mathbf{x}\in\mathbb{E}}\left\{H_\mu(\mathbf{x}) : H_\mu(\mathbf{x}) \leq H_\mu(\mathbf{x}^0)\right\}. \tag{10.66}$$

Since H_μ is closed, the feasible set $C \equiv \{\mathbf{x} \in \mathbb{E} : H_\mu(\mathbf{x}) \leq H_\mu(\mathbf{x}^0)\}$ of the right-hand side problem in (10.66) is closed. We will show that it is also bounded. Indeed, since h_μ is a $\frac{1}{\mu}$-smooth approximation of h with parameters (α, β), it follows in particular that $h(\mathbf{x}) \leq h_\mu(\mathbf{x}) + \beta\mu$ for all $\mathbf{x} \in \mathbb{E}$, and consequently $H(\mathbf{x}) \leq H_\mu(\mathbf{x}) + \beta\mu$ for all $\mathbf{x} \in \mathbb{E}$. Thus,

$$C \subseteq \{\mathbf{x} \in \mathbb{E} : H(\mathbf{x}) \leq H_\mu(\mathbf{x}^0) + \beta\mu\},$$

which by Assumption 10.56(D) implies that C is bounded and hence, by its closedness, also compact. We can therefore conclude by Weierstrass theorem for closed functions (Theorem 2.12) that an optimal solution of problem (10.65) is attained at some point $\mathbf{x}_\mu^*$ with an optimal value $H_{\mu,\mathrm{opt}}$. By Theorem 10.34, since F_μ is $(L_f + \frac{\alpha}{\mu})$-smooth,

$$H_\mu(\mathbf{x}^k) - H_{\mu,\mathrm{opt}} \leq 2\left(L_f + \frac{\alpha}{\mu}\right) \frac{\|\mathbf{x}^0 - \mathbf{x}_\mu^*\|^2}{(k+1)^2} = 2\left(L_f + \frac{\alpha}{\mu}\right) \frac{\Lambda}{(k+1)^2}, \quad (10.67)$$

where $\Lambda = \|\mathbf{x}^0 - \mathbf{x}_\mu^*\|^2$. We use again the fact that h_μ is a $\frac{1}{\mu}$-smooth approximation of h with parameters (α, β), from which it follows that for any $\mathbf{x} \in \mathbb{E}$,

$$H_\mu(\mathbf{x}) \leq H(\mathbf{x}) \leq H_\mu(\mathbf{x}) + \beta\mu. \quad (10.68)$$

In particular, the following two inequalities hold:

$$H_{\mathrm{opt}} \geq H_{\mu,\mathrm{opt}} \quad \text{and} \quad H(\mathbf{x}^k) \leq H_\mu(\mathbf{x}^k) + \beta\mu, \ k = 0, 1, \ldots, \quad (10.69)$$

which, combined with (10.67), yields

$$H(\mathbf{x}^k) - H_{\mathrm{opt}} \leq H_\mu(\mathbf{x}^k) + \beta\mu - H_{\mu,\mathrm{opt}} \leq 2L_f \frac{\Lambda}{(k+1)^2} + \left(\frac{2\alpha\Lambda}{(k+1)^2}\right)\frac{1}{\mu} + \beta\mu$$

$$\leq 2L_f \frac{\Lambda}{k^2} + \left(\frac{2\alpha\Lambda}{k^2}\right)\frac{1}{\mu} + \beta\mu.$$

Therefore, for a given $K > 0$, it holds that for any $k \geq K$,

$$H(\mathbf{x}^k) - H_{\mathrm{opt}} \leq 2L_f \frac{\Lambda}{K^2} + \left(\frac{2\alpha\Lambda}{K^2}\right)\frac{1}{\mu} + \beta\mu. \quad (10.70)$$

Minimizing the right-hand side w.r.t. μ, we obtain

$$\mu = \sqrt{\frac{2\alpha\Lambda}{\beta}} \frac{1}{K}. \quad (10.71)$$

Plugging the above expression into (10.70), we conclude that for any $k \geq K$,

$$H(\mathbf{x}^k) - H_{\mathrm{opt}} \leq 2L_f \frac{\Lambda}{K^2} + 2\sqrt{2\alpha\beta\Lambda}\frac{1}{K}.$$

Thus, to guarantee that $\mathbf{x}^k$ is an ε-optimal solution for any $k \geq K$, it is enough that K will satisfy

$$2L_f \frac{\Lambda}{K^2} + 2\sqrt{2\alpha\beta\Lambda}\frac{1}{K} \leq \varepsilon.$$

Denoting $t = \frac{\sqrt{2\Lambda}}{K}$, the above inequality reduces to

$$L_f t^2 + 2\sqrt{\alpha\beta}t - \varepsilon \leq 0,$$

which, by the fact that $t > 0$, is equivalent to

$$\frac{\sqrt{2\Lambda}}{K} = t \leq \frac{-\sqrt{\alpha\beta} + \sqrt{\alpha\beta + L_f\varepsilon}}{L_f} = \frac{\varepsilon}{\sqrt{\alpha\beta} + \sqrt{\alpha\beta + L_f\varepsilon}}.$$

We conclude that K should satisfy

$$K \geq \frac{\sqrt{2\Lambda\alpha\beta} + \sqrt{2\Lambda\alpha\beta + 2\Lambda L_f\varepsilon}}{\varepsilon}.$$

In particular, if we choose

$$K = K_1 \equiv \frac{\sqrt{2\Lambda\alpha\beta} + \sqrt{2\Lambda\alpha\beta + 2\Lambda L_f\varepsilon}}{\varepsilon}$$

and μ according to (10.71), meaning that

$$\mu = \sqrt{\frac{2\alpha\Lambda}{\beta}}\frac{1}{K_1} = \sqrt{\frac{\alpha}{\beta}}\frac{\varepsilon}{\sqrt{\alpha\beta} + \sqrt{\alpha\beta + L_f\varepsilon}},$$

then for any $k \geq K_1$ it holds that $H(\mathbf{x}^k) - H_{\mathrm{opt}} \leq \varepsilon$. By (10.68) and (10.69),

$$H(\mathbf{x}_\mu^*) - \beta\mu \leq H_\mu(\mathbf{x}_\mu^*) = H_{\mu,\mathrm{opt}} \leq H_{\mathrm{opt}} \leq H(\mathbf{x}^0),$$

which along with the inequality

$$\mu = \sqrt{\frac{\alpha}{\beta}}\frac{\varepsilon}{\sqrt{\alpha\beta} + \sqrt{\alpha\beta + L_f\varepsilon}} \leq \sqrt{\frac{\alpha}{\beta}}\frac{\varepsilon}{\sqrt{\alpha\beta} + \sqrt{\alpha\beta}} \leq \frac{\bar{\varepsilon}}{2\beta}$$

implies that $H(\mathbf{x}_\mu^*) \leq H(\mathbf{x}^0) + \frac{\bar{\varepsilon}}{2}$, and hence, by Assumption 10.56(D), it follows that $\|\mathbf{x}_\mu^*\| \leq R_\delta$, where $\delta = H(\mathbf{x}^0) + \frac{\bar{\varepsilon}}{2}$. Therefore, $\Lambda = \|\mathbf{x}_\mu^* - \mathbf{x}^0\|^2 \leq (R_\delta + \|\mathbf{x}^0\|)^2 = \Gamma$. Consequently,

$$
\begin{aligned}
K_1 \quad &= \quad \frac{\sqrt{2\Lambda\alpha\beta} + \sqrt{2\Lambda\alpha\beta + 2\Lambda L_f\varepsilon}}{\varepsilon} \\
\overset{\sqrt{\gamma+\delta} \leq \sqrt{\gamma}+\sqrt{\delta} \ \forall \gamma,\delta \geq 0}{\leq} \quad &\frac{2\sqrt{2\Lambda\alpha\beta} + \sqrt{2\Lambda L_f\varepsilon}}{\varepsilon} \\
\leq \quad &\frac{2\sqrt{2\Gamma\alpha\beta} + \sqrt{2\Gamma L_f\varepsilon}}{\varepsilon} \\
\equiv \quad &K_2,
\end{aligned}
$$

and hence for any $k \geq K_2$, we have that $H(\mathbf{x}^k) - H_{\mathrm{opt}} \leq \varepsilon$, establishing the desired result. $\square$

Remark 10.58. *Note that the smoothing parameter chosen in Theorem 10.57 does not depend on Γ, although the number of iterations required to obtain an ε-optimal solution does depend on Γ.*

Example 10.59. Consider the problem

$$\min_{\mathbf{x}\in\mathbb{E}}\{h(\mathbf{x}) : \mathbf{x}\in C\}, \tag{10.72}$$

where C is a nonempty closed and convex set and $h : \mathbb{E} \to \mathbb{R}$ is convex function, which is Lipschitz with constant ℓ_h. Problem (10.72) fits model (10.64) with $f \equiv 0$ and $g = \delta_C$. By Theorem 10.51, for any $\mu > 0$ the Moreau envelope M_h^μ is a $\frac{1}{\mu}$-smooth approximation of h with parameters $(\alpha, \beta) = (1, \frac{\ell_h^2}{2})$. In addition, by Theorem 6.60, $\nabla M_h^\mu(\mathbf{x}) = \frac{1}{\mu}(\mathbf{x} - \text{prox}_{\mu h}(\mathbf{x}))$. We will pick $h_\mu = M_h^\mu$, and therefore $F_\mu = f + M_h^\mu = M_h^\mu$. By Theorem 10.57, after employing $O(1/\varepsilon)$ iterations of the S-FISTA method with (recalling that $L_f = 0$)

$$\mu = \sqrt{\frac{\alpha}{\beta}}\frac{\varepsilon}{\sqrt{\alpha\beta} + \sqrt{\alpha\beta + L_f\varepsilon}} = \sqrt{\frac{\alpha}{\beta}}\frac{\varepsilon}{\sqrt{\alpha\beta} + \sqrt{\alpha\beta}} = \frac{\varepsilon}{2\beta} = \frac{\varepsilon}{\ell_h^2},$$

an ε-optimal solution will be achieved. The stepsize is $\frac{1}{\tilde{L}}$, where $\tilde{L} = \frac{\alpha}{\mu} = \frac{1}{\mu}$. The main update step of S-FISTA has the following form:

$$\begin{aligned}\mathbf{x}^{k+1} &= \text{prox}_{\frac{1}{\tilde{L}}g}\left(\mathbf{y}^k - \frac{1}{\tilde{L}}\nabla F_\mu(\mathbf{y}^k)\right) = P_C\left(\mathbf{y}^k - \frac{1}{\tilde{L}\mu}(\mathbf{y}^k - \text{prox}_{\mu h}(\mathbf{y}^k))\right)\\ &= P_C(\text{prox}_{\mu h}(\mathbf{y}^k)).\end{aligned}$$

The S-FISTA method for solving (10.72) is described below.

S-FISTA for solving (10.72)

Initialization: set $\mathbf{y}^0 = \mathbf{x}^0 \in C, t_0 = 1, \mu = \frac{\varepsilon}{\ell_h^2}$, and $\tilde{L} = \frac{\ell_h^2}{\varepsilon}$.

General step: for any $k = 0, 1, 2, \ldots$ execute the following steps:

(a) $\mathbf{x}^{k+1} = P_C(\text{prox}_{\mu h}(\mathbf{y}^k))$;

(b) $t_{k+1} = \frac{1+\sqrt{1+4t_k^2}}{2}$;

(c) $\mathbf{y}^{k+1} = \mathbf{x}^{k+1} + \left(\frac{t_k-1}{t_{k+1}}\right)(\mathbf{x}^{k+1} - \mathbf{x}^k)$.

■

Example 10.60. Consider the problem

$$(\text{P}) \quad \min_{\mathbf{x}\in\mathbb{R}^n}\left\{\frac{1}{2}\|\mathbf{A}\mathbf{x} - \mathbf{b}\|_2^2 + \|\mathbf{D}\mathbf{x}\|_1 + \lambda\|\mathbf{x}\|_1\right\},$$

where $\mathbf{A} \in \mathbb{R}^{m\times n}, \mathbf{b} \in \mathbb{R}^m, \mathbf{D} \in \mathbb{R}^{p\times n}$, and $\lambda > 0$. Problem (P) fits model (10.64) with $f(\mathbf{x}) = \frac{1}{2}\|\mathbf{A}\mathbf{x} - \mathbf{b}\|_2^2$, $h(\mathbf{x}) = \|\mathbf{D}\mathbf{x}\|_1$, and $g(\mathbf{x}) = \lambda\|\mathbf{x}\|_1$. Assumption 10.56 holds: f is convex and L_f-smooth with $L_f = \|\mathbf{A}^T\mathbf{A}\|_{2,2} = \|\mathbf{A}\|_{2,2}^2$, g is proper closed and convex, h is real-valued and convex, and the level sets of the objective function are bounded. To show that h is smoothable, and to find its parameters, note that $h(\mathbf{x}) = q(\mathbf{D}\mathbf{x})$, where $q : \mathbb{R}^p \to \mathbb{R}$ is given by $q(\mathbf{y}) = \|\mathbf{y}\|_1$. By Example 10.54, for any $\mu > 0$, $q_\mu(\mathbf{y}) = M_q^\mu(\mathbf{y}) = \sum_{i=1}^p H_\mu(y_i)$ is a $\frac{1}{\mu}$-smooth approximation of q with parameters $(1, \frac{p}{2})$. By Theorem 10.46(b), $q_\mu(\mathbf{Dx})$ is a $\frac{1}{\mu}$-smooth approximation of h with parameters $(\alpha, \beta) = (\|\mathbf{D}\|_{2,2}^2, \frac{p}{2})$, and we will set $h_\mu(\mathbf{x}) = M_q^\mu(\mathbf{Dx})$ and $F_\mu(\mathbf{x}) = f(\mathbf{x}) + h_\mu(\mathbf{x})$. Therefore, invoking Theorem 10.57, to obtain an ε-optimal solution of problem (P), we need to employ the S-FISTA method with

$$
\begin{aligned}
\mu &= \sqrt{\frac{\alpha}{\beta}} \frac{\varepsilon}{\sqrt{\alpha\beta} + \sqrt{\alpha\beta + L_f \varepsilon}} \\
&= \frac{2\|\mathbf{D}\|_{2,2}}{\sqrt{p}} \cdot \frac{\varepsilon}{\sqrt{\|\mathbf{D}\|_{2,2}^2 p} + \sqrt{\|\mathbf{D}\|_{2,2}^2 p + 2\|\mathbf{A}^T\mathbf{A}\|_{2,2}\varepsilon}}.
\end{aligned}
\tag{10.73}
$$

Since $F_\mu(\mathbf{x}) = f(\mathbf{x}) + M_q^\mu(\mathbf{Dx})$, it follows that

$$
\begin{aligned}
\nabla F_\mu(\mathbf{x}) &= \nabla f(\mathbf{x}) + \mathbf{D}^T \nabla M_q^\mu(\mathbf{Dx}) \\
&= \nabla f(\mathbf{x}) + \tfrac{1}{\mu}\mathbf{D}^T(\mathbf{Dx} - \mathrm{prox}_{\mu q}(\mathbf{Dx})) \quad \text{[Theorem 6.60]} \\
&= \nabla f(\mathbf{x}) + \tfrac{1}{\mu}\mathbf{D}^T(\mathbf{Dx} - \mathcal{T}_\mu(\mathbf{Dx})). \quad\quad \text{[Example 6.8]}
\end{aligned}
$$

Below we write the S-FISTA method for solving problem (P) for a given tolerance parameter $\varepsilon > 0$.

S-FISTA for solving (P)

Initialization: set $\mathbf{y}^0 = \mathbf{x}^0 \in \mathbb{R}^n, t_0 = 1$; set μ as in (10.73) and $\tilde{L} = \|\mathbf{A}\|_{2,2}^2 + \frac{\|\mathbf{D}\|_{2,2}^2}{\mu}$.

General step: for any $k = 0, 1, 2, \ldots$ execute the following steps:

(a) $\mathbf{x}^{k+1} = \mathcal{T}_{\lambda/\tilde{L}} \left(\mathbf{y}^k - \tfrac{1}{\tilde{L}}(\mathbf{A}^T(\mathbf{A}\mathbf{y}^k - \mathbf{b}) + \tfrac{1}{\mu}\mathbf{D}^T(\mathbf{Dy}^k - \mathcal{T}_\mu(\mathbf{Dy}^k)))\right)$;

(b) $t_{k+1} = \frac{1+\sqrt{1+4t_k^2}}{2}$;

(c) $\mathbf{y}^{k+1} = \mathbf{x}^{k+1} + \left(\frac{t_k - 1}{t_{k+1}}\right)(\mathbf{x}^{k+1} - \mathbf{x}^k)$.

It is interesting to note that in the case of problem (P) we can actually compute the constant Γ that appears in Theorem 10.57. Indeed, if $H(\mathbf{x}) \le \alpha$, then

$$
\lambda\|\mathbf{x}\|_1 \le \frac{1}{2}\|\mathbf{A}\mathbf{x} - \mathbf{b}\|_2^2 + \|\mathbf{Dx}\|_1 + \lambda\|\mathbf{x}\|_1 \le \alpha,
$$

and since $\|\mathbf{x}\|_2 \le \|\mathbf{x}\|_1$, it follows that R_α can be chosen as $\frac{\alpha}{\lambda}$, from which Γ can be computed. ∎

10.9 Non-Euclidean Proximal Gradient Methods

In this section, and in this section only, the underlying space will *not* be assumed to be Euclidean. We will consider two different approaches for handling this situation.

The first tackles unconstrained smooth problems through a variation of the gradient method, and the second, which is aimed at solving the composite model, is based on replacing the Euclidean prox operator by a mapping based on the Bregman distance.

10.9.1   The Non-Euclidean Gradient Method

Consider the unconstrained problem

$$\min\{f(\mathbf{x}) : \mathbf{x} \in \mathbb{E}\}, \tag{10.74}$$

where we assume that f is L_f-smooth w.r.t. the underlying norm. Recall that the gradient method (see Section 10.2) has the form

$$\mathbf{x}^{k+1} = \mathbf{x}^k - t_k \nabla f(\mathbf{x}^k). \tag{10.75}$$

As was already discussed in Section 9.1 (in the context of the mirror descent method), this scheme has a "philosophical" flaw since $\mathbf{x}^k \in \mathbb{E}$ while $\nabla f(\mathbf{x}^k) \in \mathbb{E}^*$. Obviously, as the only difference between $\mathbb{E}$ and $\mathbb{E}^*$ in this book is their underlying norm, there is no practical problem to invoke the scheme (10.75). Nonetheless, we will change the scheme (10.75) and replace $\nabla f(\mathbf{x}^k) \in \mathbb{E}^*$ with a "primal counterpart" in $\mathbb{E}$. For any vector $\mathbf{a} \in \mathbb{E}^*$, we define the *set of primal counterparts of* $\mathbf{a}$ as

$$\Lambda_{\mathbf{a}} = \operatorname{argmax}_{\mathbf{v} \in \mathbb{E}}\{\langle \mathbf{a}, \mathbf{v} \rangle : \|\mathbf{v}\| \le 1\}. \tag{10.76}$$

The lemma below presents some elementary properties of $\Lambda_{\mathbf{a}}$ that follow immediately by its definition and the definition of the dual norm.

Lemma 10.61 (basic properties of the set of primal counterparts). *Let* $\mathbf{a} \in \mathbb{E}^*$.

(a) *If* $\mathbf{a} \ne \mathbf{0}$, *then* $\|\mathbf{a}^\dagger\| = 1$ *for any* $\mathbf{a}^\dagger \in \Lambda_{\mathbf{a}}$.

(b) *If* $\mathbf{a} = \mathbf{0}$, *then* $\Lambda_{\mathbf{a}} = B_{\|\cdot\|}[\mathbf{0}, 1]$.

(c) $\langle \mathbf{a}, \mathbf{a}^\dagger \rangle = \|\mathbf{a}\|_*$ *for any* $\mathbf{a}^\dagger \in \Lambda_{\mathbf{a}}$.

We also note that by the conjugate subgradient theorem (Corollary 4.21),

$$\Lambda_{\mathbf{a}} = \partial h(\mathbf{a}), \text{ where } h(\cdot) = \|\cdot\|_*.$$

Example 10.62. Suppose that $\mathbb{E} = \mathbb{R}^n$ endowed with the Euclidean l_2-norm. In this case, for any $\mathbf{a} \ne \mathbf{0}$,

$$\Lambda_{\mathbf{a}} = \left\{ \frac{\mathbf{a}}{\|\mathbf{a}\|_2} \right\}. \qquad \blacksquare$$

Example 10.63. Suppose that $\mathbb{E} = \mathbb{R}^n$ endowed with the l_1-norm. In this case, for any $\mathbf{a} \ne \mathbf{0}$, by Example 3.52,

$$\Lambda_{\mathbf{a}} = \partial \|\cdot\|_\infty(\mathbf{a}) = \left\{ \sum_{i \in I(\mathbf{a})} \lambda_i \operatorname{sgn}(a_i) \mathbf{e}_i : \sum_{i \in I(\mathbf{a})} \lambda_i = 1, \lambda_j \ge 0, j \in I(\mathbf{a}) \right\},$$

where $I(\mathbf{a}) = \operatorname{argmax}_{i=1,2,\ldots,n} |a_i|$. $\quad \blacksquare$

Example 10.64. Suppose that $\mathbb{E} = \mathbb{R}^n$ endowed with the l_∞-norm. For any $\mathbf{a} \neq \mathbf{0}$, $\Lambda_{\mathbf{a}} = \partial h(\mathbf{a})$, where $h(\cdot) = \| \cdot \|_1$. Then, by Example 3.41,

$$\Lambda_{\mathbf{a}} = \{\mathbf{z} \in \mathbb{R}^n : z_i = \operatorname{sgn}(a_i), i \in I_{\neq}(\mathbf{a}), |z_j| \leq 1, j \in I_0(\mathbf{a})\},$$

where

$$I_{\neq}(\mathbf{a}) = \{i \in \{1, 2, \ldots, n\} : a_i \neq 0\}, I_0(\mathbf{a}) = \{i \in \{1, 2, \ldots, n\} : a_i = 0\}. \quad \blacksquare$$

We are now ready to present the non-Euclidean gradient method in which the gradient $\nabla f(\mathbf{x}^k)$ is replaced by a primal counterpart $\nabla f(\mathbf{x}^k)^\dagger \in \Lambda_{\nabla f(\mathbf{x}^k)}$.

The Non-Euclidean Gradient Method

Initialization: pick $\mathbf{x}^0 \in \mathbb{E}$ arbitrarily.
General step: for any $k = 0, 1, 2, \ldots$ execute the following steps:

(a) pick $\nabla f(\mathbf{x}^k)^\dagger \in \Lambda_{\nabla f(\mathbf{x}^k)}$ and $L_k > 0$;

(b) set $\mathbf{x}^{k+1} = \mathbf{x}^k - \frac{\|\nabla f(\mathbf{x}^k)\|_*}{L_k} \nabla f(\mathbf{x}^k)^\dagger$.

We begin by establishing a sufficient decrease property. The proof is almost identical to the proof of Lemma 10.4.

Lemma 10.65 (sufficient decrease for the non-Euclidean gradient method). *Let $f : \mathbb{E} \to \mathbb{R}$ be an L_f-smooth function, and let $\{\mathbf{x}^k\}_{k \geq 0}$ be the sequence generated by the non-Euclidean gradient method. Then for any $k \geq 0$,*

$$f(\mathbf{x}^k) - f(\mathbf{x}^{k+1}) \geq \frac{L_k - \frac{L_f}{2}}{L_k^2} \|\nabla f(\mathbf{x}^k)\|_*^2. \tag{10.77}$$

Proof. By the descent lemma (Lemma 5.7) we have

$$f(\mathbf{x}^{k+1}) \leq f(\mathbf{x}^k) + \langle \nabla f(\mathbf{x}^k), \mathbf{x}^{k+1} - \mathbf{x}^k \rangle + \frac{L_f}{2}\|\mathbf{x}^{k+1} - \mathbf{x}^k\|^2$$

$$= f(\mathbf{x}^k) - \frac{\|\nabla f(\mathbf{x}^k)\|_*}{L_k} \langle \nabla f(\mathbf{x}^k), \nabla f(\mathbf{x}^k)^\dagger \rangle + \frac{L_f \|\nabla f(\mathbf{x}^k)\|_*^2}{2L_k^2}$$

$$\stackrel{(*)}{=} f(\mathbf{x}^k) - \frac{\|\nabla f(\mathbf{x}^k)\|_*^2}{L_k} + \frac{L_f \|\nabla f(\mathbf{x}^k)\|_*^2}{2L_k^2}$$

$$= f(\mathbf{x}^k) - \frac{L_k - \frac{L_f}{2}}{L_k^2} \|\nabla f(\mathbf{x}^k)\|_*^2,$$

where $(*)$ follows by Lemma 10.61(c). $\quad\square$

Similarly to Section 10.3.3, we will consider both constant and backtracking stepsize strategies. In addition, we will also consider an exact line search procedure.

- **Constant.** $L_k = \bar{L} \in \left(\frac{L_f}{2}, \infty\right)$ for all k.

- **Backtracking procedure B4.** The procedure requires three parameters (s, γ, η), where $s > 0, \gamma \in (0,1)$, and $\eta > 1$. The choice of L_k is done as follows: First, L_k is set to be equal to the initial guess s. Then, while

$$f(\mathbf{x}^k) - f\left(\mathbf{x}^k - \frac{\|\nabla f(\mathbf{x}^k)\|_*}{L_k}\nabla f(\mathbf{x}^k)^\dagger\right) < \frac{\gamma}{L_k}\|\nabla f(\mathbf{x}^k)\|_*^2,$$

  we set $L_k := \eta L_k$. In other words, L_k is chosen as $L_k = s\eta^{i_k}$, where i_k is the smallest nonnegative integer for which the condition

$$f(\mathbf{x}^k) - f\left(\mathbf{x}^k - \frac{\|\nabla f(\mathbf{x}^k)\|_*}{s\eta^{i_k}}\nabla f(\mathbf{x}^k)^\dagger\right) \geq \frac{\gamma}{s\eta^{i_k}}\|\nabla f(\mathbf{x}^k)\|_*^2$$

  is satisfied.

- **Exact line search.** L_k is chosen as

$$L_k \in \operatorname{argmin}_{L>0} f\left(\mathbf{x}^k - \frac{\|\nabla f(\mathbf{x}^k)\|_*}{L}\nabla f(\mathbf{x}^k)^\dagger\right).$$

By the same arguments given in Remark 10.13, it follows that if the backtracking procedure B4 is used, then

$$L_k \leq \max\left\{s, \frac{\eta L_f}{2(1-\gamma)}\right\}. \tag{10.78}$$

Convergence Analysis in the Nonconvex Case

The statements and proofs of the next two results (Lemma 10.66 and Theorem 10.67) are similar those of Lemma 10.14 and Theorem 10.15.

Lemma 10.66 (sufficient decrease of the non-Euclidean gradient method). *Let f be an L_f-smooth function. Let $\{\mathbf{x}^k\}_{k\geq 0}$ be the sequence generated by the non-Euclidean gradient method for solving problem (10.74) with either a constant stepsize corresponding to $L_k = \bar{L} \in \left(\frac{L_f}{2}, \infty\right)$; a stepsize chosen by the backtracking procedure B4 with parameters (s, γ, η) satisfying $s > 0, \gamma \in (0,1), \eta > 1$; or an exact line search for computing the stepsize. Then for any $k \geq 0$,*

$$f(\mathbf{x}^k) - f(\mathbf{x}^{k+1}) \geq M\|\nabla f(\mathbf{x}^k)\|_*^2, \tag{10.79}$$

where

$$M = \begin{cases} \frac{\bar{L}-\frac{L_f}{2}}{(\bar{L})^2}, & \text{constant stepsize,} \\[3mm] \frac{\gamma}{\max\left\{s, \frac{\eta L_f}{2(1-\gamma)}\right\}}, & \text{backtracking,} \\[3mm] \frac{1}{2L_f}, & \text{exact line search.} \end{cases} \tag{10.80}$$

Proof. The result for the constant stepsize setting follows by plugging $L_k = \bar{L}$ in (10.77). If L_k is chosen by the exact line search procedure, then, in particular, $f(\mathbf{x}^{k+1}) \leq f(\tilde{\mathbf{x}}^k)$, where $\tilde{\mathbf{x}}^k = \mathbf{x}^k - \frac{\|\nabla f(\mathbf{x}^k)\|_*}{L_f} \nabla f(\mathbf{x}^k)^\dagger$, and hence

$$f(\mathbf{x}^k) - f(\mathbf{x}^{k+1}) \geq f(\mathbf{x}^k) - f(\tilde{\mathbf{x}}^k) \geq \frac{1}{2L_f} \|\nabla f(\mathbf{x}^k)\|_*^2,$$

where we used the result already established for the constant stepsize in the second inequality. As for the backtracking procedure, by its definition and the upper bound (10.78) on L_k we have

$$f(\mathbf{x}^k) - f(\mathbf{x}^{k+1}) \geq \frac{\gamma}{L_k} \|\nabla f(\mathbf{x}^k)\|_*^2 \geq \frac{\gamma}{\max\left\{s, \frac{\eta L_f}{2(1-\gamma)}\right\}} \|\nabla f(\mathbf{x}^k)\|_*^2. \quad \square$$

Theorem 10.67 (convergence of the non-Euclidean gradient method—nonconvex case). *Suppose that f is an L_f-smooth function. Let $\{\mathbf{x}^k\}_{k \geq 0}$ be the sequence generated by the non-Euclidean gradient method for solving the problem*

$$\min_{\mathbf{x} \in \mathbb{E}} f(\mathbf{x}) \tag{10.81}$$

with either a constant stepsize corresponding to $L_k = \bar{L} \in \left(\frac{L_f}{2}, \infty\right)$; a stepsize chosen by the backtracking procedure B4 with parameters (s, γ, η) satisfying $s > 0, \gamma \in (0,1), \eta > 1$; or an exact line search for computing the stepsize. Then

(a) *the sequence $\{f(\mathbf{x}^k)\}_{k \geq 0}$ is nonincreasing; in addition, $f(\mathbf{x}^{k+1}) < f(\mathbf{x}^k)$ if and only if $\nabla f(\mathbf{x}^k) \neq \mathbf{0}$;*

(b) *if the sequence $\{f(\mathbf{x}^k)\}_{k \geq 0}$ is bounded below, then $\nabla f(\mathbf{x}^k) \to \mathbf{0}$ as $k \to \infty$;*

(c) *if the optimal value of (10.81) is finite and equal to f_{opt}, then*

$$\min_{n=0,1,\ldots,k} \|\nabla f(\mathbf{x}^k)\|_* \leq \frac{\sqrt{f(\mathbf{x}^0) - f_{\text{opt}}}}{\sqrt{M(k+1)}}, \tag{10.82}$$

where M is given in (10.80);

(d) *all limit points of the sequence $\{\mathbf{x}^k\}_{k \geq 0}$ are stationary points of problem (10.81).*

Proof. (a) By Lemma 10.66,

$$f(\mathbf{x}^k) - f(\mathbf{x}^{k+1}) \geq M \|\nabla f(\mathbf{x}^k)\|_*^2, \tag{10.83}$$

where $M > 0$ is given in (10.80). The inequality (10.83) readily implies that $f(\mathbf{x}^k) \geq f(\mathbf{x}^{k+1})$ and that if $\nabla f(\mathbf{x}^k) \neq \mathbf{0}$, then $f(\mathbf{x}^{k+1}) < f(\mathbf{x}^k)$. Finally, if $\nabla f(\mathbf{x}^k) = \mathbf{0}$, then $\mathbf{x}^k = \mathbf{x}^{k+1}$, and hence $f(\mathbf{x}^k) = f(\mathbf{x}^{k+1})$.

(b) Since the sequence $\{f(\mathbf{x}^k)\}_{k \geq 0}$ is nonincreasing and bounded below, it converges. Thus, in particular $f(\mathbf{x}^k) - f(\mathbf{x}^{k+1}) \to 0$ as $k \to \infty$, which, combined with (10.83), implies that $\nabla f(\mathbf{x}^k) \to \mathbf{0}$ as $k \to \infty$.

(c) By Lemma 10.66, for any $n \geq 0$,

$$f(\mathbf{x}^n) - f(\mathbf{x}^{n+1}) \geq M \|\nabla f(\mathbf{x}^n)\|_*^2.$$

Summing the above over $n = 0, 1, \ldots, k$, we obtain

$$f(\mathbf{x}^0) - f(\mathbf{x}^{k+1}) \geq M \sum_{n=0}^{k} \|\nabla f(\mathbf{x}^n)\|_*^2 \geq (k+1)M \min_{n=0,1,\ldots,k} \|\nabla f(\mathbf{x}^n)\|_*^2.$$

Using the fact that $f(\mathbf{x}^{k+1}) \geq f_{\text{opt}}$, the inequality (10.82) follows.

(d) Let $\bar{\mathbf{x}}$ be a limit point of $\{\mathbf{x}^k\}_{k \geq 0}$. Then there exists a subsequence $\{\mathbf{x}^{k_j}\}_{j \geq 0}$ converging to $\bar{\mathbf{x}}$. For any $j \geq 0$,

$$\|\nabla f(\bar{\mathbf{x}})\|_* \leq \|\nabla f(\mathbf{x}^{k_j}) - \nabla f(\bar{\mathbf{x}})\|_* + \|\nabla f(\mathbf{x}^{k_j})\|_* \leq L_f \|\mathbf{x}^{k_j} - \bar{\mathbf{x}}\| + \|\nabla f(\mathbf{x}^{k_j})\|_*. \tag{10.84}$$

Since the right-hand side of (10.84) goes to 0 as $j \to \infty$, it follows that $\nabla f(\bar{\mathbf{x}}) = \mathbf{0}$. $\quad\square$

Convergence Analysis in the Convex Case

To establish a rate of convergence in the case where f is convex, we will require an additional boundedness-type assumption. We gather all the required assumptions in the following.

Assumption 10.68.

(A) $f : \mathbb{E} \to \mathbb{R}$ *is L_f-smooth and convex.*

(B) *The optimal set of the problem*

$$\min_{\mathbf{x} \in \mathbb{E}} f(\mathbf{x})$$

is nonempty and denoted by X^*. The optimal value is denoted by f_{opt}.

(C) *For any $\alpha > 0$, there exists $R_\alpha > 0$ such that*

$$\max_{\mathbf{x}, \mathbf{x}^*} \{\|\mathbf{x}^* - \mathbf{x}\| : f(\mathbf{x}) \leq \alpha, \mathbf{x}^* \in X^*\} \leq R_\alpha.$$

The proof of the convergence rate is based on the following very simple lemma.

Lemma 10.69. *Suppose that Assumption 10.68 holds. Let $\{\mathbf{x}^k\}_{k \geq 0}$ be the sequence generated by the non-Euclidean gradient method for solving the problem of minimizing f over $\mathbb{E}$ with either a constant stepsize corresponding to $L_k = \bar{L} \in \left(\frac{L_f}{2}, \infty\right)$; a stepsize chosen by the backtracking procedure B4 with parameters (s, γ, η) satisfying $s > 0, \gamma \in (0, 1), \eta > 1$; or an exact line search for computing the stepsize. Then*

$$f(\mathbf{x}^k) - f(\mathbf{x}^{k+1}) \geq \frac{1}{C}(f(\mathbf{x}^k) - f_{\text{opt}})^2, \tag{10.85}$$

where

$$C = \begin{cases} \frac{R_\alpha^2 \bar{L}^2}{\bar{L} - \frac{L_f}{2}}, & \text{constant stepsize,} \\ \frac{R_\alpha^2}{\gamma} \max\left\{ s, \frac{\eta L_f}{2(1-\gamma)} \right\}, & \text{backtracking,} \\ 2R_\alpha^2 L_f, & \text{exact line search,} \end{cases} \tag{10.86}$$

with $\alpha = f(\mathbf{x}^0)$.

Proof. Note that, by Theorem 10.67(a), $\{f(\mathbf{x}^k)\}_{k\geq 0}$ is nonincreasing, and in particular for any $k \geq 0$ it holds that $f(\mathbf{x}^k) \leq f(\mathbf{x}^0)$. Therefore, for any $\mathbf{x}^* \in X^*$ and $k \geq 0$,

$$\|\mathbf{x}^k - \mathbf{x}^*\| \leq R_\alpha,$$

where $\alpha = f(\mathbf{x}^0)$. To prove (10.85), we note that on the one hand, by Lemma 10.66,

$$f(\mathbf{x}^k) - f(\mathbf{x}^{k+1}) \geq M\|\nabla f(\mathbf{x}^k)\|_*^2, \tag{10.87}$$

where M is given in (10.80). On the other hand, by the gradient inequality along with the generalized Cauchy–Schwarz inequality (Lemma 1.4), for any $\mathbf{x}^* \in X^*$,

$$\begin{aligned} f(\mathbf{x}^k) - f_{\text{opt}} = f(\mathbf{x}^k) - f(\mathbf{x}^*) \\ \leq \langle \nabla f(\mathbf{x}^k), \mathbf{x}^k - \mathbf{x}^* \rangle \\ \leq \|\nabla f(\mathbf{x}^k)\|_* \|\mathbf{x}^k - \mathbf{x}^*\| \\ \leq R_\alpha \|\nabla f(\mathbf{x}^k)\|_*. \end{aligned} \tag{10.88}$$

Combining (10.87) and (10.88), we obtain that

$$f(\mathbf{x}^k) - f(\mathbf{x}^{k+1}) \geq M\|\nabla f(\mathbf{x}^k)\|_*^2 \geq \frac{M}{R_\alpha^2}(f(\mathbf{x}^k) - f_{\text{opt}})^2.$$

Plugging the expression for M given in (10.80) into the above inequality, the result (10.85) is established. □

To derive the rate of convergence in function values, we will use the following lemma on convergence of nonnegative scalar sequences.

Lemma 10.70. *Let* $\{a_k\}_{k\geq 0}$ *be a sequence of nonnegative real numbers satisfying for any* $k \geq 0$

$$a_k - a_{k+1} \geq \frac{1}{\gamma} a_k^2$$

for some $\gamma > 0$. *Then for any* $k \geq 1$,

$$a_k \leq \frac{\gamma}{k}. \tag{10.89}$$

Proof. Let k be a positive integer. If $a_k = 0$, then obviously (10.89) holds. Suppose that $a_k > 0$. Then by the monotonicity of $\{a_n\}_{n\geq 0}$, we have that $a_0, a_1, \ldots, a_k > 0$. For any $n = 1, 2, \ldots, k$,

$$\frac{1}{a_n} - \frac{1}{a_{n-1}} = \frac{a_{n-1} - a_n}{a_{n-1}a_n} \geq \frac{1}{\gamma}\frac{a_{n-1}^2}{a_{n-1}a_n} = \frac{1}{\gamma}\frac{a_{n-1}}{a_n} \geq \frac{1}{\gamma}, \tag{10.90}$$

where the last inequality follows from the monotonicity of the sequence. Summing (10.90) over $n = 1, 2, \ldots, k$, we obtain

$$\frac{1}{a_k} \geq \frac{1}{a_0} + \frac{k}{\gamma} \geq \frac{k}{\gamma},$$

proving (10.89). $\square$

Combining Lemmas 10.69 and 10.70, we can establish an $O(1/k)$ rate of convergence in function values of the sequence generated by the non-Euclidean gradient method.

Theorem 10.71 ($O(1/k)$ rate of convergence of the non-Euclidean gradient method). *Under the setting of Lemma 10.69, for any $k \geq 1$,*

$$f(\mathbf{x}^k) - f_{\mathrm{opt}} \leq \frac{C}{k}, \tag{10.91}$$

where C is given in (10.86).

Proof. By Lemma 10.69,

$$a_k - a_{k+1} \geq \frac{1}{C} a_k^2,$$

where $a_k = f(\mathbf{x}^k) - f_{\mathrm{opt}}$. Invoking Lemma 10.70 with $\gamma = C$, the inequality $a_k \leq \frac{C}{k}$, which is the same as (10.91), follows. $\square$

Remark 10.72. *When a constant stepsize $\frac{1}{L_f}$ is used (meaning that $L_k \equiv \bar{L} \equiv L_f$), (10.91) has the form*

$$f(\mathbf{x}^k) - f_{\mathrm{opt}} \leq \frac{2R_\alpha^2 L_f}{k},$$

which is similar in form to the result in the Euclidean setting in which the following bound was derived (see Theorem 10.21):

$$f(\mathbf{x}^k) - f_{\mathrm{opt}} \leq \frac{L_f \|\mathbf{x}^0 - \mathbf{x}^*\|^2}{2k}.$$

The Non-Euclidean Gradient Method in $\mathbb{R}^n$ Endowed with the l_1-Norm

Example 10.73. Suppose that the underlying space is $\mathbb{R}^n$ endowed with the l_1-norm, and let f be an L_f-smooth function w.r.t. the l_1-norm. Recall (see Example 10.63) that the set of primal counterparts in this case is given for any $\mathbf{a} \neq \mathbf{0}$ by

$$\Lambda_{\mathbf{a}} = \left\{ \sum_{i \in I(\mathbf{a})} \lambda_i \mathrm{sgn}(a_i) \mathbf{e}_i : \sum_{i \in I(\mathbf{a})} \lambda_i = 1, \lambda_j \geq 0, j \in I(\mathbf{a}) \right\},$$

where $I(\mathbf{a}) = \mathrm{argmax}_{i=1,2,\ldots,n} |a_i|$. When employing the method, we can always choose $\mathbf{a}^\dagger = \mathrm{sgn}(a_i) \mathbf{e}_i$ for some arbitrary $i \in I(\mathbf{a})$. The method thus takes the following form:

Non-Euclidean Gradient under the l_1-Norm

- **Initialization:** pick $\mathbf{x}^0 \in \mathbb{R}^n$.

- **General step:** for any $k = 0, 1, 2, \ldots$ execute the following steps:

    - pick $i_k \in \text{argmax}_i \left| \frac{\partial f(\mathbf{x}^k)}{\partial x_i} \right|$;

    - set $\mathbf{x}^{k+1} = \mathbf{x}^k - \frac{\|\nabla f(\mathbf{x}^k)\|_\infty}{L_k} \text{sgn}\left(\frac{\partial f(\mathbf{x}^k)}{\partial x_{i_k}} \right) \mathbf{e}_{i_k}$.

The constants L_k can be chosen by either one of the three options: a constant stepsize rule $L_k \equiv \bar{L} \in \left(\frac{L_f}{2}, \infty \right)$, the backtracking procedure B4, or an exact line search. Note that at each iteration only one coordinate is altered. This is a variant of a coordinate descent method that actually has an interpretation as a non-Euclidean gradient method. ∎

Example 10.74. Consider the problem

$$\min_{\mathbf{x} \in \mathbb{R}^n} \left\{ \frac{1}{2} \mathbf{x}^T \mathbf{A} \mathbf{x} + \mathbf{b}^T \mathbf{x} \right\},$$

where $\mathbf{A} \in \mathbb{S}_{++}^n$ and $\mathbf{b} \in \mathbb{R}^n$. The underlying space is $\mathbb{E} = \mathbb{R}^n$ endowed with the l_p-norm ($p \in [1, \infty]$). By Example 5.2, f is $L_f^{(p)}$-smooth with

$$L_f^{(p)} = \|\mathbf{A}\|_{p,q} = \max_{\mathbf{x}} \{ \|\mathbf{A}\mathbf{x}\|_q : \|\mathbf{x}\|_p \leq 1 \}$$

with $q \in [1, \infty]$ satisfying $\frac{1}{p} + \frac{1}{q} = 1$. Two examples of smoothness parameters are the following:

- $p = 2$. In this case, since $\mathbf{A}$ is positive definite, $L_f^{(2)} = \|\mathbf{A}\|_{2,2} = \lambda_{\max}(\mathbf{A})$.

- $p = 1$. Here $L_f^{(1)} = \|\mathbf{A}\|_{1,\infty} = \max_{i,j} |A_{i,j}|$.

The non-Euclidean gradient method for $p = 2$ is actually the Euclidean gradient method; taking a constant stepsize corresponding to $L_k = L_f^{(2)} = \lambda_{\max}(\mathbf{A})$, the method takes the following form:

Algorithm G2

- **Initialization:** pick $\mathbf{x}^0 \in \mathbb{R}^n$.

- **General step ($k \geq 0$):** $\mathbf{x}^{k+1} = \mathbf{x}^k - \frac{1}{L_f^{(2)}} (\mathbf{A}\mathbf{x}^k + \mathbf{b})$.

In the case $p = 1$ the method is a coordinate descent-type method, and with a constant stepsize corresponding to $L_k = L_f^{(1)} = \max_{i,j} |A_{i,j}|$ it takes the following form:

Algorithm G1

- **Initialization:** pick $\mathbf{x}^0 \in \mathbb{R}^n$.

- **General step** $(k \geq 0)$:

  - pick $i_k \in \mathrm{argmax}_{i=1,2,\ldots,n} |\mathbf{A}_i \mathbf{x}^k + b_i|$, where $\mathbf{A}_i$ denotes the ith row of $\mathbf{A}$.

  - update $\mathbf{x}_j^{k+1} = \begin{cases} \mathbf{x}_j^k, & j \neq i_k, \\ \mathbf{x}_{i_k}^k - \frac{1}{L_f^{(1)}}(\mathbf{A}_{i_k}\mathbf{x}^k + b_{i_k}), & j = i_k. \end{cases}$

By Theorem 10.71,[62]

$$f(\mathbf{x}^k) - f_{\mathrm{opt}} \leq \frac{2L_f^{(p)} R_{f(\mathbf{x}^0)}^2}{k}.$$

Therefore, the ratio $\frac{L_f^{(2)}}{L_f^{(1)}}$ might indicate which of the methods should have an advantage over the other. ∎

Remark 10.75. *Note that Algorithm G2 (from Example 10.74) requires $O(n^2)$ operations at each iteration since the matrix/vector multiplication $\mathbf{A}\mathbf{x}^k$ is computed. On the other hand, a careful implementation of Algorithm G1 will only require $O(n)$ operations at each iteration; this can be accomplished by updating the gradient $\mathbf{g}^k \equiv \mathbf{A}\mathbf{x}^k + \mathbf{b}$ using the relation $\mathbf{g}^{k+1} = \mathbf{g}^k - \frac{\mathbf{A}_{i_k}\mathbf{x}^k + b_{i_k}}{L_f^{(1)}}\mathbf{A}\mathbf{e}_{i_k}$ ($\mathbf{A}\mathbf{e}_{i_k}$ is obviously the i_kth column of $\mathbf{A}$). Therefore, a fair comparison between Algorithms G1 and G2 will count each n iterations of algorithm G1 as "one iteration." We will call such an iteration a "meta-iteration."*

Example 10.76. Continuing Example 10.74, consider, for example, the matrix $\mathbf{A} = \mathbf{A}^{(d)} \equiv \mathbf{J} + d\mathbf{I}$, where the matrix $\mathbf{J}$ is the matrix of all ones. Then for any $d > 0$, $\mathbf{A}^{(d)}$ is positive definite and $\lambda_{\max}(\mathbf{A}^{(d)}) = d+n$, $\max_{i,j}|A_{i,j}^{(d)}| = d+1$. Therefore, as the ratio $\rho_f \equiv \frac{L_f^{(2)}}{L_f^{(1)}} = \frac{d+n}{d+1}$ gets larger, the Euclidean gradient method (Algorithm G2) should become more inferior to the non-Euclidean version (Algorithm G1).

We ran the two algorithms for the choice $\mathbf{A} = \mathbf{A}^{(2)}$ and $\mathbf{b} = 10\mathbf{e}_1$ with initial point $\mathbf{x}^0 = \mathbf{e}_n$. The values $f(\mathbf{x}^k) - f_{\mathrm{opt}}$ as a function of the iteration index k are plotted in Figures 10.4 and 10.5 for $n = 10$ and $n = 100$, respectively. As can be seen in the left images of both figures, when meta-iterations of algorithm G1 are compared with iterations of algorithm G2, the superiority of algorithm G1 is significant. We also made the comparison when each iteration of algorithm G1 is just an update of one coordinate, meaning that we do not consider meta-iterations. For $n = 10$, the methods behave similarly, and there does not seem to be any preference to G1 or G2. However, when $n = 100$, there is still a substantial advantage of algorithm G1 compared to G2, despite the fact that it is a much cheaper method w.r.t. the number of operations performed per iteration. A possible reason for this

---

[62]Note that also $R_{f(\mathbf{x}^0)}$ might depend on the choice of norm.

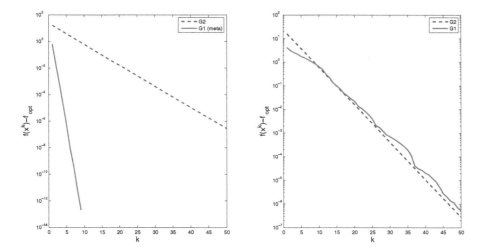

Figure 10.4. *Comparison of the Euclidean gradient method* (G2) *with the non-Euclidean gradient method* (G1) *applied on the problem from Example* 10.76 *with* $n = 10$. *The left image considers "meta-iterations" of* G1, *meaning that* 10 *iterations of* G1 *are counted as one iteration, while the right image counts each coordinate update as one iteration.*

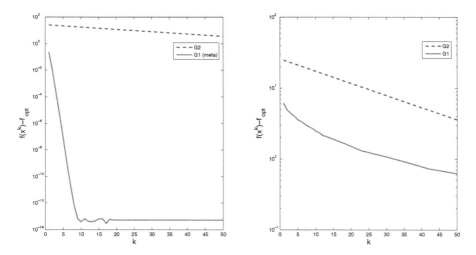

Figure 10.5. *Comparison of the Euclidean gradient method* (G2) *with the non-Euclidean gradient method* (G1) *applied on the problem from Example* 10.76 *with* $n = 100$. *The left image considers "meta-iterations" of* G1, *meaning that* 100 *iterations of* G1 *are counted as one iteration, while the right image counts each coordinate update as one iteration.*

is the fact that for $n = 10$, $\rho_f = \frac{2+10}{2+1} = 4$, while for $n = 100$, $\frac{2+100}{2+1} = 34$, and hence it is expected that the advantage of algorithm G1 over algorithm G2 will be more substantial when $n = 100$. ∎

10.9.2   The Non-Euclidean Proximal Gradient Method[63]

In this section we return to the composite model

$$\min_{\mathbf{x}\in\mathbb{E}}\{F(\mathbf{x}) \equiv f(\mathbf{x}) + g(\mathbf{x})\}, \tag{10.92}$$

where the endowed norm on $\mathbb{E}$ is not assumed to be Euclidean. Our main objective will be to develop a non-Euclidean version of the proximal gradient method. We note that when $g \equiv 0$, the method will *not* coincide with the non-Euclidean gradient method discussed in Section 10.9.1, meaning that the approach described here, which is similar to the generalization of projected subgradient to mirror descent (see Chapter 9), is fundamentally different than the approach considered in the non-Euclidean gradient method. We will make the following assumption.

Assumption 10.77.

(A) $g : \mathbb{E} \to (-\infty, \infty]$ *is proper closed and convex.*

(B) $f : \mathbb{E} \to (-\infty, \infty]$ *is proper closed and convex;* $\operatorname{dom}(g) \subseteq \operatorname{int}(\operatorname{dom}(f))$ *and* f *is* L_f*-smooth over* $\operatorname{int}(\operatorname{dom}(f))$.

(C) *The optimal solution of problem* (10.1) *is nonempty and denoted by* X^*. *The optimal value of the problem is denoted by* F_{opt}.

In the Euclidean setting, the general update rule of the proximal gradient method (see the discussion in Section 10.2) can be written in the following form:

$$\mathbf{x}^{k+1} = \operatorname{argmin}_{\mathbf{x}\in\mathbb{E}}\left\{f(\mathbf{x}^k) + \langle\nabla f(\mathbf{x}^k), \mathbf{x} - \mathbf{x}^k\rangle + g(\mathbf{x}) + \frac{L_k}{2}\|\mathbf{x} - \mathbf{x}^k\|^2\right\}.$$

We will use the same idea as in the mirror descent method and replace the half-squared Euclidean distance with a Bregman distance, leading to the following update rule:

$$\mathbf{x}^{k+1} = \operatorname{argmin}_{\mathbf{x}\in\mathbb{E}}\left\{f(\mathbf{x}^k) + \langle\nabla f(\mathbf{x}^k), \mathbf{x} - \mathbf{x}^k\rangle + g(\mathbf{x}) + L_k B_\omega(\mathbf{x}, \mathbf{x}^k)\right\},$$

where B_ω is the Bregman distance associated with ω (see Definition 9.2). The function ω will satisfy the following properties.

Assumption 10.78 (properties of ω).

- ω *is proper closed and convex.*

- ω *is differentiable over* $\operatorname{dom}(\partial\omega)$.

- $\operatorname{dom}(g) \subseteq \operatorname{dom}(\omega)$.

- $\omega + \delta_{\operatorname{dom}(g)}$ *is 1-strongly convex.*

---

[63]The non-Euclidean proximal gradient method presented in Section 10.9.2 was analyzed in the work of Tseng [121].

The proximal gradient method is defined below.

The Non-Euclidean Proximal Gradient Method

Initialization: pick $\mathbf{x}^0 \in \text{dom}(g) \cap \text{dom}(\partial \omega)$.
General step: for any $k = 0, 1, 2, \ldots$ execute the following steps:

(a) pick $L_k > 0$;

(b) compute

$$\mathbf{x}^{k+1} = \text{argmin}_{\mathbf{x} \in \mathbb{E}} \left\{ \left\langle \frac{1}{L_k} \nabla f(\mathbf{x}^k) - \nabla \omega(\mathbf{x}^k), \mathbf{x} \right\rangle + \frac{1}{L_k} g(\mathbf{x}) + \omega(\mathbf{x}) \right\}.$$
(10.93)

Our first observation is that under Assumptions 10.77 and 10.78, the non-Euclidean proximal gradient method is well defined, meaning that if $\mathbf{x}^k \in \text{dom}(g) \cap \text{dom}(\partial \omega)$, then the minimization problem in (10.93) has a unique optimal solution in $\text{dom}(g) \cap \text{dom}(\partial \omega)$. This is a direct result of Lemma 9.7 invoked with $\psi(\mathbf{x}) = \left\langle \frac{1}{L_k} \nabla f(\mathbf{x}^k) - \nabla \omega(\mathbf{x}^k), \mathbf{x} \right\rangle + \frac{1}{L_k} g(\mathbf{x})$. The two stepsize rules that will be analyzed are detailed below. We use the notation

$$V_L(\bar{\mathbf{x}}) \equiv \text{argmin}_{\mathbf{x} \in \mathbb{E}} \left\{ \left\langle \frac{1}{L} \nabla f(\bar{\mathbf{x}}) - \nabla \omega(\bar{\mathbf{x}}), \mathbf{x} \right\rangle + \frac{1}{L} g(\mathbf{x}) + \omega(\mathbf{x}) \right\}.$$

- **Constant.** $L_k = \bar{L} = L_f$ for all k.

- **Backtracking procedure B5.** The procedure requires two parameters (s, η), where $s > 0$ and $\eta > 1$. Define $L_{-1} = s$. At iteration k $(k \geq 0)$ the choice of L_k is done as follows: First, L_k is set to be equal to L_{k-1}. Then, while

$$f(V_{L_k}(\mathbf{x}^k)) > f(\mathbf{x}^k) + \langle \nabla f(\mathbf{x}^k), V_{L_k}(\mathbf{x}^k) - \mathbf{x}^k \rangle + \frac{L_k}{2} \| V_{L_k}(\mathbf{x}^k) - \mathbf{x}^k \|^2,$$

set $L_k := \eta L_k$. In other words, the stepsize is chosen as $L_k = L_{k-1} \eta^{i_k}$, where i_k is the smallest nonnegative integer for which the condition

$$f(V_{L_{k-1} \eta^{i_k}}(\mathbf{x}^k)) \leq f(\mathbf{x}^k) + \langle \nabla f(\mathbf{x}^k), V_{L_{k-1} \eta^{i_k}}(\mathbf{x}^k) - \mathbf{x}^k \rangle$$
$$+ \frac{L_k}{2} \| V_{L_{k-1} \eta^{i_k}}(\mathbf{x}^k) - \mathbf{x}^k \|^2$$

is satisfied.

Remark 10.79. *In both stepsize rules the following inequality holds:*

$$f(\mathbf{x}^{k+1}) \leq f(\mathbf{x}^k) + \langle \nabla f(\mathbf{x}^k), \mathbf{x}^{k+1} - \mathbf{x}^k \rangle + \frac{L_k}{2} \| \mathbf{x}^{k+1} - \mathbf{x}^k \|^2.$$

Remark 10.80. *By the same arguments as in Remark* 10.19 *we have that* $L_k \leq \alpha L_f$, *where* $\alpha = 1$ *for the constant stepsize case and* $\alpha = \max\left\{\eta, \frac{s}{L_f}\right\}$ *in the setting of the backtracking procedure* B5.

The rate of convergence result will now be stated and proved.

Theorem 10.81 ($O(1/k)$ rate of convergence of the non-Euclidean prox-imal gradient method). *Suppose that Assumptions* 10.77 *and* 10.78 *hold. Let* $\{\mathbf{x}^k\}_{k \geq 0}$ *be the sequence generated by the non-Euclidean proximal gradient method for solving problem* (10.92) *with either a constant stepsize rule in which* $L_k \equiv L_f$ *for all* $k \geq 0$ *or the backtracking procedure* B5. *Then*

(a) *the sequence* $\{F(\mathbf{x}^k)\}_{k \geq 0}$ *is nonincreasing;*

(b) *for any* $k \geq 1$ *and* $\mathbf{x}^* \in X^*$,

$$F(\mathbf{x}^k) - F_{\text{opt}} \leq \frac{\alpha L_f B_\omega(\mathbf{x}^*, \mathbf{x}^0)}{k},$$

where $\alpha = 1$ *in the constant stepsize setting and* $\alpha = \max\left\{\eta, \frac{s}{L_f}\right\}$ *if the backtracking rule is employed.*

Proof. (a) We will use the notation $m(\mathbf{x}, \mathbf{y}) \equiv f(\mathbf{y}) + \langle \nabla f(\mathbf{y}), \mathbf{x} - \mathbf{y} \rangle$. For both stepsize rules we have, for any $n \geq 0$ (see Remark 10.79),

$$f(\mathbf{x}^{n+1}) \leq m(\mathbf{x}^{n+1}, \mathbf{x}^n) + \frac{L_n}{2}\|\mathbf{x}^{n+1} - \mathbf{x}^n\|^2.$$

Therefore,

$$
\begin{aligned}
F(\mathbf{x}^{n+1}) &= f(\mathbf{x}^{n+1}) + g(\mathbf{x}^{n+1}) \\
&\leq m(\mathbf{x}^{n+1}, \mathbf{x}^n) + g(\mathbf{x}^{n+1}) + \frac{L_n}{2}\|\mathbf{x}^{n+1} - \mathbf{x}^n\|^2 \\
&\leq m(\mathbf{x}^{n+1}, \mathbf{x}^n) + g(\mathbf{x}^{n+1}) + L_n B_\omega(\mathbf{x}^{n+1}, \mathbf{x}^n), \qquad (10.94)
\end{aligned}
$$

where the 1-strong convexity of $\omega + \delta_{\text{dom}(g)}$ was used in the last inequality. Note that

$$\mathbf{x}^{n+1} = \operatorname{argmin}_{\mathbf{x} \in \mathbb{E}}\{m(\mathbf{x}, \mathbf{x}^n) + g(\mathbf{x}) + L_n B_\omega(\mathbf{x}, \mathbf{x}^n)\}. \qquad (10.95)$$

Therefore, in particular,

$$
\begin{aligned}
m(\mathbf{x}^{n+1}, \mathbf{x}^n) + g(\mathbf{x}^{n+1}) + L_n B_\omega(\mathbf{x}^{n+1}, \mathbf{x}^n) &\leq m(\mathbf{x}^n, \mathbf{x}^n) + g(\mathbf{x}^n) + L_n B_\omega(\mathbf{x}^n, \mathbf{x}^n) \\
&= f(\mathbf{x}^n) + g(\mathbf{x}^n) \\
&= F(\mathbf{x}^n),
\end{aligned}
$$

which, combined with (10.94), implies that $F(\mathbf{x}^{n+1}) \leq F(\mathbf{x}^n)$, meaning that the sequence of function values $\{F(\mathbf{x}^n)\}_{n \geq 0}$ is nonincreasing.

(b) Let $k \geq 1$ and $\mathbf{x}^* \in X^*$. Using the relation (10.95) and invoking the non-Euclidean second prox theorem (Theorem 9.12) with $\psi(\mathbf{x}) = \frac{m(\mathbf{x}, \mathbf{x}^n) + g(\mathbf{x})}{L_n}$, $\mathbf{b} = \mathbf{x}^n$, and $\mathbf{a} = \mathbf{x}^{n+1}$, it follows that for all $\mathbf{x} \in \text{dom}(g)$,

$$\langle \nabla \omega(\mathbf{x}^n) - \nabla \omega(\mathbf{x}^{n+1}), \mathbf{x} - \mathbf{x}^{n+1} \rangle \leq \frac{m(\mathbf{x}, \mathbf{x}^n) - m(\mathbf{x}^{n+1}, \mathbf{x}^n) + g(\mathbf{x}) - g(\mathbf{x}^{n+1})}{L_n},$$

which, combined with the three-points lemma (Lemma 9.11) with $\mathbf{a} = \mathbf{x}^{n+1}, \mathbf{b} = \mathbf{x}^n$, and $\mathbf{c} = \mathbf{x}$, yields the inequality

$$B_\omega(\mathbf{x}, \mathbf{x}^{n+1}) + B_\omega(\mathbf{x}^{n+1}, \mathbf{x}^n) - B_\omega(\mathbf{x}, \mathbf{x}^n) \leq \frac{m(\mathbf{x}, \mathbf{x}^n) - m(\mathbf{x}^{n+1}, \mathbf{x}^n) + g(\mathbf{x}) - g(\mathbf{x}^{n+1})}{L_n}.$$

Rearranging terms, we obtain that

$$m(\mathbf{x}^{n+1}, \mathbf{x}^n) + g(\mathbf{x}^{n+1}) + L_n B_\omega(\mathbf{x}^{n+1}, \mathbf{x}^n) \leq m(\mathbf{x}, \mathbf{x}^n) + g(\mathbf{x}) + L_n B_\omega(\mathbf{x}, \mathbf{x}^n)$$
$$- L_n B_\omega(\mathbf{x}, \mathbf{x}^{n+1}),$$

which, combined with (10.94), yields the inequality

$$F(\mathbf{x}^{n+1}) \leq m(\mathbf{x}, \mathbf{x}^n) + g(\mathbf{x}) + L_n B_\omega(\mathbf{x}, \mathbf{x}^n) - L_n B_\omega(\mathbf{x}, \mathbf{x}^{n+1}).$$

Since f is convex, $m(\mathbf{x}, \mathbf{x}^n) \leq f(\mathbf{x})$, and hence

$$F(\mathbf{x}^{n+1}) - F(\mathbf{x}) \leq L_n B_\omega(\mathbf{x}, \mathbf{x}^n) - L_n B_\omega(\mathbf{x}, \mathbf{x}^{n+1}).$$

Plugging in $\mathbf{x} = \mathbf{x}^*$ and dividing by L_n, we obtain

$$\frac{F(\mathbf{x}^{n+1}) - F(\mathbf{x}^*)}{L_n} \leq B_\omega(\mathbf{x}^*, \mathbf{x}^n) - B_\omega(\mathbf{x}^*, \mathbf{x}^{n+1}).$$

Using the bound $L_n \leq \alpha L_f$ (see Remark 10.80),

$$\frac{F(\mathbf{x}^{n+1}) - F(\mathbf{x}^*)}{\alpha L_f} \leq B_\omega(\mathbf{x}^*, \mathbf{x}^n) - B_\omega(\mathbf{x}^*, \mathbf{x}^{n+1}),$$

and hence

$$F(\mathbf{x}^{n+1}) - F_{\text{opt}} \leq \alpha L_f B_\omega(\mathbf{x}^*, \mathbf{x}^n) - \alpha L_f B_\omega(\mathbf{x}^*, \mathbf{x}^{n+1}).$$

Summing the above inequality for $n = 0, 1, \ldots, k-1$, we obtain that

$$\sum_{n=0}^{k-1} (F(\mathbf{x}^{n+1}) - F_{\text{opt}}) \leq \alpha L_f B_\omega(\mathbf{x}^*, \mathbf{x}^0) - \alpha L_f B_\omega(\mathbf{x}^*, \mathbf{x}^k) \leq \alpha L_f B_\omega(\mathbf{x}^*, \mathbf{x}^0).$$

Using the monotonicity of the sequence of function values, we conclude that

$$k(F(\mathbf{x}^k) - F_{\text{opt}}) \leq \alpha L_f B_\omega(\mathbf{x}^*, \mathbf{x}^0),$$

thus obtaining the result

$$F(\mathbf{x}^k) - F_{\text{opt}} \leq \frac{\alpha L_f B_\omega(\mathbf{x}^*, \mathbf{x}^0)}{k}. \qquad \square$$

Chapter 11

The Block Proximal Gradient Method

> **Underlying Spaces:** In this chapter, all the underlying spaces are Euclidean (see the details in Section 11.2).

11.1 Decomposition Methods

Many of the methods discussed in this book are *decomposition methods*, which, loosely speaking, are methods that utilize at each step only a certain portion of the problem's data or resort to solving a smaller-dimension problem at each step. One class of decomposition methods is the class of *functional decomposition methods*, in which the data of the problem comprise several functions, and at each iteration only a few of them (perhaps only one) are processed. Examples of functional decomposition methods were studied in the context of the model

$$\min_{\mathbf{x}} \left\{ \sum_{i=1}^{m} f_i(\mathbf{x}) : \mathbf{x} \in C \right\}.$$

In Example 8.36 it was shown that an implementation of the stochastic projected subgradient method amounts to a method of the form

$$\mathbf{x}^{k+1} = P_C(\mathbf{x}^k - t_k f'_{i_k}(\mathbf{x}^k)),$$

where the index i_k is picked randomly by a uniform distribution. A deterministic version of this method is the incremental projected subgradient method, which was studied in Section 8.4, in which i_k is picked by a cyclic order. In both methods, each step exploits only one of the m functions that constitute the data of the problem. The proximal gradient method is actually another example of a functional decomposition method, where the relevant model (see Chapter 10) is

$$\min_{\mathbf{x} \in \mathbb{E}} f(\mathbf{x}) + g(\mathbf{x}).$$

The general step of the proximal gradient method is of the form

$$\mathbf{x}^{k+1} = \operatorname{prox}_{t_k g}(\mathbf{x}^k - t_k \nabla f(\mathbf{x}^k)).$$

The functions f and g are treated separately in the above update formula. First, a gradient step w.r.t. f is taken, and then a prox operator w.r.t. g is computed.

Another class of decomposition methods is the class of *variables decomposition methods*, in which at each iteration only a subset of the decision variables is altered while all the other variables remain fixed. One example for such a method was given in Example 10.73, where the problem of minimizing a differentiable function over $\mathbb{R}^n$ was considered. The method described in Example 10.73 (non-Euclidean gradient method under the l_1-norm) picks one variable at each iteration by a certain greedy rule and performs a gradient step w.r.t. the chosen variable while keeping all the other variables fixed.

In this chapter we will consider additional variables decomposition methods; these methods pick at each iteration one block of variables and perform a proximal gradient step w.r.t. the chosen block.

11.2   Model and Assumptions

In this chapter we will consider methods for solving the composite model $f + g$ in the case where g has a block separable structure. More specifically, the main model of this chapter is

$$\min_{\mathbf{x}_1 \in \mathbb{E}_1, \mathbf{x}_2 \in \mathbb{E}_2, \ldots, \mathbf{x}_p \in \mathbb{E}_p} \left\{ F(\mathbf{x}_1, \mathbf{x}_2, \ldots, \mathbf{x}_p) \equiv f(\mathbf{x}_1, \mathbf{x}_2, \ldots, \mathbf{x}_p) + \sum_{j=1}^{p} g_j(\mathbf{x}_j) \right\}, \quad (11.1)$$

where $\mathbb{E}_1, \mathbb{E}_2, \ldots, \mathbb{E}_p$ are Euclidean spaces. We will denote the product space by $\mathbb{E} = \mathbb{E}_1 \times \mathbb{E}_2 \times \cdots \times \mathbb{E}_p$ and use our convention (see Section 1.9) that the product space is also Euclidean with endowed norm

$$\|(\mathbf{u}_1, \mathbf{u}_2, \ldots, \mathbf{u}_p)\|_{\mathbb{E}} = \sqrt{\sum_{i=1}^{p} \|\mathbf{u}_i\|_{\mathbb{E}_i}^2}.$$

In most cases we will omit the subscript of the norm indicating the underlying vector space (whose identity will be clear from the context). The function $g : \mathbb{E} \to (-\infty, \infty]$ is defined by

$$g(\mathbf{x}_1, \mathbf{x}_2, \ldots, \mathbf{x}_p) \equiv \sum_{i=1}^{p} g_i(\mathbf{x}_i).$$

The gradient w.r.t. the ith block ($i \in \{1, 2, \ldots, p\}$) is denoted by $\nabla_i f$, and whenever the function is differentiable it holds that

$$\nabla f(\mathbf{x}) = (\nabla_1 f(\mathbf{x}), \nabla_2 f(\mathbf{x}), \ldots, \nabla_p f(\mathbf{x})).$$

For any $i \in \{1, 2, \ldots, p\}$ we define $\mathcal{U}_i : \mathbb{E}_i \to \mathbb{E}$ to be the linear transformation given by

$$\mathcal{U}_i(\mathbf{d}) = (\mathbf{0}, \ldots, \mathbf{0}, \underbrace{\mathbf{d}}_{i\text{th block}}, \mathbf{0}, \ldots, \mathbf{0}), \quad \mathbf{d} \in \mathbb{E}_i.$$

We also use throughout this chapter the notation that a vector $\mathbf{x} \in \mathbb{E}$ can be written as

$$\mathbf{x} = (\mathbf{x}_1, \mathbf{x}_2, \ldots, \mathbf{x}_p),$$

and this relation will also be written as $\mathbf{x} = (\mathbf{x}_i)_{i=1}^p$. Thus, in our notation, the main model (11.1) can be simply written as

$$\min_{\mathbf{x} \in \mathbb{E}} \{F(\mathbf{x}) = f(\mathbf{x}) + g(\mathbf{x})\}.$$

The basic assumptions on the model are summarized below.

Assumption 11.1.

(A) $g_i : \mathbb{E}_i \to (-\infty, \infty]$ *is proper closed and convex for any* $i \in \{1, 2, \ldots, p\}$.

(B) $f : \mathbb{E} \to (-\infty, \infty]$ *is proper and closed, and* $\mathrm{dom}(f)$ *is convex;* $\mathrm{dom}(g) \subseteq \mathrm{int}(\mathrm{dom}(f))$, *and* f *is differentiable over* $\mathrm{int}(\mathrm{dom}(f))$.

(C) f *is* L_f-*smooth over* $\mathrm{int}(\mathrm{dom}(f))$ $(L_f > 0)$.

(D) *There exist* $L_1, L_2, \ldots, L_p > 0$ *such that for any* $i \in \{1, 2, \ldots, p\}$ *it holds that*

$$\|\nabla_i f(\mathbf{x}) - \nabla_i f(\mathbf{x} + \mathcal{U}_i(\mathbf{d}))\| \leq L_i \|\mathbf{d}\| \tag{11.2}$$

for all $\mathbf{x} \in \mathrm{int}(\mathrm{dom}(f))$ *and* $\mathbf{d} \in \mathbb{E}_i$ *for which* $\mathbf{x} + \mathcal{U}_i(\mathbf{d}) \in \mathrm{int}(\mathrm{dom}(f))$.

(E) *The optimal set of problem* (11.1) *is nonempty and denoted by* X^*. *The optimal value is denoted by* F_{opt}.

Remark 11.2 (block/global Lipschitz constants). *The constant* L_f *will be called the "global Lipschitz constant," while the constants* $L_1, L_2, \ldots, L_p$ *are the "block Lipschitz constants." Obviously, we can choose* $L_i = L_f$ *for all* i *since by the definition of* L_f, (11.2) *holds for* $L_i = L_f$. *However, the block Lipschitz constants can be significantly smaller than the global Lipschitz constant—a fact that might have significant influence on the performance of the derived algorithms, as well as their convergence rate.*

11.3   The Toolbox

11.3.1   The Partial Gradient Mapping

Recall that the gradient mapping associated with the functions f, g and a constant $L > 0$, as defined in Section 10.3.2, is a mapping from $\mathrm{int}(\mathrm{dom}(f))$ to $\mathbb{E}$ given by

$$G_L^{f,g}(\mathbf{x}) = L\left(\mathbf{x} - T_L^{f,g}(\mathbf{x})\right),$$

where $T_L^{f,g} : \mathrm{int}(\mathrm{dom}(f)) \to \mathbb{E}$ is the prox-grad mapping given by

$$T_L^{f,g}(\mathbf{x}) = \mathrm{prox}_{\frac{1}{L}g}\left(\mathbf{x} - \frac{1}{L}\nabla f(\mathbf{x})\right).$$

From now on we will always omit the superscripts and write T_L and G_L instead of $T_L^{f,g}$ and $G_L^{f,g}$. In the context of block variables decomposition methods, it is also important to consider the notions of *partial prox-grad mappings* and *partial gradient mappings*.

Definition 11.3 (partial prox-grad mapping). *Suppose that f and $g_1, g_2, \ldots, g_p$ satisfy properties (A) and (B) of Assumption 11.1, $L > 0$, and let $i \in \{1, 2, \ldots, p\}$. Then the **$i$th partial prox-grad mapping** is the operator $T_L^i : \mathrm{int}(\mathrm{dom}(f)) \to \mathbb{E}_i$ defined by*

$$T_L^i(\mathbf{x}) = \mathrm{prox}_{\frac{1}{L}g_i}\left(\mathbf{x}_i - \frac{1}{L}\nabla_i f(\mathbf{x})\right).$$

Definition 11.4 (partial gradient mapping). *Suppose that f and $g_1, g_2, \ldots, g_p$ satisfy properties (A) and (B) of Assumption 11.1, $L > 0$, and let $i \in \{1, 2, \ldots, p\}$. Then the **$i$th partial gradient mapping** is the operator $G_L^i : \mathrm{int}(\mathrm{dom}(f)) \to \mathbb{E}_i$ defined by*

$$G_L^i(\mathbf{x}) = L\left(\mathbf{x}_i - T_L^i(\mathbf{x})\right).$$

The ith partial prox-grad and gradient mappings depend on f and g_i, but this dependence is not indicated in our notation. If $g_i \equiv 0$ for some $i \in \{1, 2, \ldots, p\}$, then $G_L^i(\mathbf{x}) = \nabla_i f(\mathbf{x})$; that is, in this case the partial gradient mapping coincides with the mapping $\mathbf{x} \mapsto \nabla_i f(\mathbf{x})$. Some basic properties of the partial prox-grad and gradient mappings are summarized in the following lemma.

Lemma 11.5. *Suppose that f and $g_1, g_2, \ldots, g_p$ satisfy properties (A) and (B) of Assumption 11.1, $L > 0$, and let $i \in \{1, 2, \ldots, p\}$. Then for any $\mathbf{x} \in \mathrm{int}(\mathrm{dom}(f))$,*

$$\begin{aligned} T_L(\mathbf{x}) &= (T_L^1(\mathbf{x}), T_L^2(\mathbf{x}), \ldots, T_L^p(\mathbf{x})), \\ G_L(\mathbf{x}) &= (G_L^1(\mathbf{x}), G_L^2(\mathbf{x}), \ldots, G_L^p(\mathbf{x})). \end{aligned} \tag{11.3}$$

Proof. By Theorem 6.6, we have that for any $\mathbf{y} \in \mathrm{dom}(f)$,

$$\mathrm{prox}_{\frac{1}{L}g}(\mathbf{y}) = (\mathrm{prox}_{\frac{1}{L}g_i}(\mathbf{y}_i))_{i=1}^p.$$

Thus, for any $\mathbf{x} \in \mathrm{int}(\mathrm{dom}(f))$,

$$\begin{aligned} T_L(\mathbf{x}) &= \mathrm{prox}_{\frac{1}{L}g}\left(\mathbf{x} - \frac{1}{L}\nabla f(\mathbf{x})\right) = \left(\mathrm{prox}_{\frac{1}{L}g_i}\left(\left[\mathbf{x} - \frac{1}{L}\nabla f(\mathbf{x})\right]_i\right)\right)_{i=1}^p \\ &= \left(\mathrm{prox}_{\frac{1}{L}g_i}\left(\mathbf{x}_i - \frac{1}{L}\nabla_i f(\mathbf{x})\right)\right)_{i=1}^p \\ &= (T_L^i(\mathbf{x}))_{i=1}^p. \end{aligned}$$

The second identity follows immediately:

$$\begin{aligned} G_L(\mathbf{x}) &= L(\mathbf{x} - T_L(\mathbf{x})) = L\left((\mathbf{x}_i)_{i=1}^p - (T_L^i(\mathbf{x}))_{i=1}^p\right) \\ &= \left(L(\mathbf{x}_i - T_L^i(\mathbf{x}))\right)_{i=1}^p \\ &= (G_L^i(\mathbf{x}))_{i=1}^p. \quad \square \end{aligned}$$

A point $\mathbf{x}^* \in \mathrm{dom}(g)$ is a stationary point of problem (11.1) if $-\nabla f(\mathbf{x}^*) \in \partial g(\mathbf{x}^*)$ (see Definition 3.73). The following simple theorem shows that the stationarity condition for problem (11.1) can be decomposed into p conditions expressed in terms of the partial gradient mappings.

Theorem 11.6. *Suppose that f and $g_1, g_2, \ldots, g_p$ satisfy properties* (A) *and* (B) *of Assumption* 11.1. *Then*

(a) $\mathbf{x}^* \in \mathrm{dom}(g)$ *is a stationary point of problem* (11.1) *if and only if*

$$- \nabla_i f(\mathbf{x}^*) \in \partial g_i(\mathbf{x}_i^*), \ i = 1, 2, \ldots, p; \tag{11.4}$$

(b) *for any p positive numbers $M_1, M_2, \ldots, M_p > 0$, $\mathbf{x}^* \in \mathrm{dom}(g)$ is a stationary point of problem* (11.1) *if and only if*

$$G_{M_i}^i(\mathbf{x}^*) = \mathbf{0}, \ i = 1, 2, \ldots, p.$$

Proof. (a) By definition, $\mathbf{x}^* \in \mathrm{dom}(g)$ is a stationary point of problem (11.1) if and only if

$$- \nabla f(\mathbf{x}^*) \in \partial g(\mathbf{x}^*). \tag{11.5}$$

By the block separable structure of g, it is easy to show that

$$\partial g(\mathbf{x}^*) = \partial g_1(\mathbf{x}_1^*) \times \partial g_2(\mathbf{x}_2^*) \times \cdots \times \partial g_p(\mathbf{x}_p^*),$$

which, combined with the fact that $\nabla f(\mathbf{x}^*) = (\nabla_1 f(\mathbf{x}^*), \nabla_2 f(\mathbf{x}^*), \ldots, \nabla_p f(\mathbf{x}^*))$, implies that the relation (11.5) is equivalent to

$$-(\nabla_1 f(\mathbf{x}^*), \nabla_2 f(\mathbf{x}^*), \ldots, \nabla_p f(\mathbf{x}^*)) \in \partial g_1(\mathbf{x}_1^*) \times \partial g_2(\mathbf{x}_2^*) \times \cdots \times \partial g_p(\mathbf{x}_p^*),$$

that is, to (11.4).

(b) By the definition of the partial gradient mapping, $G_{M_i}^i(\mathbf{x}^*) = \mathbf{0}$ if and only if $\mathbf{x}_i^* = \mathrm{prox}_{\frac{1}{M_i} g_i} \left(\mathbf{x}_i^* - \frac{1}{M_i} \nabla_i f(\mathbf{x}^*) \right)$, which, by the second prox theorem (Theorem 6.39), is equivalent to

$$\left(\mathbf{x}_i^* - \frac{1}{M_i} \nabla_i f(\mathbf{x}^*) \right) - \mathbf{x}_i^* \in \frac{1}{M_i} \partial g_i(\mathbf{x}_i^*),$$

that is, to

$$- \nabla_i f(\mathbf{x}^*) \in \partial g_i(\mathbf{x}_i^*).$$

To summarize, $G_{M_i}^i(\mathbf{x}^*) = \mathbf{0}$ for all i if and only if $- \nabla_i f(\mathbf{x}^*) \in \partial g_i(\mathbf{x}_i^*)$ for all i, which, by part (a), is equivalent to saying that $\mathbf{x}^*$ is a stationary point of problem (11.1). $\square$

The next results shows some monotonicity properties of the partial gradient mapping w.r.t. its parameter. The result is presented without its proof, which is an almost verbatim repetition of the arguments in Theorem 10.9.

Theorem 11.7 (monotonicity of the partial gradient mapping). *Suppose that f and $g_1, g_2, \ldots, g_p$ satisfy properties* (A) *and* (B) *of Assumption* 11.1, *and let $i \in \{1, 2, \ldots, p\}$. Suppose that $L_1 \geq L_2 > 0$. Then*

$$\|G_{L_1}^i(\mathbf{x})\| \geq \|G_{L_2}^i(\mathbf{x})\|$$

and

$$\frac{\|G_{L_1}^i(\mathbf{x})\|}{L_1} \leq \frac{\|G_{L_2}^i(\mathbf{x})\|}{L_2}$$

for any $\mathbf{x} \in \mathrm{int}(\mathrm{dom}(f))$.

11.3.2 The Block Descent Lemma

The block descent lemma is a variant of the descent lemma (Lemma 5.7), and its proof is almost identical.

Lemma 11.8 (block descent lemma). *Let* $f : \mathbb{E}_1 \times \mathbb{E}_2 \times \cdots \times \mathbb{E}_p \to (-\infty, \infty]$ *be a proper function whose domain* $\mathrm{dom}(f)$ *is convex. Assume that* f *is differentiable over* $\mathrm{int}(\mathrm{dom}(f))$. *Let* $i \in \{1, 2, \ldots, p\}$. *Suppose that there exists* $L_i > 0$ *for which*

$$\|\nabla_i f(\mathbf{y}) - \nabla_i f(\mathbf{y} + \mathcal{U}_i(\mathbf{d}))\| \leq L_i \|\mathbf{d}\|$$

for any $\mathbf{y} \in \mathrm{int}(\mathrm{dom}(f))$ *and* $\mathbf{d} \in \mathbb{E}_i$ *for which* $\mathbf{y} + \mathcal{U}_i(\mathbf{d}) \in \mathrm{int}(\mathrm{dom}(f))$. *Then*

$$f(\mathbf{x} + \mathcal{U}_i(\mathbf{d})) \leq f(\mathbf{x}) + \langle \nabla_i f(\mathbf{x}), \mathbf{d} \rangle + \frac{L_i}{2} \|\mathbf{d}\|^2$$

for any $\mathbf{x} \in \mathrm{int}(\mathrm{dom}(f))$ *and* $\mathbf{d} \in \mathbb{E}_i$ *for which* $\mathbf{x} + \mathcal{U}_i(\mathbf{d}) \in \mathrm{int}(\mathrm{dom}(f))$.

Proof. Let $\mathbf{x} \in \mathrm{int}(\mathrm{dom}(f))$ and $\mathbf{d} \in \mathbb{E}_i$ such that $\mathbf{x} + \mathcal{U}_i(\mathbf{d}) \in \mathrm{int}(\mathrm{dom}(f))$. Denote $\mathbf{x}^{(t)} = \mathbf{x} + t\mathcal{U}_i(\mathbf{d})$ and define $g(t) = f(\mathbf{x}^{(t)})$. By the fundamental theorem of calculus,

$$f(\mathbf{x}^{(1)}) - f(\mathbf{x}) = g(1) - g(0) = \int_0^1 g'(t) dt$$

$$= \int_0^1 \langle \nabla f(\mathbf{x}^{(t)}), \mathcal{U}_i(\mathbf{d}) \rangle dt = \int_0^1 \langle \nabla_i f(\mathbf{x}^{(t)}), \mathbf{d} \rangle dt$$

$$= \langle \nabla_i f(\mathbf{x}), \mathbf{d} \rangle + \int_0^1 \langle \nabla_i f(\mathbf{x}^{(t)}) - \nabla_i f(\mathbf{x}), \mathbf{d} \rangle dt.$$

Thus,

$$\begin{aligned}
|f(\mathbf{x}^{(1)}) - f(\mathbf{x}) - \langle \nabla_i f(\mathbf{x}), \mathbf{d} \rangle| &= \left| \int_0^1 \langle \nabla_i f(\mathbf{x}^{(t)}) - \nabla_i f(\mathbf{x}), \mathbf{d} \rangle dt \right| \\
&\leq \int_0^1 |\langle \nabla_i f(\mathbf{x}^{(t)}) - \nabla_i f(\mathbf{x}), \mathbf{d} \rangle| dt \\
&\overset{(*)}{\leq} \int_0^1 \|\nabla_i f(\mathbf{x}^{(t)}) - \nabla_i f(\mathbf{x})\| \cdot \|\mathbf{d}\| dt \\
&\leq \int_0^1 t L_i \|\mathbf{d}\|^2 dt \\
&= \frac{L_i}{2} \|\mathbf{d}\|^2,
\end{aligned}$$

where the Cauchy–Schwarz inequality was used in $(*)$. $\square$

11.3.3 Sufficient Decrease

The basic step that will be employed by all the methods discussed in this chapter is a proximal gradient step w.r.t. a given block. Specifically, for a given $\mathbf{x} \in \mathbb{E}$ and

$i \in \{1, 2, \ldots, p\}$, the next updated vector $\mathbf{x}^+$ will have the form

$$\mathbf{x}_j^+ = \begin{cases} \mathbf{x}_j, & j \neq i, \\ T_{L_i}^i(\mathbf{x}), & j = i. \end{cases}$$

The above update formula can be compactly written as

$$\mathbf{x}^+ = \mathbf{x} + \mathcal{U}_i(T_{L_i}^i(\mathbf{x}) - \mathbf{x}_i).$$

We will now prove a variant of the sufficient decrease lemma (Lemma 10.4), in which only Lipschitz continuity w.r.t. a certain block of the gradient of the function is assumed.

Lemma 11.9 (block sufficient decrease lemma). *Suppose that f and $g_1, g_2,$ $\ldots, g_p$ satisfy properties* (A) *and* (B) *of Assumption 11.1. Let $i \in \{1, 2, \ldots, p\}$. Suppose that there exists $L_i > 0$ for which*

$$\|\nabla_i f(\mathbf{y}) - \nabla_i f(\mathbf{y} + \mathcal{U}_i(\mathbf{d}))\| \leq L_i \|\mathbf{d}\|$$

for any $\mathbf{y} \in \text{int}(\text{dom}(f))$ and $\mathbf{d} \in \mathbb{E}_i$ for which $\mathbf{y} + \mathcal{U}_i(\mathbf{d}) \in \text{int}(\text{dom}(f))$. Then

$$F(\mathbf{x}) - F(\mathbf{x} + \mathcal{U}_i(T_{L_i}^i(\mathbf{x}) - \mathbf{x}_i)) \geq \frac{1}{2L_i} \|G_{L_i}^i(\mathbf{x})\|^2 \tag{11.6}$$

for all $\mathbf{x} \in \text{int}(\text{dom}(f))$.

Proof. For the sake of simplicity, we use the shorthand notation $\mathbf{x}^+ = \mathbf{x} + \mathcal{U}_i(T_{L_i}^i(\mathbf{x}) - \mathbf{x}_i)$. By the block descent lemma (Lemma 11.8), we have that

$$f(\mathbf{x}^+) \leq f(\mathbf{x}) + \langle \nabla_i f(\mathbf{x}), T_{L_i}^i(\mathbf{x}) - \mathbf{x}_i \rangle + \frac{L_i}{2} \|T_{L_i}^i(\mathbf{x}) - \mathbf{x}_i\|^2. \tag{11.7}$$

By the second prox theorem (Theorem 6.39), since $T_{L_i}^i(\mathbf{x}) = \text{prox}_{\frac{1}{L_i} g_i}(\mathbf{x}_i - \frac{1}{L_i}\nabla_i f(\mathbf{x}))$, we have

$$\left\langle \mathbf{x}_i - \frac{1}{L_i}\nabla_i f(\mathbf{x}) - T_{L_i}^i(\mathbf{x}), \mathbf{x}_i - T_{L_i}^i(\mathbf{x}) \right\rangle \leq \frac{1}{L_i} g_i(\mathbf{x}_i) - \frac{1}{L_i} g_i(T_{L_i}^i(\mathbf{x})),$$

and hence

$$\langle \nabla_i f(\mathbf{x}), T_{L_i}^i(\mathbf{x}) - \mathbf{x}_i \rangle \leq -L_i \|T_{L_i}^i(\mathbf{x}) - \mathbf{x}_i\|^2 + g_i(\mathbf{x}_i) - g_i(\mathbf{x}_i^+),$$

which, combined with (11.7), yields

$$f(\mathbf{x}^+) + g_i(\mathbf{x}_i^+) \leq f(\mathbf{x}) + g_i(\mathbf{x}_i) - \frac{L_i}{2} \|T_{L_i}^i(\mathbf{x}) - \mathbf{x}_i\|^2.$$

Adding the identity $\sum_{j \neq i} g_j(\mathbf{x}_j^+) = \sum_{j \neq i} g_j(\mathbf{x}_j)$ to the last inequality yields

$$F(\mathbf{x}^+) \leq F(\mathbf{x}) - \frac{L_i}{2} \|T_{L_i}^i(\mathbf{x}) - \mathbf{x}_i\|^2,$$

which, by the definition of the partial gradient mapping, is equivalent to the desired result (11.6).   □

Remark 11.10.   *Under the setting of Lemma 11.9, if we denote* $\mathbf{x}^+ = \mathbf{x} + \mathcal{U}_i(T_{L_i}^i(\mathbf{x}) - \mathbf{x}_i)$, *then the sufficient decrease condition* (11.6) *can be written in the following form:*

$$F(\mathbf{x}) - F(\mathbf{x}^+) \geq \frac{L_i}{2}\|\mathbf{x} - \mathbf{x}^+\|^2.$$

11.4   The Cyclic Block Proximal Gradient Method

In the cyclic block proximal gradient (CBPG) method we successively pick a block in a cyclic manner and perform a prox-grad step w.r.t. the chosen block. The kth iterate is denoted by $\mathbf{x}^k = (\mathbf{x}_1^k, \mathbf{x}_2^k, \dots, \mathbf{x}_p^k)$. Each iteration of the CBPG method involves p "subiterations," and the by-products of these subiterations will be denoted by the following auxiliary subsequences:

$$\mathbf{x}^{k,0} = \mathbf{x}^k = (\mathbf{x}_1^k, \mathbf{x}_2^k, \dots, \mathbf{x}_p^k),$$
$$\mathbf{x}^{k,1} = (\mathbf{x}_1^{k+1}, \mathbf{x}_2^k, \dots, \mathbf{x}_p^k),$$
$$\mathbf{x}^{k,2} = (\mathbf{x}_1^{k+1}, \mathbf{x}_2^{k+1}, \mathbf{x}_3^k, \dots, \mathbf{x}_p^k),$$
$$\vdots$$
$$\mathbf{x}^{k,p} = \mathbf{x}^{k+1} = (\mathbf{x}_1^{k+1}, \mathbf{x}_2^{k+1}, \dots, \mathbf{x}_p^{k+1}).$$

We can also write the following formula for the kth member of the ith auxiliary sequence:

$$\mathbf{x}^{k,i} = \sum_{j=1}^{i} \mathcal{U}_j(\mathbf{x}_j^{k+1}) + \sum_{j=i+1}^{p} \mathcal{U}_j(\mathbf{x}_j^k). \tag{11.8}$$

We are now ready to present the method.

The Cyclic Block Proximal Gradient (CBPG) Method

Initialization: pick $\mathbf{x}^0 = (\mathbf{x}_1^0, \mathbf{x}_2^0, \dots, \mathbf{x}_p^0) \in \mathrm{int}(\mathrm{dom}(f))$.
General step: for any $k = 0, 1, 2, \dots$ execute the following steps:

- set $\mathbf{x}^{k,0} = \mathbf{x}^k$;

- for $i = 1, 2, \dots, p$, compute

$$\mathbf{x}^{k,i} = \mathbf{x}^{k,i-1} + \mathcal{U}_i(T_{L_i}^i(\mathbf{x}^{k,i-1}) - \mathbf{x}_i^{k,i-1});$$

- set $\mathbf{x}^{k+1} = \mathbf{x}^{k,p}$.

11.4.1 Convergence Analysis of the CBPG Method—The Nonconvex Case

The convergence analysis of the CBPG method relies on the following technical lemma, which is a direct consequence of the sufficient decrease property of Lemma 11.9.

Lemma 11.11 (sufficient decrease of the CBPG method—version I). *Suppose that Assumption 11.1 holds, and let* $\{\mathbf{x}^k\}_{k\geq 0}$ *be the sequence generated by the CBPG method for solving problem (11.1) with the auxiliary sequences defined in (11.8). Then*

(a) *for all* $k \geq 0$ *and* $j \in \{0, 1, \ldots, p-1\}$ *it holds that*

$$F(\mathbf{x}^{k,j}) - F(\mathbf{x}^{k,j+1}) \geq \frac{1}{2L_{j+1}} \|G_{L_{j+1}}^{j+1}(\mathbf{x}^{k,j})\|^2, \tag{11.9}$$

or equivalently,

$$F(\mathbf{x}^{k,j}) - F(\mathbf{x}^{k,j+1}) \geq \frac{L_{j+1}}{2} \|\mathbf{x}^{k,j} - \mathbf{x}^{k,j+1}\|^2; \tag{11.10}$$

(b) *for all* $k \geq 0$,

$$F(\mathbf{x}^k) - F(\mathbf{x}^{k+1}) \geq \frac{L_{\min}}{2} \|\mathbf{x}^k - \mathbf{x}^{k+1}\|^2, \tag{11.11}$$

where $L_{\min} = \min_{i=1,2,\ldots,p} L_i$.

Proof. (a) Inequality (11.9) follows by invoking Lemma 11.9 with $\mathbf{x} = \mathbf{x}^{k,j}$ and $i = j + 1$. The result (11.10) now follows by the identity $\|\mathbf{x}^{k,j} - \mathbf{x}^{k,j+1}\|^2 = \|T_{L_{j+1}}^{j+1}(\mathbf{x}^{k,j}) - \mathbf{x}_{j+1}^k\|^2 = \frac{1}{L_{j+1}^2} \|G_{L_{j+1}}^{j+1}(\mathbf{x}^{k,j})\|^2$.

(b) Summing the inequality (11.10) over $j = 0, 1, \ldots, p-1$, we obtain

$$F(\mathbf{x}^k) - F(\mathbf{x}^{k+1}) = \sum_{j=0}^{p-1}(F(\mathbf{x}^{k,j}) - F(\mathbf{x}^{k,j+1})) \geq \sum_{j=0}^{p-1} \frac{L_{j+1}}{2} \|\mathbf{x}^{k,j} - \mathbf{x}^{k,j+1}\|^2$$

$$= \sum_{j=0}^{p-1} \frac{L_{j+1}}{2} \|\mathbf{x}_{j+1}^k - \mathbf{x}_{j+1}^{k+1}\|^2 \geq \frac{L_{\min}}{2} \sum_{j=0}^{p-1} \|\mathbf{x}_{j+1}^k - \mathbf{x}_{j+1}^{k+1}\|^2$$

$$= \frac{L_{\min}}{2} \|\mathbf{x}^k - \mathbf{x}^{k+1}\|^2. \quad \square$$

A direct result of the last lemma is the monotonicity in function values of the sequence generated by the CBPG method.

Corollary 11.12 (monotonicity of the sequence generated by the CBPG method). *Under the setting of Lemma 11.11, for any* $k \geq 0$, $F(\mathbf{x}^{k+1}) \leq F(\mathbf{x}^k)$, *and equality holds if and only if* $\mathbf{x}^k = \mathbf{x}^{k+1}$.

We can now prove a sufficient decrease property of the CBPG method in terms of the (nonpartial) gradient mapping.

Lemma 11.13 (sufficient decrease of the CBPG method—version II). *Suppose that Assumption 11.1 holds, and let $\{\mathbf{x}^k\}_{k\geq 0}$ be the sequence generated by the CBPG method for solving problem (11.1). Then for any $k \geq 0$,*

$$F(\mathbf{x}^k) - F(\mathbf{x}^{k+1}) \geq \frac{C}{p}\|G_{L_{\min}}(\mathbf{x}^k)\|^2, \tag{11.12}$$

where

$$C = \frac{L_{\min}}{2(L_f + 2L_{\max} + \sqrt{L_{\min}L_{\max}})^2} \tag{11.13}$$

and

$$L_{\min} = \min_{i=1,2,\ldots,p} L_i, \; L_{\max} = \max_{i=1,2,\ldots,p} L_i.$$

Proof. Let $i \in \{0, 1, \ldots, p-1\}$. By (11.9),

$$F(\mathbf{x}^k) - F(\mathbf{x}^{k+1}) \geq F(\mathbf{x}^{k,i}) - F(\mathbf{x}^{k,i+1}) \geq \frac{1}{2L_{i+1}}\|G_{L_{i+1}}^{i+1}(\mathbf{x}^{k,i})\|^2. \tag{11.14}$$

We can bound $\|G_{L_{i+1}}^{i+1}(\mathbf{x}^k)\|$ as follows:

$$
\begin{aligned}
\|G_{L_{i+1}}^{i+1}(\mathbf{x}^k)\| &\leq \|G_{L_{i+1}}^{i+1}(\mathbf{x}^k) - G_{L_{i+1}}^{i+1}(\mathbf{x}^{k,i})\| + \|G_{L_{i+1}}^{i+1}(\mathbf{x}^{k,i})\| && \text{[triangle inequality]} \\
&\leq \|G_{L_{i+1}}(\mathbf{x}^k) - G_{L_{i+1}}(\mathbf{x}^{k,i})\| + \|G_{L_{i+1}}^{i+1}(\mathbf{x}^{k,i})\| && \text{[(11.3)]} \\
&\leq (2L_{i+1} + L_f)\|\mathbf{x}^k - \mathbf{x}^{k,i}\| + \|G_{L_{i+1}}^{i+1}(\mathbf{x}^{k,i})\| && \text{[Lemma 10.10(a)]} \\
&\leq (2L_{i+1} + L_f)\|\mathbf{x}^k - \mathbf{x}^{k+1}\| + \|G_{L_{i+1}}^{i+1}(\mathbf{x}^{k,i})\|,
\end{aligned}
$$

where the last inequality follows by the following argument:

$$\|\mathbf{x}^k - \mathbf{x}^{k,i}\| = \sqrt{\sum_{j=1}^{i}\|\mathbf{x}_j^k - \mathbf{x}_j^{k+1}\|^2} \leq \sqrt{\sum_{j=1}^{p}\|\mathbf{x}_j^k - \mathbf{x}_j^{k+1}\|^2} = \|\mathbf{x}^k - \mathbf{x}^{k+1}\|.$$

Using the inequalities (11.11) and (11.14), it follows that we can continue to bound $\|G_{L_{i+1}}^{i+1}(\mathbf{x}^k)\|$ as follows:

$$
\begin{aligned}
\|G_{L_{i+1}}^{i+1}(\mathbf{x}^k)\| \quad &\leq \quad (2L_{i+1} + L_f)\|\mathbf{x}^k - \mathbf{x}^{k+1}\| + \|G_{L_{i+1}}^{i+1}(\mathbf{x}^{k,i})\| \\
&\leq \quad \left[\frac{\sqrt{2}(2L_{i+1} + L_f)}{\sqrt{L_{\min}}} + \sqrt{2L_{i+1}}\right]\sqrt{F(\mathbf{x}^k) - F(\mathbf{x}^{k+1})} \\
&\overset{L_{i+1} \leq L_{\max}}{\leq} \quad \sqrt{\frac{2}{L_{\min}}}(L_f + 2L_{\max} + \sqrt{L_{\min}L_{\max}})\sqrt{F(\mathbf{x}^k) - F(\mathbf{x}^{k+1})}.
\end{aligned}
$$

By the monotonicity of the partial gradient mapping (Theorem 11.7), it follows that $\|G_{L_{\min}}^{i+1}(\mathbf{x}^k)\| \leq \|G_{L_{i+1}}^{i+1}(\mathbf{x}^k)\|$, and hence, for any $i \in \{0, 1, \ldots, p-1\}$,

$$F(\mathbf{x}^k) - F(\mathbf{x}^{k+1}) \geq C\|G_{L_{\min}}^{i+1}(\mathbf{x}^k)\|^2,$$

where C is given in (11.13). We can thus conclude that

$$\|G_{L_{\min}}(\mathbf{x}^k)\|^2 = \sum_{i=0}^{p-1} \|G_{L_{\min}}^{i+1}(\mathbf{x}^k)\|^2 \leq \sum_{i=0}^{p-1} \frac{F(\mathbf{x}^k) - F(\mathbf{x}^{k+1})}{C} = \frac{p}{C}(F(\mathbf{x}^k) - F(\mathbf{x}^{k+1})),$$

which is the same as (11.12). $\square$

Equipped with Lemma 11.13, it is easy to show some standard convergence properties of the CBPG method.

Theorem 11.14 (convergence of the CBPG method—nonconvex case).
Suppose that Assumption 11.1 holds, and let $\{\mathbf{x}^k\}_{k \geq 0}$ be the sequence generated by the CBPG method for solving problem (11.1). Denote

$$L_{\min} = \min_{i=1,2,\ldots,p} L_i, \ L_{\max} = \max_{i=1,2,\ldots,p} L_i,$$

and let C be given in (11.13). Then

(a) $G_{L_{\min}}(\mathbf{x}^k) \to \mathbf{0}$ *as $k \to \infty$;*

(b) $\min_{n=0,1,\ldots,k} \|G_{L_{\min}}(\mathbf{x}^n)\| \leq \dfrac{\sqrt{p(F(\mathbf{x}^0) - F_{\mathrm{opt}})}}{\sqrt{C(k+1)}}$;

(c) *all limit points of the sequence $\{\mathbf{x}^k\}_{k \geq 0}$ are stationary points of problem (11.1).*

Proof. (a) Since the sequence $\{F(\mathbf{x}^k)\}_{k \geq 0}$ is nonincreasing (Corollary 11.12) and bounded below (by Assumption 11.1(E)), it converges. Thus, in particular $F(\mathbf{x}^k) - F(\mathbf{x}^{k+1}) \to 0$ as $k \to \infty$, which, combined with (11.12), implies that $\|G_{L_{\min}}(\mathbf{x}^k)\| \to 0$ as $k \to \infty$.

(b) By Lemma 11.13, for any $n \geq 0$,

$$F(\mathbf{x}^n) - F(\mathbf{x}^{n+1}) \geq \frac{C}{p}\|G_{L_{\min}}(\mathbf{x}^n)\|^2. \tag{11.15}$$

Summing the above inequality over $n = 0, 1, \ldots, k$, we obtain

$$F(\mathbf{x}^0) - F(\mathbf{x}^{k+1}) \geq \frac{C}{p}\sum_{n=0}^{k} \|G_{L_{\min}}(\mathbf{x}^n)\|^2 \geq \frac{C(k+1)}{p} \min_{n=0,1,\ldots,k} \|G_{L_{\min}}(\mathbf{x}^n)\|^2.$$

Using the fact that $F(\mathbf{x}^{k+1}) \geq F_{\mathrm{opt}}$, the result follows.

(c) Let $\bar{\mathbf{x}}$ be a limit point of $\{\mathbf{x}^k\}_{k \geq 0}$. Then there exists a subsequence $\{\mathbf{x}^{k_j}\}_{j \geq 0}$ converging to $\bar{\mathbf{x}}$. For any $j \geq 0$,

$$\|G_{L_{\min}}(\bar{\mathbf{x}})\| \leq \|G_{L_{\min}}(\mathbf{x}^{k_j}) - G_{L_{\min}}(\bar{\mathbf{x}})\| + \|G_{L_{\min}}(\mathbf{x}^{k_j})\|$$
$$\leq (2L_{\min} + L_f)\|\mathbf{x}^{k_j} - \bar{\mathbf{x}}\| + \|G_{L_{\min}}(\mathbf{x}^{k_j})\|, \tag{11.16}$$

where Lemma 10.10(a) was used in the last inequality. Since the expression in (11.16) goes to 0 as $j \to \infty$, it follows that $G_{L_{\min}}(\bar{\mathbf{x}}) = \mathbf{0}$, which, by Theorem 10.7(b), implies that $\bar{\mathbf{x}}$ is a stationary point of problem (11.1). $\square$

11.4.2   Convergence Analysis of the CBPG Method—The Convex Case[64]

We will now show a rate of convergence in function values of the CBPG method in the case where f is assumed to be convex and a certain boundedness property of the level sets of F holds.

Assumption 11.15.

(A) f is convex.

(B) For any $\alpha > 0$, there exists $R_\alpha > 0$ such that

$$\max_{\mathbf{x},\mathbf{x}^* \in \mathbb{E}} \{\|\mathbf{x} - \mathbf{x}^*\| : F(\mathbf{x}) \leq \alpha, \mathbf{x}^* \in X^*\} \leq R_\alpha.$$

The analysis in the convex case is based on the following key lemma describing a recursive inequality relation of the sequence of function values.

Lemma 11.16. *Suppose that Assumptions 11.1 and 11.15 hold. Let $\{\mathbf{x}^k\}_{k\geq 0}$ be the sequence generated by the CBPG method for solving problem (11.1). Then for any $k \geq 0$,*

$$F(\mathbf{x}^k) - F(\mathbf{x}^{k+1}) \geq \frac{L_{\min}}{2p(L_f + L_{\max})^2 R^2}(F(\mathbf{x}^{k+1}) - F_{\text{opt}})^2,$$

where $R = R_{F(\mathbf{x}^0)}$, $L_{\max} = \max_{j=1,2,\dots,p} L_j$, and $L_{\min} = \min_{j=1,2,\dots,p} L_j$.

Proof. Let $\mathbf{x}^* \in X^*$. By the definition of the CBPG method, for any $k \geq 0$ and $j \in \{1,2,\dots,p\}$,

$$\mathbf{x}_j^{k,j} = \text{prox}_{\frac{1}{L_j}g_j}\left(\mathbf{x}_j^{k,j-1} - \frac{1}{L_j}\nabla_j f(\mathbf{x}^{k,j-1})\right).$$

Thus, invoking the second prox theorem (Theorem 6.39), for any $\mathbf{y} \in \mathbb{E}_j$,

$$g_j(\mathbf{y}) \geq g_j(\mathbf{x}_j^{k,j}) + L_j\left\langle \mathbf{x}_j^{k,j-1} - \frac{1}{L_j}\nabla_j f(\mathbf{x}^{k,j-1}) - \mathbf{x}_j^{k,j}, \mathbf{y} - \mathbf{x}_j^{k,j}\right\rangle.$$

By the definition of the auxiliary sequences given in (11.8), $\mathbf{x}_j^{k,j-1} = \mathbf{x}_j^k$, $\mathbf{x}_j^{k,j} = \mathbf{x}_j^{k+1}$, and therefore

$$g_j(\mathbf{y}) \geq g_j(\mathbf{x}_j^{k+1}) + L_j\left\langle \mathbf{x}_j^k - \frac{1}{L_j}\nabla_j f(\mathbf{x}^{k,j-1}) - \mathbf{x}_j^{k+1}, \mathbf{y} - \mathbf{x}_j^{k+1}\right\rangle.$$

Thus, in particular, if we substitute $\mathbf{y} = \mathbf{x}_j^*$,

$$g_j(\mathbf{x}_j^*) \geq g_j(\mathbf{x}_j^{k+1}) + L_j\left\langle \mathbf{x}_j^k - \frac{1}{L_j}\nabla_j f(\mathbf{x}^{k,j-1}) - \mathbf{x}_j^{k+1}, \mathbf{x}_j^* - \mathbf{x}_j^{k+1}\right\rangle.$$

---

[64]The type of analysis in Section 11.4.2 originates from Beck and Tetruashvili [22], who studied the case in which the nonsmooth functions are indicators. The extension to the general composite model can be found in Shefi and Teboulle [115] and Hong, Wang, Razaviyayn, and Luo [69].

Summing the above inequality over $j = 1, 2, \ldots, p$ yields the inequality

$$g(\mathbf{x}^*) \geq g(\mathbf{x}^{k+1}) + \sum_{j=1}^{p} L_j \left\langle \mathbf{x}_j^k - \frac{1}{L_j} \nabla_j f(\mathbf{x}^{k,j-1}) - \mathbf{x}_j^{k+1}, \mathbf{x}_j^* - \mathbf{x}_j^{k+1} \right\rangle. \quad (11.17)$$

We can now utilize the convexity of f and write

$$
\begin{aligned}
F(\mathbf{x}^{k+1}) - F(\mathbf{x}^*) &= f(\mathbf{x}^{k+1}) - f(\mathbf{x}^*) + g(\mathbf{x}^{k+1}) - g(\mathbf{x}^*) \\
&\leq \langle \nabla f(\mathbf{x}^{k+1}), \mathbf{x}^{k+1} - \mathbf{x}^* \rangle + g(\mathbf{x}^{k+1}) - g(\mathbf{x}^*) \\
&= \sum_{j=1}^{p} \langle \nabla_j f(\mathbf{x}^{k+1}), \mathbf{x}_j^{k+1} - \mathbf{x}_j^* \rangle + g(\mathbf{x}^{k+1}) - g(\mathbf{x}^*),
\end{aligned}
$$

which, combined with (11.17), implies

$$
\begin{aligned}
F(\mathbf{x}^{k+1}) - F(\mathbf{x}^*) &\leq \sum_{j=1}^{p} \langle \nabla_j f(\mathbf{x}^{k+1}), \mathbf{x}_j^{k+1} - \mathbf{x}_j^* \rangle \\
&\quad + \sum_{j=1}^{p} L_j \left\langle \mathbf{x}_j^k - \frac{1}{L_j} \nabla_j f(\mathbf{x}^{k,j-1}) - \mathbf{x}_j^{k+1}, \mathbf{x}_j^{k+1} - \mathbf{x}_j^* \right\rangle \\
&= \sum_{j=1}^{p} \langle \nabla_j f(\mathbf{x}^{k+1}) - \nabla_j f(\mathbf{x}^{k,j-1}) + L_j(\mathbf{x}_j^k - \mathbf{x}_j^{k+1}), \mathbf{x}_j^{k+1} - \mathbf{x}_j^* \rangle.
\end{aligned}
$$

Using the Cauchy–Schwarz and triangle inequalities, we can conclude that

$$
\begin{aligned}
F(\mathbf{x}^{k+1}) - F(\mathbf{x}^*) &\leq \sum_{j=1}^{p} \left(\|\nabla_j f(\mathbf{x}^{k+1}) - \nabla_j f(\mathbf{x}^{k,j-1})\| + L_j \|\mathbf{x}_j^k - \mathbf{x}_j^{k+1}\| \right) \|\mathbf{x}_j^{k+1} - \mathbf{x}_j^*\| \\
&\leq \sum_{j=1}^{p} \left(\|\nabla f(\mathbf{x}^{k+1}) - \nabla f(\mathbf{x}^{k,j-1})\| + L_j \|\mathbf{x}_j^k - \mathbf{x}_j^{k+1}\| \right) \|\mathbf{x}_j^{k+1} - \mathbf{x}_j^*\| \\
&\leq \sum_{j=1}^{p} \left(L_f \|\mathbf{x}^{k+1} - \mathbf{x}^{k,j-1}\| + L_{\max} \|\mathbf{x}^k - \mathbf{x}^{k+1}\| \right) \|\mathbf{x}_j^{k+1} - \mathbf{x}_j^*\| \\
&\leq (L_f + L_{\max}) \|\mathbf{x}^{k+1} - \mathbf{x}^k\| \sum_{j=1}^{p} \|\mathbf{x}_j^{k+1} - \mathbf{x}_j^*\|.
\end{aligned}
$$

Hence,

$$
\begin{aligned}
(F(\mathbf{x}_{k+1}) - F(\mathbf{x}^*))^2 &\leq (L_f + L_{\max})^2 \|\mathbf{x}^{k+1} - \mathbf{x}^k\|^2 \left(\sum_{j=1}^{p} \|\mathbf{x}_j^{k+1} - \mathbf{x}_j^*\| \right)^2 \\
&\leq p(L_f + L_{\max})^2 \|\mathbf{x}^{k+1} - \mathbf{x}^k\|^2 \sum_{j=1}^{p} \|\mathbf{x}_j^{k+1} - \mathbf{x}_j^*\|^2 \\
&= p(L_f + L_{\max})^2 \|\mathbf{x}^{k+1} - \mathbf{x}^k\|^2 \cdot \|\mathbf{x}^{k+1} - \mathbf{x}^*\|^2 \\
&\leq p(L_f + L_{\max})^2 R_{F(\mathbf{x}^0)}^2 \|\mathbf{x}^{k+1} - \mathbf{x}^k\|^2, \quad (11.18)
\end{aligned}
$$

where the last inequality follows by the monotonicity of the sequence of function values (Corollary 11.12) and Assumption 11.15(B). Combining (11.18) with (11.11), we obtain that

$$F(\mathbf{x}^k) - F(\mathbf{x}^{k+1}) \geq \frac{L_{\min}}{2} \|\mathbf{x}^{k+1} - \mathbf{x}^k\|^2 \geq \frac{L_{\min}}{2p(L_f + L_{\max})^2 R^2} (F(\mathbf{x}^{k+1}) - F(\mathbf{x}^*))^2,$$

where $R = R_{F(\mathbf{x}^0)}$. $\Box$

To derive the rate of convergence in function values, we will use the following lemma on the convergence of nonnegative scalar sequences satisfying a certain recursive inequality relation. The result resembles the one derived in Lemma 10.70, but the recursive inequality is different.

Lemma 11.17. *Let $\{a_k\}_{k \geq 0}$ be a nonnegative sequence of real numbers satisfying*

$$a_k - a_{k+1} \geq \frac{1}{\gamma} a_{k+1}^2, \quad k = 0, 1, \ldots, \tag{11.19}$$

for some $\gamma > 0$. Then for any $n \geq 2$,

$$a_n \leq \max \left\{ \left(\frac{1}{2}\right)^{(n-1)/2} a_0, \frac{4\gamma}{n-1} \right\}. \tag{11.20}$$

In addition, for any $\varepsilon > 0$, if $n \geq 2$ satisfies

$$n \geq \max \left\{ \frac{2}{\log(2)} (\log(a_0) + \log(1/\varepsilon)), \frac{4\gamma}{\varepsilon} \right\} + 1,$$

then $a_n \leq \varepsilon$.

Proof. Let $n \geq 2$. If $a_n = 0$, then (11.20) is trivial. We can thus assume that $a_n > 0$, from which it follows that $a_1, a_2, \ldots, a_{n-1} > 0$. For any $k \in \{0, 1, \ldots, n-1\}$,

$$\frac{1}{a_{k+1}} - \frac{1}{a_k} = \frac{a_k - a_{k+1}}{a_k a_{k+1}} \geq \frac{1}{\gamma} \frac{a_{k+1}}{a_k}. \tag{11.21}$$

For each k, there are two options:

(i) $\frac{a_{k+1}}{a_k} \leq \frac{1}{2}$.

(ii) $\frac{a_{k+1}}{a_k} > \frac{1}{2}$.

By (11.21), under option (ii) we have

$$\frac{1}{a_{k+1}} - \frac{1}{a_k} \geq \frac{1}{2\gamma}.$$

Suppose that n is a positive even integer. If there are at least $\frac{n}{2}$ indices (out of $k = 0, 1, \ldots, n-1$) for which option (ii) occurs, then

$$\frac{1}{a_n} \geq \frac{n}{4\gamma},$$

and hence

$$a_n \leq \frac{4\gamma}{n}.$$

On the other hand, if this is not the case, then there are at least $\frac{n}{2}$ indices for which option (i) occurs, and consequently

$$a_n \leq \left(\frac{1}{2}\right)^{n/2} a_0.$$

We therefore obtain that in any case, for an even n,

$$a_n \leq \max\left\{ \left(\frac{1}{2}\right)^{n/2} a_0, \frac{4\gamma}{n} \right\}. \tag{11.22}$$

If $n \geq 3$ is a positive odd integer, then

$$a_n \leq a_{n-1} \leq \max\left\{ \left(\frac{1}{2}\right)^{(n-1)/2} a_0, \frac{4\gamma}{n-1} \right\}. \tag{11.23}$$

Since the right-hand side of (11.23) is larger than the right-hand side of (11.22), the result (11.20) follows. Let $n \geq 2$. To guarantee that the inequality $a_n \leq \varepsilon$ holds, it is sufficient that the inequality

$$\max\left\{ \left(\frac{1}{2}\right)^{(n-1)/2} a_0, \frac{4\gamma}{n-1} \right\} \leq \varepsilon$$

will hold, meaning that the following two inequalities will be satisfied:

$$\left(\frac{1}{2}\right)^{(n-1)/2} a_0 \leq \varepsilon, \quad \frac{4\gamma}{n-1} \leq \varepsilon.$$

These inequalities are obviously equivalent to

$$n \geq \frac{2}{\log(2)}(\log(a_0) + \log(1/\varepsilon)) + 1, \quad n \geq \frac{4\gamma}{\varepsilon} + 1.$$

Therefore, if

$$n \geq \max\left\{ \frac{2}{\log(2)}(\log(a_0) + \log(1/\varepsilon)), \frac{4\gamma}{\varepsilon} \right\} + 1,$$

then the inequality $a_n \leq \varepsilon$ is guaranteed. $\quad\square$

Combining Lemmas 11.16 and 11.17, we can establish an $O(1/k)$ rate of convergence in function values of the sequence generated by the CBPG method, as well as a complexity result.

Theorem 11.18 ($O(1/k)$ rate of convergence of CBPG). *Suppose that Assumptions 11.1 and 11.15 hold. Let $\{\mathbf{x}^k\}_{k\geq 0}$ be the sequence generated by the CBPG method for solving problem (11.1). For any $k \geq 2$,*

$$F(\mathbf{x}^k) - F_{\mathrm{opt}} \leq \max\left\{ \left(\frac{1}{2}\right)^{(k-1)/2} (F(\mathbf{x}^0) - F_{\mathrm{opt}}), \frac{8p(L_f + L_{\max})^2 R^2}{L_{\min}(k-1)} \right\}, \tag{11.24}$$

where $L_{\min} = \min_{i=1,2,\dots,p} L_i$, $L_{\max} = \max_{i=1,2,\dots,p} L_i$, *and* $R = R_{F(\mathbf{x}^0)}$. *In addition, if* $n \geq 2$ *satisfies*

$$n \geq \max\left\{\frac{2}{\log(2)}(\log(F(\mathbf{x}^0) - F_{\mathrm{opt}}) + \log(1/\varepsilon)), \frac{8p(L_f + L_{\max})^2 R^2}{L_{\min}\varepsilon}\right\} + 1,$$

then $F(\mathbf{x}^n) - F_{\mathrm{opt}} \leq \varepsilon$.

Proof. Denote $a_k = F(\mathbf{x}^k) - F_{\mathrm{opt}}$. Then by Lemma 11.16,

$$a_k - a_{k+1} \geq \frac{1}{D}a_{k+1}^2,$$

where $D = \frac{2p(L_f + L_{\max})^2 R^2}{L_{\min}}$. The result now follows by invoking Lemma 11.17 with $\gamma = D$. $\square$

Remark 11.19 (index order). *The analysis of the CBPG method was done under the assumption that the index selection strategy is cyclic. However, it is easy to see that the same analysis, and consequently the main results (Theorems 11.14 and 11.18), hold for any index selection strategy in which each block is updated exactly once between consecutive iterations. One example of such an index selection strategy is the "cyclic shuffle" order in which the order of blocks is picked at the beginning of each iteration by a random permutation; in a sense, this is a "quasi-randomized" strategy. In the next section we will study a fully randomized approach.*

We end this section by showing that for convex differentiable functions (over the entire space) block Lipschitz continuity (Assumption 11.1(D)) implies that the function is L-smooth (Assumption 11.1(C)) with L being the sum of the block Lipschitz constants. This means that in this situation we can actually drop Assumption 11.1(C).

Theorem 11.20.[65] *Let* $\phi : \mathbb{E} \rightarrow \mathbb{R}$ *(*$\mathbb{E} = \mathbb{E}_1 \times \mathbb{E}_2 \times \cdots \times \mathbb{E}_p$*) be a convex function satisfying the following assumptions:*

(A) *ϕ is differentiable over $\mathbb{E}$;*

(B) *there exist $L_1, L_2, \dots, L_p > 0$ such that for any $i \in \{1, 2, \dots, p\}$ it holds that*

$$\|\nabla_i \phi(\mathbf{x}) - \nabla_i \phi(\mathbf{x} + \mathcal{U}_i(\mathbf{d}))\| \leq L_i \|\mathbf{d}\|$$

for all $\mathbf{x} \in \mathbb{E}$ and $\mathbf{d} \in \mathbb{E}_i$.

Then ϕ is L-smooth with $L = L_1 + L_2 + \cdots + L_p$.

Proof. Let $\mathbf{y} \in \mathbb{E}$. Define the function

$$f(\mathbf{x}) = \phi(\mathbf{x}) - \phi(\mathbf{y}) - \langle \nabla \phi(\mathbf{y}), \mathbf{x} - \mathbf{y} \rangle. \tag{11.25}$$

Then it is immediate to show that f also satisfies properties (A) and (B). In addition, the convexity of ϕ implies the convexity of f as well as the fact that f is nonnegative.

---

[65]Theorem 11.20 is a specialization of Lemma 2 from Nesterov [96].

Invoking Lemma 11.9 with $g_1 = g_2 = \cdots = g_p \equiv 0$, we obtain that for all $i \in \{1, 2, \ldots, p\}$ and $\mathbf{x} \in \mathbb{E}$,

$$f(\mathbf{x}) - f\left(\mathbf{x} - \frac{1}{L_i}\mathcal{U}_i(\nabla_i f(\mathbf{x}))\right) \geq \frac{1}{2L_i}\|\nabla_i f(\mathbf{x})\|^2,$$

which, along with the nonnegativity of f, implies that

$$f(\mathbf{x}) \geq \frac{1}{2L_i}\|\nabla_i f(\mathbf{x})\|^2.$$

Since the last inequality holds for any $i \in \{1, 2, \ldots, p\}$, it follows that

$$f(\mathbf{x}) \geq \max_{i=1,2,\ldots,p}\left\{\frac{1}{2L_i}\|\nabla_i f(\mathbf{x})\|^2\right\} \geq \sum_{i=1}^{p} \frac{L_i}{\sum_{j=1}^{p} L_j} \frac{1}{2L_i}\|\nabla_i f(\mathbf{x})\|^2$$

$$= \frac{1}{2(\sum_{j=1}^{p} L_j)}\|\nabla f(\mathbf{x})\|^2.$$

Plugging the expression (11.25) for f into the above inequality, we obtain

$$\phi(\mathbf{x}) \geq \phi(\mathbf{y}) + \langle\nabla\phi(\mathbf{y}), \mathbf{x} - \mathbf{y}\rangle + \frac{1}{2(\sum_{j=1}^{p} L_j)}\|\nabla\phi(\mathbf{x}) - \nabla\phi(\mathbf{y})\|^2.$$

Since the above inequality holds for any $\mathbf{x}, \mathbf{y} \in \mathbb{E}$, it follows by Theorem 5.8 (equivalence between (i) and (iii)) that ϕ is $(L_1 + L_2 + \cdots + L_p)$-smooth. □

11.5 The Randomized Block Proximal Gradient Method[66]

In this section we will analyze a version of the block proximal gradient method in which at each iteration a prox-grad step is performed at a randomly chosen block. The analysis is made under Assumption 11.21 given below. Note that at this point we do not assume that f is convex, but the main convergence result, Theorem 11.25, will require the convexity of f.

Assumption 11.21.

(A) $g_i : \mathbb{E}_i \to (-\infty, \infty]$ *is proper closed and convex for any* $i \in \{1, 2, \ldots, p\}$.

(B) $f : \mathbb{E} \to (-\infty, \infty]$ *is proper closed and convex,* $\mathrm{dom}(g) \subseteq \mathrm{int}(\mathrm{dom}(f))$, *and* f *is differentiable over* $\mathrm{int}(\mathrm{dom}(f))$.

(C) *There exist* $L_1, L_2, \ldots, L_p > 0$ *such that for any* $i \in \{1, 2, \ldots, p\}$ *it holds that*

$$\|\nabla_i f(\mathbf{x}) - \nabla_i f(\mathbf{x} + \mathcal{U}_i(\mathbf{d}))\| \leq L_i\|\mathbf{d}\|$$

for all $\mathbf{x} \in \mathrm{int}(\mathrm{dom}(f))$ *and* $\mathbf{d} \in \mathbb{E}_i$ *for which* $\mathbf{x} + \mathcal{U}_i(\mathbf{d}) \in \mathrm{int}(\mathrm{dom}(f))$.

---

[66]The derivation of the randomized complexity result in Section 11.5 mostly follows the presentation in the work of Lin, Lu, and Xiao [82].

(D) *The optimal set of problem* (11.1) *is nonempty and denoted by* X^**. The optimal value is denoted by* F_{opt}*.*

The Randomized Block Proximal Gradient (RBPG) Method

Initialization: pick $\mathbf{x}^0 = (\mathbf{x}_1^0, \mathbf{x}_2^0, \ldots, \mathbf{x}_p^0) \in \mathrm{int}(\mathrm{dom}(f))$.
General step: for any $k = 0, 1, 2, \ldots$ execute the following steps:

(a) pick $i_k \in \{1, 2, \ldots, p\}$ randomly via a uniform distribution;

(b) $\mathbf{x}^{k+1} = \mathbf{x}^k + \mathcal{U}_{i_k}(T_{L_{i_k}}^{i_k}(\mathbf{x}^k) - \mathbf{x}_{i_k}^k)$.

Remark 11.22. *Step* (b) *of the algorithm can also be written as*

$$\mathbf{x}^{k+1} = \mathbf{x}^k - \frac{1}{L_{i_k}}\mathcal{U}_{i_k}(G_{L_{i_k}}^{i_k}(\mathbf{x}^k)).$$

From the point of view of computational complexity, loosely speaking, each p iterations of the RBPG method are comparable to one iteration of the CBPG method.

Using the block sufficient decrease lemma (Lemma 11.9), it is easy to show a sufficient decrease property of the RBPG method.

Theorem 11.23 (sufficient decrease of the RBPG method). *Suppose that Assumption 11.21 holds, and let* $\{\mathbf{x}^k\}_{k\geq 0}$ *be the sequence generated by the RBPG method. Then for any* $k \geq 0$,

$$F(\mathbf{x}^k) - F(\mathbf{x}^{k+1}) \geq \frac{1}{2L_{i_k}}\|G_{L_{i_k}}^{i_k}(\mathbf{x}^k)\|^2.$$

Proof. Invoke Lemma 11.9 with $\mathbf{x} = \mathbf{x}^k$ and $i = i_k$. □

Remark 11.24. *A direct consequence of Theorem* 11.23 *is that the sequence of function values* $\{F(\mathbf{x}^k)\}_{k\geq 0}$ *generated by the RBPG method is nonincreasing. As a result, it is also correct that the sequence of expected function values*

$$\{\mathsf{E}_{i_0,\ldots,i_{k-1}}(F(\mathbf{x}^k))\}_{k\geq 0}$$

is nonincreasing.

In our analysis the following notation is used:

- $\xi_{k-1} \equiv \{i_0, i_1, \ldots, i_{k-1}\}$ is a multivariate random variable.

- In addition to the underlying Euclidean norm of the space $\mathbb{E}$, we define the following weighted norm:

$$\|\mathbf{x}\|_L \equiv \sqrt{\sum_{i=1}^{p} L_i \|\mathbf{x}_i\|^2}$$

and its dual norm

$$\|\mathbf{x}\|_{L,*} = \sqrt{\sum_{i=1}^{p} \frac{1}{L_i} \|\mathbf{x}_i\|^2}.$$

- We will consider the following variation of the gradient mapping:

$$\widetilde{G}(\mathbf{x}) = (G^1_{L_1}(\mathbf{x}^k), G^2_{L_2}(\mathbf{x}^k), \dots, G^p_{L_p}(\mathbf{x}^k)). \tag{11.26}$$

Obviously, if $L_1 = L_2 = \cdots = L_p = L$, then $\widetilde{G}(\mathbf{x}) = G_L(\mathbf{x})$.

The main convergence result will now be stated and proved.

Theorem 11.25 ($O(1/k)$ rate of convergence of the RBPG method). *Suppose that Assumption 11.21 holds and that f is convex. Let $\{\mathbf{x}^k\}_{k \geq 0}$ be the sequence generated by the RBPG method for solving problem (11.1). Let $\mathbf{x}^* \in X^*$. Then for any $k \geq 0$,*

$$\mathsf{E}_{\xi_k}(F(\mathbf{x}^{k+1})) - F_{\text{opt}} \leq \frac{p}{p+k+1} \left(\frac{1}{2} \|\mathbf{x}^0 - \mathbf{x}^*\|_L^2 + F(\mathbf{x}^0) - F_{\text{opt}} \right). \tag{11.27}$$

Proof. Let $\mathbf{x}^* \in X^*$. We denote for any $n \geq 0$, $r_n \equiv \|\mathbf{x}^n - \mathbf{x}^*\|_L$. Then for any $k \geq 0$,

$$
\begin{aligned}
r_{k+1}^2 &= \|\mathbf{x}^{k+1} - \mathbf{x}^*\|_L^2 \\
&= \left\| \mathbf{x}^k - \frac{1}{L_{i_k}} U_{i_k}\left(G^{i_k}_{L_{i_k}}(\mathbf{x}^k) \right) - \mathbf{x}^* \right\|_L^2 \\
&= \|\mathbf{x}^k - \mathbf{x}^*\|_L^2 - \frac{2}{L_{i_k}} L_{i_k} \langle G^{i_k}_{L_{i_k}}(\mathbf{x}^k), \mathbf{x}^k_{i_k} - \mathbf{x}^*_{i_k} \rangle + \frac{L_{i_k}}{L_{i_k}^2} \|G^{i_k}_{L_{i_k}}(\mathbf{x}^k)\|^2 \\
&= \|\mathbf{x}^k - \mathbf{x}^*\|_L^2 - 2\langle G^{i_k}_{L_{i_k}}(\mathbf{x}^k), \mathbf{x}^k_{i_k} - \mathbf{x}^*_{i_k} \rangle + \frac{1}{L_{i_k}} \|G^{i_k}_{L_{i_k}}(\mathbf{x}^k)\|^2 \\
&= r_k^2 - 2\langle G^{i_k}_{L_{i_k}}(\mathbf{x}^k), \mathbf{x}^k_{i_k} - \mathbf{x}^*_{i_k} \rangle + \frac{1}{L_{i_k}} \|G^{i_k}_{L_{i_k}}(\mathbf{x}^k)\|^2.
\end{aligned}
$$

Taking expectation w.r.t. i_k, we obtain (using the notation (11.26))

$$
\begin{aligned}
\mathsf{E}_{i_k}\left(\frac{1}{2} r_{k+1}^2 \right) &= \frac{1}{2} r_k^2 - \frac{1}{p} \sum_{i=1}^{p} \langle G^i_{L_i}(\mathbf{x}_k), \mathbf{x}^k_i - \mathbf{x}^*_i \rangle + \frac{1}{2p} \sum_{i=1}^{p} \frac{1}{L_i} \|G^i_{L_i}(\mathbf{x}^k)\|^2 \\
&= \frac{1}{2} r_k^2 - \frac{1}{p} \langle \widetilde{G}(\mathbf{x}^k), \mathbf{x}^k - \mathbf{x}^* \rangle + \frac{1}{2p} \|\widetilde{G}(\mathbf{x}^k)\|_{L,*}^2. \tag{11.28}
\end{aligned}
$$

By the block descent lemma (Lemma 11.8),

$$
f(\mathbf{x}^{k+1}) = f\left(\mathbf{x}^k - \frac{1}{L_{i_k}}\mathcal{U}_{i_k}(G^{i_k}_{L_{i_k}}(\mathbf{x}^k))\right)
$$
$$
\leq f(\mathbf{x}^k) - \frac{1}{L_{i_k}}\langle \nabla_{i_k} f(\mathbf{x}^k), G^{i_k}_{L_{i_k}}(\mathbf{x}^k)\rangle + \frac{1}{2L_{i_k}}\|G^{i_k}_{L_{i_k}}(\mathbf{x}^k)\|^2.
$$

Hence,

$$
F(\mathbf{x}^{k+1}) \leq f(\mathbf{x}^k) - \frac{1}{L_{i_k}}\langle \nabla_{i_k} f(\mathbf{x}^k), G^{i_k}_{L_{i_k}}(\mathbf{x}^k)\rangle + \frac{1}{2L_{i_k}}\|G^{i_k}_{L_{i_k}}(\mathbf{x}^k)\|^2 + g(\mathbf{x}^{k+1}).
$$

Taking expectation of both sides of the last inequality w.r.t. i_k, we obtain

$$
\mathsf{E}_{i_k}(F(\mathbf{x}^{k+1})) \leq f(\mathbf{x}^k) - \frac{1}{p}\sum_{i=1}^{p}\frac{1}{L_i}\langle \nabla_i f(\mathbf{x}^k), G^i_{L_i}(\mathbf{x}^k)\rangle + \frac{1}{2p}\|\widetilde{G}(\mathbf{x}^k)\|^2_{L,*} + \mathsf{E}_{i_k}(g(\mathbf{x}^{k+1})).
$$
$$
(11.29)
$$

Since $\mathbf{x}^{k+1}_{i_k} = \mathbf{x}^k_{i_k} - \frac{1}{L_{i_k}}G^{i_k}_{L_{i_k}}(\mathbf{x}^k) = \mathrm{prox}_{\frac{1}{L_{i_k}}g_{i_k}}\left(\mathbf{x}^k_{i_k} - \frac{1}{L_{i_k}}\nabla_{i_k} f(\mathbf{x}^k)\right)$, it follows by the second prox theorem (Theorem 6.39) that

$$
g_{i_k}(\mathbf{x}^*_{i_k}) \geq g_{i_k}\left(\mathbf{x}^k_{i_k} - \frac{1}{L_{i_k}}G^{i_k}_{L_{i_k}}(\mathbf{x}^k)\right)
$$
$$
+ L_{i_k}\left\langle \mathbf{x}^k_{i_k} - \frac{1}{L_{i_k}}\nabla_{i_k} f(\mathbf{x}^k) - \mathbf{x}^k_{i_k} + \frac{1}{L_{i_k}}G^{i_k}_{L_{i_k}}(\mathbf{x}^k), \mathbf{x}^*_{i_k} - \mathbf{x}^k_{i_k} + \frac{1}{L_{i_k}}G^{i_k}_{L_{i_k}}(\mathbf{x}^k)\right\rangle.
$$

That is,

$$
g_{i_k}(\mathbf{x}^*_{i_k}) \geq g_{i_k}\left(\mathbf{x}^k_{i_k} - \frac{1}{L_{i_k}}G^{i_k}_{L_{i_k}}(\mathbf{x}^k)\right)
$$
$$
+ \left\langle -\nabla_{i_k} f(\mathbf{x}^k) + G^{i_k}_{L_{i_k}}(\mathbf{x}^k), \mathbf{x}^*_{i_k} - \mathbf{x}^k_{i_k} + \frac{1}{L_{i_k}}G^{i_k}_{L_{i_k}}(\mathbf{x}^k)\right\rangle. \quad (11.30)
$$

Note that

$$
\mathsf{E}_{i_k}(g_{i_k}(\mathbf{x}^*_{i_k})) = \frac{1}{p}g(\mathbf{x}^*), \qquad\qquad\qquad\qquad\qquad (11.31)
$$

$$
\mathsf{E}_{i_k}(g(\mathbf{x}^{k+1})) = \frac{p-1}{p}g(\mathbf{x}^k) + \frac{1}{p}\sum_{i=1}^{p}g_i\left(\mathbf{x}^k_i - \frac{1}{L_i}G^i_{L_i}(\mathbf{x}^k)\right). \quad (11.32)
$$

Taking expectation w.r.t. i_k in (11.30) and plugging in the relations (11.31) and (11.32) leads to the following inequality:

$$
\frac{1}{p}g(\mathbf{x}^*) \geq \mathsf{E}_{i_k}(g(\mathbf{x}^{k+1})) - \frac{p-1}{p}g(\mathbf{x}^k) + \frac{1}{p}\langle -\nabla f(\mathbf{x}^k) + \widetilde{G}(\mathbf{x}^k), \mathbf{x}^* - \mathbf{x}^k\rangle
$$
$$
- \frac{1}{p}\sum_{i=1}^{p}\frac{1}{L_i}\langle \nabla_i f(\mathbf{x}^k), G^i_{L_i}(\mathbf{x}^k)\rangle + \frac{1}{p}\|\widetilde{G}(\mathbf{x}^k)\|^2_{L,*}.
$$

The last inequality can be equivalently written as

$$
\mathsf{E}_{i_k}(g(\mathbf{x}^{k+1})) - \frac{1}{p}\sum_{i=1}^{p}\frac{1}{L_i}\langle \nabla_i f(\mathbf{x}^k), G^i_{L_i}(\mathbf{x}^k)\rangle
$$
$$
\leq \frac{1}{p}g(\mathbf{x}^*) + \frac{p-1}{p}g(\mathbf{x}^k) + \frac{1}{p}\langle \nabla f(\mathbf{x}^k) - \widetilde{G}(\mathbf{x}^k), \mathbf{x}^* - \mathbf{x}^k\rangle - \frac{1}{p}\|\widetilde{G}(\mathbf{x}^k)\|^2_{L,*}.
$$

Plugging the last inequality into (11.29) we obtain that

$$\mathsf{E}_{i_k}(F(\mathbf{x}^{k+1})) \leq f(\mathbf{x}^k) - \frac{1}{2p}\|\tilde{G}(\mathbf{x}^k)\|_{L,*}^2 + \frac{1}{p}g(\mathbf{x}^*) + \frac{1}{p}\langle \nabla f(\mathbf{x}^k) - \tilde{G}(\mathbf{x}^k), \mathbf{x}^* - \mathbf{x}^k \rangle$$
$$+ \frac{p-1}{p}g(\mathbf{x}^k),$$

which, along with the gradient inequality $\langle \nabla f(\mathbf{x}^k), \mathbf{x}^* - \mathbf{x}^k \rangle \leq f(\mathbf{x}^*) - f(\mathbf{x}^k)$, implies

$$\mathsf{E}_{i_k}(F(\mathbf{x}^{k+1})) \leq \frac{p-1}{p}F(\mathbf{x}^k) + \frac{1}{p}F(\mathbf{x}^*) - \frac{1}{2p}\|\tilde{G}(\mathbf{x}^k)\|_{L,*}^2 - \frac{1}{p}\langle \tilde{G}(\mathbf{x}^k), \mathbf{x}^* - \mathbf{x}^k \rangle.$$

The last inequality, combined with (11.28), yields the relation

$$\mathsf{E}_{i_k}\left(\frac{1}{2}r_{k+1}^2\right) \leq \frac{1}{2}r_k^2 + \frac{p-1}{p}F(\mathbf{x}^k) + \frac{1}{p}F(\mathbf{x}^*) - \mathsf{E}_{i_k}(F(\mathbf{x}^{k+1})),$$

which can be rearranged as

$$\mathsf{E}_{i_k}\left(\frac{1}{2}r_{k+1}^2 + F(\mathbf{x}^{k+1}) - F_{\text{opt}}\right) \leq \left(\frac{1}{2}r_k^2 + F(\mathbf{x}^k) - F_{\text{opt}}\right) - \frac{1}{p}(F(\mathbf{x}^k) - F_{\text{opt}}).$$

Taking expectation over ξ_{k-1} of both sides we obtain (where we make the convention that the expression $\mathbb{E}_{\xi_{-1}}(F(\mathbf{x}^0))$ means $F(\mathbf{x}^0)$)

$$\mathsf{E}_{\xi_k}\left(\frac{1}{2}r_{k+1}^2 + F(\mathbf{x}^{k+1}) - F_{\text{opt}}\right) \leq \mathsf{E}_{\xi_{k-1}}\left(\frac{1}{2}r_k^2 + F(\mathbf{x}^k) - F_{\text{opt}}\right)$$
$$- \frac{1}{p}(\mathsf{E}_{\xi_{k-1}}(F(\mathbf{x}^k)) - F_{\text{opt}}).$$

We can thus conclude that

$$\mathsf{E}_{\xi_k}(F(\mathbf{x}^{k+1})) - F_{\text{opt}} \leq \mathsf{E}_{\xi_k}\left(\frac{1}{2}r_{k+1}^2 + F(\mathbf{x}^{k+1}) - F_{\text{opt}}\right)$$
$$\leq \frac{1}{2}r_0^2 + F(\mathbf{x}^0) - F_{\text{opt}} - \frac{1}{p}\sum_{j=0}^{k}\left(\mathsf{E}_{\xi_{j-1}}(F(\mathbf{x}^j)) - F_{\text{opt}}\right),$$

which, together with the monotonicity of the sequence of expected values $\{\mathsf{E}_{\xi_{k-1}}(F(\mathbf{x}^k))\}_{k\geq 0}$ (see Remark 11.24), implies that

$$\mathsf{E}_{\xi_k}(F(\mathbf{x}^{k+1})) - F_{\text{opt}} \leq \frac{1}{2}r_0^2 + F(\mathbf{x}^0) - F_{\text{opt}} - \frac{k+1}{p}\left(\mathsf{E}_{\xi_k}(F(\mathbf{x}^{k+1})) - F_{\text{opt}}\right). \quad (11.33)$$

The desired result (11.27) follows immediately from (11.33). $\quad\square$

Chapter 12

Dual-Based Proximal Gradient Methods

Underlying Spaces: In this chapter, all the underlying spaces are Euclidean.

12.1 The Primal and Dual Models

The main model discussed in this chapter is

$$f_{\text{opt}} = \min_{\mathbf{x} \in \mathbb{E}} \{f(\mathbf{x}) + g(\mathcal{A}(\mathbf{x}))\}, \tag{12.1}$$

where the following assumptions are made.

Assumption 12.1.

(A) $f : \mathbb{E} \to (-\infty, +\infty]$ *is proper closed and σ-strongly convex ($\sigma > 0$).*

(B) $g : \mathbb{V} \to (-\infty, +\infty]$ *is proper closed and convex.*

(C) $\mathcal{A} : \mathbb{E} \to \mathbb{V}$ *is a linear transformation.*

(D) *There exists $\hat{\mathbf{x}} \in \text{ri}(\text{dom}(f))$ and $\hat{\mathbf{z}} \in \text{ri}(\text{dom}(g))$ such that $\mathcal{A}(\hat{\mathbf{x}}) = \hat{\mathbf{z}}$.*

Under Assumption 12.1 the function $\mathbf{x} \mapsto f(\mathbf{x}) + g(\mathcal{A}(\mathbf{x}))$ is proper closed and σ-strongly convex, and hence, by Theorem 5.25(a), problem (12.1) has a unique optimal solution, which we denote throughout this chapter by $\mathbf{x}^*$.

To construct a dual problem to (12.1), we first rewrite it in the form

$$\begin{aligned} \min_{\mathbf{x},\mathbf{z}} \quad & f(\mathbf{x}) + g(\mathbf{z}) \\ \text{s.t.} \quad & \mathcal{A}(\mathbf{x}) - \mathbf{z} = \mathbf{0}. \end{aligned} \tag{12.2}$$

Associating a Lagrange dual vector $\mathbf{y} \in \mathbb{V}$ to the equality constraints in (12.2), the Lagrangian can be written as

$$L(\mathbf{x}, \mathbf{z}; \mathbf{y}) = f(\mathbf{x}) + g(\mathbf{z}) - \langle \mathbf{y}, \mathcal{A}(\mathbf{x}) - \mathbf{z} \rangle = f(\mathbf{x}) + g(\mathbf{z}) - \langle \mathcal{A}^T(\mathbf{y}), \mathbf{x} \rangle + \langle \mathbf{y}, \mathbf{z} \rangle. \tag{12.3}$$

Minimizing the Lagrangian w.r.t. $\mathbf{x}$ and $\mathbf{z}$, the obtained dual problem is

$$q_{\text{opt}} = \max_{\mathbf{y} \in \mathbb{V}} \left\{ q(\mathbf{y}) \equiv -f^*(\mathcal{A}^T(\mathbf{y})) - g^*(-\mathbf{y}) \right\}. \tag{12.4}$$

By the strong duality theorem for convex problems (see Theorem A.1), it follows that strong duality holds for the pair of problems (12.1) and (12.4).

Theorem 12.2 (strong duality for the pair of problems (12.1) and (12.4)).
Suppose that Assumption 12.1 holds, and let $f_{\text{opt}}, q_{\text{opt}}$ be the optimal values of the primal and dual problems (12.1) and (12.4), respectively. Then $f_{\text{opt}} = q_{\text{opt}}$, and the dual problem (12.4) possesses an optimal solution.

We will consider the dual problem in its minimization form:

$$\min_{\mathbf{y} \in \mathbb{V}} \{ F(\mathbf{y}) + G(\mathbf{y}) \}, \tag{12.5}$$

where

$$F(\mathbf{y}) \equiv f^*(\mathcal{A}^T(\mathbf{y})), \tag{12.6}$$
$$G(\mathbf{y}) \equiv g^*(-\mathbf{y}). \tag{12.7}$$

The basic properties of F and G are gathered in the following lemma.

Lemma 12.3 (properties of F and G). *Suppose that Assumption 12.1 holds, and let F and G be defined by (12.6) and (12.7), respectively. Then*

(a) *$F : \mathbb{V} \to \mathbb{R}$ is convex and L_F-smooth with $L_F = \frac{\|\mathcal{A}\|^2}{\sigma}$;*

(b) *$G : \mathbb{V} \to (-\infty, \infty]$ is proper closed and convex.*

Proof. (a) Since f is proper closed and σ-strongly convex, then by the conjugate correspondence theorem (Theorem 5.26(b)), f^* is $\frac{1}{\sigma}$-smooth. Therefore, for any $\mathbf{y}_1, \mathbf{y}_2 \in \mathbb{V}$,

$$
\begin{aligned}
\|\nabla F(\mathbf{y}_1) - \nabla F(\mathbf{y}_2)\| &= \|\mathcal{A}(\nabla f^*(\mathcal{A}^T(\mathbf{y}_1))) - \mathcal{A}(\nabla f^*(\mathcal{A}^T(\mathbf{y}_2)))\| \\
&\le \|\mathcal{A}\| \cdot \|\nabla f^*(\mathcal{A}^T(\mathbf{y}_1)) - \nabla f^*(\mathcal{A}^T(\mathbf{y}_2))\| \\
&\le \frac{1}{\sigma}\|\mathcal{A}\| \cdot \|\mathcal{A}^T(\mathbf{y}_1) - \mathcal{A}^T(\mathbf{y}_2)\| \\
&\le \frac{\|\mathcal{A}\| \cdot \|\mathcal{A}^T\|}{\sigma}\|\mathbf{y}_1 - \mathbf{y}_2\| = \frac{\|\mathcal{A}\|^2}{\sigma}\|\mathbf{y}_1 - \mathbf{y}_2\|,
\end{aligned}
$$

where we used in the last equality the fact that $\|\mathcal{A}\| = \|\mathcal{A}^T\|$ (see Section 1.14). To show the convexity of F, note that f^* is convex as a conjugate function (Theorem 4.3), and hence, by Theorem 2.16, F, as a composition of a convex function and a linear mapping, is convex.

(b) Since g is proper closed and convex, so is g^* (Theorems 4.3 and 4.5). Thus, $G(\mathbf{y}) \equiv g^*(-\mathbf{y})$ is also proper closed and convex. $\square$

12.2 The Dual Proximal Gradient Method[67]

Problem (12.5) consists of minimizing the sum of a convex L-smooth function and a proper closed and convex function. It is therefore possible to employ in this setting the proximal gradient method on problem (12.5), which is equivalent to the dual problem of (12.1). Naturally we will refer to this algorithm as the "dual proximal gradient" (DPG) method. The dual representation of the method is given below.

Dual Proximal Gradient—dual representation

- **Initialization:** pick $\mathbf{y}^0 \in \mathbb{V}$ and $L \geq L_F = \frac{\|\mathcal{A}\|^2}{\sigma}$.

- **General step $(k \geq 0)$:**

$$\mathbf{y}^{k+1} = \operatorname{prox}_{\frac{1}{L}G}\left(\mathbf{y}^k - \frac{1}{L}\nabla F(\mathbf{y}^k)\right). \tag{12.8}$$

Since F is convex and L_F-smooth and G is proper closed and convex, we can invoke Theorem 10.21 to obtain an $O(1/k)$ rate of convergence in terms of the dual objective function values.

Theorem 12.4. *Suppose that Assumption 12.1 holds, and let $\{\mathbf{y}^k\}_{k \geq 0}$ be the sequence generated by the DPG method with $L \geq L_F = \frac{\|\mathcal{A}\|^2}{\sigma}$. Then for any optimal solution $\mathbf{y}^*$ of the dual problem (12.4) and $k \geq 1$,*

$$q_{\mathrm{opt}} - q(\mathbf{y}^k) \leq \frac{L\|\mathbf{y}^0 - \mathbf{y}^*\|^2}{2k}.$$

Our goal now will be to find a primal representation of the method, which will be written in a more explicit way in terms of the data of the problem, meaning $(f, g, \mathcal{A})$. To achieve this goal, we will require the following technical lemma.

Lemma 12.5. *Let $F(\mathbf{y}) = f^*(\mathcal{A}^T(\mathbf{y}) + \mathbf{b}), G(\mathbf{y}) = g^*(-\mathbf{y})$, where f, g, and $\mathcal{A}$ satisfy properties (A), (B), and (C) of Assumption 12.1 and $\mathbf{b} \in \mathbb{E}$. Then for any $\mathbf{y}, \mathbf{v} \in \mathbb{V}$ and $L > 0$ the relation*

$$\mathbf{y} = \operatorname{prox}_{\frac{1}{L}G}\left(\mathbf{v} - \frac{1}{L}\nabla F(\mathbf{v})\right) \tag{12.9}$$

holds if and only if

$$\mathbf{y} = \mathbf{v} - \frac{1}{L}\mathcal{A}(\tilde{\mathbf{x}}) + \frac{1}{L}\operatorname{prox}_{Lg}(\mathcal{A}(\tilde{\mathbf{x}}) - L\mathbf{v}),$$

where

$$\tilde{\mathbf{x}} = \operatorname{argmax}_{\mathbf{x}}\left\{\langle \mathbf{x}, \mathcal{A}^T(\mathbf{v}) + \mathbf{b}\rangle - f(\mathbf{x})\right\}.$$

Proof. By the conjugate subgradient theorem (Corollary 4.21), since f is proper closed and convex,

$$\nabla f^*(\mathcal{A}^T(\mathbf{v}) + \mathbf{b}) = \tilde{\mathbf{x}} \equiv \operatorname{argmax}_{\mathbf{x}}\left\{\langle \mathbf{x}, \mathcal{A}^T(\mathbf{v}) + \mathbf{b}\rangle - f(\mathbf{x})\right\}.$$

---

[67]Sections 12.2 and 12.3 follow the work of Beck and Teboulle [21].

Therefore, since $\nabla F(\mathbf{v}) = \mathcal{A}(\nabla f^*(\mathcal{A}^T(\mathbf{v}) + \mathbf{b})) = \mathcal{A}(\tilde{\mathbf{x}})$,

$$y = \operatorname{prox}_{\frac{1}{L}G}\left(\mathbf{v} - \frac{1}{L}\mathcal{A}(\tilde{\mathbf{x}})\right). \qquad (12.10)$$

Invoking Theorem 6.15 with $g \leftarrow \frac{1}{L}g^*$, $\mathcal{A} = -\mathcal{I}$, $\mathbf{b} = \mathbf{0}$, we obtain that for any $\mathbf{z} \in \mathbb{V}$,

$$\operatorname{prox}_{\frac{1}{L}G}(\mathbf{z}) = -\operatorname{prox}_{\frac{1}{L}g^*}(-\mathbf{z}). \qquad (12.11)$$

Combining (12.10) and (12.11) and using the extended Moreau decomposition formula (Theorem 6.45), we finally obtain that

$$\begin{aligned}
y &= \operatorname{prox}_{\frac{1}{L}G}\left(\mathbf{v} - \frac{1}{L}\mathcal{A}(\tilde{\mathbf{x}})\right) = -\operatorname{prox}_{\frac{1}{L}g^*}\left(\frac{1}{L}\mathcal{A}(\tilde{\mathbf{x}}) - \mathbf{v}\right) \\
&= -\left[\frac{1}{L}\mathcal{A}(\tilde{\mathbf{x}}) - \mathbf{v} - \frac{1}{L}\operatorname{prox}_{Lg}(\mathcal{A}(\tilde{\mathbf{x}}) - L\mathbf{v})\right] \\
&= \mathbf{v} - \frac{1}{L}\mathcal{A}(\tilde{\mathbf{x}}) + \frac{1}{L}\operatorname{prox}_{Lg}(\mathcal{A}(\tilde{\mathbf{x}}) - L\mathbf{v}). \qquad \square
\end{aligned}$$

Equipped with Lemma 12.5, we can write a primal representation of the DPG method.

The Dual Proximal Gradient (DPG) Method—primal representation

Initialization: pick $\mathbf{y}^0 \in \mathbb{V}$, and $L \geq \frac{\|\mathcal{A}\|^2}{\sigma}$.
General step: for any $k = 0, 1, 2, \ldots$ execute the following steps:

(a) set $\mathbf{x}^k = \operatorname{argmax}_{\mathbf{x}}\left\{\langle \mathbf{x}, \mathcal{A}^T(\mathbf{y}^k)\rangle - f(\mathbf{x})\right\}$;

(b) set $\mathbf{y}^{k+1} = \mathbf{y}^k - \frac{1}{L}\mathcal{A}(\mathbf{x}^k) + \frac{1}{L}\operatorname{prox}_{Lg}(\mathcal{A}(\mathbf{x}^k) - L\mathbf{y}^k)$.

Remark 12.6 (the primal sequence). *The sequence $\{\mathbf{x}^k\}_{k \geq 0}$ generated by the method will be called "the primal sequence." The elements of the sequence are actually not necessarily feasible w.r.t. the primal problem (12.1) since they are not guaranteed to belong to* dom(g); *nevertheless, we will show that the primal sequence does converge to the optimal solution* $\mathbf{x}^*$.

To prove a convergence result in terms of the primal sequence, we will require the following fundamental primal-dual relation.

Lemma 12.7 (primal-dual relation). *Suppose that Assumption 12.1 holds. Let $\bar{\mathbf{y}} \in$ dom(G), where G is given in (12.7), and let*

$$\bar{\mathbf{x}} = \operatorname{argmax}_{\mathbf{x} \in \mathbb{E}}\left\{\langle \mathbf{x}, \mathcal{A}^T(\bar{\mathbf{y}})\rangle - f(\mathbf{x})\right\}. \qquad (12.12)$$

Then

$$\|\bar{\mathbf{x}} - \mathbf{x}^*\|^2 \leq \frac{2}{\sigma}(q_{\text{opt}} - q(\bar{\mathbf{y}})). \qquad (12.13)$$

Proof. Recall that the primal problem (12.1) can be equivalently written as the problem

$$\min_{\mathbf{x} \in \mathbb{E}, \mathbf{z} \in \mathbb{V}} \{f(\mathbf{x}) + g(\mathbf{z}) : \mathcal{A}(\mathbf{x}) - \mathbf{z} = \mathbf{0}\},$$

whose Lagrangian is (see also (12.3))

$$L(\mathbf{x}, \mathbf{z}; \mathbf{y}) = f(\mathbf{x}) - \langle \mathcal{A}^T(\mathbf{y}), \mathbf{x} \rangle + g(\mathbf{z}) + \langle \mathbf{y}, \mathbf{z} \rangle.$$

In particular,

$$L(\mathbf{x}, \mathbf{z}; \bar{\mathbf{y}}) = h(\mathbf{x}) + s(\mathbf{z}), \tag{12.14}$$

where

$$h(\mathbf{x}) = f(\mathbf{x}) - \langle \mathcal{A}^T(\bar{\mathbf{y}}), \mathbf{x} \rangle,$$
$$s(\mathbf{z}) = g(\mathbf{z}) + \langle \bar{\mathbf{y}}, \mathbf{z} \rangle.$$

Since h is σ-strongly convex and $\bar{\mathbf{x}}$ is its minimizer (see relation (12.12)), it follows by Theorem 5.25(b) that

$$h(\mathbf{x}) - h(\bar{\mathbf{x}}) \geq \frac{\sigma}{2} \|\mathbf{x} - \bar{\mathbf{x}}\|^2. \tag{12.15}$$

Since the relation $\bar{\mathbf{y}} \in \text{dom}(G)$ is equivalent to $-\bar{\mathbf{y}} \in \text{dom}(g^*)$, it follows that

$$\min_{\mathbf{z} \in \mathbb{V}} \{g(\mathbf{z}) + \langle \bar{\mathbf{y}}, \mathbf{z} \rangle\} = \min_{\mathbf{z} \in \mathbb{V}} s(\mathbf{z}) > -\infty.$$

Let $\varepsilon > 0$. Then there exists $\bar{\mathbf{z}}_\varepsilon$ for which

$$s(\bar{\mathbf{z}}_\varepsilon) \leq \min_{\mathbf{z} \in \mathbb{V}} s(\mathbf{z}) + \varepsilon. \tag{12.16}$$

Combining (12.14), (12.15), and (12.16), we obtain that for all $\mathbf{x} \in \text{dom}(f)$ and $\mathbf{z} \in \text{dom}(g)$,

$$L(\mathbf{x}, \mathbf{z}; \bar{\mathbf{y}}) - L(\bar{\mathbf{x}}, \bar{\mathbf{z}}_\varepsilon; \bar{\mathbf{y}}) = h(\mathbf{x}) - h(\bar{\mathbf{x}}) + s(\mathbf{z}) - s(\bar{\mathbf{z}}_\varepsilon) \geq \frac{\sigma}{2} \|\mathbf{x} - \bar{\mathbf{x}}\|^2 - \varepsilon.$$

In particular, substituting $\mathbf{x} = \mathbf{x}^*, \mathbf{z} = \mathbf{z}^* \equiv \mathcal{A}(\mathbf{x}^*)$, then $L(\mathbf{x}^*, \mathbf{z}^*; \bar{\mathbf{y}}) = f(\mathbf{x}^*) + g(\mathcal{A}(\mathbf{x}^*)) = f_{\text{opt}} = q_{\text{opt}}$ (by Theorem 12.2), and we obtain

$$q_{\text{opt}} - L(\bar{\mathbf{x}}, \bar{\mathbf{z}}_\varepsilon; \bar{\mathbf{y}}) \geq \frac{\sigma}{2} \|\mathbf{x}^* - \bar{\mathbf{x}}\|^2 - \varepsilon. \tag{12.17}$$

In addition, by the definition of the dual objective function value,

$$L(\bar{\mathbf{x}}, \bar{\mathbf{z}}_\varepsilon; \bar{\mathbf{y}}) \geq \min_{\mathbf{x} \in \mathbb{E}, \mathbf{z} \in \mathbb{V}} L(\mathbf{x}, \mathbf{z}; \bar{\mathbf{y}}) = q(\bar{\mathbf{y}}),$$

which, combined with (12.17), results in the inequality

$$\|\bar{\mathbf{x}} - \mathbf{x}^*\|^2 \leq \frac{2}{\sigma} (q_{\text{opt}} - q(\bar{\mathbf{y}})) + \frac{2}{\sigma} \varepsilon.$$

Since the above inequality holds for any $\varepsilon > 0$, the desired result (inequality (12.13)) follows. $\square$

Combining the primal-dual relation of Lemma 12.7 with the rate of convergence of the sequence of dual objective function values stated in Theorem 12.4, we can deduce a rate of convergence result for the primal sequence to the unique optimal solution.

Theorem 12.8 ($O(1/k)$ rate of convergence of the primal sequence of the DPG method). *Suppose that Assumption 12.1 holds, and let $\{\mathbf{x}^k\}_{k\geq 0}$ and $\{\mathbf{y}^k\}_{k\geq 0}$ be the primal and dual sequences generated by the DPG method with $L \geq L_F = \frac{\|\mathcal{A}\|^2}{\sigma}$. Then for any optimal solution $\mathbf{y}^*$ of the dual problem (12.4) and $k \geq 1$,*

$$\|\mathbf{x}^k - \mathbf{x}^*\|^2 \leq \frac{L\|\mathbf{y}^0 - \mathbf{y}^*\|^2}{\sigma k}. \qquad (12.18)$$

Proof. Invoking Lemma 12.7 with $\bar{\mathbf{y}} = \mathbf{y}^k$, we obtain by the definition of $\bar{\mathbf{x}}$ (equation (12.12)) that $\bar{\mathbf{x}} = \mathbf{x}^k$, and hence (12.13) reads as

$$\|\mathbf{x}^k - \mathbf{x}^*\|^2 \leq \frac{2}{\sigma}(q_{\text{opt}} - q(\mathbf{y}^k)),$$

which, combined with Theorem 12.4, yields the desired result. $\square$

12.3 Fast Dual Proximal Gradient

The DPG method employs the proximal gradient method on the dual problem. Alternatively, we can also employ FISTA (see Section 10.7) on the dual problem (12.4). The dual representation of the method is given below.

The Fast Dual Proximal Gradient (FDPG) Method—dual representation

- **Initialization:** $L \geq L_F = \frac{\|\mathcal{A}\|^2}{\sigma}, \mathbf{w}^0 = \mathbf{y}^0 \in \mathbb{E}, t_0 = 1$.

- **General step ($k \geq 0$):**

  (a) $\mathbf{y}^{k+1} = \text{prox}_{\frac{1}{L}G}\left(\mathbf{w}^k - \frac{1}{L}\nabla F(\mathbf{w}^k)\right)$;

  (b) $t_{k+1} = \frac{1+\sqrt{1+4t_k^2}}{2}$;

  (c) $\mathbf{w}^{k+1} = \mathbf{y}^{k+1} + \left(\frac{t_k-1}{t_{k+1}}\right)(\mathbf{y}^{k+1} - \mathbf{y}^k)$.

Since this is exactly FISTA employed on the dual problem, we can invoke Theorem 10.34 and obtain a convergence result in terms of dual objective function values.

Theorem 12.9. *Suppose that Assumption 12.1 holds and that $\{\mathbf{y}^k\}_{k\geq 0}$ is the sequence generated by the FDPG method with $L \geq L_F = \frac{\|\mathcal{A}\|^2}{\sigma}$. Then for any optimal solution $\mathbf{y}^*$ of problem (12.4) and $k \geq 1$,*

$$q_{\text{opt}} - q(\mathbf{y}^k) \leq \frac{2L\|\mathbf{y}^0 - \mathbf{y}^*\|^2}{(k+1)^2}.$$

Using Lemma 12.5 with $\mathbf{v} = \mathbf{w}^k$, $\mathbf{y} = \mathbf{y}^{k+1}$, and $\mathbf{b} = \mathbf{0}$, we obtain that step (a) of the FDPG method, namely,

$$\mathbf{y}^{k+1} = \operatorname{prox}_{\frac{1}{L}G}\left(\mathbf{w}^k - \frac{1}{L}\nabla F(\mathbf{w}^k)\right),$$

can be equivalently written as

$$\mathbf{u}^k = \operatorname{argmax}_{\mathbf{u}}\left\{\langle \mathbf{u}, \mathcal{A}^T(\mathbf{w}^k)\rangle - f(\mathbf{u})\right\},$$
$$\mathbf{y}^{k+1} = \mathbf{w}^k - \frac{1}{L}\mathcal{A}(\mathbf{u}^k) + \frac{1}{L}\operatorname{prox}_{Lg}(\mathcal{A}(\mathbf{u}^k) - L\mathbf{w}^k).$$

We can thus formulate a primal representation of the method.

The Fast Dual Proximal Gradient (FDPG) Method—primal representation

Initialization: $L \geq L_F = \frac{\|\mathcal{A}\|^2}{\sigma}, \mathbf{w}^0 = \mathbf{y}^0 \in \mathbb{V}, t_0 = 1.$
General step $(k \geq 0)$:

(a) $\mathbf{u}^k = \operatorname{argmax}_{\mathbf{u}}\left\{\langle \mathbf{u}, \mathcal{A}^T(\mathbf{w}^k)\rangle - f(\mathbf{u})\right\}$;

(b) $\mathbf{y}^{k+1} = \mathbf{w}^k - \frac{1}{L}\mathcal{A}(\mathbf{u}^k) + \frac{1}{L}\operatorname{prox}_{Lg}(\mathcal{A}(\mathbf{u}^k) - L\mathbf{w}^k)$;

(c) $t_{k+1} = \frac{1+\sqrt{1+4t_k^2}}{2}$;

(d) $\mathbf{w}^{k+1} = \mathbf{y}^{k+1} + \left(\frac{t_k-1}{t_{k+1}}\right)(\mathbf{y}^{k+1} - \mathbf{y}^k)$.

The primal sequence that we will be interested in is actually not computed during the steps of the FDPG method. The definition of the primal sequence on which a convergence result will be proved is

$$\mathbf{x}^k = \operatorname{argmax}_{\mathbf{x}\in\mathbb{E}}\left\{\langle \mathbf{x}, \mathcal{A}^T(\mathbf{y}^k)\rangle - f(\mathbf{x})\right\}. \tag{12.19}$$

The convergence result on the primal sequence is given below, and its proof is almost a verbatim repetition of the proof of Theorem 12.8.

Theorem 12.10 ($O(1/k^2)$ convergence of the primal sequence of the FDPG method). *Suppose that Assumption 12.1 holds, and let $\{\mathbf{y}^k\}_{k\geq 0}$ be the sequence generated by the FDPG method with $L \geq L_F = \frac{\|\mathcal{A}\|^2}{\sigma}$. Let $\{\mathbf{x}^k\}_{k\geq 0}$ be the sequence defined by (12.19). Then for any optimal solution $\mathbf{y}^*$ of the dual problem (12.4) and $k \geq 1$,*

$$\|\mathbf{x}^k - \mathbf{x}^*\|^2 \leq \frac{4L\|\mathbf{y}^0 - \mathbf{y}^*\|^2}{\sigma(k+1)^2}.$$

Proof. Invoking Lemma 12.7 with $\bar{\mathbf{y}} = \mathbf{y}^k$, we obtain by the definition of $\bar{\mathbf{x}}$ (equation (12.12)) that $\bar{\mathbf{x}} = \mathbf{x}^k$, and hence the result (12.13) reads as

$$\|\mathbf{x}^k - \mathbf{x}^*\|^2 \leq \frac{2}{\sigma}(q_{\mathrm{opt}} - q(\mathbf{y}^k)),$$

which, combined with Theorem 12.9, yields the desired result. ☐

12.4   Examples I

12.4.1   Orthogonal Projection onto a Polyhedral Set

Let

$$S = \{\mathbf{x} \in \mathbb{R}^n : \mathbf{A}\mathbf{x} \leq \mathbf{b}\},$$

where $\mathbf{A} \in \mathbb{R}^{p \times n}$, $\mathbf{b} \in \mathbb{R}^p$. We assume that S is nonempty. Let $\mathbf{d} \in \mathbb{R}^n$. The orthogonal projection of $\mathbf{d}$ onto S is the unique optimal solution of the problem

$$\min_{\mathbf{x} \in \mathbb{R}^n} \left\{ \frac{1}{2}\|\mathbf{x} - \mathbf{d}\|^2 : \mathbf{A}\mathbf{x} \leq \mathbf{b} \right\}. \tag{12.20}$$

Problem (12.20) fits model (12.1) with $\mathbb{E} = \mathbb{R}^n, \mathbb{V} = \mathbb{R}^p$, $f(\mathbf{x}) = \frac{1}{2}\|\mathbf{x} - \mathbf{d}\|^2$,

$$g(\mathbf{z}) = \delta_{\mathrm{Box}[-\infty\mathbf{e},\mathbf{b}]}(\mathbf{z}) = \begin{cases} 0, & \mathbf{z} \leq \mathbf{b}, \\ \infty & \text{else}, \end{cases}$$

and $\mathcal{A}(\mathbf{x}) \equiv \mathbf{A}\mathbf{x}$. We have

- $\operatorname{argmax}_{\mathbf{x}}\{\langle \mathbf{v}, \mathbf{x} \rangle - f(\mathbf{x})\} = \mathbf{v} + \mathbf{d}$ for any $\mathbf{v} \in \mathbb{R}^n$;

- $\|\mathcal{A}\| = \|\mathbf{A}\|_{2,2}$;

- $\sigma = 1$;

- $\mathcal{A}^T(\mathbf{y}) = \mathbf{A}^T\mathbf{y}$ for any $\mathbf{y} \in \mathbb{R}^p$;

- $\operatorname{prox}_{Lg}(\mathbf{z}) = P_{\mathrm{Box}[-\infty\mathbf{e},\mathbf{b}]}(\mathbf{z}) = \min\{\mathbf{z}, \mathbf{b}\}$, where $\min\{\mathbf{z}, \mathbf{b}\}$ is the vector $(\min\{z_i, b_i\})_{i=1}^p$.

Using these facts, the DPG and FDPG methods for solving problem (12.20) can be explicitly written.

Algorithm 1 [DPG for solving (12.20)]

- **Initialization:** $L \geq \|\mathbf{A}\|_{2,2}^2, \mathbf{y}^0 \in \mathbb{R}^p$.

- **General step ($k \geq 0$):**

  (a) $\mathbf{x}^k = \mathbf{A}^T\mathbf{y}^k + \mathbf{d}$;

  (b) $\mathbf{y}^{k+1} = \mathbf{y}^k - \frac{1}{L}\mathbf{A}\mathbf{x}^k + \frac{1}{L}\min\{\mathbf{A}\mathbf{x}^k - L\mathbf{y}^k, \mathbf{b}\}$.

Algorithm 2 [FDPG for solving (12.20)]

- **Initialization:** $L \geq \|\mathbf{A}\|_{2,2}^2, \mathbf{w}^0 = \mathbf{y}^0 \in \mathbb{R}^p, t_0 = 1.$

- **General step ($k \geq 0$):**

  (a) $\mathbf{u}^k = \mathbf{A}^T\mathbf{w}^k + \mathbf{d};$

  (b) $\mathbf{y}^{k+1} = \mathbf{w}^k - \frac{1}{L}\mathbf{A}\mathbf{u}^k + \frac{1}{L}\min\{\mathbf{A}\mathbf{u}^k - L\mathbf{w}^k, \mathbf{b}\};$

  (c) $t_{k+1} = \frac{1+\sqrt{1+4t_k^2}}{2};$

  (d) $\mathbf{w}^{k+1} = \mathbf{y}^{k+1} + \left(\frac{t_k-1}{t_{k+1}}\right)(\mathbf{y}^{k+1} - \mathbf{y}^k).$

The primal sequence for the FDPG method is given by $\mathbf{x}^k = \mathbf{A}^T\mathbf{y}^k + \mathbf{d}.$

12.4.2 Orthogonal Projection onto the Intersection of Closed Convex Sets

Given p closed and convex sets $C_1, C_2, \ldots, C_p \subseteq \mathbb{E}$ and a point $\mathbf{d} \in \mathbb{E}$, the orthogonal projection of $\mathbf{d}$ onto the intersection $\cap_{i=1}^p C_i$ is the optimal solution of the problem

$$\min_{\mathbf{x} \in \mathbb{E}}\left\{\frac{1}{2}\|\mathbf{x} - \mathbf{d}\|^2 : \mathbf{x} \in \cap_{i=1}^p C_i\right\}. \tag{12.21}$$

We will assume that the intersection $\cap_{i=1}^p C_i$ is nonempty and that projecting onto each set C_i is an easy task. Our purpose will be to devise a method for solving problem (12.21) that only requires computing at each iteration—in addition to elementary linear algebra operations—orthogonal projections onto the sets C_i. Problem (12.21) fits model (12.1) with $\mathbb{V} = \mathbb{E}^p, f(\mathbf{x}) = \frac{1}{2}\|\mathbf{x} - \mathbf{d}\|^2, g(\mathbf{x}_1, \mathbf{x}_2, \ldots, \mathbf{x}_p) = \sum_{i=1}^p \delta_{C_i}(\mathbf{x}_i)$, and $\mathcal{A} : \mathbb{E} \rightarrow \mathbb{V}$ given by

$$\mathcal{A}(\mathbf{z}) = \underbrace{(\mathbf{z}, \mathbf{z}, \ldots, \mathbf{z})}_{p \text{ times}} \text{ for any } \mathbf{z} \in \mathbb{E}.$$

We have

- $\text{argmax}_{\mathbf{x}}\{\langle \mathbf{v}, \mathbf{x}\rangle - f(\mathbf{x})\} = \mathbf{v} + \mathbf{d}$ for any $\mathbf{v} \in \mathbb{E}$;

- $\|\mathcal{A}\|^2 = p;$

- $\sigma = 1;$

- $\mathcal{A}^T(\mathbf{y}) = \sum_{i=1}^p y_i$ for any $\mathbf{y} \in \mathbb{E}^p;$

- $\text{prox}_{Lg}(\mathbf{v}_1, \mathbf{v}_2, \ldots, \mathbf{v}_p) = (P_{C_1}(\mathbf{v}_1), P_{C_2}(\mathbf{v}_2), \ldots, P_{C_p}(\mathbf{v}_p))$ for any $\mathbf{v} \in \mathbb{E}^p.$

Using these facts, the DPG and FDPG methods for solving problem (12.21) can be explicitly written.

Algorithm 3 [DPG for solving (12.21)]

- **Initialization:** $L \geq p, \mathbf{y}^0 \in \mathbb{E}^p$.

- **General step** $(k \geq 0)$:

  (a) $\mathbf{x}^k = \sum_{i=1}^{p} \mathbf{y}_i^k + \mathbf{d}$;

  (b) $\mathbf{y}_i^{k+1} = \mathbf{y}_i^k - \frac{1}{L}\mathbf{x}^k + \frac{1}{L}P_{C_i}(\mathbf{x}^k - L\mathbf{y}_i^k)$, $i = 1, 2, \ldots, p$.

Algorithm 4 [FDPG for solving (12.21)]

- **Initialization:** $L \geq p, \mathbf{w}^0 = \mathbf{y}^0 \in \mathbb{E}^p, t_0 = 1$.

- **General step** $(k \geq 0)$:

  (a) $\mathbf{u}^k = \sum_{i=1}^{p} \mathbf{w}_i^k + \mathbf{d}$;

  (b) $\mathbf{y}_i^{k+1} = \mathbf{w}_i^k - \frac{1}{L}\mathbf{u}^k + \frac{1}{L}P_{C_i}(\mathbf{u}^k - L\mathbf{w}_i^k)$, $i = 1, 2, \ldots, p$;

  (c) $t_{k+1} = \frac{1 + \sqrt{1 + 4t_k^2}}{2}$;

  (d) $\mathbf{w}^{k+1} = \mathbf{y}^{k+1} + \left(\frac{t_k - 1}{t_{k+1}}\right)(\mathbf{y}^{k+1} - \mathbf{y}^k)$.

To actually guarantee convergence of the method, Assumption 12.1 needs to be satisfied, meaning that we assume that $\cap_{i=1}^{p}\mathrm{ri}(C_i) \neq \emptyset$.

The primal sequence of the FDPG method is given by $\mathbf{x}^k = \sum_{i=1}^{p} \mathbf{y}_i^k + \mathbf{d}$.

Example 12.11 (orthogonal projection onto a polyhedral set revisited). Note that Algorithm 4 can also be used to find an orthogonal projection of a point $\mathbf{d} \in \mathbb{R}^n$ onto the polyhedral set $C = \{\mathbf{x} \in \mathbb{R}^n : \mathbf{A}\mathbf{x} \leq \mathbf{b}\}$, where $\mathbf{A} \in \mathbb{R}^{p \times n}, \mathbf{b} \in \mathbb{R}^p$. Indeed, C can be written as the following intersection of half-spaces:

$$C = \cap_{i=1}^{p} C_i,$$

where

$$C_i = \{\mathbf{x} \in \mathbb{R}^n : \mathbf{a}_i^T \mathbf{x} \leq b_i\}, \tag{12.22}$$

with $\mathbf{a}_1^T, \mathbf{a}_2^T, \ldots, \mathbf{a}_p^T$ being the rows of $\mathbf{A}$. The projections on the half-spaces are simple and given by (see Lemma 6.26) $P_{C_i}(\mathbf{x}) = \mathbf{x} - \frac{[\mathbf{a}_i^T\mathbf{x} - b_i]_+}{\|\mathbf{a}_i\|^2}\mathbf{a}_i$. To summarize, the problem

$$\min_{\mathbf{x} \in \mathbb{R}^n} \left\{\frac{1}{2}\|\mathbf{x} - \mathbf{d}\|_2^2 : \mathbf{A}\mathbf{x} \leq \mathbf{b}\right\}$$

can be solved by two different FDPG methods. The first one is Algorithm 2, and the second one is the following algorithm, which is Algorithm 4 specified to the case where C_i is given by (12.22) for any $i \in \{1, 2, \ldots, p\}$.

Algorithm 5 [second version of FDPG for solving (12.20)]

- **Initialization:** $L \geq p, \mathbf{w}^0 = \mathbf{y}^0 \in \mathbb{E}^p, t_0 = 1.$

- **General step $(k \geq 0)$:**

  (a) $\mathbf{u}^k = \sum_{i=1}^p \mathbf{w}_i^k + \mathbf{d}$;

  (b) $\mathbf{y}_i^{k+1} = -\frac{1}{L\|\mathbf{a}_i\|^2}[\mathbf{a}_i^T(\mathbf{u}^k - L\mathbf{w}_i^k) - b_i]_+ \mathbf{a}_i,\ i = 1, 2, \ldots, p$;

  (c) $t_{k+1} = \frac{1+\sqrt{1+4t_k^2}}{2}$;

  (d) $\mathbf{w}^{k+1} = \mathbf{y}^{k+1} + \left(\frac{t_k-1}{t_{k+1}}\right)(\mathbf{y}^{k+1} - \mathbf{y}^k).$

■

Example 12.12 (comparison between DPG and FDPG). The $O(1/k^2)$ rate of convergence obtained for the FDPG method (Theorem 12.10) is better than the $O(1/k)$ result obtained for the DPG method (Theorem 12.8). To illustrate that this theoretical advantage is also reflected in practice, we consider the problem of projecting the point $(0.5, 1.9)^T$ onto a dodecagon—a regular polygon with 12 edges, which is represented as the intersection of 12 half-spaces. The first 10 iterations of the DPG and FDPG methods with $L = p = 12$ can be seen in Figure 12.1, where the DPG and FDPG methods that were used are those described by Algorithms 3 and 4 for the intersection of closed convex sets (which are taken as the 12 half-spaces in this example) and not Algorithms 1 and 2. Evidently, the FDPG method was able to find a good approximation of the projection after 10 iterations, while the DPG method was rather far from the required solution. ■

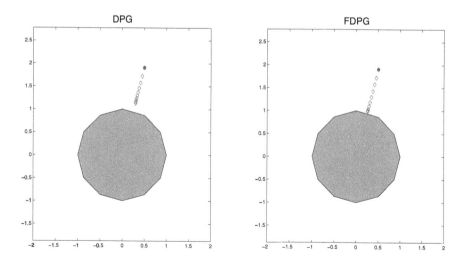

Figure 12.1. *First* 10 *iterations of the DPG method (Algorithm 3) and the FDPG method (Algorithm 4/5). The initial value of the dual vector* $\mathbf{y}$ *was the zeros vector in both methods.*

12.4.3   One-Dimensional Total Variation Denoising

In the denoising problem we are given a signal $\mathbf{d} \in \mathbb{E}$, which is contaminated by noise, and we seek to find another vector $\mathbf{x} \in \mathbb{E}$, which, on the one hand, is close to $\mathbf{d}$ in the sense that the norm $\|\mathbf{x} - \mathbf{d}\|$ is small and, on the other hand, yields a small regularization term $R(\mathcal{A}(\mathbf{x}))$, where here $\mathcal{A} : \mathbb{E} \to \mathbb{V}$ is a linear transformation that in many applications accounts for the smoothness of the signal and $R : \mathbb{V} \to \mathbb{R}_+$ is a given convex function that measures the magnitude of its argument in some sense. The denoising problem is then defined to be

$$\min_{\mathbf{x} \in \mathbb{E}} \left\{ \frac{1}{2} \|\mathbf{x} - \mathbf{d}\|^2 + R(\mathcal{A}(\mathbf{x})) \right\}. \tag{12.23}$$

In the one-dimensional total variation denoising problem, we are interested in the case where $\mathbb{E} = \mathbb{R}^n, \mathbb{V} = \mathbb{R}^{n-1}, \mathcal{A}(\mathbf{x}) = \mathbf{D}\mathbf{x}$, and $R(\mathbf{z}) = \lambda \|\mathbf{z}\|_1$ with $\lambda > 0$ being a "regularization parameter" and $\mathbf{D}$ being the matrix satisfying $\mathbf{D}\mathbf{x} = (x_1 - x_2, x_2 - x_3, \ldots, x_{n-1} - x_n)^T$ for all $\mathbf{x} \in \mathbb{R}^n$. Thus, problem (12.23) takes the form[68]

$$\min_{\mathbf{x} \in \mathbb{R}^n} \left\{ \frac{1}{2} \|\mathbf{x} - \mathbf{d}\|_2^2 + \lambda \|\mathbf{D}\mathbf{x}\|_1 \right\} \tag{12.24}$$

or, more explicitly,

$$\min_{\mathbf{x} \in \mathbb{R}^n} \left\{ \frac{1}{2} \|\mathbf{x} - \mathbf{d}\|_2^2 + \lambda \sum_{i=1}^{n-1} |x_i - x_{i+1}| \right\}.$$

The function $\mathbf{x} \mapsto \|\mathbf{D}\mathbf{x}\|_1$ is known as a one-dimensional *total variation* function and is actually only one instance of many variants of total variation functions. Problem (12.24) fits model (12.1) with $\mathbb{E} = \mathbb{R}^n, \mathbb{V} = \mathbb{R}^{n-1}, f(\mathbf{x}) = \frac{1}{2}\|\mathbf{x} - \mathbf{d}\|_2^2, g(\mathbf{y}) = \lambda\|\mathbf{y}\|_1$, and $\mathcal{A}(\mathbf{x}) \equiv \mathbf{D}\mathbf{x}$. In order to explicitly write the DPG and FDPG methods, we note that

- $\operatorname{argmax}_{\mathbf{x}}\{\langle \mathbf{v}, \mathbf{x} \rangle - f(\mathbf{x})\} = \mathbf{v} + \mathbf{d}$ for any $\mathbf{v} \in \mathbb{E}$;
- $\|\mathcal{A}\|^2 = \|\mathbf{D}\|_{2,2}^2 \leq 4$;
- $\sigma = 1$;
- $\mathcal{A}^T(\mathbf{y}) = \mathbf{D}^T\mathbf{y}$ for any $\mathbf{y} \in \mathbb{R}^{n-1}$;
- $\operatorname{prox}_{Lg}(\mathbf{y}) = \mathcal{T}_{\lambda L}(\mathbf{y})$.

The bound on $\|\mathbf{D}\|_{2,2}$ was achieved by the following argument:

$$\|\mathbf{D}\mathbf{x}\|_2^2 = \sum_{i=1}^{n-1}(x_i - x_{i+1})^2 \leq 2\sum_{i=1}^{n-1}(x_i^2 + x_{i+1}^2) \leq 4\|\mathbf{x}\|^2.$$

The DPG and FDPG methods with $L = 4$ are explicitly written below.

---

[68]Since in this chapter all underlying spaces are Euclidean and since the standing assumption is that (unless otherwise stated) $\mathbb{R}^n$ is embedded with the dot product, it follows that $\mathbb{R}^n$ is endowed with the l_2-norm.

Algorithm 6 [DPG for solving (12.24)]

- **Initialization:** $\mathbf{y}^0 \in \mathbb{R}^{n-1}$.

- **General step** $(k \geq 0)$:

  (a) $\mathbf{x}^k = \mathbf{D}^T \mathbf{y}^k + \mathbf{d}$;

  (b) $\mathbf{y}^{k+1} = \mathbf{y}^k - \frac{1}{4}\mathbf{D}\mathbf{x}^k + \frac{1}{4}\mathcal{T}_{4\lambda}(\mathbf{D}\mathbf{x}^k - 4\mathbf{y}^k)$.

Algorithm 7 [FDPG for solving (12.24)]

- **Initialization:** $\mathbf{w}^0 = \mathbf{y}^0 \in \mathbb{R}^{n-1}, t_0 = 1$.

- **General step** $(k \geq 0)$:

  (a) $\mathbf{u}^k = \mathbf{D}^T \mathbf{w}^k + \mathbf{d}$;

  (b) $\mathbf{y}^{k+1} = \mathbf{w}^k - \frac{1}{4}\mathbf{D}\mathbf{u}^k + \frac{1}{4}\mathcal{T}_{4\lambda}(\mathbf{D}\mathbf{u}^k - 4\mathbf{w}^k)$;

  (c) $t_{k+1} = \frac{1+\sqrt{1+4t_k^2}}{2}$;

  (d) $\mathbf{w}^{k+1} = \mathbf{y}^{k+1} + \left(\frac{t_k-1}{t_{k+1}}\right)(\mathbf{y}^{k+1} - \mathbf{y}^k)$.

Example 12.13. Consider the case where $n = 1000$ and the "clean" (actually unknown) signal is the vector $\mathbf{d}^{\text{true}}$, which is a discretization of a step function:

$$
d_i^{\text{true}} = \begin{cases} 1, & 1 \leq i \leq 250, \\ 3, & 251 \leq i \leq 500, \\ 0, & 501 \leq i \leq 750, \\ 2, & 751 \leq i \leq 1000. \end{cases}
$$

The observed vector $\mathbf{d}$ was constructed by adding independently to each component of $\mathbf{d}^{\text{true}}$ a normally distributed noise with zero mean and standard deviation 0.05. The true and noisy signals can be seen in Figure 12.2. We ran 100 iterations of Algorithms 6 (DPG) and 7 (FDPG) initialized with $\mathbf{y}^0 = \mathbf{0}$, and the resulting signals can be seen in Figure 12.3. Clearly, the FDPG method produces a much better quality reconstruction of the original step function than the DPG method. This is reflected in the objective function values of the vectors produced by each of the methods. The objective function values of the vectors generated by the DPG and FDPG methods after 100 iterations are 9.1667 and 8.4621, respectively, where the optimal value is 8.3031. ∎

12.4.4 Two-Dimensional Total Variation Denoising

In the two-dimensional total variation denoising problem, we are given an observed noisy matrix $\mathbf{d} \in \mathbb{R}^{m \times n}$, and we seek to solve the problem

$$
\min_{\mathbf{x} \in \mathbb{R}^{m \times n}} \left\{ \frac{1}{2}\|\mathbf{x} - \mathbf{d}\|_F^2 + \lambda \text{TV}(\mathbf{x}) \right\}. \tag{12.25}
$$

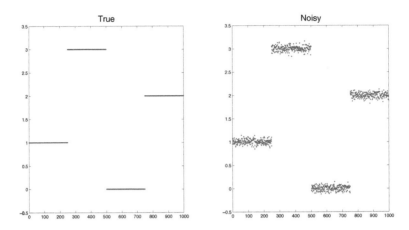

Figure 12.2. *True signal (left) and noisy signal (right).*

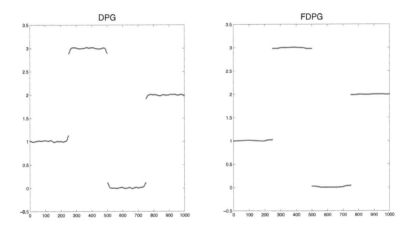

Figure 12.3. *Results of the DPG and FDPG methods.*

There are many possible choices for the two-dimensional total variation function $\mathrm{TV}(\cdot)$. Two popular choices are the isotropic TV defined for any $\mathbf{x} \in \mathbb{R}^{m \times n}$ by

$$\mathrm{TV}_I(\mathbf{x}) = \sum_{i=1}^{m-1} \sum_{j=1}^{n-1} \sqrt{(x_{i,j} - x_{i,j+1})^2 + (x_{i,j} - x_{i+1,j})^2} \qquad (12.26)$$

$$+ \sum_{j=1}^{n-1} |x_{m,j} - x_{m,j+1}| + \sum_{i=1}^{m-1} |x_{i,n} - x_{i+1,n}|$$

and the l_1-based, anisotropic TV defined by

$$\mathbf{x} \in \mathbb{R}^{m \times n}, \quad \mathrm{TV}_{l_1}(\mathbf{x}) = \sum_{i=1}^{m-1} \sum_{j=1}^{n-1} \left\{ |x_{i,j} - x_{i,j+1}| + |x_{i,j} - x_{i+1,j}| \right\}$$

$$+ \sum_{j=1}^{n-1} |x_{m,j} - x_{m,j+1}| + \sum_{i=1}^{m-1} |x_{i,n} - x_{i+1,n}|.$$

Problem (12.25) fits the main model (12.1) with $\mathbb{E} = \mathbb{R}^{m \times n}$, $\mathbb{V} = \mathbb{R}^{m \times (n-1)} \times \mathbb{R}^{(m-1) \times n}$, $f(\mathbf{x}) = \frac{1}{2}\|\mathbf{x} - \mathbf{d}\|_F^2$, and $\mathcal{A}(\mathbf{x}) = (\mathbf{p}^{\mathbf{x}}, \mathbf{q}^{\mathbf{x}})$, where $\mathbf{p}^{\mathbf{x}} \in \mathbb{R}^{m \times (n-1)}$ and $\mathbf{q}^{\mathbf{x}} \in \mathbb{R}^{(m-1) \times n}$ are given by

$$p_{i,j}^{\mathbf{x}} = x_{i,j} - x_{i,j+1}, \quad i = 1, 2, \ldots, m, j = 1, 2, \ldots, n-1,$$
$$q_{i,j}^{\mathbf{x}} = x_{i,j} - x_{i+1,j}, \quad i = 1, 2, \ldots, m-1, j = 1, 2, \ldots, n.$$

The function $g : \mathbb{V} \to \mathbb{R}$ is given in the isotropic case by

$$g(\mathbf{p}, \mathbf{q}) = g_{\mathrm{I}}(\mathbf{p}, \mathbf{q}) \equiv \sum_{i=1}^{m-1} \sum_{j=1}^{n-1} \sqrt{p_{i,j}^2 + q_{i,j}^2} + \sum_{j=1}^{n-1} |p_{m,j}| + \sum_{i=1}^{m-1} |q_{i,n}|$$

and in the anisotropic case by

$$g(\mathbf{p}, \mathbf{q}) = g_{l_1}(\mathbf{p}, \mathbf{q}) \equiv \sum_{i=1}^{m} \sum_{j=1}^{n-1} |p_{i,j}| + \sum_{i=1}^{m-1} \sum_{j=1}^{n} |q_{i,j}|.$$

Since g_{I} and g_{l_1} are a separable sum of either absolute values or l_2 norms, it is easy to compute their prox mappings using Theorem 6.6 (prox of separable functions), Example 6.8 (prox of the l_1-norm), and Example 6.19 (prox of Euclidean norms) and obtain that for any $\mathbf{p} \in \mathbb{R}^{m \times (n-1)}$ and $\mathbf{q} \in \mathbb{R}^{(m-1) \times n}$,

$$\mathrm{prox}_{\lambda g_{\mathrm{I}}}(\mathbf{p}, \mathbf{q}) = (\bar{\mathbf{p}}, \bar{\mathbf{q}}),$$

where

$$\bar{p}_{i,j} = \left(1 - \lambda / \max\left\{ \sqrt{p_{i,j}^2 + q_{i,j}^2}, \lambda \right\} \right) p_{i,j}, \quad i = 1, 2, \ldots, m-1, j = 1, 2, \ldots n-1,$$
$$\bar{p}_{m,j} = \mathcal{T}_\lambda(p_{m,j}), \quad j = 1, 2, \ldots, n-1,$$
$$\bar{q}_{i,j} = \left(1 - \lambda / \max\left\{ \sqrt{p_{i,j}^2 + q_{i,j}^2}, \lambda \right\} \right) q_{i,j}, \quad i = 1, 2, \ldots, m-1, j = 1, 2, \ldots n-1,$$
$$\bar{q}_{i,n} = \mathcal{T}_\lambda(q_{i,n}), \quad i = 1, 2, \ldots, m-1,$$

and

$$\mathrm{prox}_{\lambda g_{l_1}}(\mathbf{p}, \mathbf{q}) = (\tilde{\mathbf{p}}, \tilde{\mathbf{q}}),$$

where

$$\tilde{p}_{i,j} = \mathcal{T}_\lambda(p_{i,j}), \quad i = 1, 2, \ldots, m, j = 1, 2, \ldots n-1,$$
$$\tilde{q}_{i,j} = \mathcal{T}_\lambda(q_{i,j}), \quad i = 1, 2, \ldots, m-1, j = 1, 2, \ldots, n.$$

The last detail that is missing in order to explicitly write the DPG or FDPG methods for solving problem (12.25) is the computation of $\mathcal{A}^T : \mathbb{V} \to \mathbb{E}$ at points in $\mathbb{V}$. For that, note that for any $\mathbf{x} \in \mathbb{E}$ and $(\mathbf{p}, \mathbf{q}) \in \mathbb{V}$,

$$\langle \mathcal{A}(\mathbf{x}), (\mathbf{p}, \mathbf{q}) \rangle = \sum_{i=1}^{m} \sum_{j=1}^{n-1} (x_{i,j} - x_{i,j+1}) p_{i,j} + \sum_{i=1}^{m-1} \sum_{j=1}^{n} (x_{i,j} - x_{i+1,j}) q_{i,j}$$
$$= \sum_{i=1}^{m} \sum_{j=1}^{n} x_{i,j}(p_{i,j} + q_{i,j} - p_{i,j-1} - q_{i-1,j})$$
$$= \langle \mathbf{x}, \mathcal{A}^T(\mathbf{p}, \mathbf{q}) \rangle,$$

where we use a convention that

$$p_{i,0} = p_{i,n} = q_{0,j} = q_{m,j} = 0 \quad \text{for any } i = 1, 2, \ldots, m, j = 1, 2, \ldots, n.$$

Therefore, with the above convention in mind, for any $(\mathbf{p}, \mathbf{q}) \in \mathbb{V}$,

$$\mathcal{A}^T(\mathbf{p}, \mathbf{q})_{i,j} = p_{i,j} + q_{i,j} - p_{i,j-1} - q_{i-1,j}, \quad i = 1, 2, \ldots, m, j = 1, 2, \ldots, n.$$

We also want to compute an upper bound on $\|\mathcal{A}\|^2$. This can be done using the same technique as in the one-dimensional case; note that for any $\mathbf{x} \in \mathbb{R}^{m \times n}$,

$$\|\mathcal{A}(\mathbf{x})\|^2 = \sum_{i=1}^{m} \sum_{j=1}^{n-1} (x_{i,j} - x_{i,j+1})^2 + \sum_{i=1}^{m-1} \sum_{j=1}^{n} (x_{i,j} - x_{i+1,j})^2$$

$$\leq 2 \sum_{i=1}^{m} \sum_{j=1}^{n-1} (x_{i,j}^2 + x_{i,j+1}^2) + 2 \sum_{i=1}^{m-1} \sum_{j=1}^{n} (x_{i,j}^2 + x_{i+1,j}^2)$$

$$\leq 8 \sum_{i=1}^{n} \sum_{j=1}^{m} x_{i,j}^2.$$

Therefore, $\|\mathcal{A}\|^2 \leq 8$. We will now explicitly write the FDPG method for solving the two-dimensional anisotropic total variation problem, meaning problem (12.25) with $g = g_{l_1}$. For the stepsize, we use $L = 8$.

Algorithm 8 [FDPG for solving (12.25) with $g = \lambda \text{TV}_{l_1}$]

- **Initialization:** $\tilde{\mathbf{p}}^0 = \mathbf{p}^0 \in \mathbb{R}^{m \times (n-1)}, \tilde{\mathbf{q}}^0 = \mathbf{q}^0 \in \mathbb{R}^{(m-1) \times n}, t_0 = 1.$

- **General step $(k \geq 0)$:**

  (a) compute $\mathbf{u}^k \in \mathbb{R}^{m \times n}$ by setting for $i = 1, 2, \ldots, m, j = 1, 2, \ldots, n,$

  $$u_{i,j}^k = \tilde{p}_{i,j}^k + \tilde{q}_{i,j}^k - \tilde{p}_{i,j-1}^k - \tilde{q}_{i-1,j}^k + d_{i,j};$$

  (b) set $(\mathbf{p}^{k+1}, \mathbf{q}^{k+1})$ as

  $$p_{i,j}^{k+1} = \tilde{p}_{i,j}^k - \frac{1}{8}(u_{i,j}^k - u_{i,j+1}^k) + \frac{1}{8}\mathcal{T}_{8\lambda}(u_{i,j}^k - u_{i,j+1}^k - 8\tilde{p}_{i,j}^k),$$

  $$q_{i,j}^{k+1} = \tilde{q}_{i,j}^k - \frac{1}{8}(u_{i,j}^k - u_{i+1,j}^k) + \frac{1}{8}\mathcal{T}_{8\lambda}(u_{i,j}^k - u_{i+1,j}^k - 8\tilde{q}_{i,j}^k);$$

  (c) $t_{k+1} = \frac{1 + \sqrt{1 + 4t_k^2}}{2};$

  (d) $(\tilde{\mathbf{p}}^{k+1}, \tilde{\mathbf{q}}^{k+1}) = (\mathbf{p}^{k+1}, \mathbf{q}^{k+1}) + \left(\frac{t_k - 1}{t_{k+1}}\right)(\mathbf{p}^{k+1} - \mathbf{p}^k, \mathbf{q}^{k+1} - \mathbf{q}^k).$

12.5 The Dual Block Proximal Gradient Method

12.5.1 Preliminaries

In this section we will consider the problem

$$\min_{\mathbf{x} \in \mathbb{E}} \left\{ f(\mathbf{x}) + \sum_{i=1}^{p} g_i(\mathbf{x}) \right\}, \tag{12.27}$$

where the following assumptions are made.

Assumption 12.14.

(A) $f : \mathbb{E} \to (-\infty, +\infty]$ is proper closed and σ-strongly convex ($\sigma > 0$).

(B) $g_i : \mathbb{E} \to (-\infty, +\infty]$ is proper closed and convex for any $i \in \{1, 2, \ldots, p\}$.

(C) $\mathrm{ri}(\mathrm{dom}(f)) \cap (\cap_{i=1}^{p} \mathrm{ri}(\mathrm{dom}(g_i))) \neq \emptyset$.

Problem (12.27) is actually a generalization of the projection problem discussed in Section 12.4.2, and we can use a similar observation to the one made there and note that problem (12.27) fits model (12.1) with $\mathbb{V} = \mathbb{E}^p$, $g(\mathbf{x}_1, \mathbf{x}_2, \ldots, \mathbf{x}_p) = \sum_{i=1}^{p} g_i(\mathbf{x}_i)$, and $\mathcal{A} : \mathbb{E} \to \mathbb{V}$ given by

$$\mathcal{A}(\mathbf{z}) = (\underbrace{\mathbf{z}, \mathbf{z}, \ldots, \mathbf{z}}_{p \text{ times}}) \text{ for any } \mathbf{z} \in \mathbb{E}.$$

Noting that

- $\|\mathcal{A}\|^2 = p$;
- $\mathcal{A}^T(\mathbf{y}) = \sum_{i=1}^{p} y_i$ for any $\mathbf{y} \in \mathbb{E}^p$;
- $\mathrm{prox}_{Lg}(\mathbf{v}_1, \mathbf{v}_2, \ldots, \mathbf{v}_p) = (\mathrm{prox}_{Lg_1}(\mathbf{v}_1), \mathrm{prox}_{Lg_2}(\mathbf{v}_2), \ldots, \mathrm{prox}_{Lg_p}(\mathbf{v}_p))$ for any $\mathbf{v}_i \in \mathbb{E}$, $i = 1, 2, \ldots, p$,

we can explicitly write the FDPG method with $L = \frac{\|\mathcal{A}\|^2}{\sigma} = \frac{p}{\sigma}$.

Algorithm 9 [FDPG for solving (12.27)]

- **Initialization:** $\mathbf{w}^0 = \mathbf{y}^0 \in \mathbb{E}^p, t_0 = 1$.

- **General step ($k \geq 0$):**

  (a) $\mathbf{u}^k = \mathrm{argmax}_{\mathbf{u} \in \mathbb{E}} \left\{ \langle \mathbf{u}, \sum_{i=1}^{p} \mathbf{w}_i^k \rangle - f(\mathbf{u}) \right\}$;

  (b) $\mathbf{y}_i^{k+1} = \mathbf{w}_i^k - \frac{\sigma}{p} \mathbf{u}^k + \frac{\sigma}{p} \mathrm{prox}_{\frac{p}{\sigma} g_i}(\mathbf{u}^k - \frac{p}{\sigma} \mathbf{w}_i^k)$, $i = 1, 2, \ldots, p$;

  (c) $t_{k+1} = \frac{1 + \sqrt{1 + 4t_k^2}}{2}$;

  (d) $\mathbf{w}^{k+1} = \mathbf{y}^{k+1} + \left(\frac{t_k - 1}{t_{k+1}} \right) (\mathbf{y}^{k+1} - \mathbf{y}^k)$.

The primal sequence is given by

$$\mathbf{x}^k = \mathrm{argmax}_{\mathbf{x} \in \mathbb{E}} \left\{ \langle \mathbf{x}, \sum_{i=1}^{p} \mathbf{y}_i^k \rangle - f(\mathbf{x}) \right\}.$$

12.5.2   The Dual Block Proximal Gradient Method

Note that the stepsize taken at each iteration of Algorithm 9 is $\frac{\sigma}{p}$, which might be extremely small when the number of blocks (p) is large. The natural question is therefore whether it is possible to define a dual-based method whose stepsize is independent of the dimension. For that, let us consider the dual of problem (12.27), meaning problem (12.4). Keeping in mind that $\mathcal{A}^T(\mathbf{y}) = \sum_{i=1}^{p} \mathbf{y}_i$ and the fact that $g^*(\mathbf{y}) = \sum_{i=1}^{p} g_i^*(\mathbf{y}_i)$ (see Theorem 4.12), we obtain the following form of the dual problem:

$$q_{\text{opt}} = \max_{\mathbf{y} \in \mathbb{E}^p} \left\{ -f^* \left(\sum_{i=1}^{p} \mathbf{y}_i \right) - \sum_{i=1}^{p} \underbrace{g_i^*(-\mathbf{y}_i)}_{G_i(\mathbf{y}_i)} \right\}. \tag{12.28}$$

Since the nonsmooth part in (12.28) is block separable, we can employ a block proximal gradient method (see Chapter 11) on the dual problem (in its minimization form). Suppose that the current point is $\mathbf{y}^k = (\mathbf{y}_1^k, \mathbf{y}_2^k, \ldots, \mathbf{y}_p^k)$. At each iteration of a block proximal gradient method we pick an index i according to some rule and perform a proximal gradient step only on the ith block which is thus updated by the formula

$$\mathbf{y}_i^{k+1} = \text{prox}_{\sigma G_i} \left(\mathbf{y}_i^k - \sigma \nabla f^* \left(\sum_{j=1}^{p} \mathbf{y}_j^k \right) \right).$$

The stepsize was chosen to be σ since f is proper closed and σ-strongly convex, and thus, by the conjugate correspondence theorem (Theorem 5.26), f^* is $\frac{1}{\sigma}$-smooth, from which it follows that the block Lipschitz constants of the function $(\mathbf{y}_1, \mathbf{y}_2, \ldots, \mathbf{y}_p) \mapsto f^*(\sum_{i=1}^{p} \mathbf{y}_i)$ are $\frac{1}{\sigma}$. Thus, the constant stepsize can be taken as σ. We can now write a dual representation of the dual block proximal gradient (DBPG) method.

The Dual Block Proximal Gradient (DBPG) Method—dual representation

- **Initialization:** pick $\mathbf{y}^0 = (\mathbf{y}_1^0, \mathbf{y}_2^0, \ldots, \mathbf{y}_p^0) \in \mathbb{E}^p$.

- **General step ($k \geq 0$):**
    - pick an index $i_k \in \{1, 2, \ldots, p\}$;
    - compute $\mathbf{y}_j^{k+1} = \begin{cases} \text{prox}_{\sigma G_{i_k}} \left(\mathbf{y}_{i_k}^k - \sigma \nabla f^*(\sum_{j=1}^{p} \mathbf{y}_j^k) \right), & j = i_k, \\ \mathbf{y}_j^k, & j \neq i_k. \end{cases}$

We can utilize Lemma 12.5 to obtain a primal representation of the general step of the DBPG method.

Lemma 12.15. *Let f and $g_1, g_2, \ldots, g_p$ satisfy properties* (A) *and* (B) *of Assumption 12.14. Let $i \in \{1, 2, \ldots, p\}$ and $G_i(\mathbf{y}_i) \equiv g_i^*(-\mathbf{y}_i)$. Let $L > 0$. Then $\mathbf{y}_i \in \mathbb{E}$ and $\mathbf{v} \in \mathbb{E}^p$ satisfy the relation*

$$\mathbf{y}_i = \mathrm{prox}_{\frac{1}{L}G_i}\left(\mathbf{v}_i - \frac{1}{L}\nabla f^*\left(\textstyle\sum_{j=1}^p \mathbf{v}_j\right)\right)$$

if and only if

$$\mathbf{y}_i = \mathbf{v}_i - \frac{1}{L}\tilde{\mathbf{x}} + \frac{1}{L}\mathrm{prox}_{Lg_i}\left(\tilde{\mathbf{x}} - L\mathbf{v}_i\right),$$

where

$$\tilde{\mathbf{x}} = \mathrm{argmax}_{\mathbf{x} \in \mathbb{E}}\left\{\left\langle \mathbf{x}, \textstyle\sum_{j=1}^p \mathbf{v}_j\right\rangle - f(\mathbf{x})\right\}.$$

Proof. Follows by invoking Lemma 12.5 with $\mathbb{V} = \mathbb{E}$, $\mathcal{A} = \mathcal{I}$, $\mathbf{b} = \sum_{j \neq i}\mathbf{v}_j$, $g = g_i$, $\mathbf{y} = \mathbf{y}_i$, and $\mathbf{v} = \mathbf{v}_i$.   □

Using Lemma 12.15, we can now write a primal representation of the DBPG method.

The Dual Block Proximal Gradient (DBPG) Method—primal representation

Initialization: pick $\mathbf{y}^0 = (\mathbf{y}_1^0, \mathbf{y}_2^0, \ldots, \mathbf{y}_p^0) \in \mathbb{E}$.
General step: for any $k = 0, 1, 2, \ldots$ execute the following steps:

(a) pick $i_k \in \{1, 2, \ldots, p\}$;

(b) set $\mathbf{x}^k = \mathrm{argmax}_{\mathbf{x} \in \mathbb{E}}\left\{\langle \mathbf{x}, \sum_{j=1}^p \mathbf{y}_j^k\rangle - f(\mathbf{x})\right\}$;

(c) set $\mathbf{y}_j^{k+1} = \begin{cases} \mathbf{y}_{i_k}^k - \sigma\mathbf{x}^k + \sigma\mathrm{prox}_{g_i/\sigma}\left(\mathbf{x}^k - \mathbf{y}_{i_k}^k/\sigma\right), & j = i_k, \\ \mathbf{y}_j^k, & j \neq i_k. \end{cases}$

Note that the derived DBPG method is a functional decomposition method, as it utilizes only one of the functions $g_1, g_2, \ldots, g_p$ at each iteration, and in addition the computation involving the function f (step (b)) does not involve any other function. Thus, we obtained that in this case a variables decomposition method in the dual space gives rise to a functional decomposition method in the primal space.

What is missing from the above description of the DBPG method is the index selection strategy, meaning the rule for choosing i_k at each iteration. We will consider two variations.

- **Cyclic.** $i_k = (k \mod p) + 1$.

- **Randomized.** i_k is randomly picked from $\{1, 2, \ldots, p\}$ by a uniform distribution.

12.5.3   Convergence Analysis

The rate of convergence of the DBPG method is a simple consequence of the rates of convergence already established for the block proximal gradient method in Chapter 11 combined with the primal-dual relation presented in Lemma 12.7.

Cyclic Block Order

Recall that since the model (12.27) is a special case of the general model (12.1) (with $\mathbb{V} = \mathbb{E}^p, \mathcal{A} : \mathbf{z} \mapsto (\mathbf{z}, \mathbf{z}, \ldots, \mathbf{z}), g(\mathbf{x}) = \sum_{i=1}^p g_i(\mathbf{x}_i)$), then under Assumption 12.14 the strong duality theorem (Theorem 12.2) holds, and thus the dual problem (12.28) has a nonempty optimal set. We will denote the set of dual optimal solutions by Λ^*. The following assumption is required to present a convergence result for the DBPG method with a cyclic index selection strategy.

Assumption 12.16. *For any $\alpha > 0$, there exists $R_\alpha > 0$ such that*

$$\max_{\mathbf{y}, \mathbf{y}^* \in \mathbb{E}^p} \{\|\mathbf{y} - \mathbf{y}^*\| : q(\mathbf{y}) \geq \alpha, \mathbf{y}^* \in \Lambda^*\} \leq R_\alpha,$$

where $q(\mathbf{y}) \equiv -f^*(\sum_{i=1}^p \mathbf{y}_i) - \sum_{i=1}^p g_i^*(-\mathbf{y}_i)$.

Theorem 12.17 ($O(1/k)$ rate of convergence of DBPG with cyclic order). *Suppose that Assumptions 12.14 and 12.16 hold. Let $\{\mathbf{x}^k\}_{k\geq 0}$ and $\{\mathbf{y}^k\}_{k\geq 0}$ be the primal and dual sequences generated by the DBPG method with cyclic index selection strategy for solving problem (12.27). Then for any $k \geq 2$,*

(a) $q_{\mathrm{opt}} - q(\mathbf{y}^{pk}) \leq \max\left\{\left(\frac{1}{2}\right)^{(k-1)/2} (q_{\mathrm{opt}} - q(\mathbf{y}^0)), \frac{8p(p+1)^2 R^2}{\sigma(k-1)}\right\}$;

(b) $\|\mathbf{x}^{pk} - \mathbf{x}^*\|^2 \leq \frac{2}{\sigma} \max\left\{\left(\frac{1}{2}\right)^{(k-1)/2} (q_{\mathrm{opt}} - q(\mathbf{y}^0)), \frac{8p(p+1)^2 R^2}{\sigma(k-1)}\right\}$.

In the above two formulas $R = R_{q(\mathbf{y}^0)}$.

Proof. (a) The proof follows by invoking Theorem 11.18 while taking into account that in this case the constants in (11.24) are given by $L_{\max} = L_{\min} = \frac{1}{\sigma}, L_f = \frac{p}{\sigma}$.

(b) By the primal-dual relation, Lemma 12.7, $\|\mathbf{x}^{pk} - \mathbf{x}^*\|^2 \leq \frac{2}{\sigma}(q_{\mathrm{opt}} - q(\mathbf{y}^{pk}))$, which, combined with part (a), yields the inequality of part (b). $\square$

Randomized Block Order

A direct result of the $O(1/k)$ rate of convergence of the RBPG method presented in Theorem 11.25 along with the primal-dual relation (Lemma 12.7) yields the following result on the convergence of the DBPG method with random index selection strategy. As in Section 11.5, we will use the notation of the random variable

$\xi_k \equiv \{i_0, i_1, \ldots, i_k\}$. Note that in the randomized setting we do not require Assumption 12.16 to hold.

Theorem 12.18 ($O(1/k)$ rate of convergence of DBPG with randomized order). *Suppose that Assumption 12.14 holds. Let $\{\mathbf{x}^k\}_{k \geq 0}$ and $\{\mathbf{y}^k\}_{k \geq 0}$ be the primal and dual sequences generated by the DBPG method with randomized index selection strategy. Then for any $k \geq 0$,*

(a) $q_{\text{opt}} - \mathsf{E}_{\xi_k}(q(\mathbf{y}^{k+1})) \leq \frac{p}{p+k+1} \left(\frac{1}{2\sigma} \|\mathbf{y}^0 - \mathbf{y}^*\|^2 + q_{\text{opt}} - q(\mathbf{y}^0) \right);$

(b) $\mathsf{E}_{\xi_k} \|\mathbf{x}^{k+1} - \mathbf{x}^*\|^2 \leq \frac{2p}{\sigma(p+k+1)} \left(\frac{1}{2\sigma} \|\mathbf{y}^0 - \mathbf{y}^*\|^2 + q_{\text{opt}} - q(\mathbf{y}^0) \right).$

12.5.4 Acceleration in the Two-Block Case[69]

Both the deterministic and the randomized DBPG methods are not accelerated methods, and consequently it was only possible to show that they exhibit an $O(1/k)$ rate of convergence. In the case where $p = 2$, we will show that it is actually possible to derive an accelerated dual block proximal gradient method by using a simple trick. For that, note that when $p = 2$, the model amounts to

$$f_{\text{opt}} = \min_{\mathbf{x} \in \mathbb{E}} \{F(\mathbf{x}) \equiv f(\mathbf{x}) + g_1(\mathbf{x}) + g_2(\mathbf{x})\}. \tag{12.29}$$

We can rewrite the problem as

$$\min_{\mathbf{x} \in \mathbb{E}} \{\tilde{f}(\mathbf{x}) + g_2(\mathbf{x})\}, \tag{12.30}$$

where $\tilde{f} = f + g_1$. If Assumption 12.14 holds with $p = 2$, then $\tilde{f}$ is proper closed and σ-strongly convex, g_2 is proper closed and convex, and the regularity condition $\text{ri}(\text{dom}(\tilde{f})) \cap \text{ri}(\text{dom}(g_2)) \neq \emptyset$ is satisfied. This means that Assumption 12.1 holds for $f = \tilde{f}$, $g = g_2$, and $\mathcal{A} = \mathcal{I}$. We can now define the *accelerated dual block proximal gradient* (ADBPG), which is the FDPG method with stepsize σ employed on the model (12.1) with $f = \tilde{f}$, $g = g_2$, and $\mathcal{A} = \mathcal{I}$.

The ADBPG Method

Initialization: $\mathbf{w}^0 = \mathbf{y}^0 \in \mathbb{E}, t_0 = 1$.
General step ($k \geq 0$):

(a) $\mathbf{u}^k = \text{argmax}_{\mathbf{u}} \{\langle \mathbf{u}, \mathbf{w}^k \rangle - f(\mathbf{u}) - g_1(\mathbf{u})\}$;

(b) $\mathbf{y}^{k+1} = \mathbf{w}^k - \sigma\mathbf{u}^k + \sigma\text{prox}_{g_2/\sigma}(\mathbf{u}^k - \mathbf{w}^k/\sigma)$;

(c) $t_{k+1} = \frac{1+\sqrt{1+4t_k^2}}{2}$;

(d) $\mathbf{w}^{k+1} = \mathbf{y}^{k+1} + \left(\frac{t_k-1}{t_{k+1}}\right)(\mathbf{y}^{k+1} - \mathbf{y}^k)$.

---

[69]The accelerated method ADBPG is a different representation of the accelerated method proposed by Chambolle and Pock in [41].

A direct consequence of Theorem 12.10 is the following result on the rate of convergence of the ADBPG method.

Theorem 12.19 ($O(1/k^2)$ rate of convergence of ADBPG). *Suppose that Assumption 12.14 holds with $p = 2$, and let $\{\mathbf{y}^k\}_{k \geq 0}$ be the sequence generated by the ADBPG method. Then for any optimal solution $\mathbf{y}^*$ of the dual problem*

$$\min_{\mathbf{y} \in \mathbb{E}}\{(\tilde{f})^*(\mathbf{y}) + g_2^*(-\mathbf{y})\}$$

and $k \geq 1$, it holds that

$$\|\mathbf{x}^k - \mathbf{x}^*\|^2 \leq \frac{4\|\mathbf{y}^0 - \mathbf{y}^*\|^2}{\sigma^2(k+1)^2},$$

where $\mathbf{x}^k = \mathrm{argmax}_{\mathbf{x}}\left\{\langle \mathbf{x}, \mathbf{y}^k \rangle - f(\mathbf{x}) - g_1(\mathbf{x})\right\}$.

Remark 12.20. *When $f(\mathbf{x}) = \frac{1}{2}\|\mathbf{x} - \mathbf{d}\|^2$ for some $\mathbf{d} \in \mathbb{E}$, step (a) of the ADBPG can be written as a prox computation:*

$$\mathbf{u}^k = \mathrm{prox}_{g_1}(\mathbf{d} + \mathbf{w}^k).$$

Remark 12.21. *Note that the ADBPG is not a full functional decomposition method since step (a) is a computation involving both f and g_1, but it still separates between g_1 and g_2. The method has two main features. First, it is an accelerated method. Second, the stepsize taken in the method is σ, in contrast to the stepsize of $\frac{\sigma}{2}$ that is used in Algorithm 9, which is another type of an FDPG method.*

12.6   Examples II

Example 12.22 (one-dimensional total variation denoising). In this example we will compare the performance of the ADBPG method and Algorithm 9 (with $p = 2$)—both are FDPG methods, although quite different. We will consider the one-dimensional total variation problem (see also Section 12.4.3)

$$f_{\mathrm{opt}} = \min_{\mathbf{x} \in \mathbb{R}^n}\left\{F(\mathbf{x}) \equiv \frac{1}{2}\|\mathbf{x} - \mathbf{d}\|_2^2 + \lambda \sum_{i=1}^{n-1}|x_{i-1} - x_i|\right\}, \tag{12.31}$$

where $\mathbf{d} \in \mathbb{R}^n$ and $\lambda > 0$. The above problem can be written as

$$\min_{\mathbf{x} \in \mathbb{R}^n}\{f(\mathbf{x}) + g_1(\mathbf{x}) + g_2(\mathbf{x})\},$$

where

$$f(\mathbf{x}) = \frac{1}{2}\|\mathbf{x} - \mathbf{d}\|_2^2,$$

$$g_1(\mathbf{x}) = \lambda \sum_{i=1}^{\lfloor \frac{n}{2} \rfloor}|x_{2i-1} - x_{2i}|,$$

$$g_2(\mathbf{x}) = \lambda \sum_{i=1}^{\lfloor \frac{n-1}{2} \rfloor}|x_{2i} - x_{2i+1}|.$$

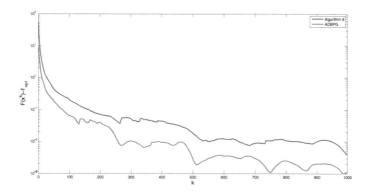

Figure 12.4. *Comparison of the ADBPG method and Algorithm 9 employed on the one-dimensional total variation denoising problem.*

By Example 6.17 we have that the prox of λ times the two-dimensional function $h(y, z) = |y - z|$ is given by

$$\text{prox}_{\lambda h}(y, z) = (y, z) + \frac{1}{2\lambda^2}(\mathcal{T}_{2\lambda^2}(\lambda y - \lambda z) - \lambda y + \lambda z)(\lambda, -\lambda)$$

$$= (y, z) + \frac{1}{2}([|y - z| - 2\lambda]_+ \text{sgn}(y - z) - y + z)(1, -1).$$

Therefore, using the separability of g_1 w.r.t. the pairs of variables $\{x_1, x_2\}$, $\{x_3, x_4\}, \dots$, it follows that

$$\text{prox}_{g_1}(\mathbf{x}) = \mathbf{x} + \frac{1}{2}\sum_{i=1}^{\lfloor \frac{n}{2} \rfloor}([|x_{2i-1} - x_{2i}| - 2\lambda]_+ \text{sgn}(x_{2i-1} - x_{2i}) - x_{2i-1} + x_{2i})(\mathbf{e}_{2i-1} - \mathbf{e}_{2i}),$$

and similarly

$$\text{prox}_{g_2}(\mathbf{x}) = \mathbf{x} + \frac{1}{2}\sum_{i=1}^{\lfloor \frac{n-1}{2} \rfloor}([|x_{2i} - x_{2i+1}| - 2\lambda]_+ \text{sgn}(x_{2i} - x_{2i+1}) - x_{2i} + x_{2i+1})(\mathbf{e}_{2i} - \mathbf{e}_{2i+1}).$$

Equipped with the above expressions for prox_{g_1} and prox_{g_2} (recalling that step (a) only requires a single computation of prox_{g_1}; see Remark 12.20), we can employ the ADBPG method and Algorithm 9 on problem (12.31). The computational effort per iteration in both methods is almost identical and is dominated by single evaluations of the prox mappings of g_1 and g_2. We ran 1000 iterations of both algorithms starting with a dual vector which is all zeros. In Figure 12.4 we plot the distance in function values[70] $F(\mathbf{x}^k) - f_{\text{opt}}$ as a function of the iteration index k. Evidently, the ADBPG method exhibits the superior performance. Most likely, the reason is the fact that the ADBPG method uses a larger stepsize (σ) than the one used by Algorithm 9 ($\frac{\sigma}{2}$). ∎

---

[70]Since the specific example is unconstrained, the distance in function values is indeed in some sense an "optimality measure."

Example 12.23 (two-dimensional total variation denoising). Consider the isotropic two-dimensional total variation problem

$$\min_{\mathbf{x} \in \mathbb{R}^{m \times n}} \left\{ \frac{1}{2} \|\mathbf{x} - \mathbf{d}\|_F^2 + \lambda \mathrm{TV}_I(\mathbf{x}) \right\},$$

where $\mathbf{d} \in \mathbb{R}^{m \times n}$, $\lambda > 0$, and TV_I is given in (12.26). It does not seem possible to decompose TV_I into two functions whose prox can be directly computed as in the one-dimensional case. However, a decomposition into three separable functions (w.r.t. triplets of variables) is possible. To describe the decomposition, we introduce the following notation. Let D_k denote the set of indices that correspond to the elements of the kth diagonal of an $m \times n$ matrix, where D_0 represents the indices set of the main diagonal, and D_k for $k > 0$ and $k < 0$ stand for the diagonals above and below the main diagonal, respectively. In addition, consider the partition of the diagonal indices set, $\{-(m-1), \ldots, n-1\}$, into three sets

$$K_i \equiv \left\{ k \in \{-(m-1), \ldots, n-1\} : (k+1-i) \mod 3 = 0 \right\}, \qquad i = 1, 2, 3.$$

With the above notation, we are now ready to write the function TV_I as

$$
\begin{aligned}
\mathrm{TV}_I(\mathbf{x}) &= \sum_{i=1}^{m} \sum_{j=1}^{n} \sqrt{(x_{i,j} - x_{i,j+1})^2 + (x_{i,j} - x_{i+1,j})^2} \\
&= \sum_{k \in K_1} \sum_{(i,j) \in D_k} \sqrt{(x_{i,j} - x_{i,j+1})^2 + (x_{i,j} - x_{i+1,j})^2} \\
&\quad + \sum_{k \in K_2} \sum_{(i,j) \in D_k} \sqrt{(x_{i,j} - x_{i,j+1})^2 + (x_{i,j} - x_{i+1,j})^2} \\
&\quad + \sum_{k \in K_3} \sum_{(i,j) \in D_k} \sqrt{(x_{i,j} - x_{i,j+1})^2 + (x_{i,j} - x_{i+1,j})^2} \\
&= \psi_1(\mathbf{x}) + \psi_2(\mathbf{x}) + \psi_3(\mathbf{x}),
\end{aligned}
$$

where we assume in the above expressions that $x_{i,n+1} = x_{i,n}$ and $x_{m+1,j} = x_{m,j}$. The fact that each of the functions ψ_i is separable w.r.t. triplets of variables $\{x_{i,j}, x_{i+1,j}, x_{i,j+1}\}$ is evident from the illustration in Figure 12.5.

The denoising problem can thus be rewritten as

$$\min_{\mathbf{x} \in \mathbb{R}^{m \times n}} \left\{ \frac{1}{2} \|\mathbf{x} - \mathbf{d}\|_F^2 + \lambda \psi_1(\mathbf{x}) + \lambda \psi_2(\mathbf{x}) + \lambda \psi_3(\mathbf{x}) \right\}.$$

It is not possible to employ the ADBPG method since the nonsmooth part is decomposed into three functions. However, it is possible to employ the DBPG method, which has no restriction on the number of functions. The algorithm requires evaluating a prox mapping of one of the functions $\lambda \psi_i$ at each iteration. By the separability of these functions, it follows that each prox computation involves several prox computations of three-dimensional functions of the form λh, where

$$h(x, y, z) = \sqrt{(x-y)^2 + (x-z)^2}.$$

$$\psi_1 \qquad\qquad \psi_2 \qquad\qquad \psi_3$$

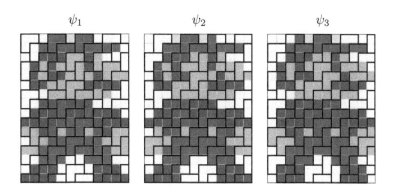

Figure 12.5. *The decomposition of a* 16×12 *pixels Mario image according to the isotropic TV into three separable functions. The images are partitioned into blocks of three pixels positioned in an r-shaped structure. Each block encompasses the three pixels that form the term* $\sqrt{(x_{i,j} - x_{i+1,j})^2 + (x_{i,j} - x_{i,j+1})^2}$. *Summing over all the terms represented by the blocks of any of the above images yields the appropriate separable function. Reprinted with permission from Elsevier.* [23]

The prox of λh can be computed using Lemma 6.68 and is given by

$$\text{prox}_{\lambda h}(\mathbf{x}) = \begin{cases} \mathbf{x} - \mathbf{A}^T(\mathbf{A}\mathbf{A}^T)^{-1}\mathbf{A}\mathbf{x}, & \|(\mathbf{A}\mathbf{A}^T)^{-1}\mathbf{A}\mathbf{x}\|_2 \leq \lambda, \\ \mathbf{x} - \mathbf{A}^T(\mathbf{A}\mathbf{A}^T + \alpha^*\mathbf{I})^{-1}\mathbf{A}\mathbf{x}, & \|(\mathbf{A}\mathbf{A}^T)^{-1}\mathbf{A}\mathbf{x}\|_2 > \lambda, \end{cases}$$

where α^* is the unique root of the decreasing function

$$g(\alpha) = \|(\mathbf{A}\mathbf{A}^T + \alpha^*\mathbf{I})^{-1}\mathbf{A}\mathbf{x}\|_2^2 - \lambda^2$$

and $\mathbf{A}$ is the matrix

$$\mathbf{A} = \begin{pmatrix} 1 & -1 & 0 \\ 1 & 0 & -1 \end{pmatrix}. \quad \blacksquare$$

Chapter 13

The Generalized Conditional Gradient Method

Underlying Spaces: In this chapter, all the underlying spaces are Euclidean.

13.1   The Frank–Wolfe/Conditional Gradient Method

Consider the problem

$$\min\{f(\mathbf{x}) : \mathbf{x} \in C\}, \tag{13.1}$$

where $C \subseteq \mathbb{E}$ is a nonempty convex and compact set and $f : \mathbb{E} \to (-\infty, \infty]$ is a convex function satisfying $C \subseteq \text{dom}(f)$. We further assume that $\text{dom}(f)$ is open and that f is differentiable over $\text{dom}(f)$. One method that can be employed in order to solve the problem is the projected gradient method (see Section 10.2) whose update step is

$$\mathbf{x}^{k+1} = P_C(\mathbf{x}^k - t_k \nabla f(\mathbf{x}^k)),$$

with t_k being an appropriately chosen stepsize. In this chapter we will consider an alternative approach that does not require the evaluation of the orthogonal projection operator at each iteration. Instead, the approach, known as the *conditional gradient* method or *Frank–Wolfe* algorithm, computes the next step as a convex combination of the current iterate and a minimizer of a linearized version of the objective function over C.

The Conditional Gradient Method

Initialization: pick $\mathbf{x}^0 \in C$.
General step: for any $k = 0, 1, 2, \ldots$ execute the following steps:

  (a) compute $\mathbf{p}^k \in \text{argmin}_{\mathbf{p} \in C} \langle \mathbf{p}, \nabla f(\mathbf{x}^k) \rangle$;

  (b) choose $t_k \in [0, 1]$ and set $\mathbf{x}^{k+1} = \mathbf{x}^k + t_k(\mathbf{p}^k - \mathbf{x}^k)$.

The conditional gradient approach is potentially beneficial in cases where computation of a linear oracle over the feasible set (that is, computation of a minimizer of a linear function over C) is a simpler task than evaluating the orthogonal projection onto C. We will actually analyze an extension of the method that tackles the problem of minimizing a composite function $f + g$, where the case $g = \delta_C$ brings us back to the model (13.1).

13.2   The Generalized Conditional Gradient Method

13.2.1   Model and Method

Consider the composite problem

$$\min \{F(\mathbf{x}) \equiv f(\mathbf{x}) + g(\mathbf{x})\}, \tag{13.2}$$

where we assume the following set of properties.

Assumption 13.1.

(A) $g : \mathbb{E} \to (-\infty, \infty]$ *is proper closed and convex and* $\mathrm{dom}(g)$ *is compact.*

(B) $f : \mathbb{E} \to (-\infty, \infty]$ *is* L_f*-smooth over* $\mathrm{dom}(f)$ $(L_f > 0)$*, which is assumed to be an open and convex set satisfying* $\mathrm{dom}(g) \subseteq \mathrm{dom}(f)$.

(C) *The optimal set of problem* (13.2) *is nonempty and denoted by* X^*. *The optimal value of the problem is denoted by* F_{opt}.

It is not difficult to deduce that property (C) is implied by properties (A) and (B). The *generalized conditional gradient method* for solving the composite model (13.2) is similar to the conditional gradient method, but instead of linearizing the entire objective function, the algorithm computes a minimizer of the sum of the linearized smooth part of f around the current iterate and leaves g unchanged.

The Generalized Conditional Gradient Method

Initialization: pick $\mathbf{x}^0 \in \mathrm{dom}(g)$.
General step: for any $k = 0, 1, 2, \ldots$ execute the following steps:

(a) compute $\mathbf{p}^k \in \mathrm{argmin}_{\mathbf{p} \in \mathbb{E}} \left\{ \langle \mathbf{p}, \nabla f(\mathbf{x}^k) \rangle + g(\mathbf{p}) \right\}$;

(b) choose $t_k \in [0, 1]$ and set $\mathbf{x}^{k+1} = \mathbf{x}^k + t_k(\mathbf{p}^k - \mathbf{x}^k)$.

13.2.2   The Conditional Gradient Norm

Throughout this chapter we will use the following notation:

$$\mathbf{p}(\mathbf{x}) \in \mathrm{argmin}_{\mathbf{p}} \left\{ \langle \mathbf{p}, \nabla f(\mathbf{x}) \rangle + g(\mathbf{p}) \right\}. \tag{13.3}$$

Of course, $\mathbf{p}(\mathbf{x})$ is not uniquely defined in the sense that the above minimization problem might have multiple optimal solutions. We assume that there exists some rule for choosing an optimal solution whenever the optimal set of (13.3) is not a singleton and that the vector $\mathbf{p}^k$ computed by the generalized conditional gradient method is chosen by the same rule, meaning that $\mathbf{p}^k = \mathbf{p}(\mathbf{x}^k)$. We can write the update step of the generalized conditional gradient method as

$$\mathbf{x}^{k+1} = \mathbf{x}^k + t_k(\mathbf{p}(\mathbf{x}^k) - \mathbf{x}^k).$$

A natural optimality measure in the context of proximal gradient methods is the gradient mapping (see Section 10.3.2). However, the analysis of the conditional gradient method relies on a different optimality measure, which we will refer to as the *conditional gradient norm*.

Definition 13.2 (conditional gradient norm). *Suppose that f and g satisfy properties* (A) *and* (B) *of Assumption* 13.1. *Then the* **conditional gradient norm** *is the function $S : \mathrm{dom}(f) \to \mathbb{R}$ defined by*

$$S(\mathbf{x}) \equiv \langle \nabla f(\mathbf{x}), \mathbf{x} - \mathbf{p}(\mathbf{x}) \rangle + g(\mathbf{x}) - g(\mathbf{p}(\mathbf{x})).$$

Remark 13.3. *The conditional gradient norm obviously depends on f and g, so a more precise notation would be $S^{f,g}(\mathbf{x})$. However, since the identities of f and g will be clear from the context, we will keep the notation $S(\mathbf{x})$.*

Remark 13.4. *By the definition of $\mathbf{p}(\mathbf{x})$ (equation* (13.3)*), we can also write $S(\mathbf{x})$ as*

$$S(\mathbf{x}) = \max_{\mathbf{p} \in \mathbb{E}} \left\{ \langle \nabla f(\mathbf{x}), \mathbf{x} - \mathbf{p} \rangle + g(\mathbf{x}) - g(\mathbf{p}) \right\}. \tag{13.4}$$

The following lemma shows how to write the conditional gradient norm in terms of the conjugate of g.

Lemma 13.5. *Suppose that f and g satisfy properties* (A) *and* (B) *of Assumption* 13.1. *Then for any $\mathbf{x} \in \mathrm{dom}(f)$,*

$$S(\mathbf{x}) = \langle \nabla f(\mathbf{x}), \mathbf{x} \rangle + g(\mathbf{x}) + g^*(-\nabla f(\mathbf{x})). \tag{13.5}$$

Proof. Follows by the definition of the conjugate function:

$$
\begin{aligned}
S(\mathbf{x}) &= \max_{\mathbf{p} \in \mathbb{E}} \left\{ \langle \nabla f(\mathbf{x}), \mathbf{x} - \mathbf{p} \rangle + g(\mathbf{x}) - g(\mathbf{p}) \right\} \\
&= \langle \nabla f(\mathbf{x}), \mathbf{x} \rangle + g(\mathbf{x}) + \max_{\mathbf{p} \in \mathbb{E}} \left\{ \langle -\nabla f(\mathbf{x}), \mathbf{p} \rangle - g(\mathbf{p}) \right\} \\
&= \langle \nabla f(\mathbf{x}), \mathbf{x} \rangle + g(\mathbf{x}) + g^*(-\nabla f(\mathbf{x})). \quad \square
\end{aligned}
$$

A direct consequence of Lemma 13.5 is that $S(\cdot)$ is an optimality measure in the sense that it is always nonnegative and is equal to zero only at stationary points of problem (13.2).

Theorem 13.6 (conditional gradient norm as an optimality measure). *Suppose that f and g satisfy properties* (A) *and* (B) *of Assumption* 13.1. *Then*

(a) $S(\mathbf{x}) \geq 0$ *for any* $\mathbf{x} \in \mathrm{dom}(f)$;

(b) $S(\mathbf{x}^*) = 0$ *if and only if* $-\nabla f(\mathbf{x}^*) \in \partial g(\mathbf{x}^*)$, *that is, if and only if* $\mathbf{x}^*$ *is a stationary point of problem* (13.2).

Proof. (a) Follows by the expression (13.5) for the conditional gradient norm and Fenchel's inequality (Theorem 4.6).

(b) By part (a), it follows that $S(\mathbf{x}^*) = 0$ if and only if $S(\mathbf{x}^*) \leq 0$, which is the same as the relation (using the expression (13.4) for $S(\mathbf{x}^*)$)

$$\langle \nabla f(\mathbf{x}^*), \mathbf{x}^* - \mathbf{p} \rangle + g(\mathbf{x}^*) - g(\mathbf{p}) \leq 0 \text{ for all } \mathbf{p} \in \mathbb{E}.$$

After some rearrangement of terms, the above can be rewritten as

$$g(\mathbf{p}) \geq g(\mathbf{x}^*) + \langle -\nabla f(\mathbf{x}^*), \mathbf{p} - \mathbf{x}^* \rangle,$$

which is equivalent to the relation $-\nabla f(\mathbf{x}^*) \in \partial g(\mathbf{x}^*)$, namely, to stationarity (see Definition 3.73). □

The basic inequality that will be used in the analysis of the generalized conditional gradient method is the following recursive inequality.

Lemma 13.7 (fundamental inequality for generalized conditional gradient). *Suppose that f and g satisfy properties of* (A) *and* (B) *of Assumption 13.1. Let $\mathbf{x} \in \mathrm{dom}(g)$ and $t \in [0, 1]$. Then*

$$F(\mathbf{x} + t(\mathbf{p}(\mathbf{x}) - \mathbf{x})) \leq F(\mathbf{x}) - tS(\mathbf{x}) + \frac{t^2 L_f}{2} \|\mathbf{p}(\mathbf{x}) - \mathbf{x}\|^2. \tag{13.6}$$

Proof. Using the descent lemma (Lemma 5.7), the convexity of g, and the notation $\mathbf{p}^+ = \mathbf{p}(\mathbf{x})$, we can write the following:

$$
\begin{aligned}
F(\mathbf{x} + t(\mathbf{p}^+ - \mathbf{x})) &= f(\mathbf{x} + t(\mathbf{p}^+ - \mathbf{x})) + g(\mathbf{x} + t(\mathbf{p}^+ - \mathbf{x})) \\
&\leq f(\mathbf{x}) - t\langle \nabla f(\mathbf{x}), \mathbf{x} - \mathbf{p}^+ \rangle + \frac{t^2 L_f}{2} \|\mathbf{p}^+ - \mathbf{x}\|^2 + g((1-t)\mathbf{x} + t\mathbf{p}^+) \\
&\leq f(\mathbf{x}) - t\langle \nabla f(\mathbf{x}), \mathbf{x} - \mathbf{p}^+ \rangle + \frac{t^2 L_f}{2} \|\mathbf{p}^+ - \mathbf{x}\|^2 + (1-t)g(\mathbf{x}) + tg(\mathbf{p}^+) \\
&= F(\mathbf{x}) - t(\langle \nabla f(\mathbf{x}), \mathbf{x} - \mathbf{p}^+ \rangle + g(\mathbf{x}) - g(\mathbf{p}^+)) + \frac{t^2 L_f}{2} \|\mathbf{p}^+ - \mathbf{x}\|^2 \\
&= F(\mathbf{x}) - tS(\mathbf{x}) + \frac{t^2 L_f}{2} \|\mathbf{p}^+ - \mathbf{x}\|^2. \quad □
\end{aligned}
$$

13.2.3   Convergence Analysis in the Nonconvex Case

Note that we do not assume at this point that f is convex, and therefore convergence (if any) will be proven to stationary points. Before we delve into the convergence analysis, we mention the different options of stepsize strategies that will be considered.

- **Predefined diminishing stepsize.** $t_k = \frac{2}{k+2}$.

- **Adaptive stepsize.** $t_k = \min\left\{1, \frac{S(\mathbf{x}^k)}{L_f \|\mathbf{p}^k - \mathbf{x}^k\|^2}\right\}$.

- **Exact line search.** $t_k \in \operatorname{argmin}_{t \in [0,1]} F(\mathbf{x}^k + t(\mathbf{p}^k - \mathbf{x}^k))$.

The motivation for considering the adaptive stepsize comes from the fundamental inequality (13.6)—it is easy to verify that $t_k = \min\left\{1, \frac{S(\mathbf{x}^k)}{L_f \|\mathbf{p}^k - \mathbf{x}^k\|^2}\right\}$ is the minimizer of the right-hand side of (13.6) w.r.t. $t \in [0,1]$ when $\mathbf{x} = \mathbf{x}^k$. Much like the analysis of the proximal gradient method, the convergence of the generalized conditional gradient method is based on a sufficient decrease property.

Lemma 13.8 (sufficient decrease for the generalized conditional gradient method). *Suppose that f and g satisfy properties (A) and (B) of Assumption 13.1, and let $\{\mathbf{x}^k\}_{k\geq 0}$ be the sequence generated by the generalized conditional gradient method for solving problem (13.2) with stepsizes chosen by either the adaptive or exact line search strategies. Then for any $k \geq 0$,*

$$F(\mathbf{x}^k) - F(\mathbf{x}^{k+1}) \geq \frac{1}{2} \min\left\{S(\mathbf{x}^k), \frac{S^2(\mathbf{x}^k)}{L_f \Omega^2}\right\}, \tag{13.7}$$

where Ω be an upper bound on the diameter of $\operatorname{dom}(g)$:

$$\Omega \geq \max_{\mathbf{x}, \mathbf{y} \in \operatorname{dom}(g)} \|\mathbf{x} - \mathbf{y}\|.$$

Proof. Let $k \geq 0$ and let $\tilde{\mathbf{x}}^k = \mathbf{x}^k + s_k(\mathbf{p}^k - \mathbf{x}^k)$, where

$$s_k = \min\left\{1, \frac{S(\mathbf{x}^k)}{L_f \|\mathbf{x}^k - \mathbf{p}^k\|^2}\right\}.$$

By the fundamental inequality (13.6) invoked with $\mathbf{x} = \mathbf{x}^k$ and $t = s_k$, we have

$$F(\mathbf{x}^k) - F(\tilde{\mathbf{x}}^k) \geq s_k S(\mathbf{x}^k) - \frac{s_k^2 L_f}{2} \|\mathbf{p}^k - \mathbf{x}^k\|^2. \tag{13.8}$$

There are two options: Either $\frac{S(\mathbf{x}^k)}{L_f \|\mathbf{x}^k - \mathbf{p}^k\|^2} \leq 1$, and in this case $s_k = \frac{S(\mathbf{x}^k)}{L_f \|\mathbf{x}^k - \mathbf{p}^k\|^2}$, and hence, by (13.8),

$$F(\mathbf{x}^k) - F(\tilde{\mathbf{x}}^k) \geq \frac{S^2(\mathbf{x}^k)}{2L_f \|\mathbf{p}^k - \mathbf{x}^k\|^2} \geq \frac{S^2(\mathbf{x}^k)}{2L_f \Omega^2}.$$

Or, on the other hand, if

$$\frac{S(\mathbf{x}^k)}{L_f \|\mathbf{x}^k - \mathbf{p}^k\|^2} \geq 1, \tag{13.9}$$

then $s_k = 1$, and by (13.8),

$$F(\mathbf{x}^k) - F(\tilde{\mathbf{x}}^k) \geq S(\mathbf{x}^k) - \frac{L_f}{2} \|\mathbf{p}^k - \mathbf{x}^k\|^2 \overset{(13.9)}{\geq} \frac{1}{2} S(\mathbf{x}^k).$$

Combining the two cases, we obtain

$$F(\mathbf{x}^k) - F(\tilde{\mathbf{x}}^k) \geq \frac{1}{2} \min\left\{ S(\mathbf{x}^k), \frac{S^2(\mathbf{x}^k)}{L_f \Omega^2} \right\}. \tag{13.10}$$

If the adaptive stepsize strategy is used, then $\tilde{\mathbf{x}}^k = \mathbf{x}^{k+1}$ and (13.10) is the same as (13.7). If an exact line search strategy is employed, then

$$F(\mathbf{x}^{k+1}) = \min_{t \in [0,1]} F(\mathbf{x}^k + t(\mathbf{p}^k - \mathbf{x}^k)) \leq F(\mathbf{x}^k + s_k(\mathbf{p}^k - \mathbf{x}^k)) = F(\tilde{\mathbf{x}}^k),$$

which, combined with (13.10), implies that also in this case (13.7) holds. □

Using Lemma 13.8 we can establish the main convergence result for the generalized conditional gradient method with stepsizes chosen by either the adaptive or exact line search strategies.

Theorem 13.9 (convergence of the generalized conditional gradient). *Suppose that Assumption 13.1 holds, and let $\{\mathbf{x}^k\}_{k \geq 0}$ be the sequence generated by the generalized conditional gradient method for solving problem (13.2) with stepsizes chosen by either the adaptive or exact line search strategies. Then*

(a) *for any $k \geq 0$, $F(\mathbf{x}^k) \geq F(\mathbf{x}^{k+1})$ and $F(\mathbf{x}^k) > F(\mathbf{x}^{k+1})$ if $\mathbf{x}^k$ is not a stationary point of problem (13.2);*

(b) *$S(\mathbf{x}^k) \to 0$ as $k \to \infty$;*

(c) *for any $k \geq 0$,*

$$\min_{n=0,1,\dots,k} S(\mathbf{x}^n) \leq \max\left\{ \frac{2(F(\mathbf{x}^0) - F_{\mathrm{opt}})}{k+1}, \frac{\sqrt{2 L_f \Omega^2 (F(\mathbf{x}^0) - F_{\mathrm{opt}})}}{\sqrt{k+1}} \right\}, \tag{13.11}$$

where Ω is an upper bound on the diameter of $\mathrm{dom}(g)$;

(d) *all limit points of the sequence $\{\mathbf{x}^k\}_{k \geq 0}$ are stationary points of problem (13.2).*

Proof. (a) The monotonicity of $\{F(\mathbf{x}^k)\}_{k \geq 0}$ is a direct result of the sufficient decrease inequality (13.7) and the nonnegativity of $S(\mathbf{x}^k)$ (Theorem 13.6(a)). As for the second claim, if $\mathbf{x}^k$ is not a stationary point of problem (13.2), then $S(\mathbf{x}^k) > 0$ (see Theorem 13.6(b)), and hence, by the sufficient decrease inequality, $F(\mathbf{x}^k) > F(\mathbf{x}^{k+1})$.

(b) Since $\{F(\mathbf{x}^k)\}_{k \geq 0}$ is nonincreasing and bounded below (by F_{opt}), it follows that it is convergent, and in particular, $F(\mathbf{x}^k) - F(\mathbf{x}^{k+1}) \to 0$ as $k \to \infty$. Therefore, by the sufficient decrease inequality (13.7), it follows that $\min\left\{ S(\mathbf{x}^k), \frac{S^2(\mathbf{x}^k)}{L_f \Omega^2} \right\} \to 0$ as $k \to \infty$, implying that $S(\mathbf{x}^k) \to 0$ as $k \to \infty$.

(c) By the sufficient decrease inequality (13.7), for all $n \geq 0$,

$$F(\mathbf{x}^n) - F(\mathbf{x}^{n+1}) \geq \frac{1}{2} \min\left\{ S(\mathbf{x}^n), \frac{S^2(\mathbf{x}^n)}{L_f \Omega^2} \right\}. \tag{13.12}$$

Summing the above inequality over $n = 0, 1, \ldots, k$,

$$F(\mathbf{x}^0) - F(\mathbf{x}^{k+1}) \geq \frac{1}{2} \sum_{n=0}^{k} \min\left\{ S(\mathbf{x}^n), \frac{S^2(\mathbf{x}^n)}{L_f \Omega^2} \right\}. \tag{13.13}$$

Using the facts that $F(\mathbf{x}^{k+1}) \geq F_{\mathrm{opt}}$ and

$$\sum_{n=0}^{k} \min\left\{ S(\mathbf{x}^n), \frac{S^2(\mathbf{x}^n)}{L_f \Omega^2} \right\} \geq (k+1) \min_{n=0,1,\ldots,k} \left[\min\left\{ S(\mathbf{x}^n), \frac{S^2(\mathbf{x}^n)}{L_f \Omega^2} \right\} \right],$$

we obtain that

$$\min_{n=0,1,\ldots,k} \left[\min\left\{ S(\mathbf{x}^n), \frac{S^2(\mathbf{x}^n)}{L_f \Omega^2} \right\} \right] \leq \frac{2(F(\mathbf{x}^0) - F_{\mathrm{opt}})}{k+1},$$

which implies in particular that there exists an $n \in \{0, 1, \ldots, k\}$ for which

$$\min\left\{ S(\mathbf{x}^n), \frac{S^2(\mathbf{x}^n)}{L_f \Omega^2} \right\} \leq \frac{2(F(\mathbf{x}^0) - F_{\mathrm{opt}})}{k+1},$$

that is,

$$S(\mathbf{x}^n) \leq \max\left\{ \frac{2(F(\mathbf{x}^0) - F_{\mathrm{opt}})}{k+1}, \frac{\sqrt{2 L_f \Omega^2 (F(\mathbf{x}^0) - F_{\mathrm{opt}})}}{\sqrt{k+1}} \right\}.$$

Since there exists $n \in \{0, 1, \ldots, k\}$ for which the above inequality holds, the result (13.11) immediately follows.

(d) Suppose that $\bar{\mathbf{x}}$ is a limit point of $\{\mathbf{x}^k\}_{k \geq 0}$. Then there exists a subsequence $\{\mathbf{x}^{k_j}\}_{j \geq 0}$ that converges to $\bar{\mathbf{x}}$. By the definition of the conditional gradient norm $S(\cdot)$, it follows that for any $\mathbf{v} \in \mathbb{E}$,

$$S(\mathbf{x}^{k_j}) \geq \langle \nabla f(\mathbf{x}^{k_j}), \mathbf{x}^{k_j} - \mathbf{v} \rangle + g(\mathbf{x}^{k_j}) - g(\mathbf{v}).$$

Passing to the limit $j \to \infty$ and using the fact that $S(\mathbf{x}^{k_j}) \to 0$ as $j \to \infty$, as well as the continuity of ∇f and the lower semicontinuity of g, we obtain that

$$0 \geq \langle \nabla f(\bar{\mathbf{x}}), \bar{\mathbf{x}} - \mathbf{v} \rangle + g(\bar{\mathbf{x}}) - g(\mathbf{v}) \text{ for any } \mathbf{v} \in \mathbb{E},$$

which is the same as the relation $-\nabla f(\bar{\mathbf{x}}) \in \partial g(\bar{\mathbf{x}})$, that is, the same as stationarity. $\square$

Example 13.10 (optimization over the unit ball). Consider the problem

$$\min\{ f(\mathbf{x}) : \|\mathbf{x}\| \leq 1 \}, \tag{13.14}$$

where $f : \mathbb{E} \to \mathbb{R}$ is L_f-smooth. Problem (13.14) fits the general model (13.2) with $g = \delta_{B_{\|\cdot\|}[0,1]}$. Obviously, in this case the generalized conditional gradient method amounts to the conditional gradient method with feasible set $C = B_{\|\cdot\|}[\mathbf{0}, 1]$. Take

$\mathbf{x} \in B_{\|\cdot\|}[\mathbf{0}, 1]$. In order to find an expression for the conditional gradient norm $S(\mathbf{x})$, we first note that

$$\mathbf{p}(\mathbf{x}) \in \operatorname{argmin}_{\mathbf{p}: \|\mathbf{p}\| \leq 1} \langle \mathbf{p}, \nabla f(\mathbf{x}) \rangle$$

is given by $\mathbf{p}(\mathbf{x}) = -\frac{\nabla f(\mathbf{x})}{\|\nabla f(\mathbf{x})\|}$ if $\nabla f(\mathbf{x}) \neq 0$ and can be chosen as $\mathbf{p}(\mathbf{x}) = \mathbf{0}$ if $\nabla f(\mathbf{x}) = \mathbf{0}$. Thus, in both cases, we obtain that for any $\mathbf{x} \in B_{\|\cdot\|}[\mathbf{0}, 1]$,

$$S(\mathbf{x}) = \langle \nabla f(\mathbf{x}), \mathbf{x} - \mathbf{p}(\mathbf{x}) \rangle = \langle \nabla f(\mathbf{x}), \mathbf{x} \rangle + \|\nabla f(\mathbf{x})\|. \tag{13.15}$$

By its definition, $S(\mathbf{x}) = \infty$ for any $\mathbf{x} \notin B_{\|\cdot\|}[\mathbf{0}, 1]$. By Theorem 13.6 the above expression (13.15) is nonnegative and is equal to zero if and only if $\mathbf{x}$ is a stationary point of (13.14), which in this case means that either $\nabla f(\mathbf{x}) = \mathbf{0}$ or $\|\mathbf{x}\| = 1$ and $\nabla f(\mathbf{x}) = \lambda \mathbf{x}$ for some $\lambda \leq 0$ (see [10, Example 9.6]).

　　Assuming that $S(\mathbf{x}^k) \neq 0$, the general update formula of the conditional gradient method for solving (13.14) is

$$\mathbf{x}^{k+1} = (1 - t_k)\mathbf{x}^k - t_k \frac{\nabla f(\mathbf{x}^k)}{\|\nabla f(\mathbf{x}^k)\|},$$

where $t_k \in [0, 1]$ is an appropriately chosen stepsize. By Theorem 13.9 if the stepsize is chosen by either an adaptive or exact line search strategies, convergence of $S(\mathbf{x}^k)$ to zero is guaranteed. ∎

Example 13.11 (the power method).[71] Continuing Example 13.10, let us consider the problem

$$\max_{\mathbf{x} \in \mathbb{R}^n} \left\{ \frac{1}{2}\mathbf{x}^T \mathbf{A}\mathbf{x} : \|\mathbf{x}\|_2 \leq 1 \right\}, \tag{13.16}$$

where $\mathbf{A} \in \mathbb{S}^n_+$. Problem (13.16) fits the model (13.14) with $f : \mathbb{R}^n \to \mathbb{R}$ given by $f(\mathbf{x}) = -\frac{1}{2}\mathbf{x}^T \mathbf{A}\mathbf{x}$. Consider the conditional gradient method for solving (13.16) and assume that $\mathbf{x}^k$ is not a stationary point of problem (13.2). Then

$$\mathbf{x}^{k+1} = (1 - t_k)\mathbf{x}^k + t_k \underbrace{\frac{\mathbf{A}\mathbf{x}^k}{\|\mathbf{A}\mathbf{x}^k\|_2}}_{\mathbf{p}^k}. \tag{13.17}$$

If the stepsizes are chosen by an exact line search strategy, then

$$t_k \in \operatorname{argmin}_{t \in [0,1]} f(\mathbf{x}^k + t(\mathbf{p}^k - \mathbf{x}^k)). \tag{13.18}$$

Since f is concave, it follows that either 0 or 1 is an optimal solution of (13.18), and by the fact that $\mathbf{x}^k$ is not a stationary point of problem (13.2), we can conclude by Theorem 13.9(a) that $t_k \neq 0$. We can thus choose $t_k = 1$, and the method (13.17) becomes

$$\mathbf{x}^{k+1} = \frac{\mathbf{A}\mathbf{x}^k}{\|\mathbf{A}\mathbf{x}^k\|_2},$$

which is the well-known *power method* for finding the eigenvector of $\mathbf{A}$ corresponding to the maximal eigenvalue. Theorem 13.9 guarantees that limit points of the method are stationary points of problem (13.16), meaning eigenvectors $\mathbf{A}$ corresponding to nonnegative eigenvalues. ∎

---

[71]The interpretation of the power method as the conditional gradient method was described in the work of Luss and Teboulle [85].

13.2.4 Convergence Analysis in the Convex Case

We will now further assume that f is convex. In this case, obviously all stationary points of problem (13.2) are also optimal points (Theorem 3.72(b)), so that Theorem 13.9 guarantees that all limit points of the sequence generated by the generalized conditional gradient method with either adaptive or exact line search stepsize strategies are optimal points. We also showed in Theorem 13.9 an $O(1/\sqrt{k})$ rate of convergence of the conditional gradient norm. Our objectives will be to show an $O(1/k)$ rate of convergence of function values to the optimal value, as well as of the conditional gradient norm to zero.

We begin by showing that when f is convex, the conditional gradient norm is lower bounded by the distance to optimality in terms of function values.

Lemma 13.12. *Suppose that Assumption* 13.1 *holds and that* f *is convex. Then for any* $\mathbf{x} \in \mathrm{dom}(g)$,

$$S(\mathbf{x}) \geq F(\mathbf{x}) - F_{\mathrm{opt}}.$$

Proof. Let $\mathbf{x}^* \in X^*$. Then for any $\mathbf{x} \in \mathrm{dom}(g)$,

$$
\begin{aligned}
S(\mathbf{x}) &= \langle \nabla f(\mathbf{x}), \mathbf{x} - \mathbf{p}(\mathbf{x}) \rangle + g(\mathbf{x}) - g(\mathbf{p}(\mathbf{x})) && \text{[definition of } S] \\
&= \langle \nabla f(\mathbf{x}), \mathbf{x} \rangle + g(\mathbf{x}) - (\langle \nabla f(\mathbf{x}), \mathbf{p}(\mathbf{x}) \rangle + g(\mathbf{p}(\mathbf{x}))) \\
&\geq \langle \nabla f(\mathbf{x}), \mathbf{x} \rangle + g(\mathbf{x}) - (\langle \nabla f(\mathbf{x}), \mathbf{x}^* \rangle + g(\mathbf{x}^*)) && \text{[definition of } \mathbf{p}(\cdot) \text{ (13.3)]} \\
&= \langle \nabla f(\mathbf{x}), \mathbf{x} - \mathbf{x}^* \rangle + g(\mathbf{x}) - g(\mathbf{x}^*) \\
&\geq f(\mathbf{x}) - f(\mathbf{x}^*) + g(\mathbf{x}) - g(\mathbf{x}^*) && \text{[convexity of } f] \\
&= F(\mathbf{x}) - F_{\mathrm{opt}}. \qquad \square
\end{aligned}
$$

The convergence analysis relies on the following technical lemma on sequences of scalars.

Lemma 13.13.[72] *Let p be a positive integer, and let $\{a_k\}_{k \geq 0}$ and $\{b_k\}_{k \geq 0}$ be nonnegative sequences satisfying for any $k \geq 0$*

$$a_{k+1} \leq a_k - \gamma_k b_k + \frac{A}{2} \gamma_k^2, \tag{13.19}$$

where $\gamma_k = \frac{2}{k+2p}$ and A is a positive number. Suppose that $a_k \leq b_k$ for all k. Then

(a) $a_k \leq \frac{2 \max\{A, (p-1)a_0\}}{k+2p-2}$ *for any $k \geq 1$;*

(b) *for any $k \geq 3$,*

$$\min_{n = \lfloor k/2 \rfloor + 2, \ldots, k} b_n \leq \frac{8 \max\{A, (p-1)a_0\}}{k-2}.$$

---

[72]Lemma 13.13 is an extension of Lemma 4.4 from Bach [4].

Proof. (a) By (13.19) and the fact that $a_k \leq b_k$, it follows that

$$a_{k+1} \leq (1 - \gamma_k)a_k + \frac{A}{2}\gamma_k^2.$$

Therefore,

$$a_1 \leq (1 - \gamma_0)a_0 + \frac{A}{2}\gamma_0^2,$$

$$a_2 \leq (1 - \gamma_1)a_1 + \frac{A}{2}\gamma_1^2 = (1 - \gamma_1)(1 - \gamma_0)a_0 + \frac{A}{2}(1 - \gamma_1)\gamma_0^2 + \frac{A}{2}\gamma_1^2,$$

$$a_3 \leq (1 - \gamma_2)a_2 + \frac{A}{2}\gamma_2^2 = (1 - \gamma_2)(1 - \gamma_1)(1 - \gamma_0)a_0$$

$$+ \frac{A}{2}\left[(1 - \gamma_2)(1 - \gamma_1)\gamma_0^2 + (1 - \gamma_2)\gamma_1^2 + \gamma_2^2\right].$$

In general,[73]

$$a_k \leq a_0 \prod_{s=0}^{k-1}(1 - \gamma_s) + \frac{A}{2}\sum_{u=0}^{k-1}\left[\prod_{s=u+1}^{k-1}(1 - \gamma_s)\right]\gamma_u^2. \qquad (13.20)$$

Since $\gamma_k = \frac{2}{k+2p}$, it follows that

$$\frac{A}{2}\sum_{u=0}^{k-1}\left[\prod_{s=u+1}^{k-1}(1 - \gamma_s)\gamma_u^2\right] = \frac{A}{2}\sum_{u=0}^{k-1}\left[\prod_{s=u+1}^{k-1}\frac{s + 2p - 2}{s + 2p}\gamma_u^2\right]$$

$$= \frac{A}{2}\sum_{u=0}^{k-1}\frac{(u + 2p - 1)(u + 2p)}{(k + 2p - 2)(k + 2p - 1)} \cdot \frac{4}{(u + 2p)^2}$$

$$= \frac{A}{2}\sum_{u=0}^{k-1}\frac{u + 2p - 1}{(k + 2p - 2)(k + 2p - 1)} \cdot \frac{4}{u + 2p}$$

$$\leq \frac{2Ak}{(k + 2p - 2)(k + 2p - 1)}. \qquad (13.21)$$

In addition,

$$a_0\prod_{s=0}^{k-1}(1 - \gamma_s) = a_0\prod_{s=0}^{k-1}\frac{s + 2p - 2}{s + 2p} = a_0\frac{(2p - 2)(2p - 1)}{(k + 2p - 2)(k + 2p - 1)}. \qquad (13.22)$$

Therefore, combining (13.20), (13.21), and (13.22),

$$a_k \leq \frac{2Ak}{(k + 2p - 2)(k + 2p - 1)} + \frac{a_0(2p - 2)(2p - 1)}{(k + 2p - 2)(k + 2p - 1)}$$

$$\leq \frac{2\max\{A, (p - 1)a_0\}(k + 2p - 1)}{(k + 2p - 2)(k + 2p - 1)}$$

$$= \frac{2\max\{A, (p - 1)a_0\}}{k + 2p - 2}.$$

---

[73]We use the convention that $\Pi_{k=\ell}^u c_k = 1$ whenever $\ell > u$.

(b) Replacing the index k with n in (13.19), we have

$$a_{n+1} \leq a_n - \gamma_n b_n + \frac{A}{2} \gamma_n^2.$$

Summing the above inequality over $n = j, j+1, \ldots, k$, we obtain that

$$a_{k+1} \leq a_j - \sum_{n=j}^{k} \gamma_n b_n + \frac{A}{2} \sum_{n=j}^{k} \gamma_n^2.$$

Thus, using the result of part (a) (assuming that $j \geq 1$),

$$\left(\sum_{n=j}^{k} \gamma_n \right) \min_{n=j,\ldots,k} b_n \leq a_j + \frac{A}{2} \sum_{n=j}^{k} \gamma_n^2$$

$$\leq \frac{2\max\{A, (p-1)a_0\}}{j + 2p - 2} + 2A \sum_{n=j}^{k} \frac{1}{(n+2p)^2}$$

$$\leq \frac{2\max\{A, (p-1)a_0\}}{j + 2p - 2} + 2A \sum_{n=j}^{k} \frac{1}{(n+2p-1)(n+2p)}$$

$$= \frac{2\max\{A, (p-1)a_0\}}{j + 2p - 2} + 2A \sum_{n=j}^{k} \left[\frac{1}{n+2p-1} - \frac{1}{n+2p} \right]$$

$$= \frac{2\max\{A, (p-1)a_0\}}{j + 2p - 2} + 2A \left[\frac{1}{j+2p-1} - \frac{1}{k+2p} \right]$$

$$\leq \frac{4\max\{A, (p-1)a_0\}}{j + 2p - 2}. \tag{13.23}$$

On the other hand,

$$\sum_{n=j}^{k} \gamma_n = 2 \sum_{n=j}^{k} \frac{1}{n+2p} \geq 2\frac{k-j+1}{k+2p},$$

which, combined with (13.23), yields

$$\min_{n=j,\ldots,k} b_n \leq \frac{2\max\{A, (p-1)a_0\}(k+2p)}{(j+2p-2)(k-j+1)}.$$

Taking $j = \lfloor k/2 \rfloor + 2$, we conclude that for any $k \geq 3$,

$$\min_{n=\lfloor k/2 \rfloor + 2, \ldots, k} b_n \leq \frac{2\max\{A, (p-1)a_0\}(k+2p)}{(\lfloor k/2 \rfloor + 2p)(k - \lfloor k/2 \rfloor - 1)}. \tag{13.24}$$

Now,

$$\frac{k+2p}{(\lfloor k/2 \rfloor + 2p)(k - \lfloor k/2 \rfloor - 1)} \leq \frac{k+2p}{(k/2 + 2p - 0.5)(k - \lfloor k/2 \rfloor - 1)}$$

$$= 2\frac{k+2p}{k+4p-1} \cdot \frac{1}{k - \lfloor k/2 \rfloor - 1}$$

$$\leq \frac{2}{k - \lfloor k/2 \rfloor - 1}$$

$$\leq \frac{2}{k/2 - 1},$$

which, combined with (13.24), yields

$$\min_{n=\lfloor k/2 \rfloor + 2, \ldots, k} b_n \leq \frac{8 \max\{A, (p-1)a_0\}}{k-2}. \qquad \Box$$

Equipped with Lemma 13.13, we will now establish a sublinear rate of convergence of the generalized conditional gradient method under the three stepsize strategies described at the beginning of Section 13.2.3: predefined, adaptive, and exact line search.

Theorem 13.14. *Suppose that Assumption* 13.1 *holds and that* f *is convex. Let* $\{\mathbf{x}^k\}_{k \geq 0}$ *be the sequence generated by the generalized conditional gradient method for solving problem* (13.2) *with either a predefined stepsize* $t_k = \alpha_k \equiv \frac{2}{k+2}$, *adaptive stepsize, or exact line search. Let* Ω *be an upper bound on the diameter of* $\mathrm{dom}(g)$:

$$\Omega \geq \max_{\mathbf{x}, \mathbf{y} \in \mathrm{dom}(g)} \|\mathbf{x} - \mathbf{y}\|.$$

Then

(a) $F(\mathbf{x}^k) - F_{\mathrm{opt}} \leq \frac{2L_f \Omega^2}{k}$ *for any* $k \geq 1$;

(b) $\min_{n=\lfloor k/2 \rfloor + 2, \ldots, k} S(\mathbf{x}^n) \leq \frac{8L_f \Omega^2}{k-2}$ *for any* $k \geq 3$.

Proof. By the fundamental inequality (13.6) invoked with $\mathbf{x} = \mathbf{x}^k$ and $t = t_k$, it follows that for any $k \geq 0$,

$$F(\mathbf{x}^k + t_k(\mathbf{p}^k - \mathbf{x}^k)) - F_{\mathrm{opt}} \leq F(\mathbf{x}^k) - F_{\mathrm{opt}} - t_k S(\mathbf{x}^k) + \frac{t_k^2 L_f}{2}\|\mathbf{p}^k - \mathbf{x}^k\|^2, \quad (13.25)$$

where $\mathbf{p}^k = \mathbf{p}(\mathbf{x}^k)$. Specifically, if a predefined stepsize is used, meaning that $t_k = \alpha_k \equiv \frac{2}{k+2}$, then

$$F(\mathbf{x}^k + \alpha_k(\mathbf{p}^k - \mathbf{x}^k)) - F_{\mathrm{opt}} \leq F(\mathbf{x}^k) - F_{\mathrm{opt}} - \alpha_k S(\mathbf{x}^k) + \frac{\alpha_k^2 L_f}{2}\|\mathbf{p}^k - \mathbf{x}^k\|^2. \quad (13.26)$$

If an exact line search is used, meaning that $t_k = u_k \in \mathrm{argmin}_{t \in [0,1]} F(\mathbf{x}^k + t(\mathbf{p}^k - \mathbf{x}^k))$, then

$$F(\mathbf{x}^k + u_k(\mathbf{p}^k - \mathbf{x}^k)) - F_{\mathrm{opt}} \leq F(\mathbf{x}^k + \alpha_k(\mathbf{p}^k - \mathbf{x}^k)) - F_{\mathrm{opt}} \qquad (13.27)$$

$$\leq F(\mathbf{x}^k) - F_{\mathrm{opt}} - \alpha_k S(\mathbf{x}^k) + \frac{\alpha_k^2 L_f}{2}\|\mathbf{p}^k - \mathbf{x}^k\|^2,$$

where the first inequality follows by the definition of u_k and the second is the inequality (13.26). Finally, in the adaptive stepsize strategy, $t_k = v_k \equiv \min\left\{1, \frac{S(\mathbf{x}^k)}{L_f\|\mathbf{p}^k - \mathbf{x}^k\|^2}\right\}$. Note that v_k satisfies

$$v_k = \operatorname{argmin}_{t\in[0,1]}\left\{-tS(\mathbf{x}^k) + \frac{t^2 L_f}{2}\|\mathbf{p}^k - \mathbf{x}^k\|^2\right\}. \qquad (13.28)$$

Thus,

$$F(\mathbf{x}^k + v_k(\mathbf{p}^k - \mathbf{x}^k)) - F_{\mathrm{opt}} \leq F(\mathbf{x}^k) - F_{\mathrm{opt}} - v_k S(\mathbf{x}^k) + \frac{v_k^2 L_f}{2}\|\mathbf{p}^k - \mathbf{x}^k\|^2$$

$$\leq F(\mathbf{x}^k) - F_{\mathrm{opt}} - \alpha_k S(\mathbf{x}^k) + \frac{\alpha_k^2 L_f}{2}\|\mathbf{p}^k - \mathbf{x}^k\|^2,$$

where the first inequality is the inequality (13.25) with $t_k = v_k$ and the second is due to (13.28). Combining the last inequality with (13.26) and (13.27), we conclude that for the three stepsize strategies, the following inequality holds:

$$F(\mathbf{x}^{k+1}) - F_{\mathrm{opt}} \leq F(\mathbf{x}^k) - F_{\mathrm{opt}} - \alpha_k S(\mathbf{x}^k) + \frac{\alpha_k^2 L_f}{2}\|\mathbf{p}^k - \mathbf{x}^k\|^2,$$

which, combined with the inequality $\|\mathbf{p}^k - \mathbf{x}^k\| \leq \Omega$, implies that

$$F(\mathbf{x}^{k+1}) - F_{\mathrm{opt}} \leq F(\mathbf{x}^k) - F_{\mathrm{opt}} - \alpha_k S(\mathbf{x}^k) + \frac{\alpha_k^2 L_f \Omega^2}{2}.$$

Invoking Lemma 13.13 with $a_k = F(\mathbf{x}^k) - F_{\mathrm{opt}}, b_k = S(\mathbf{x}^k), A = L_f\Omega^2$, and $p = 1$ and noting that $a_k \leq b_k$ by Lemma 13.12, both parts (a) and (b) follow. $\qquad\square$

13.3 The Strongly Convex Case

We will focus on the case where the nonsmooth part is an indicator of a compact and convex set C, meaning that $g = \delta_C$, so that problem (13.2) becomes

$$\min\{f(\mathbf{x}) : \mathbf{x} \in C\},$$

and the method under consideration is the conditional gradient method. In Section 10.6 we showed that the proximal gradient method enjoys an improved linear convergence when the smooth part (in the composite model) is strongly convex. Unfortunately, as we will see in Section 13.3.1, in general, the conditional gradient method does not converge in a linear rate even if an additional strong convexity assumption is made on the objective function. Later on, in Section 13.3.2 we will show how, under a strong convexity assumption on the *feasible set* (and not on the objective function), linear rate can be established.

13.3.1 The Negative Result of Canon and Cullum

The arguments go back to Canon and Cullum [37], and we follow them. We begin with some technical lemmas.

Lemma 13.15. *Let $\{a_n\}_{n \geq 0}$ be a sequence of real numbers such that $\sum_{n=0}^{\infty} |a_n|$ diverges. Then for every $\varepsilon > 0$, $\sum_{n=k}^{\infty} a_n^2 \geq \frac{1}{k^{1+\varepsilon}}$ for infinitely many k's.*

Proof. Suppose by contradiction that there is $\varepsilon > 0$ and a positive integer K such that for all $k \geq K$

$$\sum_{n=k}^{\infty} a_n^2 < \frac{1}{k^{1+2\varepsilon}}. \tag{13.29}$$

We will show that $\sum_{n=1}^{\infty} |a_n|$ converges. Note that by the Cauchy–Schwarz inequality,

$$\sum_{n=1}^{\infty} |a_n| = \sum_{n=1}^{\infty} |a_n| n^{(1+\varepsilon)/2} n^{-(1+\varepsilon)/2} \leq \sqrt{\sum_{n=1}^{\infty} n^{1+\varepsilon} a_n^2} \sqrt{\sum_{n=1}^{\infty} n^{-(1+\varepsilon)}}. \tag{13.30}$$

Since $\sum_{n=1}^{\infty} n^{-(1+\varepsilon)}$ converges, it is enough to show that $\sum_{n=1}^{\infty} n^{1+\varepsilon} a_n^2$ converges. For that, note that by (13.29), for any $m \geq K$,

$$\sum_{k=K}^{m} \left[k^{\varepsilon} \sum_{n=k}^{m} a_n^2 \right] \leq \sum_{k=K}^{m} \left[k^{\varepsilon} \sum_{n=k}^{\infty} a_n^2 \right] \leq \sum_{k=K}^{m} \frac{1}{k^{1+\varepsilon}}. \tag{13.31}$$

On the other hand,

$$\sum_{k=K}^{m} \left[k^{\varepsilon} \sum_{n=k}^{m} a_n^2 \right] = \sum_{n=K}^{m} \left[a_n^2 \sum_{k=K}^{n} k^{\varepsilon} \right],$$

which, combined with the inequality

$$\sum_{k=K}^{n} k^{\varepsilon} \geq \int_{K}^{n} x^{\varepsilon} dx = \frac{1}{1+\varepsilon} (n^{1+\varepsilon} - K^{1+\varepsilon})$$

and (13.31), implies that (taking $m \to \infty$)

$$\frac{1}{1+\varepsilon} \sum_{n=K}^{\infty} (n^{1+\varepsilon} - K^{1+\varepsilon}) a_n^2 \leq \sum_{k=K}^{\infty} \frac{1}{k^{1+\varepsilon}}.$$

Since both $\sum_{k=K}^{\infty} \frac{1}{k^{1+\varepsilon}}$ and $\sum_{n=K}^{\infty} a_n^2$ converge, it follows that $\sum_{n=K}^{\infty} n^{1+\varepsilon} a_n^2$ converges and hence, by (13.30), that $\sum_{n=1}^{\infty} |a_n|$ converges, which is a contradiction to our underlying assumptions. $\square$

We will also use the following well-known lemma.

Lemma 13.16 (see [75, Chapter VII, Theorem 4]). *Let $\{b_n\}_{n \geq 0}$ be a sequence satisfying $0 \leq b_n < 1$ for any n. Then $\prod_{n=0}^{m} (1 - b_n) \to 0$ as $m \to \infty$ if and only if $\sum_{n=0}^{\infty} b_n$ diverges.*

Our main goal will be to describe an example of a minimization problem of a strongly convex function over a nonempty compact convex set for which the conditional gradient method does not exhibit a linear rate of convergence. For that, let us consider the following quadratic problem over $\mathbb{R}^n$:

$$f_{\text{opt}} \equiv \min_{\mathbf{x} \in \mathbb{R}^n} \left\{ f_q(\mathbf{x}) \equiv \frac{1}{2}\mathbf{x}^T\mathbf{Q}\mathbf{x} + \mathbf{b}^T\mathbf{x} : \mathbf{x} \in \Omega \right\}, \tag{13.32}$$

where $\mathbf{Q} \in \mathbb{S}^n_{++}, \mathbf{b} \in \mathbb{R}^n$, and $\Omega = \text{conv}\{\mathbf{a}_1, \mathbf{a}_2, \ldots, \mathbf{a}_l\}$, where $\mathbf{a}_1, \mathbf{a}_2, \ldots, \mathbf{a}_l \in \mathbb{R}^n$. We will make the following assumption on problem (13.32).

Assumption 13.17. $\text{int}(\Omega) \neq \emptyset$ and the optimal solution of problem (13.32), denoted by $\mathbf{x}^*$, is on the boundary of Ω and is not an extreme point of Ω.

Denoting $\mathbf{A} \in \mathbb{R}^{n \times l}$ as the matrix whose columns are $\mathbf{a}_1, \ldots, \mathbf{a}_l$, we can also write problem (13.32) as

$$\min_{\mathbf{x} \in \mathbb{R}^n, \mathbf{v} \in \mathbb{R}^l} \left\{ \frac{1}{2}\mathbf{x}^T\mathbf{Q}\mathbf{x} + \mathbf{b}^T\mathbf{x} : \mathbf{x} = \mathbf{A}\mathbf{v}, \mathbf{v} \in \Delta_l \right\}.$$

The conditional gradient method with exact line search strategy for solving (13.32) reads as follows. Given the kth iterate $\mathbf{x}^k$, the next point $\mathbf{x}^{k+1}$ is computed as follows:

- Choose

$$i_k \in \text{argmin}_{i=1,2,\ldots,l}\langle \mathbf{a}_i, \nabla f_q(\mathbf{x}^k)\rangle.$$

- Define

$$\mathbf{d}^k = \mathbf{a}_{i_k} - \mathbf{x}^k. \tag{13.33}$$

If $\langle \mathbf{d}^k, \nabla f_q(\mathbf{x}^k)\rangle \geq 0$, then $\mathbf{x}^k$ is the optimal solution of problem (13.32). Otherwise, set

$$\mathbf{x}^{k+1} = \mathbf{x}^k + t_k\mathbf{d}^k,$$

where

$$t_k = \text{argmin}_{t \in [0,1]}f_q(\mathbf{x}^k + t\mathbf{d}^k) = \min\{\lambda_k, 1\},$$

with λ_k defined as

$$\lambda_k = -\frac{\langle \mathbf{d}^k, \nabla f_q(\mathbf{x}^k)\rangle}{(\mathbf{d}^k)^T\mathbf{Q}\mathbf{d}^k}. \tag{13.34}$$

We will make the following assumption on the starting point of the conditional gradient method.

Assumption 13.18. $f_q(\mathbf{x}^0) < \min_{i=1,2,\ldots,l} f_q(\mathbf{a}_i)$ and $\mathbf{x}^0 = \mathbf{A}\mathbf{v}^0 \in \Omega$, where $\mathbf{v}^0 \in \Delta_l \cap \mathbb{R}^n_{++}$. In particular, $\mathbf{x}^0 \in \text{int}(\Omega)$.

A vector $\mathbf{x}^0$ satisfying Assumption 13.18 can be easily obtained by the following procedure.

- Pick $p \in \text{argmin}_{i=1,2,\ldots,l}f_q(\mathbf{a}_i)$.

- Employ one step of the conditional gradient method starting from $\mathbf{a}_p$ and obtain a point $\tilde{\mathbf{x}}^0 \in \Omega$ for which $f_q(\tilde{\mathbf{x}}^0) < f_q(\mathbf{a}^p)$ (the latter is satisfied since $\mathbf{a}^p$ is not an optimal solution—see Theorem 13.9(a)).

- Find $\tilde{\mathbf{v}}^0 \in \Delta_l$ for which $\tilde{\mathbf{x}}^0 = \mathbf{A}\tilde{\mathbf{v}}^0$.

- If $\tilde{\mathbf{v}}^0 \in \mathbb{R}^l_{++}$, define $\mathbf{v}^0 = \tilde{\mathbf{v}}^0$ and $\mathbf{x}^0 = \tilde{\mathbf{x}}^0$. If $\tilde{\mathbf{v}}^0 \notin \mathbb{R}^l_{++}$, then take a point $\mathbf{v}^0 \in \Delta_l \cap \mathbb{R}^l_{++}$ close enough to $\tilde{\mathbf{v}}^0$ such that $\mathbf{x}^0 \equiv \mathbf{A}\mathbf{v}^0$ will satisfy $f_q(\mathbf{x}^0) < f_q(\mathbf{a}^p)$.

The following lemma gathers several technical results that will be key to establishing the slow rate of the conditional gradient method.

Lemma 13.19. *Suppose that Assumption 13.17 holds and that $\{\mathbf{x}^k\}$ is the sequence generated by the conditional gradient method with exact line search employed on problem (13.32) with a starting point $\mathbf{x}^0$ satisfying Assumption 13.18. Let $\mathbf{d}^k$ and λ_k be given by (13.33) and (13.34), respectively. Then*

(a) $\mathbf{x}^k \in \text{int}(\Omega)$ *and* $t_k = \lambda_k < 1$ *for any* $k \geq 0$;

(b) $f_q(\mathbf{x}^{k+1}) = f_q(\mathbf{x}^k) - \frac{1}{2}((\mathbf{d}^k)^T \mathbf{Q}\mathbf{d}^k)\lambda_k^2$ *for any* $k \geq 0$;

(c) $\sum_{k=0}^{\infty} \lambda_k = \infty$;

(d) *there exists* $\beta > 0$ *such that* $(\mathbf{d}^k)^T \mathbf{Q}\mathbf{d}^k \geq \beta$ *for all* $k \geq 0$.

Proof. (a) The stepsizes must satisfy $t_k = \lambda_k < 1$, since otherwise, if $t_k = 1$ for some k, then this means that $\mathbf{x}^{k+1} = \mathbf{a}_{i_k}$. But $f_q(\mathbf{x}^{k+1}) = f_q(\mathbf{a}_{i_k}) > f_q(\mathbf{x}^0)$, which is a contradiction to the monotonicity of the sequence of function values generated by the conditional gradient method (Theorem 13.9(a)). The proof that $\mathbf{x}^k \in \text{int}(\Omega)$ is by induction on k. For $k = 0$, by Assumption 13.18, $\mathbf{x}^0 \in \text{int}(\Omega)$. Now suppose that $\mathbf{x}^k \in \text{int}(\Omega)$. To prove that the same holds for $k+1$, note that since $t_k < 1$, it follows by the line segment principle (Lemma 5.23) that $\mathbf{x}^{k+1} = (1 - t_k)\mathbf{x}^k + t_k \mathbf{a}_{i_k}$ is also in $\text{int}(\Omega)$.

(b) Since $t_k = \lambda_k$, it follows that

$$\begin{aligned}
f_q(\mathbf{x}^{k+1}) &= f_q\left(\mathbf{x}^k + \lambda_k \mathbf{d}^k\right) \\
&= \frac{1}{2}(\mathbf{x}^k + \lambda_k \mathbf{d}^k)^T \mathbf{Q}(\mathbf{x}^k + \lambda_k \mathbf{d}^k) + \mathbf{b}^T(\mathbf{x}^k + \lambda_k \mathbf{d}^k) \\
&= f_q(\mathbf{x}^k) + \lambda_k(\mathbf{d}^k)^T(\mathbf{Q}\mathbf{x}^k + \mathbf{b}) + \frac{\lambda_k^2}{2}(\mathbf{d}^k)^T \mathbf{Q}\mathbf{d}^k \\
&= f_q(\mathbf{x}^k) + ((\mathbf{d}^k)^T \mathbf{Q}\mathbf{d}^k)\left(-\lambda_k^2 + \frac{\lambda_k^2}{2}\right) \\
&= f_q(\mathbf{x}^k) - \frac{1}{2}((\mathbf{d}^k)^T \mathbf{Q}\mathbf{d}^k)\lambda_k^2.
\end{aligned}$$

(c) Suppose by contradiction that $\sum_{k=0}^{\infty} \lambda_k < \infty$, then by Lemma 13.16, it follows that $\prod_{k=0}^{\infty}(1 - \lambda_k) = \delta$ for some $\delta > 0$. Note that by the definition of the method, for any $k \geq 0$, $\mathbf{x}^k = \mathbf{A}\mathbf{v}^k$, where $\{\mathbf{v}^k\}_{k \geq 0}$ satisfies

$$\mathbf{v}^{k+1} = (1 - \lambda_k)\mathbf{v}^k + \lambda_k \mathbf{e}_{i_k}.$$

Hence,

$$\mathbf{v}^{k+1} \geq (1 - \lambda_k)\mathbf{v}^k,$$

implying that

$$\mathbf{v}^k \geq \delta \mathbf{v}^0. \tag{13.35}$$

By Theorem 13.9(d), the limit points of $\{\mathbf{x}^k\}_{k\geq 0}$ are stationary points of problem (13.32). Let $\mathbf{x}^*$ be the unique optimal solution of problem (13.32). Since $\mathbf{x}^*$ is the only stationary point of problem (13.32), we can conclude that $\mathbf{x}^k \to \mathbf{x}^*$. The sequence $\{\mathbf{v}^k\}_{k\geq 0}$ is bounded and hence has a convergent subsequence $\{\mathbf{v}^{k_j}\}_{j\geq 0}$. Denoting the limit of the subsequence by $\mathbf{v}^* \in \Delta_l$, we note that by (13.35) it follows that $\mathbf{v}^* \geq \delta \mathbf{v}^0$, and hence $\mathbf{v}^* \in \Delta_l \cap \mathbb{R}^l_{++}$. Taking j to ∞ in the identity $\mathbf{x}^{k_j} = \mathbf{A}\mathbf{v}^{k_j}$, we obtain that $\mathbf{x}^* = \mathbf{A}\mathbf{v}^*$, where $\mathbf{v}^* \in \Delta_l \cap \mathbb{R}^l_{++}$, implying that $\mathbf{x}^* \in \text{int}(\Omega)$, in contradiction to Assumption 13.17.

(d) Since

$$(\mathbf{d}^k)^T \mathbf{Q}\mathbf{d}^k \geq \gamma \|\mathbf{d}^k\|_2^2 \tag{13.36}$$

with $\gamma = \lambda_{\min}(\mathbf{Q}) > 0$, it follows that we need to show that $\|\mathbf{d}^k\|_2$ is bounded below by a positive number. Note that by Assumption 13.17, $\mathbf{x}^* \notin \{\mathbf{a}_1, \mathbf{a}_2, \dots, \mathbf{a}_l\}$, and therefore there exists a positive integer K and $\beta_1 > 0$ such that $\|\mathbf{a}_i - \mathbf{x}^k\| \geq \beta_1$ for all $k > K$ and $i \in \{1, 2, \dots, l\}$. Since $\mathbf{x}^k \in \text{int}(\Omega)$ for all k, it follows that for β_2 defined as

$$\beta_2 \equiv \min\{\beta_1, \|\mathbf{a}_{i_0} - \mathbf{x}^0\|_2, \|\mathbf{a}_{i_1} - \mathbf{x}^1\|_2, \dots, \|\mathbf{a}_{i_K} - \mathbf{x}^K\|_2\} > 0,$$

it holds that $\|\mathbf{d}^k\|_2 = \|\mathbf{a}_{i_k} - \mathbf{x}^k\| \geq \beta_2$ for all $k \geq 0$, and we can finally conclude by (13.36) that for $\beta = \gamma\beta_2^2$, $(\mathbf{d}^k)^T \mathbf{Q}\mathbf{d}^k \geq \beta$ for all $k \geq 0$. $\quad\square$

The main negative result showing that the rate of convergence of the method cannot be linear is stated in Theorem 13.20 below.

Theorem 13.20 (Canon and Cullum's negative result). *Suppose that Assumption* 13.17 *holds and that* $\{\mathbf{x}^k\}$ *is the sequence generated by the conditional gradient method with exact line search for solving problem* (13.32) *with a starting point* $\mathbf{x}^0$ *satisfying Assumption* 13.18. *Then for every* $\varepsilon > 0$ *we have that* $f_q(\mathbf{x}^k) - f_{\text{opt}} \geq \frac{1}{k^{1+\varepsilon}}$ *for infinitely many* k's.

Proof. Let $\mathbf{d}^k$ and λ_k be given by (13.33) and (13.34), respectively. By Lemma 13.19(b), we have for any two positive integers satisfying $K \geq k$,

$$f_q(\mathbf{x}^K) - f_{\text{opt}} = f_q(\mathbf{x}^k) - f_{\text{opt}} - \frac{1}{2}\sum_{n=k}^{K-1}((\mathbf{d}^n)^T\mathbf{Q}\mathbf{d}^n)\lambda_n^2.$$

Taking $K \to \infty$ and using the fact that $f_q(\mathbf{x}^K) \to f_{\text{opt}}$ and Lemma 13.19(d), we obtain that

$$f_q(\mathbf{x}^k) - f_{\text{opt}} = \frac{1}{2}\sum_{n=k}^{\infty}((\mathbf{d}^n)\mathbf{Q}(\mathbf{d}^n))\lambda_n^2 \geq \frac{\beta}{2}\sum_{n=k}^{\infty}\lambda_n^2. \tag{13.37}$$

By Lemma 13.19(c), $\sum_{k=0}^{\infty}\lambda_k = \infty$, and hence by Lemma 13.15 and (13.37), we conclude that $f_q(\mathbf{x}^k) - f_{\text{opt}} \geq \frac{1}{k^{1+\varepsilon}}$ for infinitely many k's. $\quad\square$

Example 13.21. Consider the problem

$$\min\{f_q(x_1, x_2) \equiv x_1^2 + x_2^2 : (x_1, x_2) \in \operatorname{conv}\{(-1,0), (1,0), (0,1)\}\}. \qquad (13.38)$$

Assumption 13.17 is satisfied since the feasible set of problem (13.38) has a nonempty interior and the optimal solution, $(x_1^*, x_2^*) = (0,0)$, is on the boundary of the feasible set but is not an extreme point. The starting point $\mathbf{x}^0 = (0, \frac{1}{2})$ satisfies Assumption 13.18 since

$$f_q(\mathbf{x}^0) = \frac{1}{4} < 1 = \min\{f_q(-1,0), f_q(1,0), f_q(0,1)\}$$

and $\mathbf{x}^0 = \frac{1}{4}(-1,0) + \frac{1}{4}(1,0) + \frac{1}{2}(0,1)$. The first 100 iterations produced by the conditional gradient method are plotted in Figure 13.1. ∎

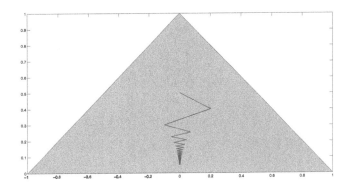

Figure 13.1. *First* 100 *iterations of the conditional gradient method employed on the problem from Example* 13.21.

13.3.2　Linear Rate under Strong Convexity of the Feasible Set

Canon and Cullum's negative result shows that different assumptions than strong convexity of the objective are required in order to establish a linear rate of convergence of the conditional gradient method. One example of such an assumption is strong convexity of the feasible set.

Definition 13.22 (strongly convex set). *A nonempty set $C \subseteq \mathbb{E}$ is called $\boldsymbol{\sigma}$-strongly convex ($\sigma > 0$) if for any $\mathbf{x}, \mathbf{y} \in C$ and $\lambda \in [0,1]$ the inclusion*

$$B\left[\lambda\mathbf{x} + (1-\lambda)\mathbf{y}, \frac{\sigma}{2}\lambda(1-\lambda)\|\mathbf{x} - \mathbf{y}\|^2\right] \subseteq C$$

holds.

A set is called strongly convex if it is σ-strongly convex for some $\sigma > 0$. Obviously, any strongly convex set is also convex. The next result states that level sets of nonnegative strongly convex and smooth functions are strongly convex sets.

Theorem 13.23 (strong convexity of level sets of strongly convex and smooth functions).[74] *Suppose that $g : \mathbb{E} \to \mathbb{R}_+$ is nonnegative, L_g-smooth, and σ_g-strongly convex. Let $\alpha > 0$. Then the set*

$$C_\alpha = \{\mathbf{x} \in \mathbb{E} : g(\mathbf{x}) \leq \alpha\}$$

is $\frac{\sigma_g}{\sqrt{2\alpha L_g}}$-strongly convex.

Proof. Let $\mathbf{x}, \mathbf{y} \in C_\alpha$ and $\lambda \in [0, 1]$. Define $\mathbf{x}_\lambda = \lambda \mathbf{x} + (1 - \lambda)\mathbf{y}$. By the nonnegativity of g and the sufficient decrease lemma (Lemma 10.4), we have

$$g(\mathbf{x}_\lambda) \geq g(\mathbf{x}_\lambda) - g\left(\mathbf{x}_\lambda - \frac{1}{L_g}\nabla g(\mathbf{x}_\lambda)\right) \geq \frac{1}{2L_g}\|\nabla g(\mathbf{x}_\lambda)\|^2.$$

Thus,

$$\|\nabla g(\mathbf{x}_\lambda)\| \leq \sqrt{2L_g g(\mathbf{x}_\lambda)}. \tag{13.39}$$

By the σ_g-strong convexity of g and the inequalities $g(\mathbf{x}), g(\mathbf{y}) \leq \alpha$,

$$g(\mathbf{x}_\lambda) \leq \lambda g(\mathbf{x}) + (1 - \lambda)g(\mathbf{y}) - \frac{\sigma_g}{2}\lambda(1 - \lambda)\|\mathbf{x} - \mathbf{y}\|^2 \leq \alpha - \beta, \tag{13.40}$$

where $\beta \equiv \frac{\sigma_g}{2}\lambda(1 - \lambda)\|\mathbf{x} - \mathbf{y}\|^2$.

Denote $\tilde{\sigma} = \frac{\sigma_g}{\sqrt{2\alpha L_g}}$. In order to show that C_α is $\tilde{\sigma}$-strongly convex, we will take $\mathbf{u} \in B[\mathbf{0}, 1]$ and show that $\mathbf{x}_\lambda + \gamma \mathbf{u} \in C_\alpha$, where $\gamma = \frac{\tilde{\sigma}}{2}\lambda(1 - \lambda)\|\mathbf{x} - \mathbf{y}\|^2$. Indeed,

$$
\begin{aligned}
g(\mathbf{x}_\lambda + \gamma \mathbf{u}) &\leq g(\mathbf{x}_\lambda) + \gamma\langle\nabla g(\mathbf{x}_\lambda), \mathbf{u}\rangle + \frac{\gamma^2 L_g}{2}\|\mathbf{u}\|^2 && \text{[descent lemma]} \\
&\leq g(\mathbf{x}_\lambda) + \gamma\|\nabla g(\mathbf{x}_\lambda)\| \cdot \|\mathbf{u}\| + \frac{\gamma^2 L_g}{2}\|\mathbf{u}\|^2 && \text{[Cauchy--Schwarz]} \\
&\leq g(\mathbf{x}_\lambda) + \gamma\sqrt{2L_g g(\mathbf{x}_\lambda)}\|\mathbf{u}\| + \frac{\gamma^2 L_g}{2}\|\mathbf{u}\|^2 && \text{[(13.39)]} \\
&= \left(\sqrt{g(\mathbf{x}_\lambda)} + \gamma\sqrt{\frac{L_g}{2}}\|\mathbf{u}\|\right)^2,
\end{aligned}
$$

which, combined with (13.40) and the fact that $\|\mathbf{u}\| \leq 1$, implies that

$$g(\mathbf{x}_\lambda + \gamma \mathbf{u}) \leq \left(\sqrt{\alpha - \beta} + \gamma\sqrt{\frac{L_g}{2}}\right)^2. \tag{13.41}$$

---

[74]Theorem 13.23 is from Journée, Nesterov, Richtárik, and Sepulchre, [74, Theorem 12].

By the concavity of the square root function $\varphi(t) = \sqrt{t}$, we have

$$\sqrt{\alpha - \beta} = \varphi(\alpha - \beta) \leq \varphi(\alpha) - \varphi'(\alpha)\beta = \sqrt{\alpha} - \frac{\beta}{2\sqrt{\alpha}}$$

$$= \sqrt{\alpha} - \frac{\sigma_g \lambda(1-\lambda)\|\mathbf{x} - \mathbf{y}\|^2}{4\sqrt{\alpha}}$$

$$= \sqrt{\alpha} - \frac{\sqrt{2\alpha L_g}\tilde{\sigma}\lambda(1-\lambda)\|\mathbf{x} - \mathbf{y}\|^2}{4\sqrt{\alpha}}$$

$$= \sqrt{\alpha} - \sqrt{\frac{L_g}{2}}\frac{\tilde{\sigma}\lambda(1-\lambda)\|\mathbf{x} - \mathbf{y}\|^2}{2}$$

$$= \sqrt{\alpha} - \gamma\sqrt{\frac{L_g}{2}},$$

which, along with (13.41), leads to the inequality $g(\mathbf{x}_\lambda + \gamma\mathbf{u}) \leq \alpha$. □

Example 13.24 (strong convexity of Euclidean balls). Consider the set[75] $C = B[\mathbf{c}, r] \subseteq \mathbb{E}$, where $\mathbf{c} \in \mathbb{E}$ and $r > 0$. Note that $C = \mathrm{Lev}(g, r^2)$, where $g(\mathbf{x}) = \|\mathbf{x} - \mathbf{c}\|^2$. Since here $L_g = \sigma_g = 2, \alpha = r^2$, it follows that the strong convexity parameter of the set is $\frac{2}{\sqrt{2\cdot 2\cdot r^2}} = \frac{1}{r}$. ∎

We will consider the problem

$$\min_{\mathbf{x}\in C} f(\mathbf{x}), \tag{13.42}$$

where we assume the following set of properties.

Assumption 13.25.

(A) C is nonempty, compact, and σ-strongly convex.

(B) $f : \mathbb{E} \to (-\infty, \infty]$ is convex L_f-smooth over $\mathrm{dom}(f)$, which is assumed to be an open and convex set satisfying $C \subseteq \mathrm{dom}(f)$.

(C) There exists $\delta > 0$ such that $\|\nabla f(\mathbf{x})\| \geq \delta$ for any $\mathbf{x} \in C$.

(D) The optimal set of problem (13.42) is nonempty and denoted by X^*. The optimal value of the problem is denoted by f_{opt}.

As usual, for any $\mathbf{x} \in C$, we use the notation

$$\mathbf{p}(\mathbf{x}) \in \mathrm{argmin}_{\mathbf{p}\in C}\langle\nabla f(\mathbf{x}), \mathbf{p}\rangle, \ S(\mathbf{x}) = \langle\nabla f(\mathbf{x}), \mathbf{x} - \mathbf{p}(\mathbf{x})\rangle.$$

We begin by establishing the following result connecting $S(\mathbf{x})$ and the distance between $\mathbf{x}$ and $\mathbf{p}(\mathbf{x})$.

---

[75]Recall that in this chapter the underlying norm is assumed to be Euclidean.

Lemma 13.26. *Suppose that Assumption 13.25 holds. Then for any* $\mathbf{x} \in C$,

$$S(\mathbf{x}) \geq \frac{\sigma\delta}{4}\|\mathbf{x} - \mathbf{p}(\mathbf{x})\|^2. \tag{13.43}$$

Proof. Let $\mathbf{x} \in C$. Define

$$\mathbf{z} = \frac{\mathbf{x} + \mathbf{p}(\mathbf{x})}{2} - \frac{\sigma}{8}\frac{\nabla f(\mathbf{x})}{\|\nabla f(\mathbf{x})\|}\|\mathbf{x} - \mathbf{p}(\mathbf{x})\|^2.$$

Then obviously $\mathbf{z} \in B\left[\frac{\mathbf{x}+\mathbf{p}(\mathbf{x})}{2}, \frac{\sigma}{8}\|\mathbf{x}-\mathbf{p}(\mathbf{x})\|^2\right]$, and hence, by the σ-strong convexity of C, $\mathbf{z} \in C$. In particular,

$$\langle \nabla f(\mathbf{x}), \mathbf{z} \rangle \geq \langle \nabla f(\mathbf{x}), \mathbf{p}(\mathbf{x}) \rangle. \tag{13.44}$$

The result (13.43) follows by the following arguments:

$$
\begin{aligned}
\langle \nabla f(\mathbf{x}), \mathbf{x} - \mathbf{p}(\mathbf{x}) \rangle &= 2\left\langle \nabla f(\mathbf{x}), \frac{\mathbf{x}+\mathbf{p}(\mathbf{x})}{2} - \mathbf{p}(\mathbf{x}) \right\rangle \\
&= 2\langle \nabla f(\mathbf{x}), \mathbf{z} - \mathbf{p}(\mathbf{x}) \rangle + 2\left\langle \nabla f(\mathbf{x}), \frac{\sigma}{8}\frac{\nabla f(\mathbf{x})}{\|\nabla f(\mathbf{x})\|}\|\mathbf{x} - \mathbf{p}(\mathbf{x})\|^2 \right\rangle \\
&\overset{(13.44)}{\geq} 2\left\langle \nabla f(\mathbf{x}), \frac{\sigma}{8}\frac{\nabla f(\mathbf{x})}{\|\nabla f(\mathbf{x})\|}\|\mathbf{x} - \mathbf{p}(\mathbf{x})\|^2 \right\rangle \\
&= \frac{\sigma}{4}\|\nabla f(\mathbf{x})\| \cdot \|\mathbf{x} - \mathbf{p}(\mathbf{x})\|^2 \\
&\geq \frac{\sigma\delta}{4}\|\mathbf{x} - \mathbf{p}(\mathbf{x})\|^2. \quad \square
\end{aligned}
$$

We will now establish the main result of this section stating that under Assumption 13.25, the conditional gradient method with either an adaptive or exact line search stepsize strategies enjoys a linear rate of convergence in function values.

Theorem 13.27. *Suppose that Assumption 13.25 holds, and let* $\{\mathbf{x}^k\}_{k\geq 0}$ *be the sequence generated by the conditional gradient method for solving problem* (13.42) *with stepsizes chosen by either the adaptive or exact line search strategies. Then for any* $k \geq 0$,

(a) $f(\mathbf{x}^{k+1}) - f_{\text{opt}} \leq (1 - \lambda)(f(\mathbf{x}^k) - f_{\text{opt}})$, *where*

$$\lambda = \min\left\{\frac{\sigma\delta}{8L_f}, \frac{1}{2}\right\}; \tag{13.45}$$

(b) $f(\mathbf{x}^k) - f_{\text{opt}} \leq (1 - \lambda)^k(f(\mathbf{x}^0) - f_{\text{opt}})$.

Proof. Let $k \geq 0$ and let $\tilde{\mathbf{x}}^k = \mathbf{x}^k + s_k(\mathbf{p}^k - \mathbf{x}^k)$, where $\mathbf{p}^k = \mathbf{p}(\mathbf{x}^k)$ and s_k is the stepsize chosen by the adaptive strategy:

$$s_k = \min\left\{1, \frac{S(\mathbf{x}^k)}{L_f\|\mathbf{x}^k - \mathbf{p}^k\|^2}\right\}.$$

By Lemma 13.7 (invoked with $\mathbf{x} = \mathbf{x}^k$ and $t = s_k$),

$$f(\mathbf{x}^k) - f(\tilde{\mathbf{x}}^k) \geq s_k S(\mathbf{x}^k) - \frac{s_k^2 L_f}{2}\|\mathbf{p}^k - \mathbf{x}^k\|^2. \tag{13.46}$$

There are two options: Either $s_k = 1$, and in this case $S(\mathbf{x}^k) \geq L_f\|\mathbf{x}^k - \mathbf{p}^k\|^2$, and thus

$$f(\mathbf{x}^k) - f(\tilde{\mathbf{x}}^k) \geq S(\mathbf{x}^k) - \frac{L_f}{2}\|\mathbf{p}^k - \mathbf{x}^k\|^2 \geq \frac{1}{2}S(\mathbf{x}^k), \tag{13.47}$$

or, on the other hand, $s_k = \frac{S(\mathbf{x}^k)}{L_f\|\mathbf{x}^k - \mathbf{p}^k\|^2}$, and then (13.46) amounts to

$$f(\mathbf{x}^k) - f(\tilde{\mathbf{x}}^k) \geq \frac{S^2(\mathbf{x}^k)}{2L_f\|\mathbf{x}^k - \mathbf{p}^k\|^2},$$

which, combined with (13.43) (with $\mathbf{x} = \mathbf{x}^k$), implies the inequality

$$f(\mathbf{x}^k) - f(\tilde{\mathbf{x}}^k) \geq \frac{\sigma\delta}{8L_f}S(\mathbf{x}^k). \tag{13.48}$$

Combining the inequalities (13.47) and (13.48) arising from the two possible cases, we obtain that

$$f(\mathbf{x}^k) - f(\tilde{\mathbf{x}}^k) \geq \lambda S(\mathbf{x}^k),$$

where λ is given in (13.45). If the method is employed with an adaptive stepsize strategy, then $\tilde{\mathbf{x}}^k = \mathbf{x}^{k+1}$, and hence $f(\tilde{\mathbf{x}}^k) = f(\mathbf{x}^{k+1})$. If the method is employed with an exact line search strategy, then $f(\mathbf{x}^{k+1}) \leq f(\tilde{\mathbf{x}}^k)$. Therefore, in both stepsize regimes, we get

$$f(\mathbf{x}^k) - f(\mathbf{x}^{k+1}) \geq f(\mathbf{x}^k) - f(\tilde{\mathbf{x}}^k) \geq \lambda S(\mathbf{x}^k). \tag{13.49}$$

On the other hand, by Lemma 13.12,

$$f(\mathbf{x}^k) - f_{\text{opt}} \leq S(\mathbf{x}^k). \tag{13.50}$$

Combining (13.49) and (13.50), we obtain that

$$\lambda(f(\mathbf{x}^k) - f_{\text{opt}}) \leq (f(\mathbf{x}^k) - f_{\text{opt}}) - (f(\mathbf{x}^{k+1}) - f_{\text{opt}}),$$

from which it readily follows that

$$f(\mathbf{x}^{k+1}) - f_{\text{opt}} \leq (1 - \lambda)(f(\mathbf{x}^k) - f_{\text{opt}}).$$

Part (b) is an immediate consequence of (a). $\square$

13.4 The Randomized Generalized Block Conditional Gradient Method[76]

In this section we will consider a block version of the generalized conditional gradient method. The model and underlying assumptions are similar to those made w.r.t.

---

[76]The randomized generalized block conditional gradient method presented in Section 13.4 is a simple generalization of the randomized block conditional gradient method introduced and analyzed by Lacoste-Julien, Jaggi, Schmidt, and Pletscher in [76].

the block proximal gradient method in Section 11.2. We will consider the problem

$$\min_{\mathbf{x}_1 \in \mathbb{E}_1, \mathbf{x}_2 \in \mathbb{E}_2, \ldots, \mathbf{x}_p \in \mathbb{E}_p} \left\{ F(\mathbf{x}_1, \mathbf{x}_2, \ldots, \mathbf{x}_p) \equiv f(\mathbf{x}_1, \mathbf{x}_2, \ldots, \mathbf{x}_p) + \sum_{j=1}^{p} g_j(\mathbf{x}_j) \right\},$$

$$(13.51)$$

where $\mathbb{E}_1, \mathbb{E}_2, \ldots, \mathbb{E}_p$ are Euclidean spaces. We will denote the product space by $\mathbb{E} = \mathbb{E}_1 \times \mathbb{E}_2 \times \cdots \times \mathbb{E}_p$ and use our convention (see Section 1.9) that the product space is also Euclidean with endowed norm

$$\|(\mathbf{u}_1, \mathbf{u}_2, \ldots, \mathbf{u}_p)\|_{\mathbb{E}} = \sqrt{\sum_{i=1}^{p} \|\mathbf{u}_i\|_{\mathbb{E}_i}^2}.$$

We will omit the subscripts of the norms indicating the underlying vector space (whose identity will be clear from the context). The function $g : \mathbb{E} \to (-\infty, \infty]$ is defined by

$$g(\mathbf{x}_1, \mathbf{x}_2, \ldots, \mathbf{x}_p) \equiv \sum_{i=1}^{p} g_i(\mathbf{x}_i),$$

and in particular $\mathrm{dom}(g) = \mathrm{dom}(g_1) \times \mathrm{dom}(g_2) \times \cdots \times \mathrm{dom}(g_p)$. The gradient w.r.t. the ith block ($i \in \{1, 2, \ldots, p\}$) is denoted by $\nabla_i f$ and is actually a mapping from $\mathrm{dom}(f)$ to $\mathbb{E}_i$. The following is satisfied:

$$\nabla f(\mathbf{x}) = (\nabla_1 f(\mathbf{x}), \nabla_2 f(\mathbf{x}), \ldots, \nabla_p f(\mathbf{x})).$$

For any $i \in \{1, 2, \ldots, p\}$ we define $\mathcal{U}_i : \mathbb{E}_i \to \mathbb{E}$ to be the linear transformation given by

$$\mathcal{U}_i(\mathbf{d}) = (\mathbf{0}, \ldots, \mathbf{0}, \underbrace{\mathbf{d}}_{i\text{th block}}, \mathbf{0}, \ldots, \mathbf{0}), \quad \mathbf{d} \in \mathbb{E}_i.$$

We also use throughout this chapter the notation that a vector $\mathbf{x} \in \mathbb{E}$ can be written as

$$\mathbf{x} = (\mathbf{x}_1, \mathbf{x}_2, \ldots, \mathbf{x}_p),$$

and this relation will also be written as $\mathbf{x} = (\mathbf{x}_i)_{i=1}^{p}$. Thus, in our notation, the main model (13.51) can be simply written as

$$\min_{\mathbf{x} \in \mathbb{E}} \{ F(\mathbf{x}) = f(\mathbf{x}) + g(\mathbf{x}) \}.$$

The basic assumptions on the model are summarized below.

Assumption 13.28.

(A) $g_i : \mathbb{E}_i \to (-\infty, \infty]$ *is proper closed and convex with compact* $\mathrm{dom}(g_i)$ *for any* $i \in \{1, 2, \ldots, p\}$.

(B) $f : \mathbb{E} \to (-\infty, \infty]$ *is convex and differentiable over* $\mathrm{dom}(f)$, *which is assumed to be an open and convex set satisfying* $\mathrm{dom}(g) \subseteq \mathrm{dom}(f)$.

(C) *There exist $L_1, L_2, \ldots, L_p > 0$ such that for any $i \in \{1, 2, \ldots, p\}$ it holds that*

$$\|\nabla_i f(\mathbf{x}) - \nabla_i f(\mathbf{x} + \mathcal{U}_i(\mathbf{d}))\| \leq L_i \|\mathbf{d}\|$$

for all $\mathbf{x} \in \mathrm{dom}(f)$ and $\mathbf{d} \in \mathbb{E}_i$ for which $\mathbf{x} + \mathcal{U}_i(\mathbf{d}) \in \mathrm{dom}(f)$.

(D) *The optimal set of problem (13.51) is nonempty and denoted by X^*. The optimal value is denoted by F_{opt}.*

For any $i \in \{1, 2, \ldots, p\}$, we denote

$$\mathbf{p}_i(\mathbf{x}) \in \mathrm{argmin}_{\mathbf{v} \in \mathbb{E}_i} \{\langle \mathbf{v}, \nabla_i f(\mathbf{x}) \rangle + g_i(\mathbf{v})\} \tag{13.52}$$

and define the *ith partial conditional gradient norm* as

$$S_i(\mathbf{x}) = \max_{\mathbf{v} \in \mathbb{E}_i} \{\langle \nabla_i f(\mathbf{x}), \mathbf{x}_i - \mathbf{v} \rangle + g_i(\mathbf{x}_i) - g_i(\mathbf{v})\} = \langle \nabla_i f(\mathbf{x}), \mathbf{x}_i - \mathbf{p}_i(\mathbf{x}) \rangle + g_i(\mathbf{x}_i) - g_i(\mathbf{p}_i(\mathbf{x})).$$

Obviously, we have

$$S(\mathbf{x}) = \sum_{i=1}^{p} S_i(\mathbf{x}).$$

There might be multiple optimal solutions for problem (13.52) and also for problem (13.3) defining $\mathbf{p}(\mathbf{x})$. Our only assumption is that $\mathbf{p}(\mathbf{x})$ is chosen as

$$\mathbf{p}(\mathbf{x}) = (\mathbf{p}_1(\mathbf{x}), \mathbf{p}_2(\mathbf{x}), \ldots, \mathbf{p}_p(\mathbf{x})). \tag{13.53}$$

The latter is not a restricting assumption since the vector in the right-hand side of (13.53) is indeed a minimizer of problem (13.3). The randomized generalized block conditional gradient method is described below.

The Randomized Generalized Block Conditional Gradient (RGBCG) Method

Initialization: pick $\mathbf{x}^0 = (\mathbf{x}_1^0, \mathbf{x}_2^0, \ldots, \mathbf{x}_p^0) \in \mathrm{dom}(g)$.
General step: for any $k = 0, 1, 2, \ldots$ execute the following steps:

(a) pick $i_k \in \{1, 2, \ldots, p\}$ randomly via a uniform distribution and $t_k \in [0, 1]$;

(b) set $\mathbf{x}^{k+1} = \mathbf{x}^k + t_k \mathcal{U}_{i_k}(\mathbf{p}_{i_k}(\mathbf{x}^k) - \mathbf{x}_{i_k}^k)$.

In our analysis the following notation is used:

- $\xi_{k-1} \equiv \{i_0, i_1, \ldots, i_{k-1}\}$ is a multivariate random variable.

- We will consider, in addition to the underlying Euclidean norm of the space $\mathbb{E}$, the following weighted norm:

$$\|\mathbf{x}\|_L \equiv \sqrt{\sum_{i=1}^{p} L_i \|\mathbf{x}_i\|^2}.$$

The rate of convergence of the RGBCG method with a specific choice of diminishing stepsizes is established in the following result.

Theorem 13.29. *Suppose that Assumption 13.28 holds, and let $\{\mathbf{x}^k\}_{k\geq 0}$ be the sequence generated by the RGBCG method for solving problem (13.51) with stepsizes $t_k = \frac{2p}{k+2p}$. Let Ω satisfy*

$$\Omega \geq \max_{\mathbf{x},\mathbf{y}\in\text{dom}(g)} \|\mathbf{x} - \mathbf{y}\|_L. \tag{13.54}$$

Then

(a) *for any $k \geq 1$,*

$$\mathsf{E}_{\xi_{k-1}}(F(\mathbf{x}^k)) - F_{\text{opt}} \leq \frac{2\max\{(p-1)(F(\mathbf{x}^0) - F_{\text{opt}}), p\Omega^2\}}{k + 2p - 2}; \tag{13.55}$$

(b) *for any $k \geq 3$,*

$$\min_{n=\lfloor k/2\rfloor+2,\ldots,k} \mathsf{E}_{\xi_{n-1}}(S(\mathbf{x}^n)) \leq \frac{8\max\{(p-1)(F(\mathbf{x}^0) - F_{\text{opt}}), p\Omega^2\}}{k - 2}. \tag{13.56}$$

Proof. We will use the shorthand notation $\mathbf{p}^k = \mathbf{p}(\mathbf{x}^k)$, and by the relation (13.53) it follows that $\mathbf{p}_i^k = \mathbf{p}_i(\mathbf{x}^k)$. Using the block descent lemma (Lemma 11.8) and the convexity of g_{i_k}, we can write the following:

$$
\begin{aligned}
F(\mathbf{x}^{k+1}) &= f(\mathbf{x}^{k+1}) + g(\mathbf{x}^{k+1}) \\
&= f(\mathbf{x}^k + t_k \mathcal{U}_{i_k}(\mathbf{p}_{i_k}^k - \mathbf{x}_{i_k}^k)) + g(\mathbf{x}^k + t_k \mathcal{U}_{i_k}(\mathbf{p}_{i_k}^k - \mathbf{x}_{i_k}^k)) \\
&\leq f(\mathbf{x}^k) - t_k \langle \nabla_{i_k} f(\mathbf{x}^k), \mathbf{x}_{i_k}^k - \mathbf{p}_{i_k}^k \rangle + \frac{t_k^2 L_{i_k}}{2} \|\mathbf{p}_{i_k}^k - \mathbf{x}_{i_k}^k\|^2 + \sum_{j=1,j\neq i_k}^{p} g_j(\mathbf{x}^k) \\
&\quad + g_{i_k}((1 - t_k)\mathbf{x}_{i_k}^k + t_k \mathbf{p}_{i_k}^k) \\
&= f(\mathbf{x}^k) - t_k \langle \nabla_{i_k} f(\mathbf{x}^k), \mathbf{x}_{i_k}^k - \mathbf{p}_{i_k}^k \rangle + \frac{t_k^2 L_{i_k}}{2} \|\mathbf{p}_{i_k}^k - \mathbf{x}_{i_k}^k\|^2 + g(\mathbf{x}^k) \\
&\quad - g_{i_k}(\mathbf{x}_{i_k}^k) + g_{i_k}((1 - t_k)\mathbf{x}_{i_k}^k + t_k \mathbf{p}_{i_k}^k) \\
&\leq f(\mathbf{x}^k) - t_k \langle \nabla_{i_k} f(\mathbf{x}^k), \mathbf{x}_{i_k}^k - \mathbf{p}_{i_k}^k \rangle + \frac{t_k^2 L_{i_k}}{2} \|\mathbf{p}_{i_k}^k - \mathbf{x}_{i_k}^k\|^2 + g(\mathbf{x}^k) \\
&\quad - g_{i_k}(\mathbf{x}_{i_k}^k) + (1 - t_k)g_{i_k}(\mathbf{x}_{i_k}^k) + t_k g_{i_k}(\mathbf{p}_{i_k}^k) \\
&= F(\mathbf{x}^k) - t_k S_{i_k}(\mathbf{x}^k) + \frac{t_k^2 L_{i_k}}{2} \|\mathbf{p}_{i_k}^k - \mathbf{x}_{i_k}^k\|^2.
\end{aligned}
$$

Taking expectation w.r.t. the random variable i_k, we obtain

$$
\begin{aligned}
\mathsf{E}_{i_k}(F(\mathbf{x}^{k+1})) &\leq F(\mathbf{x}^k) - \frac{t_k}{p} \sum_{i=1}^{p} S_i(\mathbf{x}^k) + \frac{t_k^2}{2p} \sum_{i=1}^{p} L_i \|\mathbf{p}_i^k - \mathbf{x}_i^k\|^2 \\
&= F(\mathbf{x}^k) - \frac{t_k}{p} S(\mathbf{x}^k) + \frac{t_k^2}{2p} \|\mathbf{p}^k - \mathbf{x}^k\|_L^2.
\end{aligned}
$$

Taking expectation w.r.t. ξ_{k-1} and using the bound (13.54) results with the following inequality:

$$\mathsf{E}_{\xi_k}(F(\mathbf{x}^{k+1})) \leq \mathsf{E}_{\xi_{k-1}}(F(\mathbf{x}^k)) - \frac{t_k}{p}\mathsf{E}_{\xi_{k-1}}(S(\mathbf{x}^k)) + \frac{t_k^2}{2p}\Omega^2.$$

Defining $\alpha_k = \frac{t_k}{p} = \frac{2}{k+2p}$ and subtracting F_{opt} from both sides, we obtain

$$\mathsf{E}_{\xi_k}(F(\mathbf{x}^{k+1})) - F_{\mathrm{opt}} \leq \mathsf{E}_{\xi_{k-1}}(F(\mathbf{x}^k)) - F_{\mathrm{opt}} - \alpha_k\mathsf{E}_{\xi_{k-1}}(S(\mathbf{x}^k)) + \frac{p\alpha_k^2}{2}\Omega^2.$$

Invoking Lemma 13.13 with $a_k = \mathsf{E}_{\xi_{k-1}}(F(\mathbf{x}^k)) - F_{\mathrm{opt}}, b_k = \mathsf{E}_{\xi_{k-1}}(S(\mathbf{x}^k))$, and $A = p\Omega^2$, noting that by Lemma 13.12 $a_k \leq b_k$, the inequalities (13.55) and (13.56) follow. ☐

Chapter 14

Alternating Minimization

> **Underlying Spaces:** In this chapter, all the underlying spaces are Euclidean.

14.1 The Method

Consider the problem

$$\min_{\mathbf{x}_1 \in \mathbb{E}_1, \mathbf{x}_2 \in \mathbb{E}_2, \ldots, \mathbf{x}_p \in \mathbb{E}_p} F(\mathbf{x}_1, \mathbf{x}_2, \ldots, \mathbf{x}_p), \tag{14.1}$$

where $\mathbb{E}_1, \mathbb{E}_2, \ldots, \mathbb{E}_p$ are Euclidean spaces whose product space is denoted by $\mathbb{E} = \mathbb{E}_1 \times \mathbb{E}_2 \times \cdots \times \mathbb{E}_p$. We use our convention (see Section 1.9) that the product space is also Euclidean with endowed norm

$$\|(\mathbf{u}_1, \mathbf{u}_2, \ldots, \mathbf{u}_p)\|_{\mathbb{E}} = \sqrt{\sum_{i=1}^{p} \|\mathbf{u}_i\|_{\mathbb{E}_i}^2}.$$

We will omit the subscripts of the norms indicating the underlying vector space whose identity will be clear from the context. At this point we only assume that $F : \mathbb{E} \to (-\infty, \infty]$ is proper, but obviously to assure some kind of convergence, additional assumptions will be imposed.

For any $i \in \{1, 2, \ldots, p\}$ we define $\mathcal{U}_i : \mathbb{E}_i \to \mathbb{E}$ to be the linear transformation given by

$$\mathcal{U}_i(\mathbf{d}) = (\mathbf{0}, \ldots, \mathbf{0}, \underbrace{\mathbf{d}}_{i\text{th block}}, \mathbf{0}, \ldots, \mathbf{0}), \quad \mathbf{d} \in \mathbb{E}_i.$$

We also use throughout this chapter the notation that a vector $\mathbf{x} \in \mathbb{E}$ can be written as

$$\mathbf{x} = (\mathbf{x}_1, \mathbf{x}_2, \ldots, \mathbf{x}_p),$$

and this relation will also be written as $\mathbf{x} = (\mathbf{x}_i)_{i=1}^{p}$.

In this chapter we consider the *alternating minimization method* in which we successively pick a block in a cyclic manner and set the new value of the chosen block to be a minimizer of the objective w.r.t. the chosen block. The kth iterate is denoted by $\mathbf{x}^k = (\mathbf{x}_1^k, \mathbf{x}_2^k, \ldots, \mathbf{x}_p^k)$. Each iteration of the alternating minimization method involves p "subiterations" and the by-products of these sub-iterations will be denoted by the following auxiliary subsequences:

$$
\begin{aligned}
\mathbf{x}^{k,0} &= \mathbf{x}^k = (\mathbf{x}_1^k, \mathbf{x}_2^k, \ldots, \mathbf{x}_p^k), \\
\mathbf{x}^{k,1} &= (\mathbf{x}_1^{k+1}, \mathbf{x}_2^k, \ldots, \mathbf{x}_p^k), \\
\mathbf{x}^{k,2} &= (\mathbf{x}_1^{k+1}, \mathbf{x}_2^{k+1}, \mathbf{x}_3^k, \ldots, \mathbf{x}_p^k), \\
&\;\vdots \\
\mathbf{x}^{k,p} &= \mathbf{x}^{k+1} = (\mathbf{x}_1^{k+1}, \mathbf{x}_2^{k+1}, \ldots, \mathbf{x}_p^{k+1}).
\end{aligned}
\tag{14.2}
$$

The alternating minimization method for minimizing F is described below.

The Alternating Minimization Method

Initialization: pick $\mathbf{x}^0 = (\mathbf{x}_1^0, \mathbf{x}_2^0, \ldots, \mathbf{x}_p^0) \in \mathrm{dom}(F)$.
General step: for any $k = 0, 1, 2, \ldots$ execute the following step:

- for $i = 1, 2, \ldots, p$, compute

$$
\mathbf{x}_i^{k+1} \in \mathrm{argmin}_{\mathbf{x}_i \in \mathbb{E}_i} F(\mathbf{x}_1^{k+1}, \ldots, \mathbf{x}_{i-1}^{k+1}, \mathbf{x}_i, \mathbf{x}_{i+1}^k, \ldots, \mathbf{x}_p^k).
\tag{14.3}
$$

In our notation, we can alternatively rewrite the general step of the alternating minimization method as follows:

- set $\mathbf{x}^{k,0} = \mathbf{x}^k$;

- for $i = 1, 2, \ldots, p$, compute $\mathbf{x}^{k,i} = \mathbf{x}^{k,i-1} + \mathcal{U}_i(\tilde{\mathbf{y}} - \mathbf{x}_i^k)$, where

$$
\tilde{\mathbf{y}} \in \mathrm{argmin}_{\mathbf{y} \in \mathbb{E}_i} F(\mathbf{x}^{k,i-1} + \mathcal{U}_i(\mathbf{y} - \mathbf{x}_i^k));
\tag{14.4}
$$

- set $\mathbf{x}^{k+1} = \mathbf{x}^{k,p}$.

The following simple lemma states that if F is proper and closed and has bounded level sets, then problem (14.1) has a minimizer and the alternating minimization method is well defined in the sense that the minimization problems (14.3) (or in their alternative form (14.4)) possess minimizers. In the sequel, we will impose additional assumptions on the structure of F that will enable us to establish convergence results.

Lemma 14.1 (alternating minimization is well defined). *Suppose that $F :$ $\mathbb{E} \to (-\infty, \infty]$ ($\mathbb{E} = \mathbb{E}_1 \times \mathbb{E}_2 \times \cdots \times \mathbb{E}_p$) is a proper and closed function. Assume further that F has bounded level sets; that is, $\mathrm{Lev}(F, \alpha) = \{\mathbf{x} \in \mathbb{E} : F(\mathbf{x}) \leq \alpha\}$ is bounded for any $\alpha \in \mathbb{R}$. Then the function F has at least one minimizer, and for any $\bar{\mathbf{x}} \in \mathrm{dom}(F)$ and $i \in \{1, 2, \ldots, p\}$ the problem*

$$
\min_{\mathbf{y} \in \mathbb{E}_i} F(\bar{\mathbf{x}} + \mathcal{U}_i(\mathbf{y} - \bar{\mathbf{x}}_i))
\tag{14.5}
$$

possesses a minimizer.

Proof. Take $\tilde{\mathbf{x}} \in \mathrm{dom}(F)$. Then

$$\mathrm{argmin}_{\mathbf{x} \in \mathbb{E}} F(\mathbf{x}) = \mathrm{argmin}_{\mathbf{x} \in \mathbb{E}} \{F(\mathbf{x}) : \mathbf{x} \in \mathrm{Lev}(F, F(\tilde{\mathbf{x}}))\}.$$

Since F is closed with bounded level sets, it follows that $\mathrm{Lev}(F, F(\tilde{\mathbf{x}}))$ is compact. Hence, by the Weierstrass theorem for closed functions (Theorem 2.12), it follows that the problem of minimizing the proper and closed function F over $\mathrm{Lev}(F, F(\tilde{\mathbf{x}}))$, and hence also the problem of minimizing F over the entire space, possesses a minimizer. Since the function $\mathbf{y} \mapsto F(\bar{\mathbf{x}} + \mathcal{U}_i(\mathbf{y} - \bar{\mathbf{x}}_i))$ is proper and closed with bounded level sets, the same argument shows that problem (14.5) also possesses a minimizer. $\square$

14.2 Coordinate-wise Minima

By the definition of the method, it is clear that convergence will most likely be proved (if at all possible) to *coordinate-wise minimum points*.

Definition 14.2. *A vector* $\mathbf{x}^* \in \mathbb{E}$ *is a* **coordinate-wise minimum** *of a function* $F : \mathbb{E}_1 \times \mathbb{E}_2 \times \cdots \times \mathbb{E}_p \to (-\infty, \infty]$ *if* $\mathbf{x}^* \in \mathrm{dom}(F)$ *and*

$$F(\mathbf{x}^*) \leq F(\mathbf{x}^* + \mathcal{U}_i(\mathbf{y})) \textit{ for all } i = 1, 2, \ldots, p, \mathbf{y} \in \mathbb{E}_i.$$

The next theorem is a rather standard result showing that under properness and closedness of the objective function, as well as an assumption on the uniqueness of the minimizers of the class of subproblems solved at each iteration, the limit points of the sequence generated by the alternating minimization method are coordinate-wise minima.

Theorem 14.3 (convergence of alternating minimization to coordinate-wise minima).[77] *Suppose that* $F : \mathbb{E} \to (-\infty, \infty]$ *(* $\mathbb{E} = \mathbb{E}_1 \times \mathbb{E}_2 \times \cdots \times \mathbb{E}_p$ *) is a proper closed function that is continuous over its domain. Assume that*

(A) *for each* $\bar{\mathbf{x}} \in \mathrm{dom}(F)$ *and* $i \in \{1, 2, \ldots, p\}$ *the problem* $\min_{\mathbf{y} \in \mathbb{E}_i} F(\bar{\mathbf{x}} + \mathcal{U}_i(\mathbf{y} - \bar{\mathbf{x}}_i))$ *has a unique minimizer;*

(B) *the level sets of* F *are bounded, meaning that for any* $\alpha \in \mathbb{R}$, *the set* $\mathrm{Lev}(F, \alpha) = \{\mathbf{x} \in \mathbb{E} : F(\mathbf{x}) \leq \alpha\}$ *is bounded.*

Let $\{\mathbf{x}^k\}_{k \geq 0}$ *be the sequence generated by the alternating minimization method for minimizing* F. *Then* $\{\mathbf{x}^k\}_{k \geq 0}$ *is bounded, and any limit point of the sequence is a coordinate-wise minimum.*

Proof. To prove that the sequence is bounded, note that by the definition of the method, the sequence of function values $\{F(\mathbf{x}^k)\}_{k \geq 0}$ is nonincreasing, which in particular implies that $\{\mathbf{x}^k\}_{k \geq 0} \subseteq \mathrm{Lev}(F, F(\mathbf{x}^0))$; therefore, by condition (B), it follows that the sequence $\{\mathbf{x}^k\}_{k \geq 0}$ is bounded, which along with the closedness of F

---

[77]Theorem 14.3 and its proof originate from Bertsekas [28, Proposition 2.7.1].

implies that $\{F(\mathbf{x}^k)\}_{k\geq 0}$ is bounded below. We can thus conclude that $\{F(\mathbf{x}^k)\}_{k\geq 0}$ converges to some real number $\bar{F}$. Since $F(\mathbf{x}^k) \geq F(\mathbf{x}^{k,1}) \geq F(\mathbf{x}^{k+1})$, it follows that $\{F(\mathbf{x}^{k,1})\}_{k\geq 0}$ also converges to $\bar{F}$, meaning that the sequences $\{F(\mathbf{x}^k)\}_{k\geq 0}$ and $\{F(\mathbf{x}^{k,1})\}_{k\geq 0}$ converge to the same value.

Now, suppose that $\bar{\mathbf{x}}$ is a limit point of $\{\mathbf{x}^k\}_{k\geq 0}$. Then there exists a subsequence $\{\mathbf{x}^{k_j}\}_{j\geq 0}$ converging to $\bar{\mathbf{x}}$. Since the sequence $\{\mathbf{x}^{k_j,1}\}_{j\geq 0}$ is bounded (follows directly from the boundedness of $\{\mathbf{x}^k\}_{k\geq 0}$), by potentially passing to a subsequence, we can assume that $\{\mathbf{x}^{k_j,1}\}_{j\geq 0}$ converges to some vector $(\mathbf{v}, \bar{\mathbf{x}}_2, \ldots, \bar{\mathbf{x}}_p)$ $(\mathbf{v} \in \mathbb{E}_1)$. By definition of the method,

$$F(\mathbf{x}_1^{k_j+1}, \mathbf{x}_2^{k_j}, \ldots, \mathbf{x}_p^{k_j}) \leq F(\mathbf{x}_1, \mathbf{x}_2^{k_j}, \ldots, \mathbf{x}_p^{k_j}) \text{ for any } \mathbf{x}_1 \in \mathbb{E}_1.$$

Taking the limit $j \to \infty$ and using the closedness of F, as well as the continuity of F over its domain, we obtain that

$$F(\mathbf{v}, \bar{\mathbf{x}}_2, \ldots, \bar{\mathbf{x}}_p) \leq F(\mathbf{x}_1, \bar{\mathbf{x}}_2, \ldots, \bar{\mathbf{x}}_p) \text{ for any } \mathbf{x}_1 \in \mathbb{E}_1.$$

Since $\{F(\mathbf{x}^k)\}_{k\geq 0}$ and $\{F(\mathbf{x}^{k,1})\}_{k\geq 0}$ converge to the same value, we have

$$F(\mathbf{v}, \bar{\mathbf{x}}_2, \ldots, \bar{\mathbf{x}}_p) = F(\bar{\mathbf{x}}_1, \bar{\mathbf{x}}_2, \ldots, \bar{\mathbf{x}}_p),$$

which by the uniqueness of the minimizer w.r.t. the first block (condition (A)) implies that $\mathbf{v} = \bar{\mathbf{x}}_1$. Therefore,

$$F(\bar{\mathbf{x}}_1, \bar{\mathbf{x}}_2, \ldots, \bar{\mathbf{x}}_p) \leq F(\mathbf{x}_1, \bar{\mathbf{x}}_2, \ldots, \bar{\mathbf{x}}_p) \text{ for any } \mathbf{x}_1 \in \mathbb{E}_1,$$

which is the first condition for coordinate-wise minimality. We have shown that $\mathbf{x}^{k_j,1} \to \bar{\mathbf{x}}$ as $j \to \infty$. This means that we can repeat the arguments when $\mathbf{x}^{k_j,1}$ replaces $\mathbf{x}^{k_j}$ and concentrate on the second coordinate to obtain that

$$F(\bar{\mathbf{x}}_1, \bar{\mathbf{x}}_2, \ldots, \bar{\mathbf{x}}_p) \leq F(\bar{\mathbf{x}}_1, \mathbf{x}_2, \bar{\mathbf{x}}_3, \ldots, \bar{\mathbf{x}}_p) \text{ for any } \mathbf{x}_2 \in \mathbb{E}_2,$$

which is the second condition for coordinate-wise minimality. The above argument can be repeated until we show that $\bar{\mathbf{x}}$ satisfies all the conditions for coordinate-wise minimality. $\square$

The following famous example of Powell describes a situation in which the alternating minimization method produces a sequence whose limit points are *not* coordinate-wise minima points.

Example 14.4 (Powell's example—failure of alternating minimization I).[78]
Let

$$\varphi(x, y, z) = -xy - yz - zx + [x-1]_+^2 + [-x-1]_+^2 + [y-1]_+^2 + [-y-1]_+^2 + [z-1]_+^2 + [-z-1]_+^2.$$

Note that φ is differentiable. Fixing y and z, it is easy to show that

$$\operatorname{argmin}_x \varphi(x, y, z) = \begin{cases} \operatorname{sgn}(y+z)(1 + \frac{1}{2}|y+z|), & y+z \neq 0, \\ [-1, 1], & y+z = 0, \end{cases} \qquad (14.6)$$

---

[78] Powell's example is from [106].

and similarly (by the symmetry of φ),

$$\mathrm{argmin}_y \varphi(x,y,z) = \begin{cases} \mathrm{sgn}(x+z)(1+\frac{1}{2}|x+z|), & x+z \neq 0, \\ [-1,1], & x+z = 0, \end{cases} \tag{14.7}$$

$$\mathrm{argmin}_z \varphi(x,y,z) = \begin{cases} \mathrm{sgn}(x+y)(1+\frac{1}{2}|x+y|), & x+y \neq 0, \\ [-1,1], & x+y = 0. \end{cases} \tag{14.8}$$

Suppose that $\varepsilon > 0$ and that we initialize the alternating minimization method with the point $\left(-1-\varepsilon, 1+\frac{1}{2}\varepsilon, -1-\frac{1}{4}\varepsilon\right)$. Then the first six iterations are

$$\left(1+\frac{1}{8}\varepsilon, 1+\frac{1}{2}\varepsilon, -1-\frac{1}{4}\varepsilon\right),$$

$$\left(1+\frac{1}{8}\varepsilon, -1-\frac{1}{16}\varepsilon, -1-\frac{1}{4}\varepsilon\right),$$

$$\left(1+\frac{1}{8}\varepsilon, -1-\frac{1}{16}\varepsilon, 1+\frac{1}{32}\varepsilon\right),$$

$$\left(-1-\frac{1}{64}\varepsilon, -1-\frac{1}{16}\varepsilon, 1+\frac{1}{32}\varepsilon\right),$$

$$\left(-1-\frac{1}{64}\varepsilon, 1+\frac{1}{128}\varepsilon, 1+\frac{1}{32}\varepsilon\right),$$

$$\left(-1-\frac{1}{64}\varepsilon, 1+\frac{1}{128}\varepsilon, -1-\frac{1}{256}\varepsilon\right).$$

We are essentially back to the first point, but with $\frac{1}{64}\varepsilon$ replacing ε. The process continues by cycling around the six points

$$(1,1,-1), \ (1,-1,-1), \ (1,-1,1), \ (-1,-1,1), \ (-1,1,1), \ (-1,1,-1).$$

None of these points is a stationary point of φ. Indeed,

$$\nabla\varphi(1,1,-1) = (0,0,-2), \quad \nabla\varphi(-1,1,1) = (-2,0,0), \quad \nabla\varphi(1,-1,1) = (0,-2,0),$$

$$\nabla\varphi(-1,-1,1) = (0,0,2), \quad \nabla\varphi(1,-1,-1) = (2,0,0), \quad \nabla\varphi(-1,1,-1) = (0,2,0).$$

Since the limit points are not stationary points of φ, they are also not coordinate-wise minima[79] points. The fact that the limit points of the sequence generated by the alternating minimization method are not coordinate-wise minima is not a contradiction to Theorem 14.3 since two assumptions are not met: the subproblems solved at each iteration do not necessarily possess unique minimizers, and the level sets of φ are not bounded since for any $x > 1$

$$\varphi(x,x,x) = -3x^2 + 3(x-1)^2 = -6x + 3$$

---

[79]For example, to show that $(1,1,-1)$ is not a coordinate-wise minimum, note that since $\nabla\varphi(1,1,-1) = (0,0,-2)$, then $(1,1,-1+\delta)$ for small enough $\delta > 0$ will have a smaller function value than $(1,1,-1)$.

goes to $-\infty$ as $x \to \infty$. A close inspection of the proof of Theorem 14.3 reveals that the assumption on the boundedness of the level sets in Theorem 14.3 is only required in order to assure the boundedness of the sequence generated by the method. Since the sequence in this example is in any case bounded, it follows that the failure to converge to a coordinate-wise minimum is actually due to the nonuniqueness of the optimal solutions of the subproblems (14.6),(14.7) and (14.8). ∎

Note that if the alternating minimization method reaches a coordinate-wise minimum, then it might get stuck there since the point is optimal w.r.t. each block.[80] The natural question is of course whether coordinate-wise minima are necessarily stationary points of the problem, meaning that they satisfy the most basic optimality condition of the problem. The answer is unfortunately *no* even when the objective function is convex, as the following example illustrates.

Example 14.5 (failure of alternating minimization II). Consider the convex function
$$F(x_1, x_2) = |3x_1 + 4x_2| + |x_1 - 2x_2|.$$
The function satisfies all the assumptions of Theorem 14.3: it is proper, closed, and continuous with bounded level sets and has a unique minimizer w.r.t. each variable. Therefore, Theorem 14.3 guarantees that the limit point points of the alternating minimization method are coordinate-wise minima points. We will see that for the specific problem under consideration, this result is of very little importance.

The unique minimizer of the function is $(x_1, x_2) = (0,0)$. However, for any $\alpha \in \mathbb{R}$ the point $(-4\alpha, 3\alpha)$ is a coordinate-wise minimum of f. To show this, assume first that $\alpha > 0$. Note that

$$F(-4\alpha, t) = |4t - 12\alpha| + |2t + 4\alpha| = \begin{cases} -6t + 8\alpha, & t < -2\alpha, \\ -2t + 16\alpha, & -2\alpha \le t \le 3\alpha, \\ 6t - 8\alpha, & t > 3\alpha, \end{cases}$$

and obviously $t = 3\alpha$ is the minimizer of $F(-4\alpha, t)$. Similarly, the optimal solution of

$$F(t, 3\alpha) = |3t + 12\alpha| + |t - 6\alpha| = \begin{cases} -4t - 6\alpha, & t < -4\alpha, \\ 2t + 18\alpha, & -4\alpha \le t \le 6\alpha, \\ 4t + 6\alpha, & t > 6\alpha, \end{cases}$$

is $t = -4\alpha$. A similar argument also shows that $(-4\alpha, 3\alpha)$ is a coordinate-wise minimum also for $\alpha < 0$. We conclude that $(-4\alpha, 3\alpha)$ is a coordinate-wise minimum for any $\alpha \in \mathbb{R}$ where only the value $\alpha = 0$ corresponds to the actual minimum of F; all other values correspond to nonoptimal/nonstationary[81] points of F. The severity of the situation is made clear when noting that after only one iteration

---

[80] Actually, the only situation in which the method might move away from a coordinate-wise minimum is if there are multiple optimal solutions to some of the subproblems solved at each subiteration of the method.

[81] In the sense that $\mathbf{0} \notin \partial F(\mathbf{x})$.

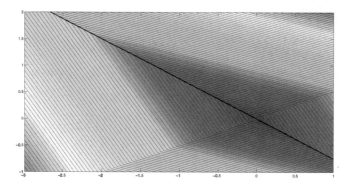

Figure 14.1. *Contour lines of the function $f(x_1, x_2) = |3x_1 + 4x_2| + |x_1 - 2x_2|$. All the points on the emphasized line $\{(-4\alpha, 3\alpha) : \alpha \in \mathbb{R}\}$ are coordinate-wise minima, and only $(0, 0)$ is a global minimum.*

of alternating minimization, the method gets stuck at a coordinate-wise minimum, which, unless the initial vector contains at least one zero element, is a nonoptimal point (easy to show). The contour lines of F, as well as the line comprising the continuum of coordinate-wise minima points is described in Figure 14.1. ∎

Example 14.5 shows that even if convexity is assumed, coordinate-wise minima points are not necessarily stationary points of the objective function; in particular, this means that the alternating minimization method will not be guaranteed to converge to stationary points (which are global minima points in the convex case). One possible reason for this phenomena is that the stationarity condition $\mathbf{0} \in \partial F(\mathbf{x})$ does not decompose into separate conditions on each block. This is why, in the next section, we present a specific model for the function F for which we will be able to prove that coordinate-wise minima points are necessarily stationary points.

14.3 The Composite Model

The model that we will analyze from now on is the composite model, which was discussed in Sections 11.2 and 13.4 in the contexts of the block proximal gradient and block conditional gradient methods. Thus, our main model is

$$\min_{\mathbf{x}_1 \in \mathbb{E}_1, \mathbf{x}_2 \in \mathbb{E}_2, \dots, \mathbf{x}_p \in \mathbb{E}_p} \left\{ F(\mathbf{x}_1, \mathbf{x}_2, \dots, \mathbf{x}_p) = f(\mathbf{x}_1, \mathbf{x}_2, \dots, \mathbf{x}_p) + \sum_{j=1}^{p} g_j(\mathbf{x}_j) \right\}. \quad (14.9)$$

The function $g : \mathbb{E} \to (-\infty, \infty]$ is defined by

$$g(\mathbf{x}_1, \mathbf{x}_2, \dots, \mathbf{x}_p) \equiv \sum_{i=1}^{p} g_i(\mathbf{x}_i).$$

The gradient w.r.t. the ith block ($i \in \{1, 2, \ldots, p\}$) is denoted by $\nabla_i f$, and the following is satisfied:

$$\nabla f(\mathbf{x}) = (\nabla_1 f(\mathbf{x}), \nabla_2 f(\mathbf{x}), \ldots, \nabla_p f(\mathbf{x})).$$

Note that in our notation the main model (14.9) can be simply written as

$$\min_{\mathbf{x} \in \mathbb{E}} \{F(\mathbf{x}) = f(\mathbf{x}) + g(\mathbf{x})\}.$$

The basic assumptions on the model are summarized below.

Assumption 14.6.

(A) $g_i : \mathbb{E}_i \to (-\infty, \infty]$ *is proper closed and convex for any* $i \in \{1, 2, \ldots, p\}$. *In addition,* g_i *is continuous over its domain.*

(B) $f : \mathbb{E} \to (-\infty, \infty]$ *is a closed function;* $\mathrm{dom}(f)$ *is convex;* f *is differentiable over* $\mathrm{int}(\mathrm{dom}(f))$ *and* $\mathrm{dom}(g) \subseteq \mathrm{int}(\mathrm{dom}(f))$.

Under the above structure of the function F, the general step of the alternating minimization method (14.3) can be compactly written as

$$\mathbf{x}_i^{k+1} \in \mathrm{argmin}_{\mathbf{x}_i \in \mathbb{E}_i} \{f(\mathbf{x}_1^{k+1}, \ldots, \mathbf{x}_{i-1}^{k+1}, \mathbf{x}_i, \mathbf{x}_{i+1}^k, \ldots, \mathbf{x}_p^k) + g_i(\mathbf{x}_i)\},$$

where we omitted from the above the constant terms related to the functions g_j, $j \neq i$.

Recall that a point $\mathbf{x}^* \in \mathrm{dom}(g)$ is a stationary point of problem (14.9) if it satisfies $-\nabla f(\mathbf{x}^*) \in \partial g(\mathbf{x}^*)$ (Definition 3.73) and that by Theorem 11.6(a), this condition can be written equivalently as $-\nabla_i f(\mathbf{x}^*) \in \partial g_i(\mathbf{x}^*)$, $i = 1, 2, \ldots, p$. The latter fact will enable us to show that coordinate-wise minima points of F are stationary points of problem (14.9).

Lemma 14.7 (coordinate-wise minimality $\Rightarrow$ stationarity). *Suppose that Assumption 14.6 holds and that* $\mathbf{x}^* \in \mathrm{dom}(g)$ *is a coordinate-wise minimum of* $F = f + g$. *Then* $\mathbf{x}^*$ *is a stationary point of problem* (14.9).

Proof. Since $\mathbf{x}^*$ is a coordinate-wise minimum of F, it follows that for all $i \in \{1, 2, \ldots, p\}$,

$$\mathbf{x}_i^* \in \mathrm{argmin}_{\mathbf{y} \in \mathbb{E}_i} \{\tilde{f}_i(\mathbf{y}) + g_i(\mathbf{y})\},$$

where

$$\tilde{f}_i(\mathbf{y}) \equiv f(\mathbf{x}^* + \mathcal{U}_i(\mathbf{y} - \mathbf{x}_i^*)) = f(\mathbf{x}_1^*, \ldots, \mathbf{x}_{i-1}^*, \mathbf{y}, \mathbf{x}_{i+1}^*, \ldots, \mathbf{x}_p^*).$$

Therefore, by Theorem 3.72(a), $-\nabla \tilde{f}_i(\mathbf{x}_i^*) \in \partial g_i(\mathbf{x}^*)$. Since $\nabla \tilde{f}_i(\mathbf{x}_i^*) = \nabla_i f(\mathbf{x}^*)$, we conclude that for any i, $-\nabla_i f(\mathbf{x}^*) \in \partial g_i(\mathbf{x}^*)$. Thus, invoking Theorem 11.6(a), we obtain that $-\nabla f(\mathbf{x}^*) \in \partial g(\mathbf{x}^*)$, namely, that $\mathbf{x}^*$ is a stationary point of problem (14.9). $\square$

Recall that Theorem 14.3 showed under appropriate assumptions that limit points of the sequence generated by the alternating minimization method are coordinate-wise minima points. Combining this result with Lemma 14.7 we obtain the following corollary.

Corollary 14.8. *Suppose that Assumption* 14.6 *holds, and assume further that* $F = f + g$ *satisfies the following:*

- *for each* $\bar{\mathbf{x}} \in \operatorname{dom}(F)$ *and* $i \in \{1, 2, \ldots, p\}$ *the problem* $\min_{\mathbf{y} \in \mathbb{E}_i} F(\bar{\mathbf{x}} + \mathcal{U}_i(\mathbf{y} - \bar{\mathbf{x}}_i))$ *has a unique minimizer;*

- *the level sets of* F *are bounded, meaning that for any* $\alpha \in \mathbb{R}$, *the set* $\{\mathbf{x} \in \mathbb{E} : F(\mathbf{x}) \leq \alpha\}$ *is bounded.*

Let $\{\mathbf{x}^k\}_{k \geq 0}$ *be the sequence generated by the alternating minimization method for solving* (14.9). *Then* $\{\mathbf{x}^k\}_{k \geq 0}$ *is bounded, and any limit point of the sequence is a stationary point of problem* (14.9).

14.4 Convergence in the Convex Case

The convergence results previously established require a rather strong assumption on the uniqueness of the optimal solution to the class of subproblems that are solved at each sub-iteration of the alternating minimization method. We will show how this assumption can be removed if we assume convexity of the objective function.

Theorem 14.9.[82] *Suppose that Assumption* 14.6 *holds and that in addition*

- f *is convex;*

- f *is continuously differentiable*[83] *over* $\operatorname{int}(\operatorname{dom}(f))$;

- *the function* $F = f + g$ *satisfies that the level sets of* F *are bounded, meaning that for any* $\alpha \in \mathbb{R}$, *the set* $\operatorname{Lev}(F, \alpha) = \{\mathbf{x} \in \mathbb{E} : F(\mathbf{x}) \leq \alpha\}$ *is bounded.*

Then the sequence generated by the alternating minimization method for solving problem (14.9) *is bounded, and any limit point of the sequence is an optimal solution of the problem.*

Proof. Let $\{\mathbf{x}^k\}_{k \geq 0}$ be the sequence generated by the alternating minimization method, and let $\{\mathbf{x}^{k,i}\}_{k \geq 0}$ $(i = 0, 1, \ldots, p)$ be the auxiliary sequences given in (14.2). We begin by showing that $\{\mathbf{x}^k\}_{k \geq 0}$ is bounded. Indeed, by the definition of the method, the sequence of function values is nonincreasing, and hence $\{\mathbf{x}^k\}_{k \geq 0} \subseteq \operatorname{Lev}(F, F(\mathbf{x}^0))$. Since $\operatorname{Lev}(F, F(\mathbf{x}^0))$ is bounded by the premise of the theorem, it follows that $\{\mathbf{x}^k\}_{k \geq 0}$ is bounded.

Let $\bar{\mathbf{x}} \in \operatorname{dom}(g)$ be a limit point of $\{\mathbf{x}^k\}_{k \geq 0}$. We will show that $\bar{\mathbf{x}}$ is an optimal solution of problem (14.9). Since $\bar{\mathbf{x}}$ is a limit point of the sequence, there exists a subsequence $\{\mathbf{x}^{k_j}\}_{j \geq 0}$ for which $\mathbf{x}^{k_j} \to \bar{\mathbf{x}}$. By potentially passing to a subsequence, the sequences $\{\mathbf{x}^{k_j, i}\}_{j \geq 0}$ $(i = 1, 2, \ldots, p)$ can also be assumed to be convergent and $\mathbf{x}^{k_j, i} \to \bar{\mathbf{x}}^i \in \operatorname{dom}(g)$ as $j \to \infty$ for all $i \in \{0, 1, 2, \ldots, p\}$. Obviously, the following three properties hold:

- **[P1]** $\bar{\mathbf{x}} = \bar{\mathbf{x}}^0$.

---

[82]Theorem 14.9 is an extension of Proposition 6 from Grippo and Sciandrone [61] to the composite model.

[83] "Continuously differentiable" means that the gradient is a continuous mapping.

- **[P2]** for any i, $\bar{\mathbf{x}}^i$ is different from $\bar{\mathbf{x}}^{i-1}$ only at the ith block (if at all different).

- **[P3]** $F(\bar{\mathbf{x}}) = F(\bar{\mathbf{x}}^i)$ for all $i \in \{0,1,2,\ldots,p\}$ (easily shown by taking the limit $j \to \infty$ in the inequality $F(\mathbf{x}^{k_j}) \geq F(\mathbf{x}^{k_j,i}) \geq F(\mathbf{x}^{k_j+1})$ and using the continuity of F over its domain).

By the definition of the sequence we have for all $j \geq 0$ and $i \in \{1,2,\ldots,p\}$,

$$\mathbf{x}_i^{k_j,i} \in \operatorname{argmin}_{\mathbf{x}_i \in \mathbb{E}_i} F(\mathbf{x}_1^{k_j+1},\ldots,\mathbf{x}_{i-1}^{k_j+1},\mathbf{x}_i,\mathbf{x}_{i+1}^{k_j},\ldots,\mathbf{x}_p^{k_j}).$$

Therefore, since $\mathbf{x}_i^{k_j,i}$ is a stationary point of the above minimization problem (see Theorem 3.72(a)),

$$-\nabla_i f(\mathbf{x}^{k_j,i}) \in \partial g_i(\mathbf{x}_i^{k_j,i}).$$

Taking the limit[84] $j \to \infty$ and using the continuity of ∇f, we obtain that

$$-\nabla_i f(\bar{\mathbf{x}}^i) \in \partial g_i(\bar{\mathbf{x}}_i^i). \tag{14.10}$$

Note that for any $\mathbf{x}_{i+1} \in \operatorname{dom}(g_{i+1})$,

$$F(\mathbf{x}^{k_j,i+1}) \leq F(\mathbf{x}_1^{k_j+1},\ldots,\mathbf{x}_i^{k_j+1},\mathbf{x}_{i+1},\mathbf{x}_{i+2}^{k_j},\ldots,\mathbf{x}_p^{k_j}).$$

Taking the limit $j \to \infty$ and using [P3], we conclude that for any $\mathbf{x}_{i+1} \in \operatorname{dom}(g_{i+1})$,

$$F(\bar{\mathbf{x}}^i) = F(\bar{\mathbf{x}}^{i+1}) \leq F(\bar{\mathbf{x}}_1^i,\ldots,\bar{\mathbf{x}}_i^i,\mathbf{x}_{i+1},\bar{\mathbf{x}}_{i+2}^i,\ldots,\bar{\mathbf{x}}_p^i),$$

from which we obtain, using Theorem 3.72(a) again, that for any $i \in \{0,1,\ldots,p-1\}$,

$$-\nabla_{i+1} f(\bar{\mathbf{x}}^i) \in \partial g_{i+1}(\bar{\mathbf{x}}_{i+1}^i). \tag{14.11}$$

We need to show that the following implication holds for any $i \in \{2,3,\ldots,p\}, l \in \{1,2,\ldots,p-1\}$ such that $l < i$:

$$-\nabla_i f(\bar{\mathbf{x}}^l) \in \partial g_i(\bar{\mathbf{x}}_i^l) \Rightarrow -\nabla_i f(\bar{\mathbf{x}}^{l-1}) \in \partial g_i(\bar{\mathbf{x}}_i^{l-1}). \tag{14.12}$$

To prove the above implication, assume that $-\nabla_i f(\bar{\mathbf{x}}^l) \in \partial g_i(\bar{\mathbf{x}}_i^l)$ and let $\boldsymbol{\eta} \in \mathbb{E}_i$. Then

$$\begin{aligned}
\langle \nabla f(\bar{\mathbf{x}}^l), \bar{\mathbf{x}}^{l-1} + \mathcal{U}_i(\boldsymbol{\eta}) - \bar{\mathbf{x}}^l \rangle &\overset{(*)}{=} \langle \nabla_l f(\bar{\mathbf{x}}^l), \bar{\mathbf{x}}_l^{l-1} - \bar{\mathbf{x}}_l^l \rangle + \langle \nabla_i f(\bar{\mathbf{x}}^l), \boldsymbol{\eta} \rangle \\
&\overset{(**)}{\geq} g_l(\bar{\mathbf{x}}_l^l) - g_l(\bar{\mathbf{x}}_l^{l-1}) + \langle \nabla_i f(\bar{\mathbf{x}}^l), \boldsymbol{\eta} \rangle \\
&\overset{(***)}{=} g_l(\bar{\mathbf{x}}_l^l) - g_l(\bar{\mathbf{x}}_l^{l-1}) + \langle \nabla_i f(\bar{\mathbf{x}}^l), (\bar{\mathbf{x}}_i^{l-1} + \boldsymbol{\eta}) - \bar{\mathbf{x}}_i^l \rangle \\
&\overset{(****)}{\geq} g_l(\bar{\mathbf{x}}_l^l) - g_l(\bar{\mathbf{x}}_l^{l-1}) + g_i(\bar{\mathbf{x}}_i^l) - g_i(\bar{\mathbf{x}}_i^{l-1} + \boldsymbol{\eta}) \\
&= g(\bar{\mathbf{x}}^l) - g(\bar{\mathbf{x}}^{l-1} + \mathcal{U}_i(\boldsymbol{\eta})), \tag{14.13}
\end{aligned}$$

---

[84]We use here the following simple result: if $h : \mathbb{V} \to (-\infty,\infty]$ is proper closed and convex and $\mathbf{a}^k \in \partial h(\mathbf{b}^k)$ for all k and $\mathbf{a}^k \to \bar{\mathbf{a}}, \mathbf{b}^k \to \bar{\mathbf{b}}$, then $\bar{\mathbf{a}} \in \partial h(\bar{\mathbf{b}})$. To prove the result, take an arbitrary $\mathbf{z} \in \mathbb{V}$. Then since $\mathbf{a}^k \in \partial h(\mathbf{b}^k)$, it follows that $h(\mathbf{z}) \geq h(\mathbf{b}^k) + \langle \mathbf{a}^k, \mathbf{z} - \mathbf{b}^k \rangle$. Taking the liminf of both sides and using the closedness (hence lower semicontinuity) of h, we obtain that $h(\mathbf{z}) \geq h(\bar{\mathbf{b}}) + \langle \bar{\mathbf{a}}, \mathbf{z} - \bar{\mathbf{b}} \rangle$, showing that $\bar{\mathbf{a}} \in \partial h(\bar{\mathbf{b}})$.

where $(*)$ follows by [P2], $(**)$ is a consequence of the relation (14.10) with $i = l$, $(***)$ follows by the fact that for any $l < i$, $\bar{\mathbf{x}}_i^l = \bar{\mathbf{x}}_i^{l-1}$, and $(****)$ is due to our underlying assumption that $-\nabla_i f(\bar{\mathbf{x}}^l) \in \partial g_i(\bar{\mathbf{x}}_i^l)$. Using inequality (14.13) and the gradient inequality on the function f (utilizing its convexity), we obtain

$$
\begin{aligned}
F(\bar{\mathbf{x}}^{l-1} + \mathcal{U}_i(\boldsymbol{\eta})) &= f(\bar{\mathbf{x}}^{l-1} + \mathcal{U}_i(\boldsymbol{\eta})) + g(\bar{\mathbf{x}}^{l-1} + \mathcal{U}_i(\boldsymbol{\eta})) \\
&\geq f(\bar{\mathbf{x}}^l) + \langle \nabla f(\bar{\mathbf{x}}^l), \bar{\mathbf{x}}^{l-1} + \mathcal{U}_i(\boldsymbol{\eta}) - \bar{\mathbf{x}}^l \rangle + g(\bar{\mathbf{x}}^{l-1} + \mathcal{U}_i(\boldsymbol{\eta})) \\
&\geq F(\bar{\mathbf{x}}^l) \\
&\overset{[P3]}{=} F(\bar{\mathbf{x}}^{l-1}).
\end{aligned}
$$

We thus obtain that

$$
\bar{\mathbf{x}}_i^{l-1} \in \operatorname{argmin}_{\mathbf{x}_i \in \mathbb{E}_i} F(\bar{\mathbf{x}}_1^{l-1}, \ldots, \bar{\mathbf{x}}_{i-1}^{l-1}, \mathbf{x}_i, \bar{\mathbf{x}}_{i+1}^{l-1}, \ldots, \bar{\mathbf{x}}_p^{l-1}),
$$

which implies that $-\nabla_i f(\bar{\mathbf{x}}^{l-1}) \in \partial g_i(\bar{\mathbf{x}}_i^{l-1})$, establishing the implication (14.12). We are now ready to prove that $\bar{\mathbf{x}} = \bar{\mathbf{x}}^0$ is an optimal solution of problem (14.9). For that, we will show that for any $m \in \{1, 2, \ldots, p\}$ it holds that

$$
-\nabla_m f(\bar{\mathbf{x}}) \in \partial g_m(\bar{\mathbf{x}}_m). \tag{14.14}
$$

By Theorem 11.6 these relations are equivalent to stationarity of $\bar{\mathbf{x}}$, and using Theorem 3.72(b) and the convexity of f, we can deduce that $\bar{\mathbf{x}}$ is an optimal solution of problem (14.9). For $m = 1$ the relation (14.14) follows by substituting $i = 0$ in (14.11) and using the fact that $\bar{\mathbf{x}} = \bar{\mathbf{x}}^0$ (property [P1]). Let $m > 1$. Then by (14.11) we have that $-\nabla_m f(\bar{\mathbf{x}}^{m-1}) \in \partial g_m(\bar{\mathbf{x}}_m^{m-1})$. We can now utilize the implication (14.12) several times and obtain

$$
-\nabla_m f(\bar{\mathbf{x}}^{m-1}) \in \partial g_m(\bar{\mathbf{x}}_m^{m-1})
$$
$$
\Downarrow
$$
$$
-\nabla_m f(\bar{\mathbf{x}}^{m-2}) \in \partial g_m(\bar{\mathbf{x}}_m^{m-2})
$$
$$
\Downarrow
$$
$$
\vdots
$$
$$
\Downarrow
$$
$$
-\nabla_m f(\bar{\mathbf{x}}^0) \in \partial g_m(\bar{\mathbf{x}}_m^0),
$$

and thus, since $\bar{\mathbf{x}} = \bar{\mathbf{x}}^0$ (property [P1]), we conclude that $-\nabla_m f(\bar{\mathbf{x}}) \in \partial g_m(\bar{\mathbf{x}}_m)$ for any m, implying that $\bar{\mathbf{x}}$ is an optimal solution of problem (14.9). $\square$

14.5   Rate of Convergence in the Convex Case

In this section we will prove some rates of convergence results of the alternating minimization method in the convex setting. We begin by showing a general result that holds for any number of blocks, and we will then establish an improved result for the case $p = 2$.

14.5.1 General p

We will consider the model (14.9) that was studied in the previous two sections. The basic assumptions on the model are gathered in the following.

Assumption 14.10.

(A) $g_i : \mathbb{E}_i \to (-\infty, \infty]$ *is proper closed and convex for any* $i \in \{1, 2, \ldots, p\}$.

(B) $f : \mathbb{E} \to \mathbb{R}$ *is convex and* L_f-*smooth.*

(C) *For any* $\alpha > 0$, *there exists* $R_\alpha > 0$ *such that*

$$\max_{\mathbf{x}, \mathbf{x}^* \in \mathbb{E}} \{ \| \mathbf{x} - \mathbf{x}^* \| : F(\mathbf{x}) \leq \alpha, \mathbf{x}^* \in X^* \} \leq R_\alpha.$$

(D) *The optimal set of problem* (14.9) *is nonempty and denoted by* X^*. *The optimal value is denoted by* F_{opt}.[85]

Theorem 14.11 ($O(1/k)$ rate of convergence of alternating minimization).[86] *Suppose that Assumption* 14.10 *holds, and let* $\{\mathbf{x}^k\}_{k \geq 0}$ *be the sequence generated by the alternating minimization method for solving problem* (14.9). *Then for all* $k \geq 2$,

$$F(\mathbf{x}^k) - F_{\text{opt}} \leq \max \left\{ \left(\frac{1}{2} \right)^{(k-1)/2} (F(\mathbf{x}^0) - F_{\text{opt}}), \frac{8 L_f p^2 R^2}{k-1} \right\}, \qquad (14.15)$$

where $R = R_{F(\mathbf{x}^0)}$.

Proof. Let $\mathbf{x}^* \in X^*$. Since the sequence of function values $\{F(\mathbf{x}^k)\}_{k \geq 0}$ generated by the method is nonincreasing, it follows that $\{\mathbf{x}^k\}_{k \geq 0} \subseteq \text{Lev}(F, F(\mathbf{x}_0))$, and hence, by Assumption 14.10(C),

$$\| \mathbf{x}^{k+1} - \mathbf{x}^* \| \leq R, \qquad (14.16)$$

where $R = R_{F(\mathbf{x}^0)}$. Let $\{\mathbf{x}^{k,j}\}_{k \geq 0}$ $(j = 0, 1, \ldots, p)$ be the auxiliary sequences given in (14.2). Then for any $k \geq 0$ and $j \in \{0, 1, 2, \ldots, p-1\}$,

$$F(\mathbf{x}^{k,j}) - F(\mathbf{x}^{k,j+1})$$
$$= f(\mathbf{x}^{k,j}) - f(\mathbf{x}^{k,j+1}) + g(\mathbf{x}^{k,j}) - g(\mathbf{x}^{k,j+1})$$
$$\geq \langle \nabla f(\mathbf{x}^{k,j+1}), \mathbf{x}^{k,j} - \mathbf{x}^{k,j+1} \rangle + \frac{1}{2L_f} \| \nabla f(\mathbf{x}^{k,j}) - \nabla f(\mathbf{x}^{k,j+1}) \|^2 + g(\mathbf{x}^{k,j}) - g(\mathbf{x}^{k,j+1})$$
$$= \langle \nabla_{j+1} f(\mathbf{x}^{k,j+1}), \mathbf{x}_{j+1}^k - \mathbf{x}_{j+1}^{k+1} \rangle + \frac{1}{2L_f} \| \nabla f(\mathbf{x}^{k,j}) - \nabla f(\mathbf{x}^{k,j+1}) \|^2$$
$$+ g_{j+1}(\mathbf{x}_{j+1}^k) - g_{j+1}(\mathbf{x}_{j+1}^{k+1}), \qquad (14.17)$$

where the inequality follows by the convexity and L_f-smoothness of f along with Theorem 5.8 (equivalence between (i) and (iii)). Since

$$\mathbf{x}_{j+1}^{k+1} \in \text{argmin}_{\mathbf{x}_{j+1}} F(\mathbf{x}_1^{k+1}, \ldots, \mathbf{x}_j^{k+1}, \mathbf{x}_{j+1}, \mathbf{x}_{j+2}^k, \ldots, \mathbf{x}_p^k),$$

---

[85]Property (D) actually follows from properties (A), (B), and (C); see Lemma 14.1.

[86]The proof of Theorem 14.11 follows the proof of Theorem 3.1 from the work of Hong, Wang, Razaviyayn, and Luo [69].

it follows that

$$-\nabla_{j+1}f(\mathbf{x}^{k,j+1}) \in \partial g_{j+1}(\mathbf{x}_{j+1}^{k+1}), \tag{14.18}$$

and hence, by the subgradient inequality,

$$g_{j+1}(\mathbf{x}_{j+1}^k) \geq g_{j+1}(\mathbf{x}_{j+1}^{k+1}) - \langle \nabla_{j+1}f(\mathbf{x}^{k,j+1}), \mathbf{x}_{j+1}^k - \mathbf{x}_{j+1}^{k+1} \rangle,$$

which, combined with (14.17), yields

$$F(\mathbf{x}^{k,j}) - F(\mathbf{x}^{k,j+1}) \geq \frac{1}{2L_f} \|\nabla f(\mathbf{x}^{k,j}) - \nabla f(\mathbf{x}^{k,j+1})\|^2.$$

Summing the above inequality over $j = 0, 1, \ldots, p-1$, we obtain that

$$F(\mathbf{x}^k) - F(\mathbf{x}^{k+1}) \geq \frac{1}{2L_f} \sum_{j=0}^{p-1} \|\nabla f(\mathbf{x}^{k,j}) - \nabla f(\mathbf{x}^{k,j+1})\|^2. \tag{14.19}$$

On the other hand, for any $k \geq 0$,

$$\begin{aligned}
F(\mathbf{x}^{k+1}) - F(\mathbf{x}^*) &= f(\mathbf{x}^{k+1}) - f(\mathbf{x}^*) + g(\mathbf{x}^{k+1}) - g(\mathbf{x}^*) \\
&\leq \langle \nabla f(\mathbf{x}^{k+1}), \mathbf{x}^{k+1} - \mathbf{x}^* \rangle + g(\mathbf{x}^{k+1}) - g(\mathbf{x}^*) \\
&= \sum_{j=0}^{p-1} \left[\langle \nabla_{j+1}f(\mathbf{x}^{k+1}), \mathbf{x}_{j+1}^{k+1} - \mathbf{x}_{j+1}^* \rangle + (g_{j+1}(\mathbf{x}_{j+1}^{k+1}) - g_{j+1}(\mathbf{x}_{j+1}^*)) \right] \\
&= \sum_{j=0}^{p-1} \left[\langle \nabla_{j+1}f(\mathbf{x}^{k,j+1}), \mathbf{x}_{j+1}^{k+1} - \mathbf{x}_{j+1}^* \rangle + (g_{j+1}(\mathbf{x}_{j+1}^{k+1}) - g_{j+1}(\mathbf{x}_{j+1}^*)) \right] \\
&\quad + \sum_{j=0}^{p-1} \langle \nabla_{j+1}f(\mathbf{x}^{k+1}) - \nabla_{j+1}f(\mathbf{x}^{k,j+1}), \mathbf{x}_{j+1}^{k+1} - \mathbf{x}_{j+1}^* \rangle \\
&\leq \sum_{j=0}^{p-1} \langle \nabla_{j+1}f(\mathbf{x}^{k+1}) - \nabla_{j+1}f(\mathbf{x}^{k,j+1}), \mathbf{x}_{j+1}^{k+1} - \mathbf{x}_{j+1}^* \rangle, \tag{14.20}
\end{aligned}$$

where the first inequality follows by the gradient inequality employed on the function f, and the second inequality follows by the relation (14.18). Using the Cauchy–Schwarz and triangle inequalities, we can continue (14.20) and obtain that

$$F(\mathbf{x}^{k+1}) - F(\mathbf{x}^*) \leq \sum_{j=0}^{p-1} \|\nabla_{j+1}f(\mathbf{x}^{k+1}) - \nabla_{j+1}f(\mathbf{x}^{k,j+1})\| \cdot \|\mathbf{x}_{j+1}^{k+1} - \mathbf{x}_{j+1}^*\|. \tag{14.21}$$

Note that

$$\begin{aligned}
\|\nabla_{j+1}f(\mathbf{x}^{k+1}) - \nabla_{j+1}f(\mathbf{x}^{k,j+1})\| &\leq \|\nabla f(\mathbf{x}^{k+1}) - \nabla f(\mathbf{x}^{k,j+1})\| \\
&\leq \sum_{t=j+1}^{p-1} \|\nabla f(\mathbf{x}^{k,t}) - \nabla f(\mathbf{x}^{k,t+1})\| \\
&\leq \sum_{t=0}^{p-1} \|\nabla f(\mathbf{x}^{k,t}) - \nabla f(\mathbf{x}^{k,t+1})\|,
\end{aligned}$$

which, combined with (14.21), yields the inequality

$$F(\mathbf{x}^{k+1}) - F(\mathbf{x}^*) \le \left(\sum_{t=0}^{p-1} \|\nabla f(\mathbf{x}^{k,t}) - \nabla f(\mathbf{x}^{k,t+1})\| \right) \left(\sum_{j=0}^{p-1} \|\mathbf{x}_{j+1}^{k+1} - \mathbf{x}_{j+1}^*\| \right).$$

Taking the square of both sides and using (14.16), we obtain

$$(F(\mathbf{x}^{k+1}) - F(\mathbf{x}^*))^2 \le \left(\sum_{t=0}^{p-1} \|\nabla f(\mathbf{x}^{k,t}) - \nabla f(\mathbf{x}^{k,t+1})\| \right)^2 \left(\sum_{j=0}^{p-1} \|\mathbf{x}_{j+1}^{k+1} - \mathbf{x}_{j+1}^*\| \right)^2$$

$$\le p^2 \left(\sum_{t=0}^{p-1} \|\nabla f(\mathbf{x}^{k,t}) - \nabla f(\mathbf{x}^{k,t+1})\|^2 \right) \left(\sum_{j=0}^{p-1} \|\mathbf{x}_{j+1}^{k+1} - \mathbf{x}_{j+1}^*\|^2 \right)$$

$$= p^2 \left(\sum_{t=0}^{p-1} \|\nabla f(\mathbf{x}^{k,t}) - \nabla f(\mathbf{x}^{k,t+1})\|^2 \right) \|\mathbf{x}^{k+1} - \mathbf{x}^*\|^2$$

$$\le p^2 R^2 \sum_{t=0}^{p-1} \|\nabla f(\mathbf{x}^{k,t}) - \nabla f(\mathbf{x}^{k,t+1})\|^2. \tag{14.22}$$

We can thus conclude by (14.19) and (14.22) that for any $k \ge 0$,

$$(F(\mathbf{x}^{k+1}) - F_{\mathrm{opt}})^2 \le 2L_f p^2 R^2 (F(\mathbf{x}^k) - F(\mathbf{x}^{k+1})).$$

Denoting $a_k = F(\mathbf{x}^k) - F_{\mathrm{opt}}$, the last inequality can be rewritten as

$$a_k - a_{k+1} \ge \frac{1}{\gamma} a_{k+1}^2,$$

where $\gamma = 2L_f p^2 R^2$. Invoking Lemma 11.17, we obtain that for all $k \ge 2$,

$$a_k \le \max \left\{ \left(\frac{1}{2} \right)^{(k-1)/2} a_0, \frac{8L_f p^2 R^2}{k-1} \right\},$$

which is the desired result (14.15). $\square$

14.5.2 $p = 2$

The dependency of the efficiency estimate (14.15) on the global Lipschitz constant L_f is problematic since it might be a very large number. We will now develop a different line of analysis in the case where there are only two blocks ($p = 2$). The new analysis will produce an improved efficiency estimate that depends on the smallest block Lipschitz constant rather than on L_f. The general model (14.9) in the case $p = 2$ amounts to

$$\min_{\mathbf{x}_1 \in \mathbb{E}_1, \mathbf{x}_2 \in \mathbb{E}_2} \{ F(\mathbf{x}_1, \mathbf{x}_2) \equiv f(\mathbf{x}_1, \mathbf{x}_2) + g_1(\mathbf{x}_1) + g_2(\mathbf{x}_2) \}. \tag{14.23}$$

As usual, we use the notation $\mathbf{x} = (\mathbf{x}_1, \mathbf{x}_2)$ and $g(\mathbf{x}) = g_1(\mathbf{x}_1) + g_2(\mathbf{x}_2)$. We gather below the required assumptions.

Assumption 14.12.

(A) *For $i \in \{1,2\}$, the function $g_i : \mathbb{E}_i \to (-\infty, \infty]$ is proper closed and convex.*

(B) *$f : \mathbb{E} \to \mathbb{R}$ is convex. In addition, f is differentiable over an open set containing $\mathrm{dom}(g)$.*

(C) *For any $i \in \{1,2\}$ the gradient of f is Lipschitz continuous w.r.t. $\mathbf{x}_i$ over $\mathrm{dom}(g_i)$ with constant $L_i \in (0, \infty)$, meaning that*

$$\|\nabla_1 f(\mathbf{x}_1 + \mathbf{d}_1, \mathbf{x}_2) - \nabla_1 f(\mathbf{x}_1, \mathbf{x}_2)\| \leq L_1 \|\mathbf{d}_1\|,$$
$$\|\nabla_2 f(\mathbf{x}_1, \mathbf{x}_2 + \mathbf{d}_2) - \nabla_2 f(\mathbf{x}_1, \mathbf{x}_2)\| \leq L_2 \|\mathbf{d}_2\|$$

for any $\mathbf{x}_1 \in \mathrm{dom}(g_1), \mathbf{x}_2 \in \mathrm{dom}(g_2)$, and $\mathbf{d}_1 \in \mathbb{E}_1, \mathbf{d}_2 \in \mathbb{E}_2$ such that $\mathbf{x} + \mathbf{d}_1 \in \mathrm{dom}(g_1), \mathbf{x}_2 + \mathbf{d}_2 \in \mathrm{dom}(g_2)$.

(D) *The optimal set of (14.23), denoted by X^*, is nonempty, and the corresponding optimal value is denoted by F_{opt}.*

(E) *For any $\alpha > 0$, there exists $R_\alpha > 0$ such that*

$$\max_{\mathbf{x},\mathbf{x}^* \in \mathbb{E}} \{\|\mathbf{x} - \mathbf{x}^*\| : F(\mathbf{x}) \leq \alpha, \mathbf{x}^* \in X^*\} \leq R_\alpha.$$

The alternating minimization method for solving problem (14.23) is described below.

The Alternating Minimization Method

Initialization: $\mathbf{x}_1^0 \in \mathrm{dom}(g_1), \mathbf{x}_2^0 \in \mathrm{dom}(g_2)$ such that

$$\mathbf{x}_2^0 \in \mathrm{argmin}_{\mathbf{x}_2 \in \mathbb{E}_2} f(\mathbf{x}_1^0, \mathbf{x}_2) + g_2(\mathbf{x}_2).$$

General step ($k = 0, 1, \ldots$):

$$\mathbf{x}_1^{k+1} \in \mathrm{argmin}_{\mathbf{x}_1 \in \mathbb{E}_1} f(\mathbf{x}_1, \mathbf{x}_2^k) + g_1(\mathbf{x}_1), \qquad (14.24)$$
$$\mathbf{x}_2^{k+1} \in \mathrm{argmin}_{\mathbf{x}_2 \in \mathbb{E}_2} f(\mathbf{x}_1^{k+1}, \mathbf{x}_2) + g_2(\mathbf{x}_2). \qquad (14.25)$$

Note that, as opposed to the description of the method so far, we assume that "half" an iteration was performed prior to the first iteration (that is, $\mathbf{x}_2^0 \in \mathrm{argmin}_{\mathbf{x}_2 \in \mathbb{E}_2} f(\mathbf{x}_1^0, \mathbf{x}_2) + g_2(\mathbf{x}_2)$). We will also utilize the auxiliary sequence $\{\mathbf{x}^{k,1}\}_{k \geq 0}$ as defined in (14.2) but use the following simpler notation:

$$\mathbf{x}^{k+\frac{1}{2}} = (\mathbf{x}_1^{k+1}, \mathbf{x}_2^k).$$

We will adopt the notation used in Section 11.3.1 and consider for any $M > 0$ the partial prox-grad mappings

$$T_M^i(\mathbf{x}) = \mathrm{prox}_{\frac{1}{M} g_i}\left(\mathbf{x}_i - \frac{1}{M} \nabla_i f(\mathbf{x})\right), \quad i = 1, 2,$$

as well as the partial gradient mappings

$$G_M^i(\mathbf{x}) = M\left(\mathbf{x}_i - T_M^i(\mathbf{x})\right), \quad i = 1, 2.$$

Obviously, for any $M > 0$,

$$T_M(\mathbf{x}) = (T_M^1(\mathbf{x}), T_M^2(\mathbf{x})), \ G_M(\mathbf{x}) = (G_M^1(\mathbf{x}), G_M^2(\mathbf{x})),$$

and from the definition of the alternating minimization method we have for all $k \geq 0$,

$$G_M^1(\mathbf{x}^{k+\frac{1}{2}}) = \mathbf{0}, G_M^2(\mathbf{x}^k) = \mathbf{0}. \tag{14.26}$$

We begin by proving the following sufficient decrease-type result.

Lemma 14.13. *Suppose that Assumption 14.12 holds. Let $\{\mathbf{x}^k\}_{k \geq 0}$ be the sequence generated by the alternating minimization method for solving problem (14.23). Then for any $k \geq 0$ the following inequalities hold:*

$$F(\mathbf{x}^k) - F(\mathbf{x}^{k+\frac{1}{2}}) \geq \frac{1}{2L_1}\|G_{L_1}^1(\mathbf{x}^k)\|^2, \tag{14.27}$$

$$F(\mathbf{x}^{k+\frac{1}{2}}) - F(\mathbf{x}^{k+1}) \geq \frac{1}{2L_2}\|G_{L_2}^2(\mathbf{x}^{k+\frac{1}{2}})\|^2. \tag{14.28}$$

Proof. Invoking the block sufficient decrease lemma (Lemma 11.9) with $\mathbf{x} = \mathbf{x}^k$ and $i = 1$, we obtain

$$F(\mathbf{x}_1^k, \mathbf{x}_2^k) - F(T_{L_1}^1(\mathbf{x}^k), \mathbf{x}_2^k) \geq \frac{1}{2L_1}\|G_{L_1}^1(\mathbf{x}_1^k, \mathbf{x}_2^k)\|^2.$$

The inequality (14.27) now follows from the inequality $F(\mathbf{x}^{k+\frac{1}{2}}) \leq F(T_{L_1}^1(\mathbf{x}^k)), \mathbf{x}_2^k)$. The inequality (14.28) follows by invoking the block sufficient decrease lemma with $\mathbf{x} = \mathbf{x}^{k+\frac{1}{2}}$, $i = 2$, and using the inequality $F(\mathbf{x}^{k+1}) \leq F(\mathbf{x}_1^{k+1}, T_{L_2}^2(\mathbf{x}^{k+\frac{1}{2}}))$. $\Box$

The next lemma establishes an upper bound on the distance in function values of the iterates of the method.

Lemma 14.14. *Let $\{\mathbf{x}^k\}_{k \geq 0}$ be the sequence generated by the alternating mini-mization method for solving problem (14.23). Then for any $\mathbf{x}^* \in X^*$ and $k \geq 0$,*

$$F(\mathbf{x}^{k+\frac{1}{2}}) - F(\mathbf{x}^*) \leq \|G_{L_1}^1(\mathbf{x}^k)\| \cdot \|\mathbf{x}^k - \mathbf{x}^*\|, \tag{14.29}$$

$$F(\mathbf{x}^{k+1}) - F(\mathbf{x}^*) \leq \|G_{L_2}^2(\mathbf{x}^{k+\frac{1}{2}})\| \cdot \|\mathbf{x}^{k+\frac{1}{2}} - \mathbf{x}^*\|. \tag{14.30}$$

Proof. Note that

$$T_{L_1}(\mathbf{x}^k) = (T_{L_1}^1(\mathbf{x}^k), T_{L_1}^2(\mathbf{x}^k)) = \left(T_{L_1}^1(\mathbf{x}^k), \mathbf{x}_2^k - \frac{1}{L_1}G_{L_1}^2(\mathbf{x}^k)\right) = (T_{L_1}^1(\mathbf{x}^k), \mathbf{x}_2^k),$$

where in the last equality we used (14.26). Combining this with the block descent lemma (Lemma 11.8), we obtain that

$$f(T_{L_1}(\mathbf{x}^k)) - f(\mathbf{x}^*) \leq f(\mathbf{x}^k) + \langle \nabla_1 f(\mathbf{x}^k), T_{L_1}^1(\mathbf{x}^k) - \mathbf{x}_1^k \rangle$$
$$+ \frac{L_1}{2} \|T_{L_1}^1(\mathbf{x}^k) - \mathbf{x}_1^k\|^2 - f(\mathbf{x}^*)$$
$$= f(\mathbf{x}^k) + \langle \nabla f(\mathbf{x}^k), T_{L_1}(\mathbf{x}^k) - \mathbf{x}^k \rangle$$
$$+ \frac{L_1}{2} \|T_{L_1}^1(\mathbf{x}^k) - \mathbf{x}_1^k\|^2 - f(\mathbf{x}^*). \qquad (14.31)$$

Since f is convex, it follows that $f(\mathbf{x}^k) - f(\mathbf{x}^*) \leq \langle \nabla f(\mathbf{x}^k), \mathbf{x}^k - \mathbf{x}^* \rangle$, which, combined with (14.31), yields

$$f(T_{L_1}(\mathbf{x}^k)) - f(\mathbf{x}^*) \leq \langle \nabla f(\mathbf{x}^k), T_{L_1}(\mathbf{x}^k) - \mathbf{x}^* \rangle + \frac{L_1}{2} \|T_{L_1}^1(\mathbf{x}^k) - \mathbf{x}_1^k\|^2. \qquad (14.32)$$

Since $T_{L_1}(\mathbf{x}^k) = \text{prox}_{\frac{1}{L_1} g}\left(\mathbf{x}^k - \frac{1}{L_1}\nabla f(\mathbf{x}^k)\right)$, then by invoking the second prox theorem (Theorem 6.39) with $f = \frac{1}{L_1} g, \mathbf{x} = \mathbf{x}^k - \frac{1}{L_1}\nabla f(\mathbf{x}^k)$, and $\mathbf{y} = \mathbf{x}^*$, we have

$$g(T_{L_1}(\mathbf{x}^k)) - g(\mathbf{x}^*) \leq L_1 \left\langle \mathbf{x}^k - \frac{1}{L_1}\nabla f(\mathbf{x}^k) - T_{L_1}(\mathbf{x}^k), T_{L_1}(\mathbf{x}^k) - \mathbf{x}^* \right\rangle. \qquad (14.33)$$

Combining inequalities (14.32) and (14.33), along with the fact that $F(\mathbf{x}^{k+\frac{1}{2}}) \leq F(T_{L_1}^1(\mathbf{x}^k), \mathbf{x}_2^k) = F(T_{L_1}(\mathbf{x}^k))$, we finally have

$$F(\mathbf{x}^{k+\frac{1}{2}}) - F(\mathbf{x}^*) \leq F(T_{L_1}(\mathbf{x}^k)) - F(\mathbf{x}^*)$$
$$= f(T_{L_1}(\mathbf{x}^k)) + g(T_{L_1}(\mathbf{x}^k)) - f(\mathbf{x}^*) - g(\mathbf{x}^*)$$
$$\leq L_1\langle \mathbf{x}^k - T_{L_1}(\mathbf{x}^k), T_{L_1}(\mathbf{x}^k) - \mathbf{x}^* \rangle + \frac{L_1}{2} \|T_{L_1}^1(\mathbf{x}^k) - \mathbf{x}_1^k\|^2$$
$$= \langle G_{L_1}(\mathbf{x}^k), T_{L_1}(\mathbf{x}^k) - \mathbf{x}^* \rangle + \frac{1}{2L_1}\|G_{L_1}(\mathbf{x}^k)\|^2$$
$$= \langle G_{L_1}(\mathbf{x}^k), T_{L_1}(\mathbf{x}^k) - \mathbf{x}^k \rangle + \langle G_{L_1}(\mathbf{x}^k), \mathbf{x}^k - \mathbf{x}^* \rangle + \frac{1}{2L_1}\|G_{L_1}(\mathbf{x}^k)\|^2$$
$$= -\frac{1}{L_1}\|G_{L_1}(\mathbf{x}^k)\|^2 + \langle G_{L_1}(\mathbf{x}^k), \mathbf{x}^k - \mathbf{x}^* \rangle + \frac{1}{2L_1}\|G_{L_1}(\mathbf{x}^k)\|^2$$
$$\leq \langle G_{L_1}(\mathbf{x}^k), \mathbf{x}^k - \mathbf{x}^* \rangle$$
$$\leq \|G_{L_1}(\mathbf{x}^k)\| \cdot \|\mathbf{x}^k - \mathbf{x}^*\|$$
$$= \|G_{L_1}^1(\mathbf{x}^k)\| \cdot \|\mathbf{x}^k - \mathbf{x}^*\|,$$

establishing (14.29). The inequality (14.30) follows by using the same argument but on the sequence generated by the alternating minimization method with starting point $(\mathbf{x}_1^1, \mathbf{x}_2^0)$ and assuming that the first index to be updated is $i = 2$. $\quad\square$

With the help of Lemmas 14.13 and 14.14, we can prove a sublinear rate of convergence of the alternating minimization method with an improved constant.

Theorem 14.15 ($O(1/k)$ rate of alternating minimization—improved result). *Suppose that Assumption 14.12 holds, and let $\{\mathbf{x}^k\}_{k \geq 0}$ be the sequence generated by the alternating minimization method for solving problem (14.23). Then* *for all $k \geq 2$,*

$$F(\mathbf{x}^k) - F_{\text{opt}} \leq \max \left\{ \left(\frac{1}{2} \right)^{(k-1)/2} (F(\mathbf{x}^0) - F_{\text{opt}}), \frac{8 \min\{L_1, L_2\} R^2}{k - 1} \right\}, \quad (14.34)$$

where $R = R_{F(\mathbf{x}^0)}$.

Proof. By Lemma 14.14 and Assumption 14.12(E),

$$F(\mathbf{x}^{k+\frac{1}{2}}) - F_{\text{opt}} \leq \|G_{L_1}^1(\mathbf{x}^k)\| R,$$

where $R = R_{F(\mathbf{x}^0)}$. Now, by Lemma 14.13,

$$\begin{aligned}
F(\mathbf{x}^k) - F(\mathbf{x}^{k+1}) \geq F(\mathbf{x}^k) - F(\mathbf{x}^{k+\frac{1}{2}}) &\geq \frac{1}{2L_1} \|G_{L_1}^1(\mathbf{x}^k)\|^2 \\
&\geq \frac{(F(\mathbf{x}^{k+\frac{1}{2}}) - F_{\text{opt}})^2}{2L_1 R^2} \\
&\geq \frac{1}{2L_1 R^2} (F(\mathbf{x}^{k+1}) - F_{\text{opt}})^2.
\end{aligned} \quad (14.35)$$

Similarly, by Lemma 14.14 and Assumption 14.12(E),

$$F(\mathbf{x}^{k+1}) - F_{\text{opt}} \leq \|G_{L_2}^2(\mathbf{x}^{k+\frac{1}{2}})\| R.$$

Thus, utilizing Lemma 14.13 we obtain

$$F(\mathbf{x}^k) - F(\mathbf{x}^{k+1}) \geq F(\mathbf{x}^{k+\frac{1}{2}}) - F(\mathbf{x}^{k+1}) \geq \frac{1}{2L_2} \|G_{L_2}^2(\mathbf{x}^{k+\frac{1}{2}})\|^2 \geq \frac{(F(\mathbf{x}^{k+1}) - F_{\text{opt}})^2}{2L_2 R^2},$$

which, combined with (14.35), yields the inequality

$$F(\mathbf{x}^k) - F(\mathbf{x}^{k+1}) \geq \frac{1}{2 \min\{L_1, L_2\} R^2} (F(\mathbf{x}^{k+1}) - F_{\text{opt}})^2. \quad (14.36)$$

Denoting $a_k = F(\mathbf{x}^k) - F_{\text{opt}}$ and $\gamma = 2 \min\{L_1, L_2\} R^2$, we obtain that for all $k \geq 0$,

$$a_k - a_{k+1} \geq \frac{1}{\gamma} a_{k+1}^2,$$

and thus, by Lemma 11.17, it holds that for all $k \geq 2$

$$a_k \leq \max \left\{ \left(\frac{1}{2} \right)^{(k-1)/2} a_0, \frac{8 \min\{L_1, L_2\} R^2}{k - 1} \right\},$$

which is the desired result (14.34). $\quad \square$

Remark 14.16. *Note that the constant in the efficiency estimate (14.34) depends on $\min\{L_1, L_2\}$. This means that the rate of convergence of the alternating minimization method in the case of two blocks is dictated by the smallest block Lipschitz constant, meaning by the smoother part of the function. This is not the case for the efficiency estimate obtained in Theorem 14.11 for the convergence of alternating minimization with an arbitrary number of blocks, which depends on the global Lipschitz constant L_f and is thus dictated by the "worst" block w.r.t. the level of smoothness.*

Chapter 15

ADMM

Underlying Spaces: In this chapter all the underlying spaces are Euclidean $\mathbb{R}^n$ spaces endowed with the dot product and the l_2-norm.

15.1 The Augmented Lagrangian Method

Consider the problem

$$H_{\text{opt}} = \min\{H(\mathbf{x}, \mathbf{z}) \equiv h_1(\mathbf{x}) + h_2(\mathbf{z}) : \mathbf{A}\mathbf{x} + \mathbf{B}\mathbf{z} = \mathbf{c}\}, \qquad (15.1)$$

where $\mathbf{A} \in \mathbb{R}^{m \times n}, \mathbf{B} \in \mathbb{R}^{m \times p}$, and $\mathbf{c} \in \mathbb{R}^m$. For now, we will assume that h_1 and h_2 are proper closed and convex functions. Later on, we will specify exact conditions on the data $(h_1, h_2, \mathbf{A}, \mathbf{B}, \mathbf{c})$ that will guarantee the validity of some convergence results. To find a dual problem of (15.1), we begin by constructing a Lagrangian:

$$L(\mathbf{x}, \mathbf{z}; \mathbf{y}) = h_1(\mathbf{x}) + h_2(\mathbf{z}) + \langle \mathbf{y}, \mathbf{A}\mathbf{x} + \mathbf{B}\mathbf{z} - \mathbf{c} \rangle.$$

The dual objective function is therefore given by

$$
\begin{aligned}
q(\mathbf{y}) &= \min_{\mathbf{x} \in \mathbb{R}^n, \mathbf{z} \in \mathbb{R}^p} \{h_1(\mathbf{x}) + h_2(\mathbf{z}) + \langle \mathbf{y}, \mathbf{A}\mathbf{x} + \mathbf{B}\mathbf{z} - \mathbf{c} \rangle\} \\
&= -h_1^*(-\mathbf{A}^T \mathbf{y}) - h_2^*(-\mathbf{B}^T \mathbf{y}) - \langle \mathbf{c}, \mathbf{y} \rangle,
\end{aligned}
$$

and the dual problem is given by

$$q_{\text{opt}} = \max_{\mathbf{y} \in \mathbb{R}^m} \{-h_1^*(-\mathbf{A}^T \mathbf{y}) - h_2^*(-\mathbf{B}^T \mathbf{y}) - \langle \mathbf{c}, \mathbf{y} \rangle\} \qquad (15.2)$$

or, in minimization form, by

$$\min_{\mathbf{y} \in \mathbb{R}^m} \{h_1^*(-\mathbf{A}^T \mathbf{y}) + h_2^*(-\mathbf{B}^T \mathbf{y}) + \langle \mathbf{c}, \mathbf{y} \rangle\}. \qquad (15.3)$$

The proximal point method was discussed in Section 10.5, where its convergence was established. The general update step of the proximal point method employed on problem (15.3) takes the form ($\rho > 0$ being a given constant)

$$\mathbf{y}^{k+1} = \text{argmin}_{\mathbf{y} \in \mathbb{R}^m} \left\{ h_1^*(-\mathbf{A}^T \mathbf{y}) + h_2^*(-\mathbf{B}^T \mathbf{y}) + \langle \mathbf{c}, \mathbf{y} \rangle + \frac{1}{2\rho} \|\mathbf{y} - \mathbf{y}^k\|^2 \right\}. \qquad (15.4)$$

Assuming that the sum and affine rules of subdifferential calculus (Theorems 3.40 and 3.43) hold for the relevant functions, we can conclude by Fermat's optimality condition (Theorem 3.63) that (15.4) holds if and only if

$$0 \in -\mathbf{A}\partial h_1^*(-\mathbf{A}^T\mathbf{y}^{k+1}) - \mathbf{B}\partial h_2^*(-\mathbf{B}^T\mathbf{y}^{k+1}) + \mathbf{c} + \frac{1}{\rho}(\mathbf{y}^{k+1} - \mathbf{y}^k). \qquad (15.5)$$

Using the conjugate subgradient theorem (Corollary 4.21), we obtain that $\mathbf{y}^{k+1}$ satisfies (15.5) if and only if $\mathbf{y}^{k+1} = \mathbf{y}^k + \rho(\mathbf{A}\mathbf{x}^{k+1} + \mathbf{B}\mathbf{z}^{k+1} - \mathbf{c})$, where $\mathbf{x}^{k+1}$ and $\mathbf{z}^{k+1}$ satisfy

$$\mathbf{x}^{k+1} \in \operatorname{argmin}_{\mathbf{x}\in\mathbb{R}^n}\{\langle\mathbf{A}^T\mathbf{y}^{k+1}, \mathbf{x}\rangle + h_1(\mathbf{x})\},$$
$$\mathbf{z}^{k+1} \in \operatorname{argmin}_{\mathbf{z}\in\mathbb{R}^p}\{\langle\mathbf{B}^T\mathbf{y}^{k+1}, \mathbf{z}\rangle + h_2(\mathbf{z})\}.$$

Plugging the update equation for $\mathbf{y}^{k+1}$ into the above, we conclude that $\mathbf{y}^{k+1}$ satisfies (15.5) if and only if

$$\mathbf{y}^{k+1} = \mathbf{y}^k + \rho(\mathbf{A}\mathbf{x}^{k+1} + \mathbf{B}\mathbf{z}^{k+1} - \mathbf{c}),$$
$$\mathbf{x}^{k+1} \in \operatorname{argmin}_{\mathbf{x}\in\mathbb{R}^n}\{\langle\mathbf{A}^T(\mathbf{y}^k + \rho(\mathbf{A}\mathbf{x}^{k+1} + \mathbf{B}\mathbf{z}^{k+1} - \mathbf{c})), \mathbf{x}\rangle + h_1(\mathbf{x})\},$$
$$\mathbf{z}^{k+1} \in \operatorname{argmin}_{\mathbf{z}\in\mathbb{R}^p}\{\langle\mathbf{B}^T(\mathbf{y}^k + \rho(\mathbf{A}\mathbf{x}^{k+1} + \mathbf{B}\mathbf{z}^{k+1} - \mathbf{c})), \mathbf{z}\rangle + h_2(\mathbf{z})\},$$

meaning if and only if (using the properness and convexity of h_1 and h_2, as well as Fermat's optimality condition)

$$\mathbf{y}^{k+1} = \mathbf{y}^k + \rho(\mathbf{A}\mathbf{x}^{k+1} + \mathbf{B}\mathbf{z}^{k+1} - \mathbf{c}), \qquad (15.6)$$
$$0 \in \mathbf{A}^T(\mathbf{y}^k + \rho(\mathbf{A}\mathbf{x}^{k+1} + \mathbf{B}\mathbf{z}^{k+1} - \mathbf{c})) + \partial h_1(\mathbf{x}^{k+1}), \qquad (15.7)$$
$$0 \in \mathbf{B}^T(\mathbf{y}^k + \rho(\mathbf{A}\mathbf{x}^{k+1} + \mathbf{B}\mathbf{z}^{k+1} - \mathbf{c})) + \partial h_2(\mathbf{z}^{k+1}). \qquad (15.8)$$

Conditions (15.7) and (15.8) are satisfied if and only if $(\mathbf{x}^{k+1}, \mathbf{z}^{k+1})$ is a coordinate-wise minimum (see Definition 14.2) of the function

$$\tilde{H}(\mathbf{x}, \mathbf{z}) \equiv h_1(\mathbf{x}) + h_2(\mathbf{z}) + \frac{\rho}{2}\left\|\mathbf{A}\mathbf{x} + \mathbf{B}\mathbf{z} - \mathbf{c} + \frac{1}{\rho}\mathbf{y}^k\right\|^2.$$

By Lemma 14.7, coordinate-wise minima points of $\tilde{H}$ are exactly the minimizers of $\tilde{H}$, and therefore the system (15.6), (15.7), (15.8) leads us to the following primal representation of the dual proximal point method, known as the *augmented Lagrangian method*.

The Augmented Lagrangian Method

Initialization: $\mathbf{y}^0 \in \mathbb{R}^m, \rho > 0$.
General step: for any $k = 0, 1, 2, \ldots$ execute the following steps:

$$(\mathbf{x}^{k+1}, \mathbf{z}^{k+1}) \in \operatorname*{argmin}_{\mathbf{x}\in\mathbb{R}^n, \mathbf{z}\in\mathbb{R}^p}\left\{h_1(\mathbf{x}) + h_2(\mathbf{z}) + \frac{\rho}{2}\left\|\mathbf{A}\mathbf{x} + \mathbf{B}\mathbf{z} - \mathbf{c} + \frac{1}{\rho}\mathbf{y}^k\right\|^2\right\} \quad (15.9)$$

$$\mathbf{y}^{k+1} = \mathbf{y}^k + \rho(\mathbf{A}\mathbf{x}^{k+1} + \mathbf{B}\mathbf{z}^{k+1} - \mathbf{c}). \qquad (15.10)$$

Naturally, step (15.9) is called the *primal update step*, while (15.10) is the *dual update step*.

Remark 15.1 (augmented Lagrangian). *The augmented Lagrangian associated with the main problem (15.1) is defined to be*

$$L_\rho(\mathbf{x}, \mathbf{z}; \mathbf{y}) = h_1(\mathbf{x}) + h_2(\mathbf{z}) + \langle \mathbf{y}, \mathbf{A}\mathbf{x} + \mathbf{B}\mathbf{z} - \mathbf{c} \rangle + \frac{\rho}{2} \|\mathbf{A}\mathbf{x} + \mathbf{B}\mathbf{z} - \mathbf{c}\|^2.$$

Obviously, $L_0 = L$ is the Lagrangian function, and L_ρ for $\rho > 0$ can be considered as a penalized version of the Lagrangian. The primal update step (15.9) can be equivalently written as

$$(\mathbf{x}^{k+1}, \mathbf{z}^{k+1}) \in \operatorname{argmin}_{\mathbf{x} \in \mathbb{R}^n, \mathbf{z} \in \mathbb{R}^p} L_\rho(\mathbf{x}, \mathbf{z}; \mathbf{y}^k).$$

The above representation of the primal update step as the outcome of the minimization of the augmented Lagrangian function is the reason for the name of the method.

15.2 Alternating Direction Method of Multipliers (ADMM)

The augmented Lagrangian method is in general not an implementable method since the primal update step (15.9) can be as hard to solve as the original problem. One source of difficulty is the coupling term between the $\mathbf{x}$ and the $\mathbf{z}$ variables, which is of the form $\rho(\mathbf{x}^T \mathbf{A}^T \mathbf{B}\mathbf{z})$. The approach used in the *alternating direction method of multipliers* (ADMM) to tackle this difficulty is to replace the exact minimization in the primal update step (15.9) by one iteration of the alternating minimization method; that is, the objective function of (15.9) is first minimized w.r.t. $\mathbf{x}$, and then w.r.t. $\mathbf{z}$.

ADMM

Initialization: $\mathbf{x}^0 \in \mathbb{R}^n$, $\mathbf{z}^0 \in \mathbb{R}^p$, $\mathbf{y}^0 \in \mathbb{R}^m$, $\rho > 0$.
General step: for any $k = 0, 1, \ldots$ execute the following:

(a) $\mathbf{x}^{k+1} \in \operatorname{argmin}_{\mathbf{x}} \left\{ h_1(\mathbf{x}) + \frac{\rho}{2} \left\| \mathbf{A}\mathbf{x} + \mathbf{B}\mathbf{z}^k - \mathbf{c} + \frac{1}{\rho}\mathbf{y}^k \right\|^2 \right\}$;

(b) $\mathbf{z}^{k+1} \in \operatorname{argmin}_{\mathbf{z}} \left\{ h_2(\mathbf{z}) + \frac{\rho}{2} \left\| \mathbf{A}\mathbf{x}^{k+1} + \mathbf{B}\mathbf{z} - \mathbf{c} + \frac{1}{\rho}\mathbf{y}^k \right\|^2 \right\}$;

(c) $\mathbf{y}^{k+1} = \mathbf{y}^k + \rho(\mathbf{A}\mathbf{x}^{k+1} + \mathbf{B}\mathbf{z}^{k+1} - \mathbf{c})$.

15.2.1 Alternating Direction Proximal Method of Multipliers (AD-PMM)

We will actually analyze a more general method than ADMM in which a quadratic proximity term is added to the objective in the minimization problems of steps

(a) and (b). We will assume that we are given two positive semidefinite matrices $\mathbf{G} \in \mathbb{S}_+^n, \mathbf{Q} \in \mathbb{S}_+^p$, and recall that $\|\mathbf{x}\|_{\mathbf{G}}^2 = \mathbf{x}^T \mathbf{G} \mathbf{x}, \|\mathbf{x}\|_{\mathbf{Q}}^2 = \mathbf{x}^T \mathbf{Q} \mathbf{x}$.

AD-PMM

Initialization: $\mathbf{x}^0 \in \mathbb{R}^n, \mathbf{z}^0 \in \mathbb{R}^p, \mathbf{y}^0 \in \mathbb{R}^m, \rho > 0$.
General step: for any $k = 0, 1, \ldots$ execute the following:

(a) $\mathbf{x}^{k+1} \in \operatorname{argmin}_{\mathbf{x} \in \mathbb{R}^n} \left\{ h_1(\mathbf{x}) + \frac{\rho}{2} \left\| \mathbf{A}\mathbf{x} + \mathbf{B}\mathbf{z}^k - \mathbf{c} + \frac{1}{\rho}\mathbf{y}^k \right\|^2 + \frac{1}{2} \|\mathbf{x} - \mathbf{x}^k\|_{\mathbf{G}}^2 \right\}$;

(b) $\mathbf{z}^{k+1} \in \operatorname{argmin}_{\mathbf{z} \in \mathbb{R}^p} \left\{ h_2(\mathbf{z}) + \frac{\rho}{2} \left\| \mathbf{A}\mathbf{x}^{k+1} + \mathbf{B}\mathbf{z} - \mathbf{c} + \frac{1}{\rho}\mathbf{y}^k \right\| + \frac{1}{2} \|\mathbf{z} - \mathbf{z}^k\|_{\mathbf{Q}}^2 \right\}$;

(c) $\mathbf{y}^{k+1} = \mathbf{y}^k + \rho(\mathbf{A}\mathbf{x}^{k+1} + \mathbf{B}\mathbf{z}^{k+1} - \mathbf{c})$.

One important motivation for considering AD-PMM is that by using the proximity terms, the minimization problems in steps (a) and (b) of ADMM can be simplified considerably by choosing $\mathbf{G} = \alpha \mathbf{I} - \rho \mathbf{A}^T \mathbf{A}$ with $\alpha \geq \rho \lambda_{\max}(\mathbf{A}^T \mathbf{A})$ and $\mathbf{Q} = \beta \mathbf{I} - \rho \mathbf{B}^T \mathbf{B}$ with $\beta \geq \rho \lambda_{\max}(\mathbf{B}^T \mathbf{B})$. Then obviously $\mathbf{G}, \mathbf{Q} \in \mathbb{S}_+^n$, and the function that needs to be minimized in the $\mathbf{x}$-step can be simplified as follows:

$$h_1(\mathbf{x}) + \frac{\rho}{2} \left\| \mathbf{A}\mathbf{x} + \mathbf{B}\mathbf{z}^k - \mathbf{c} + \frac{1}{\rho}\mathbf{y}^k \right\|^2 + \frac{1}{2} \|\mathbf{x} - \mathbf{x}^k\|_{\mathbf{G}}^2$$

$$= h_1(\mathbf{x}) + \frac{\rho}{2} \left\| \mathbf{A}(\mathbf{x} - \mathbf{x}^k) + \mathbf{A}\mathbf{x}^k + \mathbf{B}\mathbf{z}^k - \mathbf{c} + \frac{1}{\rho}\mathbf{y}^k \right\|^2 + \frac{1}{2} \|\mathbf{x} - \mathbf{x}^k\|_{\mathbf{G}}^2$$

$$= h_1(\mathbf{x}) + \frac{\rho}{2} \|\mathbf{A}(\mathbf{x} - \mathbf{x}^k)\|^2 + \left\langle \rho\mathbf{A}\mathbf{x}, \mathbf{A}\mathbf{x}^k + \mathbf{B}\mathbf{z}^k - \mathbf{c} + \frac{1}{\rho}\mathbf{y}^k \right\rangle$$

$$+ \frac{\alpha}{2} \|\mathbf{x} - \mathbf{x}^k\|^2 - \frac{\rho}{2} \|\mathbf{A}(\mathbf{x} - \mathbf{x}^k)\|^2 + \text{constant}$$

$$= h_1(\mathbf{x}) + \rho \left\langle \mathbf{A}\mathbf{x}, \mathbf{A}\mathbf{x}^k + \mathbf{B}\mathbf{z}^k - \mathbf{c} + \frac{1}{\rho}\mathbf{y}^k \right\rangle + \frac{\alpha}{2} \|\mathbf{x} - \mathbf{x}^k\|^2 + \text{constant},$$

where by "constant" we mean a term that does not depend on $\mathbf{x}$. We can therefore conclude that step (a) of AD-PMM amounts to

$$\mathbf{x}^{k+1} = \operatorname{argmin}_{\mathbf{x} \in \mathbb{R}^n} \left\{ h_1(\mathbf{x}) + \rho \left\langle \mathbf{A}\mathbf{x}, \mathbf{A}\mathbf{x}^k + \mathbf{B}\mathbf{z}^k - \mathbf{c} + \frac{1}{\rho}\mathbf{y}^k \right\rangle + \frac{\alpha}{2} \|\mathbf{x} - \mathbf{x}^k\|^2 \right\},$$
$$(15.11)$$

and, similarly, step (b) of AD-PMM is the same as

$$\mathbf{z}^{k+1} = \operatorname{argmin}_{\mathbf{z} \in \mathbb{R}^p} \left\{ h_2(\mathbf{z}) + \rho \left\langle \mathbf{B}\mathbf{z}, \mathbf{A}\mathbf{x}^{k+1} + \mathbf{B}\mathbf{z}^k - \mathbf{c} + \frac{1}{\rho}\mathbf{y}^k \right\rangle + \frac{\beta}{2} \|\mathbf{z} - \mathbf{z}^k\|^2 \right\}.$$
$$(15.12)$$

The functions minimized in the update formulas (15.11) and (15.12) are actually constructed from the functions minimized in steps (a) and (b) of ADMM by linearizing the quadratic term and adding a proximity term. This is the reason why the resulting method will be called the *alternating direction linearized proximal method of multipliers* (AD-LPMM). We can also write the update formulas (15.11) and

(15.12) in terms of proximal operators. Indeed, (15.11) can be rewritten equivalently as

$$\mathbf{x}^{k+1} = \text{argmin}_{\mathbf{x}} \left\{ \frac{1}{\alpha} h_1(\mathbf{x}) + \frac{1}{2} \left\| \mathbf{x} - \left(\mathbf{x}^k - \frac{\rho}{\alpha} \mathbf{A}^T \left(\mathbf{A}\mathbf{x}^k + \mathbf{B}\mathbf{z}^k - \mathbf{c} + \frac{1}{\rho} \mathbf{y}^k \right) \right) \right\|^2 \right\}.$$

That is,

$$\mathbf{x}^{k+1} = \text{prox}_{\frac{1}{\alpha} h_1} \left[\mathbf{x}^k - \frac{\rho}{\alpha} \mathbf{A}^T \left(\mathbf{A}\mathbf{x}^k + \mathbf{B}\mathbf{z}^k - \mathbf{c} + \frac{1}{\rho} \mathbf{y}^k \right) \right].$$

Similarly, the $\mathbf{z}$-step can be rewritten as

$$\mathbf{z}^{k+1} = \text{prox}_{\frac{1}{\beta} h_2} \left[\mathbf{z}^k - \frac{\rho}{\beta} \mathbf{B}^T \left(\mathbf{A}\mathbf{x}^{k+1} + \mathbf{B}\mathbf{z}^k - \mathbf{c} + \frac{1}{\rho} \mathbf{y}^k \right) \right].$$

We can now summarize and write explicitly the AD-LPMM method.

AD-LPMM

Initialization: $\mathbf{x}^0 \in \mathbb{R}^n$, $\mathbf{z}^0 \in \mathbb{R}^p$, $\mathbf{y}^0 \in \mathbb{R}^m$, $\rho > 0$, $\alpha \geq \rho\lambda_{\max}(\mathbf{A}^T\mathbf{A})$, $\beta \geq \rho\lambda_{\max}(\mathbf{B}^T\mathbf{B})$.
General step: for any $k = 0, 1, \dots$ execute the following:

(a) $\mathbf{x}^{k+1} = \text{prox}_{\frac{1}{\alpha} h_1} \left[\mathbf{x}^k - \frac{\rho}{\alpha} \mathbf{A}^T \left(\mathbf{A}\mathbf{x}^k + \mathbf{B}\mathbf{z}^k - \mathbf{c} + \frac{1}{\rho} \mathbf{y}^k \right) \right]$;

(b) $\mathbf{z}^{k+1} = \text{prox}_{\frac{1}{\beta} h_2} \left[\mathbf{z}^k - \frac{\rho}{\beta} \mathbf{B}^T \left(\mathbf{A}\mathbf{x}^{k+1} + \mathbf{B}\mathbf{z}^k - \mathbf{c} + \frac{1}{\rho} \mathbf{y}^k \right) \right]$;

(c) $\mathbf{y}^{k+1} = \mathbf{y}^k + \rho(\mathbf{A}\mathbf{x}^{k+1} + \mathbf{B}\mathbf{z}^{k+1} - \mathbf{c})$.

15.3 Convergence Analysis of AD-PMM

In this section we will develop a rate of convergence analysis of AD-PMM employed on problem (15.1). Note that both ADMM and AD-LPMM are special cases of AD-PMM. The following set of assumptions will be made.

Assumption 15.2.

(A) $h_1 : \mathbb{R}^n \to (-\infty, \infty]$ and $h_2 : \mathbb{R}^p \to (-\infty, \infty]$ are proper closed convex functions.

(B) $\mathbf{A} \in \mathbb{R}^{m \times n}, \mathbf{B} \in \mathbb{R}^{m \times p}, \mathbf{c} \in \mathbb{R}^m, \rho > 0$.

(C) $\mathbf{G} \in \mathbb{S}_+^n, \mathbf{Q} \in \mathbb{S}_+^p$.

(D) For any $\mathbf{a} \in \mathbb{R}^n, \mathbf{b} \in \mathbb{R}^p$ the optimal sets of the problems

$$\min_{\mathbf{x} \in \mathbb{R}^n} \left\{ h_1(\mathbf{x}) + \frac{\rho}{2} \|\mathbf{A}\mathbf{x}\|^2 + \frac{1}{2} \|\mathbf{x}\|_{\mathbf{G}}^2 + \langle \mathbf{a}, \mathbf{x} \rangle \right\}$$

and

$$\min_{\mathbf{z} \in \mathbb{R}^p} \left\{ h_2(\mathbf{z}) + \frac{\rho}{2}\|\mathbf{Bz}\|^2 + \frac{1}{2}\|\mathbf{z}\|_{\mathbf{Q}}^2 + \langle \mathbf{b}, \mathbf{z} \rangle \right\}$$

are nonempty.

(E) *There exists* $\hat{\mathbf{x}} \in \mathrm{ri}(\mathrm{dom}(h_1))$ *and* $\hat{\mathbf{z}} \in \mathrm{ri}(\mathrm{dom}(h_2))$ *for which* $\mathbf{A}\hat{\mathbf{x}} + \mathbf{B}\hat{\mathbf{z}} = \mathbf{c}$.

(F) *Problem* (15.1) *has a nonempty optimal set, denoted by* X^*, *and the corresponding optimal value is* H_{opt}.

Property (D) guarantees that the AD-PMM method is actually a well-defined method.

By the strong duality theorem for convex problems (see Theorem A.1), under Assumption 15.2, it follows that strong duality holds for the pair of problems (15.1) and (15.2).

Theorem 15.3 (strong duality for the pair of problems (15.1) and (15.2)).
Suppose that Assumption 15.2 *holds, and let* $H_{\mathrm{opt}}, q_{\mathrm{opt}}$ *be the optimal values of the primal and dual problems* (15.1) *and* (15.2), *respectively. Then* $H_{\mathrm{opt}} = q_{\mathrm{opt}}$, *and the dual problem* (15.2) *possesses an optimal solution.*

We will now prove an $O(1/k)$ rate of convergence result of the sequence generated by AD-PMM.

Theorem 15.4 ($O(1/k)$ rate of convergence of AD-PMM).[87] *Suppose that Assumption* 15.2 *holds. Let* $\{(\mathbf{x}^k, \mathbf{z}^k)\}_{k \geq 0}$ *be the sequence generated by AD-PMM for solving problem* (15.1). *Let* $(\mathbf{x}^*, \mathbf{z}^*)$ *be an optimal solution of problem* (15.1) *and* $\mathbf{y}^*$ *be an optimal solution of the dual problem* (15.2). *Suppose that* $\gamma > 0$ *is any constant satisfying* $\gamma \geq 2\|\mathbf{y}^*\|$. *Then for all* $n \geq 0$,

$$H(\mathbf{x}^{(n)}, \mathbf{z}^{(n)}) - H_{\mathrm{opt}} \leq \frac{\|\mathbf{x}^* - \mathbf{x}^0\|_{\mathbf{G}}^2 + \|\mathbf{z}^* - \mathbf{z}^0\|_{\mathbf{C}}^2 + \frac{1}{\rho}(\gamma + \|\mathbf{y}^0\|)^2}{2(n+1)}, \quad (15.13)$$

$$\|\mathbf{A}\mathbf{x}^{(n)} + \mathbf{B}\mathbf{z}^{(n)} - \mathbf{c}\| \leq \frac{\|\mathbf{x}^* - \mathbf{x}^0\|_{\mathbf{G}}^2 + \|\mathbf{z}^* - \mathbf{z}^0\|_{\mathbf{C}}^2 + \frac{1}{\rho}(\gamma + \|\mathbf{y}^0\|)^2}{\gamma(n+1)}, \quad (15.14)$$

where $\mathbf{C} = \rho\mathbf{B}^T\mathbf{B} + \mathbf{Q}$ and

$$\mathbf{x}^{(n)} = \frac{1}{n+1} \sum_{k=0}^{n} \mathbf{x}^{k+1}, \quad \mathbf{z}^{(n)} = \frac{1}{n+1} \sum_{k=0}^{n} \mathbf{z}^{k+1}.$$

Proof. By Fermat's optimality condition (Theorem 3.63) and the update steps (a) and (b) of AD-PMM, it follows that $\mathbf{x}^{k+1}$ and $\mathbf{z}^{k+1}$ satisfy

$$-\rho\mathbf{A}^T\left(\mathbf{A}\mathbf{x}^{k+1} + \mathbf{B}\mathbf{z}^k - \mathbf{c} + \frac{1}{\rho}\mathbf{y}^k\right) - \mathbf{G}(\mathbf{x}^{k+1} - \mathbf{x}^k) \in \partial h_1(\mathbf{x}^{k+1}), \quad (15.15)$$

$$-\rho\mathbf{B}^T\left(\mathbf{A}\mathbf{x}^{k+1} + \mathbf{B}\mathbf{z}^{k+1} - \mathbf{c} + \frac{1}{\rho}\mathbf{y}^k\right) - \mathbf{Q}(\mathbf{z}^{k+1} - \mathbf{z}^k) \in \partial h_2(\mathbf{z}^{k+1}). \quad (15.16)$$

---

[87]The proof of Theorem 15.4 on the rate of convergence of AD-PMM is based on a combination of the proof techniques of He and Yuan [65] and Gao and Zhang [58].

We will use the following notation:

$$\tilde{\mathbf{x}}^k = \mathbf{x}^{k+1},$$
$$\tilde{\mathbf{z}}^k = \mathbf{z}^{k+1},$$
$$\tilde{\mathbf{y}}^k = \mathbf{y}^k + \rho(\mathbf{A}\mathbf{x}^{k+1} + \mathbf{B}\mathbf{z}^k - \mathbf{c}).$$

Using (15.15), (15.16), the subgradient inequality, and the above notation, we obtain that for any $\mathbf{x} \in \mathrm{dom}(h_1)$ and $\mathbf{z} \in \mathrm{dom}(h_2)$,

$$h_1(\mathbf{x}) - h_1(\tilde{\mathbf{x}}^k) + \left\langle \rho\mathbf{A}^T\left(\mathbf{A}\tilde{\mathbf{x}}^k + \mathbf{B}\mathbf{z}^k - \mathbf{c} + \frac{1}{\rho}\mathbf{y}^k\right) + \mathbf{G}(\tilde{\mathbf{x}}^k - \mathbf{x}^k), \mathbf{x} - \tilde{\mathbf{x}}^k \right\rangle \geq 0,$$

$$h_2(\mathbf{z}) - h_2(\tilde{\mathbf{z}}^k) + \left\langle \rho\mathbf{B}^T\left(\mathbf{A}\tilde{\mathbf{x}}^k + \mathbf{B}\tilde{\mathbf{z}}^k - \mathbf{c} + \frac{1}{\rho}\mathbf{y}^k\right) + \mathbf{Q}(\tilde{\mathbf{z}}^k - \mathbf{z}^k), \mathbf{z} - \tilde{\mathbf{z}}^k \right\rangle \geq 0.$$

Using the definition of $\tilde{\mathbf{y}}^k$, the above two inequalities can be rewritten as

$$h_1(\mathbf{x}) - h_1(\tilde{\mathbf{x}}^k) + \left\langle \mathbf{A}^T\tilde{\mathbf{y}}^k + \mathbf{G}(\tilde{\mathbf{x}}^k - \mathbf{x}^k), \mathbf{x} - \tilde{\mathbf{x}}^k \right\rangle \geq 0,$$

$$h_2(\mathbf{z}) - h_2(\tilde{\mathbf{z}}^k) + \left\langle \mathbf{B}^T\tilde{\mathbf{y}}^k + (\rho\mathbf{B}^T\mathbf{B} + \mathbf{Q})(\tilde{\mathbf{z}}^k - \mathbf{z}^k), \mathbf{z} - \tilde{\mathbf{z}}^k \right\rangle \geq 0.$$

Adding the above two inequalities and using the identity

$$\mathbf{y}^{k+1} - \mathbf{y}^k = \rho(\mathbf{A}\tilde{\mathbf{x}}^k + \mathbf{B}\tilde{\mathbf{z}}^k - \mathbf{c}),$$

we can conclude that for any $\mathbf{x} \in \mathrm{dom}(h_1)$, $\mathbf{z} \in \mathrm{dom}(h_2)$, and $\mathbf{y} \in \mathbb{R}^m$,

$$H(\mathbf{x}, \mathbf{z}) - H(\tilde{\mathbf{x}}^k, \tilde{\mathbf{z}}^k) + \left\langle \begin{pmatrix} \mathbf{x} - \tilde{\mathbf{x}}^k \\ \mathbf{z} - \tilde{\mathbf{z}}^k \\ \mathbf{y} - \tilde{\mathbf{y}}^k \end{pmatrix}, \begin{pmatrix} \mathbf{A}^T\tilde{\mathbf{y}}^k \\ \mathbf{B}^T\tilde{\mathbf{y}}^k \\ -\mathbf{A}\tilde{\mathbf{x}}^k - \mathbf{B}\tilde{\mathbf{z}}^k + \mathbf{c} \end{pmatrix} - \begin{pmatrix} \mathbf{G}(\mathbf{x}^k - \tilde{\mathbf{x}}^k) \\ \mathbf{C}(\mathbf{z}^k - \tilde{\mathbf{z}}^k) \\ \frac{1}{\rho}(\mathbf{y}^k - \mathbf{y}^{k+1}) \end{pmatrix} \right\rangle \geq 0,$$

$$(15.17)$$

where $\mathbf{C} = \rho\mathbf{B}^T\mathbf{B} + \mathbf{Q}$. We will use the following identity that holds for any positive semidefinite matrix $\mathbf{P}$:

$$(\mathbf{a} - \mathbf{b})^T\mathbf{P}(\mathbf{c} - \mathbf{d}) = \frac{1}{2}\left(\|\mathbf{a} - \mathbf{d}\|_{\mathbf{P}}^2 - \|\mathbf{a} - \mathbf{c}\|_{\mathbf{P}}^2 + \|\mathbf{b} - \mathbf{c}\|_{\mathbf{P}}^2 - \|\mathbf{b} - \mathbf{d}\|_{\mathbf{P}}^2\right).$$

Using the above identity, we can conclude that

$$(\mathbf{x} - \tilde{\mathbf{x}}^k)^T\mathbf{G}(\mathbf{x}^k - \tilde{\mathbf{x}}^k) = \frac{1}{2}\left(\|\mathbf{x} - \tilde{\mathbf{x}}^k\|_{\mathbf{G}}^2 - \|\mathbf{x} - \mathbf{x}^k\|_{\mathbf{G}}^2 + \|\tilde{\mathbf{x}}^k - \mathbf{x}^k\|_{\mathbf{G}}^2\right)$$

$$\geq \frac{1}{2}\|\mathbf{x} - \tilde{\mathbf{x}}^k\|_{\mathbf{G}}^2 - \frac{1}{2}\|\mathbf{x} - \mathbf{x}^k\|_{\mathbf{G}}^2, \qquad (15.18)$$

as well as

$$(\mathbf{z} - \tilde{\mathbf{z}}^k)^T\mathbf{C}(\mathbf{z}^k - \tilde{\mathbf{z}}^k) = \frac{1}{2}\|\mathbf{z} - \tilde{\mathbf{z}}^k\|_{\mathbf{C}}^2 - \frac{1}{2}\|\mathbf{z} - \mathbf{z}^k\|_{\mathbf{C}}^2 + \frac{1}{2}\|\mathbf{z}^k - \tilde{\mathbf{z}}^k\|_{\mathbf{C}}^2 \qquad (15.19)$$

and

$$2(\mathbf{y} - \tilde{\mathbf{y}}^k)^T(\mathbf{y}^k - \mathbf{y}^{k+1})$$
$$= \|\mathbf{y} - \mathbf{y}^{k+1}\|^2 - \|\mathbf{y} - \mathbf{y}^k\|^2 + \|\tilde{\mathbf{y}}^k - \mathbf{y}^k\|^2 - \|\tilde{\mathbf{y}}^k - \mathbf{y}^{k+1}\|^2$$
$$= \|\mathbf{y} - \mathbf{y}^{k+1}\|^2 - \|\mathbf{y} - \mathbf{y}^k\|^2 + \rho^2\|\mathbf{A}\tilde{\mathbf{x}}^k + \mathbf{B}\mathbf{z}^k - \mathbf{c}\|^2$$
$$- \|\mathbf{y}^k + \rho(\mathbf{A}\tilde{\mathbf{x}}^k + \mathbf{B}\mathbf{z}^k - \mathbf{c}) - \mathbf{y}^k - \rho(\mathbf{A}\tilde{\mathbf{x}}^k + \mathbf{B}\tilde{\mathbf{z}}^k - \mathbf{c})\|^2$$
$$= \|\mathbf{y} - \mathbf{y}^{k+1}\|^2 - \|\mathbf{y} - \mathbf{y}^k\|^2 + \rho^2\|\mathbf{A}\tilde{\mathbf{x}}^k + \mathbf{B}\mathbf{z}^k - \mathbf{c}\|^2 - \rho^2\|\mathbf{B}(\mathbf{z}^k - \tilde{\mathbf{z}}^k)\|^2.$$

Therefore,

$$\frac{1}{\rho}(\mathbf{y}-\tilde{\mathbf{y}}^k)^T(\mathbf{y}^k-\mathbf{y}^{k+1}) \geq \frac{1}{2\rho}\left(\|\mathbf{y}-\mathbf{y}^{k+1}\|^2 - \|\mathbf{y}-\mathbf{y}^k\|^2\right) - \frac{\rho}{2}\|\mathbf{B}(\mathbf{z}^k-\tilde{\mathbf{z}}^k)\|^2. \quad (15.20)$$

Denoting

$$\mathbf{H} = \begin{pmatrix} \mathbf{G} & \mathbf{0} & \mathbf{0} \\ \mathbf{0} & \mathbf{C} & \mathbf{0} \\ \mathbf{0} & \mathbf{0} & \frac{1}{\rho}\mathbf{I} \end{pmatrix},$$

as well as

$$\mathbf{w} = \begin{pmatrix} \mathbf{x} \\ \mathbf{z} \\ \mathbf{y} \end{pmatrix}, \quad \mathbf{w}^k = \begin{pmatrix} \mathbf{x}^k \\ \mathbf{z}^k \\ \mathbf{y}^k \end{pmatrix}, \quad \tilde{\mathbf{w}}^k = \begin{pmatrix} \tilde{\mathbf{x}}^k \\ \tilde{\mathbf{z}}^k \\ \tilde{\mathbf{y}}^k \end{pmatrix},$$

we obtain by combining (15.18), (15.19), and (15.20) that

$$\left\langle \begin{pmatrix} \mathbf{x}-\tilde{\mathbf{x}}^k \\ \mathbf{z}-\tilde{\mathbf{z}}^k \\ \mathbf{y}-\tilde{\mathbf{y}}^k \end{pmatrix}, \begin{pmatrix} \mathbf{G}(\mathbf{x}^k-\tilde{\mathbf{x}}^k) \\ \mathbf{C}(\mathbf{z}^k-\tilde{\mathbf{z}}^k) \\ \frac{1}{\rho}(\mathbf{y}^k-\mathbf{y}^{k+1}) \end{pmatrix} \right\rangle \geq \frac{1}{2}\|\mathbf{w}-\mathbf{w}^{k+1}\|_{\mathbf{H}}^2 - \frac{1}{2}\|\mathbf{w}-\mathbf{w}^k\|_{\mathbf{H}}^2$$

$$+ \frac{1}{2}\|\mathbf{z}^k-\tilde{\mathbf{z}}^k\|_{\mathbf{C}}^2 - \frac{\rho}{2}\|\mathbf{B}(\mathbf{z}^k-\tilde{\mathbf{z}}^k)\|^2$$

$$\geq \frac{1}{2}\|\mathbf{w}-\mathbf{w}^{k+1}\|_{\mathbf{H}}^2 - \frac{1}{2}\|\mathbf{w}-\mathbf{w}^k\|_{\mathbf{H}}^2.$$

Combining the last inequality with (15.17), we obtain that for any $\mathbf{x} \in \mathrm{dom}(h_1)$, $\mathbf{z} \in \mathrm{dom}(h_2)$, and $\mathbf{y} \in \mathbb{R}^m$,

$$H(\mathbf{x},\mathbf{z}) - H(\tilde{\mathbf{x}}^k,\tilde{\mathbf{z}}^k) + \langle \mathbf{w}-\tilde{\mathbf{w}}^k, \mathbf{F}\tilde{\mathbf{w}}^k + \tilde{\mathbf{c}} \rangle \geq \frac{1}{2}\|\mathbf{w}-\mathbf{w}^{k+1}\|_{\mathbf{H}}^2 - \frac{1}{2}\|\mathbf{w}-\mathbf{w}^k\|_{\mathbf{H}}^2, \quad (15.21)$$

where

$$\mathbf{F} = \begin{pmatrix} \mathbf{0} & \mathbf{0} & \mathbf{A}^T \\ \mathbf{0} & \mathbf{0} & \mathbf{B}^T \\ -\mathbf{A} & -\mathbf{B} & \mathbf{0} \end{pmatrix}, \quad \tilde{\mathbf{c}} = \begin{pmatrix} \mathbf{0} \\ \mathbf{0} \\ \mathbf{c} \end{pmatrix}.$$

Note that

$$\langle \mathbf{w}-\tilde{\mathbf{w}}^k, \mathbf{F}\tilde{\mathbf{w}}^k + \tilde{\mathbf{c}} \rangle = \langle \mathbf{w}-\tilde{\mathbf{w}}^k, \mathbf{F}(\tilde{\mathbf{w}}^k-\mathbf{w}) + \mathbf{F}\mathbf{w} + \tilde{\mathbf{c}} \rangle$$
$$= \langle \mathbf{w}-\tilde{\mathbf{w}}^k, \mathbf{F}\mathbf{w} + \tilde{\mathbf{c}} \rangle,$$

where the second equality follows from the fact that $\mathbf{F}$ is skew symmetric (meaning $\mathbf{F}^T = -\mathbf{F}$). We can thus conclude that (15.21) can be rewritten as

$$H(\mathbf{x},\mathbf{z}) - H(\tilde{\mathbf{x}}^k,\tilde{\mathbf{z}}^k) + \langle \mathbf{w}-\tilde{\mathbf{w}}^k, \mathbf{F}\mathbf{w} + \tilde{\mathbf{c}} \rangle \geq \frac{1}{2}\|\mathbf{w}-\mathbf{w}^{k+1}\|_{\mathbf{H}}^2 - \frac{1}{2}\|\mathbf{w}-\mathbf{w}^k\|_{\mathbf{H}}^2.$$

Summing the above inequality over $k = 0, 1, \ldots, n$ yields the inequality

$$(n+1)H(\mathbf{x}, \mathbf{z}) - \sum_{k=0}^{n} H(\tilde{\mathbf{x}}^k, \tilde{\mathbf{z}}^k) + \left\langle (n+1)\mathbf{w} - \sum_{k=0}^{n} \tilde{\mathbf{w}}^k, \mathbf{F}\mathbf{w} + \tilde{\mathbf{c}} \right\rangle \geq -\frac{1}{2}\|\mathbf{w} - \mathbf{w}^0\|_{\mathbf{H}}^2.$$

Defining

$$\mathbf{w}^{(n)} = \frac{1}{n+1} \sum_{k=0}^{n} \tilde{\mathbf{w}}^k, \mathbf{x}^{(n)} = \frac{1}{n+1} \sum_{k=0}^{n} \mathbf{x}^{k+1}, \mathbf{z}^{(n)} = \frac{1}{n+1} \sum_{k=0}^{n} \mathbf{z}^{k+1}$$

and using the convexity of H, we obtain that

$$H(\mathbf{x}, \mathbf{z}) - H(\mathbf{x}^{(n)}, \mathbf{z}^{(n)}) + \langle \mathbf{w} - \mathbf{w}^{(n)}, \mathbf{F}\mathbf{w} + \tilde{\mathbf{c}} \rangle + \frac{1}{2(n+1)}\|\mathbf{w} - \mathbf{w}^0\|_{\mathbf{H}}^2 \geq 0.$$

Using (again) the skew-symmetry of $\mathbf{F}$, we can conclude that the above inequality is the same as

$$H(\mathbf{x}, \mathbf{z}) - H(\mathbf{x}^{(n)}, \mathbf{z}^{(n)}) + \langle \mathbf{w} - \mathbf{w}^{(n)}, \mathbf{F}\mathbf{w}^{(n)} + \tilde{\mathbf{c}} \rangle + \frac{1}{2(n+1)}\|\mathbf{w} - \mathbf{w}^0\|_{\mathbf{H}}^2 \geq 0.$$

In other words, for any $\mathbf{x} \in \mathrm{dom}(h_1)$ and $\mathbf{z} \in \mathrm{dom}(h_1)$,

$$H(\mathbf{x}^{(n)}, \mathbf{z}^{(n)}) - H(\mathbf{x}, \mathbf{z}) + \langle \mathbf{w}^{(n)} - \mathbf{w}, \mathbf{F}\mathbf{w}^{(n)} + \tilde{\mathbf{c}} \rangle \leq \frac{1}{2(n+1)}\|\mathbf{w} - \mathbf{w}^0\|_{\mathbf{H}}^2. \quad (15.22)$$

Let $(\mathbf{x}^*, \mathbf{z}^*)$ be an optimal solution of problem (15.1). Then $H(\mathbf{x}^*, \mathbf{z}^*) = H_{\mathrm{opt}}$ and $\mathbf{A}\mathbf{x}^* + \mathbf{B}\mathbf{z}^* = \mathbf{c}$. Plugging $\mathbf{x} = \mathbf{x}^*, \mathbf{z} = \mathbf{z}^*$, and the expressions for $\mathbf{w}^{(n)}, \mathbf{w}, \mathbf{w}^0, \mathbf{F}, \mathbf{H}, \tilde{\mathbf{c}}$ into (15.22), we obtain (denoting $\mathbf{y}^{(n)} = \frac{1}{n+1}\sum_{k=0}^{n} \tilde{\mathbf{y}}^k$)

$$H(\mathbf{x}^{(n)}, \mathbf{z}^{(n)}) - H_{\mathrm{opt}} + \langle \mathbf{x}^{(n)} - \mathbf{x}^*, \mathbf{A}^T \mathbf{y}^{(n)} \rangle + \langle \mathbf{z}^{(n)} - \mathbf{z}^*, \mathbf{B}^T \mathbf{y}^{(n)} \rangle$$
$$+ \langle \mathbf{y}^{(n)} - \mathbf{y}, -\mathbf{A}\mathbf{x}^{(n)} - \mathbf{B}\mathbf{z}^{(n)} + \mathbf{c} \rangle$$
$$\leq \frac{1}{2(n+1)} \left\{ \|\mathbf{x}^* - \mathbf{x}^0\|_{\mathbf{G}}^2 + \|\mathbf{z}^* - \mathbf{z}^0\|_{\mathbf{C}}^2 + \frac{1}{\rho}\|\mathbf{y} - \mathbf{y}^0\|^2 \right\}.$$

Cancelling terms and using the fact that $\mathbf{A}\mathbf{x}^* + \mathbf{B}\mathbf{z}^* = \mathbf{c}$, we obtain that the last inequality is the same as

$$H(\mathbf{x}^{(n)}, \mathbf{z}^{(n)}) - H_{\mathrm{opt}} + \langle \mathbf{y}, \mathbf{A}\mathbf{x}^{(n)} + \mathbf{B}\mathbf{z}^{(n)} - \mathbf{c} \rangle \leq \frac{\|\mathbf{x}^* - \mathbf{x}^0\|_{\mathbf{G}}^2 + \|\mathbf{z}^* - \mathbf{z}^0\|_{\mathbf{C}}^2 + \frac{1}{\rho}\|\mathbf{y} - \mathbf{y}^0\|^2}{2(n+1)}.$$

Since the above inequality holds for any $\mathbf{y} \in \mathbb{R}^m$, we can take the maximum of both sides over all $\mathbf{y} \in B_2[\mathbf{0}, \gamma]$ and obtain the inequality

$$H(\mathbf{x}^{(n)}, \mathbf{z}^{(n)}) - H_{\mathrm{opt}} + \gamma\|\mathbf{A}\mathbf{x}^{(n)} + \mathbf{B}\mathbf{z}^{(n)} - \mathbf{c}\| \leq \frac{\|\mathbf{x}^* - \mathbf{x}^0\|_{\mathbf{G}}^2 + \|\mathbf{z}^* - \mathbf{z}^0\|_{\mathbf{C}}^2 + \frac{1}{\rho}(\gamma + \|\mathbf{y}^0\|)^2}{2(n+1)}.$$

Since $\gamma \geq 2\|\mathbf{y}^*\|$ for some optimal dual solution $\mathbf{y}^*$ and strong duality holds (Theorem 15.3), it follows by Theorem 3.60 that the two inequalities (15.13) and (15.14) hold. □

15.4   Minimizing $f_1(\mathbf{x}) + f_2(\mathbf{Ax})$

In this section we consider the model

$$\min_{\mathbf{x}\in\mathbb{R}^n} \{f_1(\mathbf{x}) + f_2(\mathbf{Ax})\}, \tag{15.23}$$

where f_1, f_2 are proper closed convex functions and $\mathbf{A} \in \mathbb{R}^{m\times n}$. As usual, $\rho > 0$ is a given constant. An implicit assumption will be that f_1 and f_2 are "proximable," which loosely speaking means that the prox operator of λf_1 and λf_2 can be efficiently computed for any $\lambda > 0$. This is obviously a "virtual" assumption, and its importance is only in the fact that it dictates the development of algorithms that rely on prox computations of λf_1 and λf_2.

Problem (15.23) can be rewritten as

$$\min_{\mathbf{x}\in\mathbb{R}^n, \mathbf{z}\in\mathbb{R}^m} \{f_1(\mathbf{x}) + f_2(\mathbf{z}) : \mathbf{Ax} - \mathbf{z} = \mathbf{0}\}. \tag{15.24}$$

This fits the general model (15.1) with $h_1 = f_1, h_2 = f_2$, $\mathbf{B} = -\mathbf{I}$, and $\mathbf{c} = \mathbf{0}$. A direct implementation of ADMM leads to the following scheme ($\rho > 0$ is a given constant):

$$\mathbf{x}^{k+1} \in \operatorname{argmin}_{\mathbf{x}\in\mathbb{R}^n} \left[f_1(\mathbf{x}) + \frac{\rho}{2}\left\|\mathbf{Ax} - \mathbf{z}^k + \frac{1}{\rho}\mathbf{y}^k\right\|^2 \right], \tag{15.25}$$

$$\mathbf{z}^{k+1} = \operatorname{argmin}_{\mathbf{z}\in\mathbb{R}^m} \left[f_2(\mathbf{z}) + \frac{\rho}{2}\left\|\mathbf{Ax}^{k+1} - \mathbf{z} + \frac{1}{\rho}\mathbf{y}^k\right\|^2 \right],$$

$$\mathbf{y}^{k+1} = \mathbf{y}^k + \rho(\mathbf{Ax}^{k+1} - \mathbf{z}^{k+1}).$$

The $\mathbf{z}$-step can be rewritten as a prox step, thus resulting in the following algorithm for solving problem (15.23).

Algorithm 1   [ADMM for solving (15.23)—version 1]

- **Initialization:** $\mathbf{x}^0 \in \mathbb{R}^n, \mathbf{z}^0, \mathbf{y}^0 \in \mathbb{R}^m, \rho > 0$.

- **General step ($k \geq 0$):**

  (a) $\mathbf{x}^{k+1} \in \operatorname{argmin}_{\mathbf{x}\in\mathbb{R}^n} \left[f_1(\mathbf{x}) + \frac{\rho}{2}\left\|\mathbf{Ax} - \mathbf{z}^k + \frac{1}{\rho}\mathbf{y}^k\right\|^2 \right]$;

  (b) $\mathbf{z}^{k+1} = \operatorname{prox}_{\frac{1}{\rho}f_2}\left(\mathbf{Ax}^{k+1} + \frac{1}{\rho}\mathbf{y}^k\right)$;

  (c) $\mathbf{y}^{k+1} = \mathbf{y}^k + \rho(\mathbf{Ax}^{k+1} - \mathbf{z}^{k+1})$.

Step (a) of Algorithm 1 might be difficult to compute since the minimization in step (a) is more involved than a prox computation due to the quadratic term $\frac{\rho}{2}\mathbf{x}^T\mathbf{A}^T\mathbf{Ax}$. We can actually employ ADMM in a different way that will refrain from the type of computation made in step (a). For that, we will rewrite problem (15.23) as

$$\min_{\mathbf{x},\mathbf{w}\in\mathbb{R}^n,\mathbf{z}\in\mathbb{R}^m} \{f_1(\mathbf{w}) + f_2(\mathbf{z}) : \mathbf{Ax} - \mathbf{z} = \mathbf{0}, \mathbf{x} - \mathbf{w} = \mathbf{0}\}.$$

The above problem fits model (15.1) with $h_1 \equiv 0$, $h_2(\mathbf{z},\mathbf{w}) = f_1(\mathbf{z}) + f_2(\mathbf{w})$, $\mathbf{B} = -\mathbf{I}$, and $\begin{pmatrix}\mathbf{A}\\\mathbf{I}\end{pmatrix}$ taking the place of $\mathbf{A}$. The dual vector $\mathbf{y} \in \mathbb{R}^{m+n}$ is of the form $\mathbf{y} = (\mathbf{y}_1^T, \mathbf{y}_2^T)^T$, where $\mathbf{y}_1 \in \mathbb{R}^m$ and $\mathbf{y}_2 \in \mathbb{R}^n$. In the above reformulation we have two blocks of vectors: $\mathbf{x}$ and $(\mathbf{z},\mathbf{w})$. The $\mathbf{x}$-step is given by

$$\begin{aligned}
\mathbf{x}^{k+1} &= \operatorname{argmin}_{\mathbf{x}\in\mathbb{R}^n} \left[\left\|\mathbf{Ax} - \mathbf{z}^k + \frac{1}{\rho}\mathbf{y}_1^k\right\|^2 + \left\|\mathbf{x} - \mathbf{w}^k + \frac{1}{\rho}\mathbf{y}_2^k\right\|^2 \right] \\
&= (\mathbf{I} + \mathbf{A}^T\mathbf{A})^{-1}\left(\mathbf{A}^T\left[\mathbf{z}^k - \frac{1}{\rho}\mathbf{y}_1^k\right] + \mathbf{w}^k - \frac{1}{\rho}\mathbf{y}_2^k \right).
\end{aligned}$$

The $(\mathbf{z},\mathbf{w})$-step is

$$\begin{aligned}
\mathbf{z}^{k+1} &= \operatorname{prox}_{\frac{1}{\rho}f_2}\left(\mathbf{Ax}^{k+1} + \frac{1}{\rho}\mathbf{y}_1^k\right), \\
\mathbf{w}^{k+1} &= \operatorname{prox}_{\frac{1}{\rho}f_1}\left(\mathbf{x}^{k+1} + \frac{1}{\rho}\mathbf{y}_2^k\right).
\end{aligned}$$

The method is summarized in the following.

Algorithm 2 [ADMM for solving (15.23)—version 2]

- **Initialization:** $\mathbf{x}^0, \mathbf{w}^0, \mathbf{y}_2^0 \in \mathbb{R}^n$, $\mathbf{z}^0, \mathbf{y}_1^0 \in \mathbb{R}^m$, $\rho > 0$.

- **General step ($k \geq 0$):**

$$\begin{aligned}
\mathbf{x}^{k+1} &= (\mathbf{I} + \mathbf{A}^T\mathbf{A})^{-1}\left(\mathbf{A}^T\left[\mathbf{z}^k - \frac{1}{\rho}\mathbf{y}_1^k\right] + \mathbf{w}^k - \frac{1}{\rho}\mathbf{y}_2^k\right), \\
\mathbf{z}^{k+1} &= \operatorname{prox}_{\frac{1}{\rho}f_2}\left(\mathbf{Ax}^{k+1} + \frac{1}{\rho}\mathbf{y}_1^k\right), \\
\mathbf{w}^{k+1} &= \operatorname{prox}_{\frac{1}{\rho}f_1}\left(\mathbf{x}^{k+1} + \frac{1}{\rho}\mathbf{y}_2^k\right), \\
\mathbf{y}_1^{k+1} &= \mathbf{y}_1^k + \rho(\mathbf{Ax}^{k+1} - \mathbf{z}^{k+1}), \\
\mathbf{y}_2^{k+1} &= \mathbf{y}_2^k + \rho(\mathbf{x}^{k+1} - \mathbf{w}^{k+1}).
\end{aligned}$$

Algorithm 2 might still be too computationally demanding since it involves the evaluation of the inverse of $\mathbf{I} + \mathbf{A}^T\mathbf{A}$ (or at least the evaluation of $\mathbf{A}^T\mathbf{A}$ and a solution of a linear system at each iteration), which might be a difficult task in large-scale problems. We can alternatively employ AD-LPMM on problem (15.24) and obtain the following scheme that does not involve any matrix inverse calculations.

Algorithm 3 [AD-LPMM for solving (15.23)]

- **Initialization:** $\mathbf{x}^0 \in \mathbb{R}^n, \mathbf{z}^0, \mathbf{y}^0 \in \mathbb{R}^m$, $\rho > 0$, $\alpha \geq \rho \lambda_{\max}(\mathbf{A}^T \mathbf{A}), \beta \geq \rho$.

- **General step $(k \geq 0)$:**

$$\mathbf{x}^{k+1} = \text{prox}_{\frac{1}{\alpha} f_1} \left[\mathbf{x}^k - \frac{\rho}{\alpha} \mathbf{A}^T \left(\mathbf{A} \mathbf{x}^k - \mathbf{z}^k + \frac{1}{\rho} \mathbf{y}^k \right) \right],$$

$$\mathbf{z}^{k+1} = \text{prox}_{\frac{1}{\beta} f_2} \left[\mathbf{z}^k + \frac{\rho}{\beta} \left(\mathbf{A} \mathbf{x}^{k+1} - \mathbf{z}^k + \frac{1}{\rho} \mathbf{y}^k \right) \right],$$

$$\mathbf{y}^{k+1} = \mathbf{y}^k + \rho (\mathbf{A} \mathbf{x}^{k+1} - \mathbf{z}^{k+1}).$$

The above scheme has the advantage that it only requires simple linear algebra operations (no more than matrix/vector multiplications) and prox evaluations of λf_1 and λf_2 for different values of $\lambda > 0$.

Example 15.5 (l_1-regularized least squares). Consider the problem

$$\min_{\mathbf{x} \in \mathbb{R}^n} \left\{ \frac{1}{2} \|\mathbf{A}\mathbf{x} - \mathbf{b}\|_2^2 + \lambda \|\mathbf{x}\|_1 \right\}, \tag{15.26}$$

where $\mathbf{A} \in \mathbb{R}^{m \times n}, \mathbf{b} \in \mathbb{R}^m$ and $\lambda > 0$. Problem (15.26) fits the composite model (15.23) with $f_1(\mathbf{x}) = \lambda \|\mathbf{x}\|_1$ and $f_2(\mathbf{y}) \equiv \frac{1}{2} \|\mathbf{y} - \mathbf{b}\|_2^2$. For any $\gamma > 0$, $\text{prox}_{\gamma f_1} = \mathcal{T}_{\gamma \lambda}$ (by Example 6.8) and $\text{prox}_{\gamma f_2}(\mathbf{y}) = \frac{\mathbf{y} + \gamma \mathbf{b}}{\gamma + 1}$ (by Section 6.2.3). Step (a) of Algorithm 1 (first version of ADMM) has the form

$$\mathbf{x}^{k+1} \in \text{argmin}_{\mathbf{x} \in \mathbb{R}^n} \left[\lambda \|\mathbf{x}\|_1 + \frac{\rho}{2} \left\| \mathbf{A}\mathbf{x} - \mathbf{z}^k + \frac{1}{\rho} \mathbf{y}^k \right\|^2 \right],$$

which actually means that this version of ADMM is completely useless since it suggests to solve an l_1-regularized least squares problem by a sequence of l_1-regularized least squares problems.

Algorithm 2 (second version of ADMM) has the following form.

ADMM, version 2 (Algorithm 2):

$$\mathbf{x}^{k+1} = (\mathbf{I} + \mathbf{A}^T \mathbf{A})^{-1} \left(\mathbf{A}^T \left[\mathbf{z}^k - \frac{1}{\rho} \mathbf{y}_1^k \right] + \mathbf{w}^k - \frac{1}{\rho} \mathbf{y}_2^k \right),$$

$$\mathbf{z}^{k+1} = \frac{\rho \mathbf{A} \mathbf{x}^{k+1} + \mathbf{y}_1^k + \mathbf{b}}{\rho + 1},$$

$$\mathbf{w}^{k+1} = \mathcal{T}_{\frac{\lambda}{\rho}} \left(\mathbf{x}^{k+1} + \frac{1}{\rho} \mathbf{y}_2^k \right),$$

$$\mathbf{y}_1^{k+1} = \mathbf{y}_1^k + \rho (\mathbf{A} \mathbf{x}^{k+1} - \mathbf{z}^{k+1}),$$
$$\mathbf{y}_2^{k+1} = \mathbf{y}_2^k + \rho (\mathbf{x}^{k+1} - \mathbf{w}^{k+1}).$$

An implementation of the above ADMM variant will require to compute the matrix $\mathbf{A}^T \mathbf{A}$ in a preprocess and to solve at each iteration an $n \times n$ linear system

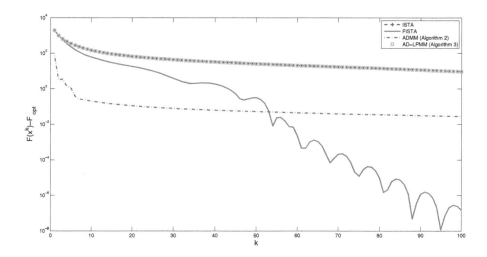

Figure 15.1. *Results of 100 iterations of ISTA, FISTA, ADMM (Algorithm 2) and AD-LPMM (Algorithm 3) on an l_1-regularized least squares problem.*

(or, alternatively, compute the inverse of $\mathbf{I} + \mathbf{A}^T\mathbf{A}$ in a preprocess). These operations might be difficult to execute in large-scale problems.

The general step of Algorithm 3 (which is essentially AD-LPMM) with $\alpha = \lambda_{\max}(\mathbf{A}^T\mathbf{A})\rho$ and $\beta = \rho$ takes the following form (denoting $L = \lambda_{\max}(\mathbf{A}^T\mathbf{A})$).

AD-LPMM (Algorithm 3):

$$\mathbf{x}^{k+1} = \mathcal{T}_{\frac{\lambda}{L\rho}}\left[\mathbf{x}^k - \frac{1}{L}\mathbf{A}^T\left(\mathbf{Ax}^k - \mathbf{z}^k + \frac{1}{\rho}\mathbf{y}^k\right)\right],$$

$$\mathbf{z}^{k+1} = \frac{\rho\mathbf{Ax}^{k+1} + \mathbf{y}^k + \mathbf{b}}{\rho + 1},$$

$$\mathbf{y}^{k+1} = \mathbf{y}^k + \rho(\mathbf{Ax}^{k+1} - \mathbf{z}^{k+1}).$$

The dominant computations in AD-LPMM are matrix/vector multiplications.

To illustrate the performance of the above two methods, we repeat the experiment described in Example 10.38 on the l_1-regularized least squares problem. We ran ADMM and AD-LPMM on the exact same instance, and the decay of the function values as a function of the iteration index k for the first 100 iterations is described in Figure 15.1. Clearly, ISTA and AD-LPMM exhibit the same performance, while ADMM seems to outperform both of them. This is actually not surprising since the computations carried out at each iteration of ADMM (solution of linear systems) are much heavier than the computations per iteration of AD-LPMM and ISTA (matrix/vector multiplications). In that respect, the comparison is in fact not fair and biased in favor of ADMM. What is definitely interesting is that FISTA significantly outperforms ADMM starting from approximately 50 iterations despite the fact that it is a simpler algorithm that requires substantially less computational effort per iteration. One possible reason is that FISTA is a method with a provably

$O(1/k^2)$ rate of convergence in function values, while ADMM is only guaranteed to converge at a rate of $O(1/k)$.   ∎

Example 15.6 (robust regression). Consider the problem

$$\min_{\mathbf{x}} \|\mathbf{A}\mathbf{x} - \mathbf{b}\|_1, \tag{15.27}$$

where $\mathbf{A} \in \mathbb{R}^{m \times n}$ and $\mathbf{b} \in \mathbb{R}^m$. Problem (15.27) fits the composite model (15.23) with $f_1 \equiv 0$ and $f_2(\mathbf{y}) = \|\mathbf{y} - \mathbf{b}\|_1$. Let $\rho > 0$. For any $\gamma > 0$, $\text{prox}_{\gamma f_1}(\mathbf{y}) = \mathbf{y}$ and $\text{prox}_{\gamma f_2}(\mathbf{y}) = \mathcal{T}_\gamma(\mathbf{y} - \mathbf{b}) + \mathbf{b}$ (by Example 6.8 and Theorem 6.11). Therefore, the general step of Algorithm 1 (first version of ADMM) takes the following form.

ADMM, version 1 (Algorithm 1):

$$\mathbf{x}^{k+1} = \text{argmin}_{\mathbf{x} \in \mathbb{R}^m} \left\| \mathbf{A}\mathbf{x} - \mathbf{z}^k + \frac{1}{\rho}\mathbf{y}^k \right\|^2,$$

$$\mathbf{z}^{k+1} = \mathcal{T}_{\frac{1}{\rho}} \left(\mathbf{A}\mathbf{x}^{k+1} + \frac{1}{\rho}\mathbf{y}^k - \mathbf{b} \right) + \mathbf{b},$$

$$\mathbf{y}^{k+1} = \mathbf{y}^k + \rho(\mathbf{A}\mathbf{x}^{k+1} - \mathbf{z}^{k+1}).$$

The general step of Algorithm 2 (second version of ADMM) reads as follows:

$$\mathbf{x}^{k+1} = (\mathbf{I} + \mathbf{A}^T\mathbf{A})^{-1} \left(\mathbf{A}^T \left[\mathbf{z}^k - \frac{1}{\rho}\mathbf{y}_1^k \right] + \mathbf{w}^k - \frac{1}{\rho}\mathbf{y}_2^k \right),$$

$$\mathbf{z}^{k+1} = \mathcal{T}_{\frac{1}{\rho}} \left(\mathbf{A}\mathbf{x}^{k+1} + \frac{1}{\rho}\mathbf{y}_1^k - \mathbf{b} \right) + \mathbf{b},$$

$$\mathbf{w}^{k+1} = \mathbf{x}^{k+1} + \frac{1}{\rho}\mathbf{y}_2^k,$$

$$\mathbf{y}_1^{k+1} = \mathbf{y}_1^k + \rho(\mathbf{A}\mathbf{x}^{k+1} - \mathbf{z}^{k+1}),$$
$$\mathbf{y}_2^{k+1} = \mathbf{y}_2^k + \rho(\mathbf{x}^{k+1} - \mathbf{w}^{k+1}).$$

Plugging the expression for $\mathbf{w}^{k+1}$ into the update formula of $\mathbf{y}_2^{k+1}$, we obtain that $\mathbf{y}_2^{k+1} = \mathbf{0}$. Thus, if we start with $\mathbf{y}_2^0 = 0$, then $\mathbf{y}_2^k = \mathbf{0}$ for all $k \geq 0$, and consequently $\mathbf{w}^k = \mathbf{x}^k$ for all k. The algorithm thus reduces to the following.

ADMM, version 2 (Algorithm 2):

$$\mathbf{x}^{k+1} = (\mathbf{I} + \mathbf{A}^T\mathbf{A})^{-1} \left(\mathbf{A}^T \left[\mathbf{z}^k - \frac{1}{\rho}\mathbf{y}_1^k \right] + \mathbf{x}^k \right),$$

$$\mathbf{z}^{k+1} = \mathcal{T}_{\frac{1}{\rho}} \left(\mathbf{A}\mathbf{x}^{k+1} + \frac{1}{\rho}\mathbf{y}_1^k - \mathbf{b} \right) + \mathbf{b},$$

$$\mathbf{y}_1^{k+1} = \mathbf{y}_1^k + \rho(\mathbf{A}\mathbf{x}^{k+1} - \mathbf{z}^{k+1}).$$

Algorithm 3 (which is essentially AD-LPMM) with $\alpha = \lambda_{\max}(\mathbf{A}^T\mathbf{A})\rho$ and $\beta = \rho$ takes the following form (denoting $L = \lambda_{\max}(\mathbf{A}^T\mathbf{A})$).

AD-LPMM (Algorithm 3):

$$\mathbf{x}^{k+1} = \mathbf{x}^k - \frac{1}{L}\mathbf{A}^T\left(\mathbf{Ax}^k - \mathbf{z}^k + \frac{1}{\rho}\mathbf{y}^k\right),$$

$$\mathbf{z}^{k+1} = \mathcal{T}_{\frac{1}{\rho}}\left[\left(\mathbf{Ax}^{k+1} - \mathbf{b} + \frac{1}{\rho}\mathbf{y}^k\right)\right] + \mathbf{b},$$

$$\mathbf{y}^{k+1} = \mathbf{y}^k + \rho(\mathbf{Ax}^{k+1} - \mathbf{z}^{k+1}). \quad \blacksquare$$

Example 15.7 (basis pursuit). Consider the problem

$$\begin{aligned} \min \quad & \|\mathbf{x}\|_1 \\ \text{s.t.} \quad & \mathbf{Ax} = \mathbf{b}, \end{aligned} \tag{15.28}$$

where $\mathbf{A} \in \mathbb{R}^{m \times n}$ and $\mathbf{b} \in \mathbb{R}^m$. Problem (15.28) fits the composite model (15.23) with $f_1(\mathbf{x}) = \|\mathbf{x}\|_1$ and $f_2 = \delta_{\{\mathbf{b}\}}$. Let $\rho > 0$. For any $\gamma > 0$, $\text{prox}_{\gamma f_1} = \mathcal{T}_\gamma$ (by Example 6.8) and $\text{prox}_{\gamma_2 f_2} \equiv \mathbf{b}$. Algorithm 1 is actually not particularly implementable since its first update step is

$$\mathbf{x}^{k+1} \in \text{argmin}_{\mathbf{x} \in \mathbb{R}^n}\left\{\|\mathbf{x}\|_1 + \frac{\rho}{2}\left\|\mathbf{Ax} - \mathbf{z}^k + \frac{1}{\rho}\mathbf{y}^k\right\|^2\right\},$$

which does not seem to be simpler to solve than the original problem (15.28). Algorithm 2 takes the following form (assuming that $\mathbf{z}^0 = \mathbf{b}$).

ADMM, version 2 (Algorithm 2):

$$\mathbf{x}^{k+1} = (\mathbf{I} + \mathbf{A}^T\mathbf{A})^{-1}\left(\mathbf{A}^T\left[\mathbf{b} - \frac{1}{\rho}\mathbf{y}_1^k\right] + \mathbf{w}^k - \frac{1}{\rho}\mathbf{y}_2^k\right),$$

$$\mathbf{w}^{k+1} = \mathcal{T}_{\frac{1}{\rho}}\left(\mathbf{x}^{k+1} + \frac{1}{\rho}\mathbf{y}_2^k\right),$$

$$\mathbf{y}_1^{k+1} = \mathbf{y}_1^k + \rho(\mathbf{Ax}^{k+1} - \mathbf{b}),$$
$$\mathbf{y}_2^{k+1} = \mathbf{y}_2^k + \rho(\mathbf{x}^{k+1} - \mathbf{w}^{k+1}).$$

Finally, assuming that $\mathbf{z}^0 = \mathbf{b}$, Algorithm 3 with $\alpha = \lambda_{\max}(\mathbf{A}^T\mathbf{A})\rho$ and $\beta = \rho$ reduces to the following simple update steps (denoting $L = \lambda_{\max}(\mathbf{A}^T\mathbf{A})$).

AD-LPMM (Algorithm 3):

$$\mathbf{x}^{k+1} = \mathcal{T}_{\frac{1}{\rho L}}\left[\mathbf{x}^k - \frac{1}{L}\mathbf{A}^T\left(\mathbf{Ax}^k - \mathbf{b} + \frac{1}{\rho}\mathbf{y}^k\right)\right],$$

$$\mathbf{y}^{k+1} = \mathbf{y}^k + \rho(\mathbf{Ax}^{k+1} - \mathbf{b}). \quad \blacksquare$$

Example 15.8 (minimizing $\sum_{i=1}^p g_i(\mathbf{A}_i\mathbf{x})$). Consider now the problem

$$\min_{\mathbf{x} \in \mathbb{R}^n} \sum_{i=1}^p g_i(\mathbf{A}_i\mathbf{x}), \tag{15.29}$$

where $g_1, g_2, \ldots, g_p$ are proper closed and convex functions and $\mathbf{A}_i \in \mathbb{R}^{m_i \times n}$ for all $i = 1, 2, \ldots, p$. Problem (15.29) fits the composite model (15.23) with

- $f_1 \equiv 0$;

- $f_2(\mathbf{y}) = \sum_{i=1}^{p} g_i(\mathbf{y}_i)$, where we assume that $\mathbf{y} \in \mathbb{R}^{m_1+m_2+\cdots+m_p}$ is of the form $\mathbf{y} = (\mathbf{y}_1^T, \mathbf{y}_2^T, \ldots, \mathbf{y}_p^T)^T$, where $\mathbf{y}_i \in \mathbb{R}^{m_i}$;

- the matrix $\mathbf{A} \in \mathbb{R}^{(m_1+m_2+\cdots+m_p) \times n}$ given by $\mathbf{A} = (\mathbf{A}_1^T, \mathbf{A}_2^T, \ldots, \mathbf{A}_p^T)^T$.

For any $\gamma > 0$, $\mathrm{prox}_{\gamma f_1}(\mathbf{x}) = \mathbf{x}$ and $\mathrm{prox}_{\gamma f_2}(\mathbf{y})_i = \mathrm{prox}_{\gamma g_i}(\mathbf{y}_i)$, $i = 1, 2, \ldots, p$ (by Theorem 6.6). The general update step of the first version of ADMM (Algorithm 1) has the form

$$\mathbf{x}^{k+1} \in \mathrm{argmin}_{\mathbf{x} \in \mathbb{R}^n} \sum_{i=1}^{p} \left\| \mathbf{A}_i \mathbf{x} - \mathbf{z}_i^k + \frac{1}{\rho} \mathbf{y}_i^k \right\|^2, \tag{15.30}$$

$$\mathbf{z}_i^{k+1} = \mathrm{prox}_{\frac{1}{\rho} g_i} \left(\mathbf{A}_i \mathbf{x}^{k+1} + \frac{1}{\rho} \mathbf{y}_i^k \right), \quad i = 1, 2, \ldots, p,$$

$$\mathbf{y}_i^{k+1} = \mathbf{y}_i^k + \rho(\mathbf{A}_i \mathbf{x}^{k+1} - \mathbf{z}_i^{k+1}), \quad i = 1, 2, \ldots, p.$$

In the case where $\mathbf{A}$ has full column rank, step (15.30) can be written more explicitly, leading to the following representation.

ADMM, version 1 (Algorithm 1):

$$\mathbf{x}^{k+1} = \left(\sum_{i=1}^{p} \mathbf{A}_i^T \mathbf{A}_i \right)^{-1} \sum_{i=1}^{p} \mathbf{A}_i^T \left(\mathbf{z}_i^k - \frac{1}{\rho} \mathbf{y}_i^k \right),$$

$$\mathbf{z}_i^{k+1} = \mathrm{prox}_{\frac{1}{\rho} g_i} \left(\mathbf{A}_i \mathbf{x}^{k+1} + \frac{1}{\rho} \mathbf{y}_i^k \right), \quad i = 1, 2, \ldots, p,$$

$$\mathbf{y}_i^{k+1} = \mathbf{y}_i^k + \rho(\mathbf{A}_i \mathbf{x}^{k+1} - \mathbf{z}_i^{k+1}), \quad i = 1, 2, \ldots, p.$$

The second version of ADMM (Algorithm 2) is not simpler than the first version, and we will therefore not write it explicitly. AD-LPMM (Algorithm 3) invoked with the constants $\alpha = \lambda_{\max}(\sum_{i=1}^{p} \mathbf{A}_i^T \mathbf{A}_i)\rho$ and $\beta = \rho$ reads as follows (denoting $L = \lambda_{\max}(\sum_{i=1}^{p} \mathbf{A}_i^T \mathbf{A}_i)$).

AD-LPMM (Algorithm 3):

$$\mathbf{x}^{k+1} = \mathbf{x}^k - \frac{1}{L} \sum_{i=1}^{p} \mathbf{A}_i^T \left(\mathbf{A}_i \mathbf{x}^k - \mathbf{z}_i^k + \frac{1}{\rho} \mathbf{y}_i^k \right),$$

$$\mathbf{z}_i^{k+1} = \mathrm{prox}_{\frac{1}{\rho} g_i} \left(\mathbf{A}_i \mathbf{x}^{k+1} + \frac{1}{\rho} \mathbf{y}_i^k \right), \quad i = 1, 2, \ldots, p,$$

$$\mathbf{y}_i^{k+1} = \mathbf{y}_i^k + \rho(\mathbf{A}_i \mathbf{x}^{k+1} - \mathbf{z}_i^{k+1}), \quad i = 1, 2, \ldots, p. \quad \blacksquare$$

Appendix A

Strong Duality and Optimality Conditions

The following strong duality theorem is taken from [29, Proposition 6.4.4].

Theorem A.1 (strong duality theorem). *Consider the optimization problem*

$$
\begin{aligned}
f_{\text{opt}} = \quad &\min \quad f(\mathbf{x}) \\
&s.t. \quad g_i(\mathbf{x}) \le 0, \quad i = 1, 2, \dots, m, \\
&\qquad h_j(\mathbf{x}) \le 0, \quad j = 1, 2, \dots, p, \\
&\qquad s_k(\mathbf{x}) = 0, \quad k = 1, 2, \dots, q, \\
&\qquad \mathbf{x} \in X,
\end{aligned}
\tag{A.1}
$$

where $X = P \cap C$ with $P \subseteq \mathbb{E}$ being a convex polyhedral set and $C \subseteq \mathbb{E}$ convex. The functions $f, g_i, i = 1, 2, \dots, m : \mathbb{E} \to (-\infty, \infty]$ are convex, and their domains satisfy $X \subseteq \operatorname{dom}(f), X \subseteq \operatorname{dom}(g_i), i = 1, 2, \dots, m$. The functions $h_j, s_k, j = 1, 2, \dots, p, k = 1, 2, \dots, q$, are affine functions. Suppose there exist

(i) *a feasible solution $\bar{\mathbf{x}}$ satisfying $g_i(\bar{\mathbf{x}}) < 0$ for all $i = 1, 2, \dots, m$;*

(ii) *a vector satisfying all the affine constraints $h_j(\mathbf{x}) \le 0, j = 1, 2, \dots, p, s_k(\mathbf{x}) = 0, k = 1, 2, \dots, q$, and that is in $P \cap \operatorname{ri}(C)$.*

Then if problem (A.1) has a finite optimal value, then the optimal value of the dual problem

$$
q_{\text{opt}} = \max\{q(\boldsymbol{\lambda}, \boldsymbol{\eta}, \boldsymbol{\mu}) : (\boldsymbol{\lambda}, \boldsymbol{\eta}, \boldsymbol{\mu}) \in \operatorname{dom}(-q)\},
$$

where $q : \mathbb{R}^m_+ \times \mathbb{R}^p_+ \times \mathbb{R}^q \to \mathbb{R} \cup \{-\infty\}$ is given by

$$
\begin{aligned}
q(\boldsymbol{\lambda}, \boldsymbol{\eta}, \boldsymbol{\mu}) &= \min_{\mathbf{x} \in X} L(\mathbf{x}, \boldsymbol{\lambda}, \boldsymbol{\eta}, \boldsymbol{\mu}) \\
&= \min_{\mathbf{x} \in X} \left[f(\mathbf{x}) + \sum_{i=1}^m \lambda_i g_i(\mathbf{x}) + \sum_{j=1}^p \eta_j h_j(\mathbf{x}) + \sum_{k=1}^q \mu_k s_k(\mathbf{x}) \right],
\end{aligned}
$$

is attained, and the optimal values of the primal and dual problems are the same:

$$f_{\text{opt}} = q_{\text{opt}}.$$

We also recall some well-known optimality conditions expressed in terms of the Lagrangian function in cases where strong duality holds.

Theorem A.2 (optimality conditions under strong duality). *Consider the problem*

$$\min \quad f(\mathbf{x})$$

$$\text{(P)} \qquad \text{s.t.} \quad g_i(\mathbf{x}) \leq 0, i = 1, 2, \ldots, m,$$

$$h_j(\mathbf{x}) = 0, j = 1, 2, \ldots, p,$$

$$\mathbf{x} \in X,$$

where $f, g_1, g_2, \ldots, g_m, h_1, h_2, \ldots, h_p : \mathbb{E} \to (-\infty, \infty]$, *and* $X \subseteq \mathbb{E}$. *Assume that* $X \subseteq \text{dom}(f)$, $X \subseteq \text{dom}(g_i)$, *and* $X \subseteq \text{dom}(h_j)$ *for all* $i = 1, 2, \ldots, m$, $j = 1, 2, \ldots, p$. *Let* (D) *be the following dual problem:*

$$\text{(D)} \qquad \begin{array}{c} \max \quad q(\boldsymbol{\lambda}, \boldsymbol{\mu}) \\ \text{s.t.} \quad (\boldsymbol{\lambda}, \boldsymbol{\mu}) \in \text{dom}(-q), \end{array}$$

where

$$q(\boldsymbol{\lambda}, \boldsymbol{\mu}) = \min_{\mathbf{x} \in X} \left\{ L(\mathbf{x}; \boldsymbol{\lambda}, \boldsymbol{\mu}) \equiv f(\mathbf{x}) + \sum_{i=1}^{m} \lambda_i g_i(\mathbf{x}) + \sum_{j=1}^{p} \mu_j h_j(\mathbf{x}) \right\},$$

$$\text{dom}(-q) = \{ (\boldsymbol{\lambda}, \boldsymbol{\mu}) \in \mathbb{R}_+^m \times \mathbb{R}^p : q(\boldsymbol{\lambda}, \boldsymbol{\mu}) > -\infty \}.$$

Suppose that the optimal value of problem (P) *is finite and equal to the optimal value of problem* (D). *Then* $\mathbf{x}^*, (\boldsymbol{\lambda}^*, \boldsymbol{\mu}^*)$ *are optimal solutions of problems* (P) *and* (D), *respectively, if and only if*

(i) $\mathbf{x}^*$ *is a feasible solution of (P);*

(ii) $\boldsymbol{\lambda}^* \geq \mathbf{0};$

(iii) $\lambda_i^* g_i(\mathbf{x}^*) = 0, i = 1, 2, \ldots, m;$

(iv) $\mathbf{x}^* \in \text{argmin}_{\mathbf{x} \in X} L(\mathbf{x}; \boldsymbol{\lambda}^*, \boldsymbol{\mu}^*).$

Proof. Denote the optimal values of problem (P) and (D) by f_{opt} and q_{opt}, respectively. An underlying assumption of the theorem is that $f_{\text{opt}} = q_{\text{opt}}$. If $\mathbf{x}^*$ and $(\boldsymbol{\lambda}^*, \boldsymbol{\mu}^*)$ are the optimal solutions of problems (P) and (D), then obviously (i) and

(ii) are satisfied. In addition,

$$
\begin{aligned}
f_{\mathrm{opt}} = q_{\mathrm{opt}} &= q(\boldsymbol{\lambda}^*, \boldsymbol{\mu}^*) \\
&= \min_{\mathbf{x} \in X} L(\mathbf{x}, \boldsymbol{\lambda}^*, \boldsymbol{\mu}^*) \\
&\le L(\mathbf{x}^*, \boldsymbol{\lambda}^*, \boldsymbol{\mu}^*) \\
&= f(\mathbf{x}^*) + \sum_{i=1}^{m} \lambda_i^* g_i(\mathbf{x}^*) + \sum_{j=1}^{p} \mu_j^* h_j(\mathbf{x}^*) \\
&\le f(\mathbf{x}^*),
\end{aligned}
$$

where the last inequality follows by the facts that $h_j(\mathbf{x}^*) = 0$, $\lambda_i^* \ge 0$, and $g_i(\mathbf{x}^*) \le 0$. Since $f_{\mathrm{opt}} = f(\mathbf{x}^*)$, all of the inequalities in the above chain of equalities and inequalities are actually equalities. This implies in particular that $\mathbf{x}^* \in \operatorname{argmin}_{\mathbf{x} \in X} L(\mathbf{x}, \boldsymbol{\lambda}^*, \boldsymbol{\mu}^*)$, meaning property (iv), and that $\sum_{i=1}^{m} \lambda_i^* g_i(\mathbf{x}^*) = 0$, which by the fact that $\lambda_i^* g_i(\mathbf{x}^*) \le 0$ for any i, implies that $\lambda_i^* g_i(\mathbf{x}^*) = 0$ for any i, showing the validity of property (iii).

To prove the reverse direction, assume that properties (i)–(iv) are satisfied. Then

$$
\begin{aligned}
q(\boldsymbol{\lambda}^*, \boldsymbol{\mu}^*) \quad &= \min_{\mathbf{x} \in X} L(\mathbf{x}, \boldsymbol{\lambda}^*, \boldsymbol{\mu}^*) && \text{[definition of } q] \\
&= L(\mathbf{x}^*, \boldsymbol{\lambda}^*, \boldsymbol{\mu}^*) && \text{[property (iv)]} \\
&= f(\mathbf{x}^*) + \sum_{i=1}^{m} \lambda_i^* g_i(\mathbf{x}^*) + \sum_{j=1}^{p} \mu_j^* h_j(\mathbf{x}^*) \\
&= f(\mathbf{x}^*). && \text{[property (iii)]}
\end{aligned}
$$

By the weak duality theorem, since $\mathbf{x}^*$ and $(\boldsymbol{\lambda}^*, \boldsymbol{\mu}^*)$ are primal and dual feasible solutions with equal primal and dual objective functions, it follows that they are the optimal solutions of their corresponding problems. □

Appendix B

Tables

Support Functions

C	$\sigma_C(\mathbf{y})$	Assumptions	Reference
$\{\mathbf{b}_1, \mathbf{b}_2, \ldots, \mathbf{b}_n\}$	$\max_{i=1,2,\ldots,n}\langle \mathbf{b}_i, \mathbf{y}\rangle$	$\mathbf{b}_i \in \mathbb{E}$	Example 2.25
K	$\delta_{K^\circ}(\mathbf{y})$	K – cone	Example 2.26
$\mathbb{R}^n_+$	$\delta_{\mathbb{R}^n_-}(\mathbf{y})$	$\mathbb{E} = \mathbb{R}^n$	Example 2.27
Δ_n	$\max\{y_1, y_2, \ldots, y_n\}$	$\mathbb{E} = \mathbb{R}^n$	Example 2.36
$\{\mathbf{x} \in \mathbb{R}^n : \mathbf{Ax} \leq \mathbf{0}\}$	$\delta_{\{\mathbf{A}^T\boldsymbol{\lambda}:\boldsymbol{\lambda}\in\mathbb{R}^m_+\}}(\mathbf{y})$	$\mathbb{E} = \mathbb{R}^n,\ \mathbf{A} \in \mathbb{R}^{m\times n}$	Example 2.29
$\{\mathbf{x} \in \mathbb{R}^n : \mathbf{Bx} = \mathbf{b}\}$	$\langle \mathbf{y}, \mathbf{x}_0\rangle + \delta_{\mathrm{Range}(\mathbf{B}^T)}(\mathbf{y})$	$\mathbb{E} = \mathbb{R}^n,\ \mathbf{B} \in \mathbb{R}^{m\times n},\ \mathbf{b} \in \mathbb{R}^m,\ \mathbf{Bx}_0 = \mathbf{b}$	Example 2.30
$B_{\|\cdot\|}[\mathbf{0}, 1]$	$\|\mathbf{y}\|_*$	-	Example 2.31

Weak Subdifferential Results

Function	Weak result	Setting	Reference
$-q$ = negative dual function	$-\mathbf{g}(\mathbf{x}_0) \in \partial(-q)(\boldsymbol{\lambda}_0)$	$q(\boldsymbol{\lambda}) = \min_{\mathbf{x}\in X} f(\mathbf{x}) + \boldsymbol{\lambda}^T\mathbf{g}(\mathbf{x})$, $f: \mathbb{E} \to \mathbb{R}$, $\mathbf{g}: \mathbb{E} \to \mathbb{R}^m$, $\mathbf{x}_0 = $ a minimizer of $f(\mathbf{x}) + \boldsymbol{\lambda}_0^T\mathbf{g}(\mathbf{x})$ over X	Example 3.7
$f(\mathbf{X}) = \lambda_{\max}(\mathbf{X})$	$\mathbf{vv}^T \in \partial f(\mathbf{X})$	$f: \mathbb{S}^n \to \mathbb{R}$, $\mathbf{v} = $ normalized maximum eigenvector of $X \in \mathbb{S}^n$	Example 3.8
$f(\mathbf{x}) = \|\mathbf{x}\|_1$	$\mathrm{sgn}(\mathbf{x}) \in \partial f(\mathbf{x})$	$\mathbb{E} = \mathbb{R}^n$	Example 3.42
$f(\mathbf{x}) = \lambda_{\max}(\mathbf{A}_0 + \sum_{i=1}^m x_i\mathbf{A}_i)$	$(\tilde{\mathbf{y}}^T\mathbf{A}_i\tilde{\mathbf{y}})_{i=1}^m \in \partial f(\mathbf{x})$	$\tilde{\mathbf{y}} = $ normalized maximum eigenvector of $\mathbf{A}_0 + \sum_{i=1}^m x_i\mathbf{A}_i$	Example 3.56

Strong Subdifferential Results

$f(\mathbf{x})$	$\partial f(\mathbf{x})$	Assumptions	Reference
$\|\mathbf{x}\|$	$B_{\|\cdot\|_*}[\mathbf{0}, 1]$	$\mathbf{x} = \mathbf{0}$	Example 3.3
$\|\mathbf{x}\|_1$	$\left\{ \sum_{i \in I_{\neq}(\mathbf{x})} \mathrm{sgn}(x_i)\mathbf{e}_i + \sum_{i \in I_0(\mathbf{x})} [-\mathbf{e}_i, \mathbf{e}_i] \right\}$	$\mathbb{E} = \mathbb{R}^n$, $I_{\neq}(\mathbf{x}) = \{i \;:\; x_i \neq 0\}$, $I_0(\mathbf{x}) = \{i \;:\; x_i = 0\}$.	Example 3.41
$\|\mathbf{x}\|_2$	$\begin{cases} \left\{ \frac{\mathbf{x}}{\|\mathbf{x}\|_2} \right\}, & \mathbf{x} \neq \mathbf{0}, \\ B_{\|\cdot\|_2}[\mathbf{0}, 1], & \mathbf{x} = \mathbf{0}. \end{cases}$	$\mathbb{E} = \mathbb{R}^n$	Example 3.34
$\|\mathbf{x}\|_\infty$	$\left\{ \sum_{i \in I(\mathbf{x})} \lambda_i \mathrm{sgn}(x_i)\mathbf{e}_i \;:\; \begin{array}{c} \sum_{i \in I(\mathbf{x})} \lambda_i = 1 \\ \lambda_i \geq 0 \end{array} \right\}$	$\mathbb{E} = \mathbb{R}^n$, $I(\mathbf{x}) = \{i : \|\mathbf{x}\|_\infty = |x_i|\}$, $\mathbf{x} \neq \mathbf{0}$	Example 3.52
$\max(\mathbf{x})$	$\left\{ \sum_{i \in I(\mathbf{x})} \lambda_i \mathbf{e}_i \;:\; \sum_{i \in I(\mathbf{x})} \lambda_i = 1, \lambda_i \geq 0 \right\}$	$\mathbb{E} = \mathbb{R}^n$, $I(\mathbf{x}) = \{i : \max(\mathbf{x}) = x_i\}$	Example 3.51
$\max(\mathbf{x})$	Δ_n	$\mathbb{E} = \mathbb{R}^n$, $\mathbf{x} = \alpha\mathbf{e}$ for some $\alpha \in \mathbb{R}$	Example 3.51
$\delta_S(\mathbf{x})$	$N_S(\mathbf{x})$	$\emptyset \neq S \subseteq \mathbb{E}$	Example 3.5
$\delta_{B[\mathbf{0},1]}(\mathbf{x})$	$\begin{cases} \{\mathbf{y} \in \mathbb{E}^* : \|\mathbf{y}\|_* \leq \langle \mathbf{y}, \mathbf{x} \rangle\}, & \|\mathbf{x}\| \leq 1, \\ \emptyset, & \|\mathbf{x}\| > 1. \end{cases}$		Example 3.6
$\|\mathbf{A}\mathbf{x} + \mathbf{b}\|_1$	$\sum_{i \in I_{\neq}(\mathbf{x})} \mathrm{sgn}(\mathbf{a}_i^T\mathbf{x} + b_i)\mathbf{a}_i + \sum_{i \in I_0(\mathbf{x})} [-\mathbf{a}_i, \mathbf{a}_i]$	$\mathbb{E} = \mathbb{R}^n$, $\mathbf{A} \in \mathbb{R}^{m \times n}$, $\mathbf{b} \in \mathbb{R}^m$, $I_{\neq}(\mathbf{x}) = \{i : \mathbf{a}_i^T\mathbf{x} + b_i \neq 0\}$, $I_0(\mathbf{x}) = \{i : \mathbf{a}_i^T\mathbf{x} + b_i = 0\}$	Example 3.44
$\|\mathbf{A}\mathbf{x} + \mathbf{b}\|_2$	$\begin{cases} \frac{\mathbf{A}^T(\mathbf{A}\mathbf{x}+\mathbf{b})}{\|\mathbf{A}\mathbf{x}+\mathbf{b}\|_2}, & \mathbf{A}\mathbf{x} + \mathbf{b} \neq \mathbf{0}, \\ \mathbf{A}^T B_{\|\cdot\|_2}[\mathbf{0}, 1], & \mathbf{A}\mathbf{x} + \mathbf{b} = \mathbf{0}. \end{cases}$	$\mathbb{E} = \mathbb{R}^n$, $\mathbf{A} \in \mathbb{R}^{m \times n}$, $\mathbf{b} \in \mathbb{R}^m$	Example 3.45
$\|\mathbf{A}\mathbf{x} + \mathbf{b}\|_\infty$	$\left\{ \sum_{i \in I_{\mathbf{x}}} \lambda_i \mathrm{sgn}(\mathbf{a}_i^T\mathbf{x} + b_i)\mathbf{a}_i \;:\; \begin{array}{c} \sum_{i \in I_{\mathbf{x}}} \lambda_i = 1 \\ \lambda_i \geq 0 \end{array} \right\}$	$\mathbb{E} = \mathbb{R}^n$, $\mathbf{A} \in \mathbb{R}^{m \times n}$, $\mathbf{b} \in \mathbb{R}^m$, $I_{\mathbf{x}} = \{i : \|\mathbf{A}\mathbf{x} + \mathbf{b}\|_\infty = |\mathbf{a}_i^T\mathbf{x} + b_i|\}$, $\mathbf{A}\mathbf{x} + \mathbf{b} \neq \mathbf{0}$	Example 3.54
$\|\mathbf{A}\mathbf{x} + \mathbf{b}\|_\infty$	$\mathbf{A}^T B_{\|\cdot\|_1}[\mathbf{0}, 1]$	same as above but with $\mathbf{A}\mathbf{x} + \mathbf{b} = \mathbf{0}$	Example 3.54
$\max_i\{\mathbf{a}_i^T\mathbf{x} + b\}$	$\left\{ \sum_{i \in I(\mathbf{x})} \lambda_i \mathbf{a}_i \;:\; \sum_{i \in I(\mathbf{x})} \lambda_i = 1, \lambda_i \geq 0 \right\}$	$\mathbb{E} = \mathbb{R}^n$, $\mathbf{a}_i \in \mathbb{R}^n$, $b_i \in \mathbb{R}$, $I(\mathbf{x}) = \{i : f(\mathbf{x}) = \mathbf{a}_i^T\mathbf{x} + b_i\}$	Example 3.53
$\frac{1}{2}d_C(\mathbf{x})^2$	$\{\mathbf{x} - P_C(\mathbf{x})\}$	C = nonempty closed and convex, $\mathbb{E}$ = Euclidean	Example 3.31
$d_C(\mathbf{x})$	$\begin{cases} \left\{ \frac{\mathbf{x} - P_C(\mathbf{x})}{d_C(\mathbf{x})} \right\}, & \mathbf{x} \notin C, \\ N_C(\mathbf{x}) \cap B[\mathbf{0}, 1] & \mathbf{x} \in C. \end{cases}$	C = nonempty closed and convex, $\mathbb{E}$ = Euclidean	Example 3.49

Conjugate Calculus Rules

$g(\mathbf{x})$	$g^*(\mathbf{y})$	Reference
$\sum_{i=1}^m f_i(\mathbf{x}_i)$	$\sum_{i=1}^m f_i^*(\mathbf{y}_i)$	Theorem 4.12
$\alpha f(\mathbf{x})\ (\alpha > 0)$	$\alpha f^*(\mathbf{y}/\alpha)$	Theorem 4.14
$\alpha f(\mathbf{x}/\alpha)\ (\alpha > 0)$	$\alpha f^*(\mathbf{y})$	Theorem 4.14
$f(\mathcal{A}(\mathbf{x}-\mathbf{a})) + \langle \mathbf{b}, \mathbf{x}\rangle + c$	$f^*\left((\mathcal{A}^T)^{-1}(\mathbf{y}-\mathbf{b})\right) + \langle \mathbf{a}, \mathbf{y}\rangle - c - \langle \mathbf{a}, \mathbf{b}\rangle$	Theorem 4.13

Conjugate Functions

f	$\mathrm{dom}(f)$	f^*	Assumptions	Reference
e^x	$\mathbb{R}$	$y\log y - y\ (\mathrm{dom}(f^*) = \mathbb{R}_+)$	–	Section 4.4.1
$-\log x$	$\mathbb{R}_{++}$	$-1 - \log(-y)\ (\mathrm{dom}(f^*) = \mathbb{R}_{--})$	–	Section 4.4.2
$\max\{1-x, 0\}$	$\mathbb{R}$	$y + \delta_{[-1,0]}(y)$	–	Section 4.4.3
$\frac{1}{p}\lvert x\rvert^p$	$\mathbb{R}$	$\frac{1}{q}\lvert y\rvert^q$	$p > 1, \frac{1}{p} + \frac{1}{q} = 1$	Section 4.4.4
$-\frac{x^p}{p}$	$\mathbb{R}_+$	$-\frac{(-y)^q}{q}\ (\mathrm{dom}(f^*) = \mathbb{R}_{--})$	$0 < p < 1, \frac{1}{p} + \frac{1}{q} = 1$	Section 4.4.5
$\frac{1}{2}\mathbf{x}^T\mathbf{A}\mathbf{x} + \mathbf{b}^T\mathbf{x} + c$	$\mathbb{R}^n$	$\frac{1}{2}(\mathbf{y}-\mathbf{b})^T\mathbf{A}^{-1}(\mathbf{y}-\mathbf{b}) - c$	$\mathbf{A} \in \mathbb{S}_{++}^n,\ \mathbf{b} \in \mathbb{R}^n, c \in \mathbb{R}$	Section 4.4.6
$\frac{1}{2}\mathbf{x}^T\mathbf{A}\mathbf{x} + \mathbf{b}^T\mathbf{x} + c$	$\mathbb{R}^n$	$\frac{1}{2}(\mathbf{y}-\mathbf{b})^T\mathbf{A}^\dagger(\mathbf{y}-\mathbf{b}) - c$ $(\mathrm{dom}(f^*) = \mathbf{b} + \mathrm{Range}(\mathbf{A}))$	$\mathbf{A} \in \mathbb{S}_+^n,\ \mathbf{b} \in \mathbb{R}^n, c \in \mathbb{R}$	Section 4.4.7
$\sum_{i=1}^n x_i \log x_i$	$\mathbb{R}_+^n$	$\sum_{i=1}^n e^{y_i - 1}$	–	Section 4.4.8
$\sum_{i=1}^n x_i \log x_i$	Δ_n	$\log\left(\sum_{i=1}^n e^{y_i}\right)$	–	Section 4.4.10
$-\sum_{i=1}^n \log x_i$	$\mathbb{R}_{++}^n$	$-n - \sum_{i=1}^n \log(-y_i)$ $(\mathrm{dom}(f^*) = \mathbb{R}_{--}^n)$	–	Section 4.4.9
$\log\left(\sum_{i=1}^n e^{x_i}\right)$	$\mathbb{R}^n$	$\sum_{i=1}^n y_i \log y_i$ $(\mathrm{dom}(f^*) = \Delta_n)$	–	Section 4.4.11
$\max_i\{x_i\}$	$\mathbb{R}^n$	$\delta_{\Delta_n}(\mathbf{y})$	–	Example 4.10
$\delta_C(\mathbf{x})$	C	$\sigma_C(\mathbf{y})$	$\emptyset \neq C \subseteq \mathbb{E}$	Example 4.2
$\sigma_C(\mathbf{x})$	$\mathrm{dom}(\sigma_C)$	$\delta_{\mathrm{cl}(\mathrm{conv}(C))}(\mathbf{y})$	$\emptyset \neq C \subseteq \mathbb{E}$	Example 4.9
$\lVert \mathbf{x}\rVert$	$\mathbb{E}$	$\delta_{B_{\lVert\cdot\rVert_*}[\mathbf{0},1]}(\mathbf{y})$	–	Section 4.4.12
$-\sqrt{\alpha^2 - \lVert\mathbf{x}\rVert^2}$	$B[\mathbf{0},\alpha]$	$\alpha\sqrt{\lVert\mathbf{y}\rVert_*^2 + 1}$	$\alpha > 0$	Section 4.4.13
$\sqrt{\alpha^2 + \lVert\mathbf{x}\rVert^2}$	$\mathbb{E}$	$-\alpha\sqrt{1 - \lVert\mathbf{y}\rVert_*^2}$ $(\mathrm{dom}f^* = B_{\lVert\cdot\rVert_*}[\mathbf{0},1])$	$\alpha > 0$	Section 4.4.14
$\frac{1}{2}\lVert\mathbf{x}\rVert^2$	$\mathbb{E}$	$\frac{1}{2}\lVert\mathbf{y}\rVert_*^2$	–	Section 4.4.15
$\frac{1}{2}\lVert\mathbf{x}\rVert^2 + \delta_C(\mathbf{x})$	C	$\frac{1}{2}\lVert\mathbf{y}\rVert^2 - \frac{1}{2}d_C^2(\mathbf{y})$	$\emptyset \neq C \subseteq \mathbb{E}, \mathbb{E}$ Euclidean	Example 4.4
$\frac{1}{2}\lVert\mathbf{x}\rVert^2 - \frac{1}{2}d_C^2(\mathbf{x})$	$\mathbb{E}$	$\frac{1}{2}\lVert\mathbf{y}\rVert^2 + \delta_C(\mathbf{y})$	$\emptyset \neq C \subseteq \mathbb{E}$ closed convex. $\mathbb{E}$ Euclidean	Example 4.11

Conjugates of Symmetric Spectral Functions over $\mathbb{S}^n$ (from Example 7.16)

$g(\mathbf{X})$	$\operatorname{dom}(g)$	$g^*(\mathbf{Y})$	$\operatorname{dom}(g^*)$
$\lambda_{\max}(\mathbf{X})$	$\mathbb{S}^n$	$\delta_{\Upsilon_n}(\mathbf{Y})$	Υ_n
$\alpha\|\mathbf{X}\|_F \ (\alpha > 0)$	$\mathbb{S}^n$	$\delta_{B_{\|\cdot\|_F}[0,\alpha]}(\mathbf{Y})$	$B_{\|\cdot\|_F}[0,\alpha]$
$\alpha\|\mathbf{X}\|_F^2 \ (\alpha > 0)$	$\mathbb{S}^n$	$\frac{1}{4\alpha}\|\mathbf{Y}\|_F^2$	$\mathbb{S}^n$
$\alpha\|\mathbf{X}\|_{2,2} \ (\alpha > 0)$	$\mathbb{S}^n$	$\delta_{B_{\|\cdot\|_{S_1}}[0,\alpha]}(\mathbf{Y})$	$B_{\|\cdot\|_{S_1}}[0,\alpha]$
$\alpha\|\mathbf{X}\|_{S_1} \ (\alpha > 0)$	$\mathbb{S}^n$	$\delta_{B_{\|\cdot\|_{2,2}}[0,\alpha]}(\mathbf{Y})$	$B_{\|\cdot\|_{2,2}}[0,\alpha]$
$-\log\det(\mathbf{X})$	$\mathbb{S}_{++}^n$	$-n-\log\det(-\mathbf{Y})$	$\mathbb{S}_{--}^n$
$\sum_{i=1}^n \lambda_i(\mathbf{X})\log(\lambda_i(\mathbf{X}))$	$\mathbb{S}_+^n$	$\sum_{i=1}^n e^{\lambda_i(\mathbf{Y})-1}$	$\mathbb{S}^n$
$\sum_{i=1}^n \lambda_i(\mathbf{X})\log(\lambda_i(\mathbf{X}))$	Υ_n	$\log\left(\sum_{i=1}^n e^{\lambda_i(\mathbf{Y})}\right)$	$\mathbb{S}^n$

Conjugates of Symmetric Spectral Functions over $\mathbb{R}^{m\times n}$ (from Example 7.27)

$g(\mathbf{X})$	$\operatorname{dom}(g)$	$g^*(\mathbf{Y})$	$\operatorname{dom}(g^*)$
$\alpha\sigma_1(\mathbf{X}) \ (\alpha > 0)$	$\mathbb{R}^{m\times n}$	$\delta_{B_{\|\cdot\|_{S_1}}[0,\alpha]}(\mathbf{Y})$	$B_{\|\cdot\|_{S_1}}[0,\alpha]$
$\alpha\|\mathbf{X}\|_F \ (\alpha > 0)$	$\mathbb{R}^{m\times n}$	$\delta_{B_{\|\cdot\|_F}[0,\alpha]}(\mathbf{Y})$	$B_{\|\cdot\|_F}[0,\alpha]$
$\alpha\|\mathbf{X}\|_F^2 \ (\alpha > 0)$	$\mathbb{R}^{m\times n}$	$\frac{1}{4\alpha}\|\mathbf{Y}\|_F^2$	$\mathbb{R}^{m\times n}$
$\alpha\|\mathbf{X}\|_{S_1} \ (\alpha > 0)$	$\mathbb{R}^{m\times n}$	$\delta_{B_{\|\cdot\|_{S_\infty}}[0,\alpha]}(\mathbf{Y})$	$B_{\|\cdot\|_{S_\infty}}[0,\alpha]$

Smooth Functions

$f(\mathbf{x})$	$\operatorname{dom}(f)$	Parameter	Norm	Reference
$\frac{1}{2}\mathbf{x}^T\mathbf{A}\mathbf{x} + \mathbf{b}^T\mathbf{x} + c$ $(\mathbf{A}\in\mathbb{S}^n, \mathbf{b}\in\mathbb{R}^n, c\in\mathbb{R})$	$\mathbb{R}^n$	$\|\mathbf{A}\|_{p,q}$	l_p	Example 5.2
$\langle\mathbf{b},\mathbf{x}\rangle + c$ $(\mathbf{b}\in\mathbb{E}^*, c\in\mathbb{R})$	$\mathbb{E}$	0	any norm	Example 5.3
$\frac{1}{2}\|\mathbf{x}\|_p^2, \ p\in[2,\infty)$	$\mathbb{R}^n$	$p-1$	l_p	Example 5.11
$\sqrt{1+\|\mathbf{x}\|_2^2}$	$\mathbb{R}^n$	1	l_2	Example 5.14
$\log(\sum_{i=1}^n e^{x_i})$	$\mathbb{R}^n$	1	l_2, l_∞	Example 5.15
$\frac{1}{2}d_C^2(\mathbf{x})$ $(\emptyset \neq C \subseteq \mathbb{E} \text{ closed convex})$	$\mathbb{E}$	1	Euclidean	Example 5.5
$\frac{1}{2}\|\mathbf{x}\|^2 - \frac{1}{2}d_C^2(\mathbf{x})$ $(\emptyset \neq C \subseteq \mathbb{E} \text{ closed convex})$	$\mathbb{E}$	1	Euclidean	Example 5.6
$H_\mu(\mathbf{x}) \ (\mu > 0)$	$\mathbb{E}$	$\frac{1}{\mu}$	Euclidean	Example 6.62

Strongly Convex Functions

$f(\mathbf{x})$	$\text{dom}(f)$	Strongly convex parameter	Norm	Reference
$\frac{1}{2}\mathbf{x}^T\mathbf{A}\mathbf{x} + 2\mathbf{b}^T\mathbf{x} + c$ ($\mathbf{A} \in \mathbb{S}^n_{++}, \mathbf{b} \in \mathbb{R}^n, c \in \mathbb{R}$)	$\mathbb{R}^n$	$\lambda_{\min}(\mathbf{A})$	l_2	Example 5.19
$\frac{1}{2}\|\mathbf{x}\|^2 + \delta_C(\mathbf{x})$ ($\emptyset \neq C \subseteq \mathbb{E}$ convex)	C	1	Euclidean	Example 5.21
$-\sqrt{1 - \|\mathbf{x}\|_2^2}$	$B_{\|\cdot\|_2}[\mathbf{0}, 1]$	1	l_2	Example 5.29
$\frac{1}{2}\|\mathbf{x}\|_p^2 \;\; (p \in (1, 2])$	$\mathbb{R}^n$	$p - 1$	l_p	Example 5.28
$\sum_{i=1}^n x_i \log x_i$	Δ_n	1	l_2 or l_1	Example 5.27

Orthogonal Projections

Set (C)	$P_C(\mathbf{x})$	Assumptions	Reference
$\mathbb{R}^n_+$	$[\mathbf{x}]_+$	$-$	Lemma 6.26
$\text{Box}[\boldsymbol{\ell}, \mathbf{u}]$	$P_C(\mathbf{x})_i = \min\{\max\{x_i, \ell_i\}, u_i\}$	$\ell_i \leq u_i$	Lemma 6.26
$B_{\|\cdot\|_2}[\mathbf{c}, r]$	$\mathbf{c} + \frac{r}{\max\{\|\mathbf{x}-\mathbf{c}\|_2, r\}}(\mathbf{x} - \mathbf{c})$	$\mathbf{c} \in \mathbb{R}^n, r > 0$	Lemma 6.26
$\{\mathbf{x} : \mathbf{A}\mathbf{x} = \mathbf{b}\}$	$\mathbf{x} - \mathbf{A}^T(\mathbf{A}\mathbf{A}^T)^{-1}(\mathbf{A}\mathbf{x} - \mathbf{b})$	$\mathbf{A} \in \mathbb{R}^{m \times n}$, $\mathbf{b} \in \mathbb{R}^m$, $\mathbf{A}$ full row rank	Lemma 6.26
$\{\mathbf{x} : \mathbf{a}^T\mathbf{x} \leq b\}$	$\mathbf{x} - \frac{[\mathbf{a}^T\mathbf{x} - b]_+}{\|\mathbf{a}\|^2}\mathbf{a}$	$\mathbf{0} \neq \mathbf{a} \in \mathbb{R}^n, b \in \mathbb{R}$	Lemma 6.26
Δ_n	$[\mathbf{x} - \mu^*\mathbf{e}]_+$ where $\mu^* \in \mathbb{R}$ satisfies $\mathbf{e}^T[\mathbf{x} - \mu^*\mathbf{e}]_+ = 1$		Corollary 6.29
$H_{\mathbf{a},b} \cap \text{Box}[\boldsymbol{\ell}, \mathbf{u}]$	$P_{\text{Box}[\boldsymbol{\ell},\mathbf{u}]}(\mathbf{x} - \mu^*\mathbf{a})$ where $\mu^* \in \mathbb{R}$ satisfies $\mathbf{a}^T P_{\text{Box}[\boldsymbol{\ell},\mathbf{u}]}(\mathbf{x} - \mu^*\mathbf{a}) = b$	$\mathbf{a} \in \mathbb{R}^n\backslash\{\mathbf{0}\}, b \in \mathbb{R}$	Theorem 6.27
$H^-_{\mathbf{a},b} \cap \text{Box}[\boldsymbol{\ell}, \mathbf{u}]$	$\begin{cases} P_{\text{Box}[\boldsymbol{\ell},\mathbf{u}]}(\mathbf{x}), & \mathbf{a}^T\mathbf{v_x} \leq b, \\ P_{\text{Box}[\boldsymbol{\ell},\mathbf{u}]}(\mathbf{x} - \lambda^*\mathbf{a}), & \mathbf{a}^T\mathbf{v_x} > b, \end{cases}$ $\mathbf{v_x} = P_{\text{Box}[\boldsymbol{\ell},\mathbf{u}]}(\mathbf{x}), \mathbf{a}^T P_{\text{Box}[\boldsymbol{\ell},\mathbf{u}]}(\mathbf{x} - \lambda^*\mathbf{a}) = b, \lambda^* > 0$	$\mathbf{a} \in \mathbb{R}^n\backslash\{\mathbf{0}\}, b \in \mathbb{R}$	Example 6.32
$B_{\|\cdot\|_1}[\mathbf{0}, \alpha]$	$\begin{cases} \mathbf{x}, & \|\mathbf{x}\|_1 \leq \alpha, \\ \mathcal{T}_{\lambda^*}(\mathbf{x}), & \|\mathbf{x}\|_1 > \alpha, \end{cases}$ $\|\mathcal{T}_{\lambda^*}(\mathbf{x})\|_1 = \alpha, \lambda^* > 0$	$\alpha > 0$	Example 6.33
$\{\mathbf{x} : \boldsymbol{\omega}^T\|\mathbf{x}\| \leq \beta,$ $-\boldsymbol{\alpha} \leq \mathbf{x} \leq \boldsymbol{\alpha}\}$	$\begin{cases} \mathbf{v_x}, & \boldsymbol{\omega}^T\|\mathbf{v_x}\| \leq \beta, \\ \mathcal{S}_{\lambda^*\boldsymbol{\omega},\boldsymbol{\alpha}}(\mathbf{x}), & \boldsymbol{\omega}^T\|\mathbf{v_x}\| > \beta, \end{cases}$ $\mathbf{v_x} = P_{\text{Box}[-\boldsymbol{\alpha},\boldsymbol{\alpha}]}(\mathbf{x}),$ $\boldsymbol{\omega}^T\|\mathcal{S}_{\lambda^*\boldsymbol{\omega},\boldsymbol{\alpha}}(\mathbf{x})\| = \beta, \lambda^* > 0$	$\boldsymbol{\omega} \in \mathbb{R}^n_+,\; \boldsymbol{\alpha} \in [0,\infty]^n,\; \beta \in \mathbb{R}_{++}$	Example 6.34
$\{\mathbf{x} > \mathbf{0} : \Pi x_i \geq \alpha\}$	$\begin{cases} \mathbf{x}, & \mathbf{x} \in C, \\ \left(\frac{x_j + \sqrt{x_j^2 + 4\lambda^*}}{2}\right)^n_{j=1}, & \mathbf{x} \notin C, \end{cases}$ $\Pi_{j=1}^n\left((x_j + \sqrt{x_j^2 + 4\lambda^*})/2\right) = \alpha, \lambda^* > 0$	$\alpha > 0$	Example 6.35
$\{(\mathbf{x}, s) : \|\mathbf{x}\|_2 \leq s\}$	$\begin{cases} \left(\frac{\|\mathbf{x}\|_2 + s}{2\|\mathbf{x}\|_2}\mathbf{x}, \frac{\|\mathbf{x}\|_2 + s}{2}\right) & \text{if } \|\mathbf{x}\|_2 \geq |s| \\ (\mathbf{0}, 0) \text{ if } s < \|\mathbf{x}\|_2 < -s, \\ (\mathbf{x}, s) \text{ if } \|\mathbf{x}\|_2 \leq s. \end{cases}$	$-$	Example 6.37
$\{(\mathbf{x}, s) : \|\mathbf{x}\|_1 \leq s\}$	$\begin{cases} (\mathbf{x}, s), & \|\mathbf{x}\|_1 \leq s, \\ (\mathcal{T}_{\lambda^*}(\mathbf{x}), s + \lambda^*), & \|\mathbf{x}\|_1 > s, \end{cases}$ $\|\mathcal{T}_{\lambda^*}(\mathbf{x})\|_1 - \lambda^* - s = 0, \lambda^* > 0$	$-$	Example 6.38

Orthogonal Projections onto Symmetric Spectral Sets in $\mathbb{S}^n$

set (T)	$P_T(\mathbf{X})$	Assumptions
$\mathbb{S}^n_+$	$\mathbf{U}\text{diag}([\boldsymbol{\lambda}(\mathbf{X})]_+)\mathbf{U}^T$	$-$
$\{\mathbf{X}:\ell\mathbf{I}\preceq\mathbf{X}\preceq u\mathbf{I}\}$	$\mathbf{U}\text{diag}(\mathbf{v})\mathbf{U}^T,$ $v_i=\min\{\max\{\lambda_i(\mathbf{X}),\ell\},u\}$	$\ell\le u$
$B_{\|\cdot\|_F}[\mathbf{0},r]$	$\frac{r}{\max\{\|\mathbf{X}\|_F,r\}}\mathbf{X}$	$r>0$
$\{\mathbf{X}:\text{Tr}(\mathbf{X})\le b\}$	$\mathbf{U}\text{diag}(\mathbf{v})\mathbf{U}^T,\ \mathbf{v}=\boldsymbol{\lambda}(\mathbf{X})-\frac{[\mathbf{e}^T\boldsymbol{\lambda}(\mathbf{X})-b]_+}{n}\mathbf{e}$	$b\in\mathbb{R}$
Υ_n	$\mathbf{U}\text{diag}(\mathbf{v})\mathbf{U}^T,\ \mathbf{v}=[\boldsymbol{\lambda}(\mathbf{X})-\mu^*\mathbf{e}]_+$ where $\mu^*\in\mathbb{R}$ satisfies $\mathbf{e}^T[\boldsymbol{\lambda}(\mathbf{X})-\mu^*\mathbf{e}]_+=1$	$-$
$B_{\|\cdot\|_{S_1}}[\mathbf{0},\alpha]$	$\begin{cases}\mathbf{X}, & \|\mathbf{X}\|_{S_1}\le\alpha,\\ \mathbf{U}\text{diag}(\mathcal{T}_{\beta^*}(\boldsymbol{\lambda}(\mathbf{X})))\mathbf{U}^T, & \|\mathbf{X}\|_{S_1}>\alpha,\\ \|\mathcal{T}_{\beta^*}(\boldsymbol{\lambda}(\mathbf{X}))\|_1=\alpha,\ \beta^*>0\end{cases}$	$\alpha>0$

Orthogonal Projections onto Symmetric Spectral Sets in $\mathbb{R}^{m\times n}$ (from Example 7.31)

set (T)	$P_T(\mathbf{X})$	Assumptions
$B_{\|\cdot\|_{S_\infty}}[\mathbf{0},\alpha]$	$\mathbf{U}\text{diag}(\mathbf{v})\mathbf{V}^T,\ v_i=\min\{\sigma_i(\mathbf{X}),\alpha\}$	$\alpha>0$
$B_{\|\cdot\|_F}[\mathbf{0},r]$	$\frac{r}{\max\{\|\mathbf{X}\|_F,r\}}\mathbf{X}$	$r>0$
$B_{\|\cdot\|_{S_1}}[\mathbf{0},\alpha]$	$\begin{cases}\mathbf{X}, & \|\mathbf{X}\|_{S_1}\le\alpha,\\ \mathbf{U}\text{diag}(\mathcal{T}_{\beta^*}(\boldsymbol{\sigma}(\mathbf{X})))\mathbf{V}^T, & \|\mathbf{X}\|_{S_1}>\alpha,\\ \|\mathcal{T}_{\beta^*}(\boldsymbol{\sigma}(\mathbf{X}))\|_1=\alpha,\ \beta^*>0\end{cases}$	$\alpha>0$

Prox Calculus Rules

$f(\mathbf{x})$	$\text{prox}_f(\mathbf{x})$	Assumptions	Reference
$\sum_{i=1}^m f_i(\mathbf{x}_i)$	$\text{prox}_{f_1}(\mathbf{x}_1)\times\cdots\times\text{prox}_{f_m}(\mathbf{x}_m)$	$-$	Theorem 6.6
$g(\lambda\mathbf{x}+\mathbf{a})$	$\frac{1}{\lambda}\left[\text{prox}_{\lambda^2 g}(\lambda\mathbf{x}+\mathbf{a})-\mathbf{a}\right]$	$\lambda\ne 0,\mathbf{a}\in\mathbb{E},\ g$ proper	Theorem 6.11
$\lambda g(\mathbf{x}/\lambda)$	$\lambda\text{prox}_{g/\lambda}(\mathbf{x}/\lambda)$	$\lambda>0,\ g$ proper	Theorem 6.12
$g(\mathbf{x})+\frac{c}{2}\|\mathbf{x}\|^2+\langle\mathbf{a},\mathbf{x}\rangle+\gamma$	$\text{prox}_{\frac{1}{c+1}g}\left(\frac{\mathbf{x}-\mathbf{a}}{c+1}\right)$	$\mathbf{a}\in\mathbb{E},c>0,\gamma\in\mathbb{R},\ g$ proper	Theorem 6.13
$g(\mathcal{A}(\mathbf{x})+\mathbf{b})$	$\mathbf{x}+\frac{1}{\alpha}\mathcal{A}^T(\text{prox}_{\alpha g}(\mathcal{A}(\mathbf{x})+\mathbf{b})-\mathcal{A}(\mathbf{x})-\mathbf{b})$	$\mathbf{b}\in\mathbb{R}^m,$ $\mathcal{A}:\mathbb{V}\to\mathbb{R}^m,$ g proper closed convex, $\mathcal{A}\circ\mathcal{A}^T=\alpha I,$ $\alpha>0$	Theorem 6.15
$g(\|\mathbf{x}\|)$	$\begin{cases}\text{prox}_g(\|\mathbf{x}\|)\frac{\mathbf{x}}{\|\mathbf{x}\|}, & \mathbf{x}\ne\mathbf{0}\\ \{\mathbf{u}:\|\mathbf{u}\|=\text{prox}_g(0)\}, & \mathbf{x}=\mathbf{0}\end{cases}$	g proper closed convex, $\text{dom}(g)\subseteq[0,\infty)$	Theorem 6.18

Prox Computations

$f(\mathbf{x})$	$\mathrm{dom}(f)$	$\mathrm{prox}_f(\mathbf{x})$	Assumptions	Reference
$\frac{1}{2}\mathbf{x}^T\mathbf{A}\mathbf{x} + \mathbf{b}^T\mathbf{x} + c$	$\mathbb{R}^n$	$(\mathbf{A}+\mathbf{I})^{-1}(\mathbf{x}-\mathbf{b})$	$\mathbf{A} \in \mathbb{S}^n_+,\ \mathbf{b} \in \mathbb{R}^n,\ c \in \mathbb{R}$	Section 6.2.3
λx^3	$\mathbb{R}_+$	$\frac{-1+\sqrt{1+12\lambda[x]_+}}{6\lambda}$	$\lambda > 0$	Lemma 6.5
μx	$[0,\alpha] \cap \mathbb{R}$	$\min\{\max\{x-\mu,0\},\alpha\}$	$\mu \in \mathbb{R},\ \alpha \in [0,\infty]$	Example 6.14
$\lambda\|\mathbf{x}\|$	$\mathbb{E}$	$\left(1 - \frac{\lambda}{\max\{\|\mathbf{x}\|,\lambda\}}\right)\mathbf{x}$	$\|\cdot\|$—Euclidean norm, $\lambda > 0$	Example 6.19
$-\lambda\|\mathbf{x}\|$	$\mathbb{E}$	$\left(1 + \frac{\lambda}{\|\mathbf{x}\|}\right)\mathbf{x}, \quad \mathbf{x} \neq \mathbf{0},$ $\{\mathbf{u}: \|\mathbf{u}\| = \lambda\}, \quad \mathbf{x} = \mathbf{0}.$	$\|\cdot\|$—Euclidean norm, $\lambda > 0$	Example 6.21
$\lambda\|\mathbf{x}\|_1$	$\mathbb{R}^n$	$\mathcal{T}_\lambda(\mathbf{x}) = [|\mathbf{x}| - \lambda\mathbf{e}]_+ \odot \mathrm{sgn}(\mathbf{x})$	$\lambda > 0$	Example 6.8
$\|\boldsymbol{\omega} \odot \mathbf{x}\|_1$	$\mathrm{Box}[-\boldsymbol{\alpha},\boldsymbol{\alpha}]$	$\mathcal{S}_{\boldsymbol{\omega},\boldsymbol{\alpha}}(\mathbf{x})$	$\boldsymbol{\alpha} \in [0,\infty]^n, \boldsymbol{\omega} \in \mathbb{R}^n_+$	Example 6.23
$\lambda\|\mathbf{x}\|_\infty$	$\mathbb{R}^n$	$\mathbf{x} - \lambda P_{B_{\|\cdot\|_1}[\mathbf{0},1]}(\mathbf{x}/\lambda)$	$\lambda > 0$	Example 6.48
$\lambda\|\mathbf{x}\|_a$	$\mathbb{E}$	$\mathbf{x} - \lambda P_{B_{\|\cdot\|_{a,*}}[\mathbf{0},1]}(\mathbf{x}/\lambda)$	$\|\mathbf{x}\|_a$—norm, $\lambda > 0$	Example 6.47
$\lambda\|\mathbf{x}\|_0$	$\mathbb{R}^n$	$\mathcal{H}_{\sqrt{2\lambda}}(x_1) \times \cdots \times \mathcal{H}_{\sqrt{2\lambda}}(x_n)$	$\lambda > 0$	Example 6.10
$\lambda\|\mathbf{x}\|^3$	$\mathbb{E}$	$\frac{2}{1+\sqrt{1+12\lambda\|\mathbf{x}\|}}\mathbf{x}$	$\|\cdot\|$—Euclidean norm, $\lambda > 0$,	Example 6.20
$-\lambda\sum_{j=1}^n \log x_j$	$\mathbb{R}^n_{++}$	$\left(\frac{x_j+\sqrt{x_j^2+4\lambda}}{2}\right)_{j=1}^n$	$\lambda > 0$	Example 6.9
$\delta_C(\mathbf{x})$	$\mathbb{E}$	$P_C(\mathbf{x})$	$\emptyset \neq C \subseteq \mathbb{E}$	Theorem 6.24
$\lambda\sigma_C(\mathbf{x})$	$\mathbb{E}$	$\mathbf{x} - \lambda P_C(\mathbf{x}/\lambda)$	$\lambda > 0,\ C \neq \emptyset$ closed convex	Theorem 6.46
$\lambda\max\{x_i\}$	$\mathbb{R}^n$	$\mathbf{x} - P_{\Delta_n}(\mathbf{x}/\lambda)$	$\lambda > 0$	Example 6.49
$\lambda\sum_{i=1}^k x_{[i]}$	$\mathbb{R}^n$	$\mathbf{x} - \lambda P_C(\mathbf{x}/\lambda),$ $C = H_{\mathbf{e},k} \cap \mathrm{Box}[\mathbf{0},\mathbf{e}]$	$\lambda > 0$	Example 6.50
$\lambda\sum_{i=1}^k |x_{\langle i\rangle}|$	$\mathbb{R}^n$	$\mathbf{x} - \lambda P_C(\mathbf{x}/\lambda),$ $C = B_{\|\cdot\|_1}[\mathbf{0},k] \cap \mathrm{Box}[-\mathbf{e},\mathbf{e}]$	$\lambda > 0$	Example 6.51
$\lambda M_f^\mu(\mathbf{x})$	$\mathbb{E}$	$\mathbf{x} + \frac{\lambda}{\mu+\lambda}\left(\mathrm{prox}_{(\mu+\lambda)f}(\mathbf{x}) - \mathbf{x}\right)$	$\lambda,\mu > 0,\ f$ proper closed convex	Corollary 6.64
$\lambda d_C(\mathbf{x})$	$\mathbb{E}$	$\mathbf{x} + \min\left\{\frac{\lambda}{d_C(\mathbf{x})},1\right\}(P_C(\mathbf{x}) - \mathbf{x})$	$\emptyset \neq C$ closed convex, $\lambda > 0$	Lemma 6.43
$\frac{\lambda}{2}d_C^2(\mathbf{x})$	$\mathbb{E}$	$\frac{\lambda}{\lambda+1}P_C(\mathbf{x}) + \frac{1}{\lambda+1}\mathbf{x}$	$\emptyset \neq C$ closed convex, $\lambda > 0$	Example 6.65
$\lambda H_\mu(\mathbf{x})$	$\mathbb{E}$	$\left(1 - \frac{\lambda}{\max\{\|\mathbf{x}\|,\mu+\lambda\}}\right)\mathbf{x}$	$\lambda,\mu > 0$	Example 6.66
$\rho\|\mathbf{x}\|_1^2$	$\mathbb{R}^n$	$\left(\frac{v_i x_i}{v_i+2\rho}\right)_{i=1}^n,\ \mathbf{v} =$ $\left[\sqrt{\frac{\rho}{\mu}}|\mathbf{x}| - 2\rho\right]_+, \mathbf{e}^T\mathbf{v} = 1\ (\mathbf{0}$ when $\mathbf{x} = \mathbf{0})$	$\rho > 0$	Lemma 6.70
$\lambda\|\mathbf{A}\mathbf{x}\|_2$	$\mathbb{R}^n$	$\mathbf{x} - \mathbf{A}^T(\mathbf{A}\mathbf{A}^T + \alpha^*\mathbf{I})^{-1}\mathbf{A}\mathbf{x},$ $\alpha^* = 0$ if $\|\mathbf{v}_0\|_2 \leq \lambda$; otherwise, $\|\mathbf{v}_{\alpha^*}\|_2 = \lambda$; $\mathbf{v}_\alpha \equiv (\mathbf{A}\mathbf{A}^T+\alpha\mathbf{I})^{-1}\mathbf{A}\mathbf{x}$	$\mathbf{A} \in \mathbb{R}^{m\times n}$ with full row rank, $\lambda > 0$	Lemma 6.68

Prox of Symmetric Spectral Functions over $\mathbb{S}^n$ (from Example 7.19)

$F(\mathbf{X})$	$\mathrm{dom}(F)$	$\mathrm{prox}_F(\mathbf{X})$	Reference
$\alpha\|\mathbf{X}\|_F^2$	$\mathbb{S}^n$	$\frac{1}{1+2\alpha}\mathbf{X}$	Section 6.2.3
$\alpha\|\mathbf{X}\|_F$	$\mathbb{S}^n$	$\left(1-\frac{\alpha}{\max\{\|\mathbf{X}\|_F,\alpha\}}\right)\mathbf{X}$	Example 6.19
$\alpha\|\mathbf{X}\|_{S_1}$	$\mathbb{S}^n$	$\mathbf{U}\mathrm{diag}(\mathcal{T}_\alpha(\boldsymbol{\lambda}(\mathbf{X})))\mathbf{U}^T$	Example 6.8
$\alpha\|\mathbf{X}\|_{2,2}$	$\mathbb{S}^n$	$\mathbf{U}\mathrm{diag}(\boldsymbol{\lambda}(\mathbf{X})-\alpha P_{B_{\|\cdot\|_1}[\mathbf{0},1]}(\boldsymbol{\lambda}(\mathbf{X})/\alpha))\mathbf{U}^T$	Example 6.48
$-\alpha\log\det(\mathbf{X})$	$\mathbb{S}^n_{++}$	$\mathbf{U}\mathrm{diag}\left(\frac{\lambda_j(\mathbf{X})+\sqrt{\lambda_j(\mathbf{X})^2+4\alpha}}{2}\right)\mathbf{U}^T$	Example 6.9
$\alpha\lambda_1(\mathbf{X})$	$\mathbb{S}^n$	$\mathbf{U}\mathrm{diag}(\boldsymbol{\lambda}(\mathbf{X})-\alpha P_{\Delta_n}(\boldsymbol{\lambda}(\mathbf{X})/\alpha))\mathbf{U}^T$	Example 6.49
$\alpha\sum_{i=1}^k\lambda_i(\mathbf{X})$	$\mathbb{S}^n$	$\mathbf{X}-\alpha\mathbf{U}\mathrm{diag}(P_C(\boldsymbol{\lambda}(\mathbf{X})/\alpha))\mathbf{U}^T,$ $C=H_{\mathbf{e},k}\cap\mathrm{Box}[\mathbf{0},\mathbf{e}]$	Example 6.50

Prox of Symmetric Spectral Functions over $\mathbb{R}^{m\times n}$ (from Example 7.30)

$F(\mathbf{X})$	$\mathrm{prox}_F(\mathbf{X})$
$\alpha\|\mathbf{X}\|_F^2$	$\frac{1}{1+2\alpha}\mathbf{X}$
$\alpha\|\mathbf{X}\|_F$	$\left(1-\frac{\alpha}{\max\{\|\mathbf{X}\|_F,\alpha\}}\right)\mathbf{X}$
$\alpha\|\mathbf{X}\|_{S_1}$	$\mathbf{U}\mathrm{dg}(\mathcal{T}_\alpha(\boldsymbol{\sigma}(\mathbf{X})))\mathbf{V}^T$
$\alpha\|\mathbf{X}\|_{S_\infty}$	$\mathbf{X}-\alpha\mathbf{U}\mathrm{dg}(P_{B_{\|\cdot\|_1}[\mathbf{0},1]}(\boldsymbol{\sigma}(\mathbf{X})/\alpha))\mathbf{V}^T$
$\alpha\|\mathbf{X}\|_{\langle k\rangle}$	$\mathbf{X}-\alpha\mathbf{U}\mathrm{dg}(P_C(\boldsymbol{\sigma}(\mathbf{X})/\alpha))\mathbf{V}^T,$ $C=B_{\|\cdot\|_1}[\mathbf{0},k]\cap B_{\|\cdot\|_\infty}[\mathbf{0},1]$

Appendix C

Symbols and Notation

Vector Spaces

$\mathbb{E}, \mathbb{V}$		underlying vector spaces
$\mathbb{E}^*$	p. 9	dual space of $\mathbb{E}$
$\|\cdot\|_*$	p. 9	dual norm
$\dim(V)$	p. 2	dimension of a vector space V
$\mathrm{aff}(S)$	p. 3	affine hull of a set S
$\|\cdot\|$	p. 2	norm
$\|\cdot\|_{\mathbb{E}}$	p. 2	norm of a vector space $\mathbb{E}$
$\langle \mathbf{x}, \mathbf{y} \rangle$	p. 2	inner product of $\mathbf{x}$ and $\mathbf{y}$
$\mathbb{R}^n$	p. 4	space of n-dimensional real column vectors
$[\mathbf{x}, \mathbf{y}]$	p. 3	closed line segment between $\mathbf{x}$ and $\mathbf{y}$
$(\mathbf{x}, \mathbf{y})$	p. 3	open line segment between $\mathbf{x}$ and $\mathbf{y}$
$B(\mathbf{c}, r), B_{\|\cdot\|}(\mathbf{c}, r)$	p. 2	open ball with center $\mathbf{c}$ and radius r
$B[\mathbf{c}, r], B_{\|\cdot\|}[\mathbf{c}, r]$	p. 2	closed ball with center $\mathbf{c}$ and radius r
$\mathbb{R}^{m \times n}$	p. 6	space of $m \times n$ real-valued matrices
$\mathcal{A}^T$	p. 11	adjoint of the linear transformation $\mathcal{A}$
$\mathcal{I}$	p. 8	identity transformation

The Space $\mathbb{R}^n$

$\mathbf{e}_i$	p. 4	ith vector in the standard basis of $\mathbb{R}^n$
$\mathbf{e}$	p. 4	vector of all ones
$\mathbf{0}$	p. 4	vector of all zeros
$\|\cdot\|_p$	p. 5	l_p-norm
Δ_n	p. 5	unit simplex
$\mathrm{Box}[\boldsymbol{\ell}, \mathbf{u}]$	pp. 5, 147	box with lower bounds $\boldsymbol{\ell}$ and upper bounds $\mathbf{u}$
$\mathbb{R}^n_+$	p. 5	nonnegative orthant
$\mathbb{R}^n_{++}$	p. 5	positive orthant
$H_{\mathbf{a},b}$	p. 3	the hyperplane $\{\mathbf{x} : \langle \mathbf{a}, \mathbf{x} \rangle = b\}$
$H^-_{\mathbf{a},b}$	p. 3	the half-space $\{\mathbf{x} : \langle \mathbf{a}, \mathbf{x} \rangle \leq b\}$
$[\mathbf{x}]_+$	p. 5	nonnegative part of $\mathbf{x}$
$|\mathbf{x}|$	p. 5	absolute values vector of $\mathbf{x}$
$\mathrm{sgn}(\mathbf{x})$	p. 5	sign vector of $\mathbf{x}$
$\mathbf{a} \odot \mathbf{b}$	p. 5	Hadamard product
$\mathbf{x}^\downarrow$	p. 180	$\mathbf{x}$ reordered nonincreasingly

The Space $\mathbb{R}^{m \times n}$

$\mathbb{S}^n$	p. 6	set of all $n \times n$ symmetric matrices
$\mathbb{S}^n_+$	p. 6	set of all $n \times n$ positive semidefinite matrices
$\mathbb{S}^n_{++}$	p. 6	set of all $n \times n$ positive definite matrices
$\mathbb{S}^n_-$	p. 6	set of all $n \times n$ negative semidefinite matrices
$\mathbb{S}^n_{--}$	p. 6	set of all $n \times n$ negative definite matrices
$\mathbb{O}_n$	p. 6	set of all $n \times n$ orthogonal matrices
Υ_n	p. 183	spectahedron
$\|\mathbf{A}\|_F$	p. 6	Frobenius norm of $\mathbf{A}$
$\|\mathbf{A}\|_{S_p}$	p. 189	Schatten p-norm of $\mathbf{A}$
$\|\mathbf{A}\|_{\langle k \rangle}$	p. 190	Ky Fan k-norm of $\mathbf{A}$
$\|\mathbf{A}\|_{ab}$	p. 7	induced norm of $\mathbf{A} \in \mathbb{R}^{m \times n}$ when $\mathbb{R}^n$ and $\mathbb{R}^m$ the norms $\|\cdot\|_a$ and $\|\cdot\|_b$ respectively
$\|\mathbf{A}\|_2$	p. 7	spectral norm of $\mathbf{A}$
$\lambda_{\max}(\mathbf{A})$		maximum eigenvalue of a symmetric matrix $\mathbf{A}$
$\lambda_{\min}(\mathbf{A})$		maximum eigenvalue of a symmetric matrix $\mathbf{A}$

Sets

$\mathrm{int}(S)$		interior of S
$\mathrm{cl}(S)$		closure of S
$\mathrm{conv}(S)$		convex hull of S
$A + B$	p. 26	Minkowski sum of A and B
K°	p. 27	polar cone of K
$N_S(\mathbf{x})$	p. 36	normal cone of S at $\mathbf{x}$
$\mathrm{ri}(S)$	p. 43	relative interior of S
$\#A$		number of elements in A
Λ_n	p. 180	$n \times n$ permutation matrices
Λ_n^G	p. 180	$n \times n$ generalized permutation matrices

Functions and Operators

$\log x$		natural logarithm of x
$\text{dom}(f)$	p. 14	(effective) domain of f
δ_C	p. 14	indicator function of the set C
$\text{epi}(f)$	p. 14	epigraph of f
$\text{Lev}(f, \alpha)$	p. 15	α-level set of f
d_C	p. 22	distance function to C
σ_C	p. 26	support function of C
$h_1 \square h_2$	p. 24	infimal convolution of h_1 and h_2
$\partial f(\mathbf{x})$	p. 35	subdifferential set of f at $\mathbf{x}$
$f'(\mathbf{x})$	p. 202	subgradient of f at $\mathbf{x}$
$\text{dom}(\partial f)$	p. 40	set of points of differentiability
$f'(\mathbf{x}; \mathbf{d})$	p. 44	directional derivative of f at $\mathbf{x}$ in the direction $\mathbf{d}$
$\nabla f(\mathbf{x})$	p. 48	gradient of f at $\mathbf{x}$
$\nabla^2 f(\mathbf{x})$		Hessian of a function over $\mathbb{R}^n$ at $\mathbf{x}$
P_C	p. 49	orthogonal projection on C
$f \circ g$		f composed with g
f^*	p. 87	conjugate of f
$C_L^{1,1}(D)$	p. 107	class of L-smooth functions over D
$\text{prox}_f(\mathbf{x})$	p. 129	proximal mapping of f evaluated at $\mathbf{x}$
$\mathcal{T}_\lambda(\mathbf{x})$	p. 136	soft thresholding with level λ evaluated at $\mathbf{x}$
$\mathcal{S}_{\mathbf{a},\mathbf{b}}$	p. 151	two-sided soft thresholding
H_μ	p. 163	Huber function with smoothing parameter μ
$T_L^{f,g}(\mathbf{x}), T_L(\mathbf{x})$	p. 271	prox-grad mapping evaluated at $\mathbf{x}$
$G_L^{f,g}(\mathbf{x}), G_L(\mathbf{x})$	p. 273	gradient mapping evaluated at $\mathbf{x}$

Matrices

$\mathbf{A}^\dagger$		Moore–Penrose pseudoinverse
$\lambda_{\max}(\mathbf{A})$		maximum eigenvalue of $\mathbf{A}$
$\lambda_{\min}(\mathbf{A})$		minimum eigenvalue of $\mathbf{A}$
$\sigma_{\max}(\mathbf{A})$		maximum singular of $\mathbf{A}$
$\mathrm{Range}(\mathbf{A})$		range of $\mathbf{A}$—all linear combinations of the columns of $\mathbf{A}$
$\mathrm{Null}(\mathbf{A})$		null space/kernel of $\mathbf{A}$
$\mathrm{diag}(\mathbf{x})$		diagonal matrix with diagonal $\mathbf{x}$
$\mathrm{dg}(\mathbf{x})$	p. 188	generalized diagonal matrix with diagonal $\mathbf{x}$

Appendix D

Bibliographic Notes

Chapter 1. For a comprehensive treatment of finite-dimensional vector spaces and advanced linear algebra topics, the reader can refer to the classical book of Halmos [64], as well as to the textbooks of Meyer [86] and Strang [117].

Chapters 2, 3, 4. Most of the material in these chapters is classical. Additional materials and extensions can be found, for example, in Bauschke and Combettes [8], Bertsekas [29], Borwein and Lewis [32], Hiriart-Urruty and Lemaréchal [67], Nesterov [94] and Rockafellar [108]. Example 2.17 is taken from the book of Hiriart-Urruty and Lemaréchal [67, Example 2.1.4]. Example 2.32 is from Rockafellar [108, p. 83]. The proof in Example 3.31 follows Beck and Teboulle [20, Theorem 4.1]. Section 3.5, excluding Theorem 3.60, follows Hiriart-Urruty and Lemaréchal [67, Section VII.3.3]. Theorem 3.60 is a slight extension of Lemma 6 from Lan [78]. The optimality conditions derived in Example 3.66 are rather old and can be traced back to Sturm, who proved them in his work from 1884 [118]. Actually, (re)proving these conditions was the main motivation for Weiszfeld to devise the (now-called) Weiszfeld's method in 1937 [124]. For more information on the Fermat–Weber problem and Weiszfeld's method, see the review paper of Beck and Sabach [14] and references therein.

Chapter 5. The proof of the descent lemma can be found in Bertsekas [28]. The proof of Theorem 5.8 follows the proof of Nesterov in [94, Theorem 2.1.5]. The equivalence between claims (i) and (iv) in Theorem 5.8 is also known as the Baillon-Haddad theorem [5]. The analysis in Example 5.11 of the smoothness parameter of the squared l_p-norm follows the derivation in the work of Ben-Tal, Margalit, and Nemirovski [24, Appendix 1]. The conjugate correspondence theorem can be deduced from the work of Zalinescu [128, Theorem 2.2] and can also be found in the paper of Azé and Penot [3] as well as Zalinescu's book [129, Corollary 3.5.11]. In its Euclidean form, the result can be found in the book of Rockafellar and Wets [111, Proposition 12.60]. Further characterizations appear in the paper of Bauschke and Combettes [7]. The proof of Theorem 5.30 follows Beck and Teboulle [20, Theorem 4.1].

Chapter 6. The seminal 1965 paper of Moreau [87] already contains much of the properties of the proximal mapping discussed in the chapter. Excellent references for the subject are the book of Bauschke and Combettes [8], the paper of Combettes and Wajs [44], and the review paper of Parikh and Boyd [102]. The computation of the prox of the squared l_1-norm in Section 6.8.2 is due to Evgeniou, Pontil, Spinellis, and Nassuphis [54].

Chapter 7. The notion of symmetry w.r.t. a given set of orthogonal matrices was studied by Rockafellar [108, Chapter 12]. A variant of the symmetric conjugate theorem (Theorem 7.9) can be found in Rockafellar [108, Corollary 12.3.1]. Fan's inequality can be found in Theobald [119]. Von Neumann's trace inequality [123], as well as Fan's inequality, are often formulated over the complex field, but the adaptation to the real field is straightforward. Sections 7.2 and 7.3, excluding the spectral proximal theorem, are based on the seminal papers of Lewis [80, 81] on unitarily invariant functions. See also Borwein and Lewis [32, Section 1.2], as well as Borwein and Vanderwerff [33, Section 3.2]. The equivalence between the convexity of spectral functions and their associated functions was first established by Davis in [47]. The spectral proximal formulas can be found in Parikh and Boyd [102].

Chapter 8. Example 8.3 is taken from Vandenberghe's lecture notes [122]. Wolfe's example with $\gamma = \frac{16}{9}$ originates from his work [125]. The version with general $\gamma > 1$, along with the support form of the function, can be found in the set of exercises [35]. Studies of subgradient methods and extensions can be found in many books; to name a few, the books of Nemirovsky and Yudin [92], Shor [116] and Polyak [104] are classical; modern accounts of the subject can be found, for example, in Bertsekas [28, 29, 30], Nesterov [94], and Ruszczyński [113]. The analysis of the stochastic and deterministic projected subgradient method in the strongly convex case is based on the work of Lacoste-Julien, Schmidt, and Bach [77]. The fundamental inequality for the incremental projected subgradient is taken from Nedić and Bertsekas [89], where many additional results on incremental methods are derived. Theorem 8.42 and Lemma 8.47 are Lemmas 1 and 3 from the work of from Nedić and Ozdaglar [90]. The latter work also contains additional results on the dual projected subgradient method with constant stepsize. The presentation of the network utility maximization problem, as well as the distributed subgradient method for solving it, originates from Nedić and Ozdaglar [91].

Chapter 9. The mirror descent method was introduced by Nemirovsky and Yudin in [92]. The interpretation of the method as a non-Euclidean projected subgradient method was presented by Beck and Teboulle in [15]. The rate of convergence analysis of the mirror descent method is based on [15]. The three-points lemma was proven by Chen and Teboulle in [43]. The analysis of the mirror-C method is based on the work of Duchi, Shalev-Shwartz, Singer, and Tewari [49], where the algorithm is introduced in an online and stochastic setting.

Chapter 10. The proximal gradient method can be traced back to the forward-backward algorithm introduced by Bruck [36], Pasty [103], and Lions and Mercier [83]. More modern accounts of the topic can be found, for example, in Bauschke and Combettes [8, Chapter 27], Combettes and Wajs [44], and Facchinei and Pang

[55, Chapter 12]. The proximal gradient method is a generalization of the gradient method, which goes back to Cauchy [38] and was extensively studied and generalized by many authors; see, for example, the books of Bertsekas [28], Nesterov [94], Polyak [104], and Nocedal and Wright [99], as well as the many references therein. ISTA and its variations was studied in the literature in several contexts; see, for example, the works of Daubechies, Defrise, and De Mol [46]; Hale, Yin, and Zhang [63]; Wright, Nowak, and Figueiredo [127]; and Elad [52]. The analysis of the proximal gradient method in Sections 10.3 and 10.4 mostly follows the presentation of Beck and Teboulle in [18] and [19]. Lemma 10.11 was stated and proved for the case where g is an indicator of a nonempty closed and convex set in [9]; see also [13, Lemma 2.3]. Theorem 10.9 on the monotonicity of the gradient mapping is a simple generalization of [10, Lemma 9.12]. The first part of the monotonicity result was shown in the case where g is an indicator of a nonempty closed and convex set in Bertsekas [28, Lemma 2.3.1]. Lemma 10.12 is a minor variation of Lemma 2.4 from Necoara and Patrascu [88]. Theorem 10.26 is an extension of a result of Nesterov from [97] on the convergence of the gradient method for convex functions. The proximal point method was studied by Rockafellar in [110], as well as by many other authors; see, for example, the book of Bauschke and Combettes [8] and its extensive list of references. FISTA was developed by Beck and Teboulle in [18]; see also the book chapter [19]; the convergence analysis presented in Section 10.7 is taken from these sources. When the nonsmooth part is an indicator function of a closed and convex set, the method reduces to the optimal gradient method of Nesterov from 1983 [93]. Other accelerated proximal gradient methods can be found in the works of Nesterov [98] and Tseng [121]—the latter also describes a generalization to the non-Euclidean setting, which is an extension of the work of Auslender and Teboulle [2]. MFISTA and its convergence analysis are from the work of Beck and Teboulle [17]. The idea of using restarting in order to gain an improved rate of convergence in the strongly convex case can be found in Nesterov's work [98] in the context of a different accelerated proximal gradient method, but the idea works for any method that gains an $O(1/k^2)$ rate in the (not necessarily strongly) convex case. The proof of Theorem 10.42 follows the proof of Theorem 4.10 from the review paper of Chambolle and Pock [42]. The idea of solving nonsmooth problems through a smooth approximation was studied by many authors; see, for example, the works of Ben-Tal and Teboulle [25], Bertsekas [26], Moreau [87], and the more recent book of Auslender and Teboulle [1] and references therein. Lemma 10.70 can be found in Levitin and Polyak [79]. The idea of producing an $O(1/\varepsilon)$ complexity result for nonsmooth problems by employing an accelerated gradient method was first presented and developed by Nesterov in [95]. The extension to the three-part composite model and to the setting of more general smooth approximations was studied by Beck and Teboulle [20], where additional results and extensions can also be found. The non-Euclidean gradient method was proposed by Nutini, Schmidt, Laradji, Friendlander, and Koepke [100], where its rate of convergence in the strongly convex case was analyzed; the work [100] also contains a comparison between two coordinate selection strategies: Gauss–Southwell (which is the one considered in the chapter) and randomized selection. The non-Euclidean proximal gradient method was presented in the work of Tseng [121], where an accelerated non-Euclidean version was also analyzed.

Chapter 11. The version of the block proximal gradient method in which the nonsmooth functions g_i are indicators was studied by Luo and Tseng in [84], where some error bounds on the model were assumed. It was shown that under the model assumptions, the CBPG method with each block consisting of a single variable has a linear rate of convergence. Nesterov studied in [96] a randomized version of the method (again, in the setting where the nonsmooth functions are indicators) in which the selection of the block on which a gradient projection step is performed at each iteration is done randomly via a pre-described distribution. For the first time, Nesterov was able to establish global nonasymptotic rates of convergence in the convex case without any strict convexity, strong convexity, uniqueness, or error bound assumptions. Specifically, it was shown that the rate of convergence to the optimal value of the expectation sequence of the function values of the sequence generated by the randomized method is sublinear under the assumption of Lipschitz continuity of the gradient and linear under a strong convexity assumption. In addition, an accelerated $O(1/k^2)$ was devised in the unconstrained setting. Probabilistic results on the convergence of the function values were also provided. In [107] Richtarik and Takac generalized Nesterovs results to the composite model. The derivation of the randomized complexity result in Section 11.5 mostly follows the presentation in the work of Lin, Lu, and Xiao [82]. The type of analysis in the deterministic convex case (Section 11.4.2) originates from Beck and Tetruashvili [22], who studied the case in which the nonsmooth functions are indicators. The extension to the general composite model can be found in Shefi and Teboulle [115] as well as in Hong, Wang, Razaviyayn, and Luo [69]. Lemma 11.17 is Lemma 3.8 from [11]. Theorem 11.20 is a specialization of Lemma 2 from Nesterov [96]. Additional related methods and discussions can be found in the extensive survey of Wright [126].

Chapter 12. The idea of using a proximal gradient method on the dual of the main model (12.1) was originally developed by Tseng in [120], where the algorithm was named "alternating minimization." The primal representations of the DPG and FDPG methods, convergence analysis, as well as the primal-dual relation are from Beck and Teboulle [21]. The DPG method for solving the total variation problem was initially devised by Chambolle in [39], and the accelerated version was considered by Beck and Teboulle [17]. The one-dimensional total variation denoising problem is presented as an illustration for the DPG and FDPG methods; however, more direct and efficient methods exist for tackling the problem; see Hochbaum [68], Condat [45], Johnson [73], and Barbero and Sra [6]. The dual block proximal gradient method was discussed in Beck, Tetruashvili, Vaisbourd, and Shemtov [23], from which the specific decomposition of the isotropic two-dimensional total variation function is taken. The accelerated method ADBPG is a different representation of the accelerated method proposed by Chambolle and Pock in [41]. The latter work also discusses dual block proximal gradient methods and contains many other suggestions for decompositions of total variation functions.

Chapter 13. The conditional gradient algorithm was presented by Frank and Wolfe [56] in 1956 for minimizing a convex quadratic function over a compact polyhedral set. The original paper of Frank and Wolfe also contained a proof of an $O(1/k)$ rate of convergence in function values. Levitin and Polyak [79] showed that this $O(1/k)$ rate can also be extended to the case where the feasible set is a general compact convex set and the objective function is L-smooth and convex. Dunn and Harshbarger [50] were probably the first to suggest a diminishing stepsize rule for the conditional gradient method and to establish a sublinear rate under such a strategy. The generalized conditional gradient method was introduced and analyzed by Bach in [4], where it was shown that under a certain setting, it can be viewed as a dual mirror descent method. Lemma 13.7 (fundamental inequality for generalized conditional gradient) can be found in the setting of the conditional gradient method in Levitin and Polyak [79]. The interpretation of the power method as the conditional gradient method was described in the work of Luss and Teboulle [85], where many other connections between the conditional gradient method and the sparse PCA problem are explored. Lemma 13.13 is an extension of Lemma 4.4 from Bach's work [4], and the proof is almost identical. Similar results on sequences of nonnegative numbers can be found in the book of Polyak [104, p. 45]. Section 13.3.1 originates from the work of Canon and Cullum [37]. Polyak in [104, p. 214, Exercise 10] seems to be the first to mention the linear rate of convergence of the conditional gradient method under a strong convexity assumption on the feasible set. Theorem 13.23 is from Journée, Nesterov, Richtárik, and Sepulchre [74, Theorem 12]. Lemma 13.26 and Theorem 13.27 are from Levitin and Polyak [79], and the exact form of the proof is due to Edouard Pauwels. Another situation, which was not discussed in the chapter, in which linear rate of converge can be established, is when the objective function is strongly convex and the optimal solution resides in the interior of the feasible set (Guélat and Marcotte [62]). Epelman and Freund [53], as well as Beck and Teboulle [16], showed a linear rate of convergence of the conditional gradient method with a special stepsize choice in the context of finding a point in the intersection of an affine space and a closed and convex set under a Slater-type assumption. The randomized generalized block conditional gradient method presented in Section 13.4 is a simple generalization of the randomized block conditional gradient method introduced and analyzed by Lacoste-Julien, Jaggi, Schmidt, and Pletscher in [76]. A deterministic version was analyzed by Beck, Pauwels, and Sabach in [12]. An excellent overview of the conditional gradient method, including many more theoretical results and applications, can be found in the thesis of Jaggi [72].

Chapter 14. The alternating minimization method is a rather old and fundamental algorithm. It appears in the literature under various names such as the block-nonlinear Gauss-Seidel method or the block coordinate descent method. Powell's example appears in [106]. Theorem 14.3 and its proof originate from Bertsekas [28, Proposition 2.7.1]. Theorem 14.9 and its proof are an extension of Proposition 6 from Grippo and Sciandrone [61] to the composite model. The proof of Theorem 14.11 follows the proof of Theorem 3.1 from the work of Hong, Wang, Razaviyayn, and Luo [69], where more general schemes than alternating minimization are also considered. Section 14.5.2 follows [11].

Chapter 15 The augmented Lagrangian method can be traced back to Hestenes [66] and Powell [105]. The method and its many variants was studied extensively in the literature, see, for example, the books of Bertsekas [27] and Bertsekas and Tsitsiklis [31] and references therein. Rockafellar [109] was first to establish the duality between the proximal point and the augmented Lagrangian methods; see also additional discussions in the work of Iusem [71]. ADMM is equivalent to an operator splitting method called Douglas–Rachford splitting, which was introduced in the 1950s for the numerical solution of partial differential equations [48]. ADMM, as presented in the chapter, was first introduced by Gabay and Mercier [57] and Glowinski and Marrocco [59]. An extremely extensive survey on ADMM method can be found in the work of Boyd, Parikh, Chu, Peleato, and Eckstein [34]. AD-PMM was suggested by Eckstein [51]. The proof of Theorem 15.4 on the rate of convergence of AD-PMM is based on a combination of the proof techniques of He and Yuan [65] and Gao and Zhang [58]. Shefi and Teboulle provided in [114] a unified analysis for general classes of algorithm that include AD-PMM as a special instance. Shefi and Teboulle also showed the relation between AD-LPMM and the Chambolle–Pock algorithm [40].

Bibliography

[1] A. AUSLENDER AND M. TEBOULLE, *Asymptotic cones and functions in optimization and variational inequalities*, Springer Monographs in Mathematics, Springer-Verlag, New York, 2003. (Cited on p. 459)

[2] ——, *Interior gradient and proximal methods for convex and conic optimization*, SIAM J. Optim., 16 (2006), pp. 697–725, https://doi.org/10.1137/S1052623403427823. (Cited on p. 459)

[3] D. AZÉ AND J. PENOT, *Uniformly convex and uniformly smooth convex functions*, Ann. Fac. Sci. Toulouse Math. (6), 4 (1995), pp. 705–730. (Cited on p. 457)

[4] F. BACH, *Duality between subgradient and conditional gradient methods*, SIAM J. Optim., 25 (2015), pp. 115–129, https://doi.org/10.1137/130941961. (Cited on pp. 387, 461)

[5] J. B. BAILLON AND G. HADDAD, *Quelques propriétés des opérateurs angle-bornés et n-cycliquement monotones*, Israel J. Math., 26 (1977), pp. 137–150. (Cited on p. 457)

[6] A. BARBERO AND S. SRA, *Modular proximal optimization for multidimensional total-variation regularization*. Available at https://arxiv.org/abs/1411.0589. (Cited on p. 460)

[7] H. H. BAUSCHKE AND P. L. COMBETTES, *The Baillon-Haddad theorem revisited*, J. Convex Anal., 17 (2010), pp. 781–787. (Cited on p. 457)

[8] ——, *Convex analysis and monotone operator theory in Hilbert spaces*, CMS Books in Mathematics/Ouvrages de Mathématiques de la SMC, Springer, New York, 2011. With a foreword by Hédy Attouch. (Cited on pp. 457, 458, 459)

[9] A. BECK, *Convergence Rate Analysis of Gradient Based Algorithms*, Ph.D. thesis, School of Mathematical Sciences, Tel-Aviv University, 2003. (Cited on p. 459)

[10] ——, *Introduction to Nonlinear Optimization: Theory, Algorithms, and Applications with MATLAB*, MOS-SIAM Series on Optimization, SIAM, Philadelphia, PA, 2014, https://doi.org/10.1137/1.9781611973655. (Cited on pp. 24, 28, 31, 45, 49, 63, 108, 112, 147, 195, 256, 386, 459)

[11] ——, *On the convergence of alternating minimization for convex programming with applications to iteratively reweighted least squares and decomposition schemes*, SIAM J. Optim., 25 (2015), pp. 185–209, https://doi.org/10.1137/13094829X. (Cited on pp. 460, 461)

[12] A. BECK, E. PAUWELS, AND S. SABACH, *The cyclic block conditional gradient method for convex optimization problems*, SIAM J. Optim., 25 (2015), pp. 2024–2049, https://doi.org/10.1137/15M1008397. (Cited on p. 461)

[13] A. BECK AND S. SABACH, *A first order method for finding minimal norm-like solutions of convex optimization problems*, Math. Program., 147 (2014), pp. 25–46. (Cited on p. 459)

[14] ——, *Weiszfeld's method: Old and new results*, J. Optim. Theory Appl., 164 (2015), pp. 1–40. (Cited on p. 457)

[15] A. BECK AND M. TEBOULLE, *Mirror descent and nonlinear projected subgradient methods for convex optimization*, Oper. Res. Lett., 31 (2003), pp. 167–175. (Cited on p. 458)

[16] ——, *A conditional gradient method with linear rate of convergence for solving convex linear systems*, Math. Methods Oper. Res., 59 (2004), pp. 235–247. (Cited on p. 461)

[17] ——, *Fast gradient-based algorithms for constrained total variation image denoising and deblurring problems*, IEEE Trans. Image Process., 18 (2009), pp. 2419–2434. (Cited on pp. 296, 459, 460)

[18] ——, *A fast iterative shrinkage-thresholding algorithm for linear inverse problems*, SIAM J. Imaging Sci., 2 (2009), pp. 183–202, https://doi.org/10.1137/080716542. (Cited on pp. 272, 290, 459)

[19] ——, *Gradient-based algorithms with applications to signal-recovery problems*, in Convex Optimization in Signal Processing and Communications, Cambridge University Press, Cambridge, 2010, pp. 42–88. (Cited on pp. 272, 459)

[20] ——, *Smoothing and first order methods: A unified framework*, SIAM J. Optim., 22 (2012), pp. 557–580, https://doi.org/10.1137/100818327. (Cited on pp. 49, 304, 457, 459)

[21] ——, *A fast dual proximal gradient algorithm for convex minimization and applications*, Oper. Res. Lett., 42 (2014), pp. 1–6. (Cited on pp. 355, 460)

[22] A. BECK AND L. TETRUASHVILI, *On the convergence of block coordinate descent type methods*, SIAM J. Optim., 23 (2013), pp. 2037–2060, https://doi.org/10.1137/120887679. (Cited on pp. 342, 460)

[23] A. BECK, L. TETRUASHVILI, Y. VAISBOURD, AND A. SHEMTOV, *Rate of convergence analysis of dual-based variables decomposition methods for strongly convex problems*, Oper. Res. Lett., 44 (2016), pp. 61–66. (Cited on pp. 377, 460)

[24] A. Ben-Tal, T. Margalit, and A. Nemirovski, *The ordered subsets mirror descent optimization method with applications to tomography*, SIAM J. Optim., 12 (2001), pp. 79–108, https://doi.org/10.1137/S1052623499354564. (Cited on pp. 112, 457)

[25] A. Ben-Tal and M. Teboulle, *A smoothing technique for nondifferentiable optimization problems*, in Optimization (Varetz, 1988), vol. 1405 of Lecture Notes in Math., Springer, Berlin, 1989, pp. 1–11. (Cited on p. 459)

[26] D. P. Bertsekas, *Nondifferentiable optimization via approximation: Nondifferentiable optimization*, Math. Programming Stud., (1975), pp. 1–25. (Cited on p. 459)

[27] ——, *Constrained optimization and Lagrange multiplier methods*, Computer Science and Applied Mathematics, Academic Press. [Harcourt Brace Jovanovich], New York, London, 1982. (Cited on p. 461)

[28] ——, *Nonlinear Programming*, Athena Scientific, Belmont, MA, second ed., 1999. (Cited on pp. 407, 457, 458, 459, 461)

[29] ——, *Convex Analysis and Optimization*, Athena Scientific, Belmont, MA, 2003. With Angelia Nedić and Asuman E. Ozdaglar. (Cited on pp. 41, 439, 457, 458)

[30] ——, *Convex Optimization Algorithms*, Athena Scientific, Belmont, MA, 2015. (Cited on p. 458)

[31] D. P. Bertsekas and J. N. Tsitsiklis, *Parallel and Distributed Computation: Numerical Methods*, Prentice-Hall, Upper Saddle River, NJ, 1989. (Cited on p. 461)

[32] J. M. Borwein and A. S. Lewis, *Convex Analysis and Nonlinear Optimization: Theory and Examples*, CMS Books in Mathematics/Ouvrages de Mathématiques de la SMC, 3, Springer, New York, second ed., 2006. (Cited on pp. 183, 457, 458)

[33] J. M. Borwein and J. D. Vanderwerff, *Convex Functions: Constructions, Characterizations and Counterexamples*, vol. 109 of Encyclopedia of Mathematics and Its Applications, Cambridge University Press, Cambridge, 2010. (Cited on p. 458)

[34] S. Boyd, N. Parikh, E. Chu, B. Peleato, and J. Eckstein, *Distributed optimization and statistical learning via the alternating direction method of multipliers*, Found. Trends Mach. Learn., 3 (2011), pp. 1–122. (Cited on p. 462)

[35] S. Boyd and L. Vandenberghe, *Additional exercises for convex optimization*. Available at http://www.stanford.edu/~boyd/cvxbook/bv_cvxbook. (Cited on p. 458)

[36] R. E. Bruck, *On the weak convergence of an ergodic iteration for the solution of variational inequalities for monotone operators in Hilbert space*, J. Math. Anal. Appl., 61 (1977), pp. 159–164. (Cited on p. 458)

[37] M. D. CANON AND C. D. CULLUM, *A tight upper bound on the rate of convergence of the Frank-Wolfe algorithm*, SIAM J. Control, 6 (1968), pp. 509–516, https://doi.org/10.1137/0306032. (Cited on pp. 391, 461)

[38] A. L. CAUCHY, *Méthode generales pour la résolution des systèmes d'equations simultanées*, Comptes Rendues Acad. Sci. Paris, 25 (1847), pp. 536–538. (Cited on p. 459)

[39] A. CHAMBOLLE, *An algorithm for total variation minimization and applications*, J. Math. Imaging Vision, 20 (2004), pp. 89–97. Special issue on mathematics and image analysis. (Cited on p. 460)

[40] A. CHAMBOLLE AND T. POCK, *A first-order primal-dual algorithm for convex problems with applications to imaging*, J. Math. Imaging Vision, 40 (2011), pp. 120–145. (Cited on p. 462)

[41] ——, *A remark on accelerated block coordinate descent for computing the proximity operators of a sum of convex functions*, SMAI J. Comput. Math., 1 (2015), pp. 29–54. (Cited on pp. 373, 460)

[42] ——, *An introduction to continuous optimization for imaging*, Acta Numerica, 25 (2016), 161–319. (Cited on pp. 302, 459)

[43] G. CHEN AND M. TEBOULLE, *Convergence analysis of a proximal-like minimization algorithm using Bregman functions*, SIAM J. Optim., 3 (1993), pp. 538–543, https://doi.org/10.1137/0803026. (Cited on pp. 252, 458)

[44] P. L. COMBETTES AND V. R. WAJS, *Signal recovery by proximal forward-backward splitting*, Multiscale Model. Simul., 4 (2005), pp. 1168–1200, https://doi.org/10.1137/050626090. (Cited on p. 458)

[45] L. CONDAT, *A direct algorithm for 1-d total variation denoising*, IEEE Signal Process. Lett., 20 (2013), pp. 1054–1057. (Cited on p. 460)

[46] I. DAUBECHIES, M. DEFRISE, AND C. DE MOL, *An iterative thresholding algorithm for linear inverse problems with a sparsity constraint*, Comm. Pure Appl. Math., 57 (2004), pp. 1413–1457. (Cited on p. 459)

[47] C. DAVIS, *All convex invariant functions of hermitian matrices*, Arch. Math., 8 (1957), pp. 276–278. (Cited on p. 458)

[48] J. DOUGLAS AND H. H. RACHFORD, *On the numerical solution of heat conduction problems in two and three space variables*, Trans. Amer. Math. Soc., 82 (1956), pp. 421–439. (Cited on p. 462)

[49] J. C. DUCHI, S. SHALEV-SHWARTZ, Y. SINGER, AND A. TEWARI, *Composite objective mirror descent*, in COLT 2010—The 23rd Conference on Learning Theory, 2010, pp. 14–26. (Cited on pp. 260, 458)

[50] J. C. DUNN AND S. HARSHBARGER, *Conditional gradient algorithms with open loop step size rules*, J. Math. Anal. Appl., 62 (1978), pp. 432–444. (Cited on p. 461)

[51] J. ECKSTEIN, *Some saddle-function splitting methods for convex programming*, Optim. Methods Softw., 4 (1994), pp. 75–83. (Cited on p. 462)

[52] M. ELAD, *Why simple shrinkage is still relevant for redundant representations?*, IEEE Trans. Inform. Theory, 52 (2006), pp. 5559–5569. (Cited on p. 459)

[53] M. EPELMAN AND R. M. FREUND, *Condition number complexity of an elementary algorithm for computing a reliable solution of a conic linear system*, Math. Program., 88 (2000), pp. 451–485. (Cited on p. 461)

[54] T. EVGENIOU, M. PONTIL, D. SPINELLIS, AND N. NASSUPHIS, *Regularized robust portfolio estimation*, in Regularization, Optimization, Kernels, and Support Vector Machines, CRC Press, Boca Raton, FL, 2015. (Cited on pp. 173, 458)

[55] F. FACCHINEI AND J. S. PANG, *Finite-dimensional variational inequalities and complementarity problems. Vol. II*, Springer Series in Operations Research, Springer-Verlag, New York, 2003. (Cited on p. 459)

[56] M. FRANK AND P. WOLFE, *An algorithm for quadratic programming*, Naval Res. Logist. Quart., 3 (1956), pp. 95–110. (Cited on p. 460)

[57] D. GABAY AND B. MERCIER, *A dual algorithm for the solution of nonlinear variational problems via finite element approximations*, Comp. Math. Appl., 2 (1976), pp. 17–40. (Cited on p. 462)

[58] X. GAO AND S.-Z. ZHANG, *First-order algorithms for convex optimization with nonseparable objective and coupled constraints*, J. Oper. Res. Soc. China, 5 (2017), pp. 131–159. (Cited on pp. 428, 462)

[59] R. GLOWINSKI AND A. MARROCO, *Sur l'approximation, par éléments finis d'ordre un, et la résolution, par pénalisation-dualité d'une classe de problèmes de dirichlet non linéaires*, ESAIM: Mathematical Modelling and Numerical Analysis—Modélisation Mathématique et Analyse Numérique, 9 (1975), pp. 41–76. (Cited on p. 462)

[60] G. H. GOLUB AND C. F. VAN LOAN, *Matrix Computations*, Johns Hopkins Studies in the Mathematical Sciences, Johns Hopkins University Press, Baltimore, MD, third ed., 1996. (Cited on p. 188)

[61] L. GRIPPO AND M. SCIANDRONE, *On the convergence of the block nonlinear Gauss-Seidel method under convex constraints*, Oper. Res. Lett., 26 (2000), pp. 127–136. (Cited on pp. 413, 461)

[62] J. GUÉLAT AND P. MARCOTTE, *Some comments on Wolfe's "away step,"* Math. Program., 35 (1986), pp. 110–119. (Cited on p. 461)

[63] E. T. HALE, W. YIN, AND Y. ZHANG, *Fixed-point continuation for ℓ_1-minimization: Methodology and convergence*, SIAM J. Optim., 19 (2008), pp. 1107–1130, https://doi.org/10.1137/070698920. (Cited on p. 459)

[64] P. R. HALMOS, *Finite-Dimensional Vector Spaces*, Undergraduate Texts in Mathematics, Springer-Verlag, New York, Heidelberg, second ed., 1974. (Cited on p. 457)

[65] B. HE AND X. YUAN, *On the $O(1/n)$ convergence rate of the Douglas–Rachford alternating direction method*, SIAM J. Numer. Anal., 50 (2012), pp. 700–709, https://doi.org/10.1137/110836936. (Cited on pp. 428, 462)

[66] M. R. HESTENES, *Multiplier and gradient methods*, J. Optimization Theory Appl., 4 (1969), pp. 303–320. (Cited on p. 461)

[67] J. B. HIRIART-URRUTY AND C. LEMARÉCHAL, *Convex analysis and minimization algorithms. I*, vol. 305 of Grundlehren der Mathematischen Wissenschaften [Fundamental Principles of Mathematical Sciences], Springer-Verlag, Berlin, 1996. Second Printing. (Cited on pp. 22, 67, 119, 457)

[68] D. S. HOCHBAUM, *An efficient algorithm for image segmentation, Markov random fields and related problems*, J. ACM, 48 (2001), pp. 686–701. (Cited on p. 460)

[69] M. HONG, X. WANG, M. RAZAVIYAYN, AND Z. Q. LUO, *Iteration complexity analysis of block coordinate descent methods*. Available at http://arxiv.org/abs/1310.6957. (Cited on pp. 342, 416, 460, 461)

[70] R. A. HORN AND C. R. JOHNSON, *Matrix Analysis*, Cambridge University Press, Cambridge, second ed., 2013. (Cited on p. 189)

[71] A. N. IUSEM, *Augmented Lagrangian methods and proximal point methods for convex optimization*, Investigacion Operativa, 8 (1999), pp. 11–49. (Cited on p. 461)

[72] M. JAGGI, *Sparse Convex Optimization Methods for Machine Learning*, Ph.D. thesis, ETH Zurich, 2011. (Cited on p. 461)

[73] N. A. JOHNSON, *A dynamic programming algorithm for the fused lasso and L_0-segmentation*, J. Comput. Graph. Statist., 22 (2013), pp. 246–260. (Cited on p. 460)

[74] M. JOURNÉE, Y. NESTEROV, P. RICHTÁRIK, AND R. SEPULCHRE, *Generalized power method for sparse principal component analysis*, J. Mach. Learn. Res., 11 (2010), pp. 517–553. (Cited on pp. 397, 461)

[75] K. KNOPP, *Theory and Application of Infinite Series*, Blackie & Son Limited, 1951. (Cited on p. 392)

[76] S. LACOSTE-JULIEN, M. JAGGI, M. SCHMIDT, AND P. PLETSCHER, *Block-coordinate Frank-Wolfe optimization for structural SVMs*, in Proceedings of the 30th International Conference on Machine Learning (ICML-13), vol. 28, 2013, pp. 53–61. (Cited on pp. 400, 461)

[77] S. LACOSTE-JULIEN, M. SCHMIDT, AND F. BACH, *A simpler approach to obtaining an $O(1/t)$ convergence rate for the projected stochastic subgradient method*, ArXiv e-prints, 2012. (Cited on pp. 219, 458)

[78] G. LAN, *An optimal method for stochastic composite optimization*, Math. Program., 133 (2011), pp. 365–397. (Cited on pp. 70, 457)

[79] E. S. LEVITIN AND B. T. POLYAK, *Constrained minimization methods*, U.S.S.R. Comput. Math. Math. Phys., 6 (1966), pp. 787–823. (Cited on pp. 459, 460, 461)

[80] A. S. LEWIS, *The convex analysis of unitarily invariant matrix functions*, J. Convex Anal., 2 (1995), pp. 173–183. (Cited on pp. 182, 458)

[81] ——, *Convex analysis on the Hermitian matrices*, SIAM J. Optim., 6 (1996), pp. 164–177 https://doi.org/10.1137/0806009. (Cited on pp. 182, 458)

[82] Q. LIN, Z. LU, AND L. XIAO, *An accelerated randomized proximal coordinate gradient method and its application to regularized empirical risk minimization*, SIAM J. Optim., 25 (2015), pp. 2244–2273, https://doi.org/10.1137/141000270. (Cited on pp. 347, 460)

[83] P. L. LIONS AND B. MERCIER, *Splitting algorithms for the sum of two nonlinear operators*, SIAM J. Numer. Anal., 16 (1979), pp. 964–979, https://doi.org/10.1137/0716071. (Cited on p. 458)

[84] Z. Q. LUO AND P. TSENG, *On the convergence of the coordinate descent method for convex differentiable minimization*, J. Optim. Theory Appl., 72 (1992), pp. 7–35. (Cited on p. 460)

[85] R. LUSS AND M. TEBOULLE, *Conditional gradient algorithms for rank-one matrix approximations with a sparsity constraint*, SIAM Rev., 55 (2013), pp. 65–98, https://doi.org/10.1137/110839072. (Cited on pp. 386, 461)

[86] C. D. MEYER, *Matrix Analysis and Applied Linear Algebra*, SIAM, Philadelphia, PA, 2000. (Cited on p. 457)

[87] J. J. MOREAU, *Proximité et dualité dans un espace hilbertien*, Bull. Soc. Math. France, 93 (1965), pp. 273–299. (Cited on pp. 458, 459)

[88] I. NECOARA AND A. PATRASCU, *Iteration complexity analysis of dual first-order methods for conic convex programming*, Optim. Methods Softw., 31 (2016), pp. 645–678. (Cited on pp. 277, 459)

[89] A. NEDIĆ AND D. BERTSEKAS, *Convergence rate of incremental subgradient algorithms*, in Stochastic Optimization: Algorithms and Applications, Springer, Boston, MA, 2001, pp. 223–264. (Cited on pp. 230, 458)

[90] A. NEDIĆ AND A. OZDAGLAR, *Approximate primal solutions and rate analysis for dual subgradient methods*, SIAM J. Optim., 19 (2009), pp. 1757–1780, https://doi.org/10.1137/070708111. (Cited on pp. 233, 238, 458)

[91] A. NEDIĆ AND A. OZDAGLAR, *Distributed multi-agent optimization*, in Convex Optimization in Signal Processing and Communications, D. Palomar and Y. Eldar, eds., Cambridge University Press, Cambridge, 2009, pp. 340–386. (Cited on p. 458)

[92] A. S. NEMIROVSKY AND D. B. YUDIN, *Problem Complexity and Method Efficiency in Optimization*, A Wiley-Interscience Publication, New York, 1983. (Cited on p. 458)

[93] Y. NESTEROV, *A method for solving the convex programming problem with convergence rate* $O(1/k^2)$, Dokl. Akad. Nauk SSSR, 269 (1983), pp. 543–547. (Cited on p. 459)

[94] ——, *Introductory Lectures on Convex Optimization: A Basic Course*, vol. 87 of Applied Optimization, Kluwer Academic Publishers, Boston, MA, 2004. (Cited on pp. 457, 458, 459)

[95] ——, *Smooth minimization of non-smooth functions*, Math. Program., 103 (2005), pp. 127–152. (Cited on pp. 304, 459)

[96] ——, *Efficiency of coordinate descent methods on huge-scale optimization problems*, SIAM J. Optim., 22 (2012), pp. 341–362, https://doi.org/10.1137/100802001. (Cited on pp. 346, 460)

[97] ——, *How to make the gradients small*, Optima, 88 (2012), pp. 10–11. (Cited on p. 459)

[98] ——, *Gradient methods for minimizing composite functions*, Math. Program., 140 (2013), pp. 125–161. (Cited on p. 459)

[99] J. NOCEDAL AND S. J. WRIGHT, *Numerical Optimization*, Springer Series in Operations Research and Financial Engineering, Springer, New York, second ed., 2006. (Cited on p. 459)

[100] J. NUTINI, M. SCHMIDT, I. H. LARADJI, M. FRIENDLANDER, AND H. KOEPKE, *Coordinate descent converges faster with the Gauss-Southwell rule than random selection*, in Proceedings of the 32nd International Conference on Machine Learning, Lille, France, 2015. (Cited on p. 459)

[101] J. M. ORTEGA AND W. C. RHEINBOLDT, *Iterative Solution of Nonlinear Equations in Several Variables*, vol. 30 of Classics in Applied Mathematics, SIAM, Philadelphia, PA, 2000. Reprint of the 1970 original, https://doi.org/10.1137/1.9780898719468. (Cited on p. 112)

[102] N. PARIKH AND S. BOYD, *Proximal algorithms*, Found. Trends Optim., 1 (2014), pp. 123–231. (Cited on pp. 182, 458)

[103] G. B. PASSTY, *Ergodic convergence to a zero of the sum of monotone operators in Hilbert space*, J. Math. Anal. Appl., 72 (1979), pp. 383–390. (Cited on p. 458)

[104] B. T. POLYAK, *Introduction to Optimization*, Translations Series in Mathematics and Engineering, Optimization Software Inc., New York, 1987. (Cited on pp. 204, 458, 459, 461)

[105] M. J. D. POWELL, *A method for nonlinear constraints in minimization problems*, in Optimization (Sympos., Univ. Keele, Keele, 1968), Academic Press, London, 1969, pp. 283–298. (Cited on p. 461)

[106] ——, *On search directions for minimization algorithms*, Math. Program., 4 (1973), pp. 193–201. (Cited on pp. 408, 461)

[107] P. RICHTÁRIK AND M. TAKÁČ, *Iteration complexity of randomized block-coordinate descent methods for minimizing a composite function*, Math. Program., 144 (2014), pp. 1–38. (Cited on p. 460)

[108] R. T. ROCKAFELLAR, *Convex Analysis*, vol. 28 of Princeton Mathematical Series, Princeton University Press, Princeton, NJ, 1970. (Cited on pp. 30, 43, 44, 45, 56, 102, 119, 181, 457, 458)

[109] ——, *A dual approach to solving nonlinear programming problems by unconstrained optimization*, Math. Program., 5 (1973), pp. 354–373. (Cited on p. 461)

[110] ——, *Monotone operators and the proximal point algorithm*, SIAM J. Control Optim., 14 (1976), pp. 877–898, https://doi.org/10.1137/0314056. (Cited on p. 459)

[111] R. T. ROCKAFELLAR AND R. J. B. WETS, *Variational Analysis*, vol. 317 of Grundlehren der Mathematischen Wissenschaften [Fundamental Principles of Mathematical Sciences], Springer-Verlag, Berlin, 1998. (Cited on p. 457)

[112] W. RUDIN, *Principles of Mathematical Analysis*, International Series in Pure and Applied Mathematics, McGraw-Hill, New York, Auckland, Düsseldorf, third ed., 1976. (Cited on pp. 59, 113)

[113] A. RUSZCZYŃSKI, *Nonlinear Optimization*, Princeton University Press, Princeton, NJ, 2006. (Cited on p. 458)

[114] R. SHEFI AND M. TEBOULLE, *Rate of convergence analysis of decomposition methods based on the proximal method of multipliers for convex minimization*, SIAM J. Optim., 24 (2014), pp. 269–297, https://doi.org/10.1137/130910774. (Cited on p. 462)

[115] ——, *On the rate of convergence of the proximal alternating linearized minimization algorithm for convex problems*, EURO J. Comput. Optim., 4 (2016), pp. 27–46. (Cited on pp. 342, 460)

[116] N. Z. SHOR, *Minimization Methods for Nondifferentiable Functions*, vol. 3 of Springer Series in Computational Mathematics, Springer-Verlag, Berlin, 1985. Translated from the Russian by K. C. Kiwiel and A. Ruszczyński. (Cited on p. 458)

[117] G. STRANG, *Introduction to Linear Algebra*, Wellesley-Cambridge Press, fourth ed., 2009. (Cited on p. 457)

[118] R. STURM, *Ueber den Punkt kleinster Entfernungssumme von gegebenen Punkten*, J. Reine Angew. Math., 97 (1884), pp. 49–61. (Cited on p. 457)

[119] C. M. THEOBALD, *An inequality for the trace of the product of two symmetric matrices*, Math. Proc. Cambridge Philos. Soc., 77 (1975), pp. 265–267. (Cited on pp. 183, 458)

[120] P. TSENG, *Applications of a splitting algorithm to decomposition in convex programming and variational inequalities*, SIAM J. Control Optim., 29 (1991), pp. 119–138, https://doi.org/10.1137/0329006. (Cited on p. 460)

[121] ———, *Approximation accuracy, gradient methods, and error bound for structured convex optimization*, Math. Program., 125 (2010), pp. 263–295. (Cited on pp. 326, 459)

[122] L. VANDENBERGHE. *Optimization Methods for Large-Scale Systems*, EE236C lecture notes, UCLA, 2016. (Cited on pp. 196, 458)

[123] J. VON NEUMANN, *Some matrix inequalities and metrization of matric space*, Tomsk. Univ. Rev., 1 (1937), pp. 286–300. (Cited on pp. 190, 458)

[124] E. V. WEISZFELD, *Sur le point pour lequel la somme des distances de n points donnés est minimum*, Tôhoku Math. J., 43 (1937), pp. 355–386. (Cited on p. 457)

[125] P. WOLFE, *Note on a method of conjugate subgradients for minimizing non-differentiable functions*, Math. Program., 7 (1974), pp. 380–383. (Cited on p. 458)

[126] S. J. WRIGHT, *Coordinate descent algorithms*, Math. Program., 151 (2015), pp. 3–34. (Cited on p. 460)

[127] S. J. WRIGHT, R. D. NOWAK, AND M. A. T. FIGUEIREDO, *Sparse reconstruction by separable approximation*, IEEE Trans. Signal Process., 57 (2009), pp. 2479–2493. (Cited on p. 459)

[128] C. ZALINESCU, *On uniformly convex functions*, J. Math. Anal. Appl., 95 (1983), pp. 344 – 374. (Cited on p. 457)

[129] C. ZALINESCU, *Convex Analysis in General Vector Spaces*, World Scientific, River Edge, NJ, 2002. (Cited on p. 457)

Index